# Lecture Notes in Computer Science

*Commenced Publication in 1973*
Founding and Former Series Editors:
Gerhard Goos, Juris Hartmanis, and Jan van Lee

# Preface

In the past few years, intelligence and security informatics (ISI) research, which is concerned with the study of the development and use of advanced information technologies and systems for national and international security-related applications, has experienced tremendous growth and attracted substantial interest from academic researchers in related fields as well as practitioners from both government agencies and industry. The ISI community is maturing, and a core set of research methodologies and technical approaches has emerged and is becoming the underpinning of ISI research.

The first two meetings (ISI 2003 and ISI 2004) in the ISI symposium and conference series were held in Tucson, Arizona. With sponsorship by the IEEE Intelligent Transportation Systems Society, ISI 2005 was held in Atlanta, Georgia. Building on the momentum of these ISI meetings, we held ISI 2006 in San Diego, California, in May 2006. In addition to the established and emerging ISI technical research topics, ISI 2006 included a track on terrorism informatics, which is a new stream of terrorism research leveraging the latest advances in social science methodologies, and information technologies and tools.

ISI 2006 was jointly hosted by the University of California, Irvine (UCI); the University of Texas at Dallas (UTD); and the University of Arizona (UA). The two-day program included one plenary panel discussion session focusing on the perspectives and future research directions of the government-funding agencies, several invited panel sessions, 69 regular papers, and 56 posters. In addition to the main sponsorship from the National Science Foundation, the Intelligence Technology Innovation Center, and the U.S. Department of Homeland Security, the conference was also co-sponsored by several units within the three hosting universities, including: the ResCUE project at the California Institute of Telecommunications and Information Technology (Calit2) at UCI, the Database Research Group in the Bren School of Information and Computer Sciences at UCI; the Eller College of Management and the Management Information Systems Department at UA; the NSF COPLINK Center of Excellence at UA; the Artificial Intelligence Laboratory at UA; the Intelligent Systems and Decisions Laboratory at UA; and the Program for Advanced Research in Complex Systems at UA. We also thank the Public Health Foundation Enterprises (PHFE) Management Solutions and the Chesapeake Innovation Center for their generous support.

We wish to express our gratitude to all members of the ISI 2006 Program Committee and additional reviewers who provided high-quality, constructive review comments under an unreasonably short lead-time. Our special thanks go to Edna Reid, who recruited high-caliber contributors from the terrorism informatics research community and helped process submissions in the terrorism informatics area. We wish to express our gratitude to Quent Cassen, Jean Chin, Catherine Larson, Priscilla Rasmussen, and Shing Ka Wu for providing excellent conference logistics support. ISI 2006 was co-located with the 7th Annual National Conference on Digital Government Research (DG.O). We wish to thank the DG.O organizers and support staff for their cooperation and assistance. We also would like to thank the Springer LNCS editorial and production staff for their professionalism and continuous support of the ISI symposium and conference series.

Our sincere gratitude goes to all of the sponsors. Last, but not least, we thank Larry Brandt, Art Becker, Robert Ross, Valerie Gregg, and Joshua Sinai for their strong and continuous support of the ISI series and other related ISI research.

May 2006

Sharad Mehrotra
Daniel Zeng
Hsinchun Chen
Bhavani Thuraisingham
Fei-Yue Wang

# Organization

## ISI 2006 Organizing Committee

*Conference Co-chairs:*

| | |
|---|---|
| Hsinchun Chen | University of Arizona |
| Bhavani Thuraisingham | University of Texas at Dallas |
| Feiyue Wang | Chinese Academy of Sciences and University of Arizona |

*Program Co-chairs:*

| | |
|---|---|
| Sharad Mehrotra | University of California, Irvine |
| Daniel Zeng | University of Arizona |

*Government Liaisons:*

| | |
|---|---|
| Larry Brandt | National Science Foundation |
| Art Becker | Intelligence Technology Innovation Center |
| Valerie Gregg | University of Southern California |
| Joshua Sinai | Logos Technologies |

*Local Committee Arrangements Co-chairs:*

| | |
|---|---|
| Quent Cassen | University of California, Irvine |
| Cathy Larson | University of Arizona |
| Priscilla Rasmussen | Academic and Research Conference Services |

*Terrorism Informatics Track Coordinator:*

| | |
|---|---|
| Edna Reid | University of Arizona |

# ISI 2006 Program Committee

| | |
|---|---|
| Yigal Arens | University of Southern California |
| Homa Atabakhsh | University of Arizona |
| Antonio Badia | University of Louisville |
| Pierre Baldi | University of California, Irvine |
| Judee Burgoon | University of Arizona |
| Carter Butts | University of California, Irvine |
| Guoray Cai | Pennsylvania State University |
| Michael Chau | University of Hong Kong |
| Sudarshan S. Chawathe | University of Maine |
| Lee-Feng Chien | Academia Sinica, Taiwan |
| Wingyan Chung | University of Texas at El Paso |
| Ruwei Dai | Chinese Academy of Sciences |
| Chris Demchak | University of Arizona |
| James Ellis | National Memorial Institute for the Prevention of Terrorism |
| Johannes Gehrke | Cornell University |
| Jason Geng | Chinese Academy of Sciences |
| Mark Goldberg | Rensselaer Polytechnic Institute |
| Bob Grossman | University of Illinois at Chicago |
| Jiawei Han | University of Illinois at Urbana-Champaign |
| Alan R. Hevner | University of South Florida |
| Paul Hu | University of Utah |
| Zan Huang | Pennsylvania State University |
| Paul Kantor | Rutgers University |
| Hillol Kargupta | University of Maryland, Baltimore County |
| Moshe Koppel | Bar-Ilan University, Israel |
| Don Kraft | Louisiana State University |
| Seok-Won Lee | University of North Carolina at Charlotte |
| Leslie Lenert | University of California, San Diego |
| Gondy Leroy | Claremont Graduate University |
| Ee-peng Lim | Nanyang Technological University, Singapore |
| Chienting Lin | Pace University |
| Ruqian Lu | Chinese Academy of Sciences |
| Cecil Lynch | University of California at Davis |
| Brinton Milward | University of Arizona |
| Pitu Mirchandani | University of Arizona |
| Gheorghe Muresan | Rutgers University |
| Clifford Neuman | University of Southern California |
| Greg Newby | University of Alaska, Fairbanks |
| Jay Nunamaker | University of Arizona |
| Joon S. Park | Syracuse University |
| Ganapati P. Patil | Pennsylvania State University |
| Peter Probst | ISTPV |
| Ram Ramesh | State University of New York at Buffalo |
| H. Raghav Rao | State University of New York at Buffalo |

# Additional Reviewers

| | |
|---|---|
| Ahmed Abbasi | University of Arizona |
| Naveen Ashish | University of California, Irvine |
| Wei Chang | University of Arizona |
| Stella Chen | University of California, Irvine |
| Amit Deokar | University of Arizona |
| Mayur Deshpande | University of California, Irvine |
| Joel Helquist | University of Arizona |
| Bijit Hore | University of California, Irvine |
| Daning Hu | University of Arizona |
| Hojjat Jafarpour | University of California, Irvine |
| Ravi Jammalamadaka | University of California, Irvine |
| Dmitri Kalashnikov | University of California, Irvine |
| Siddharth Kaza | University of Arizona |
| Jiexun Li | University of Arizona |
| Xin Li | University of Arizona |
| Ming Lin | University of Arizona |
| Hsin-Min Lu | University of Arizona |
| Jian Ma | University of Arizona |
| Yiming Ma | University of California, Irvine |
| Dani Massaguer | University of California, Irvine |
| Tom Meservy | University of Arizona |
| Mirko Montanari | University of California, Irvine |
| Mark Patton | University of Arizona |
| Jialun Qin | University of Arizona |
| Tiantian Qin | University of Arizona |
| Rob Schumaker | University of Arizona |
| Dawit Seid | University of California, Irvine |
| Aaron Sun | University of Arizona |
| Alan Wang | University of Arizona |
| Jinsu Wang | University of California, Irvine |
| Bo Xing | University of California, Irvine |
| Ping Yan | University of Arizona |
| Xingbo Yu | University of California, Irvine |
| Yilu Zhou | University of Arizona |

# Table of Contents

## Access Control, Privacy, and Cyber Trust

## Surveillance and Emergency Response

## Infrastructure Protection and Cyber Security

## Terrorism Informatics and Countermeasures

# Emerging Applications

# Part II: Short Papers

# Data Analysis, Knowledge Discovery, and Information Dissemination

## Access Control, Privacy, and Cyber Trust

## Surveillance, Bioterrorism, and Emergency Response

## Infrastructure Protection and Cyber Security

## Terrorism Informatics

## Emerging Applications

## Part III: Extended Abstracts for Posters and Demos

## Data Analysis and Knowledge Discovery

# Data, Information, and Knowledge Management

# Threat Detection, Surveillance, and Emergency Response

## Infrastructure Protection and Cyber Security

## Terrorism Informatics

## Emerging Applications

# Computer-Mediated Collaborative Reasoning and Intelligence Analysis*

Douglas Yeung[1] and John Lowrance[2]

[1] Department of Psychology, Rutgers University – Newark,
101 Warren St., Newark, NJ 07102, USA
dcyeung@psychology.rutgers.edu
[2] Artificial Intelligence Center, SRI International,
333 Ravenswood Avenue, Menlo Park, CA 94205, USA
lowrance@ai.sri.com

**Abstract.** Problems of bias in intelligence analysis may be reduced by the use of web-based cognitive aids. We introduce a framework spanning the entire collaborative thought process using the Angler and SEAS (Structured Evidential Argumentation System) applications. Angler encourages creative brainstorming while SEAS demands analytical reasoning. The dual nature of this approach suggests substantial benefits from using computer-mediated collaborative and structured reasoning tools for intelligence analysis and policymaking.

Computer-mediated communication (CMC) may be impacted by many factors, including group dynamics and cultural and individual differences between participants. Based on empirical research, potential enhancements to Angler and SEAS are outlined, along with experiments to evaluate their worth. The proposed methodology may also be applied to assess the value of the suggested features to other such CMC tools.

## 1 Introduction

The accuracy and effectiveness of intelligence analysis must first contend with the cognitive biases inherent to any subjective undertaking. To address these flaws in reasoning, the practice can benefit from increased cooperation and an infusion of rigor and structured thinking, which computer-mediated communication tools such as Angler and SEAS (Structured Evidential Argumentation System) provide.

Angler is designed to support collaborative divergent and convergent thinking [1], and SEAS to support and capture collaborative analytic reasoning [2]. When the two are used in conjunction, the end product of Angler workshops – clusters of thoughts – can be employed to develop analytic objectives for SEAS. Conversely, these objectives may be used to identify and flag potential problems for which a solution can be collectively brainstormed, using Angler workshops.

Thus a framework spanning the entire collaborative thought process using the Angler and SEAS applications will be introduced. Empirical research also suggests additional studies that could result in new Angler and SEAS features as well as

---
* This work was partially supported by SRI International. The authors would like to thank Kent D. Harber and Eric Yeh for their helpful comments on an earlier draft.

S. Mehrotra et al. (Eds.): ISI 2006, LNCS 3975, pp. 1 – 13, 2006.

advantages to using these tools in a larger process of collaborative reasoning, exploiting the principal advantages of each.

Indeed, computer-mediated communication (CMC) has been a growing area of research, as the advent of asynchronous communication media such as email and text messaging has focused attention on its influence on human behavior. The types of communication supported by Angler and SEAS may be impacted by many factors, including group dynamics and cultural and individual differences between participants.

This report will cover general theories of group dynamics that affect ease of communication, productivity, and satisfaction, as well as their effects on the individual. Subsequently, the impact of electronic communication on groups will be examined, including benefits of web-based tools such as Angler, which is relatively new, and the more mature SEAS.

The proposed system is intended to support collaborative decision making and scenario planning, for which Angler itself was originally developed [1]. However, the inclusion of SEAS should produce a more robust overall process, allowing for more timely assessments of opportunities and threats. Angler encourages creative brainstorming while SEAS demands analytical reasoning. In this manner the characteristics of one mode of reasoning may compensate for the limitations of the other. The dual nature of this approach suggests substantial benefits from using computer-mediated collaborative and structured reasoning tools for intelligence analysis and policymaking.

## 2   Problems of Bias in Intelligence Analysis

Intelligence analysis is, at its heart, the art of prognostication. Pattern recognition, cultural and behavioral insight, and even simple intuition are employed to make enough sense of partial and vague data points to generate an informed report on their significance. In this process, analysts are subject to well-known biases and flaws in reasoning when making judgments and predictions.

Foremost among these is the tendency to distill information into preexisting notions. Given its inherent complexity and ambiguity, analysts rely upon mental models to simplify and manage the onslaught of incoming information [3]. Intelligence is shoehorned into preconceived concepts and often disregarded if it cannot be made to fit existing models or beliefs [4]. An overwhelming inflow of information can also lead to the simple inability to process it without the aid of structuring or organization [5].

Moreover, analysis is personally risky. Presenting a forecast or specific recommendation puts the analyst at risk of being proven wrong, damaging self-esteem and feelings of competence [6], [7]. Thus analysts may hesitate to deliver alarming or disturbing reports to their superiors or to policymakers [8]. Conversely, recipients may be just as reluctant to accept such information [9].

Together, this unwillingness to share troubling information may contribute to the intelligence community's cultural tendency towards an obsession with secrecy, which has been criticized of late [10]. Clearly, some level of secrecy must be maintained. However, overzealousness in this regard squanders the power of collaborative reasoning, in doing so opening the door for potentially deleterious effects of individual biases and cultural worldviews on information processing. To combat these problems, some rather ambitious solutions have been advanced [11] along with smaller-scale recommendations, such as the implementation of methods to inject rigor into critical thinking [3].

Tools intended to aid collaboration, force structure upon reasoning, and leverage organizational knowledge bases can help offset these biases and improve intelligence analysis. For example, simple awareness of cognitive biases may not suffice to counteract them [3], and an active effort to do so may even be counterproductive [12].

## 3  Social Psychology Theories of Group Behavior

Much of the social psychology literature on group behavior presents a similarly bleak view of groups and their power over an individual. Evidence indicates that people conform to majority views and accepted norms, implicit and explicit [13], [14], [15], [16]. Collectivist cultures have been found to imply greater conformity, e.g., "groupthink" [17], than in more individualist cultures [18]. The anonymity possible within a group can lead to deindividuation [19], [20], resulting in loss of self-awareness and individual responsibility.

Individually, anxiety over personally disturbing events may have a toxic effect on cognitive processing and social perception, leading to increasingly biased thinking that may affect social interactions and, eventually, group dynamics. However, emotional disclosure, the process of putting thoughts and feelings about such events into language, has been shown to reduce these effects [21], even for electronic communication [22].

In sum, the psychological research covering group behavior can have largely negative implications for collaborative brainstorming sessions, which depend on free-flowing exchanges of often-unconventional ideas. However, evidence provides reason for optimism that group behavior may in fact be positively impacted by electronic communication media, as discussed in the following sections.

### 3.1  Virtual Group Dynamics

*Communication apprehension* is anxiety regarding the use of communication technology. Users may fear a large, lurking audience, inhibiting their willingness to bring up points of dispute [23]. One possible reason is that, face-to-face, feedback is immediate. Silence does not necessarily equate to lack of response, as nonverbal reactions may be conveyed. Online, however, any response is generally interpreted as success, while silence is failure.

Thus for electronic communication, silence is akin to rejection. Cyberostracism, the online "act of ignoring and exclusion," results in greater conformity to group norms [24]. Speed and spontaneity of information flow may also be impaired, resulting in higher cognitive workload [25]. Such issues make it difficult to establish cohesion and thus achieve consensus in virtual groups [23].

However, an asynchronous, anonymous paradigm may allow collaborators to express greater disagreement and eventually reach greater consensus [26].

Disagreement is desirable for collaboration. It is evidence of the divergent thinking that is encouraged in the brainstorming phase of Angler. Anonymity may free participants to contribute more frequently and meaningfully than they might otherwise feel comfortable with.

Also, new members in virtual groups may be unable to contribute meaningful thoughts until they become more established within the group [27]. Increased identification with and attachment to a virtual group may be exacerbated by lack of physical cues [28].

Although CMC has been suggested to cause some difficulty in communication, it might also make group processes more egalitarian, thus overcoming other challenges in forming virtual groups [29]. Together, these findings imply that CMC can be an obstacle to developing cohesive groups but may allow fairer participation, thus potentially avoiding biased thinking according to group norms or polarization.

### 3.2 Technology Facilitates Communication

Technology can both help and hinder communication. For example, it has been argued that CMC technology amplifies the impact of cultural differences, as social cues are reduced, increasing the relative importance of more explicit forms of communication [30]. From this it was suggested that relative anonymity or perceived remoteness may introduce greater cultural biases. In the absence of contextual information, participants may lean more heavily on their own culturally formed mental schema in computer-mediated social interaction.

Delivering bad news or other negative information is difficult in any medium. Bearers of bad news using CMC distort less, reducing potential for misinterpretation, and are more comfortable and satisfied with the process than either face-to-face or phone [8]. This work may have broader implications for intelligence analysis or policymaking, where subordinates may be hesitant to deliver bad news to superiors. Such effects are already seen in testing of SEAS (E. Yeh, personal communication, January, 2006).

### 3.3 CMC and Individual Differences

Individual differences between participants, such as gender and personality, can also affect communication styles when using electronic media. Gender differences may affect writing formality [31], apparent social presence (level of immersion in a technology-mediated environment [32]) [33], and satisfaction [34].

Personality dimensions also play a role. For example, an agreeable writer is more likely to be perceived as conscious of a shared context between self and reader [31]. Also, those who desire interaction while working independently may find cue-lean media more objectionable than those who prefer less interaction [23].

The foregoing discussion illustrated general effects of computer-mediated communication on group biases and individual differences. The next sections will focus more strictly on how CMC technology, Angler and SEAS in particular, may reduce problems of bias in intelligence analysis.

# 4   Angler and SEAS

Angler and SEAS were developed as web-based tools to aid threat assessment and scenario planning for policy formation and intelligence analysis. Angler supports collaboration on a focus topic, facilitating cognitive expansion by using divergent (brainstorming) and convergent (clustering or ranking) techniques. Virtual workshops are organized by a facilitator to bring a group of people together to accomplish a knowledge task. As more workshops are stored in the knowledge base, a corporate memory is formed.

In the brainstorming phase, participants contribute *thoughts* (ideas) to answer a focused question. Angler provides a convenient interface for participants to author such thoughts, review and respond to other thoughts, and organize the growing set of shared contributions.

After sufficient input and review, the facilitator moves the workshop into the clustering phase, where participants group thoughts into coherent themes. This process promotes a rich interchange of ideas and perspectives. Finally, in a consensus and ranking phase, participants come to understand their differing views and vote on names for the consensus clusters [1]. The end result is a set of diverse, reasoned ideas, which may then be used for scenario planning, among other things.

In contrast, SEAS is based on the concept of a *structured argument*, a hierarchically organized set of questions (tree), used to monitor intelligence and to assess whether an opportunity or threat is imminent. This hierarchy of questions is called a *template*, as opposed to the *argument*, an instantiation of the template that answers the questions posed. The problem at hand is broken into a hierarchical set of questions. Each question is multiple-choice, with answers along a scale at one end representing strong support for a particular opportunity or threat and the other end representing strong refutation.

Arguments are formed by answering the supporting questions posed by the template and attaching the evidence used to arrive at those selected answers. In this manner SEAS reminds the intelligence analyst of key indicators and warning signs and records the analyst's reasoning in applying an argument template to the target situation. The resulting instantiated argument may then be browsed and critiqued by other analysts [2].

## 4.1   Advantages of Angler and SEAS

Angler and SEAS each offer distinct advantages to collaboration in accordance with those inherent in CMC technologies, characteristics that have proven advantageous for intelligence analysis. Text-based web tools such as Angler allow users to participate across different times and locations and provide a sense of control and real-time feedback [35] while maintaining individual or cultural differences [30].

Angler, however, moves beyond other such tools by offering asynchronous and anonymous contributions to collaboration, balanced by a live facilitator to ensure a smooth process. Anonymous brainstorming leads to higher productivity, improves communication [30], and encourages expression of thoughts and feelings [28].

Virtual groups also profit from the coordinator and liaison roles that the existing Angler facilitator fills by managing flow of information [27]. The facilitator moderates discussion by ensuring that everyone's thoughts are heard, suggesting unexplored topics, and maintaining socialization and civility as necessary.

A particularly illustrative account that demonstrates the facilitator's value finds that minor turf wars can ensue during face-to-face brainstorming sessions. Participants may develop territorial attachments, either when returning from lunch to find someone else sitting in "their" seat, or when asked as a group by the facilitator to switch seats to break out of calcified mindsets (T. Boyce, personal communication, 2005). Virtual groups, such as those formed in Angler, are unaffected by such issues [28].

Structured reasoning, when applied to analysis undertaken more intuitively than rigorously, can also demonstrate concrete gains. A tool such as SEAS allows users to quickly understand lines of reasoning, promotes best practices by creating templates, and captures corporate knowledge [2], [36].

Finally, SEAS supports the same asynchronous collaboration as Angler. Both template authors and analysts have simultaneous read-write access, benefiting from the increased flexibility and sense of control that computer-mediated groups enjoy.

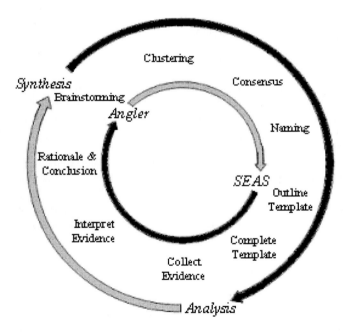

**Fig. 1.** A collaborative thought process encompassing Angler and SEAS allows analysts to consider focus topics as a group and then observe those situations in a structured fashion. In the first phase (*Synthesis*), issues raised and discussed in Angler workshops are used to develop SEAS templates. In the *Analysis* phase, SEAS templates are used as arguments to monitor impending situations. This information in turn motivates further discussion in Angler workshops, leading to another cycle of collaborative reasoning.

## 4.2  Collaborative Process

Because Angler and SEAS provide relatively discrete feature sets, the combination may be extremely powerful in exploiting collaboration to reduce bias while supporting diversity of thought. The scenarios and significant themes resulting from Angler sessions are subsequently used to form the structure of SEAS templates. Arguments formed from these templates may then motivate further topics to be examined with an additional Angler group. Figure 1 outlines the phases in Angler and SEAS composing the overall collaborative process.

The resulting cycle of reasoning provides concrete benefits for intelligence analysis and policy formation by reducing dependence on mental models, encouraging information sharing, and creating a knowledge base that may then be leveraged in potentially unforeseen ways.

Another advantage of this approach is ease of implementation – no new software is required, as benefits are realized by simply modifying patterns of usage and incorporating the results of one tool into the other.

# 5   Potential Features

The collaborative process adds value to intelligence analysis even with both products in their current form. In Angler, participants gain from both web-based anonymity and facilitated fairness. SEAS introduces structure to analysis, organizing thinking that may have been dominated by heuristics and models.

However, CMC theories can suggest improvements to increase adoption of these tools and to enhance user experience. Reticence due to communication anxiety may be reduced by increased socialization. Lack of access to the tools may prevent the assembly of an appropriate mixture of expertise. Increased flexibility in when and how to participate, such as on a mobile platform, is a step toward resolving the difficulty of finding enough participants to hold a meaningful brainstorming workshop. Finally, creating an effective knowledge base or corporate memory against which to critique reasoning requires a relatively comprehensive slice of data. Synthetic participants, facilitators, or critics could begin to fill these gaps.

Thus Angler and, to a lesser extent, SEAS may be extended by adding features accordingly. The following sections examine such enhancements, each of which seeks to address a range of the known issues.

## 5.1  Increased Socialization

Candid discussion may be the first casualty when group members are not comfortable enough to share their thoughts. With increasing saturation and ubiquity of CMC, communication apprehension should remain evident, coexisting with normal anxiety over socializing and fitting in on the "first day of school." To create a more open and supportive environment to counteract communication apprehension, Angler could include more greetings, vocatives (addressing participants by name), and feedback between group members, as well as descriptions of shared context [23].

This could suggest some use for a "meet-and-greet" session, or for "cafes," subconferences designated for social interaction [23]. A short bio for each participant could be made available, even if names were not associated to each specific contribution later. Synthetic agents or any other system features could address participants by name: *"John, do you understand this thought?"* or *"Sally, please choose a name for this cluster."* A synthetic aid could remind the facilitator to do so as well. These synthetic agents are discussed in a later section.

Socialization is currently handled informally, such as by going out to dinner or mingling over drinks (T. Boyce, personal communication, June 2005). A more structured method of achieving group cohesion may increase productivity. Partnering newcomers with a more experienced member would provide a ready source of information about group norms and expectations, integrating new members more quickly and encouraging them to contribute sooner. Increased socialization in this manner would also improve personal relationships [26], [28] and minimize hostile behavior in response to perceived cyberostracism [37].

## 5.2  Technology-Use Mediation

The cognitive bias of technology apprehension may be another impediment to effective usage of Angler and SEAS. People who once traveled across the globe for meetings may still be getting used to replacements such as videoconferencing or real-time chatting, remaining unconvinced as to their merits. Thus it may not be a technological advance that would result in the greatest improvement for Angler and SEAS in terms of results and user satisfaction, but rather, a real-world advocate. This person(s) would act as a consultant of sorts to promote the tools' benefits, help with implementation, and ease the transition into regular usage.

Organizations wishing to implement these tools or increase usage could thus employ *technology-use mediation*: "deliberate, organizationally-sanctioned intervention…which helps to adapt a new communication technology…, modifies the context as appropriate to accommodate use of the technology, and facilitates the ongoing usefulness of the technology over time" [38].

In each Angler session, the facilitator temporarily fills this role, coaxing and cajoling to get people to buy into ideas, to stimulate discussion and encourage participation. However, it may be helpful to have a position within an organization dedicated to this task.

## 5.3  Cathartic Exercise

A "cathartic" exercise prior to brainstorming where participants could freely express thoughts and feelings could similarly prove useful, reducing inhibition of thoughts and overreliance on mental models [21]. The active suppression of thoughts and feelings, as when dealing with classified information, has significant implications for policymakers and intelligence analysts. It may prevent productive group discussion between committee members. It can produce biased thinking in an individual analyst, as traumatic or stress-inducing information cannot be organized and processed without conscious confrontation [39]. Providing Angler participants or SEAS authors and analysts with the opportunity to first anonymously convey their emotion, and not necessarily the substance of the information, could reduce dependence on biases and allow them to contribute more readily to discussion [28].

## 5.4 Synthetic Agents – Participants, Facilitators, and Critics

Although the asynchronous nature should minimize problems due to scheduling constraints, getting the right mix of people with appropriate areas of expertise may still be impossible. Development of synthetic agents that could contribute thoughts to brainstorming and participate in clustering could go a long way in extending both Angler and SEAS. Such a participant could leverage knowledge bases or corporate memory to suggest thoughts. Using semantic indexing [1], the "participant" could contribute thoughts to Angler brainstorming either related to existing contributions or of topics that had not yet been mentioned. Furthermore, agent participants could access various knowledge bases to simulate area experts in different fields, thus increasing realism and more closely approximating a process with human participants. They might vary their behavior according to the participants involved, as cultural differences may affect the way people relate to a computer agent [40].

A synthetic agent could also aid the live facilitator or even fill its role entirely. Again leveraging knowledge bases or corporate memory, it could suggest potential participants based on historical contributions prior to the session, or during the session, as-yet unexplored topics that the facilitator could propose to the participants. It might help the facilitator track participation. To avoid overreliance on culturally based viewpoints, the agent could use semantic closeness in conjunction with logical rules to identify potentially biased thinking [41].

To accomplish this, an agent would analyze a contributed thought against other contributions. Determining its thematic closeness to and alignment with those contributions, it could use logic built in to identify and flag a "groupthink" bias, for example. This alert would indicate that the participant may have been adjusting his thoughts to align with his view of the consensus. Similarly, the agent could attempt to identify cultural differences. Logical rules to identify known biases could be built in along with functionality to allow end users to write in their individual observed tendencies. Once alerted to such biases, the facilitator could take steps to tease out more diversity in thought.

A synthetic SEAS critic could also analyze completed templates and arguments for bias and logicality. As SEAS critics are currently limited to checking for completeness and grammar, an extension to determine bias in questions, evidence, and rationales could result in improved templates and arguments.

## 6 Experiments

Prior empirical evidence can suggest potential upgrades to Angler and SEAS and provide support for their value. However, experiments conducted specifically to evaluate these features would offer more concrete substantiation for the enhancements. The experiments presented in Table 1 can help in assessing the value of, for example, holding "meet and greet" sessions to improve participation, or the role of a dedicated advocate in encouraging usage of web-based collaborative reasoning tools.

To measure both quality and satisfaction, a collaborative session (Angler workshop leading to development of SEAS template) incorporating the proposed enhancements could be compared against another session as currently implemented. Participants using the upgraded tools would constitute the experimental group, while those using unchanged versions of Angler and SEAS would serve as controls.

The resulting differences should indicate the effectiveness of these features, for which a mapping of semantic diversity could be the appropriate metric. For example, clusters of thoughts with greater semantic distance from each other might indicate a greater diversity in thought, implying that the enhanced collaborative process provided the intended support. To measure participant satisfaction, surveys or interviews could be conducted.

**Table 1.** Experiments to evaluate proposed upgrades to Angler and SEAS are summarized, along with methodologies and metrics to assess effectiveness

| Topic of Interest | Approach | Methodology | Metrics |
|---|---|---|---|
| Benefits of collaborative process & proposed enhancements | **Compare collaborative processes** | – Hold separate collaborative sessions – with and without enhancements <br> – Compare and contrast results | – Semantic diversity of clusters <br> – Self-reported attitudes and satisfaction |
| Effectiveness of technology usage advocate | **Instantiate SEAS Information Campaign Argument** | – Create structured reasoning argument to analyze effectiveness <br> – Gather evidence <br> – Write rationale | – Positive assessment from SEAS argument <br> – Observed increase in tool usage |
| Virtual group processes and conformity to norms | **Replicate social psychology group dynamics experiments** | – Conduct experiments with CMC <br> – Use different paradigm | – % participants who conform <br> – % trials in which participants conform |

Other methods would explore how CMC technologies are introduced to often-skeptical audiences. The SEAS Sociopsychological Assessment of an Information Campaign template [42] assesses whether a message in an ongoing information campaign was received as intended. An argument created from this template would determine whether bad news or criticism was received as intended, that the target audience interpreted the information correctly and believed what was said. The same SEAS argument could also test the resulting difference between official, organizationally sanctioned champions, and those operating informally.

To specifically observe whether electronic communications lessen group biases, a simple approach would involve replicating classic social psychology experiments [13], [14], using computer-mediated rather than face-to-face interaction. As many social psychology studies have become fairly well-known in popular culture, different paradigms employing the same general principles might yield even more compelling results. For example, adherence to virtual group norms may be moderated by the ability of pressuring group members to project social presence, an individual's perceived inclusion in a group, or social identity.

## 7  Conclusion

The power of CMC technology may be reliably harnessed in tools such as Angler and SEAS to improve collaboration and reduce biased thinking. When jointly implemented, these tools form a potent overall process that benefits intelligence analysis and policy formation by assisting collaborative analysis in scenario planning and assessment of opportunities and threats.

Research across related fields such as social psychology, human-computer interaction, and artificial intelligence can contribute significantly to the future direction of collaborative reasoning. Although these findings may suggest some potential improvements, the predictive power of any such advice may be modest.

Thus the empirical research on this matter should inform and suggest directions for future study. By increasing understanding of medium-dependent communication styles, it becomes possible to test specifically for relevant behaviors under the overall paradigm of interest – a collaborative process consisting of Angler workshops and SEAS arguments. The resulting knowledge may then be used to expand the capability of asynchronous web-based collaboration and structured reasoning to improve intelligence analysis.

## References

1. Murray, K., Lowrance, J., Appelt, D., & Rodriguez, A. (2005). Fostering collaboration with a semantic index over textual contributions. *AI Technologies for Homeland Security, Papers from the 2005 AAAI Spring Symposium, 3*, 99-106.
2. Lowrance, J.D., Harrison, I.W., & Rodriguez, A.C. (2000). Structured argumentation for analysis. *Proceedings of the 12th International Conference on Systems Research, Informatics, and Cybernetics: Focus Symposia on Advances in Computer-Based and Web-Based Collaborative Systems.* Baden-Baden, Germany.
3. Center for the Study of Intelligence, Central Intelligence Agency. (1999). *Psychology of Intelligence Analysis.* Washington, D.C.: Heuer, R.J., Jr.
4. Lord, C., Ross, L., & Lepper, M. (1979). Biased assimilation and attitude polarization: The effects of prior theories on subsequently considered evidence. *Journal of Personality and Social Psychology, 37*, 2098-2109.
5. Popp, R. L. (2005, March). *Exploiting AI, information and computational social science technology to understand the adversary.* Slide presentation. 2005 AAAI Spring Symposium: AI Technologies for Homeland Security.

6. Crook, R.H., Healy, C.C., & O'Shea, D.W. (1984). The linkage of work achievement to self-esteem, career maturity, and college achievement. *Journal of Vocational Behavior, 25(1),* 70-79.
7. Mutran, E.J., Reitzes, D.J., Bratton, K.A., & Fernandez, M.E. (1997). Self-esteem and subjective responses to work among mature workers: similarities and differences by gender. *Journal of Gerontology Series B: Psychological Sciences and Social Sciences, 52(2),* S89-96.
8. Sussman, S.W. & Sproull, L. (1999). Straight talk: Delivering bad news through electronic communication. *Information Systems Research, 10,* 150-166.
9. Reed, M.B. & Aspinwall, L.G. (1998). Self-affirmation reduces biased processing of health-risk information. *Motivation and Emotion, 22,* 99-132.
10. Steele, R.D. (2001). *The new craft of intelligence.* Advance review draft, OSS Inc.
11. Kean, T.H., Hamilton, L.H., Ben-Veniste, R., Kerrey, B., Fielding, F.F., Lehman, J.F., Gorelick, J.S., Roemer, T.J., Gorton, S., & Thompson, J.R. (2004). *The 9-11 commission report: Final report of the national commission on terrorist attacks upon the United States.* Retrieved Sept 13, 2005, from National Commission on Terrorist Attacks Upon the United States Web site, http://www.9-11commission.gov/report/911Report.pdf.
12. Wegner, D.M. (1994). Ironic processes of mental control. *Psychological Review, 101,* 34-52.
13. Asch, S.E. (1951). Effects of group pressure upon the modification and distortion of judgment. In H. Guetzkow (Ed.), *Groups, leadership, and men.* (pp. 177-190). Pittsburgh, PA: Carnegie Press.
14. Sherif, M. (1936). *The psychology of social norms.* New York: Harper Brothers.
15. Sherif, M., Harvey, O.J., White, B.J., Hood, W.R., & Sherif, C.W. (1961). *Intergroup conflict and cooperation: The Robber's Cave experiment.* Norman, OK: University of Oklahoma Book Exchange.
16. Tajfel, H. & Turner, J. (1986). The social identity theory of intergroup behavior. In S. Worchel & W.G. Austin (Eds.), *Psychology of Intergroup Relations* (pp. 7-24). Chicago, IL: Nelson.
17. Janis, I. (1972). *Victims of groupthink: A psychological study of foreign-policy decisions and fiascoes.* Boston: Houghton Mifflin.
18. Bond, R. & Smith, P. B. (1996). Culture and conformity: A meta-analysis of studies using Asch's (1952b, 1956) line judgment task. *Psychological Bulletin, 119(1),* 111-137.
19. Festinger, L., Pepitone, A., & Newcomb, T. (1952). Some consequences of de-individuation in a group. *Journal of Abnormal and Social Psychology, 47,* 382-389.
20. Zimbardo, P.G. (1969). The human choice: Individuation, reason, and order vs. deindividuation, impulse, and chaos. In W.J. Arnold & D. Levine (Eds.). *Nebraska Symposium on Motivation, 17,* (pp.237-307). Lincoln, NE: University of Nebraska Press.
21. Pennebaker, J.W. (1989). Confession, inhibition, and disease. *Advances in Experimental Social Psychology, 22,* 211-244.
22. Sheese, B.E., Brown, E.L., & Graziano, W.G. (2004). Emotional expression in cyberspace: Searching for moderators of the Pennebaker Disclosure Effect via e-mail. *Health Psychology, 23,* 457-464.
23. Rourke, L. & Anderson, T. (2000). Exploring social communication in computer conferencing. *Journal of Interactive Learning Research, 13(3),* 259-275.
24. Williams, K.D., Cheung, C.K.T., & Choi, W. (2000). Cyberostracism: Effects of being ignored over the Internet. *Journal of Personality and Social Psychology, 79(5),* 748-762.
25. Campbell, J.A. (1999). Communication apprehension and participation in videoconferenced meetings. *Proceedings of the 10th Australasian Conference on Information Systems.* Wellington, New Zealand.

26. Lowry, P.B. & Nunamaker, Jr., J.F. (2002). Synchronous, distributed collaborative writing for policy agenda setting using Collaboratus, an Internet-based collaboration tool. *Proceedings of the 35th Hawaii International Conference on System Sciences.* Waikoloa, HI.
27. Ahuja, M.K. & Galvin, J.E. (2003). Socialization in Virtual Groups. *Journal of Management, 29(2),* 161-185.
28. McKenna, K.Y.A. & Green, A.S. (2002). Virtual group dynamics. *Group Dynamics: Theory, Research and Practice, 6(1),* 116-127.
29. Corbitt, G., Gardiner, L.R., & Wright, L.K. (2004). A comparison of team developmental stages, trust and performance for virtual versus face-to-face teams. *Proceedings of the 37th Hawaii International Conference on System Sciences.* Waikoloa, HI.
30. Kersten, G.E., Koszegi, S.T., & Vetschera, R. (2003). The effects of culture in computer-mediated negotiations. *The Journal of Information Technology Theory and Application, 5(2),* 1-28.
31. Nowson, S., Oberlander, & J., Gill, A.J. (2005). Weblogs, genres, and individual differences. *Proceedings of the 27th Annual Conference of the Cognitive Science Society.* Stresa, Italy.
32. Coman, E. & Rauh, C. (2003) The impact of imagination on computer mediated telepresence. *Presence panel: Information Systems Division, International Communication Association.* San Diego, CA.
33. Nowak, K.L. (2003). Sex categorization in computer mediated communication (CMC): Exploring the utopian promise. *Media Psychology, 5,* 83-103.
34. Olaniran, B.A. (1993). Individual differences and computer mediated communication: The role of perception. *The Electronic Journal of Communication, 3:2.*
35. Suh, K.-Won, Couchman, P.K., Park, J.-Won, & Hasan, H. (2003). The application of activity theory to WMC. In H. Hasan, E. Gould, I. Verenikina (Eds.), *Information Systems and Activity Theory Volume 3: Expanding the Horizon. (pp.122-140).* Wollongong: University of Wollongong Press.
36. Mani, I. & Klein, G.L.(2005). Evaluating intelligence analysis arguments in open-ended situations. *Proceedings of the 2005 International Conference on Intelligence Analysis.* McLean, VA.
37. Williams, K.D., Govan, C.L., Croker, V., Tynan, D., Cruickshank, M., & Lam, A. (2002). Investigations into differences between social- and cyberostracism. *Group Dynamics: Theory, Research and Practice, 6(1),* 65-77.
38. Orlikowski, W.J., Yates, J., Okamura, K., & Fujimoto, M. (1994). *Shaping electronic communication: The metastructuring of technology in use.* Center for Coordination Science Technical Report #155.
39. Harber, K.D. & Pennebaker, J.W. (1992). Overcoming traumatic memories. In S.A. Christianson (Ed.). *The Handbook of Emotion and Memory Research; Theory and Research.* Hillsdale, N.J.: Lawrence Erlbaum Associates.
40. King, W.J. (1997). Human-computer dyads? A survey of nonverbal behavior in human-computer systems. *Proceedings of the Workshop on Perceptual User Interfaces.* Los Alamitos, CA.
41. Yeung, D.C. & Yoshida, N. (2005). *Algorithms for identifying cognitive biases.* Unpublished manuscript.
42. Yeung, D.C. & Lowrance, J.D. (2005). *Sociopsychological assessment of an information campaign EZ.* In SEAS Multi-dimensional Templates. Available at http://seas.ai.sri.com.

# Using Importance Flooding to Identify Interesting Networks of Criminal Activity

Byron Marshall[1] and Hsinchun Chen[2]

[1] Accounting, Finance, and Information Management Department,
Oregon State University, Corvallis, OR 97331, USA
byron.marshall@bus.oregonstate.edu
[2] Department of Management Information Systems, The University of Arizona,
Tucson, AZ 85721, USA
hchen@eller.arizona.edu

**Abstract.** In spite of policy concerns and high costs, the law enforcement community is investing heavily in data sharing initiatives. Cross-jurisdictional criminal justice information (e.g., open warrants and convictions) is important, but different data sets are needed for investigational activities where requirements are not as clear and policy concerns abound. The community needs sharing models that employ obtainable data sets and support real-world investigational tasks. This work presents a methodology for sharing and analyzing investigation-relevant data. Our importance flooding application extracts interesting networks of relationships from large law enforcement data sets using user-controlled investigation heuristics and spreading activation. Our technique implements path-based interestingness rules to help identify promising associations to support creation of investigational link charts. In our experiments, the importance flooding approach outperformed relationship-weight-only models in matching expert-selected associations. This methodology is potentially useful for large cross-jurisdictional data sets and investigations.

## 1 Introduction

Events in the last several years have brought new attention to the need for cross-jurisdictional data sharing to support investigations. A number of technology-related initiatives have been undertaken. For example, the FBI sunk $170 million into a "Virtual Case File" system which was, unfortunately, considered dead on arrival [1]. It will likely be scrapped although lessons learned will benefit future systems. This high profile system failure highlights the difficulty of sharing investigational data across localities. It is even more difficult when multiple agencies are involved, as when local police departments have data of value to national or regional agencies. Computer-supported investigational models are needed to guide the development of policies, protocols, and procedures intended to increase the flow of useful information.

An effective cross-jurisdictional investigation model needs to support real analysis tasks and use data sets that can be realistically collected and shared. In previous work with the BorderSafe consortium, we developed a model for organizing local data into a network of annotated relationships between people, vehicles, and locations [2]. The

S. Mehrotra et al. (Eds.): ISI 2006, LNCS 3975, pp. 14–25, 2006.
© Springer-Verlag Berlin Heidelberg 2006

proposed methodology considers administrative, policy, and security restrictions aiming to identify a useful data representation that can be collected from existing data sets in spite of administrative and technical challenges. In this paper we explore an importance flooding approach intended to extract interesting CANs (criminal activity networks) from large collections of law enforcement data. Useful analysis models are crucial for the community because without knowing how shared data can be effectively employed, costly resources will likely be wasted in expensive but un-workable integration efforts.

Network-based techniques are commonly used in real-world investigational processes. Criminals who work together in a pattern of criminal activity can be charged with conspiracy and taken off the street for a longer period of time. While many traditional data mining techniques produce un-explainable results, criminal association networks are understandable and actionable. Many networks of associations are "drawn" only in the minds of the investigators, but visual network depictions called link charts are commonly used in important cases. Link charts combine multiple events to depict a focused set of criminal activity. Selected associations may be focused on particular crime types, localities, or target individuals. Link charts are used to focus investigations, communicate within law enforcement agencies, and present data in court. Link chart creation is a manual, expensive, but valuable investigational technique.

An analysis support technique needs to be adaptable because investigational resources are limited and investigational assignments are distributed. Investigators come to a case with specific concerns and relevant experience. Because criminal records are incomplete [3] and missing or ambiguous data such as family relationships are important, rules of thumb (heuristics) need to play a role in analysis if the results are to be accepted by the investigational community. For example, a fraud investigation unit may be only incidentally concerned with drug trafficking. When a crime analyst makes a link chart manually, they look up individual cases, make a judgment as to the importance of particular bits of information, and add information that is not recorded in the regular police records. These investigational parameters change over time. For instance, if the fraud unit realizes that many fraud cases are related to methamphetamine trafficking, they might seek to re-analyze data with an emphasis on this important correlation. Policy concerns also impact analysis. For example, because investigators need to respect individual privacy, law enforcement prefers to focus on individual target(s) rather than "fishing" for patterns in public records.

In any case, one key function of the investigation process is the generation of useful leads. Within this broader context, this paper studies a methodology for increasing the efficiency of link chart creation to (1) save time and money, (2) allow the technique to be used in more investigations, and (3) employ large quantities of available data. Such a model can be used to support investigations and to guide the implementation of data sharing systems. Our research focus can be summarized in a single research question: *How can we effectively identify interesting sub networks useful for link chart creation from associations found in a large collection of criminal incidents employing domain knowledge to generate useful investigational leads and support criminal conspiracy investigations?*

## 2   Literature Review

Network analysis has a long history in criminal investigation [4-6]. In [3], Sparrow highlights the importance of social network analysis techniques in this important domain, identifying a wide variety of network structure measures and logically connecting those measures with investigational implications. For example, he points out that questions such as " *'who is central to the organization?', 'which names in this database appear to be aliases?', 'which three individuals' removal or incapacitation would sever this drug-supply network?', 'what role or roles does a specific individual appear to play within a criminal organization?' or 'which communications links within a international terrorist fraternity are likely to be most worth monitoring?' "* (p 252)  would all be familiar to social network analysis practitioners.

Some of the analysis techniques anticipated by Sparrow have been explored in more recent work. [6] categorized criminal network analysis tools into three generations. First generation tools take a manual approach allowing investigators to depict criminal activity as a network of associations. Second generation systems include Netmap, Analyst's Notebook, Watson, and the COPLINK Visualizer [7-9]. These tools provide various levels of interaction and pattern identification, representing information using various visual clues and algorithms to help the user understand charted relationships. Third generation tools would possess advanced analytical capabilities. This class of tool has yet to be widely deployed but techniques and methodologies have been explored in the research literature. [5] introduces genetic algorithms to implement subgraph isomorphism and classification via social network analysis metrics for intelligence analysis. Network analysis tools to measure centrality, detect subgroups, and identify interaction patterns were used in [10], and the topological characteristics of cross-jurisdictional criminal networks are studied in [11].

Shortest path measures have received particular attention. One important consideration in an investigation is the identification of the closest associates of target individuals. A variation of this analysis tries to identify the shortest path between two target individuals. These ideas, closest associates and shortest path, are clearly relevant in link chart analysis. CrimeLink Explorer employed relation strength heuristics to support shortest-path analysis [12]. Based on conversations with domain experts, they weighted associations by: (1) crime-type and person-role, (2) shared addresses or phones, and (3) incident co-occurrence. An algorithm for shortest path analysis for criminal networks was implemented and tested in [13]. Because criminal networks can be very large and very dense, the computational burden required to identify the shortest path between two individuals can be significant. [13] addresses this using a carefully crafted computational strategy.

Building on this research, we want to help identify "interesting" subsets of large criminal activity networks. The interestingness (or importance) issue is a well recognized problem in the association rule mining field. Interestingness measures seek to assign a ranking to discovered associations based on some interestingness calculation methodology [14]. The various measures of interestingness can be classified into two categories: objective measures and subjective measures [15]. Objective measures are generally statistical and include confidence and support. Subjective interestingness measures, on the other hand, can be classified into two groups: actionable and unexpected. [16] notes that beliefs are important in identifying interesting associations.

Results can be filtered by encoding user beliefs (e.g., expected or potentially action-able relationship or patterns) using some "grammar" and comparing extracted rela-tionships to that grammar [17, 18]. A way to incorporate beliefs is important for automatic interestingness analysis.

Notions of interestingness have received special attention in the context of data that can be represented as a network. Some researchers emphasize that interestingness is relative. For example, a "root set of nodes" within a larger network are used to en-hance relevance searching in [19]. They describe a general class of algorithms that use explicit definitions of relative importance. The two main intuitions behind the ap-proach are that 1) two nodes are related according to the paths that connect them, and 2) the longer a path is, the less importance is conferred along that path. Using a scalar coefficient, White and Smyth pass smaller amounts of importance as the distance be-tween a pair of nodes increases. They note several ways of choosing non-overlapping paths between node pairs. These notions of relative importance align well with the cognitive model described by investigators we have talked with. Investigations begin with some target suspect(s) and look for close associates to identify leads.

In [20] novel network paths (not just nodes or links) are identified to reveal inter-esting information. This was a novel way of analyzing the HEP-Th bibliography data set from the Open Task of the 2003 KDD Cup [21]. Bibliographic citation data was analyzed to answer questions such as "which people are interestingly connected to C.N. Pope?" The basic notion of their analysis was to detect interesting short paths through a network rather than to detect interesting nodes. They categorized link types and used multiple node types in their network. So, for instance, universities were as-sociated with authors who had published a paper while affiliated with the university, and authors were associated with their co-authors. Without putting in specific rules defining "interesting" their algorithm discovered that Mr. H. Lu. was the most inter-esting person relative to C.N. Pope because he interacted with Pope along a variety of network paths. These paths take the following form:

[Lu]-writes-[Paper1]-cites-[Paper2]-written_by-[Pope]
[Lu]-authors-[Paper1]-authored_by-[Pope], and
[Lu]-authors-[Paper1]-authored_by-[Person1]-authors-[Paper2]-authored_by-[Pope].

This notion that interestingness is path-based rather than node-based is applicable to criminal investigations. For example, one analyst working on a Fraud/Meth link chart noted that she was more interested in people who sold drugs and were associ-ated both with people who sold methamphetamines and people who committed fraud. This kind of association pattern is a short path through the criminal activity network.

## 3   Creating Link Charts by Filtering CANs

Previous work has shown that criminal records can be usefully depicted in a link chart but more advanced methodologies such as criminal network analysis and shortest path evaluation have not been used to directly address the important task of link chart crea-tion. The association rule mining literature suggests several approaches intended to identify interesting items in networks but previous criminal association computations simplify criminal networks using some single measure of association strength.

Our goal is to combine and adapt criminal network and interestingness techniques to support investigational tasks while allowing for the real-world challenges of this important domain. If effective, we expect such a methodology to be useful in a variety of real-world network evaluation applications. Based on our review of the literature and our conversations with investigators we developed a list of design goals:

1. Allow query-specific information to fill in missing data.
2. Incorporate domain-appropriate heuristics (or beliefs) to support analysis, encoding these heuristics in a format that can be adjusted at query time for new insights.
3. Tolerate missing and ambiguous data. While missing information is expected to hamper analysis, a good methodology for this domain needs to be somewhat tolerant of data limitations.
4. Be target focused.

Importantly, these goals are applicable to smaller local investigations but are also relevant to large-scale inter-jurisdictional investigations.

We propose the use of an importance flooding algorithm to identify interesting sub networks within larger CANs to help detectives interactively construct investigational link charts. This represents one phase of a larger process in which police records are organized for sharing as described in [2]. Police records from local jurisdictions are converted into a common schema. Person records are matched to form a network of incident-based associations. Then, with a target list of suspects and sets of link weight rules and importance heuristics, individuals are importance ranked for inclusion in investigation-specific link charts. The basic intuitions of the algorithm are (1) associates of interesting people become relatively more interesting and (2) both a person's past activity and their involvement in interesting association patterns establish initial importance. The algorithm considers two key network elements in its calculation (1) association closeness and (2) importance evaluation. The calculation leverages association closeness measures as suggested by [12], scalar coefficients as in [19], and leverages a path-based notion of interestingness reminiscent of the methodology used in [20]. The algorithm proceeds in four basic steps:

1. Weights are assigned to network links.
2. Initial importance values are assigned to network nodes.
3. Importance is passed to nearby nodes generating a final score for each node.
4. A network subset is selected starting with target nodes and best first search.

Our algorithm employs 6 components: a set of nodes, a set of associations such that each association connects two of the nodes and is described by a set of properties, a set of rule-based relation weights consisting of a single link weight for each unique pair of nodes connected in the associations, initial importance rules, a decaying distribution function, and a set of starting nodes.

In this paper, we test our approach by comparing the output of an importance flooding computation with two link charts which had previously been created by a crime analyst from the Tucson Police Department (TPD). The nodes in the network we test in this work are individuals found in an integrated TPD/Pima County Sheriff's Department data set. We used only people as nodes although the algorithm could also evaluate location or vehicle entities. The association properties we considered include crime type, from role (the role of the first of the two nodes in the association), to role (the role of the second node in the association), and crime date. These properties were selected so that we could use a close approximation of the association strength formula presented in [12].

Relation weights ranging from 0 to 1 are assigned to each association found in the records. Relation weights are assigned to node pairs by evaluating the corresponding associations as a function of the number of associations and properties of those associations. We used relatively simple heuristics in the testing presented here. For example, our rules expressed a strong relational weight for a pair of individuals who were both recorded as arrestees in the same incident, but a lower weight for associations where the two individuals were considered investigational leads in the same incident. In addition to these initial link weights, frequency of association was considered. As suggested by [11], when a pair of individuals appears together in four or more police incidents a maximal relation weight of 1 is assigned regardless of crime role or incident type. When less than four incidents connect two individuals, we multiply the strongest association weight by 3/5, the second strongest by 1/5, and the third strongest by 1/5 and sum the products. The 3/5, 1/5, 1/5 distribution is somewhat arbitrary but it is reasonable in light of previous research.

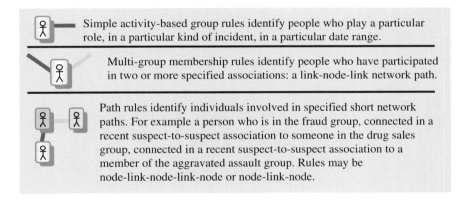

**Fig. 1.** Three Types of Initial Importance Rules

Initial importance values are assigned to nodes using path-based importance heuristics. In our current implementation, we accept three kinds of importance rules: (1) activity-based group rules, (2) multi-group membership rules, and (3) path rules. Figure 1 describes the three types of rules. Weight values are assigned to each rule, each node is evaluated for group membership based on the rule, and a node is assigned an initial importance score equal to the sum of the weights of all groups to which the node belongs. Importance values are normalized to fall between 0 and 1 and target nodes are always assigned a score of 1. The link weight and importance values assigned in our implementation were derived from previous research or developed in conversation with crime analysts and require only information that is likely to be available in a cross-jurisdictional setting.

In these experiments, our decaying distribution function used .5 for any directly connected nodes and .25 for transitively connected nodes and the target nodes are identified by the analyst. Pseudo code for the iterative importance flooding calculation is shown below. Each node N1 of N has: a unique "ID," an initial score "INIT," a previous score "PREV," and an accumulated amount of importance added in this iteration "ADD." The algorithm includes a main loop and a recursive path tracing method. A maximum node importance score of Init+Prev+Add "MAXVAL" is maintained for each iteration as each node and path is processed. This score is used to normalize the values at the end of each iteration. A Decaying Distribution Depth "DDD" is used by the computation and is set equal to the number of terms in the scalar coefficient (e.g., if the scalar coefficient is [.5, .25], DDD is 2).

```
Main Process:
Initialize all nodes N1 in N: N1.PREV= 0, N1.ADD = 0
For each iteration
   For each node N1 in N    // Call recursive path tracing
      PassAmt = N1.PREV + N1.INIT
      PathList = N1.ID, PathLen = 1
      pathTrace (PassAmount, PathList, PathLen)
   For each node N1 in N // Normalize and re-initialize
      N1.PREV = (N1.PREV + N1.INIT + N1.ADD) / MAXVAL
      N1.ADD = 0
   // reinforce the importance investigational targets
   For each node T1 in the TargetNode List: T1.PREV = 1


Recursive Path Tracing:
pathTrace (PassAmount, PathList, PathLen)
   PassingNode = The last node included in PathList
   NumOfAssoc = The # of nodes associated with PassingNode
   For each node Na associated with PassingNode
   if Na is not already included in PathList
      RELWGT = the relation weight for the pair [PassingNode,Na]
      DECAYRATE = the decay coefficient for PathLength
      PASSONAMT = PassAmt * RELWGT * DECAYRATE * (1 / NumOfAssoc)
      Na.ADD = Na.ADD + PASSONAMT
   if PathLen < DDD  // traverse paths to length DDD
      pathTrace (PASSONAMT, PathList + Na.ID, PathLen + 1)
```

Finally, a best first search algorithm uses the resulting importance scores to expand the network from the target nodes to a network of some specified size. The nodes in the starting list of target nodes are placed into a list of visited nodes and into a priority queue with a priority value of 2. Nodes are sequentially popped from the queue until enough nodes have been selected. As each node is popped, the algorithm adds it to a list of selected nodes and then searches for all other nodes associated with that node. If the associated node is not already in the visited node list, it is added to the priority queue with its importance score (which can range from 0 to 1) as its priority value. Intuitively, the algorithm asks: of all the nodes attached to any of the selected nodes, which has the highest importance score? An analyst using the output might well consider which node to add to a link chart next using a similar procedure.

# 4  Experimentation

To explore the usefulness of our methodology we needed a human-generated link chart and a large criminal activity network, along with heuristics and targets for a particular investigation. We obtained access to a large link chart prepared for the TPD fraud unit. It depicts key people involved in both methamphetamine trafficking and fraud. The chart includes 110 people and originally took 6 weeks to create.

We drew our network from incidents recorded by the Tucson Police Department and the Pima County Sheriff's Department. The records were converted to a common schema (COPLINK) and associations were created whenever two people were listed in an incident. We recorded "crime type," "from role" (the 1st person's role), "to role" (the 2nd person's role), and "crime date." Using practitioner-suggested guidelines, individuals were matched on first name, last name, and date of birth. Some correct matches were missed due to data entry errors or intentional deception. The combined set includes records from 5.2 million incidents involving 2.2 million people. To approximate the search space considered by the analyst, we include only people within 2 associational hops of the targets. Investigators tell us they are generally not interested past that limit. We ignored records added after the chart was drawn. This filtering process resulted in 4,877 individuals for the fraud/meth investigation, including 73 of the 110 "correct" individuals depicted in the manually created link chart.

The heuristic components came from two sources: previous research guided the development of the very general link weight heuristics and case priorities dictated the importance rules. Each association between a pair of individuals was evaluated: Suspect/Suspect Relationships = .99; Suspect/Not Suspect = .5, Not Suspect/Not Suspect = .3. A single association strength was then assigned as follows: 4 or more associations, weight = 1; else, $\sum$ (strongest relation * .6, 2nd * .2 , and 3rd * .2). Initial importance calculations included group, multi-group, and path rules. Several relevant groups were identified by the analyst: Aggravated Assault (A), Drug Sales (S), Drug Possession (P), Fraud (F). Membership in any of these groups added an importance value of 3 to an individual's total initial importance score. Membership in any two groups added 3 more, and membership in all three groups added 5. Participation in an (A)-(D)-(F) added 5 and participation in paths (A)-(D), (A)-(F), (D)-(F), or (P)-(F) added 3. For example, in cases where the suspect in an assault (A) was connected in some incident to a suspected drug seller (D) who was connected to a suspected check washer (F), an initial importance value of 5 was added to each of the nodes.

We compared our algorithm's results to the human-drawn link chart, considering how the algorithm might impact the effectiveness of time spent working on the link chart. When an analyst creates a chart, they begin with one or more target individuals, look for associations involving those individuals, and evaluate each potential associate to see if they are important enough to be included in the chart. Reviewing more promising associates first would allow creation of a good chart in less time. In our tests we started with the same information considered by the human analyst and produced an ordered list of individuals such that selecting them in order forms a network. Selection methodologies that listed the "correct" individuals (those selected by the human analyst) earlier in the list were considered to be "better." We compared several methods of ordering the lists, including several variations of importance flooding:

- *Breadth First Search* provides a baseline for comparison. Start with the target(s) and choose direct associates, then choose indirect associates.
- *Closest Associate* is a link-chart application of previously proposed shortest path algorithms. New individuals are added to the network in order of association closeness to someone already included in the network.
- *Importance Flooding* was used to rank all the individuals. New individuals are added to the network by choosing the highest ranked individual associated with any of the people already included in the network.
- *Path Heuristics with No Flooding* employed the path-based heuristics to rank importance but did not flood importance to nearby nodes. This was intended to show that both the initial importance of a node and its structural place in the network impact its chart-worthiness.
- *Node-only Importance Flooding* demonstrated that the path-based heuristics add to the algorithm's effectiveness as a supplement to node-only analysis.

For comparison we used measuring function *A* which operates for a ranking method (technique) over a size range. As each node is added to a network, we can compute the total number of nodes added divided by the number of "correct" nodes added. This ratio computes the number of nodes an analyst would have to consider for each correct node considered. A smaller number is better in that the analyst would have spent less time on un-interesting nodes. Our measure *A* is the average of the ratio over a range. For example, consider *A (importance flooding) at 250* = average ratio of selected nodes to "correct" nodes, selected by the importance flooding algorithm, when the number of selected nodes is 1,2,3…250. Our hypotheses are shown in Table 1.

**Table 1.** Hypotheses

| Techniques: | |
|---|---|
| • BFS = breadth first (rank by # of hops)<br>• CA = closest associates | • IMP = importance flooding<br>• PATH = path heuristics, no flooding<br>• NO = only node heuristics, flooding |
| All techniques improve on BFS | |
| • H1a: A(IMP) < A(BFS) *Accepted* | • H1b: A(CA) < A(BFS) *Accepted* |
| Importance flooding outperforms closest associates | |
| • H2: A(IMP) < A(CA) *Accepted* | |
| Importance flooding outperforms path heuristics with no flooding | |
| • H3: A(IMP) < A(PATH) *Accepted at 500,1000 & 2000 but NOT for 100,250* | |
| Importance flooding outperforms node only heuristics | |
| • H4: A(IMP) < A(NO) *Accepted* | |
| Hypotheses are expected to hold for 100, 250, 500, 1000, and 2000 selected nodes.<br>*Accepted Hypotheses were significant at p=.01* | |

Performance results for the basic methods (breadth first, closest associate, and importance flooding) are reported in Figure 2. The importance flooding approach consistently found more of the correct nodes for any given number of nodes selected. The closest associate method seems to have generally outperformed breadth first search. In addition, based on the acceptance of hypotheses 3 and 4, we observe that both the flooding and the path heuristics added something to the effectiveness of our final result because omitting either part reduced accuracy. When a second link chart was also analyzed, the importance flooding algorithm again outperformed the best first search and closest associate methods. Detailed results are omitted because of space limitations.

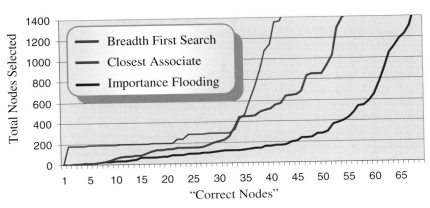

**Fig. 2.** Comparison of Ranking Methods for the Fraud/Meth Link Chart. The importance flooding algorithm (blue) consistently outperformed other methods.

## 5  Discussion and Future Directions

Our approach differs from previous work in several ways. (1) It is applied directly to the task of link chart generation. Previous work has hinted at this kind of application but has not experimented with actual charts. (2) We combine structure (closeness-weighted associations) and activity-based importance heuristics (e.g. "people who have been involved in fraud") in our computation instead of social network measures based on closeness-weighted associations. (3) We encode the users' importance notions as short network paths. This can be simple grouping (e.g. people who have been suspects in fraud incidents) but we also leverage relational patterns. For example, one of the heuristics we use in our testing process captures the analyst's input that she was more interested in people who sold drugs and were associated both with people who sold methamphetamines and people who committed fraud. (4) Our approach is target-directed. These advances have both theoretical and practical implications.

We tested our methodology using data that could be realistically generated in the law enforcement domain. The network representation used in our study can be (and was) generated from actual criminal records systems recorded in different records management systems in different jurisdictions. Our methodology does not require analysis of difficult to process items such as MO (modus operandi) or physical descriptions. What's more, our current representation categorizes crimes using standard crime types which do not differentiate, for instance, between drug crimes involving methamphetamines vs. drug crimes involving heroine or marijuana. Certainly these features can play an important investigational role but extraction of such details might be expensive, inconsistent, and subject to additional administrative and privacy restrictions in a cross-jurisdictional environment. Our results demonstrate analysis value in spite of limited representational detail. With all that being said, additional features could be used by the algorithm simply by changing the initial input rules. We believe the association model we propose (entities connected in labeled associations including roles, types, and dates) is flexible enough to support various investigational tasks, yet simple enough to be readily sourced from different underlying records management systems. Different analysis implementations could leverage different feature sets when the needed data was relevant and available. But even when association details cannot be shared because of policy, financial, or technical limitations, we believe many organizations would find it possible to share high level association data (e.g. Bob and Fred were both involved in a drug investigation last June) with certified law enforcement personnel from other jurisdictions.

While promising, our results need further validation. Because of restrictions on the sharing of information about old investigations, we only tested on two link charts. Even then, the nodes included in the manually prepared link chart are a "bronze standard" rather than a "gold standard." It may be that some people "should" have been included but were not because they were missed by the analyst or left off for a variety of reasons. If an individual was in prison or was working with the police as an informant, they may have been omitted from the chart. Thus we have no real objective standard to say that one chart is "correct" while all others are "incorrect." Instead we would argue that some charts are clearly better than others. Also, sensitivity to variations in computational parameters and user-provided heuristics should be explored.

More work can certainly be done in the law enforcement domain. We would like to study test cases more deeply to address several practical questions. Are some of the nodes we "suggest" good ones for analysis but left off the charts for a specific reason? How much can we improve results by adding query specific data to the importance ranking calculations? Is the technique useful for creating link charts with various purposes? Does inclusion of locations, vehicles, and border crossings enhance analysis? We plan to implement some version of the algorithm in a real-time, real-data criminal association visualization tool to support this kind of detailed work. The value of the approach may increase as data sets grow larger. In our results, the use of path heuristics with no flooding (technique PATH in Table 1) was not significantly different from the complete treatment (technique IMP) until more than 250 nodes were selected. Thus, while the path-based heuristics seem to contribute to selection value in smaller applications, flooding adds even more value in a larger context.

We plan to test importance flooding in other informal node-link knowledge representations. The algorithm is designed to overcome link and identifier ambiguity, leveraging a network's structure and semantics. The technique presented here allows us to test this basic notion in other application domains. For example, we plan to explore the use of this algorithm in selecting interesting subsets of a network of biomedical pathway relations extracted from the text of journal abstracts.

## Acknowledgements

This work was supported in part by the NSF, Knowledge Discovery and Dissemination (KDD) # 9983304. NSF, ITR: "COPLINK Center for Intelligence and Security Informatics Research - A Crime Data Mining Approach to Developing Border Safe Research". Department of Homeland Security (DHS) / Corporation for National Research Initiatives (CNRI): "Border Safe". We are also grateful to Kathy Martinjak, Tim Petersen, and Chuck Violette for their input.

# References

1. Schmitt, R.B., New FBI Software May Be Unusable, in Los Angeles Times. 2005: Los Angeles, CA.
2. Marshall, B., et al. Cross-Jurisdictional Criminal Activity Networks to Support Border and Transportation Security. in 7th International IEEE Conference on Intelligent Transportation Systems. 2004. Washington D.C.
3. Sparrow, M.K., The Application of Network Analysis to Criminal Intelligence: An Assessment of the Prospects. Social Networks, 1991. **13**(3): p. 251-274.
4. Coady, W.F., Automated Link Analysis - Artificial Intelligence-Based Tool for Investigators. Police Chief, 1985. **52**(9): p. 22-23.
5. Coffman, T., S. Greenblatt, and S. Marcus, Graph-Based Technologies for Intelligence Analysis. Communications of the ACM, 2004. **47**(3): p. 45-47.
6. Klerks, P., The Network Paradigm Applied to Criminal Organizations: Theoretical nitpicking or a relevant doctrine for investigators? Recent developments in the Netherlands. Connections, 2001. **24**(3): p. 53-65.
7. Chabrow, E., Tracking The Terrorists: Investigative skills and technology are being used to hunt terrorism's supporters, in Information Week. 2002.
8. I2. I2 Investigative Analysis Software. 2004 [cited 2004 November 29]; Available from: http://www.i2inc.com/Products/Analysts_Notebook/#.
9. KCC. COPLINK from Knowledge Computing Corp. 2004 [cited 2004 November 29]; Available from: http://www.coplink.net/vis1.htm.
10. Xu, J. and H. Chen. Untangling Criminal Networks: A Case Study. in NSF/NIJ Symp. on Intelligence and Security Informatics (ISI). 2003. Tucson, AZ: Springer.
11. Kaza, S., et al., Topological Analysis of Criminal Activity Networks: Enhancing Transportation Security. IEEE Transactions on Intelligent Transportation Systems, forthcoming, 2005.
12. Schroeder, J., J. Xu, and H. Chen. CrimeLink Explorer: Using Domain Knowledge to Facilitate Automated Crime Association Analysis. in Intelligence and Security Informatics, Proceedings of ISI-2004, Lecture Notes in Computer Science. 2003: Springer.
13. Xu, J. and H. Chen, Fighting Organized Crime: Using Shortest-Path Algorithms to Identify Associations in Criminal Networks. Decision Support Systems, 2004. **38**(3): p. 473-487.
14. Hilderman, R.J. and H.J. Hamilton, Evaluation of Interestingness Measures for Ranking Discovered Knowledge. Lecture Notes in Computer Science, 2001. **2035**: p. 247-259.
15. Silberschatz, A. and A. Tuzhilin, What Makes Patterns Interesting in Knowledge Discovery Systems. IEEE Transactions on Data and Knowledge Engineering, 1996. **8**: p. 970-974.
16. Padmanabhan, B. and A. Tuzhilin, Unexpectedness as a Measure of Interestingness in Knowledge Discovery. Decision Support Systems, 1999. **27**(3): p. 303-318.
17. Sahar, S. On Incorporating Subjective Interestingness into the Mining Process. in Data Mining, 2002. ICDM 2002. Proceedings. 2002 IEEE International Conference on. 2002.
18. Sahar, S. Interestingness Preprocessing. in Data Mining, 2001. ICDM 2001, Proceedings IEEE International Conference on. 2001.
19. White, S. and P. Smyth. Algorithms for Estimating Relative Importance in Networks. in ACM SIGKDD internt'l conference on knowledge discovery and data mining. 2003. Washington, D. C.: ACM Press.
20. Lin, S.-d. and H. Chalupsky, Using Unsupervised Link Discovery Methods to Find Interesting Facts and Connections in a Bibliography Dataset. SIGKDD Explor. Newsl., 2003. **5**(2): p. 173-178.
21. Gehrke, J., P. Ginsparg, and P. Ginsparg, Overview of the 2003 KDD Cup. SIGKDD Explor. Newsl., 2003. **5**(2): p. 149-151.

# Towards Automatic Event Tracking

Clive Best, Bruno Pouliquen, Ralf Steinberger, Erik Van der Goot, Ken Blackler,
Flavio Fuart, Tamara Oellinger, and Camelia Ignat

Institute for Protection and Security of the Citizen, Joint Research Centre,
European Commission, Italy
Clive.best@jrc.it

**Abstract.** An automatic news tracking and analysis system which records world events over long time periods is described. It allows to track country specific news, the activities of individual persons and groups, to derive trends, and to provide data for further analysis and research. The data source is the Europe Media Monitor (EMM) which monitors news from around the world in real time via the Internet and from various News Agencies. EMM's main purpose is to provide rapid feedback of press coverage and breaking news for European Policy Makers. Increasingly, however it is being used for security applications and for foreign policy monitoring. This paper describes how language technologies and clustering techniques have been applied to the 30,000 daily news reports to derive the top stories in each of 13 languages, to locate events geospatially, and to extract and record entities involved. Related stories have been linked across time and across languages, allowing for national comparisons and to derive name variants. Results and future plans are described.

## 1 Introduction

Like most governmental and international organizations, the European Union monitors media reports concerning EU policies and potential threats. A major challenge since 2004 for the EU has been the need to handle some 25 different languages. The Europe Media Monitor [1] was developed to meet that challenge by scanning over 800 web sites and 15 national news agencies 24/7. About 30,000 articles are detected and processed each day in over 30 languages. The full text of each article is filtered against 10,000 multilingual keyword combinations to sort each article into one or more of 600 topic definitions. Alerts keep subscribers informed of immediate updates on key subjects by email and SMS. Each alert is a predefined combination of keywords conditions which describe one of the 600 topics. However this doesn't cover the unexpected "Breaking News" story. For this purpose a real-time breaking news system was developed which tracks the occurrence of capitalized keywords across languages and can detect sudden increases of existing keywords or the sudden emergence of new keywords. The system is very successful at quickly detecting major breaking news stories. EMM results are published through an automatically generated NewsBrief, a public version of which can be seen at http://press.jrc.it and through electronically edited reviews which are distributed internally in the European Commission. The NewsBrief has a similar functionality to Google News and Yahoo News, but a much wider topic coverage which includes all countries of the world.

S. Mehrotra et al. (Eds.): ISI 2006, LNCS 3975, pp. 26–34, 2006.

Increasingly EMM is being asked to review and analyse past events to produce situation reports for conflicts and crises in various parts of the world. Monitoring Avian Flu reports is an example of the type of issue EMM is being asked to study. Similarly, terrorism is of particular concern for the EU following the London and Madrid attacks. Therefore research was started in 2003 into automated methods to improve the news analysis and to derive additional information in as many languages as possible.

## 2  EMM

The Europe Media Monitor uses an XML/XSLT technique to detect headlines published on monitored web sites. Each site is checked upto every 10 minutes. Individual web pages are first converted to XHTML and then transformed to an RSS (Really Simple Syndication) 2.0 format using a stylesheet for each site. New headlines are detected by comparing the current content to a cache.

EMM's Alert system is it's most unique feature. It drives most of the content and adds value to news monitored. The overall objective is to process as rapidly as possible each discovered article and decide which subjects (Alert definitions) are mentioned. If an alert criterion is satisfied the article is appended to a result RSS file [2], one for each alert definition. If a user has subscribed to an immediate email alert for that topic then a processor is called to send the article summary by email. If a special alert called SMSauto has been satisfied and certain timing criteria are satisfied then an automatic SMS message is sent to a small number of persons.

A number of technical challenges have been overcome in implementing the alert system. Firstly, the real textual content from web pages needs to be extracted from raw HTML. It is no good triggering alerts on adverts or on sidebar menu items which have nothing to do with the content of the web page. Secondly the alert system must be extremely fast to keep up with incoming articles and to alert interested persons as required. Specialised algorithms have been developed for EMMalert system. The alert processor can scan a text of a thousand words against combinations of 10,000 keywords and trigger conditions in 100 msec an a modern PC.

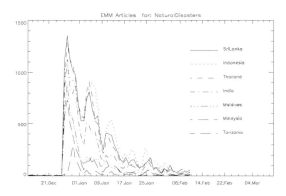

**Fig. 1.** Raw alert statistics showing number of articles per day for S.E. Asian countries following the 2004 Tsunami

The alert system keeps hourly statistics of the number of articles detected for each Alert in the system. This is stored in XML files accessible on the web server. One file is stored every day containing the hourly values and taken together form long term time series of event statistics. As major events occur – so their development is recorded in the statistics files. As an example Figure 1 shows the number of articles per day for different countries following the Asian Tsunami as recorded by EMM's alert system. It can be seen that "breaking news" within a given topic area can be defined as a large positive time differential in the statistics plot for that alert.

A more detailed analysis of daily news is performed after midnight GMT. All detected articles in each of currently 13 languages are processed together in order to automatically deduce the top stories and derive related information. In particular keyword and entity extraction from news, place name identification, multilingual thesaurus indexing, and the recording of EMM topic alerts allow to track news topics across time and language.

Often a top story will describe one single event, but just as often it will describe a reaction to an event, or an ongoing investigation. Research is therefore beginning on identifying individual events and recording their attributes. This will improve event logging, trend analysis and conflict analysis. However, the results achieved so far by the existing analysis are already greatly improving analysis and trend recording. This analysis is described below

### 2.1  News Keyword Identification

The objective is to numerically identify clusters of similar news items in order to identify the major news items each day. All articles processed by EMM are collected together in each language for processing after midnight GMT. For English this represents something like 4000 articles per day. A signature for each article is then derived using a large reference corpus of news articles in the given language. This consists of a weighted list of keywords calculated as follows. After removing stop words from the text frequency word list is calculated and compared with frequency lists in the long term corpus. This corpus consists of 6 months of information in each of the languages. The most relevant keywords are then identified for each article using a Log-Likelihood test [3]. The result of the keyword identification process is thus a representation of each incoming news article in a vector space.

### 2.2  Geographic Place Name Recognition and Geocoding

Place name recognition is achieved using a multilingual gazetteer [4], which includes exonyms (foreign language equivalents) and disambiguates between places with the same name (e.g. Paris in France rather than the other 13 places called Paris in the World). The purpose of this exercise is two fold. Firstly each place name adds to the country score for that article, which is then used for cross language linking, and secondly the place names themselves serve to "geocode" articles for map displays. The normalized country score per article is calculated by summing each country score and then performing the same log-likelihood test against the corpus for these countries.

## 2.3  Article Clustering

A bottom up algorithm is used for the clustering process. A similarity measure is defined as the cosine of the two keyword vectors for each article. Each pair of articles is compared for similarity. The vector for each pair of articles consists of its keywords and their log-likelihood values, enhanced with the country profile values. If two or more documents have a similarity > 90% they are considered duplicates. The two most similar articles are then combined as a cluster with vector equal to the sum of both. The intra-cluster similarity is then defined as the cosine between members of a cluster and overall vector. For the clustering process the new cluster node is treated as any other article, but the weight will increase accordingly. The process is repeated until all articles have been paired off either into growing clusters or single articles.

In a next step, the tree of clusters is searched for the major news clusters of the day, by identifying all subclusters which fulfill the following conditions : 1) intra-cluster similarity above a threshold of 50% 2) the number of feeds is at 2 (news is considered significant when published in two different newspapers). This is to avoid dominance from a single source and ensure coherent clusters. The results are very good, yielding 10- 20 major (> 10 articles) clusters for each day in each language. The centroid article in each cluster is taken as the most representative for display purposes. Figure 2 shows such a cluster tree after applying these rules.

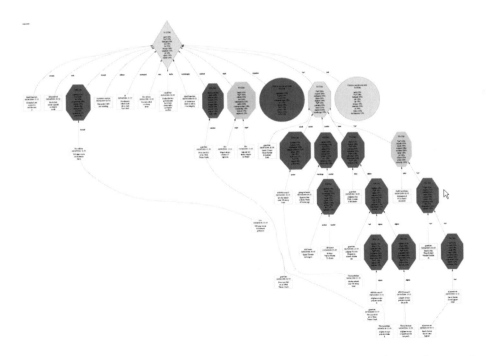

**Fig. 2.** An example of a cluster tree derived by the algorithm. The tree is cut whenever the intra-cluster similarity is <50%.

## 2.4  Entity Extraction

The text of all articles in a cluster is scanned for occurrences of named entities recorded in a database. This database of known entities is a growing resource through a procedure for entity recognition using lexical patterns. These are of two types. Firstly "title" patterns like "former president" and "Doctor" are identified Secondly common first names in different languages also trigger the name recognition algorithm. Disambiguation rules are applied to help distinguish between places and persons.

Once a new named entity has been identified, a check is made to see if this is a potential name variant of an existing entity in the database. Small language variants of names are common, as are spelling variants in a single language. A fuzzy match based on a percentage of letter n-gram changes will store the new name as a variant of an existing name. The on-line resource Wikipedia [6] also provides a ready made list of language variants covering famous persons. The identification of name variants is also important for the next stage in the analysis – cross-lingual cluster linking. This algorithm is described in [7].

## 2.5  Cross Lingual Temporal Cluster Matching

The cross-lingual linking of daily news clusters is based on three criteria. Firstly the use of a multilingual thesaurus classifier, secondly on comparing identified countries, and thirdly using name variants of referenced entities. Previous work [5] has identified document profiles (keyword rankings) which represent Eurovoc [8] classifiers (thesaurus nodes) in currently 6 EU languages. The keywords from each language cluster are compared to these profiles to match potential Eurovoc IDs. Potential links are then detected when clusters in different languages match the same Eurovoc IDs. The second criterion uses the country scores for clusters. described above, matched against country IDs. The third criterion uses matching name variants from different language clusters. These three criteria are combined in the ratios 50% Eurovoc IDs, 30% Countries and 20% Entities to trigger a cluster match – currently score > 30%.

Temporal matching in the same language is an easier problem and  only cluster keywords are compared. Currently clusters from the previous day are matched if Keyword score > 50%.

## 2.6  Results and Current Status

The daily cluster analysis has been running since beginning 2003, with continuous improvements. Today it is performed in 13 languages including Russian, Farsi and Arabic. There are usually 10-15 large clusters with over 5 members per major language, and many (over 100 in English) small ones. Each cluster is represented by the centroid article of the cluster. This is the article with the closest cosine similarity to the vector sum of all members. The results are then published daily on the "News Explorer" website http://press.jrc.it/NewsExplorer.  All clusters are "geocoded" using the place names identified and a gazetteer [4] and then presented in a map interface using Worldkit [12]. Clusters can be navigated across languages and time giving a very broad overview on world news reporting both by country of origin and places mentioned.

About 300,000 entities (persons and organizations) have been automatically identified since 2003. All cluster related information including places, EMM can be linked to individual entities. This allows for a number of novel analyses to be done.

## 2.7  Entity Tracking

A number of relationships can be identified about an individual entity over long time periods. Firstly all related news clusters mentioning a given person can be identified, and these can then be tracked back over long. Secondly other persons and organizations mentioned within the same news clusters can then be linked together. One problem with blindly linking persons mentioned in the same news article, is that certain persons, for example George W Bush, tend to be mentioned in many different contexts. Therefore a method to enhance the most associated persons was invented [11]. This enhances links most associated with a single cluster, topic or person and is defined as:

$$w_{e_1,e_2} = \ln(C_{e_1,e_2}) \cdot \frac{2 \cdot C_{e_1,e_2}}{\left(C_{e_1} + C_{e_2}\right)} \cdot \frac{1}{1 + \ln(A_{e_1} \cdot A_{e_2})}$$

where $C_{e_1,e_2}$ is the number of clusters the two entities appear together and $C_{e_1}$ and $C_{e_2}$ are the total number of clusters for each individual entity. $A_{e_1}$ and $A_{e_2}$ are the number of other entities each is associated with.

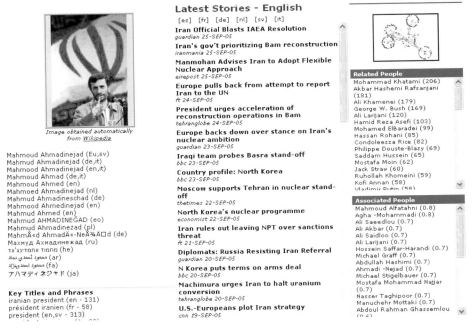

**Fig. 3.** Automatic Profile generation for Iranian President: Mahmoud Ahmadinejad. Shown on the left are the various name variants, in the centre the latest news reports and on the right related and associated entities.

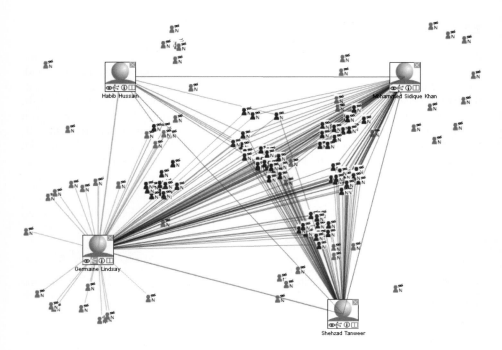

**Fig. 4.** London Bombers Network. Individual entities linked to each of the bombers are displayed. Common entities between two or more bombers are highlighted. Each can be investigated further through their news reports or through their relationships.

A searchable index of all entities has also been generated and is available through the web site to find any named identity and to visualize the derived information. Identified name variants are displayed together with most recent news topics, related and associated persons (Figure 3). A social network can be visualized showing these relationships graphically and allows further navigation options to open further relationships. The searchable index also allows locating any two or more random entities and then visualising whether these entities are linked through common clusters. Figure 4 shows part of the automatically derived network for the July 7th London Bombers.

## 2.8   Linking Entities to EMM Alerts

The EMM Alert system records articles which mention a particular topic. Each country in the world forms a single topic. Furthermore certain topics are defined as "themes" and articles are logged which trigger both a country and a theme as are statistics on these combinations. This allows EMM to produce automated news maps [9] and also to define normalised thematic indicators for countries [10]. Applying the entity analysis has now allowed us to also identify the most associated persons for each country and indeed for any other EMM Alert. This is being applied initially for automatic country tracking as shown for Pakistan in Figure 4. Similarly persons most in the news each day and their media coverage comparisons across different national media also become possible since the sources are known. This can be important to compare the impact of a statement for example by a world leader in different parts of the world.

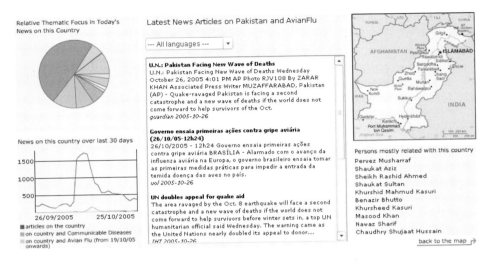

**Fig. 5.** Automatic VIP identification associated with Pakistan combined with EMM Alert statistics trends. The peak is the recent earthquake.

## 3   Future Work

Work is now beginning on deriving details of individual events by applying rule based algorithms to lead sentences in news clusters. The idea is to automate the quantitative deduction and recording of "who did what to whom where and with what consequences". One of the motivations for this work is to automatically log violent events, namely: the location where they occurred, the number of casualties and who was involved. This will then supply data for country conflict assessment studies, terrorism knowledge bases and general situation monitoring. Although human editors may give more accurate results, variations between individuals and their selection criteria means that biases can influence comparisons and trends. Automatic event extraction has the advantage of being objective, quantitative and time independent even if absolute accuracy is less.

## 4   Conclusions

An automatic news analysis and recording system is in operation and can be referenced on the Internet. Novel features are the cross-lingual linkage of news, entities and places. 300,000 persons have been derived from just over 2 years of news analysis and automatic name variants deduced. Linking this with the existing EMM alert system has made possible automated country, topic and person tracking.

# References

1. Clive Best et al. Europe Media Monitor – System Description, EUR Report 22173 EN 2006, http://press.jrc.it
2. Really Simple Syndication V 2.0 Specifications: http://blogs.law.harvard.edu/tech/rss
3. Dunning T. (1994). *Statistical Identification of Language*. Computing Research Laboratory Technical Memo MCCS 94-273, New Mexico State University, Las Cruces, New Mexico, USA, 31 p. Also available at http://citeseer.nj.nec.com/dunning94statistical.html
4. Multilingual Gazetteer - KNAB project (http://www.eki.ee/knab/knab.htm) of the Institute of the Estonian Language
5. Steinberger Ralf, Pouliquen Bruno & Camelia Ignat (2004) *Exploiting Multilingual Nomenclatures and Language-Independent Text Features as an Interlingua for Cross-lingual Text Analysis Applications*. In: Information Society 2004 (IS'2004) - Proceedings B of the 7th International Multiconference - Language Technologies, pages 2-12. Ljubljana, Slovenia, 13-14 October 2004.
6. Wikipedia, the free encyclopedia - http://www.wikipedia.org/
7. Pouliquen Bruno, Ralf Steinberger, Camelia Ignat, Irina Temnikova, Anna Widiger, Wajdi Zaghouani & Jan Žižka (2005). *Multilingual person name recognition and transliteration*. Journal CORELA - Cognition, Représentation, Langage. (available at http://edel.univ-poitiers.fr/corela/document.php?id=490 )
8. Eurovoc Multilingual Thesaurus see: http://europa.eu.int/celex/eurovoc/
9. Clive Best, Erik ven der Goot, Ken Blackler, Teofilo Garcia, David Horby, Ralf Steinberger, Bruno Pouliquen, Mapping World Events, Proceedings of Geo-Information for Disaster Management, Springer ISBN 3-540-24988-5, May 2005
10. Clive Best, Erik Van der Goot, Monica de Paola: Thematic Indicators Derived from World News Reports. Intelligence and Security Informatics, Proceedings of ISI-2005, pages 436-447 (2005)
11. Bruno Pouliquen, Ralf Steinberger, Camelia Ignat, Tamara Oellinger (forthcoming) Building and Displaying Name Relations using Automatic Unsupervised Analysis of Newspaper Articles, JADT 2006 proceedings, Besancon, France, 19-21/04/2006.
12. Worldkit Web mapping system see: http://worldkit.org/

# Interactive Refinement of Filtering Queries on Streaming Intelligence Data*

Yiming Ma and Dawit Yimam Seid

School of Information and Computer Science,
University of California, Irvine, USA
{maym, dseid}@ics.uci.edu

**Abstract.** Intelligence analysis involves routinely monitoring and correlating large amount of data streaming from multiple sources. In order to detect important patterns, the analyst normally needs to look at data gathered over a certain time window. Given the size of data and rate at which it arrives, it is usually impossible to manually process every record or case. Instead, automated filtering (classification) mechanisms are employed to identify information relevant to the analyst's task. In this paper, we present a novel system framework called FREESIA (Filter REfinement Engine for Streaming InformAtion) to effectively generate, utilize and update filtering queries on streaming data.

## 1   Introduction

Intelligence analysis involves routinely monitoring and correlating large amount of data streaming from multiple sources. In order to detect important patterns, the analyst normally needs to look at data gathered over a certain time window. However not all data is relevant for the analysts task; the relevant set of data needs to be selected from the streaming data. The task of monitoring involves a combination of automated filtering system to identify candidate cases and human analysis of cases and their related data. The filtering system is typically part of a data aggregation server to which transaction data are fed from numerous agencies in near real time. An analyst stores his task or goal specific filters that are matched to incoming data as it flows. Multiple filters may be needed to extract information from different sources.

Formulating the right filtering queries is an iterative and evolutionary process. Initially the analyst may draw from his domain knowledge to express a filter. But this filter needs to be refined based on how well it performs. Besides, it needs to be refined to capture the changes over time in the emphasis given to various attributes. In this paper we consider how to enable the filtering system to perform automatic query refinement based on minimal and continuous feedback gathered from the user. Below we give examples drawn from two intelligence related tasks that illustrate how such a system can be employed:

---

* This research was supported by the National Science Foundation under Award Numbers 0331707 and 0331690.

S. Mehrotra et al. (Eds.): ISI 2006, LNCS 3975, pp. 35–47, 2006.

*Example 1 (Intelligence Report Monitoring).* Massive amount of incident reports are continuously generated by law enforcement agencies which are monitored by analysts at different levels to detect trends and correlations. For instance, an analyst at federal level may want to continuously filter and analyze all relevant incident reports from local agencies that relates to multi-housing (e.g. rental apartment or condominium) and lodging (e.g. hotels or motels) facilities that have national monuments in their proximity. The analyst may also express detailed preferences on the attributes related to the suspects described in the incident report. To achieve this, the analyst draws from his domain knowledge to specify an initial (imprecise) filter to the data reporting server. The server matches the filter with incoming reports. In cases where matching reports can be large, it will be useful if the system can also rank the reports based on how strongly they match the given filter. To refine both the classification and ranking capabilities of the filter over time, the system offers the analyst a feature to provide feedback on the relevance of the reports. Based on the feedback the system automatically refines the filter.

*Example 2 (Intelligence Information Dissemination).* Large amount of intelligence information is gathered everyday from various sensors. For instance, US custom services use various sensing technologies (e.g., cameras, finger-print reader) to gather passenger information from airports and seaports. Different feature extraction tools are used to extract features from these data. Data matching given multi-feature criteria, watch-lists or archived data must be disseminated to analysts in different agencies for further processing. Analysts register filtering queries to the central system that gathers the data which then disseminates relevant information in a prioritized manner to analysts. Similar to the previous example, feedback from the analyst can be used to automatically adjust filtering queries stored in the system.

Technically, filtering queries can be considered as *classifiers* since their purpose is to classify each incoming data item as relevant (i.e. belong to the target class) or non-relevant. However, the following three important requirements distinguish our filtering queries from traditional classifiers:

**1. Ranking and Scoring.** For the purpose of filtering data instances belonging to a target class from massive volumes of streaming data, classifiers that merely make binary decisions are inadequate. The classifiers need to also score and rank records based on how strongly they match the filters. Ranking is useful for two reasons: (1) it enables the analyst to prioritize the processing of records, and (2) in cases where rigid binary partitioning of relevant and non-relevant data is undesirable, it facilitates the prioritization of records that are highly likely to be in the target class while at the same time not eliminating records. The latter issue is particularly important due to the fact that in most situations the filters are not crisp rules but rather fuzzy and approximate. This makes classifiers that score and rank data instances more appropriate than classifiers that only make binary decisions on class membership.

**2. Incorporating Analyst's Domain knowledge.** In a great majority of intelligence applications, analyst's domain knowledge (e.g. about features of suspects, etc.) forms a critical component. Hence, it is imperative that the system provides a mechanism to readily incorporate domain knowledge-induced filtering rules. However, while filtering rules representing domain knowledge are normally vague and imprecise, current database systems on which much of data filtering is carried out require crisp expressions. In order to express filtering rules on such systems, analysts are forced to convert their rules to very complex crisp expressions. To avoid this problem, the filtering system needs to allow direct execution of inexact filtering queries.

**3. Interactive Refinement.** As illustrated in the above examples, allowing the analyst to refine filters through relevance feedback (a.k.a. supervised learning) is an important requirement. This becomes necessary when the rules expressed by the analyst fail to capture the desired domain knowledge, or rules change over time. An important issue to notice here is that unlike traditional approaches where a classifier is learned and then applied in distinct phases, here the classifier needs to be incrementally refined using a feedback loop. Also notice that human domain knowledge is incorporated in two ways: first, through submission of domain knowledge in the form of initial filtering queries, and second, through feedback on the classified records.

In this paper, we propose a framework called FREESIA (Filter REfinement Engine for Streaming InformAtion) that meets the above requirements. FREESIA achieves ranking of streaming data by representing filtering queries (classifiers) as multi-parametric similarity queries which allow the analyst to express his imprecise filtering rules. Then, in the course of data analysis, the analyst can refine and update these filters through example-based training so as to achieve required accuracy and meet evolving demands. To efficiently support such dynamic adaptation of filters, FREESIA provides a set of algorithms for refining filters based on continuous relevance feedback.

## 2    Definitions and Preliminaries

### 2.1    Data Model

Filters in FREESIA assume a structured multi-dimensional data. However, originally the data can be either a set of relational tables or in any unstructured/semi-structured format. If the data is unstructured, data extraction tools[1] can be first applied to extract relevant values (e.g. names, places, time, etc.). The extracted data is then represented in the form of attribute-value pairs and fed into filtering modules.

### 2.2    Filtering Query Model

In this section we define a flexible query model that is powerful enough to capture human supplied filters and domain knowledge in addition to enabling incremental refinement. A filtering query or rule, henceforth simply referred to as *filter* or

---

[1] For example, Attensity's Extraction Engines: www.attensity.com

*classifier*, consists of four components: a set of similarity predicates structured in DNF form (Disjunctive Normal Form), a set of weights assigned to each similarity predicate, a ranking function and a cut-off value.

**Definition 1.** *A filter (classifier) is represented as a quadruple* $\langle \rho, \omega, \phi, \alpha \rangle$ *where* $\rho$ *is a conditional expression,* $\omega$ *is a set of weights,* $\phi$ *is a ranking function and* $\alpha$ *is a cut-off value. Below we give a brief description of these four elements.*

**Conditional Expression:** A conditional expression, $\rho$, is a DNF (Disjunctive Normal Form) expression over similarity predicates. Formally, an expression $Q = C_1 \vee C_2 \vee \ldots \vee C_n$ is a DNF expression where $C_i = C_{i1} \wedge C_{i2} \ldots, C_{in}$ is a conjunction, and each $C_{ij}$ is a similarity predicate. A *similarity predicate* is defined over the domain of a given data type (attribute type). A similarity predicate takes three inputs: (1) an attribute value from a data record, $t$, (2) a target value that can be a *set* of points or ranges, and (3) a similarity function, $f$, that computes the similarity between a data value and the target value. A similarity function is a mapping from two data attribute values, $v_1$ and $v_2$, to the range [0,1], $f : v_1 \times v_2 \rightarrow [0, 1]$. The values $v_1$ and $v_2$ can be either point values or range values. Similarity functions can be defined for data types or for specific attributes as part of the filtering system.

**DNF Ranking Functions, Weights and Cut-off:** A *DNF ranking function*, $\phi$, is a domain-specific function used to compute the score of an incoming record by aggregating scores from individual similarity predicates according to the DNF structure of $\rho$ and its corresponding set (template) of *weights* that indicate the importance of each similarity predicate. The template of weights, $\omega$, corresponds to the structure of the search condition and associates a weight to each predicate in a conjunction and also to each conjunction in the overall disjunction.

A DNF ranking function first uses *predicate weights* to assign aggregate scores for each conjunction, and it then uses *conjunction weights* to assign an overall score for the filter. A conjunction weight is in the range of [0, 1]. All predicate weights in a conjunction add up to 1 while all conjunction weights in a disjunction may not add up to 1. We aggregate the scores from predicates in a conjunction with a weighted $L_1$ metric (weighted summation). Using weighted $L_1$ metric as a conjunction aggregation function has been widely used in text IR query models where a query is typically expressed as a single conjunction [12, 10]. To compute an overall score of a query (disjunction), we use the $MAX$ function over the weighted conjunction scores. $MAX$ is one of the most popular disjunction aggregation functions [4].

### 2.3   Filter Refinement Model

The similarity conditions constituting a filter are refined using relevance feedback that is used as real-time training example to adapt the predicates, condition structure and corresponding weights to the information needs of the analyst. More formally, given a filter, $Q$, a set $R$ of the top $k$ records returned by $Q$, and relevance feedback $F$ on these records (i.e., a triple $\langle Q, R, F \rangle$), the refinement problem is to transform $Q$ into $Q'$ in such a way that, when $Q'$ is used to filter future streaming information or is re-executed on archival information, it will return more relevant records. Section 3.2 will discuss in detail the types of feedback that are gathered by the system and how they are represented.

# 3   Our Approach

In this section, we present our proposed approach for applying and refining filters on streaming data. We first present an overall architecture of our system FREESIA followed by a description of how the analyst interacts with FREESIA (i.e. the feedback loop). We then propose algorithms that implement the classifier refinement and scoring/ranking model refinement components of FREESIA.

## 3.1   The FREESIA System Architecture

FREESIA's schematic design is depicted in Figure 1. The following four main components constitute the system.

**Filter Processing Component.** When a new data group is received by the system, the filters that are represented as similarity queries are executed by the Filter Processing Component in order to score and filter relevant target records. This component can be implemented in any commercial database system using common similarity query processing techniques (e.g. [5, 1]). To readily apply the similarity queries in this context, we use an SQL equivalent of the weighted DNF query defined in 2.2.

If the similarity query has been modified (refined) since its last execution, the system will also evaluate it on the *archived data store* which is used to store the *unseen* (but matching) records as well as *filtered out* records. Re-evaluating the query on the archive allows the identification of previously excluded records that match the current filter. The scored list of records that results from the filter processing component is passed to the ranking component.

*Example 3.* Consider the incident report analysis application from example 1. For simplicity suppose that a data instance consists of only the location coordinates, incident type, location type and number of suspects. Then one possible query that filters potential analyst is given below.

```
SELECT Location, IncidentType, LocType, NumSuspects, RankFunc(w1,s1, w2, s2, w12) AS S,
FROM IncidentReports
WHERE LocNear(location, National_Monument, s1) AND LocTypeLike(LocType, {multi-housing,
   lodging}, s2)
ORDER BY S desc
```

The label "National_Monument" stands for a set of national monuments stored separately. LocNear takes a given location and computes its distance from the nearest national monument. LocTypeLike implements heuristic techniques to match similarity of a location type to a classification hierarchy of places.

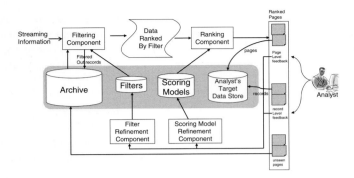

**Fig. 1.** FREESIA system overview

**Ranking Component.** This component applies scoring rules to produce a ranking of data instances. We employ two types of scoring methods. The first is the similarity scoring rule (i.e. the ranking function defined in Section 2.2) that is used by the Filter Processing Component. This represents the *long-term* filter of the analyst. In addition to this scoring rule, FREESIA also incorporates other scoring models that represent *short-term* (or special-case) rules that may not participate in the filtering process (i.e. are not evaluated as similarity queries) but are used for ranking. This, for instance, allows the analyst to temporarily force the system to rank reports that fulfill a given complex criteria at the top. Also, such rule can be specified by giving a record as a sample and asking "give me records like this". Many data mining methods can be used (e.g. [11]) to model such samples to produce scores for incoming records (more details on this will be given in Section 3.3). Given the scores from the similarity match and the scoring rules, the *Ranking Component* applies a combination method to produce the final ranking. As we mentioned in Section 2.3, the resulting ranked list of records is partitioned into pages for presentation to the analyst.

**Filter Refinement Component.** As discussed before, it is often necessary to interactively refine the analyst's initial filtering queries. This is achieved in FREESIA by collecting relevance feedback on the outputs of a filter. Upon seeing the ranked list of records, the analyst can submit feedback on the relevance (or otherwise) of the records - i.e. whether the records belong to the target class or not. Based on this feedback, the Filter Refinement Component refines the similarity queries. Section 3.3 will give details on the refinement process.

**Scoring Model Refinement Component.** In addition to its use for filter refinement, the feedback from the analyst is also utilized to refine the additional scoring rules. Section 3.3 will give details of this refinement process.

## 3.2   Gathering and Representing Feedback

Various types of feedback are gathered in FREESIA. One type of feedback is what we call *record-level feedback* where the analyst provides feedback on particular records. However, in cases where the analyst receives large amount of matching reports, FREESIA also provides feature to provide group feedback. For this we exploit the fact that the system presents the results in pages (groups) of a certain size which enables *page-level feedback*. Often, when an analyst looks at a page, he can tell whether most of the records in the page are relevant in his initial scanning of the results. If some level of error in a page is tolerable, the analyst may want to accept all the records in a page for further processing. On the contrary, in cases where the analyst determines that a page contains only some relevant records, she may want to give record-level feedback.

For feedback gathering purposes, we distinguish three types of pages:

- *Highly relevant pages:* almost all the records in these pages are relevant. In other words, the analyst will use *all* the record in these pages for further actions despite the fact that there could be a few records in these page which are not relevant.
- *Relevant pages:* only some of the records in these pages are relevant. For these pages, the analyst provides feedback on each record.
- *Unseen pages:* these are the pages returned by the filter but are not viewed by the analyst. We assume that these are deemed to be non-relevant.

Despite the availability of page-level feedback, providing record-level feedback may still be a time consuming operation in some cases. To deal with this, FREESIA provides a parameter to specify the number of pages the analyst wants to give record-level feedback on. The remaining pages are considered unseen pages.

### 3.3   Filter Refinement

**Feedback Preprocessing.** The refinement strategies used by the Query Refinement and the Scoring Model Refinement components require two sets of data: contents of records on which the analyst gave relevance feedback (for e.g. to modify target values in predicates), and the feedback itself. We initially capture these two types of information in the following two tables:

(1) A *Result Table* contains the ranked list of records returned by the filter as well as the score assigned to each by the system.
(2) A *Feedback Table* contains the relevance feedback given by the analyst on records that are a subset of those in the Result Table. Particularly, this table contains record-level feedback given on *Relevant Pages*. Table 1 shows a sample feedback table from the intelligence report monitoring example.

Since data attributes can have complex and non-ordinal attributes, performing query refinement directly on the *result* and *feedback* tables is difficult as this will require specialized refinement method for each attribute type. To circumvent this problem, we transform the diverse data types and similarity predicates defined on them into a homogeneous similarity space on which a single refinement method can operate. We refer to the resulting table as *Scores Table*. It

**Table 1.** Example feedback table (I=Irrel,R=Rel)

| ID | Location | Incident Type | LocType | #Suspect | FB |
|----|----------|---------------|---------|----------|-----|
| 4 | Irvine | photographing | retail center | 2 | I |
| 1 | Irvine | Bomb threat | hotel | 0 | R |
| 7 | LA | Request for building blueprints | apartment | 1 | R |
| 10 | LA | Unauthorized access | hotel | 2 | R |
| 60 | LA | Arson | Inn | 5 | I |
| 2 | San Diego | suspicious package delivery | office | 1 | I |
| 3 | San Diego | Larceny | Fed. Building | 5 | I |

contains the following five columns that store statistical information useful for the refinement process:

(1) Entry Identifier:– This identifier is a triple $\langle AttributeID, ValueID, ConjunctionID \rangle$. The first two entries show the attribute-value pair. The Conjunction ID, which comes from the filter, identifies the conjunction that is satisfied by the attribute-value pair. Since we use a DNF representation, a conjunction contains one or more predicates.
(2) Counts of relevant records having the value in this entry.
(3) Count of non-relevant records having the value in this entry.
(4) Proximity to other values (of same attribute) of relevant records.
(5) Proximity to other values (of same attribute) of non-relevant records.

For every distinct value $v_i$ in the scores table, we compute its weighted proximity to other relevant values of the same attribute *in the scores table* using the following formula:

$$v_i.RelevantCount + \sum_{j=1}^{k-1}(v_j.RelevantCount * sim(v_i, v_j))$$

where $v_i.RelevantCount$ is the count of relevant records (second column in the scores table), $k$ is the total number of distinct values of the attribute corresponding to $v_i$ that also have the same $conjID$, and $sim(v_i, v_j)$ is the similarity between $v_i$ and $v_j$ as computed by the similarity function corresponding to the attribute. In the same fashion, we compute proximity to non-relevant values using the above formula with $v_i.nonRelevantCount$ and $v_j.nonRelevantCount$ values. The intuition behind the proximity values is to bolster the exact counts of every distinct attribute-value pair in the scores table with the counts of other values of the same attribute weighted by their similarity to the attribute value at hand. This in essence allows us to capture the query region which the user is giving an example of. Table 2 shows an example scores table with one conjunction ($C1$) of one predicate on the attribute *location*.

**Table 2.** Example scores table

| OBJ ID | Rel Count | Irrel Count | AggRel Count | AggIrrel Count |
|--------|-----------|-------------|--------------|----------------|
| < Location, Irvine, C1 > | 1 | 1 | 1+2*0.8 =2.6 | 1 + 1 * 0.8 +2 * 0.2 = 2.2 |
| < Location, LA, C1 > | 2 | 1 | 2+1*0.8 =2.8 | 1+1*0.8 +2*0.2=2.2 |
| < Location, SD, C1 > | 0 | 2 | 0+1*0.2 +2*0.2=0.6 | 2+1*0.2 +1*0.2=2.4 |

**Refinement Algorithms.** In principle, the feedback given by the analyst can potentially result in one of three types of filter refinement. A filter that is too specific can be made more general (called *filter expansion*), a filter that is too general can be made more specific (called *filter contraction*) and finally the target values of predicates can be shifted to a new value (called *filter movement*).

The refinement algorithm in figure 2 performs all three kinds of refinements and adjusts weights. The algorithm starts by pruning insignificant predicates (entries) from scores table using the *pruneInsigEntires* function. Due to limited space, we skip the detailed discussion of this function. In short, it uses statistical method to measure the performance of each candidate predicate, and deletes the useless ones. The output of this function is a subset of the scores table, $ST_{pruned}$, whose entries are used as *candidates* to refine the filter.

Using the pruned scores table, $ST_{pruned}$, the algorithm next tries to determine whether the filter should be updated (line 3 to line 13). For each predicate in each conjunction, the algorithm first extracts the relevant entries, $ST_{Pj}$. This is performed by matching the *conjunctionID* and attribute name in the filter with $ST_{pruned}$ entries. This matching may result in many candidate predicates. Hence, we need a mechanism to select those that represent the right values to which we should move the filter. We do this selection by first clustering the candidate predicates and then choosing the cluster centroid as a representation of the new target value of $P_j$. For this, we use hierarchical agglomerative clustering (HAC) [2] method where the distance measure is computed based on the similarity between predicates in $ST_{Pj}$.

Once we get a set of candidate target points using HAC clustering, the algorithm tests whether each candidate is actually a new target value (line 7). The *isNewPoint* function determines the closeness of each candidate to each of the existing filter predicate. If a candidate is not near any of the existing target points, we add it as a new target value of the current predicate (line 8).

Next, the algorithm updates the weights of the predicates and conjunctions in the query. The predicate weight is computed as the average confidence level

```
ComputeNewQuery()
Input: Filter (Q), Scores_table(ST)
NumCase, NumRelCase, HACThresh
Output: NewFilter
1.   ST_pruned = pruneInsigEntries (NumCase, NumRelCase)
2.   Foreach Conjunction (C_i) in Query
3.     Foreach Predicate (P_j) in C_i
4.        ST_Pj = filterScoreTable (ST_pruned, P_j.attribute, C_i)
5.        Clusters_Pj = computeHACCluster (ST_Pj, HACThresh)
6.        Foreach Cluster (Cl_k) in Clusters_Pj
7.           if P_j.isNewPoint(Cl_k.centroid, P_j)
8.              P_j.addQueryPoint (Cl_k.centroid)
9.           endif
10.        endFor
11.        P_j.weight = averageConf(P_j.queryPoints)
12.     endFor
13.     C_i.weight = ( Σ_{j=1}^{|C_i|} P_j.weight ) / |C_i|
14.     NewFilter.addConjunction(C_i)
15.     NewFilter.normalizeWeight()
16. endFor
```

**Fig. 2.** ComputeNewFilter Algorithm

of the query points in the updated predicate. The confidence value of a predicate is computed based on its proximity values stored in the scores table as: $\frac{ProximityToRelevant}{ProximityToRelevant+ProximityToIrrelevant}$. The weight for a conjunction is computed as the *average* of the weights of its constituent predicates.

**Refining The Scoring Model.** The primary task of FREESIA's ranking component is to assign an accurate ranking score to each record. This component uses the maximum of the scores from the Filtering Component and the score from the short-term scoring model to be a record's final ranking score. When the analyst provides samples to form the scoring rules, many general incremental learning methods can be applied. In FREESIA, we use a pool based active learning method [11] which is suited to streaming data and is able to capture sample based *short-term* user model. It is a three-step procedure:

- Train a Naive Bayes classifier – *short-term* model – using sampled feedback records.
- Apply the *short-term* model to score the records returned by the Filter Component.
- Merge the scores from *long-term* model (i.e., filter score) and from *short-term* model.

## 4      Experiments

In this section, we present the results of the experiments we conducted to evaluate the effectiveness of our refinement method.

**Table 3.** Dataset Descriptions and Parameters

| Dataset | # Cases | # Cls. attrs | # cont attrs | # disc | Page size | Data Group size |
|---------|---------|--------------|--------------|--------|-----------|-----------------|
| adult | 32,561 | 2 | 6 | 8 | 40 | 1,000 |
| covertype | 10,000 | 7 | 10 | 40 | 40 | 1,000 |
| hypo | 3,163 | 2 | 7 | 18 | 20 | 316 |
| waveform21 | 5,000 | 2 | 21 | 0 | 20 | 500 |

We used four real-life datasets from the UCI machine learning repository [8]. The datasets are a good ensemble to some intelligence data. They are reasonable in size and have predefined target (classes); they also cover some portions of US census data (adult), environmental data (covertype), disease data (hypo) and scientific analysis data (waveform21). Table 3 shows the characteristics of the datasets. There are two types of attributes in the datasets (viz. continuous and discrete). We manually generate 20 initial and target query pairs for each dataset.

Our evaluation process closely follows the FREESIA architecture(Section 3.1). Table 3 shows two of the parameters we used for each dataset, namely *page size* and *data group size*. Page size specifies the number of records in each page. Data group size shows the number of records streaming into the system at each iteration. In addition, we set two more parameters, namely *precision threshold* and *record-level feedback page threshold*. Precision threshold shows that if the precision in a page is higher than this number, the page will be treated as a highly relevant page. We use 80% for all data sets. For all data sets, record-level feedback is gathered for 2 page.

The initial query is executed in the first iteration. The system then presents the data in pages. If a page is a *highly relevant* page, the system continues fetching the next page, and no feedback will be given to the system. This is to simulate the page-level feedback. If a page is not a highly relevant page, then in reality record-level feedback will be given on this page. Since we are using a pre-labeled dataset, we simulate this feedback process by assigning the respective true label of each record in the page. If the number of record-level feedback pages is beyond the page limit of record-level feedback specified above, the system will dump the remaining pages to the data archive (i.e. they are unseen pages).

**Tested Strategies.** Four approaches were compared in our experiments:

(1) *Baseline method (Q).* This uses only the initial query.
(2) *Query and Scoring Model Refinement (QM+).* This refines the scoring model, but the similarity query is not refined. This, in effect, simply makes the query more specific.
(3) *Query Refinement (Q+).* This refines the similarity query only. This performs all three types of refinement.
(4) *Query Refinement and Scoring Model Refinement (Q+M+).* This refines both the query and the scoring models. This also refines all three types of refinement but is capable of producing much more focused queries.

## 4.1   Results

Figures 3 to 6 show the precision and recall measures across different refinement iterations. In the first two datasets (*adult* and *hypo*), we show results where the desired refinement of the initial queries is achieved in the first few iterations (around two or three iterations). Moreover, the system was able to maintain the high precision and recall measures across the subsequent iterations. As can be clearly seen in these two figures, the two algorithms that perform similarity

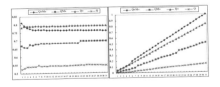

**Fig. 3.** Adult: Prec-Rec over 31 iters 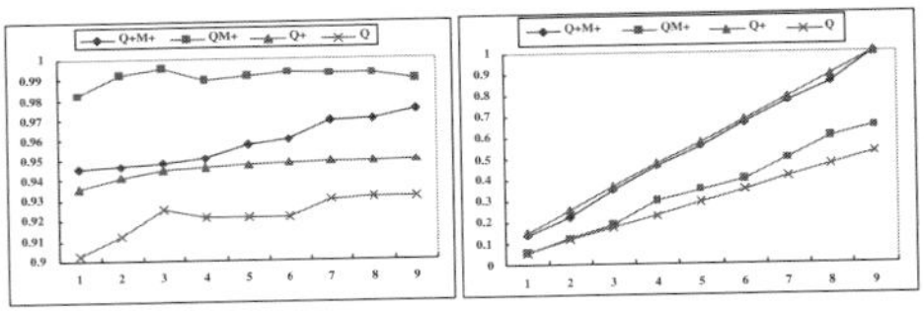         **Fig. 4.** Hypo: Prec-Rec over 9 iters

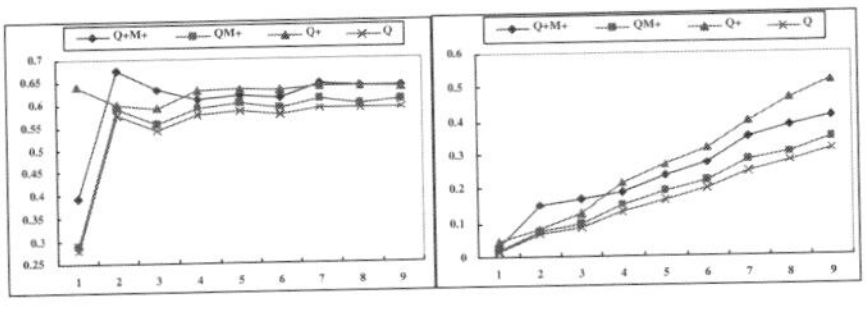

**Fig. 5.** Wave21: Prec-Rec over 9 iters 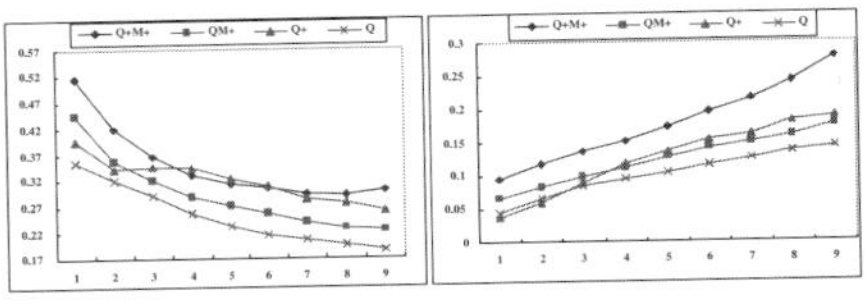        **Fig. 6.** Covertype: Prec-Rec over 9 iters

query refinement (i.e. $Q+$ and $Q + M+$) have much better performance compared to the other two which do not perform query refinement. For the dataset ($waveform21$), to achieve the desired refinements, more refinement iterations are required compared to the above two datasets (see the recall graph). Here as well $Q + M+$ and $QM+$ achieved the best precision and recall. The last dataset ($covertype$) shows cases where the initial query is very different from the desired target. As shown in the graph, precision declines as more iterations are needed (i.e. relatively more non-relevant records are retrieved). Still, $Q + M+$ performs better than the rest. The above results clearly show the effectiveness of FREESIA's refinement algorithms.

## 5   Related Work

The filtering process studied in this paper is related to target data selection techniques proposed in data mining on static data warehouses. However, unlike data mining on data warehouses (where a relevant subset of the database is filtered out for data mining tasks by carrying out as much refinement on the filters as required), in streaming data filtering has to be done continuously to allow data mining to occur as soon as the data arrives. There has been some research to address the problem of target subset selection from static data using classifiers [7, 9]. This body of research, however, only dealt with the problem of automatic classifier generation and the data considered were static. Recently, [3, 6] have considered the problem of data mining on streaming data. These works considered dynamic construction and maintenance of general models in a precise data environment. Whereas, our work deals with user predefined imprecise selection filters, and exploits the user knowledge to improve the accuracy of the filtering process.

## 6    Conclusions

In this paper, we have proposed a novel filtering framework called FREESIA, which enables analysts to apply the classifiers directly on database systems (in the form of similarity queries) to filter data instances that belong to a desired target class on a continuous basis. We believe our system can be used in many intelligence related tasks.

**Acknowledgments.** We would like to thank Prof. Sharad Mehrotra for giving us valuable feedback on this work.

## References

1. S. Chaudhuri and L. Gravano. Evaluating top-k selection queries. In *Proc. of the Twenty-fifth International Conference on Very Large Databases (VLDB99)*, 1999.
2. W. Day and H. Edelsbrunner. Efficient algorithms for agglomerative hierarchical clustering methods. 1(1):7–24, 1984.

3. P. Domingos and G. Hulten. Mining high-speed data streams. In *Knowledge Discovery and Data Mining*, pages 71–80, 2000.
4. R. Fagin. Combining Fuzzy Information from Multiple Systems. *Proc. of the 15th ACM Symp. on PODS*, 1996.
5. R. Fagin, A. Lotem, and M. Naor. Optimal aggregation algorithms for middleware. In *PODS'2001, Santa Barnara, California*, pages 83 – 99, May 2001.
6. D. Lambert and J. C. Pinheiro. Mining a stream of transactions for customer patterns. In *Knowledge Discovery and Data Mining*, pages 305–310, 2001.
7. C. Ling and C. Li. Data mining for direct marketing: problems and solutions. In *Proceedings of ACM SIGKDD (KDD-98)*, pages 73–79, 1998.
8. C. J. Merz and P. Murphy. UCI Repository of Machine Learning Databases. http://www.cs.uci.edu/ mlearn/MLRepository.html, 1996.
9. G. Piatetsky-Shapiro and B. Masand. Estimating campaign benefits and modeling lift. In *Proceedings of ACM SIGKDD (KDD-99)*, pages 185–193, 1999.
10. J. Rocchio. Relevance feedback in information retrieval. In G. Salton, editor, *The SMART Retrieval System: Experiments in Automatic Document Processing*, pages 313–323. Prentice Hall, 1971.
11. N. Roy and A. McCallum. Toward optimal active learning through sampling estimation of error reduction. In *Proceedings of ICML'01*, pages 441–448, 2001.
12. R. B. Yates and R. Neto. Modern information retrieval. In *ACM Press Series Addison Wesley*, 1999.

# Semantic Analytics Visualization

Leonidas Deligiannidis[1,2], Amit P. Sheth[2], and Boanerges Aleman-Meza[2]

[1] Virtual Reality Lab and [2]LSDIS Lab, Computer Science,
The University of Georgia, Athens, GA 30602, USA
{ldeligia, amit, boanerg}@cs.uga.edu

**Abstract.** In this paper we present a new tool for semantic analytics through 3D visualization called "Semantic Analytics Visualization" (SAV). It has the capability for visualizing ontologies and meta-data including annotated web-documents, images, and digital media such as audio and video clips in a synthetic three-dimensional semi-immersive environment. More importantly, SAV supports visual semantic analytics, whereby an analyst can interactively investigate complex relationships between heterogeneous information. The tool is built using Virtual Reality technology which makes SAV a highly interactive system. The backend of SAV consists of a Semantic Analytics system that supports query processing and semantic association discovery. Using a virtual laser pointer, the user can select nodes in the scene and either play digital media, display images, or load annotated web documents. SAV can also display the ranking of web documents as well as the ranking of paths (sequences of links). SAV supports dynamic specification of sub-queries of a given graph and displays the results based on ranking information, which enables the users to find, analyze and comprehend the information presented quickly and accurately.

## 1 Introduction

National security applications, such as aviation security and terrorist threat assessments, represent significant challenges that are being addressed by information and security informatics research [25]. As the amount of information grows, it is becoming crucial to provide users with flexible and effective tools to retrieve, analyze, and comprehend large information sets. Existing tools for searching and retrieving information (such as search engines) typically focus on unstructured text and some may be adapted to support display of the results of text analytics. However, semantics is considered to be the best framework to deal with the heterogeneity and dynamic nature of the resources on the Web and within enterprise systems [35]. Issues pertaining to semantics have been addressed in many fields such as linguistics, knowledge representation, artificial intelligence, information systems and database management. Semantic Analytics involves the application of techniques that support and exploit the semantics of information (as opposed to just syntax and structure/schematic issues [32] and statistical patterns) to enhance existing information systems [30].

Semantic analytics techniques for national security applications have addressed a variety of issues such as aviation safety [33], provenance and trust of data sources [15], and the document-access problem of Insider Threat [3]. Ranking, or more specifically "context-aware semantic association ranking" [4], is very useful as it finds

S. Mehrotra et al. (Eds.): ISI 2006, LNCS 3975, pp. 48–59, 2006.

and presents to the end-user the most relevant information of his/her search. The presentation of these results is normally done via a list of paths (i.e., sequences of links). Sometimes these results also include documents ranked according to their relevance to the results. These interconnections of ranked links and documents can be viewed as a graph or a network. Visualization of large networks has always been challenging. There is an increasing need for tools to graphically and interactively visualize such modeling structures to enhance their clarification, verification and analysis [2, 38]. Effective presentation of such data plays a crucial role because it helps the end-user analyze and comprehend the data. As a result, data is transformed into information and then into knowledge [33]. Efficient understanding of semantic information leads to more actionable and timely decision making. Thus, without an effective visualization tool, analysis and understanding of the results of semantic analytics techniques is difficult, ineffective, and at times, impossible.

The fundamental goal of visualization is to present, transform and convert data into a visual representation. As a result, humans, with their great visual pattern recognition skills, can comprehend data tremendously faster and more effectively through visualization than by reading the numerical or textual representation of the data [12]. Interfaces in 2D have been designed for visualization results of queries in dynamic and interactive environments (e.g., InfoCrystal [6]). Even though the textual representation of data is easily implemented, it fails to capture conceptual relationships. Three-dimensional (3D) interactive graphical interfaces are capable of presenting multiple views to the user to examine local detail while maintaining a global representation of the data (e.g., SemNet [18]). Using virtual environments, the user is able to visualize the data and to apply powerful manipulation techniques. In addition, the user of such systems is able to view and listen to associated metadata for each subject of interest at a given location such as a suspicious phone call or an image of a handwritten message. Thus, we address the challenge of visualization in the context of semantic analytic techniques, which are increasingly relevant to national security applications. For example, semantic data allows rich representation of the movements of an individual such as a person P that traveled from city A to city B taking bus X, in which a terrorist Q was also traveling.

The contribution of this paper is a highly interactive tool for semantic analysis through 3D visualization (in a semi-immersive environment) built using Virtual Reality technology with the goal of enabling analysts to find and better comprehend the information presented. The main features of the "Semantic Analytics Visualization" (SAV) tool are three. First, SAV visualizes ontologies, metadata and heterogeneous information including annotated text, web-documents and digital media, such as audio and video clips and images. Second, interaction is facilitated by using a virtual laser pointer for selection of nodes in the scene and either play digital media, display images, or open annotated web documents. Third, SAV can display the results of semantic analytics techniques such as ranking of web documents as well as the ranking of paths (i.e., sequences of links).

## 2  Background

Industry and academia are both focusing their attention on information retrieval over semantic metadata extracted from the Web (i.e., collection of dots). In addition, it is increasingly possible to analyze such metadata to discover interesting relationships (i.e., connect the dots). However, just as data visualization is a critical component in today's text analytics tools, the visualization of complex relationships (i.e., the different ways the dots are connected) will be an important component in tomorrow's semantic analytics capabilities. For example, visualization is used in tools that support the development of ontologies such as ontology extraction tools (OntoLift [39], Text-to-Onto [28]) or ontology editors (Protégé (protege.stanford.edu), OntoLift). These tools employ visualization techniques that primarily focus on the structure of the ontology, or in other words, its concepts and their relationships.

The Cluster Map visualization technique [1] bridges the gap between complex semantic structures and their intuitive presentation. It presents semantic data without being burdened with the complexity of the underlying metadata. For end users, information about the population of the ontology (entities, instance data) is often more important than the structure of the ontology that is used to describe these instances. Accordingly, the Cluster Map technique focuses on visualizing instances and their classifications according to the concepts of the ontology. However, some knowledge bases and ontologies like WordNet [29], TAP [22] or SWETO (lsdis.cs.uga.edu/projects/semdis/sweto/) cannot be easily visualized as a graph, as they consist of a large number of nodes and edges. Similarly, there are many large bio-informatics ontologies like Gene ontology [20] and GlycO [21] which have several hundred classes at the schema level and a few thousand instances.

TouchGraph (www.touchgraph.com) is a spring-embedding algorithm and tool to implement customizable layouts. It is a nice tool but can be annoying to users because it keeps re-adjusting the graph to a layout it determines to be best. TGVizTab [2] is a visualization plug-in for Protégé based on TouchGraph. Large graphs can be cluttered and the user may need to manually move some nodes away from her/his point of interest to see clearly the occluded nodes or read a label on a node successfully. However, even while the user is trying to move a node out of her/his view, s/he ends up dragging the graph while TouchGraph is readjusting it. People are used to placing things where they want and coming back later to find them still there. This is quite difficult to do with TouchGraph. OWLViz, part of the CO-ODE project (www.co-ode.org), is a plug-in for Protégé to visualize ontologies but it only shows *is-a* (i.e., subsumption) relationships among concepts.

Many ontology based visualization tools are, at least partially, based on the Self-Organizing Map (SOM) [27] technique/algorithm. WEBCOM [26] is a tool that utilizes SOM to visualize document clusters where semantically similar documents are placed in a cluster. The order of document clustering helps in finding related documents. ET-Map [10] is also used to visualize a large number of documents and websites. It uses a variation of SOM called Multilayer SOM to provide a concept-based categorization for web servers.

Spectable [38] visualizes ontologies as taxonomic clusters. These clusters represent groups on instances of individual classes or multiple classes. Spectable displays class hierarchical relations while it hides any relations at the instance level. It presents each instance by placing it into a cluster based on its class membership; instances that are members of multiple classes are placed in overlapping clusters. This visualization provides a clear and intuitive depiction of the relationships between instances and classes.

In [37] a holistic "imaging" is produced of the ontology which contains a semantic layout of the ontology classes where instances and their relations are also depicted. Coloring is also employed to show which classes have more instances. However, this approach is not suitable to visualize instance overlap like in Spectable.

Our previous research on Semantic Discovery [7] has focused on finding complex relationships including paths and relevant sub-graphs in graphs representing metadata and ontological terms and then present the information to the user as a list of paths (i.e., sequences of links). We have also implemented algorithms that perform ranking based on semantic associations [4, 8], and have studied applications in national/homeland security [3, 33], bioinformatics and detection of conflict of interest using social networks [5]. We experimented with a variety of visualization tools, including Protégé, TouchGraph and Jambalaya [36], to present the results to the user in a non-textual form. In this paper, we propose SAV as a virtual reality tool that better allows visualization of results from semantic analytics techniques.

## 3   The Virtual Reality Prototype

The interface presented in this paper is to be used in front of a group of people where only one person interacts with the tool. Images are drawn on a projection screen via a rear-projector system.

One of the major capabilities of SAV is to assist users in comprehending and analyzing complex relations of the semantic web. With SAV, the user can navigate, select and query the semantic information and select web documents. More interesting capabilities of SAV include the visualization of hundreds of web documents and other digital media and providing an environment where a user can easily and naturally interact with the environment such as finding related documents and at the end reading the documents. The documents in our experiments are annotated documents, such as web pages (the automatic semantic annotation system we used is described in [23]). The user (e.g., intelligence analyst) is interested not only in finding the documents in the Virtual Environment (VE) but also reading these documents. Hence, upon selecting a document, the document is loaded in a conventional browser where the user can read the annotated pages the same way s/he reads conventional web pages.

### 3.1   Software and Hardware

The prototype was designed using Java3D, the JWSU toolkit [14] and the GraphViz system [17, 19]. The application was running on a PC with 1GB of memory and an ATI Radeon 9800 video card. The user can interact with the VE using a PinchGlove – for selection of objects and navigation. We also used a Polhemus FastRak to track the user's head and hand in space. One of the problems with such an interface, however, is that the user may need to simply turn her head to the left or right to see the rest of the environment and therefore, the user cannot possibly look at the display. For this reason, we used 3 sensors on our Polhemus Fastrak. The first sensor is used to track the position and orientation of the user's head. The second sensor is used to track the user's hand. In Figure 1(a) the user is looking straight and the third sensor held by her left hand does not provide any additional rotation. The third sensor provides additional rotation of the camera (the view) around the Y axis – the vertical axis. Thus, instead of the user turning to the left as shown in Figure 1(b), the user can rotate the sensor that is held by her second (non-dominant) hand as shown in Figure 1(c). Users were easily adapting to this mechanism almost immediately, within seconds.

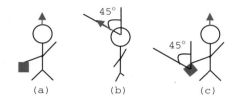

**Fig. 1.** Rotation sensor for the Virtual Environment

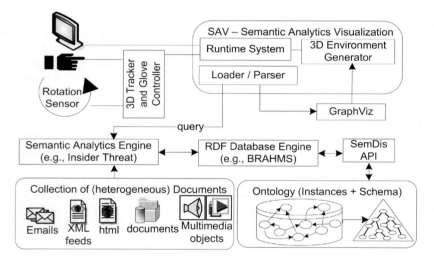

**Fig. 2.** System architecture of SAV

### 3.1.1  Software Architecture

The application loads the ontology result using BRAHMS [24] and the SemDis API [31]. The result is fed to GraphViz's layout algorithm(s) and then we generate the Virtual Environment (VE). The system architecture of SAV is shown in figure 2. After we generate the 3D environment based on the output of GraphViz and the weight (ranking) information of the documents, the user can interact with the VE using a 3D tracker and PinchGloves.

### 3.2  Retrieving and Loading the Data

The visualization of sequences of links and relevant documents for a query is built upon our previous work on Insider Threat analysis [3]. The ontology of this application captures the domain of National Security and Terrorism. It contains relevant metadata extracted from different information sources such as government watch-lists, sanction-lists, gazetteers, and lists of organizations. These sources were selected for their semi-structured format, information richness and their relationship to the domain of terrorism. The ontology population contains over 32,000 instances and over 35,000 relationships among them. For ontology design and population, the Se-magix Freedom toolkit (www.semagix.com) was used. Freedom is a commercial software toolkit based on a technology developed at and licensed from the LSDIS lab [34].

A query can be a selection of a concept (i.e., class) or a particular entity from the ontology. The results of a search are related entities which are discovered by means of traversing links to other entities (in a graph representation of the ontology). Different documents are relevant to a query depending upon which entities appear within the content of the documents. The final result is a group of entities (or nodes) intercon-nected by different named relationships (such as 'located in'), together with a set of documents that are related to the entities. The interconnections of the entities can be viewed as sequences of links where each sequence has a ranking score. The docu-ments also have a rank score based on their relevance to the query. For visualization purposes, a cached version of each document is placed in a separate web server to provide quick and persistent access from SAV. These documents are often web pages but can also include images, audio, or video clips whereby meta-data annotations provide the connections to entities in the ontology.

SAV accesses data to be visualized by loading the results from the query module of the application for detection of Insider Threat mentioned earlier. Note that this appli-cation exemplifies a semantic analytics technique. The architecture of SAV considers data independence of any particular semantic analytics technique. The relevant com-ponents of results fed into and visualized by SAV are: (i) each entity represents a node in the results graph; (ii) nodes are connected by named relationships; (iii) each path contains a ranking score; (iv) each document contains a relevance score and is related to one or more nodes.

## 3.3  Semantic Visualization

One of the more complex ontology searches we visualized is presented in the remain-der of this paper as our main illustrative example. The data to be visualized (i.e., search results) includes information about entities and relationships among them, relevant annotated documents associated with entities, media associated with each entity, ranking of web pages and path ranking. To visualize the results, we partition the space into two volumes, the foreground and background volumes. In the fore-ground we visualize the entities and their relationships and in the background we visualize the documents. Figure 3 illustrates the foreground of SAV.

SAV runs the "dot" filter of the GraphViz product to generate the coordinates of every visible node in the scene along with the splines' control points. GraphViz uses splines to connect entities, not straight lines, in order to minimize edge crossing, gen-erate a symmetric layout and make the graph more readable. Generating splines in space requires the creation of objects with complex geometry. Instead, we create multiple cylinder objects and we connect them together to form a line that connects the control points of each spline.

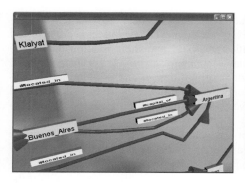 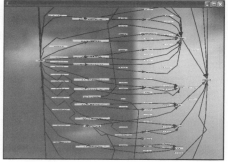

**Fig. 3.** (Left) Entities (bluish rectangles) and relationships (arrows between entities – a yellow rectangle above the arrow is the relationship's label) visualized in SAV. (Right) the entities and their relationships from a distance; we removed the document nodes to make the figure more readable.

GraphViz is invoked twice, once for the foreground and once for the background layout. Then, the generated output of GraphViz is loaded and 3D objects are created and attached in the scene. As illustrated in figure 3, we represent entities as rectangles and their relationships to other entities as directional splines in space; each relationship has a label attached on it. Each entity and relationship has a textual label. We dynamically generate PNG images (using Java2D) out of the textual label (with anti-aliasing enabled) of each node and then we apply the un-scaled generated images as textures on the nodes (entities and relationships). We found that by doing this the labels are readable even from a distance. Text anti-aliasing must be enabled while the images are generated and when applying the textures no scaling should be done – the images should have dimensions of power of two.

The documents are represented as red spheres in the background as shown in figure 5. The position of a document changes depending on its ranking. The higher the ranking, or else the more important a document is, the closer to the foreground it is placed. The intensity of the red color also becomes higher when the ranking is higher (redder spheres indicate higher ranking). Additionally, depending on a document's ranking, the width of the sphere representing the document becomes bigger, in which case a sphere becomes a 3D oval shape (wider 3D ovals indicate higher ranking). Since the most relevant documents are closer to the foreground, the user can select them more easily because they are closer to the user and the objects (the spheres) are bigger in size.

The number of documents relative to a search could range from one hundred to several thousand. As a result, we visualized the entities and their relationships in the foreground while the document information stays in the background without cluttering the user's view.

## 4   User Interaction

The user can interact and navigate in the VE using her hand while wearing a Pinch-Glove to inform the system of her actions. The user can change the speed of travel

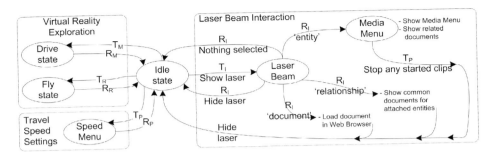

**Fig. 4.** State machine of SAV

using 3D menus similar to the ones in [13]. The state diagram that describes the functionality of SAV is shown in figure 4.

There are six states in the state machine. Initially the user is in the *Idle* state. The user can choose the "drive" or "fly" technique to explore the VE. "Drive" means that the user can travel in the VE at the direction of her hand while staying at the ground level where the ground level is defined by the horizontal plane of where the user is at the initiation of the traveling technique. "Fly", on the other hand, means that the user can freely travel in space at the direction of her hand.

On the state transition edges we place a label for which "pinch" (the contact of two fingers) moves the user to different states. A "T" indicates that the thumb and another finger are touching and an "R" indicates the release of the two fingers. The subscript indicates the second finger; the finger that touches the thumb ("I" for index, "M" for middle, "R" for ring, and "P" for pinky). For example, $T_R$ means that the thumb and the "ring" fingers are touching.

When the user moves in the *Speed* menu state, s/he can increase or decrease the speed of travel. While in the *Idle* state, the user can activate the laser beam to select an entity, a relationship, or a document. Upon selecting a document, we load the document in a web browser and the user can read the annotated web page, click on links, and so on. Upon selecting an entity, all documents become semi-transparent with the exception of the documents that are related to the selected entity. Edges that connect documents to other entities become fully transparent. Additionally, all entities and relationships become semi-transparent except for the selected entity. This helps the user to easily find the related documents associated with the selected entity, and also focus on the detail presented currently while keeping the overview of the entire scene. Thus, the user's attention is on the selection while s/he is still capable of looking around to see the rest of the environment that is transparent but still visible. The transparency provides a solution to the "detail" and "overview" problem where the query result stays in focus while the rest of the VE becomes transparent but still visible. Additionally, by means of head rotations, the user can still get an overview of the environment while also being capable of seeing the detail of the selection.

Entities, relationships and documents can be selected using the user's virtual laser pointer. The user can activate the virtual laser pointer by touching her/his thumb and index finger when in the *Idle* state. We implemented a ray casting technique for remote object selection (selectable objects are away for the user's hand reach), since this is one of the best techniques for selecting remote objects [9]. The laser beam

stays activated until the user initiates a release of the two fingers at which time a selection is performed.

Entities at the leaf level may contain digital media while some entities represent
concepts in the ontology and do not have any associated media attached to them. That
is, after the selection of an entity, we display the digital media menu (the current state
becomes *Media*). The user can then play video and audio clips, and load in images in
the VE. To implement this aspect of the application we used the Java Media Framework (JMF).

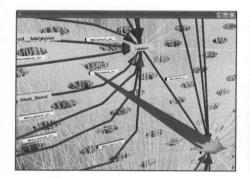 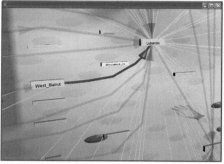

**Fig. 5.** (Left) Remote object selection using ray casting. A laser bean extends from the user's
hand to infinity. The first object that is penetrated by the laser is selected. (Right) After a selection of a relationship, all entities and relationships become semi-transparent but the selected
relationship and the attached entities. Additionally, all documents become semi-transparent but
the common documents attached to the entities.

Selecting a relationship (e.g. an edge) is similar to selecting an entity. However,
when selecting a relationship, all nodes in the scene become semi-transparent except
the selected relationship, its attached entities and the common documents of the attached entities as shown in figure 5 (right). Selection of a relationship is performed by
selecting the (yellowish) label of the line that connects two entities.

By making the non-relevant entities, relationships and documents semi-transparent,
we un-clutter the visualization space in order to assist the user in the exploration of
related documents and help her/him focus on the detail of a sub-query [16]. Since the
non-relevant portion of the environment is still visible but semi-transparent, the user
can keep a view of the whole data available, while pursuing detailed analysis of a sub-
selection.

## 5  Conclusions and Future Work

We presented a highly interactive tool, SAV, for visualizing ontologies, metadata and
documents or digital media. SAV is based on VR technology and its primary goal is
to display the information to the user in a simple and intuitive way within a Virtual
Environment. SAV builds a dynamic environment where users are able to focus on

different sub-queries (detail) while still keeping them in context with the rest of the environment (overview).

SAV provides an environment where users can select a small set of objects to examine, dynamically and in real-time, providing better contextual information. The users can select and manipulate objects directly and naturally via skills gained in real life as it is described in [11]. Such a system will be of increasing importance for interactive activities in semantic analytics.

Throughout our preliminary studies and demonstrations, users and observers showed a high interest in SAV. Their comments and suggestions will be considered in future releases. Usability studies and experiments are planned to observe how SAV is used and how we can improve upon its interactivity. This will help us discover any further requirements needed to improve the functionality and use of this tool.

## Acknowledgments

This research was principally supported by "SemDis: Discovering Complex Relationships in Semantic Web" funded by the National Science Foundation (NSF) grant IIS-0325464, projects funded by ARDA and the Office of Instructional Support and Development at UGA. Any opinions, findings, and conclusions or recommendations expressed in this material are those of the author(s) and do not necessarily reflect the views of the NSF, ARDA or UGA.

## References

1.  Aduna Cluster Map Library version 2005.1 (Integration Guide), 2005.
2.  Alani, H., TGVizTab: An Ontology Visualization Extension for Protégé. In *Knowledge Capture, Workshop on Visualization Information in Knowledge Engineering*, (2003).
3.  Aleman-Meza, B., Burns, P., Eavenson, M., Palaniswami, D. and Sheth, A.P., An Ontological Approach to the Document Access Problem of Insider Threat. In *IEEE International Conference on Intelligence and Security Informatics (ISI-2005)*, (Atlanta, Georgia, USA, 2005), Springer, 486-491.
4.  Aleman-Meza, B., Halaschek, C., Arpinar, I.B. and Sheth, A., Context-Aware Semantic Association Ranking. In *First International Workshop on Semantic Web and Databases*, (Berlin, Germany, 2003), 33-50.
5.  Aleman-Meza, B., Nagarajan, M., Ramakrishnan, C., Ding, L., Kolari, P., Sheth, A.P., Arpinar, I.B., Joshi, A. and Finin, T., Semantic Analytics on Social Networks: Experiences in Addressing the Problem of Conflict of Interest Detection. In *15th International World Wide Web Conference*, (Edinburgh, Scotland, 2006).
6.  Anselm, S., InfoCrystal: A Visual Tool for Information Retrieval. In *IEEE Visualization Conference*, (San Jose, California, USA, 1993), 150-157.
7.  Anyanwu, K. and Sheth, A.P., r-Queries: Enabling Querying for Semantic Associations on the Semantic Web. In *Twelfth International World Wide Web Conference*, (Budapest, Hungary, 2003), 690-699.
8.  Anyanwu, K., Sheth, A.P. and Maduko, A., SemRank: Ranking Complex Relationship Search Results on the Semantic Web. In *14th International World Wide Web Conference*, (Chiba Japan, 2005), 117-127.

9.  Bowman, D. and Hodges, L., An Evaluation of Techniques for Grabbing and Manipulating Remote Objects in Immersive Virtual Environments. In *1997 Symposium on Interactive 3D Graphics*, (1997), 35-38.

10. Chen, H., Schuffels, C. and Orwig, R. Internet Categorization and Search: A Self-Orginizing Approach. *Journal of Visual Communication and Image Representation, 7* (1). 88-102.

11. Chuah, M.C., Roth, S.F., Mattis, J. and Kolojejchick, J., SDM: Selective Dynamic Manipulation of Visualizations. In *ACM Symposium on User Interface Software and Technology*, (1995), 61-70.

12. DeFanti, T.A., Brown, M.D. and McCormick, B.H. Visualization: Expanding Scientific and Engineering Research Opportunities. *IEEE Computer, 22* (8). 12-25.

13. Deligiannidis, L. and Jacob, R.J.K., The London Walkthrough in an Immersive Digital Library Environment. In *2005 International Conference on Modeling, Simulation and Visualization Methods*, (2005), 179-185.

14. Deligiannidis, L., Weheba, G., Krishnan, K. and Jorgensen, M., JWSU: A Java3D Framework for Virtual Reality. In *International Conference on Imaging Science, Systems, and Technology*, (2003).

15. Ding, L., Kolari, P., Finin, T., Joshi, A., Peng, Y. and Yesha, Y., On Homeland Security and the Semantic Web: A Provenance and Trust Aware Inference Framework. In *AAAI Spring Symposium on AI Technologies for Homeland Security*, (Stanford University, California, USA, 2005).

16. Eick, S.G. and Wills, G.J., Navigating Large Networks with Hierarchies. In *IEEE Visualization Conference*, (San Jose, California, USA, 1993), 204-210.

17. Ellson, J., Gansner, E.R., Koutsofios, E., North, S.C. and Woodhull, G., Graphviz - Open Source Graph Drawing Tools. In *Graph Drawing, 9th International Symposium*, (Vienna, Austria, 2001), 483-484.

18. Fairchild, K.M., Poltrock, S.E. and Furnas, G.W., SemNet: Three-dimensional graphic representation of large knowledge bases. In *Cognitive Science and its Application for Human-Computer Interface*, (Erlbaum, Hillsdale, NJ, USA, 1988), 201-233.

19. Gansner, E.R. and North, S.C. An Open Graph Visualization System and Its Applications to Software Engineering. *Software - Practice and Experience, 30* (11). 1203-1233.

20. Gene-Ontology. http://www.geneontology.org.

21. Glyco-Ontology. http://lsdis.cs.uga.edu/Projects/Glycomics.

22. Guha, R.V. and McCool, R. TAP: A Semantic Web Test-bed. *Journal of Web Semantics, 1* (1). 81-87.

23. Hammond, B., Sheth, A. and Kochut, K. Semantic Enhancement Engine: A Modular Document Enhancement Platform for Semantic Applications over Heterogeneous Content. In Kashyap, V. and Shklar, L. eds. *Real World Semantic Web Applications*, Ios Press Inc, 2002, 29-49.

24. Janik, M. and Kochut, K., BRAHMS: A WorkBench RDF Store and High Performance Memory System for Semantic Association Discovery. In *Fourth International Semantic Web Conference*, (Galway, Ireland, 2005).

25. Kantor, P.B., Muresan, G., Roberts, F., Zeng, D.D., Wang, F.-Y., Chen, H. and Merkle, R.C. (eds.). *Intelligence and Security Informatics, IEEE International Conference on Intelligence and Security Informatics (ISI 2005)*. Springer, Atlanta, GA, USA, 2005.

26. Kohonen, T., Self-organization of very large document collections: State of the art. In *8th International Conference on Artificial Neural Networks*, (1998), 65-74.

27. Kohonen, T. *Self Organizing Maps*. Springer, Espoo, Finland, 1994.

28. Maedche, A. and Staab, S., The Text-To-Onto Ontology Learning Environment (Software Demonstration at ICCS-2000). In *Eight International Conference on Conceptual Structures*, (Darmstadt, Germany, 2000).

29. Miller, G.A. WordNet: A Lexical Database for English. *Communications of the ACM, 38* (11). 39-41.

30. Polikoff, I. and Allemang, D. Semantic Technology - TopQuadrant Technology Briefing v1.1, 2003.

31. SemDis. http://lsdis.cs.uga.edu/projects/semdis/.

32. Sheth, A.P. Semantic Meta Data for Enterprise Information Integration, *DM Review*, 2003.

33. Sheth, A.P., Aleman-Meza, B., Arpinar, I.B., Halaschek, C., Ramakrishnan, C., Bertram, C., Warke, Y., Avant, D., Arpinar, F.S., Anyanwu, K. and Kochut, K. Semantic Association Identification and Knowledge Discovery for National Security Applications. *Journal of Database Management, 16* (1). 33-53.

34. Sheth, A.P., Bertram, C., Avant, D., Hammond, B., Kochut, K. and Warke, Y. Managing Semantic Content for the Web. *IEEE Internet Computing, 6* (4). 80-87.

35. Sheth, A.P. and Ramakrishnan, C. Semantic (Web) Technology in Action: Ontology Driven Information Systems for Search, Integration and Analysis. *IEEE Data Engineering Bulletin, 26* (4). 40-47.

36. Storey, M.A.D., Noy, N.F., Musen, M.A., Best, C., Fergerson, R.W. and Ernst, N., Jambalaya: An Interactive Environment for Exploring Ontologies. In *International Conference on Intelligent User Interfaces*, (2002).

37. Tu, K., Xiong, M., Zhang, L., Zhu, H., Zhang, J. and Yu, Y., Towards Imaging Large-Scale Ontologies for Quick Understanding and Analysis. In *Fourth International Semantic Web Conference*, (Galway, Ireland, 2005), 702-715.

38. van Harmelen, F., Broekstra, J., Fluit, C., ter Horst, H., Kampman, A., van der Meer, J. and Sabou, M., Ontology-based Information Visualization. In *International Conference on Information Visualisation*, (London, England, UK, 2001), 546-554.

39. Volz, R., Oberle, D., Staab, S. and Studer, R. OntoLiFT Prototype - WonderWeb: Ontology Infrastructure for the Semantic Web, *WonderWeb Deliverable*.

# Visualizing Authorship for Identification

Ahmed Abbasi and Hsinchun Chen

Department of Management Information Systems, The University of Arizona,
Tucson, AZ 85721, USA
aabbasi@email.arizona.edu, hchen@eller.arizona.edu

**Abstract.** As a result of growing misuse of online anonymity, researchers have begun to create visualization tools to facilitate greater user accountability in online communities. In this study we created an authorship visualization called *Writeprints* that can help identify individuals based on their writing style. The visualization creates unique writing style patterns that can be automatically identified in a manner similar to fingerprint biometric systems. *Writeprints* is a principal component analysis based technique that uses a dynamic feature-based sliding window algorithm, making it well suited at visualizing authorship across larger groups of messages. We evaluated the effectiveness of the visualization across messages from three English and Arabic forums in comparison with Support Vector Machines (SVM) and found that *Writeprints* provided excellent classification performance, significantly outperforming SVM in many instances. Based on our results, we believe the visualization can assist law enforcement in identifying cyber criminals and also help users authenticate fellow online members in order to deter cyber deception.

## 1 Introduction

The rapid proliferation of the Internet has facilitated the increasing popularity of computer mediated communication. Inevitably, the numerous benefits of online communication have also allowed the realization of several vices. The anonymous nature of the Internet is an attractive medium for cybercrime; ranging from illegal sales and distribution of software [11] to the use of the Internet as a means of communication by extremist and terrorist organizations [20, 1].

In addition to using the internet as an illegal sales and communication medium, there are several trust related issues in online communities that have surfaced as a result of online anonymity [13]. Internet-based deception is rampant when interacting with online strangers [5]. With widespread cybercrime and online deception, there is a growing need for mechanisms to identify online criminals and to provide authentication services to deter abuse of online anonymity against unsuspecting users.

We propose the use of authorship visualization techniques to allow the identification and authentication of online individuals. In order to accomplish this task we developed a visualization called *Writeprints*, which can automatically identify authors based on their writing style. Due to the multilingual nature of online communication and cybercrime, the visualization was designed to handle text in multiple languages. *Writeprints* is adept at showing long-term author writing patterns over larger quantities of text. We tested the

S. Mehrotra et al. (Eds.): ISI 2006, LNCS 3975, pp. 60–71, 2006.

effectiveness of the technique on a test bed consisting of messages from three web forums composed of English and Arabic messages. Our results indicate that *Writeprints*
can provide a high level of accuracy and utility which may greatly aid online users and
law enforcement in preventing online deception and cybercrime.

## 2  Related Work

### 2.1  Visualizing Authors in Online Communities

Kelly et al. [8] suggested the notion that collecting user activity data in online communities and feeding it back to the users could lead to improved user behavior. Erickson and
Kellogg [7] also contended that greater informational transparency in online communities would likely lead to increased user accountability. Due to the copious amounts of
data available in online forums and newsgroups, information visualization techniques
can present users with relevant information in a more efficient manner [17].

There have been several visualizations created using participant activity information for the purpose of allowing online users to be more informed about their fellow
members [7, 14, 6, 17]. Most of the author information provided by each of these
visuals is based on their interaction patterns derived from message threads. Hence,
there is little evaluation of author message content. From the perspective of cybercrime and online deception, viewing author posting patterns alone is not sufficient to
safeguard against deceit. Individuals can use multiple usernames or copycat/forge
other users with the intention of harassing or deceiving unsuspecting members. Thus,
there is also a need for authentication techniques based on message content. Specifically, authorship visualizations can provide additional mechanisms for identification
and authentication in cyberspace.

### 2.2  Authorship Analysis

Authorship Analysis is grounded in Stylometry, which is the statistical analysis of
writing style. Currently authorship analysis has become increasingly popular in identification of online messages due to augmented misuse of the Internet. De Vel et al. [4]
applied authorship identification to email while there have been several studies that
have applied the techniques to web forum messages [20, 1, 10].

Online content poses problems for authorship identification as compared to conventional forms of writing (literary works, published articles). Perhaps the biggest
concern is the shorter length of online messages. Online messages tend to be merely a
couple of hundred words on average [20] with great variation in length. In light of the
challenges associated with cyber content, the ability to identify online authorship
signifies a dramatic leap in the effectiveness of authorship identification methodologies in recent years. Much of this progress can be attributed to the evolution of the
two major parameters for authorship identification which are the writing style markers
(features) and classification techniques incorporated for discrimination of authorship.

#### 2.2.1  Authorship Features
Writing style features are characteristics that can be derived from a message in order
to facilitate authorship attribution. Numerous types of features have been used in

previous studies including n-grams and the frequency of spelling and grammatical errors, however four categories used extensively for online material are lexical, syntactic, structural, and content specific features [20].

*Lexical* features include total number of words, words per sentence, word length distribution, vocabulary richness, characters per sentence, characters per word, and the usage frequency of individual letters. *Syntax* refers to the patterns used for the formation of sentences. This category of features is comprised of punctuation and function/stop words. *Structural* features deal with the organization and layout of the text. This set of features has been shown to be particularly important for online messages [4]. Structural features include the use of greetings and signatures, the use of phone numbers or email addresses for contact information, and the number of paragraphs and average paragraph length. *Content-specific* features are key words that are important within a specific topic domain.

### 2.2.2 Authorship Techniques

The two most commonly used analytical techniques for authorship attribution are statistical and machine learning approaches. Many multivariate statistical approaches such as principal component analysis [2, 3] have been shown to provide a high level of accuracy. Statistical techniques have the benefit of providing greater explanatory potential which can be useful for evaluating trends and variances over larger amounts of text.

Drastic increases in computational power have caused the emergence of machine learning techniques such as support vector machines, neural networks, and decision trees. These techniques have gained wider acceptance in authorship analysis studies in recent years [16, 4]. Machine learning approaches provide greater scalability in terms of the number of features that can be handled and are well suited to cope with the shorter lengths of online messages. Specifically, SVM has emerged as perhaps the most powerful machine learning technique for classification of online messages. In comparisons, it outperformed other machine learning techniques for classification of web forum messages [20, 1].

### 2.3 Authorship Visualization

There has been a limited amount of work on authorship visualization. Kjell et al. [9] used statistical techniques such as principal component analysis (PCA) and cosine similarity to visualize writing style patterns for Hamilton and Madison's Federalist papers. The study created writing style patterns based on usage frequencies of the ten n-grams with the greatest variance between the two authors. Shaw et al. [15] used latent semantic indexing (LSI) for authorship visualization of biblical texts based on n-gram usage. Their visualization tool, called SFA, allows authorship tendencies to be viewed based on visualization of eigenvectors (principal components) in multidimensional space. Ribler and Abrams [12] used an n-gram based visualization called Patterngrams to compare the similarity between documents for plagiarism detection in student computer programs.

There are several important things to note about these studies: (1) they all used n-gram features to discriminate authorship, (2) they all used manual observation to evaluate the visualizations, (3) none of them were applied to online media, and (4) there is no indication of whether the techniques can be successfully applied in a multilingual setting.

# 3   Visualization Requirements

Based on gaps in previous visualization tools created for online communities and authorship analysis, we have identified some requirements for our authorship visualizations. We would like to create visualizations that can automatically identify authors based on writing style patterns, using a set of features specifically designed and catered towards identification of authorship in cyberspace. A detailed description of our requirements is given below:

## 3.1   Visualizing Cyber Authorship

As we previously mentioned, there has been significant work relating to the creation of visualizations to improve user awareness and accountability in online settings. However, there have not been any visualization tools created specifically with the intention of diminishing cybercrime and online deception. We believe that there is a dire need for such tools and that authorship visualizations can facilitate identification of cyber criminals and lessen online deception.

## 3.2   Automatic Recognition

Previous authorship visualization studies used observation to determine authorship similarity. Manual inspection was sufficient since these studies only compared a few authors; however this is not possible for online authorship identification. It is infeasible to visually compare large numbers of writing style patterns manually. In addition to being overly time consuming, it is beyond the boundaries of human cognitive abilities. To overcome these deficiencies, Li et al. [10] called for the creation of authorship visualizations that can be automatically identified in a manner analogous to fingerprint biometric systems.

## 3.3   Online Authorship Features

Previous studies have used n-grams. It is unclear whether or not such an approach would be scalable when applied to a larger number of authors in an online setting. In contrast, lexical, syntactic, structural, and content-specific features have demonstrated their ability to provide a high level of discriminatory potential in online settings [4] featuring multilingual message corpora [20, 1]. Thus, the authorship visualizations created for identification of online messages should incorporate a feature set encompassing these feature types.

# 4   Process Design

We propose the creation of a visualization techniques designed for authorship identification and authentication called *Writeprints*. The visualization uses dimensionality reduction to create a more coherent representation of authorship style. *Writeprints* is a principal component analysis based visualization technique that uses a dynamic feature-based sliding window algorithm. Principal component analysis is a powerful technique that has been used in several previous authorship analysis and visualization studies [3, 9]. The *Writeprint* visualization is aimed at providing greater power for lengthier amounts of text by visualizing the writing style variation, which can create powerful patterns that are highly differentiable.

Figure 1 provides a description of the processes entailed towards the creation of *Writeprints* beginning with the collection of messages and extraction of writing style features from the collected content. The authorship visualizations are created by transforming the feature usage values into writing style patterns using dimensionality reduction techniques and specific algorithms designed to accentuate the important writing style patterns of the various authors. These patterns can uniquely identify authors using automatic recognition techniques.

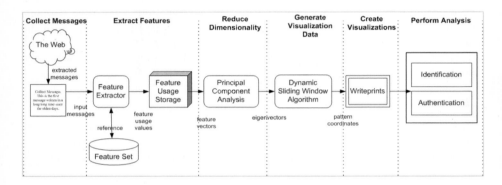

**Fig. 1.** Authorship Visualization Process Design

## 4.1   Collection and Extraction

Messages are automatically collected from the forums using web spidering programs that can retrieve all the messages for a particular author or authors. The messages are then cleaned to remove noise such as forwarded and re-quoted content. Automated feature extraction programs can then compute the feature usage values and extract the feature usage vectors. The list of features designed for online messages (based on previous online authorship studies) is presented below.

### 4.1.1   Feature Set: English and Arabic
We believe that the use of a more in depth feature set can provide greater insight for the assessment of content for authorship identification as compared to simple word or n-gram based features. Our English feature set consists of 270 writing style markers including lexical, syntactic, structural, and content-specific features. Figure 2 shows an overview of the complete feature set. In this particular feature set, the content specific words belong to messages related to software sales and distribution; however these words differ depending on the domain. A description of each feature can be found in Zheng et al. [20].

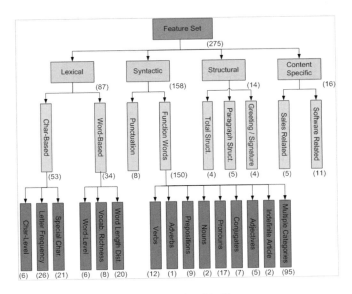

**Fig. 2.** Online Authorship Features

## 4.2 Dimensionality Reduction

Principal Component Analysis (PCA) is an unsupervised learning approach for feature selection and dimensionality reduction. It is identical to the self-featuring information compression variation of Karhunen-Loeve transforms that is often used in pattern recognition studies [18, 19]. The feature usage vectors for a specific group of features (e.g., punctuation) were transformed by using the two principal components (the two eigenvectors with the largest eigenvalues). Only the first two principal components were used since our analysis found that this many components were sufficient to capture the variance in the writing explained by each feature group. The extracted eigenvectors were then used by the dynamic sliding window algorithm to generate data points for the purpose of creating the *Writeprints*.

## 4.3 Dynamic Sliding Window Algorithm

The sliding window algorithm, originally used by Kjell et al. [9], is an iterative algorithm used to generate more data points for the purpose of creating writing style patterns. The algorithm can create powerful writing patterns by capturing usage variations at a finer level of granularity across a text document.

Figure 3 shows how the sliding window algorithm works. Once the eigenvectors have been computed using principal component analysis (Step 1) the algorithm extracts the feature usage vector for the text region inside the window, which slides over the text (Step 2). For each window instance, the sum of the product of the principal component (primary eigenvector) and the feature vector represents the x-coordinate of the pattern point while the sum of the product of the second component (secondary eigenvector) and the feature vector represents the y-coordinate of the data point (Step 3).

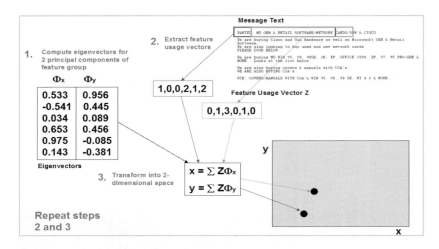

**Fig. 3.** Sliding Window Algorithm Illustration

Each data point generated is then plotted onto a 2-dimensional space to create the *Writeprint*. Steps 2 and 3 are repeated while the window slides over the text.

The dynamic sliding window algorithm features a couple of amendments over the original version [9], added specifically for the purpose of dealing with online material. Firstly, due to the challenging nature of cyber content and the shorter length of online messages, we applied the algorithm to our feature set sub-groups (e.g., punctuation, content-specific words, word length distribution, letter usage, etc.). Using multiple feature groups may provide better scalability to cope with the larger pool of potential authors associated with online messages. Secondly, we used dynamic window and overlap sizes based on message lengths. Online message lengths pose a challenge for authorship identification, with messages typically ranging anywhere from 20 to 5,000 characters in length (as compared to literary texts which can easily surpass lengths of 200,000 characters).

### 4.3.1 Selecting Feature Groups

Certain groups of features are not suitable for use with the dynamic sliding window algorithm. Ideal features are "frequency-based" features, which can easily be measured across a window, such as the usage of punctuation. Vocabulary richness, average, and percentage-based features (e.g., % characters per word, average word length) are not suitable since these are more effective across larger amounts of data and less meaningful when measured across a sliding window. Based on these criteria, we incorporated punctuation, letter frequencies, special characters, word length distributions, content specific words, and structural features. Structural features could not be captured using the sliding window, so they were transformed using feature vectors at the message level. This exception was made for structural features since they have been shown to be extremely important for identification of online messages [4]. Excluding them would result in weaker classification power for the *Writeprint* visualization.

### 4.3.2  Dynamic Window and Overlap Sizes

Our algorithm uses dynamic window and overlap sizes based on message lengths. This feature was incorporated in order to compensate for fluctuations in the sizes of online messages and to provide better support for shorter messages. We varied our window size between 128-1024 characters and interval between 4-16 characters.

## 4.4  Writeprints

Figure 4 shows an example of an author *Writeprint*. Each of the two regions shows the pattern for a particular feature group created using principal component analysis and the dynamic sliding window algorithm. Each point within a pattern represents an instance of feature usage captured by a particular window.

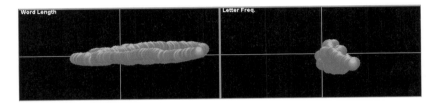

**Fig. 4.** Example Author Writeprint

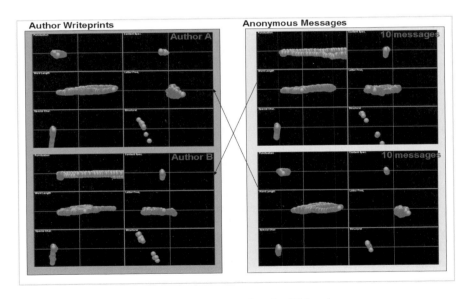

**Fig. 5.** Identification Example using Writeprints

### 4.4.1  Using Writeprints for Identification

Figure 5 presents an example of how *Writeprints* can be used for identification. The left column shows the writing style patterns for two authors (authors A-B) created using 20 messages. After creating these *Writeprints*, we then extracted 10 additional messages for each author as anonymous messages. By comparing the anonymous patterns to the ones known to belong to authors A and B, we can clearly attribute correct authorship of the anonymous messages. The anonymous messages on top belong to Author B and the ones on the bottom belong to Author A.

### 4.4.2  Limitations of Writeprints

While *Writeprints* provides a powerful visualization technique for authorship identification when given larger amounts of text, it is constrained when dealing with shorter individual messages (i.e., messages less than 30-40 words). This is due to the minimum length needs of the sliding window algorithm.

## 5   Evaluation

We believe that the *Writeprints* is better suited for larger quantities of information. In order to evaluate the viability of this visualization, we need to create automatic recognition mechanisms and conduct experiments on messages from different forums to evaluate our hypotheses.

### 5.1  Automatic Recognition

An automatic recognition technique is essential for the use of *Writeprints* in an online authorship identification setting. We created a Writeprint Comparison Algorithm in order to compare author/message writing style patterns created by *Writeprints*. The Writeprint algorithm compares the anonymous message(s) against all potential authors and determines the best author-message fit based on a similarity score.

The evaluation algorithm, consists of three parts. The first part (Step 1) attempts to determine the degree of similarity based on the shape and location of patterns for each feature group. The second part (Step 2) attempts to account for differences in the sizes of the two patterns that may occur due to large variations in the number of underlying data points that exist in the two *Writeprints* being compared. The final part (Step 3) involves computing the overall score which is the sum of the average distances between points in the two patterns as calculated based on Steps 1 and 2 taken across all feature groups (e.g., punctuation, content specific words, etc.).

### 5.2  Test Bed

Our test bed consisted of data taken from three online forums that were used based on their relevance to cybercrime research. The forums used included a USENET forum consisting of software sales and distribution messages (misc.forsale.computers.*), a Yahoo group forum for Al-Aqsa Martyrs (an Arabic speaking extremist group), and a website forum for the White Knights (a chapter of the Ku Klux Klan). For each forum, 30 messages were collected for each of 10 authors (300 messages per forum).

## 5.3  Experiment

In order to evaluate the discriminatory potential of Writeprints, we conducted an experiment on our test bed which consisted of messages from the three forums. For each author, 20 messages were used for training. The remaining 10 messages per author were used to test the visualizations.

The experiment was designed to evaluate what we perceived to be the strengths of our visualization. The experiment tested the ability of Writeprints to discriminate authorship across a group of messages. Support Vector Machines (SVM) was used as a baseline since it has established itself as an effective technique for online authorship identification. The classification accuracy (# correctly classified / # total classifications) was used to evaluate performance.

Principal component analysis was performed on our training messages (20 per author) for each forum in order to compute our eigenvectors. The three sets of eigenvectors were then used with the sliding window algorithm to create our "existing" author Writeprints. The testing messages were then compared against these Writeprints in order to determine authorship.

Three different scenarios were used for the test messages. We assumed that the anonymous messages from each author were received in groups of 10 messages, 5 messages, and individual messages. Thus, given 100 test messages total, we had 10 groups of 10 messages (1 group per author), 20 groups of 5 messages (2 groups per author), or 100 individual messages (10 per author). Varying cluster sizes of messages were used in order to test the effectiveness of *Writeprints* when presented with different amounts of text. For each scenario, the classification accuracy of *Writeprints* was compared against SVM, with the results presented in Table 1.

**Table 1.** Writeprints and SVM Classification Accuracy

| Forum | 10-Message Groups | | 5-Message Groups | | Single Messages* | |
|---|---|---|---|---|---|---|
| | WP | SVM | WP | SVM | WP | SVM |
| Software | 100.00% | 50.00% | 95.00% | 55.00% | 75.47% | 93.00% |
| White Knights | 100.00% | 60.00% | 100.00% | 65.00% | 85.00% | 94.00% |
| Al-Aqsa | 100.00% | 50.00% | 90.00% | 60.00% | 68.92% | 87.00% |

It should be noted that for individual messages, *Writeprints* was not able to perform on messages shorter than 250 characters (approximately 35 words) due to the need to maintain a minimum sliding window size and gather sufficient data points for the evaluation algorithm.

Pair wise t-tests were conducted to show the statistical significance of the results presented. The t-test results indicated that all experiment results were significant at an alpha level of 0.01 or 0.05. Thus, *Writeprints* significantly outperformed SVM when presented with a group of 5 or 10 messages and SVM significantly outperformed *Writeprints* on individual messages.

Based on the results, it is evident that SVM is better suited for classifying individual messages while *Writeprints* performs better for a group of anonymous messages that are known to belong to a single author. Thus, *Writeprints* may be a better alternative when provided a group of messages belonging to an anonymous author, as is quite common in computer mediated conversation. CMC conversations can result in a large group of messages written by an individual in a short period of time. Treating these messages as a single entity (as done in *Writeprints*) makes sense as compared to evaluating each as a separate short message, resulting in improved accuracy.

## 5.4   Results Discussion and Limitations

Based on the experimental evaluation of *Writeprints*, we believe that this technique is useful for authorship identification. Specifically, *Writeprints* is strong for identifying a group of messages. While the techniques isn't powerful enough to replace machine learning approaches such as SVM for authorship identification of individual online messages, it could provide significant utility if used in conjunction. Furthermore, *Writeprints* can provide invaluable additional information and insight into author writing patterns and authorship tendencies. While we feel that this work represents an important initial exploration into the use of information visualization for authorship identification, there is still a need for further experimentation to evaluate the scalability of these techniques across different online domains and languages, using a larger number of authors.

## 6   Conclusions and Future Directions

In this research we proposed a technique for authorship identification of online messages called *Writeprints*. The use of a writing style feature set specifically tailored towards multilingual online messages and automatic recognition mechanisms makes our proposed visualizations feasible for identification of online messages. The visualization provides unique benefits that can improve identification and authentication of online content. We believe that this technique represents an important and essential contribution towards the growing body of tools geared towards facilitating online accountability.

## References

1.  Abbasi, A. & Chen, H. Applying Authorship Analysis to Extremist-Group Web Forum Messages. IEEE Intelligent Systems, 20(5): (2005), 67-75.
2.  Baayen, R. H., Halteren, H. v., & Tweedie, F. J. Outside the cave of shadows: using syntactic annotation to enhance authorship attribution. Literary and Linguistic Computing, 2: (1996), 110-120.
3.  Burrows, J. F. Word patterns and story shapes: the statistical analysis of narrative style. Literary and Linguistic Computing, 2: (1987), 61 -67.
4.  De Vel, O., Anderson, A., Corney, M., & Mohay, G. Mining E-mail content for author identification forensics. SIGMOD Record, 30(4): (2001), 55-64.
5.  Donath, J. Identity and Deception in the Virtual Community. In Communities in Cyberspace, London, Routledge Press, 1999.
6.  Donath, J., Karahalio, K. & Viegas, F. Visualizing Conversation. Proceedings of the 32nd Hawaii International Conference on System Sciences (HICSS, 99), Hawaii, USA, 1999.

7. Erickson, T. & Kellogg, W. A. Social Translucence: An Approach to Designing Systems that Support Social Processes. ACM Transactions on Computer-Human Interaction, 7(1): (2001), 59-83.

8. Kelly, S. U., Sung, C., Farnham, S. Designing for Improved Social Responsibility, User Participation and Content in On-Line Communities. Proceedings of the Conference on Human Factors in Computing Systems (CHI '02), 2002.

9. Kjell, B., Woods, W.A., & Frieder, O. Discrimination of authorship using visualization. Information Processing and Management, 30 (1): (1994), 141-150.

10. Li, J., Zeng, R., & Chen, H. From Fingerprint to Writeprint. Communications of the ACM, (2006) Forthcoming.

11. Moores, T., & Dhillon, G. Software Piracy: A View from Hong Kong. Communications of the ACM, 43(12): (2000), 88-93.

12. Ribler, R. L., & Abrams, M. Using visualization to detect plagiarism in computer science classess. Proceedings of the IEEE Symposium on Information Vizualization, 2000.

13. Rocco, E. Trust Breaks Down in Electronic Contexts but can be repaired by some Initial Face-to-Face Contact. Proceedings of the Conference on Human Factors in Computing Systems (CHI '98), (1998), 496-502.

14. Sack, W. Conversation Map: An Interface for Very Large-Scale Conversations. Journal of Management Information Systems, 17(3): (2000), 73-92.

15. Shaw, C.D., Kukla, J.M., Soboroff, I., Ebert, D.S., Nicholas, C.K., Zwa, A., Miller, E.L., & Roberts, D.A. Interactive volumetric information visualization for document corpus management. International Journal on Digital Libraries, 2: (1999), 144–156.

16. Tweedie, F. J., Singh, S., & Holmes, D. I. Neural Network applications in stylometry: the Federalist papers. Computers and the Humanities, 30(1): (1996), 1-10.

17. Viegas, F.B., & Smith, M. Newsgroup Crowds and AuthorLines: Visualizing the Activity of Individuals in Conversational Cyberspaces Proceedings of the 37th Hawaii International Conference on System Sciences (HICSS, 04), Hawaii, USA, 2004.

18. Watanabe, S. Pattern Recognition: Human and Mechanical. John Wiley and Sons, Inc., New York, NY, 1985.

19. Webb, A. Statistical Pattern Recognition. John Wiley and Sons, Inc., New York, NY, 2002.

20. Zheng, R., Qin, Y., Huang, Z., & Chen, H. A Framework for Authorship Analysis of Online Messages: Writing-style Features and Techniques. Journal of the American Society for Information Science and Technology 57(3): (2006), 378-393.

# A Dictionary-Based Approach to Fast and Accurate Name Matching in Large Law Enforcement Databases

Olcay Kursun[1], Anna Koufakou[2], Bing Chen[2], Michael Georgiopoulos[2], Kenneth M. Reynolds[3], and Ron Eaglin[1]

[1] Department of Engineering Technology
[2] School of Electrical Engineering and Computer Science
[3] Department of Criminal Justice and Legal Studies,
University of Central Florida, Orlando, FL 32816
{okursun, akoufako, bchen,michaelg,
kreynold, reaglin}@mail.ucf.edu

**Abstract.** In the presence of dirty data, a search for specific information by a standard query (e.g., search for a name that is misspelled or mistyped) does not return all needed information. This is an issue of grave importance in homeland security, criminology, medical applications, GIS (geographic information systems) and so on. Different techniques, such as soundex, phonix, n-grams, edit-distance, have been used to improve the matching rate in these name-matching applications. There is a pressing need for name matching approaches that provide high levels of accuracy, while at the same time maintaining the computational complexity of achieving this goal reasonably low. In this paper, we present ANSWER, a name matching approach that utilizes a prefix-tree of available names in the database. Creating and searching the name dictionary tree is fast and accurate and, thus, ANSWER is superior to other techniques of retrieving fuzzy name matches in large databases.

## 1  Introduction

With the advances in computer technologies, large amounts of data are stored in data warehouses (centralized or distributed) that need to be efficiently searched and analyzed. With the increased number of records that organizations keep the chances of having "dirty data" within the databases (due to aliases, misspelled entries, etc.) increases as well [1,2]. Prior to the implementation of any algorithm to analyze the data, the issue of determining the correct matches in datasets with low data integrity must be resolved.

The problem of identifying the correct individual is indeed of great importance in the law enforcement and crime analysis arenas. For example, when detectives or crime analysts query for individuals associated with prior burglary reports, they need to be able to examine all the records related to these individuals, otherwise they might miss important clues and information that could lead to solving these cases. As mentioned earlier, missing names (and thus records) becomes a problem mainly due to common typing and misspelling errors. However, in the case of crime related

S. Mehrotra et al. (Eds.): ISI 2006, LNCS 3975, pp. 72–82, 2006.
© Springer-Verlag Berlin Heidelberg 2006

applications, this problem becomes even bigger due to other reasons, most important of which being that criminals try to modify their name and other information in order to deceive the law enforcement personnel and thus evade punishment. The other reason is that for a large number of cases, the name information might come from witnesses, informants, etc., and therefore this information (for example the spelling of a name) is not as reliable as when identification documents are produced. This is also true in the field of counterterrorism, where a lot of information comes from sources that might be unreliable, but which still needs to be checked nevertheless. It is evident then that it is imperative to have an efficient and accurate name matching technique that will guarantee to return all positive matches of a given name. On the other hand, the returned matches should not have too many false-positives, as the person who is investigating a crime is likely to be overwhelmed by unrelated information, which will only delay the solution of a case.

In this paper, we focus on the problem of searching proper nouns (first and last names) within a database. The application of interest to us is in law enforcement; however, there are many other application domains where availability of accurate and efficient name search tools in large databases is imperative, such as in medical, commercial, or governmental fields [3, 4].

There are two main reasons for the necessity of techniques that return fuzzy matches to name queries: (1) the user does not know the correct spelling of a name; (2) names are already entered within the database with errors because of typing errors, misreported names, etc [5]. For example, record linkage, defined as finding duplicate records in a file or matching different records in different files [6, 7], is a valuable application where efficient name matching techniques must be utilized.

## 2  Existing Methods

The main idea behind all name matching techniques is comparing two or more strings in order to decide if they both represent the same string. The main string comparators found in the literature can be divided in phonetic and spelling based. *Soundex* [8] is used to represent words by phonetic patterns. Soundex achieves this goal by encoding a name as the first letter of the name, followed by a three-digit number. These numbers correspond to a numerical encoding of the next three letters (excluding vowels and consonants h, y, and w) of the name [11]. The number code is such that spelled names that are pronounced similar will have the same soundex code, e.g., "Allan" and "Allen" are both coded as "A450". Although soundex is very successful and simple, it often misses legitimate matches, and at the same time, detects false matches. For instance, "Christie" (C623) and "Kristie" (K623) are pronounced similarly, but have different soundex encodings, while "Kristie" and "Kirkwood" share the same soundex code but are entirely different names.

On the contrary, spelling string comparators check the spelling differences between strings instead of phonetic encodings. One of the well-known methods that is used to compare strings is measuring their "edit distance", defined by Levenshtein [9]. This can be viewed as the minimum number of characters that need to be inserted into, deleted from, and/or substituted in one string to create the other (e.g., the edit distance of "Mich*a*el" and "Mi*t*chel*l*" is three). Edit-distance approaches can be extended in a variety of ways, such as taking advantage of phonetic similarity of substituted characters (or proximity of the corresponding keys on the keyboard) or checking for transposition of neighboring characters as another kind of common typographical error [10] (e.g., "Baldwin" vs. "Badlwin"). The name-by-name comparison by edit distance methods throughout the entire database renders the desired accuracy, at the expense of exhibiting high complexity and lack of scalability.

In this paper, we propose a string-matching algorithm, named ANSWER (Approximate Name Search With ERrors), that is fast, accurate, scalable to large databases, and exhibiting low variability in query return times (i.e., robust). This string comparator is developed to establish the similarity between different attributes, such as first and last names. In its application to name matching, ANSWER is shown to be even faster than phonetic-based methods in searching large databases. It is also shown that ANSWER's accuracy is close to those of full exhaustive searches by spelling-based comparators. Similar work to ours has been described by Wang et. al. [4], which focuses in identifying deceptive criminal identities, i.e. in matching different records that correspond to the same individual mainly due to false information provided by these individuals.

## 3  The Operational Environment -- FINDER

One of the major advantages of our research is that we have a working test-bed to experiment with (FINDER – the Florida Integrated Network for Data Exchange and Retrieval). FINDER (see Fig. 1) has been a highly successful project in the state of Florida that has addressed effectively the security and privacy issues that relate to information sharing between above 120 law enforcement agencies. It is operated as a partnership between the University of Central Florida and the law-enforcement

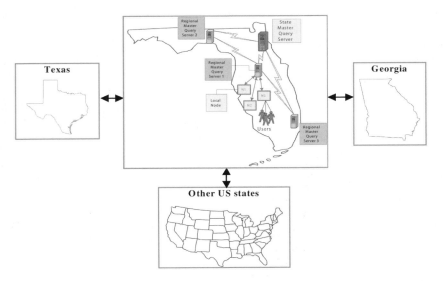

**Fig. 1.** The general overview of the FINDER network in Florida and expanded to other states

agencies in Florida sharing data – referred to as the Law Enforcement Data Sharing Consortium. Detailed information about the organization of the data sharing consortium and the FINDER software is available at http://finder.ucf.edu.

Part of the constraints of the FINDER system and also most law enforcement records management systems is that once the data has entered into the system it must remain intact in its current form. This includes data that have been erroneously entered, and consequently they contain misspellings. This problem was identified by the FINDER team and has also been substantiated in the literature [1, 12, 13, 14]. A simple illustration related to name matching, utilizing dirty data available in the FINDER system, is shown in Table 1, which emphasizes both the level of data integrity and the challenges of using standard SQL queries to retrieve records from a law enforcement database (also known as merge/purge problems [14]). In Table 1, we are depicting the results of an SQL query on "Joey Sleischman". An SQL query will miss all the records but the first one. The other records could be discovered only if we were to apply an edit distance algorithm on all the existing records in the database, an unsuitable approach though, due to its high computational complexity, especially in large databases. In particular, the rest of the records (besides the exact match), shown in Table 1 were identified by comparing the queried record ("Joey Sleischman") against all records in the database (by applying the edit distance approach). The Last Name, First Name, DOB (Date of Birth), and Sex were used as parameters in this search. In order to detect the matching records, we assigned weights to the fields: Last Name (40%), First Name (20%), DOB (30%), and Sex (10%). We used the edit distance algorithm [9] for determining the degree of match between fields.

**Table 1.** Example of the Data Integrity Issues within the FINDER data

| Last Name | First Name | DOB | Sex | Match |
|-----------|-----------|-----|-----|-------|
| INPUT QUERY: | | | | |
| *SLEISCHMAN* | *JOEY* | *1/21/1988* | *M* | *≥ 85%* |
| MATCHING RECORDS: | | | | |
| SLEISCHMAN | JOEY | 1/21/1988 | M | 100% |
| SLEICHMAN | JOEY | 7/21/1988 | M | 91% |
| SLEISCHMANN | JOSEPH | 1/21/1988 | M | 88% |
| SLEISCHMANN | JOSPEH | 1/21/1988 | M | 88% |
| SLEISHMAN | JOEY | | M | 87% |
| SLEISCHMANN | JOEY | | M | 87% |
| SLEISHCHMANN | JOSEPH | 1/21/1988 | M | 86% |
| SLESHMAN | JOEY | | M | 85% |

As it can be seen in Table 1, the edit distance algorithm provides an excellent level of matching, but the algorithm requires a full table scan (checking all records in the database). This level of computational complexity makes it unsuitable as a technique for providing name matching in applications, such as FINDER, where the number of records is high and consistently increasing. In the next sections, we are discussing in detail a name matching approach that alleviates this computational complexity.

## 4  The PREFIX Algorithm

In order to reduce the time complexity of the full-search of partially matching names in the database (of crucial importance in homeland security or medical applications), we propose a method that constructs a structured dictionary (or a tree) of prefixes corresponding to the existing names in the database (denoted PREFIX). Searching through this structure is a lot more efficient than searching through the entire database.

The algorithm that we propose is dependent on a maximum edit distance value that is practically reasonable. Based on experimental evidence, it has been stated that edit distance up to three errors performs reasonably well [15]. For example, "Michael" and "Miguel" are already at an edit distance of three. Let $k$ represent the maximum number of errors that is tolerated in the name matching process. Using a minimal $k$ value that works well in the application at hand would make the search maximally fast. Setting $k$ to zero would equal to an exact search which is currently available in any query system. Increasing $k$ increases the recall (i.e., it will not miss any true matches), even though this implies a very slow search and an increase in the number of false positives.

PREFIX relies on edit distance calculations. Its innovation though lies on the fact that it is not searching the entire database to find names that match the query entry but accomplishes this goal by building a dictionary of names. One might think that it would not be very efficient to have such a dictionary due to the fact that we would still need to search the whole dictionary, as the spelling error could happen anywhere in the string, such as "Smith" vs. "Rmith". However, our algorithm can search the dictionary very fast, using a tree-structure, by eliminating the branches of the tree that have already been found to differ from the query string by more than $k$.

There are two key points to our approach: (1) Constructing a tree of prefixes of existing names in the database and searching this structure can be much more efficient than a full scan of all names (e.g., if "Jon" does not match "Paul", one should not consider if "Jonathan" does); (2) such a prefix-tree is feasible and it will not grow unmanageably big. This is due to the fact that many substrings would hardly ever be encountered in valid names (e.g., a name would not start with a "ZZ"); consequently, this cuts down significantly the number of branches that can possibly exist in the tree. Similar data structures are proposed in the literature [16, 17] but they are not as suitable as ours when it comes to DBMS implementation (see Section 7).

The PREFIX algorithm creates a series of prefix-tables $T_1, T_2, T_3\ldots$, where $T_n$ will link (index) $T_{n+1}$. $T_n$ will contain all $n$-symbol-long prefixes of the names in the database. These tables correspond to the levels of the prefix-tree. The reason that we use tables is to facilitate the implementation of this approach in any database system. $T_n$ will have the following fields: current symbol (the $n^{th}$ symbol), previous symbol ($n$-$1^{st}$ symbol), next symbol ($n$+$1^{st}$ symbol), its links (each link will point to the index of an entry in the prefix-table $T_{n+1}$ with this current entry as the prefix, followed by the symbol in the "next symbol" field), and a field called Name that indicates whether or not the prefix itself is already a name (e.g., Jimm is a prefix of Jimmy but it may not be a valid name). Note that in the links field we cannot have more than 26 links because there are only 26 letters in the English alphabet. Also note that the first prefix-table ($T_0$) will not utilize the previous symbol field.

Suppose that our database contains "John", "Jon", "Jonathan", "Olcay", "Jim", "Oclay", and "Jimmy". After building the prefix-dictionary shown in Fig. 2, it can be used as many times as needed for subsequent queries. It is very simple to update the dictionary when new records are added (the same procedure explained above, when creating the tables in the first place, is used to add records one by one). Each level $i$ in Fig. 2 is a depiction of the prefix-table $T_i$ (for example the third table consists of JOH, JON, OLC, JIM, OCL). The dark-colored nodes in Fig. 2 are the prefixes that are actually valid names as well.

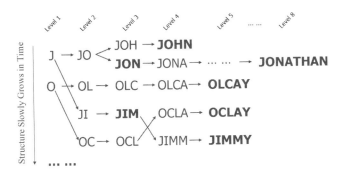

**Fig. 2.** The tree obtained by processing "John", "Jon", "Jonathan", "Olcay", "Jim", "Oclay", and "Jimmy"

The advantage of PREFIX is that when we search for approximate name matches, we can eliminate a sub-tree of the above-depicted tree (a sub-tree consists of a node and all of its offspring nodes and branches). Suppose that we search for any similar names with no more than one edit-error to the name "Olkay". When the algorithm examines level two of the tree, (i.e., the prefix-table $T_2$), it will find that the node JI is already at a minimum edit distance of two from "Olkay". Therefore any node that extends from JI-node should not be considered any further. That is, any name that starts with a JI is not going to be within the allowable error margin.

## 5   The ANSWER Algorithm

To use the PREFIX algorithm for a full name query rather than a single string query (such as a last name or a first name only), we apply the following steps: (1) build prefix-dictionary for the last names; (2) for a given full name query, search the tree for similar last names; (3) apply edit-distance algorithm on the returned records to obtain the ones that also have matching first names. In step 1, we could have built a prefix-tree for first names and in step 2, we could have obtained matching first names by scanning this tree; however, it would not have been as efficient as the stated PREFIX algorithm because first names are, in general, less distinct; consequently, by using first names at the beginning of the search process would have reduced our capability of filtering out irrelevant records.

The PREFIX algorithm offers a very efficient search of names. Nevertheless, it does not provide any direct way of utilizing a given first name along with the last name of a query because it does not use the first name information during the search of the tree. We propose the ANSWER (Approximate Name Search With ERrors) algorithm for fast and still highly accurate search of full names based on the PREFIX idea. In the process of building the prefix-dictionary, ANSWER takes every full name in the database, and using the PREFIX algorithm, it creates required nodes and links for the last names in the tree. It also augments each node in the tree by 26 bits, each bit representing whether any last name on that branch has an associated first name starting with the corresponding letter in the alphabet. For example, if the last name "Doe" could be found in the database only with the first names "Jon", "John", and "Michael", the corresponding nodes in the "Doe" branch in the tree would be "linked" with "J" and "M", meaning that the last name "Doe" can only have first names starting with "J" or "M".

This architecture allows early (before the edit-distance exceeds the predefined threshold $k$) pruning of tree nodes based on the first letter of the first name of the query. For example, if the query name was "John Doe", ANSWER would prune, say the F-node, if there were no last names starting with letter "F" associated with a first name that starts with "J", the first letter of "John". Based on our preliminary experiments and what we deduced from the literature [5, 11], it is unlikely that both first name and last name initials are incorrect (e.g., "Zohn Foe" is not an expectable match for "John Doe"). On the other hand, PREFIX would not prune the F-node right away because it does not take into consideration the first name at all, and there could be a last name similar to DOE that starts with "F" (e.g., "Foe"). Thus, PREFIX would scan more branches and take longer than ANSWER. Moreover, even though ANSWER is not an exhaustive search algorithm, it exhibits high hit rate as explained in the following section.

## 6   Experimental Results

In order to assess the performances of our exhaustive search engine PREFIX and its heuristic version ANSWER, we conducted a number of experiments. After creating the prefix-dictionary tree, we queried all distinct full names available in the FINDER database and measured the *time* taken by PREFIX and ANSWER in terms of the number of columns computed in the calculation of edit-distance calls (how edit-distance computation works was explained in Section 4.2). This way, the effect of factors such as operating system, database server, programming language, are alleviated. Furthermore, we compared PREFIX's and ANSWER's performance with other name matching techniques. In particular, we compared PREFIX and ANSWER with two other methods: Filtering-based soundex approach applied on (1) only last name (SDXLAST); (2) first or last names (SDXFULL). SDXLAST is a simple method that is based on the commonly used soundex schema that returns records with soundex-wise-matching last names, and then applies the edit-distance procedure (just as in our methods, the edit-distance calls terminate the computation once the maximum allowable edit errors $k$ is exceeded) to the last names to eliminate the false positives, and applies the edit-distance procedure once more on the first names of the remaining last names, in order to obtain the final set of matching full names.

It is worth noting though, that the hit rate obtained by using only the soundex-matches for the last names is insufficient due to inherent limitations of the soundex scheme [11]. For example, searching for "Danny Boldwing" using SDXLAST would not return "Danny Bodlwing" because the soundex code for "Boldwing" does not match the soundex code for "Bodlwing". Therefore, we devised an extension of SDXLAST in order to enhance its hit rate. We called this new method SDXFULL. SDXFULL selects records with soundex-wise-matching last names *or* soundex-wise-matching first names. As a result, if "Danny Boldwing" is the input query, SDXFULL would return not only "Danny Bodlwing" and "Dannie Boldwing" as possible true positives, but it would also return many false positives such as "Donnie Jackson" or "Martin Building". These false positives will be eliminated (by applying edit distance calculations to all these returned records) as in the SDXLAST method. Thus, it is expected that SDXFULL will have a higher recall (true positives) than SDXLAST but longer run-time since it also returns a larger number of false positives). The low recall rate of soundex is the reason for not comparing our methods with other phonetic-type matching methods, such as *Phonix* [11]. Phonix assigns unique numerals to even smaller groups of consonants than soundex, and it is thus expected to have an even lower recall rate than the already unacceptable recall rate observed in SDXLAST [11].

Our database contains about half a million (414,091 to be exact) records of full names, out of which 249,899 are distinct. In order to evaluate the behavior of these four name matching methods as the number of records in the database increases, we have applied each one of the aforementioned methods (PREFIX, ANSWER, SDXLAST, and SDXFULL) to the database at different sizes. For our experiments, we have chosen 25% (small), 50% (medium), 75% (large), and 100% (x-large) of records as the working set sizes. Note that a different prefix-dictionary is used for different set sizes, as the number of records in the database expands from the small to x-large sizes. We used the PREFIX algorithm as the baseline for our algorithm comparisons, since it performs an exhaustive search. For our experiments we used a maximum number of allowable edit-distance of 2 ($k=2$), for both last and first names. Thus, for every query by the exhaustive search, we have selected from the database all the available full names of which neither the last nor the first name deviates by more than two errors from the last and the first names, respectively, of the query. Of course, this does not mean all of these records with an edit distance of two or less refer to the same individual but this was the best that we could use as a baseline for comparisons because these names were at least interesting in respect that they were spelled similarly.

Fig. 3a plots the graph of average run-times for queries of each approach as a function of the database size. Note that in some applications, the hit-rate of the search can be as important as (if not more important than) the search time. Therefore, in order to quantify the miss rate, we have also computed the average hit-rates (the ratio of the true positives identified versus the total number of actual positives) for these methods (Fig. 3b). SDXLAST is the fastest search; however, it has the lowest hit-rate amongst all the algorithms. Furthermore, SDXLAST's hit-rate is unacceptably low for many applications [5, 11]. The ANSWER search is the next fastest for large databases (except for SDXLAST, which has a small hit rate). ANSWER is also significantly more accurate than the SDXFULL search. SDXFULL executes a simple search that fails when there are errors in both the last and the first names (this happens in increasingly more than 15% of the records). For instance, some of the records that are found by ANSWER but missed by SDXFULL are "Samantha Etcheeson" versus "Samatha Etcheenson" or "Yousaf Kodyxr" versus "Youse Rodyxr".

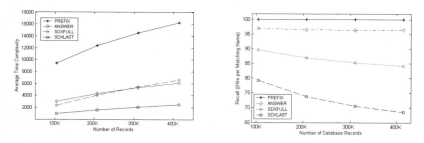

**Fig. 3.** Scalability versus database size. **(a)** Run-times; **(b)** Recall rates.

# 7   DBMS Implementation

ANSWER offers a very efficient search of names. Its database system implementation is not as fast, however it still remains to be a crucial tool of querying because it is a full search tool. Other techniques we could use are either partial searches with 60%-70% recall rates (such as soundex or phonix), or very slow (e.g. one pass over all the distinct full names with Levenshtein comparison takes about 10 minutes in database implementation). Soundex takes about half a second to query a name. However, it misses matching records due to its weak heuristicity.

This does not come as a surprise because it is a problem in general that algorithms implemented offline that use data outside the database system can employ efficient structures that reside in memory and a minimal number of database scans, and thus exhibit better performance than the equivalent database implementations. From the performance perspective, data mining algorithms that are implemented with the help of SQL are usually considered inferior to algorithms that process data outside the database systems. One of the important reasons is that offline algorithms employ sophisticated in-memory data structures and can scan the data as many times as needed without much cost due to speed of random access to memory [18]. Our initial experiments with early efforts of DBMS implementation resulted that the run time for ANSWER for $k=1$ is under a second. For k=2, the search time is in order of 5 seconds.

Disk-access is a very costly operation in database systems. Therefore, we will have to reduce the number of database accesses needed for searching the tree. One idea is to use the breadth-first search algorithm. For a query with a searched name of length $n$ and *MaxError* tolerable edit distance, the upper bound of the number of database accesses is, therefore, $n + MaxError$.

In order to further reduce database access, when we import the names into prefix tables, we can load the names in partial order so that the similar names are stored together in prefix name tables. Names whose initial letters are "AA" are firstly imported, then those with "AB", "AC", and until "ZZ". This way, when we query names, database server will automatically load and cache the data blocks with similar prefixes, thus we can facilitate I/O accesses by reducing the number of memory blocks to be retrieved.

# 8  Summary, Conclusions and Future Work

Dirty data is a necessary evil in large databases. Large databases are prevalent in a variety of application fields such as homeland security, medical, among others. In that case, a search for specific information by a standard query fails to return all the relevant records. The existing methods for fuzzy name matching attain variable levels of success related to performance measures, such as speed, accuracy, consistency of query return times (robustness), scalability, storage, and even ease of implementation.

Name searching methods using name-by-name comparisons by edit distance (i.e., the minimum number of single characters that need to be inserted into, deleted from, and/or substituted in one string to get another) throughout the entire database render the desired accuracy, but they exhibit high complexity of run time and thus are non-scalable to large databases. In this paper, we have introduced a method (PREFIX) that is capable of an exhaustive edit-distance search at high speed, at the expense of some additional storage for a prefix-dictionary tree constructed. We have also introduced a simple extension to it, called ANSWER that has run-time complexity comparable to soundex methods, and it maintains robustness and scalability, as well as a comparable level of accuracy compared to an exhaustive edit distance search. ANSWER has been tested, and its advantages have been verified, on real data from a law-enforcement database (FINDER).

# References

1. Kim, W. (2002) "On Database Technology for US Homeland Security", *Journal of Object Technology*, vol. 1(5), pp. 43–49.
2. Taipale, K.A. (2003) "Data Mining & Domestic Security: Connecting the Dots to Make Sense of Data", *The Columbia Science & Technology Law Review*, vol. 5, pp. 1–83.
3. Bilenko, M., Mooney, R., Cohen, W., Ravikumar, P., Fienberg, S. (2003) "Adaptive name matching in information integration", *IEEE Intelligent Systems*, vol. 18(5), pp. 16–23.
4. Wang, G., Chen, H., Atabakhsh, H. (2004) "Automatically detecting deceptive criminal identities", *Communications of the ACM*, March 2004, vol. 47(3), pp. 70–76.
5. Pfeifer, U., Poersch, T., Fuhr, N. (1995) "Searching Proper Names in Databases", *Proceedings of the Hypertext - Information Retrieval – Multimedia (HIM 95)*, vol. 20, pp. 259–276.
6. Winkler, W.E. (1999) "The state of record linkage and current research problems", *Proceedings of the Section on Survey Methods of the Statistical Society of Canada*.
7. Monge, A.E. and Elkan, C.P. (1997) "An Efficient Domain-Independent Algorithm for Detecting Approximately Duplicate Database Records", Proceedings of the ACM-SIGMOD Workshop on Research Issues on Knowledge Discovery and Data Mining, Tucson, AZ.
8. Newcombe, H.B., Kennedy J.M., Axford S.J., James, A.P. (1959) "Automatic linkage of vital records", *Science,* vol. 3381, pp. 954–959.
9. Levenshtein, V.L. (1966) "Binary codes capable of correcting deletions, insertions, and reversals", *Soviet Physics*, Doklady, vol. 10, pp. 707–710.

10. Jaro, M.A. (1976) "UNIMATCH: A Record Linkage System: User's Manual. Technical Report", *U.S. Bureau of the Census*, Washington, DC.
11. Zobel, J., Dart, P. (1995) "Finding approximate matches in large lexicons", *Software-Practice and Experience,* vol. 25(3), pp. 331–345.
12. Wilcox, J. (1997) "Police Agencies Join Forces To Build Data-Sharing Networks: Local, State, and Federal Crimefighters Establish IT Posses", *Government Computer News*, Sept. 1997.
13. Maxwell, T. (2005) "Information, Data Mining, and National Security: False Positives and Unidentified Negatives", *Proceedings of the 38th Hawaii International Conference on System Science.*
14. Hernandez, M., and Stolfo, S. (1998) "Real-world Data is Dirty: Data Cleansing and the Merge/purge Problems", *Data Mining Knowledge Discovery*, vol. 2, pp. 9-37, 1998.
15. Mihov, S., Schulz, K.U. (2004) "Fast Approximate Search in Large Dictionaries", *Journal of Computational Linguistics*, vol. 30(4), pp. 451–477.
16. Aoe, J., Morimoto, K., Shishibori M., Park, K. (2001) "A Trie Compaction Algorithm for a Large Set of Keys", *IEEE Transactions on Knowledge and Data Engineering*, vol. 8(3), pp. 476–491.
17. Navarro, G. (2001) "A Guided Tour to Approximate String Matching", *ACM Computing Surveys,* vol. 33(1), pp.31-88.

# Iterative Relational Classification Through Three–State Epidemic Dynamics

Aram Galstyan and Paul R. Cohen

Information Sciences Institute,
University of Southern California,
Marina del Rey, CA, USA
{galstyan, cohen}@isi.edu

**Abstract.** Relational classification in networked data plays an important role in many problems such as text categorization, classification of web pages, group finding in peer networks, *etc.* We have previously demonstrated that for a class of label propagating algorithms the underlying dynamics can be modeled as a two-state epidemic process on heterogeneous networks, where infected nodes correspond to classified data instances. We have also suggested a binary classification algorithm that utilizes non–trivial characteristics of epidemic dynamics. In this paper we extend our previous work by considering a three–state epidemic model for label propagation. Specifically, we introduce a new, intermediate state that corresponds to "susceptible" data instances. The utility of the added state is that it allows to control the rates of epidemic spreading, hence making the algorithm more flexible. We show empirically that this extension improves significantly the performance of the algorithm. In particular, we demonstrate that the new algorithm achieves good classification accuracy even for relatively large overlap across the classes.

**Keywords:** Relational learning, binary classification.

## 1 Introduction

Relational learning has attracted a great deal of attention in recent years. In contrast to traditional machine learning where data instances are assumed to be independent and identically distributed, relational learning techniques explicitly take into account interdependence of various instances. This allows them to make inferences based on not only intrinsic attributes of data but also its relational structure, thus enhancing inference accuracy. Recently a number of authors[10, 5, 1] have successfully used relational learning algorithms for classifying papers in CORA data–set [6] into topics. Other relevant applications of relational learning techniques include hypertext classification [4], link prediction[11], classification of web pages [9, 5], studying relational structures in scientific publications [7], etc.

Most relational learning algorithms are iterative and work by propagating either class labels or corresponding probabilities [8, 5]. One important issue with

S. Mehrotra et al. (Eds.): ISI 2006, LNCS 3975, pp. 83–92, 2006.

iterative classifiers is that false inferences made at some point in iteration might propagate further causing an "avalanche" [8]. Hence, it is very desirable to have some indicators showing when this happens. In our previous work we have shown that for a class of label propagating algorithms such an indicator can be obtained by looking at the dynamics of newly classified instances [1, 2]. We have demonstrated that these dynamics can be modeled as an epidemic spreading in heterogeneous population. Furthermore, if the coupling between two sub–populations is sufficiently weak, then the epidemics has a non-trivial two–tier structure. This is due to the fact that *true* class labels propagate at faster rate than *false* ones. We have also indicated how to use this dynamical signature for obtaining a robust and virtually parameter–free classifier.

Although the two–tier dynamics based classifier works well for relatively weak coupling between the classes, its performance deteriorates with increasing the overlap between them. This is because for large overlap there is a high probability that the infection will spread outside the class at the early stages of iterative process. In this paper we address this shortcoming by adding a new, intermediate state and extending the analogy of label propagation scheme to an epidemic system with three states: "healthy", "susceptible", and "infected". Initially all the nodes (e.g., data instances) are in the "healthy" state, except the nodes with known class labels that are in the "infected" state. At each iteration, a node will become susceptible if it is connected to super–threshold number of infected nodes. In contrast to the previous algorithm, however, not all susceptible nodes will make a transition to "infected" state at once. Instead, at each time step only a certain fraction of susceptible nodes will actually become infected. The main utility of the added state is that it slows down the rate of epidemic spreading, hence allowing to control the spread of infection from one sub–population to the other. We demonstrate that this added flexibility provides significant improvement over the original algorithm. In particular, we present empirical evidence that the new algorithm consistently outperforms the previous one, and achieves a good classification accuracy even when the overlap across two classes is relatively large.

## 2   Problem Settings

Generally speaking, relational learning algorithms use both intrinsic and relational characteristics of the data for inference. In this paper, however, we will neglect any intrinsic attributes and concentrate on solely relational aspect of classification. In this context, the relational data–set can be represented as a graph, where nodes represent data instances, and edges (possibly weighted) describe relationship between them. For instance, in CORA data–set of categorized computer science papers [6], each node represents a paper, while a link between two papers describes their relationship (e.g., common authors, cross–references, etc.). The main assumption of relational classification on such data is *homophily*, i.e., the notion that the data instances that are similar tend to be better connected (e.g., for the CORA data–set the homophily assumption means that papers that share authors and/or common references are likely to be similar).

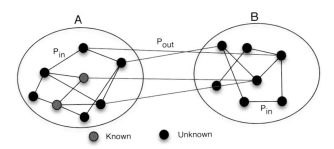

**Fig. 1.** Schematic representation of relational data–set

Throughout this paper we will evaluate our algorithms on synthetic data–sets as one schematically depicted in Fig. 1. Namely, each data instance belongs to one of two possible classes, $A$ and $B$, with $N_a$ and $N_b$ nodes in each class, respectively. These two classes are characterized by two loosely coupled subgraphs in Fig. 1. Initially we are given the class labels of small fraction of data instances of type $A$ (red nodes). The problem is then to find other members of $A$ based on the pattern of links in the graph. The graph itself is constructed as follows. Within each group, we randomly establish a link between two nodes with probability $p_{in}^{a,b}$. Probability of a link between two nodes across the groups is $p_{out}$. We also define average connectivities between respective types of nodes, $z_{aa} = p_{in}^a N_a$, $z_{bb} = p_{in}^b N_b$, $z_{ab} = p_{out} N_b$ and $z_{ba} = p_{out} N_a$. Note that generally speaking $z_{ab} \neq z_{ba}$ if the sizes of two groups are not equal, $N_a \neq N_b$. In this paper, we will characterize the intra– and inter–group connectivities through $z_{aa} = z_{bb} \equiv z_{in}$, and $z_{ab} \equiv z_{out}$. Clearly, the ratio $z_{out}/z_{in}$ characterizes the difficulty of the classification task. For small values of this ratio, the coupling between two sub–graphs is weak so most classification algorithms should do a good job of assigning correct class labels. If one increases this ratio, however, then the difference between in– and out–group link patterns decreases, hence making it difficult to classify nodes correctly.

## 3   Two–Tier Dynamics in Iterative Classification

The idea behind iterative classification is that inferences made at some point might be used for drawing further inferences. Although iterative classifiers are superior to one–shot classification techniques, there is a certain risk involved. Indeed, if one makes incorrect inferences at some point then there is a possibility that it will "snowball" and cause an avalanche of further incorrect inferences [8]. Moreover, since most of the algorithm rely on parameters, then the issue of parameter sensitivity becomes very important. Indeed, if small adjustment in parameters result in even a small number of incorrect inferences, then there is a chance that the iterative procedure will propagate these erroneous inferences further, causing instabilities. Hence, it is very important to be able to detect such instabilities, and prevent them from happening.

In our previous work we have suggested heuristics for detecting such undesired avalanches [1, 2]. This is done by looking at the dynamics of newly classified instances. The key for detection the instability is a phenomenon that we call two–tier dynamics. Namely, we characterize the dynamics of an iterative classifier by fraction of newly classified instances at each time step., e.g., if $\rho(t)$ is the fraction of classified instances at time $t$, then the relevant variable is $\Delta\rho(t) = \rho(t) - \rho(t - 1)$. As it will be clear later, two–tiered dynamics arises whenever $\Delta\rho(t)$ has two temporally separated peaks, that characterize epidemic spreading in separate sub–populations of nodes.

To be concrete, let us consider a relational data–set where each data instance belongs to one of two classes $A$ and $B$, as one depicted in Fig. 1 . We assume that the relational structure is fully characterized by the adjacency matrix $M$ so that the entry $M_{ij}$ describes the strength of the relationship between the $i$–th and $j$–th instances. Our algorithm relies on a threshold to decide when to propagate labels. Namely, a node will be classified as type $A$ if it is connected to super–threshold number of type $A$ nodes. Let us associate a state variable with each node, $s_i = 0, 1$ so that the state value $s_i = 1$ corresponds to type $A$. Initially, only the nodes with known class labels have $s_i = 1$ while the rest are in state $s = 0$. At each iteration step, for each non–classified node we calculate the cumulative weight of the links of that instance with known instances of type $A$. If this cumulative weight is greater or equal than a certain threshold $H$ , that node will be classified as a type $A$ itself. The pseudo–code for this iterative scheme is shown in Fig. 2. Note that this mechanism asymmetric in the sense that if a node was classified as type $A$ it will remain in that class until the end of iteration. This implies that the total number of classified $A$ node is a monotonically non–decreasing function of time. If the duration of iteration, $T_{max}$, is sufficiently long, then a steady state will be achieved, e.g., none of the nodes changes its state upon further iterations. Obviously, the final state of the system will depend on the threshold value and the graph properties as characterized by adjacency matrix. Specifically, if the threshold $H$ is set sufficiently low then the system will evolve to a state where every node is in state $s = 1$, i.e., every instance has been classified as type $A$. On the other hand, if threshold is too high, then no additional node will change its state to $s = 1$ at all.

```
input adjacency matrix M
initialize sᵢ = 1, for initially known instances,
initialize sᵢ = 0 for unknown instances
initialize a threshold H
iterate t = 0 : Tₘₐₓ
      for i–th node with sᵢ(t) = 0
            calculate wᵢ = Σ Mᵢⱼsⱼ(t)
            if wᵢ ≥ H ⇒ sᵢ(t + 1) = 1
      end for loop
end
```

**Fig. 2.** Pseudo–code of the iterative procedure

Before proceeding further, we note that our iterative procedure can be viewed as an epidemic process on a network. Indeed, let us treat the initially known data instances of type $A$ as "infected". Then the dynamical scheme above describes an epidemic spreading throughout the network. If there were no links between data instances of different type, then clearly the epidemics would be contained in the $A$ sub–population. Hence, one could relax the classification criterion by reducing the threshold $H$ so that all the data instances of type $A$ will be infected, i.e., correctly classified. If there is a non–zero coupling between two classes, however, then there is a chance that the epidemic will "leak" to the second sub–population too, hence causing an avalanche of wrong inferences. Our main observation is that if the coupling is not very strong, then one can choose a threshold value so that the epidemic spreading in separate sub–populations is well–separated in time. In other words, the epidemic infects most of the nodes in population $A$ before spreading through the second population. Then, one can look at the dynamics of newly classified instances and detect the onset of the avalanche.

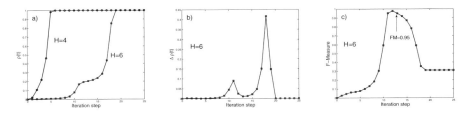

**Fig. 3.** Simulation results for $\rho(t)$ (a), $\Delta\rho(t) = \rho(t) - \rho(t-1)$ (b) and F measure (c) for a random network

To demonstrate this, in Fig. 3 we present the results of the iterative procedure on randomly generated graphs for the same network parameters but two different values of the threshold parameter. The parameters of the network are $N_a = 1000$, $N_b = 4000$, $z_{aa} = z_{bb} = 20$, $z_{ab} = 8$. Initially, only 10% of $A$ nodes are classified. For $H = 4$ all of the nodes are classified as type $A$ after a short period of time. For $H = 6$, however, the dynamics is drastically different as it has a distinctly bimodal shape. Indeed, after a sharp initial spread the dynamics seems to be saturating around $t = 13$. However, upon further iteration the number of classified nodes increases rapidly and after short transient all the nodes are infected. Clearly, this corresponds to the onset of the "avalanche" where certain wrong inferences propagate and infect rest of the system. This is especially clear in Fig. 3 (b) where we plot the the fraction of newly classified instances vs time, and observe two well separated maxima, which characterize the peak infection rates in respective population.

Note that this bimodal shape suggest a natural criterion for stopping the iteration. Namely, the iteration should be stopped when the second peaks starts to develop, e.g., before infection starts to spread into the second population. Indeed, in Fig. 3 (c) we plot the F measure of classification accuracy vs iteration step. One can see that at the point where the second peak starts to develop the F measure is $\sim 0.95$, which is only slightly less than the maximum value 0.97.

We now consider the effect of the overlap between two populations by increasing the inter–group connectivity $z_{ab}$. As we mentioned before, increasing the overlap should make the classification task more difficult. In particular, we expect that for large $z_{ab}$ the two–tier dynamics should be less pronounced. Indeed, in Fig. 4 a) we plot the fraction of newly infected nodes for $z_{ab} = 12$ and $z_{ab} = 16$. One can see that for $z_{ab} = 12$, although there are still two peaks, the separation between them has decreased drastically. Increasing $z_{ab}$ further leads to gradual disappearance of two–tier structure, as it shown for $z_{ab} = 16$. In the terminology of epidemic dynamics, this is due the fact that for large inter–group connectivity the epidemic starts to spread into the $B$ nodes before infecting majority of $A$ nodes.

To explain this phenomenon, we now provide a qualitative assessment of two–tier dynamics (a more detailed study will be presented elsewhere [3]). Let us first consider epidemic spreading in a single population, e.g., among $A$ nodes, and neglect inter–group links. It can be demonstrated that for a fixed fraction of initially infected nodes, there is a critical intra–group connectivity $z_{in}^c$ so that for $z_{in} < z_{in}^c$ the epidemic will be contained within a small fraction of nodes, while for $z_{in} > z_{in}^c$ it will spread throughout a system. Put conversely, we can say that for any fixed connectivity $z_{in}$, there is a critical fraction of initially infected nodes $\rho_0^c$ so that for $\rho_0 > \rho_0^c$ the epidemic will spread globally. We also note that at the critical point, the transient time (i.e., time to reach the steady state) of the epidemic process diverges. Now let us consider the full system with two populations. Let us again assume that all initially infected nodes are contained in the $A$ population. For sufficiently weak coupling between the groups, the the epidemic dynamics among $A$ nodes will be virtually unaffected by the $B$ nodes. In particular, whether the epidemic will infect all of the $A$ nodes will depend on the fraction of initially infected nodes and the connectivity $z_{in}$. Assume that these parameters are chosen such that the epidemic process indeed infects all of the $A$ nodes. Let us now ask under what conditions the infection will spread through $B$ population. It is easy to see that the infected $A$ nodes play the role of infection "seeds" for $B$ nodes. Moreover, the effective fraction of these seed nodes depend

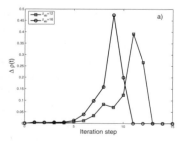 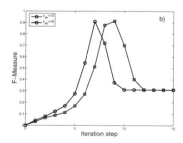

**Fig. 4.** (a)The fraction of newly classified nodes and (b) F measure vs iteration step for $z_{ab} = 12$ and $z_{ab} = 16$.

on the inter–group connectivity $z_{out}$. Hence, by extending the reasoning about critical phenomenon to $B$ nodes, one can demonstrate that for a given fraction of infected $A$ nodes $\rho_a$ and an intra–group connectivity $z_{in}$, there is a critical inter–group connectivity $z_{out}^c(\rho_a, z_{in})$ so that for $z_{out} > z_{out}^c$ the infection will spread globally to $B$ nodes. Assuming that $z_{in}$ is fixed, this relation is characterized by a critical line in $z_{out} - \rho_a$ plane. Now we can assess when the two tier–dynamics will be most pronounced. Indeed, if we take $\rho_a = 1$ (meaning that all $A$ nodes have been affected) then the maximum separation between two activity peaks will be infinite for $z_{out} = z_{out}^c(1, z_{in})$, since the transient time of epidemic among $B$ nodes diverges at the critical point. Moreover, for values of $z_{out}$ slightly above the critical value, one should still expect a significant separation between two peaks.

We now consider the effect of increasing the inter–group connectivity $z_{out}$. Clearly, this will decrease the critical fraction of $A$ nodes for which the epidemics will spread to $B$ nodes. Specifically, let us define $\rho_a^c(z_{out})$ as the minimum fraction of infected $A$ nodes required to cause a global epidemic among $B$ nodes. In other words, for a fixed $z_{out}$ the infection will spread to $B$ population only after infecting the fraction $\rho_a^c(z_{out})$ of $A$ nodes. Now, if this fraction is close to 1, then the epidemic will spread to $B$ nodes only after infecting the majority of $A$ nodes, hence, giving rise to two–tier dynamics. On the other hand, if this fraction is considerably less than one, the the epidemic will leak to $B$ nodes prematurely. To be more precise, consider again Fig. 3 (b). If at the height of the first peak the density of infected $A$ nodes is considerably greater than the threshold $\rho_a^c(z_{out})$ , then at the next iteration there will be a large number of infected $B$ nodes . As a consequence, the fraction of newly infected nodes will still increase, and there will be no two–tier dynamics.

It is worthwhile to note that even in the absence of two–tier dynamics, our main assumption that *true* class labels propagate faster than the *false* ones still holds to some degree. Indeed, in Fig. 4 we plot the F measure vs iteration step, and note that it still attains a maximum value that is close to 0.95. Hence, if we somehow knew where to stop the iteration, we would still be able to obtain good classification accuracy. The problem is, however, that without a clear two–tier signature we do not have any criterion as when to stop the iteration.

## 4    Three–State Epidemic Model for Label Propagation

As we explained above, the two-tier dynamics is not present for sufficiently strong coupling between two populations. At the same time, we saw that the true class labels still propagate faster than the false ones. This suggests that the two–state epidemic mechanism is somehow rigid as it does not allow one to control the rate of epidemic spreading. Indeed, recall that there is a threshold fraction of $A$ nodes $\rho_a^c$ so that for $\rho_a > \rho_a^c$ the epidemic starts to spread among $B$ nodes. Thus, if we could control the rate of epidemic among $A$ nodes, we should in principle be able to infect up to $\rho_a^c$ fraction of $A$ nodes without worrying that the infection will leak to $B$ nodes . However, in the absence of such a control mechanism, there is a chance that at some point in the iteration the fraction of infected $A$ nodes will "overshoot" this threshold significantly, hence causing epidemic among $B$ nodes.

To account for this shortcoming, we now consider an extension of the previous algorithm by adding another, intermediate state. In the terminology of relational classification this intermediate state describes a node that has been "marked" for infection, but has not been infected yet. We term this intermediate state as "susceptible". At a given iteration step, a node will become susceptible if it is connected to super-threshold number of infected nodes. However, we will now allow only a maximum number, $N_{max}$, of susceptible nodes to become infected at each iteration step. By choosing $N_{max}$ sufficiently small, we can expect that the fraction of infected $A$ nodes will approach its critical value $\rho_a^c$ smoothly, without the risk of overshooting[1]. Note that in practice this can be done by keeping a queue of susceptible nodes, and processing the queue according to some priority mechanism. The priority mechanism used in this paper is FIFO (first–in–first–out). However, other mechanism can be used too.

Before presenting our results, we now address the question of what kind of criterion should be used for stopping the iteration. Clearly, since at each time step only a handful of nodes are classified as infected, one should not expect any two–tier dynamics in the number of infected nodes. However, as we will see below, the number of newly susceptible nodes does in fact have the two–tier structure, e.g., if $s(t)$ is the fraction of susceptible nodes at time $t$, then the relevant quantity is $\Delta s(t) = s(t) - s(t-1)$. As in the case of previous two-state algorithm, the onset of the "avalanche" is then indicated by a second developing peak. Once this onset is found (e.g., by finding the iteration step for which the curve has its minimum), then we can backtrack trough class–label assignments, and "un–impeach" nodes that became susceptible after the onset.

To test our new algorithm, we have performed extensive empirical studies of new classification scheme for data-sets of varying overlap. We found that the new algorithm consistently outperforms the old one for all considered data–sets. Even for relatively small overlap across the classes, when the two–tier dynamics in two–state model is present, the classification accuracy of the new algorithm is significantly better. Indeed, in Fig. 5 (a) we plot the time series of $F$ measure for the new classification scheme, for a inter–group connectivities $z_{ab} = 8$ and $z_{ab} = 20$. For $z_{ab} = 8$, the F measure attains a maximum value very close to 1, while for $z_{ab} = 20$ the maximum is close to 0.9. Note that the behavior of both curves is relatively smooth around the maxima. This suggests that even if one stops the iteration within some interval around the optimal stopping time, one can still obtain relatively good classification. Indeed, in Fig. 5 (b) we plot the differential fraction of susceptible nodes, $\Delta s(t)$. Because of large dispersion, we also plot the running averages of each curve using a window of size 20, and use this average for examining two–tier structure. Note that for $z_{ab} = 8$, $\Delta s(t)$ is rather flat for a time interval between $t = 50$ and $t = 80$. Remarkably, we

---

[1] Our experiments suggest that the exact value of $N_{max}$ does not affect the results much, if it is not chosen too high. In the results reported below, we used $N_{max} = 10$.

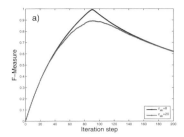 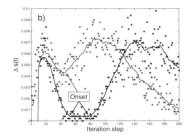

**Fig. 5.** The F measure (a) and the fraction of newly "susceptible" nodes (b) vs iteration step for $z_{ab} = 8$ (blue) and $z_{ab} = 20$ (red). The solid line in (b) is the moving average of respective scatter–plots using a window of size 20.

found that even if we choose the stopping time randomly from this interval, the resulting F measure will be contained in the interval $0.985 - 0.99$, which is higher than the F measure 0.95 achieved by the previous algorithm. Most importantly, however, the new algorithm allows to achieve significant classification accuracy even when the previous two-state scheme fails, e.g., does not demonstrate two–tier dynamics. Indeed, determining the onset for $z_{ab} = 20$ at $t \approx 50$, one is able to achieve an F measure around 0.85.

## 5   Conclusion and Future Work

In conclusion, we have presented a binary relational classification algorithm based on a three state epidemic process. This algorithm extends our previous two–state model by by adding a new, intermediate state. The addition of this state allows us to control the rate of epidemic spreading across the networked data, hence preventing premature leak of epidemic into the second sub–population. Our experiments demonstrate that this extension improves significantly the performance of the algorithm. In particular, the algorithm is remarkably accurate even when the overlap between two classes in relational data is relatively large.

As future work, we intend to test different priority mechanisms while processing the queue of susceptible nodes. For instance, one could define a priority scheme that depends on the degree of the nodes. The reason for this is as follows: if a certain nodes has super–threshold number of links to infected nodes, but has less links in total as other susceptible nodes, then it should be a better candidate for classification. We do not think that such a priority mechanism would make difference on the empirical studies on random graphs presented here. Indeed, the number of links of a node within and outside of a group are uncorrelated by our construction. However, this mechanism might be important in other scenarios where such a correlation exists.

We also intend to validate our algorithm on real world data–sets. We have previously demonstrated that the two–tier dynamics based algorithm performs well on certain subtopics from CORA archive of categorized computer science papers. However, one of the issues with the previous algorithms was that it did not perform well for classes with large number of members. The reason for poor performance is that for a large class the chances that the epidemic will leak outside before infecting the correct class instances are greater. Since our new algorithm allows better control over the rate of epidemic spredading, we we expect that it will perform well on large classes too.

# References

1. A. Galstyan and P. R. Cohen, "Inferring Useful Heuristics from the Dynamics of Iterative Relational Classifiers, International Joint Conference on Artificial Intelligence, Edinburgh, Scotland, (2005).
2. A. Galstyan and P. R. Cohen, "Identifying Covert Sub-Networks Through Iterative Node Classification", in Proc. of International Conference on Intelligence Analysis, McLean, VA, (2005).
3. A. Galstyan and P. R. Cohen, "Global Cascades in Modular Networks, working paper, (2006).
4. L. Getoor, E. Segal, B. Taskar, and D. Koller, "Probabilistic models of text and link structure for hypertext classification", In IJCAI Workshop on Text Learning: Beyond Supervision, 2001.
5. S. A. Macskassy, and F. J. Provost, "A Simple Relational Classifier", Workshop on Multi-Relational Data Mining in conjunction with KDD-2003, (2003).
6. Andrew McCallum, Kamal Nigam, Jason Rennie, and Kristie Seymore, "Automating the construction of internet portals with machine learning", *Information Retrieval Journal*, 3:127–163, 2000.
7. A. McGovern, L. Friedland, M. Hay, B. Gallagher, A. Fast, J. Neville, and D. Jensen, "Exploiting relational structure to understand publication", 2003.
8. J. Neville and D. Jensen, "Iterative classification in relational data", Proc. AAAI-2000 Workshop on Learning Statistical Models from Relational Data, pages 13–20. AAAI Press, 2000.
9. Seán Slattery and Mark Craven, "Discovering test set regularities in relational domains", In Pat Langley, editor, *Proceedings of ICML-00, 17th International Conference on Machine Learning*, pages 895–902, Stanford, US, 2000. Morgan Kaufmann Publishers, San Francisco, US.
10. B. Taskar, E. Segal and D. Koller, "Probabilistic Classification and Clustering in Relational Data", In Proceedings of IJCAI-01, 17th International Joint Conference on Artificial Intelligence, Seattle, US, 2001.
11. B. Taskar, M. Wong, P. Abbeel, and D. Koller, "Link prediction in relational data", In Proceedings of Neural Information Processing Systems, 2004.

# Analyzing Entities and Topics in News Articles Using Statistical Topic Models

David Newman[1], Chaitanya Chemudugunta[1],
Padhraic Smyth[1], and Mark Steyvers[2]

[1] Department of Computer Science,
UC Irvine, Irvine, CA
{newman, chandra, smyth}@uci.edu
[2] Department of Cognitive Science,
UC Irvine, Irvine, CA
msteyver@uci.edu

**Abstract.** Statistical language models can learn relationships between topics discussed in a document collection and persons, organizations and places mentioned in each document. We present a novel combination of statistical topic models and named-entity recognizers to jointly analyze entities mentioned (persons, organizations and places) and topics discussed in a collection of 330,000 New York Times news articles. We demonstrate an analytic framework which automatically extracts from a large collection: topics; topic trends; and topics that relate entities.

## 1   Introduction

The ability to rapidly analyze and understand large sets of text documents is a challenge across many disciplines. Consider the problem of being given a large set of emails, reports, technical papers, news articles, and wanting to quickly gain an understanding of the key information contained in this set of documents. For example, lawyers frequently need to analyze the contents of very large volumes of evidence in the form of text documents during the discovery process in legal cases (e.g., the 250,000 Enron emails that were made available to the US Justice Department [1]). Similarly, intelligence analysts are faced on a daily basis with vast databases of intelligence reports from which they would like to quickly extract useful information.

There is increasing interest in text mining techniques to solve these types of problems. Supervised learning techniques classify objects such as documents into predefined classes [2]. While this is useful in certain problems, in many applications there is relatively little knowledge *a priori* about what the documents may contain.

Unsupervised learning techniques can extract information from sets of documents without using predefined categories. Clustering is widely used to group

S. Mehrotra et al. (Eds.): ISI 2006, LNCS 3975, pp. 93–104, 2006.
© Springer-Verlag Berlin Heidelberg 2006

documents into $K$ clusters, where the characteristics of the clusters are determined in a data-driven fashion [3]. By representing each document as a vector of word or term counts (the "bag of words" representation), standard vector-based clustering techniques can be used, where the learned cluster centers represent "prototype documents." Another set of popular unsupervised learning techniques for document collections are based on matrix approximation methods, i.e. singular value decomposition (or principal components analysis) of the document-word count matrix [4, 5]. This approach is often referred to as latent semantic indexing (LSI).

While both clustering and LSI have yielded useful results in terms of reducing large document collections to lower-dimensional summaries, they each have their limitations. For example, consider a completely artificial data set where we have three types of documents with equal numbers of each type: in the first type each document contains only two words *wordA, wordB*, in the second type each document contains only the words *wordC, wordD*, and the third type contains a mixture, namely the words *wordA, wordB, wordC, wordD*.

LSI applied to this toy data produces two latent topic vectors with orthogonal "directions": *wordA + wordB + wordC + wordD* and *wordA + wordB - wordC - wordD*. These two vectors do not capture the fact that each of the three types of documents are mixtures of two underlying "topics", namely *wordA + wordB* and *wordC + wordD*. This limitation is partly a reflection of the fact that LSI must use negative values in its basis vectors to represent the data, which is inappropriate given that the underlying document-word vectors (that we are representing in a lower-dimensional space) consist of non-negative counts. In contrast, as we will see later in the paper, probabilistic representations do not have this problem. In this example the topic model would represent the two topics *wordA + wordB* and *wordC + wordD* as two multinomial probability distributions, $[\frac{1}{2}, \frac{1}{2}, 0, 0]$ and $[0, 0, \frac{1}{2}, \frac{1}{2}]$, over the four-word vocabulary, capturing the two underlying topics in a natural manner. Furthermore, the topic model would correctly estimate that these two topics are used equally often in the data set, while LSI would estimate that its first topic direction is used approximately twice as much as its second topic direction.

Document clustering techniques, such as k-means and agglomerative clustering, suffer from a different problem, that of being forced to assume that each document belongs to a single cluster. If we apply the k-means algorithm to the toy data above, with $K = 2$ clusters it will typically find one cluster to be centered at $[1, 1, 0, 0]$ and the other at $[\frac{1}{2}, \frac{1}{2}, 1, 1]$. It is unable to capture the fact that there are two underlying topics, corresponding to *wordA + wordB* and *wordC + wordD* and that that documents of type 3 are a combination of these two topics.

A more realistic example of this effect is shown in Table 1. We applied k-means clustering with $K = 100$ and probabilistic topic models (to be described in the next section) with $T = 100$ topics to a set of 1740 papers from 12 years of the Neural Information Processing (NIPS) Conference[1]. This data set contains

---

[1] Available on-line at http://www.cs.toronto.edu/~roweis/data.html

a total of $N = 2,000,000$ word tokens and a vocabulary size of $W = 13,000$ unique words. Table 1 illustrates how two different papers were interpreted by both the cluster model and the probabilistic topic model. The first paper discussed an analog circuit model for auditory signal processing—in essence it is a combination of a topic on circuits and a topic on auditory modeling. The paper is assigned to a cluster which fails to capture either topic very well—shown are the most likely words in the cluster it was assigned to. The topic model on the other hand represents the paper as a mixture of topics. The topics are quite distinct (the highest probability words in each topic are shown), capturing the fact that the paper is indeed a mixture of different topics. Similarly, the second paper was an early paper in bioinformatics, again combining topics that are somewhat different, such as protein modeling and hidden Markov models. Again the topic model can separate out these two underlying topics, whereas the clustering approach assigns the paper to a cluster that is somewhat mixed in terms of concepts and that does not summarize the semantic content of the paper very well.

The focus of this paper is to extend our line of research in probabilistic topic modeling to analyze persons, organizations and places. By combining named entity recognizers with topic models we illustrate how we can analyze the relationships between these entities (persons, organizations, places) and topics, using a large collection of news articles.

**Table 1.** Comparison of topic modeling and clustering

| Abstract from Paper | Topic Mix | Cluster Assignment |
|---|---|---|
| Temporal Adaptation in a Silicon Auditory Nerve (**J Lazzaro**) Many auditory theorists consider the temporal adaptation of the auditory nerve a key aspect of speech coding in the auditory periphery. Experiments with models of auditory localization ... I have designed an analog integrated circuit that models many aspects of auditory nerve response, including temporal adaptation. | [**topic 80**] analog circuit chip current voltage vlsi figure circuits pulse synapse silicon implementation cmos output mead hardware design [**topic 33**] auditory sound localization cochlear sounds owl cochlea song response system source channels analysis location delay | [**cluster 8**] circuit figure time input output neural analog neuron chip system voltage current pulse signal circuits networks response systems data vlsi |
| Hidden Markov Models in Molecular Biology: New Algorithms and Applications (**P Baldi, Y Chauvin, T Hunkapiller, M McClure**) Hidden Markov Models (HMMs) can be applied to several important problems in molecular biology. We introduce a new convergent learning algorithm for HMMs ...that are trained to represent several protein families including immunoglobulins and kinases. | [**topic 10**] state hmm markov sequence models hidden states probabilities sequences parameters transition probability training hmms hybrid model likelihood modeling [**topic 37**] genetic structure chain protein population region algorithms human mouse selection fitness proteins search evolution generation function sequence sequences genes | [**cluster 88**] model data models time neural figure state learning set parameters network probability number networks training function system algorithm hidden markov |

## 2    A Brief Review of Statistical Topic Models

The key ideas in a statistical topic model are quite simple and are based on a probabilistic model for each document in a collection. A topic is a multinomial probability distribution over the $V$ unique words in the vocabulary of the corpus, in essence a $V$-sided die from which we can generate (in a memoryless fashion) a "bag of words" or a set of word counts for a document. Thus, each topic $t$ is a probability vector, $p(w|t) = [p(w_1|t), \ldots, p(w_V|t)]$, where $\sum_v p(w_v|t) = 1$, and there are $T$ topics in total, $1 \leq t \leq T$.

A document is represented as a finite mixture of the $T$ topics. Each document $d$, $1 \leq d \leq N$, is assumed to have its own set of mixture coefficients, $[p(t = 1|d), \ldots, p(t = T|d)]$, a multinomial probability vector such that $\sum_t p(t|d) = 1$. Thus, a randomly selected word from document $d$ has a conditional distribution $p(w|d)$ that is a mixture over topics, where each topic is a multinomial over words:

$$p(w|d) = \sum_{t=1}^{T} p(w|t)p(t|d).$$

If we were to simulate $W$ words for document $d$ using this model we would repeat the following pair of operations $W$ times: first, sample a topic $t$ according to the distribution $p(t|d)$, and then sample a word $w$ according to the distribution $p(w|t)$.

Given this forward or generative model for a set of documents, the next step is to learn the topic-word and document-topic distributions given observed data. There has been considerable progress on learning algorithms for these types of models in recent years. Hofmann [6] proposed an EM algorithm for learning in this context using the name "probabilistic LSI" or pLSI. Blei, Ng and Jordan [7] addressed some of the limitations of the pLSI approach (such as the tendency to overfit) and recast the model and learning framework in a more general Bayesian setting. This framework is called Latent Dirichlet allocation (LDA), essentially a Bayesian version of the model described above, and the accompanying learning algorithm is based on an approximation technique known as variational learning. An alternative, and efficient, estimation algorithm based on Gibbs sampling was proposed by Griffiths and Steyvers [9], a technique that is closely related to earlier ideas derived independently for mixture models in statistical genetics [10]. Since the Griffiths and Steyvers paper was published in 2004, a number of different groups have successfully applied the topic model with Gibbs sampling to a variety of large corpora, including large collections of Web documents [11], a collection of 250,000 Enron emails [12], 160,000 abstracts from the CiteSeer computer science collection [13], and 80,000 news articles from the 18th-century Pennsylvania Gazette [14]. A variety of extensions to the basic topic model have also been developed, including author-topic models [15], author-role-topic models [12], topic models for images and text [16, 7], and hidden-Markov topic models for separating semantic and syntactic topics [17].

In this paper all of the results reported were obtained using the topic model outlined above with Gibbs sampling, as described originally in [9]. Our description of the model and the learning algorithm is necessarily brief: for a more detailed tutorial introduction the reader is recommended to consult [18].

# 3   Data Set

To analyze entities and topics, we required a text dataset that was rich in entities including persons, organizations and locations. News articles are ideal because they have the primary purpose of conveying information about who, what, when and where. We used a collection of New York Times news articles taken from the Linguistic Data Consortium's English Gigaword Second Edition corpus (www.ldc.upenn.edu). We used all articles of type "story" from 2000 through 2002, resulting in 330,000 separate articles spanning three years. These include articles from the NY Times daily newspaper publication as well as a sample of news from other urban and regional US newspapers.

We automatically extracted named entities (i.e. proper nouns) from each article using one of several named entity recognition tools. We evaluated two tools including GATE's Information Extraction system ANNIE (gate.ac.uk), and Coburn's Perl Tagger (search.cpan.org/ acoburn/Lingua-EN-Tagger). ANNIE is rules-based and makes extensive use of gazetteers, while Coburn's tagger is based on Brill's HMM part-of-speech tagger [19]. ANNIE tends to be more conservative in identifying a proper noun. For this paper, entities were extracted using Coburn's tagger. For this 2000-2002 period, the most frequently mentioned people were: George Bush; Al Gore; Bill Clinton; Yasser Arafat; Dick Cheney and John McCain. In total, more than 100,000 unique persons, organizations and locations were extracted. We filtered out 40,000 infrequently occurring entities by requiring that an entity occur in at least ten different news articles, leaving 60,000 entities in the dataset.

After tokenization and removal of stopwords, the vocabulary of unique words was also filtered by requiring that a word occur in at least ten different news articles. We produced a final dataset containing 330,000 documents, a vocabulary of 40,000 unique words, a list of 60,000 entities, and a total of 110 million word tokens. After this processing, entities occur at the rate of 1 in 6 words (not counting stopwords).

# 4   Experiments

In this section we present the results from a $T = 400$ topic model run on the three years of NY Times news articles. After showing some topics and topic trends, we show how the model reveals topical information about particular entities, and relationships between entities. Note that entities are just treated as regular words in the learning of the topic models, and the topic-word distributions are separated out into entity and non-entity components as a postprocessing step. Models that treat entity and non-entity words differently are also of interest, but are beyond the scope of this paper.

## 4.1   Topics and Topic Trends

Upon completion of a topic model run, the model saves data to compute the likelihood of words and entities in a topic, $p(w|t)$ and $p(e|t)$, the mix of topics in each document, $p(t|d)$, and $z_i$ the topic assigned to the $i^{th}$ word in the corpus.

For each topic, we print out the most likely words and most likely entities. We then review the list of words and entities to come up with a human-assigned topic label that best summarizes or captures the nature of the topic. It is important to point out that these topic labels are created *after* the model is run; they are not *a priori* defined as fixed or static subject headings.

Unsurprisingly, our three-years of NY Times includes a wide range of topics: from renting apartments in Brooklyn to diving in Hawaii; from Tiger Woods to PETA liberating tigers; from voting irregularities to dinosaur bones. From a total of 400 diverse topics, we selected a few to highlight. Figure 1 shows four seasonal topics which we labeled Basketball, Tour de France, Holidays and Oscars. Each of these topics shows a neat division within the topic of *what* (the words in lowercase), and *who* and *where* (the entities in uppercase). The Basketball topic appears to focus on the Lakers; the Tour de France topic tell us that it's all about Lance Armstrong; Barbie trumps the Grinch in Holidays; and Denzel Washington most likely had a good three years in 2000-2002.

Figure 2 shows four "event" topics which we labeled September 11 Attacks, FBI Investigation, Harry Potter/Lord of the Rings, and DC Sniper. This Sept. 11 topic – one of several topics that discuss the terrorist attacks on Sept 11 – is clearly about the breaking news. It discusses what and where, but not who (i.e. no mention of Bin Laden). The FBI Investigation topic lists 9/11 hijackers

| Basketball | | Tour de France | | Holidays | | Oscars | |
|---|---|---|---|---|---|---|---|
| team | 0.028 | tour | 0.039 | holiday | 0.071 | award | 0.026 |
| play | 0.015 | rider | 0.029 | gift | 0.050 | film | 0.020 |
| game | 0.013 | riding | 0.017 | toy | 0.023 | actor | 0.020 |
| season | 0.012 | bike | 0.016 | season | 0.019 | nomination | 0.019 |
| final | 0.011 | team | 0.016 | doll | 0.014 | movie | 0.015 |
| games | 0.011 | stage | 0.014 | tree | 0.011 | actress | 0.011 |
| point | 0.011 | race | 0.013 | present | 0.008 | won | 0.011 |
| series | 0.011 | won | 0.012 | giving | 0.008 | director | 0.010 |
| player | 0.010 | bicycle | 0.010 | special | 0.007 | nominated | 0.010 |
| coach | 0.009 | road | 0.009 | shopping | 0.007 | supporting | 0.010 |
| playoff | 0.009 | hour | 0.009 | family | 0.007 | winner | 0.008 |
| championship | 0.007 | scooter | 0.008 | celebration | 0.007 | picture | 0.008 |
| playing | 0.006 | mountain | 0.008 | card | 0.007 | performance | 0.007 |
| win | 0.006 | place | 0.008 | tradition | 0.006 | nominees | 0.007 |
| LAKERS | 0.062 | LANCE-ARMSTRONG | 0.021 | CHRISTMAS | 0.058 | OSCAR | 0.035 |
| SHAQUILLE-O-NEAL | 0.028 | FRANCE | 0.011 | THANKSGIVING | 0.018 | ACADEMY | 0.020 |
| KOBE-BRYANT | 0.028 | JAN-ULLRICH | 0.003 | SANTA-CLAUS | 0.009 | HOLLYWOOD | 0.009 |
| PHIL-JACKSON | 0.019 | LANCE | 0.003 | BARBIE | 0.004 | DENZEL-WASHINGTON | 0.006 |
| NBA | 0.013 | U-S-POSTAL-SERVICE | 0.002 | HANUKKAH | 0.003 | JULIA-ROBERT | 0.005 |
| SACRAMENTO | 0.007 | MARCO-PANTANI | 0.002 | MATTEL | 0.003 | RUSSELL-CROWE | 0.005 |
| RICK-FOX | 0.007 | PARIS | 0.002 | GRINCH | 0.003 | TOM-HANK | 0.005 |
| PORTLAND | 0.006 | ALPS | 0.002 | HALLMARK | 0.002 | STEVEN-SODERBERGH | 0.004 |
| ROBERT-HORRY | 0.006 | PYRENEES | 0.001 | EASTER | 0.002 | ERIN-BROCKOVICH | 0.003 |
| DEREK-FISHER | 0.006 | SPAIN | 0.001 | HASBRO | 0.002 | KEVIN-SPACEY | 0.003 |

**Fig. 1.** Selected seasonal topics from a 400-topic run of the NY Times dataset. In each topic we first list the most likely words in the topic, with their probability, and then the most likely entities (in uppercase). The title above each box is a human-assigned topic label.

| September 11 Attacks | |
|---|---|
| attack | 0.033 |
| tower | 0.025 |
| firefighter | 0.020 |
| building | 0.018 |
| worker | 0.013 |
| terrorist | 0.012 |
| victim | 0.012 |
| rescue | 0.012 |
| floor | 0.011 |
| site | 0.009 |
| disaster | 0.008 |
| twin | 0.008 |
| ground | 0.008 |
| center | 0.008 |
| fire | 0.007 |
| plane | 0.007 |
| WORLD-TRADE-CTR | 0.035 |
| NEW-YORK-CITY | 0.020 |
| LOWER-MANHATTAN | 0.005 |
| PENTAGON | 0.005 |
| PORT-AUTHORITY | 0.003 |
| RED-CROSS | 0.002 |
| NEW-JERSEY | 0.002 |
| RUDOLPH-GIULIANI | 0.002 |
| PENNSYLVANIA | 0.002 |
| CANTOR-FITZGERALD | 0.001 |

| FBI Investigation | |
|---|---|
| agent | 0.029 |
| investigator | 0.028 |
| official | 0.027 |
| authorities | 0.021 |
| enforcement | 0.018 |
| investigation | 0.017 |
| suspect | 0.015 |
| found | 0.014 |
| police | 0.014 |
| arrested | 0.012 |
| search | 0.012 |
| law | 0.011 |
| arrest | 0.011 |
| case | 0.010 |
| evidence | 0.009 |
| suspected | 0.008 |
| FBI | 0.034 |
| MOHAMED-ATTA | 0.003 |
| FEDERAL-BUREAU | 0.001 |
| HANI-HANJOUR | 0.001 |
| ASSOCIATED-PRESS | 0.001 |
| SAN-DIEGO | 0.001 |
| U-S | 0.001 |
| FLORIDA | 0.001 |

| Harry Potter/Lord Rings | |
|---|---|
| ring | 0.050 |
| book | 0.015 |
| magic | 0.011 |
| series | 0.007 |
| wizard | 0.007 |
| read | 0.007 |
| friend | 0.006 |
| movie | 0.006 |
| children | 0.006 |
| part | 0.005 |
| secret | 0.005 |
| magical | 0.005 |
| kid | 0.005 |
| fantasy | 0.005 |
| fan | 0.004 |
| character | 0.004 |
| HARRY-POTTER | 0.024 |
| LORD OF THE RING | 0.013 |
| STONE | 0.007 |
| FELLOWSHIP | 0.005 |
| CHAMBER | 0.005 |
| SORCERER | 0.004 |
| PETER-JACKSON | 0.004 |
| J-K-ROWLING | 0.004 |
| TOLKIEN | 0.004 |
| HOGWART | 0.002 |

| DC Sniper | |
|---|---|
| sniper | 0.024 |
| shooting | 0.019 |
| area | 0.010 |
| shot | 0.009 |
| police | 0.007 |
| killer | 0.006 |
| scene | 0.006 |
| white | 0.006 |
| victim | 0.006 |
| attack | 0.005 |
| case | 0.005 |
| left | 0.005 |
| public | 0.005 |
| suspect | 0.005 |
| killed | 0.005 |
| car | 0.005 |
| WASHINGTON | 0.053 |
| VIRGINIA | 0.019 |
| MARYLAND | 0.013 |
| D-C | 0.012 |
| JOHN-MUHAMMAD | 0.008 |
| BALTIMORE | 0.006 |
| RICHMOND | 0.006 |
| MONTGOMERY-CO | 0.005 |
| MALVO | 0.005 |
| ALEXANDRIA | 0.003 |

**Fig. 2.** Selected event topics from a 400-topic run of the NY Times dataset. In each topic we first list the most likely words in the topic, with their probability, and then the most likely entities (in uppercase). The title above each box is a human-assigned topic label.

Mohamed Atta and Hani Hanjour. The Harry Potter/Lord of the Rings topic combines these same-genre runaway successes, and the DC Sniper topic shows specific details about John Muhammad and Lee Malvo including that they were in a white van.

What year had the most discussion of the Tour de France? Is interest in football declining? What was the lifetime of Elian Gonzalez story? These questions can be answered by examining the time trends in the topics. These trends are easily computed by counting the the topic assignments $z_i$ of each word in each time period (monthly). Figure 3 uses the topics already presented plus additional topics to show some seasonal/periodic time trends and event time trends. We see from the trends on the left that Basketball gets 30,000 in May; discussions of football are increasing; 2001 was a relatively quiet year for the Oscars; but 2001 had the most buzz over quarterly earnings. The trends on the right on the other hand shows some very peaked events: from Elian Gonzalez in April 2000; thru the September 11 Attacks in 2001; to the DC Sniper killing spree and the collapse of Enron in 2002.

## 4.2   Entity-Entity Relationships

We use the topic model to determine topic-based entity-entity relationships. Unlike social networks created from co-mentions – which would not link two entities that were never co-mentioned – our topic-based approach can potentially link a pair of entities that were never co-mentioned. A link is created when the entity-entity "affinity", defined as $(p(e_1|e_2) + p(e_2|e_1))/2$, is above some threshold. The graph in Figure 4, constructed using this entity-entity affinity was created in two steps. First we selected key entities (e.g. Yasser Arafat, Sad-

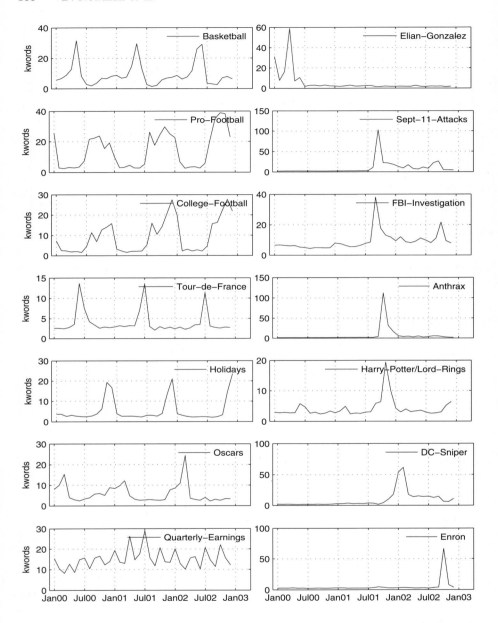

**Fig. 3.** Selected topic-trends from a 400-topic run of the NY Times dataset. Seasonal/periodic topics are shown on the left, and event topics are shown on the right. Each curve shows the number of words (in thousands) assigned to that topic for the month (on average there are 9,000 articles written per month containing 3 million words, so if the 400 topics were equally likely there would be 8 kwords per topic per month). The topic words and entities for Basketball, Tour de France, Holidays and Oscars are given in Figure 1, and Sept 11 Attacks, FBI Investigation, Harry Potter/Lord of the Rings and DC Sniper are given in Figure 2.

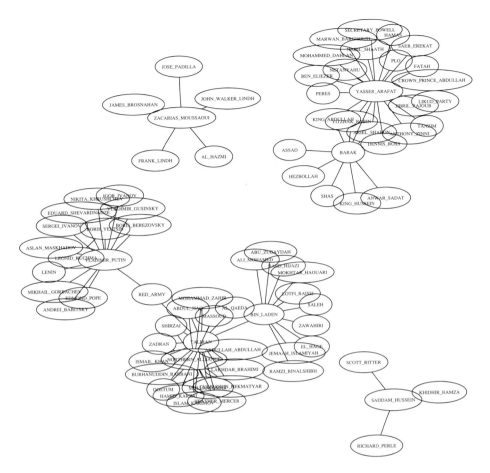

**Fig. 4.** Social network showing topic-model-based relationships between entities. A link is present when the entity-entity "affinity" $(p(e_1|e_2) + p(e_2|e_1))/2$ is above a threshold.

dam Hussien, Osama Bin Laden, Zacarias Moussaoui, Vladamir Putin, Ariel Sharon, The Taliban ) and determined what other entities had some level of affinity to these. We then took this larger list of 100 entities, computed all 10,000 entity-entity affinities, and thresholded the result to produce the graph. It is possible to annotate each link with the topics that most contribute to the relationship, and beyond that, the original documents that most contribute to that topic.

A related but slightly different representation is shown in the bipartite graph showing relationships between entities and topics in Figure 5. A link is present when the likelihood of an entity in a particular topic $p(e|t)$, is above a threshold. This graph was created by selecting 15 entities from the graph shown in Figure 4 and computing all $15 \times 400$ entity-given-topic probabilities, and thresholding

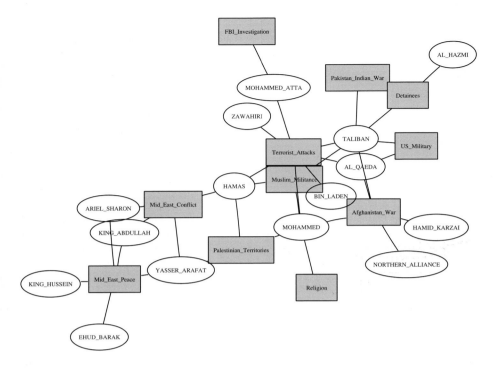

**Fig. 5.** Bipartite graph showing topic-model-based relationships between entities and topics. A link is present when the likelihood of an entity in a particular topic $p(e|t)$ is above a threshold.

the result to plot links. Again, with this bipartite graph, the original documents associated with each topic can be retrieved.

## 5    Conclusions

Statistical language models, such as probabilistic topic models, can play an important role in the analysis of large sets of text documents. Representations based on probabilistic topics go beyond clustering models because they allow the expression of multiple topics per document. An additional advantage is that the topics extracted by these models are invariably interpretable, facilitating the analysis of model output, in contrast to the uninterpretable directions produced by LSI.

We have applied standard entity recognizers to extract names of people, organizations and locations from a large collection of New York Times news articles. Probabilistic topic models were applied to learn the latent structure behind these named entities and other words that are part of documents, through a set of interpretable topics. We showed how the relative contributions of topics changed over time, in lockstep with major news events. We also showed how the model was able to automatically extract social networks from documents by connecting persons to other persons through shared topics. The social networks produced in this way are different from social networks produced by co-reference data where persons are connected only if they co-appear in documents. One advantage over these co-reference methods is that a set of topics can be used as labels to explain *why* two people are connected. Another advantage is that the model leverages the latent structure between the other *words* present in document to better estimate the latent structure between *entities*. This research has shown the benefits of applying simple statistical language models to understand the latent structure between entities.

## Acknowledgements

Thanks to Arthur Asuncion and Jason Sellers for their assistance. This material is based upon work supported by the National Science Foundation under award number IIS-0083489 (as part of the Knowledge Discovery and Dissemination Program) and under award number ITR-0331707.

## References

1. Klimt, B., and Yang, Y.: A New Dataset for Email Classification Research. 15th European Conference on Machine Learning (2004)
2. Yang, Y.: An Evaluation of Statistical Approaches to Text Categorization. Journal of Information Retrieval, Vol. 1 (1999) 67–88
3. Chakrabarti, S: Mining the Web: Discovering Knowledge from Hypertext Data. Morgan Kaufmann Publishers (2002)
4. Deerwester, S.C. , Dumais, S.T. , Landauer, T.K. , Furnas, G.W. , Harshman, R.A.: Indexing by Latent Semantic Analysis. American Society of Information Science, 41(6) (1990) 391–407
5. Berry, M.W., Dumais, S.T., O'Brien G.W.: Using Linear Algebra for Intelligent Information Retrieval. SIAM Review 37 (1994) 573–595
6. Hofmann, T.: Probabilistic Latent Semantic Indexing. 22nd Int'l. Conference on Research and Development in Information Retrieval (1999)
7. Blei, D.M., Ng, A.Y., Jordan, M.I.: Latent Dirichlet Allocation. Journal of Machine Learning Research, **1** (2003) 993–1022
8. Minka, T., and La, J.: Expectation-Propagation for the Generative Aspect Model. 18th Conference on Uncertainty and Artificial Intelligence (2002)
9. Griffiths, T.L., and Steyvers, M.: Finding Scientific Topics. National Academy of Sciences, 101 (suppl. 1) (2004) 5228–5235
10. Pritchard, J.K., Stephens, M., Donnelly, P.: Inference of Population Structure using Multilocus Genotype Data. Genetics 155 (2000) 945–959
11. Buntine, W. , Perttu, S. , Tuulos, V.: Using Discrete PCA on Web Pages. Proceedings of the Workshop W1 on Statistical Approaches for Web Mining (SAWM). Italy (2004) 99-110
12. McCallum, A., Corrada-Emmanuel, A., Wang, X.: Topic and Role Discovery in Social Networks. 19th Joint Conference on Artificial Intelligence (2005)
13. Steyvers, M., Smyth, P., Rosen-Zvi, M., Griffiths, T.: Probabilistic Author-Topic Models for Information Discovery. 10th ACM SIGKDD (2004)

14. Newman, D. J., and Block, S.: Probabilistic Topic Decomposition of an Eighteenth-Century Newspaper. Journal American Society for Information Science and Technology (2006)
15. Rosen-Zvi, M., Griffiths, T., Steyvers, M., Smyth, P.: The Author-Topic Model for Authors and Documents. 20th Int'l. Conference on Uncertainty in AI (2004)
16. Blei, D., and Jordan, M.: Modeling Annotated Data. 26th International ACM SIGIR (2003) 127-134
17. Griffiths, T., Steyvers, M., Blei, D. M., Tenenbaum, J. B.: Integrating Topics and Syntax. Advances in Neural Information Processing Systems, 17 (2004)
18. Steyvers, M., and Griffiths, T.L.: Probabilistic Topic Models. T. Landauer et al. (eds), Latent Semantic Analysis: A Road to Meaning: Laurence Erlbaum (2006)
19. Brill E.: Some Advances in Transformation-Based Part of Speech Tagging. National Conference on Artificial Intelligence (1994)

# The Hats Simulator and Colab: An Integrated Information Fusion Challenge Problem and Collaborative Analysis Environment

Clayton T. Morrison and Paul R. Cohen

Center for Research on Unexpected Events (CRUE)
Information Sciences Institute
University of Southern California
4676 Admiralty Way, Suite 1001
Marina del Rey, California, USA
{clayton, cohen}@isi.edu
http://crue.isi.edu/

**Abstract.** We present an overview of our work in information fusion for intelligence analysis. This work includes the Hats Simulator and the COLAB system. The Hats Simulator is a parameterized model of a virtual world in which hundreds of thousands of agents engage in individual and collective activities. Playing against the simulator, the goal of the analyst is to identify and stop harmful agents before they carry out terrorist attacks on simulated landmarks. The COLAB system enables multiple human analysts in different physical locations to conduct collaborative intelligence analysis. COLAB consists of two components: an instrumented analysis working environment built on a blackboard system, and a web-based user interface that integrates the Trellis hypothesis authoring and management tool with a query language. COLAB is integrated with the Hats Simulator to provide a complete end-to-end analysis environment with challenging problem domain.

## 1 Introduction

The COLAB Project brings together the Hats Simulator, a collaborative intelligence analysis environment, and a user interface to produce a prototype end-to-end system for intelligence analysis. Hats has been operational for three years and has been used in several studies, including providing data for part of the AFRL EAGLE project and assessing algorithms for relational data mining [1, 2]. The prototype intelligence analysis environment [3] and interface are implemented. The complete system has three intended applications:

1. A testbed for studying distributed intelligence analysis and information fusion tools.
2. An environment for training intelligence analysts.

S. Mehrotra et al. (Eds.): ISI 2006, LNCS 3975, pp. 105–116, 2006.

3. A configurable laboratory to test models of command and control organization structure in an intelligence analysis setting.

Consider the following scenario. Several human analysts[1] work together in the COLAB environment to develop an interpretation of events in the Hats Simulator world. Their goal is to identify and stop terrorist agent activities in the simulator while trying to keep their costs low. Obtaining information about the simulation is expensive and there are penalties for making false arrests and failing to identify terrorist plots. By design, each player has a different view of the information in the simulated world and none has all the relevant information. Each player has her own workspace where she can store and process information that she gathers from the simulator. The players collaborate via a shared workspace where they can post hypotheses and data they think is relevant to the larger analysis. This shared space becomes the collective interpretation of the state of the simulator. By monitoring this interpretation a player can identify trends, patterns, and gaps in the corporate intelligence. She will also develop trust (or mistrust) in her colleagues by noting the quality of their analyses.

In the following sections, we present the Hats Simulator and the components of the COLAB system. We begin in Section 2 by describing the Hats Simulator, including the Hats domain, the Information Broker interface, and scoring. In Section 3 describe the blackboard system that serves as the integration model for the COLAB analysis working environment, the web-based interface to COLAB that incorporates the Trellis argument authoring tool for hypothesis representation, and the query and agent definition language for accessing and manipulating information on the blackboard.

## 2   The Hats Simulator

The Hats Simulator [1, 2] is home to hundreds of thousands of agents (hats) which travel to meetings. Some hats are covert terrorists and a very few hats are known terrorists. All hats are governed by plans generated by a planner. Terrorist plans end in the destruction of landmarks. The object of a game against the Hats simulator is to find terrorist task forces before they carry out their plans. One pays for information about hats, and also for false arrests and destroyed landmarks. At the end of a game, one is given a score, which is the sum of these costs. The goal is to play Hats rationally, that is, to catch terrorist groups with the least combined cost of information, false arrests, and destroyed landmarks. Thus Hats serves as a testbed not only for analysts' tools but also for new theories of rational information fusion that take into account information source assessment and cost in the context of analysis goals and decisions. Hats encourages players to ask only for the information they need, and to not accuse hats or issue alerts without justification.

---

[1] In the rest of this paper, we will use the terms "analyst" and "user" interchangeably to refer to a human analyst using the COLAB system.

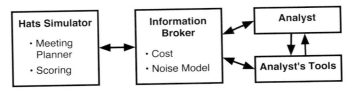

**Fig. 1.** Information Broker Interface to the Hats Simulator

The Hats Simulator consists of the core simulator and an Information Broker. The Information Broker is responsible for handling requests for information about the state of the simulator and thus forms the interface between the simulator and the analyst and her tools (see Figure 1). Some information has a cost, and the quality of information returned is a function of the "algorithmic dollars" spent. Analysts may also take actions: they may raise beacon alerts in an attempt to anticipate a beacon attack, and they may arrest agents believed to be planning an attack. Together, information requests and actions form the basis of scoring analyst performance in identifying terrorist threats. Scoring is assessed automatically and serves as the basis for analytic comparison between different analysts and tools. The simulator is implemented and manages the activities of hundreds of thousands of agents.

### 2.1   The Hats Domain

The Hats Simulator models a "society in a box" consisting of many very simple agents, hereafter referred to as hats. (Hats get its name from the classic spaghetti western, in which heroes and villains are identifiable by the colors of their hats.) The Hats society also has its heroes and villains, but the challenge is to identify which color hat they should be wearing, based on how they behave. Some hats are known terrorists; others are covert and must be identified and distinguished from the benign hats in the society.

Hats is staged in a two-dimensional grid on which hats move around, go to meetings and trade capabilities. The grid consists of two kinds of locations: those that have no value, and high-valued locations called beacons that terrorists would like to attack. All beacons have a set of attributes, or vulnerabilities, corresponding to the capabilities which hats carry. To destroy a beacon, a task force of terrorist hats must possess capabilities that match the beacon's vulnerabilities, as a key matches a lock. In general, these capabilities are not unique to terrorists, so one cannot identify terrorist hats only on the basis of the capabilities they carry.

The Hats society is structured by organizations. All hats belong to at least two organizations and some hats belong to many. Terrorist organizations host only known and covert terrorist hats. Benign organizations, on the other hand, may contain any kind of hat, including known and covert terrorists.

**Population Generation.** Hats populations may be built by hand or generated by the Hats Simulator. Because the constitution of a population affects the difficulty of identifying covert terrorists, population generation is parameterized. There are four sets of population parameters. The first set specifies the total number of known terrorists, covert terrorists and benign hats in the population. Another set defines the number of benign and terrorist organizations. Not all organizations have the same number of members, so a third set of parameters assigns the relative numbers of hats that are members of each organization, represented as a ratio among organizations. Finally, hats may be members of two or more organizations. An overlap parameter determines the percentage of hats in each organization that are members of two or more other organizations. Since hat behaviors are governed by their organization membership, as we will see in the next section, organization overlap affects how difficult it is to identify covert terrorist hats. To generate populations with hundreds of thousands of hats and thousands of organizations, we use a randomization algorithm that estimates organization overlap percentage and membership ratios while matching the total number of organizations and hats in the population. An efficient, approximate population generation algorithm is described in [4].

**Meeting Generation.** Hats act individually and collectively, but always planfully. In fact, the actions of hats are planned by a generative planner. Benign hats congregate at locations including beacons. Terrorist hats meet, acquire capabilities, form task forces, and attack beacons. The purpose of the planner is to construct an elaborate "shell game" in which capabilities are passed among hats in a potentially long sequence of meetings, culminating in a final meeting at a target. By moving capabilities among hats, the planner masks its intentions. Rather than directing half a dozen hats with capabilities required for a task to march purposefully up to a beacon, instead hats with required capabilities pass them on to other hats, and eventually a capable task force appears at the beacon.

Each organization has a generative planner that plans tasks for its members. At each tick, each organization has a chance of beginning a new task. When a new task is started, the Hats meeting planner creates a task force, the size of which is controlled by a parameter. The planner next selects a target location in the Hats world. If a beacon is selected as the target, the goal of the task is to bring to that location the set of required capabilities that match the vulnerabilities of the beacon. If the location is not a beacon, a random set of required capabilities is selected as the set to bring to the location.

Task force members may or may not already possess the required capabilities; usually they dont. The planner creates a set of meetings designed to ensure that the task force acquires all of the required capabilities before going to the target location. This is accomplished by constructing a meeting tree that specifies meetings and their temporal order. Figure 2 shows an example meeting tree, where boxes represent planned meetings among hats and arrows represent the planned temporal partial order of meetings. The tree is "inverted" in the sense that the arrows point from leaves inward toward the root of the tree. Parent meetings, where arrows originate, are executed first. When all of the parent meetings of a child meeting have completed, then the child meeting happens.

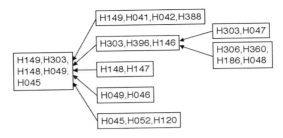

**Fig. 2.** Example of a generated meeting tree. Each box represents a meeting and contains a list of participating hats. Arrows indicate planned temporal order of meetings.

## 2.2   The Information Broker

As an analyst playing the game, your job is to protect the Hats society from terrorist attacks. You need to identify terrorist task forces before they attack beacons, but you also need to avoid falsely accusing innocent hats. The only way to do this successfully is to gather information about hats, identify meetings, track capability trades and form hypotheses about the intentions of groups of hats. The information broker provides information about the state of the Hats world. The information broker will respond to questions such as "Where is $Hat_{27}$ right now?" It will also provide information by subscription to analysts' tools, which in turn make information broker requests. For example, a tool might process requests like, "Identify everyone $Hat_{27}$ meets in the next 100 steps," or, "Tell me if $Hat_{27}$ approaches a beacon with capabilities $C_1$, $C_7$ or $C_{29}$."

   Some information is free, but information about states of the simulator that change over time is costly. The quality of the information obtained is determined by the amount paid.

   Eight basic information requests can may be made: the hats at the location (if any), participants in a meeting, capabilities carried by a hat, capability trades, meeting times, hat death time, meeting locations and hat locations. The first five requests return lists of things, such as hats, capabilities, times, etc. The latter three are scalar values.

## 2.3   Actions

In addition to requesting information, the analyst playing the Hats game can also change a beacon's alert level and arrest hats. Both actions affect an analyst's performance score (discussed in Section 2.4).

**Raising Alerts.** We may not be able to stop an attack, but if we know it is coming, we can prepare and minimize loss. This is the inspiration behind modeling *beacon alerts*. Each beacon can be in one of three alert levels: off (default), low, or high. These correspond to the conditions of no threat, a chance of an attack, and attack likely. The analyst decides which level a beacon alert is set to, but the Hats Simulator keeps track of alert states over time and whether an actual attack occurs while the state is elevated. The goal of the analyst is to minimize the time beacon alerts are elevated. High alerts are more costly than low ones. On the other hand, if an attack does occur on a beacon, a high alert is better than a low alert, and a low alert is better than none.

**Arresting Hats.** Analysts can also issue arrest warrants for hats in order to prevent beacon attacks. Arrests are successful only when the targeted hat is currently a member of a terrorist task force. Attempted arrests under any other conditions, including hats that are terrorists but not currently part of a terrorist task force, result in a false arrest (a false positive). Under this model, a hat can be a terrorist but not be guilty of any crime. Unless terrorist hats are engaged in *ongoing* terrorist activities, their arrest incurs penalties. While this is a simple model, it places realistic constraints on the analyst's choice of actions.

### 2.4   Scoring Analyst Performance

The Hats Simulator and Information Broker together provide an environment for testing analyst tools. The object of the game is to identify terrorist task forces before they attack beacons. Three kinds of costs are accrued:

1. The cost of acquiring and processing information about a hat. This is the "government in the bedroom" or intrusiveness cost.
2. The cost of falsely arresting benign hats.
3. The cost of harm done by terrorists.

The skill of analysts and the value of analysis tools can be measured in terms of these costs, and they are assessed automatically by the Hats Simulator as analysts play the Hats game.

## 3   The COLAB Analysis Environment

The Hats game is very challenging. There is a vast amount of information to keep track of. There are hundreds of thousands of entities. The properties of these entities change from one time step to the next. There is considerable hidden structure, including organization membership, task force membership, coordinated task goals, and benign or malevolent intention. Identifying any of this structure will require keeping track of individual and group behavioral histories. Interacting with the Information Broker alone makes the task nearly impossible. Any analysis environment worth its salt must help the analyst manage and explore this information. This is the goal of COLAB analysis environment.

The COLAB analyst environment is built on a blackboard architecture designed to represent relational data and integrate a variety of intelligence analysis algorithms as problem solving components. We first introduce the blackboard system architecture and why we believe it is well-suited for this kind of task, and then describe the COLAB blackboard components.

## 3.1   Blackboard Systems

Blackboard systems are knowledge-based problem solving environments that work through the collaboration of independent reasoning modules [5, 6]. More recently blackboards have been recognized as platforms for data fusion [7]. They were developed in the 1970s and originally applied to signal-processing tasks. The first, HEARSAY-II [8], was used for speech recognition, employing acoustic, lexical, syntactic, and semantic knowledge. Other systems were applied to problems as diverse as interpretation of sonar data, protein folding, and robot control [5].

Blackboard systems have three main components: the blackboard itself, knowledge sources, and control. The *blackboard* is a global data structure that contains hypotheses or partial solutions to problems. The blackboard is typically organized into *spaces* representing levels of abstraction of the problem domain. For example, HEARSAY-II had different levels for phrases, words, syllables, and so forth. *Knowledge sources* (KSs) are modular, self-contained programs which post results of local computations to the blackboard. Different KSs use different types of knowledge: for example, one might use a grammar to generate words which are likely to occur next, while another might detect phonemes directly from the acoustic signal. While no single knowledge source can solve the problem, working together they can. Getting knowledge sources to "work together" is the task of blackboard *control* [9].

## 3.2   The COLAB Blackboard

The COLAB blackboard follows the same architectural principles of a standard blackboard except that human users interact with the blackboard, playing the same role as other domain and control knowledge sources. The COLAB blackboard is the analyst's "workspace," representing and managing information that the analyst gathers from the Hats Information Broker. In this workspace, the analyst views, manipulates and processes Information Broker reports to extract evidence supporting hypotheses about ongoing on potential future events. Analysts are also provided an interface to define and manage their own KS assistants, *agents* that can handle routine querying, watching for user-defined conditions of interest, and sending alerts or reminders when conditions are satisfied.

## 3.3   COLAB Knowledge Sources

A class of KSs called *report triage* KSs handle processing information broker reports and updating the Labels and Processed Reports spaces. Another class consists of KS interfaces or wrappers for algorithms available to the analyst as analysis tools or "services." The beauty of the blackboard architecture is that it is specifically designed to facilitate collaborative software [7]; as long as these algorithms can read representations on the blackboard and write output to the blackboard that is interpretable by other KSs, they can participate in blackboard processing. Some examples of analysis services include algorithms for assigning suspicion scores to hats [10], identifying community structure [11, 12], and reasoning about behaviors over time. Some services may require their own blackboard spaces for specialized processing, such as a graph representation used for community finding, but the results of any service are reported to the Raw Reports space as a report, just like a report from the Hats Information Broker.

Another class of KSs consists of the user-defined "agents" that perform simple tasks. Like other KSs, agents have a trigger condition and action that is taken if the condition is met, but triggers and actions are restricted to what can be expressed in components of the COLAB query language, described in Section 3.4. These agents may issue there own queries, check for conditions, and either trigger other KSs or send messages to the users. They may be scheduled for repeated activation and run in the background, automating routine checks of conditions such as whether a hat on a watchlist has moved within some distance of a beacon.

## 3.4   The COLAB Interface

Up to this point we have described the problem domain and the core architecture supporting the analyst working environment. We now describe the third component of COLAB: the web-based user interface. The goal of COLAB interface design is intuitive information management. This means making information stored on the blackboard as accessible as possible and providing mechanisms for analysts to author and manage their hypotheses. Information management is an open research challenge that includes issues in knowledge engineering, query languages, data mining and data visualization. Our design philosophy is to start simple and start with existing technologies. For hypothesis representation, CO-LAB uses the Trellis argument authoring tool. For information access we have implemented a subset of standard SQL with small extensions. And our initial interface for browsing blackboard contents will be hypertext-based.

**Trellis.** Trellis [13] is an interactive web-based application for argumentation and decision-making. Trellis has its roots in the Knowledge Capture AI community, whose aim is to make it possible for unassisted users to represent their knowledge in a form that can be use by knowledge-base AI systems. Trellis takes a step in this direction by allowing the user to express herself using a combination of semi-formal argument terms and relations to structured combinations of free text and documents found on the web (including text, images, video and other media). Users individually or collaboratively author structured arguments and analyses. The tool is domain independent, permitting general structured argumentation about any topic.

We have chosen to adopt Trellis as the COLAB hypothesis authoring tool because it expresses the basic hierarchical support/dissent relationships between statements that we believe will be useful to analysts. Trellis also provides a well-designed, intuitive user interface. The left half of the COLAB browser window in Figure 3 shows an example of the Trellis Discussion interface. The interface currently displays an argument supporting the hypothesis that beacon B012 is threatened. The top-level statement (the "target hypothesis") asserts that Task-force-34 threatens beacon B012. This claim is supported by three additional

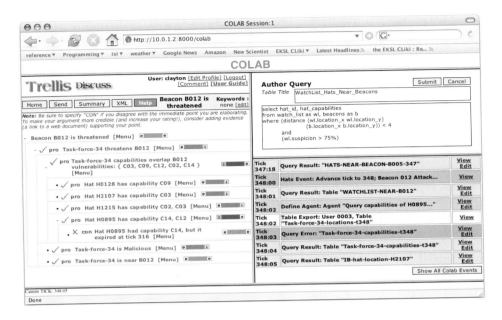

**Fig. 3.** The COLAB web interface. The left half of the browser window contains the interface to the Trellis argument authoring tool. An argument about whether beacon B12 is threatened is currently being edited. The upper right of the browser window contains the field for entering commands and queries. The Author Query command template is currently selected. The bottom right provides a history of COLAB events, including events created by user input, events initiated by other users (such as making a table public) and Hats Simulator world-state events, such as advancing a tick.

statements, that `Task-force-34` has capabilities that overlap the vulnerabilities of the beacon, that `Task-force-34` is malicious, and that the members of `Task-force-34` are near the beacon. Capability overlap is further elaborated by evidence that the capabilities are carried by individual hats in the group. The example also includes a "Con" relationship, expressing a statement against the group having the required overlapping capabilities: hat `H0895` is no longer carrying the remaining required capability `C14`, having apparently expired at tick 316. The Trellis window also represents, by the colored bars to the right of each statement, a tally of votes provided by other analysts indicating whether they agree or disagree with the statement. In this case, only one other analyst has voted; green indicates they agree, red indicates they do not agree with the statement.

**Query Language.** During an analysis session, the blackboard will rapidly fill with many reports about events in the Hats world, the results of analysis tools and analyst-authored hypotheses. In order to gather, manipulate and manage this data, we have implemented a subset of SQL, an intuitive, well-studied language with a long, successful history in practical database applications [14]. In the relational model, an individual fact is represented as a set of attribute values. Facts are collected in tables in which each row represents a fact, each column corresponds to an attribute, and the cell at the row/column intersection holds the the attribute value for the fact. Queries specify what information to extract from tables, and the results of queries are expressed in new tables. The upper-right frame of the browser window in Figure 3 shows the query entry field. The query example in the window requests a table containing the `hat_ids` and `hat_capabilities` for hats from the `watch_list` table – but only for those hats that are within distance 4 of a beacon and have a suspicion greater than 75%. The table has also been assigned the name `WatchList_Hats_Near_Beacons` by the user.

**Agents: User-defined KSs.** Knowledge sources provide another facility for analyst information management. As mentioned in Section 3.3, users may use the query language to specify KS triggers and actions.

The following is a set of example tasks that can be expressed as agents, to help with routine monitoring of events in the Hats Simulator:

- **Meeting Alert.** Any time two or more hats from a specified set of hats (e.g., all hats whose locations have just been reported) meet at the same location for more than two ticks, send an alert to the user that a meeting may have just taken place (Along with location and time). Another agent may be defined to trigger when the meeting alert is issued; this sensor may then send a query to the Information Broker asking whether a meeting has taken place at that location.
- **Watchlist Scheduled Query.** This KS updates a "watchlist" dynamic table to include any hats whose number of meetings with known terrorists is above some threshold. Alternatively, the KS may schedule execution of a suspicion scoring analysis service and the suspicion scores of hats above some threshold are included in the Watchlist table.
- **Beacon Vulnerability Sensor.** After each update to the watchlist above, check whether any hats on the watchlist have capabilities that overlap a specified beacon's vulnerabilities. If so, trigger a beacon threat alert KS.
- **Beacon Threat Alert.** Triggered by the Beacon Vulnerability Sensor, this KS tests whether hat(s) triggering the vulnerability sensor are within some distance of the beacon. If so, then send an alert to the analyst.

## 3.5   COLAB Implementation

COLAB is was developed in Macintosh Common Lisp[2] (MCL) 5.1 and open-MCL[3] 1.0 running on Macintosh OS X. For the blackboard we used the GB-Bopen[4] blackboard framework. The web interface server is also written in Common Lisp, built on top of the lightweight Araneida[5] server. Except for MCL and Mac OS X, all of these software packages are open source.

---

[2]  http://www.digitool.com/
[3]  http://www.openmcl.org/
[4]  http://gbbopen.org/
[5]  http://www.cliki.net/araneida

# 4   Concluding Remarks

In the introduction we described three target uses for the Hats Simulator in conjunction with COLAB: an environment for studying analyst collaboration and analysis tools, an environment for training analysts, and a configurable laboratory to study varying command and control structures for network-centric, distributed intelligence analysis. All three are very ambitious goals and COLAB is still an early prototype. However, the facilities described in this paper are implemented and we are beginning user testing. COLAB provides and interesting, novel information fusion architecture for intelligence analysis that is unique in its pairing of a hypothesis authoring tool, provided in Trellis, a configurable multiuser information management system, provided by the COLAB blackboard, and a challenging, discrete-time simulated problem domain that can be played online.

## Acknowledgements

The Hats Simulator was conceived of by Paul Cohen and Niall Adams at Imperial College in the summer of 2002. Dr. Cohen implemented the first version of Hats. Work on the Hats Simulator was funded by the Air Force Research Laboratory, account number 53-4540-0588. Work on the COLAB project was supported by the Office of the Assistant Secretary of Defense for Networks and Information Integration (OASD/NII), through its Command & Control Research Program (CCRP), USC subcontract CCRP-COLAB 53-4540-7723. We are indebted to Dr. David S. Alberts, Dr. Mark Nissen and the Naval Postgraduate School's Center for Edge Power for leading and coordinating the Edge Power Projects. We thank Dr. Yolanda Gil, Dr. Tim Chklovski and Varun Ratnakar for discussions and help with integrating COLAB with Trellis, and Dr. Dan Corkill and Gary W. King for help with GBBopen and Ijara. The U.S. Government is authorized to reproduce and distribute reprints for governmental purposes notwithstanding any copyright notation hereon.

## References

1. Cohen, P.R., Morrison, C.T.: The hats simulator. In: Proceedings of the 2004 Winter Simulation Conference. (2004)
2. Morrison, C.T., Cohen, P.R., King, G.W., Moody, J.J., Hannon, A.: Simulating terrorist threat with the hats simulator. In: Proceedings of the First International Conference on Intelligence Analysis. (2005)
3. Morrison, C.T., Cohen, P.R.: Colab: A laboratory environment for studying analyst sensemaking and collaboration. In: Proceedings of the Tenth International Command and Control Research and Technology Symposium (10th ICCRTS). (2005)
4. Hannon, A.C., King, G.W., Morrison, C.T., Galstyan, A., Cohen, P.R.: Population generation in large-scale simulation. In: Proceedings of AeroSense 2005. (2005)
5. Nii, H.P.: Blackboard systems. In Barr, A., Cohen, P.R., Feigenbaum, E.A., eds.: The Handbook of Artificial Intelligence, Volume IV. Addison-Wesley Publishing Company, Inc. (1989) 1–82

6. Corkill, D.D.: Blackboard systems. AI Expert **6** (1991) 40–47
7. Corkill, D.D.: Collaborating software: Blackboard and multi-agent systems & the future. In: Proceedings of the International Lisp Conference, New York (2003)
8. Erman, L.D., Hayes-Roth, F., Lesser, V.R., Reddy, D.R.: The hearsay-ii speech understanding system: Integrating knowledge to resolve uncertainty. ACM Computing Survey **12** (1980) 213–253
9. Carver, N., Lesser, V.: The evolution of blackboard control architectures. Expert Systems with Applications–Special Issue on the Blackboard Paradigm and Its Applications **7** (1994) 1–30
10. Galstyan, A., Cohen, P.R.: Identifying covert sub-networks through iterative node classification. In: Proceedings of the First International Conference on Intelligence Analysis. (2005)
11. Adibi, J., Cohen, P.R., Morrison, C.T.: Measuring confidence intervals in link discovery: a bootstrap approach. In: Proceedings of the ACM Special Interest Group on Knowledge Discovery and Data Mining (ACM-SIGKDD-04). (2004)
12. Newman, M.E.J.: Fast algorithm for detecting community structure in networks. Phys. Rev. E **69** (2003)
13. Chklovski, T., Ratnakar, V., Gil, Y.: User interfaces with semi-formal representations: a study of designing argumentation structures. In: Under Review for the Intelligent User Interfaces Conference 2005. (2005)
14. Elmasri, R., Navathe, S.B.: Fundamentals of Database Systems. 4th edn. Boston: Addison Wesley (1999)

# Cost-Sensitive Access Control for Illegitimate Confidential Access by Insiders

Young-Woo Seo and Katia Sycara

Robotics Institute
Carnegie Mellon University
Pittsburgh PA 15213, USA
{ywseo, katia}@cs.cmu.edu

**Abstract.** In many organizations, it is common to control access to confidential information based on the need-to-know principle; The requests for access are authorized only if the content of the requested information is relevant to the requester's current information analysis project. We formulate such content-based authorization, i.e. whether to accept or reject access requests as a binary classification problem. In contrast to the conventional error-minimizing classification, we handle this problem in a cost-sensitive learning framework in which the cost caused by incorrect decision is different according to the relative importance of the requested information. In particular, the cost (i.e., damaging effect) for a false positive (i.e., accepting an illegitimate request) is more expensive than that of false negative (i.e., rejecting a valid request). The former is a serious security problem because confidential information, which should not be revealed, can be accessed. From the comparison of the cost-sensitive classifiers with error-minimizing classifiers, we found that the costing with a logistic regression showed the best performance, in terms of the smallest cost paid, the lowest false positive rate, and the relatively low false negative rate.

## 1  Introduction

Illegitimate access to confidential information by insiders poses a great risk to an organization. Since malicious insiders are well aware of where the valuable information resides and which cause damaging effects, the results of illegitimate confidential access are far more costly. Illegitimate access is difficult to effectively prohibit or detect because malevolent actions are done by already trusted persons.

One of the most common approaches to handle this problem is access control based on the need-to-know principle; The requests for access are authorized only if the content of the requested information is relevant to the requester's project. For example, if an information analyst's current project concerns the development of nuclear weapon by Iran, it would be illegitimate for the analyst to have access to documents on other aspects, e.g., feminist activities in Iran. However, since documents on these different aspects of Iranian politics and welfare are not

S. Mehrotra et al. (Eds.): ISI 2006, LNCS 3975, pp. 117–128, 2006.

necessarily a priori separated in different secured data bases, the issue of allowing access on a need-to-know basis on particular documents is very challenging.

Requests to access the confidential information may occur, for example, when an employee is assigned to a new project and needs to access background knowledge. The project manager will either hand select only those confidential information that he will let the employee see, or completely bar access to the entire collection rather than exposing information that should not be exposed. However this approach is quite inflexible. It does not allow easy adjustment to frequent changes of a user's task assignment. Project assignments for an employee may be changed quite often and hence the employee needs to access confidential information related to the newly assigned project. Alternatively, since the organization wants to make sure that the employee accesses only pertinent information, a set of access control lists (ACL) may be compiled manually to control those requests. Each item of confidential information is associated with an ACL, which ensures a corresponding level of security and can be accessed by anyone who has been authorized. However this approach has a crucial security weakness. Since, for the purpose of indexing and security, confidential information is grouped into containers by project-basis, a user who is authorized to a segment of confidential information in a container is actually able to access the entire container.

As a solution for these problems, we developed a multi-agent system that handles the authorization of requests for confidential information as a binary classification problem [9]. Instead of relying on hand-picked information or coarse-grained ACLs, our system classifies on-the-fly the content of each requested information access as positive or negative with respect to the content of the requester's project and authorizes the request if the requested information is classified as positive to the requester's project. Otherwise the request is rejected because the requester's project description is not similar to the information. Our approach is quite flexible and adaptive to changes of project assignment because only an updated description of newly assigned projects is necessary to re-train the classifiers, instead of re-compiling the ACL on all changing relevant information. Therefore, it is much less expensive, both computationally, and also in terms of human time and effort, than an ACL-based approach.

Although our approach showed a relatively good performance [9], we believe there is room for improvement. Previously we made use of five different error-minimizing classifiers for authorizing the requests to access confidential information. However, in domains where there is differential cost for misclassification of examples, an error-minimizing approach may not give results that reflect the reality of the domain. For example, suppose that there are 100 medical cases that are comprised of 5 cancer cases and 95 flu cases. Without considering the cost for misclassification (e.g., compensation for misdiagnosis), an error-minimizing classifier would simply achieve the lower error rate by ignoring the minority class, even though the actual result of misdiagnosis on cancer is far worse than that of flu. Thus, it is undesirable to use an error-minimizing classification method, which treats all mis-classification costs equally for such a cost-sensitive scenario because primarily it classifies every example as belonging to the most probable class.

In this paper we present our works for testing the effectiveness of cost-sensitive learning for the problem of confidential access control. Section 2 compares cost-sensitive classification with error-minimizing classification in terms of the optimal decision boundary. In addition, it describes two cost-sensitive learning methods for the process of confidential access control. Section 3 describes experimental settings and empirical evaluation of cost-sensitive learners. Section 4 presents related work and section 5 presents conclusion and future work.

## 2   Cost-Sensitive Classification

A classification method is a decision rule that assigns one of (or more than one) predefined classes to given examples. The optimal decision boundary is a decision criterion that allows a classifier to produce the best performance. Let us consider a hypothetical example in figure 1 which shows two classes with overlapping boundaries due to their intrinsic randomness – their actual values are random variables. In this example, the class-conditional density for each class is a normal distribution, that is, $f_0(x|class = 0) \sim N(\mu_0, \sigma_0^2)$ and $f_1(x|class = 1) \sim N(\mu_1, \sigma_1^2)$ (i.e., $\mu_0 = 0.3500, \sigma_0 = 0.1448, \mu_1 = 0.7000, \sigma_1 = 0.1736$).

Under the equal cost for misclassification, the optimal decision boundary (the solid line in the figure 1) lies in the center of two class distributions. An example randomly generated will be assigned to class 1 if its value is greater than 0.52 (the actual value of the optimal decision boundary in figure 1 is $xe^* = 0.52$). Otherwise it is assigned to class 0. According to the optimal boundary, a classifier can generate four possible classification outcomes for a given example; $a$: true positive, $b$: false positive, $c$: false negative, and $d$: true negative [4]. Table 1 captures this information as well as the cost $(\lambda_{ij})$ involved in those four outcomes.

If the cost for misclassification is unequal, where then would be the optimal decision boundary? Let us consider the case that there are text documents belonging to "class 0" and "class 1," and all of them are confidential information of which careless release may have a damaging effect. An employee is newly

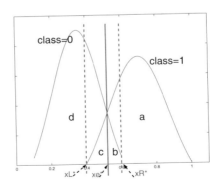

**Fig. 1.** The optimal decision boundary for a binary classification may vary according to the cost for misclassification

**Table 1.** A cost matrix represents four possible classification outcomes and their associated costs. In particular, for a given example, $x$, "a" means true positive, i.e., the example belongs to class 1 and is classified as class 1. " c" is false negative if $x$ is classified as class 0. "d" is true negative if $x$ belongs to class 0 and is classified as class 0. Finally, "b" is false positive if $x$ is classified as positive. $\lambda_{ij}$ is the cost for classifying an example belonging to $j$ as $i$.

|  | true $class = 1$ | true $class = 0$ |
|---|---|---|
| output $class = 1$ | a ($\lambda_{11}$) | b ($\lambda_{10}$) |
| output $class = 0$ | c ($\lambda_{01}$) | d ($\lambda_{00}$) |

assigned to a project for which records are labeled as "class 1." He is authorized to access only documents in "class 1" because he needs to know background knowledge of the project. Assuming that a zero cost is assigned to the correct classification [1] (i.e., $\lambda_{11} = \lambda_{00} = 0$), the costs for two types of error should be considered carefully for providing a reliable confidential access control; false negative ($\lambda_{01}$) – reject the valid request (e.g., reject the request that the employee asks to access a "class 1" document); false positive ($\lambda_{10}$) – accept the invalid request (e.g., accept the request that the employee asks to access a "class 0" document). In particular, a false negative causes the employee to be inconvenienced because he is not able to access need-to-know information. However, not approving valid requests does not cause a serious problem from the security perspective. On the contrary, a false positive is a serious problem because confidential information, which should not be revealed, can be accessed. Therefore, for a need-to-know basis confidential authorization, the cost for false positive (i.e., the damaging effect) is much higher than that of false negative.

Thus the decision boundary for uniform-cost must be re-located, in order to minimize the cost for misclassifications. For example, if the cost of false positive is higher than that of false negative, the decision line should be moved toward the right (e.g., $xe^* \rightarrow xR^*$). Two dashed lines in figure 1 represent the optimal decision boundaries for non-uniform misclassification cost assigned to each example. However a tradeoff must be considered because choosing one of the extremes (e.g., $xL^*$ or $xR^*$ ) will not consider the error. In particular, the classifier could reduce the false negative close to zero if we would choose $xL^*$ as a decision line, but with higher false positive. If either of extremes is not the solution, the optimal decision line should be chosen somewhere between extremes by considering the tradeoff.

## 2.1   Methods for Cost-Sensitive Classification

In the problem of unequal misclassificaiton cost, the goal of cost-sensitive learning is to find the boundary between the regions that divide optimally the example space. Obviously the misclassification cost, particularly a cost table

---

[1] We assume that the employee is authorized to access if the requested documents is classified by the system as "class 1".

(e.g., table 1), is the dominant factor for the optimal boundaries. That is, the region where class $j$ must be predicted will expand at the expense of the regions of other classes if misclassifying examples of class $j$ is more expensive relative to misclassifying others, even though the class probabilities remain unchanged.

In this paper, we utilize two methods that convert arbitrary error-minimizing classifiers into cost-sensitive ones without modifying classification rules: costing [13] and metacost [2]. These methods make use of sampling techniques that change the original example distribution $D$ to $\hat{D}$ by incorporating the relative misclassification cost of each instance, according to a given cost matrix. This changes the proportion of a certain class (e.g., documents that are "need-to-know" to perform a given project) by re-sampling of the original examples. Then the methods make any cost-insensitive error-minimizing classifiers to perform cost minimization on the newly generated distribution, $\hat{D}$.

**Costing.** Costing (cost proportionate rejection sampling with aggregation) is a wrapper for cost-sensitive learning that trains a set of error-minimizing classifiers by a distribution, which is the original distribution with the relative cost of each example, and outputs a final classifier by taking the average over all learned classifiers [13]. Costing is comprised of two processes: rejection sampling and bagging. Rejection sampling has been used to generate independently and identically distributed (i.i.d.) samples that are used as a proxy distribution to achieve simulation from the target distribution. Rejection sampling for the costing assigns each example in the original distribution with a relative cost [2] and draws a random number $r$ from a uniform distribution $U(0,1)$. It will keep the example if $r > \frac{c}{Z}$. Otherwise it discards the example and continues sampling until certain criteria are satisfied. The accepted examples are regarded as a realization of the altered distribution, $\hat{D} = \{S'_1, S'_2, ..., S'_k\}$. With the altered distribution, $\hat{D}$, costing trains $k$ different hypotheses, $h_i \equiv Learn(S'_i)$, and predicts the label of a test example, $\mathbf{x}$, by combining those hypotheses, $h(\mathbf{x}) = sign\left(\sum_{i=1}^{k} h_i(\mathbf{x})\right)$.

**MetaCost.** MetaCost is another method for converting an error-minimizing classifier into cost-sensitive classifier by re-sampling [2]. The underlying assumption is that an error-minimizing classifier could learn the optimal decision boundary based on the cost matrix if each training example is relabeled with the cost. MetaCost's learning process is also comprised of two processes: bagging for re-labeling and retraining the classifiers with cost. In particular, it generates a set of samples with replacement from the training set and estimates the class of each instance by taking the average of votes over all the trained classifiers. Then MetaCost re-labels each training example with the estimated optimal class and re-trains the classifier to the relabeled training set.

---

[2] $\hat{x}_i = \frac{c}{Z} \times x_i$, where $c$ is a cost assigned to $x_i$ and $Z$ is a normalization factor, satisfying $\max_{c \in S} c$.

## 3    Experiments

The scenario which we are particularly interested in is a process of confidential access control based on the need-to-know principle. We model the decision whether to reject or accept the access request as a binary classification. In particular, our system classifies the content of the requested information as positive or negative with respect to the content of the requester's project and authorizes the request if the requested information is classified as positive to the requester's project. Otherwise the request is rejected. To this end, we choose three different classification methods, linear discriminant analysis (LDA), logistic regression (LR), and support vector machines (SVM), because of their relative good performance, particularly in text classification [7], [8], [11].

The purpose of the experiments is two-fold; (1) to find a good classification method that minimizes the cost and the false positive rate while holding the false negative rate reasonably low, (2) to verify that the cost-sensitive learning methods reduce the total cost for misclassification in comparison with error-minimizing classifiers. From these objectives, three performance metrics are primarily used to measure the usefulness of classifiers; false negative, defined as $fn = \frac{c}{a+c}$ by using the values in the table 1, false positive, $fp = \frac{b}{b+d}$, and cost for misclassification. These metrics are better matched to our purpose because we are interested in primarily reducing the error and the cost.

Since there are no datasets available that are comprised of confidential information, we choose the Reuters-21578 document collections for experiments. This data set, which consists of world news stories from 1987, has become a benchmark in text categorization evaluations. It has been partially labelled by human experts with respect to a list of categories. Since our task is a binary classification task where each document must be assigned to either positive or negative, we discarded documents that are assigned no topic or multiple topics. Moreover, classes with fewer than 10 documents are discarded. The resulting data set is comprised of 9,854 documents as a training set and 4,274 documents as a test set with 67 categories.

The experimental setting is as follows. All the documents are regarded as confidential. Documents belonging to the selected category are regarded as confidential information that the requester needs to know. Conversely the rest of test documents are confidential information that should not be revealed. A false positive occurs when a method classifies a document as positive that should have not been revealed whereas a false negative occurs when the method classifies a request as negative that should have been accepted. For both errors, the system pays the cost for misclassification. In the next section, we describe a method for cost assignment.

### 3.1    Cost Assignment

According to the class assignment – not the original Reuters-21578 category label, but the artificially assigned class label, such as need-to-know confidential or otherwise (simply, positive or negative) – each of the documents in both the training and testing sets is assigned a cost, ensuring that the mis-classification cost of a need-to-know confidential information is higher than that of the remaining confidential documents (i.e., $\lambda_{10} > \lambda_{01}$, $\lambda_{10} > \lambda_{00}$, $\lambda_{01} > \lambda_{11}$) [3].

Since the Reuters-21578 document collection does not have cost information, we devised a heuristic for cost assignment. There is a cost involved in incorrect classification. Moreover, a higher cost is assigned to a false positive than a false negative. Particularly, the cost for misclassifying a confidential document, $\mathbf{d}_i$, is computed by:

$$cost(\mathbf{d}_i) = \begin{cases} [s, s + |c_j|] & \text{if } \mathbf{d}_i \in c_j \text{ and } c_j = \text{positive} \\ \left[0, \dfrac{\sum_{s \in positive} cost(\mathbf{d}_s)}{|\text{number of negative documents}|}\right] & \text{Otherwise} \end{cases}$$

where $s = \ln\left(\frac{N}{|c_j|}\right) \times 100$, $N$ is the total number of documents and $|c_j|$ is the number of documents belonging to the $j$th category. The total cost for misclassification is added to the cost of confidential documents misclassed if a classifier is not able to predict any of the positive cases, in order to prevent the case that a low cost is simply achieved by ignoring the class with a low frequency. For example, there are 15 out of 10,000 documents belonging to the positive class. The cost assignment ensures that the total cost for misclassifying those 15 examples should be either equal to or higher than that of the remaining documents [3].

## 3.2   Experimental Results

From the 67 selected categories of the Reuters-21578 dataset, we choose the five different categories as representative ones according to their category frequencies: small ("livestock" and "corn"), medium ("interest"), and large ("acq" and "earn"). There are 70% of documents in a category (e.g., the "livestock" category) used as "training" and the remaining 30% documents are used for "testing", respectively. There are nine different classifiers tested: LDA, LR, and SVMs, and the combination of those three classifiers with two methods for cost-sensitive learning: metacost and costing. A binary classifier was trained for each of the selected categories by considering the category as positive (i.e., documents that an employee needs to know) with the rest of the data as negative examples. We made use of the LIBSVM[4] and tested three different kernels, such as linear, polynomial, and Gaussian. The Gaussian kernel (i.e., $width = \frac{1}{\text{max feature dimension}}$) was chosen due to its best performance and the different cost factors are assigned [5], $C = 10 \sim 100$. Those values are chosen optimally by 10-fold cross validation.

---

[3] For this case, the cost for misclassifying a positive document is 650.0789 ($= \ln\left(\frac{9985}{15}\right) \times 100$) and the sum of the cost is 9751.1835 ($=650.0789 \times 15$). Accordingly the cost of misclassification of a negative document is 0.9765 ($= \frac{9751.1835}{9985}$) and the cost sums to 9751.1835 ($= 0.9765 \times 9985$).

[4] http://www.csie.ntu.edu.tw/~cjlin/libsvm/

[5] The cost of constrain violation is set to 100 if there are relatively small amount of positive examples available. Otherwise it is set to about 10.

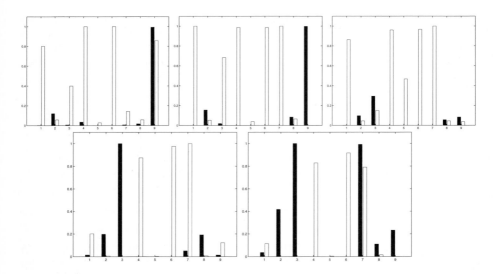

**Fig. 2.** Pairs of false positive (filled bar) and false negative (empty bar) for three selected categories by nine different classifiers, which are numbered from the left to right: (1) SVM, (2) SVM with costing, (3) SVM with metacost, (4) LR, (5) LR with costing, (6) LR with metacost, (7) LDA, (8) LDA with costing, and (9) LDA with metacost, respectively. From the top left, the results for "livestock," "corn," "interest," "acq," and "earn" are presented

As mentioned earlier, the experimental results are primarily analyzed by "false positive," "false negative," and "cost." The procedure of experiments is as follows: firstly, pick one of five selected categories; secondly, assign the cost to each of documents according to its importance using the heuristic described in section 3.1; then, train each of nine classifiers by training examples with cost; finally compute three performance measure (i.e., false positive, false negative, and cost for incorrect classification). Figure 2 shows pairs of false positive and false negative for the three selected categories by nine different classifiers. Except the "interest" category, LR with the costing showed the best results that minimize false positive while holding false negative low. In particular, for the "livestock" category, LR trained by only 18% training data (i.e., 1,781 out of 9,854 documents) resulted 0% false positive and 2.8% false negative rate. For the costing, we carried out five different sampling trials for each category (i.e., 1, 3, 5, 10, and 15) and represented the trial for the best performance. For this category, a newly generated distribution by 10 rejection sampling trials is used to achieve this result. Each resampled set has only about 178 documents. LDA with the costing showed the smallest error for the "interest" category that is comprised of 5.6% false positive and 4.5% false negative.

Table 2 replicates this trend in terms of the total cost for misclassification. The number in parenthesis next to topic name in table 2 is the total number of text documents belonging to that category. The results reported for the costing

**Table 2.** The cost for misclassification by nine different classifiers are presented. The values in bold face are the best for corresponding category.

| Methods | livestock (114) | corn (253) | interest (513) | acq (2448) | earn (3987) |
|---------|-----------------|------------|----------------|------------|-------------|
| SVM | 13967 | 66453 | 54065 | 83141 | 108108 |
| SVM (w/costing) | 4035 ± 30 | 8851 ± 52 | 9058 ± 159 | 40009 ± 252 | 96007 ± 331 |
| SVM (w/mc) | 7147 ± 50 | 23596 ± 64 | 32011 ± 321 | 194165 ± 451 | 228612 ± 453 |
| LR | 35809 | 32759 | 60031 | 349080 | 710631 |
| LR (w/costing) | **484 ± 11** | **1333 ± 44** | 29614 ± 110 | **606 ± 145** | **2521 ± 191** |
| LR (w/mc) | 34980 ± 35 | 32759 ± 79 | 60374 ± 154 | 386859 ± 1185 | 788819 ± 263 |
| LDA | 2638 | 66453 | 124733 | 591300 | 908690 |
| LDA (w/costing) | 1461 ± 28 | 6092 ± 89 | **7301 ± 152** | 39354 ± 205 | 41478 ± 159 |
| LDA (w/mc) | 40079 ± 57 | 45778 ± 71 | 8955 ± 157 | 51789 ± 285 | 54084 ± 244 |
| Cost for base line | 42625 | 79084 | 139113 | 591357 | 1090498 |

and the metacost are the average of 5 different runs. The bottom line entitled "cost for base line" is the total cost for a category if a classifier classifies all the testing examples incorrectly (e.g., the misclassification cost of a classifier for "livestock" will be 42,625 if the classifier classifies all incorrectly). For the "earn" category, LR with the costing caused only 0.002 out of the total cost (2,521 out of 1,090,498). For the remaining categories, the best-performer paid only less than 0.05 out of the total cost.

From the comparison with error-minimizing classifiers, the costing proved its effectiveness in that it requires relatively small amount of training data for a better performance. For the "corn" category, LR with the costing, which only used 10% of the training data (i.e., 986 out of 9,854 documents) showed the best result in terms of the smallest loss (1,333 out of 79,084), zero false positive, and lower false negative rate (0.039). The LR classifier was trained by a sample set by three rejection sampling trials that is comprised of 458 positive and 528 negative examples. The smallest cost implies that it is expected to pay 1.1% of the total cost caused by incorrect confidential access control (i.e., misclassification). From the false positive perspective (zero false alarm), there is no leaking of confidential information. 39% false negative rate means that there would be 39 out of 1,000 valid requests to the confidential information that are mistakenly rejected. This inconveniences employees because they have to access particular information for their projects, but the system does not authorize their access requests. This trend holds good for the remaining four categories.

## 4   Related Work

Weippl and Ibrahim [12] proposed content-based management of text document access control. They applied a self-organized map (SOM) to cluster a given collection of text documents into groups which have similar contents. This approach also allowed humans to impose dynamic access control to identified text document groups. However they did not address a potential problem that occurs when the security policy for individual documents of a cluster does not match with the security policy for that cluster. Giuri and Iglio [5] proposed an approach that determines a user's access to confidential information, which is based on the content of the information and the role of the user. For example, they consider subdividing medical records into several different categories (e.g., pediatrics), and allow that only relevant physicians (e.g., pediatrician) can access them. Since they do not mention automatic techniques in their paper, one is left with the suspicion that they manually categorize content and roles. Aleman-Meza and his colleagues proposed an ontological approach to deal with the legitimate document access problem of insider threat [1]. An attempt to access document is regarded as legitimate if the job assignment of a requester (e.g., an intelligence analyst) has a semantic association with the documents that are accessed. This approach is quite similar to ours in that they enforce the need-to-know principle by using a predefined ontology. A well-defined ontology might be useful to determine the semantic associations between the existing documents and the analysts' assignments, but regular updates are required to accommodate the change of the document collections and the topics of assignments. Symonenko and his colleagues propose a hybrid approach that combines role-based access monitoring, social network analysis, and semantic analysis of insiders' communications, in order to detect inappropriate information exchange [10]. Lee and his colleagues [6] introduced a cost-sensitive framework for the intrusion detection domain and analyzed cost factors in detail. Particularly, they identify the major cost factors (e.g., costs for development, operation, damages and responding to intrusion) and then applied a rule induction learning technique (i.e., RIPPER) to this cost model, in order to maximize security while minimizing costs. However their cost model needs to be changed manually if a system's cost factors are changed.

## 5   Conclusion and Future Work

In the scenario of confidential access control based on the need-to-know principle, a false positive occurs when the system accepts a request that should not have been accepted whereas a false negative occurs when the system rejects a request that should have been accepted. For both errors, the system pays the cost for misclassification. From the security perspective, it is more tolerable to have an authorization process with a high false negative rather than one with a high false positive rate because the latter is a serious security problem since confidential information, which should not be revealed, can be accessed.

In this paper we test the effectiveness of cost-sensitive learning for confidential access control and improve our previous results by taking into consideration the cost caused by misclassification. To this end, we model the binary decision whether to reject or accept the request in a cost-sensitive learning framework, where the cost caused by incorrect decision for the request is different according to the relative importance of the requested information. In addition, we invented a cost assignment method that ensures that the mis-classification cost of a need-to-know confidential information is higher than that of the other confidential information. Finally we tested three different error-minimizing classification methods.

From the comparison of the cost-sensitive learning methods with the error-minimizing classification methods, we found that the costing with a logistic regression showed the best performance. In particular, it requires far less training data for much better results, in terms of the smallest cost paid, the lowest false positive rate, and the relatively low false negative rate. The smallest cost implies that it is expected to pay 1.1% of the total cost caused by incorrect confidential access control. The nearly zero false positive rate means that there is no leaking of confidential information. The benefit of smaller training data is two-fold; First, obviously it takes less time to train the classifier; Second, it enables a human administrator to conveniently identify arbitrary subsets of confidential information, in order to train the initial classifier. In other words, through our proposed methods, it becomes easier for a human administrator to define, assign, and enforce an effective access control for a particular subset of confidential information. Although our approach demonstrates a promising result, we believe that such a content-based approach should be used as a complementary tool for a human administrator.

Although to our knowledge, the cost-sensitive learning approach is a novel one for confidential access control, it would be very interesting if we compare the effectiveness of our framework with conventional document management systems (e.g., ACL-based systems) and knowledge-intensive approaches (e.g., ontology-based systems) as future work.

## Acknowledgement

This research was partially supported by award BAA-03-02-CMU from Computer Technology Associates to Carnegie Mellon University and in part by AFOSR contract number F49640-01-1-0542.

## References

1. Aleman-Meza, B., Burns, P., Eavenson, M., Palaniswami, D., and Sheth, A., An ontological approach to the document access problem of insider threat, In *Proceedings of IEEE International Conference on Intelligence and Security Informatics* (ISI-05), pp. 486-491, 2005.
2. Domingos, P., MetaCost: A general method for making classifiers cost-sensitive, In *Proceedings of International Conference on Knowledge Discovery and Data Mining* (KDD-99), pp. 155-164, 1999.
3. Elkan, C., The foundations of cost-sensitive learning, In *Proceedings of International Joint Conference on Artificial Intelligence* (IJCAI-01), pp. 973-978, 2001.
4. Fawcett, T., ROC graphs: Notes and practical considerations for researchers, HP Lab Palo Alto, *HPL-2003-4*, 2003.
5. Giuri, L. and Iglio, P., Role templates for content-based access control, In *Proceedings of ACM Workshop on Role Based Access Control*, pp. 153-159, 1997.

6. Lee, W., Miller, M., Stolfo, S., Jallad, K., Park, C., Zadok, E., and Prabhakar, V., Toward cost-sensitive modeling for intrusion detection, *ACM Journal of Computer Society*, Vol. 10, No. 1-2, pp. 5-22, 2002.

7. Joachims, T., Text categorization with support vector machines: Learning with many relevant features, In *Proceedings of European Conference on Machine Learning* (ECML-98), 1998.

8. Schutze, H., Hull, D.A., and Pedersen, J.O., A comparison of classifiers and document representations for the routing problem, In *Proceedings of International ACM Conference on Research and Development in Information Retrieval* (SIGIR-95), pp. 229-237, 1995.

9. Seo, Y.-W., Giampapa, J., and Sycara, K., A multi-agent system for enforcing Need-To-Know security policies, In *Proceedings of International Conference on Autonomous Agents and Multi Agent Systems (AAMAS) Workshop on Agent Oriented Information Systems* (AOIS-04), pp. 163-179, 2004.

10. Symonenko, S., Liddy, E.D., Yilmazel, O., Semantic analysis for monitoring insider threats, In *Proceedings of Symposium on Intelligence and Security Informatics*, 2004.

11. Torkkola, T., Linear discriminant analysis in document classification, In *IEEE Workshop on TextMining*, 2001.

12. Weippl, E. and Ibrahim, K., Content-based management of document access control, In *Proceedings of the 14th International Conference on Applications of Prolog*, 2001.

13. Zadrozny, B., Langford, J., and Abe, N., A simple method for cost-sensitive learning, *IBM Tech Report*, 2002.

# Design and Implementation of a Policy-Based Privacy Authorization System*

HyangChang Choi[1], SeungYong Lee[1], and HyungHyo Lee[2],**

[1] Dept. of Information Security, Chonnam National University, Gwangju, Korea, 500-757
{hcchoi, birch}@lsrc.jnu.ac.kr
[2] Div. of Information and EC, Wonkwang University, Iksan, Korea, 570-749
hlee@wonkwang.ac.kr

**Abstract.** In the Internet era, enterprises want to use personal information of their own or other enterprises' subscribers, and even provide it to other enterprises for their profit. On the other hand, subscribers to Internet enterprises expect their privacy to be securely protected. Therefore, a conflict between enterprises and subscribers can arise in using personal information for the enterprises' benefits. In this paper, we introduce a privacy policy model and propose a policy-based privacy authorization system. The privacy policy model is used for authoring privacy policies and the privacy authorization system renders the authorization decision based on the privacy policies. In the proposed system, policies for enterprises and subscribers are described in XACML, an XML-based OASIS standard language for access control policies. In addition, we show the details of how the procedure of the privacy authorization and conflict resolution is processed in the proposed system.

## 1 Introduction

Subscribers' personal information (PI) stored and managed in enterprise information systems is usually used both for the subscribers' convenience such as eliminating the re-entering process of their PI when they perform transactions and for the profit of the enterprise. During using enterprises' services, the subscribers want to make sure that their PI is not utilized nor transferred beyond the relevant enterprise perimeter. Sometimes, however, it is reported that the subscriber's PI is used or leaked against his/her privacy policy [1, 2, 3]. As a consequence, the uninformed use of PI by an enterprise may cause a privacy breach and hinder services that utilize PI [3, 4].

In terms of privacy, enterprises should inform their subscribers which personal information is collected and for which purposes it is used [3, 7]. For example, if an electronic commercial transaction analyzes the subscribers' preference for products with the purpose of advertisement it would be effective from enterprises' standpoint, while it would be considered as a privacy violation from users' standpoint. In order to solve the problem, several non-technical regulations were proposed; privacy protection guidelines

---

* This research was supported by the MIC(Ministry of Information and Communication), Korea, under the ITRC(Information Technology Research Center) support program supervised by the IITA(Institute of Information Technology Assessment).
** Corresponding author.

S. Mehrotra et al. (Eds.): ISI 2006, LNCS 3975, pp. 129–140, 2006.

of OECD and Fair Information Practice from the US are the most important examples. As technology-based privacy protection methods, W3C's P3P (Platform for Privacy Preferences) and IBM's EPAL (Enterprise Privacy Authorization Language) were proposed. But, P3P is mainly for automating the privacy policy verification process between user agents and web servers and EPAL is a formal language for writing enterprise privacy policies to govern personal information. And there is no general privacy authorization model encompassing both user and enterprise privacy policies.

In this paper, we introduce a privacy policy model and propose a Policy-based Privacy Authorization System (PPAS). The privacy policy model is used for authoring privacy policies on which the privacy authorization system is based. In the proposed system, policies for enterprises and subscribers are described in XACML [6], an OASIS standard language for access control policies. In addition, we show the details of how the procedure of privacy authorization and a conflict resolution is processed in the proposed system.

The rest of this paper is organized as follows: in section 2, re-searches on the privacy-enhancing techniques are briefly reviewed. In section 3, a model for privacy policies and the procedure of the privacy authorization system are described. Section 4 illustrates the implementation of the policy-based privacy authorization system and conflict resolution procedure. Finally, the conclusion and future research plans are presented.

## 2   Related Work

Alan Westin, Samuel Warren, and Louis Brandeis have defined privacy in a manner that has been accepted by many researches [7]. They recommend that when information associated to a user or an organization has been disclosed, there should be no material loss or emotional damage to be suffered by the users or system administrators of organizations. Moreover, it constitutes the privacy principles that should be maintained as a foundation for security and their business. The privacy principles include accountability, identifying purpose, consent, limiting collection, limiting use, accuracy, openness, individual access, challenging compliance, and safeguards [9].

The important researches on describing privacy protection principles are W3C's P3P (the Platform for Privacy Preferences) [10] and IBM's E-P3P (the Platform for Enterprise Privacy Practices)[13]. P3P is a platform designed to give users more control of their personal information when browsing Internet Websites. Nonetheless, P3P does have its limitations [11]. Most importantly, it does not include a mechanism for enforcement. It can not ensure that enterprises or organizations will actually follow the privacy policies on their websites. E-P3P performs authorization according to a privacy protection policy established by an enterprise privacy manager [8]. The privacy policy of E-P3P is expressed in EPAL (the Enterprise Privacy Authorization Language), which is designed for formulating privacy authorization rules that allow or deny actions on data by users for certain purposes under certain conditions while mandating certain obligations. E-P3P is yet a promising solution from the enterprise's point of view to provide privacy for user information. However, there exists a fundamental vulnerability since EPAL only takes the enterprise privacy policy into account [8].

In order to solve the problems, a new privacy authorization system encompassing both the enterprise and user privacy policies and supporting the privacy authorization decision process as well as a conflict resolution are needed.

## 3   A Privacy Policy Model and the Design of a Privacy Authorization System

### 3.1   A Privacy Policy Model

In the Internet environment, Internet users subscribe to services of enterprises with a lot of his/her PI such as his/her name and incomes and the enterprise provides the subscribers' information to other enterprises and accesses to PI of subscribers of other enterprises. Enterprises create a lot of privacy policies to protect subscribers' privacy and each subscriber also composes his/her own privacy policies for his/her privacy protection. Like this, in order to protect PI, privacy-enhancing technologies compose privacy policies and determine whether access requests for PI can be permitted or denied. Elements composing a privacy policy are a user who is about to access PI, a group of which the user is a member, PI which the user accesses, a purpose for which the user access to PI, an access mode which is a type of access operations such as *read, write, create* and *delete*. There are two types of privacy policies: a privacy policy for administration (PPA) and a privacy policy for enforcement (PPE). PPA is used for administrators to access mode a privacy policy while PPE is used for privacy authorization systems to render the authorization decision.

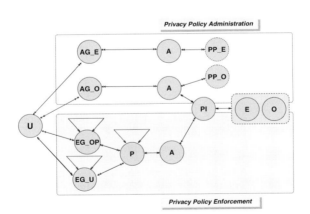

**Fig. 1.** A Privacy Policy Model

Our proposed privacy policy model presented in figure 1 consists of two models: a privacy policy administration model and a privacy policy enforcement model. A privacy policy administration model (PPAM) is for PPA, while a privacy policy enforcement model (PPEM) is for PPE. In this paper, only the PPEM is considered

**Table 1.** Components of the Privacy Policy Model

| Components | Definition and Description |
|---|---|
| **U (Users)** | A set of users and enterprises who want to access to PI. U is referred to as a *subject* in access control. U = *PI_O ∪ PI_E ∪ PI_OP ∪ PI_U* |
| **PI_E** | A set of privacy administrators for PI in an enterprise |
| **PI_O** | A set of PI owners |
| **PI_OP** | A set of PI operators in an enterprise |
| **PI_U** | A set of PI requesters. |
| **G (Groups)** | A set of user groups G = *AG_O ∪ AG_E ∪ EG_OP ∪ EG_U* |
| **AG_ E** | A set of PI _E groups |
| **AG_ O** | A set of PI_O groups |
| **EG_ OP** | A set of PI _OP groups |
| **EG_ U** | A set of PI _U groups |
| **PI       (Personal Information)** | A set of personal information of subscribers to an enterprise. PI is referred to a *resource* to which a subject wants to access. |
| **P (Purposes)** | A set of purposes of using PI |
| **A (Access modes)** | A set of access modes to PI A = *{r, w, c, d}* , *r: read, w: write, c: create, d: delete* |
| **E (Effects)** | A set of effects which are the intended consequence of a satisfied policy E = *{ permit, deny, indeterminate, not applicable }* |
| **O (Obligations)** | A set of obligations which must be observed in conjunction with the enforcement of an authorization decision |

because PPE is applied to determine whether an access requests for PI is authorized or not.

Based on the privacy policy model, a privacy policy can be created, which is a rule to determine if a user who wants to do an operation on PI with a purpose and whether a member of a group is permitted or denied with an obligation. The components of the privacy policy model are described in table 1 with details. Groups and purposes in the model are hierarchically structured.

### 3.1.1  A Privacy Policy Based on the Privacy Policy Enforcement Model

A privacy policy based on the PPEM is used for rendering the authorization decision to access requests for PI. Privacy policies are divided into two types of privacy policies: an *enterprise privacy policy* (PP_E) which is created by PI_E of an enterprise and an *owner privacy policy* (PP_O) which is composed by the owner of personal information. Both the privacy policies are composed by the Cartesian production of six sets: *subject, resource, purpose, access_mode, effect* and *obligation*. The combination of a *purpose* and *access_mode* is reffered to as an *action* in XACML. The difference between the two privacy policies is who crates the privacy policies. While PP_O created by PI owners is for expressing which PI of owner is permitted to be accessed by which enterprises for a specific purpose, PP_E created by an enterprise is for describing which PI of subscribers is granted to its applications and other enterprises. The formal definition of privacy policies and their descriptions are illustrated in table 2.

**Table 2.** The Formal Definitions and Descriptions of Privacy Policy

| Privacy Policy types | | Definition and Description |
|---|---|---|
| **PP** | | PP = *PP_E* ∪ *PP_O* |
| | **PP_E** | A set of privacy policy created by PI_E<br>PP_E = $(U \cup G) \times PI \times P \times A \times E \times O$,<br>*subject × resource × purpose × access_mode × effect × obligation* |
| | **PP_O** | A set of privacy policy created by PI_O<br>PP_O = $(U \cup G) \times PI \times P \times A \times E \times O$<br>*subject × resource × purpose × access_mode × effect × obligation* |

## 3.2  Design of the Policy-Based Privacy Authorization System

### 3.2.1  Privacy Authorization System

We design the policy-based privacy authorization system based on the privacy policy model, which makes an authorization decision when a *subject (i.e. U ∪ G)* requests *resource (i.e. PI)* of subscribers of other enterprises with an *action (i.e. P × A)*. The PPAS analyses an access request for *PI*, retrieves privacy policies applicable to the request, applies privacy policies to access requests for *PI* and decide whether the requests can be permitted or denied. Privacy policies used in the PPAS and access requests for *PI* are written in XACML. Privacy policies must be authored and stored in privacy authorization systems before privacy authorization decisions. Privacy policies are created and administrated based on the policy elements of XACML.

There are three policy types: Enterprise policy, Enterprise exception policy and User policy. Both Enterprise policy and Enterprise exception policy types are created by enterprises and applied to all the subscribers' PI. Enterprise exception policy type is for exceptional cases such as emergencies. User policy type includes policies which

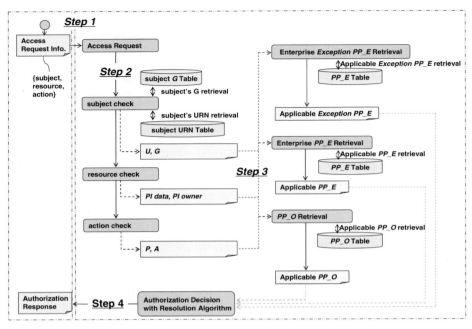

**Fig. 2.** Authorization Procedure of PI Access Requests

owners of PI individually create for their fine-grained protection. Enterprise policy and Enterprise exception policy shown in figure 2 correspond to PP_E, because they are manipulated and managed by PI_E. User policy which is created by owners of PI corresponds to PP_O.

### 3.2.2   Authorization Procedure of Privacy Access Requests

The authorization decision to access requests is processed with the applicable privacy policies through the 4 steps shown in figure 2. The first step is to receive an access request for PI from an information requestor and to convert the request into XACML. In the second step, the request which is represented in XACML is analyzed and the necessary information is extracted. One or more policies applicable to the request are retrieved from enterprise policies, enterprise exception policies and user policies in the third step. In the final step, the permission to the access request is determined with the applicable policies and the result of the access decision is returned in XACML. Each step is described with details as follows.

**Step1: Analyzing an Access Request for Personal Information**

An access request for PI must be submitted with three elements: *subject*, *resource* and *action*, because a subject accesses a resource in order to perform a specific action. In the elements, the subject element is referred to as a user who requests PI, the resource element is referred to as an object which the user wants to access and the action element is behavior of which the user does to the object. The resource element is consists of a resource itself and owner of the resource and the action element

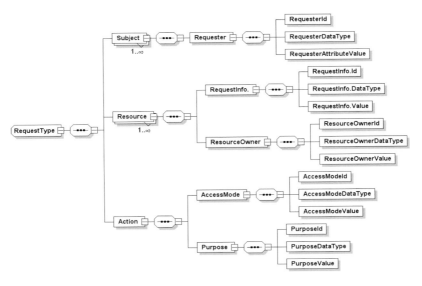

**Fig. 3.** Schema for a Personal Information Request

consists of access modes and purposes. A subject and a resource can be uniquely distinguished and administrated by introducing the URN indication method. The PPAS converts an access request into an XACML document based on the subject, resource and action of the request. Figure 3 shows the schema for personal information requests, which is represented by Design View of XML SPY [12] for our privacy authorization system. The XML document shown in figure 4 is an example of a personal information request.

**Step2: Processing an Access Request for Personal Information**
A received access request for PI, which is written in XACML, is processed in the second step as followings. First, it is checked if the subject of the request and the group of the subject are valid by retrieving the *subject URN* table and the *subject G* table which maintains valid subject URNs and groups of the subjects respectively. With the similar method, it is checked if the requested resource is a single type or category type by analyzing the URN of PI, which PI is and who the owner of the PI is. Finally, it is checked what the access mode to PI and the purpose of using it are. Information including subjects, resources and actions which are extracted in this step are used for retrieving privacy policies applicable to the request in the third step.

**Step3: Retrieving Privacy Policies Applicable to an Access Request**
Each enterprise maintains its own privacy policies and each subscriber to an enterprise can compose his/her own privacy policies for his/her own PI. Therefore, the privacy authorization system maintains a lot of enterprise and owner privacy policies. Some of the privacy policies are applicable to an access request according to the subjects, resources and actions of the request. A privacy policy is applicable to an access request only when the subjects, resources and actions of the privacy policy

```
<?xml version="1.0" encoding="UTF-8"?>
<Request xmlns="urn:oasis:names:tc:xacml:1.0:context" xmlns:xsi="http://www.w3.org/2001/XMLSchema-instance">
  <Subject>
    <Attribute AttributeId="urn:oasis:names:tc:xacml:1.0:subject:Group-Name-urn" DataType="http://www.w3.org/2001/XMLSchema#String">
      <AttributeValue>urn:IDSP:ETRI:Highly_Trust_Group:www.nhic.or.kr</AttributeValue>
    </Attribute>
  </Subject>

  <Resource>
    <Attribute AttributeId="urn:oasis:names:tc:xacml:1.0:resource:Group-Name-urn" DataType="http://www.w3.org/2001/XMLSchema#string">
      <AttributeValue>urn:ETRI-PP:Contact_Info:Home:Phone:AreaCode</AttributeValue>
    </Attribute>
    <Attribute AttributeId="urn:oasis:names:tc:xacml:1.0:resource:Owner" DataType="http://www.w3.org/2001/XMLSchema#string">
      <AttributeValue>alice@abcmail.or.kr</AttributeValue>
    </Attribute>
  </Resource>

  <Action>
    <Attribute AttributeId="urn:oasis:names:tc:xacml:1.0:action:Purpose-type" DataType="http://www.w3.org/2001/XMLSchema#string">
      <AttributeValue>Credit_inquiry</AttributeValue>
    </Attribute>
    <Attribute AttributeId="urn:oasis:names:tc:xacml:1.0:action:Accessmode-type" DataType="http://www.w3.org/2001/XMLSchema#string">
      <AttributeValue>r</AttributeValue>
    </Attribute>
  </Action>
</Request>
```

**Fig. 4.** An Example of an Access Request in XACML

include or is equal to the subjects, resources, and action of the access request respectively. In this step, the PPAS retrieves privacy policies applicable to access requests for PI by comparing them respectively so as to render the authorization decision to the requests. In each policy type, which is one of *Enterprise policy*, *Enterprise Exception policy* and *User policy*, two or more policies can be applicable to a request, but only one policy is selected with the 'policy- or rule-combining-algorithm' attributes of the policy or rule elements in XACML.

**Step4: Authorization and Conflict Resolution**

After retrieving the applicable privacy policies, the PPAS must determine whether the access request can be permitted or denied based on the applicable privacy policies. If two or more privacy policies are applicable to an access request then a policy conflict occurs because the privacy authorization system cannot decide which policy must be applied to the request. In order to solve the problem, the PPAS select only one policy of them by applying a resolution algorithm such as *EnterpriseExceptionPolicy_First*, *EnterprisePolicy_First, UserPolicy_First, Deny_Overrides and Permit_Overrides*. For example, if several policies including an enterprise privacy policy are applicable and the resolution algorithm is UserPolicy_First, an owner policy takes precedence over an enterprise policy and an enterprise exception policy. After selecting privacy policy, the PPAS applies it to access requests and decides the authorization. The authorization decision to access requests is one of *permit, deny, indeterminate* and *not_applicable* as defined in XACML [6].

## 4   Implementation

The privacy authorization system was implemented to make the privacy authorization decision by modifying the XACML1.2 package that was developed in Java language [5]. For the efficient authorization decision, the PPAS stores and retrieves privacy policies in the Oracle 9i database with the SYS.XMLTYPE format.

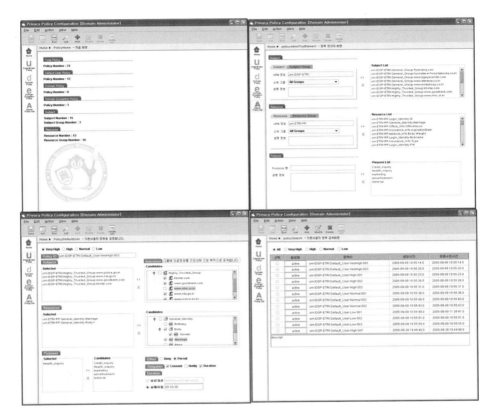

**Fig. 5.** Snapshots of PPAS

**An example privacy information request:** Assume that there is an e-mail site (abcmail.or.kr) holding information of its customers including Alice and that the resolution algorithm of the PPAS of the site is UserPolicy_First. When an enterprise, whose subject-urn is *"urn:IDSP:ETRI:Highly_Trust_Group:www.nhic.or.kr"*, is about to read the areacode of Alice's mobile phone, which is identified by *"urn: ETRI-PP:Contact_info:Home:Phone:Areacode"*, with the *"Credit_inquiry"* purpose, the PPAS executes making a decision for the request through the authorization process such as in figure 6.

Example privacy policies of the PPAS are shown in table 2 and only *E_771* and *Alice_5* are applicable to the example request because the subject, resource and action of the privacy policies are equal to or include those of the example request.

The authorization decision procedure of the example access request is described step by step in figure 6. The request is denied by applying the *Alice_5* policy.

The PPAS applies the *Alice_5* privacy policy to the example request and returns *"Deny"* with *"Notify"* obligation, because the resolution algorithm of the PPAS is *UserPolicy_First* and *Alice_5* is applicable. A PI access request and the authorization decision to the request are shown in figure 7. The access request is presented in the *Request XACML box* in figure 7 in XML and the result of the request is provided in the *Response box* with *"Deny"* decision after rendering the authorization decision. The PPAS protects privacy by authorizing PI based on privacy policies for its request and permission.

**Table 3.** An Example of Privacy Policies applicable to the Scenario

| PPType _No | Access Request | | | | Response | |
|---|---|---|---|---|---|---|
| | subject | resource | action | | effect | obligation |
| | U ∪ G | PI | P | A | | |
| E_771 | TG | A002 | ALL | r, w, c, d | Permit | Consent |
| EE_59 | abcmail.or.kr | A002 | Credit_inquiry | r | Deny | Notify |
| Alice_5 | www.nhic.or.kr | A001 | Credit_inquiry | r | Deny | Notify |

※ **Note**
- **PPType** = {E, EE, O}, *E= Enterprise PP_E, EE= Enterprise Exception PP_E, O= PP_O*
- **G** = {HTG, TG, GG, NG}, *HTG= Highly Trusted Group, TG= Trusted Group, GG= General Group, NG= No Group, HTG > TG > GG > NG*
- **PI** = {A001, A002}, *A001= urn:ETRI-PP:Contact_info: Home:Phone:Areacode, A002= urn:ETRI-PP:Contact_info: Home*
- **P** = {ALL, Credit_inquiry, Health_Info_Inquiry, Marketing}
- **effect** = {Permit, Deny, Indeterminate, Not_applicable}
- **obligation** = {Consent, Notify}

---

*Step 1:* **Access Request:** *Figure 3*

*Step 2:* **Subject:**
U = *"www.nhic.or.kr"*;
G = *"HTG"*;

**Resource:**
PI Data = *"A001"*;
PI Owner = *"alice@abcmail.or.kr"*;

**Action:**
P = *"Credit_inquiry"*;
A = *"r"*;

*Step 3:* **Applicable Privacy Policies:**
E_771 = {*"TG"* × *"A002"* × *"ALL"* × *"r, w, c, d"* × *"Permit"* × *"Consent"*};
Alice_5 = {*"www.nhic.or.kr"* × *"A001"* × *"Credit_inquiry"* × *"r"* × *"Deny"* × *"Notify"*};

*Step 4:* **Authorization**
= **UserPolicy_First**(E_771, **Alice_5**)
➔ *Effect= Deny, Obligation= Notify*

**Fig. 6.** An Example of Privacy Authorization Procedure of PI Access Request

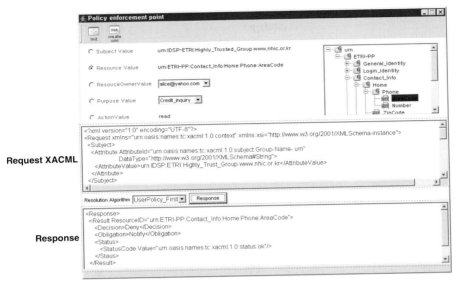

**Fig. 7.** Example of a Personal Information Access Request

# 5   Conclusions

Enterprises create a lot of privacy policies to protect subscribers' privacy and each subscriber also composes his/her own privacy policies for his/her privacy protection. Like this, in order to protect personal information, privacy-enhancing technologies using privacy policies are needed to determine whether access requests for PI can be permitted or denied.

In this paper, we have introduced a privacy policy model which is used for composing a privacy policy. The type of a privacy policy is the Cartesian production of six sets: subject, resource, purpose, access_mode, effect and obligation. And, we also have proposed a policy-based privacy authorization system which renders the authorization decision of access request for personal information. The privacy authorization system retrieves applicable policies and applies them to access requests based on the proposed privacy policy model. For the portability and interoperability, privacy polices and access request for personal information is described in XACML, an XML based OASIS standard language for expressing access control policy, in the privacy authorization system.

In the proposed privacy authorization system, we have applied only simple conflict resolution algorithms to make a privacy decision when the results of applicable privacy policies are not consistent. In the future, we will improve our privacy authorization system to support various resolution algorithms. And we will provide a method how to check privacy policy conflicts in advance during authoring privacy policies.

# References

1. Magnuson, G., Reid, P.: Privacy and Identity Management Survey. IAPP Conference (2004)
2. Privacy and Security Best Practices. Liberty Alliance Project (2003)
3. Who Goes There?: Authentication Through the Lens of Privacy. Computer Science and Telecommunications Board (2003). http://www.nap.edu/catalog/10656.html
4. PRIME: Privacy and Identity Management for Europe Date of preparation. PRIME Project (2004). http://www.prime- project.eu.org/
5. Sun's XACML Implementation. SUN (2005). http://sunxacml.sourcefor ge.net/
6. eXtensible Access Control Markup Language. OASIS (2005). http://www.oasis-open.org
7. Hyang-Chang Choi, Seung-Yong Lee, Hyung-Hyo Lee: PIMS: An Access-Control based Privacy Model for Identity Management Systems. GESTS International Transaction on Computer Science and Engineering Vol.9 and No.1(ISSN 1738-6438) (2005)
8. Paul Ashley, Satoshi Hada, Günter Karjoth, Calvin Powers, Matthias Schunter: Enterprise Privacy Authorization Language (EPAL 1.2). W3C (2003). http://www.w3.org /Submission/2003/SUBM-EPAL-20031110
9. George Yee, Larry Korba: An Agent Architecture for E-Services Privacy Policy Compliance. Advanced Information Networking and Application (2005)
10. Lorrie Faith Cranor: Web Privacy with P3P. O'Reilly (2002)
11. Charlin Lu: P3P in the Context of Legislation and Education. Sensitive Information in a Wired World (2003)
12. XML SPY. Altova (2004). http://www.xml.com/pub/p/15
13. P. Ashley, S. Hada, G. Karjoth, M. Schunter: E-P3P, "Privacy Policies and Privacy Authorization. WPES November (2002)

# Privacy Preserving *DBSCAN* for Vertically Partitioned Data

Artak Amirbekyan and V. Estivill-Castro

School of ICT, Griffith University,
Nathan QLD 4111, Brisbane, Australia

**Abstract.** Clustering algorithms are attractive for the core task of class identification in large databases. In recent years privacy issues also became important for data mining. In this paper, we construct a privacy preserving version of the popular clustering algorithm *DBSCAN*. This algorithm is density-based. Such notion of clustering allows us to discover clusters of arbitrary shape. *DBSCAN* requires only two input parameters, but it offers some support in determining appropriate values. Originally, *DBSCAN* uses *R*-Trees to support efficient associative queries. Thus, one solution for privacy preserving *DBSCAN* requires to have privacy preserving *R*-Trees. We achieve this here.

## 1 Introduction

This paper considers clustering. However, application to large databases raises the requirement for little or no human intervention or domain knowledge when supplying input parameters to allow the discovery process to be exploratory and free of human bias. While efficiency on large databases is also a factor, flexible modeling to allow for arbitrary shape of clusters and enable potentially meaningful subclasses is also important. The task here is not only to have clustering algorithms satisfying the above requirements, but to enable clustering algorithms to ensure a level of privacy. With the current emphasis on intelligence for safeguarding modern societies from crime and terrorism, data mining is to be applied to analyze large amounts of digitally recorded data about the activities and operations of individuals and organization for spotting out the potentially dangerous [11]. This threatens privacy and values of democratic societies. Privacy preserving clustering is more apparent in settings where different data holders have different data about the same individuals (vertically partitioned data [14]). For example, a government agency classifies individuals as law obeying citizens, potentially dangerous individuals, and certainly dangerous individuals based on attributes available to the law enforcing agencies. However, a more accurate classification (clustering) could be obtained if data about the financial transactions of individuals was available as well. Then, police resources could be more focused for more promising (and perhaps preventive) investigations. But financial transactions or phone records may be in the ownership of banks or phone companies that may or may not be obliged to disclose (in some countries these records are not to be made available unless the individual is charged).

S. Mehrotra et al. (Eds.): ISI 2006, LNCS 3975, pp. 141–153, 2006.

The *DBSCAN* algorithm is one of the most popular algorithms for clustering because it almost completely satisfies the requirements described before. If the data is already stored in an *R*-Tree, the algorithm is very efficient exhibiting sub-quadratic time complexity for large databases. As opposed to *k*-means or *k*-medoids, which can be considered simplifications of the parametric statistical inference of clustering by identifying a mixture by Expectation Maximization, *DBSCAN* seems to fit more closely the exploratory nature of data mining. However, very few clustering methods have been enabled for the privacy preserving (PP) context and it is urgent to migrate *DBSCAN*, so that this powerful tool can be used in such context. Recently, such clustering algorithms as *k*-means [15] and *k*-medoids [5][1] have been presented in the security context, but clusters in these algorithms are always spherical. Non-convex clusters are detected with *DBSCAN*. In this paper we present privacy preserving *DBSCAN*. We will achieve this by some already existing privacy preserving operations, such as a secure protocol for the scalar product, and also some new methods to secure data structures for associative queries. In particular, this paper presents the first privacy preserving version of *R*-Trees. Thus, we enable many other applications demanding privacy besides clustering. We study privacy preserving collaboration between several parties [10]. Each party holds a private data set, and all will conduct clustering on the joint dataset, that is the union of all datasets.

We develop efficient methods that enable this type of computation while minimizing the private information each party reveals.

We adopt the common assumption that the data records of the database $\mathbb{D}$ have been numerically coded and we identify them with their corresponding numerical multidimensional key $\boldsymbol{p} = (x_1, \ldots x_k)$. Thus,clustering is to be performed on the proximity on the keys. Each $x_j$ is an element of some totally ordered domain $D_j$, and $\boldsymbol{p}$ is an element of $D = D_1 \times \cdots \times D_k$.Vertically partitioned data among several parties, means that each party holds the knowledge of all values in a range of attributes and only that party knows these values.

To illustrate the partition of the data and the description of the algorithms, we will usually focus in the privacy preserving collaboration of two parties we name Alice and Bob. Of course, our algorithms allow for more than two parties, but for simplicity of presentation, where there is no loss of generality, we will use Alice and Bob. We will point out if there are additional steps for more than 2 parties, but typically, more parties make things simpler under the common assumption no two will collude against a third [2]. We can illustrate vertically partitioned data with the example in Fig. 1. Every record in the database is an attribute-value vector. One part of that vector is owned by Alice and

---

[1] In algorithms like *k*-means, the variable *k* identifies the number of clusters and must be supplied by the user. In *DBSCAN*, the algorithm finds the number of clusters, so we reserve *k* for the dimension of the data records, or the dimension of vectors.

[2] If the third party Charles has reason to suspect two other parties will collude, then Charles should treat them as one party (and again the problem of *k* parties comes down to $k - 1$).

the other part by Bob. In the case of more than two parties, then every party will own some part (a number of attributes) from the attribute-value vector.

For vertically partitioned data, a direct use of clustering algorithms on the union of the data requires one party to receive data (every record) from all other parties, or all parties to send their data to a trusted central place. The recipient of the data would conduct the computation in the resulting union. In settings where each party must keep their data private, this is unacceptable. We identify each domain with one

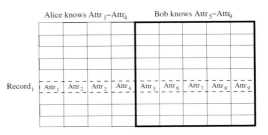

**Fig. 1.** Vertically partitioned data, Alice knows four attributes while Bob knows five

party (so the dimension $k$ of the records is also as the number or parties). Typically there would be less parties than dimensions (as in Fig. 1 where two parties have data for 9-dimensional records). However, we consider Alice as 4 virtual parties (one for each of the columns) and Bob as 5 virtual parties each controlling one of Bob's column. This simplifies the notation in the algorithms (and communication between two virtual parties of the same party just does not need to occur).

## 2   *DBSCAN*

*DBSCAN*'s notion of cluster [4] is a region of high density[3]. *DBSCAN* has two parameters, $\epsilon$ (for the granularity of the histogram) and *MinPts* (for the threshold on the height of the density). For *DBSCAN* those points that have high density around them are called core-points. *DBSCAN* is interested not only in collecting all core points, but also all points in $N_\epsilon(\boldsymbol{p})$, for all core points $\boldsymbol{p}$.

**Definition 1.** *We write $N_\epsilon(\boldsymbol{p}) = \{\boldsymbol{q} \in \mathbb{D} \mid dist(\boldsymbol{p}, \boldsymbol{q}) \leq \epsilon\}$ for the $\epsilon$-neighborhood of a point $\boldsymbol{p}$. We say a point $\boldsymbol{q}$ is a core point if $|N_\epsilon(\boldsymbol{q})| \geq MinPts$.*

**Lemma 1.** *[4] Let $\boldsymbol{p}$ be core. Then, the set of all points $\boldsymbol{q}$ such that $\exists\,\boldsymbol{p} = \boldsymbol{p}_0, \boldsymbol{p}_1, \ldots, \boldsymbol{p}_n = \boldsymbol{q}$, so that $\boldsymbol{p}_i \in N_\epsilon(\boldsymbol{p}_{i-1})$ and $|N_\epsilon(\boldsymbol{p}_{i-1})| \geq MinPts$, (for $i = 1, \ldots, n$) is a cluster. If $C$ is a cluster and $\boldsymbol{p} \in C$ is a core point, then $C$ equals all the points $\boldsymbol{q}$ such that $\boldsymbol{p} = \boldsymbol{p}_0, \boldsymbol{p}_1, \ldots, \boldsymbol{p}_n = \boldsymbol{q}$ with $\boldsymbol{p}_i \in N_\epsilon(\boldsymbol{p}_{i-1})$ and $|N_\epsilon(\boldsymbol{p}_{i-1})| \geq MinPts$, for $i = 1, \ldots, n$.*

*DBSCAN* finds all clusters defined by Lemma 1 [4]. Therefore, *DBSCAN* works essentially by finding a core point and then all points that can be reached by a sequence of $\epsilon$-neighborhoods [4]. It starts with an arbitrary point $\boldsymbol{p}$ and checks

---

[3] In a statistical sense this is a loose notion of what is a cluster, as those areas in a histogram with density above a certain threshold, but illustrates the flavor of *DBSCAN* as it is closer to descriptive statistics than parametric inference.

whether $p$ is a core point. If it is, $p$ becomes $p_0$ and then all points in $N_\epsilon(p_0)$ are examined to see if they are core points (while $N_\epsilon(p_0)$ is added to the cluster). All points $p_i$ found to have $N_\epsilon(p_i) \geq MinPts$ are included to the cluster as core points and also their $\epsilon$-neighbors until no more points can be added. Thus, the fundamental operation in $DBSCAN$ is "Given a point $p \in \mathbb{D}$, retrieve all points $q \in N_\epsilon(p)$". From the central operation, the following operations are readily implemented.

- OP1 (*Is $p$ core?*): Given a point $p$ in the database $\mathbb{D}$, is $|N_\epsilon(p)| \geq MinPts$?
- OP2 (*Find neighborhood of core*): Given a point $p$ in the database $\mathbb{D}$ with $|N_\epsilon(p)| \geq MinPts$, retrieve all other points $q \in N_\epsilon(p)$.
- OP3 (*Core neighbors of core*): Given a core point $q$, retrieve a list of core points in $N_\epsilon(q) \setminus \{q\}$?[4]

The fundamental operation can be performed efficiently using data structures for associative queries, like $KD$-Trees, $R$-Trees or other multidimensional access methods [6]. We now focus on how the central operation can be performed in the context of several parties with vertically partitioned data.

## 3    Privacy Preserving Operations

We use some tools originally developed as "secure multiparty computation" (SMC) [7]. Here, Alice holds one input vector $x$ and Bob holds an input vector $y$. They both want to compute a function $f(x, y)$ without each other learning anything about each other's input except what can be inferred from $f(x, y)$. Yao's Millionaires Problem [16] provides the origin for SMC. In the Millionaires, Alice holds a number $a$ while Bob holds $b$. They want to identify who holds the larger value (they compute if $a > b$) without neither learning anything else about the others value. The function $f(x, y)$ is the predicate $f(x, y) = x > y$. In this paper, we adopt the common assumption identified as *the semi-trusted model* where by each party is so interested in the outcomes that it will follow the protocol without supplying false information or unnecessary transmission of data (for example asking queries repeatedly is not possible). However, parties are entitled to unlimited computation on the values they hold (and obtain) while following the protocol in order to discover the values of other parties.

The secure multiparty add-vector protocol [5] (this is the case when $f(x, y)$ is $x + y$) can be performed, even in the case of two parties, but in such case, the output is owned by one party with perturbations added by some permutation $\pi$ (to ensure privacy). More specifically, one of the two will receive $\pi(x+y)$, so that knowledge of $x$ is insufficient to find $y$ (or knowing $y$ is not enough to disclose $x$). For $k \geq 3$ parties, the secure add-vector protocol can be extended to the $\sum$ of $k$ vectors, where each party owns a vector and in this case there is no need

---

[4] While this operation is technically different to OP2 or OP1 and this is useful for the correctness of the pseudocode, in practical implementations of the pseudocode, when OP3 follows an OP2 or and OP1, the work of the previous operation would be used for a fast implementation of the OP3.

to permute with $\pi$. For 2 parties, the scalar product for vectors of dimension greater than 2 can also be computed under SMC. Because of space limitations we only show how to compute a secure multiparty Euclidean distance. Suppose for a moment that we need to know the Euclidean distance between two points $p$ and $q$ in the database. Also, the $i$-th party knows a common range of the attributes of the vectors $p$ and $q$. It is not hard to see that

$$Euclidean^2(p, q) = \sum_{i=1}^{k} \sum_{\substack{\text{attributes known} \\ \text{by party } i}} \left( \begin{matrix} j\text{-th attr. in} \\ p \text{ own by } i \end{matrix} - \begin{matrix} j\text{-th attr. in} \\ q \text{ own by } i \end{matrix} \right)^2.$$

Letting $v_i^2$ be the square of the Euclidean distance of those attributes known to the $i$-party, then $Euclidean^2(p, q) = v_1^2 + \cdots + v_k^2$, and the problem reduces to finding the value of the sum of values distributed among $k$ parties(each contributes the Euclidean distance squared in the projection that they own). This can be performed as before. The only case that may raise concerns could be $k = 2$ parties. In this case, one of the parties learns the Euclidean distance between two data points in the projection owned by the other party. However, only if the first party owns only one attribute can the second party reduce the possibilities to learn the first party's data value. When each party owns several attributes, even in the two party case, one party can not infer significantly beyond that what would be inferred from the cluster information.

The protocol to add the $k$ values among the $k \geq 3$ parties is as follows.

**VC1.** The $1^{st}$ party uses a random number $r$ and sends $r + v_1^2$ to the $2^{nd}$.

**VC2.** The $2^{nd}$ party adds $r + v_1^1 + v_2^2$ and sends to the $3^{rd}$ party.

**VC3.** Continue until the $k^{th}$ party has the sum $r + (v_1^2 + v_2^2 + \cdots + v_{k-1}^2 + v_k^2)$ and sends it to the $1^{st}$ party.

**VC4.** Then the first party takes away $r$. and announces the result to all parties.

## 4    PP-$R$-Trees

Lemma 1 is the density-based model that *DBSCAN* uses for what is a cluster. This partition can be found by *DBSCAN* using R-Trees or by any other algorithm that constructs the clusters as per these lemmas. The page limit prevents us from presenting a simpler privacy solution using *KD*-Trees for the fundamental associative query and its variants, OP1, OP2, and OP3. For large databases, efficient implementations of these operations are achieved using $R$-Trees, (and that is what *DBSCAN* uses). Thus, we focus on the algorithms for privacy preserving $R$-Trees. An $R$-Tree [8] is a height-balanced tree. For *DBSCAN*, the $R$-Tree is used with spatial objects that are points. Leaf nodes in an $R$-Tree for *DBSCAN* contain entries $(I, p)$ where $p$ refers to the point (or key) in the database and $I$ can be identified with $p$. Internal nodes contain entries $(I, child\_pointer)$ where $child\_pointer$ is the address of a lower node in the $R$-Tree and $I = I_0 \times I_1 \times \ldots \times I_{k-1}$ is a $k$-dimensional box. The intervals $I_i$ are closed

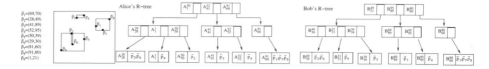

**Fig. 2.** Example of shared $R$-Tree structure, but different bounding boxes per domain, where Alice knows the first coordinate and Bob the second

bounded intervals describing the extent in the $i$-th domain. Most importantly, $I$ is the smallest box that spatially contains the boxes in all its descendant nodes. Fig. 2 illustrates a 2D $R$-Tree with the containment and overlapping relationship that can exist between rectangles. The entire structure of the privacy preserving $R$-Tree is known to all parties (that is, which nodes are pointed to which, which is the root and where all pointers points to). However, in leaves of the form $(I, \boldsymbol{p})$, because $\boldsymbol{p}$ is essentially $I$, each party will only know the attributes in the domain it controls. In internal nodes $(I, child\_pointer)$, each party will know those closed intervals $I_i$ in the domain of its control for each $I = I_0 \times I_1 \times \ldots \times I_{k-1}$. For illustration, we use two parties in Fig. 2. It shows two mirror $R$-Trees that exist for Alice and Bob. Each of them only knows his/her domain intervals in internal nodes. They also know the identifier of those attribute-value vectors at the leaves of the $R$-Tree. What they do not share is the boxes $I$ on the internal nodes. Because we are dealing in 2D, Fig. 2 uses bounding boxes of the form $BB = A_i^l \times B_r^s$, where $A_i^l = [i, l]$ is an interval known by Alice and only Alice, and $B_r^s = [r, s]$ is an interval known by Bob and only Bob. For each of the points $\boldsymbol{p}_i = (a_i, b_i)$, Alice and only Alice knows $a_i$ and Bob and only Bob knows $b_i$. To operate a preserving privacy $R$-Tree all parties will become aware of outcomes of comparisons, but no party will learn the values of the other parties. We explain our methods with two parties not only to get the main ideas across, but because this is usually the difficult case. When the details differ for more parties, we will make a note of it. The operations for a PP-$R$-Tree are insertions, deletions and associative queries. In $R$-Trees, these operations are built upon other operations. As with B-trees, in order to keep the tree balanced, the value $M$ denotes maximum number of entries that will fit in one node while $m \le \frac{M}{2}$ denotes the minimum number of entries. A split happens when a node reaches its capacity $M$, and then two new bounding boxes need to be selected, and the $M+1$ boxes of the original node must be distributed among the new boxes. Thus, the algorithm for the operation to split a node relays in the operation **PickSeeds** (in order to select two new boxes) and **PickNext** (in order to distribute children of the split node into the new boxes). We start with the splitting and then go into its two sub-operations.

### 4.1   Splitting a Node or Algorithm SplitNode

The literature includes many ways to split nodes in $R$-Trees and each way has its advantages and disadvantages. Here, we are more interested in splitting while preserving privacy of the parties involved. Thus, we focus on the classical splitting algorithm [8] with quadratic cost. This algorithm heuristically finds a small-volume split. The split algorithm uses Algorithm **PickSeeds** to choose two of the $M+1$ entries to be the first elements of the two new groups by choosing the pair that would use the most volume. The remaining entries are then assigned to groups one at a time using Algorithm **PickNext**. In **PickNext**, the volume expansion required to add each remaining entry to each group is calculated, and the entry assigned is the one showing the greatest difference between the two groups. Naturally, the parties can split nodes preserving privacy provided that they can apply **PickSeeds** and **PickNext** preserving privacy. Lets look at these two building blocks now.

**Algorithm PickSeeds.** selects two entries to be the first respective element of two new groups as follows. For each pair of entries $E_1$ and $E_2$, we compose a bounding box $J$ for $E_1$ and $E_2$ and calculate $V = Vol(J)$, the volume of $J$. We choose the pair with the largest $V$.

To achieve privacy here, we need to know how to calculate $Vol(J)$. For security reasons, we will separate the two party case from the multiparty ($k \geq 3$) case. Note, that even if one party owns more than one attribute, computing the volume is the product of the volume values on the projections. First let us see how we can calculate the volume when $k \geq 3$ (three or more parties are involved). It is not hard to reduce computing the bounding box of two entries to computing the bounding box of two extreme points (each party just needs to find the extreme values under the domain it controls for all the points involved in the entries). Let us assume we are given two extreme points $\boldsymbol{p}_1 = (v_1^x, v_2^x, \cdots, v_k^x)$ and $\boldsymbol{p}_2(v_1^y, v_2^y, \cdots, v_k^y)$. The goal is to calculate the $k$-dimensional volume which includes these two points (when each party controls one and only one of the dimension). The volume is $|v_1^x - v_1^y| \times |v_2^x - v_2^y| \times \cdots \times |v_k^x - v_k^y|$. This multiplication can be performed in the same way as the circular sum (but using products) along the parties with the first masking with a random number and dividing the product at the end by the random number. In this algorithm, because with the semi-trusted model parties do not collude, no party learns each others data. Since we have to calculate for all possible pairs $E_i$ and $E_j$ and then take the one with largest $V$ (see Algorithm **PickSeeds** Step 1), the only thing left is to calculate the largest value of the obtained $k$-dimensional volumes. This can be performed securely as the first party (who already has all volumes possible) can calculate the largest of the volumes and send to the other parties, so all parties learn which pair ($E_i$ and $E_j$) produces the largest volume. However, the case with only two parties does not have Step VC3, and needs more machinery. Note that the previous protocol is unsuitable for 2 parties because the first party obtains private data of the second party by dividing the product by $r|v_1^x - v_1^y|$. To avoid this security risk we use the secure scalar product [3] which produces $|v_1^x - v_1^y| \times |v_2^x - v_2^y| = V_1 + V_2$, where $V_1$ is known by Alice (first party) and $V_2$ is known by Bob (second party). Now, the secure scalar product among two parties converts a distributed multiplication into a distributed addition. Since there are $M + 1$ bounding boxes for the entries been considered in the splitting of the node, there are

$\binom{M+1}{2}$ pairs. The task is to find $\max_{\forall i,j}(vol(Bounding\_Box(E_i, E_j)))$, where $i, j$ denotes the indices to identify one of the possible pairs of boxes. Note that

$$V_A + V_B, = Vol(Pr_V(\text{Bounding\_Box}(E_i, E_j))) \times Vol(Pr_B(\text{Bounding\_Box}(E_i, E_j)))$$
$$= Vol(Bounding\_Box(E_i, E_j))$$

where $Pr_A$ and $Pr_B$ are the projections only known by Alice and Bob respectively, $V_A$ and $V_B$ the vectors obtained after secure scalar product [3]. For two parties, the question of the largest value of distributed products becomes the largest value of distributed sums. To calculate $\max_{l=l(i,j)}(V_A(l) + V_B(l))$ we can use again the "add vector" protocol. Thus, Alice will obtain $\pi(V_A + V_B)$ and then find the largest value of the entries. Say $l_0$ is the index where $\pi(V_A(l_0) + V_B(l_0)) = \max_l (\pi(V_A(l) + V_B(l)))$. Alice sends $l_0$ to Bob, so now they know which pair $E_i$ and $E_j$ gives the largest joint area. Hence, neither Alice nor Bob learn the values of their data records but they learn which pair of records has the largest area.

**Algorithm PickNext.** Select one remaining entry for classification in a group. For each entry $E$ not yet in a group, calculate $d_1 = $ the volume increase required if the covering box of Group 1 includes $E$. Calculate $d_2$ using Group 2. Choose the entry with the largest difference between $d_1$ and $d_2$. The question is now how to calculate securely the increased volume $\Delta Vol$ when we want to include one additional point or entry into already existed box? Thus, the problem is given a box with corner points $p_1$ and $p_2$, calculate the volume that will be added when we increase the box so that it includes the new point $p_3$. It is clear that, in $k$ dimensions, the increase in volume $\Delta Vol$ can be calculated in the following way.

$$\Delta Vol = Vol(\text{New box}) - Vol(\text{Old box}) = [v_1 + V_1] \times \cdots \times [v_k + V_k] - [v_1] \times \cdots \times [v_k],$$

where $v_i = |v_i^x - v_i^y|$ is the projection of the $k$-dimensional volume in the $i^{th}$ direction, $V_i$ is the increased projection, again in the $i^{th}$ domain. Now, the only thing left is to apply the secure multiplication algorithm we used for calculating $Vol(J)$ in the **PickSeeds** algorithm. Again, the two party case should be separated, because of privacy concerns. However, in the $k = 2$ case (as in the algorithm **PickSeeds**), we can take advantage of operations in vectors. When the first call to **PickNext**, we decide which among $M + 1 - 2$ entries is assigned to Group 1 or Group 2. Then, on the second call to **PickNext**, we decide which entry is to be assigned to Group 1 or Group 2 among $M + 1 - 3$ entries (because the bounding box of at least one of the groups changes every time an entry is assigned to a group). Moreover, Alice and Bob never perform this exercise for less than $m$ entries (thus, they are always operating with permuted vectors). That is, in the case of two parties, Alice and Bob compute simultaneously for all entries $E_i$ (not assigned to a group) the values $d_1^i = \Delta Vol(Group1(E_i))$ and $d_2^i = \Delta Vol(Group2(E_i))$ (see Step 1 in **PickNext**). As a result, they obtain the index of the entry for which $|d_2^i - d_1^i|$ is largest with high privacy.

## 4.2   Algorithm Search

In the following, we denote the box part of an index entry $E$ by $EI$, and the *child_pointer* part by $Ep$. The associative queries is, given a simple shape $S$ (like a box or a $\epsilon$-neighborhood) and an $R$-Tree whose root node is $T$, find all points contained by the search shape $S$. When $T$ is not a leaf, we check each entry $E$ to determine whether $EI$ overlaps $S$. For all overlapping entries, the search algorithm descends the tree ($R$-Trees do not to guarantee logarithmic worst-case performance) recursively invoking **Search** on the tree whose root node is pointed to by $Ep$. When a leaf is reached, we check all entries $E$ to determine whether $EI$ overlaps $S$. If so, $E$ is qualifying point. In the searching algorithm we have to find all boxes $EI$ who overlap the given shape $S$. When $S$ is a box, every party checks appropriate projections ($Proj_i(EI)$ and $Pr_i(S)$, for the $i^{th}$ party). All parties must report an intersection in their domain for box $S$ to overlap $EI$. If any party misses an overlap, then $S$ and $EI$ do not overlap. The case for an $\epsilon$-neighborhood is slightly more delicate and also typically a slightly different algorithm is used. In such algorithm, the point $p$ that is the center of the neighborhood is found first (using standard search with $S = p$). Then, the algorithm proceeds from the leaf where $p$ was found up the tree invoking the **Search** algorithm with $S = \epsilon$-neighborhood on all nodes not already searched. In this case, the overlap at each non-leaf involves testing if $[Pr_i(p) - \epsilon, Pr_i(p) + \epsilon]$ intersects the projection on the $i$-th domain; while for leafs, a secure distance computation is required. We also note that the case where the shape $S$ is a point $p$ essentially works as we described before treating $S$ as box with the upper limit equal the lower limit in all projections. However, when we expect to find $p$ exactly once, the algorithm is called **FindLeaf**. We do not feel it is necessary to reproduce further details for this more specific search algorithm. Moreover, in clustering it may be possible that a point $p$ appears more than once; however, the name **FindLeaf** is used by the deletion algorithm.

## 4.3   Insertion and Deletion

For insertion it is not possible to invoke **FindLeaf** because we may not find the point (that is probably the main reason it is being inserted). Although **FindLeaf** may find a leaf where it can be inserted if not found, it may cause to enlarge the overlap between sibling nodes up the tree. Keeping the overlap to a minimum is crucial to ensure good performance on searches (recall that the depth of a tree is the logarithm of its size, with the value of the base equal to the arity of nodes). Searches go down siblings that overlap causing extra work besides a path from the root to a leaf. Heuristically, overlap during insertion is minimized by the sub-algorithm **ChooseLeaf**, while the possible overload of a node when inserting a new value is handled by the **SplitNode** (which we deal with already). The propagation of splits up the tree is the responsibility of **AdjustTree**. These pieces compose the insertion algorithm.

1. Invoke **ChooseLeaf** to select a leaf node $L$ in which to place $E$.
2. If $L$ has room for another entry, install $E$. Otherwise invoke **SplitNode** to obtain $L$ and $LL$ containing $E$ and all the old entries of $L$.
3. Invoke **AdjustTree** on $L$, also passing $LL$ if a split was performed.
4. If node split propagation caused the root to split, create a new root whose children are the two resulting nodes.

**Algorithm ChooseLeaf.** To select a leaf in which to place a new entry $E$ we set $N$ to be the root node and while $N$ is not a leaf we let $F$ be the entry in $N$ whose box $FI$ needs least enlargement to include $EI$. We resolve ties by choosing the entry with the box of smallest volume. We set $N$ to be the child node pointed to by $Fp$. The only step that applies operations on private data by parties is evaluating enlargements in a box. However, in $DBSCAN$ clustering, the data inserted is a point $\boldsymbol{p}$ (and not a spatial object with non-zero volume). The parties can compute the enlargement it would produce for all entries on $N$. We have already shown how to achieve this securely for 3 or more parties. The delicate case is 2 parties. If $N$ is not the root, it has at least $m$ entries. Using the simultaneous computation on these $m$ entries by first the scalar product (which converts a product into sum) and then the maximum of a secure add-vectors operation, this can be achieved for two parties. The only problem is for the first $m$ data records ever inserted. For the first $m$ records, two parties using a simple protocol can tell if the point being inserted is different than the already inserted ones. After $m$ insertions, the root will have at least $m$ entries and computation will proceed preserving privacy as described by the previous algorithms for evaluating the enlargement that a point causes on a node.The **AdjustTree** Algorithm ascends from a leaf node $L$ to the root, adjusting covering boxes and propagating node splits as necessary. Recall that the structure of the tree is shared by all parties, and that **SplitNode** has now been developed to the privacy preserving setting. So the only privacy concern is to compute (preserving privacy) the box that tightly encloses all of a given a number of boxes. We have already argued that finding this corresponds to finding extremes in each domain. For example, with two parties, given a set of $n$ boxes

$$r_1 = [a_{11}, a_{12}] \times [b_{11}, b_{12}], \cdots, r_n = [a_{n1}, a_{n2}] \times [b_{11}, b_{12}]$$

we must find $R = [A_1, A_2] \times [B_1, B_2]$ such that $\bigcup_{i=1..n} r_i \subset R$ and no smaller box $R$ has this property. Let $A_1 = \min(a_{11}, ...a_{n1})$, $A_2 = \max(a_{12}, ...a_{n2})$, $B_1 = \min(b_{11}, ...b_{n1})$, and $B_2 = \max(b_{12}, ...b_{n2})$. This is clearly a solution and each max and min operation here can be performed by each party in isolation (the best assurance possible that privacy is preserved). Deletions are not necessary for $DBSCAN$ but are part of a full dynamic data structure. **FindLeaf** locates the leaf node $L$ containing $E$ and we remove $E$ from $L$. This may cause the merging of nodes and is handled by Algorithm **CondenseTree**. Given a leaf node $L$ from which an entry has been deleted, **CondenseTree** eliminates the node if it has too few entries and relocate its entries. It propagates node elimination upward as necessary, adjusting all covering rectangles on the path to the root, making them smaller if possible. All steps are tree structure steps, except adjusting boxes to a tighter box. However, we again face the situation where we need to find a tight box for a set of entries (we have demonstrated this can be done securely).

## 5   Analysis

The requirements of a privacy preserving *DBSCAN* can not be obtained without a cost. We will first analyze the overhead on the time resources (i.e. the additional operations relative to the naive alternative of concentrating the data with only one party who then performs the clustering). Observe first that **SplitNode** is described in terms of **PickSeeds** and **PickNext** with no overhead. **PickSeeds**/ does need the private calculation of volumes. However, if all data was sent to one party, the multiplications to compute the volume will still be required. In the case $k \geq 3$, the generation of a random number in a large enough range, the $k$ data exchanges among the values of partial products masked by the random number, the initial masking (a multiplication) with the random number, and the division (by a random number) to obtain the result are all overhead. However, in terms of CPU operations, these are just 2 more floating point products. Because we have $k \geq 3$ dimensions, this is insignificant. What is costly is the $k$ sequential data exchanges between the parties. On the other hand, **PickNext** incurs an overhead of 2 volume computations every time it is executed. It also cost as many as $\binom{M+1}{2}$ secure scalar products (of vectors of dimension 2) in order to translate into a sum, plus one secure add-vector for a vector of dimension $\binom{M+1}{2}$. For clustering, we may assume that all data items are inserted into an initially empty tree. The number of **SplitNode** operations is linear on the size of the tree. Thus, the number of **SplitNode** operations for a database with $n$ items is $O(n/m)$. Note also that on insertion the algorithm **ChooseLeaf** has no privacy overhead except a volume calculation for each level when an entry whose box needs the least enlargement is sought. Again, classical results on analysis of algorithms show that in a tree that grows from empty to a balanced tree with $O(n/m)$ leafs, the cost of the executions of **ChooseLeaf** is $O(n \log(n/m)/m)$. Thus, the total overhead for all insertions is subquadratic in the number of nodes.

Now we analyze the overhead of the associative queries in *DBSCAN*. Algorithm **FindLeaf** requires the public calculation of a conjunction of $k$ Boolean values. Relative to the naive alternative of all the data, the cost is not the Boolean conjunction but the data exchanges of $k$ boolean variables. Secure distance computations only occur at the leaves. Thus once again, the total overhead for all associative queries in linear on the number of nodes of the $R$-Tree. This analysis demonstrates that the time cost for the overhead caused by computations is perfectly reasonable and in fact very much affordable relative to running *DBSCAN* on one party with the union of the data from all parties. The concern may be the cost of data exchanges which is $O(kn/m)$ real values. However, if one takes into account that a solution that concentrates the data on one party needs to transmit $k-1$ databases of $n$ records from the other parties to the data concentration party, then one realizes that the privacy preserving computation is in fact even a more efficient solution in terms of data exchanges.

Consider now the overhead in space. Each party has the structural information of the $R$-Tree. This are $k$ copies of the $R$-Tree. However, each copy is only of the dimension of the data has at that party and therefore, it is only the pointer information that constitutes overhead (relative to the space that the concentration party would require to store in an $R$-Tree the data of all parties). The pointer size (i.e. space) is proportional to the external path length and thus also linear on the number of leaves in the $R-Tree$. Thus, the total overhead is $O(kn/m)$ pointers, which is a very reasonable price to pay for privacy. The last cost is for the generation of random numbers (this is also linear on the number of nodes). Hence, the total overhead is perfectly within the bounds of a practical efficient implementation.

## 6    Final Remarks

We have extended the work for other metrics besides Euclidean, but space restrictions prevent their discussion. However, $R$-Trees are mainly used for indexing data in low-dimensional space. The exploratory clustering of $DBSCAN$ is based on associative queries and in particular nearest neighbor queries and range queries. We do not have the space to present a solution using $KD$-Trees. For high-dimensional spaces, other data structures are common in practice (TV-tree [9] and X-trees [1], for example). Our illustration here that the core operations needing privacy are the metric calculations are indicative that these other data structures should become private along the path shown in this paper.

## References

1. S. Berchtold, D. A. Keim, and H.-P. Kriegel. The X-tree : An index structure for high-dimensional data. *VLDB'96, 22th VLDB, 1996, Bombay* , 28–39. Morgan Kaufmann, 1996.
2. W. Du and M.J. Atallah. Privacy-preserving cooperative statistical analysis. *17th ACSAC*, 102–110, New Orleans, 2001. ACM SIGSAC, IEEE Computer Society.
3. W. Du and Z. Zhan. Building decision tree classifier on private data. *Privacy, Security and Data Mining*, 1–8, 2002. IEEE ICDM Workshop Vol 14 CRPIT.
4. M. Ester, H.P. Kriegel, S. Sander, and X. Xu. A density-based algorithm for discovering clusters in large spatial databases with noise. 2nd KDD-96, 226–231, Menlo Park, 1996. AAAI Press.
5. V. Estivill-Castro. Private representative-based clustering for vertically partitioned data. *5th ENC-04*, 160–167, Colima, 2004. IEEE Computer Society.
6. V. Gaede and O. Günther. Multidimensional access methods. *ACM Computing Surveys*, 30(2):170–231, June 1998.
7. O Goldreich. Secure multi-party computation. Working draft, Department of Computer Science and Applied Mathematics, Weizmann Institute of Science, Rehevolt, Israel, June 9 1998. www.citeseer.ist.psu.edu/goldreich98secure.html.
8. A. Guttmann. R-trees: a dynamic index structure for spatial searching. *ACM SIGMOD* , 47–57, 1984.
9. K.-I. Lin, H. V. Jagadish, and C. Faloutsos. The TV-tree: An index structure for high-dimensional data. *VLDB J.*, 3(4):517–542, 1994.

10. Y Lindell and Pinkas B. Privacy preserving data mining. *CRYPTO-00*, 36–54, Santa Barbara, 2000. LNCS 1880.
11. J. Mena. *Investigative Data Mining for Security and Criminal Detection.* Butterworth-Heinemann, US, 2003.
12. D. Naccache and J. Stern. A new public key cryptosystem based on higher residues. *5th ACM Conference on Computer and Communications Security*, pages 59–66, San Francisco, SIGSAC, ACM Press.
13. T. Okamoto and S.: Uchiyama. A new public-key cryptosystem as secure as factoring. *EUROCRYPT '98* , 308–318, Espoo, 1998. LNCS 1403.
14. J. Vaidya and C. C. Clifton. Privacy preserving association rule mining in vertically partitioned data. *8th ACM SIGKDD* . SIGKDD, 2002.
15. J. Vaidya and C. C. Clifton. Privacy-preserving $k$-means clustering over vertically partitioned data. *SIGKDD-ACM* , Washington, D.C., 2003.
16. A.C. Yao. Protocols for secure computation. *IEEE Symposium of Foundations of Computer Science*, 1982.

# Inferring Privacy Information from Social Networks[*]

Jianming He[1], Wesley W. Chu[1], and Zhenyu (Victor) Liu[2]

[1] Computer Science Department UCLA, Los Angeles, CA 90095, USA
[2] Google Inc. USA

**Abstract.** Since privacy information can be inferred via social relations, the privacy confidentiality problem becomes increasingly challenging as online social network services are more popular. Using a Bayesian network approach to model the causal relations among people in social networks, we study the impact of prior probability, influence strength, and society openness to the inference accuracy on a real online social network. Our experimental results reveal that personal attributes can be inferred with high accuracy especially when people are connected with strong relationships. Further, even in a society where most people hide their attributes, it is still possible to infer privacy information.

## 1   Introduction

With the increasing popularity of Social Network Services (SNS), more and more online societies such as Friendster, Livejournal, Blogger and Orkurt have emerged. Unlike traditional personal homepages, people in these societies publish not only their personal attributes (e.g., age, gender, and interests), but also their relationships with friends. As social networks grow rapidly, many interesting research topics [3, 6, 13] arise. Unfortunately, among these topics, privacy has not been fully addressed yet. Given the huge amount of personal data and social relations available in online social networks (for example, Friendster owns over 24 million personal profiles), it is foreseeable that privacy may be compromised if people are not careful in releasing their personal information.

Information privacy has become one of the most urgent research issues in building next-generation information systems. A great deal of research effort has been devoted to protecting people's privacy. Aside from recent developments in cryptography and security protocols that provide secure data transfer capabilities, there has been work on enforcing industry standards (e.g., P3P [12]) and government policies (e.g., the HIPAA Privacy Rule [11]) to grant individuals control over their own privacy. These existing techniques and policies aim to effectively block *direct* disclosure of sensitive personal information. However, to the best of our knowledge, none of the existing techniques handle *indirect* disclosure which can often be achieved by intelligently combining pieces of seemingly innocuous or unrelated information. Specifically, in scenarios like social networks,

---

[*] This research is in part supported by NSF grant # IIS-03113283.

S. Mehrotra et al. (Eds.): ISI 2006, LNCS 3975, pp. 154–165, 2006.

we realize that individuals connected in social networks often share common attributes. For instance, in a dance club, people come together due to their common interest; in an office, people connect to each other because of similar professions. Therefore, it is possible that one may be able to infer someone's attribute from the attributes of his/her friends. In such cases, privacy is indirectly disclosed by their social relations rather than from the owner directly.

In this paper, we study the privacy disclosure in social networks. We want to analyze under what conditions and to what extent privacy might be disclosed by social relations. In order to perform privacy inference, we propose an approach to map Bayesian networks to social networks. We discuss prior probability, influence strength and society openness which might affect the inference, and conduct extensive experiments on a real online social network structure.

The paper is organized as follows. In Section 2, we briefly introduce the background and related work. In Section 3, we explain the target scenarios, propose an approach to model social networks with Bayesian networks and perform Bayesian inference on personal attributes. In Section 4, we present three key characteristics of social networks and conduct experiments to investigate their impact on privacy inference. In Section 5, we discuss the issue of society openness and explain why Bayesian inference performs well even with little evidence of friends' attributes. Finally, we summarize this paper.

## 2    Background and Related Work

### 2.1    Social Networks

Social network analysis has been conducted in many areas. Milgram's classic paper [8] in 1967 estimates that every person in the world is only six hops away from each other. The recent success of the Google search engine [2], which applies social network ideas to the Internet, draws great attention on social network analysis again. For instance, Newman [10] reviews the relationship between graph structure and dynamical behavior of large networks. The ReferralWeb project mined social networks from a wide variety of public-available information [6]. A work similar to ours is [3], which realizes that one's decision to buy products may be influenced by his/her friends, and they model social network as a Markov random field to find the customers' network value. In contrast, we believe a person's attribute can be reflected from his/her friends' attributes, and we view a social network as a Bayesian network.

### 2.2    Bayesian Networks

A Bayesian network [4, 5, 9] is a graphic representation of the joint probability distribution over a set of variables. It consists of a network structure and a collection of *conditional probability tables* (CPT). The network structure is represented as a *Directed Acyclic Graph* (DAG) in which each node corresponds to a random variable and each edge indicates a dependent relationship between connected variables. In addition, each variable (node) in a Bayesian network is associated with a CPT, which enumerates the conditional probabilities for this variable, given all the combinations of its parents' value. Thus, for a Bayesian network, the DAG captures causal relationships among random variables, and CPTs quantify these relationships.

Bayesian networks have been extensively applied to fields such as medicine, image processing, and decision support systems. Since Bayesian networks include the consideration of network structure, we use them as our inference model. Individuals in a social network can be represented as nodes and the relations between individuals can be modelled as edges in Bayesian networks.

## 3   Bayesian Inference Via Social Relations

### 3.1   Problem Statement

Intuitively, friends often share common attributes (e.g., hobbies and professions); thus, it is possible to predict someone's attributes by looking at the types of friends he/she has. In this paper, we want to investigate the effect of social relations on privacy inference. However, in the real world, people are acquainted with each other via all types of relations, and a personal attribute may only be sensitive to certain types of relations. For example, in order to predict someone's age, it is more appropriate to consider the ages of his/her classmates rather than officemates. Therefore, to infer people's privacy from social relations, one must be able to filter out other types of relations between two connected people. To simplify this problem, we investigate privacy inference in *homogeneous societies* where individuals are connected by a single type of social relations (referred to as "friendship") and the impact of every person on his/her friends is the same. Homogenous societies reflect small closely related groups (such as offices, classes or clubs), where people are connected by a relatively pure relationship. Real social networks can be regarded as the combinations of many homogeneous societies.

To perform inference, we use Bayesian networks to model the causal relations among people in social networks. Specifically, if we want to infer the value of attribute $A$ for a person (referred to as *query node $X$*), we first construct a Bayesian network from $X$'s social network, and then analyze the Bayesian network to obtain the probability that $X$ has attribute $A$. In Section 3.2, we start from a simple case in which privacy inference only involves the direct friends of the query node. In Section 3.3, we treat the more complex case where attribute values from friends at multiple hops away are considered.

### 3.2   Single Hop Inference

Let us consider the case in which we know the attribute values for *all* the direct friends of the query node $X$. We define $Y_{ij}$ as the $j$th friend of $X$ at $i$ hops away. If a friend can be reached via more than one route from $X$, we use the depth of the shortest path as the value of $i$. Let $Y_i$ be the set of $Y_{ij}$ $(1 \leq j \leq n_i)$, where $n_i$

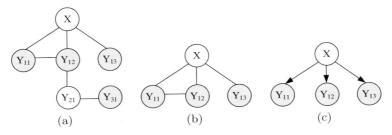

**Fig. 1.** Reduction of a social network (a) into a Bayesian network to infer X from his friends Y via Localization assumption (b) and via Naive Bayesian Assumption (c). The shaded nodes represent friends whose attribute values are known.

is the number of $X$'s friends at $i$ hops away. For instance, $Y_1 = \{Y_{11}, Y_{12}, ..., Y_{1n_1}\}$ is the set of $X$'s direct friends which are one hop away.

An example of a social network with six friends is shown in Fig. 1(a). In this figure, $Y_{11}$, $Y_{12}$ and $Y_{13}$ are direct friends of $X$. $Y_{21}$ and $Y_{31}$ are the direct friends of $Y_{12}$ and $Y_{21}$ respectively. In this scenario, the attribute values of $Y_{11}$, $Y_{12}$ and $Y_{13}$ are known (represented as shaded nodes).

**Bayesian Network Construction.** To facilitate the construction of the Bayesian network, we make two assumptions.

Intuitively, the direct friends of an individual have more influence on this person than friends who are two or more hops away. We assume that it is sufficient to consider only the attribute values of direct friends $Y_1$ to infer $X$'s attribute. Once all the attribute values of $Y_1$ are known, knowing the attribute values of any other friends at multiple hops away provides no additional information for predicting $X$'s attribute. Formally, we state this assumption as follows.

**Localization Assumption.** Given the attribute values of the direct friends $Y_1$ of the query node $X$, then friends at more than one hop away (i.e., $Y_i$ for $i > 1$) are conditionally independent of $X$.

Based on this assumption, $Y_{21}$ and $Y_{31}$ in Fig. 1(a) can be pruned, and the inference of $X$ only involves $X$, $Y_{11}$, $Y_{12}$ and $Y_{13}$ (Fig. 1(b)). Then the next question is how to decide a DAG linking the remaining nodes. If the resulting social network does not contain cycles, a Bayesian network can be obtained immediately. Otherwise, one must employ more sophisticated techniques to remove cycles, such as the use of auxiliary variables to capture non-causal constraints (*exact conversion*) and the deletion of edges with the weakest relations (*approximation conversion*). We adopt the latter approach and make a *Naive Bayesian* Assumption. That is, the attribute value of $X$ influences that of $Y_{1j}$ ($1 \leq j \leq n_1$), and there is a direct link pointing from $X$ to each $Y_{1j}$. By making this assumption, we consider the inference paths from $X$ to $Y_{1j}$ as the *primary* correlations, and disregard the correlations among the nodes in $Y_1$. Formally, we have:

**Naive Bayesian Assumption.** Given the attribute value of the query node $X$, the attribute values of direct friends $Y_1$ are conditionally independent of each other.

This Naive Bayesian model has been used in many classification/prediction applications including textual-document classification. Even though it simplifies the correlation among variables, this model has been shown to be quite effective [7]. Thus, we adopted this assumption in our study. In Fig. 1(c), we obtain a final DAG by removing the connection between $Y_{11}$ and $Y_{12}$ in Fig. 1(b).

**Bayesian Inference.** We use the Bayes Decision Rule to predict the attribute value of $X$. For a general Bayesian network with maximum depth $i$, let the value for $X$, $\bar{x}$, be the attribute value with the maximum conditional probability given the observed attribute values of other nodes in the network (i.e., the maximum posterior probability):

$$\bar{x} = \arg \max_{x} P(X = x \mid Y_1, Y_2, ..., Y_i) \qquad x \in \{t, f\}. \qquad (1)$$

Since single hop inference involves only the direct friends $Y_1$ that are independent of each other, the posterior probability can be further reduced using the conditional independence encoded in the Bayesian network:

$$
\begin{aligned}
P(X = x \mid Y_1) &= P(X = x \mid Y_{11} = y_{11}, ..., Y_{1n_1} = y_{1n_1}) \\
&= \frac{P(X = x, Y_{11} = y_{11}, ..., Y_{1n_1} = y_{1n_1})}{P(Y_{11} = y_{11}, ..., Y_{1n_1} = y_{1n_1})} \\
&= \frac{P(X = x) \cdot P(Y_{11} = y_{11}, ..., Y_{1n_1} = y_{1n_1} \mid X = x)}{\sum_{x}[P(X = x) \cdot P(Y_{11} = y_{11}, ..., Y_{1n_1} = y_{1n_1} \mid X = x)]} \\
&= \frac{P(X = x) \cdot \prod_{i=1}^{n_1} P(Y_{1i} = y_{1i} \mid X = x)}{\sum_{x}[P(X = x) \cdot \prod_{i=1}^{n_1} P(Y_{1i} = y_{1i} \mid X = x)]},
\end{aligned}
\qquad (2)
$$

where $x$ and $y_{1j}$ are the attribute values of $X$ and $Y_{1j}$ respectively ($1 \le j \le n_1$, $x, y_{1j} \in \{t, f\}$) and the value of $y_{1j}$ is known.

Since we assumed that the network is homogeneous, the CPT for each node is the same. Thus, we use $P(Y = y \mid X = x)$ to represent $P(Y_{1j} = y_{1j} \mid X = x)$. For this reason, direct friends of $X$ are equivalent to each other, and the posterior probability now depends on $N_{1t}$, which is the number of friends with attribute value $t$, rather than the individual attribute value. Therefore, we rewrite the posterior probability $P(X = x \mid Y_1)$ as $P(X = x \mid N_{1t} = n_{1t})$. If $N_{1t} = n_{1t}$, we obtain:

$$P(X = x \mid N_{1t} = n_{1t}) = \frac{P(X = x) \cdot P(Y = t \mid X = x)^{n_{1t}} \cdot P(Y = f \mid X = x)^{n_1 - n_{1t}}}{\sum_{x}[P(X = x) \cdot P(Y = t \mid X = x)^{n_{1t}} \cdot P(Y = f \mid X = x)^{n_1 - n_{1t}}]}. \qquad (3)$$

To compute (3), we need to further learn the conditional probability $P(Y = y \mid X = x)$. We apply the *parameter estimation* [9] technique and obtain:

$$P(Y = y \mid X = x) = \frac{\text{\# of friendship links connecting people with } X = x \text{ and } Y = y}{\text{\# of friendship links connecting a person with } X = x}. \qquad (4)$$

Substituting (4) and (3) into (1) yields $\bar{x}$.

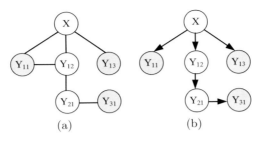

**Fig. 2.** Reduction of a social network (a) into a Bayesian network to infer X from his friends Y via Generalized Localization assumption (b). The shaded nodes represent friends whose attribute values are known.

### 3.3 Multiple Hops Inference

In real world, the attribute values of all the direct friends may not be observed because people may hide their sensitive information. Therefore, the Localization Assumption in Section 3.2 is no longer applicable. To incorporate more attribute information into our Bayesian network, we propose a *generalized localization assumption* as follows.

**Generalized Localization Assumption.** Given the attribute value of the $j$th friend of $X$ at $i$ hops away, $Y_{ij}$ $(1 \leq j \leq n_i)$, the attribute of $X$ is conditionally independent of the descendants of $Y_{ij}$.

This assumption states that if the attribute value for the $X$'s direct friend, $Y_{1j}$, is unknown, then the attribute value of $X$ is conditionally dependent on the attribute values for the direct friends of $Y_{1j}$. This process continues until we reach a descendent of $Y_{1j}$ whose attribute value is known. For example, the network structure in Fig. 2(a) is the same as in Fig. 1(a), but the attribute value of $Y_{12}$ is unknown. Based on the Generalized Localization Assumption, we extend the network by branching to $Y_{12}$'s direct child $Y_{21}$. Since $Y_{21}$'s attribute is unknown, we further branch to $Y_{21}$'s direct friend $Y_{31}$. The branch terminates here because the attribute of $Y_{31}$ is known. Thus, the inference network for $X$ includes all the nodes in the graph. After applying Naive Bayesian assumption, we obtain the DAG shown in Fig. 2(b). Similar to single hop inference, the resulting DAG in multiple hops inference is also a tree rooted at the query node $X$. One interpretation of this model is that when we predict the attribute value of $X$, we always treat him/her as an egocentric person who influences his/her friends but not vice versa. Thus, the attribute value of $X$ can be reflected by those of his/her friends.

For multiple hops inference, we still apply the Bayes Decision Rule. Due to additional unknown attribute values such as $Y_{12}$, the calculation of the posterior probability becomes more complicated. One common technique to solve this equation is through variable elimination [14]. We adopt the same technique to derive the value of $\bar{x}$ in (1).

# 4     Experimental Study of Inference Accuracy

In this section, we define three characteristics of social networks that might affect Bayesian inference and evaluate their impact. The performance metric that we consider is *inference accuracy*, which is defined as the percentage of nodes predicted correctly by inference.

## 4.1     Characteristics of Social Networks

**Prior Probability** $P(X = t)$ is the probability that people in the social network have attribute $A$. When no additional information is provided, we could use prior probability to naively predict attribute values for the query nodes: if $P(X = t) \geq 0.5$, we predict that every query node has value $t$; otherwise, we predict that it has value $f$. We call this method *naive inference*. The average naive inference accuracy that can be obtained is $max(P(X = t), 1 - P(X = t))$. In our study, we use it as a reference to compare with our Bayesian inference approach.

**Influence Strength** $P(Y = t \mid X = t)$ is defined as the conditional probability that $Y$ has attribute $A$ given that its direct friend $X$ has the same attribute. This conditional probability measures how $X$ influence its friend $Y$. A higher influence strength implies that there is a higher probability that $X$ and $Y$ will have attribute $A$.[1]

**Society Openness** $O(A)$ is defined as the percentage of people in a society who release their values of attribute $A$. The more people release their attribute values, the higher the society openness is, and the more evidence about attribute $A$ is observed.

## 4.2     Data Set

For the experiment, we collect $66,766$ personal profiles from an online weblog service provider Livejournal [1], which owns 2.6 million active members. For each member, Livejournal generates a personnel profile which specifies the member's personal information as well as the URLs for the profiles of this member's friends. Among the collected profiles, there are $4,031,348$ friend relations. The number of friends per member v.s. the number of members follows the power law distribution. About half of the population have less than 10 direct friends.

In order to evaluate the inference behaviors for a wide range of parameters, we use a hypothetical attribute and synthesize the attribute values: for each member, we assign a CPT and determine the actual attribute value based on the parent's value and the assigned CPT. The attribute assignment starts from the set of nodes whose in-degree is 0 and explores the rest of the network following

---

[1] There is another type of influence strength $P(Y = t \mid X = f)$, which is the conditional probability that two friends have opposite values of attribute $A$. In an equilibrium state, the value of $P(Y = t \mid X = f)$ can be derived from $P(X = t)$ and $P(Y = t \mid X = t)$, so we do not introduce it as an additional characteristic.

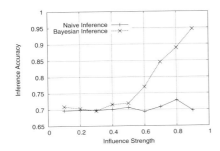
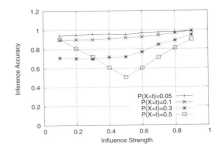

**Fig. 3.** Inference accuracy of Bayesian vs. naive inference when $P(X = t) = 0.3$

**Fig. 4.** Inference accuracy of Bayesian inference for different prior probabilities

friendship links. Since we are investigating homogeneous societies, all the members are assigned with the same CPT. We evaluate the inference performance by using different CPTs.

After the attribute assignment, we obtain a social network. To infer each individual, we built a corresponding Bayesian network, and then conducted Bayesian inference as described in Section 3.

### 4.3   Experimental Results

**Comparison of Bayesian and Naive Inference.** In the first set of experiments, we compare the performance of Bayesian inference with naive inference. We want to study whether we can utilize the social relations to improve inference accuracy. We fix the prior probability to 0.3 and vary the influence strength from 0.1 to 0.9. Fig. 3 shows the inference accuracy of the two methods. It is clear that Bayesian inference outperforms naive inference. The curve for naive inference fluctuates around 70%, because with the prior probability being 0.3, the average accuracy we can achieve is 70%. The performance of Bayesian inference varies with influence strength. We achieve a very high accuracy, especially at high influence strength. The accuracy even reaches 95% for the influence strength 0.9, which is much higher than the 70% accuracy of the naive inference. We observed the same trend for other prior probabilities as well.

**Effect of Influence Strength and Prior Probability.** Fig. 4 shows the inference accuracy of Bayesian inference when the prior probability is 0.05, 0.1, 0.3 and 0.5, and the influence strength varies from 0.1 to 0.9. As the prior probability varies, the inference accuracy yields different trends with the influence strength. The lowest inference accuracy always occurs when the influence strength is equal to the prior probability. For example, the lowest inference accuracy (approximately 70%) at the prior probability 0.3 is achieved when the influence strength is 0.3. This is because when the influence strength is equal to the prior probability, knowing friend relations provide no more information than just knowing the prior probability; thus, people in the network are actually independent of each other. Furthermore, the higher the difference between the influence strength and the prior probability, the stronger the influence (no

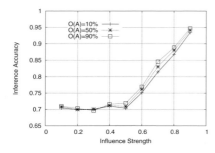
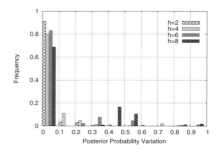

**Fig. 5.** Inference accuracy of Bayesian inference for different society openness.

**Fig. 6.** Frequency of posterior probability variation for single hop inference.

matter positive or negative) of parent on children, and the better the Bayesian inference performs.

**Society Openness.** In the previous experiments, we assume the society openness is 100%. That is, all the friends' attribute values of the query node are known. In this set of experiments, we study the inference behavior at different levels of society openness. We randomly hide the attributes of a certain percentage of members, ranging from 10% to 90%, and then perform Bayesian inference on those nodes.

Fig. 5 shows the experimental results for the prior probability $P(X = t) = 0.3$ and the society openness $O(A) = 10\%, 50\%$ and 90%. The inference accuracy decreases as more members hide their attributes. For instance, at influence strength 0.7, when the openness is decreased from 90% to 10%, the accuracy reduces from 84.6% to 81.5%. However, the reduction in inference accuracy is relatively small (on average less than 5%). We also observe similar trends for other prior probabilities. This phenomenon is quite counterintuitive. Generally, when the society openness is small, the observed evidence on friends' attributes is low and the inference accuracy should drop drastically. To better understand the impact of openness, we perform some analysis in the next section.

## 5   Discussions on Society Openness

In this section, we want to obtain some insight about the impact that society openness has on the inference accuracy through analysis and simulations in simple regular social network structures. We consider single hop inference in two-level trees and multiple hops inference in complete $k$-ary trees.

### 5.1   Single Hop Inference

As mentioned earlier, the Bayesian network for single hop inference is a two-level tree. Given a general two-level tree with the query node $X$ as the root and $n_1$ direct friends $Y_{11}, ..., Y_{1n_1}$ as leaves, we want to derive the probability distribution of the posterior probability variation due to the change of openness, i.e., the difference of the posterior probability and the probability that this difference occurs. We change the openness by randomly hiding a certain percentage of friends' attributes.

Let random variables $N_{1t}$ and $N'_{1t}$ be the number of friends having attribute value $t$ before and after hiding the attribute values of $h$ friends, where $0 \leq h \leq n_1$ and $max(0, N_{1t} - h) \leq N'_{1t} \leq min(N_{1t}, n_1 - h)$. If $N_{1t} = n_{1t}$ and $N'_{1t} = n'_{1t}$, we can compute the posterior probabilities $P(X = t \mid N_{1t} = n_{1t})$ and $P(X = t \mid N'_{1t} = n'_{1t})$ from (3) respectively. Note that for Bayesian inference, hiding friends' attribute values in a two-level tree has the same effect as removing these nodes. Therefore, the posterior probability variation caused by hiding $h$ attribute values is:

$$\Delta P(X = t \mid N_{1t} = n_{1t}, N'_{1t} = n'_{1t}) = |P(X = t \mid N_{1t} = n_{1t}) - P(X = t \mid N'_{1t} = n'_{1t})|. \quad (5)$$

Now we want to derive the probability that each possible value of $\Delta P(X = t \mid N_{1t} = n_{1t}, N'_{1t} = n'_{1t})$ occurs. In other words, we want to compute the probability of the joint event $N_{1t} = n_{1t}$ and $N'_{1t} = n'_{1t}$ (before and after hiding nodes), which is equal to:

$$P(N_{1t} = n_{1t}, N'_{1t} = n'_{1t}) = P(N_{1t} = n_{1t}) \cdot P(N'_{1t} = n'_{1t} \mid N_{1t} = n_{1t}). \quad (6)$$

Thus, we need to compute the two terms on the right-hand side of the equation.

Initially, if we know $X$'s attribute value is $x$ ($x \in \{t, f\}$), the probability that $N_{1t} = n_{1t}$ follows the Binomial distribution:

$$P(N_{1t} = n_{1t} \mid X = x) = \binom{n_1}{n_{1t}} \cdot P(Y = t \mid X = x)^{n_{1t}} \cdot P(Y = f \mid X = x)^{n_1 - n_{1t}}. \quad (7)$$

By unconditioning on $X$, we obtain:

$$P(N_{1t} = n_{1t}) = P(X = t) \cdot P(N_{1t} = n_{1t} \mid X = t) + P(X = f) \cdot P(N_{1t} = n_{1t} \mid X = f). \quad (8)$$

We define $h_t$ and $h_f$ as the numbers of hidden nodes with attribute $t$ and $f$, respectively ($h_t = n_{1t} - n'_{1t}$ and $h_f = h - h_t$). Then we can compute the conditional probability that $N'_{1t} = n'_{1t}$ given $N_{1t} = n_{1t}$ as:

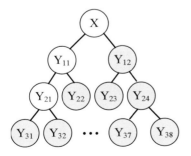

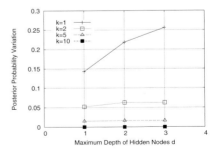

**Fig. 7.** An example for multiple hops inference when $k=2$ and $d=2$

**Fig. 8.** Posterior probability variation for multiple hops inference

$$P(N'_{1t} = n'_{1t} \mid N_{1t} = n_{1t}) = \frac{\binom{n_{1t}}{h_t} \cdot \binom{n_1 - n_{1t}}{h_f}}{\binom{n_1}{h}}. \tag{9}$$

In this equation, the numerator represents the number of ways to hide $h_t$ friends with value $t$ and $h_f$ friends with value $f$, and the denominator represents the number of combinations to choose any $h$ nodes from a total of $n_1$ nodes. Substituting (8) and (9) into (6), we obtain $P(N_{1t} = n_{1t}, N'_{1t} = n'_{1t})$.

In the simulation study, we fix $n_1$ to be 10. To obtain the posterior probability variation $\Delta P(X = t \mid N_{1t} = n_{1t}, N'_{1t} = n'_{1t})$ and its corresponding probability for each possible combination of $n_{1t}$ and $n'_{1t}$, we vary $h$ from 2 to 8. We plot the histogram of the posterior probability variation as follows. We divide the range of posterior probability variation into 10 equal width intervals. Then we compute the probability that the posterior probability variation falls in each interval.

Fig. 6 shows the histogram of the posterior probability variation when the prior probability is 0.3 and the influence strength is 0.7. The x axis represents the intervals and the y axis represents the frequency of the posterior probability variation within the interval. We observe that for 70% to 90% of the cases, the variation is less than 0.1. Thus, in single hop inference, the posterior probability is unlikely to be varied greatly due to hiding nodes randomly.

### 5.2   Multiple Hops Inference

For multiple hops inference, we use complete $k$-ary trees, in which all the internal nodes have $k$ children. We hide a node with all of its ancestors in the tree, and check how the posterior probability varies with $k$ and the maximum depth of the hidden nodes $d$. Fig. 7 depicts an example of when $k = 2$ and $d = 2$. The attribute values of $Y_{11}$ and $Y_{21}$ are hidden.

Fig. 8 plots the posterior probability variation when we vary $k$ and $d$ in a $k$-ary tree. The prior probability is 0.3 and the influence strength is 0.7. As $k$ increases, the posterior probability variation before and after hiding nodes decreases, because there are increasingly more direct friends and the inference result will depend less on the hidden nodes. Moreover, when $k = 1$, the posterior probability varies more significantly when the maximum depth of hidden nodes is larger. For $k > 1$, the posterior probability does not vary much with the depth. These two observations show that, if there are many closer friends to the query node, a friend that is further away has little impact on the posterior probability. For our experiments in Section 4, the majority of the nodes have multiple direct friends. For example, about half of the population have more than 10 direct friends. As a result, openness in such an environment yields small variations of posterior probability which result in small changes in inference accuracy.

## 6   Conclusions

In this paper, we investigated the problem of privacy inference in social networks. Using Bayesian networks to model the causal relations among people in social networks, we performed a series of experiments on the real social network structures. We showed that privacy may be indirectly released via social relations, and the inference accuracy of privacy information is closely related to the inference strength between friends. Further, we observed that even in a society where people hide their attributes, privacy still could be inferred from Bayesian inference.

To protect privacy disclosure in social networks, we could either hide our friendship relations or ask our friends to hide their attributes. However, our analysis showed that randomly hiding friends' attributes and hiding people's attributes at multiple hops away have a small impact on privacy inference. Therefore, effective privacy protection should selectively hide friendship relations or friends' attributes. To achieve this, we should take both social network structures and influence strength of social relations into consideration. We plan to investigate this issue in our future work.

# References

1. *Livejournal.* http://www.livejournal.com.
2. S. Brin and L. Page. The anatomy of a large-scale hypertextual Web search engine. In *Proceedings of the Seventh International World Wide Web Conference*, 1998.
3. P. Domingos and M. Richardson. Mining the network value of customers. In *Proceedings of the 7th International Conference on Knowledge Discovery and Data Mining*, 2001.
4. D. Heckerman. A Tutorial on Learning Bayesian Networks. Technical Report MSR-TR-95-06, March 1995.
5. D. Heckerman, D. Geiger, and D. M. Chickering. Learning bayesian networks: The combination of knowledge and statistical data. In *KDD Workshop*, pages 85–96, 1994.
6. H. Kautz, B. Selman, and M. Shah. Referral Web: Combining social networks and collaborative filtering. *Communications of the ACM*, 40(3):63–65, 1997.
7. D. Lowd and P. Domingos. Naive bayes models for probability estimation. In *Proceedings of the Twenty-Second International Conference on Machine Learning (ICML)*, Bonn, Germany, 2005. ACM Press.
8. S. Milgram. The small world problem. *Psychology Today*, 1967.
9. D. K. A. P. N. Friedman, L. Getoor. Learning probabilistic relational models. In *Proceedings of the 16th International Joint Conference on Artificial Intelligence (IJCAI)*, Stockholm, Sweden, August 1999.
10. M. Newman. The structure and function of complex networks. *SIAM Review*, 45(2):167–256, 2003.
11. U. D. of Health and O. for Civil Rights Human Services. *Standards for Privacy of Individually Identifiable Health Information*, 2003. http://www.hhs.gov/ocr/combinedregtext.pdf.
12. W. W. W. C. (W3C). *The platform for privacy preferences 1.1 (P3P1.1)*, 2004. http://www.w3.org/TR/P3P11/.
13. D. J. Watts and S. H. Strogatz. Collective dynamics of "small-world" networks. *Nature*, 1998.
14. N. L. Zhang and D. Poole. Exploiting causal independence in bayesian network inference. *Journal of Artificial Intelligence Research*, 5:301–328, 1996.

# Motion-Alert: Automatic Anomaly Detection in Massive Moving Objects*

Xiaolei Li, Jiawei Han, and Sangkyum Kim

Department of Computer Science, University of Illinois at Urbana-Champaign

**Abstract.** With recent advances in sensory and mobile computing technology, enormous amounts of data about *moving objects* are being collected. With such data, it becomes possible to automatically identify suspicious behavior in object movements. *Anomaly detection* in massive sets of moving objects has many important applications, especially in surveillance, law enforcement, and homeland security.

Due to the sheer volume of spatiotemporal and non-spatial data (such as weather and object type) associated with moving objects, it is challenging to develop a method that can efficiently and effectively detect anomalies in complex scenarios. The problem is further complicated by the fact that anomalies may occur at various levels of abstraction and be associated with different time and location granularities. In this paper, we analyze the problem of anomaly detection in moving objects and propose an efficient and scalable classification method, *Motion-Alert*, which proceeds with the following three steps.

1. Object movement features, called *motifs*, are extracted from the object paths. Each path consists of a sequence of motif expressions, associated with the values related to time and location.
2. To discover anomalies in object movements, motif-based generalization is performed that clusters similar object movement fragments and generalizes the movements based on the associated motifs.
3. With motif-based generalization, objects are put into a multi-level feature space and are classified by a classifier that can handle high-dimensional feature spaces.

We implemented the above method as one of the core components in our moving-object anomaly detection system, *motion-alert*. Our experiments show that the system is more accurate than traditional classification techniques.

## 1 Introduction

In recent years, gathering data on *moving objects*, *i.e.*, the objects that change their spatial locations with time, has become an easy and common task. The

* The work was supported in part by the U.S. National Science Foundation NSF IIS-03-08215/05-13678. Any opinions, findings, and conclusions or recommendations expressed in this paper are those of the authors and do not necessarily reflect the views of the funding agencies.

S. Mehrotra et al. (Eds.): ISI 2006, LNCS 3975, pp. 166–177, 2006.

tracking of mobile objects, whether it be a tiny cellphone or a giant ocean liner, is becoming increasingly accessible with embedded GPS devices and other sensors. In cases where direct recording is unavailable, particle tracking techniques are available using RADAR or satellite images. Such enormous amounts of data on moving objects pose great challenges on effective and scalable analysis and applications. One application which is of particular interest in homeland security is the *detection of suspicious or anomalous moving objects*: i.e., automatic identification of the abnormal or suspicious moving objects from among a massive set of object movements.

**Example 1.** There is a large number of vessels traveling near American coasts. It is unrealistic to manually trace such an enormous number of moving objects and identify suspicious ones. But there is likely to exist a number of previous case studies on suspicious vessels. Training for manual inspection of ships provided by experts would be a good source of such examples. Thus it is possible and highly desirable to develop automated tools that can evaluate the behavior of *all* maritime vessels and flag the suspicious ones. This will allow human agents to focus their monitoring more efficiently and accurately.                    ∎

In this paper, we take vessels in Example 1 as a typical type of moving objects and study how to develop scalable and effective methods for automated detection of anomalous moving objects. We believe such methods can be easily extended to other applications. In general, there are two general mechanisms for anomaly detection: *classification*, which relies on training data sets, and *clustering*, which performs automated grouping without using training sets. Here we focus our study on *classification*, because it is not hard to find a set of training examples. With good quality training data, classification often leads to higher accuracy than clustering-based methods in anomaly detection.

There are several major challenges in anomaly detection of moving objects. First, tracking moving objects can generate an enormous amount of high precision and complex data, consisting of both spatiotemporal and non-spatial information. For example, the time and location of a vessel might be recorded every few seconds, and non-spatial information such as the vessel's weight, speed, shape, and paint-color may be included in the recordings. Second, there exist substantial complexities of possible abnormal behavior, which may occur at arbitrary levels of abstraction and be associated with different time and location granularities. The massive amount of data and complexity of abnormal patterns make efficient and effective anomaly detection very challenging.

In this study, we systematically study this problem and propose Motion-Alert, an effective and scalable classification method for detecting anomalous behavior in moving objects. It features the following components.

1. **Motif-based representation:** Instead of viewing the movement path of an object as a sequence of low-level spatiotemporal points, we view it as a sequence of movement motifs.
2. **Motif-oriented feature space transformation:** The movement paths are transformed into a feature space that is oriented on the movement motif expressions.

**Table 1.** Original input data

| | Non-Spatiotemporal Features | | | Path | Class |
|---|---|---|---|---|---|
| | Size | . . . | Type | | |
| 1 | Cruiser | . . . | Military | $\langle \ldots \rangle$ | $-$ |
| 2 | Cruiser | . . . | Commercial | $\langle \ldots \rangle$ | $-$ |
| 3 | Cruiser | . . . | Civilian | $\langle \ldots \rangle$ | $+$ |
| 4 | Sailboat | . . . | Commercial | $\langle \ldots \rangle$ | $-$ |
| 5 | Sailboat | . . . | Civilian | $\langle \ldots \rangle$ | $-$ |

3. **Clustering-based motif feature extraction:** Generalized motif features are extracted from the movement paths. We perform micro-clustering to extract higher level features.
4. **High-dimensional, generalized motif-based classification:** A classifier is learned using the extracted generalized motif features.

The rest of the paper is organized as follows. In Section 2, we describe the representation of moving object data based on movement motifs. In Section 3, we describe the extraction of higher level features from the motif expressions. Experimental results are shown in Section 4. We discuss some related works in Section 5 and conclude the study in Section 6.

## 2   Movement Motifs

We assume that the input data consists of a set of labeled *movement paths*, $\mathcal{P} = \{p_1, p_2, \ldots\}$, where each path is a sequence of time-related points of an object, and each object is associated with a set of non-spatiotemporal attributes that describe non-motion-related properties. Table 1 shows such a data set extracted from a naval surveillance example, where each ship has non-spatiotemporal attributes, such as "size" and "type", along with the movement path. The "class" column labels the case as either positive (suspicious) or negative (normal).

### 2.1   Extraction of Movement Motifs

Although the concrete spatiotemporal data could be in the precision of seconds and inches, it is necessary to extract *movement motifs* at certain higher abstraction level in order to perform efficient and semantically meaningful analysis. Consider the two ship movements shown in Fig. 1. They share similar movements except an extra loop in the dashed path. To make semantically meaningful comparisons between moving objects, we propose to extract movement motifs at a proper level for further reasoning and classification.

A **movement motif** is a prototypical movement pattern of an object in either 2D or 3D space. They could be pre-defined by domain experts. Typical examples include *straight line*, *right turn*, *u-turn*, *loop*, etc. Let there be $M$ defined motifs: $\{m_1, m_2, \ldots, m_M\}$. A movement path is then transformed to a sequence of motifs

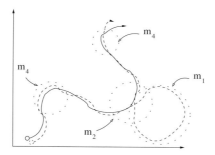

**Fig. 1.** Extracting motif expressions in raw paths

with other pieces of information associated. Fig. 1 shows this extraction process. Expressed by a sequence of motifs, the two paths now have much in common: They share one $m_2$ and two $m_4$'s, and their only difference is an extra $m_1$ in the dashed path.

We can assume there is a *movement motif extractor* (as preprocessing) that recognizes a pre-defined set of motifs modulo some geometric transformations (*e.g.*, rotation, translation, resizing, etc). Normalization methods to smooth out differences due to speed, direction, etc. are also needed. In general, each path takes the form,

$$\langle (m_i, t_{start}, t_{end}, l_{start}, l_{end}), (m_j, t_{start}, t_{end}, l_{start}, l_{end}), \ldots \rangle \qquad (1)$$

where $m_i$ is an expressed motif, $t_{start}$ and $t_{end}$ are the starting and ending times, and $l_{start}$ and $l_{end}$ are the starting and ending locations in 2D or 3D space. In a single motif expression, $t_{start} < t_{end}$ since each motif must take some non-zero time to execute. In a full path, motifs may be expressed in overlapping times and/or locations. A single motif maybe expressed multiple times within a single movement path.

## 2.2   Motif-Oriented Feature Space

Recall that the motif extractor is able to extract some preliminary spatiotemporal information about the motif expressions. Using such information, we can derive a set of **attributes**, *e.g.*, `duration`, `avg_speed`, and `generalized_location`. These attributes, with proper generalization, will be very useful in analysis. Take Fig. 2 as an example. There are three ships moving in an area that contains an important landmark. The left and right ships have the same movement shapes except that the left one makes its circle around a landmark. This extra piece of information (*i.e.*, general location) combined with the movement motif can be crucial in decision making. If we had the information that the left ship made its movement late at night and at very slow speeds, the combination of all such features is very telling in anomaly detection.

Let there be $A$ such interesting attributes: $\{a_1, a_2, \ldots, a_A\}$. For each $a_i$, we map the set of distinct values (*e.g.*, intervals, location coordinates, *etc.*) to a

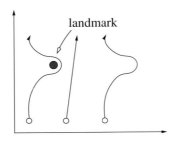

**Fig. 2.**

**Table 2.** Motif-oriented database

| | Motif Expressions | Class |
|---|---|---|
| 1 | $(\texttt{Right-Turn}, 3am, l_7), (\texttt{U-Turn}, 4pm, l_2), (\texttt{U-Turn}, 10pm, l_1)$ | − |
| 2 | $(\texttt{U-Turn}, 10am, l_2)$ | − |
| 3 | $(\texttt{Left-Turn}, 6am, l_7), (\texttt{U-Turn}, 11am, l_3), (\texttt{Right-Turn}, 1pm, l_7), (\texttt{Right-Turn}, 4pm, l_7)$ | + |
| 4 | $(\texttt{Right-Turn}, 1am, l_1), (\texttt{U-Turn}, 9am, l_1), (\texttt{Left-Turn}, 3pm, l_3), (\texttt{U-Turn}, 3pm, l_3)$ | − |
| 5 | $(\texttt{Right-Turn}, 2am, l_1), (\texttt{Left-Turn}, 9pm, l_3)$ | − |

set of integers between 1 and $V$, where $V$ is the largest needed value. We now represent each movement path in the following form,

$$\langle (m_i, v_1, v_2, \ldots, v_A), (m_j, v_1, v_2, \ldots, v_A), \ldots \rangle \tag{2}$$

where each tuple is a **motif expression** and $v_i$ is the value of attribute $a_i$. The set of all possible motif expressions, $(m_i, v_1, v_2, \ldots, v_A)$, plus the non-spatiotemporal features, define the **motif-oriented feature space**.

Table 2 shows a sample transformation from Table 1 to a **motif-oriented database**. For space consideration, we did not include the non-spatiotemporal features. The "Path" feature in Table 1 has been transformed to sets of motif expressions here. In this particular case, we have three motifs: `Right-Turn`, `Left-Turn`, and `U-Turn`. Each motif has two attributes: `Time` and `Location`. Notice that this model is still a simplified one for illustration of the major concepts. In some analysis, additional attributes, such as average, maximum, or minimum speed of the vessel, may need to be associated with a motif for successful anomaly detection.

One could try to feed the motif-oriented database into some learning machine. But such attempts may prove to be futile. In the raw database, motif expressions can be recorded with high granularity values, *i.e.*, the number of distinct values for each attribute is very large. And since each distinct expression is mapped to a feature in the motif-oriented feature space, this makes generalization difficult. Take the time-of-the-day attribute as an example. If it is stored at the second level, almost all motif expressions will have different values. Because these different values are stored as different features, generalization becomes essentially impossible. Learning on a feature that is at `10:30:01am` will have no bearing on a feature that is at `10:30:02am`.

Thus, a different approach is needed to overcome this problem. We propose an extraction process named **Motif Feature Extraction** which will smooth out the high granularity values and extract higher level features. For example, the *exact* distance from a ship to a landmark is unimportant, and it is enough to consider "rather close_to it" in comparison with most other ships. We explain this process in detail in the following section.

## 3  Motif Feature Extraction

The **Motif Feature Extraction** (MFE) process *clusters* the features belonging to each motif attribute and extracts higher level features. Recall that each feature in the motif-oriented feature space is a tuple of the form $(m_i, v_1, v_2, \ldots, v_A)$, where $v_j$ is the value of attribute $a_j$. For each $m_i$ and $a_j$ combination, MFE independently clusters the values for $a_j$. For example, suppose we are dealing with the time-of-the-day attribute, MFE will extract representative time concepts based on the data distribution. The result may correspond to a special period in the time of the day, such as *1-3am*, or *late_night*.

These newly found clusters can be seen as higher level features in the data. And thus they will replace the original high granularity values in each $a_j$. As a result, each feature in the motif-oriented feature space will be a tuple of the form $(m_i, c_1, c_2, \ldots, c_A)$, where $c_j$ is the cluster for attribute $a_j$. Because the number of clusters will be much smaller than the number of original values for each attribute, the feature space will be greatly reduced. We term this new reduced feature space the **MFE Feature Space**.

In order to cluster the attribute values, we have to define a distance metric for each attribute. In general, a distance metric might not exist for an attribute (e.g., categorical data). Fortunately, because the attributes here are spatiotemporal, distance metrics are naturally defined. For example, attributes related to speed or time are just one-dimensional numerical values. Attributes related to spatial location can be measured with 2D or 3D Euclidean distance metrics.

### 3.1  Feature Clustering

Now that we have the distance metric for each attribute, we wish to find clusters in the attribute value space. These clusters will replace the original features and form a more compact feature space. We use a hierarchical micro-clustering technique similar to BIRCH [33] for this task. The reason we chose a "micro-clustering" technique is because we only want to extract some small, tight clusters. Higher level semantics are captured in the hierarchies.

**CF Vector & Tree.** First, we introduce some basic concepts. Given $n$ features (motif-expressions) in the meta-feature space: $\{f_1, f_2, \ldots, f_n\}$, the centroid $C$ and radius $R$ are defined as follows. Recall that each feature $f_i$ is a $A$-dimensional vector in the meta-feature space.

$$C = \frac{\sum_{i=1}^{n} f_i}{n} \tag{3}$$

$$R = \left( \frac{\sum_{i=1}^{n} ||f_i - C||^2}{n} \right)^{\frac{1}{2}} \tag{4}$$

Next, we define the **clustering feature** (CF) vector: given $n$ features in a cluster, the CF vector is a triplet defined as: $CF = (n, LS, SS)$, where $n$ is the number of features in the cluster, $LS$ is the linear sum vector of the $n$ features, i.e., $\sum_{i=1}^{n} f_i$, and $SS$ is the square sum vector of the $n$ features, i.e., $\sum_{i=1}^{n} f_i^2$.

A CF tree is a height-balanced tree with two parameters: branching factor $b$ and radius threshold $t$. The tree is hierarchical in the following sense: the CF at any node contains information for all data points in that node's subtree. All leaf entries have to satisfy the threshold $t$ constraint, which restricts the radius of an entry to be less than $t$. Building the CF tree is efficient, the cost of constructing a CF tree from $N$ points is $O(N)$. More properties are described in [33].

### 3.2    MFE Feature Space

After building the CF tree from the features belonging to a single motif attribute, we perform hierarchical agglomerative clustering on the leaves in the CF tree to form the final clustering. This step is needed because irregularities in the data could cause the CF tree to misplace nodes or split nodes that should belong together [33]. The leaf nodes of the resultant hierarchical clustering are then the micro-clusters and their centroids are the *extracted features*. They will *replace* the original features to form a new feature space. We term this feature space the **MFE feature space**.

### 3.3    Classification

After MFE has performed some primitive generalization in the individual dimensions, we employ the use of a classifier to learn more complex generalizations on the database. Since the MFE feature space is fairly high dimensional, we make use of the support vector machine [10, 8] in this learning task.

## 4    Experiments

In this section, we test our classification system's performance in a variety of settings.

### 4.1    Data Generation

To systematically study the performance of the method under different data distributions, we generated our own test data sets. Each data set consists of a set of paths divided into two classes: positive and negative. Both classes use the same background model to generate a sequence of motif expressions. The positive class model has an additional model to insert "abnormal" motif patterns. The models did not include non-spatiotemporal features because we only wanted to test the motif expression components. But note that the feature space can handle all general features.

The background model is a Gaussian mixture distribution over the possible motif expressions. It randomly chooses a set of seeds from this space and generates a Gaussian distribution (independently for each attribute) for each expression. During path generation, a length is randomly generated and motif expressions are then randomly generated according to the Gaussian mixture model. The abnormal class has an additional model to generate "abnormal" motif patterns which make it different. Each pattern consists of one or more motif expressions. This additional model is another Gaussian mixture distribution over the motif expression space. During path generation, one or more abnormal motif pattern(s) are inserted into the positive paths.

## 4.2   Experiments

For comparison, we constructed a simple baseline model, Plain-SVM. It is an SVM trained on the motif-oriented database without MFE (i.e., Table 2). Our model is named MFE-SVM. The branching factor $b$ of the CF tree is set to 4 in all experiments.

Table 3 shows experimental results in a variety of settings. The first column lists the different data sets. All data sets had 2000 normal paths and 2000 suspicious paths. Each path's average length was 50 motif expressions. Each suspicious path had one additional abnormal motif pattern (randomly generated from the model), which consisted of 2 normally correlated motif expressions.

The other parameters are shown in the table. Each data set's name is in the form of "$\#M\#A\#V\#T\#S$", where $M$ is the number of motifs, $A$ is the number of attributes, $V$ is the number of values, $T$ is the number of abnormal patterns in the abnormal model, and $S$ is the standard deviation in the Gaussian mixture distributions. For the MFE-SVM, we tried 2 different numbers for the parameter $t$, which adjusts the granularity of the CF tree. All SVMs used a radial kernel and all accuracy values were the average of 5 random data sets, each with 10-fold cross validation.

As the experiments show, classification accuracies with the MFE features were much better than the plain method. This is easy to justify since generalization in the plain case was essentially impossible (i.e., the SVM functioned as a simple rote learner). In the MFE features, similar spatiotemporal motif expressions were clustered together to allow the SVM to generalize.

**Clustering Parameter.** In Table 3, we see that when the $t$ parameter (radius threshold) was adjusted higher, classification accuracies decreased. Recall $t$ controls the size of the micro-clusters in the CF trees (i.e., bigger $t$ means bigger clusters). In terms of motifs, a larger $t$ means rougher granularities, or higher generalizations, in the attribute measurements. For example, using *late_night* (low granularity feature) vs. {*1-2am, 2-3am, ...*} (high granularity features) to represent the time measurement. Also, note that setting $t$ to 0 is equivalent to using the Plain-SVM.

**Table 3.** Classification accuracy: on plain data sets vs. on motif-oriented data sets

| Dataset | Plain-SVM | MFE-SVM $(t = 40)$ | MFE-SVM $(t = 150)$ |
|---|---|---|---|
| $10M3A1000V20T2.0S$ | 52% | 74% | 74% |
| $10M3A1000V20T1.0S$ | 57% | 72% | 73% |
| $10M3A1000V20T0.5S$ | 80% | 73% | 73% |
| $20M5A1000V20T2.0S$ | 50% | 92% | 72% |
| $20M5A1000V20T1.0S$ | 51% | 93% | 71% |
| $20M5A1000V20T0.5S$ | 58% | 96% | 72% |
| $20M10A1000V20T2.0S$ | 51% | 95% | 97% |
| $20M10A1000V20T1.0S$ | 51% | 97% | 97% |
| $20M10A1000V20T0.5S$ | 57% | 99% | 96% |
| $40M10A1000V20T2.0S$ | 50% | 96% | 96% |
| $40M10A1000V20T1.0S$ | 53% | 99% | 96% |
| $40M10A1000V20T0.5S$ | 58% | 99% | 98% |
| $40M10A1000V50T2.0S$ | 50% | 89% | 85% |
| $40M10A1000V50T1.0S$ | 51% | 95% | 92% |
| $40M10A1000V50T0.5S$ | 62% | 95% | 93% |
| *Average* | *55.4%* | *90.9%* | *85.6%* |

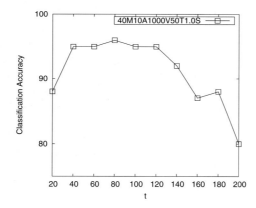

**Fig. 3.** The effect of the $t$ parameter on classification

Fig. 3 shows the effects of $t$ on classification accuracies on one particular data set. As the curve shows, accuracy peaks in the middle ranges and dips at the two ends. In terms of generalization, the two ends denote not enough generalization and too much generalization. The optimal setting of $t$ is closely tied to the data. It would be difficult to choose an optimal value a priori. One possibility is to dynamically adjust $t$, on a motif-by-motif basis, using feedback from the classifier. This is a direction for future research.

# 5   Related Work

Research on moving object databases (MOD) [15, 14] has been an emerging field. There are several areas in this field that relate to our work. First is nearest neighbor (NN) search [25, 5, 26, 16, 23, 12]. [25] uses a data structure similar to R-Tree to store samplings of the moving objects. [5] uses TPR-tree [22, 27] to do NN and also reverse NN. [26] uses R-Tree with a different metric to perform continuous NN queries. However, these works are only concerned with the proximity of moving objects in physical space. They are not concerned with higher level concepts of movement patterns or associations to time and location values.

There are some approaches for pattern existence queries over time series data [35, 2]. These approaches converted data into strings and used string matching algorithms to find patterns. This is related to our motif-extraction procedure. However, they do not address issues associated with higher-level analysis.

Clustering of moving objects [13, 18] is another area in MOD. Closely related is clustering of time series, which can be viewed as a special case of one-dimensional spatiotemporal data [4]. There is also a work to cluster high-dimensional data stream [1]. These works are mainly focused on clustering the data itself, while we try to find the clusters in the meta-feature space to form a compact and generalized feature space.

There have been many works in the spatiotemporal domain which touch on related topics. Data structures such as TPR-tree [22], TPR*-tree [27], and STRIPES [21] index spatiotemporal data efficiently. Query processing and nearest neighbor queries are studied in [17, 20, 31, 29, 32, 5, 9]. These studies are focused on indexing and query processing at the level of raw points and edges. Our study is on data mining at higher semantic levels of motif-based micro-clusters.

In data mining, there have been works which focus on finding frequent patterns. [28] mines sequential patterns in spatial locations. The mined patterns are frequent sequences of events that occur at the locations. Another data mining problem is co-location mining. Each frequent co-location pattern is a set of frequent locations associated closely by some neighborhood function. [19, 24, 30] are works that focus on this problem. [24, 30] use Apriori-based [3] approaches to join smaller co-location patterns together. [30] performs a more complicated process by looking additionally at partial joins. [34] is a recent work that quickly finds co-location patterns by using multiway joins. In comparison with such studies, this study is on building up classification models by motif feature extraction and aggregation.

Another related field is vision [11]. In cases where direct tracking of objects is unavailable, particle tracking techniques are appropriate. [6] provides a good overview including tracking with RADAR. For the task of motif extraction, there is an abundance of work under the title of segmentation and recognition [7].

# 6   Conclusion

In this paper, we have investigated the problem of anomaly detection in moving objects. With recent advances in surveillance technology and the imminent need for better protection of homeland security, automated solutions for detecting abnormal behavior in moving objects, such as ships, planes and vehicles, have become an important issue in intelligence and security informatics. This is a hard problem since the pattern of movement linked with the environment can become very complex. A primitive approach which analyzes the raw data will have a hard time making efficient and generalized decisions.

Instead, we propose a higher-level approach which views object paths as motif expressions, where a motif is a prototypical movement pattern. By linking the motifs with other features (both spatiotemporal and regular), we automatically extract higher level features that better represent the moving objects. In experimental testing, we see that classification using the higher level features produced better accuracies than that without using such features.

# References

1. C. Aggarwal, J. Han, J. Wang, and P. S. Yu. A framework for projected clustering of high dimensional data streams. In *VLDB'04*.
2. R. Agrawal, G. Psaila, E. L. Wimmers, and M. Zait. Querying shapes of histories. In *VLDB'95*.
3. R. Agrawal and R. Srikant. Fast algorithm for mining association rules in large databases. In *Research Report RJ 9839*, IBM Almaden Research Center, 1994.
4. A. J. Bagnall and G. J. Janacek. Clustering time series from arma models with clipped data. In *KDD'04*.
5. R. Benetis, C. S. Jensen, G. Karciauskas, and S. Saltenis. Nearest neighbor and reverse nearest neighbor queries for moving objects. In *Proc. IDEAS*, 2002.
6. S. Blackman and R. Popoli. *Design and Analysis of Modern Tracking Systems*. Artech House, 1999.
7. R. J. Campbell and P. J. Flynn. A survey of free-form object representation and recognition techniques. *Computer Vision and Image Understanding*, 81:166–210, 2001.
8. Chih-Chung Chang and Chih-Jen Lin. *LIBSVM: a library for support vector machines*, 2001. Software available at http://www.csie.ntu.edu.tw/~cjlin/libsvm.
9. H. D. Chon, D. Agrawal, and A. E. Abbadi. Range and knn query processing for moving objects in grid model. In *ACM/Kluwer MONET*, 2003.
10. N. Cristianini and J. Shawe-Taylor. *An Introduction to Support Vector Machines: And Other Kernel-Based Learning Methods*. Cambridge Univ. Press, 2000.
11. D.A. Forsyth and J. Ponce. *Computer Vision - A Modern Approach*. Prentice-Hall, 2002.
12. E. Frentzos, K. Gratsias, N. Pelekis, and Y. Theodoridis. Nearest neighbor search on moving object trajectories. In *SSTD'05*.
13. S. Gaffney and P. Smyth. Trajectory clustering with mixtures of regression models. In *KDD'99*.
14. G. H. Güting and M. Schneider. *Moving Objects Databases*. Morgan Kaufmann, 2005.
15. R. H. Güting, et al. A foundation for representing and querying moving objects. In *ACM Trans. Database Systems (TODS)*, March 2000.
16. G. S. Iwerks, H. Samet, and K. Smith. Continuous k-nearest neighbor queries for continuously moving points with updates. In *VLDB'03*.

17. C. S. Jensen, D. Lin, and B. C. Ooi. Query and update efficient b+-tree based indexing of moving objects. In *VLDB'04*.
18. Panos Kalnis, Nikos Mamoulis, and Spiridon Bakiras. On discovering moving clusters in spatio-temporal data. In *SSTD'05*.
19. K. Koperski and J. Han. Discovery of spatial association rules in geographic information databases. In *SSD'95*.
20. M. F. Mokbel, X. Xiong, and W. G. Aref. Sina: Scalable incremental processing of continuous queries in spatio-temporal databases. In *SIGMOD'04*.
21. J. M. Patel, Y. Chen, and V. P. Chakka. Stripes: An efficient index for predicted trajectories. In *SIGMOD'04*.
22. S. Saltenis, C. Jensen, S. Leutenegger, and M. Lopez. Indexing the positions of continuously moving objects. In *SIGMOD'00*.
23. C. Shahabi, M. Kolahdouzan, and M. Sharifzadeh. A road network embedding technique for k-nearest neighbor search in moving object databases. In *GeoInformatica*, 2003.
24. S. Shekhar and Y. Huang. Discovering spatial co-location patterns: A summary of results. In *SSTD'01*.
25. Z. Song and N. Roussopoulos. K-nearest neighbor search for moving query points. In *SSTD'01*.
26. Y. Tao, D. Papadias, and Q. Shen. Continuous nearest neighbor search. In *VLDB'02*.
27. Y. Tao, D. Papadias, and J. Sun. The tpr*-tree: An optimized spatio-temporal access method for predictive queries. In *VLDB'03*.
28. I. Tsoukatos and D. Gunopulos. Efficient mining of spatiotemporal patterns. In *SSTD'01*.
29. X. Xiong, M. F. Mokbel, and W. G. Aref. Sea-cnn: Scalable processing of continuous k-nearest neighbor queries in spatio-temporal databases. In *ICDE'05*.
30. J. S. Yoo and S. Shekhar. A partial join approach to mining co-location patterns. In *GIS'04*.
31. X. Yu, K. Q. Pu, and N. Koudas. Monitoring k-nearest neighbor queries over moving objects. In *ICDE'05*.
32. J. Zhang, M. Zhu, D. Papadias, Y. Tao, and D. Lee. Location-based spatial queries. In *SIGMOD'03*.
33. T. Zhang, R. Ramakrishnan, and M. Livny. BIRCH: an efficient data clustering method for very large databases. In *SIGMOD'96*.
34. X. Zhang, N. Mamoulis, D. W. Cheung, and Y. Shou. Fast mining of spatial collocations. In *KDD'04*.
35. Y. Zu, C. Wang, L. Gao, and X. S. Wang. Supporting movement pattern queries in user-specified scales. *IEEE Trans. Knowledge and Data Engineering*, 2003.

# Adaptive Method for Monitoring Network and Early Detection of Internet Worms

Chen Bo, Bin Xing Fang, and Xiao Chun Yun

The Department of Computer Science and Engineering, Harbin Institute of Technology, Harbin, 150001, China
{chenbo, bxf, yxc}@pact518.hit.edu.cn

**Abstract.** After many Internet-scale worm incidents in recent years, it is clear that a simple self-propagation worm can quickly spread across the Internet. And every worm incidents can cause severe damage to our society. So it is necessary to build a system that can detect the presence of worm as quickly as possible. This paper first analyzes the worm's framework and its propagation model. Then, we describe a new algorithm for detecting worms. Our algorithm first monitors the computers on network and gets the number of abnormal computers. Then based on the monitoring result, we detect an unknown worm by using recursive least squares estimation. The experiments result proves that our approach is effective to detect unknown worm.

## 1 Introduction

Now, more and more people log on the internet to chat with others, download files or read WebPages. The Internet becomes an important role for the economy of country and life of people. Once the network breaks down, it will cause an enormous economic loss. In 1988, Moriis worm breaks out and 6000 servers are infected and stop working in a few days. This incident makes loss be over 10 million dollars. After that, Code Red, Code Red II, Nimda, Slammer, Blaster, Sasser, and Witty have repeatedly attacked the Internet and caused great damage to our society. So more and more people and organizations pay attention to detect and defend against worm.

In the worm detection research area, Dagon *et al.* [12] presented a "honeystat" worm detection method by correlating infection statistics provided by local honeypots when a worm tries to infect them. The CounterMalice quarantine device [13] also tries to detect infected hosts in local enterprise networks. Stainford-Chen et al. [5] presented "GrIDS", which can detect worm-infected hosts in a local network through building the worms infection graph. C.C.Zou et al. [1] present a method which detect worm using Kalman filter. The method can detect un-known worm. But its detection time is long. In this paper, we present a new detection methodology. The detection methodology is based on these characteristic: 1) when a computer is infected by worm, it will send out a lot of connection request; 2) the number of infected computers can be modeled by (1). The rest of this paper is organized as follows. Section II introduces the worm's general framework and its propagation models. Section III presents a new methodology to monitor the network. In Section IV, we

S. Mehrotra et al. (Eds.): ISI 2006, LNCS 3975, pp. 178 – 189, 2006.

present an adaptive method to detect worm. Section V, we do a set of experiments to evaluate our detection methodology. In the end, Section VI concludes this paper.

## 2  Worm's General Framework and Its Propagation Model

A network worm is a special of virus that can replicate itself to remote computers. It can actively scan computers on network and detect if it has vulnerability. When the worm find a remote computational machine has vulnerability. It will replicate itself through network. Fig.1 describes the general framework of network worm.

```
while(1){
  h = GetTarget();
  checkConnect(h);
  if h can't connect then
   continue;
  Exploit e = checkVULN(h);
  If h has not vulnerable then
   continue;
  acquirePrivs(h,e);
  if can't acquire privilege then
   continue;
  infect(h);

}
```

**Fig. 1.** Framework of worm

From figure 1, we can know that the worm can be divided into three phases: 1) Target Acquisition Phase; 2) Elevating privilege phase; 3) Infection phase. The *Target Acquisition Phase* describes the worm agent how to select hosts that will be targeted for infection. We call the set of all hosts that will eventually be targeted for infection is target set. This set may be a very large set and usually is not explicitly encoded in a worm agent. Now the Target Acquisition Function has following algorithm to select a target: random selecting algorithm; sequent selecting algorithm; half random selecting algorithm. The *elevating privilege phase* firstly judge whether the selected host has vulnerability. If the selected host exist the vulnerability, worm agent will elevate its privilege through the vulnerability and make itself have an ability to write file, execute process and so on. In *infection phase*, the worm agent will replicate itself to remote computer through the elevated privilege.

When a worm agent start on a computer, for infect other computer on network, worm agent will select a different host to infect. So in a short time, the agent will contact a lot of different host and generate a lot of number of connection. Fig.2 shows some typical worms' connection states in 30 seconds. Fig.3 shows a normal host's

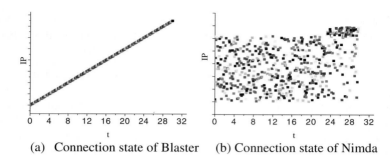

(a)  Connection state of Blaster     (b) Connection state of Nimda

**Fig. 2.** Typical worms' connection state

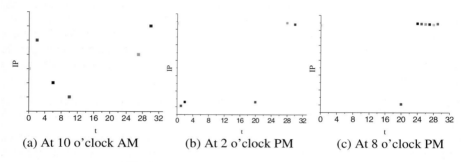

(a) At 10 o'clock AM          (b) At 2 o'clock PM          (c) At 8 o'clock PM

**Fig. 3.** Normal computers' connection state

connection stats in 30 seconds in the morning, noon and evening. Comparing Fig.2 and Fig.3 we can find that the number of connection of a infected host is far greater than a normal host.

When a worm breaks out in network, worm's propagation will follows fluid models because of its large-scale distributed infection. The model can be written as [1]:

$$\frac{dI_t}{dt} = \beta I_t [N - I_t] \tag{1}$$

where $I_t$ is the number of infected hosts at time $t$; $N$ is the size of vulnerable population; and $\beta$ is called the *pairwise rate of infection* in epidemic studies.

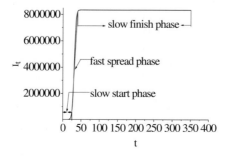

**Fig. 4.** Worm propagation model

Fig.4 shows the dynamics of $I_t$ as time goes on for one set of parameters. We can roughly partition a worm's propagation into three phases: the slow start phase, the fast spread phase, and the slow finish phase [1]. Our task is to detect the presence of a worm in the Internet in its slow start phase or in its beginning of the fast spread phase.

## 3  Network Monitoring

### 3.1  Network Monitoring Algorithm

Network operators principally monitor two finds of data in network. The first is data available from Simple Network Management Protocol (SNMP) queried from network nodes. This Management Information Base (MIB) data is quite broad, and mainly consists of counts of activity (such as the number of packets transmitted) on a node. The second type of data available is from IP flow monitor. This data includes protocol level information about specific end-to-end packet flows which make it more specific than SNMP data. But because of the characteristic of worm, In this paper, we present a new method to monitor network.

**Definition 1.** Connection Degree In a time interval $t$, host $i$ contact $n$ different IP host computers. Then $n$ is defined the connection degree of host $i$ in time interval $t$.

From above analysis, we can know that the number of different connection of the host infected by worm is far greater than a normal host's. That is to say, the connection degree of host infected by worm is far higher than a normal host's. So we can design a monitoring system to monitor computers' connection degree.

As a computer $i$, it should have three states: 1) sending packets; 2) receiving packets; 3) not sending or receiving. Because of the character of a worm, we don't need to pay attention to the receiving packets state. So we can define binary time series $\{ W(t), t \geq 0 \}$. $W(t)=1$ means that the computer is sending packets at time $t$ and $W(t)=0$ means that the computer don't send packets at time $t$. Let $\{ D(t,t_1,t_2), t_1 \leq t < t_2 \}$ denote a series of different computers' IP, which computer $i$ is sending packets to from time $t_1$ to time $t_2$. And let $Dst(t)$ denote the destination computer's IP which computer $i$ is sending packets to at time $t$. Using Under the definition of connection degree, we can get

$$C_t^i = \int_{(t-1)T}^{tT} W(t)K(t)dt \tag{2}$$

where $C_t^i$ is the computer $i$'s connection degree at time t. And $K(t)$ is a decision function. It can be expressed

$$K(t) = Dst(t) \oplus D(t,0,t-1) \tag{3}$$

In (3), we define a new operator $\oplus$. It is an operation between a variable and a vector. Supposing there is a variable and a vector $A$. we define that

$$a \oplus A = \begin{cases} 0 & a \in A \\ 1 & a \notin A \end{cases} \tag{4}$$

Using (2), we can record each computer's connection degree.

## 3.2  General Framework of Worm Detection

The general framework of worm detection is shown in Fig.5. The whole system is composed of two parts: a Date Processing Center (DPC) and distributed monitors. These monitors are located on gateways or border routers of local networks. It can be set up as a part of the egress filter on the routers of a local network. The job of distributed monitors is to monitor the network and find how many computers are abnormal. When Distributed monitors get the number of abnormal computers, they are required to send these results to remote DPC continuously without serious delay; The DPC's main task is judge whether the worm is breaking out based on the data sent by monitors.

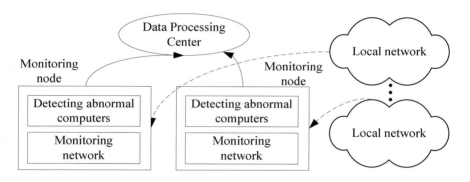

**Fig. 5.** General framework of Worm Detection

## 4  Adaptive Method to Early Detecting Worm

In this section, we describe an adaptive method to detect worm. The method can be divided into two parts: 1) In distributed monitors, we detect abnormal computers and get a time series $A(t)$. In our paper, the series is consist of number of abnormal computers at different time; 2) In DPC, we verify there is worm attack using RLS(recursive least squares).

## 4.1  Detection of Abnormal Computers

If $x_n^i$ is the connection degree of computer $i$ in the $n$-th time interval, and $\overline{\mu}_n$ is the mean rate estimated from measurements prior to n, then we predict the computer is anomaly based on the following condition:

$$x_n^i \geq (1+\gamma)\overline{\mu}_{n-1} \qquad (5)$$

where $\gamma > 0$ is a parameter that indicate the percentage above the mean value that we consider to be an indication of anomalous behaviour. The mean $\overline{\mu}_n$ can be computed over some past time window or using an exponential weighted moving average (EWMA) of previous measurements.

$$\overline{\mu}_n = \lambda\overline{\mu}_{n-1} + (1-\lambda)\frac{1}{A}\sum_{i=1}^{A} x_n^i \qquad (6)$$

where $\lambda$ is the EWMA factor. And $A$ is number of computers which are monitored.

Direct application of the above algorithm would yield high numbers of false detection. So we modify the algorithm to improve its performance. We detect anomalous behaviour after a minimum number of consecutive violations of the threshold [14].

$$\sum_{j=n-k+1}^{n} 1_{x_j^i \geq (1+\gamma)\overline{\mu}_{j-1}} \geq k \qquad (7)$$

where $k > 1$ is a parameter that indicates the number of consecutive intervals the threshold must be violated for an detection to be raised. Then $A(n)$ can be written as:

$$A(n) = |\{i \mid \sum_{j=n-k+1}^{n} 1_{x_j^i \geq (1+\gamma)\overline{\mu}_{j-1}} \geq k\}| \qquad (8)$$

## 4.2  Worm Attack Verification

From above analysis, we can know that if a worm breaks out, the $A(t)$ should follow model (1). Based on this conclusion, we can verify worm attack using recursive least squares (RLS) to judge whether the time serial $A(t)$ follows the model (1). First we describe the preliminaries of recursive least squares. And then we describe our approach to detect worm using RLS.

Supposing the output $z(t)$ at time $t$ of a time series is a linear combination of $p$ input measurements at time $t$, $h(t) = [h_1(t), h_2(t) \cdots h_p(k)]^\tau$. Therefore we have:

$$z(t) = h^\tau(t)\theta + n(t) \qquad (9)$$

where $\theta$ is the vector of model parameters and $n(t)$ is a random–variable (white noise). Given a sequence of $z(i)$ and $h(i)$ for $i = 1,2,3 \cdots t$ (the offline case where all the data points are available before hand), the RLS method estimates a constant $\theta$, given $h(t)$, so that the mean squared error of the estimated output,

$$V_t(\theta) = \frac{1}{t}\sum_{k=1}^{t}[z(k) - h^\tau(k)\theta]^2 \qquad (10)$$

is minimized. In the offline version of RLS, the estimated model parameters are

$$\hat{\theta}(t) = \overline{R}(t)^{-1}B(t) \tag{11}$$

where $R(t) = \sum_{k=1}^{t} h^{\tau}(k)h(k)$ is the variance covariance matrix of the inputs, and

$B(t) = \sum_{k=1}^{t} h(k)z(k)$ is the cross-covariance between the inputs and output. The RLS

estimate $\hat{\theta}(t)$ can also be obtained recursively [9].

$$\hat{\theta}(t) = \hat{\theta}(t-1) + \frac{1}{t}R^{-1}(t)h(t)[z(t) - h(t)\hat{\theta}(t-1)] \tag{12}$$

$$R(t) = R(t-1) + \frac{1}{t}[h(t)h^{\tau}(t) - R(t-1)] = \frac{1}{t}\overline{R}(t) \tag{13}$$

Computing the inverse $R^{-1}(t)$ , which is expensive and sensitive to numerical errors, can be avoided by using the *matrix–inversion* lemma [9]: given matrices A, B, C and D of compatible dimensions, so that the product BCD and the sum A+BCD exist:

$$[A+BCD]^{-1} = A^{-1} - A^{-1}B[DA^{-1}B + C^{-1}]^{-1}DA^{-1} \tag{14}$$

provided all the required matrix inverses exist. Using the matrix inversion lemma in equation 12, and letting $P(t) = \overline{R}^{-1}(t) = \frac{1}{t}R^{-1}(t)$ .The *recursive least squares* (RLS) algorithm [10] can be obtained:

$$\begin{cases} \hat{\theta}(k) = \hat{\theta}(k-1) + K(k)[z(k) - h^{\tau}(k)\hat{\theta}(k-1)] \\ K(k) = P(k-1)h(k)[h^{\tau}(k)P(k-1)h(k) + \frac{1}{\tau}]^{-1} \\ P(k) = \frac{1}{\tau}[I - K(k)h^{\tau}(k)]P(k-1) \end{cases} \tag{15}$$

Where $\tau$ is the forgetting factor. It specifies how quickly the algorithm forgets past the sample information. We can use it to adjust whether our estimation should rely more on recently monitored data or equally on all monitored data. $P(0)$ can be initialized to a diagonal matrix with large positive diagonal elements, or to the matrix that corresponds to the first few input/output elements of the time series. Note that if $P(t) \approx 0$ then the RLS algorithm stops learning/adapting; typically, when this happens, $P(t)$ is reset appropriately.

In this paper, we use the discrete-time model for early detection. Time is divided into intervals of length $\Delta$ where $\Delta$ is the discrete time unit. To simplify the notations, we use "$t$" as the discrete time index from now on. For example, $I_t$ means the number of infected hosts at the real time $t$. The discrete-time version of the simple epidemic model (1) can be written as:

$$\begin{cases} I_t = (1+\alpha\Delta)I_{t-1} - \beta\Delta I_{t-1}^2 \\ \partial = \beta N \end{cases} \quad (16)$$

We call $\partial$ the infection rate, because it is an average number of vulnerable hosts that can be infected per unit of time by one infected host during the early stage of a worm's propagation. Let $y_1, y_2 \cdots y_t$ be the measured data used by RLS, then $y_t$ can be written as:

$$y_t = I_t + e_t \quad (17)$$

Substituting (17) into the worm epidemic model (14) yields an equation:

$$y_t = (1+\alpha\Delta)y_{t-1} - \beta\Delta y_{t-1}^2 + \zeta_t \quad (18)$$

where the $\zeta_t$ is

$$\zeta_t = e_t - (1+\alpha\Delta)e_{t-1} + \beta\Delta(2y_{t-1}e_{t-1} - e_{t-1}^2) \quad (19)$$

If we denote $h(t) = [y_{t-1}, y_{t-1}^2]^{\tau}$ and $\theta = \begin{pmatrix} 1+\alpha\Delta \\ -\beta\Delta \end{pmatrix}$, then we can estimate $\alpha$ Using (15). When the $\theta$ is convergent and stable, it shows that $y_t$ follows the model (1). So we can determine that the worm breaks.

## 5 Simulation Experiments

In this section, we describe a set of simulation experiments to evaluate our detection method. In our simulation experiments, we do not simply use the epidemic model (1) to numerically generate a worm's propagation curve. Instead, we have programmed discrete-time worm propagation simulator. The simulation platform is shown in Fig.6. It is composed of four parts: the module of sending background noise, the module of sending worm's packets, controlling module and our worm detection algorithm. The controlling module monitors the packets on network. If it finds a packet sent by module of sending worm's packets, it will start another module to send worm's packets with a possibility of $\mu$. The $\mu$ is not constant. It can be expressed by $\mu = N\eta/2^{32}$, where $\eta$ is scan rate of worm.

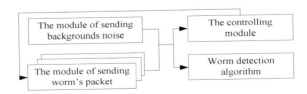

**Fig. 6.** Simulation platform of experiment

In our simulation experiments, we will show the network state when Code Red breaks out. In the case of Code Red, its scan rate is 358 per minute and more than 359,000 hosts had been infected by Code Red on July 19th 2001. So we can consider that the number of all host which can be infected by Code Red are 360,000 [1]. And we also need to consider background noise in our simulation experiments. Fortunately cliff zou et al [1] proposes a normal distribution model for the number of scans and number of hosts that send noise. For each hour the number of noise scans follows $N(110.5, 30^2)$ and the number of hosts send noise follows $N(17.4, 3.3^2)$.

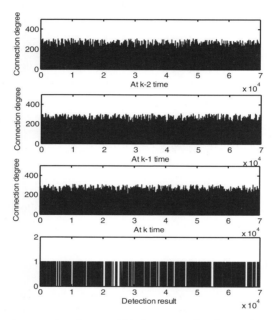

**Fig. 7.** Computers' connection degree within k-consecutive time and our detection result

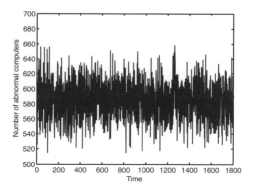

**Fig. 8.** Time serial $A(t)$ at no worm

Time $t_1$ is defined the time point of Red Code breaking. So When time $t < t_1$, there is no worm in network. Using (2) we can monitor computers' connection degree. Fig.7 (a)-(c) show the monitoring result within k-consecutive time. Using formula (7), we can get the abnormal computer at this time which is shown in Fig.7 (d). In Fig.7 (d), the x-axis is computer number, and the y-axis denotes the according computer is abnormal. 1 means the computer is abnormal and 0 means the computer is normal. At different time, using the formula (7) and formula (8), we can get the time serial $A(t)$ which is shown in Fig.8 . if we use the RLS algorithm to track the $A(t)$ and judge whether the $A(t)$ follows epidemic model, we can get the results shown in Fig.9. From Fig.9, we can know that even if the error of RLS is small, the estimated infection rate can't converge. This means that our detection algorithm detects no worm appears in the network.

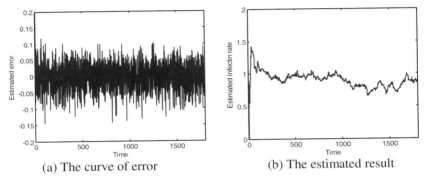

(a) The curve of error                    (b) The estimated result

**Fig. 9.** Result of RLS algorithm when no worm breaks out

After a lapse of time, it is $t_1$. The Red Code was breaking. Now the network state has changed and the worm propagated on the network. Using our algorithm, we can get the time serial $A(t)$ which is shown in Fig.10. In Fig.10, the time serial $A(t)$ is divided into two parts to be shown: a) $A(t)$ at the Code Red propagation being slow start phase; b) $A(t)$ at the Code Red propagation being fast spread phase；

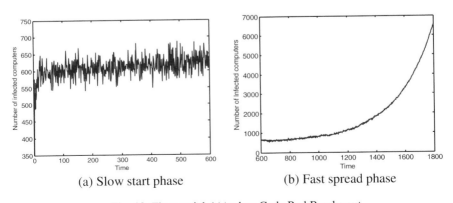

(a) Slow start phase                    (b) Fast spread phase

**Fig. 10.** Time serial $A(t)$ when Code Red Breaks out

Alike to the experiment above, we use RLS to track *A(t)*. Fig.11(a) shows the error of RLS. Through the error shown, it is easy to know our RLS can reveal the *A(t)* state. Fig.11(b) shows the estimated infection rate. From Fig.11(b), we can know that the estimated infection rate $\partial$ has already stabilized at a positive constant value at time 1500. by that time, the worm Red Code only infects 0.672% of all vulnerable population in the Internet. That is to say our approach can detect the worm at the beginning fast spread phase.

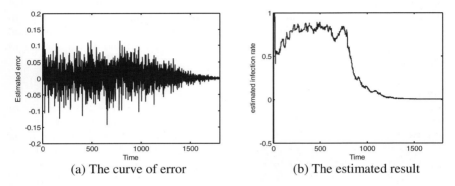

(a) The curve of error                    (b) The estimated result

**Fig. 11.** Result of RLS algorithm when worm breaks out

## 6   Conclusions

This paper proposed new method to detect worms. Our detection algorithm is based on two following facts: 1) the connection degree of a computer which is infected by worm will be abnormal. 2) The number of infected computers can be modeled. Our detection first monitor network to find abnormal computers. When our detection algorithm detect there are abnormal computers in network, it will use RLS to verify worm attack. The evaluation experimentsïprove that our detection algorithm can detect unknown worm effectively and quickly.

## References

1. Cliff C. Zou., Weibo Gong.: Monitoring and Early Detection of Internet Worms. Proceeding of th 10th ACM symposium on computer and communication security. Washington DC, USA: ACM. (2003) 190-199
2. C. C. Zou., W. Gong., D. Towsley.: Worm Propagation Modeling and Analysis under Dynamic Quarantine Defense. Proceedings of ACM CCS Workshop on Rapid Malcode. (2003) 51-60
3. V. H. Berk., R.S. Gray., and G. Bakos.: Using Sensor Networks and Data Fusion for Early Detection of Active Worms. Proceedings of the SPIE AeroSense. (2003)
4. J.O. Kephart., S.R. White.: Directed-graph Epidemiological Models of Computer Viruses. Proceedings of IEEE Symposium on Security and Privacy. (1991) pages 343–359

5.  S. Staniford-Chen., S. Cheung, R., Crawford., M. Dilger, J. Frank., J. Hoagland., K. Levitt., C. Wee., R. Yip., D. Zerkle.: GrIDS a Graph Based Intrusion Detection System for Large Networks. Proceedings of the 19th National Information Systems Security Conference. (1996) 361-370
6.  Dan Ellis.: Worm Anatomy and Model. Proceedings of the ACM workshop on Rapid Malcode. (2003) 43-50
7.  C. C. Zou., W. Gong., D. Towsley.: Code Red Worm Propagation Modeling and Analysis. Proceedings of 9th ACM Conference on Computer and Communications Security. (2002) 138-147
8.  D.J. Daley., J. Gani.: Epidemic Modeling: An Introduction. Cambridge University Press, 1999.
9.  L. Ljung.: System Identification: Theory for the User. Prentice Hall, Upper Saddle River. (1999.)
10. L. Ljung and T. Soderstrom.: Theory and Practice of Recursive Identification. M.I.T. Press, Cambridge, MA. (1983)
11. Jun Zheng, Mingzeng HU.: An Anomaly Intrusion Detection System Based on Vector Quantization. IEICE TRANS INF. & SYST., VOL.E89-D, NO.1 (2006) 201-210
12. D. Dagon., X. Qin., G. Gu., W. Lee., J. Grizzard., J. Levin., H. Owen.: Honeystat: Local worm detection using honeypots. Proceedings of the 7th International Symposium on Recent Advances in Intrusion Detection (RAID). (2004)
13. S. Staniford.: Containment of Scanning Worms in Enterprise Networks. Journal of Computer Security. (2003)

# Measures to Detect Word Substitution in Intercepted Communication

S.W. Fong[1], D.B. Skillicorn[1], and D. Roussinov[2]

[1] School of Computing,
Queen's University
[2] W.P. Carey School of Business,
Arizona State University

**Abstract.** Those who want to conceal the content of their communications can do so by replacing words that might trigger attention by other words or locutions that seem more ordinary. We address the problem of discovering such substitutions when the original and substitute words have the same natural frequency. We construct a number of measures, all of which search for local discontinuities in properties such as string and bag-of-words frequency. Each of these measures individually is a weak detector. However, we show that combining them produces a detector that is reasonably effective.

## 1 Motivation

Terrorists and criminals must be aware of the possibility of interception whenever they communicate by phone or email. In particular, terrorists must be aware of systems such as Echelon [3] that examine a very large number of messages and select some for further analysis based on a watchlist of significant words.

Given that it may not be possible to evade some examination of their messages, terrorists and criminals have two defensive strategies: encryption and obfuscation. The problems with encryption are that it draws immediate attention to messages and so permits at least meta-analysis; and it may be that there are backdoors to commonly available encryption methods. Obfuscation tries to hide messages in the background of the vast number of other messages, replacing words that might trigger attention by other innocent-sounding words or locutions. For example, al Qaeda, for a time, used the word 'wedding' to mean 'attack'.

When a word is replaced by a word of substantially different natural frequency, Skillicorn [10] showed that a different kind of potentially detectable signature is created. This is because most collections of messages represent an agglomeration of conversations, and conversations are always about something. Rare topics only appear in rare conversations. When a word substitution occurs, a rare topic begins to appear more frequently than it 'should'. An increase in both the frequency difference between original and substituted words and the frequency of messages that contain the substitution both increase the detectability of the presence of a substitution.

S. Mehrotra et al. (Eds.): ISI 2006, LNCS 3975, pp. 190–200, 2006.

However, substitution by a word of approximately similar frequency is possible, given either a predefined codebook or access to a frequency-ranked word list (on the internet perhaps). In this paper, we address the detection of messages in which a word has been replaced by a word of similar frequency.

Consider the sentence "the attack will be tomorrow". Using the al Qaeda substitution, we get "the wedding will be tomorrow" which is designedly a natural-sounding sentence. However, 'attack' is the 1072nd most common English word according to the site www.wordcount.org/main.php, while 'wedding' is the 2912th most common, so the substantial frequency difference might make this substitution detectable using the approach described above. On the other hand, if the word 'attack' is replaced by the word 'complex' which has similar frequency, than any human will be able to detect that the sentence "the complex will be tomorrow" is extremely unusual. However, detecting this kind of substitution automatically using software has not been attempted, except in a very preliminary way [4].

The contribution of this paper is to show that a number of techniques using only syntactic properties such as word frequencies can detect such word substitutions, although only weakly. Most techniques are either good at detecting substitutions with a high false positive rate, or have a low false positive rate but do not detect substitutions well. However, combining the best of these techniques produces a detector whose detection rate, on an individual sentence basis, is close to 82% with a false positive rate of only 20%.

## 2   Related Work

The problem of detecting a word that is somehow out of context occurs in a number of settings. For example, speech recognition algorithms model the expected next word, and back up to a different interpretation when the next word becomes sufficiently unlikely [1]. This problem differs from the problem addressed here because of the strong left context that is used to decide on how unlikely the next word is, and the limited amount of resources that can be applied to detection because of the near-realtime performance requirement.

Detecting words out of context can also be used to detect (and correct) misspellings [5]. This problem differs from the problem addressed here because the misspelled words are nonsense, and often nonsense predictably transformed from the correctly spelled word, for example by letter reversal.

Detecting words out of context has also been applied to the problem of spam detection. For example, SpamAssassin uses rules that will detect words such as 'V!agra'. The problem is similar to detecting misspellings, except that the transformations have properties that preserve certain visual qualities rather than reflecting lexical formation errors. Lee and Ng [7] detect word-level manipulations typical of spam using Hidden Markov Models. As part of their work, they address the question of whether an email contains examples of obfuscation at all. They expected this to be simpler than the problem they set out to address – recovering the text that had been obfuscated – but remark that detecting obfuscation at all is 'surprisingly difficult' [7, Section 5] and achieve prediction accuracies of around 70% using word-level features.

The task of detecting replacements can be considered as the task of detecting words that are "out of context," which means surrounded by the words with which they typically do not co-occur. The task of detecting typical co-occurrences of words in the specific contexts was considered in [9, 8].

## 3   Strategies

We wish to detect places where word substitutions have occurred, without any access to direct semantic information. The techniques we use are all based on the intuition that a substitution creates a local 'bump' in the frequencies of substrings or sentences containing the substitute.

An obvious starting point might be the 2-gram (or n-gram) frequencies of adjacent pairs (or n-tuples) of words in the sentence. A 2-gram that contain the substituted word might have lower frequency than expected. There are two problems with this simple idea. First, what *is* the expected frequency, given that we don't know what the original word was? Second, Ferrer i Cancho and Solé [6] have shown that the graph of English word adjacencies has a small-world property. In other words, most rare words are surrounded by common words, and the pairwise frequencies of pairs that include rare words do not differ much from the rare word single-word frequencies. This can be seen in the example sentence above: there is nothing unusual about the fragment "the complex will be"; it is not until the word 'tomorrow' is appended that the sentence becomes unusual. It is the pair of non-stopwords (complex, tomorrow) whose frequency is significant, and these may be separated by many stopwords.

We determine frequencies by querying large repositories such as Google. Such repositories implicitly contain information about the frequencies of fragments of text, of bags of words, and of sets of words with stopwords deleted. However, it is not always possible to get this implicit information directly, which forces us to use subtle measures to obtain the scores we want.

We concentrate on nouns, since these represent the most likely targets of substitution, there is more information available about their frequencies than about other parts of speech, and there are fewer variant forms in English than for verbs.

### 3.1   k-Gram Frequencies

In examining a sentence for potential substitutions, we consider each noun in sequence. In our initial work we considered the region surrounding each noun extending to the left until the first non-stopword was encountered, and extending to the right until the first non-stopword was encountered. For example, in the sentence "A nine mile walk is no joke", the region surrounding 'walk' is "mile walk is no joke". However, we discovered that, in real, informal text, these regions are long enough that there are typically *no* instances of them, even at Google. This is partly because they are long enough to capture author idiosyncrasies, partly because of the grammatical oddities of informal text, and partly because texts in limited domains also tend to use limited vocabulary, such as technical terms which are not well represented in general-purpose repositories.

However, what we call the *left k-gram*, the text from the considered noun leftwards up to and including the first non-stopword; and the *right k-gram*, the text from the considered noun rightwards up to and including the first non-stopword, seem to produce more useful fragments. In the example sentence above, the left k-gram of 'walk' is "mile walk" ($f = 50$ at Google) and the right k-gram is "walk is no joke" ($f = 876{,}000$). Intuitively, each of these fragments considered separately is more natural, and so more likely, than the complete k-gram above ($f = 33$). Surprisingly, the left and right k-grams detect substantially different properties of sentences, presumably because word order is important in English, both to convey meaning and style (observe the different frequencies above).

## 3.2   Sentence Oddity

Sentence oddity measures are designed to measure the frequency of an entire sentence. Because most sentences do not appear verbatim even once in a large text repository, obtaining such frequencies comes at the expense of ignoring the order of the sentence words.

In general, if a word is discarded from a bag of words, the frequency of the smaller bag should be greater than that of the original bag. However, if the bag of words was a sentence with the word order ignored, and the discarded word was meaningful in the context of the sentence, then we might expect that the difference in frequency to be moderate. If the discarded word was *not* meaningful in the context of the sentence, then the difference in frequency might be much greater. Hence we define sentence oddity as:

$$\text{sentence oddity} = \frac{\text{frequency of bag of words with word discarded}}{\text{frequency of entire bag of words}}$$

The more unusual the discarded word was in the context of its sentence, the greater we expect the sentence oddity to be.

## 3.3   Semantic Oddity

If a word is a substitution, then we expect that word not to fit into the context well. If the substituted word is, in turn, replaced by a related word, the frequency of the resulting sentence will change, and this change will reflect something about how unusual the original substitution was. This requires a way to find related words, which is fundamentally a semantic issue, but there are sources of such words, for example Wordnet.

The hypernym of a noun is the word immediately above it in the ordinary ontology of meanings; for example, the hypernym of 'car' is 'motor vehicle'. We had expected that, when a normal word is replaced by its hypernym, the frequency of the resulting sentence would stay the same or increase; while when a substituted word is replaced by its hypernym the frequency of the resulting sentence would decrease.

This turns out to be exactly wrong – the actual behavior is the other way around, and considerably more subtle. The hypernym of a word has its own hypernym, and original word also has a hyponym, a more specialized word, so that there are a chain of hypernyms and hyponyms passing through any given noun. The place on this chain that best represents the entire chain is called the *class word*. An example of a chain is (from the bottom): "broodmare, mare, horse, equine, odd-toed ungulate, hoofed mammal, mammal, vertebrate". Here the class word is 'horse'. What happens when a word is replaced by its hypernym depends on where in such a chain the word appears. If the word is below the class word, then the hypernym is probably more common, and the frequency of the new sentence greater; if the word is above the class word, then the hypernym is probably more technical and less common, and the frequency of the new sentence is smaller. For example, the hypernym of 'rabbit' is the biological term 'leporid', which is unlikely to be used in ordinary sentences.

In fact, the chain of hypernyms for many words exhibits an oscillating structure, moving from technical terms to common terms and then back to technical terms, and so on. For example, a chain containing 'attack" is (from the bottom): "foray, incursion, attack, operation, activity, act, event" in which 'attack' and 'act' are simpler words than the others. Another chain is "comprehension, understanding, knowing, higher cognitive process, process, cognition", in which 'understanding', 'knowing, and 'process' are ordinary words while the other words in the chain are more technical.

In ordinary informal text, the nouns in use are likely to be close to the appropriate class words – using non-class words tends to sound pompous. Substitution by a hypernym is likely to produce a more technical sentence, and so a lower frequency. If the noun under consideration is already a substitution, however, it is less likely to be a simple word. Substitution by a hypernym may therefore move *towards* a simpler word, producing a less technical sentence, and so one with a greater frequency. The chain containing 'complex' is: "hybrid, complex, whole, concept, idea, mental object". In our example sentence, "the complex is tomorrow", hypernym replacement produces "the whole is tomorrow" which is a much more common bag of words.

We define the *hypernym oddity* to be:

$$\text{hypernym oddity} \;=\; f_H - f$$

where $f$ is the frequency of a sentence, regarded as a bag of words; and $f_H$ is the frequency of a bag of words in which the noun under consideration has been replaced by its hypernym. We expect this measure to be close to zero or negative for ordinary sentences, but positive for sentences that contain a substitution.

These three strategies, looking for frequencies of exact substrings of the sentence under consideration, looking for changes in frequency between the entire sentence and the sentence without the word under consideration, and looking for changes in frequency when the word under consideration is replaced by its hypernym (or other related words) can all suggest when a substitution has occurred. In the next section, we describe the exact measures we have used in our experiments.

# 4   Techniques

## 4.1   Usable Frequency Data

In order to be able to measure the frequencies of sentences, sentence fragments, and bags of words, we must use data about some repository of text. The choice of repository makes a great deal of difference, since the better the match between the repository and the style of text in which substitutions may have occurred, the more accurate the prediction of substitutions will be. It is well known, for example, that perplexity, which measures a one-sided 2-gram frequency, is considerably reduced in sets of documents from a particular domain.

We use Google as the source of frequency data, on the grounds that it indexes a very large number of English documents, and so provides a good picture of frequencies of English text. That said, it is surprising how often an apparently ordinary phrase occurs zero times in Google's document collection.

There are also particular idiosyncrasies of Google's techniques that have some impact on our results. First, the frequencies returned via the Google API and via the Google web interface are substantially different; the API frequency values are used in all programs here. Second, the Google index is updated every 10 days or so, but this is not easily detectable, so frequencies may be counted from different instantiations of the index (large frequencies are rounded so this makes little difference, except for rare strings). Third, the way Google handles stop words is not transparent, and makes it impossible to invoke exactly the searches we might have wished. For example, "chase the dog" occurs 9,580 times whereas "chase dog" occurs 709 times, so quoted string searches clearly do not ignore stopwords. On the other hand, the bag of words search {chase the dog} occurs 6,510,000 times while {chase dog} occurs only 6,490,000 times, which seems counterintuitive. Fourth, the order of words seems to be significant, even in bag-of-word searches. For example, searches for {natural language processing} and {natural processing language} consistently produce different frequencies.

We use the number of pages returned by Google as a surrogate for word frequency. This fails to take into account intraword frequencies within each individual document. It also fails to take into account whether two words appear, say, adjacently or at opposite ends of a given returned document, which we might expect to be relevant information about their relationship. We have experimented with using locality information of this kind, but it does not improve performance.

## 4.2   Usable Semantic Data

The only semantic information we use is the hypernyms of nouns being considered. We get this information from Wordnet (wordnet.princeton.edu). In general, a word can have several hypernyms, so we collect the entire set and use them as described below. For example, the direct hypernyms of 'complex' are 'whole', 'compound', 'feeling', and 'structure', derived from the different meanings of 'complex'.

## 4.3   Experimental Data

In order to evaluate measures to detect substitutions, we need sets of reasonable sentences to use as data. Standard grammatical sentences, for example from news articles, are not compelling test data because the kinds of sentences intercepted from email and (even more so) from speech will not necessarily be complete or formal grammatical sentences.

A large set of emails was made public as the result of the prosecution of the Enron corporation. This set of emails was collected over three and a half years and contains emails from and to a large set of individuals who never imagined that they would be made public. This set of emails is therefore a good surrogate for the kinds of texts that might be collected by systems such as Echelon, and we use it as a source of informal, and so realistic, sentences.

Enron emails contain many strings that are not English words, for example words in other languages, acronyms, and highly technical terms relating to energy. We use the British National Corpus (BNC) [2] to discard strings that do not appear to be English words, and also as our source for the natural frequencies of English words.

We extracted all strings ending with periods as possible sentences, except when the BNC corpus indicated the possibility of periods as integral parts of words, e.g. 'Mr.'. Sentences with fewer than 5 words or more than 15 words were discarded, leaving a total of 712,662 candidate sentences. A random sample of 3000 sentences were drawn from this set.

We detected the first noun in each sentence, and replaced it with an adjacent word in the BNC frequency ranking for nouns. Sentences for which the selected noun either did not have a hypernym known to Wordnet, or occurred with zero frequency at Google were discarded.

The resulting set of sentences still contained sentences that did not make good test examples because they contained unusual word use (i.e., they were too informal), because they contained typos at the level of words, or because they used technical vocabulary for which Google frequencies were too low ($f < 10$) to be useful. Some examples are: "not unless you count having two refrigerators to be a constitutionally protected right"; "do you mind returning this please let me know"; and "first that would help you sorry should have given it to you this morning".

To remove such sentences, we computed the sentence oddity for each original sentence and for the sentence derived from it by substitution. This measure should increase when a replacement is made; when it did not, we discarded the pair of sentences, since this means that the original sentence was *more* unusual that the one containing the substitution. This reduced the available set of sentences by approximately a further 25%. Of course, this means that the set of sentences is biased towards successful detection using sentence oddity, so the further results using this measure are included for interest only.

Our test set is therefore a set of 554 sentences from the Enron corpus, and a set of 554 sentences derived from them by substituting a word of equal frequency. The original set of sentences is useful because it lets us measure the false positive rate of the various measures. Also using a set in which the only difference is the occurrence of a substitution guarantees that performance differences do not arise from other features of the sentences.

For each measure defined below, we train a decision tree on the measured values for original sentences and sentences containing substitutions to learn the best boundary between the two classes. For all of these measures, there is considerable overlap between the measured values for the two classes (that is, there are many examples on the wrong side of the boundary), reflecting the complex possibilities for informal English sentences. It is therefore not surprising that the error rates of each individual measure are quite high.

## 4.4   Experiments

We applied the measures described previously to the sentence set.

For the family of k-gram measures, we compute the left k-gram frequency, the right k-gram frequency, and the average of these two measures.

There are often several hypernyms for a given word. We had observed, in previous work [4], that trying to choose a single hypernym could lead to poor results. We compute the hypernym oddities for all of the possible hypernyms of the noun under consideration, and compute: the *minimum* hypernym oddity over all hypernyms, the *maximum* hypernym oddity over all hypernyms, and the *average* hypernym oddity over all hypernyms.

# 5   Results

Even though we have used sentence oddity to select the set of sentences used as data, it is still reasonable to see how well this measure separates original and substituted sentences. The decision tree trained on both sets of sentences choose the boundary sentence oddity $> 2.5$ to predict sentences with substitutions. In other words, removing a substituted word from a sentence typically makes the frequency of the remaining bag of words more the double, while the change in frequency is smaller than this when an ordinary word is removed.

Figure 1 summarizes the performance of the various measures on the sentence dataset. In general, each of these techniques makes errors on different sentences, and so combining measures produces better results than using each measure alone. This is clear for the k-gram measures: the average k-gram measure has a much lower false positive rate than either of its two components; but the right k-gram detects substitutions very strongly. Notice that the left k-gram measure detects substitutions only weakly – this suggests that adapting techniques from speech recognition is not likely to work well for this problem. The three hypernym measures also show divergent properties: the minimum hypernym measure does not detect sentences with substitutions well, but has a low false positive rate. The boundaries for all of these measures were determined automatically using a decision tree, but it is clear that there is some scope for altering these boundaries to get better substitution detection at the expense of higher false positive rates (and *vice versa*). However, it is not clear how to do this in a principled way.

| Measure | Detection Rate (%) | False Positive Rate (%) | Boundary score |
|---|---|---|---|
| Sentence oddity | 71 | 20 | 2.5 |
| Left k-gram | 51 | 28 | 461 |
| Right k-gram | 89 | 48 | 722 |
| Average k-gram | 51 | 13 | 418 |
| Minimum hypernym | 40 | 15 | 10 |
| Maximum hypernym | 68 | 31 | 10 |
| Average hypernym | 59 | 22 | 0 |
| Combined | 82 | 20 | see Figure 2 |

**Fig. 1.** Detection performance results

A decision tree was trained using all of the measures as attributes. The resulting decision tree is shown in Figure 2. It is clear from the Table that the combined tree uses only the sentence oddity, average and right k-gram measures and minimum hypernym semantic oddity; but that these measures make their errors on different sentences, so that the overall accuracies are higher than those of the component measures. The high false positive rate is a problem, given that ordinary sentences are much more likely in intercepts than sentences with substitutions.

```
SO <= 2.48
|   KGRAM_AVG <= 4271.5
|   |   SO <= 1.27: 0
|   |   SO > 1.27
|   |   |   KGRAM_R <= 623: 1
|   |   |   KGRAM_R > 623
|   |   |   |   Hyp_MIN <= 5000: 0
|   |   |   |   Hyp_MIN > 5000: 1
|   KGRAM_AVG > 4271.5: 0
SO > 2.48
|   KGRAM_R <= 1380: 1
|   KGRAM_R > 1380
|   |   KGRAM_R <= 173000: 0
|   |   KGRAM_R > 173000: 1
```

**Fig. 2.** Structure of the decision tree, combining measures (0 – normal sentence, 1 – sentence containing a substitution; SO – sentence oddity, KGRAM – k-gram, Hyp – Hypernym)

It might be argued that the decision tree above performs well because the training sentences were selected so that the sentence oddity measure behaves appropriately. Figure 3 shows a combined decision tree in which only the k-gram and hypernym measures are used. The performance is only slight worse (accuracy for sentences containing a substitution: 78%, and false positive rate: 22%). A slightly smaller set of 884 sentences in which the sentence oddity criterion was not used to discard sentences shows comparable results (accuracy for sentences containing a substitution: 79%, and false positive rate: 23%). Overall performance results shows little sensitivity to choice of data or measures used, as long as several different measures are combined. This probably reflects the complexity of informal English, exhibited by any sufficiently large set of examples, and the lack of any single signature for word substitution.

```
KGRAM_R <= 722
|   Hyp_AVG <= 0
|   |   KGRAM_AVG <= 332: 1
|   |   KGRAM_AVG > 332: 0
|   Hyp_AVG > 0: 1
KGRAM_R > 722
|   KGRAM_L <= 15
|   |   Hyp_AVG <= -151
|   |   |   Hyp_MIN <= -1889000: 1
|   |   |   Hyp_MIN > -1889000: 0
|   |   Hyp_AVG > -151: 1
|   KGRAM_L > 15: 0
```

**Fig. 3.** Decision tree, without sentence oddity measures (0 – normal sentence, 1 – sentence containing a substitution; KGRAM – k-gram, Hyp – Hypernym)

The performance results and the boundaries were computed for smaller sets of sentences and were remarkably stable as the size of the dataset grew.

## 6  Conclusions

We have tested how word substitutions within textual communication can be detected. Our technique allows us to automatically flag suspicious messages, so that they can be further investigated, either by a more sophisticated data-mining techniques or manually. The task of detecting substitutions is becoming important since terrorists, criminals, spies and other adversarial parties may use substitution in order to avoid being flagged because of the use of certain words (e.g. 'bomb', 'explosives', 'attack', etc.). Our technique extends prior work, which was not able to detect substitutions when a word is replaced by another word with similar frequency of use. This is because our approach is grounded in the semantics of word usage rather than in the frequency ranks. We mine the necessary semantic information from World Wide Web through analyzing the frequency of use of specially constructed phrases obtained by transforming sentences from a message or communication. We have been able to demonstrate empirically that such detection is possible and, when several indicators are combined into one model, can be performed with practically useful accuracy.

Since our model is the first formulation of the task of substitution detection through semantic relationships, we were able only to investigate a simple heuristic model. We are leaving for future research the creation of a more fine-grained model (e.g. based on popular language models) and testing with a wider variety of test sets. It will be also interesting to investigate how the correlation between substitutions can be exploited to increase the accuracy and even to guess what original words were obfuscated.

# References

1. J.A. Bilmes and K. Kirchhoff. Factored language models and generalized parallel backoff. In *Proceedings of HLT/NACCL*, 2003.
2. British National Corpus (BNC), 2004. **www.natcorp.ox.ac.uk**.
3. European Parliament Temporary Committee on the ECHELON Interception System. Final report on the existence of a global system for the interception of private and commercial communications (ECHELON interception system), 2001.
4. SW. Fong, D.B. Skillicorn, and D. Roussinov. Detecting word substitution in adversarial communication. In *Workshop on Link Analysis, Counterterrorism and Security at the SIAM International Conference on Data Mining*, to appear, 2006.
5. A. R. Golding and D. Roth. A Winnow-based approach to context-sensitive spelling correction. *Machine Learning, Special issue on Machine Learning and Natural Language*, 1999.
6. R. Ferrer i Cancho and R.V. Solé. The small world of human language. *Proceedings of the Royal Society of London Series B – Biological Sciences*, pages 2261–2265, 2001.
7. H. Lee and A.Y. Ng. Spam deobfuscation using a Hidden Markov Model. In *Proceedings of the Second Conference on Email and Anti-Spam*, 2005.
8. D. Roussinov and L. Zhao. Automatic discovery of similarity relationships through web mining. *Decision Support Systems*, pages 149–166, 2003.
9. D. Roussinov, L. Zhao, and W. Fan. Mining context specific similarity relationships using the World Wide Web. In *Proceedings of the 2005 Conference on Human Language Technologies*, 2005.
10. D.B. Skillicorn. Beyond keyword filtering for message and conversation detection. In *IEEE International Conference on Intelligence and Security Informatics (ISI2005)*, pages 231–243. Springer-Verlag Lecture Notes in Computer Science LNCS 3495, May 2005.

# Finding Hidden Group Structure in a Stream of Communications*

J. Baumes[1], M. Goldberg[1], M. Hayvanovych[1], M. Magdon-Ismail[1],
W. Wallace[2], and M. Zaki[1]

[1] CS Department, RPI, Rm 207 Lally, 110 8th Street, Troy, NY 12180, USA
{baumej, goldberg, hayvam, magdon, zaki}@cs.rpi.edu
[2] DSES Department, RPI, 110 8th Street, Troy, NY 12180, USA
wallaw@rpi.edu

**Abstract.** A *hidden group* in a communication network is a group of
individuals planning an activity over a communication medium without announcing their intentions. We develop algorithms for separating
non-random planning-related communications from random background
communications in a streaming model. This work extends previous results related to the identification of hidden groups in the cyclic model.
The new statistical model and new algorithms do not assume the existence of a planning time-cycle in the stream of communications of a
hidden group. The algorithms construct larger hidden groups by building them up from smaller ones. To illustrate our algorithms, we apply
them to the Enron email corpus in order to extract the evolution of
Enron's organizational structure.

## 1 Introduction

Modern communication networks (telephone, email, Internet chat room, etc.)
facilitate rapid information exchange among millions of users around the world.
This vast communication activity provides the ideal environment for groups to
plan their activity undetected: the related communications are embedded (hidden) within the myriad of random background communications, making them
difficult to discover. When a number of individuals in a network exchange communications related to a common goal, or a common activity, they form a group;
usually, the presence of the coherent communication activity imposes a certain
structure on the communications of that set (group) of actors. A group of actors
may communicate in a structured way while not being forthright in exposing
its existence and membership. In this paper, we describe a novel statistical and
algorithmic approach to discovering such hidden groups. Our work extends previous results related to the identification of hidden groups in the cyclic model.

* This material is based upon work partially supported by the National Science Foundation under Grant No. 0324947. Any opinions, findings, and conclusions or recommendations expressed in this material are those of the author(s) and do not
necessarily reflect the views of the National Science Foundation.

S. Mehrotra et al. (Eds.): ISI 2006, LNCS 3975, pp. 201–212, 2006.
© Springer-Verlag Berlin Heidelberg 2006

The new statistical model and new algorithms do not assume the existence of a planning time-cycle in the stream of communications of a hidden group.

The tragic events of September 11, 2001 underline the need for algorithmic tools (and corresponding software implementations) which facilitate the discovery of hidden (malicious) groups during their *planning* stage, before they move to implement their plans. A generic way of discovering such groups is based on discovering *correlations* among the communications of the actors in the communication network. Although the content of the messages can be informative and natural language processing may be brought to bear in its analysis, such an analysis is generally time consuming and intractable for large datasets. The research presented here makes use of only three properties of a message: its time, the name of the sender and the name of the recipient of the message.

Our approach is based on the observation that a pattern of communications exhibited by actors in a social group pursuing a common objective is different from that of a randomly selected set of actors. Specifically, we focus on the discovery of such groups whose communications during the observation time-period exhibit statistical *correlations*. Since any group, even one which tries to hide itself, must communicate regularly, hidden groups will have communications that display statistically significant structure, as compared to a group formed at random. This is related to the social concept of homophily, which states that individuals will tend to communicate with those similar to themselves [1].

Identifying structure in networks has been studied in [2,3,4,5,6], which focuses on static non-planning hidden groups. The study of identifying planning hidden groups was initiated in [7] using Hidden Markov models. In [2,3], algorithms were established for detecting groups which are correlated in time, given certain assumptions. In particular, it was assumed that the group communicates among all members at least once over consecutive disjoint time in-

| | |
|---|---|
| 00 **A→C** Golf tomorrow? Tell everyone. | 00 **A→C** |
| 05 **C→F** Alice mentioned golf tomorrow. | 05 **C→F** |
| 06 **A→B** Hey, golf tomorrow? Spread the word | 06 **A→B** |
| 12 **A→B** Tee time: 8am; Place: Pinehurst. | 12 **A→B** |
| 13 **F→G** Hey guys, golf tomorrow . | 13 **F→G** |
| 13 **F→H** Hey guys, golf tomorrow . | 13 **F→H** |
| 15 **A→C** Tee time: 8am; Place: Pinehurst. | 15 **A→C** |
| 20 **B→D** We're playing golf tomorrow. | 20 **B→D** |
| 20 **B→E** We're playing golf tomorrow. | 20 **B→E** |
| 22 **C→F** Tee time: 8am; Place: Pinehurst. | 22 **C→F** |
| 25 **B→D** Tee time: 8am; Place: Pinehurst. | 25 **B→D** |
| 25 **B→E** Tee time 8am, Pinehurst. | 25 **B→E** |
| 31 **F→G** Tee time 8am, Pinehurst. | 31 **F→G** |
| 31 **F→H** Tee off 8am,Pinehurst. | 31 **F→H** |
| (a) | (b) |

**Fig. 1.** (a) Streaming hidden group with two waves of planning. (b) Streaming group without message content – only time, sender id and receiver id are available.

tervals of a given length – the *cycle* model. The contribution of this paper is the formulation of the problem of finding hidden groups in a streaming model (*streaming* hidden groups), together with algorithms for finding such hidden groups. In this model, hidden groups do not necessarily display a fixed time-cycle, during which all members of group members exchange messages.

An example of a streaming hidden group is illustrated in Figure 1(a) – a group planning a golf game. Given the message content, it is easy to identify two "waves" of communication. The first wave (in darker font) establishes the golf game; and, the second wave (in lighter font) finalizes the game details. Based on this data, it is not hard to identify the group and conclude that the "organizational structure" of the group is represented in Figure 2 to the right (each actor is represented by their first initial). The challenge is to deduce this same information from the communication stream *without* the message contents (Figure 1(b)). There are two main features that distinguish the stream model from the cycle model:

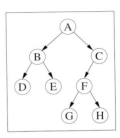

**Fig. 2.** Group structure for Figure 1

(i) communication waves may overlap, as in Figure 1(a);
(ii) waves may different durations, some considerably longer than others.

The first feature may result in bursty waves of intense communication (many overlapping waves) followed by periods of silence. Such a type of communication dynamics is hard to detect in the cycle model, since all the (overlapping) waves of communication may fall in one cycle. The second can be quantified by a propagation delay function which specifies how much time may elapse between a hidden group member receiving the message and forwarding it to the next member; sometimes the propagation delays may be large, and sometimes small. One would typically expect that such a streaming model would be appropriate for hidden groups with some organizational structure as illustrated in the tree. We present algorithms which not only discover the streaming hidden group, but also its organizational structure *without the use of message content.*

We use the notion of communication frequency in order to distinguish non-random behavior. Thus, if a group of actors communicates unusually often using the same chain of communication, i.e. the structure of their communications persists through time, then we consider this group to be statistically significant and indicative of a hidden group. We present algorithms to detect small frequent tree-like structures, and build hidden structures starting from the small ones.

*Paper Organization.* We begin in Section 2 by formally describing the problem and the data representation. We present our algorithms and statistical models for discovering streaming hidden groups in Sections 3, 4 and 5. In Section 6, we give some experimental results on the evolution of the Enron organizational structure using the Enron e-mail corpus, and conclude in Section 7 with some future directions.

## 2    Problem Statement

A communication stream is a set of tuples of the form $\langle \mathsf{senderID}, \mathsf{receiverID}, \mathsf{t}, \mathsf{msg} \rangle$, where $\mathsf{senderID}$ sends the message $\mathsf{msg}$ to receiverID at time $\mathsf{t}$. In our approach to detecting hidden groups, we do not rely on any semantic information (message content) contained in the communications. The reason is that communications on a public network are usually encrypted in some way and can be quite complex to analyze, hence the message information may be either misleading or unavailable.

A hidden group communication structure can be represented by a directed graph. Each vertex is an actor and every edge shows the direction of the communication. For example a hierarchical organization structure could be represented by a directed tree. The graph in Figure 3 to the right is an example of a communication structure, in which actor $A$ "simultaneously" sends messages to $B$ and $C$; then, after receiving the message from $A$, $B$ sends messages to $C$ and $D$; $C$ sends a message to $D$ after receiving the messages from $A$ and $B$. Every graph has two basic types of communication structures: *chains* and *siblings*. A *chain* is a path of length at least 3, and a *sibling* is a tree with a root and two or more children,

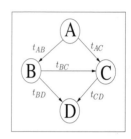

**Fig. 3.**    Hypothetical Group Structure

but no other nodes. Of particular interest are chains and sibling trees with three nodes, which we denote *triples*. For example, the chains and sibling trees of size three (triples) in the communication structure above are: $A \rightarrow B \rightarrow D$; $A \rightarrow B \rightarrow C$; $A \rightarrow C \rightarrow D$; $B \rightarrow C \rightarrow D$; $A \rightarrow B, C$; and, $B \rightarrow C, D$. We suppose that a hidden group employs a communication structure that can be represented by a directed graph as above. If the hidden group is hierarchical, the communication graph will be a tree. The task is to discover such a group and its structure based solely on the communication data.

If a communication structure appears in the data many times, then it is likely to be non-random, and hence represent a hidden group. To discover hidden groups, we will discover the communication structures that appear many times. We thus need to define what it means for a communication structure to "appear". Specifically, we consider chain and sibling triples (trees of size three). For a chain $A \rightarrow B \rightarrow C$ to appear, there must be communication $A \rightarrow B$ at time $t_{AB}$ and a communication $B \rightarrow C$ at time $t_{BC}$ such that $(t_{BC} - t_{AB}) \in [\tau_{min}, \tau_{max}]$. This intuitively represents the notion of causality, where $A \rightarrow B$ "causes" $B \rightarrow C$ within some time interval specified by $\tau_{min}, \tau_{max}$. A similar requirement holds for the sibling triple $A \rightarrow B, C$; the sibling triple appears if there exists $t_{AB}$ and $t_{AC}$ such that $(t_{AB} - t_{AC}) \in [-\delta \ \delta]$. This constraint represents the notion of $A$ sending messages "simultaneously" to $B$ and $C$ within a small time interval of each other, as specified by $\delta$. For an entire graph (such as the one above) to appear, every chain and sibling triple in the graph must appear using a single set of times. For example, in the graph example above, there must exist a set of times, $\{t_{AB}, t_{AC}, t_{BC}, t_{BD}, t_{CD}\}$, which satisfies all the six chain and sibling constraints. A graph appears multiple times if there are disjoint sets of times each of which is an appearance of the graph. A set of times *satisfies* a graph if all chain and sibling constraints are satisfied by the set of times. The number of times a graph appears is the maximum number of disjoint sets of times that can be found, where each set satisfies the graph. Causality requires that multiple occurrences of a graph should monotonically increase in time. Specifically, if $t_{AB}$ "causes" $t_{BC}$ and $t'_{AB}$ "causes" $t'_{BC}$ with $t'_{AB} > t_{AB}$, then it should be that $t'_{BC} > t_{BC}$. In general, if we have two disjoint occurrences (sets of times) $\{t_1, t_2, \ldots\}$ and $\{s_1, s_2, \ldots\}$ with $s_1 > t_1$, then it should be that $s_i > t_i$ for all $i$.

A communication structure which occurs frequently enough becomes statistically significant when its frequency of occurrence exceeds the expected frequency of such a structure from the random background communications. The goal is to find all statistically significant communication structures, which is formally stated in the following algorithmic problem statement.

**Input:** A communication data stream; $\delta$, $\tau_{min}$, $\tau_{max}$, $h$, $\kappa$.
**Output:** All communication structures of size $\geq h$, which appear at least $\kappa$ times, where the appearance is defined with respect to $\delta$, $\tau_{min}$, $\tau_{max}$.

The statistical task is to determine $h$ and $\kappa$ to ensure that all output communication structures are statistically significant. We will first consider small trees, specifically chain and sibling triples. We then develop a heuristic algorithm to build up larger hidden groups from clusters of triples. We will also obtain evolving hidden groups by using a sliding window.

## 3    Algorithms for Chain and Sibling Trees

We will start by introducing a technique to find chain and sibling triples, i.e. trees of type $A \rightarrow B \rightarrow C$ (chain) and trees of type $A \rightarrow B, C$ (sibling). To accomplish this, we will enumerate all the triples and count the number of times each triple occurs. Enumeration can be done by brute force, i.e. considering each possible triple in the stream of communications. We have developed a general algorithm for counting the number of occurrences of chains of length $\ell$, and siblings of width $k$. These algorithms proceed by posing the problem as a multi-dimensional matching problem, which in the case of tipples becomes a two-dimensional matching problem. Generally multi-dimensional matching is hard to solve, but in our case the causality constraint imposes an ordering on the matching which allows us to construct a linear time algorithm. Finally we will introduce a heuristic to build larger graphs from statistically significant triples using overlapping clustering techniques [8].

### 3.1    Computing the Frequency of a Triple

Consider the triple $A \rightarrow B \rightarrow C$ and the associated time lists $L_1 = \{t_1 \leq t_2 \leq \ldots \leq t_n\}$ and $L_2 = \{s_1 \leq s_2 \leq \cdots \leq s_m\}$, where $t_i$ are the times when $A$ sent to $B$ and $s_i$ the times when $B$ sent to $C$. An occurrence of the triple $A \rightarrow B \rightarrow C$

is a pair of times $(t_i, s_i)$ such that $(s_i - t_i) \in [\tau_{min} \; \tau_{max}]$. Thus, we would like to find the maximum number of such pairs which satisfy the causality constraint. It turns out that the causality constraint does not affect the size of the maximum matching, however it is an intuitive constraint in our context.

We now define a slightly more general maximum matching problem: for a pair $(t_i, s_i)$ let $f(t_i, s_i)$ denote the score of the pair. Let $M$ be a matching $\{(t_{i_1}, s_{i_1}), (t_{i_2}, s_{i_2}) \dots (t_{i_k}, s_{i_k})\}$ of size $k$. We define the score of $M$ to be

$$Score(M) = \sum_{j=1}^{k} f(t_{i_j}, s_{i_j}).$$

The maximum matching problem is to find a matching with a maximum score. The function $f(t, s)$ captures how likely a message from $B \to C$ at time $s$ was "caused" by a message from $A \to B$ at time $t$. In our case we are using a hard threshold function

$$f(t, s) = f(t - s) = \begin{cases} 1 \text{ if } t - s \in [\tau_{min}, \tau_{max}], \\ 0 \text{ otherwise.} \end{cases}$$

The matching problem for sibling triples is identical with the choice

$$f(t, s) = f(t - s) = \begin{cases} 1 \text{ if } t - s \in [-\delta, \delta], \\ 0 \text{ otherwise.} \end{cases}$$

We can generalize to chains of arbitrary length and siblings of arbitrary width as follows. Consider time lists $L_1, L_2, \dots, L_{\ell-1}$ corresponding to the chain $A_1 \to A_2 \cdots \to A_\ell$, where $L_i$ contains the sorted times of communications $A_i \to A_{i+1}$. An occurrence of this chain is now an $\ell-1$ dimensional matching $\{t_1, t_2, \dots, t_{\ell-1}\}$ satisfying the constraint $(t_{i+1} - t_i) \in [\tau_{min} \; \tau_{max}] \; \forall \; i = 1, \cdots, \ell - 2$.

The sibling of width $k$ breaks down into two cases - ordered siblings which obey constraints similar to the chain constraints, and unordered siblings. Consider the sibling tree $A_0 \to A_1, A_2, \cdots A_k$ with corresponding time lists $L_1, L_2, \dots, L_k$, where $L_i$ contains the times of communications $A_0 \to A_i$. Once again, an occurrence is a matching $\{t_1, t_2, \dots, t_k\}$. In the ordered case the constraints are $(t_{i+1} - t_i) \in [-\delta \; \delta]$. This represents $A_0$ sending communications "simultaneously" to its recipients in the order $A_1, \dots, A_k$. The unordered sibling tree obeys the stricter constraint $(t_i - t_j) \in [-(k-1)\delta, (k-1)\delta], \; \forall \; i, j$ pairs, $i \neq j$. This stricter constraint represents $A_0$ sending communications to its recipients "simultaneously" without any particular order.

Both problems can be solved with a greedy algorithm. The detailed algorithms for arbitrary chains and siblings are given in Figure 4(a). Here we sketch the algorithm for triples. Given two time lists $L_1 = \{t_1, t_2, \dots, t_n\}$ and $L_2 = \{s_1, s_2, \dots, s_m\}$ the idea is to find first valid match $(t_{i_1}, s_{i_1})$, which is the first pair of times that obey the constraint $(s_{i_1} - t_{i_1}) \in [\tau_{min} \; \tau_{max}]$. Then, recursively find the maximum matching on the remaining sub lists $L'_1 = \{t_{i_1+1}, \dots, t_n\}$ and $L'_2 = \{s_{i_1+1}, \dots, s_m\}$.

The case of general chains and ordered sibling trees is similar. The first valid match is defined similarly. Every pair of entries $t_{L_i} \in L_i$ and $t_{L_{i+1}} \in L_{i+1}$ in the maximum matching must obey the constraint $(t_{L_{i+1}} - t_{L_i}) \in [\tau_{min} \ \tau_{max}]$. To find the first valid match, we begin with the match consisting of the first time in all lists. Denote these times $t_{L_1}, t_{L_2}, \ldots, t_{L_\ell}$. If this match is valid (all consecutive pairs satisfy the constraint) then we are done. Otherwise consider the first consecutive pair to violate this constraint. Suppose it is $(t_{L_i}, t_{L_{i+1}})$; so either $(t_{L_{i+1}} - t_{L_i}) > \tau_{max}$ or $(t_{L_{i+1}} - t_{L_i}) < \tau_{min}$. If $(t_{L_{i+1}} - t_{L_i}) > \tau_{max}$ $(t_{L_i}$ is too small), we advance $t_{L_i}$ to the next entry in the time list $L_i$; otherwise $(t_{L_{i+1}} - t_{L_i}) < \tau_{min}$ $(t_{L_{i+1}}$ is too small) and we advance $t_{L_{i+1}}$ to the next entry in the time list $L_{i+1}$. This entire process is repeated until a valid first match is found. An efficient implementation of this algorithm is given in Figure 4. The algorithm for unordered siblings follows a similar logic.

In the algorithms below, we initialize $i = 0; j = 1$ ($i, j$ are time list indices), and $P_1, \ldots, P_n = 0$ ($P_k$ is an index within $L_k$ ). Let $t_i = L_i[P_i]$ and $t_j = L_j[P_j]$.

| | |
|---|---|
| 1: **Algorithm Chain** | 1: **Algorithm Sibling** |
| 2: **while** $P_k \leq \|L_k\| - 1, \forall k$ **do** | 2: **while** $P_k \leq \|L_k\| - 1, \forall k$ **do** |
| 3:     **if** $(t_j - t_i) < \tau_{min}$ **then** | 3:     **if** $(t_j - t_i) < -(k-1)\delta$ **then** |
| 4:       $P_j \leftarrow P_j + 1$ | 4:       $P_j \leftarrow P_j + 1$ |
| 5:     **else if** $(t_j - t_i) \in [\tau_{min}, \tau_{max}]$ **then** | 5:     **else if** $(t_j - t_i) > (k-1)\delta, \forall i < j$ **then** |
| 6:       **if** $j = n$ **then** | 6:       $P_i \leftarrow P_i + 1; j \leftarrow i + 1$ |
| 7:         $(P_1, \ldots, P_n)$ is the next match | 7:     **else** |
| 8:         $P_k \leftarrow P_k + 1, \forall k; i \leftarrow 0; j \leftarrow 1$ | 8:       **if** $j = n$ **then** |
| 9:       **else** | 9:         $(P_1, \ldots, P_n)$ is the next match |
| 10:         $i \leftarrow j; j \leftarrow j + 1$ | 10:         $P_k \leftarrow P_k + 1, \forall k; i \leftarrow 0; j \leftarrow 1$ |
| 11:     **else** | 11:       **else** |
| 12:       $P_i \leftarrow P_i + 1; j \leftarrow i; i \leftarrow i - 1$ | 12:         $j \leftarrow j + 1$ |
| (a) | (b) |

**Fig. 4.** (a) maximum matching algorithm for chains and ordered siblings; (b) maximum matching algorithm for unordered siblings

The next theorem gives the correctness of the algorithms.

**Theorem 1.** *Algorithm-Chain and Algorithm-Sibling find maximum matchings.*

*Proof.* By induction. Given a set of time lists $L = (L_1, L_2, \ldots, L_n)$ our algorithm produces a matching $M = (m_1, m_2, \ldots, m_k)$, where each matching $m_i$ is a sequence of $n$ times from each of the $n$ time lists $m_i = (t_1^i, t_2^i, \ldots, t_n^i)$. Let $M^* = (m_1^*, m_2^*, \ldots, m_{k^*}^*)$ be a maximum matching of size $k^*$. We prove that $k = k^*$ by induction on $k^*$. We will need the next two lemmas which follow by construction in the Algorithms (we postpone the detailed proofs).

**Lemma 1.** *If there is a valid matching our algorithm will find one.*

**Lemma 2.** *Algorithm-Chain and Algorithm-Sibling find an earliest valid matching: let the first valid matching found by either algorithm be $m_1 = (t_1, t_2, \ldots, t_n)$. Then for any other valid matching $m' = (s_1, s_2, \ldots, s_n)$ $t_i \leq s_i \ \forall \ i = 1, \cdots, n$.*

If $k^* = 0$, then $k = 0$ as well. If $k^* = 1$, then there exists a valid matching and by Lemma 1 our algorithm will find it.

Suppose that for all sets of time lists for which $k^* = M$, the algorithm finds matchings of size $k^*$. Now consider a set of time lists $L = (L_1, L_2, \ldots, L_n)$ for which an optimal algorithm produces a maximum matching of size $k^* = M + 1$ and consider the first matching in this list (remember that by the causality constraint, the matchings can be ordered). Our algorithm constructs the earliest matching and then recursively processes the remaining lists. By Lemma 2, our first matching is not later than optimal's first matching, so the partial lists remaining after our first matching contain the partial lists after optimal's first matching. This means that the optimal matching for our partial lists must be $M$. By the induction hypothesis our algorithm finds a matching of size $M$ on these partial lists for a total matching of size $M + 1$.

For a given set of time lists $L = (L_1, L_2, \ldots, L_n)$ as input, where each $L_i$ has a respective size $d_i$, define the total size of the data as $\|D\| = \sum_{i=1}^{n} d_i$.

**Theorem 2.** *Algorithm-Chain runs in $O(\|D\|)$ time.*

*Proof.* When looking for a matching, we compare a pair of elements from two time lists. For each comparison, we increment at least once in a time list if the comparison failed. After $n - 1$ successful comparisons, we increment in every time list by one. Thus there can be at most $O(\|D\|)$ failed comparisons and $O(\|D\|)$ successful comparisons, since the are $\|D\|$ list advances in total.

**Theorem 3.** *Algorithm-Sibling runs in $O(n \cdot \|D\|)$ time.*

*Proof.* As in Algorithm-Chain a failed comparison leads to at least one increment, but now $\binom{n}{2}$ successful comparisons are needed before incrementing in every time list. Therefore, in the worst case $O(n^2)$ comparisons lead to $O(n)$ list advances. Since there are at most $\|D\|$ list advances, the maximum number of comparisons is $O(n \cdot \|D\|)$

### 3.2    Finding all Triples

Assume the data are stored in a vector. Each component in the vector corresponds to a sender id and stores a balanced search tree of receiver lists (indexed by a receiver id). And $S$ is the whole set of the distinct senders. The algorithm for finding chain triples considers sender id $s$ and its list of receivers $\{r_1, r_2, \cdots, r_d\}$. Then for each such receiver $r_i$ that is also a sender, let $\{\rho_1, \rho_2, \cdots, \rho_f\}$ be the receivers to which $r_i$ sent messages. All chains begining with $s$ are of the form $s \rightarrow r_i \rightarrow \rho_j$. This way we can more efficiently enumerate the triples (since we ignore triples which do not occur). For each sender $s$ we count the frequency of each triple $s \rightarrow r_i \rightarrow \rho_j$. Assuming all time lists of approximately the same size, the total runtime is $O(d_{max}\|D\|)$, where $d_{max}$ is the size of the longest possible list of receivers and $\|D\|$ is the total dataset size.

## 4    Statistically Significant Triples

In order to determine the minimum frequency $\kappa$ that makes a triple statistically significant, we build a statistical model that mimics certain features of the data. In particular we model the inter-arrival time distribution and receiver id probability conditioned on sender id. Using this model, we generate synthetic data and find all randomly occurring triples to determine the threshold frequency $\kappa$.

### 4.1    A Model for the Data

We estimate directly from the data the message inter-arrival time distribution $f(\tau)$, the conditional probability distribution $P(r|s)$, and the marginal distribution $P(s)$ using simple histograms (one for $f(\tau)$, $S$ for $P(r|s)$ and $S$ for $P(s)$, i.e. one conditional and marginal distribution histogram for each sender, where $S$ is the number of senders). One may also model additional features (eg. $P(s|r)$), to obtain more accurate models. One should however bear in mind that the more accurate the model, the closer the random data is to the actual data, hence the less useful the statistical analysis will be - it will simply reproduce the data.

*Generating a Synthetic Data Set.* Suppose one wishes to generate $N$ messages using $f(\tau)$, $P(r|s)$ and $P(s)$. First we generate $N$ inter-arrival times independently, which specifies the times of the communications. We now must assign sender-receiver pairs to each communication. The senders are selected independently from $P(s)$. We then generate each receiver independently, but conditioned on the sender of that communication, according to $P(r|s)$.

### 4.2    Determining Significance Threshold

To determine the significance threshold $\kappa$, we generate $M$ (as large as possible) synthetic data sets and determine the triples together with their frequencies of occurrence in each synthetic data set. The threshold $\kappa$ may be selected as the average plus two standard deviations, or (more conservatively) as the maximum frequency of occurrence of a triple.

## 5    Constructing Larger Graphs Using Heuristics

Now we discuss a heuristic method for building larger communication structures, using only statistically significant triples. We will start by introducing the notion of an overlap factor. We will then discuss how the overlap factor is used to build a larger communication graph by finding clusters, and construct the larger communication structures from these clusters.

### 5.1    Overlap Between Triples

Given two statistically significant triples $(A, B, C)$ and $(D, E, F)$ of chain or sibling type, let their maximum matchings occur respectively at the times $M_1 = \{(t_1, s_1), \ldots, (t_k, s_k)\}$ and $M_2 = \{(t'_1, s'_1), \ldots, (t'_p, s'_p)\}$.

We define an overlap weighting function $W(M_1, M_2)$ to capture the degree of coincidence between the matchings $M_1$ and $M_2$. The simplest such overlap weighting function is the extent to which the two time intervals of communication overlap. Specifically, $W(M_1, M_2)$ is the percentage overlap between the two intervals $[t_1, s_k]$ and $[t_1', s_p']$, if they overlap, and otherwise zero:

$$W(M_1, M_2) = \max \left\{ \frac{\min(s_k, s_p') - \max(t_1, t_1')}{\max(s_k, s_p') - \min(t_1, t_1')}, 0 \right\}$$

A large *overlap factor* suggests that both triples are part of the same hidden group. More sophisticated overlap factors could take into account intermittent communication but for our present purpose, we will use this simplest version.

### 5.2   The Weighted Overlap Graph and Clustering

We construct a weighted graph by taking all significant triples to be the vertices in the graph. Let $M_i$ be the maximum matching corresponding to vertex (triple) $v_i$. Then, we define the weight of the edge $e_{ij}$ to be $\omega(e_{ij}) = W(M_i, M_j)$. Thus, we have an undirected complete graph (some weights may be 0). By thresholding the weights, one could obtain a sparse graph. Dense subgraphs in this graph correspond to triples that were all active at about the same time, and are a candidate hidden group. Thus, we want to cluster the graph into dense possibly overlapping subgraphs. Given the triples in a cluster we can build a directed graph which will represent a communication structure within that cluster. The graph built will be constructed to be consistent with all the triples in the cluster, and will usually be a single connected component. If a cluster contains multiple connected components, this may imply the existence of some hidden structure connecting them. Here is an outline of the entire algorithm:

1:  Obtain the significant triples.
2:  Construct a weighted graph by computing overlap factors between every pair of significant triples.
3:  Perform clustering on the weighted graph.
4:  Use each cluster to determine a candidate hidden group structure.

The analysis of each step of this algorithm has already been presented except for the clustering. For the clustering, since we allow overlapping clusters, we use the algorithms presented in [8], [9].

## 6   Experimental Results

### 6.1   Finding Triples in Enron Data

For our experiments we considered the Enron email corpus. We took $\tau_{min}$ to be 1 hour and $\tau_{max}$ to be 1 day. Figure 5 compares the number of triples occurring in the data to the number that occur randomly in the synthetically generated data using the model derived from the Enron data. As can be observed, the number

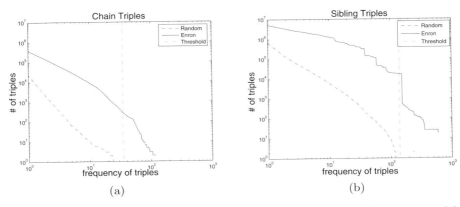

**Fig. 5.** Abundance of triples occurring as a function of frequency of occurrence. (a) chain triples; (b) sibling triples.

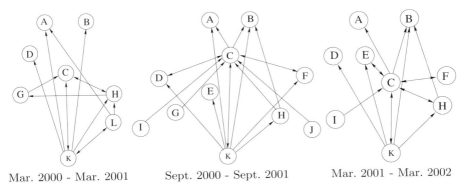

**Fig. 6.** Evolution of part of the Enron organizational structure from 2000 - 2002

of triples in the data by far exceeds the random triples. After some frequency threshold, no random triples of higher frequency appear - i.e., all the triples appearing in the data at this frequency are significant. We used $M = 1000$ data sets to determine the random triple curve in Figure 5. For chains the significance threshold frequency was $\kappa_{chain} = 35$ and for siblings it was $\kappa_{sibling} = 160$. We used a sliding window of one year to obtain evolving hidden groups. On each window we obtained the significant chains (frequency $> \kappa_{chain}$) and significant siblings (frequency $> \kappa_{sibling}$) and the clusters in the corresponding weighted overlap graph. We use the clusters to build the communication structures and show the evolution of one of the hidden groups in Figure 6.

## 7   Conclusions

In this paper we have given algorithms for finding significant chain and sibling triples from streaming communication data. Using a heuristic to build from triples, we find hidden groups of larger sizes. Using a moving window we can track the evolution of the organizational structure as well as hidden group membership.

Our algorithms do not use communication content and do not differentiate between the natures of the hidden groups discovered, i.e. some of the hidden groups may be expected and some may not. Further work, perhaps using human analysts may be needed to identify the trully suspicious groups. This is the content of future work. Our statistical algorithms serve to narrow down the set of possible hidden groups that need to be analysed further.

Future work includes exact efficient algorithms to obtain the frequency of general trees and to enumerate all statistically significant general trees of a specified size. In addition, other scoring functions for the matching and overlap weighting functions for the clustering may yield interesting results.

# References

1. Monge, P., Contractor, N.: Theories of Communication Networks. Oxford University Press (2002)
2. Baumes, J., Goldberg, M., Magdon-Ismail, M., Wallace, W.: Discovering hidden groups in communication networks. Intelligence and Security Informatics ISI) (2004) 378–389
3. Baumes, J., Goldberg, M., Magdon-Ismail, M., Wallace, W.: On hidden groups in communication networks. Technical report, TR 05-15, CS Dept., RPI (2005)
4. Capocci, A., Servedio, V.D.P., Caldarelli, G., Colaiori, F.: Detecting communities in large networks. Workshop on Algorithms and Models for the Web-Graph (WAW) (2004) 181–188
5. Newman, M.E.J.: The structure and function of complex networks. SIAM Review **45** (2003) 167–256
6. Girvan, M., Newman, M.E.J.: Community structure in social and biological networks. Proc. Natl. Acad. Sci. **99** (2002) 7821–7826
7. Magdon-Ismail, M., Goldberg, M., Wallace, W., Siebecker, D.: Locating hidden groups in communication networks using Hidden Markov Models. In: International Conference on Intelligence and Security Informatics (ISI 2003), Tucson, AZ (2003)
8. Baumes, J., Goldberg, M., Krishnamoorthy, M., Magdon-Ismail, M., Preston, N.: Finding comminities by clustering a graph into overlapping subgraphs. Proceedings of IADIS Applied Computing (2005) 97–104
9. Baumes, J., Goldberg, M., Magdon-Ismail, M.: Efficient identification of overlapping communities. Intelligence and Security Informatics (ISI) (2005) 27–36

# Collective Sampling and Analysis of High Order Tensors for Chatroom Communications

Evrim Acar, Seyit A. Çamtepe, and Bülent Yener [*]

Department of Computer Science, Rensselaer Polytechnic Institute
110 8$^{th}$ Street, Troy, NY 12180
{acare, camtes, yener}@cs.rpi.edu

**Abstract.** This work investigates the accuracy and efficiency tradeoffs between centralized and collective (distributed) algorithms for (i) sampling, and (ii) n-way data analysis techniques in multidimensional stream data, such as Internet chatroom communications. Its contributions are threefold. First, we use the Kolmogorov-Smirnov goodness-of-fit test to show that statistical differences between real data obtained by collective sampling in time dimension from multiple servers and that of obtained from a single server are insignificant. Second, we show using the real data that collective data analysis of 3-way data arrays *(users x keywords x time)* known as *high order tensors* is more efficient than centralized algorithms with respect to both space and computational cost. Furthermore, we show that this gain is obtained without loss of accuracy. Third, we examine the sensitivity of collective constructions and analysis of high order data tensors to the choice of server selection and sampling window size. We construct 4-way tensors *(users x keywords x time x servers)* and analyze them to show the impact of server and window size selections on the results.

## 1 Introduction and Background

Chatroom communications are attractive sources of information since they are in public domain and *real identities* are decoupled from the *virtual identities* (i.e., nicknames). However, chatroom communications generate real-time stream data that may have nonlinear structure [1] which is difficult to extract without semantic interpretation of the messages. Thus, data analysis techniques, such as Singular Value Decomposition (SVD) [2] that rely on linear relationships in a matrix representation of data, may fail to capture important structure information [1]. In particular, we showed that constructing multiway data arrays known as *high order tensors* such as data cubes with (users x keywords x time) modes can discover the subgroups that cannot be detected by SVD [1].

In this work, we extend centralized data collection and analysis of multiway data arrays to collective sampling and analysis. In particular, we consider how to

[*] This research is supported in part by NSF ACT Award # 0442154 and NSF ITR Award # 0324947.

S. Mehrotra et al. (Eds.): ISI 2006, LNCS 3975, pp. 213–224, 2006.

build and analyze three-way and four-way data arrays from chatroom communications collected by sampling the data from multiple servers in time dimension. We discuss and compare collective sampling and analysis approach to a centralized one. Our motivations are twofold. First, a distributed (collective) approach would be more suitable to real-time data streams. Furthermore, it can eliminate the drawbacks of a centralized approach including being a single point of failure and becoming a performance bottleneck. Second, collective n-way data analysis may reduce the time and space complexity of a centralized one. In this work, we verify by using the real data that collective n-way data analysis provides significant saving with respect to space and computational cost.

## 1.1   Our Contributions

In this paper we report following contributions:

i. We present a simple distributed sampling approach, and analyze the statistical properties of data obtained by this approach. Sampling is done in time domain. Statistical comparison, based on Kolmogorov-Smirnov goodness-of-fit test, between data collected from multiple servers and data collected from a single server is provided. Thus we report that collective sampling method can produce chatroom logs which are statistically good fit to centralized ones.

ii. We construct 3-way tensors with modes of (users x keywords x time) at each server, and employ Tucker3 model to analyze them. We collect summaries of data generated by Tucker3 analysis at different servers and analyze them collectively using SVD at a central location.

iii. We compare the performance of collective tensor analysis approach with central tensor analysis in terms of space complexity, ease of determining model parameters and computation cost. We emphasize that same user clusters are identified by using both collective and central analysis of chatroom tensors.

iv. We rearrange 3-way tensors from multiple servers into a 4-way tensor with modes of (users x keywords x time x servers) to inspect the sensitivity of Tucker3 analysis with respect to server selection.

**Organization of the paper:** This paper is organized as follows. Section 2 discusses data collection and the statistical comparisons of data obtained from a single server with data constructed from multiple servers. Section 3 explains the methodology for collective 3-way data analysis. In this section we also provide a cost comparison between centralized analysis and collective one with respect to space and computations cost. In Section 4 we present a sensitivity study for the collective data analysis. Finally, we conclude in Section 5.

## 2   Collective Sampling of Chatroom Data

In this work, we collected *philosophy* chatroom data from eight Undernet IRC servers located in USA, Canada, Netherland, Austria, and Croatia. We used eight

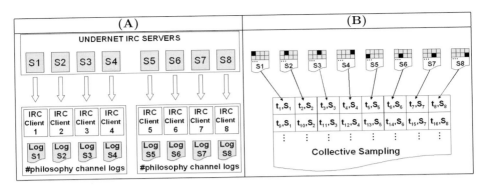

**Fig. 1.** (A) Centralized collection of *philosophy* chatroom data from eight *Undernet* IRC servers ($S_1$, $S_2$, ..., $S_8$) which are located in USA, Canada, Netherland, Austria, and Croatia. Eight copies of IRC clients running on two computers connected to servers and generated individual log files for 17 days (Jan 4th - 20th, 2006). (B) Collective sampling of *philosophy* chatroom data from eight *Undernet* IRC servers. Time is divided into time windows (150, 180, 210, 240, 270 and 300 seconds), and at each time window chatroom data coming from a specific server are accepted; at time window $T_i$, chatroom data coming from server $S_j$ where $j = ((i - 1) \ mod \ 8) + 1$ are accepted.

copies of IRC clients running on two computers as described in Figure 1-A. There are several challenges for collecting data from multiple servers. First of all, chatroom operators don't like silent listeners. Therefore, they frequently *disconnect* such users. They can *ban* IP addresses of such users, even sometimes whole IP domain. Use of public proxy servers or any other anonymity networks may sometimes be useless because of two reasons: (i) most of the servers permit only three or four connections from each IP address, (ii) a proxy or anonymity server may get banned because of the offensive acts of another IRC client sharing the same proxy. It is also possible that one or more servers are disconnected from the remaining IRC servers in which case views of the same chatroom will be completely different in terms of users and their messages. Due to these reasons, data collected from each server are different then the others. Table 1 lists number of messages collected from each server for 17 days (Jan 4th - 20th, 2006). We collected 23530 messages from the server $S_7$ while we collected 59320 messages from the server $S_4$. In a centralized approach, where chatroom data are collected only from server $S_7$, it would not be possible to obtain a good view of chatroom data. Instead of centralized data collection where an IRC client connects one IRC server, we use collective sampling technique where chatroom data are collected from multiple IRC servers.

In Figure 1-B, collective sampling technique is illustrated. In this work, we use several different time window values to analyze effectiveness of collective sampling. We first use centralized data collection technique to collect chatroom logs from eight servers for 17 days as illustrated in Figure 1-A. We simulate collective sampling on these chatroom logs to obtain collective chatroom data for different time windows (150, 180, 210, 240, 270 and 300 seconds). Number of messages for both centralized and collective chatroom data are given in Table 1. In the next section, we statistically compare centralized chatroom data with collective ones.

## 2.1   Statistical Comparison of Collective vs. Centralized Data Collection

We first try to find suitable upper and lower bounds on time windows for collective sampling of chatroom data. Interarrival time distribution, as given in Table 1, states that 99% of the interarrival times are less than 150 seconds. When chatroom data are divided into time windows larger than 150 seconds, we expect more than one message in each time window with high probability. For the upper bound of 300 seconds, we consider the gaps in the centralized chatroom data due to connection problems. When we use collective sampling, too big time windows may cause such gaps to be transferred to collective chatroom data. Therefore we use time windows of 150, 180, 210, 240, 270 and 300 seconds. As shown in Table 1, collective data provide similar percentages as centralized data for these time windows.

Table 2 provides interarrival time and message size (in word count) statistics for centralized and collective data. Mean, median, standard deviation, skewness and kurtosis statistics for centralized and collective data are provided. Our first observation is that in both data sets, mean and standard deviation values are very close; this highlights distributions such as exponential where mean and standard deviation are the same. Positive skewness values for both data sets indicate a distribution with an asymmetric tail extending towards more positive values. Positive kurtosis values indicate a distribution with a peak. As the kurtosis statistic gets larger with a positive value, it indicates the possibility of a tall distribution. These statistics support findings in [1] that interarrival and message size fit to exponential distributions. Table 3 provides results of statistical comparison between collective and centralized data based on Kolmogorov-Smirnov goodness-of-fit test (kstest). Centralized data are compared to collective data in terms of interarrival time and message size distributions.

**Table 1.** Number of messages and percentage of interarrival times smaller than 150, 180, 240, and 300 seconds for centralized and collective data. Analysis made over 17 days of data (Jan 4th - 20th, 2006).

| Centralized Chatroom Data | | | | | | Collective Chatroom Data | | | | | |
|---|---|---|---|---|---|---|---|---|---|---|---|
| Server | # Mess. | < 150 | < 180 | < 240 | < 300 | Time Win. | # Mess. | < 150 | < 180 | < 240 | < 300 |
| S1 | 49179 | 0.995 | 0.996 | 0.997 | 0.998 | 150 sec. | 45497 | 0.965 | 0.976 | 0.983 | 0.985 |
| S2 | 48626 | 0.994 | 0.995 | 0.997 | 0.997 | 180 sec. | 45340 | 0.970 | 0.971 | 0.985 | 0.987 |
| S3 | 41862 | 0.994 | 0.995 | 0.997 | 0.997 | 210 sec. | 45057 | 0.973 | 0.974 | 0.982 | 0.987 |
| S4 | 59320 | 0.994 | 0.996 | 0.997 | 0.998 | 240 sec. | 44982 | 0.976 | 0.977 | 0.978 | 0.987 |
| S5 | 46679 | 0.994 | 0.995 | 0.996 | 0.997 | 270 sec. | 45233 | 0.979 | 0.980 | 0.981 | 0.987 |
| S6 | 42728 | 0.994 | 0.995 | 0.996 | 0.997 | 300 sec. | 45076 | 0.981 | 0.981 | 0.983 | 0.983 |
| S7 | 23530 | 0.995 | 0.996 | 0.997 | 0.998 | | | | | | |
| S8 | 49630 | 0.995 | 0.996 | 0.997 | 0.998 | | | | | | |

**Table 2.** Interarrival time and message size (in word count) statistics (mean, median, standard deviation, skewness and kurtosis) for centralized and collective data. Analysis made over 17 days of data (Jan 4th - 20th, 2006). Only the messages in time interval 17 : 00 and 19 : 00 of each day is considered for the analysis because these are the times when eight Undernet IRC servers have minimum connectivity problem throughout 17 days of data.

|  | Centralized Chatroom Data | | | | | Collective Chatroom Data | | | | |
|---|---|---|---|---|---|---|---|---|---|---|
|  | Server | Mean | Med | Std | Skew | Kurt | Time Win. | Mean | Med | Std | Skew | Kurt |
| Inter-<br>arrival<br>Time | S1 | 15 | 10 | 17 | 3 | 13 | 150 sec. | 17 | 11 | 21 | 3 | 17 |
| | S2 | 16 | 11 | 19 | 2 | 11 | 180 sec. | 16 | 11 | 19 | 3 | 14 |
| | S3 | 18 | 12 | 20 | 2 | 11 | 210 sec. | 17 | 11 | 19 | 2 | 11 |
| | S4 | 16 | 11 | 18 | 2 | 11 | 240 sec. | 16 | 11 | 18 | 2 | 12 |
| | S5 | 17 | 12 | 20 | 2 | 9 | 270 sec. | 17 | 11 | 19 | 2 | 11 |
| | S6 | 20 | 13 | 22 | 2 | 8 | 300 sec. | 17 | 11 | 19 | 3 | 13 |
| | S7 | 18 | 12 | 20 | 3 | 13 | | | | | | |
| | S8 | 17 | 11 | 19 | 2 | 12 | | | | | | |
| Message<br>Size<br>in word<br>counts | S1 | 11 | 9 | 10 | 2 | 6 | 150 sec. | 11 | 8 | 10 | 2 | 5 |
| | S2 | 11 | 9 | 10 | 2 | 5 | 180 sec. | 11 | 8 | 10 | 2 | 6 |
| | S3 | 11 | 8 | 10 | 1 | 5 | 210 sec. | 11 | 8 | 9 | 1 | 5 |
| | S4 | 11 | 8 | 10 | 1 | 5 | 240 sec. | 11 | 8 | 10 | 1 | 5 |
| | S5 | 10 | 8 | 9 | 1 | 5 | 270 sec. | 11 | 8 | 10 | 1 | 5 |
| | S6 | 11 | 8 | 10 | 2 | 5 | 300 sec. | 11 | 8 | 10 | 1 | 5 |
| | S7 | 10 | 8 | 10 | 2 | 7 | | | | | | |
| | S8 | 11 | 8 | 10 | 2 | 6 | | | | | | |

## 2.2 Collective Construction of Chatroom Tensors

3-way (users × keywords × time) and 4-way (users × keywords × time × servers) tensors of Figure 3 are generated from centralized and collective data for 2-hour interval from 17 : 00 to 19 : 00 on Jan 07, 2006. For tensor generation, first step is to generate list of keywords and users active in 2-hour time interval. We used a dictionary of 5000 most frequent words to eliminate frequently used words (i.e. the, they, etc.). Next, simple forms of the irregular verbs and verbs with -ed, -ing, -s are found by using online *webster* dictionary. *Webster* is also used to fix simple typos. Once the list of keywords is obtained, a user list is generated. Finally, 2-hour data are divided into time window intervals. Each time window corresponds to a time slot in *time* dimension of (user × keywords × time) tensor. Entry *(i,j,k)* of the tensor indicates the number of times keyword $j$ is used in time slot $k$ by user $i$. Once 3-way tensors for centralized data (chatroom logs from eight IRC servers) and collective data are generated, 4-way tensor is obtained by the join of these nine tensors.

Collective chatroom data are obtained by receiving data from server $S_j$ in time window $T_i$ if $j = ((i-1) \bmod 8) + 1$. When 3-way tensor is generated from the collective data, values for time slot $T_i$ in the tensor corresponds to messages coming from the server $S_j$. We used the same time window value for collective sampling chatroom data and tensor generation. Matrix slice for collective data

**Table 3.** Centralized data are compared to collective data with time windows 150, 180, 210, 240, 270 and 300 seconds. Table lists resulting P values of Kolmogorov-Smirnov Goodness-of-fit tests (kstest) for interarrival time and message size (in word count). P values: (i) $> 0.05$ mean difference between two data sets is statistically insignificant, (ii) 0.01 to 0.05 mean difference is significant, (iii) 0.001 to 0.01 mean difference is very significant, and (iv) $< 0.001$ mean difference is extremely significant. P values should be $> 0.05$ to be able to conclude that there is no sufficient evidence to reject the hypothesis that two data sets are coming from the same distribution. For interarrival time, P values $> 0.05$ for the servers $S_1$, $S_2$, $S_4$ and $S_8$ which have highest message counts as given in Table 1. There is no sufficient evidence to reject that interarrival time distributions of these pairs of data sets are the same. For message size, all P values are $> 0.05$, meaning that, difference between two data sets is statistically insignificant and there is no sufficient evidence to reject that message size distributions of these pairs of data sets are the same.

| | Interarrival Time | | | | | | | Message Size (in word counts) | | | | | |
|------|--------|--------|--------|--------|--------|--------|------|--------|--------|--------|--------|--------|--------|
| | 150 s. | 180 s. | 210 s. | 240 s. | 270 s. | 300 s. | | 150 s. | 180 s. | 210 s. | 240 s. | 270 s. | 300 s. |
| S1 | 0.12 | 0.4 | 0.09 | 0.23 | 0.09 | 0.05 | S1 | 0.9 | 0.94 | 0.88 | 1 | 0.96 | 0.99 |
| S2 | 0.99 | 0.96 | 1 | 0.99 | 0.99 | 0.7 | S2 | 0.79 | 0.67 | 0.56 | 0.96 | 0.73 | 0.65 |
| S3 | 0.17 | 0.03 | 0.13 | 0.04 | 0.22 | 0.18 | S3 | 0.99 | 1 | 0.91 | 1 | 0.99 | 0.99 |
| S4 | 0.8 | 1 | 0.9 | 0.99 | 0.92 | 0.49 | S4 | 1 | 1 | 1 | 0.99 | 1 | 1 |
| S5 | 0.29 | 0.03 | 0.25 | 0.09 | 0.34 | 0.33 | S5 | 0.97 | 0.96 | 0.99 | 0.71 | 0.96 | 0.97 |
| S6 | 0.01 | 2e-4 | 0.01 | 6e-4 | 0.02 | 0.04 | S6 | 0.99 | 0.99 | 0.99 | 0.98 | 0.99 | 0.99 |
| S7 | 0.1 | 0.01 | 0.09 | 0.03 | 0.1 | 0.12 | S7 | 0.63 | 0.65 | 0.71 | 0.32 | 0.46 | 0.75 |
| S8 | 0.90 | 0.23 | 0.89 | 0.44 | 0.82 | 0.97 | S8 | 0.92 | 0.97 | 0.99 | 0.71 | 0.91 | 0.95 |

tensor for time slot $T_i$ will be equivalent to matrix slice for centralized data tensor of server $S_j$ for time slot $T_i$. Thus, the server $S_j$ may send its matrix slice for time slot $T_i$ instead of messages, and collective chatroom data tensor can be collectively constructed.

# 3     Collective 3-Way Analysis of Chatroom Data

## 3.1     Methodology

**Tucker Model/ HOSVD:** We employ one of the most common multiway analysis models, i.e. Tucker [9], in chatroom data analysis. For a 3-way tensor $T$ of size I x J x K, Tucker3 model decomposes the tensor in the following form:

$$T_{ijk} = \sum_{r_1=1}^{R_1} \sum_{r_2=1}^{R_2} \sum_{r_3=1}^{R_3} G_{r_1 r_2 r_3} \mathbf{A}_{ir_1} \mathbf{B}_{jr_2} \mathbf{C}_{kr_3} + E_{ijk}$$

where $\mathbf{A} \in R^{I x R_1}$, $\mathbf{B} \in R^{J x R_2}$, $\mathbf{C} \in R^{K x R_3}$ are component matrices for first, second and third mode, respectively, $G \in R^{R_1 x R_2 x R_3}$ is the core tensor and $E \in R^{I x J x K}$ represents the error term. Tucker model is not limited to 3-way arrays and can be generalized to high-order datasets. Different constraints such as non-negativity, unimodality or orthogonality can also be enforced on the component matrices. We constrain component matrices to be orthogonal. Tucker3 model with orthogonality constraints is rather referred as High-Order Singular Value Decomposition (HOSVD) or multilinear SVD [6].

**Collective Tensor Analysis:** Collective Tensor Analysis approach analyzes multiple tensors simultaneously and then transfers summaries of data from each tensor to a central location. Those summaries are combined together to capture the structure in the mode, which we want to explore. In the context of chatroom communications, collective method assumes that data are sampled by different servers and arranged as a tensor at each sampling site. These tensors are locally analyzed at each sampling site by fitting a multiway model, i.e. Tucker3. Summaries of data representing the user space are collected at a central location. Matrix formed by gathering user space summaries from each server is then analyzed using SVD to capture the structure in the whole user space.

Let $T_i$ be an n-way tensor constructed at the $i^{th}$ server by rearranging sampled data as a tensor. Each $T_i$, for $i = 1, 2, ...s$, is decomposed by Tucker3, whose structural model can also be represented as $\mathbf{T}_i = \mathbf{A}_i \mathbf{G}_i (\mathbf{C}_i \otimes \mathbf{B}_i)^T$. $\mathbf{T}_i$ and $\mathbf{G}_i$ are matrices, which are matricized forms of tensors $T_i$ and $G_i$ in the first mode and $\mathbf{A}_i$, $\mathbf{B}_i$ and $\mathbf{C}_i$ are the component matrices corresponding to first, second and third mode, respectively. We are interested in extracting the structure of first (user) mode so we collect $\mathbf{A_i}$'s, the singular vectors for the first mode and $\Sigma_i^{\,n}$, the singular values corresponding to first mode ($n = 1$) to construct matrix M [6]. This matrix is then analyzed using SVD and significant left singular vectors, U, and corresponding singular values, S, are used to extract the structure in user space.

$$\mathbf{T}_i = \mathbf{A}_i \mathbf{G}_i (\mathbf{C}_i \otimes \mathbf{B}_i)^T \text{ where i=1,2,...s}$$
$$\Sigma_i^{\,n} = diag(\sigma_1^{\,n}, \sigma_2^{\,n}, ..., \sigma_R^{\,n}) \text{ where R is the rank of } n^{th} \text{ mode} \qquad (1)$$
$$\mathbf{M} = [\mathbf{A_1} * \Sigma_1 | \mathbf{A_2} * \Sigma_2 | ... | \mathbf{A_s} * \Sigma_s] = \mathbf{U} * \mathbf{S} * \mathbf{V^T}$$

Steps of collective analysis of multiple tensors are listed in Equation 1. This approach is a generalized version of Collective Principal Component Analysis (CPCA)[3] to high-order datasets. Collective tensor analysis employs the same approach used in multiway multiblock component models [8] except for the minimization of a common objective function. The objective function is defined to be the sum of the residuals in multiple tensor decompositions and residual of the final step: 2-way component analysis in [8]. We, on the other hand, handle modeling of each tensor independently at each sampling site.

## 3.2   Collective Analysis of Chatroom Data Cubes

Tensors constructed at different servers contain only a specific portion of the data depending on the sampling scheme. Therefore, these tensors may not contain information regarding to every user. Table 4 shows how many users are logged as active users by different servers. We decompose these small tensors, sizes of which are given in Table 4 using Tucker3 model. Around $85 - 90\%$ percent of the data fits the model at each sampling site.

Tensor decomposition at each sampling site provides component matrices and singular values corresponding to the singular vectors in the user mode. Since

**Table 4.** Size of the tensors collected at each server for time window = 300 seconds. Maximum number of possible Tucker3 models that can be fit in collective tensor analysis is much smaller than maximum number of Tucker3 models for the complete tensor. Maximum number of Tucker3 models for tensor $X$ is the number of all possible component number combinations $[R_1 R_2 R_3]$ such that $R_1 \leq R_2 * R_3$, $R_2 \leq R_1 * R_3$ and $R_3 \leq R_1 * R_2$. Total number of entries in collective tensors are around 8% of the entries in complete tensor.

| Server Id | # Users (m1) | # Keywords (m2) | # Time Samples (m3) | # Tucker3 Models | # Entries |
|---|---|---|---|---|---|
| 1 | 12 | 77 | 3 | 350 | 2772 |
| 2 | 13 | 91 | 3 | 406 | 3549 |
| 3 | 16 | 99 | 3 | 601 | 4752 |
| 4 | 11 | 100 | 3 | 297 | 3300 |
| 5 | 14 | 80 | 3 | 467 | 3360 |
| 6 | 15 | 68 | 3 | 532 | 3060 |
| 7 | 13 | 61 | 3 | 406 | 2379 |
| 8 | 14 | 79 | 3 | 467 | 3318 |
| | | | *Total* | *3526* | *26490* |
| Complete Tensor | 28 | 501 | 24 | 117847 | 336672 |

different sets of users are logged at different servers, we pad the rows of $\mathbf{A}_i^* \mathbf{\Sigma}_i$ with zeros for the users which are not in the set of users logged by server i. Matrix $\mathbf{M}$, is then formed as in Equation 1 and decomposed by SVD.

An alternative analysis approach is to collect the tensors constructed by different servers at a central location and then decompose one large tensor containing data for the logs of all users during whole period of conversation. We apply Tucker3 analysis on the large tensor and determine the component numbers such that Tucker model fits around 80% of the data compatible with the percent of the data modeled using reduced SVD of matrix $\mathbf{M}$. Let $\mathbf{A}$ be the component matrix for the user mode obtained by the decomposition of large tensor. We also find the singular values corresponding to the singular vectors in this component matrix ($\mathbf{\Sigma}$) as we have done in small tensor analysis and compute $\mathbf{A}^* \mathbf{\Sigma}$.

Last step of the analysis is to cluster user groups. We use $\mathbf{U}^* \mathbf{S}$ from SVD of matrix $\mathbf{M}$ and $\mathbf{A}^* \mathbf{\Sigma}$ from Tucker3 decomposition of the large tensor to find and compare the user groups identified by collective and central analysis of chatroom tensors. We apply K-means algorithm [7] with different number of clusters, $k = 1, 2, ..6$ and observe that both central and collective analysis of 2-hour chatroom data for time windows 150 and 300 seconds identify the same user clusters. Complete procedure for central and collective tensor analysis is summarized in Figure 2.

### 3.3   Performance Comparison

Collective analysis of chatroom tensors has several advantages over central analysis of one large tensor. First of all, small tensors do not store the user entries if users do not speak in sampled time windows. Keywords, which are not used

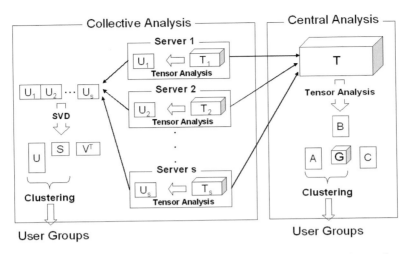

**Fig. 2.** Collective and Central Analysis of Tensors. In collective analysis of a tensor, partitions of the tensor are decomposed by tensor decomposition locally at different servers. User clusters are found by analyzing the collection of data summaries. On the other hand, central analysis decomposes one large tensor and user groups are determined using data summaries obtained from tensor analysis.

during those time windows, are not stored, either. Since most of the zero-entries in complete tensor are omitted, total number of entries shrinks in collective tensor analysis. Table 4 demonstrates that number of entries we keep track of in collective tensor analysis is approximately 8 % of the entries we use in centralized analysis.

Second, determining number of components for Tucker3 model is much easier compared to the central case. Techniques such as residual analysis, DIFFIT [4, 5] etc. determine the right number of components in Tucker3 model based on model fit values. For a 3-way tensor of size I x J x K, model fit should be computed only for the component number combinations, where $IJ \geq K$ and $IK \geq J$ and $JK \geq I$. For the cases, when $IJ < K$, we obtain the same model fit as $IJ = K$ [10]. Number of components are easily determined in collective tensor analysis because total number of Tucker3 models that can be fit to small tensors drops dramatically compared to the number of possible Tucker models for the central tensor. In Table 4, we show that total number of possible models for collective analysis is around 3% of the models that can be fit to the large tensor. Third, tensor analysis of multiple tensors is computationally more efficient than multiway analysis of one large tensor. Computational cost of Tucker3 model using ALS (Alternating Least Square) algorithm is $\prod_{j=1}^{n} m_j * 3R^2$ per iteration, where $m_j$ is the number of dimensions in the $j^{th}$ mode, n is the number of modes and R is the maximum of the component numbers used in Tucker3 analysis. We clearly observe:

$$\overset{\text{\# of servers}}{\underset{i=1}{\sum}} ((\prod_{j=1}^{3} m_{ij} * 3r_i^2) * (\# \text{ of iterations})) < \prod_{j=1}^{3} M_j * 3R^2 * (\# \text{ of iterations})$$

where $m_{ij}$ is the dimension of the $j^{th}$ mode of the tensor constructed in server i, $M_j$ is the dimensionality of the $j^{th}$ mode in the complete tensor and $r_i$ is the maximum of component numbers in Tucker3 analysis in server i. Iteration numbers are observed to be approximately the same in both central and collective analysis of tensors.

## 4   4-Way Analysis of Chatroom Data for Sensitivity

### 4.1   Impact of Server Selection

We construct 3-way tensors with users, keywords and time samples using the chatroom data logged during a specific time period at different servers. Our goal is to explore how tensors formed by different servers compare to each other. At this step, unlike collective tensor analysis, each server logs total chatroom conversation for a specific time period.

Data collected by different servers are arranged into a 4-way tensor, where first, second, third and fourth modes are users, keywords, time samples and servers, respectively (Figure 3 B). We are particularly interested in extracting the structure in the server mode. Therefore, after fitting Tucker model to 4-way tensor, we examine the component matrix corresponding to server mode.

2-hour chatlog is arranged into a 3-way tensor for each server and these are used to construct a 4-way dataset. Server mode also contains the tensor formed by combining partial data from several servers. It is essential to compare this tensor formed from data samples from different servers to all other tensors collected at a single server in order to show the validity of collective partial chatroom analysis.

We fit Tucker model to the 4-way data such that model explains around 95% of the data. This fit value can be achieved by extracting only one component from the server mode. Singular value corresponding to that single singular vector captures 96.97%, 99.88%, 97.40% and 96.36% of the variation for time window sizes of 150 sec., 180 sec., 240 sec. and 300 sec., respectively. Explained variations demonstrate that rank-one reduction in the server mode is enough and coefficients in the extracted singular vector reveal that each server contributes

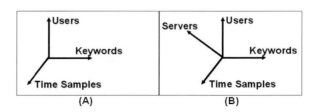

**Fig. 3.** Chatroom Tensors. 3-way tensors with modes of users, keywords and time samples are constructed at each server. 4-way tensors with modes of users, keywords, time samples and servers are used in sensitivity analysis of chatroom data with respect to different servers.

almost equally to the first component. The results also indicate that collection of chatroom data at different servers does not make any difference in terms of the analysis of chatroom tensors.

### 4.2  Impact of Sampling Window Size

In order to inspect the effect of time window size in the comparison of tensors constructed at different servers, 2-hour chatroom log is arranged as a 4-way tensor using different time window sizes. Our analyses with different time window sizes give the same strong rank-one reduction in the server mode as we have indicated in the previous section. Therefore, we demonstrate that collection of chatroom data at different servers with the given time window sizes does not make any difference in terms of constructed chatroom tensors.

## 5  Conclusions

In this paper we consider how to collect and analyze multilinear stream data from multiple servers in a distributed way. As an example of such data we consider Internet chatroom communications as our case study to demonstrate the results. We show that sampling in time domain by multiple servers can be used to obtain data with no statistical difference from the data obtained by a centralized approach. Consequently, we discuss how to construct 3-way data arrays and how to analyze the structure of multilinear data represented as high order tensors. Our collective analysis algorithm is based on constructing smaller tensors at each server (sampling site) and applying a tensor decomposition technique to obtain component matrices. The component matrix of interest (e.g., corresponding user groups) from each site is combined into a one larger component matrix which is then analyzed using SVD. We show that this approach compared to constructing a single tensor with full information and analyzing it with the same tensor decomposition technique gives the same structural information for the data. Since we establish the accuracy of the collective approach, we also compare the space and computation cost of collective analysis to the centralized one. We show that on our chatroom communication data, collective analysis provides significant savings. We define an equation that shows the computational cost relationship between centralized and collective analysis approach.

## References

1. Acar E., Camtepe S. A., Krishnamoorthy M. and Yener, B. Modeling and Multiway Analysis of Chatroom Tensors. IEEE ISI 2005.
2. Golub G.H. and Loan C.F.V. Matrix Computations. 3rd edn. The Johns Hopkins University Press, Baltimore, MD (1996).
3. Kargupta H., Huang W., Sivakumar K. and Johnson, E. Distributed Clustering Using Collective Principal Component Analysis Knowledge and Information Systems Journal, 3 (2001), 4, pp. 422-448.

4. Timmerman M. and Kiers H.A.L. Three-mode principal component analysis: Choosing the numbers of components and sensitivity to local optima British Journal of Mathematical and Statistical Psychology, 53 (2000), pp.1-16.
5. Kiers H.A.L. and der Kinderen A. A fast method for choosing the numbers of components in Tucker3 analysis British Journal of Mathematical and Statistical Psychology, 56 (2003), pp.119-125.
6. Lathauwer L.D., Moor B. D. and Vanderwalle J. A Multilinear Singular Value Decomposition. SIAM Journal on Matrix Analysis and Applications, Vol 21, No.4, (2000), pp. 1253-1278.
7. MacQueen J.B. Some Methods for classification and Analysis of Multivariate Observations Proceedings of 5-th Berkeley Symposium on Mathematical Statistics and Probability, Berkeley, University of California Press, 1 (1967), pp.281-297.
8. Smilde Age K., Westerhuis J.A. and Boque R. Multiway Multiblock Component and Covariates Regression Models J. Chemometrics, 14 (2000), pp. 301-331.
9. Tucker L. Some mathematical notes on three mode factor analysis. Psychometrika, 31 (1966), pp. 279-311.
10. Wansbeek T. and Verhees J. Models for multidimensional matrices in econometrics and psychometrics R.Coppi and S. Bolasco (Eds.), Multiway Data Analysis, Amsterdam: North Holland.

# Naturally Occurring Incidents as Facsimiles for Biochemical Terrorist Attacks

Jamie L. Griffiths, Donald J. Berndt, and Alan R. Hevner

University of South Florida,
Tampa, FL 33620
{jgriffit, dberndt, ahevner}@coba.usf.edu

**Abstract.** Research on techniques for effective bioterrorism surveillance is limited by the availability of data from actual bioterrorism incidents. This research explores the potential contribution of naturally occurring incidents, such as Florida wildfires, as reasonable facsimiles for airborne bioterrorist attacks. Hospital discharge data on respiratory illnesses are analyzed to uncover patterns that might resemble the effects of an aerosolized biological or chemical attack. Previous research [3] is extended by (1) utilizing Geographic Information Systems (GIS) to introduce appropriate spatial data and (2) increasing the sophistication of the spatial analysis by applying the retrospective space-time permutation model available through SaTScan$^{TM}$. Initial results are promising and lead to a confirmation that Florida wildfires are potentially interesting surrogates for aerosolized biochemical terrorist attacks. Research implications are discussed in reference to the on-going development of effective bioterrorism surveillance systems.

## 1 Introduction

The abilities to identify and react effectively to a biological or chemical attack are of concern to all nations. Research on techniques for effective bioterrorism surveillance is limited by the availability of data from actual bioterrorism incidents. This research explores the potential contribution of naturally occurring incidents, such as Florida wildfires, as reasonable facsimiles for airborne bioterrorist attacks. Our previous research in this area [3] is extended by: (1) utilizing a Geographic Information Systems (GIS) to introduce more appropriate spatial data [38]; and (2) increasing the sophistication of the spatial analysis by applying the retrospective space-time permutation model available through SaTScan$^{TM}$ [23, 35, 36].

The University of South Florida has an on-going research program to investigate bioterrorism surveillance systems that utilize the Comprehensive Assessment for Tracking Community Health (CATCH) data warehouse as a basis for identifying abnormal patterns of disease related to biological or chemical agents [3, 4, 5, 6]. The State of Florida provides a particularly interesting case for the development of a bioterrorism surveillance system, especially given the large tourism industry. Florida's population has increased by more than 700% from 1950 to 2000, and Florida is projected to overtake Texas as the third most populous state by the year 2011. Florida

S. Mehrotra et al. (Eds.): ISI 2006, LNCS 3975, pp. 225–236, 2006.

is also the "oldest state" and is expected to maintain this standing with more than 26% of its population projected to be over 65 by the year 2025 [7]. Lastly, Florida was one of four states affected by the first episode of bioterrorist-related anthrax in the fall of 2001 which resulted in a total of 22 cases and 5 fatalities [34].

This paper focuses on three key issues. First, naturally occurring wildfires are considered as surrogates for airborne biochemical terrorist attacks. If supported by various analyses, unusual illness patterns in hospital admissions, emergency room visits, and other "routinely collected data" could be useful in developing and calibrating surveillance algorithms [44]. Second, realistic data from events such as wildfires may provide components for training exercises and scenarios that include unfolding events in surveillance systems. Finally, the paper considers a particular analytic technique, SaTScan$^{TM}$, for uncovering respiratory illness patterns associated with Florida wildfires. The resulting data set and analytic results form an intriguing benchmark for assessing detection techniques.

## 2   Data Exploration – Wildfires and the CATCH Data Warehouse

Two major data sources are used in this study, roughly two decades of detailed Florida wildfire data and data on respiratory illnesses drawn from a pre-existing healthcare data warehouse, the CATCH data warehouse. Wildfire smoke, a combination of gases and particulate matter, can cause respiratory irritation and worsen preexisting heart and lung conditions. These effects are not likely to closely resemble a pathogen such as the Category A-C disease/agents cataloged by the CDC, which may involve person-to-person transmission. However, several chemical agents can cause respiratory symptoms, including ammonia, chlorine, vinyl chloride, phosgene, sulfur dioxide, nitrogen dioxide, tear gas, and zinc chloride [13]. Wildfires may provide realistic scenarios that can be used as proxies for chemical attacks. As other researchers have noted, such biochemical attacks can disrupt local infrastructures, cause mass anxiety, and undermine our confidence in personal security [1]. Clearly such attacks represent a serious threat and a reasonable context for investigating surveillance systems.

### 2.1  Florida Wildfires

Florida wildfires are naturally occurring events that may have the potential to provide an interesting facsimile for biochemical terrorist attacks. A geo-coded wildfire layer was obtained from the Florida Division of Forestry. This layer contains the geographic location of over 100,000 wildfires over the period 1981 to 2001 and associated attributes. These attributes include fire ID, cause of fire, date discovered, date contained, and acres burned at containment, among others. As can be seen in Figure 1, the total acres burned by Florida wildfires vary significantly from year to year. The addition of geo-coded wildfires affords the opportunity for multi-year time series analysis in addition to advanced spatial analytics.

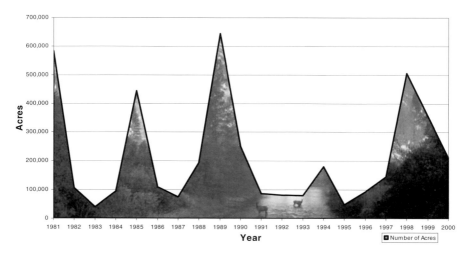

**Fig. 1.** Annual Acres Burned by Wildfires in Florida, 1981 to Early 2001

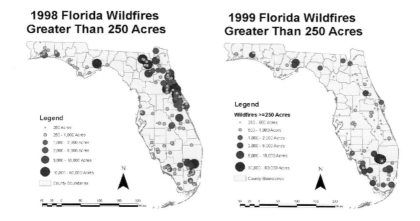

**Fig. 2.** Significant Florida Wildfires (>250 Acres)

Figure 2 compares the size and spatial distribution of wildfires over a two year period from 1998 to 1999. As can be seen, 1998 was a particularly active year with many wildfires occurring near densely populated areas. In addition to smoke closing a 48 mile section of I-95, connecting Jacksonville to Cocoa Beach, there were large scale evacuations and events such as the NASCAR Pepsi 400 in Daytona Beach had to be rescheduled [10]. From 1996 to 2001, the number of fires larger than 250 acres ranged from 79 in 1996 to 159 in 1998. Total acres burned ranged from 73,304 acres in 1997 to 509,733 acres in 1998.

Figure 3 displays a NOAA satellite image from July 2, 1998 adjacent to calculated burn scars of the 1998 wildfires. Given total burned acres at containment as an attribute and assuming circular growth from the start of a fire, radii were calculated and buffers were created to represent burn scars. As can be seen, the circular shape is appropriate but depending on wind conditions there may be a directional shift, in this case to the west, when compared to the actual fire or burn scar. Cities affected by the 1998 wildfires include Daytona Beach, Ormond Beach, Oak Hill and Titusville, among others.

As noted earlier, the wildfire data obtained from the Florida Department of Forestry includes all wildfires from 1981 to early 2001. The authors have recently obtained wildfire data for the period 2003 to 2005 and are in the process of obtaining data from early 2001 to 2003. This will provide a complete dataset for an expanded spatial-temporal analysis.

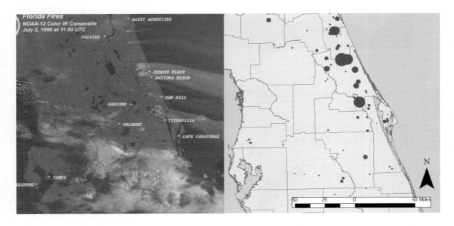

**Fig. 3.** NOAA Satellite Image, 2 July 2001, and Corresponding Wildfire Burn Scar Map

## 2.2  Health Data and the CATCH Data Warehouse

Respiratory data extracted from the CATCH data warehouse [5] included quarterly hospital discharge data with three diagnosis code groupings (acute respiratory infections, pneumonia, and respiratory problems from external agents) at both the ZIP code and county levels. Asthma was later included based upon preliminary findings associated with the 1998 wildfires by the Volusia County Health Department. As can be seen in Table 1, the health department compared the frequency of emergency room department visits and hospital visits for selected conditions for two 6 day periods in 1997 and 1998 (June 1 to July 6, 1997 and June 1 to July 6, 1998). The data were collected and analyzed in near real time during the 1998 wildfires. They found that emergency department visits increased for Asthma (91%), Bronchitis with acute exacerbation (132%), Chest Pain (37%), Conjunctivitis (32%), and Shortness of Breath/Wheezing (32%). Hospital admissions increased for Asthma (46%), and Chest Pain (24%). This illustrates that rapid surveillance of non-reportable diseases and conditions is possible during a public health disaster [37]. In addition, patient level demographics including age bands were extracted for each diagnosis.

**Table 1.** Emergency Room and Hospital Admissions, Volusia and Flagler Counties [37]

| Diagnosis | ICD-9 | Emergency Visits | | | Hospital Admissions | | |
|---|---|---|---|---|---|---|---|
| | | 1997 | 1998 | %Change | 1997 | 1998 | %Change |
| Asthma | 493-493.91 | 77 | 147 | +91% | 13 | 19 | +46% |
| Chest Pain | 786.50-786.59 | 218 | 299 | +37% | 63 | 78 | +24% |
| Bronchitis with acute exacerbation | 491.21 | 28 | 65 | +132% | 56 | 56 | -- |
| Heat Exhaustion | 992.3-992.5 | 7 | 19 | +171% | 2 | 1 | -50% |
| Shortness of Breath/Wheezing | 786.09 | 68 | 90 | +32% | 1 | 1 | -- |
| Conjunctivitis | 372.30-372.39 | 59 | 79 | +34% | 0 | 0 | 0% |

Although the CATCH data warehouse is currently limited to hospital discharge data the State of Florida recently began collecting data at the emergency room level. This will provide an opportunity for further development and evaluation of bioterrorism surveillance methods. Since it is likely that spikes in emergency room admissions will be more pronounced and include more general signs and symptoms than hospitalizations, this analysis will be improved with the addition of emergency room data.

For privacy reasons, the hospital discharge data utilized for this analysis lacks an exact date, but includes the quarter of admission. Currently daily, weekly or monthly data have to be obtained by taking all discharges for a hospital and assigning dates assuming a uniform distribution within a quarter. Since hospitalizations are likely to be seasonal, with more hospitalizations occurring in the winter when there is an increase due to Florida's migratory population, this estimation method is limited. Though including hospital discharge data with exact dates may improve results, clusters should still be preserved in the ordering of hospitalizations. We are currently pursuing the special request process to obtain hospitalization data with exact dates.

# 3  Pattern Recognition

Although global cluster tests are widely available, pinpointing locations of clusters in space-time is of greater utility for disease surveillance. This section introduces SaTScan<sup>TM</sup> and associated space-time cluster detection applications. SaTScan<sup>TM</sup> is freely available from www.satscan.org  and has recently gained attention in the surveillance community.

## 3.1  SaTScan<sup>TM</sup>

SaTScan™ software, developed by Martin Kulldorff and Information Management Services, Inc. with assistance from the Alfred P. Sloan Foundation, the National Cancer Institute, and the Centers for Disease Control and Prevention, is designed to analyze space-time data using the spatial, temporal, or space-time scan statistics. It is designed for any of the following interrelated purposes: (1) to evaluate reported spatial or space-time disease clusters, to see if they are statistically significant; (2)  to test whether a disease is randomly distributed over space, over time, or over space and time; (3) to perform geographical surveillance of disease, to detect areas of significantly high or low rates; and (4) to perform repeated time-periodic disease surveillance for the early detection of disease outbreaks [18, 30].

SaTScan™ Version 6.0 [35, 36] has the following features: Bernoulli and Poisson Models, Retrospective Space-Time Scan Statistic; Prospective Space-Time Scan Statistic; Space-Time Permutation Model; Ordinal Model; Multivariate Scan Statistic; Monte Carlo Hypothesis Testing; Recurrence Intervals; and an Exponential Model [9, 14, 15, 16, 17, 18, 20, 21, 22]. The Space-Time Permutation Model introduced by Kulldorff in 2005 for the early detection of disease outbreaks is unique in that it does not require population-at-risk data, it simply needs case numbers. This is useful in situations where population-at-risk information is unavailable or irrelevant [23]. Population-at-risk data may be problematic in a state like Florida with large sunbird, snowbird, and tourist populations.

Several surveillance systems and have been developed from techniques available in SaTScan™. These include the New York State Department of Health Information Network (HIN), the National Bioterrorism Syndromic Surveillance Demonstration Program, and the first and second generation of the Electronic Surveillance System for Early Notification of Community-based Epidemics (ESSENCE I & ESSENCE II), among others [8, 12, 23, 24, 25, 26, 27, 28, 29, 31, 39].

## 3.2  Recent SaTScan™ Applications

Hearne [14] and Montashari [31, 32] call for the effective use of bioterrorism surveillance systems [14, 30, 32]. Uses of syndromic surveillance systems in New York City have included the early detection of a gastrointestinal (norovirus) outbreak, using residential and hospital level data, and the development of an early warning system for the detection of West Nile virus activity utilizing dead bird clusters, mosquito trap data, and human case patients at the census tract level [14, 15, 31, 32]. A similar retrospective gastrointestinal outbreak system was developed in Minnesota [41, 42]. Nordin [33] simulated an Anthrax attack at the Mall of America and utilized SaTScan™ statistics along with data from the HealthPartners Medical Group, which provides approximately 9% of medical care in the Minneapolis-St-Paul area, to test surveillance methods. This study provided an interesting application utilizing private physician data rather than relying solely on hospital level data. These recent applications of SaTScan™ techniques reveal that it has gained attention in the surveillance community.

## 4  Analysis and Results

For our study, we analyzed respiratory illness data annually at the county level over the period 1998 to 2000. Annual data are utilized for two reasons. First, although respiratory data are available at the quarterly level, SaTScan™ restricts analysis to daily, monthly, and yearly levels. Second, the space-time permutation statistic is sensitive to population increases therefore analyzing at the yearly level will minimize the effect of seasonal migration [23, 24, 36]. Although county level data were utilized for this analysis, future analyses will need to be conducted at a finer spatial resolution and unique issues associated with ZIP code level data must be addressed [6, 19, 23, 45].

SaTScan™'s Retrospective Space-Time Permutation Model is utilized to detect clusters of respiratory illness in hospital admissions. The model was first run at the county level for all asthma cases. The model was then restricted to patients over 65 years of age which resulted in a primary space-time cluster in 1999 and two secondary space-time clusters in 1998 significant at 95%. The health threats from wildfire smoke are more likely to affect older adults, young children, and those with pre-existing conditions such as heart or lung disease [40].

Figure 4 displays the clusters along with the burn scars of all fires greater than 250 acres for the years 1998 and 1999. The primary cluster in 1999 consists of Palm Beach and Broward Counties and is associated with three extremely large fires along with dozens of smaller fires. The largest of the three fires burned a total of 173,000 acres, the largest single fire in the dataset (satellite images included in Figure 5), and the smaller two burned over 25,000 acres each. For comparison, the largest single fire in 1998 burned 61,500 acres. Figure 4B displays secondary clusters, the first of which is associated with intense fire activity throughout the fifteen counties included in the cluster.

Table 2 displays both significant and non-significant clusters associated with the Figure 4. It is interesting to note that Cluster 1 (1999) and Cluster 2 (1998) contain more than 700 cases while clusters 3 through 5 contain less than 100 cases. Clusters 3 through 5 have observed to expected ratios higher than the first two clusters.

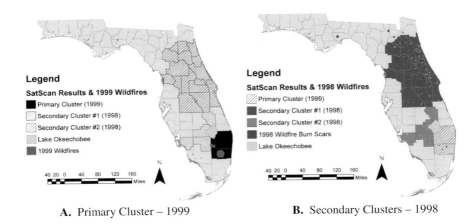

**A.** Primary Cluster – 1999          **B.** Secondary Clusters – 1998

**Fig. 4.** SaTScan™ Space-Time Cluster Results and Associated Wildfire Burn Scars

**Table 2.** Asthma Clusters in Florida Counties, 1998 to 2000

| Cluster (Year) | Approximate Location | | Cases | Exp | Observed/ Expected | Test Statistic | P-Value |
|---|---|---|---|---|---|---|---|
| 1 (1999) | 26.1388530 N | 80.220032 W | 1133 | 1026.26 | 1.104 | 6.063339 | 0.006 |
| 2 (1998) | 29.0839040 N | 81.115273 W | 726 | 646.36 | 1.23 | 5.008701 | 0.02 |
| 3 (1999) | 26.7161600 N | 81.203453 W | 87 | 62.20 | 1.399 | 4.419553 | 0.045 |
| 4 (2000) | 27.5511610 N | 81.813843 W | 47 | 31.04 | 1.514 | 3.551211 | 0.185 |
| 5 (2000) | 27.3591540 N | 80.343491 W | 66 | 48.06 | 1.373 | 3.010146 | 0.377 |

Smoke from the 1999 wildfires in South Florida caused a 60 mile stretch of I-75 between Ft. Myers and the outskirts of Miami, known as Alligator Alley, to be closed for several days [39]. Firefighters dubbed this particular fire the "Deceiving Fire" because of frequently shifting winds [39]. Figure 5 contains NOAA satellite images of fires and smoke plumes for the 1999 "Deceiving Fire". These images reveal the size, extent, directional shifts and rapid movement of both wildfires and related smoke plumes. Figure 5 also displays the location and shape of the actual burn scar, the estimated burn scar, and the primary cluster which is shaded in black.

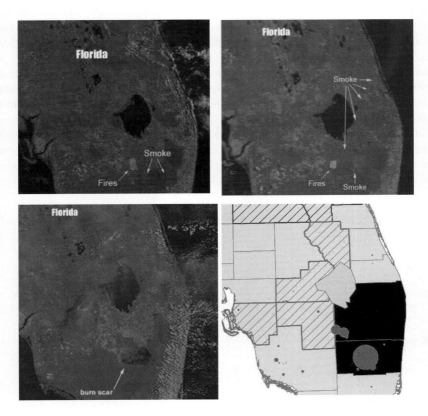

**Fig. 5.** Florida's 1999 "Deceiving" Wildfire (#216) – 173,000 Acres Burned

Asthma counts for hospital patients over 65 years of age in primary cluster counties plus Miami-Dade County are included in Table 3. Although Miami-Dade County was not detected for inclusion in the primary cluster by the retrospective space-time permutation model, it shows a similar trend. Miami-Dade County is south of the main cluster and adjacent to Broward County. Miami-Dade County asthma counts increased from 656 cases in 1998 to 858 cases in 1999 and then decreased to 735 cases in 2000.

**Table 3.** Asthma Cases for Patients over 65 in Primary Cluster & Miami-Dade Counties

|  | 1998 | 1999 | 2000 |
|---|---|---|---|
| **Broward County** | 412 | **645** | 540 |
| **Palm Beach County** | 321 | **488** | 362 |
| **Miami-Dade County\*** | 656 | **858** | 735 |
| \* Miami-Dade County is directly south of the primary cluster. | | | |

# 5  Conclusions and Future Research

The primary goal of this research is to analyze the potential contribution of naturally occurring incidents, such as Florida wildfires, as reasonable facsimiles for biochemical terrorist attacks. Wildfire events resemble most closely attacks using respiratory irritants such as ammonia, chlorine, vinyl chloride and other gaseous agents. For this study, SaTScan™ software is utilized to detect respiratory illness clusters associated with wildfire activity. The results, as presented and discussed in Section 4, look promising. We find clear indications of increased incidences of asthma among the elderly in Florida counties near the 1999 primary burn cluster.

Thus, further analyses of naturally-occurring events may be retroactively used for simulating bio-chemical attacks. The Florida wildfire data sets vary significantly from year-to-year and provide a relatively large volume of data for assessing surveillance algorithms. The data may also be useful for constructing realistic training exercises and scenarios that include surveillance systems. Our future research will address the several limitations discussed in the paper, such as expanding the window of analysis, obtaining more timely data, including multiple sources, and increasing the sophistication of the spatial analysis.

In particular, one consideration for future study is related to the use of residence rather than hospital location. As Nordin and Ostroff [33, 34] point out, some outbreaks may not be clustered at residences, as is the case of an exposure occurring at the workplace. If we assume that people go to the nearest hospital when they feel ill, analyzing hospital location data in addition to residential ZIP code or county may provide higher power to detect non-residential related outbreaks. This is particularly relevant in Florida with tourist and migratory populations.

Another consideration is that the wildfire data are geo-coded to the center of the Section of the Township-Range System, basically a one mile by one mile area, where each wildfire ignited. A point is provided with various attributes but there is little information regarding how the fire spread over time. Although this limitation should have little impact in our current study, the addition of data from plume models, such as the Environmental Protection Agency's Aloha Model, could potentially improve results. In addition, remote sensing techniques for monitoring wildfire evolution [2] could provide increasingly accurate boundaries and an application for examining near real-time surveillance.

With regard to the use of analytic techniques, Zeng [43] compares three hot spot techniques utilizing West Nile Virus data: (a) the spatial scan statistic using SaTScan™ with the Bernoulli Model option; (b) RNNH using CrimeSTAT; and (c) a

SVM-based clustering method implemented in the MATLAB programming environment. Zeng notes that all three of these methods "are driven by the locations of the baseline and cases of interest and are not capable of incorporating relevant factors such as natural land features, land-use elements, and temperatures, into model development and outbreak detection." This reveals a particularly interesting research extension that can be addressed in future analysis.

Finally, Graham-Rowe [11] state that someday large databases managed by intelligent software agents may be used to predict (terrorist) attacks before they happen. Potential future research in this area might focus on detecting a bioterrorism attack in space-time for quick containment. Intelligent agents could provide a framework for running complex spatial analyses from a variety of distributed data sources and reporting unexpected spikes to community health practitioners across the State of Florida. These avenues for further investigation seem well-suited to the general CATCH data warehouse infrastructure used for this study, as well as the more specific case of wildfires proxies for biochemical attacks.

## Acknowledgements

We gratefully acknowledge the insightful comments of the two reviewers which led to important paper improvements. We also acknowledge the many contributors who have helped develop the CATCH data warehouse.

## References

1. Alexander, D.A. and Klein, S.: Biochemical Terrorism: Too Awful to Contemplate, Too Serious to Ignore," British Journal of Psychiatry, 183 (2003): 491-497.
2. Al-Rawi, K.R., Casinova, J.L., and Romo, A.: IFEMS: a new approach for monitoring wild fire evolution with NOAA-AVHRR imagery. *International Journal of Remote Sensing*, 22 10 (2001), 2033-2042.
3. Berndt, D.J., Bhat, S., Fisher, J.W., Hevner, A.R., and Studnicki, J.: Data Analytics for Bioterrorism Surveillance. *Proceedings of the Second Symposium on Intelligence and Security Informatics (ISI 2004)*, June 10-11 (2004), Tucson, Arizona
4. Berndt, D.J., Fisher, J., Hevner, A., and Studnicki, J.: Data Warehousing and Quality Assurance. *IEEE Computer,* 34 12 (2001), 33-42.
5. Berndt, D.J., Hevner, A., and Studnicki, J.: The CATCH Data Warehouse: Support for Community Health Care Decision Making. *Decision Support Systems*, 35 (2003), 367-384.
6. Berndt, D.J., Hevner, A.J., and Studnicki, J.: Bioterrorism Surveillance with Real-Time Data Warehousing. *Proceedings of the first NSF/NIJ Symposium on Intelligence and Security Informatics (ISI 2003)*, Lecture Notes in Computer Science, LNCS 2665, Springer-Verlag (2003), 322-335.
7. Cambel, P.: Current Population Reports: Population Projections: 1995-2025. *US Bureau of the Census,* (1997)
8. Burkom, H.S., Elbert, Y., Feldman, A., and Lin, J.: Role of Data Aggregation in Biosurveillance Detection Strategies with Applications from ESSENSE. *MMWR.* 53 (2004), 67-73.
9. Dwass, M.: Modified randomization tests for nonparametric hypothesis. *Annals of Mathematical Statistics.* 28 (1957), 181-187.

10. Florida Wildfires Threaten all of Flagler County, CNN.com 3 July (1998)
    < www.cnn.com/US/9807/03/florida.fires.01/ >
11. Grahm-Rowe: Intelligence analysis software could predict attacks. *New Scientist* (2001)
12. Green, M.S. and Kaufmann, Z.: Surveillance for Early Detection Monitoring of Infectious Disease Outbreak Associated with Bioterrorism. *The Israeli Medical Association Journal.* 4 (2002), 503-506.
13. Greenfield, R.A., Brown, B.R., Hutchins, J.B., Iandolo, J.J., Jackson, R., Slater, L.N., and Bronze, M.S.: Microbiologica, Biological, and Chemical Weapons of Warfare and Terrorism. *The American Journal of Medical Sciences*, 323 6 (2002): 326-340.
14. Hearne, S.A., Segal, L.M.: Leveraging the Nation's Bioterrorism Investments: Foundation Efforts to Ensure A Revitalized Public Health System. *Health Affairs.* 22 4 (2003), 230-234.
15. Heffernan, R., Mostashari, F., Das, D., Karpati, A., Kulldorff, M.., Weiss, D., Syndromic Surveillance in Public Health Practice: The New York City emergency department system. *Emerging Infectious Diseases.* 10 (2004), 858-864.
16. Huang, L., Kulldorff, M., Kassen, A. A Spatial Scan Statistic for Survival Data. Manuscript (2005)
17. Jung, I., Kulldorff, M., Klassen, A.: A spatial scan statistic for ordinal data. Manuscript (2005)
18. Kleinman, K., Abrams, A., Kulldorff, M., Platt, R.: A model-adjusted space-time scan statistic with an application to syndromic surveillance. *Epidemiology and Infectious Disease*, 133 (2003), 409-419.
19. Krieger, N., Weterman, P., Chen, J, and May-Jabeen, S.: Zip Code Caveat: Bias Due to Spatio-Temporal Mismatches Between Zip Codes and US Census – Defined Geographic Areas – The Public Health Disparities Project. *American Journal of Public Health*, 92 7 (2002), 1100-1103.
20. Kulldorff, M. A spatial scan statistic. *Communications in Statistics: Theory and Methods.* 26 (1997), 1481-1496.
21. Kulldorff, M. Prospective time-periodic geographical disease surveillance using a scan statistic. *Journal of the Royal Statistical Society.* (2001), 61-72.
22. Kulldorff, M., Athas, W., Feuer, E., Miller, B., and Key, C.: Evaluating Cluster Alarms: A space-time scan statistic and brain cancer in Los Alamos. *American Journal of Public Health.* 88 (1998), 1377-1380.
23. Kulldorff, M., Heffernan, R., Hartman, J., Assuncao, R.M., Mostashari, F.: A space-time permutation statistic for the early detection of disease outbreaks. *PLoS Medicine.* 2 (2005), 216-224.
24. Kulldorff, M. and Information Management Services, Inc.: SaTScan™. Software for spatial and space-time scan statistics (computer program). Version 2.1 Bethesda, MD: *National Cancer Institute* (2005). < www.satscan.org >
25. Kulldorff, M., Mostashari, F., Duczmal, L., Yih, K., Kleinman, K., Platt, R.: Multivariate spatial scan statistics for disease surveillance. Manuscript (2005)
26. Kulldorff, K., Nagarwalla, N.: Spatial disease clusters: Detection and Inference. *Statistics in Medicine*, 14 (1995), 799-810.
27. Kulldorff, K., Lazarus, R., Platt, R.: A generalized linear mixed models approach for detecting incident clusters of disease in small areas with application to biological terrorism. *American Journal of Epidemiology* (2004), 217-224.
28. Minnesota Department of Health: Syndromic Surveillance: A New Tool to Detect Disease Outbreaks. *Disease Control Newsletter*, 32 (2004), 16-17.

29. Lombardo, J., Burkom, H., Elbert, E., Magruder, S., Lewis, S.H., Loschen, W., Sari, J., Sniegoski, C., Wojcik, R., and Pavilin, J.: A Systems Overview of the Electronic Surveillance System for the Early Notification of Community-Based Epidemics (ESSENCE II). *Journal of Urban Health,* 80 2 (2003), 32-41.
30. Mandl, K., Overhage, J., Wagner, M., Lober, W., Sebastiani, P., Mostashari, F., Pavlin, J., Gestland, P., Tradwell, T., Koki, E., Hutwagner, L., Buckeridge, D., Aller, R., Grannis, S.: Implementing Synromic Surveillance: A Practical Guide Informed by Early Experience. *Journal of the American Medical Informatics Association,* 11 2 (2004), 141-150.
31. Mostashari, F. and Hartman, J. Syndromic Surveillance: A Local Perspective. *Journal of Urban Health,* 80 2 (2003).
32. Mostashari, F., Kulldorff, M., Hartman, J.J., Miller, J.R., Kulasekera, V.: Dead bird clustering: A potential early warning system for West Nile virus activity. *Emerging Infectious Diseases.* 9 (2003), 641-646.
33. Nordin, J.D., Goodman, M.J., Kulldorff, M., Ritzwoller, D.P., Abrams, A.M., Kleinman, K., Levitt, M.J., Donahue, J., Platt, R. Simulated anthrax attacks and syndromic surveillance. *Emerging Infectious Diseases,* 11 (2005), 1394-1398.
34. Ostroff, S. The CDC and Emergency Preparedness for the Elderly and Disabled: *Testimonly before the Senate Special Committee on Aging – NY Field Hearing,* February 22 (2002), < http://www.cdc.gov/mmwr/preview/mmwrhtml/00056377.htm >
35. SaTScan<sup>TM</sup> Version History. Viewed November 7 (2005), Version 6. October 24 (2005) < http://www.satscan.org/techdoc.html >
36. SaTScan<sup>TM</sup> web site. Viewed November 7 (2005), < http://www.satscan.org >
37. Surveillance of Morbidity during Wildfires – Central Florida 1998. *MMWR,* 48 40 (1999)
38. United States Geological Survey (USGS), Geographic Information Systems (GIS) Poster < http://erg/isgs/gpv/isb/pubs/gis_poster/ >
39. Wildfires burn 70,000 acres in Everglades. April 19 (1999), < www.cnn.com >
40. Wildfires Fact Sheet: Health Threat from Wildfire Smoke. Department of Health and Human Services. Center for Disease Control and Prevention (2003) < www.bt.cdc.gov. firesafety >
41. Yih, W.K., Caldwell, B., Harmon, R., Kleinman, K., Lazarus, K., Lazarus, R., Nelson, A., Nordin, J., Rehm, B. National Bioterrorism Syndromic Surveillance Demonstration Program. *MMWR.* 53 (2004), 43-46.
42. Yih, K., Abrams, A., Kleinman, K., Kulldorff, M., Nordin, J., and Platt, R. Ambulatory-care diagnosis as potential indicators of outbreaks of gastrointestinal illness – Minnesota. *MMWR.* 54 suppl. (2004), 157-162.
43. Zeng, D., Hsinchun, C. Lynch, C., Edson, M., and Gotham, I. Infectious Disease Informatics and Outbreak Detection. *Medical Informatics,* Chapter 13 (2006), 359-395.
44. Zeng, X., Wagner, M. Modeling Effects of Epidemics on Routinely Collected Data, Journal of the American Medical Informatics Association, 9 Supplement (2002), s17-s22.
45. ZipCode Data. Great Data Frequently Asked Questions < http://www.greatdata.com/ zipcodefaqs.php >

# DrillSim: A Simulation Framework for Emergency Response Drills*

Vidhya Balasubramanian, Daniel Massaguer,
Sharad Mehrotra, and Nalini Venkatasubramanian

Donald Bren School of Information and Computer Science,
University of California, Irvine
Irvine, CA 92697, USA
{vbalasub, dmassagu, sharad, nalini}@ics.uci.edu

**Abstract.** Responding to natural or man-made disasters in a timely
and effective manner can reduce deaths and injuries, contain or prevent
secondary disasters, and reduce the resulting economic losses and social
disruption. Appropriate IT solutions can improve this response. However, exhaustive and realistic validation of these IT solutions is difficult;
proofs are not available, simulations lack realism, and drills are expensive
and cannot be reproduced. This paper presents DrillSim: a simulation
environment that plays out the activities of a crisis response (e.g., evacuation). It has capabilities to integrate real-life drills into a simulated
response activity using an instrumented environment with sensing and
communication capabilities. IT solutions can be plugged in the simulation system to study their effectiveness in disaster management and
response. This way, by using a simulation coupled with an on-going drill,
IT solutions can be tested in a less expensive but realistic scenario.

## 1 Introduction

Organized crisis response activities include measures undertaken to protect life
and property immediately before (for disasters where there is at least some
warning period), during, and immediately after disaster impact. Depending upon
the scale of the disaster, crisis response may be a large-scale, multi-organizational
operation involving many layers of government, utility companies, commercial
entities, volunteer organizations, media, and the public. In a crisis, these entities
work together as a virtual organization to save lives, preserve infrastructure and
community resources, and reestablish normalcy within the community. During
a crisis, responding organizations confront grave uncertainties in making critical
decisions. They need to gather situational information (e.g., state of the civil,
transportation and information infrastructures) and information about available
resources (e.g., medical facilities, rescue and law enforcement units). Timely
and accurate information can radically transform the ability of organizations

---

* This research has been supported by the National Science Foundation under award
numbers 0331707 and 0331690.

S. Mehrotra et al. (Eds.): ISI 2006, LNCS 3975, pp. 237–248, 2006.

to gather, manage, analyze and disseminate information when responding to man-made and natural catastrophes.

While innovations in information technology are being made to support awareness in a crisis, a key issue that must be addressed is evaluating the efficacy of the developed solutions in an actual response process. In other words, strategies must be developed to translate IT metrics into meaningful emergency response metrics that help us analyze the cost-effectiveness of the technologies before deployment. One approach is to mimic a crisis by conducting emergency drills over a sample region, incorporating the IT innovations in the process of response during the drill, and measuring the improvements in the process as compared to some pre-existing baseline. Organizing and conducting emergency drills is a challenging proposition due to several reasons. Drills are expensive in terms of time and resources, significant planning is required to instrument drills. Participation of multiple response organizations, businesses and individuals might need to be coordinated making frequent spot-testing of technology solutions impossible. Furthermore, drills are often carefully scripted making it impossible to test out response to a range of scenarios using "what-if" analysis. In addition, scalability testing of solutions (e.g. evacuation of an entire city) is close to impossible to test via drills.

An alternate solution is to use simulation tools and techniques to understand disasters, their evolution, and the potential impact of IT solutions on the outcome of the response. A simulation based approach allows us to create what-if scenarios dynamically and determine the ability of the response to adapt to the changing disaster landscape. Simulations are also useful for training response personnel and in evaluating solutions and plans for emergency response. The need for sophisticated tools and techniques for the modeling, simulation, and visualization of emergency activities has been articulated in recent reports [17]. Much of the efforts in the area of crisis simulations have focused on modeling disasters and their effects–techniques for radioactive plume modeling, modeling the spread of biological agents, fire modeling, earthquake impact modeling help in understanding the characteristics of the specific type of disaster itself.

What has not been studied in as much detail are simulation tools that help understand the response activity itself (e.g. evacuation, medical triaging, fire fighting, rubble removal) as it unfolds. Commercial evacuation simulators [5, 8, 2] help establish bounds on evacuation of regions and buildings under ideal knowledge conditions; these tools model movement and behavior of people during evacuation. However, they do not capture the interactions between people or the impact of technology in such scenarios.

In this paper, we discuss the design and implementation of a simulation environment for crisis response that addresses the aforementioned gap. A simulation framework for crisis response activities must address the modeling of human behavior (and decisions made by humans) in a changing environment. The proposed simulation framework is a multi-agent system for crisis response activities that mainly (a) embodies agents that drive the simulation in different roles and make decisions and (b) captures the environment under which agents make decisions through the use of a pervasive infrastructure. In addition, the framework incorporates a variety of models that drive the activity and decision making, captures information flow between different entities/agents and integrates the abilities of the infrastructure with respect to the information flow. In addition to scalability (supporting large numbers of entities) and flexibility (extensibility to various crises), the emphasis of our simulation framework is on being able to accurately calibrate the crisis environment and behavior of agents in that environment.

A key aspect of our approach is the incorporation of real-world instrumented framework [6], i.e. a pervasive environment, that can capture physical reality during an activity as it occurs. The instrumented smart space consists of a variety of sensing technologies (video, audio, RFID people sensors) and is used to conduct and monitor emergency drills. This extends the scope of the simulation framework into an augmented reality environment for IT testing in the context of a crisis. Such an integration allows humans to assume specific roles in the multi-agent simulator (e.g. first responder in an evacuation process within a building) and capture decisions made by humans (evacuees, response personnel) involved in the response process. Capturing people's behavior during a drill also allows calibrating the simulation both in terms of physical and cognitive agent response (e.g., speed of movement and decisions taken).

The rest of the paper is organized as follows. Section 2 presents the design details and concepts behind the system. A prototype is presented in Section 3. Given the implementation framework we describe how this system serves to test IT solutions and disaster response methodologies in Section 4. Conclusions and future research directions are discussed in Section  5.

## 2   Design Details of DrillSim

Figure  1 illustrates the basic methodology of the DrillSim environment which consists of a multi-agent simulator driven by an instrumented smart space. An activity in DrillSim occurs in a *hybrid world* that is composed of (a) the **simulated world** generated by a multi-agent simulator and (b) a **real world** captured by a smart space.

The purpose of this environment is to play out a crisis response activity where agents might be either computer agents or real people playing diverse roles (actors). In order to capture real actors in the virtual space we utilize a sensing infrastructure that monitors and extracts information from real actors that is needed by simulator (such as agent location, agent state, etc.); in other words, we infuse actions and state of human actors in the virtual space. Likewise, to enable a real-actor to participate in a simulated reality, we use appropriate display devices and modalities to provide the real-actor with awareness of the virtual world. While our main goal is to evaluate new techniques for crisis response, one important byproduct of the hybrid world approach is that it becomes an immersive training environment for first responders. Another design consideration of DrillSim is to be able to run DrillSim with other simulators (e.g., communication simulators, crisis simulators). Such simulators are often developed by domain experts and the ability to integrate relevant input to DrillSim from these simulators allows us to model a wider range of aspects more accurately. For instance a crisis simulator can be plugged into DrillSim by translating the crisis parameters to the impact. In the remainder of this section, we describe our approach to modeling the various components of the DrillSim world and in enabling interactions between the two worlds (real to simulated and vice-versa).

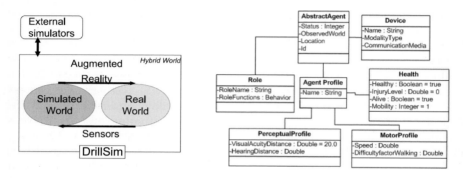

**Fig. 1.** Methodology                    **Fig. 2.** UML of Agent

## 2.1   Conceptual Modeling of DrillSim

Two key concepts that drive the design and implementation of DrillSim are *entities* and *scenario*. Together these concepts capture the overall activity over space and time as well as the observed world of each agent (real or virtual) participating in the activity.

**DrillSim Entities:** The primary entities modeled in DrillSim are the agents, space, resources, crisis, and infrastructure. In our model, entities can either be real or virtual.

*Agents* are autonomous participants that drive the crisis response simulation and can be real or virtual. Agents may represent an evacuee, a firefighter, a building captain, etc. Every agent has a set of properties associated with it. A UML representation of some sample agent properties is shown in Figure 2. The properties of an agent include its role (e.g., evacuee, fire fighter), the agents physical and perceptual profile (e.g., range of sight, speed of walking), the current health status of the agent(e.g. injured, unconscious), and the devices carried by the agent (e.g. cellphone). At any given time, agents are associated with a given location in the geographical space.

*Space* is where the response activity is played out and includes both indoor space and outdoor space. Indoor space consists of floors, rooms, corridors, stairways, elevators, etc., while outdoor space consists of buildings, roads, walkways, open spaces of different terrains, parking lots and other external structures.

The *Crisis* models physical phenomena such as spreading fire and spread of a hazardous material. Instead of modeling a crisis, our simulator represents crisis via its impact. Specifically, it represents at any time, for each location the impact of the crisis to other entities (the intensity of fire, the toxicity of chemical spill at the location, etc).

*Infrastructure* represents the sensing and communication components used to capture the context in which an activity occurs. The components can be a fire alarm within a building that is used by an agent. Again, infrastructure is modeled via its impact to the pervasive space. For instance, instead of modeling WiFi communication using a set of access points, we model whether WiFi communication is available to a particular agent at a particular location.

**Scenario Representation:** A scenario is essentially the state of the real and virtual entities modeled at a given point of time. We specifically represent scenario as a snapshot taken at every time unit. This snapshot is represented using a grid based representation which is expanded to include information about obstacles, hazards, and occupancy. In this representation we divide the space into equal sized grid cells and every cell contains a tuple of the form $G_{i,j} = <Obstacle, Occupied, Hazard>$. *Obstacle* is a value between 0 and 1 and represents the difficulty an agent faces in traversing a cell. *Occupied* contains a list of agents occupying the cell. Hazard contains a list of hazards present on that cell. While the cell-based representation is simplistic it is rich enough to capture a variety of crisis activities. Our future plans are to expand the representation further to capture other entities like cell tower, fire extinguishers etc.

## 2.2   Virtual Reality/Augmented Reality Integration

Virtual reality/augmented reality integration requires projection of the simulated world to the real world and vice versa. To augment the real world with the simulated world, the necessary Virtual Reality/Augmented Reality (VR/AR) interfaces have to be designed, such that real persons taking part in a drill can interact with the hybrid world and take decisions based on their observation of this hybrid world. This immersion is achieved via the appropriate GUIs on portable devices (cellphone, PDA, etc) carried by the person. There are several challenges in bringing the simulated world to the real world. The first set of challenges arise from limitations in the device such as processing, storage, and energy capabilities. To address the restrictions imposed by hand-held devices, the interface at the hand-held device is simplified to contain a minimal set of functions that enable the user to effectively communicate with the agents in the simulation. Furthermore, synchronization issues also arise due to communication delays between server and clients and due to the different processing capabilities of different clients. The second set of challenges emphasize the need for a customized view of the simulation based on user location and orientation. This has to be done in real-time so that appropriate contextual information is sent to the user as and when needed. Key technologies to enable this include quality-aware localization [12] and adaptive content customization.

To capture a real agent participating in the activity we must have a mechanism to observe the real agents and their actions in space. We have instrumented a *smart space* within our campus that allows us to capture phenomena taking place in the real world. The smart space consists of integrated sensing and communication infrastructure that includes video and audio sensors, people counters, built-in RFID technology, powerline, ethernet, and wireless communications. Specifically, real sensors and communication devices are used to capture physical space and phenomena, and to monitor people positions and actions. This instrumentation also enables calibrating both the agent's action parameters (e.g., speed of movement) and decision-making mechanisms. Furthermore, this smart space provides an infrastructure for IT researchers to test their solutions (e.g., 802.11-based localization [10]). One of the key issues in the collection of dynamic multimodal data is in aggregating and interpreting the collected data in real time. Also, incompatibility and unreliability of multi-sensor data has to be addressed using suitable sensor fusion (e.g. probabilistic) techniques. Additionally there are privacy issues regarding collected data about real people participating in a drill. Our research within the RESCUE [18] project addresses several of these challenges.

## 2.3   DrillSim Operational Dynamics

We begin the simulation by generating the current scenario on a chosen geographical space using the pervasive infrastructure, i.e. the current state of real world entities (e.g. location of people, state of resources) is used to calibrate an initial scenario generator. The current crisis, which is generated by the crisis generator, represents both the disaster as well as the changes that occur as an effect of the disaster. These changes are reflected both in the geographical space and the scenario, and updated as the simulation progresses through the shared cell-based representation of space.

The main entities that drive the simulation are the agents. Agents wake up every $t$ time units and execute some actions. Specifically, on waking up, an agent acquires awareness of the world around it, transforms the acquired data into information relevant to decision making, and makes decisions based on this information. The acquired awareness is stored as the observed world of the agent (and may be augmented using information from the instrumented smart space). An agent takes decisions using the awareness acquired. Based on the decisions, it (re)generates a set of action plans. These plans dictate the actions the agents attempt before going to sleep again. For example, hearing a fire alarm may result in the decision of exiting a floor, which in turn may result in a navigation plan to attempt to go from the current location to an exit location on the floor. Given this navigation plan, the agent executes one action of the plan every time, e.g. it walks one step towards the exit of the room. An impact of changing global environment, crisis, and actions of other agents is the possible change of plan or even a change of decision. Decisions, plans, and actions are logged by the agents as and when they change.

# 3   DrillSim: System Implementation

We now describe the architecture and implementation of the DrillSim simulation framework. The prototype of the simulator models a multi-agent evacuation activity at a campus level. In this system there are two types of agents–the evacuee and the floor warden–whose role is to evacuate the floor during an emergency. The architecture of DrillSim is shown in Figure  3. The primary components are the I/O interfaces, simulation engine, data management module, and the VR/AR modules. In addition there is a database server which holds the spatial data. These components are described in the sections below.

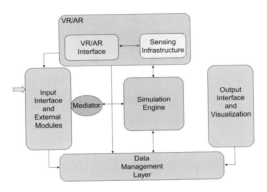

**Fig. 3.** Software architecture of DrillSim

## 3.1   I/O Interfaces of DrillSim

Figure 4 shows a sample screenshot of the I/O interface of the system. The interface allows a set of inputs to be provided to the simulation, outputs the results of the simulation, and also allows users to interact with the simulation environment. The user can start the simulation, start the crisis when needed, turn on the fire alarm once a crisis starts, communicate with other agents, and control an agent. The user interfaces are built using Java and Java3D.

*Inputs to DrillSim*: allow users to initialize parameters to the properties of Drill-Sim entities, specified in Section 2.1, and the initial scenario. Agent inputs include the definition of roles and their behavior, definition of profiles to be associated with the different agents, location of different people at the beginning of the simulation, the devices agents carry, etc. In the current implementation the geography, roles of agents, agent behavior definitions and profiles are pre-defined. Location of agents at the beginning of the simulation is entered by the user. Inputs pertaining to resources, crisis and infrastructure are entered by the user as a spatial layer on a geographical map. Users can also input response procedure plans to the system. The inputs to DrillSim come both from users who instantiate parameters and from external models that relate to the actual event (crisis and its response) and the entities in the event (the resources, people, devices, etc). The inputs can be dynamic as in the scenario generated by external

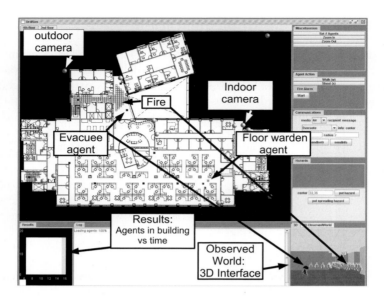

**Fig. 4.** Snapshot of DrillSim User Interface

modules (e.g., crisis model, scenario generator) or static parameters initializing
the scenario (e.g, time of start of simulation, total number of people in building,
location of resources). In addition, inputs can be derived from the sensors in
the pervasive space, which dynamically feed back user counts, user locations,
resource locations, and so on. There is a mediator for every external model that
translates the data to the grid representation format understood by the simulator. The inputs are either sent directly to the engine or stored in the database.
The geography is stored in the database. Also embedded within the DrillSim are
the geography (in the database) and the response plan which outlines the basic
response rules followed in our campus.

*Outputs of DrillSim*: While the other modules in DrillSim model and generate
the response activity, it is also essential to generate output of the activity so that
the end user can observe the simulation and evaluate the results. The output
modules capture the results of the simulation through a 2D/3D visualization
or as statistics. The visualization is a hybrid output with both the real world
and simulated world overlapping and can be both in 2D and 3D. While the 2D
visualization provides a birds-eye view of the entire activity or of the observed
reality of a specific agent, the 3D observed reality is the view of a camera set
in any arbitrary position or on top of any agent. The latter is useful both to
understand what a simulated agent decides based on its observed world and to
be able to take the role one of the agents by controlling it. The statistics of
the simulation include disaster response metrics such as speed of evacuation and
number of people injured. These metrics help to study the effectiveness of the
solutions plugged into our system. Recall the primary purpose of this simulator is
to evaluate IT solutions by translating IT metrics to disaster metrics. At every

instance of time, the simulator updates a graph of *time* versus *agents in the building*. This graph is an example of a method to show the impact of different IT solutions in the context of an evacuation.

## 3.2 DrillSim Simulation Engine and Data Management Module

The *simulation engine* is the principal component that drives DrillSim by playing out an evacuation activity. The simulation engine is driven by different agents and, in our current implementation, is developed using Java and JADE [11]. It consists of the simulated geographic space, the current evacuation scenario (i.e. where people are and what they are doing), and the current crisis as it unfolds. The functionality of the engine is supported by different agents that represent the human population involved in the response. In our engine the two agents represented are evacuees and floor warden. Their representation also conveys when they are receiving messages from other agents and when the floor warden agent is activated. The agents follow the operational dynamics as described in Section 2.4. Decision-making in an agent is modeled as a stochastic neural network. In particular, it is a recurrent neural network [13] that outputs the probability of taking each decision (e.g., evacuate the floor, exit the building). The input to the neural network is the agent's information, the probability of taking each decision, and the decisions made. The weights of the neural network (i.e. the weights given to every input) are set according to the agent's profile and calibrated by running real emergency response drills within the smart space. Modeling decision-making as a neural network allows for explicitly modeling the importance of each piece of information on each decision, setting the emphasis on the impact of information on decision making rather than on the reasoning process itself. The engine is the most computationally intensive module in DrillSim which results in scalability issues (i.e., as more agents are added, they compete for limited resources). We are working on strategies to distribute the computation uniformly to improve the efficiency of the system.

The data management module manages the data exchange between other components. The data relevant to the simulator is stored in a database. The geography of both indoor and outdoor spaces are converted to the GIS format and stored in the database. There is a JDBC interface available for agents to access this spatial information in order to make decisions. The data management module is responsible for 1.- managing continuous queries from agents regarding the environment, other agents etc, 2.- managing highly frequent updates, and 3.- logging the events as they happen. An important aspect of this module is the representation of the spatial and temporal data so as to adequately support functioning of the simulated activity.

## 3.3 Virtual Reality/Augmented Reality Integration in DrillSim

In order to allow the projection of the virtual world to real people, the visualization interface is extended to allow the user both to observe the simulation and to participate in it. Specifically there are three versions of the interface implemented. The EOC version of this interface is running on a laptop or a PC and can be connected to a 5x11 multi-tier display. The EOC version also allows a user to manage the entire simulation, see what an agent (real or virtual) is seeing, send messages to other agents, and control the actions of an agent. In the current implementation the PDA version is a low resolution version of the same interface. The output of the computer is connected to a pair of MicroOptical SV-6 VR glasses [1]. In order to provide the customized output for the user carrying the PDA we need to track and localize the user. This is achieved using the instrumented smart space covering one quarter of our campus. Indoor localization is achieved via WiFi based localization technologies such as the Ekahau Positioning Engine [3]. Sensor fusion based techniques using WiFi, Bluetooth, RFID triangulation and GSM are also being implemented and tested. In addition, people counting technologies (video-based counting) also help feed the real time data of location of people to generate more realistic dynamic scenarios.

## 4    Testing and Validation

An important purpose of the simulator is for advancing research in human behavior, emergency response processes, and developing IT solutions in the context of emergency response. This section describes how DrillSim can be used to test impact of IT techniques and response procedures on disaster response. Note that the experiments are here included for illustration purposes only, since the validity of the results depends on the validity of the behavior model. Studying the validity of the behavior model and calibrating the behavior model remains part of our future work.

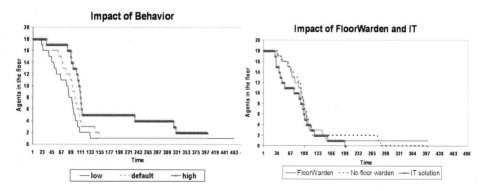

**Fig. 5.** Impact of Human Behavior          **Fig. 6.** Impact of FloorWarden and IT

The prototype simulates an evacuation activity in one building with four floors. Specifically, the experiments are performed on the 4th floor of the building, with 20 agents evacuating the floor due to a fire. There are two roles taken by agents: floor warden and evacuees. The floor warden is responsible for evacuating the floor by going to every room and making sure the evacuees leave the building, and is the last to leave the floor. The evacuee agents' decisions include exiting the building, and telling others to exit the building. The relevance each evacuee gives to the fire alarm or to each other agent requesting to evacuate (including the floor warden) depends on the obstinacy level–the higher the obstinacy level the less likely the agent will evacuate.

In the first set of experiments given the activity chosen (evacuation in the presence of fire) we study the impact of human behavior by studying the impact of obstinacy of agents in such situations. Figure 5 shows the relationship between evacuation time and agent obstinacy levels. As expected, the more obstinate the agents, the longer time it takes to evacuate them. The second set of experiments demonstrate the impact of floor warden on the process of evacuation as shown in Figure 6. We can notice that those agents who are obstinate even after hearing the fire alarm leave earlier due to the presence of fire alarm. However we can see that the floor warden is in the building long after people have left in order to search the entire floor. An IT solution that can tell the floor warden when the floor has been evacuated, he can leave earlier The plot labelled IT Solution indicates the impact of this IT solution in the evacuation process, and shows the floor warden leaving earlier.

## 5   Related Work and Concluding Remarks

Evacuation simulation tools like Myriad, Simulex, and Egress and others [5, 8, 2] model movement and behavior of people during evacuation. Multi-agent simulators like the efforts in Robocup-Rescue Simulation Project [7] and the evacuation simulator developed as part of the Digital city project in Kyoto, Japan [19] simulate not only the civilian movement but also the activities of the response personnel. While the efforts mentioned address individual aspects of disaster management these tools do not address the overall emergency response activity. A few efforts have been directed towards integrating different tools [9, 4, 14]. For instance the SOFIA project at Los Alamos National Laboratory is aimed at developing actor-based software for analyzing infrastructures that are interdependent. The Integrated Emergency Response Framework from National Institute of Standards and Technology [14, 15, 16] targets integration of different simulation tools to address overall emergency response. Our simulator not only simulates activities but also integrates the actual instrumented infrastructure, enabling us to immerse real people in the simulation. The primary goal is to use this emergency response activity view in order to integrate IT solutions at appropriate interface points in the simulator and test the effectiveness of IT solutions in disaster response.

In this paper, we described DrillSim. Such a simulation framework that merges reality and simulation opens up opportunities to recreate more realistic response activities and test solutions and models in this context. Designing such a simulator opens many research challenges related to modeling and data management. Mixing of real with virtual worlds, dynamic data management, modeling the geographical space and representing events on it, and modeling agents to mimic human behavior in crisis are some of these challenges. We have addressed a few of them in this paper. We have also demonstrated how DrillSim can be used to test solutions for disaster response. We are focussing on modeling spatial data and agent behaviors as part of ongoing work. There are scalability and synchronization issues when designing a large scale crisis response simulator. Our eventual goal is to support scalable plug and play of crisis response activities over a variety of scenarios and geographies.

# References

1. MicroOptical-SV-6 PC Viewer specification, 2003.
2. EGRESS. http://www.aeat-safety-and-risk.com/html/egress.html, 2005.
3. Ekahau Positioning Engine. http://www.ekahau.com/, 2005.
4. Interdependent Infrastructure Modeling, Simulation, and Analysis Project (SOFIA), Los Alamos National Laboratory. http://www.lanl.gov/orgs/d/d4/infra/sofia.html, 2005.
5. Myriad. http://www.crowddynamics.com, 2005.
6. Responsphere. http://www.responsphere.org, 2005.
7. Robocup-Rescue Simulation Project. http://www.rescuesystem.org/robocuprescue/, 2005.
8. Simulex: Simulation of Occupant Evacuation. http://www.iesve.com, 2005.
9. The Urban Security Initiative, Los Alamos National Laboratory. http://www.lanl.gov/orgs/d/d4/infra/urban.html, 2005.
10. BAHL, P., AND PADMANABHAN, V. N. RADAR: An In-Building RF-Based User Location and Tracking System. In *INFOCOM (2)* (2000), pp. 775–784.
11. BELLIFEMINE, F., POGGI, A., RIMASSA, G., AND TURCI, P. "An object oriented framework to realize agent systems". In *WOA 2000* (May "2000").
12. CRISTOFORETTI, J. Multimodal Systems in the Management of Emergency Situations. Master's thesis, Universita de Bologna, 2005.
13. HAYKIN, S. *Neural Networks - A Comprehensive Foundation*. Prentic Hall, 1999.
14. JAIN, S., AND MCLEAN, C. R. A Framework for Modeling and Simulation for Emergency Response. *Winter Simulation Conference* (2003).
15. JAIN, S., AND MCLEAN, C. R. An Integrating Framework for Modeling and Simulation of Emergency Response. *Simulation Journal: Transactions of the Society for Modeling and Simulation International* (2003).
16. JAIN, S., AND MCLEAN, C. R. An Architecture for Modeling and Simulation of Emergency Response. *Proceedings of the 2004 IIE Conference* (2004).
17. JOHN L. HENNESSY, D. A. P., AND S.LIN, H.
18. MEHROTRA, S., BUTTS, C., KALASHNIKOV, D., VENKATASUBRAMANIAN, N., RAO, R., CHOCKALINGAM, G., EGUCHI, R., ADAMS, B., AND HUYCK, C. Project rescue: Challenges in responding to the unexpected. *SPIE Journal of Electronic Imaging, Displays, and Medical Imaging*, 5304 (2004), 179–192.
19. YOHEI MURAKAMI, KAZUHISA MINAMI, E. A. Multi-Agent Simulation for Crisis Management. *KMN* (2002).

# A Review of Public Health Syndromic Surveillance Systems

Ping Yan, Daniel Zeng, and Hsinchun Chen

Department of Management Information Systems,
University of Arizona, Tucson, Arizona
pyan@email.arizona.edu, {zeng, hchen}@eller.arizona.edu

**Abstract.** In response to the critical need of early detection of potential infectious disease outbreaks or bioterrorism events, public health syndromic surveillance systems have been rapidly developed and deployed in recent years. This paper surveys major research and system development issues related to syndromic surveillance systems and discusses recent advances in this important area of security informatics study.

## 1 Introduction

Syndromic surveillance is gaining wide acceptance in public health and bioterrorism event detection and response [35]. A syndromic surveillance system is aimed at detecting and characterizing a possible epidemic (either naturally-occurring or man-made) early on and can provide timely information to help prompt public health intervention and mitigate the event's impact. While traditional disease surveillance relies on physicians to report suspicious cases, contemporary syndromic surveillance research and development focuses on automating bioterrorism and public health preparedness and response to greatly improve surveillance capacity, significantly speed up in detection of disease outbreaks, and provide timely, suggestive information of epidemics to hospitals as well as to state, local, and federal health officials.

This paper surveys the existing technical literature and system development efforts in syndrome surveillance research and implementation. In comparison with current review articles that exist in the area [13][29][32], this review focuses on an in-depth description of technical components of syndromic surveillance systems and frames the related research questions from an IT and security informatics perspective.

In the literature, the discussion of syndromic surveillance systems usually falls under the following functional areas: 1) data acquisition, 2) syndrome classification, 3) anomaly detection, and 4) data visualization and data access. The surveillance data are first collected from the data providers to a centralized data repository where the raw data are categorized into syndrome categories to indicate certain disease threats. Anomaly detection employing time and space data analysis algorithms characterizes the syndormic data to detect the anomalies (for example, the surge of counts of clinic visits aggregated by days, or anomalous spatial clusters of medical records aggregated by ZIP codes). The data visualization and data access module is used to facilitate case investigations and support data exploration and summarization in a visual environment.

S. Mehrotra et al. (Eds.): ISI 2006, LNCS 3975, pp. 249–260, 2006.
© Springer-Verlag Berlin Heidelberg 2006

Sections 2 to 5 are dedicated to these four functional areas, respectively. Section 6 concludes the paper by highlighting the key issues and research challenges for future syndromic surveillance research and system development.

## 2 Data Acquisition

### 2.1 Data Sources

Syndromic surveillance is a data-driven public health surveillance approach which collects and processes a wide array of data sources. These data sources include chief complaints, emergency department (ED) visits, ambulatory visits, hospital admissions, triage nurse calls, 911 calls, work or school absenteeism data, veterinary health records, laboratory test orders, health department requests for influenza testing, among others [16][30]. For instance, one of the most established syndromic surveillance projects, the Real-time Outbreak Detection system (RODS), uses laboratory orders, dictated radiology reports, dictated hospital reports, poison control center calls, chief complaints data, and daily sales data for over-the-counter (OTC) medications for syndromic surveillance [39].

Preliminary investigations have evaluated the effectiveness of different data sources in syndromic surveillance and studied the difference among them in terms of information timeliness and characterization ability for outbreak detection, as they represent various aspects of patient health-care-seeking behavior [16][27][31]. For example, school absenteeism comes to notice relatively earlier as individuals take leave before seeking health care in hospitals or clinics, but specific disease evidence provided by the absenteeism type of data is limited. Table 1 provides a rough-cut classification of different data sources used for syndromic surveillance organized by their timeliness and the capability to characterize epidemic events.

**Table 1.** Data sources organized by data timeliness and epidemic characterization

| Characterization / Timeliness | High | Low |
|---|---|---|
| High | Chief complaints from ED visits and ambulatory visits [7][20][30][39] Hospital admission [51][52] Test orders [16][30] Triage nurse calls, 911 calls [34] Prescription medication data | OTC medication sales School or work absenteeism Veterinary health records |
| Low | ICD-9 code Laboratory test results Clinical reports | Public sources (local or regional events) |

### 2.2 Data Collection and Storage

Data collection is a critical early step when developing a syndromic surveillance system. The particular data collection strategy is obviously dependent on the data providers' information system infrastructure. Such strategies range from direct manual entry on paper or using hand-held devices [49] to automated data transmission, archiving, query and messaging [20][21].

Many practical challenges exist hindering the data collection effort. 1) Different coding conventions among the health facilities need to be reconciled when integrating the different data sources. CDC has led the way in the push for data standardization through the National Electronic Disease Surveillance System (NEDSS) and the Public Health Information Network (PHIN) initiatives. These initiatives define a set of vocabularies, messaging standards, message and data formats and so on [3]. 2) Providing and transmission of data either requires staff intervention or dedicated network infrastructure with relatively high security level, which are often viewed as extra cost to data providers. 3) Data sharing and transmission must comply with HIPAA and others, to be secure and assure privacy. 4) There is a time lag getting data from data providers to syndromic surveillance systems. Data quality challenges (e.g., incompleteness and duplications) often pose additional challenges.

## 3   Syndrome Classification

The onset of a number of syndromes can indicate certain diseases that are viewed as threats to the public health. For example, influenza-like syndrome could be due to an anthrax attack, which is of particular interest in detection of bioterrorism events.

Syndrome classification thus is one of the first and most important steps in syndromic data processing. Currently the syndrome classification process is implemented into syndromic surveillance systems either manually or through an automated system. The BioSense system initiated by CDC [16] basically relies on a working group that work on syndrome mapping converging with CDC definitions. However, automated, computerized syndrome classification is essential to real-time syndromic surveillance. The software application that evaluates the patient's chief complaint or ICD-9 codes and then assigns it a syndrome category is often known as syndrome classifier. Classification methods that have been studied and employed can largely be categorized into four groups: 1) Natural language processing; 2) Bayesian classifiers; 3) Text string searching; and 4) Vocabulary abstraction. We summrize existing classification methods in Table 2.

Evaluations have been conducted to compare various classifiers' performance for certain selected syndrome types. For instance, experiments conducted on two Bayesian classifiers for acute gastrointestinal syndrome demonstrate a 68 percent mapping success against expert classification of ED reports[18]. The classifiers are usually designed to work on a limited number of syndrome groups (for example, in RODS system, there are 7 syndrome groups of interest for purposes of biosurveillance, while EARS defines a more detailed list of 43 syndromes). Some syndromes are of common interest, such as respiratory or gastrointestinal syndromes; however, studies are to be done for other syndrome categories where the data set has relatively low availability.

In addition, there is no standardized syndrome definitions employed universally by different syndromic surveillance systems. Different computerized classifiers, or human chief complaint coders, are trained to prioritize and code symptoms differently

**Table 2.** Syndrome classification approaches

| Approach | Description | Example Systems |
|---|---|---|
| Manual grouping | 1. In Biosense project, a working group comprised of experts in surveillance, infectious diseases, and medical informatics performs the mapping of laboratory test orders into 11 syndrome categories according to CDC definition [16].<br>2. Triage nurses can also do the grouping when recording the symptoms. | The BioSense system [7][28] and Syndromal Surveillance Tally Sheet program used in ED of Santa Clara County, California. |
| Natural language processing | MPLUS system, a Bayesian network (BN)-based natural language processing system, originally used to analyze narrative and descriptive medical records [4] was adapted by RODS group for classifying free-text CC with simplified grammar containing rules for nouns, adjectives, prepositional phrases, and conjunctions. | Chapman et al. adapted the MPLUS to RODS system for classifying the free-text chief complaints [33][42]. |
| Bayesian classifiers | Bayesian classifiers, including naïve Bayesian classifier, bigram Bayes, and their variations, as supervised learning method classify CC learned from the training data of tagged CC. | The CoCo Bayesian classifier from RODS laboratory |
| Text string searching | A rule-based method that first uses keyword matching and synonym lists to standardize CC. In the second step, predefined rules are used to classify CCs or ICD-9 codes into syndrome categories. | EARS# employs this method, named TSS[17]. ESSENSE* developed a mapping of ICD-9 codes syndrome categories, which has been widely distributed[7]. |
| Vocabulary abstraction | This approach creates a series of intermediate abstractions up to a syndrome category from the individual level primitive data (e.g., signs, lab tests) according to a syndrome ontology that describes how primitive data relate to syndromes indicative of illness due to an agent of bioterrorism [9]. | The BioStorm System [34] [9][38] |

*ESSENSE: Electronic Surveillance System for the Early Notification of Community-Based Epidemics; #EARS: Early Aberration Reporting System.

following different coding conventions. As a result, there exists an obstacle for public health surveillance efforts to converge over a broader geographic scale. The comparison conducted by Christina et al. [5] between two syndrome coding systems shows low agreement in most of the syndrome classifications.

## 4 Data Analysis and Outbreak Detection

Automated data analysis for aberration detection is essential to real-time syndromic surveillance. These algorithms, spanning from classic statistical methods to artificial intelligence approaches, are used to quantify the possibility of an outbreak observed from the surveillance data. Usually, a detection system employs more than one algorithms, as no single algorithm can cover the wide spectrum of possible situations. Table 3 summarizes related outbreak detection algorithms organized as temporal, spatial, and temporal-spatial methods [11][32]. Note that it is not our intention to cover all existing detection algorithms. Rather we selected representative methods to illustrate the basic types of approaches that have been developed in the context of syndromic surveillance.

Another category, which is not shown in Table 3, includes "data-fusion" approaches where multiple data sources (e.g., ED visits and OTC sales data) are combined to perform outbreak detection. The majority of detection algorithms monitor individual data sources and do not cross reference between them. In the study conducted by the BioStorm research group, different analytical methods are assigned to different types of surveillance data with different settings [9][34]. The idea of such "data-fusion" approaches is that multiple data streams are analyzed with the extensions of analytical techniques, such as MCUSUM or MEWMA, to increase detection sensitivity while limiting the number of false alarms. Multiple univariate statistical techniques and multivariate methods are used in the literature based on different assumptions of independence among the data streams: multiple univariate methods assume independence among the data, while multivariate methods establish the covariance matrix typically estimated from a baseline period [11]. However, to model the multiple univariate signals from different data streams, an in-depth investigation and characterization of health-care–seeking behavior is necessary. In the ESSENSE II project, chief complaints data and sales of OTC medications are treated as covariates in SaTScan analytics [30]. The corresponding performance analysis shows substantial gain in the detection probabilities [2][44]. However, rigorous comparative evaluation to quantify the gain of using covariates from multiple data sources in surveillance is not reported yet.

Another challenging issue for real time outbreak detection is that the surveillance algorithms rely on historic datasets that span a considerable length of time (e.g., EARS relies on the past 3-5 years historic data in their long-term implementation [17]) against which to measure the anomaly of observed data. Few methods demonstrate reliable detection capability with short-term baseline data. This is a particular concern for event-based surveillance systems (also referred to as drop-in models) that have to be implemented against bioterrorism attacks or natural disease outbreaks in settings such as international and national sports events or meetings which involve a large population. EARS were used for syndromic surveillance at several large public events in the United States, including the Democratic National Convention of 2000, the 2001 Super Bowl, and the 2001 World Series [17]. The RODS system demonstrated its surveillance capacity during the 2002 Olympic Winter Games [14]. LEADERS (Lightweight Epidemiology Advanced Detection and Emergency Response System) often serves as a drop-in surveillance system intended to facilitate communication and coordination within and between the public health facilities [37]. The question is how analytics can be conducted with the limited availability of historic data to model normal patterns. CUSUM and its variation methods, as employed in EARS short-term surveillance implementation [17], allows a baseline data within 1-9 days.

Measurements on timeliness, specificity, and sensitivity of the detection algorithms have been reported; however, existing evaluation studies are quite limited, as they are either reliable only for one specific disease [23] or are biased by simulation settings as very few bioterrorism attacks for real testing are available [12].

**Table 3.** Algorithms for outbreak detection

| Algorithm | Description | Remarks |
|---|---|---|
| Time series analysis | | |
| Serfling method | A static cyclic regression model with predefined parameters optimized through the training data | Available from RODS [40]; used by CDC for flu detection |
| ARIMA | Autoregressive Integrated Moving Average method; Linear function with parameters learned from historical data [36]; seasonal effect can be adjusted | Available from RODS |
| EWMA | Exponentially Weighted Moving Average; Predictions based on exponential smoothing of previous several weeks of data with recent days having the highest weight. | Available from ESSENCE |
| CUSUM | A control chart method to monitor the departure of the mean of the observed data's time series from a theoretical mean [10][15]; It allows for limited baseline data | Widely used in current surveillance systems including Biosense, EARS [17] and ESSENSE among others |
| Spatial clustering analysis | | |
| SMART (Small Area Regression and Testing) | An adaptation of a generalized linear mixed modeling (GLMM) technique which takes into account multiple comparisons and includes parameters for ZIP code, day of the week, holiday, day after a holiday, and seasonal cyclic variation; Parameters are updated weekly [7] | Available in Biosense [7][16] and National Bioterrorism syndromic surveillance demonstration program[47] |
| GLMM | A generalized linear mixed modeling approach for evaluating whether observed counts in relatively small areas are larger than would be expected on the basis of a history of naturally occurring disease [24][25]. | Used in Minnesota [43] |
| RLS (Recursive Least Square) | A dynamic autoregressive linear model that predicts current count of each prodrome within a region based on the historical data and adjusts its model coefficients based on prediction errors; An alert is triggered when RLS finds the current count is greater than the 95% confidence interval of its predicted count; continuously updating its parameters | Available from RODS |
| Modified spatial scan statistics | It takes into account the different addresses of persons between home and workplace, which might improve the detection of disease outbreaks when exposure occurs in the workplace. | Proposed in [31] |

**Table 3.** (*continue*)

| Temporal, spatial, and temporal-spatial | | |
|---|---|---|
| SatScan™ software | Including space-time scan statistics and temporal scan statistic; Searching all the subregions for likely clusters in space and time [26] | Widely-used in many community surveillance systems including the National Bioterrorism Syndromic Surveillance Demonstration Program [47]; Related visualization available from BioPortal |
| WSARE (What is Strange About Recent Event) | Searching for groups with specific characteristics (e.g., a recent pattern of place, age, and diagnosis associated with illness that is anomalous when compared with historic patterns) [32][48]; Addressing the limitations of traditional analytical methods' incapability of defining representative features combination of multi-dimensional data to monitor [45][46] | Available from RODS; performance evaluated in Israel, June 2004 [48] |
| PANDA (Population-wide Anomaly Detection and Assessment) | Using a causal Bayesian network to model a population of persons and infer the spatio-temporal probability distribution of disease for the population as a whole or each patient in the population [1][8] | Under development in RODS |
| Risk-Adjusted Support Vector Clustering | Combining the risk adjustment idea with Support Vector Clustering to improve the quality of spatio-temporal clustering analysis | Available from BioPortal [50] |

# 5   Data Access and Visualization

In most cases anomaly detection is only suggestive not conclusive. Due to the presence of false alarms and a scarcity of real outbreak events, initiating a response, especially against bioterrorism attacks, is a difficult decision to make. How to interpret the computerized surveillance outcomes and how to differentiate a real threat from an explainable anomaly are critical issues. These are system functionality issues which are also related to the experience of responsible officials, communication mechanisms, and collaborations within and outside the public health domain [19][22].

To facilitate interactive data exploration, maps, graphs, and tables are common forms of helpful visualization tools. Below we provide examples of such tools implemented in various research prototypes and deployed surveillance systems. The RODS system employs the GIS (geographical information system) module to depict data spatially [20]. In Biosense and ESSENSE, a geographical map consisting of individual zip code is marked with different colors to represent the threat level. Stratification can be applied for different syndrome categories, and individual case details can be accessed by "drill down" functions. A more sophisticated case manager as a functional module for investigation of anomalies and to reduce false positives is also proposed [6]. Such a case manager includes a logic-rich engine and two configurable tools for case organization and dynamic data visualization. The BioPortal project makes available an advanced visualization module, called the Spatial Temporal Visualizer (STV) [41] to facilitate exploration of infectious disease case data and to summarize query results. STV is a generic visualization environment that can be used to visualize a number of spatial temporal datasets simultaneously. It allows the user to load and save spatial temporal data in a dynamic manner for exploration and dissemination. The Biosense working group presents a basic road map for abnormal event inquiry to support the decision of whether to initiate a response [16]. The process consists of data quality evaluation, aberration extent estimation, comparison with other data sources, and supplemental facts gathering.

## 6 Discussion and Conclusion

This paper provides a brief survey of the emerging field of syndromic surveillance that involves identifying, collecting, and analyzing public heath data for early outbreak detection. Traditional disease surveillance systems are based on confirmed diagnoses, whereas syndromic surveillance makes use of pre-diagnosis information for timely data collection and analysis. The main IT-related research topics and challenges in syndromic surveillance are presented in this survey.

With regards to future research in syndromic surveillance, we see a lot of opportunities for informatics studies on topics ranging from data visualization, further development and comprehensive evaluation of outbreak detection algorithms, data interoperability, and further development of response and event management decision models based on data and predictions provided by syndromic surveillance systems. From an application domain perspective, the following trends can potentially lead to new interesting research questions. First, public health surveillance can be a truly global effort for pandemic diseases such as avian influenza. Issues concerning global data sharing (including multilingual information processing) and the development of models that work over a wide geographical area need to be addressed. Second, although syndromic surveillance systems have been developed and deployed in many state public health departments, there is a critical need to create a cross-jurisdictional data sharing infrastructure to maximize the potential benefit and practice impact of syndromic surveillance. Third, syndromic surveillance concepts, techniques, and systems are equally applicable to animal health besides public health. We expect to see significant new work to be done to model animal health-specific issues and deal with zoonotic diseases.

## References

1. Andrew W. Moore, G.C., Rich Tsui, Mike Wagner: Summary of Biosurveillance-relevant Statistical and Data Mining Techniques. RODS Laboratory Technical Report, 2002.
2. Burkom, H.S.: Biosurveillance Applying Scan Statistics with Multiple Disparate Data Sources. Journal Urban Health 2003. 80(2), pp. 57-65, 2003.

3.  CDC: National Electronic Disease Surveillance System: the surveillance and monitoring component of the Public Health Information Network. Atlanta, GA: US Department of Health and Human Services, 2004.
4.  Christensen L, H.P., Fiszman M: MPLUS: a Probabilistic Medical Language Understanding System. in Workshop on Natural Language Processing in the Biomedical Domain. 2002.
5.  Christina A. Mikosz, J.S., S. Black, G. Gibbs, I. Cardenas: Comparison of Two Major Emergency Department-Based Free-Text Chief-Complaint Coding Systems. Morbidity and Mortality Weekly Report, the Epidemiology Program Office, Centers for Disease Control and Prevention (CDC). 53(Suppl), 2004.
6.  Colin R. Goodall, A.L., S. Halasz, E. Koski, D. Agarwal, S. Tse, G. Jacobson: Performance-Critical Anomaly Detection — United States, December 2002–March 2004. Morbidity and Mortality Weekly Report, the Epidemiology Program Office, Centers for Disease Control and Prevention (CDC). 54(Suppl), pp. 188, 2005.
7.  Colleen A. Bradley, H.R., D. Walker, J. Loonsk: BioSense: Implementation of a National Early Event Detection and Situational Awareness System. Morbidity and Mortality Weekly Report, the Epidemiology Program Office, Centers for Disease Control and Prevention (CDC), 54(Suppl), pp. 11-20, 2005.
8.  Cooper GF, D.D., Levander JD, Wong WK, Hogan WR, Wagner MM: Bayesian Biosurveillance of Disease Outbreaks. In the Twentieth Conference on Uncertainty in Artificial Intelligence. 2004. Banff, Alberta, Canada.
9.  D. L. Buckeridge, J.G., M. J. O'Connor, M. K. Choy, S. W. Tu, M. A.: Musen: Knowledge-Based Bioterrorism Surveillance. in American Medical Informatics Association Symposium. 2002. San Antonio, TX.
10.  Das D, W.D., Mostashari F: Enhanced Drop-in Syndromic Surveillance in New York City Following September 11, 2001. J Urban Health. 80(1), pp. 176-188, 2003.
11.  David L. Buckeridge, H.B., Murray Campbell, William R. Hogan, Andrew W. Moore: Algorithms for Rapid Outbreak Detection: a Research Synthesis. Journal of Biomedical Informatics. 38, pp. 99-113, 2005.
12.  David L. Buckeridge, P.S., D. Owens, D. Siegrist, J. Pavlin, M. Musen: An Evaluation Model for Syndromic Surveillance: Assessing the Performance of a Temporal Algorithm. Morbidity and Mortality Weekly Report, the Epidemiology Program Office, Centers for Disease Control and Prevention (CDC). 54(Suppl), pp. 109-115, 2005.
13.  Dena M. Bravata, K.M.M., Wendy M. Smith, Chara Rydzak, Herbert Szeto, David L Buckeridge, Corinna Haberland, Douglas K. Owens: Systematic Review: Surveillance Systems for Early Detection of Bioterrorism-Related Diseases. Ann Intern Med. 140, pp. 910-922, 2004.
14.  Gesteland PH, W.M., Chapman WW, et al.: Rapid Deployment of an Electronic Disease Surveillance System in the State of Utah for the 2002 Olympic Winter games. in Proc AMIA Symp 2002. 2002.
15.  Grigoryan VV, W.M., Waller K, Wallstrom GL, Hogan WR: The Effect of Spatial Granularity of Data on. Reference Dates for Influenza Outbreaks. RODS Laboratory Technical Report, 2005
16.  Haobo Ma, H.R., K. Mandl, D. Buckeridge, A. Fleischauer, J. Pavlin: Implementation of Laboratory Order Data in BioSense Early Event Detection and Situation Awareness System. Morbidity and Mortality Weekly Report, the Epidemiology Program Office, Centers for Disease Control and Prevention (CDC). 54(Suppl), pp. 27-30, 2005.
17.  Hutwagner L, T.W., Seeman GM, Treadwell T: The Bioterrorism Preparedness and Response Early Aberration Reporting System (EARS). J Urban Health. 80(2), pp. 89-96, 2003.

18. Ivanov O, W.M., Chapman WW, Olszewski RT: Accuracy of Three Classifiers of Acute Gastrointestinal Syndrome for Syndromic Surveillance. in AMIA Symp. 2002.
19. James B. Daniel, D.H.-G., P. Gadam, W. Yih, K. Mandl, A. DeMaria, Jr., R. Platt: Connecting Health Departments and Providers: Syndromic Surveillance's Last Mile. Morbidity and Mortality Weekly Report, the Epidemiology Program Office, Centers for Disease Control and Prevention (CDC). 54(Suppl), pp. 147-51, 2005.
20. Jeremy U. Espino, M.W., C. Szczepaniak, F-C. Tsui, H. Su, R. Olszewski, Z. Liu, W. Chapman, X. Zeng, L. Ma, Z. Lu, J. Dara: Removing a Barrier to Computer-Based Outbreak and Disease Surveillance — The RODS Open Source Project. Morbidity and Mortality Weekly Report, the Epidemiology Program Office, Centers for Disease Control and Prevention (CDC). 53(Suppl), pp. 34-41, 2004.
21. Joseph Lombardo, H.B., Eugene Elbert, Steven Magruder, Sheryl Happel Lewis, Wayne Loschen, James Sari, Carol Sniegoski, Richard Wojcik, and Julie Pavlin: A systems overview of the Electronic Surveillance System for the Early Notification of Community-based Epidemics (ESSENCE II). Journal of Urban Health: Bulletin of the New York Academy of Medicine. 80(2), pp. 32-42, 2003.
22. Kathy J. Hurt-Mullen, J.C.: Syndromic Surveillance on the Epidemiologist's Desktop: Making Sense of Much Data. Morbidity and Mortality Weekly Report, the Epidemiology Program Office, Centers for Disease Control and Prevention (CDC), 54(Suppl), pp. 141-147, 2005.
23. Ken P. Kleinman, A.A., K. Mandl, R. Platt: Simulation for Assessing Statistical Methods of Biologic Terrorism Surveillance. Morbidity and Mortality Weekly Report, the Epidemiology Program Office, Centers for Disease Control and Prevention (CDC). 54(Suppl), pp. 103-110, 2005.
24. Kleinman K, A.A., Kulldorff M, Platt R: A Model-adjusted Spacetime Scan Statistic with an Application to Syndromic Surveillance. Epidemiol Infect 2005, (119), pp. 409-19, 2005.
25. Kleinman K, L.R., Platt R: A Generalized Linear Mixed Models Approach for Detecting Incident Cluster/signals of Disease in Small Areas, with an Application to Biological Terrorism (with Invited Commentary). Am J Epidemiol 2004. 159, pp. 217-24, 2004.
26. Kulldorff, M.: Prospective Time Periodic Geographical Disease Surveillance Using a Scan Statistic. Journal of the Royal Statistical Society, Series A, (164), pp. 61-72, 2001.
27. Lazarus R, K.K., Dashevsky I, DeMaria A, Platt R: Using Automated Medical Records for Rapid Identification of Illness Syndromes (Syndromic Surveillance): the Example of Lower Respiratory Infection. BMC Public Health 1(9), 2001.
28. Leslie Z. Sokolow, N.G., H. Rolka, D. Walker, P. McMurray, R. English-Bullard, J. Loonsk: Deciphering Data Anomalies in BioSense. Morbidity and Mortality Weekly Report, the Epidemiology Program Office, Centers for Disease Control and Prevention (CDC). 54(Suppl), pp. 133-140, 2005.
29. Lober WB, K.B., Wagner MM: Roundtable on Bioterrorism Detection: Information System-based Surveillance. J Am Med Inform Assoc 2003. 9, pp. 105-15, 2002.
30. Lombardo J, B.H., Pavlin J: Electronic Surveillance System for the Early Notification of Community-Based Epidemics (ESSENCE II), Framework for Evaluating Syndromic Surveillance Systems. Syndromic surveillance: report from a national conference, 2003. MMWR 2004. 53(Suppl), pp. 159-65, 2004.
31. Luiz Duczmal, D.B.: Using Modified Spatial Scan Statistic to Improve Detection of Disease Outbreak When Exposure Occurs in Workplace — Virginia, 2004. Morbidity and Mortality Weekly Report, the Epidemiology Program Office, Centers for Disease Control and Prevention (CDC). 54(Suppl), pp. 187, 2005.

32. Mandl KD, O.J., Wagner MM, Lober WB, Sebastiani P, Mostashari F, Pavlin JA, Gesteland PH, Treadwell T, Koski E, Hutwagner L, Buckeridge DL, Aller RD, Grannis S: Implementing Syndromic Surveillance: a Practical Guide Informed by the Early Experience. J Am Med Inform Assoc. 11(2), pp. 141-50, 2004.

33. Michael M. Wagner, J.E., F-C. Tsui, P. Gesteland, W. Chapman, O. Ivanov, A. Moore, W. Wong, J. Dowling, J. Hutman: Syndrome and Outbreak Detection Using Chief-Complaint Data — Experience of the Real-Time Outbreak and Disease Surveillance Project. MMWR, Centers for Disease Control and Prevention (CDC). 53(Suppl), pp. 28-32, 2004.

34. Monica Crubézy, M.O.C., Zachary Pincus, and Mark A. Musen: Ontology-Centered Syndromic Surveillance for Bioterrorism. IEEE INTELLIGENT SYSTEMS. 20(5), pp. 26-35, 2005.

35. CDC.: Syndromic Surveillance for Bioterrorism Following the Attacks on the World Trade Center–New York City, 2001. MMWR. 51, pp. 13-5, 2002.

36. Reis BY, M.K. (2003) Time Series Modeling for Syndromic Surveillance. BMC Medical Informatics and Decision Making.

37. Ritter, T.: LEADERS: Lightweight Epidemiology Advanced Detection and Emergency Response System. In SPIE. 2002.

38. Shahar Y, M.M.: Knowledge-based Temporal Abstraction in Clinical Domains. Artificial Intelligence in Medicine. 8, pp. 267-98, 1996.

39. Tsui FC, E.J., Dato VM, Gesteland PH, Hutman J, Wagner MM: Technical Description of RODS: a Real-time Public Health Surveillance System. J Am Med Inform Assoc 2003. 10, pp. 399-408, 2003.

40. Tsui, F.C.R., Wagner, M., Dato, V., & Chang, H. C.: Value of ICD-9–Coded Chief Complaints for Detection of Epidemics. Symposium of Journal of American Medical Informatics Association, 2001.

41. Ty Buetow, L.G.C., Christopher D. O'Toole, Tom Cushna, Damien Daspit, Tim Petersen, Homa Atabakhsh, Hsinchun Chen: A Spatio Temporal Visualizer for Law Enforcement. In ISI. 2003.

42. W. Chapman, L.C., M. Wagner, P. Haug, O. Ivanov, J. Dowling, R. Olszewski: Classifying Free-text Triage Chief Complaints into Syndromic Categories with Natural Language Processing. Artificial Intelligence in Medicine. 33(1), pp. 31-40, 2005.

43. W. Katherine Yih, A.A., R. Danila, K. Green, K. Kleinman, M. Kulldorff, B. Miller, J. Nordin, R. Platt: Ambulatory-Care Diagnoses as Potential Indicators of Outbreaks of Gastrointestinal Illness — Minnesota. MMWR, Centers for Disease Control and Prevention (CDC). 54(Suppl), pp. 157-162, 2005.

44. Weng-Keen Wong, G.C., D. Dash, J. Levander, J. Dowling, W. Hogan, M. Wagner Use of Multiple Data Streams to Conduct Bayesian Biologic Surveillance. MMWR, the Epidemiology Program Office, Centers for Disease Control and Prevention (CDC). 54(Suppl), pp. 63-70, 2005.

45. Wong W-K, M.A., Cooper G, Wagner M: Rule-based Anomaly Pattern Detection for Detecting Disease Outbreaks. In AAAI-02. 2002. Edmonton, Alberta

46. Wong WK, M.A., Cooper G, Wagner M.: WSARE: What's Strange about Recent Events? Journal of Urban Health. 80(2), pp. 66-75, 2003.

47. Yih WK, C.B., Harmon R: The National Bioterrorism Syndromic Surveillance Demonstration Program. MMWR 2004. 53(Suppl). pp. 43-6, 2004.

48. Zalman Kaufman, E.C., T. Peled-Leviatan, C. Lavi, G. Aharonowitz, R. Dichtiar, M. Bromberg, O. Havkin, and R.M. Y. Shalev, V. Shalev, J. Shemer, M. Green: Using Data on an Influenza B Outbreak To Evaluate a Syndromic Surveillance System — Israel, June 2004 [abstract]. MMWR, Centers for Disease Control and Prevention (CDC). 54(Suppl), pp. 191, 2005.

49. Zelicoff A, B.J., Forslund DW, et al.: The rapid syndrome validation project (RSVP). In AMIA Symp. 2001.
50. Zeng, D., W. Chang, H. Chen: Clustering-based Spatio-Temporal Hotspot Analysis Techniques in Security Informatics. In IEEE Transactions on Intelligent Transportation Systems. 2004.
51. Zygmunt F. Dembek, K.C., A. Siniscalchi, J. Hadler: Hospital Admissions Syndromic Surveillance — Connecticut, September 2001–November 2003. MMWR, Centers for Disease Control and Prevention (CDC). 53(Suppl), pp. 50-52, 2004.
52. Zygmunt F. Dembek, K.C., J. Hadler: Guidelines for Constructing a Statewide Hospital Syndromic Surveillance Network. MMWR, Centers for Disease Control and Prevention (CDC). 54(Suppl), pp. 21-26, 2005.

# A Novel Mechanism to Defend Against Low-Rate Denial-of-Service Attacks*

Wei Wei[1], Yabo Dong[1], Dongming Lu[1], Guang Jin[1,2], and Honglan Lao[3]

[1] College of Computer Science and Technology, Zhejiang University,
Hangzhou 310027, P.R. China
[2] College of Information Science and Engineering, Ningbo University,
Ningbo 315211, P.R. China
[3] Department of Electrical Engineering, University of Southern California,
Los Angeles CA 90089-2564, USA
{weiwei_tc, dongyb, ldm, d05jinguang}@zju.edu.cn,
hlao@usc.edu

**Abstract.** Low-rate TCP-targeted Denial-of-Service (DoS) attack (shrew) is a new kind of DoS attack which is based on TCP's Retransmission Timeout (RTO) mechanism and can severely reduce the throughput of TCP traffic on victim. The paper proposes a novel mechanism which consists of effective detection and response methods. Through analyzing sampled attack traffic, we find that there is a stable difference between attack and legitimate traffic in frequency field, especially in low frequency. We use Sum of Low Frequency Power spectrum (SLFP) for detection. In our algorithm the destination IP address is used as flow label and SLFP is applied to every flow traversing edge router. If shrew is found, all flows to the destination are processed by Aggregated Flows Balance (AFB) at a proper upstream router. Simulation shows that attack traffics are restrained and TCP traffics can obtain enough bandwidth. The result indicates that our mechanism is effective and deployable.

## 1 Introduction

### 1.1 Denial-of-Service Attack

Denial-of-Service (DoS) is a major threat to Internet security. Attack packets often assemble to victim to disturb the legitimate use of a service. These attack packets consume some key resources, confuse applications or protocols on the victim and make it inefficient or even disabled. In current Internet, DoS is usually detected as Distributed DoS (DDoS) in which distributed DoS flows assemble in target network and result in an overwhelming destruction.

---

* Funded by National Natural Science Foundation of China (60503061); Zhejiang Provincial Natural Science Foundation (Y104437); Zhejiang Provincial Science and Technology Program (2005C33034); The Program for New Century Excellent Talents in University (NCET-04-0535); The Program for New Century 151 Outstanding Scholar of Zhejiang Province.

S. Mehrotra et al. (Eds.): ISI 2006, LNCS 3975, pp. 261–271, 2006.

The focus of the paper is to defend against a new kind of DoS attack: low-rate TCP-targeted DoS attack (shrew) [1]. It does not make use of leaks of systems and protocols, but TCP's RTO mechanism. In shrew, periodical traffic bursts are sent to victim and induce packet losses in neck link. Then the TCP flows to victim enter repeated timeout and the throughput decreases to a very low fraction of bandwidth.

## 1.2 TCP's RTO Mechanism

In one TCP connection, one end sends out one or several packets and then waits for acknowledgement. If the sender does not receive any response from the receiver after a certain time span, RTO, the sender will resend the packets and wait for acknowledgement again. For one TCP connection, if above phenomenon lasts then it indicates probable congestion in networks. RTO should be increased every time in order to escape the congestion and usually exponential back-off is used. For example, in usual RTO implementation, with integer value, initial RTO is 1 second, and will increase to 3 seconds after first timeout. If the next retransmissions still result in timeout, RTO will orderly increase to 6, 12, 24, 48 seconds and finally stays in a maximum value which is often 64 seconds. If the process lasts long enough, the sender will give up.

RTO, Round Trip Time (RTT) and other related values are computed periodically according to RFC793 [2]. The formula is given as follows.

$$R' = \alpha R + (1 - \alpha)M$$
$$RTO = \beta R' \tag{1}$$

Here $\alpha$ is a filter gain constant with suggested value of 0.9 and $R'$ is the estimated RTT. $R$ is the estimated RTT of last estimation and $M$ is the measured RTT of this time. $\beta$ is the disperse coefficient and the suggested value is 2.

V. Jacobson et al found that if RTT fluctuated with large variance, the computation in (1) would cause unnecessary retransmission and be inefficient [3]. They suggested computing the variance of old RTTs to adjust estimated RTT. The variance of RTTs is approximated by mean deviation and the updated formula is shown in (2):

$$E = M - R$$
$$R' = R + gE$$
$$D' = D + h(|E| - D)$$
$$RTO = \max(\min RTO, R' + 4D') \tag{2}$$

In (2) $R$ is the estimated RTT of last estimation. $M$ is the measured RTT of this time and $R'$ is the estimated RTT. $D$ and $D'$ are the mean deviations of last and current estimations respectively. And $minRTO$ is the lower bound of RTO. V. paxson et al considered that if there was a lower bound of RTO with about 1 second, TCP would have best performance [4].

### 1.3  Low-Rate TCP-Targeted DoS Attack

Low-rate TCP-targeted DoS attack is also named "shrew" and was firstly proposed and confirmed through experiments by A. Kuzmanovic et al [1]. In shrew, the target is the TCP traffics on victim. Since most applications are based on TCP protocol which accounts for large fraction of traffic in networks, shrew will have severe impact on victim.

The mechanism of shrew is to bring most TCP flows to victim into periodical timeout and sharply decrease the TCP throughput. For one TCP flow, if a packet or the corresponding ACK is dropped due to network congestion, the sender retransmits this packet after RTO and updates RTO value. If the loss happens again, the sender repeats this action while the TCP throughput is zero. If one malicious user sends a series of traffic bursts to the victim and produces network congestion synchronized with retransmission process of one TCP flow to the victim, the TCP flow will be halted. If the bursts occur in the upstream link of the victim, most of the TCP flows to it will repeatedly time out and the TCP throughput decreases drastically. If the burst period is around 1 second and the burst length is around RTT, nearly all TCP flows to victim will be halted. The standard pattern of attack traffic is shown in Fig. 1(a). Because of background traffic and the low rate of shrew, it is hard to detect by traditional methods.

### 1.4  Distributed Shrew Attack

It is possible to observe attack pattern of single source shrew attack in the source network. However, for a distributed shrew attack, attack patterns will not likely be detected until multiple attack flows converge in the destination network. And for one of the attack flows, the mean rate is lower and pattern is harder to detect. The distributed shrew attacks can be classified into three kinds: temporal overlay, spatial overlay and mixed overlay. The first is shown in Fig. 1(b) where the burst period of single attack flow expands to times of original period. The second in Fig. 1(c) shows that the finally converged burst consists of multiple bursts of single flows. The third is a mixture of above two kinds and is illustrated in Fig. 1(d).

The rest of this paper is organized as follows. An overview of related work is given in section 2 and our detection algorithm SLFP is presented in section 3. In section 4 the response strategy AFB is provided. Simulations are shown and explained in section 5 and then conclusions are given in section 6.

## 2  Related Work

Shrew attack was firstly proposed by A. Kuzmanovic et al [1] and many discussions appeared subsequently. Based on the idea that big router cache could smooth traffic burst, S. Sarat et al [5] discussed the effect of router cache size on shrew attack. Considering that the efficiency of shrew attack mainly relies on the homogeneity of RTO, J. Tsao et al tried using RTO-randomization [6]. G. Yang et al discussed the effect of randomized RTO and found that RTO-randomization not only restrained shrew attack but also reduced the performance of legitimate TCP traffic [7].

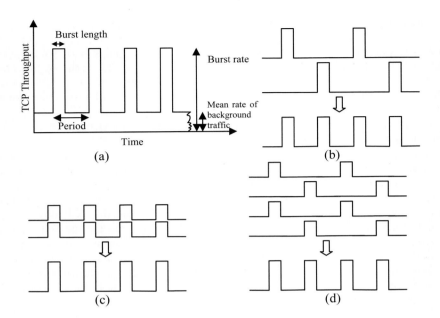

**Fig. 1.** Shrew attacks. (a) Typical single flow shrew. (b) Temporal overlay shrew. (c) Spatial overlay shrew. (d) Mixed overlay attack.

For the detection and response, A. Shevtekar et al pointed out the rate of shrew attack flow had square-wave pattern in samples of edge routers [8]. X. Luo et al used wavelet transformation to detect abnormal fluctuation of incoming TCP and outgoing TCP ACK traffics [9]. Y. Chen et al suggested tracking shrew pattern in a transport-level flow and drop the flow if shrew attack was detected [10]. They found that the pattern in attack traffic caused a deviation from legitimate spectrum in frequency field and could be used for detection. H. Sun et al [11] presented detection in edge router and supposed that the congestion happens in the router's downstream link. They transformed temporal attack pattern to correlation sequence which eliminated the time shift starting from the initial point of measurement to the beginning of the attack pulse. Then the legitimate traffic can be differentiated.

## 3   The Detection: SLFP

Shrew attack can escape most of current DoS detection methods. However, the attack effect is sensitive to the changes of attack parameters and the attack pattern is similar to the standard pattern in Fig. 1(a) [1] which the detection may rely on.

Periodical and non-periodical sequences in time field should have different properties in corresponding sequences of frequency field. Although it is challenging to detect shrew attack in time field, it is feasible to implement detection in frequency field. There has been some related work in [10] where DFT is used to get amplitude spectrum. Here we use Power Spectrum Density (PSD) which has been used in detection, e.g., A. Hussain et al used PSD to differentiate single-source DoS and multi-source DDoS [12] and C. M. Cheng et al found there was a difference in peak position of PSD between DoS and legitimate traffics [13]. One time sequence's PSD can be computed using DFT of its auto-correlation sequence and also can be approximated by periodogram. Here we use the periodogram. For a discrete sequence $\{x_1, x_2, \ldots x_n\}$, its periodogram could be computed as follows:

$$S(e^{j\omega}) = \frac{1}{n}\left|\sum_{l=1}^{n} x_l e^{-j\omega l}\right|^2 \tag{3}$$

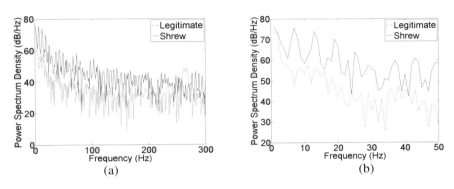

**Fig. 2.** PSD sequences of legitimate and attack traffics

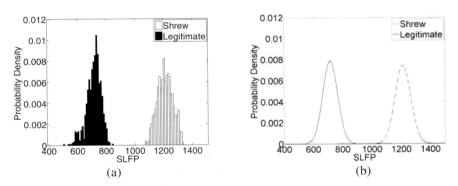

**Fig. 3.** Distribution of total power

To illustrate the effectiveness of PSD, we compare the PSD sequences of typical legitimate and shrew attack traffics. Fig. 2(a) is the 1-300 Hz PSD sequences. We can see there are obvious differences between the two sequences, especially in low frequency. Fig. 2(b) is the corresponding comparison in 1-50 Hz.

Considering the difference is caused by different power distribution, we use the summation of power in 1-50 Hz. We call it Sum of Low Frequency Power spectrum (SLFP). To illustrate that SLFPs of attack and legitimate traffics are localized in different ranges that can be clearly differentiated, we collect respective 5000 3.5 seconds long sequences for legitimate and shrew traffics with sampling unit of 0.01

second and the 5000 attack sequences are from shrew with period of 1 second and burst length of 50, 100, 150, 200, 250 milliseconds respectively. The distribution of total power of 1-50 Hz is given in Fig. 3(a).Then we use normal distribution to fit above samples. The fitted curve is shown in Fig. 3(b) and the parameters are:

Legitimate: Average ($\mu$) is 715.3, standard deviation ($\sigma$) is 50.5.
Shrew: Average ($\mu$) is 1212.1, standard deviation ($\sigma$) is 53.6.

Here the summation of power is a stable value and is perfect for classification. SLFP can be implemented in edge routers of victim. Before detection, a table is allocated to save samples for all protected downstream servers and flows to different servers are recorded periodically into corresponding table entries. If one sampling cycle is over, SLFP is applied to samples in every table entry and if an attack exists in traffic to one server and no previous response has been given, a message is sent to an appropriate upstream router with most of attack traffic is from the router. The router will decide whether to start the balancing algorithm or continually trace back. In the contrary, if attack does not exist and sign of previous detection was set T seconds before, an undo message is sent and the sign of detection is unset. The balancing algorithm is given in next chapter.

# 4   The Response: AFB

## 4.1   Algorithms

Since TCP traffic is the target of shrew attack, we consider reserving most bandwidth for TCP with the remaining for other traffics and give a response method called Aggregated Flow Balance (AFB). All TCP flows are classified and each class is given a reasonable fraction of bandwidth in order to restrict the burst rate from single shrew source.

AFB is implemented at the edge router and more upstream routers. How to locate the edge router is beyond our consideration and can be found in [14]. Using SLFP the edge router spots a shrew attack in the traffic to one server and then traces back the attack traffic by sending messages to the upstream router which forwards attack flows. If one appropriate upstream router can not determine, AFB is started. The router classifies flows by the router's incoming ports, i.e. classifies all UDP and other protocol flows to the destination as one class, and then divide TCP flows from different incoming ports into different classes. If there are $N$ incoming ports on the router, there will be $N+1$ traffic classes, i.e. $N$ TCP flows from $N$ incoming ports and one class for other flows from all incoming ports. We use an array to allocate the bandwidth, i.e. array $AFB\_Buckets$, which is updated periodically and its each element represents the bytes allocated for the corresponding traffic class in current update period. The elements of $AFB\_Buckets$ are initialized to preseted value in the beginning. If a packet with length of $L$ arrives in incoming port $i$, the router checks the corresponding value of $AFB\_Buckets[i-1]$. If $AFB\_Buckets[i-1] \geq L$, then the packet is forwarded and $L$ is subtracted from $AFB\_Buckets[i-1]$, else if $AFB\_Buckets[i-1] < L$, the packet is dropped. And the value of one period will not cumulate to next period. The bandwidth allocated to class $i$ in the beginning of one period is in proportion to the throughput of traffic class $i$ in last period. The AFB algorithm is given below.

Get bandwidth allocated to the attacked server as $B$;
Setup two arrays, *AFB_Buckets* for bandwidth allocation and *Hist* for recording historical rate in last update period;
    For every arrived packet {
    Record the length of packet using $L$, and the class it belongs to using $i$;
    $Hist[i-1]=Hist[i-1]+L$;
    If $L <= AFB\_Buckets[i-1]$ { forward the packet;
    $AFB\_Buckets[i-1]=AFB\_Buckets[i-1]-L$; }
    Else Drop the packet;
    If it is the end of update period {
    For $i = 1$ to $N+1$
        $AFB\_Buckets[i-1]=B * Hist[i-1] / $ (summation of *Hist*);
    }}

**Fig. 4.** AFB algorithm

## 4.2  Considerations of Realization

We prototype SLFP using a 2.66GHz Pentium 4 machine and it costs averagely about 1.05 ms to compute a SLFP value from a 3.5-second sample. Meanwhile AFB can be implemented based on bucket mechanism and its cost is neglectable when compared with SLFP. From above information we can see that the processing overhead for protecting one target host is about 1.05 ms every 3.5 seconds. On the other hand, the memory requirement can be concluded from Fig. 4 and it needs less than 1 KB for one protected host. So we consider, as long as the involved routers are not too busy, it is applicable to use these routers to shelter one class C network.

# 5  Simulations

To validate the effectiveness of above algorithms, we insert several attack agents *Shrew_Agent* to send shrew packets and classifiers *AFB_Classifier* into the entry of NS2 nodes to implement SLFP and AFB. The simulation network topology is in Fig. 5. There are 5 clients, 4 attackers and 5 servers connected by core router A and B. The bandwidth of the link between A and B is 100Mbps, and the bandwidth of every link from B to downstream routers is 20Mbps, other links are all with bandwidth of 10Mbps. The attacked server is "victim" and attack causes packet dropping in the link between victim and S. TCP NewReno is used and we have completed three typical shrew attack scenarios which are given as below.

## 5.1  Simulation 1: Single Attack Flow and Single Legitimate TCP Flow

There is only one legitimate TCP flow between one client and the victim and an attacker sends shrew flow to the victim. The attack period is 1 second and the burst rate is 10Mbps with burst length of 200 milliseconds. The attack lasts 30 seconds. Fig. 6(a) and Fig. 6(b) show the throughput of TCP flow without and with AFB. The throughput in Fig. 6(a) is only 11.3% and is 63.2% in Fig. 6(b).

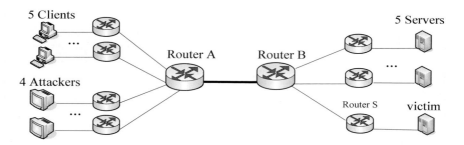

**Fig. 5.** Simulation network topology

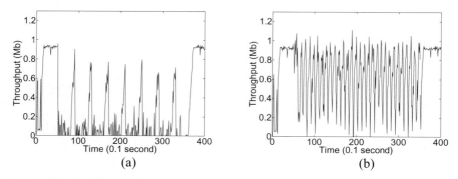

**Fig. 6.** The result of simulation 1. (a) is the TCP throughput without AFB and (b) is the TCP throughput with AFB.

### 5.2 Simulation 2: Single Attack Flow and Multiple Legitimate TCP Flows

There are 7 legitimate TCP flows between clients and servers. The first 3 clients connect to the victim with 3 legitimate flows and 4 clients connect to other 4 servers with 4 legitimate flows. Here there is still one attacker. The attack period is 1 second with burst rate of 10Mbps and burst length of 200 milliseconds. The attack lasts 30 seconds. Fig. 7(a) and Fig. 7(b) shows the throughput of TCP flow without and with AFB. The throughput is respectively 11.6% and 95.6%.

### 5.3 Simulation 3: Multiple Attack Flows and Multiple Legitimate TCP Flows

There are 7 legitimate TCP flows from 5 clients and a distributed mixed overlay (Fig.1(d)) shrew attack from 4 attackers to victim. For every attack flow, the attack period is 2 seconds with burst rate of 5Mbps and burst length of 200 milliseconds. When attack flows converged in incoming ports of A, the converged attack period is 1 second and the expected burst rate is 10Mbps and the burst length is 200 milliseconds. The attack lasts about 30 seconds. Fig. 8(a) and Fig. 8(b) are the throughputs of TCP flow without and with AFB. The throughput is 29.0% and 75.3% respectively.

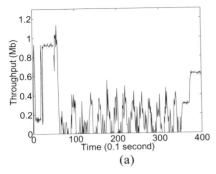 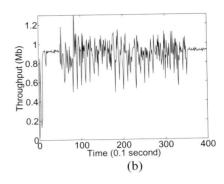

(a)                                              (b)

**Fig. 7.** The result of simulation 2. (a) is the TCP throughput without AFB and (b) is the TCP throughput with AFB.

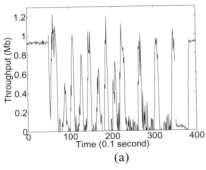 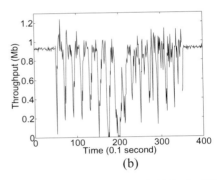

(a)                                              (b)

**Fig. 8.** The result of simulation 3. (a) is the TCP throughput without AFB and (b) is the TCP throughput with AFB.

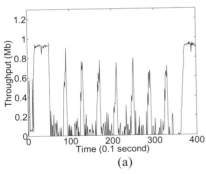 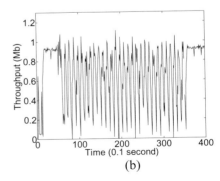

(a)                                              (b)

**Fig. 9.** The comparison between shrew filtering and AFB. (a) is the TCP throughput with shrew filtering and (b) is the TCP throughput with AFB.

Compared to shrew-filtering method using NCAS in [10] where the algorithm does not work well when attacker used forged addresses or ports, AFB with SLFP will not be affected by this confusion. We illustrate this difference by simulating an attack where one shrew flow vs. one legitimate TCP flow. The shrew flow sends out UDP attack packets with random head content except destination IP address and comparison between shrew-filtering and ours is given in Fig. 9 where (a) is the effect of shrew filtering and (b) is that of AFB. We can see shrew-filtering nearly is nearly useless while AFB is effective as before.

Additionally, the method in [11] only detects bursts happening in the downstream link of the edge router and that is unrealistic in real-life network. Yet our mechanism can be deployed in any upstream edge router and can achieve satisfying legitimate throughput.

## 6  Conclusions

Shrew attack is a newly proposed attack which could achieve similar effect as traditional DoS but with lower mean flow rate. In this paper we propose an effective detection algorithm SLFP and a feasible response method AFB that can be deployed in edge router. Theoretical analyses and simulation results are provided in detail. We consider our mechanism have advantages over some former methods.

## References

1. A. Kuzmanovic, E. Knightly.: Low-rate TCP-targeted denial of service attacks (the shrew vs. the mice and elephants). In Proceedings of ACM SIGCOMM 2003, Aug 2003.
2. J. Postel.: Transmission control protocol. Internet RFC 793, Sep 1981.
3. V. Jacobson.: Congestion avoidance and control. Computer Communication Review, Vol. 18(4), 314-329, Aug 1988.
4. M. Allman, V. Paxson.: On estimating end-to-end network path properties. Computer Communication Review, Vol. 29(4), 263-274, Oct 1999.
5. S. Sarat, A. Terzis.: On the effect of router buffer sizes on low-rate denial of service attacks. In Proceedings of 14th International Conference on Computer Communications and Networks (ICCCN 2005), 281-286, Oct 2005.
6. J. Tsao, P. Efstathopoulos.: Low-rate TCP-targeted denial of service attack defense. Advanced Computer Networks, 2003.
7. G. Yang, M. Gerla, M. P. Sanadidi.: Defense against low-rate TCP targeted denial-of-service attacks. In proceedings of 9th International Symposium on Computers and Communications (ISCC 2004), Vol. 1, 345-350, 2004.
8. A. Shevtekar, A. Karunakar, N. Ansari.: Low rate TCP denial-of-service attack detection at edge routers. IEEE Communications Letters, Vol. 9(4), 363-365, Apr 2005.
9. X. Luo, and R. K. C. Chang.: On a new class of pulsing denial-of-service attacks and the defense. In proceedings of Network and Distributed System Security Symposium (NDSS 2005), Feb 2005.
10. Y. Chen, Y. K. Kwok, K. Hwang.: Filtering shrew DDoS attacks using a new frequency-domain approach. In proceedings of 1st IEEE LCN Workshop on Network Security (WoNS 2005), June 2005.
11. H. Sun, J. C .S. Lui, D. K. Y. Yau.: Defending against low-rate TCP attacks: dynamic detection and protection. In proceedings of 12th IEEE International Conference on Network Protocols (ICNP 2004), 196-205, 2004.

12. A. Hussain, J. Heidemann, C. Papadopoulos.: Distinguishing between single and multi-source attacks using signal processing. Computer Networks, Vol. 46(4), 479-503, Nov 2004.
13. C. M. Cheng, K. S. Tan, H. T. Kung.: Use of spectral analysis in defense against DoS attacks. In proceedings of IEEE Global Telecommunications Conference (Globecom 2002), Vol. 3, 2143-2148, 2002.
14. G. Jin and J. Yang.: Deterministic Packet Marking based on Redundant Decomposition for IP Traceback. IEEE Communications Letters, Vol. 10(3), 204-206, Mar 2006.

# Integrating IDS Alert Correlation and OS-Level Dependency Tracking

Yan Zhai, Peng Ning, and Jun Xu

North Carolina State University

**Abstract.** Intrusion alert correlation techniques correlate alerts into meaningful groups or attack scenarios for the ease to understand by human analysts. However, the performance of correlation is undermined by the imperfectness of intrusion detection techniques. Falsely correlated alerts can be misleading to analysis. This paper presents a practical technique to improve alert correlation by integrating alert correlation techniques with OS-level object dependency tracking. With the support of more detailed and precise information from OS-level event logs, higher accuracy in alert correlation can be achieved. The paper also discusses the application of such integration in improving the accuracy of hypotheses about possibly missed attacks while reducing the complexity of the hypothesizing process. A series of experiments are performed to evaluate the effectiveness of the methods, and the results demonstrate significant improvements on correlation results with the proposed techniques.

## 1 Introduction

Intrusion detection has received a lot of attention in the past two decades. However, current intrusion detection systems (IDSs) often generate huge numbers of alerts as well as numerous false positives and false negatives. These problems make the reports from IDSs very hard to understand and manage. Many researchers and vendors have proposed various alert correlation techniques (e.g., [15,6,7]) to make large numbers of IDS alerts more understandable and at the same time reduce the impact of false positives and false negatives.

Recent alert correlation techniques can be classified into three categories: similarity-based correlation (e.g., [15, 5, 3]), correlation by matching with pre-defined attack scenarios (e.g., [7, 6]), and correlation based on the prerequisite (preconditions) and consequence (postconditions) of individual attacks (e.g., [11, 4]). Each technique has its advantages and disadvantages. However, the correctness of correlation results is strongly affected by the false positives and false negatives among IDS alerts.

Several researchers recently investigated integrating additional information sources into alert correlation to improve its quality. In [10], a formal model named M2D2 was proposed to represent data relevant to alert correlation. The technique in [13] reasons about the relevancy of alerts by fusing alerts with the targets' topology and vulnerabilities, and ranks alerts based on their relationships with critical resources and users' interests. In [16] a statistical reasoning framework is proposed to combine IDS alert correlation with local system state information from tools such as system scanners and

S. Mehrotra et al. (Eds.): ISI 2006, LNCS 3975, pp. 272–284, 2006.

system monitors. These approaches can improve the performance of correlation by integrating different sources of security-related information. However, the correlation results are still not yet satisfactory. For example, neither of the approaches can deal with false negatives quite well. Thus, it is desirable to find additional ways to integrate other information sources to further improve alert correlation.

In this paper, we propose to harness OS-level event logging and dependency tracking to improve the accuracy of alert correlation. OS-level dependency tracking is a recently developed technique to analyze the system operation history toward a given object. It tracks dependency-causing events such as process forking and file operations in the system event log, and spans up a tree of system objects connected by these events from the target object. Though a very useful tool for forensics applications, backtracker has two limitations. Firstly, because it is system call oriented, the complexity of tracking and tracking results can be very high. For example, during a normal system run, the resulting dependency graph of such a tracking (using *Backtracker* [8]) can contain up to tens of thousands of objects and hundreds of thousands of edges. Such complexity with tracking is obviously time and resource consuming, while the tracking results are also hard to understand. Secondly, the tracking is highly dependent on the availability of so-called "detection points", which are significant evidence of system being attacked. However, such "detection points" are not usually available, making it inconvenient to use in security administration. Integrating event logging and dependency tracking tools with alert correlation can potentially address the above limitations, and at the same time improve the performance of alert correlation.

Our integration method is based on the following observations: Firstly, most attacks have corresponding operations on specific OS-level objects. Secondly, other than a few exceptions, if one attack prepares for another, the later attack's corresponding operations would be dependent on the earlier one's. Because logging these system calls is more straightforward than detecting attacks using rules and signatures, such information is considerably more accurate and trustworthy than the IDS alerts. Utilizing such information will improve the performance of alert correlation.

Given the alert correlation results and an OS-level dependency tracking tool, the integration is done in two phases. The first phase is to identify the system objects corresponding to the IDS alerts based on their semantics. The second phase is to verify the relationships demonstrated in the correlation result or discover the missed relationships among the alerts by tracking the dependencies among their corresponding system objects using a dependency tracking tool such as Backtracker.

The contribution of this paper is the development of a framework to integrate the information from OS-level event logging and dependency tracking into IDS alert correlation. With the support of OS-level event logs, we can achieve better accuracy in the final result than the original alert correlation method. We also discuss how such integration can facilitate the hypotheses about possibly missed attacks. Finally, we evaluate the effectiveness of this scheme by performing a series of experiments. Our experiment results show that the integration can greatly improve the correctness of correlation and help making hypotheses about possibly missed attacks. For example, in our experiment, our approach can totally remove the false correlations in all three attack scenarios.

The remainder of this paper is structured as below. Section 2 briefly introduces the background of alert correlation and OS-level dependency tracking. Section 3 discusses the details on how to integrate OS-level object dependency tracking into alert correlation. Section 4 gives experimental results used to evaluate our approach. Section 5 discusses related work. Section 6 concludes and points out some future directions.

## 2   Background

As discussed earlier, our goal is to improve intrusion alert analysis by integrating OS-level event logging and object dependency tracking into IDS alert correlation. In this section, we give a brief introduction to the alert correlation and OS-level dependency tracking techniques to be used in our method. For alert correlation, we use the method based on attack's prerequisite and consequence [11], due to the ease to make connections between alert correlation and OS-level objects in this method. The dependency tracking technique used in this paper is *Backtracker* [8], which to our best knowledge is the only such tool available.

### 2.1   Alert Correlation Based on Prerequisites and Consequences of Attacks

Here we give a brief overview of the alert correlation method in [11]. This method correlates intrusion alerts using the prerequisites and consequences of attacks. Intuitively, the prerequisite of an attack is the necessary condition for the attack to be successful. For example, the existence of a vulnerable service is the prerequisite of a remote buffer overflow attack against the service. The consequence of an attack is the possible outcome of the attack. For example, gaining certain privilege on a remote machine. In a series of attacks, there are usually connections between the consequences of the earlier attacks and the prerequisites of the later ones. Accordingly, we identify the prerequisites and the consequences of attacks, and correlate the detected attacks (i.e., alerts) by matching the consequences of previous alerts to the prerequisites of later ones.

The correlation method uses logical formulas, which are logical combinations of predicates, to represent the prerequisites and consequences of attacks. The correlation model represents the attributes, prerequisites, and consequences of known attacks as alert types. The correlation process is to identify the *prepare-for* relations between alerts, which is done with the help of prerequisite sets and expanded consequence sets of alerts. Given an alert, its prerequisite set is the set of all predicates in the its prerequisite, and its expanded consequence set is the set of all predicates in or implied by its consequence. An earlier alert $t_1$ *prepares for* a later alert $t_2$ if the expanded consequence set of $t_1$ and the prerequisite set of $t_2$ share some common predicates. An alert correlation graph is used to represent a set of correlated alerts. An alert correlation graph $CG = (N, E)$ is a connected directed acyclic graph, where $N$ is a set of alerts, and for each pair $n_1, n_2 \in N$, there is a directed edge from $n_1$ to $n_2$ in $E$ if and only if $n_1$ prepares for $n_2$.

The advantage of this method is that the correlation result is easy to understand and directly reflects the possible attack scenarios. However, as the correlation is solely based on IDS alerts, the result highly depends on the quality of the IDS alerts. For example, the result may contain false correlations when there are false alerts.

## 2.2 Backtracker

*Backtracker* is an OS-level dependency tracking tool [8]. Backtracker monitors specific types of OS-level objects, i.e., processes and files. The objects are kept in a log with their properties such as the $uid$ of the objects. It also monitors specific dependency-causing system calls like process forking, file reading, and memory sharing, which together are called "high-control events" in [8]. Given the information of a specific object such as the $pid$ of a process or the $inode$ number of a file, Backtracker identifies the previous objects and system calls that could have potentially affected a target object, and displays chains of events in a dependency graph. In a Backtracker dependency graph, each node $A$ represents an OS-level object, and each edge $A \rightarrow B$ represents that object B is dependent on object A. Moreover, an edge $A \leftrightarrow B$ is used to represent that objects A and B are potentially dependent on each other. As mentioned earlier, the major limitations of Backtracker are the complexity of its results and the inconvenience to use because of its dependency on the availability of "detection points". In its later version [9], the tool can also track dependencies between remote hosts by tracking the logged socket ids.

# 3 Integrating Alert Correlation and OS-Level Dependency Tracking

Our integration is to identify the relevancy between the relationships among IDS alerts and the dependencies among OS-level objects, and then use the OS-level dependencies to verify or discover the relationships among IDS alerts. To identify such relationships, we first look into attacks' OS-level behaviors.

From the operating system's point of view, an attack is a set of OS-level events that access or modify a set of system objects. The OS-level objects and operations corresponding to an attack can be derived from the semantics of the attack. In our model, such semantics consist of two parts: one is the prerequisites and consequences of attacks, and the other is the correspondence between the predicates in attacks prerequisites or consequences and the OS-level objects on the host. With such information, we can identify the OS-level objects corresponding to the attacks on the host. For example, given an attack that exploits a vulnerable service as its prerequisite and yields a shell as its consequence, we can identify the corresponding service process and shell process.

Accordingly, the OS-level objects corresponding to an attack can be divided into two sets: the *prerequisite object set*, which are the objects derived from the attack's prerequisite, and the *consequence object set*, which are the objects derived from the attack's consequence. These two sets may overlap, because some attacks' consequences may affect their prerequisite objects. By backtracking among the OS-level objects, we can also find dependencies among those objects at the OS level. Though different from the *prepare-for* relation used in alert correlation, such OS-level dependencies can be utilized to verify or discover the *prepare-for* relations among the alerts.

In our framework, we first extract necessary information from the alerts to identify the corresponding OS-level objects. We then verify the dependencies among alerts by using the OS-level dependencies among their corresponding objects, and thus improve the alert correlation based on the causal relationship. Moreover, by identifying the OS-level objects corresponding to the evidence of possibly missed attacks, and tracking back from those objects, we can improve the performance of existing methods [12, 16] for hypothesizing about possibly missed attacks.

An attack has to have impacts on the local system in order to be observable in the OS-level log. Thus, our method only guarantees improvement of alert correlation for the alerts of successful attacks, though it may provide positive results for some failed attack attempts.

### 3.1   Identifying OS-Level Objects Corresponding to Intrusion Alerts

Now we discuss how to find the OS-level objects accessed by the attacks which trigger IDS alerts. We call this process the mapping of IDS alerts to OS-level objects. We summarize the semantics carried by an alert that can be used to identify the corresponding OS-level objects. Firstly, an IDS alert comes with a timestamp, which indicates when the attack happens. Secondly, given an alert, we have the knowledge about how the attack works and how the system should behave in response to it. For example, given a Snort alert "FTP EXPLOIT wu-ftpd 2.6.0", we know that the corresponding attack exploits a vulnerable wu-ftpd server and forks a root shell. Finally, given local system's configuration, we can identify which OS-level objects correspond to each predicate in attacks' prerequisites and consequences. For example, a predicate "Samba server" may correspond to "/usr/sbin/smbd" process on a given computer. Below we discuss how each type of knowledge is used to map the alerts.

Though the number of logged events and objects is large in system logs, the timestamp of each alert can be used to easily narrow down the potentially relevant system objects. In Backtracker's log, each OS-level object or event is associated with a time period, which is the lifetime of the object or event. (The original Backtracker toolkit does not provide exact timestamp information. We slightly modified Backtracker's source code to add this functionality.) Given a fixed time period $T = [t_1, t_2]$, an object $o$ can be accessed during $T$ if $o's$ lifetime $[t_s, t_e]$ overlaps with $T$. Given the timestamp of an alert, we can estimate an approximate time window during which all the relevant OS-level activities occur, and then narrow down the scope of OS-level objects that need to be examined. Such a time window has to be relaxed to accommodate delays in OS-level operations and the clock discrepancy between the IDS sensor and the OS.

Given the name of an alert, we have the corresponding attack's prerequisite and consequence from experts' knowledge. According to [11], the prerequisite of an attack is a logical combination of predicates, and the consequence of an attack is a set of predicates. Each of those predicates is associated with some OS-level objects such as services, processes, and files. Thus, for each predicate in attacks' prerequisites and consequences, we can identify the corresponding file or process on the host computer, and represent them as $(predicate, OS\text{-}level\ object)$ pairs in the knowledge base. For example, given a pair $(Samba\_service(host\_IP), "/usr/sbin/smbd")$ in the knowledge base, whenever there is predicate of $Samba\_service(host\_IP)$, we can locate its corresponding process of "/user/sbin/smbd". Thus, after identifying the predicates in an attack's prerequisite and consequence, we can identify the OS-level objects corresponding to those predicates on the host computer. Based on whether the corresponding predicate belongs to attack's prerequisite or consequence, those objects can be divided into prerequisite objects and consequence objects.

There are additional constraints for the mapped objects. Firstly, some predicate implies constraints on the properties of its corresponding OS-level objects. For example, the predicate $Root\_shell(host\_IP)$ implies the privilege of its corresponding OS-level object is root, which is represented by $uid = 0$ for the corresponding object in Backtracker's log. We represent such a constraint along with the object mapping information in the knowledge base in the form of $(predicate, OS\text{-}level\ object, constraint)$. In the above example, we may have a triple $(Root\_shell(host\_IP), /usr/bin/sh, uid = 0)$ to indicate that the predicate $Root\_shell$ is mapped to a process $/usr/bin/sh$, and the process's $uid$ should be 0.

Secondly, if we focus on successful attacks, we expect to see the prerequisite and consequence of a successful attack at the OS level. In other words, for each predicate $p$ in an attack's prerequisite and consequence, there must be at least one object $o$ in the mapped object set corresponding to $p$, unless the logging tool does not monitor objects corresponding to such predicates. For example, assume the prerequisite and the consequence of a Samba buffer overflow attack are $Vulnerable\_Samba\_service(dstIP)$ and $Root\_shell\ (dstIP)$, respectively. If this attack is successful, there must be OS-level objects corresponding to these predicates in the object sets. Thus, if such OS-level objects do not exist, the alert must represent a false alert or a failed attack.

Finally, the system activities corresponding to an attack should all be related in Backtracker dependency graph. Moreover, the consequence of an attack should be dependent on the prerequisite of the attack at the OS-level. Thus, for each consequence object corresponding to an attack, it should be a prerequisite object, or dependent on some prerequisite objects of the attack. Thus, we have the dependency constraint: Given alert $A$ and its mapped prerequisite object set $P_A$ and consequence object set $C_A$, for each consequence object $o$ in $C_A$, if $P_A$ is not empty, there should exist paths from objects in $P_A$ to $o$ in Backtracker's dependency graph unless $o$ is also in $P_A$. If such paths do not exist, the corresponding consequence object $o$ should not be associated with the given alert. For example, given an alert with prerequisite object set $\{service\_process\}$ and consequence object set $\{shell\_process, file\_foo\}$, if $service\_process$ is not connected to $shell\_process$ in the Backtracker dependency graph, the consequence object $shell\_process$ should not be included in the consequence object set.

After mapping IDS alerts to OS-level objects and with OS-level dependency tracking tools, the number of false correlations can be potentially reduced by verifying the dependencies between the corresponding objects. Below we discuss in detail how to identify the OS-level dependencies among alerts with OS-level dependency tracking, and how to use such dependencies to achieve better accuracy in alert correlation.

### 3.2   OS-Level Dependencies Among IDS Alerts

After IDS alerts are mapped to groups of objects within particular time periods in the Backtracker dependency graph, some groups are connected with each other through objects and events in the dependency graph while others are not. It is not difficult to see that an later object is dependent on an earlier object if there exists a path in the dependency graph from the earlier object to the later object. Such paths among these object groups reveal the dependencies between their corresponding alerts. However, such dependencies can be not only malicious attack behaviors but also normal system activities, which makes it different from the prepare-for relations used in alert correlation. To find out the security-relevant dependencies interested by alert correlation, below we discuss in further detail about these dependencies.

As we have mentioned, the OS-level objects corresponding to an alert can be divided into two subsets: the prerequisite object set $O_P$, which are derived from the attack's prerequisite, and the consequence object set $O_C$, which are derived from the attack's consequence. As discussed earlier, the consequence objects in $O_C$ should be dependent on the prerequisite objects in $O_P$. Moreover, two alerts being correlated with each other means the earlier attack's consequence "contributes" to the later attack's prerequisite. Thus, at the OS level, such a prepare-for relation should be reflected by the paths from the earlier attack's consequence object set to the later attack's prerequisite object set (i.e., the later attack's prerequisite objects are dependent on the earlier attack's consequence objects). To distinguish such dependencies from other dependencies, we say alert $A$ is *strongly connected* with alert $B$ if, in the Backtracker dependency graph, there exists a path from one of $A$'s consequence objects to one of $B$'s prerequisite objects. Thus, if alert $A$ prepares for alert $B$, $A$ should be strongly connected with $B$.

### 3.3   Verifying the Dependencies Among Correlated IDS Alerts

Except for a few types of attacks (e.g., attacks utilizing guest kernels or hidden channels), which are relatively rare as discussed in [8], backtracker is capable of tracking OS-level dependencies among most attacks. In other words, in normal cases, if two alerts are not found strongly connected with each other, there should not be prepare-for relations between them.

Given an alert correlation graph, we can map the alerts to OS-level objects and check whether the correlated alerts are strongly connected. If two correlated alerts are not found strongly connected, the correlation between them is considered false. For example, assume $A \rightarrow B$ are a pair of correlated alerts. To verify this correlation, we first map them into OS-level object sets. If the mappings are successful, there will be corresponding prerequisite and consequence object sets: $P_A$ and $C_A$ of alert $A$, as well as $P_B$ and $C_B$ of alert $B$. By tracking back from the objects in $P_B$ with Backtracker, we can verify whether the two alerts are strongly connected. If there does not exist a path between objects in $C_A$ and objects in $P_B$, we consider the correlation $A \rightarrow B$ false.

Note that two alerts being strongly connected in the dependency graph does not guarantee that the earlier one prepares for the other. This is because OS-level dependencies can be operations of benign programs. That being said, being strongly connected on OS-level dependency graph indicates that the involved attacks have higher possibility to be causally related. Thus, we can use this information to discover attacks missed by IDSs, which lead to missing correlations among alerts.

### 3.4   Facilitating Hypotheses of Missed Attacks

Integrating IDS alert correlation and OS-level event logging can also help in making hypotheses about possibly missed attacks. Several approaches [12, 16] have been proposed in making hypotheses about possibly missed attacks. Given evidence of attacks being missed, these methods search among known attack types of attacks to fill in the gaps between their correlation graphs and the evidence based on attacks' prerequisites and consequences. However, such search processes can be computationally expensive considering the size of the attack type knowledge base and the number of steps that could have been missed.

Integrating IDS alert correlation with OS-level dependency tracking can facilitate hypothesizing of missed attacks. Signs (evidence) of missing attacks, such as IDS alerts and observed system modifications, can usually be mapped to groups of system objects. Assume a piece of evidence $E$ is mapped to a set of OS-level objects. By tracking backward from those objects, a forest of system objects connected via various events can be generated. For any missed attack, unless it can evade the OS-level dependency tracking, part of its mapped objects must be in this spanned forest. Using the information of the correspondence between predicates and OS-level objects, such a forest of objects can be converted to predicates. Thus, the searching space for possibly missed attacks can be greatly reduced to only the attacks related to the predicates.

For example, an attacker takes the following attack steps: (1) Launch a buffer overflow attack toward a vulnerable Samba server, which yields a root shell; (2) Delete the web page files via the shell. Assume all those activities are missed by the IDS, while the file deletion is detected by some file system integrity monitoring tool, which is taken as evidence indicating previous attacks being missed. By tracking back from the deleted file, the file is found dependent on the following objects in the OS-level event log: a smbd process and a shell process forked by the smbd process. Thus, when searching for possibly missed attacks, we can limit the search within attacks related to Samba and shell. Since only Samba is an initial system service, we hypothesize there is a Samba-related attack missed. By trying to map each candidate attack to OS-level objects, we can eliminate the majority of invalid hypotheses. The uncertainty within the remaining results is affected by the knowledge we have about the local system (e.g., the version of Samba) and the attacks (e.g., the number of attack types in the knowledge base).

## 4   Experimental Results

We have performed a series of experiments to validate the effectiveness of our method. Since our method requires actual system responses to real attacks, we developed three attack scenarios in our lab, in which an attacker launches a sequence of attacks against a computer monitored by both the Backtracker and the Snort IDS.

The Backtracker was configured on the target server and slightly modified to log system calls with their timestamps. Two vulnerable services were running on the server: Samba 2.2.8 and icecast 1.3.11. Snort 2.40 was installed on the server to monitor the network traffic as an IDS sensor. To detect more attacks, we used the "Bleeding Snort Rulesets" [1] with Snort. Clock drifting is not considered in our experiments because both programs were running on the same computer. We also injected background traffic during the experiments to mimic an operational network. The background traffic was collected on the target machine when it was connected to our campus network, and was manually verified to contain no attacks toward the target machine. We also injected some failed attempts of wu-ftpd buffer overflow attacks into the background traffic.

Due to space reasons, we only discuss in detail the experimental results on Scenario 1 here in this paper. Description of the other two scenarios and additional information about these experiments can be found in the full version of this paper [17].

## 4.1   Details of Scenario 1

Our first attack scenario exploits a vulnerable Samba server. It includes the following attack steps:

1. Two remote buffer overflow attack attempts exploiting the vulnerable Samba server (resulting 2 remote root shells).
2. Uploading and starting a server daemon of a DDoS tool called TFN (Tribe Flood Network) on the target host.
3. Using TFN's client program to direct the TFN server daemon on the victim server to start SYN flood and UDP flood attacks against another computer.

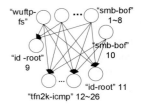

**Fig. 1.** Original Correlation Graph

The above attacks took about 5 minutes. During the period, Backtracker logged 81,613 events. Moreover, the Snort sensor raised 9 "NETBIOS SMB trans2open buffer overflow attempt" ("smb-bof") alerts (No. 1–8 and No.10), 15 "DDOS tfn2k icmp possible communication" ("tfn2k-icmp") alerts (No. 12–26), and 2 "ATTACK-RESPONSES id check returned root" ("id-root") alerts (No.9 and No.11). The background traffic triggered 32 alerts related to the target server, which include 8 "SCAN nmap TCP" ("nmap-tcp") alerts, 23 "SNMP public access udp" ("snmp-udp") alerts, and 1 "FTP EXPLOIT wu-ftpd 2.6.0 site exec format string overflow Linux" ("wuftp-fs") alert. Among the 3 types of alerts, the third one is triggered by the failed attempt of wu-ftpd buffer overflow attack injected into the background traffic.

Using the alert correlation method proposed in [11], we generated the correlation graph shown in Fig. 1. Obviously, it contains many false correlations due to the false positives within the alerts. Using the Backtracker's log and the semantics of these alerts, we mapped these alerts to a number of OS-level objects, as listed in Table 1.

For each alert prepared by other alerts in Fig. 1, we generated Backtracker dependency graphs by tracking back from their prerequisite objects. In these graphs, we look for paths from an earlier alerts' consequence objects to a later alert's prerequisite objects if the former prepares for the later. Examples of such paths found in our experiments are shown in Fig.2(a). According to our previous discussion, when such

**Table 1.** OS-level Objects Corresponding to the Alerts in Scenario 1

| Alert | Prerequisite Objects | Consequence Objects |
|---|---|---|
| "smb-bof" 8 | {smbd_2717} | {sh_2720} |
| "smb-bof" 10 | {smbd_2717} | {sh_2725} |
| "id-root" 9 | {sh_2722, /usr/bin/id_324551} | Null |
| "id-root" 11 | {sh_2727, /usr/bin/id_324551} | Null |
| "tfn2k-icmp" 12 26 | {td_2737} | Null |

a path exists, the two alerts are strongly connected and thus the correlations between them are verified at the OS level. Otherwise, the correlation would be considered false.

In this way, we can verify each of the correlations in the original correlation graph, remove those that are verified to be false, and finally come up with a new correlation graph. The new correlation graph for scenario 1 is shown in Fig. 3(a). We can see it is the correct correlation graph of the reported Snort alerts based on the actual attack scenario.

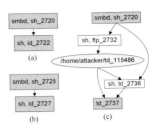

Fig. 2. Paths Between Alerts' Mapped Objects

In the correlation graph, the "smb-bof" alerts prepare for the "tfn2k-icmp" alerts because the consequence of the former (i.e., root_shell (dstIP)) implies the prerequisite of the later (i.e., tfn2k_server_daemon ()). This implication indicates that some activities are missed between the two alerts.

By backtracking from the prerequisite object set $\{td\_2737\}$ of the tfn2k alert, a tree of OS-level objects are spanned. Because the consequence object set $\{sh\_2720\}$ of the "smb-bof" alert is among them, we focus on the paths linking the two object sets. Along the path shown in Fig. 2(c), we find the following OS-level objects being involved: process object "$ftp\_2732$", file object "$/home/attacker/td\_115486$", and process object "$td\_2736$". Thus, we can limit the searching within the activities related to the ftp and tfn2k server program. It is easy to see that the attacker downloaded the tfn2k server program via ftp and launched it via the shell. These hypotheses are shown in dotted circles and lines in Fig. 3(b).

## 4.2   Overall Evaluation

Assume an alert correlation method outputs that an alert $A$ prepares for another alert $B$. If both alerts are detections of actual attacks, and the attack corresponding to alert $A$ is indeed used to prepare for the later attack corresponding to alert $B$, we consider this correlation as a *true correlation*. Otherwise, it is considered a *false correlation*. Moreover, if one attack is used to prepare for another attack, but there is no correlation corresponding to these attacks (due to missing detection or incorrect correlation), we say there is a *missing correlation*. In our experiments, since we know the details of the attack scenarios, we can easily identify true, false, and missing correlations.

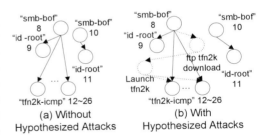

Fig. 3. New Correlation Graphs

We use two metrics, false correlation rate and missing correlation rate, to evaluate the overall performance of alert correlation before and after integrating Backtracker's results. Given a set of correlated alerts, the *false correlation rate* is the ratio between the number of false correlations over the total number of correlations generated by alert

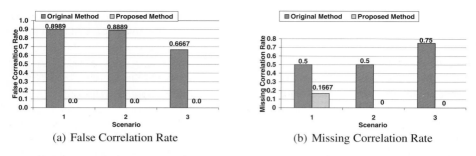

(a) False Correlation Rate                    (b) Missing Correlation Rate

**Fig. 4.** Compare between the Original Correlation Method [11] and the Proposed Method

correlation. The *missing correlation rate* is the ratio between the number of missing-correlations over the total number of correlations between *attacks*. Intuitively, these two metrics show the degrees of correctness and completeness of the correlation. Obviously, the smaller these two metrics are, the better performance alert correlation has.

Fig. 4(a) shows the false correlation rates in all three attack scenarios. As we can see, our proposed method reduces the false correlation rate significantly in all three scenarios. Indeed, false correlations are completely removed in all scenarios. This is not surprising, because OS-level dependency provides another way to properly verify the correlation between alerts through trustworthy information kept in OS-level logs.

Fig. 4(b) shows the missing correlation rates in the three scenarios. We can see significant reduction in missing correlation rate in all three scenarios. While the missing correlation rate is reduced to 0 in scenarios 2 and 3, the missing correlation rate of the first scenario is still non-zero after making hypotheses. This is because the DDoS attack (via the tfn server) is neither detected by Snort, nor hypothesized by our approach.

Our experiments confirmed that OS-level object dependency graphs can often be too complicated to understand in reality. For example, during the 30 minutes' period of the third scenario, Backtracker logged more than $410,000$ events, resulting a dependency graph of more than $4,000$ nodes. Manually analyzing such a complicated graph requires lots of time and very detailed knowledge about attacks' OS-level behaviors. Our proposed method solves this problem because: 1. our method tries to *verify* alert correlations instead of to *detect* attacks, only moderate information about attacks' OS-level behaviors is required,and 2. the verification processes can be done automatically by computer programs instead of human experts.

The experiment results also showed how the proposed method can help make hypotheses about possibly missed attacks. In the attack scenarios, one type of attacks are hard to be detected by any IDS, which are the attackers' "legitimate" activities after the break-in. It is very difficult to guess about such activities without the OS-level dependency information.

## 5   Related Work

Our technique is closely related to the alert correlation techniques based on prerequisites (pre-conditions) and consequences (post-conditions) of attacks proposed in [11, 14, 4] as well as OS-level dependency tracking techniques proposed in [8,9], which have been discussed in the Introduction and Section 2. The work closest to ours is [9]. In [9], King et al. proposed to use the dependency information from Backtracker to study attacks within and across the hosts, as well as prospected the application of Backtracker in alert correlation. Although they demonstrated the potential benefit of combining backtracker analysis and IDS alert analysis with some heuristic case studies, the main focus of [9] is the backtracking among remote hosts. It does not give any specific method for combining the two different analyses. All the analyses in citeEnrichAlerts are done manually, which is computationally expensive and difficult in practice. In our approach, after discussing the difference and resemblance between the OS-level dependencies and the dependencies among attacks, we proposed a specific method to automatically combine the analyses.

Several techniques also use local system information to reason about the causal relationships between IDS alerts. In [16], local system state information is used to reason about the correlation of alerts. In [2], such information is used to analyze the vulnerability of the system and study the potential attacks that could compromise the system. These techniques are complementary to the approach proposed in this paper.

Some approaches have been proposed in [12, 16] to make hypotheses about attacks possibly missed by IDSs. [12] makes hypotheses based on the prerequisite and consequences of attack types when similarities are found between alerts in separate correlation graphs. [16] uses similar attack type knowledge to make hypotheses upon inconsistencies between observed facts and alert correlation graph. Our techniques can facilitate the hypothesis process by bringing additional information from OS-level dependency tracking, thus to reduce the search space for the possibly missed attacks.

## 6   Conclusion and Future work

In this paper, we developed a series of techniques to integrate the alert correlation method (based on prerequisites and consequences of attacks) and OS-level object dependency tracking. A critical step in this integration is to map IDS alerts to OS-level objects, so that connections between alert correlation and OS-level objects can be established. We also identified a number of constraints that the OS-level objects should satisfy if they are relevant to the IDS alerts (or attacks) that are correlated. By using these constraints, we can verify the IDS alerts as well as the correlation between IDS alerts, and reduce false correlations. Moreover, the dependency between OS-level objects can also facilitate the hypotheses of attacks possibly missed by the IDSs. Our experimental evaluation gave favorable results, showing that OS-level dependency tracking can significantly reduce false correlations when integrated with the alert correlation method.

Several issues are worth doing in our future research. First, we will investigate more techniques to integrate OS-level dependency tracking with techniques to hypothesize about possibly missed attacks. Second, we want to investigate the possibility of learning "normal" patterns of dependencies among OS-level objects from training period to improve the verification of correlations and making hypotheses.

# References

1. Bleedingsnort. www.bleedingsnort.com.
2. P. Ammann, D. Wijesekera, and S. Kaushik. Scalable, graph-based network vulnerability analysis. In *Proceedings of the 9th ACM CCS*, 2002.
3. F. Cuppens. Managing alerts in a multi-intrusion detection environment. In *Proceedings of the 17th Annual Computer Security Applications Conference*, December 2001.
4. F. Cuppens and A. Miege. Alert correlation in a cooperative intrusion detection framework. In *Proceedings of the 2002 IEEE Symposium on Security and Privacy*, May 2002.
5. O. Dain and R. Cunningham. Building scenarios from a heterogeneous alert stream. In *Proceedings of the 2001 IEEE Workshop on Information Assurance and Security*, June 2001.
6. O. Dain and R. Cunningham. Fusing a heterogeneous alert stream into scenarios. In *Proceedings of the 2001 ACM Workshop on Data Mining for Security Applications*, Nov. 2001.
7. H. Debar and A. Wespi. Aggregation and correlation of intrusion-detection alerts. In *Recent Advances in Intrusion Detection*, LNCS 2212, pages 85 – 103, 2001.
8. S. King and P. Chen. Backtracking intrusions. In *Proceedings of the 2003 Symposium on Operating Systems Principles (SOSP)*, October 2003.
9. S. King, Z. Mao, D. Lucchetti, and P. Chen. Enriching intrusion alerts through multi-host causality. In *Proceedings of the 12th NDSS*, 2005.
10. B. Morin, L. Mé, H. Debar, and M. Ducassé. M2D2: A formal data model for IDS alert correlation. In *Proceedings of RAID 2002)*.
11. P. Ning, Y. Cui, and D. S. Reeves. Constructing attack scenarios through correlation of intrusion alerts. In *Proceedings of the 9th ACM CCS*, 2002.
12. P. Ning, D. Xu, C. Healey, and R. St. Amant. Building attack scenarios through integration of complementary alert correlation methods. In *Proceedings of the 11th Annual Network and Distributed System Security Symposium (NDSS '04)*, pages 97–111, February 2004.
13. P. Porras, M. Fong, and A. Valdes. A mission-impact-based approach to INFOSEC alarm correlation. In *Proceedings of RAID 2002*.
14. S. Templeton and K. Levitt. A requires/provides model for computer attacks. In *Proceedings of New Security Paradigms Workshop*, pages 31 – 38. ACM Press, September 2000.
15. A. Valdes and K. Skinner. Probabilistic alert correlation. In *Proceedings of the 4th International Symposium on Recent Advances in Intrusion Detection*, pages 54–68, 2001.
16. Y. Zhai, P. Ning, P. Iyer, and D. Reeves. Reasoning about complementary intrusion evidence. In *Proceedings of the 20th Annual Computer Security Applications Conference*, Dec. 2004.
17. Y. Zhai, P. Ning, and J. Xu. Integrating IDS alert correlation and OS-level depdendency tracking. Technical Report TR-2005-27, Department of Computer Science, North Carolina State University, 2005.

# Attacking Confidentiality: An Agent Based Approach

Kapil Kumar Gupta[1], Baikunth Nath[2], Kotagiri Ramamohanarao[3], and Ashraf U. Kazi[4]

[1,2,3] Department of Computer Science and Software Engineering
National ICT Australia
The University of Melbourne
{kgupta, bnath, rao}@csse.unimelb.edu.au
[4] Department of Business Law and Taxation
Monash University
ashraf.kazi@buseco.monash.edu.au

**Abstract.** A network is not secure unless it can ensure the three basic security concepts; confidentiality, integrity and availability. Attack on confidentiality and integrity of data are emerging trends in network intrusion. In this paper we primarily focus on the confidentiality aspect. With more and more sophisticated tools being easily available the number of security incidents has been rapidly increasing. Such tools reduce the attack preparation time thereby increasing attack frequency. The use of such tools also makes it difficult to discover attacks at an early stage before substantial damage has been done. Here we show a highly personalized attack by the use of specialized agents whose purpose is to search and transmit specific information from a private network without authorized access. This information may be in the form of a competitor's marketing strategy, customers' personal details, true financial status of an organization or any other information. We discuss that such an agent and its activity is different from common malware, describe its characteristics and design and show that such a scenario is a real possibility. We also discuss the related issues and the alarming effects posed by such an agent. It is possible that the agent we are discussing may already be in existence but are unreported.

## 1 Introduction

Protecting a private network connected to the internet is a challenge and nightmare for network security analysts, particularly when the attackers frequently come up with more and more sophisticated and previously unseen attacks. Most common are the Distributed Denial of Service (DDoS) attacks and the attacks by the malicious code [3] including worms and spywares. However, these are mainly directed towards the loss of availability [19]. Starting with the Morris worm of 1988 the list goes on unending with Code Red, Nimda, and SQL Slammer as some of the devastating ones. Further, securing the ever increasing digital data on a network and ultimately on the web is a major concern [11].

S. Mehrotra et al. (Eds.): ISI 2006, LNCS 3975, pp. 285–296, 2006.

In this paper we show that obtaining private and sensitive information from a protected network without authorized access represents an emerging trend and is relatively hard to discover when the attack is carried out by experts with the motive to hide the entire attack and hence protect their identity from being discovered. We discuss one such unseen scenario where specialized agents are used to accomplish this task.

This paper is organized as follows. We discuss the background for such an agent in Sect. 2. Section 3 describes the characteristics and flow of the system. In Sect. 4 we discuss the design related issues. Section 5 describes the effects of such an activity. In Sect. 6 we discuss some of the possible future directions in intrusion and intrusion detection. We discuss the legal issues related to such an activity in Sect. 7. In Sect. 8 we propose a possible response and finally we summarize and conclude in Sect. 9.

## 2   Background

Internet today is stormed by newer and even more sophisticated attacks than ever seen before. These attacks may include DDoS, malicious code (including worms, virus and spyware along with others), scanning, root compromise, session highjack and many more [24]. The purpose of a Denial of Service (DoS) attack is to simply flood any service provider with non legitimate requests so that it is unable to provide its services to normal users, thus leading to loss of availability. Similarly internet worms target a specific vulnerability, setting up a vast network, ultimately leading to a DoS attack. No Intrusion Detection System (IDS) vendor can guarantee complete security; confidentiality (sometimes used interchangeably with privacy), integrity and availability of data and resources, the three security concepts [24]. Violation of any of these is a major security incident.

IDS today are based on two concepts; first is the matching of the previously seen and hence known anomalous patterns from an internal database of signatures and the second is building profiles based on normal data and detecting deviations from the expected behaviour. The first one is termed as Misuse Detection or Signature Based IDS and the second is called as Anomaly Detection or Behaviour based IDS. Both have certain merits and demerits. The Signature based IDS's though have very high detection accuracy but they fail when an attack is previously unseen. On the other hand Behaviour based IDS may have the ability to detect new unseen attacks but have the problem of low detection accuracy [14].

The deployment of an Intrusion Detection System is also critical. Based on their deployment, the IDS are classified as; Network based, Host based and Application based. Each of these also have limited capabilities depending on the level of deployment since attacks directed towards a particular host or application may be hidden to a Network based IDS while others directed towards a network may be invisible to a Host based or Application based IDS. The Network based IDS though are easy to deploy and manage, but are limited to monitor network packets as they fail to identify the semantics. On the other hand Host based and Application based IDS are effective for special hosts and applications but are difficult to deploy and manage and can be exploited as part of the attack [14].

Recent trend shows that there is an increasing concern over confidentiality and integrity along with persistent concerns over availability [3] [30] [11]. The claim is confirmed by past worms such as witty and sircam. The witty worm of 2004 was the first widely propagated worm that led to the loss of information as it carried a destructive payload [29], attacking at the integrity aspect. With earlier attempts by worms such as W32/sircam which transmitted random files from the machine [21] [1] and with the vulnerability discovered in Oracle [9], we expect more incidents in the future which would be more damaging, difficult to identify and solely targeted towards loss of confidentiality.

Here we are not talking of a simple spyware [22] [13] [6] or a worm [2] [31] [33]. A spyware is a program that monitors users' activity such as typing of passwords, pin numbers; credit card numbers etc. and send them outside by a back channel. Such a spyware generally hides itself in some freely available software [22] [6]. More importantly any spyware is confined to a single machine as by definition spyware do not replicate and do not create a network. It depends on a user to install them, generally unknowingly, on a machine. Hence though same spyware may exist on different machines, they act individually and do not cooperate [6]. A spyware is the lowest level implementation of what we propose.

A worm is a malicious code that self propagates on a network by exploiting various security flaws generally in a widely used and deployed service(s) or software(s). It is primarily meant to spread very fast and disrupt the normal internet activities mainly by consuming large bandwidth hence leading to DoS attacks [33] [3]. Worms are not specifically targeted to a particular network and are not intended to hide their identity. Recently worms such as sircam have been discovered that attempt to delete files from machines and more importantly transmit random files [21] [1] thus exploiting confidentiality. However, worms show their presence very fast since they are primarily meant for launching DoS attacks.

Agents have been used for various purposes including online shopping assistance, customization of news reports, filling of webpage forms, competitors' price check, information retrieval from the World Wide Web and many more [5]. They have seldom been employed for unauthorized information access though security and privacy concerns are central to agents [26].

In this paper we talk about smart agents [5] [27] that searches for specific information, in a private network connected to the internet. The information required is not simple such as getting the competitors' price checks but is more related to marketing and pricing strategy, actual financial status of an organization etc. The agent is able to hide itself from being discovered by resorting to stealth scan [32], replicate itself in limited numbers depending upon the situation, transmit the identified information and destroy itself and its traces after completing its task. The whole idea is that such an agent is invisible to the network monitors and it performs its task without being discovered and exposing its identity.

A cursory look at these properties might lead us to believe that there is little difference between a worm and the intruding agent. However, though they might share some of the structural properties their behaviour is very much different. Taking an analogy from the biological virus, there are mainly two modes of virus spread. One in which the spread is very fast with a high infection/time ratio and the other in which the spread is extremely slow with a low infection/time ratio. Both the cases, however, eventually end up with massive infections. The intruding agent on the other hand is not meant to spread large-scale infections, rather it infects a very limited number of nodes in an attempt to remain undiscovered. The virus in the first category shows their presence at an early stage of their life while those in the second category may not show their presence at all or until their objective is fulfilled. Very fast spreading worms falls in the first category and the slow spreading worms as discussed in [32] fits into the second. While the worms make a lot of rapid infections showing their presence very soon, their spread can be controlled by isolation but the intruding agent as shown here is slow spreading without affecting any of the normal routine tasks and hence is very difficult to be detected. There is no question of containment of an undiscovered intruding agent. Thus, such an agent differs from common worms and spywares. We summarize and further differentiate their properties in table 1.

**Table 1.** Comparison between Worm, Spyware and Intruding Agent

| | Worm | Spyware | Intruding Agent |
|---|---|---|---|
| Primary Purpose | Consume available bandwidth leading to DoS attack | Monitor user activity to obtain useful credentials such as passwords, credit card details | Search for and transmit specific information |
| Target Specific | No | No | Yes |
| Entry Point | n parallel Zombies; Exploit vulnerable software/service already installed | n parallel Zombies; Enter by hiding in a freely available software (generally in disguise) | Only a single Zombie or any launching vehicle that can hide the identity |
| Self Replication | Yes | No | Yes |
| Replication Volume | Extremely High | N.A. | Controlled |
| Cooperation Among Replicated Copies | Possible | N.A. | Yes |
| Information Search | No | Select a random file rather than performing a specific search | Yes |
| Need to Hide | No | Yes | Yes |
| Degrades System Performance | Yes | Yes | No |
| Self Destruction | No | No | Yes |

# 3   Characteristics and Flow

We have identified the characteristics of such an intruding agent and in this section we discuss all of these in detail.

To achieve the target of information gathering the agent needs to search and control a machine known as "zombie" to start with. It does not require a collection of such zombies but only one compromised machine is sufficient, to hide the original identity of the attacker.

Once a zombie is available, it starts its actual task. The agent makes repeated attempts, if required, to enter the target network. In order to enter the target network Social Engineering, which is manipulating the legitimate users to obtain confidential information [4] [22], can be one of the many other possibilities. The point worth considering here is that the successive attempts to enter the target network are spread over a large time interval so as to avoid detection by an Intrusion Detection System deployed on the target network. If there is little success, and certain predefined time elapses, the agent suspends its current task to resume it after it controls a new zombie. This is required since the firewall might have introduced a rule to stop any traffic from that particular source. Hence until successful the agent repeats the process to ultimately fool the firewall and any Network based Intrusion Detection System running on the target network. Since the agent is interested to search for specific information it does not send any probe outside the local network and remains confined to the network until its final stages. As a result it can now move forward with its task without any concerns from the Network based IDS. However, it still has to hide itself from the Host based and Application based IDS and internal network monitors.

Once the agent enters the network, it gathers and updates its prior knowledge about the network to adjust its actions and finish its task as early as possible. This, however, is required only in case of an external attack.

Depending upon the nature and amount of task and the collected information of the network, the agent decides the amount of replication. The point worth taking care of is, whatever the situation is, the agent replicates only in a limited number as replication will result in communication between the agents which can be noticed by the network monitors. Time constraint is one of the deciding factors in this decision but there is a compromise between the two; requirement to prevent the detection of the agent and the time within which the agent needs to accomplish the task. Further, the time constraint is governed by the purpose of intrusion. Some of the intrusive activities require quick response while others may have a waiting time for as long as many years. This gives rise to a special feature of an agent to stop its activity when a node becomes active, which helps in deterring detection, and re-launch after certain time of inactivity of the node.

The network of agents thus established is used to search for the specific information in the network. The agent always hides its communication by spreading it in large intervals of time to prevent detection. Since the required information may not be freely available the agent might resort to root compromise, session hijack and other hacking methods described in [24].

Once the agent is successful in securing the desired information, it must send the information outside the network, back to the controlled zombie that helped the agent to enter the network rather than sending it directly to the attacker. This ensures that the attackers' identity is still hidden. Finally the agent needs to be informed that the information is received and is one that was expected so that it can perform clean up tasks. However, if the information was not the one that was required the agent continues to search for the information until successful. This, however, does not go on indefinitely as after a particular stage the required information may be of little use. So after a particular time the agent abandons its task and performs the clean up operation as described next.

In order to prevent any trace back the agent must ensure that all the traces, in the form of system and database logs must be removed successfully [12] [18]. This is required not only to hide the attacker's identity but to hide what information is compromised. The attacker's identity can not be traced as the task was performed by controlling a zombie. Entirely removing the footprints might be a challenge as it would be difficult to remove the entire logs without authorized access. However, this too is achievable as mentioned in [12] [18]. Once all this is done, the agent destroys its complete network.

The agent is intelligent to respond to unseen situations and is capable of completely destroying itself once it suspects that its identity is being exposed. Figure 1 represents a typical behaviour of the proposed intruding agent.

We have studied the feasibility of such a system and found that this is possible as the attackers have access to more and more sophisticated tools that not only leads

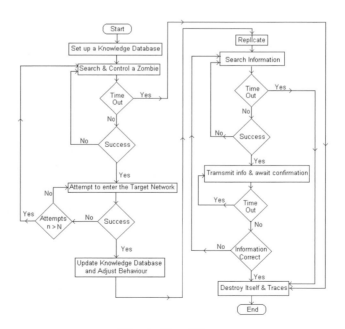

**Fig. 1.** Flow Diagram

to more severe types of attacks but also helps them to speed up their tasks [3]. We devote Sect. 4 to discuss the related issues.

# 4   Design and Issues; Is This Really Possible?

We now discuss each of the desired characteristics as identified in Sect. 3 to see whether such a system is feasible and to what extent the protection and detection mechanisms, such as Firewalls and Intrusion Detection Systems respectively, can be useful.

The agent starts by setting up a knowledge database, which is the most expected layout of the network the agent is supposed to enter. This may or may not be an exact layout depending upon the availability of some prior knowledge of the network. At this point there is a trade off; the more specific the prior information is, the faster and easier it is for the agent to finish its task as it does not require analyzing the network once it enters there; but on the other hand repeated intrusive attempts might be discovered. Hence starting with limited and basic knowledge is a preferred option. As discussed in Sect. 3 Social Engineering might come out to be useful in this case [4] [28].

Searching and controlling a zombie is not a big problem when an attacker has the available tools at hand [3]. Moreover, increasing number of vulnerabilities are identified and not all systems are suitably patched to remove the same, making it easier to gain complete control of a system. Using a zombie for launching the attack is essential to reduce the risk of trace back. It is from this zombie that the agent attempts to enter the target network by disguising as the normal traffic [3].

Once the agent gets control of a zombie it requires to enter the target network. Entering a target is simple when the network is connected to the internet. Probes and scans and a known vulnerability are simple methods of entering. This was, however, required when the attack was initiated outside the private network but the situation is much different and simple when the attack originates from within the network. In case of an internal attack, the agent has the complete knowledge of the layout of the network setup beforehand and is free from being detected by Firewalls and Network based Intrusion Detection Systems. In order to hide identity, the attacker may originate the attack from some general purpose machines available in the network. The only thing that the agent has to be aware of is the detection by a Host based Intrusion Detection Systems and internal network monitors. This, however, applies to the externally originated attacks as well.

Once the agent is in the network it decides whether to replicate or not depending upon the time constraint. In most cases it would be better to do so; hence the basic question is the number of replications. No matter what the case, this number of replication is always limited. Once replicated there is a small network of agents that is set up. The agents hide by minimizing the communication and by hiding in the network devices from where they can slowly scan the entire network for required information.

The agents can obtain passwords and other information by monitoring key-strokes and other monitoring approaches. This is the most effective method as it provides direct authorized access to the information. Moreover, once the access is provided the monitoring systems (primarily the Host based Intrusion Detection Systems) can be turned down or manipulated so as to hide the detection.

When successful in securing information the agent transmits it back to the zombie so that the information can be verified for its relevance. If the informa-tion is not found to be relevant the agent again searches for the information keeping track of the deadline and continues the search. Finally if it is successful or it encounters a situation of time out, the agent tries to eliminate its foot-prints. This is done by modifying the audit logs which may be maintained by the host systems. This too is possible as stated in [12] [18]. For this, the agent would require root access which might again be possible by session highjack or exploiting a vulnerability leading to root compromise and hence modifying the logs. The agents and their entire network finally ends with self destruction.

The success of such an agent lies in the ability to hide its identity from being discovered. However, there is no state of the art Intrusion Detection System that can lead to the detection of such an attack. Also the current Intrusion Detection Systems are either Signature based or Anomaly based. The Signature based systems suffer from the problem of not being able to detect new type of attacks while the Anomaly based systems are either based on threshold or timing window; hence are not able to detect very slow attacks. Moreover, if a Network based Intrusion Detection System is deployed, it monitors only the network packets as a result the agent is free from detection once it is inside the network. On the other hand if a Host based Intrusion Detection System is deployed it can be controlled by the agent to inhibit its detection as discussed in Sect. 2.

At this stage we do not intend to provide an implementation of such an agent based system. However, we would like to strengthen our point that such an agent based attack is possible in future or it might already be in existence but none of the in place security systems have reported such an activity. This calls for an extra effort to identify the possible attack scenarios and provide a solution to prevent possible attacks based on the identified scenarios, rather than only protecting the systems from known attacks.

## 5   Effects of Such an Agent

The proposed scenario shows that such an agent based system can be extremely powerful in compromising confidentiality. Its strength can be realized from the fact that the agent has the ability to select and distinguish between the required information. It also takes every possible step to protect itself from being discov-ered. This shows that in order to completely protect the networks we not only need to build strong external defenses that protects the malicious external traffic from entering inside the network but we also need to provide sufficient internal traffic and status monitoring, particularly relating to the access of data, so that any unauthorized access can be detected and hence confidentiality of data can be ensured.

# 6  Future Directions in Intrusion and Intrusion Detection

We are still at the beginning of the intrusion era and we are yet to discover highly personalized and more damaging attacks. This paper is an attempt to show that such personalized attacks are possible and can be highly damaging. The future of attacks is not in large scale disruption of services over the internet, though they will coexist, but the future will witness tremendous increase in the attacks which are highly localized and driven by profit and other motives.

Increasing interest in the agent technology and parallel advances in the intrusion activities using advanced attack methodologies opens the door for more sophisticated and previously unseen attack scenarios which can be more damaging in terms of loss of confidential information rather than in only wide scale disruption of services. We believe that to detect such highly specific attacks, along with other conventional attacks, we need to model our Detection Systems to focus on the attack target and work in conjunction with the network periphery security devices such as the Firewalls.

# 7  Legal Issues

Law is central to any matter related to Intrusion. In this section we discuss the related legal aspects which are of prime concern. The legal issues concerning, in general, the internet security overlap with privacy and pose problems about how to balance freedom of speech, government regulation and the role of private companies [20]. Unauthorized access is considered as the most important offence in the field of computer crime, because, access is the fundamental predicate of the misuse, leading further to a series of cyber crimes [17]. Legal analysis of Internet security exhibits three tiers which are generally put together but must be well understood independently to deal with cyber crime and security [10]. The three tiers consists of the Internet as a network at the topmost layer, which is also the weakest point. The second layer consists of the Transactional Security, also known as the commerce and personal identity. Finally the third layer consists of the Personal Privacy. Alarmed by the increasing number of Denial of Service attacks, a special computer security summit was convened at the White House which resulted in expanding the American Federal Government role to monitor Internet activity [7]. However, such and similar efforts [8] have rather failed to some extent as the users prefer not to let the government know every little thing they do.

The problem further complicates when it comes to the an organization connected to the internet where most of the employers have access to the emails of their employees' [15]. This indicates that the privacy of the employee is weighed against the business needs of an employer. Even the courts have been more protective of the business needs of the employer than the privacy of the employee

[23]. In an attempt to provide security by constant monitoring, personal privacy is sacrificed [16]. The fact, that the local government in the United States of America has a legal right to read the email and watch web surfing of its employees including the judges and the courts, further confirms this [25].

However, when we talk of inter organization security breeches, as we have represented, the situation is much different. Any form of unauthorized access is considered as a criminal offence and is punishable, but the intention and the role of the organizations involved are worth considering. When such a task is business driven and performed for personal profit motive, it is likely to be prosecuted. However, when the task is performed by the intruding agent it is difficult to identify and hence prosecute the attacker as the agent leaves no traces and in emergency situations it destroys itself to evade identification. On the other hand when the task is performed by an government agency or any non-profit organization, in an attempt to expose off some scandal the situation is not the same. The agency takes ownership of the task performed to prove its claim. In this case, however, the issue is whether it is justified to access private confidential information without authorized access.

Nonetheless if such a tool is possible, and as we have shown it is, it cannot be guaranteed that it is used for communal interest, neglecting personal gains. It can be available to the attacker who is driven by self profit motive. Hence there is a need to be able to detect such an agent so as to avoid any loss of private information.

## 8   Action Against the Intrusive Agent

To deter any kind of intrusion the basic requirement is of an online system that can effectively block any intrusion attempt in real time. However, it should also provide strong and reliable evidence of the correct source of intrusion so that legal action can be taken against the intruder. We introduced a new type of intrusion possible with current technology which is very likely to appear soon or might already be in existence (but not yet reported). The current detection systems, however, are inadequate to detect such an activity of the intruding agent. Hence in order to deter such intrusive activities we require to build strong defence systems as well as an equally strong legal system that would discourage such attacks. For the legal system to be effective it requires the source to be correctly identified and then collecting strong evidence against the identified source. However, more work is required to correctly identify the source of intrusion as the proposed agent takes every step to hide its identity. One possible method to detect an agent activity is to take a periodic snapshot of activities of the processes in a secure media such as write once only media which can be used for further analysis and for building evidence of intrusion.

## 9   Conclusions and Future Work

In this paper we proposed and evaluated a new agent based system that is able to collect specific information from a private network without authorized access.

We also discussed the legal implications in various situations that arises due to such an activity. Examining the log files manually after the incident is reported, fails to protect confidentiality. We also argued that the future of intrusion lies in highly personalized attacks which would be very difficult to identify and hence to react to. This paper also highlights the point that the security systems in use today are not adequate to cater to all aspects of security viz. confidentiality, integrity and availability. As part of our future work we plan to expand on the shortcomings of present IDS techniques and develop a system which is robust and free (virtually) from all kinds of attacks and is not confined to detecting some special type of attacks. We also plan to work on the Application based IDS particularly in database applications.

# References

[1] Cert advisory ca-2001-22 w32/sircam malicious code, august 2001. Online Reference: http://www.cert.org/advisories/CA-2001-22.html.

[2] Computer worm. Wikipedia, the free encyclopedia. Online Reference: http://en.wikipedia.org/wiki/Computer_worm.

[3] Overview of attack trends, 2002. Online Reference: http://www.cert.org/archive/pdf/attack_trends.pdf.

[4] Social engineering. Wikipedia, the free encyclopedia. Online Reference: http://en.wikipedia.org/wiki/Social_engineering_(computer_security).

[5] Software agent. Wikipedia, the free encyclopedia. Online Reference: http://en.wikipedia.org/wiki/Software_agent.

[6] Spyware. Wikipedia, the free encyclopedia. Online Reference: http://en.wikipedia.org/wiki/Spyware.

[7] Report on Privacy and Security, The Federal Trade Commission Advisory Committee on Online Access and Security, May 2000.

[8] The G8 Internet Security Conference, Paris, France, May 2000.

[9] Oracle http server vulnerability, 2005. Online Reference: http://www.kb.cert.org/vuls/id/890940.

[10] Michael Adler. Cyberspace, General Searches and Digial Conraband: The Fourth Amendment and the Net-Wite Search. *Yale Law Journal*, 105:1093–1120, 1996.

[11] R. Agarwal, J. Kiernan, R. Srikant, and Y. Xu. Hippocratic databases. In *Proceedings of the 28th International Conference on Very Large Databases, 2002*, 2002.

[12] Julia Allen, Alan Christie, William Fithen, John McHugh, Jed Pickel, and Ed Stoner. State of practice of intrusion detection technologies. Technical Report CMU/SEI-99-TR-028 ESC-99-028, 1999. Online Reference: http://www.sei.cmu.edu/pub/documents/99.reports/pdf/99tr028.pdf.

[13] Wes Ames. Understanding spyware: risk and response. *IT Professional*, 6(5):25–29, September/October 2004. Published by IEEE Computer Society.

[14] Rebecca Bace and Peter Mell. *Intrusion Detection Systems*. Gaithersburg, MD : Computer Security Division, Information Technology Laboratory, National Institute of Standards and Technology, 2001, 2001.

[15] S. Bronitt. Complementary Comment: Electronic Surveillance and Informers: Infringing the Right to Silence and Privacy. *Criminal Law Journal*, 20:144–152, 1996.

[16] S. Bronitt. Electronic Surveillance, Human Rights and Criminal Justice. *Australian Journal of Human Rights*, 3:183–207, 1997.

[17] Michael Carroll and Robert Schrader. Computer Related Crimes. (Tenth Survey of White Collar Crime). *American Criminal Law Review*, 32(2):185–211, 1995.

[18] S. Castano, M. Fugini, G. Martella, and P. Samarati. *Database Security*. Addison Wesley, 1994.

[19] Stephen D. Crocker. Protecting the internet from distributed denial-of-service attacks: a proposal. *Proceedings of the IEEE. September 2004*, 92(9), 2004.

[20] Mark C. Dearing. Personal Jurisdiction and the Internet: Can the Traditional Principles and Landmark Cases Guide the Legal System Into the 21st Centuary? *Journal of Technology, Law and Policy*, 4(1), 1999.

[21] Peter Ferrie and Peter Szor. W32.sircam.worm@mm. Online Reference: http://www.symantec.com/avcenter/venc/data/w32.sircam.worm@mm.html.

[22] Aaron Hackworth. Spyware. CERT Coordination Center Report, 2005. Online Reference: http://www.cert.org/archive/pdf/spyware2005.pdf.

[23] Lee Hochberg. E-Avesdropping. Online News, January 2000. http://www.pbs.org/newshour/bb/cyberspace/jan-june00/email_1-7.html

[24] Thomas A. Longstaff, James T. Ellis, Shawn V. Hernan, Howard F. Lipson, Robert D. Mcmillan, Linda Hutz Pesante, and Derek Simmel. Security of the internet. The Froehlich/Kent Encyclopedia of Telecommunications vol. 15, Marcel Dekker, New York. CERT Coordination Center Report, 1997, pages 231-255. Online Reference: http://www.cert.org/encyc_article/tocencyc.html.

[25] B. Marlowe. You are Being Watched. ZDNet Magazine, December 1999.

[26] Murch and Johnson. Intelligent software agents, 1999.

[27] H.S. Nwana. Software agents: An overview. Online Reference: http://www.sce.carleton.ca/netmanage/docs/AgentsOverview/ao.html.

[28] Linda Dailey Paulson. Spike in phishing and malware a danger to it. *IT Professional*, 7(3), May/June 2005. Published by IEEE Computer Society.

[29] Colleen Shannon and David Moore. The spread of the witty worm. CAIDA analysis for the spread of Witty worm. Online Reference: http://www.caida.org/analysis/security/witty/

[30] Joel Sommers, Vinod Yegneswaran, and Paul Barford. A framework for malicious workload generation. In *Internet Measurement Conference, October 25 - 27, 2004, Taormina, Sicily, Italy*, 2004. Online Reference: http://www.cs.wisc.edu/~pb/mace_final.pdf.

[31] E. Spafford. The internet worm program: An analysis. Technical Report CSD-TR-823, Purdue University, November 1988.

[32] S. Staniford, V. Paxson, and N. Weaver. How to own the internet in your spare time. In *11th Usenix Security Symposium, San Francisco, August, 2002*, 2002.

[33] Nicholas Weaver, Vern Paxson, Stuart Staniford, and Robert Cunningham. A taxonomy of internet worms. Online Reference: http://www.cs.berkeley.edu/~nweaver/papers/taxonomy.pdf.

# Viability of Critical Mission of Grid Computing

Fangfang Liu[1], Yan Chi[2], and Yuliang Shi[1]

[1] Department of Computing and Information Technology, FUDAN University, Handan Road 220, Shanghai, China, 200433
{041021055, 031021056}@fudan.edu.cn
[2] Shifang Research, Bibo Road 456, Shanghai, China, 201203
chiyan@shifang.com.cn

**Abstract.** Grid computing is a kind of important paradigm for networked applications and information technology. Many critical infrastructure applications of our daily life are built on gird systems. Then, survivability becomes a necessary property of grid computing. In dynamic and complex network environment, grid systems face different kinds of attacks, failures and accidents that appear frequently. And At the same time new challenges for survivability arise with characteristics of grid system. To resolve them, we focus on continuous providing of critical mission, which determines survivability of the whole grid system. We utilize PVA, methods of conservation biology, for viability analysis of critical mission and some parameters, which are helpful for predicating viability. Hence, we can achieve survivability of grid system using results of viability.

## 1 Introduction

Grid is "Coordinated resource sharing and problem solving in dynamic, multi-institutional virtual organizations (VO)[1]". Grid computing has emerged as an important new paradigm distinguished from conventional distributed computing by its focus on large-scale resource sharing, innovative applications, and in some cases, high-performance orientation [1]. Applications of grid computing have reached many aspects of life and most of these systems are used in critical infrastructures of society, such as telecom communication services, health care services. Survivability of grid systems becomes very important.

Survivability is "a necessary facet of system dependability" [3] and is relatively a new research area. Generally, survivability is defined as "the ability of a system to fulfill its mission, in a timely manner, in the presence of attacks, failures or accidents [2]". Survivability is different from reliability, security or other properties of a system. It focuses on continuity of service (degraded, less dependable or different) which can satisfy user's requirement when various events cause damages to the system. Instead of assuring every part of a system, survivability only aims at critical mission of it. Critical mission plays an important role in survivability of the whole system. Grid computing paradigm naturally requires survivability as strong support for its dependability. A lot of work for survivability has been done on attack types that system faces and enforcement of components of system. However, some new challenges arise with characteristics of grid computing. For example, a grid system is composed of resources/applications, or entities located worldwide. Improvement of every entity participating

S. Mehrotra et al. (Eds.): ISI 2006, LNCS 3975, pp. 297–307, 2006.

in critical mission is not appropriate. And that different types of attacks may occur to different entities makes it hard for system to have consistent treatment with attacks. In addition, applications/resources in/out of gird system (virtual organization) dynamically and freely also have impact on ability of system, while this case is not caused by attacks or failures. Since grid system is composed of entities coming from different organizations and different plat-forms, system has no central control mechanism and only has limit knowledge about its component and itself. All these new situations have to be taken into consideration to assure that ability of critical mission provided by applications/resources conforms to bottom line of users' requirement.

In this paper, we present our method for survivability of critical mission of grid system. Different from other research works, which focus on replication of components or alternate services according to faults or attacks, we work on viability of critical mission in grid environment. Viability refers to capability of living and surviving from outside attacks. Instead of solving survivability by analyzing attack or failure types and improve ability of individual entity, viability of critical mission cares about predictions of whether critical mission can live and survive or not. Our work is based on a kind of ecological conservation analysis method——PVA (population viability analysis) [4,5]. Ideally, conservation organizations would seek to preserve every rare, endangered species. But it is not feasible in practice for financial consideration. PVA is just the method focusing on preserving critical species to meet conservation requirement. Broadly defined, PVA refers to the use of quantitative methods to predict the likely future status of a population or collection of populations of conservation concern [18].

For a grid system, users determine critical mission of system and also give their requirement when system meets failures, attacks or accidents. Many factors can lead to degradation of critical mission and we do not need to consider them one by one. In turn, inspired by ecological conservation, we focus on viability of critical mission. Critical mission is just like critical species. Services dynamically in and out of the system can be seen as reproduction and survival of species, and timing constraints of service providing is like in a period of time, population size should be kept in a predicted level. Then, we can utilize model of PVA to analyze viability of critical mission and also some important measures for critical mission using methods of PVA.

The remainder of the paper is organized as follows. Section 2 is related work about survivability. Section 3 introduces our main point. Section 4 provides simulation experiment. And section 5 concludes the paper.

## 2   Related Work

Survivability is important to modern IT system. It is a relatively new research area. And it is a necessary branch of dependability. We have mentioned a kind of definition of survivability. In fact, there have been different definitions about survivability [6, 7]. These definitions are centered on continuity of system's function. In fact, the content of the definition of survivability depends on domain. The survivability requirements of systems vary substantially, depending on the scope of the system, and the criticality and consequences of failure and interruption of service [2]. The definition and analysis of survivability requirements is a first step in achieving system survivability. Authors in [2] presented key properties of survivable system and categorize requirements definitions of survivability into several types.

Survivability is not only a plug-in property of system. It should be taken into account at the system design phase [3]. And some works have been done on analysis and design of survivability architectures and prototypes have been proposed. In [7, 11, 12], issues met in developing survivability architecture have been discussed and approaches for those problems are put forward. Researches in [2, 13, 14] offer another design method for survivability SSA (Survivable System Analysis), which is based on intrusion usage Scenario. For this method, survivability is integrated into software development life cycle. In [8], a survivability architecture called SAMBER is presented. SABER blocks, evades and reacts to a variety of attacks by using several security and survivability mechanisms in an automated and coordinated fashion. Intrusion Tolerant Distributed Object System (ITDOS) [9] is also survivability architecture. It discusses some of the challenging technical issues related to intrusion tolerance in heterogeneous middleware systems. A middleware-based mobile C4I (Command, Control, Communications, Computers, &Intelligence) architecture is discussed in [10]. Design of prototype ITDB [15] is based on intrusion tolerance. This method doesn't need to develop a new survivable system.

Survivability is closely related to security. In [16], reasoning frameworks are presented to be able to predictably determine how architecture responds to security threats and be able to improve that response. As to survivability of grids, authors in [17] describe the Grid Dependability and Survivability Architecture (GDSA). In GDSA a series of instruments continuously monitor application and system behavior. The raw monitoring data are processed, collected and distributed to appropriate dependability services, analyzed, and then appropriate corrective actions are taken.

These researches mainly focus on issues of architecture level. As to specific mechanisms for enforcement of critical mission, most works on survivability tackle it from the point that survivability of systems should be achieved by dealing with different kinds of attacks, failures and accidents. However, in gird computing environment, without central control and only part knowledge of component applications/ resources, it is inappropriate to take same measures for every component. And on the other side, component applications/resources from different organizations or different plat-forms have their own ability and behavior. It is also hard to get accurate data about components and have survival analysis on them to achieve survivability of critical mission.. To avoid cases above, we try to resolve survivability from a top point of view. Since survivability of critical missions determines survivability of system, in this paper, we work on survivability with the main idea that viability of critical mission is much important. And no matter what happens, if we can guarantee viability of critical mission, we can achieve our goal, system survivability. Thus, we can use model of PVA in ecological system to analyze viability of critical mission and infer measures from the model, which are useful for viability.

## 3   Survivability of Critical Mission of Grid Computing

Survivability of grid system depends on its architecture and requirement of specific application. In this section, we introduce OGSA, architecture of grid computing and model of viability of critical mission based on OGSA.

## 3.1  Architecture of Grid Computing

Open Grid Service Architecture (OGSA) is a kind of important architecture for grid. Its goal is to provide a service-oriented infrastructure that leverages standardized protocols and services to enable pervasive access to, and coordinated sharing of geographically distributed hardware, software, and information resources. The fundamental concept underlying OGSA is the virtualization of applications, resource or any kind of entities, as services and the seamless interactions and integration of these services. OGSA specification [19] defines standard interfaces and mechanisms for describing, invoking and managing grid services. A service is defined as a network enabled entity that provides some capability and communicates through the exchange of messages. In OGSA, entities on the grid are represented as services and new higher-level services and applications can be constructed from the available services.

OGSA has two backup technologies: grid technology (GLOBUS software packages) and Web service [20]. Web services are encapsulated, self-descriptive, modular, internet applications that may be accessible by the users via the network. Web Service is a promising way to solve interoperability and integration of distributed applications on the network. Web Service architecture consists of service providers, service consumers and service registry. Service providers register their services on service registry, service consumers query services from service registry, and then service consumers can invoke services offered by service providers. OGSA is Web Service. In OGSA, services entering VO should be registered. Scheduling mechanism of OGSA picks up suitable services from registry to perform tasks. And grid system is composed of just services.

## 3.2  Survivability of Grid Computing

Survivability of a grid system depends on application type and specific requirements of users. To achieve survivability of the system, the first step is to define critical mission, which is determined by users. The ability of critical mission may be guaranteed by degraded services or migration to new services. Here, we consider only the case of offering degraded services and assume that there is no migration. Then, viability of the system just rests on critical mission.

For example, in application of a data grid (Fig. 1), thousands of physicists, which are service providers, at hundreds of labs and universities worldwide, come together to resolve some big scientific problems. They pool computing, storage and networking resources, all of which are called services, to process a lot of data of scientific problems. From users' point, computing ability is critical to accomplishment of the system. Then computing ability is critical mission and guaranteeing computing ability is one of main goals of survivability of this gird system. Data are decomposed to suitable sub-parts and distributed to different services selected from service registry to compute. Efficiency of data processing depends on capability of services in the system. Cyber-attacks, failures or accidents may happen to services and services may leave VO freely. In that case, sub-tasks can be reallocated to new services joining VO and becoming parts of critical mission.

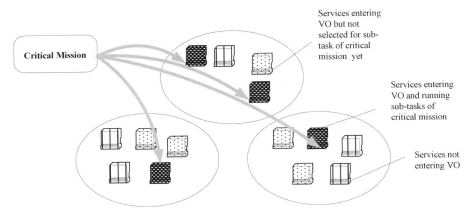

**Fig. 1.** In a data grid, services from different organizations are registered and picked up to perform sub-tasks of critical mission. Component service may become unavailable and new services may join and perform subtasks. Number of services for critical mission is 4.

Methods of PVA analyze viability of critical species. Viability is directly reflected by population size of species. Population size does not increase of decrease smoothly over time. Variation in the environment, which causes the rates of reproduction and survival to vary over time, contributes to fluctuations in population size. And the potential sources of environment-driven variations are too numerous to be analyzed individually. Thus, it is impossible to predict exact population size. The methods of PVA are, given threshold of population size, to build model for predicating the probability of population reaching threshold, therefore to infer mean time to extinction, mean growth of population and other measures of viability.

Critical mission of data grid system in Fig. 1 has huge impact on survivability of the whole system. Compared to PVA, we can see that analyzing viability of computing mission can help to accomplish survivability of system. Since there are hundreds or thousands of services provide their computing ability to the system, individual service is not our object for analysis. The computing power offered by all of them plays an important role. Naturally, quantity of services can reflect change of computing ability. Assume that services are all registered. Then, in example of Fig. 1, services are divided into three types: registered services in VO running sub-tasks of critical mission; services in VO but not selected for critical mission; services not in VO. Not all of services with computing capability in the registry are counted and only services selected to really run sub-tasks of the critical mission are taken into consideration. That is because states of services in the registry not working have no effect on ability of computing mission. But, services already in the registry, not used previously, once are picked up by scheduling mechanism to do sub-tasks, will also be added to services count. And reasons like services leaving the VO or cyber attack, failures and accidents also contribute to fluctuation of services size. Thus, in example of Fig. 1, there are already 4 services entering VO and executing sub-tasks. That is, number of services size is 4. While, as reasons we have mentioned above, number of services is not constant. It changes with time.

### 3.3  Viability of Critical Mission

We have mentioned that quantity can represent ability of a critical mission. However, the number of services fulfilling the mission is not constant. Cyber-attacks may bring damages to services and make them unavailable. Services may be broken down and unable to work. Services may enter the virtual organizations and begin to perform sub-job or leave the VO freely. Or leases of some services are overdue and services providers do not continue their services any more. There are many other reasons and we do not list here. Because of these reasons, the number of services does not increase or decrease smoothly over time, but instead show considerable variation around long-term trends.

In this part, we apply basic PVA to grid computing. We mainly refer to model and methods of PVA mentioned in [18, 21]. Assuming that $N(t)$ denotes the number of individuals performing sub-tasks of critical mission at time t, $N_0$ is the initial size of services for critical mission in the system and contributing to computing mission and $\lambda$ is the growth rate of the number of services. Then, the conceptual model of services growth is:

$$N(t+1) = \lambda N(t) \tag{1}$$

When there is no other variation, just services leaving or entering VO, the services growth rate $\lambda$ is constant. And given that threshold is $N_e$, only three qualitative types of $\lambda$ are possible: $\lambda$ is more than one, the number of services grows geometrically; $\lambda$ is less than one, the number of services declines geometrically below threshold; and if $\lambda$ exactly equals one, the number of services neither increases or decreases, but maintain at its initial size in subsequent time. But, as we have listed that, variation in the environment, that is network, may drive changes in services growth unpredictably and we must face the fact that we cannot predicate exactly what the future services size will be. We can only make statements on probability of services size in subsequent time. To make this point more clearly, we use computer programs to simulate random variation of $\lambda$. Results are presented in Fig. 2. From it, we can learn that when service growth rate is in a "stochastic" environment, the further into the future predictions about number of services are made, the less precise they become and change of sequence of $\lambda$ do not follow very well the predicted trend based on some average value. Some points are far below the average values, while many others may be above it. That's because in general cases, services size can always grows, while catastrophe reduces it hugely. Anyway, if we want to make predications about likely abundance of services, we have to lay our attention on probability distribution of numbers of services.

Just like in PVA [18], we can make the statement that the natural log of services size will be normally distributed. That is to say, quantity $X(t) = \log N(t)$, will have, as t becomes large, an approximate normal distribution with mean $x_0 + \mu \cdot t$ and variance $\sigma^2 t$, where $x_0 = \log N_0$, or $X(t) \doteq N(x_0 + \mu \cdot t, \sigma^2 t)$, where $\doteq$ is distributed as, and dot indicates that the distribution is approximate. Here, $\mu$ is a real-value constant and $\sigma^2$ is a positive, real-value constant. And $\mu$ determines how quickly the mean of the number of services increases or decreases and $\sigma^2$ determines how quickly

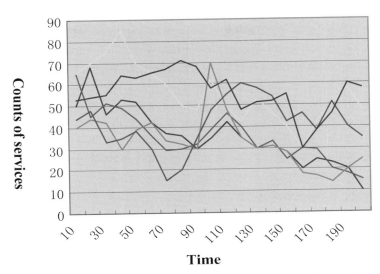

**Fig. 2.** Simulation of Random Change of Services Growth Rate. Service growth rate doesn't change smoothly. Many points are high above or low below average value. The further into future predications about change rate is made, the less precise they are.

the variance increases. If $\mu$ is less than zero, services size down to threshold is certain, but even if $\mu$ is positive, there will be some chance that size still falls below threshold in case that $\sigma^2$ increase rapidly. Thus, we must know the estimated values of $\mu$ and $\sigma^2$.

Estimates of $\mu$ and $\sigma^2$ can be obtained with just a single series of observations on services size at times $0, t_1, t_2, ..., t_q$. Accordingly, the services sizes observed are $N(0) = N_0, N(1) = N_1, ..., N(q) = N_q$. Parameters $\mu$ and $\sigma^2$ can be estimated using maximum likelihood (ML) estimates or linear regression approach (more details referred to [21]). We prefer to the ML which is simple to perform. The results of ML yield estimation, $\hat{\mu}$ and $\hat{\sigma}^2$, for parameters $\mu$ and $\sigma^2$ respectively. Furthermore, various quantities related to viability analysis are functions of $\mu$ and $\sigma^2$, such as the probability of the critical mission reaching threshold, the mean time to reach threshold and other parameters able to reflecting viability of critical missions. And these measures can be straightforward estimated. Here, we choose the most important ones.

Given threshold $N_e$, $x_e = \log N_e$ and $x_d = x_0 - x_e = \log N_0 / N_e$,

- the probability of services reaching threshold
  We have known that if $\mu$ is less than zero, then reaching threshold is certain. Otherwise, the probability of reaching threshold depends on $\mu$ and $\sigma^2$.

  Since quantity $X(t)$ is normally distributed, according to [21], then the probability density function of $X(t)$ is:

$$p_x(x,t \mid x_0) = (2\pi\sigma^2 t)^{-1/2} \exp[-(x - x_0 - \mu \cdot t)^2 / 2\sigma^2 t] \tag{2}$$

$$-\infty < x < \infty$$

As explained in many researches about PVA like [22, 23], the probability of services reaching threshold is:

$$\pi(x_d, \mu, \sigma^2) = \begin{cases} 1, \mu \leq 0 \\ \exp(-2\mu \cdot x_d / \sigma^2), \mu > 0 \end{cases} \tag{3}$$

From estimation $\hat{\mu}$ and $\hat{\sigma}^2$, estimate for probability of reaching threshold is:

$$\hat{\pi} = \begin{cases} 1, \mu \leq 0 \\ (x_e / x_0)^{2q\hat{\mu}/(q-1)\hat{\sigma}^2}, \mu > 0 \end{cases} \tag{4}$$

- mean time to threshold

The lower and upper 95% confidence for mean time to threshold is:

$$\left( \hat{\theta} \pm z_{0.025/2} \sqrt{\frac{\ln(n_0 / n_e)\hat{\sigma}^2}{\hat{\mu}^4 \cdot t_q}} \right) \tag{5}$$

where $\hat{\theta} = \dfrac{\ln(n_0 / n_e)}{|\hat{\mu}|}$

We must be careful to use mean time to threshold. It is always overestimated because though catastrophe rarely happen, once appears, it can make services size reduce rapidly below threshold. Thus, mean time to threshold should only be used as a measure when $\hat{\mu}$ is negative.

- Cumulative Distribution Function (CDF) of the conditional time to threshold and median time to threshold

Since meant time to threshold is always overestimated, we use probability of the conditional time to threshold. If threshold is attained, the amount of time $T$, elapsed before the threshold is first reached is a positive, real-valued random variable with a continuous probability distribution. The CDF of the distribution is:

$$\Pr[T \leq t] = \Phi\left( \frac{-x_d + |\mu| \cdot t}{\sigma\sqrt{t}} \right) + \exp(2x_d |\mu| / \sigma^2)\Phi\left( \frac{-x_d + |\mu| \cdot t}{\sigma\sqrt{t}} \right) \tag{6}$$

$$0 < t < \infty$$

And estimate of CDF is,

$NORMDIST(y) + \exp(2a)MORMDIST(-z)$

where

$$a = \ln(n_0 / n_e)/\sqrt{\sigma^2}, b = |\mu|/\sqrt{\sigma^2},$$
$$y = (bt - a)/\sqrt{t}, z = (bt + a)/\sqrt{t}$$

Median time to threshold is the time when CDF reaches 50%. And median time is always more accurate than mean time to threshold.

# 4  Simulation Experiment Analysis

One of the backup technologies for OGSA is GLOBUS packages. We setup GLOBUS as experimental platform. And through some simulation programs, we imitate case of services in/out of system and get data about counts of services which participate in a computing application. In experiment, we assume that the application is critical mission and $S(t)$ is count of services for critical mission, $S(0) = S_0$ is initial size. $S(t)$ is defined as follow:

$$S(t+1) = S(t) + a_t - l_t \tag{7}$$

Where

$a_t$ : number of services joining application between time unit $t$ and $t+1$.

$l_t$ : number of services which don't provide services for application anymore between time unit $t$ and $t+1$.

We choose an hour as time unit to take counts of services for the simulation. Collected data are presented in Table 1. The initial number of services size is 50, assuming that threshold is 20, we can get parameters of model and calculate measures for viability of critical mission by equations (2)-(5). Using data of table 1, estimates of parameters and $\mu$ and $\sigma^2$ are: 0.003223 and 0.033491 respectively. The probability of services reaching threshold is 0.783547. And the meant time to threshold is 374 hours with lower bound 0 and higher bound 943 of 95% confidence.

The meant time to threshold is always overestimated. Then, we compute the probability to reach threshold using Cumulative Distribution Function using (6). Figure 3 gives the final results. From it, we know that after 150 hours, the probability that threshold is reached is 50%, or the median time to threshold is 150.

Experiments show that viability of this computing is optimistic. And if users want that services size is still above threshold after median time to threshold, it can be achieved by increasing initial services size. We have to mentioned that here we haven't consider the case that catastrophe may happen and cause number of services fall rapidly. Hence, it is likely that result of viability of application may be over-optimistic.

**Table 1.** Data of Count of Services In Simulation Experiment. Time unis is hour. Services count is taken per hour. We take 20 hour counts of services as our estimation data.

| time(/h) | count | time(/h) | count | Time(/h) | count | time(/h) | Count |
|----------|-------|----------|-------|----------|-------|----------|-------|
| 1 | 53 | 6 | 65 | 11 | 62 | 16 | 30 |
| 2 | 54 | 7 | 67 | 12 | 48 | 17 | 38 |
| 3 | 55 | 8 | 71 | 13 | 51 | 18 | 46 |
| 4 | 64 | 9 | 68 | 14 | 52 | 19 | 60 |
| 5 | 63 | 10 | 58 | 15 | 55 | 20 | 58 |

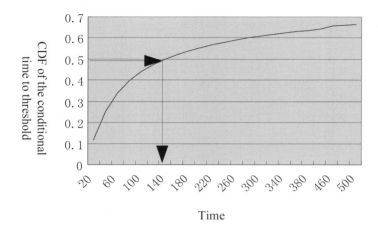

**Fig. 3.** Cumulative Distributed Function of the Conditional to Threshold. The curve represents with time changing, probability of reaching threshold is become large. In nearly 150 hour, the probability that threshold is 0.5.

## 5   Conclusion

In this paper, we study issue on critical mission of survivability of grid computing. Aiming at features of gird computing and inspired by one of the most important ecological conservation techniques——PVA, we focus on viability of critical mission of grid computing and analyze them to achieve survivability of system. We utilize model and methods of PVA and apply results of PVA to component services size of critical mission. The services size includes services which really participate in grid system and perform sub-jobs decomposed from critical mission. Some other measures that can reflect viability of critical mission are also presented.

There are some directions deserving studied and many works needed to be done in the future. In this paper, we only use basic model of PVA and there are some more complex model. And though viability of critical mission has been analyzed, we want to know that in what kind of cases we can assure that ability of critical mission is beyond threshold and be kept in a predicted time. And in our analysis, we ignore catastrophe that may happen and cause huge effect on viability. Viability is changed by many factors in the environment. Though it is difficult to analyze them one by one, factors may be categorized and compared. Then determinant ones can be found to take measure to improve viability of critical mission and hence, survivability of whole system. We will try to find resolutions for these problems.

## References

1.  Foster, I., Kesselman, C. and Tuecke, S.: The Anatomy of the Grid: Enabling scalable visited organizations. International Journal of Supercomputer Applications, 2001
2.  Ellision, R.J., Fisher, D.A., Linger, R.C., Lipson, H.F., Longstaff, T.A. and Mead, N.R.: An Approach to Survivable Systems. Technical Report, CERT Coordination Center, Software Engineering Institute, Carnegie Mellon University, 1999

3. Tarvainen, P.: Survey of the Survivability of IT Systems. http://virtual.vtt.fi/merlin/pub/survey_ of_the_survivability_of_it_systems.pdf

4. Soule'E M. Introduction. In :M E Soule'(ed. ) , Viable population for conservation. Cambridge : Cambridge University Press ,1987 ,1~9

5. Soule'M E , Simberloff, D.: What do genetics and ecology tell us about the design of nature reserve?. Biological Conservation , 1986 ,35 :19~40

6. Knight, J.C. and Sullivan, K.J.: On the Definition of Survivability. University of Virginia, Department of Computer Science, Technical Report CS-TR-33-00, 2000

7. Knight, J.C., Sullivan, K.J., Elder, M.C. and Wang, C.: Survivability Architectures: Issues and Approaches. DARPA Information Survivability Conference and Exposition, Jan. 2000.

8. Keromytis, A.D., PAreckh, J., Gross, P.N., Kaiser, G., Misra, V., Nieh, J., Rubenstein, D. and Stolfo, S.: A Holistic Approach to Service Survivability. Technical Report CUSU-021-03, Dep. Of Computer Science, Columbia University, 2003.

9. Sames, D., Matt, B., Niebuhr, B., Tally, G., Whitmore B. and Bakken, D.: Developing a heterogeneous Intrusion Tolerant CORBA System. International Conference on Dependable Systems and Networks (DSN'02), 2002

10. Browne, R., Valente J. and Hariri. S.: An Advanced Middleware Architecture for Secure and Survivable Mobile C4I Systems", Military Communications Conference Proceedings, MILCOM 1999, IEEE, Volume: 1, pp. 506-513, 1999

11. Knight, J.C., Lubinsky, R.W., McHugh J. and Sullivan, K.J.: Architectural Approaches to Information Survivability. Technical Report CS-97-25, Department of Computer Science, University of Virginia, Charlottesville, VA 22903, 1997.

12. Knight J.C. and Strunk E.A.: Achieving Critical System Survivability through Software Architectures. http://www.cs.virginia.edu/~jck/publications/ knight.strunk.architecture.pdf

13. Lipson, H.F.: Survivability-A New Security Paradigm for Protecting Highly Distributed Mission Critical Systems. 38th Meeting of IFIP Working Group Dependable Computing and Fault Tolerance, 2000

14. Mead, N.R, Ellison, R.J., Linger, R.C.: Survivable Network Analysis Method. Technical Report, CMU/SEI-200-TR-013, ESC-2000-TR-013, Software Engineering Institute, Carnegie Mellon University, 2000

15. Peng, L.. "Research Directions in Survivable Systems and Networks". http://www.is.ac.cn/pliu-talk-beijing-2.

16. Ellison, R.J., Moore, A.P., Bass, L., Klein, M. and Bachmann, F.: Security and Survivability Reasoning Frameworks and Architectural Design Tactics. Technical Note CMU/SEI-2004-TN-022

17. Grimshaw, A., Humphrey, M., Knight, J.C., Tuong, A.N., Rowanhill, J., Wasson, G. and Basney, J.: The Development of Dependable and Survivable Grids. ICCS 2005, LNCS 3515, pp. 729-737

18. Morris, W., Doak, D., Groom, M., Kareiva, P., Fiegerg, J., Gerber, L., Murphy, P. and Thomson, D.: A Practical Handbook for Population Viability Analysis. The Nature Conservancy., April, 1999

19. Foster, I., Kesselman, C., Nick, J. and Tuecke, S.: The Physiology of the Grid: An Open Grid Services Architecture for Distributed Systems Integration. In Open Grid Service Infrastructure, WG, Global Grid Forum, June 22, 2002

20. Champion, M., Fessis, C. and Newcomer, E.: Web Service Architecture. http://www.w3.org/TR/ws-arch/, Feb. 11, 2004

21. Dennis, B., Munholland, P.L. and Scott, J.M.: Estimation of Growth and Extinction Parameters for Endangered Species. Ecological Monographs, 61(2), 1991, pp. 115-143

22. Ginzburg, L.R., Slobodkin, B., Johnson, K. and Bindman, A.G.: Quasiextinction Probabilities as A Measure of Impact on Population Growth. Risk Analysis. 1982 2: 171-181

23. Lande, R. and Orzack, S.H.: Extinction Dynamics of Age-structured Populations in a Fluctuating Environment. Proceeding of the National Academy of Sciences, 1988, 85: 7418-7421.

# Suspect Vehicle Identification for Border Safety with Modified Mutual Information

Siddharth Kaza, Yuan Wang, and Hsinchun Chen

Department of Management Information Systems, University of Arizona
sidd@u.arizona.edu, ywang@email.arizona.edu,
hchen@eller.arizona.edu

**Abstract.** The Department of Homeland Security monitors vehicles entering and leaving the country at land ports of entry. Some vehicles are targeted to search for drugs and other contraband. Customs and Border Protection agents believe that vehicles involved in illegal activity operate in groups. If the criminal links of one vehicle are known then their border crossing patterns can be used to identify other partner vehicles. We perform this association analysis by using mutual information (MI) to identify pairs of vehicles that are potentially involved in criminal activity. Domain experts also suggest that criminal vehicles may cross at certain times of the day to evade inspection. We propose to modify the mutual information formulation to include this heuristic by using cross-jurisdictional criminal data from border-area jurisdictions. We find that the modified MI with time heuristics performs better than classical MI in identifying potentially criminal vehicles.

## 1 Introduction

In recent years border safety has been identified as a critical part of homeland security. The national strategy for homeland security [1] calls for the creation of "smart borders" that provide "greater security through better intelligence and coordinated national efforts." In addition, the report also emphasizes that information sharing systems are the foundations to improve the nation's infrastructure.

The Department of Homeland Security (DHS) monitors vehicles entering and leaving the country, recording their license plates with a date and time of entry using license plate readers. Customs and Border Protection (CBP) agents search vehicles for drugs and other contraband. These thorough checks are done for vehicles on watch lists (target vehicles) and on random vehicles as well. This process is time consuming and if the waiting times become too long, the flow of people, vehicles, and commerce is impaired.

CBP agents believe that vehicles involved in illegal activity (especially smuggling) operate in groups. If the criminal links of one vehicle in a group are known, then the group's crossing patterns and frequency can be used to identify other partner vehicles. In a previous study [10] we found that the criminal associations of vehicles crossing the border may be recorded in local law enforcement databases in border-area jurisdictions. However, Customs and Border Protection does not always have access to criminal records of vehicles and sometimes lacks the methods to perform this analysis.

S. Mehrotra et al. (Eds.): ISI 2006, LNCS 3975, pp. 308 – 318, 2006.

We perform this association analysis by using mutual information (MI) to identify pairs of vehicles crossing together and potentially involved in criminal activity. Our previous study [7] had found that the use of MI may be a promising solution to this problem. In this paper we do an evaluation of MI in this problem domain and also attempt to modify the measure to incorporate domain heuristics. Domain experts (CBP agents, police detectives and analysts) suggest that groups of criminal vehicles may cross at certain times during the day to try and evade inspection. It is difficult to identify these heuristics with border crossing information alone since it does not contain clear indications of criminal history or possible intent. We use law enforcement information from border-area jurisdictions to identify times that criminal vehicles prefer and incorporate this knowledge in the MI formulation.

This study attempts to answer the following questions:

- Can law enforcement information from border-area jurisdictions be used to identify target vehicles at the border?
- How can we include domain heuristics to enhance the performance of mutual information?

In the next section we discuss background information and previous studies using mutual information. Section 3 presents the research testbed and explains the research design. Experimental results are shown and discussed in Section 4. Section 5 concludes and presents future directions.

## 2  Literature Review

In this section we review previous studies that have used association mining and mutual information in various domains. We also briefly discuss the challenges of using information from multiple data sources.

### 2.1  Information from Multiple Sources

In order to explore the criminal links of border-crossing vehicles it is necessary to extract data from multiple sources. To triangulate information about a vehicle, all the instances of the vehicle across datasets have to be reconciled, which is a challenging task. Matching of entities and their relationships is a task that is hampered by problems that include [4]: *name differences*: similar  entities in different databases have different names, *missing and conflicting data*: incomplete data or different values in different sources, and *object identification*: lack of global identifiers.

We use the BorderSafe information sharing and analysis framework [10] for accessing information from multiple datasets. These datasets include border crossing and local law enforcement records. Information on border crossing vehicles is located in local law enforcement datasets using their license plates and issue authorities (states). This enables us to extract the criminal histories for border crossing vehicles. More details about the datasets and their use are presented in Section 3.

## 2.2  Association Rule Mining

Inferring associations between items in a database was motivated by decision support problems faced by retail organizations [14]. Retail stores needed information on which items their customers were likely to buy together. The problem spawned a method in data mining known as association rule mining. An association rule is a relationship of the form $A \rightarrow B$, where $A$ is the antecedent item-set and $B$ is the consequent item-set. The antecedent and consequent item-sets can contain multiple items. $A \rightarrow B$ holds in a transaction set $T$ with confidence '$c$' if $c\%$ of transactions in $T$ that contain $A$, also contain $B$. $A \rightarrow B$ holds with support '$s$' if $s\%$ of transactions in $T$ contain both $A$ and $B$. To find associations between two item-sets, the association mining procedures identify all relationships (rules) that have support and confidence greater than user-specified thresholds.

Association rule mining has been applied in many domains including 'market basket' data [2], web log analysis (to identify online user behavior) [11], network intrusion detection [8], and gene regulatory network extraction (to identify cause-effect relationships between genes) [3].

## 2.3  Mutual Information

Mutual Information is an information theoretic measure that can be used to identify interesting co-occurrences of objects. The earliest definition of MI was given by Fano [6]. It was defined as the amount of information provided by the occurrence of an event ($y$) about the occurrence of another event ($x$). They formulated it as:

$$I(x; y) = \log_2 \frac{P(x, y)}{P(x)P(y)}$$

Intuitively, this concept measures if the co-occurrence of $x$ and $y$ ($P(x,y)$) is more likely than their independent occurrences ($P(x).P(y)$). This formula is referred to as the classical mutual information in the rest of the paper. Classical MI can be considered a subset of association rule mining with 1-item antecedent and 1-item consequent item-sets.

The MI measure has been applied to problems in many domains. It works well for phrase extraction from text documents. This is because text documents can be considered as a set of events (words), and the probability of the occurrence of a word can be calculated over the entire document. Previous studies in this area have used MI to study association between words in English texts and identify commonly occurring phrases [5]. It has also been used for key phrase extraction in Chinese texts [12].

Pantel et al. [13] used MI to match database columns containing similar information. In the bioinformatics domain, MI has been used to extract protein motif patterns from sequences [15]. However, the above studies have not modified the classical MI measure to include domain heuristics.

Work on extending or modifying the classical MI measure to add domain heuristics includes studies in natural language processing: Magerman and Marcus [9] modified the MI measure (bi-gram) to include n-grams and bioinformatics: Wren [16] extended the measure to calculate transitive MI scores for biological associations.

Border-crossing records can be considered as a stream of text (license plates) ordered by the time of crossing. So, MI can be used to identify frequent co-occurrence between a pair of vehicle crossings. If one vehicle in the pair has a criminal record, some inferences may be made about the second vehicle if they cross together frequently. In a previous study [7] we found that the time of crossing may be an important heuristic for improving the performance of MI in this domain. We propose to use conditional probability to include these domain heuristics in the MI formulation (Section 3.1.5).

## 3 Research Testbed and Design

The testbed for this study includes datasets obtained from the Tucson Police Department (TPD) and Pima County Sheriff's Department (PCSD). Data from these agencies is referred to as police data throughout this paper. In addition, we also use data from the Tucson Customs and Border Protection (CBP). These datasets were provided to us through the BorderSafe project funded by the Department of Homeland Security. The TPD and PCSD datasets include information on police incidents over 15 years (1990-2005). These incidents include individuals and vehicles that are involved in illegal activity in southern Arizona. A summary of these datasets is shown in Table 1.

**Table 1.** Key statistics of TPD and PCSD data

|                    | TPD         | PCSD        |
| ------------------ | ----------- | ----------- |
| Date Range         | 1990 – 2005 | 1990 – 2004 |
| Recorded Incidents | 3.3 million | 2.18 million |
| Vehicles           | 800, 656    | 520, 539    |

CBP data includes information on vehicles crossing the border between Arizona and Mexico at six ports of entry. This data includes the license plate, state, date, port, and time for crossings between 2003 and 2005. Details of this dataset are shown in Table 2.

**Table 2.** Key statistics of CBP border crossing data

| Recorded crossings | 10.7 million |
| ------------------ | ------------ |
| Number of vehicles | 1.7 million  |

### 3.1 Research Design

Prior to presenting the research design we need to define the terms *criminal vehicle* and *police contact*. A criminal vehicle is a vehicle that has been suspected, arrested, or has a warrant (with its occupant) for crimes that include narcotics (sale, possession, etc.), violence (homicide, aggravated assault, armed robbery, etc.), larceny and theft (property, vehicles, etc.), and other serious crimes in the TPD/PCSD datasets. Police detectives and analysts consider these crimes and roles (suspect, arrestee) as strong indications of involvement in criminal activity. A vehicle that has had a police contact is one that is recorded in the law enforcement databases; this may be for serious crimes (as listed above) or for other activities that may include forgery and counterfeiting, suspicious activity, and others. Vehicles with police contacts are also referred to as *potentially criminal* vehicles in this paper. These definitions are used in the description of the design and the evaluation process.

To identify interesting pairs of vehicles that cross the border together we use the *time of crossing* as a heuristic to enhance mutual information. The time of crossing heuristic suggests that vehicle pairs that cross during certain times of the day/night are more interesting than others. Domain experts (CBP agents, police detectives and analysts) and our previous study [7] suggest that criminal vehicles regularly cross at odd times during the night. The mutual information measure modified to include the time heuristic is referred to as '*MIT*' (Equation 2, shown in Section 3.1.5) and classical mutual information (without heuristics) is referred to as '*MIC*' (Equation 1, shown in Section 3.1.4).

Fig. 1 shows the research design and the process of utilizing information from multiple sources, heuristic calculation, and identification of potential target vehicles at the border. Different parts of the figure are explained in the following sub-sections.

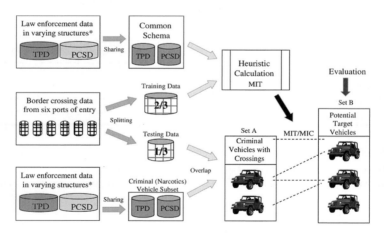

**Fig. 1.** Research design and process

### 3.1.1 Heuristic Calculation

The TPD and PCSD datasets were consolidated by transforming them to a single schema [10]. The common schema contained information on all vehicles that had police contacts along with information on the incidents that they were involved in. This was done to simplify access to multiple sources of information. To evaluate the performance of MIT and MIC, the CBP border crossing records were divided into training and testing datasets. This was done using a 2/3 – 1/3 hold out procedure. The training dataset contained 6.5 million ($\approx$2/3 of total) crossing records from March 2004 to November 2004.

To calculate the time heuristic the day was divided into six time periods corresponding to office travel (5am to 10am), travel for lunch (10am to 2am), night time (8pm to 12pm, 12pm – 5am), and others. These time periods were defined with the help of domain experts. For each of these time periods the ratio of vehicles with police contacts to the total number of crossings was calculated. This value was used to inform the mutual information score between vehicles in a given time period (as shown in Section 3.1.5).

### 3.1.2  Testing

The testing data contained 3.5 million ($\approx$1/3 of total) crossings from November 2004 to June 2005. Police data and the border crossings in the testing dataset were used to identify two sets of vehicles:

> *Set A*: 140 criminal vehicles that had been arrested or suspected for narcotics sale in the TPD/PCSD jurisdiction since January 2003.
> *Set B*: All the border crossing vehicles crossing *within one hour* of vehicles in *Set A* at the same port and in the same direction (i.e., both vehicles are either entering the U.S. or leaving it).

MIT and MIC were calculated between vehicles in *Set A* and *Set B*. The vehicles with high scores were considered potential target vehicles.

### 3.1.3  Evaluation

The potential target vehicles identified were evaluated by measuring their overlap with police datasets. This was done by measuring the number of vehicles with police contacts that were contained in the set of potential target vehicles. The number of potentially criminal vehicles identified by MIT and MIC were compared to each other to ascertain the performance of the modified measures. Since the aim of CBP is to target potentially criminal vehicles, a greater number of such vehicles in the target vehicle set indicates a higher quality result.

### 3.1.4  Classical Mutual Information (MIC) Formulation

The classical mutual information score between any two vehicles is defined as:

$$MIC(A, B) = \log_2 \frac{P(A, B)}{P(A)P(B)} \qquad (1)$$

Here $A$ is a vehicle in *Set A*, and $B$ is a vehicle in *Set B*. $P(A)$ and $P(B)$ are the probabilities of the vehicles $A$ and $B$ crossing the border, these are calculated from the border crossing datasets. $P(A,B)$ is the probability of $B$ crossing within one hour of $A$, this is calculated based on the number of times $A$ and $B$ are seen crossing together.

### 3.1.5  Mutual Information with Time Heuristics (MIT)

In the MIT formulation, we use conditional probability to modify the definition of $P(A)$, $P(B)$, and $P(A,B)$.

> $P'(A)$: Probability that vehicle $A$ crosses the border and has a police contact.
> $P'(B)$: Probability that vehicle $B$ crosses the border and has a police contact.
> $P'(A,B)$: Probability that vehicles $A$ and $B$ cross the border together and have police contacts.

Thus, a high $MI'(A,B)$ indicates that the vehicles are likely to cross the border and potentially commit crimes together.

Given this, we can now modify the classical MI formulation to include the time heuristic: Let $P_c(a)$ be the probability that vehicle '$a$' has contact with the police, and $P_b(a)$ be the probability that '$a$' crosses the border. The probability of vehicles with police contacts crossing during the six time periods is calculated using historical information in the police databases. So, we can obtain $P_c(V|t)$, which is the probability that *any* vehicle $V$ in time period $t$ ($1 \leq t \leq 6$) will have a contact with the police.

Now, by definition of $P'(A)$,

$$P'(A) = \sum_{t=1}^{6} P[(A_b \text{ and } A_c)|t]$$

In the above equation $A_b$ refers to vehicle $A$ crossing the border, and $A_c$ refers to vehicle $A$ having contact with the police. This equation reduces to

$$P'(A) = \sum_{t=1}^{6} P_b(A|t)P_c(V|t)$$

since the probability that a vehicle crosses the border and having police contact are independent (so they are multiplied to obtain $P'(A)$). In addition, $A$ is replaced by $V$ in the second term since the probability that a vehicle in time period $t$ has a police contact is the same for all vehicles in that time period. So the above process basically utilizes historical information (about crime) in the police datasets as a weight to modify $P'(A)$. Similar derivations can be used to obtain $P'(B)$, $P'(A,B)$, and thus $MIT(A,B)$ as shown in the following equations:

$$P'(B) = \sum_{t=1}^{6} P_b(B|t)P_c(V|t)$$

$$P'(A,B) = \sum_{t=1}^{6} P[((AB)_b \text{ and } (AB)_c)|t] = \sum_{t=1}^{6} P_b((AB)|t)P_c(V|t)P_c(V|t)$$

$$MIP(A,B) = \log_2 \frac{P'(A,B)}{P'(A)P'(B)} \qquad (2)$$

## 4   Experimental Results

To ascertain whether law enforcement information can be used to identify potential criminal vehicles, we first measured the overlap between border-crossing vehicles and police records in border-area jurisdictions. There were 45,091 border crossing vehicles that had police incident records in TPD/PCSD datasets. The number suggests that many vehicles crossing the border have incidents recorded in local law enforcement databases. This is a positive sign since it allows us to identify target vehicles at the border by exploring their criminal links. The existence of the overlap is also important for the calculation of heuristics based on law enforcement information.

### 4.1.1  Temporal Patterns of Border Crossings

Studying the temporal patterns of border crossings helps better understand the crossing activity. Fig. 2(a) shows the time distribution of border crossings for all vehicles entering and leaving the country over six time periods. Each slice of the pie shows the percentage of the total crossings that take place in the respective time period. It can be seen that a majority (about 65%) of the border crossings occur due to work and lunch/dinner related traffic during working hours (approximately 6am to 8pm). The chart also shows that about 37% of all crossings take place during the night or after dark (approximately 7pm to 6am).

Fig. 2(b) shows the time distribution of border crossings by vehicles with police contacts. Each slice of the pie shows the percentage of total crossings by such vehicles that took place in the respective time-period. For instance, 27% of all the border crossings by police contact vehicles took place between 8pm and midnight. The chart suggests that a large percentage (about 48%) of crossings by these vehicles take place after dark. MIT incorporates this information to assign more weight to time periods with high percentage of crossings by vehicles with police contacts. The weights also discount work travel related periods since they have a lower percentage of such crossings. Such information can also be used by CBP to increase or decrease enforcement in certain time periods.

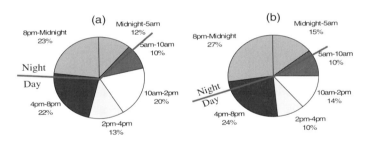

**Fig. 2.** Temporal distribution of crossings - (a) percentage of total crossings (b) percentage of crossings with police contacts

### 4.1.2  Comparative Evaluation of MIT and MIC

Mutual information scores (MIT and MIC) were calculated for 230,000 pairs of vehicles (the first vehicle from *Set A* and the second from *Set B*). To compare the two measures, the number of police contact vehicles identified by each was counted. The results are shown in Fig. 3. On the X-axis are top-*n* pairs (*n* ranging from 10-2500) of vehicles ordered by their MIT and MIC scores. On the Y-axis is the number of vehicles with police contacts identified by the two measures. For instance, three vehicles of the top-100 vehicles identified by MIT had previous police contacts. As can be seen in the figure MIT consistently identified more potentially criminal vehicles (vehicles with prior police contacts) than MIC.

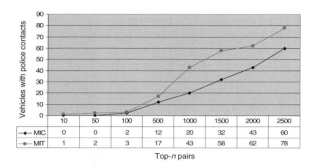

**Fig. 3.** Number of vehicles with police contacts identified by MIT and MIC

Even though the top-$n$ pairs contained a few potentially criminal vehicles, they also contained other vehicles that had no past criminal records. This might not look promising in other domains, but has positive connotations in this one. It suggests that many of the vehicles postulated to be criminal by the algorithms were not known to have police records before. So the new measure can be used to identify potentially new criminal vehicles that can be targeted at the border. The low number of police contacts might also be a result of properties of the datasets. A more accurate evaluation of the algorithm is possible if a larger dataset was available for training and testing. We commit this to future work.

## 6   Conclusions and Future Directions

Exploring the criminal links of border crossing vehicles in local law enforcement databases can be used to enhance border security. In this study we used mutual information to identify pairs of border crossing vehicles that may be involved in criminal activity. We found that mutual information may be used to identify potential target vehicles at the border. In addition, we concluded that the mutual information measure modified to include domain heuristics like time of crossing performs better than classical mutual information in the identification of potentially criminal vehicles.

In the future, we plan to incorporate other domain heuristics like port of crossing, traffic at the port of entry, and makes of vehicles in the mutual information formulation. In addition we plan to use larger datasets for training and testing of the new measures. We also plan to design a more comprehensive evaluation scheme (including cross-validation) to test the effectiveness of the modified measures as compared to classical mutual information.

## Acknowledgements

This research was supported in part by the NSF Digital Government (DG) program: "COPLINK Center: Information and Knowledge Management for Law Enforcement" #9983304, NSF Knowledge Discovery and Dissemination (KDD) program:

"COPLINK Border Safe Research and Testbed" #9983304, NSF Information Technology Research (ITR) program: "COPLINK Center for Intelligence and Security Informatics Research - A Crime Data Mining Approach to Developing Border Safe Research" #0326348, and Department of Homeland Security (DHS) through the "BorderSafe" initiative #2030002.

We thank our BorderSafe project partners: Tucson Police Department, Pima County Sheriff's Department, Tucson Customs and Border Protection, ARJIS (Automated Regional Justice Information Systems), San Diego Super Computer Center (SDSC), SPAWAR, Department of Homeland Security, and Corporation for National Research Initiatives (CNRI). We also thank Homa Atabakhsh and Hemanth Gowda of the AI Lab at the University of Arizona, Tim Petersen and Chuck Violette of the Tucson Police Department, and Ron Friend of Tucson Customs and Border Protection for their contributions to this research.

# References

1. National Strategy for Homeland Security. Office of Homeland Security. (2002)
2. R. Agrawal, T. Imielinski, and A. Swami: Mining Association Rules between Sets of Items in large Databases. In: Proc. of ACM SIGMOD Conference on Management of Data (1993)
3. D. Berrar, W. Dubitzky, M. Granzow, and R. Eils: Analysis of Gene Expression and Drug Activity Data by Knowledge-Based Association Mining. In: Proc. of Critical Assessment of Microarray Data Analysis Techniques (CAMDA '01) (2001)
4. I.-M. A. Chen and D. Rotem: Integrating Information from Multiple Independently Developed Data Sources. In: Proc. of 7th International Conference on Information and Knowledge Management, Bethesda, Maryland (1998)
5. K. W. Chruch and P. Hanks: Word Association Norms, Mutual Information, and Lexicography. Computational Linguistics 16 (1990) 22-29
6. R. M. Fano: Transmission of Information. MIT Press, Cambridge, MA (1961)
7. S. Kaza, T. Wang, H. Gowda, and H. Chen: Target Vehicle Identification for Border Safety using Mutual Information. In: Proc. of 8th International IEEE Conference on Intelligent Transportation Systems, Vienna, Austria (2005)
8. W. Lee and S. J. Stolfo: Data Mining Approaches for Intrusion Detection. In: Proc. of 7th USENIX Security Symposium (1998)
9. D. M. Magerman and M. P. Marcus: Parsing a Natural Language using Mutual Information Statistics. In: Proc. of Eight National Conference on Artificial Intelligence (1990)
10. B. Marshall, S. Kaza, J. Xu, H. Atabakhsh, T. Petersen, C. Violette, and H. Chen: Cross-Jurisdictional Criminal Activity Networks to Support Border and Transportation Security. In: Proc. of 7th International IEEE Conference on Intelligent Transportation Systems, Washington D.C. (2004)
11. B. Mobasher, N. Jain, E. H. Han, and J. Srivastava: Web mining: Pattern discovery from world wide web transactions. Department of Computer Science, University of Minnesota. Minneapolis, Technical Report (1996)
12. T. Ong and H. Chen: Updateable PAT-Tree Approach to Chinese Key Phrase Extraction Using Mutual Information: A Linguistic Foundation for Knowledge Management. In: Proc. of Second Asian Digital Library Conference, Taipei, Taiwan (1999)

13. P. Pantel, A. Philpot, and E. Hovy: Aligning Database Columns using Mutual Information. In: Proc. of The 6th National Conference on Digital Government Research (dg.o), Atlanta, GA (2005)
14. M. Stonebraker, R. Agrawal, U. Dayal, E. Neuhold, and A. Reuter: The DBMS Research at Crossroads. In: Proc. of The VLDB Conference, Dublin (1993)
15. T. Tao, C. X. Zhai, X. Lu, and H. Fang: A study of statistical methods for function prediction of protein motifs. Applied Bioinformatics 3 (2004) 115-124
16. J. D. Wren: Extending the Mutual Information Measure to Rank Inferred Literature Relationships. BMC Bioinformatics 5 (2004)

# Experimental Analysis of Sequential Decision Making Algorithms for Port of Entry Inspection Procedures

Saket Anand, David Madigan, Richard Mammone, Saumitr Pathak, and Fred Roberts[*]

Rutgers University, Piscataway, NJ 08854
froberts@dimacs.rutgers.edu

**Abstract.** Following work of Stroud and Saeger, we investigate the formulation of the port of entry inspection algorithm problem as a problem of finding an optimal binary decision tree for an appropriate Boolean decision function. We report on an experimental analysis of the robustness of the conclusions of the Stroud-Saeger analysis and show that the optimal inspection strategy is remarkably insensitive to variations in the parameters needed to apply the Stroud-Saeger method.

## 1 Introduction

As a stream of containers arrives at a port, a decision maker has to decide how to inspect them, which to subject to further inspection, which to allow to pass through with only minimal levels of inspection, etc. We look at this as a complex sequential decision making problem. Stroud and Saeger [8] have formulated this problem, in an important special case, as a problem of finding an optimal binary decision tree for an appropriate binary decision function. In this paper, we report on experimental analysis of the Stroud-Saeger method that has led us to the conclusion that the optimal inspection strategy is remarkably insensitive to variations in the parameters needed to apply the method.

## 2 Sequential Diagnosis

Sequential decision problems arise in many areas, including communication networks (testing connectivity, paging cellular customers, sequencing tasks, etc.), manufacturing (testing machines, fault diagnosis, routing customer service calls, etc.), artificial intelligence and computer science (optimal derivation strategies in knowledge bases, best-value satisfying search, coding decision tables, etc.), and medicine (diagnosing patients, sequencing treatments, etc.). A selected list of references for such applications includes [4, 6, 7].

Sequential diagnosis is an old subject, but one that has become increasingly important with the need for new models and algorithms as the traditional methods for making decisions sequentially do not scale.

---

[*] Communicating author.

S. Mehrotra et al. (Eds.): ISI 2006, LNCS 3975, pp. 319–330, 2006.

# 3  Problem Formulation

The problem we investigate is to find algorithms for sequential diagnosis that minimize the total "cost" of the inspection procedure, including the cost of false positives and false negatives. To make the problem precise, we imagine a stream of containers arriving at the port with the goal of classifying each of them into one of several categories. In the simplest case, these are "ok" (0) or "suspicious" (1). There are several possible tests that can be performed and an inspection scheme specifies which test to perform next based on outcomes of previous tests. We can think of the containers as having certain attributes, such as levels of certain kinds of chemical or biological materials, whether or not certain types of cargo are present in the cargo list, and whether cargo was picked up in a certain port. At present, inspectors use attributes such as: Does the container's ship's manifest set off an "alarm"? Is the neutron or Gamma emission count above threshold? Does a radiograph image come up positive? Does an induced fission test come up positive? We can imagine many other attributes. Our study is concerned with general algorithmic approaches. We seek a methodology that is not necessarily tied to today's technology. Detectors are evolving quickly and so this approach makes sense to us.

## 3.1  Boolean Decision Functions and Corresponding Binary Decision Trees

In the simplest case, the attributes can be described as being in one of two states, either 0 ("absent") or 1 ("present"), and we can think of a container as corresponding to a binary string such as 011001. Classification then corresponds to a binary decision function $F$ that assigns each binary string to a category. For instance, $F(011001) = 1$ means that we say that a package is suspicious if it has the second, third, and sixth attributes. If the category must be 0 or 1, $F$ is a *Boolean decision function (BDF)*. An inspection scheme tells us in which order to calculate the binary string so as to be able to compute the Boolean function $F$. Stroud and Saeger look at this as the problem of finding an optimal *binary decision tree (BDT)* for calculating $F$. In the BDT, the nodes are sensors or categories (0 or 1). Two arcs exit from each sensor node, labeled left and right. Take the right arc when the sensor says the attribute is present, the left arc otherwise. For instance, in Figure 1, we reach category 1 from the root only through the path $a_0$ to $a_1$ to 1. A container is classified in category 1 iff it has both attributes $a_0$ and $a_1$. The corresponding Boolean function is given by $F(11) = 1$, $F(10) = F(01) = F(00) = 0$. In Figure 2, we reach category 1 from the root by $a_0$ left to $a_1$, then right to $a_2$, then right to 1, or $a_0$ right to $a_2$ right to 1. A container is classified in category 1 iff it has $a_1$ and $a_2$ and not $a_0$ or $a_0$ and $a_2$ and possibly $a_1$. The corresponding Boolean function is given by $F(111) = F(101) = F(011) = 1$, $F(abc) = 0$ otherwise. Figure 3 gives a BDT corresponding to the same Boolean function. However, it has one less observation node $a_i$. So, it is more efficient if we simply count number of observation nodes.

Even if the Boolean function $F$ is fixed, the problem of finding the "optimal" BDT for it is very hard (NP-complete) [5]. One can try to solve it by brute force enumeration. However, even if the number of attributes $n$ is 4, this is not practical. In present-day practice in the Port of Long Beach/Los Angeles, the nation's busiest port, $n = 4$.

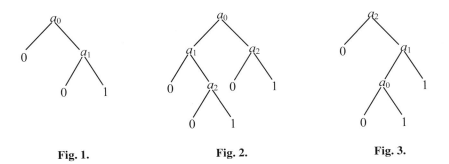

**Fig. 1.**                    **Fig. 2.**                    **Fig. 3.**

Several classes of BDFs have been found for which an efficient solution is possible. This is the case for $k$-out-of-$n$ systems, certain series-parallel systems, read-once systems, "regular systems", and Horn systems.

### 3.2 Complete, Monotone Boolean Functions

One approach to the problem, therefore, is to make special assumptions about the Boolean function $F$. For "monotone" Boolean functions, integer programming formulations give promising heuristics. A Boolean function is *monotone* if given two strings $x_1,x_2...x_n$, $y_1,y_2...y_n$ with $x_i \geq y_i$ for all $i$, then $F(x_1,x_2...x_n) \geq F(y_1,y_2...y_n)$. Stroud and Saeger limit their analysis to complete, monotone Boolean functions, where a Boolean function F is incomplete if $F$ can be calculated by finding at most $n-1$ attributes and knowing the value of the input string on those attributes. The rationale for limiting the analysis is that sensors detect "bad" things so a positive reading should make things worse (monotonicity) and that all sensors should be in a BDT (completeness). Stroud and Saeger enumerate all complete, monotone Boolean functions and then calculate the least expensive corresponding BDTs under assumptions about various costs associated with the trees. Their method is practical for $n$ up to 4, but not $n = 5$.

The problem is exacerbated by the number of BDFs. For example, for $n = 2$, there are 6 monotone Boolean functions; only 2 are complete and monotone; and there are 4 binary decision trees for calculating these 2 complete, monotone Boolean functions. For $n = 3$, there are 9 complete, monotone Boolean functions and 60 distinct binary trees for calculating them. For $n = 4$, there are 114 complete, monotone Boolean functions and 11,808 distinct corresponding BDTs. Compare this with 1,079,779,602 BDTs for all Boolean functions! For $n = 5$, there are 6894 complete, monotone Boolean functions and 263,515,920 corresponding BDTs. Even worse: compare $5 \times 10^{18}$ BDTs corresponding to all Boolean functions. (Counts are from Stroud-Saeger.)

### 3.3 Cost of a BDF

We seek a least-cost Boolean function and in particular a least-cost corresponding BDT. How does one calculate cost? The cost of an inspection scheme is not just measured by the number of sensors in the BDT. Using a sensor has several costs: the unit cost of inspecting one item with it, the fixed cost of purchasing and deploying it, and the delay cost from queuing up at the sensor station. In our study, we have disregarded the fixed and delay costs and so sought to minimize unit costs. Of course, unit costs should be looked at probabilistically. How many nodes of the decision tree are actually visited during the "average" container's inspection? This depends on the "distribution" of containers. In this study, we assume this distribution has been used to obtain the probability of sensor errors, we also assume we know the probability of a bomb in a container, and we seek to estimate the expected cost of utilizing a tree, the expected sum of unit costs. We denote this expected utilization cost by $C_{util}$. More sophisticated models would include models of the distribution of attributes of containers and a more refined analysis of expected cost of utilizing the tree, bringing in delay costs. The other key costs associated with a BDF or corresponding BDT are the cost of a false positive and of a false negative. The former is the cost of additional tests. If it means opening the container, it is relatively expensive. The latter involves complex issues such as estimating the cost of a bomb going off in a large city.

### 3.4  Sensor Errors

A more refined analysis models sensor errors. In the simplest model, we assume that all sensors checking for attribute $a_i$ have the same fixed probability of saying $a_i$ is 0 if in fact it is 1, and similarly saying it is 1 if in fact it is 0. A more sophisticated analysis later will describe a model for determining probabilities of sensor errors. In what follows, we use the notation $X$ for state of nature (bomb or no bomb) and $Y$ for the outcome 0 or 1 of a sensor inspection or of the entire inspection process. The total (expected) cost of utilizing a tree is given by

$$C_{Tot} = C_{FP}*P_{FP} + C_{FN}*P_{FN} + C_{util} \tag{1}$$

where $C_{FP}$ is the cost of false positive (Type I error); $C_{FN}$ is the cost of false negative (Type II error); $P_{FP}$ is the probability of a false positive occurring; $P_{FN}$ is the probability of a false negative occurring; $C_{util}$ is the expected cost of utilization of the tree.

## 4  The Stroud-Saeger Calculations

Stroud and Saeger ranked all trees formed from three or four sensors according to increasing tree costs. We denote sensors by A, B, C and D. Stroud and Saeger used the cost function defined in Equation (1). Assumptions in their work were specific values for the properties of the sensors, i.e., cost of utilizing them and probabilities of false positive and false negative sensor outcomes. Specifically, the values used in their analysis were as follows, where $C_A$ is the unit cost of utilizing a sensor of type A, $Y_A$ the outcome of inspection on a container by sensor A, etc.

$C_A = .25$        $P(Y_A=1|X=1) = .9856$        $P(Y_A=1|X=0) = .0144$

$C_B = 10$        $P(Y_B=1|X=1) = .7779$        $P(Y_B=1|X=0) = .2221$

$C_C = 30$        $P(Y_C=1|X=1) = .9265$        $P(Y_C=1|X=0) = .0735$

$C_D = 1$        $P(Y_D=1|X=1) = .9893$        $P(Y_D=1|X=0) = .0107$

Also fixed were the three parameters we call ***base parameters***: $C_{FN}$, $C_{FP}$, $P(X=1)$. The purpose of our work was to explore the sensitivity of the Stroud-Saeger conclusions about optimal BDTs to changes in values of the parameters defining the problem. In this paper, we explore changes in the base parameters.

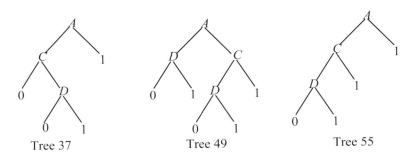

Tree 37                    Tree 49                    Tree 55

**Fig. 4.** Trees that attained top rank for experiments with n = 3

## 5  Sensitivity Analysis for the Case of Three Attributes

We started by looking at the case $n = 3$ and used sensors A, C and D in our BDTs. In our computer experiments, we used ranges for the values of base parameters. $C_{FN}$ was varied between $25 million and $500 billion. These are low and high estimates of the direct and indirect costs incurred due to a false negative - interpreted as the cost of a bomb going off in a large city. Stroud and Saeger used the value $50 billion and we sought to use numbers that were much higher and much lower than this. $C_{FP}$ was varied between $180 and $720. This is interpreted as the cost incurred due to a false positive, which requires opening the container with 4 men working on it. The estimates ranged from a low of 4 men working 3 hours at a salary of $15/hour to 4 men working 6 hours at a salary of $30/hour. Stroud and Saeger used the value $600. Finally, $P(X=1)$ was varied between $3 \times 10^{-9}$ and $1 \times 10^{-5}$. These numbers were chosen to give a wide range around the Stroud-Saeger-assumed value of $3 \times 10^{-8}$.

In the first sets of experiments, we chose a fixed value for one of the base parameters. In one set of experiments, the value was chosen at random from its interval, and in another, the value was fixed at that used by Stroud and Saeger. In each of 10,000 runs, we picked the values of the other two base parameters randomly and uniformly from their interval of values and then found the highest ranked tree. Results of the experiments are shown in Table 1.

In all of these experiments, only three trees out of a possible 60 ever came out ranked first: Trees numbered 37, 49, and 55 in the Stroud-Saeger enumeration. They are shown in Figure 4. Tree 55 was predominantly the top-ranked tree, except in the runs when $P(X=1)$ was fixed at the Stroud-Saeger value, in which case tree 37 was predominantly first. Tree 49 never appeared more than 1.21% of the time in any one of the experiments.

**Table 1.** Frequency that trees attained top rank when n = 3. One parameter was fixed at a randomly selected value from its interval and then at Stroud and Saeger values, and the other two parameters were assigned 10,000 randomly chosen values from their intervals.

| Variables | Fixed | Randomly Selected Values | | | Stroud and Saeger Values | | |
|---|---|---|---|---|---|---|---|
| | | Value | Tree No. | Frequency | Value | Tree No. | Frequency |
| P(X=1) | $C_{FN}$ | $8.2737 \times 10^{10}$ | 37 | 343 | $5 \times 10^{10}$ | 37 | 441 |
| | | | 49 | 37 | | 49 | 66 |
| $C_{FP}$ | | | 55 | 9620 | | 55 | 9493 |
| $C_{FN}$ | P(X=1) | $0.5538 \times 10^{-5}$ | 37 | 99 | $3 \times 10^{-8}$ | 37 | 9923 |
| | | | 49 | 8 | | | |
| $C_{FP}$ | | | 55 | 9893 | | 55 | 77 |
| P(X=1) | $C_{FP}$ | 668.1793 | 37 | 412 | 600 | 37 | 541 |
| | | | 49 | 121 | | 49 | 53 |
| $C_{FN}$ | | | 55 | 9467 | | 55 | 9406 |

**Table 2.** Frequency that trees attained top rank when $n$ = 3. Two parameters were fixed at randomly selected values from their intervals and then at Stroud and Saeger values, and the third parameter was assigned 10,000 randomly chosen values from its interval.

| Variables | Fixed | Randomly Selected Values | | | Stroud and Saeger Values | | |
|---|---|---|---|---|---|---|---|
| | | Value | Tree No. | Frequency | Value | Tree No. | Frequency |
| $C_{FN}$ | P(X=1) | $0.1281 \times 10^{-5}$ | 37 | 568 | $3 \times 10^{-8}$ | 37 | 10000 |
| | $C_{FP}$ | 492.6116 | 55 | 9432 | 600 | | |
| P(X=1) | $C_{FN}$ | $4.747 \times 10^{11}$ | 37 | 54 | $5 \times 10^{10}$ | 37 | 694 |
| | $C_{FP}$ | 351.9526 | 55 | 9946 | 600 | 49 | 108 |
| | | | | | | 55 | 9198 |
| $C_{FP}$ | P(X=1) | $0.8373 \times 10^{-5}$ | 55 | 10000 | $3 \times 10^{-8}$ | 37 | 10000 |
| | $C_{FN}$ | $4.2681 \times 10^{11}$ | | | $5 \times 10^{10}$ | | |

Similar experiments were performed by fixing two of the base parameters and varying the third, with fixed values either being chosen (independently) randomly in their intervals or at the Stroud-Saeger values. Results are shown in Table 2. Again, only the same three trees, 37, 49, and 55, were ever ranked first, with trees 37 and 55 again dominating and tree 49 only appearing once more than 1% of the time. The robustness of the results of the experiments with $n$ = 3 is quite surprising.

A comparison of the BDF corresponding to trees 37, 49, and 55 is also interesting. Tree 37 corresponds to the Boolean expression 00011111, which represents the sequence $F(000)F(001)...F(110)F(111)$. Tree 49 corresponds to the Boolean expression 01010111 and tree 55 to the Boolean expression 01111111. Thus, in Tree 55, a container is called suspicious if it fails at least one test. In Tree 37, a container is called suspicious if it fails the first test or if it fails both the remaining tests. In Tree 49, a container is called suspicious if it fails at least two tests or fails only the third one.

## 6  Sensitivity Analysis for the Case of Four Attributes

Turning to the case $n = 4$, we used sensors A, B, C, and D in our BDTs and used the same interval of values for the parameters $C_{FP}$, $C_{FN}$ and $P(X=1)$ as before. We ran the same kinds of experiments as in the case $n = 3$. Tables 3 and 4 show the results (omitting trees that were rarely ranked first). When one base parameter was fixed, only five trees ever appeared first more than 1% of the time in an experiment: Trees numbered 6797, 8965, 9133, 11605, and 11785 in the Stroud-Saeger numbering. Each appeared first at least 5% of the time in at least one experiment. These trees are shown in Figure 5. If we consider trees appearing first at least .99% of the time, only tree 11305 gets added to the list. In each experiment, one tree dominated first place, except in the experiment where $P(X=1)$ was fixed at the Stroud-Saeger value, when two trees dominated. Considering the fact that there are 11,808 candidate trees, this is remarkable stability of results.

In the case where two base parameters were held fixed, again the same five trees dominated as the only trees appearing first at least 1% of the time in any experiment. Indeed, only they appeared first at least .02% of the time in any experiment. Only a sixth tree, 11305, which also appeared in the experiments with one base parameter held fixed, appeared if we consider trees that were ranked first in at least .017% of the runs in some experiment. Again, the stability of the top-ranked trees is quite striking.

For the five top trees, it is interesting the compare the Boolean expression corresponding to $F(0000)F(0001)...F(1011)F(1111)$. Tree 6797 corresponds to expression 0001000101111111, tree 8965 to 0001010101111111, tree 9133 to 0001010111111111, tree 11605 to 0101011111111111, and tree 11785 to 0111111111111111. The expressions for trees 11605 and 11785 differ in only two places, as do those for trees 9133 and 11605. There can be quite a difference in Boolean expressions, however. Those for trees 6797 and 11785 differ in six places.

**Table 3.** Frequency that trees attained top rank when $n = 4$. One parameter was fixed at a randomly selected value from its interval and then at Stroud and Saeger values, and the other two parameters were assigned 10,000 randomly chosen values from their intervals. Trees with small frequency of top rank are not shown.

| Variables | Fixed | Randomly Selected Values | | | Stroud and Saeger Values | | |
|---|---|---|---|---|---|---|---|
| | | Value | Tree No. | Frequency | Value | Tree No. | Frequency |
| P(X=1) | $C_{FN}$ | $4.7485 \times 10^{10}$ | 8965 | 121 | $5 \times 10^{10}$ | 8965 | 117 |
| | | | 9133 | 392 | | 9133 | 374 |
| $C_{FP}$ | | | 11305 | 99 | | 11305 | 96 |
| | | | 11605 | 9351 | | 11605 | 9381 |
| $C_{FN}$ | P(X=1) | $0.6344 \times 10^{-5}$ | 9133 | 65 | $3 \times 10^{-8}$ | 6797 | 558 |
| | | | 11605 | 7928 | | 8965 | 3833 |
| $C_{FP}$ | | | 11785 | 1979 | | 9133 | 5406 |
| P(X=1) | $C_{FP}$ | 453.6849 | 9133 | 235 | 600 | 9133 | 184 |
| | | | 11605 | 8621 | | 11605 | 9232 |
| $C_{FN}$ | | | 11785 | 1062 | | 11785 | 333 |

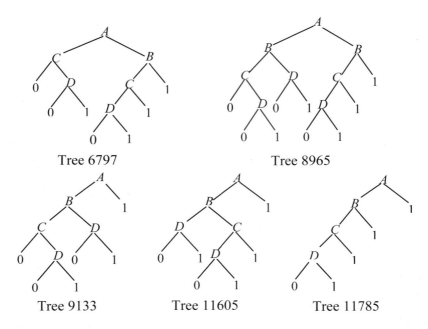

Tree 6797          Tree 8965

Tree 9133          Tree 11605          Tree 11785

**Fig. 5.** Trees that attained top rank most frequently for the experiments with n = 4

**Table 4.** Frequency that trees attained top rank when $n = 4$. Two parameters were fixed at randomly selected values from their intervals and then at Stroud and Saeger values, and the third parameter was assigned 10,000 randomly chosen values from its interval. Trees with small frequency of attaining top rank for $n = 4$ are not shown.

| Variables | Fixed | Randomly Selected Values | | | Stroud and Saeger Values | | |
|---|---|---|---|---|---|---|---|
| | | Value | Tree No. | Frequency | Value | Tree No. | Frequency |
| $C_{FN}$ | P(X=1) | $0.6284 \times 10^{-5}$ | 9133 | 47 | $3 \times 10^{-8}$ | 6797 | 897 |
| | | | 11605 | 3614 | | 8965 | 8671 |
| | $C_{FP}$ | 188.5681 | 11785 | 6339 | 600 | 9133 | 309 |
| P(X=1) | $C_{FN}$ | $4.0624 \times 10^{11}$ | 9133 | 44 | $5 \times 10^{10}$ | 8965 | 237 |
| | | | 11605 | 4551 | | 9133 | 357 |
| | $C_{FP}$ | 297.5277 | 11785 | 5405 | 600 | 11305 | 170 |
| | | | | | | 11605 | 9156 |
| $C_{FP}$ | P(X=1) | $0.5992 \times 10^{-5}$ | 11605 | 9087 | $3 \times 10^{-8}$ | 6797 | 2336 |
| | $C_{FN}$ | $2.4041 \times 10^{11}$ | 11785 | 913 | $5 \times 10^{10}$ | 8965 | 3942 |
| | | | | | | 9133 | 3722 |

## 7 Modeling Sensor Errors Using Thresholds

One approach to sensor errors involves modeling sensor operation/interpretation of sensor readings. A natural model, one used by Stroud and Saeger, is a threshold model using counts (e.g., Gamma radiation counts). If the count exceeds some threshold, we conclude that the attribute being tested for is present. To describe such a threshold model, suppose that sensor $i$ has discriminating power $K_i$ and let the threshold for sensor $i$ be denoted by $T_i$. We calculate the fraction of containers in each category whose readings exceed the threshold. While sensor characteristics are a function of design and environmental conditions, the thresholds can be set by the decision maker.

The Stroud-Saeger approach is to seek threshold values that minimize all costs: inspection, false positive/negative. The readings of sensors are also determined by their design and environmental conditions. Let us assume that readings of category 0 containers (those not containing a bomb) follow a Gaussian distribution and similarly category 1 containers (those containing a bomb). See Figure 6, in which $\Sigma_i$ is the

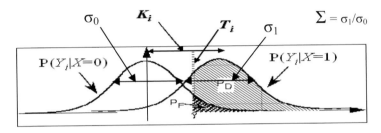

**Fig. 6.** Typical sensor characteristics

**Table 5.** Frequency that trees attained top rank when thresholds were varied. The base parameters were fixed at randomly selected values from their intervals. For n = 3 sensors, 15 out of 60 trees came out to be top rank. For $n$ = 4 sensors, only 244 out of 11,808 trees attained top rank. Trees with small frequency of attaining top rank for $n$ = 4 are not shown.

| n=3, number of experiments = 68,921 | | | n=4, number of experiments = 194481 | | |
|---|---|---|---|---|---|
| Constants | Tree No. | Frequency | Constants | Tree No. | Frequency |
| | 1 | 5828 | | 87 | 3402 |
| | 2 | 183 | | 145 | 11143 |
| | 7 | 13392 | | 325 | 5574 |
| | 15 | 2437 | | 386 | 4018 |
| $C_{FN} =$ | 19 | 5256 | $C_{FN} =$ | 445 | 13012 |
| $5.0125 \times 10^9$ | 23 | 1475 | $4.8668 \times 10^{11}$ | 505 | 10545 |
| | 25 | 957 | | 506 | 5249 |
| $P(X=1) =$ | 27 | 114 | $P(X=1) =$ | 2617 | 10139 |
| $5.05 \times 10^{-6}$ | 29 | 146 | $7.5361 \times 10^{-6}$ | 5761 | 5942 |
| | 37 | 17515 | | 8003 | 4539 |
| and $C_{FP} =$ | 38 | 4572 | and $C_{FP} =$ | 9133 | 9280 |
| 450 | 45 | 5873 | 499.75 | 10783 | 4496 |
| | 49 | 264 | | 11605 | 10958 |
| | 51 | 322 | | 11785 | 5910 |
| | 55 | 10587 | | 11791 | 5196 |

relative spread factor and $P_D$ is the probability of detection by the $i^{th}$ sensor $P(Yi=1|X=1)$ while $P_F$ is the probability of a false positive at the $i$th sensor $P(Yi=1|X=0)$. The probability of false positive for the $i^{th}$ sensor is computed as:

$$P(Y_i=1|X=0) = 0.5 \ erfc[T_i/\sqrt{2}], \qquad (2)$$

while the probability of detection for the $i$th sensor is computed as

$$P(Y_i=1|X=1) = 0.5 \ erfc[(T_i-K_i)/(\Sigma\sqrt{2})], \qquad (3)$$

where $erfc$, the complementary error function, is given by

$$erfc(x) = \Gamma(\tfrac{1}{2},x^2)/\sqrt{\pi}. \qquad (4)$$

We ran experiments with this model by choosing the following values of sensor parameters also used by Stroud-Saeger: $K_A = 4.37$, $\Sigma_A = 1$; $K_B = 1.53$, $\Sigma_B = 1$; $K_C = 2.9$, $\Sigma_C = 1$; $K_D = 4.6$, $\Sigma_D = 1$. We then varied the individual sensor thresholds $T_A$, $T_C$ and $T_D$ (for $n = 3$) from -4.0 to +4.0 in steps of 0.4. These values were chosen since they gave us an "ROC curve" (see Section 8) for the individual sensors over a complete range $P(Y_i=1|X=0)$ and $P(Y_i=1|X=1)$. The base parameters were chosen at randomly selected values in these intervals.

In the case $n = 3$, 68,921 experiments were conducted, as each $T_i$ was varied through its entire range. As seen from Table 5, a total of 15 different trees were ranked first in these experiments, more than were obtained in our earlier experiments. Tree 37 had the highest frequency of attaining rank one, appearing first 17,515 times. A few of the other trees that ranked first a relatively large number of times were trees numbered 7 and 55. Note that 37 and 55 also predominated in our other experiments.

In the case $n = 4$, 194,481 similar experiments were conducted. A total of 244 trees ranked first, with tree 445 the most frequent (13,012 times). Other trees often ranked first in our other experiments were here too: 9133, 11605, and 11785. Results for these experiments with $n = 4$ are summarized in Table 5.

## 8   Using the ROC Curve

We can use Receiver Operating Characteristic (ROC) curves to identify optimal thresholds for sensors. The ROC curve is the plot of the probability of correct detection ($P_D$) vs. the probability of a false positive ($P_F$). The ROC curve is used to select an operating point, which provides the tradeoff between $P_D$ and $P_F$. Each sensor has a ROC curve and the combination of the sensors into a decision tree has a composite ROC curve. We seek operating characteristics of sensors that place us in the upper left hand corner of the ROC curve. Here, $P_F$ is small and $P_D$ is large.

The parameter that is varied to get different operating points on the ROC curve is the sensor threshold and a combination of thresholds for the decision tree. The Equal Error Rate (EER) is the operating point on the ROC curve where $P_F = 1 - P_D$. By studying the performance characteristics $(P(Y=1|X=0), P(Y=1|X=1))$ of the tree over all combinations of sensor thresholds $(T_i)$ and studying the region of high detection probabilities and low false positive probabilities, we can use the ROC curve to choose threshold values in practice. Assuming performance probabilities $(P(Y=1|X=1)$ and $P(Y=1|X=0))$ to be monotonically related (in the sense that $P(Y=1|X=1)$ can be called a monotonic function of $P(Y=1|X=0)$), we can find an ROC curve for the tree consisting of the set containing maximum $P(Y=1|X=1)$ value corresponding to given $P(Y=1|X=0)$ value.

## 9 Conclusions, Discussion, and Further Work

Our work has shown a remarkable robustness in the conclusions about optimal binary decision trees in sequential decision making applications in inspection applications. Very few trees arise as optimal over a wide range of choices of values for the key parameters in the model. Moreover, there is also considerable robustness in the optimal Boolean decision function – very few decision functions correspond to the optimal trees and those that do often are closely related. We do not yet have a good theoretical explanation for these conclusions about robustness. We also do not have a good understanding, as yet, of the relations between the different optimal trees, in particular their tree structure. Our results should be regarded as preliminary, though intriguing and suggesting many questions.

As Stroud and Saeger have noted, their method does not scale very well. We have already reached limits of computation for the case of $n = 4$ types of inspections. With $n = 5$, similar experiments seem infeasible. We did these calculations with Matlab on a Pentium IV 3 GHz processor, with 1GB of RAM. Other methods are needed to find optimal trees if we have more types of sensors and to investigate the sensitivity of the conclusions.

There are more experiments that we propose to do to test sensitivity of the Stroud-Saeger conclusions. In particular, our experiments have fixed the characteristics of the sensors through such parameters as $C_A$, $K_A$, $P(Y_A = 1|X = 0)$, etc. We only did experiments by using specific values of parameters. The optimal tree is certainly related to these characteristics of the available sensors. We will do other experiments in which these values are varied.

We have not done a lot of analysis of the robustness of the second, third, and fourth-ranked trees, though initial results show a great deal of robustness akin to that reported here. In practical applications, a near-optimal tree might very well be a perfectly acceptable solution to the inspection problem. In this case, there might be more efficient methods for finding near-optimal trees than the brute force methods described by Stroud and Saeger and tested here.

The methods here and in Stroud-Saeger depend heavily on being able to limit the number of possible Boolean decision functions and hence the number of possible BDTs. In particular, they depend on the monotonicity and completeness assumptions. More work is needed to explore alternative assumptions that are relevant to the port of entry inspection applications.

In practice, one thinks of $n$ types of sensors that measure presence or absence of the $n$ attributes. There are many copies of each sensor. A complication is that different sensor types have different characteristics. As containers arrive for inspection, we have to decide which sensor of a given type to use. The containers are sent to different inspection lanes, each having a particular test (sensor), and the containers form queues. Recall that the "cost" of inspection includes the cost of failure, including failure to foil a terrorist plot. There are many ways to lower the total "cost" of inspection.

Only one is to use more efficient orders of inspection. Others are to find ways to inspect more containers, to find ways to cut down on delays at inspection lanes, etc. More complicated cost models would bring in costs of delays and also consider the limits on delays that are imposed by the need to keep the port operating. Besides efficient inspection schemes, one could decrease costs by buying more sensors or changing the allocation of containers to sensor lanes.

Another variant of the Stroud-Saeger model would have us go to more than two values of an attribute, e.g., present, absent, present with probability > 75%, absent with probability at least 75%; or ok, not ok, ok with probability > 99%, ok with probability between 95% and 99%. Still another approach would have us infer the Boolean function from observations. There is a considerable literature that deals with partially defined Boolean functions (see for example [1, 2, 3]). Still another approach would use machine learning methods to learn the thresholds of the sensors in order to minimize the misclassification error of the entire tree, subject to the constraint of minimizing the total cost of the generated tree.

*Acknowledgement.* Supported by ONR grant number N00014-05-1-0237 and NSF grant number NSFSES 05-18543 to Rutgers University. The authors thank Kevin Saeger and Phillip Stroud for providing values of parameters and code to assist us in the analysis in this paper.

# References

1. Boros, E., Ibaraki, T. and Makino, K., *"Logical Analysis of Binary Data with Missing Bits,"* Artificial Intelligence, 107 (1999), 219-263.
2. Boros, E., Ibaraki, T. and Makino, K., *"Variations on Extending Partially Defined Boolean Functions with Missing Bits,"* Information and Computation, 180 (2003), 53-70.
3. Chiu, S.Y., Cox, L.A. and Sun, X., *"Least-Cost Failure Diagnosis in Uncertain Reliability Systems,"* Reliability Engineering and System Safety, 54 (1996), 203-216.
4. Duffuaa, S. O., and Raouf, A., *"An Optimal Sequence in Multicharacteristics Sequence,"* Journal of Optimization Theory and Applications, 67 (1990), 79-87.
5. Hyafil, L. and Rivest, R. L., *"Constructing Optimal Binary Decision Trees is NP-Complete,"* Information Processing Letters, 5 (1976), 15-17.
6. Lauritzen, S. N., and Nilsson, D., *"Representing and Solving Decision Problems with Limited Information,"* Management Science, 47 (2001), 1238-1251.
7. Simon, H. A. and Kadane, J. B., *"Optimal Problem-Solving Search: All-or-None Solutions,"* Artificial Intelligence, 6 (1975), 235-247.
8. Stroud, P. D. and Saeger K. J., *"Enumeration of Increasing Boolean Expressions and Alternative Digraph Implementations for Diagnostic Applications,"* Proceedings Volume IV, Computer, Communication and Control Technologies, (2003), 328-333

# Analyzing the Terrorist Social Networks with Visualization Tools

Christopher C. Yang[1], Nan Liu[1], and Marc Sageman[2]

[1] Department of Systems Engineering and Engineering Management
The Chinese University of Hong Kong
[2] The Solomon Asch Center for Study of Ethnopolitical Conflict
The University of Pennsylvania

**Abstract.** Analysis of terrorist social networks is essential for discovering knowledge about the structure of terrorist organizations. Such knowledge is important for developing effective combating strategies against terrorism. Visualization of a network with the support of social network analysis techniques greatly facilitates the inspection of the network global structure. However, its usefulness becomes limited when the size and complexity of the network increase. In this work, we develop two interactive visualization techniques for complex terrorist social networks: fisheye views and fractal views. Both techniques facilitate the exploration of complex networks by allowing a user to select one or more focus points and dynamically adjusting the graphical layout and abstraction level to enhance the view of regions of interest. Combining the two techniques can effectively help an investigator to recognize patterns previously unreadable in the normal display due to the network complexity. Case studies are presented to illustrate how such visualization tools are capable to extract the hidden relationships among terrorists in the network through user interactions. Experiment was conducted to evaluate the performance of the visualization techniques.

**Keywords:** Terrorist social networks, social network analysis, information visualization, fisheye views, fractal views.

## 1 Introduction

As a type of organized crime, terrorism requires the collaboration among a number of terrorists. The relationships among different terrorists form the basis of a terrorist organization and are essential for its operations [11]. An effective model for capturing the structure of a terrorist organization is the network model in which terrorists and their relationships are represented by nodes and links respectively. Terrorist social networks fall into the large category of social networks. While social networks have been successfully used to model the structure of communication networks and the World Wide Web, it is also especially appropriate for investigations in terrorism [1]. An investigator of a terrorist social network typically performs three major tasks [2]: (a) subgroup detection [4], (b) identification of important actors and their roles, (c) discovery of patterns of interaction [4].

S. Mehrotra et al. (Eds.): ISI 2006, LNCS 3975, pp. 331 – 342, 2006.

Traditional terrorist social network analysis and social network analysis in general is mainly a manual process. An investigator has to spend a large amount of time performing database searches and reading reports in an attempt to identify useful entities and relationships in a large network. This is both time-consuming and labor-intensive. To facilitate social network analysis, modern systems such as COPLINK [3] employs visualizations such as a 2D graph to present a network. In a 2D graphical portrayal of a social network, the stronger the association between two nodes or two groups, the closer they appear on the graph; the weaker the association, the farther apart. Xu and Chen [5] has adopted the metric multidimensional scaling algorithm to visualize the criminal social networks. While a static graphical layout suffices to reveal the structure of relatively small and simple networks, it is usually not effective enough for the manual exploration of large and complex networks. In this work, we propose interactive visualization techniques such as fisheye views and fractal views for facilitating the analysis of complex social networks and demonstrate its application in the analysis of a large terrorist network, the global Salafi Jihad (the violent, revivalist social movement of which al Qaeda is a part) [11].

## 2   Terrorist Social Network – Global Salafi Jihad

A social network is typically represented by a weighted graph $G = (V, E; w)$, where $V$ corresponds to the set of nodes, $E$ is the set of links, $w$ is a function mapping each link $(u,v) \in E$ to a weight $w_{uv}$ in the range [0,1] that indicates the strength of association between $u$ and $v$. Each node, $v$, is corresponding to a person, which is a terrorist in a terrorist social network (TSN).    A link between two nodes (terrorists), $(u,v)$, represents that there are some kinds of relationships between the corresponding terrorists, $u$ and $v$.    The weight $w_{uv}$ is determined by the number of types of relationships existing between $u$ and $v$. Two terrorists can be related through different types of associations. We have heuristically assigned an importance score $s_r$ to each type of relationship $r$ and compute a total score $s_{uv}$ for each link $(u, v)$ as the total score of the relationships between $u$ and $v$, i.e.,

$$s_{uv} = \sum_{r \in R(u,v)} s_r$$

where $R(u,v)$ denotes the set of relationships existing between $u$ and $v$. The link weight $w_{uv}$ is then computed as the normalized link score, i.e.,

$$w_{uv} = \frac{s_{uv}}{\max_{u,v \in V}(s_{uv})}$$

In this work, we have adopted the data available from an authoritative terrorism monograph, authored by Sageman [11], to build the terrorist social network of the global Salafi Jihad.  Sageman is a forensic psychiatrist and an expert on Al-Qaeda. He is a former CIA case officer, who has worked closely with Afghanistan's mujahedin.  He has advised various branches of the U.S. government in the war of terror. In the global Salafi Jihad social network, there are totally 366 terrorists described in the data set, which is given as a list of records with the same schema, one record for each terrorist. Each record includes two types of information: terrorist's properties such as name, alias, date of birth, etc. and his relationships with other terrorists, which include 6 types: acquaintance $(r_1)$, friends $(r_2)$, relatives $(r_3)$, nuclear family member $(r_4)$, teachers $(r_5)$, and religious leader $(r_6)$. Based on the data set, the resulted terrorist social network consists of a total of 366 nodes and 1275 links.

## 3 Visualization of Terrorist Social Networks

The computation of initial node coordinates and sizes is the most important step in representing the terrorists and their relationships as a weighted graph $G = (V, E; w)$ on a two-dimensional space. In the computation, we map a node $v \in V$ of the terrorist social network to a point $p_v = (x_v, y_v) \in \mathbb{R}^2$, the coordinates of $v$ on the plot are computed.

There are several desirable properties of an effective visualization: (1) Nodes should be separated by an optimal distance in order to fully utilize the two-dimensional space instead of being cluttered (2) The length of a link should reflect the strength of association between the two end nodes, i.e., two connected nodes should appear closer if they are strongly associated, and distant if the association is weak. (3) The crossing of edges should be minimized so that the user can clearly see the relationships between nodes. (4) The size of a node should be proportional to the importance of the corresponding terrorist.

### 3.1 Computing Node Coordinates

We utilize the spring embedder algorithm [6] to initialize the coordinates of the nodes in the terrorist social network to achieve objectives (1) and (2) as described above. The spring embedder algorithm models nodes as charged particles with mutual repulsion and links as springs attached to their end nodes. It produces a 2D layout of the network by finding a (locally) minimum energy state of this physical system. The repulsive force is introduced to avoid having the nodes cluttered together while spring force tries to maintain a desirable distance between nodes.

Spring Embedder Algorithm:

1. Specify natural length of spring $l_{uv}$ for each $(u,v) \in E$ which controls the desirable distance between $u$ and $v$

   $l_{uv} = l_{max}(1-w_{uv})$             where $l_{max}$ is an upper limit on the length of links
2. Randomly initialize the node position $p_v$ of node $v$ for all $v \in V$
3. Compute the force acting on nodes $F(v)$

$$F(v) = \sum_{u \in V \setminus \{v\}} F_{repulsion}(u,v) + \sum_{u \in N(v)} F_{spring}(u,v)$$

where $N(v)$ denotes the set of nodes linked to $v$ in the network.

$$F_{repulsion}(u,v) = \frac{R}{\|p_u - p_v\|^2} \cdot \overrightarrow{p_u p_v}$$

where $R$ is a repulsion constant

$$F_{spring}(u,v) = S \cdot (\|p_u - p_v\| - l_{uv}) \cdot \overrightarrow{p_u p_v}$$

where $S$ is the stiffness parameter of the spring

4. Update node positions $p_v$

$$p_v = p_v + \mu \cdot F(v)$$

where the step length $\mu$ is usually a very small number

5. Repeat Step 3 and 4 until $F(v) = 0$

### 3.2   Computing Node Size

Each node $v$ is displayed as a circle, whose size is controlled by its radius $r_v$. For the purpose of terrorist social network analysis, a node's prominence is largely determined by its centrality [4]. In particular, we employed two centrality measures: degree and closeness. A node's degree $c_{degree}(v)$ is the number of links attached to it. An individual having a high degree may imply leadership while an individual with high closeness is more likely to serve as a mediator in the network. A node's closeness $c_{closeness}(v)$ is the inverse of the sum of its distances to all other nodes in the network,

i.e., $$c_{closeness}(v) = \frac{1}{\sum\limits_{v \neq u \in V} \|p_u - p_v\|}.$$

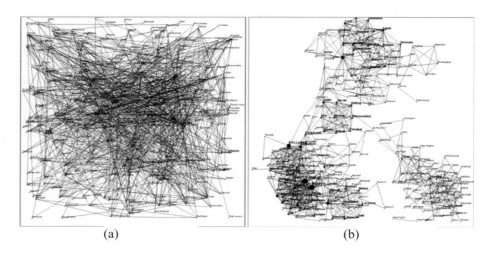

(a)                                        (b)

**Fig. 1.** (a) Initial Layout (b) Layout after applying the spring embedder algorithm

In Fig. 1 (a), the Global Salafi Jihad social network without using the spring embedder algorithm for initialization is presented. The nodes are spread out to optimize the usage of the rectangular space. However, the natural clusters of the terrorist groups cannot be found and the distance between any two terrorists does not correspond to their strength of associations. After utilizing the spring embedded algorithm, four natural clusters can be identified as shown in Fig. 1 (b). These clusters correspond to the central staff of al Qaeda, Core Arabs, Maghreb Arabs, and Southeast Asians. Using the measurement of degree and closeness of the nodes to compute their sizes, as illustrated in Fig. 1 (b), the important persons or leaders of each cluster can be extracted visually.

## 4   Focus-Plus-Context Based Visualization of Social Networks

The focus-plus-context visualization [12] is a type of interactive visualization. It allows a user to select one or more *focuses*, which are nodes in the case of social networks, and dynamically adjust the layout of the network based on the focuses in order to enhance the view of the focuses and their surrounding context. Fisheye views and fractal views are two particular kinds of focus-plus-context visualization techniques [13]. Both techniques have been applied to visualize the self-organize maps for Internet browsing. Fisheye view is a kind of nonlinear magnification technique. It maintains the same screen size by magnifying the region surrounding the focus while compressing the distant regions without losing the global structure of the network. Fractal view identifies a focus's context based on its associations with other nodes. It enhances the view of focus and its context by reducing less relevant information. Fisheye views and fractal views are complements of each other. Combining the two techniques produce effective focus-plus-context view of complex networks. It is proven that fisheye views and fractal view are successful to support users in exploring the details of the self organizing maps which are impossible before such techniques are applied. However, they have not been applied to visualize a network structure such as terrorist social networks. It has not been investigated how fisheye views and fractal views perform in analyzing the relationships among the nodes in a high density social network. In addition, the fractal views for self-organizing maps are developed based on the adjacency of the two-dimensional regions; however, the fractal views for terrorist social networks are developed based on the links and shortest paths of the networks.

### 4.1   Fisheye View

Fisheye views was first proposed by Furnas [7] and further enhanced by Marchionini and Brown [8]. It is known as a distortion technique in information visualization. Regions of interest are enlarged and the other regions are diminished so that one or more parts of a view are emphasized. Both local details of the regions of interest and global structure of the overall display are maintained. By specifying the focus point(s), users may enhance the views of particular regions of the two dimensional network.

Using fisheye views, we transform a node's normal coordinates, $(x_{norm}, y_{norm})$ into the fisheye coordinates, $(x_{feye}, y_{feye})$ based on the focus point, $(x_{focus}, y_{focus})$ using polar transformation. Equation (1) presents the polar transformation.

$$< x_{feye}, y_{feye} > \; = \; < x_{focus} + r_{feye} \cos \theta, y_{focus} + r_{feye} \sin \theta > \tag{1}$$

where

$$r_{feye} = r_{norm} \cdot \frac{d+1}{d \cdot \frac{r_{norm}}{r_{max}} + 1}$$

$$r_{norm} = \sqrt{(x_{norm} - x_{focus})^2 + (y_{norm} - y_{focus})^2}$$

$$\theta = \tan^{-1}\left(\frac{y_{norm} - y_{focus}}{x_{norm} - x_{focus}}\right)$$

The constant $d$ is the *distortion factor*. When $d$ equals to zero, no magnification of the focus area is applied. As $d$ increases, the focus and its context will be magnified and the further regions will be diminished. $r_{max}$ corresponds to the maximum possible value of r in the same direction as $\theta$. Fig. 2 (a) and (b) present the fisheye views using polar transformation with distortion factors as 2 and 6, respectively.

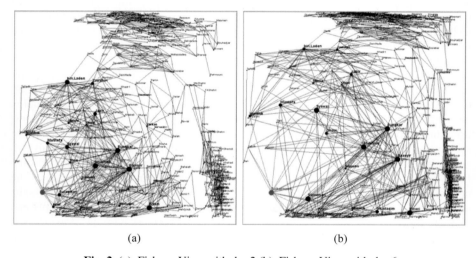

(a)                                        (b)

**Fig. 2.** (a) Fisheve View with d = 2 (b) Fisheye View with d = 6

### 4.2   Fractal View

Fractal view belongs to another class of information visualization techniques known as information reduction. It controls the amount of information displayed by focusing on the syntactic structure of the information. Fractal view [9] utilizes the concept of Fractal [10] to abstract complex objects and controls the amount of information displayed with a threshold set by users. In order to apply the fractal views, we first generate a hierarchical structure capturing the syntactic relationships between the focus and other nodes. The network topology is transformed into a hierarchy by extracting a tree from the network that has the focus at its root and other nodes at the branches and the leaves. Each path from the focus to another node in this tree should establish the strongest association between the two nodes. As the length of each in the network corresponds to the strength of association between two connected nodes, the total length of a path is a good indicator of the strength of the association along the path. Therefore, we generate this tree structure by finding the shortest paths from the focus to every other node in the network using the shortest path algorithm. The fractal values of the nodes in the tree are determined by propagation from the root to other nodes based on the following procedure:

1. Fractal value of the focus = $F_{focus} = 1$
2. Other nodes' fractal values are determined based on the fractal value of their parent node as follows:

$$F_c = (\frac{w_{cp}}{\sum_{c' \in children\_of\,(p)} w_{c'p}})^{-1/D} F_p$$

where $c$ is a child of $p$; $w_{cp}$ denote the association weight between c and p; the constant $D$ corresponds to the fractal dimension. The association weights are taken into account so that a parent node will propagate more fractal value down to the child nodes which are more strongly associated with the parent.

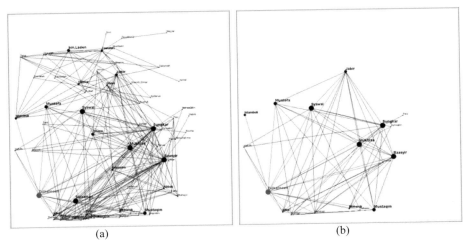

(a)                                                         (b)

**Fig. 3.** Fractal Views  (a) Fractal Value Threshold = 0.3 (b)Fractal Value Threshold = 0.7

A higher fractal value indicates the node is more closely related to the focus. The degree of abstraction can be controlled by a threshold on the fractal value. Only nodes with a fractal value above the threshold will be kept visible while those with fractal values below the threshold are considered less relevant to the current focus and are not displayed. Fig. 3 illustrates the effect of fractal view with different thresholds. The number of nodes filtered increases as the threshold increases. By hiding nodes with low fractal values, the complexity of the network could be effectively simplified, which enables a user to focus more on the relationships between the focus and those closely related nodes. Fig. 3 (a) and (b) illustrate the fractal views of the network in **Fig. 1** (b) with factual value thresholds as 0.3 and 0.7, respectively.

### 4.3  Fisheye Views and Fractal Views with Multiple Focuses

Multiple focuses can be useful when a user wants to magnify several local regions or to uncover the associations between indirectly connected nodes. To determine a node's fisheye coordinates and radius under multiple focus points, we first compute a node's fisheye coordinate $(x^i_{feye}, y^i_{feye})$ and radius $r^i_{feye}$ when focus $i$ is effective. The set of $(x^i_{feye}, y^i_{feye})$ and $r^i_{feye}$ are then averaged to obtain the node's final coordinate and radius.

$$(x_{feye}, y_{feye}) = \sum_i^K (x^i_{feye}, y^i_{feye}) \Big/ K \qquad r_{feye} = \sum_i^K r^i_{feye} \Big/ K$$

where $K$ is the number of focuses selected by the user.

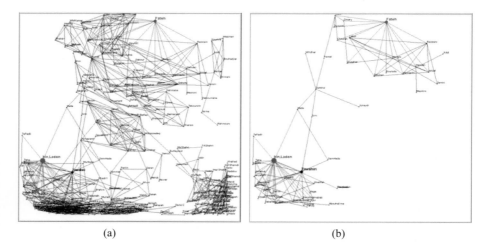

|     (a)     |     (b)     |

**Fig. 4.** (a) Fisheye view with both Fateh and Bin Laden as focuses (b) Combined fisheye and fractal view with both Fateh and Bin Laden as focus and a fractal value threshold of 0.6

The fisheye view in Fig. 4(a) is produced with Fateh and Bin Laden as focuses. The regions around both Fateh and Bin Laden are magnified. To determine a node's fractal value under multiple focuses, we generate a shortest path tree for each of the focuses. A node's fractal value is computed as the average of the fractal values propagated to it based on this set of trees. Accordingly, a node with a high fractal value under multiple focuses must be strongly connected with all or most of the selected focuses and could be considered as good intermediaries between the focuses. Fig. 4(b) illustrates the effect of fractal view with two focus points.

## 5  Case Study

In this section, we present two case studies on how the proposed visualization tools support the analysis of two terrorist cells in the global Salafi Jihad network: the plotters of the unsuccessful millennial bombing at the Los Angeles airport and the Hamburg cell responsible for the 9/11 attacks. In particular, we show how the visualization techniques facilitate the exploration of the inner structures of the two terrorist cells, which are originally embedded in the global network. All the background information used in our analysis was detailed in [11].

## 5.1 The U.S. Millennial Plot

In Fig. 5, Fateh Kamel (the focus) was the hub around which the network responsible for millennial plot grew. After applying fisheye views and fractal views (Fig. 5 (b)), most of the other important figures related to Fateh are clearly revealed: Omary set up the network of supporters with Fateh for the Bosnia jihad, Atmani and Ouzghar were invited to Canada by Fateh, Ressam carried out the bomb mission and failed.

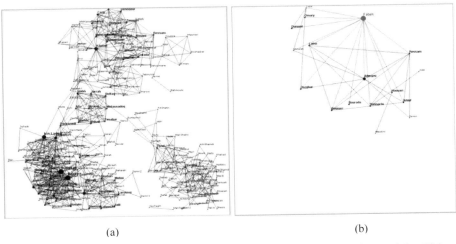

(a)                                                    (b)

**Fig. 5.** The view of the network with Fateh selected as Focus before and after applying Fisheye and Fractal View

Ressam and Meskini were the two terrorists who carried out the operation. Ressam attempted to infiltrate from Canada to U.S. but failed. Meskini, who lived in U.S., was supposed to assist Ressam after he crossed the border. After reduction of most less relevant nodes using fractal view and magnification with Fisheye View (Fig. 6(b)), an association path between them through Haouari and Fateh is clearly seen. In [11], it was reported that that Haouari is a childhood friend of Meskini and Meskini also bought Fateh's store from him. Fateh was the leader of the group.

## 5.2 The Hamburg Cell

The Hamburg Cell is a closely tied group, who carried out the 9/11 attack. Of its members, Atta, Jarrah and al-Shehhi received training in the U.S. and carried out the

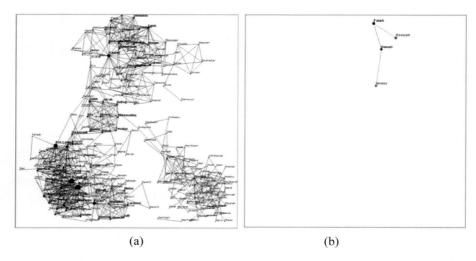

**Fig. 6.** Applying Fisheye and Fractal View to analyze linkages between Ressam and Meskini

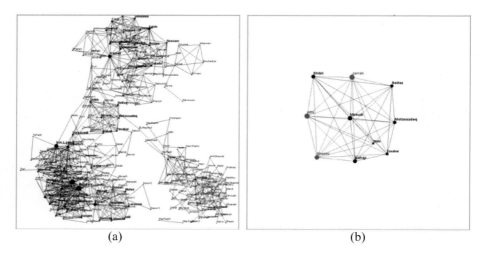

**Fig. 7.** View of the Hamburg Cell

operation. Fig. 7 shows the display when selecting these three nodes as focuses. After applying fisheye and fractal view, the inner structure of this group is more clearly shown. Shibh was responsible for coordination while Mzoudi, Motassadeq, Essabar and Bahaji played supporting roles and took care of affairs back in Germany.

## 6   Experiments

To evaluate the performance of the proposed visualization techniques for the terrorist social networks, we have conducted a user evaluation with ten subjects.  Each subject was first given a training session to demonstrate the functionality of the visualization tools and gains hands-on experience with the system. The training session took about 30 minutes. After the training session, the subjects were randomly assigned twenty tasks. The tasks include identifying the key person in the terrorist groups and the interaction patterns of the terrorists, similar to the tasks as presented in the above case studies. For each of the tasks, the subjects were also randomly asked to use the visualization tools without fisheye views and fractal views, with zoom-in windows, with fisheye views only, with fractal views only, or with combination of fisheye views and fractal views. We measure the effectiveness by the number of correct answers a subject provided for the tasks and measure the efficiency by the average time a subject needed to complete the tasks.

The experimental results are presented in Fig. 8. It is shown that using fractal views only or combination of fisheye views and fractal views obtain the highest effectiveness and efficiency. The effectiveness and efficiency of using fisheye views only is substantially lower than using fractal views only or combination of fisheye and fractal views. However, we only observe substantially higher effectiveness when we compare fisheye views with zoom-in windows.

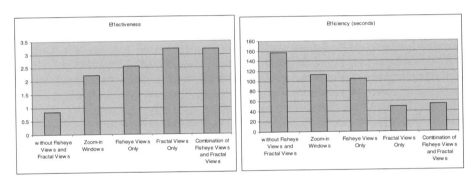

**Fig. 8.** Experimental Results

## 7   Conclusion

In the recent years, we have seen frequent reports of terrorist attacks all around the world. A good understanding of the terrorist organizations and their social networks is helpful to combat the potential terrorist attacks. Visualization tools are capable to support the analysis of terrorist social networks especially when the networks are large and complex. In this work, we have utilized the spring embedded algorithm to initialize the coordinates of nodes in terrorist social networks and applied the fisheye views and fractal views for visualizing and exploring the global Salafi Jihad network interactively. The spring embedded algorithm optimizes the usage of the two dimensional space. The distance between nodes represents the strength of their associations. The fisheye views are developed based on a distortion approach to magnify the area of interests selected by users. On the other hand, the fractal views are developed based on an information reduction approach to filter the less relevant information from the overloaded visualization space. Two case studies, the US

Millennial Plot and the Hamburg Cell, are presented to demonstrate how the proposed visualization tool identify the key persons in the terrorist groups and discovering specific patterns of interaction among the terrorists. The experimental result shows that the combination of fisheye views and fractal views or fractal views alone have the best performance in terms of effectiveness and efficiency.

# References

[1] M. K. Sparrow, The application of network analysis to criminal intelligence: An assessment of the prospects, *Social Network*, 13, 1991.
[2] S. Wasserman, K. Fause, "Social Network Analysis: Methods and Applications," Cambridge, Cambridge University Press, 1994
[3] J. Xu, B. Marshall, S. Kaza, and H. Chen, "Analyzing and Visualizing Criminal Network Dynamics: A Case Study," *Proceedings of ISI'04*, Tucson, AZ, June 10-11, 2004.
[4] J. Xu and H. Chen, "Criminal Network Analysis and Visualization," *CACM*, 48(6), 2005.
[5] J. Xu and H. Chen, "CrimeNet Explorer: A Framework for Criminal Network Knowledge Discovery," *ACM Transactions on Information Systems*, 23(2), April, 2005, pp. 201-226.
[6] P. Eades, "A Heuristic for Graph Drawing," *Congressus Numerantium*, 42, 1984.
[7] G.W. Furnas, "Generalized Fisheye Views," *Proceedings of the SIGCHI Conference on Human Factors in Computing System*, 1986.
[8] S. Manojit and M.H Brown, "Graphical Fisheye Views," *CACM*, 37, 1994.
[9] H. Koike, "Fractal Views: a Fractal-based Method for Controlling Information Display," *ACM Transactions on Information Systems*, 13(3), 1995.
[10] J. Feder, "Fractals", Plenum, New York, 1988.
[11] M. Sageman, *Understanding Terror Networks*, University of Pennsylvania Press, 2004.
[12] Y. K. Leung and M. D. Apperley, "A review and taxonomy of distortion-oriented presentation techniques", *ACM Transactions on Computer-Human Interaction (TOCHI)*, 1(2), 1994.
[13] C. C. Yang, H. Chen, and K. Hong, "Visualization of Large Category Map for Internet Browsing," *Decision Support Systems,* 35(1), 2003, pp.89-102

# Tracing the Event Evolution of Terror Attacks from On-Line News

Christopher C. Yang[1], Xiaodong Shi[1], and Chih-Ping Wei[2]

[1] Department of Systems Engineering and Engineering Management
The Chinese University of Hong Kong
[2] Institute of Technology Management
National Tsing Hua University, Taiwan

**Abstract.** Since the September 11th terror attack at New York in 2001, the frequency of terror attacks around the world has been increasing and it draws more attention of the public. On January 20 of 2006, CNN reported that al Qaeda leader Osama bin Laden had released a tape claiming that a series of terror attacks were planned in US. These attacks and messages from terrorists are threatening everyone in the world. As an intelligence officer or a citizen in any countries, we are interested in the development of the terror attacks around us. We can easily extract hundreds or thousands of news stories of any terror attack incidents from newswires such as CNN.com but the volume of information is too large to capture the information we need. Information retrieval techniques such as Topic Detection and Tracking are able to organize the news stories as events within a topic of terror attack. However, they are incapable to present the complex evolution relationships between the events. We are interested to learn what the major events but also how they develop within the topic of a terror attack. It is beneficial to identify the starting and ending events, the seminal events and the evolution of these events. In this work, we propose to utilize the temporal relationship, event similarity, temporal proximity and document distributional proximity to identify the event evolution relationships between events in a terror attack incident. An event evolution graph is utilized to present the underlying structure of events for efficient browsing and extracting information. Case study and experiment are presented to illustrate and show the performance of our proposing technique.

**Keywords:** Security informatics, topic detection and tracking, event evolution.

## 1 Introduction

Terror attacks are occurring frequently in the recent years and they draw attention of the public. We are threatened and anxious to obtain more information about these incidents. Due to the popularity of the Internet, news stories are now available online at the news information providers' Web sites. We can easily go to any newswires such as CNN, BBC, CBS, etc. or infomediaries such as Google and Yahoo to retrieve news stories for any terror attack incidents in the past. However, the popularity of the online news creates the information overloading problem at the same time. We can retrieve hundreds or thousands of news stories for any single terror attack incident

S. Mehrotra et al. (Eds.): ISI 2006, LNCS 3975, pp. 343–354, 2006.

without much difficulty; yet it is impossible for users to capture the flow of stories efficiently and effectively from a large volume of news stories.

In the research of topic detection and tracking (TDT), techniques are developed to monitor news stories, spot news events, and track the progress of previously spotted events [1]-[3], [11]-[14]. It clusters news stories as a hierarchical structure as shown in Fig. 1. Although users are able to capture the major events in a terror attack incident, it is difficult to capture the development of events within an incident. For example, the out break of a war may evolve to the economic crisis and then evolve to the problem of refugees. In order to capture such evolution relationships, we must consider the temporal information in addition to the content of the news stories.

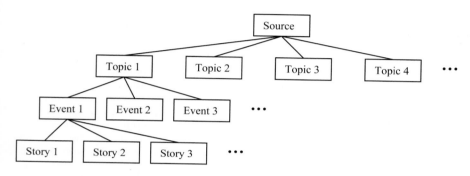

**Fig. 1.** Document organization in topic detection and tracking

In the research of temporal text mining (TTM), techniques are developed to discover temporal patterns in text information over time based on the timestamps of the text streams [7]. In this technique, text steams are partitioned into a number of non-overlapping sliced time intervals. The theme of each interval is identified and the evolution of theme between successive intervals is extracted. However, the events of the incident are not identified. An event in the terror attack incident may take more than one interval or only part of an interval. The theme extracted from an interval may be part of an event or a combination of several events that occur in the interval. Such technique is not ideal for users to capture the flow of major events in a terror attack incident.

Event evolution is a new concept developed recently. Makkonen [6] was the first to conduct investigation on event evolution as a subtopic of TDT. The news documents within a topic are temporally linearly ordered. A narrative begins when the first story of the topic is detected. A seminal event may lead to several other events. The events at the beginning may have more influence on the events coming immediately after than the events at the later time. As we go through the event in the temporal order, we may see the evolution of events within a terror attack incident. The events and the event evolution relationship can be represented as a graph structure (Fig. 2). Nallapati et al. [8] have investigated the dependencies among events and developed a few simple models to determine the event threading relationships from a small number of documents. However, the existing model is rather too simple to capture the complex relationships among the events in a large collection of documents within a topic. The concept of event evolution has not been well defined. Wei and Chang [9] proposed an event evolution pattern discovery technique that identifies event episodes together with their temporal relationships that occur frequently in a collection of events of the same type. Their work differs from prior studies in that they focus on segmenting a sequence of news stories of a specific event into event episodes and generalizing event episodes across different events of similar topics. However, they only consider temporal relationship in their technique. In this work, we formally define the event evolution by three logical rules. Besides, we introduce the temporal relationship, event similarity, temporal proximity and document distributional proximity to identify the event evolution relationships to construct the event evolution graphs. Given such graphical representation of the underlying structure of events in a terror attack incident, users can easily navigate the development of the incident and extract specific information for their needs.

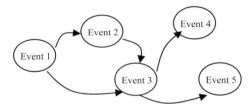

**Fig. 2.** Event evolution graph

## 2   Event Evolution

Event evolution describes the relationship between two events in a news topic. In order to have a better understanding of event evolution, we must first understand the definitions of story, event, and topic as defined in the research area of topic detection and tracking (TDT). A *story* is a news article delivering some information to users. An *event* is something that happens at a specific time but may or may not at a specific place. Although event is defined with a specific place in typical definition in TDT, some events do not have a specific place practically. An event may happen at many places at the same time. A *topic* is a set of events that are strongly interconnected with each other.

Event evolution is a new concept developed by Makkonen [6], Nallapati et al. [8], and Wei and Chang [9] recently. Makkonen described event evolution as the changing nature of a topic. Nallapati el al. described event threading as the dependencies between events, while Wei and Chang viewed event evolution as temporal dependencies between episodes (i.e., stages or subevents) with an event. We formally define event evolution as a relationship between the events within a topic such that the relationships are narrating the changes of events from the seminal events to the terminal events along the timeline. Such relationship is known as event evolution relationship [10]. We define that the **event evolution relationship** between event A and event B must follow *3 rules* if event A evolves to event B: (1) event A must temporally precede event B, (2) event A must be the necessary and/or the sufficient condition of event B, (3) the event evolution relationship must coincide with the user information needs.

## 2.1 Event Evolution Graphs

To represent the changes of nature within a terror attack incident, we use an event evolution graph to represent the underlying structure of the events and their relationships. Given such event evolution graphs, we can easily identify the seminal events of the terror attack incident and the evolution from the seminal events to other events. For example, the terrorists seizing the Beslan school is the starting event of the "Beslan School Hostage Crisis". The starting event evolves to the event of the attack of Russian special task force. Such Russian attack event is the seminal event that causes the death of the hostages, the investigation of the suspects, the counterterrorism responses from other countries and some other events.

An event evolution graph is a directed acyclic graph (DAG) consisting of events as the nodes and event evolution relationships as the directed edges between nodes. Given a set of $n$ distinct news stories $\mathbf{S} = \{s_1, s_2, \cdots, s_n\}$ on a given news topic, we have a set of $m$ events $\mathbf{E} = \{e_1, e_2, \cdots, e_m\}$ and their event timestamps $\mathbf{T} = \{t_1, t_2, \cdots, t_m\}$. $t_i = \tau(e_i)$. Each story is assigned to one of the $m$ events. A directed edge from vertex $e_i$ to $e_j$ is created in the event evolution graph if there is an event evolution relationship from $e_i$ to $e_j$. Event $e_i$ is the parent of event $e_j$ and event $e_j$ is the child of event $e_i$. $\mathbf{L}$ is the set of event evolution relationships, $\mathbf{L} = \{(e_i, e_j)$ where $e_i, e_j \in \mathbf{E}$. Therefore, the event evolution graph $\mathbf{G}$ is a directed acyclic graph, $\mathbf{G} = \{\mathbf{E}, \mathbf{L}\}$. The most important task in constructing the event evolution graph is identifying the event evolution relationships from the events of the terror attack incident.

**Table 1.** Eight temporal relationships that satisfy the first rule of event evolution relationship

| | Temporal Relationships | Illustration |
|---|---|---|
| 1 | $t_A < t_B$ ($t_A$ before $t_B$) | $s_A \quad e_A \quad s_B \quad e_B$ |
| 2 | $t_A \, m \, t_B$ ($t_A$ meets $t_B$) | $s_A \quad e_A$ / $s_B \quad e_B$ |
| 3 | $t_A \, o \, t_B$ ($t_A$ overlaps $t_B$) | $s_A \quad e_A$ / $s_B \quad e_B$ |
| 4 | $t_A \, di \, t_B$ ($t_A$ contains $t_B$) | $s_A \quad e_A$ / $s_B \quad e_B$ |
| 5 | $t_A \, s \, t_B$ ($t_A$ starts $t_B$) | $s_A \quad e_A$ / $s_B \quad e_B$ |
| 6 | $t_A \, si \, t_B$ ($t_A$ started by $t_B$) | $s_A \quad e_A$ / $s_B \quad e_B$ |
| 7 | $t_A \, fi \, t_B$ ($t_A$ finished by $t_B$) | $s_A \quad e_A$ / $s_B \quad e_B$ |
| 8 | $t_A = t_B$ ($t_A$ equal to $t_B$) | $s_A \quad e_A$ / $s_B \quad e_B$ |

In order to satisfy the first rule of event evolution relationship that event A must temporally precede event B, we adopt eight temporal relationships among the thirteen temporal relationships as defined by Allen [4]. An event has a timestamp $t$ which is a time interval. Given two events, event A and event B, and their timestamps, $t_A = [s_A, e_A]$ and $t_B = [s_B, e_B]$, the eight temporal relationships between event A and event B that satisfy the first rule of event evolution relationship are illustrated in Table 1. The distance between $t_A$ and $t_B$, $d(t_A, t_B)$, is measured as $e_A - s_B$ if $e_A$ is before or equal to $s_B$; otherwise $d(t_A, t_B)$ equals to 0.

We utilize the event similarity to identify the pairs of events that satisfy the second and third rules of event evolution relationships. The events that follow the second and third rules share some common information in their content, such as keywords, person and location names. Stories in the pair of events which possess the event evolution relationship usually discuss closely related matters. The authors of the news stories tend to refer the parent event when they are writing the stories of the child event. In our work, we utilize the cosine similarity of term vectors to represent the relatedness of events.

Define a k-term feature space for **S** as $\omega = \{\omega_1, \omega_2, ..., \omega_k\}$, then a story $i$ can be represented as a weighting vector $\omega_i = \{\omega_{i1}, \omega_{i2}, ..., \omega_{ik}\}$. The traditional TF-IDF function is

$$\omega_{ik} = \frac{tf_{ik}}{\max_l tf_{il}} \log \frac{N}{df_k} \tag{1}$$

where $tf_{ik}$ is the frequency of term $k$ in document $i$. $N$ is the total number of documents in that topic and $df_k$ is the number of documents which contains term $k$ in that topic.

We compute the event term vector of event $j$ using the average of the document term vectors of stories that belong to event $j$. We define the event term vector for event $j$ as $\omega'_j = \{\omega'_{j1}, \omega'_{j2}, ..., \omega'_{jk}\}$ where,

$$\omega'_{jk} = \frac{1}{n_j} \sum_{\forall s_i \in e_j} \omega_{ik} \tag{2}$$

where $n_j$ is the number of stories in **S** that belongs to event $j$.

The event content similarity is computed as followed.

$$cos\_sim(e_i, e_j) = \frac{\sum_{x=1}^{k} \omega'_{ix} \omega'_{jx}}{\sqrt{\left[\sum_{x=1}^{k} (\omega'_{ix})^2\right]\left[\sum_{x=1}^{k} (\omega'_{jx})^2\right]}} \tag{3}$$

In addition to the event similarity, we also adopt the temporal proximity and document distributional proximity to measure the strength of event evolution relationships. If two events are distant from each other along the timeline, then the event evolution relationship is less likely to exist between them than those events occur closely with each other. The longer the temporal distance between the two events is, the less likely the event evolution between them exists and vice versa. On the other hand, the document distributional proximity supplements the weakness of temporal proximity when there is a burst of number of events in a relatively short period which usually happens at the beginning of the incident. We utilize two decaying functions to reflect the temporal proximity and document distributional proximity.

$$tp(e_i, e_j) = e^{-\alpha \left[ \frac{d(\tau(e_i), \tau(e_j))}{T} \right]} \tag{4}$$

where $T$ is the *event horizon* defined as the temporal distance between the start time of the earliest event timestamp and the end time of the latest event timestamp in the same topic. $\tau(e_i)$ is the timestamp of $e_i$. $\alpha$ is the time decaying factor which is between 0 and 1.

$$df(e_i, e_j) = e^{-\beta \frac{m}{N}} \tag{5}$$

where $m$ is the number of documents that belong to the events happening in-between event $e_1$ and $e_2$. $N$ is the total number of documents in the topic. $\beta$ is the document distribution decay factor which is between 0 and 1.

To measure the strength of the event evolution relationship between two events, we integrate the event similarity function and the two decaying functions to compute the event evolution score as follow:

$$score(e_i, e_j) = \begin{cases} \cos\_sim(e_i, e_j) tp(e_i, e_j) df(e_i, e_j) & if \ e_i \ procede\ e_j \\ 0 & otherwise \end{cases} \tag{6}$$

In this work, we utilize a static threshold $\lambda$ $(0 < \lambda < 1)$ on the event evolution scores to identify the event evolution relationships. If the event evolution score of a pair of events is higher than or equal to the static threshold, we consider that there is an event evolution relationship between this pair of events. The event evolution graph is constructed as

$$G = \{E, L\}$$

where $L = \{(e_i, e_j) \mid score(e_i, e_j) \geq \lambda\}$. $\tag{7}$

The size of the event evolution graph depends on the granularity of the events. If we decrease the granularity of the events, there will be more number of events. As a result, the complexity of the event evolution graph increases. That means the number of event evolution relationships increase. For example, considering the four events, "Chechen terrorists seized the Beslan school with hostages" (Event A), "Negotiation with terrorists broke down" (Event B), "26 women and infants freed but most hostages were still held" (Event C), and "Special task force assaulted terrorists" (Event D), we may identify the event evolution relationships from Event A to Event B, Event A to Event C, and Event B to Event D. However, if we increase the granularity, we may merge Event A, Event B and Event C as one single event because these events occur in a short period of time and there is only one story in each of the first two events. In this case, the event evolution relationships from Event A to Event B and Event A to Event C are gone but there is one event evolution relationship from the merged event to Event D. The granularity of the event evolution graph should be controlled by users depending on their information needs. Some users may want to have a brief picture of the overall incident at the beginning. Some other users may want to explore more and decrease the granularity when they find interests in the specific events.

## 3   Case Study

In this section, we illustrate the event evolution graph of the terror attack incident. The news stories in our corpus are all extracted from the CNN News website. All stories are written in English. The corpus is generated by automatic crawling and searching with the support of filtering by human annotator. Given the URL of a beginning news story, the crawler analyzed the hyperlinks in the "related stories" section on each page of news story. It eliminated invalid links and crawl the linked news stories. The crawler repeated this process until there were no more links available or it reached a predefined depth. Since the section of "related stories" is often manually created, it is a good indicator of related stories. Alternatively, the human annotator submitted a query containing topic-specified keywords and obtained the searching results. The system analyzed the hyperlinks in the searching results and crawled related news stories on the submitted topic. Unrelated stories collected in these processes were then filtered out manually.

After the generation of the corpus and filtering of unrelated stories, the human annotator was also instructed to create the truth data of the event evolution graphs. The annotator was first asked to read through the news stories within a specific topic several times and formed a general picture of event evolution graph. In the second step, he was asked to identify the events and assigned each story to one of the events. Given the events, the annotator identified the evolution relationship based on the three rules of event evolution relationships. The annotator reviewed and revised the event evolution graph until no further revision could be made.

In the following subsection, we use the terror attack incident of Chechen Terrorist Seizing Beslan School as an illustration. As discussed in the earlier section, the complexity of event evolution graphs increases as we decrease the granularity of the events. For illustration purpose, we choose a higher granularity in order to present the ideas of event evolutions and the impact of the event evolution scores on the performance of the automatic generated event evolution graphs.

### 3.1   Chechen Terrorists Seizing Beslan School

In the terror attack case of Chechen Terrorist Seizing Beslan School, there are 32 news documents collected from CNN. We have identified 8 events. The details of the events are presented in Table 2.

**Table 2.** Events in Chechen Terrorists Seizing Beslan School terrorist attach case

| Event no. | Label | Number of doc. | Start time | End time |
|---|---|---|---|---|
| 1 | Chechen terrorists seized the Beslan school with hostages, negotiation and some hostages freed | 5 | 2004-09-02 01:46 | 2004-09-03 07:08 |
| 2 | Special task force assaulted terrorists and hundreds of hostages were dead | 3 | 2004-09-03 14:46 | 2004-09-05 05:14 |
| 3 | The responses of different parties on the Beslan school hostage tragic | 5 | 2004-09-04 15:45 | 2004-09-07 13:04 |
| 4 | Russia approached to identify the suspects of Beslan tragic | 6 | 2004-09-06 01:07 | 2004-09-08 17:54 |
| 5 | Russia conducted investigation and was determined to put terrorists on trial | 4 | 2004-09-08 15:44 | 2004-09-24 11:36 |
| 6 | Beslan school resumed classes after the hostage tragic | 3 | 2004-09-14 08:12 | 2004-09-15 12:33 |
| 7 | Russia claimed to strike Chechen terrorism | 3 | 2004-09-14 08:52 | 2004-09-17 12:38 |
| 8 | Russia's successive efforts against terrorism | 3 | 2004-09-29 12:01 | 2004-12-17 13:53 |

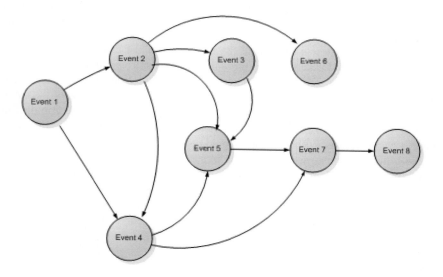

**Fig. 3.** Event evolution graph of Chechen Terrorists Seizing Beslan School terror attack case

Fig. 3 presents the event evolution graph of Chechen Terrorists Seizing Beslan School terror attack case generated by a professional annotator. There are 11 event evolution relationships. Event 2 "Special task force assaulted terrorists and hundreds of hostages were dead" has 4 out-links which is the maximum in the event evolution graph. It can be considered as a seminal event that causes the sequences of events such as the responses of anti-terrorism from different countries, the investigation of the attack and striking the terrorists. Event 6 "Beslan school resumed classes after the hostage" and event 8 "Russia's successive efforts against terrorism" are the terminal events. They can be considered as the final results of the events.

Fig. 4 presents the result of the event evolution graph generated with the threshold of event evolution score as 0.55. The precision is 0.73 and the recall is 0.73. Fig. 5 presents the result of the event evolution graph generated with the threshold of event evolution score as 0.60. The precision is 0.85 and the recall is 0.55. When we increase the threshold, we reduce the number of incorrect event evolution relationship; however, we increase the number of missed event evolution relationship. As a result, the precision increases but the recall decreases.

As we observe in the automatic generated event evolution graphs, some event evolution relationships from Event 2 are missed. It is mainly because the temporal distance between Event 2 and the child events are relatively large. The influence of Event 2 to the child events is considered less in our proposed techniques. As a result, they are easily missed. On the other hand, incorrect event evolution relationship from Event 3 to Event 4 is identified by our proposed techniques. It is because there are some overlapping content in the stories of both events and the temporal distance between the two events is small. It is difficult to achieve perfect precision and recall; however, the proposed techniques are promising in producing a meaningful and useful event evolution graph to support user navigation and extraction of information to satisfy their information needs.

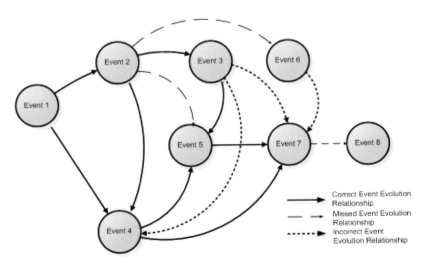

**Fig. 4.** Automatic generated event evolution graph with the threshold of event similarity as 0.55

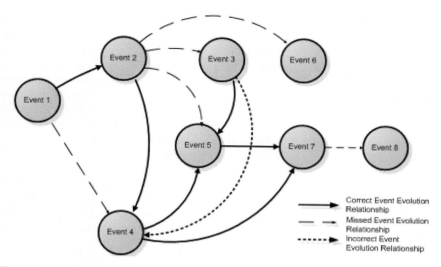

**Fig. 5.** Automatic generated event evolution graph with the threshold of event similarity as 0.60

## 4   Experiment

We have conducted an experiment to evaluate the performance of our proposed techniques in constructing the event evolution graph. 10 news topics are collected in our corpus. On average, there are 78 news stories per topic, 17.6 events per topic and 4.44 stories per event. From the event evolution graphs we generated manually, there are 24.4 event evolution relationships per topic and 1.4 event evolution relationships per event.

We tested the evolution score function with different parameters:

- *CS*: Cosine similarity of event term vectors only, without temporal proximity and document distributional proximity. This is equivalent to setting $\alpha = 0$ and $\beta = 0$ in our suggested event evolution score function;
- *CS*TP*: Cosine similarity of event term vectors multiplied by temporal proximity. This is equivalent to setting $\alpha = 1$ and $\beta = 0$;
- *CS*DF*: Cosine similarity of event term vectors multiplied by document distributional proximity. This is equivalent to setting $\alpha = 0$ and $\beta = 1$;
- *CS*sqrt(TP*DF)*: Cosine similarity of event term vectors multiplied by the square root of the product of temporal proximity and document distributional proximity. This is equivalent to setting $\alpha = \frac{1}{2}$ and $\beta = \frac{1}{2}$.

In Fig. 6, we observe that both *CS*TP* approach and *CS*DF* approach are better than *CS* approach substantially. This proves that both the temporal proximity and document distributional proximity are helpful in evaluating event evolution relationships. However, it is also interesting to observe that *CS*sqrt(TP*DF)* approach which incorporates both temporal proximity and document distributional proximity does not significantly outperform the *CS*DF* approach. It may due to the overlapping effect of the temporal

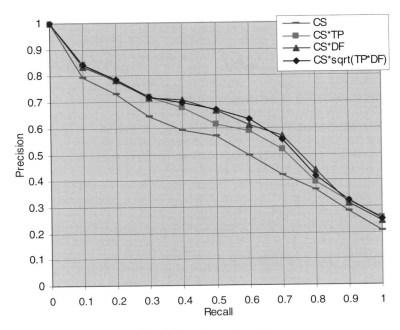

**Fig. 6.** Experimental result

proximity and document distributional proximity have some overlapping effects. When they are both included, they cancel the effects of each other in some degree.

## 5  Conclusion

There is a large volume of news stories reporting the terror attack incidents on the Web. This information is of great interest to us due to the recent threat of terrorism. In order to capture the development of the events in these terror attack incidents efficiently and effectively, we develop the techniques to identify the event evolution relationships of the events and represent the underlying structure as event evolution graphs. Illustration has been presented. An experiment has been conducted to report the impact of the parameters of the proposed event evolution score function. The performance of the proposed technique is promising. It supports users in efficient navigation of the related events and effectively extracts the specific information that satisfies user information needs.

## References

1. James Allan, editor. Topic Detection and Tracking: Event Based Information Organization. Kluwer Academic Publishers, 2000.
2. James Allan, Jaime Carbonell, George Doddington, Jonathan Yamron, Yiming Yang. Topic Detection and Tracking Pilot Study Final Report. In Proceedings of the Broadcast News Transcription and Understanding Workshop, 1998.

3. James Allan, Ron Papka, and Victor Lavrenko. On-line New Event Detection and Iracking. In Proceedings of the 21st Annual International ACM SIGIR Conference on Research and Development in Information Retrieval, ACM Press, pp. 37–45, 1998

4. James F. Allen. Maintaining Knowledge about Temporal Intervals. In Communications of the ACM, Vol. 26, No. 11, pp. 832–843, 1983.

5. J. Carthy. Lexical Chains for Topic Detection. Technical Report in Department of Computer Science: National University of Dublin, 2002

6. Juha Makkonen. Investigations on Event Evolution in TDT. In Proceedings of HLT-NAACL 2003 Student Workshop, pp. 43–48, 2004.

7. Qiaozhu Mei and Chengxiang Zhai. Discovering Evolutionary Theme Patterns from Text: An Exploration of Temporal Text Mining. In *Proceeding of the 11th ACM SIGKDD International Conference on Knowledge Discovery in Data Mining*, pp. 198-207, 2005.

8. Ramesh Nallapati, Ao Feng, Fuchun Peng, and James Allan. Event Threading within News Topics. In *Proceedings of the 2004 Thirteenth ACM Conference on Information and Knowledge Management*, pp. 446-453, 2004.

9. Chih-Ping Wei and Yu-Hsiu Chang. Discovering Event Evolution Patterns from Document Sequences. In IEEE Transactions on Systems, Man, and Cybernetics Part A: Systems and Humans, forthcoming.

10. C. C. Yang and X. Shi, "Tracking the Evolution of News Events," Proceedings of the Workshop on the Science of the Artificial, Taiwan, December, 2005.

11. Yiming Yang, Jaime Carbonell, Ralf Brown, Thomas Pierce, Brian T. Archibald, and Xin Liu. Learning Approaches for Detecting and Tracking News Events. In IEEE Intelligent Systems, Vol. 14, No. 4, pp. 32–43, 1999.

12. Y. Yang, T. Ault, T. Pierce, and C. W. Lattimer. Improving Text Categorization Methods for Event Tracking. In Proceedings of the 23rd International ACM SIGIR Conference on Research and Development in Information Retrieval, Athens, Greece, 2000.

13. Y. Yang, J. Carbonell, R. Brown, J. Lafferty, T. Pierce, and T. Ault. Multi-Strategy Learning for TDT. In Topic Detection and Tracking: Event-based Information Organization, J. Allan, Ed. Norvell: Kluwer Academic Publishers, 2002, pp. 85-114.

14. Y. Yang, J. Zhang, J. Carbonell, and C. Jin. Topic-conditioned Novelty Detection. In Proceedings of the 8th ACM SIGKDD International Conference on Knowledge Discovery and Data Mining, 2002.

# Measuring Effectiveness of Anti-terrorism Programs Using Performance Logic Models

Robert G. Ross

Deputy Director, Office of Comparative Studies
Science and Technology Directorate
Department of Homeland Security

The views expressed in this paper are those of the author and do not necessarily reflect the views of the Department of Homeland Security or the U.S. government.

**Abstract.** For many government agencies, measuring effectiveness has proven to be extremely problematic. There are several reasons for this, but the manner in which government agencies have implemented the Government Performance and Results Act (GPRA) has not helped. Rather than create a rich suite of appropriate data to support decision-making at all levels of the organization, most agencies have been content to report a small number of high-level outcome measures whose relationship to more effective management is unclear. Despite clear requirements for measures of different types and at every level from specific program activities and products up to societal outcomes, existing GPRA guidance actually encourages agencies to misinterpret what is required. As a result, GPRA performance reporting is now little more than an exercise in satisfying checklist requirements. This paper presents a new approach for developing agency and program appropriate measurement and data schemas to support decision-making at every level of an organization. The approach presented integrates a number of existing management tools, such as Program Logic Models and Activity-Based Costing, and adds a new concept – Outcome-Oriented Activity Impact Measures. Several anti-terrorism functions are used to illustrate the concepts presented. A fundamental premise underlying this approach is that government agencies and programs impact societal outcomes only by performing activities for which there is an expectation of beneficial impact. The paper does not tell any agency what to measure. Rather, it provides a sound approach through which agency managers can identify measures of effectiveness and other data appropriate to their specific programs.

## 1 Introduction

The federal landscape is littered with failed efforts at improving government program effectiveness and efficiency with "new" managerial methods. Included among the wreckage are Management by Objectives (MBO), Zero-Based Budgeting (ZBB), and Total Quality Management (TQM). The most recent effort, the Government Performance and Results Act (GPRA) is also failing to meet expectations and has arguably devolved into a bureaucratic exercise of checklists and the reporting of easily obtained statistics rather than being the transformational force intended. One

S. Mehrotra et al. (Eds.): ISI 2006, LNCS 3975, pp. 355 – 366, 2006.

obvious response to this statement is "*Why* has government reform failed so badly?" Another might be "If those other efforts didn't work, what would?" This paper provides one federal manager's partial and perhaps even simplistic answers to the second question, with the hope that efforts that do work can contribute to upgrading our understanding of measuring effectiveness in anti-terrorism programs.

## 2   For-Profit and Not-for-Profit Measurement Environments

Without significant adaptation, some measurement concepts developed for the for-profit sector frequently do not work well when applied to government. There are several reasons for this but two are paramount. First, desired outcomes in the for-profit sector (profit rather than loss, high return on investment) are internal to the enterprise, can generally be expressed in terms of a single unit of measurement – dollars – and can be determined with some precision. Outcomes sought by government programs are felt in society as a whole and come in many different forms – a sense of security from crime, safety on the highways, equitable protection of property and personal rights, etc. Some have attempted to express outcomes of this kind in dollars but such figures do not have widespread credibility. As a result, it is difficult to meaningfully measure outcomes in the government and not-for-profit sectors in an aggregate way. Rather, selected data sets (usually selected for the simple reason that they are available) are used to make inferences about overall outcome goals, but the linkages and proof can be very weak.

The other major difference is time. In the for-profit sector, products and services exist *for a time*, after which they disappear. This process can be extremely rapid. In the government sector, efforts in pursuit of societal outcomes generally exist *for all time*. This is not the result of bureaucratic self-perpetuation. It is because most government programs respond to enduring facts of life. For example, the societal need for highway safety will continue to exist so long as we have highways. Government products and services will change over time but facts of life endure. Additionally, many government programs aim to change behavior, but behavior changes slowly. Thus, government can seem to be plodding in comparison to the for-profit sector. Outcome measures for government programs must be tailored to the timeframes over which they operate.

## 3   Data, Information, Knowledge, Understanding and Wisdom

There is a logical and hierarchal relationship between data, information, knowledge, understanding and wisdom. As shown Figure 1, the DIKUW Hierarchy[1], there is a place for numerical and other "factual" observations (i.e., data) on conditions existing within the "problem space" of concern. Moreover, data can be placed in context, processed and combined in ways that make it more meaningful. Thus, data becomes information. However, data and information are not enough. We must move beyond our preoccupation with the quantitative (data and information) and move to the more important qualitative levels of the hierarchy (knowledge, understanding and, hopefully, wisdom).

---

[1] "The Data, Information, Knowledge, Wisdom Chain: The Metaphorical Link": Jonathan Hey, December, http://best.me.berkeley.edu/~jhey03/files/reports/IS290_Finalpaper_HEY.pdf

**The DIKUW Hierarchy**

**Fig. 1.**

# 4   Managerial Decision-Making in an Organizational Context

A number of propositions underlay the approach presented. Complete justifications for each of these propositions could be provided but, in the interest of brevity, they will be presented here in tabular form in two broad categories: (1) Management and Decision-Making and (2) Organizational Objectives and Effectiveness.

**Table 1.** Propositions on Management and Decision-Making

1. The defining role of managers is making decisions.
2. Decision-makers are found at all levels of any given organization.
3. Decision-makers in a given organization, while linked by common organizational objectives, will have differing spheres of responsibility within which they make decisions.
4. Acting within his or her sphere of responsibility, a manager's duty is to make decisions that will maximize program Effectiveness and/or Efficiency, and thereby improve Cost-Effectiveness.[2]
5. Decision-makers with differing spheres of responsibility have differing information needs.[3]

---

[2] Effectiveness measures the impact on outcomes of a given activity, product or service. Efficiency measures the cost per unit of performance of a given activity, product or service. Cost-Effectiveness measures the impact on outcomes per dollar expended producing a given class of activity, product or service.

[3] To understand this point, consider a car manufacturer. The CEO will manage the corporate bottom line by using high level/aggregated data from the major divisions within the company. That's appropriate. But someone will be responsible for automotive brakes. That individual cannot make decisions about brake system designs and suppliers using high level or aggregated information from the brake or any other division. This individual needs information on costs of materials and labor, warranty repair rates, supplier performance, results of accident investigations, pending lawsuits alleging brake failure, etc. Decisions made about brake systems will affect both the division and corporate bottom lines, and should be made with the intent of maximizing both bottom lines, but such decisions require information that is specific, detailed and pertinent to brake systems. This info would be available to the CEO if needed, but would ordinarily be below the CEO's level of attention.

6.  Decisions are made on some basis of support. Possible bases include information, misinformation, disinformation, personal experience, prejudice, ideology, political considerations, personal (and maybe organizational) value systems, perceived personal benefit and others.
7.  Decisions will be made, with or without adequate supporting information, due to political pressure and/or decision deadlines (e.g., the annual federal budget cycle and OMB due-dates) as well as other possible factors.
8.  Tactical, operational and strategic decisions are required at all levels of an organization, with the balance between these types of decision being different at each organizational level.

**Table 2.** Propositions on Organizational Objectives & Effectiveness

1.  Every organization seeks to achieve its objectives within an external system or societal context (i.e., group, local, national, industry, etc.)
2.  All organizations perceive their objectives as "value-adding," with "value" being determined primarily by the organization. The organization's "values" need not conform to those of its target.
3.  Organizations do not seek their objectives in a vacuum. Other entities and factors will act on an organization's target(s) in ways that can reinforce or counter the organization's efforts and impact.
4.  No organization controls the outcomes it seeks. Rather, an organization can only influence the outcomes it seeks.
5.  Organizations influence outcomes only by the actions they take.
6.  Every action taken by an organization is taken with an expectation (not necessarily rational) that it will create a specific beneficial impact.
    a.  External/operational actions are undertaken with the expectation that the actions will directly or indirectly influence a societal outcome in a manner consistent with the organization's objectives.
    b.  Internal/support actions are undertaken with the expectation that the actions will positively influence the organization's ability to carry out its external/operational actions.

# 5  The Management Decision-Making Process

In order to create a measurement schema to support the decision-making process, it is helpful to have an idea of what that process entails. Figure 2 presents managerial decision-making as a cycle with five major steps. This generic cycle addresses many of the propositions listed above and captures the critical steps in making any kind of decision. It may require a bit of word-smithing but "Identify Opportunity…" can be completed to accommodate many different kinds of decisions that might be thought of as somehow different. For example, "Identify Opportunity to mitigate an identified risk" makes this a risk management cycle, while "Identify Opportunity to market a new product to satisfy _____ need" makes this a business planning cycle. If carried out in keeping with the implications of the DIKUW Hierarchy and the propositions above, the steps shown in Figure 2 should lead to a good decision.

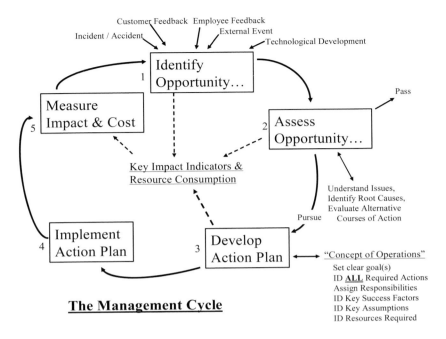

**Fig. 2.**

## 6  Effectiveness and Efficiency in Government Programs

Readers jaundiced about government will scoff, but the reality is that most government programs are highly successful. For example, more than 99.99+% of the oil shipped by water safely gets where it is going. Similarly, significant accidents in commercial aviation are exceedingly rare and the vast majority of automobile trips are completed safely. Other examples could be provided but there are more important points to be made. One is that government is not solely responsible for *any* of these cited public outcomes. Many others also influence these positive outcomes. Among them are responsible ship and airline operators, the vast majority of the driving public and others too numerous to mention. In fact, what may anger more people about government is not its lack of *Effectiveness* but rather its perceived lack of *Efficiency*. Another important point is that, when dealing with issues such as potential incidents involving oil tankers and airliners, a success rate of 99.99999+% can result in public outrage. Concerns over Efficiency may cause a slow public or Congressional burn, but shortcomings in Effectiveness are what really get things stirred up.

Responsible managers will seek excellence in effectiveness, efficiency and cost-effectiveness, and will set goals accordingly. Thus, while a goal of reducing already low accident rates by __% over the next year would be appropriate under some circumstances, a more appropriate goal under other conditions might be to reduce program operating costs by __% without letting failures rise. Finally, for programs operating at or near a tipping point (i.e., where marginal increases in performance come only at the expense of extraordinary increases in cost or, conversely, where marginal reductions in program expenditures result in significant increases in program failure) it may be most appropriate to simply concentrate on maintaining a satisfactory and cost-effective status-quo. Sometimes, good enough really is good enough.

## 7  The Performance Logic Model

There are a number of thoughts captured above that must be taken into account when designing a suite of decision-support data and information: outcome orientation, external context for outcomes sought, impact only through actions taken, expectation of beneficial impact for actions taken, influence over outcomes rather than control, managerial spheres of responsibility, decision support information tailored to the needs of individual managers, complete Concepts of Operation, Effectiveness, Efficiency and the Law of Unintended Consequences. The measurement approach outlined below is an attempt to satisfy the implications of each of these key thoughts.

Lying at the heart of this approach is something called a Performance Logic Model[4] (Figure 3). A Performance Logic Model (PLM) consists of a series of logical *How*? and *Why*? questions that link, at one end, the activities performed by an organization and, at the opposite end, the outcomes sought by the organization. Once the logical How/Why structure is built, an appropriate set of internal and external data and other information can be identified, collected and used to support managerial decisions.

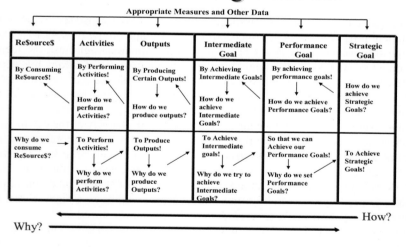

Fig. 3.

---

[4] The Performance Logic Model concept is adapted from Program Logic Models used for a number of years in various organizations. A Performance Logic Model is a Program Logic Model with measurement added.

Viewed from the outcome end, a PLM helps an organization answer the question "How do we achieve our objectives?" or for government, "How do we influence the societal outcome for which we have been assigned responsibility?" Viewed from the activities end, a PLM will enable a member of the organization to answer the question "Why am I doing this?" At a higher level of understanding, a PLM will help a worker identify the societal outcome he or she is working to bring about. At a lower level, a PLM answers a more immediate question: "What impact will my work have?" Borrowing from the parable used in almost every leadership seminar over the last few decades, a PLM would help the stonecutter recognize that he is both building a cathedral **and** cutting a stone. Understanding does not have to be an either/or proposition.

When appropriate measures of effectiveness at the activity level and higher-level outcome measures are considered together, a PLM helps answer questions such as "Are our activities creating the intended impact?" With cost of performance data, a PLM can help answer the efficiency or cost-effectiveness question "Is the impact created by this activity commensurate with its cost of performance?" With the right external data (e.g., the number of ____ will increase sharply over the next decade), a PLM can become a tool for forecasting future demand for services or products.

# 8  A Performance Logic Model Case Study

Developing and explaining a full-blown Performance Logic Model for a complex activity is beyond the scope of this paper but a partial Coast Guard model illustrates some of the key points. Fortunately for the purposes of this paper, there are significant similarities between many of the activities carried out by the Coast Guard in pursuit of its pre-9/11 objectives and the activities carried out by DHS and others in post-9/11 anti- and counter-terrorist programs. In its pre-9/11 GPRA efforts the Coast Guard identified 5 high level societal outcomes sought through its missions. One was to "Eliminate deaths, injuries and property damage associated with maritime transportation, fishing and recreational boating." Few would question that this is a desirable societal outcome goal. The real question, however, is how to achieve it.

The Coast Guard's highest-level strategic approach to achieving its outcome goals is Risk Management. As Risk results from the combination of Probability and Consequence, Risk Management consists of measures taken to reduce Probability (i.e., Prevention) and to mitigate Consequences when Prevention fails (i.e., Response). Prevention and Response are both logical and intuitively appealing, but they are still far too broad for effective execution. Enter the Performance Logic Model.

There are many separate things that have to happen if marine accidents are to be prevented and the full range of measures is far too extensive to list here. However, even a single branch of the Prevention How/Why logic model will serve to illustrate the process. Figure 5[5] traces the deconstruction of the nation's transportation safety

---

[5] Observant readers will have noted that Figure 4 is horizontal while Figure 5 is vertical. Either way works.

goal[6] into a Coast Guard goal and then into a goal for the Coast Guard's Merchant Marine Safety Program, which focuses on marine transportation. These goals are all high-level outcome goals. The next level down consists of intermediate goals. Getting the intermediate goals right is the key to building a useful How/Why logic model. Doing this requires both developing a solid logical How/Why structure and using the right words to express intermediate goals. Note that, as shown here, there may be several levels of intermediate goals needed to capture a complete logical structure. The salient common characteristic of the intermediate goals shown in Figure 5 is that each is *necessary but not sufficient* to attain the supported outcome goal. Intermediate goals are pursued by producing outputs – products and services – which are, in turn, delivered through the activities performed by Coast Guard men and women across the nation. This is where the Coast Guard, or any other agency, adds value – by performing activities that impact societal outcomes.

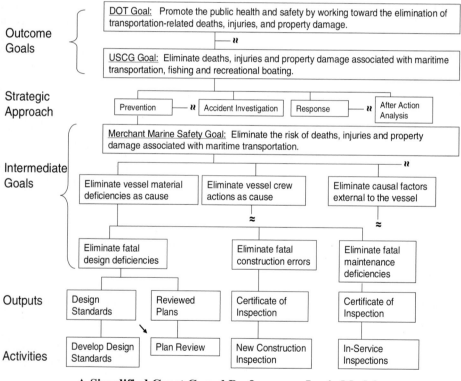

**A Simplified Coast Guard Performance Logic Model**

**Fig. 5.**

---

[6] The highest level outcome goal shown in Figure 5 is a Department of Transportation (DOT) goal. The Homeland Security Act of 2002 (P.L. 107-296) specified that the Coast Guard's non-homeland security missions were to continue without change in the new Department. Thus, this goal remains relevant today.

# 9  Selecting Appropriate Measures

There are a number of factors that have to be considered when deciding what kinds of measures to use when crafting a Performance Logic Model. Many of these are actually determined by the nature of the work being measured. In every case, however, it is vital that those selecting measures of effectiveness and other data understand the purposes to which it will be put.

The Government Performance and Results Act of 1973[7] (GPRA) governs measuring performance in federal programs. GPRA has forced agencies to think in terms of the societal outcomes for which they are responsible but it has not lived up to expectations. A major reason for that may be that GPRA implementation has been focused on judging effectiveness only, and then only in terms of highest-level outcomes.

The first substantive statements in GPRA are contained in Section 2 - Findings and Purposes. This section opens by talking about "...waste and inefficiency in federal programs..." and goes on to mention efficiency and inefficiency as often as it mentions "performance and results." Despite this, in 50+ pages, GAO Guidance on GPRA implementation[8] mentions the word efficiency only twice and inefficiency only once. Similarly, GPRA talks in various sections to measuring "...results...service quality... *customer satisfaction*..." and the need for "...performance indicators to be used in measuring or assessing the relevant *outputs*, *service levels*, and *outcomes* of *each* program *activity*..." (emphasis added). Despite the importance given to these performance indicators, the GAO guidance mentions *outputs* only 3 times, *customer satisfaction* only once and *service levels* not at all! The document is effectively silent on meaningful measurement of program activities. Even though government programs create, or fail to create, benefit at the activity level, GAO appears to be actively discouraging measurement at any level below the overall program! Guidance issued by the Office of Management and Budget on its Program Assessment Rating Technique, also aimed at GPRA requirements, is similarly focused on high level outcomes[9].

This GAO and OMB exclusive focus on high-level outcomes has had adverse consequences. For example, I was once told by a senior Coast Guard manager that GPRA actually **forbids** any measurement below the highest level outcomes! That is not only factually wrong, it is also complete nonsense. Measuring overall program outcomes is absolutely necessary, but decision-makers also need more detailed information on the activities by which they seek to influence those high-level societal outcomes in order to manage programs and activities for effectiveness and efficiency. Denying them this information cannot be what GPRA's drafters intended.

GPRA's call for capturing managerially meaningful information down to the program activity level is in keeping with Propositions 2 through 5 in Table 1 and

---

[7] Text available at http://www.whitehouse.gov/omb/mgmt-gpra/gplaw2m.html#h2 and other sources.

[8] "Executive Guide: Effectively Implementing the Government Performance and Results Act": Government Accountability Office, 1996: Washington, DC; available at www.gao.gov/cgi-bin/getrpt?GGD-96-118

[9] See http://www.whitehouse.gov/omb/part/index.html for OMB's guidance on the PART process.

Propositions 5 and 6 in Table 2. Further, the brake system manufacturing example in Footnote 3 illustrates and validates the necessity of using outcome-oriented information that is both different from and far more granular than high-level outcome measures. With this solid foundation for the necessity of capturing useful data at the activity level, we can now turn to the issue of the kinds and characteristics of data that would be useful.

In general, there are three basic categories of information that would be useful in managing an activity in detail: (1) environmental data that describes the context within which the activity will be conducted; (2) the cost of actually performing the activity; and (3) the outcome-oriented impact achieved in performing the activity. The specific information captured in each of these categories for a given activity, particularly outcome-oriented impact data, will depend on the nature of the activity in question. These can be illustrated by looking at TSA's passenger screening function.

Environmental data pertinent to TSA screening would include factors such as the number of airports and screening points within them, the number of passengers in each who require screening and leading indicators of future demand, such as industry growth trends and airport construction plans. Activity cost data would primarily be the direct point of performance costs - labor and pro-rated equipment costs. Indirect overhead costs such as space, utilities, training and oversight, both immediate and at higher levels, should also be captured. Finally, there is effectiveness. An incident would reveal ineffectiveness but, as is true for many security and safety programs, we can't wait for incidents to find out if TSA screening is being effective. Proxies and indirect measures are needed. These could include the numbers of forbidden items detected and the number of times trusted agents were able to get past security. Such measures might not be definitive but they would be indicative and useful.

## 10  Outcome-Oriented Activity Impact Measures

If an agency's mission or functions relate to a societal outcome over which the involved agency has some influence but no true control, the normal case for most government agencies and not-for-profit organizations[10], measuring effectiveness is especially problematic. Was the desired societal outcome achieved because of something the agency did? Or were the agency's actions irrelevant? Was the desired outcome not realized in spite of properly executed agency efforts? Were the agency's efforts merely inadequate or, in the worst case, were the agency's efforts actually harmful? These questions can be boiled down to "Is the agency doing the right things?" and "Is the agency doing the right things right?"[11] In either case, how can we tell?

---

[10] For-profit entities don't actually control their outcomes either. Customers have the final say. However, measurement may be more easily conducted in the for-profit sector than in government and not-for-profits.

[11] Those who survived the government's TQM fad of the early 1990s will recognize these as the first two elements of the TQM triplet: "Do the right thing. Do the right thing right. Do the right thing better." A properly developed Performance Logic Model helps to satisfy all three TQM commandments.

The answer to that question is provided by Propositions 4, 5 and 6 in Table 2. Taken together, these propositions imply that the best way to assess the effectiveness of most government programs may be by identifying the specific impacts expected from individual activities, products and services, and then seeing if those impacts are, in fact, being created.

Outcome-Oriented Activity Impact Measures must be chosen with consideration for the nature of the activity in question (is the activity expansive or retractive, case work or process flow work?), the specific outcome-oriented impact expected from the activity and the operational concept on which the activity is based. Providing detailed instructions on how to select appropriate measures is beyond the scope of this paper. However, a few comments can be offered and first among them is that merely counting the times an activity has been performed is not sufficient. Neither are other simple numerical tallies, such as the number of defects identified in an inspection process or the number of intelligence sources recruited. The significance of the defects identified and the value of the sources recruited are far more important. One major defect identified or one major intelligence source recruited may be vastly more important than hundreds or even thousands of the less significant. Evaluating such qualitative outcome-oriented activity impact may not be easy, especially in a field as subjective as intelligence, but that does not mean that it should not be attempted.

If the activity involves a customer interaction, then customer satisfaction is probably an appropriate measure. If the customer interaction in question is an in-depth encounter, such as applying for a permit or license, then an individual questionnaire might be appropriate. On the other hand, if customer encounters are brief and occur in large numbers, periodic surveys are the better bet. Of course, there is also a question of how customer satisfaction should be measured. This will be driven by the nature of the customer interaction. For example, if the interaction is a permit application, the applicant should not be asked an open-ended question such as "Are you satisfied?" If the applicant was properly denied a permit for which the applicant was clearly unqualified, the answer will be both "No" and irrelevant. More appropriate questions would relate to level of service such as "Was your appointment time met?" and "Were your questions answered?" and possibly "If the permit you asked for was denied, were you told what you will need to do to receive it in the future?"

## 11   Deciding What to Measure and How

Attempting to give managers a specific pre-determined list of what they should measure and how would be a fool's mission. The reason for this is simple – no outside consultant or "expert" will understand an agency's mission or management concerns as well as the agency's managers. Rather, the most that should be attempted is to provide concepts and guidelines that will assist managers as they decide for themselves what to measure and how. That is what this paper is intended to accomplish – provide concepts and guidelines that will help managers identify measures and data that will best meet their needs. Thus, the final thoughts to be offered are a list of the characteristics that a well designed measurement schema will satisfy.

**Table 3.** Characteristics of Quality Data and Measurements

1. Selected by managers based on relevance to their responsibilities.
2. Appropriate to the issue or activity being measured.
3. Simple – Easily Collected – Affordable.
4. Objective to the maximum extent feasible.
5. Subjective, when appropriate or when suboptimal but unavoidable, with variability minimized by structured and well-anchored descriptors.
6. Standardized and consistently applied across all like products and services of a widely distributed activity or broad program.
7. Adequate to describe a program's purpose, target and the environment in which that target and program exist.
8. Inclusive of both direct and indirect program costs and presented in terms appropriate to the agency's budget process.
9. Accurate in capturing effectiveness in terms of both high level outcomes *and* the impact of activities performed in pursuit of those outcomes.

## 12  Conclusion

According to the late Peter Drucker, the guru of modern American management, "You cannot manage what you do not measure." This is no less true in government than it is elsewhere. A government manager who doesn't measure outcomes may get lost in the minutia of activities, products and services. However, managers will have no informational basis from which to manage if they don't measure, in some detail, relevant aspects of the activities, products and services for which they are responsible. By effectively integrating Program Logic Models, Outcome-Oriented Activity Impact Measures, Activity-Based Cost Management concepts, and appropriate environmental data, Performance Logic Models offer an innovative and potentially fruitful way to provide improved decision-support information to government managers.

# On the Topology of the Dark Web of Terrorist Groups

Jennifer Xu[1], Hsinchun Chen[2], Yilu Zhou[2], and Jialun Qin[2]

[1] Computer Information Systems Department, Bentey College, 175 Forest Street,
Waltham, MA 02452, USA
jxu@bentley.edu
[2] Department of Management Information Systems, Eller College of Management,
The University of Arizona, Tucson, AZ 85721, USA
{hchen, yiluz, qin}@eller.arizona.edu

**Abstract.** In recent years, terrorist groups have used the WWW to spread their ideologies, disseminate propaganda, and recruit members. Studying the terrorist websites may help us understand the characteristics of these websites and predict terrorist activities. In this paper, we propose to apply network topological analysis methods on systematically collected the terrorist website data and to study the structural characteristics at the Web page level. We conducted a case study using the methods on three collections of Middle-Eastern, US domestic, and Latin-American terrorist websites. We found that these three networks have the small-world and scale-free characteristics. We also found that smaller size websites which share same interests tend to make stronger inter-website linkage relationships.

## 1 Introduction

Terrorism and terrorist activities substantially threaten national security. Although authorities have taken extensive counter-terrorism measures, terrorist groups remain active, using all kinds of media to disseminate propaganda, seek support, and recruit new members. The WWW, an effective information presentation and dissemination tool, has been widely used by terrorist groups as a communication medium. The Web presence of these terrorist groups reflects their different characteristics and may provide information about planned terrorist activities. Thus, monitoring and studying the content and structural characteristics of terrorist websites may help us analyze and even predict the activities of terrorist groups.

Recently, research on terrorism and terrorist groups on the Web has become an important topic in intelligence and security informatics. Researchers have employed content analysis and Web structure mining to reveal the characteristics of terrorist websites at site level. In this research, we analyze the structural characteristics of terrorist websites at a lower granularity—page level. Based on a systematically collected "Dark Web" data set, we conducted topological analysis to compare the hyperlink structures of terrorist websites from three geographical regions: Middle-East, the United States, and Latin-America.

The remainder of the paper is organized as follows. Section 2 reviews previous work on the structure of terrorist websites and the topological analysis methods. In

S. Mehrotra et al. (Eds.): ISI 2006, LNCS 3975, pp. 367–376, 2006.
© Springer-Verlag Berlin Heidelberg 2006

section 3, we present our data collection methods and the "Dark Web" dataset. In section 4, we report and discuss our findings from the analysis. Section 5 concludes the paper with implications and future research directions.

## 2  Literature Review

In this section, we review prior research on the structure of terrorist websites, and the network topology analysis methodology, which has been widely employed in other domains.

### 2.1  Web Mining Studies on Terrorist Websites

The World Wide Web has been increasingly used by terrorists to spread their ideologies [1]. According to the Southern Poverty Law Center (SPLC) [2], there were 708 active extremist and hate groups in the US in 2002. These groups had 443 websites in 2002 and this number increased to 497 in 2003.

Researchers and watchdog organizations such as SPLC have started monitoring, tracing and studying terrorist websites. The traditional approach is to study the contents and structure of these websites [3]. This approach is limited in the size of dataset and cannot be used to keep track of the dynamic characteristics of terrorist websites. Like other websites, terrorist websites usually suddenly emerge; the content and hyperlinks are frequently modified, and they may also swiftly disappear [4]. In recent years, Web mining techniques have been used in cyber crime and terrorism research [5].

Web mining combines data mining, text mining, and information retrieval techniques in the Web context to discover knowledge from the content of Web pages (content analysis), the structure of hyperlinks (structure analysis), and the visit and usage patterns of websites (usage analysis). In the terrorism domain, content analysis and structure analysis are the most frequently used techniques.

Studies on the content analysis of terrorist websites have shown that terrorist websites present different characteristics from other ordinary websites. For example, Gerstenfeld et al. found that many terrorist websites contain multimedia contents and racist symbols [6]. Gustavson and Sherkat found that terrorist groups used the Internet mainly for ideological resource sharing [7, 8]. This finding was also supported by a few other studies such as Zhou et al. [9], which analyzed the contents of terrorist websites in the United States and found that sharing ideology was one of the most important purposes for building these websites.

Structure analysis based on hyperlinks has also been seen in several previous studies. It is reported that website interconnection relations provide reasonably accurate representation of terrorist groups' interorganizational structure [9, 10]. However, most of these studies focus on the hyperlink structures at the site level. There are few studies that analyze the hyperlink structure of websites among different terrorist groups at the page level, which may provide insight into the structure of terrorist groups. The topological characteristics of these websites at a lower granularity (page level) remain unknown.

## 2.2  Network Topological Analysis

Statistical analysis of network topology [11] is a recent development in network structure analysis research. In network topological analysis, entities, regardless of their contents, are treated as nodes and their relations are treated as links. The result is a graph representation of the network. Three topologies have been widely studied recently, namely, random network [12], small-world network [13], and scale-free network [14]. Different topologies have different structural characteristics and implications.

It has been found that most empirical networks such as social networks, biological networks, and the Web are nonrandom networks [11]. Actually, many of these networks are found to be small-world networks, which are characterized by small average path length and relatively large clustering coefficient compared to a random network. Moreover, many of these networks are also scale-free, meaning that a large percentage of nodes have just a few links, while a small percentage of nodes have a large number of links. Studies have shown that the WWW, in general, is both a small-world and a scale-free network [11].

A number of measures and approaches, many of which are borrowed from Social Network Analysis research [15], can be employed to reveal the structural patterns of a network. For example, nodes with high degrees may act as hubs or leaders, where the degree of a node is the number of links it has. The patterns found often have important implications to the functioning of the network.

The topological analysis has been used in previous studies on terrorist networks [16-18] and terrorist website structural studies at the site level [9]. In this research, we analyze the topological characteristics of "Dark Web" to reveal the structural properties of terrorist websites at the page level.

# 3   The Dark Web Dataset

We call the special section of the Web that is used by terrorists, extremist groups, and their supporters the "Dark Web." As a long-term research project, we have kept collecting and tracing the content and hyperlinks of several terrorist groups' websites and created a Dark Web test bed. [19]

## 3.1  Collection Building

In our research, we focused on terrorist groups from three geographical areas: the United States, Latin-America, and Middle-Eastern countries. By November 2004, we had collected three batches of Dark Web data by spidering these websites. To identify the correct terrorist groups to spider, we used the reports from authoritative sources suggested by a domain expert with 13 years of experience. The sources include: Anti-Defamation League, FBI, Southern Poverty Law Center, Militia Watchdog, United States Committee for a Free Lebanon, Counter-Terrorism Committee of the UN Security Council, and etc. From these resources, a total of 224 US domestic terrorist groups and 440 international terrorist groups were identified.

We then identified an initial set of terrorist group URLs and expanded them. In the initial set of URLs, all US domestic group URLs and some international group URLs were directly obtained from US State Department reports and FBI reports. Additional international group URLs were identified through online searches. We constructed three terrorism keyword lists in terrorist groups' native languages, which contain terrorist organization name(s), leader(s)' and key members' names, slogans, special words used by terrorists, etc. From the search results, those websites that were explicitly purported to be official sites of terrorist organizations and that contained praise of or adopt ideologies espoused by a terrorist group were added to the initial URL set. The initial URL set is expanded by adding the URLs' in-link and out-link websites. Manual filtering was performed on the expanded links to ensure their quality.

After the URL of a terrorist group website was identified, we used a digital library building toolkit to collect the contents and hyperlinks from the sites.

We identified 108 US domestic terrorist websites, 68 Latin-American terrorist websites, and 135 Middle-Eastern terrorist websites.

### 3.2  Network Creation

After we collected the Web pages, the static HTML files and dynamic files were parsed and the hyperlinks in the files were extracted. We created a Dark Web page network, whose nodes were Web pages in the Dark Web collection and links were hyperlinks between these pages. For the US domestic collection, the network contained 97,391 nodes. The Latin-American collections contained 152,414 nodes. The Middle-Eastern collection contained 298,761 nodes.

## 4  Dark Web Page Level Topological Analysis

### 4.1  Network Topological Analysis

In this research, we ignored the directions of hyperlinks, and studied topological characteristics of the resulting non-directional networks. Table 1 shows the basic statistics of the three networks. We defined clustering coefficient as [20]:

$$C = \frac{3 \times number\ of\ triangles\ on\ the\ graph}{number\ of\ connected\ triples\ of\ nodes} \tag{1}$$

Because these networks were rather large, we employed an approximation algorithm called ANF to calculate the average path length [21]. To estimate the diameter of the three networks, we randomly selected 400 nodes in each network and calculated the shortest path length between them.

Comparing the topological characteristics of the three networks we found that the Middle-Eastern network is much larger than the US domestic network and the Latin American Network. The number of nodes in the Middle-Eastern network (298,761) is almost three times of that in the US domestic network (97,391) and two times of that in the Latin-American network (152,414). Among the three networks, the Middle-Eastern network has the highest average degree (12.66), indicating that their Web pages tend to point to each other more often than those in the US domestic network and in the Latin-American network. The size of the Middle-Eastern network and the high average degree may indicate their relatively active status and strong intention to cooperate with each other.

**Table 1.** Basic statistics of the three collections of Dark Web page level networks

| Collections | US domestic | Latin-American | Middle-Eastern |
|---|---|---|---|
| *No. of Nodes* | 97,391 | 152,414 | 298,761 |
| *No. of Links* | 296,330 | 586,115 | 1,914,099 |
| *No. of N-Links* | 239,572 | 475,748 | 1,890,728 |
| *<k>* | 4.92 | 6.24 | 12.66 |
| *C* | 0.32 | 0.31 | 0.06 |
| *$C_{rand}$* | 5.05E-05 | 4.1E-05 | 4.24E-05 |
| *l (by ANF)* | 3.33 | 4.70 | 3.52 |
| *$l_{rand}$* | 7.21 | 6.52 | 4.97 |
| *D (by simulation)* | $\geq 39$ | $\geq 46$ | $\geq 38$ |
| *NC* | 4,134 | 1,110 | 674 |
| *$Node_C$* | 81,803 | 22,175 | 255,699 |
| *$Link_C$* | 239,982 | 95,346 | 1,718,626 |

*N-Links*: Non-directional links; *<k>*: average degree; *l*: average path length; *$l_{rand}$*: average path length of a random network; *C*: clustering coefficient; *$C_{rand}$*: clustering coefficient of a random network; *D*: network diameter; *NC*: number of components; *$Node_C$*: number of nodes in the largest component; *$Link_C$*: number of links in the largest component

All the three networks have rather high clustering coefficients and small average path length comparing with their random network counterparts. The high clustering coefficient indicates that the networks contain dense and strongly connected local clusters. In this case, it is obvious that the Web pages are more likely to point to pages within the same site, resulting in local clusters. Note that the clustering coefficient of the Middle-Eastern network is smaller than those of the other two networks. This may be caused by two reasons. First, the US domestic and Latin-American networks have a much larger number of components than the Middle-Eastern network. These components serve as local clusters, causing the overall clustering coefficients of the whole networks to be higher. Second, it may be because that the pages in the giant component of the Middle-Eastern network are more decentralized.

Figure 1 shows the in-degree distribution and out-degree distribution of the three networks in log-log plots. All the six degree distributions have a long tail which is often observed in large empirical networks. The in-degree distributions of the Middle-Eastern network and the US domestic network follow a power law degree distribution. The out-degree distribution of the three networks and the in-degree distribution of the Latin American network show two power law parts with a tail.

The power-law distribution takes the form of $P(k) \sim k^{-\gamma}$, where P(k) is the probability that a node has exactly $k$ links. The values of the exponents of the six distributions are shown in Table 2. The special shape of the out-degree distributions of the three networks may be because a Web page normally does not contain so many hyperlinks to the other pages. Thus, the likelihood of such high out-degree pages will quickly drop as degree increases. For the in-degree distribution, as the Latin-American network contains several small components and very few large components, it is difficult for the high in-degree nodes to emerge. As the in-degree increases, the number of nodes with high in-degrees decreases quickly.

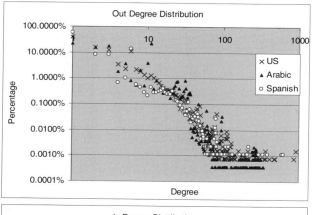

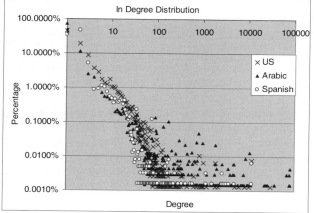

**Fig. 1.** Degree distributions of the three networks

**Table 2.** Exponents of the three networks' degree distributions

| Collections | US domestic | Latin-American | Middle-Eastern |
|---|---|---|---|
| In degree exponent | 1.94 | 2.16/2.53 | 1.60 |
| Out degree exponent | 1.95/2.30 | 2.24/2.26 | 1.88/ 2.44 |

## 4.2 Giant Component Analysis

Although the Middle-Eastern network is the largest network, it has fewer components than the other two networks. Table 3 shows the three networks' top five components' node percentage in their networks. The three networks all have a giant component (The Latin-American network's largest component has 22.77% of the nodes. But it is still very big compared with the other components in the network.). We also observed that these giant components usually are composed of several terrorist websites.

**Table 3.** The node percentages of the top 5 components in the three networks

| Component Size Rank | US domestic | Latin-American | Middle-Eastern |
|---|---|---|---|
| *1* | 53.67% pages | 22.77% pages | 85.62% pages |
|  | 54 websites | 9 websites | 68 websites |
| *2* | 2.31% pages | 6.58% pages | 2.73% pages |
|  | 1 website | 1 website | 1 website |
| *3* | 0.68% pages | 5.84% pages | 1.66% pages |
|  | 1 website | 10 websites | 1 website |
| *4* | 0.56% pages | 4.61% pages | 1.35% pages |
|  | 1 website | 11 websites | 2 websites |
| *5* | 0.43% pages | 2.79% pages | 1.13% pages |
|  | 1 website | 1 website | 10 websites |
| *Other Components* | 42.35% pages | 57.41% pages | 7.51% pages |

The giant component of the Latin-American network contains fewer websites than the giant components in the other two networks. This may be because that these Latin-American terrorist groups have diverse ideologies and beliefs. As a result, it is less likely for them to refer to each other on their websites or to seek cooperation.

The three giant components compose the bulk of the three networks. We thus focused only on the giant components of the three networks.

In general, there is a positive correlation between a website's size (number of pages) and number of internal links. This is also observed in the websites and pages included in the giant components of the three networks (Figure 2). However, these terrorist networks show special characteristics on inter-site links. Figure 3 presents the relationship between the website sizes and the number of inter-site links of the three networks. In this figure, the vertical axis represents the number of hyperlinks between a pair of websites in the giant component and the other two axes represent the number

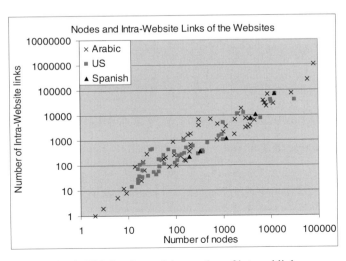

**Fig. 2.** Website size and the number of internal links

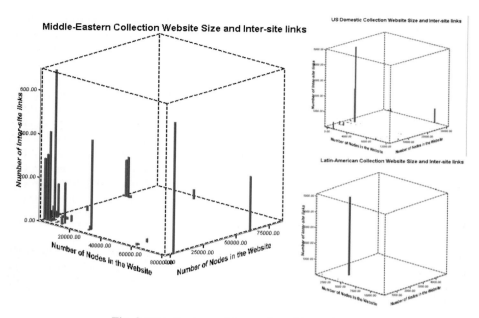

**Fig. 3.** Website size and the number of inter-site links

of pages in the two websites. For all three networks, we observe that most of the inter-site links are not present between large websites. For example, in the Middle-Eastern network, most of the inter-site links appear between websites that have less than 10,000 pages. It is normal for large websites to share a large number of inter-links. However, if two websites with relatively small number of pages are connected by many inter-links, it means that the two websites must have a close relationship.

To further study the relationships between the small and middle sized websites, which usually are connected by many inter-site links, we selected and examined some of these websites. For example, in the US domestic network, there are 4,875 inter-site links between www.resistance.com (12,188 pages) and www.natall.com (943 pages), 2,173 links between www.resistance.com and www.natvan.com (814 pages), and 414 links between www.natvan.com and www.natall.com. After we examined their websites, we found that the three websites have very close relationship. www.natall.com is the official Website of the National Alliance, a white supremacist group. www.natvan.com is another domain name of www.natall.com. www.resistance.com is an e-commerce website owned by Resistance Records, which is a music production company affiliated with National Alliance. Therefore, the dense inter-site hyperlinks may reflect the close relationship between the organizations.

In the Latin-American Eastern network, clajadep.lahaine.org (3,796 pages) and www.carteleralibertaria.org (1,177 pages) are connected by 4,979 links. The Clajadep group (clajadep.lahaine.org) is focused more on broadcasting affairs in Mexico, while the Cartelera Libertaria group (www.carteleralibertaria.org) more on Spain. These two groups all belong to a terrorist alliance called "La Haine," which has people from different Spanish-speaking and Latin America countries. The dense inter-site links may result from the fact that members in La Haine share similar ideologies, beliefs and interests.

Similarly, in the Middle-Eastern network, there are some small websites of close relationship. For example, www.daymohk.info (737 pages) and www.chechen.org (7,042 pages) have 676 links, which are both websites for extremists in Chechnya. www.palestine-info.info (3,698 nodes) and www.infopalestina.com (550 nodes) shared 410 interlinks, which are both news websites for Palestinians.

These cases show that the similarities in terrorist groups' ideologies, beliefs, interests, and geographical closeness may cause their websites to frequently point to each other. From Figure 3, we can see that the Middle-Eastern giant component has many more and denser inter-site links than the other two giant components. It implies that the terrorist groups in Middle-Eastern have relatively closer relationships and more interconnections than those in the United States and Latin-American. Such dense inter-site links also enable the emergence of the giant component in the network.

## 5   Conclusions and Future Directions

In this research, we analyzed the structural properties of the Dark Web at the page level based on systematically connected terrorist websites data. Our goal was to reveal the characteristics of these websites. We conducted a case study based on a "Dark Web" test bed of US domestic, Latin-American, and Middle-Eastern terrorist websites. From the case study we found that:

- The three networks are small worlds.
- The three networks' in-degree and out-degree distributions roughly follow a power-law degree distribution, indicating that they have the scale-free characteristics. In addition as degree increases in the three networks, the probability of having nodes with high degrees decreases more quickly than in scale free networks.
- The giant components of the three networks contain several websites, which are not very large and share the same interests. They also have more inter-site links and closer relationships.

A limitation of our study is that focused only on the structural properties of the Dark Web without performing content analysis that might reveal important insights into the ideology, mission, and other information about these terrorists groups. Cautions must be made when any interpretation is drawn based solely on the structure of the Dark Web. In the future, we plan to perform in-depth content analysis on these terrorist web sites and combine it with other structural analysis methods such as cluster analysis from the network structural perspective to advance our knowledge of the Dark Web.

## References

1. E. Lee and L. Leets, "Persuasive storytelling by hate groups online - Examining its effects on adolescents," American Behavioral Scientist, vol. 45, pp. 927-957, 2002.
2. S. P. L. Center, "Hate Groups, Militias on Rise as Extremists Stage Comeback," 2004, pp. www.splcenter.org/center/splcreport/article.jsp?aid=71.

3. M. Whine, "Far Right on the Internet," in Governance of Cyberspace, B. Loader, Ed.: Routledge, 1997, pp. 209-227.

4. G. Weimann, "How Modern Terrorism Uses the Internet," United States Institute of Peace, www.terror.net Special Report 116, 2004.

5. H. Chen, W. Chung, J. Xu, G. Wang, Y. Qin, and M. Chau, "Crime data mining: A general framework and some examples," Computer, vol. 37, pp. 50-+, 2004.

6. P. B. Gerstenfeld, D. R. Grant, and C.-P. Chiang, "Hate Online: A Content Analysis of Extremist Internet Sites," Analyses of Social Issues and Public Policy, vol. 3, pp. 29, 2003.

7. A. T. Gustavson and D. E. Sherkat, "Elucidating the Web of Hate: The Ideological Structuring of Network Ties among White Supremacist Groups on the Internet," presented at presented at Ann. Meeting Am. Sociological Assoc., 2004.

8. C. C. Demchak, C. Friis, and T. M. L. Porte, "Webbing Governance: National Differences in Constructing the Face of Public Organizations," in Handbook of Public Information Systems, G. D. Garson, Ed.: Marcel Dekker, 2000.

9. Y. Zhou, J. Qin, G. Lai, E. Reid, and H. Chen, "Building Knowledge Management System for Researching Terrorist Groups on the Web," presented at Proceedings of the Eleventh Americas Conference on Information Systems, Omaha, NE, USA, 2005.

10. V. Burris, E. Smith, and A. Strahm, "White Supremacist Networks on the Internet," Sociological Focus, vol. 33, pp. 215?35, 2000.

11. R. Albert and A. L. Barabasi, "Statistical mechanics of complex networks," Reviews of Modern Physics, vol. 74, pp. 47-97, 2002.

12. P. Erdos and A. Renyi, "On random graphs," Publ Math-Debrecen, vol. 6, pp. 290-297, 1959.

13. D. J. Watts and S. H. Strogatz, "Collective dynamics of 'small-world' networks," Nature, vol. 393, pp. 440-2, 1998.

14. A. L. Barabasi and R. Albert, "Emergence of scaling in random networks," Science, vol. 286, pp. 509-12, 1999.

15. S. Wasserman and K. Faust, Social Network Analysis: Methods and Applications. Cambridge: Cambridge University Press, 1994.

16. D. McAndrew, "The structural analysis of criminal networks," in The Social Psychology of Crime: Groups, Teams, and Networks, I, Offender Profiling Series, II, D. Canter, Alison, L., Ed. Aldershot, Dartmouth, 1999, pp. 53-94.

17. J. S. McIllwain, "Organized crime: A social network approach," Crime, Law & Social Change, vol. 32, pp. 301-323, 1999.

18. M. K. Sparrow, "The application of network analysis to criminal intelligence: An assessment of the prospects," Social Networks, vol. 13, pp. 251-274, 1991.

19. J. Qin, Y. Zhou, G. Lai, E. Reid, M. Sageman, and H. Chen, "The Dark Web portal project: Collecting and analyzing the presence of terrorist groups on the web," Intelligence and Security Informatics, Proceedings, vol. 3495, pp. 623-624, 2005.

20. M. E. Newman, D. J. Watts, and S. H. Strogatz, "Random graph models of social networks," Proc Natl Acad Sci U S A, vol. 99 Suppl 1, pp. 2566-72, 2002.

21. C. Palmer, P. Gibbons, and C. Faloutsos, "ANF: A fast and scalable tool for data mining in massive graphs," presented at In Proc. of the 8th ACM SIGKDD Internal Conference on Knowlege Discovery and Data Mining, 2002.

# Indicators of Threat: Reflecting New Trends

Yael Shahar

Senior Researcher, Institute for Counter-Terrorism, Interdisciplinary Center Herzliya

**Abstract.** The Venue-Specific Threat Assessment model has been used by researchers at ICT to estimate the "attractiveness" of specific facilities to terrorist organizations. This paper will explore some of the issues that must be addressed in order to make this threat assessment model more widely applicable. In particular, we will examine the considerations used to generate one of the most crucial components of the model: the threat indices used for determining the dangers posed by terrorist organizations.

## 1 Overview of Current Threat Assessment Model

For several years, the Institute for Counter-Terrorism has used an analytical tool called the "Venue-Specific Threat Assessment Model" for the purposes of building an overall picture of terrorist threats to specific installations. This model combines information on known terrorist organizations and their target-selection methods with an exhaustive on-site analysis of target vulnerabilities. The result is a statistical comparison of potential scenarios by those terrorist organizations seen as most likely to endanger the installation.

The methodology used has been discussed elsewhere, so I will provide only a brief overview. This paper will explore some of the issues that must be addressed in order to make this threat assessment model more widely applicable. In particular, I will examine the considerations used to generate one of the most crucial components of the model—the threat indices used for determining the danger posed by terrorist organizations.

### 1.1 Methodology: Existing Threat Assessment Framework

The venue-specific threat assessment model assumes that the probability of a terror attack on a particular target is dependent not only on the characteristics of the target—its symbolic or strategic value and its vulnerabilities—but also on the ambition, capabilities, and sensitivities of the relevant terrorist organizations.

Data on the terrorist organizations active in the region in question comes from a database developed by the Institute for Counter-Terrorism. The model combines this information with the characteristics of each potential *modus operandi* to arrive at the probability that a particular type of attack will be carried out by a particular organization.

The stages used in the threat assessment are:

1. *Determination of Organization-specific factors* – We determine which organizations present the greatest threat to the venue in question, based on the

S. Mehrotra et al. (Eds.): ISI 2006, LNCS 3975, pp. 377–388, 2006.

motivations, capabilities, and ideologies of the organizations. Each organization is given a Risk Score, based on the relative score of each index applied to that organization. The analysts running the model determine the threshold above which organizations will be included in the model.

2. *Determination of Venue-specific factors* – An exhaustive analysis of the vulnerabilities of the venue in question is carried out by a professional security team. For most high-profile venues, this analysis will already have been performed by the installation's security personnel as part of their routine duties. Care must be taken to examine the vulnerabilities of the venue in question from the point of view of the potential attacker—seeking weaknesses that might be exploited to carry out an attack.

3. *Scenario building* – the information on venue vulnerabilities is combined with data on potential scenarios. In our model, the list of scenarios is taken from a database of hundreds of potential terror attacks, chosen in accordance with the vulnerabilities of the venue in question. Each scenario will be given a score based on the difficulty of carrying it out and the potential damage of a successful attack.

4. *Numerical synthesis* – Combining the results of the last three stages, we arrive at a numerical evaluation of the likelihood that any particular type of attack will be carried out by a particular terrorist organization. We do this by categorizing the various scenarios according to the target-selection methods of the different organizations: for example, the difficulty of successfully perpetrating the attack and the desirability of the outcome of the attack from the point of view of the terrorist organization. For each terrorist organization, we include factors to weigh the terrorists' sensitivity to these attack-specific factors. The result is a score that indicates the net "attractiveness" of a particular type of attack to a particular type of organization. For example, some organizations may be more deterred by physical difficulty or by attacks requiring years of planning, while others would be undeterred by these factors. Some may see achieving maximal casualties as a central goal, while others may be unwilling to risk causing high casualties.

## 1.2 Limitations of the Current Model

The threat-assessment model described above has provided credible results when used with comprehensive on-site risk analysis reports. It has in fact been successful in predicting *modus operandi* and organizational affiliation for two actual attacks. Its strength is that it provides a way of estimating overall probabilities of particular scenarios against the venue under consideration.

However, its results are only as good as the information that goes into it. In order to reach credible and useful results, a high degree of familiarity with the motivations and target-selection criteria of the relevant organizations is needed. In short, the model is dependent on the human element to produce meaningful results. In particular, the organizations seen as most dangerous to the venue are chosen according to a pre-determined list of threat indicators. Both the selection of indicators and their application requires a high level of expertise on the part of the analyst carrying out the study. So while our risk-assessment model is useful for providing an overview of threats, its use is limited to highly-trained security professionals; it is virtually inaccessible to the people who would find it most useful, such as installation-protection personnel and local law-enforcement agencies.

In order for this model to become more accessible to those responsible for protecting particular venues, a means must be found to "automate" to some degree the function of the analyst in the process. In the current model, this function is primarily the determination and application of threat indices, i.e. the choice of which organizations and entities pose the greatest danger to the venue in question. Apart from this, the model is fairly well "automated;" the input of target vulnerabilities is based on existing security surveys, while the scenarios are generated from a database of possible scenarios, based on a history of past attacks on similar installations.

In theory, the organization-specific indicators—currently generated "on-the-fly" by analysts—could be calculated by applying computational methods, provided the dataset used is large enough to provide a sufficient statistical basis. The system could then be programmed to "flag" certain organizations as soon as venue-specific data is entered into the system.

In what follows, we will examine some of the primary assumptions used in developing organization-specific threat indices. This discussion will not deal with the technical aspects of building the computational algorithms, but will instead deal with some of the issues that must be addressed in order to come up with such indicators. This in turn will give us some idea of the kinds of considerations that would go into "automating" this function.

## 2   Developing Threat Indicators: Basic Assumptions

**Assumption 1: Threat indicators are venue-specific**

One of the fundamental assumptions behind the venue-specific threat assessment is that the degree of threat posed by any terrorist organization is not an absolute; different organizations will pose varying degrees of threat to different venues. It is impossible to gauge the threat posed by a terrorist organization in and of itself. Terrorism is a tactic—defined for the purposes of this analysis as "the intentional use, or threat of use, of violence against civilian personnel or installations." In general, it makes no sense to state that such a tactic poses such and such a risk, without referring to the venue which might be targeted. By the same token, one cannot say that the risk that organization Y will employ a given *modus operandi* is X, without referring to the potential target. The characteristics of the venue in question will determine the kind of threat posed by each organization to that venue. For this reason, an on-site risk analysis plays an integral role in determining what type of terrorist organization would be interested in exploiting the venue's symbolic value and vulnerabilities.

**Assumption 2: Statistic data can bridge the gap in precise intelligence**

Our knowledge of what organizations are present in the area of concern gives no hint as to their intentions to target the particular venue under consideration. Often, the kind of specific intelligence that would enable us to know the precise target of a planned attack is not only unavailable, but may not even *exist* in the usual sense. In other words, the terrorists themselves may not settle on a particular target until the last moment, making preventive intelligence-gathering extremely difficult, if not impossible.

Short of penetrating the organizations and learning of their plans, the best that we can do is to apply what is known of the organizations' target-selection criteria to the venue in question. This requires that we understand how the terrorists think—how they themselves would view the target and its vulnerabilities. Is it a soft target or a heavily-guarded one; what are the chances of a successful attack using the organization's usual *modus operandi;* is the target's symbolic value worth risking a more complicated attack despite a higher risk of failure?

To find answers to such questions requires that we either understand the mindset of the terrorist organizations, or else that we have a large enough dataset that their behavior can be inferred from past incidents, failed attacks, statements of organization leaders, etc. Ideally, our analysis should be based on both.

## Assumption 3: Threat Indicators must by dynamic

Terrorism is a dynamic and continually changing phenomenon. Almost every aspect of international terrorism—from the make-up of the organizations, to their tactics, to their overall goals—has undergone major changes over the past two decades. These factors need to be reflected in the threat indicators attached to the terrorist organizations and entities in the database. Following are some of the more notable changes that must be taken into account.

### Higher casualty attacks

Even before September 11, it was recognized that terror attacks were, in general, becoming more lethal. This went hand-in-hand with a shift in the underlying motives of the terrorist organizations themselves. The organizations active in the 1970's and 1980's were mostly secular organizations with clearly-defined political objectives. Their attacks were calculated to create sufficient casualties to produce shock value, to gain media attention, and to coerce a target population to alter its political views. However, these organizations were cognizant of the fact that too much bloodshed would only alienate their prospective supporters, and could lead to a backlash or otherwise undermine their cause.

From the early 1990s, a change could be seen in the overall strategies of terrorism. Rather than merely killing enough people to call attention to his political demands, the modern terrorist is interested in mass-casualty attacks. He no longer wants merely to influence political processes; his goal is now likely to be to create a completely new political reality. An analysis of recent terror chronologies shows that terrorist attacks in the 1990's had nearly a 20% greater probability of resulting in death or injury than did those of the previous two decades.

The many terrorist bombings since the September 11 attacks have shown beyond doubt that this trend continues. Of the many attacks thwarted in the United States and Europe in recent years, almost all were meant to kill hundreds, if not thousands, of people.

### Religious motivation and suicide

This trend toward higher-casualty attacks reflects, in part, the changing motivation of the terrorists. Today's terrorist is much more likely to be driven by extremist religious beliefs than by a wish to gain political concessions; the al-Qaida network is a prime example of this trend. The aim of such groups is to win converts among potential supporters, to intimidate potential enemies, and to punish perceived enemies.

While the traditional terrorist attack was a means to an end—a way to induce a desired response in the targeted population—the religiously-motivated terrorist of the new type sees the act as an end in itself. The terror attack is meant to bring the war to the enemy, and is often seen as a kind of religious act.

The rise of religiously-motivated terrorism has been accompanied by a rise in suicide attacks. This is particularly true of extremist Islamist terrorism, where the image of the suicide bomber, or "Shahid," carries great power and prestige. The most devastating of the recent attacks around the world have been suicide attacks, and all were carried out by groups motivated by extremist Islamic ideologies.

*Loose networks united by a common ideology*

This shift in motivation has been accompanied by a change in the structure and make-up of the terrorist organizations themselves. Gone, for the most part, are the days of clearly delineated, hierarchically-organized terrorist groups. Today's terrorist organization is more likely to be a network of loosely connected cells, bound by a common ideology, than a rigid military-style hierarchy with a clear-cut political goal. While the hierarchies of leadership still do exist, the modern terrorist can act with much greater autonomy than ever before.

*Use of modern communications*

The development of unifying communications technologies—particularly the Internet—allows a terrorist cell to operate without the support of a large terrorist organization or a wealthy state sponsor. Cryptography and global telecommunications technologies have provided terrorist networks with new tools to communicate in a secure fashion with members scattered across the globe. This allows members to be distributed around the world with little physical contact between them. Such a situation presents grave difficulties to counter-terrorist forces. The investigation into the September 11 attacks has revealed how difficult it can be to uncover a small number of plotters, even when they spend substantial time in the target country before the attack. The prospect of tracking a widely scattered group of individuals, who can be anywhere in the world, and who can communicate in a secure and instantaneous fashion with each other, presents a daunting challenge to security services.

*From state-sponsorship to sub-state sponsorship*

During the 1980's and 90's, almost every major terrorist attack had the backing, to one degree or another, of a sovereign state. Likewise, every international terrorist organization that left its mark on history was backed by a state; those that did not have state sponsorship remained purely local phenomena, and rarely carried out significant attacks outside of their sphere of influence. However, in recent years the support of nations has increasingly been replaced by the support of a multi-national "terrorist conglomerate".

Sub-state entities are increasingly providing the financial and logistical support needed for international terrorism to operate. Such sub-state terrorism sponsors tend to group together in united fronts in order to assist one another in their operations. Osama bin Ladin's International Islamic Front for Jihad against the U.S. and Israel brings together nearly a dozen Islamic terrorist organizations of different countries. Such conglomerations are independent of state sponsorship, forming loose, transnational affiliations based on religious or ideological affinity and their common hatred of the West in general.

*Individual extremism and domestic terrorism*

To make matters even more complicated, today's terrorist may not even be affiliated with any known group. He can be an individual motivated by rage or hatred, whose operational knowledge is gleaned from the Internet and whose inspiration and marching orders come from an extremist website. Many of the most recent terror attacks were organized from the bottom up. Marc Sageman, who researches terrorist networks, notes:

> The [jihad] movement has now degenerated into something like the internet. Spontaneous groups of friends, as in Madrid and Casablanca, who have few links to any central leadership, are generating sometimes very dangerous terrorist operations, notwithstanding their frequent errors and poor training[1].

In some cases, a group of individuals, motivated by religious zeal, expresses a desire to act on jihadist internet forums, and thus comes to the attention of jihad "talent spotters". After ascertaining the group's commitment, the talent spotter puts them in contact with operational leaders, who facilitate the attack.

These individuals, with no history of terrorist activities, pose perhaps the greatest risk; they have no defined place in an established hierarchy and are on no government's watch-list of possible terrorists.

# 3   Main Focus of Threat Indicators

## 3.1   Capability

The capabilities of a terrorist organization comprise both military or operational capabilities and existential, or organizational capabilities—those resources which enable the terrorist group to exist as a viable entity.

By existential capabilities, we mean all those activities which enhance or sustain the terrorist organization's routine operations. These include its ability to finance its activities, to recruit members and garner support among its internal constituency, and to communicate quickly and securely across national borders.

In addition, there are the organization's operational capabilities: its ability to mount successful attacks on its chosen targets. Such capabilities include military training of members, technical expertise, ability to blend in with a local population while planning and executing the attacks, ability to gather pre-operational intelligence, etc.[2]

As the network of global jihad fragments and metastasizes, the capabilities of cells have come to overshadow the capabilities of "meta-organizations" in determining the degree of threat. This, in turn has led to the increasing importance of the human element in terrorists' operational capabilities: the talents and capabilities of individual members. In traditional threat-assessment models, the makeup of the terrorist group's

---

[1] Marc Sageman. "Understanding Terror Networks." November 1, 2004. http://www.fpri.org/enotes/20041101.middleeast.sageman.understandingterrornetworks.html

[2] For a discussion of "organizational activities" vs. "operational activities," see The RAND Corporation's "The Dynamic Terrorist Threat: An Assessment of Group Motivations and Capabilities in a Changing World," by Kim Cragin and Sara A. Daly.

rank and file was given less weight than the character of the group's leadership. Due to the fact that today's terrorist attack is likely to be organized from the bottom up, the characteristics of individual cell members play a significant role in determining both the cell's choice of targets and its choice of *modus operandi.*

## 3.2  Motivation

It is usual when analyzing terrorists' motivation to focus on hostile intent—whether stated or actively demonstrated—toward the target country. However, such an analysis may miss key factors in terrorist psychology. The motivations to carry out an attack may have little to do with enmity toward a perceived enemy, and everything to do with the organization's own constituency. Thus, throughout the current "intifada," the various Palestinian terrorist organizations have competed in carrying out attacks against Israel, not because of any desire to change Israeli policies, but in order to win status among their own constituencies. The equation: successful attacks = political and/or social power, is the main motivating factor in this kind of activity.

What is needed is not merely an indicator to measure hostile intent, but an indicator—or more realistically a whole suite of indicators—to measure perceived social benefits of an attack to the attacking organization.

In addition, the ideological motivation of the organization will play a role in determining the degree of threat it poses. In general, organizations promoting a religious or apocalyptic agenda should be viewed with more concern than those with more limited nationalistic goals.

## 3.3  Past Activities

While our model makes extensive use of an organization's operational "portfolio" and history, past attacks should not be used as the sole indicator of an organization's present capabilities. Since terrorist organizations are dynamic entities, it is important to take into consideration the threat posed by organizations that are transient entities, with no prior history of hostile activity. For example, the London subway bombings were carried out by individuals with no history of terrorist activities, even though the coordinator of the attacks may have been involved in previous terrorist activities[3].

In addition, we should not neglect groups with a well-founded radical ideology, but which hitherto have not carried out any actual attacks. For example, Hizb al-Tahrir does not directly advocate violence, but instead serves as a kind of recruiting agency for the global jihad. The organization's radical ideology is well thought-out and internally consistent, and often serves as an initiation into the ideas of radical jihad for jihad "newbies". Organizations like this not only exert a tremendous influence on individuals and cells, but also espouse an ideology that, while not calling for activity at this stage, nonetheless reserves the right to move from words to actions at a later stage. Indeed, Hizb al-Tahrir's long-term strategy foresees the use of open warfare (jihad) as soon as a "critical mass" of loyal members has been reached[4].

---

[3] "Terror Ruling Favors the U.S.: A British judge says a man suspected of plotting to set up an Oregon training camp can be extradited," *LA Times*, January 6, 2006.

[4] Ariel Cohen, "Hizb ut-Tahrir: An Emerging Threat to U.S. Interests in Central Asia." The Heritage Foundation. http://www.heritage.org/Research/RussiaandEurasia/BG1656.cfm

## 3.4  Intergroup Influences and Group Dynamics

Other factors that must be taken into account when determining threat indicators are the ways in which terrorist groups and individuals influence one another. This is particularly important due to the interconnectedness of modern terror organizations, notably the global jihad movement[5].

### 3.4.1  Operational Influences

Operational influence can be either indirect, as in the case of "copy cat" attacks, or direct, as when organizations share technical expertise with other organizations. Generally, such direct influence will take place between organizations that already share a common ideology.

In addition, the cell-based nature of modern jihadist groups means that the sharing of operational expertise will depend on other factors, among them the cell's ability to exploit technical means of information sharing. For example, cell members have access to a variety of technical information derived from internet forums, jihadist websites, etc. However, the ability to download files on bomb-making does not in itself convey a high level of technical expertise. In the words of internet terror tracker Adrian Weisburd, "Using internet instructions to learn how to make TATP is a singularly Bad Idea™"[6].

The sharing of technical expertise takes on greater significance when organizations not only share information, but also share the services of technical personnel. The RAND publication "Aptitude for destruction: organizational learning in terrorist groups and its implications for combating terrorism" makes a useful distinction between "explicit knowledge" and "tacit knowledge":

> *Explicit* knowledge—e.g., recipes for explosive materials, blueprints for attractive targets, weapons or other technologies—can be transferred readily to a terrorist group, provided it can find an appropriate and willing source. *Tacit* knowledge—e.g., proficiency in mixing explosives safely or the military expertise and operational intuition needed to plan an operation well—is more difficult to transfer from one group to another.[7]

The true measure of increased operational capabilities based on sharing of information will thus depend as much on the sharing of technical personnel as on the sharing of information. For this reason, it is necessary to develop an indicator of "connectedness", i.e. some measure of how well a specific cell is connected to other like-minded cells or groups. This indicator will need to be based on the kind of social network analysis done by researchers like Marc Sageman, who analyzed family and

---

[5] See also: *"The Dynamic Terrorist Threat* An Assessment of Group Motivations and Capabilities in a Changing World." Prepared for the United States Air Force. RAND Corporation.

[6] A. Aaron Weisburd, "Global Jihad, the Internet and Opportunities for Counter-Terror Operations." http://haganah.org.il/harchives/004824.html.

[7] Brian A. Jackson et al. "Aptitude for destruction: organizational learning in terrorist groups and its implications for combating terrorism". RAND Corporation 2005.

friendship bonds, group dynamics, and sociological factors among a sample of some 400 jihadi terrorists[8].

### 3.4.2 Ideological Influence

It is also true that the cross-pollination of ideas can take place in the realm of ideology, and this can be even more consequential than the sharing of operational information. In essence, this is precisely what has transformed al-Qaida from an organization (or network of organizations) into a movement. And while much of the groundwork for spreading Wahabbism was laid in the early 1980's by global Saudi-funded institutions, the radicalization of these institutions by al-Qaida-trained ideologues is one of the factors in spawning independent terrorist cells around the world.

Due to economic and social isolation in some countries—especially in Europe—young Muslims are particularly at risk of radicalization. Thus, it will be necessary to develop some measure of radicalization and "ideological influence" in the host society: For every X moderate Muslims, we can find Y adherents of radical Jihad. Of those Y adherents, we can expect to find Z individuals who are ready and willing to go beyond expressing extremist ideas on an internet forum.

## 4  Organization-Specific Indicators: An Example

All of the factors discussed above are helpful in generating a set of organization-specific threat indicators, once the venue is known. For purposes of illustration, we will base the following example on a tourist venue in the United States. Using the considerations outlined previously, we can come up with a partial list of threat indicators. For example, we might conclude that the greatest threat to tourist sites in the United States is likely to be posed by groups or cells having the following characteristics:

### Structure and Reach

- *Supported by a state or sub-state entity.* The stronger such support, the greater the resources at the disposal of the group, and the more ambitious a potential attack is likely to be.
- *Loose network affiliated with other like-minded cells or groups around the world.* Such international connections are particularly useful in the planning stages of an attack, and facilitate the escape of those directly involved in supervising and perpetrating the attack. Groups posing the greatest danger are those with a broad-based support system around the world. Such a support system often consists of fundraising and political activists living outside the group's normal sphere of operations.
- *Is able to blend in with immigrant groups in the target country.* Because of the need for extensive planning and pre-operational intelligence, the members of a

---

[8] See for example, Sageman's book, Understanding Terror Networks. University of Pennsylvania Press (2004).

potential attack cell would be required to spend long periods under cover inside the target country. Connections with a particular ethnic group within that country could greatly facilitate the existence of "sleeper" cells.

**Motivation**

- *Motivated by religion or quasi-religious ideology.* This entails a preference for mass-casualty attacks, as well as the potential to carry out suicide attacks. Such organizations may share some of the characteristics of apocalyptic cults.
- *Shows past history of hatred of the target country/countries.* Most terrorist groups are fairly vocal about their agenda, in order to recruit like-minded individuals to their camp. Although not all vocally anti-Western groups pose a threat, it is probable that those that do pose a threat will make no secret of their intentions.
- *Motivated by desire to win points among an internal constituency.* Organizations that have "something to prove" to their supporters are more likely to use terrorist attacks as a means of demonstrating their viability as a force to be reckoned with. Likewise, organizations that are jockeying for position among others espousing the same general goals may compete with one another in carrying out attacks.

**Characteristics of Past Attacks**

- *Has carried out attacks outside its local sphere of influence.* Often, this is a function of how much assistance the group receives from a state or sub-state sponsor. Those foreign-based organizations that have demonstrated capability to act far from their home ground are naturally to be considered of greater threat.
- *Has carried out attacks against similar targets.* For example, an organization that has singled out tourism targets for attack is one whose goals generally include inflicting economic damage on the target country. This is true of some domestic groups, such as ETA, as well as of international terrorist groups. However, organizations that single out tourist sites popular with international travelers generally have a more globe-spanning goal. International tourism-related targets are often chosen because they represent the antithesis of the terrorists' own worldview: they stand for openness, diversity, and globalization.
- *Has carried out attacks against targets or interests belonging to the country under consideration.* For example, a history of attacks on American targets indicates not only a pre-existing enmity toward the United States, but more importantly, a readiness to transform this enmity into action.

## 5   Directions for Future Development

In order to "automate" the selection of indicators such as those listed above, an extensive dataset is needed which will allow these factors to be calculated from statistical trends. For the system to be truly dynamic, it should include open source data-mining abilities. This would help in tracking the activities of the different organizations in order to discover meaningful patterns and trends, which could impact on the organization's target selection criteria and modus operandi. In addition, it would provide the basis for a continual reevaluation of the organizational factors that enter into the equation, as well as the availability of resources that could be used in the perpetration of certain types of attack. The result will be a dynamic threat assessment apparatus which could be programmed to "flag" certain types of incidents and organization when the relevant threat indices reach a critical level. The system could also be programmed to apply a set of pre-determined indicators when data on particular venues was entered, in order to match organizational capabilities, motivations, and targeting patterns to particular scenarios.

The enhancement of the model to include advanced data-mining technologies will enable it to become self-adjusting to changes in terrorist organization make-up, local circumstances, and political realities.

# 6   Conclusion: Threat Assessment as an Element in Effective Defense

Clearly, the very nature of the threat of religious and ideological terrorism places severe limitations on effective intelligence gathering and evaluation. This, in turn, places an even greater burden of responsibility on the last link in the chain of counter-terrorism—the defensive measures in place at any given installation. In many cases, these anti-terrorism measures may not be merely the last line of defense; they may be the *only* line of defense.

Lacking the necessary resources to plan for every eventuality, those responsible for installation protection all too often fall back on planning for "worst case" scenarios. However, this often entails the over-allocation of resources to some of the least likely scenarios. Preparing for the "low risk / high consequence" attack is not the only (or even the best) response. Scarce resources can be better exploited if a way is found to classify threats according to likelihood, and not just according to the severity of consequences.

Yet the breadth of knowledge gained by years of academic study of terrorist organizations is usually not available to most law-enforcement agencies or installation protection forces; there are only so many professional analysts to go around. At times, decisions regarding the protection of a particular installation will need to be taken quickly, based on vague warnings from the national or state level, with little time for an in-depth analysis of the organizations that might pose a risk.

What is needed is a way to reproduce, or "automate" this expertise using advanced data-mining and artificial intelligence, with the goal of producing a model that could be used by law-enforcement agencies and installation-protection personnel, who may not have the extensive knowledge that experienced intelligence analysts and terrorism researchers could bring to the problem.

It is clear that our model must take into account the dynamic nature of terrorist organizations, and that the end product should offer some guidelines as to the kind of modus operandi that the organizations under consideration might favor.

For such an automated system to be useful, the dataset should be extensive enough to allow statistical trends to be extracted. The composite of these trends would help determine which organizations (or types of organization) pose the greatest threat to the venue in question. This information could then be applied to the specific venue based on the known characteristics of the installation—data which would already be in the hands of installation security planners.

The end product would be a risk-assessment model that would allow security planners to combine what they know of their installation's vulnerabilities and "symbolic profile" with indices of threat based on a comprehensive dataset of known terrorist entities. The combined data would give some idea of the types of attack that might be employed against the installation, and a profile of the most likely attackers. In effect, the output would provide planners with a statistical basis for allocation of resources according to considerations of high consequence / low probability vs. low consequence / high probability. The goal is not so much to give a precise prediction of who, how, and where; but rather to provide a better basis for deciding how best to allocate finite counter-terrorism resources.

# Practical Algorithms for Destabilizing Terrorist Networks

Nasrullah Memon and Henrik Legind Larsen

Software Intelligence Security Research Center,
Department of Software and Media Technology
Aalborg University Niels Bohrs Vej 8
6700 Esbjerg Denmark
{nasrullah, legind}@cs.aaue.dk

**Abstract.** This paper uses centrality measures from complex networks to discuss how to destabilize terrorist networks. We propose newly introduced algorithms for constructing hierarchy of covert networks, so that investigators can view the structure of terrorist networks / non-hierarchical organizations, in order to destabilize the adversaries. Based upon the degree centrality, eigenvector centrality, and dependence centrality measures, a method is proposed to construct the hierarchical structure of complex networks. It is tested on the September 11, 2001 terrorist network constructed by Valdis Krebs. In addition we also propose two new centrality measures i.e., position role index (which discovers various positions in the network, for example, leaders / gatekeepers and followers) and dependence centrality (which determines who is depending on whom in a network). The dependence centrality has a number of advantages including that this measure can assist law enforcement agencies in capturing / eradicating of node (terrorist) which may disrupt the maximum of the network.

## 1 Introduction

Many diverse systems in different research fields can be described as complex networks, that is, connecting the nodes together by the edges with nontrivial topological structures (Strogatz, S. H., 2001). Detailed works have been focused on several distinctive statistical properties sharing among a large amount of real world networks, to cite examples, the clustering effect (Albert, R. and Barabási, A.L., 2002, Dorogovtsev, S.N.; Mendes,J.F.F., 2002) and the right-skewed degree distribution (Albert, R. and Barabási, A.L., 1999). In this paper we consider another property sharing among many networks, the hierarchical structure of a complex network.

Hierarchy, as one common feature for many real world networks has attracted special attention in recent years (Ravasz, E., Barabási, A.L., 2003). In a network, there are usually some groups of nodes where the nodes in each group are highly interconnected with each other, while there are few or no links between the groups. These groups can induce a high degree of clustering, which can be measured with the connectivity probability for a pair of the neighbors of one node. This property coexists usually with the right-skewed degree distributions. The coexistence of these two properties tells us that the groups should combine in a hierarchical manner. Hierarchy is one of the key aspects of a theoretical model (Ravasz, E., Barabási, A.L., 2003) to

S. Mehrotra et al. (Eds.): ISI 2006, LNCS 3975, pp. 389–400, 2006.

capture the statistical characteristics of a large number of real networks, including some social networks (Newman, M. E. J., 2003).

As covert networks share some features with innocent individuals (overt networks), they are harder to identify because they mask their transactions. Another complicating factor is that covert / terrorist networks are often embedded in a much larger population. Hence, it is desirable to have tools to correctly classify individuals in covert networks so that the resources for destabilizing them will be used more efficiently.

To assist law enforcement and intelligence agencies to ascertain terrorist network knowledge efficiently and effectively, we proposed a framework of automated analysis, visualization and destabilization of terrorist networks (Memon, N. et al., 2004). Based on this framework, we developed a prototype called *iMiner* that incorporated several advanced techniques, for automatically detecting cells from a network, identifying various roles in a network (e.g., central members, gatekeepers, and followers), and may also assist law enforcement about the effect on the network after capturing a terrorist in a network.

The three innovative points of our paper are:

- The use of new measure Position Role Index (PRI) on the pattern of efficiency introduced by Vito Latora and Massimo Marchiori. This measure identifies leaders / gatekeepers and followers in the network. The algorithms for efficiency, importance of critical nodes in a network and PRI are also presented.
- The use of another measure known as Dependence Centrality (DC) which discovers who is depending on whom in a network. The algorithm of DC is also presented.
- Estimate possible hierarchical structure of a complex network by applying degree centrality and Eigenvector centrality from social network analysis (SNA) literature and combining it with new measure dependence centrality. The algorithm for estimating the possible hierarchical structure of the terrorist network is also shown. The all the algorithms presented in the paper are designed and developed by the authors.

The remainder of the paper is organized as follows: Section 2 briefly describes the motivation of this research and existing destabilizing approaches for terrorist networks; Section 3 describes fundamentals of networks analysis; whereas Section 4 discusses algorithms and techniques for destabilizing terrorist networks. Section 5 shows how hierarchy is constructed from covert networks and Section 6 concludes the paper.

## 2   Motivation

When intelligence agencies arrest a few members of a terrorist cell, how can they know if the cell has been disabled?

Social scientists have imagined individual terrorists as nodes on a graph, most of them are connected to only one or two other nodes. Using such cellular graphs, researchers have proposed ways of estimating whether a chain of relationships has been effectively shattered, even when some of its members elude capture.

There is a growing amount of literature on modeling terrorist networks as graphs, an outgrowth of the existing literature concerning other types of criminal networks (Krebs, V., 2002, Klerks, P., 2001). There is also a small amount of literature on destabilizing networks, modeled as graphs, by seeing how connections do or do not dissipate when nodes are removed (Carley, K. M., Lee, J-S. and Krackhardt, D., 2002; Carley, K. M. et al., 2003).

A graph model, however, may not be the best one available for representing a typical terrorist organization (Farley, J. D., 2003). His views are that modeling terrorist networks as graphs does not give us enough information to deal with the threat. Lattice theory is the abstract study of order and hierarchy. In terrorist organizations, hierarchy appears to matter. "Modeling terrorist cells as graphs ignores an important aspect of their structure, namely their hierarchy, and the fact that they are composed of leaders and followers" (Farley, J. D., 2003).

We have related the concept of hierarchy and graph and predicted the structure of a non hierarchical network so that it can be viewed as a hierarchy. Our results for September 11 terrorist network (Krebs, V., 2002), are in excellent agreement to reality.

## 3  Social Network Analysis (SNA)

In general, the network studied in this paper can be represented by an undirected and un-weighted graph $G = (V, E)$, where $V$ is the set of vertices (or nodes) and $E$ is the set of edges (or links). Each edge connects exactly one pair of vertices, and a vertex pair can be connected by (a maximum of) one edge, i.e., multi-connection is not allowed.

A terrorist network consists of $V$ set of actors (nodes) and $E$ relations (ties or edges) between these actors. The nodes may be individuals, groups (terrorist cells), organizations, or terrorist camps. The ties may fall within a level of analysis (e.g. individual to individual ties) or may cross levels of analysis (individual-to-group analysis). A terrorist network can change in its nodes, links, groups, and even the overall structure. In this paper, we focus on detection and description of node level dynamics.

Mathematically, a network can be represented by a matrix called the *adjacency matrix* $\mathbf{A}$, which in the simplest case is an $n \times n$ symmetric matrix, where $n$ is the number of vertices in the network. The adjacency matrix has elements.

$A_{ij} = 1$, if there is an edge between vertices i and j, and 0 otherwise.

The matrix is symmetric since if there is an edge between $i$ and $j$ then clearly there is also an edge between $j$ and $i$. Thus $A_{ij} = A_{ji}$.

### 3.1  Node Level Measures

As terrorists establish new relations or break existing relations with others, their position roles, and power may change accordingly. These node dynamics resulting from relation changes can be captured by a set of centrality measures from SNA. The centrality measures address the question, "Who is the most important or central person in the network?"

There are many answers to this question, depending on what we mean by important. Perhaps the simplest of centrality measures is *degree centrality*, also called simply *degree*. The degree of a vertex in a network is the number of edges attached to it. In mathematical terms, the degree $k_i$ of a vertex $i$ is (Newman, M. E. J., 2003):

$$k_i = \sum_{j=1}^{n} A_{ij} \tag{1}$$

Though simple, *degree* is often a highly effective measure of the influence or importance of a node: in many social settings people with more connections tend to have more power.

A more sophisticated version of the same idea is the so-called *eigenvector centrality*. Where degree centrality gives a simple count of the number of connections a vertex has, eigenvector centrality acknowledges that not all connections are equal. If we denote the centrality of vertex $i$ by $x_i$, then we can allow for this effect by making $x_i$ proportional to the average of the centralities of $i$'s network neighbors (Newman, M. E. J., 2003):

$$x_i = \frac{1}{\lambda} \sum_{i=1}^{n} A_{ij} x_j \tag{2}$$

where $\lambda$ is a constant. Defining the vector of centralities $\mathbf{x} = (x1; x2; : : :)$, we can rewrite this equation in matrix form as:

$$\lambda x = A \bullet x \tag{3}$$

Hence we see that $\mathbf{x}$ is an eigenvector of the adjacency matrix with eigenvalue $\lambda$. Assuming that we wish the centralities to be non-negative, it can be shown that $\lambda$ must be the largest eigenvalue of the adjacency matrix and $\mathbf{x}$ the corresponding eigenvector.

## 4   Destabilizing Terrorist Networks

### 4.1   The Efficiency E(G) of a Network

The network efficiency E (G) is a measure to quantify how efficiently the nodes of the network exchange information (Latora, V., Marchiori, M., 2004). To define efficiency of G first we calculate the shortest path lengths $\{d_{ij}\}$ between two generic points $i$ and $j$. Let us now suppose that every vertex sends information along the network, through its edges. The efficiency $\varepsilon_{ij}$ in the communication between vertex i and j is inversely proportional to the shortest distance: $\varepsilon_{ij} = 1/d_{ij} \ \forall \ i, j$ when there is no path in the graph between i, and $j$, we get $d_{ij} = +\infty$ and consistently $\varepsilon_{ij} = 0$. N is known as the size of the network or the numbers of nodes in the graph. Consequently the average efficiency of the graph of G can be defined as (Latora V., Marchiori, M., 2004):

$$E(G) = \frac{\sum_{i \neq j \in G} \varepsilon_{ij}}{N(N-1)} = \frac{1}{N(N-1)} \sum_{i \neq j \in G} \frac{1}{d_{ij}} \tag{4}$$

The above formula gives a value of E that can vary in the range $[0, \infty]$, while it be more practical to normalize E in the interval of $[0, 1]$.

## 4.2  The Critical Components of a Network

Latora V. et al recently proposed a method to determine network critical components based on the efficiency of the network briefly discussed in the previous subsection. This method focuses on the determination of the critical nodes. The general theory and all the details can be found in Ref. (Latora V., Marchiori, M., 2004).

The main idea is to use as a measure of the centrality of a node i the drop in the network efficiency caused by deactivation of the node. The importance I (node$_i$) of the $_i$th node of the graph G is therefore:

$$I\,(node_i) \equiv \Delta E = E\,(G) - E\,(G - node_i)\,,\, i = 1,...,N, \tag{5}$$

Where $G - node_i$ indicates the network obtained by deactivating node$_i$ in the graph G. The most important nodes, i.e. the critical nodes are the ones causing the highest $\Delta E$. The results of deactivation of nodes for 9-11 hijackers and their affiliates are shown in figure 1 and figure 2.

## 4.3  Position Role Index (PRI)

The PRI is our proposed measure which highlights a clear distinction between followers and gatekeepers (It is a fact that leaders may act as gatekeepers). It depends on the basic definition of efficiency as discussed in equation (4). It is also a fact that the efficiency of a network in presence of followers is low in comparison to their absence in the network. This is because they are usually less connected nodes and their presence increases the number of low connected nodes in a network, thus decreasing its efficiency.

If we plot the values on the graph, the nodes which are plotted below x-axis are followers, whereas the nodes higher than remaining nodes with higher values on positive y axis are the gatekeepers. While the nodes which are on the x-axis usually central nodes, which can easily bear the loss of any node. The leaders tend to hide on x-axis there.

We applied this measure on the network of alleged 9-11 hijackers, (Krebs, V., 2002) and results are shown in figure 1. The algorithms for PRI, efficiency of network and critical components of network are described in Exhibit 1.

## Exhibit 1. Algorithms for Efficiency, Delta Efficiency and Position Role Index

### Algorithm for Efficiency E(G)

Let G be a graph, N is a set of nodes which are contained by G and E is the set of edges through which the nodes of graph are connected. Let m is the number of elements in N

Input:
Graph G, N set of its nodes
Output:
Efficiency of Graph G
Let s=0 and e=0
For each element n1 in N
    For each element n2 in N
    Let s = s + 1/ d (n1, n2)
    Next n1
    Let e= e + s
Next n2
Let e=1/ (m * (m− 1)) * e
Return e
Where "e" is the efficiency of the graph and d(n1, n2) is the function which gives us the distance of shortest path from n1 to n2.

### Algorithm for Finding Delta Efficiency:

Suppose n is the node for which we are finding delta efficiency. Let G' be a sub-graph similar to G, only the difference is that E is the set of edges through which the nodes of graph are connected except the edges which originate or point to n. (G' does not contain any edge to or from n). Let N is a set of Nodes in G' and m is the number of elements in N.

Input:
Graph G, N set of its nodes, n is the node for which we are finding the value of Delta Efficiency and remove edges to or from n in G to get G'
Output:

Delta Efficiency of n in G.
Let s=0 and de=0
For each element n1 in N
    For each element n2 in N
    Let s = s + 1/ d (n1, n2)
    Next n1
    Let de= de + s
Next n2
Let de=1/ (m * (m − 1)) * de
Let efficiency=E (G)
Let de = ((efficiency − de) / efficiency)
Return de

### Algorithm for Finding Position Role Index

Suppose n is the node for which we are finding delta efficiency. Let G' be the sub-graph that is similar to G − n1. (G' does not contain any edge to or from n and also it does not contain n). Let N is a set of Nodes in G' and m is the number of elements in N.

Input:
Graph G, N set of its nodes, n is the node for which we are finding the value of NI and remove n and all the edges coming from or to n in G to get G'
Output:
NI of n in G.
Let s=0 and ni=0
For each element n1 in N
    ni=0
    For each element n2 in N
    Let s = s + 1/ d (n1, n2)
    Next n1
    Let ni= ni + s
Next n2
Let ni = 1/ (m * (m − 1)) * ni
Let efficiency = E (G)
Let ni=((efficiency − ni)/efficiency)
Return ni

## 4.4  Dependence Centrality (DC)

The DC is the recently introduced measure by the authors (Memon, N., Legind, H.L., 2006). The dependence centrality of a node is defined as how much that node is dependent on any other node in the network.  Mathematically it can be written as:

$$DC_{mn} = \sum_{m \neq p, p \in G} \frac{d_{mn}}{N_p} + \Omega \qquad (6)$$

Where **m** is the root node which depends on **n** by **DC$_{mn}$** centrality and **N$_p$** actually is the Number of geodesic paths coming from **m** to **p** through **n**, and **d$_{mn}$** is geodesic distance from **m** to **n**. The $\Omega$ is taken 1 if graph is connected and 0 in case it is disconnected. In this paper we take $\Omega$ as 1, because we consider that graph is connected. The first part of the formula tells us that:

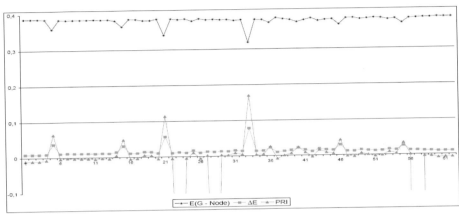

**Fig. 1.** The efficiency of the original network is E (G) = 0.395. The removed node is shown on x-axis; the efficiency of the graph once the node is removed is reported as E (G – Node$_i$), while the importance of the node (drop of efficiency) is shown as $\Delta$ E. While position role index shown as PRI of the removed node. The results prove important aspects of the network and confirmed that Mohammed Atta (node # 33) was the ring leader.

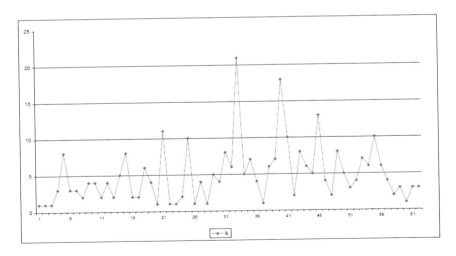

**Fig. 2.** An alternative measure of the importance of the node (k), the degree of (i.e. the number of links incident with) the removed node

How many times **m** uses **n** to communicate other node **p** of the network? In simple words **p** is every node of the network, to which **m** is connected through **n** (The connection represents the shortest path of node **m** to **p**, and **n** is in between). $N_p$ represents the number of alternatives available to **m** to communicate to **p** and $d_{mn}$ is the multiplicative inverse of geodesic distance (**1/d**).

## Algorithm for Dependence Centrality

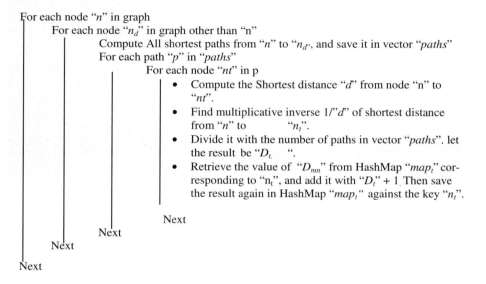

For each node "$n$" in graph
    For each node "$n_d$" in graph other than "$n$"
        Compute All shortest paths from "$n$" to "$n_d$", and save it in vector "*paths*"
        For each path "$p$" in "*paths*"
            For each node "$nt$" in p
- Compute the Shortest distance "$d$" from node "$n$" to "$nt$".
- Find multiplicative inverse $1/$"$d$" of shortest distance from "$n$" to "$n_t$".
- Divide it with the number of paths in vector "*paths*". let the result be "$D_t$".
- Retrieve the value of "$D_{mn}$" from HashMap "*map*," corresponding to "$n_t$", and add it with "$D_t$" + 1. Then save the result again in HashMap "*map_t*" against the key "$n_t$".

            Next
        Next
    Next
Next

This measure shows that how much node **m** is dependent on the node **n**. We can also say that how much node **n** is useful to node **m** in order to communicate with other nodes of the network.

The node which has less in summation of *dependence centrality might be key player* i.e., leader / gatekeeper, who usually direct many other peripherals and control communication. The key players have low *dependence centrality* (DC) as they have large number of direct links with other nodes of the network and they do not depend on others to communicate with those nodes.

When we tabulate the Dependence Centrality (DC), a matrix is obtained; where each row corresponds to a particular node, its DC against all the nodes are represented in the form of values (1 $\leq$ values $\geq$ (total nodes – 1)) at different columns in the same row. When we sum up all of these values in a row, the sum shows how much the node is dependent on other nodes. The lower the sum, the less will be the node *dependent* on other nodes or that node is said to be an *independent* node. Similarly if we sum each column, it will show how much all the nodes depend on that particular node which is associated with that column. The dependence centralities of the hijackers and their affiliates as shown in figure 3 can be seen at http://cs.aue.aau.dk/~nasrullah/DC_9_11.htm. There are some interesting results from this 62x62 matrix that shows, if *node 33* is removed, *nodes 23 and 28* will also be *isolated completely* from the network. Similarly if *node 38* is eradicated/captured, *nodes 20, 22, and 26* are *totally isolated* from the network. The rationale behind that is the nodes (for example, 23, 28; 20, 22, 26) are completely depending on the nodes (for example, 33 and 38 respectively). If the nodes are completely depending on the other nodes, they will be isolated (cut-off from the network completely) by capturing the node on which those nodes are depending.

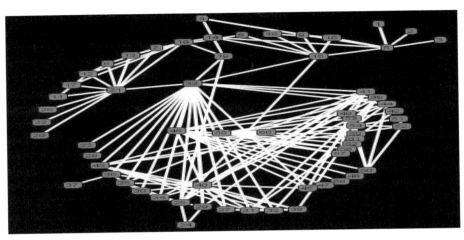

**Fig. 3.** 9/11 hijackers and their affiliates dataset. The names of terrorists shown in Appendix A at the end of paper.

## 5   Construction of Hierarchy for 9-11 Terrorists' Network

By using algorithms shown in Exhibit 2, we have constructed the *hierarchy* shown in figure 4 (using *iMiner*), of the hijackers involved in 9/11 terrorist attack and their affiliates (from the publicly available dataset as shown in figure 3).

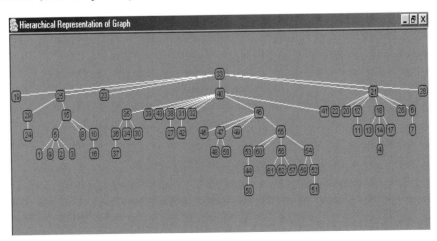

**Fig. 4.** Hierarchy discovered by iMiner from graph shown in figure 3, using Algorithms shown in Exhibit 2

The hierarchy clearly suggests that *Muhammad Atta* (33) was the key leader of the plot. While *Marvan Al Shehhi* (40) was assisting him as he is below in the hierarchy. They both were suggested as potential leaders in 9/11 attack and led their respective groups. They were also both members of Hamburg Cell. *Fayez Ahmed* (31), and *Mohand Al Shehhi* (42), who were in the same hijacked plane with *Marvan Al Shehhi,* are below Marvan Al Shehhi. While *Abdul Aziz Alomari* (39), *Waleed Al Shehhi* (38) are in 3rd level in the hierarchy.

The intelligence agencies can easily detect who are potential leaders / gatekeepers and even peripheries by using these new algorithms.

### Exhibit 2. Algorithms for Constructing Hierarchy

### Algorithm. Converting undirected graph G into directed D

1. Take any node "n" of graph G, and find its neighbors "N".
2. Take a node "s" such that s ∈ N (N is set of neighbors of n.). Compare Degree Centrality of s to Degree Centrality of n,
   - if Degree Centrality of s > Degree Centrality of n, Mark a directed edge from s to n.
   - if Degree Centrality of s < Degree Centrality of n, Mark a directed edge from n to s.
   - if Degree Centrality of s = Degree Centrality of n
     1. Compare Eigen-Vector Centrality of s to Eigen-Vector Centrality of n,
        - If Eigen-Vector Centrality of s > Eigen-Vector Centrality of n, Mark a directed edge from s to n.
        - If Eigen-Vector Centrality of s < Eigen-Vector Centrality of n, Mark a directed edge from s to n.
        - If Eigen-Vector Centrality of s = Eigen-Vector Centrality of n, Ignore the link.
3. Repeat Step 2 for every member of N.
4. Repeat Step 1 for every node of graph G.

### Algorithm. To make Tree T from Directed Graph D

1. Take any node "n" of directed Graph "D", and find all the nodes "N(n)" adjacent to edges originating from node n. and mark them as Children of n. Here N(n) is neighbors N of node n.
2. Find all the nodes (parents) "P" adjacent to edges pointing to node n and mark them as Parents of n.
3. Repeat step 1 and 2 for all nodes of Directed Graph D.
4. Again take any node "n" of directed Graph "D",
5. If number of elements in P (where P is the set of Parents of n) is 0, then add "root "of Tree "T" as its parent and mark node n as children of "root".
6. If number of elements in P > 1, Remove all the nodes except "p1" from P, such that (N (p1) ∩ N (n)) is maximum.(Where N (p1) is the set of Neighbors of p1). Also mark n as Children of p1.

7. If number of elements in P is still > 1, remove all the nodes from P except the node p1, for which the n has highest Dependence Centrality. Also mark n as Children of p1.
8. If number of elements in P is still > 1, Remove all of its parents and then add "root" of Tree T as its parent and also mark node n as children of "root".
9. Repeat Step 4 to 8, for all nodes of directed graph D.
10. Draw Tree T.

## 6  Conclusions

In this paper we have proposed new practical algorithms which can assist law enforcement agencies to discover who is under the influence of whom in a network by visualizing the hierarchal chart. The position role index measure assists in finding about who is who in a network. The dependence centrality determines which individuals are depending on which nodes, in order to help investigators to disrupt the network. All the algorithms discussed in the paper are implemented in the prototype *iMiner*. The prototype can provide assistance to law enforcement agencies, indicating when the *capture* of a *specific* terrorist will likely disrupt the terrorist network. Moreover, using *iMiner* an investigator has the power to estimate the network's size, determine its membership structure, find who the most important terrorist in the network is, determine the efficiency of the network, unearth the leaders / gatekeepers / followers, and determine on which node the maximum nodes in the network depends.

## References

1. Albert, R. and A.L. Barabási, (2002) *Dynamics of complex systems: scaling laws for the period of boolean networks*, Physics Reviews. **47**
2. Albert, R. and A.L. Barabási, (1999) *Emergence of scaling in random networks*, Science, **286**:509-512
3. Carley, Kathleen M., Lee Ju-Sung, Krackhardt, D. (2002) Destabilizing Networks. *Connections* 24 (3) 79-92
4. Carley, K. M. et al. (2003) Destabilizing Dynamic Covert Networks. In *Proceedings of 8th International Command and Control Research and Technology Symposium.* Conference held at National Defense War College, Washington, DC. Evidence Based Research Vienna, VA.
5. Dorogovtsev, S.N. and J.F.F. Mendes, (2002) Evolution of Networks *Adv. Phys.* **51**, 1079
6. Farely, David J. (2003) Breaking Al Qaeda Cells: A Mathematical analysis of counterterrorism *Operations Studies in conflict terrorism.* **26**:399–411
7. Klerks, P. (2001) The network paradigm applied to criminal organizations", *Connections* **24** (3)
8. Krebs, V. (2002) Mapping Terrorist Networks, *Connections* **24**(3)
9. Latora, V., Massimo Marchiori  (2004) How Science of Complex Networks can help in developing Strategy against Terrorism, *Chaos, Solitons and Fractals* **20**, 69-75
10. Memon Nasrullah, Daniel Ortiz Arroyo, Henrik Legind Larsen (2004) *Investigative* Data Mining: A General Framework. In *Proceedings* of *International Conference on Computational Intelligence*, Istanbul, Turkey  384-387
11. Memon Nasrullah, Henrik Legind Larsen (2006) Practical Approaches for Analysis, Visualization and Destabilizing Terrorist Networks. In *Proceedings of ARES 2006: The First*

*International Conference on Availability, Reliability and Security*, Vienna University of Technology Austria.

12. Newman, M. E. J. (2003) The structure and function of complex networks, *SIAM Review* **45**, 167- 256
13. Ravasz, E. A.L. Barabási, (2003) Hierarchical organization in complex networks, *Phys. Rev. E*, **67**, 261121
14. Strogatz, S. H. (2002) Exploring Complex Networks, *Nature 410*, 268-276
15. Trusina, A. S.; Maslov, P. Minnhagen and K. Sneppen, (2004) Hierarchy and Anti-Hierarchy in Real and Scale Free Networks *Phys. Rev. Lett.* **92**, 178702

# Appendix A. Names of 9/11 Hijackers and Their Affiliates

1. Jean Marc Grandvisir
2. Abu Zubaida
3. Nizar Trabelsi
4. Abu Walid
5. Djamal Beghal
6. Mehdi Khammoun
7. Hyder Abu Doha
8. Ahmed Ressam
9. Kamel Dauod
10. Jerome Courtailler
11. Lased Ben Heni
12. Mohamed Bensakhria
13. Essoussi Laaroussi
14. Abu Qatada
15. Zaoarias Moussaoui
16. David Courtailler
17. Seifallah ben hassine
18. Tarek Maaroufi
19. Imdad Eddin Barakat Yarkas
20. Fahid al sharki
21. Essid Sami Ben Khemais

22. Madjid Sahoune
23. Abdelghani Mzoudi
24. Mohamed Belfas
25. Ramzi Bin al Shibh
26. Samir Kishk
27. Mustafa Ahmed Al Hissaw
28. Ahmed Khalil Ibrahim Samir
29. Agus Badim
30. Mounir el motassaeq
31. Fayez Ahmed
32. Wail Al Shehhi
33. Mohamed Atta
34. Zakariya Essabar
35. Said Bahaji
36. Mamoun Darkazanali
37. Mamduh Mahmud Salim
38. Waleed Al Shehhi
39. Abdul Aziz Al Omari
40. Marwan Al Shehhi
41. Ziad Jarrah

42. Mohand Al Shehhi
43. Satam Suqami
44. Ahmed Al Haznawi
45. Lotfi Raissi
46. Hani Hunjor
47. Rayed Mohammed Abdullah
48. Bandar Alhazmi
49. Salem Alhazmi
50. Ahmed Alghamdi
51. Raed Hijazi
52. Nabil al Marabh
53. Hamza Alghamdi
54. Saeed Alghamdi
55. Nawaf Al hazmi
56. Khalid Al Mindhar
57. Majed Moqed
58. Faisal al salmi
59. Ahmed alnami
60. Mohamed Abidi
61. Abdussattar Shaikh
62. Ossama Awadallah

# Combating Terrorism Insurgency Resolution Software: A Research Note

Joshua Sinai

Logos Technologies
jsinai@logos-technologies.net

This is a research note to propose the development of a combating terrorism (CbT)[1] insurgency resolution software that would operationalize and visualize all the processes involved in resolving terrorist-type insurgencies, including metrics for measures of success. Such a computerized CbT application is not currently available in the non-governmental, open source community, so this research note is intended to stimulate the development of such a prototype through collaboration between combating terrorism subject matter experts and software developers. When it is finally developed, the CbT software is intended to guide a user to formulate coordinated and integrated response strategies and tactics, whether at the governmental or analytical levels, to resolve a hypothetical or actual terrorist insurgency using a spectrum of possible responses. Of particular relevance to contemporary CbT concerns, the software program would also have the capability to respond to the spectrum of terrorist warfare, ranging from "conventional" low impact to "unconventional" high impact chemical, biological, radiological, and nuclear (CBRN) terrorist tactics and weaponry.[2]

Once developed as an operating system, the tool's objective is to enable the user—whether in government, law enforcement, intelligence, the military, or the public policy/academic communities—to use it either as an educational and training or operational application in which structured argumentation is used to formulate all the steps and processes involved in planning and executing a CbT campaign, as well as assessing the effectiveness of previous or on-going CbT campaigns in order to draw lessons and applications for future CbT responses.

Such a software program will assist the user through all phases, missions and roles not only of a prototypical, generic CbT campaign but actual on-going campaigns, from the initial response phase of the outbreak of the terrorist rebellion to conflict termination and the post-conflict reconstruction phase.

A CbT software program is required because of the absence of such tools, at least in the open source community, to enable government planners or academic analysts to use standardized templates (with the capability for adjustment to unique circumstances) to formulate counteraction campaign plans against the escalation in warfare against states by groups such as al Qaeda and its affiliates, the protracted nature of many of the internal conflicts around the world, such as in Sri Lanka and the

---

[1] Combating Terrorism is the umbrella concept for anti-terrorism, which is defensive, and countering terrorism, which is offensive.

[2] Cyber warfare is another tool in the terrorist arsenal, but this threat is not discussed in the research note, although any combating terrorism tool should have the capability to address it.

S. Mehrotra et al. (Eds.): ISI 2006, LNCS 3975, pp. 401–406, 2006.
© Springer-Verlag Berlin Heidelberg 2006

Palestinian-Israeli arena. As demonstrated by these and other cases, CbT methodo-logical frameworks need to be flexible and adaptable to take into account the fact not all terrorist insurgencies are alike, thus requiring different responses. Some terrorist insurgencies are internal (e.g., in the Palestinian-Israeli arena), while others are transnational (e.g., al Qaeda and its affiliates), and even here the nature and characteristics of terrorist rebellions differ from country to country. Moreover, some terrorist insurgencies can be resolved only through military means, whereas others can be resolved peacefully. Peace accords, for example, have been reached between governments and insurgents in El Salvador, Guatemala, and Northern Ireland, whereas in other cases, such as Israel and the Palestinians, provisional peace accords were reached in which both sides failed to strictly adhere to their provisions, resulting in partial breakdowns and violence by rejectionist Palestinian groups. In other cases (e.g., al Qaeda and its affiliates) only a military or law enforcement solution is possible because the terrorist insurgents' actions and demands are so politically extremist, undemocratic, or criminal that no compromise or conciliation is possible. Finally, terrorist insurgencies may become protracted because neither governments nor insurgents are incapable of military or peaceful resolution of their conflict.

The CbT software program will be grounded in the leading concepts and approaches in the disciplines of combating terrorism and conflict resolution, and illustrated by empirical cases of past and current terrorist insurgencies. Examples of peace treaties or accords that succeeded or failed to resolve terrorist insurgencies will be included (e.g., the 1993 Oslo Peace Accord, the 1998 Northern Ireland Accord, etc.). These peace accords would be used as models and templates by the user to formulate new peace agreements to propose resolution of hypothetical or actual terrorist insurgencies.

## Project Overview

Once operationalized, the software program will consist of two parts: first, an **overview** of generic CbT campaigns, based on previous campaigns and analytical literature about those campaigns, highlighting their strategic, operational, and tactical components, including attempts to resolve those conflicts; and second, a **series of templates** for the user to input data, ordered around the CbT plan's components and segments, including qualitative and quantitative metrics for success in resolving such conflicts. These templates are intended to serve as a decision making roadmap and a forecasting tool to provide the necessary criteria and metrics to plan, manage, measure and evaluate the results of the CbT campaign, including planning for the post-conflict, reconstruction nation building phases.

As an operational tool to manage an on-going CbT campaign, the tool will have two components. The first is **a templated tracking and reporting interface** to provide the user with situational awareness, including status summaries, of the sequencing of counter-terrorism measures in order to track the results of the CbT campaign. The second component would provide **real time or near real time, operational "situational management" of the CbT campaign** to serve as a **decision making tool**, encompassing data input and analysis from a government's overseas diplomatic, military, and intelligence reporting posts to national level CbT planners.

In such a way, the CbT tool is envisioned as an automated, easy-to-use planning, forecasting, managing, and evaluating application that will guide the user through the CbT planning process, such as conceptualizing strategically about a government's position vis-à-vis the terrorist insurgent compared to other, non-combatant parties to the conflict, building forecasts with multiple levels of detail, and creating and managing CbT action plans and conflict resolution proposals.

## Project Description

The computerized CbT working model is intended to guide the user through the entire process—from the initial steps of responding to the outbreak of a terrorist insurgency to the end-point of military victory, defeat, stalemate or peaceful conflict resolution, with each step involving, in a typical conflict, the full spectrum of options, situation reports, and ideal- and worst-case scenarios; strategic, operational, and tactical planning and execution, including coercive (military) and conciliatory (peaceful) responses; addressing the conflict's root causes; interaction between governmental, insurgent, and third party actors, including the post-conflict reconstruction of the violent-torn society.

The tool is intended to highlight the **strategic, operational, and tactical components of the CbT plan**, with sub-menus, tracking lists, and to do tasks. A series of adjustable screens will sequence the CbT campaign's components.

The tool will also include templates to guide the user to effectively **respond to terrorist insurgent grievances** that would differentiate actionable grievances versus irresolvable demands by insurgents. New criteria will be defined to distinguish between legitimate and illegitimate grievances (e.g., whether they are anchored in international law), as well as the differing perspectives of governments and insurgents towards grievances and demands. The templates would provide an ordered range of intervention points for governments. The goal is to enable decision-makers to make plausible responses at appropriate points to plausible grievances.

The tool will include a series of **templates to plan, manage, forecast, and evaluate** an actual CbT campaign's attempt to resolve an ongoing conflict, with all its components and sequences (which could be adjusted), and a capability to qualitatively and quantitatively assess the results.

The templates will also include a **representative sample of peace plans and treaties** agreed to by governments and terrorist insurgents, whose features could be integrated by the user in planning or evaluating ways to resolve their own CbT campaigns. These representative samples will be drawn from the resolution or attempted resolution of the insurgencies in El Salvador, Cambodia, Israel vis-à-vis the Palestinians, Northern Ireland, Mozambique, Sri Lanka, etc.

The templates used in the program would specify as much or as little detail as required, and could be accompanied with comments by the participants and evaluators, with one sentence or more of elaboration.

Every screen will include a **definition of terminology**. A tutorial will help to explain what is on the screen.

Once the initial CbT plan is formulated, based on the program's templates, which the program will move to the strategic, operational, and tactical components of the campaign. The **operational execution** of the plan is the primary focus of the model because it links strategic objectives and tactical actions. Thus, at the **operational level** political, diplomatic, military, judicial and law enforcement agencies are employed to achieve strategic goals through the execution of a CbT campaign. The **strategic portion** of the CbT plan consists of the plan description, a mission statement, and the plan's objectives and end-states. The **tactical portion** consists of the plan's programs, activities, and operations, including promotional actions (a variety of programs to win the targeted population's "hearts and minds," such as psychological operations and various conciliatory programs, such as civic action and nation building). The estimated cost of each of the tactical programs will be shown on a cost-benefit/return on investment screen.

The system will automatically generate **segment wrap ups** that will summarize in one screen the strategic, operational, and tactical components to make it convenient for reference later on when writing action and after-action programs and lessons learned reports.

The system will create **action to do lists and task assignments** (start and end dates for assignment, persons responsible, and the base cost of action). The to-do lists will help track actions that need to be done on a weekly, monthly, or quarterly basis and the status of actions.

For each portion of the plan, a **summary chart** will be generated to show the overall resource allocation by the plan's strategic, operational and tactical components. The summary will sort all actions according to criteria listed at the top of the chart by segment, program, CbT components, staff responsible, or specific dates to accomplish tasks.

The system will create a **planning calendar** that would serve as a mini forecasting system. Target dates will enable forecasting. **Critical target dates** will become **opportunity dates** in order to identify **need periods**. These will be shown as color coded dates on the calendar. The calendar will appear simultaneously as a small box on the screen.

In the model's concluding section, the **actual,** or in the case of a simulated campaign, the **hypothetical**, **results** of the CbT campaign will be filled in, ranging from a military to a peaceful resolution of the terrorism conflict, or a political or military stalemate. The input of data into the templates will generate information to assess the strengths and weaknesses in the **overall CbT plan**, as well as its **segments**, which will be scored in terms of their effectiveness and return on investment. The system will generate a total score for each segment. The system will then generate effectiveness graphs in black and white or color. Graphs will automatically be created on display or be manually generated.

The **concluding section** will include a provision for **outside comments** to help in **evaluating the CbT campaign** as well as in planning future CbT campaigns, such as what is likely to go right or wrong in implementing and executing the plan. A **program summary** also will be created to summarize all key components and segments of the plan for future reference.

The concluding portion will also include a section on **implementation requirements for negotiated peace settlements** that would assess the factors that are likely to make peace accords effective or ineffective in resolving terrorist conflicts in the long-term. Among the factors to be assessed in peace accord effectiveness are whether they are based on all-inclusive or partial societal consensus; the extensiveness of the treaty's details; the nature of the agreement's implementation phase, including the demobilization, disarmament, and restructuring of the armed forces (including the terrorist insurgents), police, and any paramilitary forces; the capacity of the state to perform basic administrative functions; the willingness of the state to establish the rule of law, including holding free and fair elections, promoting human rights, and creating an impartial and independent judiciary; and, if applicable, reforming socioeconomic institutions. The model would apply these effectiveness factors to assess what other factors may be necessary to resolve cases where peace accords have been reached but remain far from being fully implemented.

The grouping of segment and component screens could be arranged in different orders, and could be printed, or saved in a file. Import and export buttons would allow files to be e-mailed and posted on a password-protected web site. The comments about particular aspects of the CbT campaign could be disseminated to appropriate officials responsible for planning and executing the campaign. Anyone needing to review these screens or the whole plan will be able to write a comment on every screen individually without altering the original plan. Multiple comments would be able to be stored for each screen, and a combination of screens could be generated for appropriate officials, or, in the case of a hypothetical campaign, with the linked analytical community of participants.

Although the following matrix does not display all the components discussed above, the CbT tool would be based on such an analytical framework, which sequences the categories of government responses and hierarchically decomposes the measures accompanying each response category, including an evaluation of the CbT campaign.

| Outbreak Of Insurgency | Initial Gov't Response | Threshold Level for Conciliation | Outcome of CbT Campaign | Evaluation of CbT Campaign (Metrics of Effectiveness) |
|---|---|---|---|---|
| Root Causes: Societal Conditions | Coercive Measures | Can Insurgency Be Resolved Militarily or Peacefully? | Defeat of Government Forces | Political Impact on Targeted Society |
| Facilitating Causes: Radical Subcultures | Conciliatory Measures | Are the Group's Grievances Legitimate or Illegitimate? | Victory of Government Forces | Economic Impact on Targeted Society |
| Characteristics of Terrorist Group | Political-Military Plan: Strategic, Operational & Tactical Measures | Role of External State Sponsors in Facilitating or Exacerbating the Rebellion | Protracted "Hurting" Stalemate | Military Impact on Targeted Society |
| Nature of Group's | | Role of External | | Psychological Impact on Targeted Society |

| Leadership | | States or NGOs in Facilitating Conflict Resolution | | |
|---|---|---|---|---|
| Insurgent Grievances/ Demands | | | | Impact of CbT Campaign on Terrorist Group's Military Capability |
| Group Strategies | | | | Impact of CbT Campaign on Terrorist Group's Political Influence |
| Front Groups | | | | Impact of CbT Campaign on Terrorist Group's Finances |
| Type of Warfare Conducted by Group: "Conventional" to CBRN/Cyber | | | | Impact of CbT Campaign on Terrorist Group's Constituency and Supporters |

# A First Look at Domestic and International Global Terrorism Events, 1970–1997

Laura Dugan, Gary LaFree, and Heather Fogg

Department of Criminology and the National Center for the Study of Terrorism and the Response to Terrorism, University of Maryland, 2220 LeFrak Hall, College Park, MD 20742
{ldugan, glafree, hfogg}@crim.umd.edu

**Abstract.** While the study of terrorism has expanded dramatically since the 1970s, most analyses are limited to qualitative case studies or quantitative analyses of international incidents only—which comprise a very small proportion of all terrorist events. Until now, empirical data on both domestic and international terrorist events have not existed. We have compiled information from more than 69,000 terrorism global incidents from 1970 to 1997. Most of these data were originally collected from a private intelligence service agency using open-source data. Since we completed coding the original data in 2005, we have been continually updating and validating the data and we now call the Global Terrorism Database (GTD). We begin this paper by describing the data collection efforts and the strengths and weaknesses of relying on open-source data. We then summarize completed research projects and end by listing on-going efforts to better understand the dynamics of world-wide terrorism events.

## 1   Introduction

Although the research literature on terrorism has expanded dramatically since the 1970s, the number of studies based on systematic empirical analysis is surprisingly limited. One of the main reasons for this lack of cutting-edge empirical analysis on terrorism is the low quality of available statistical data. To remedy this, we coded and verified a previously unavailable data set composed of 67,165 terrorist events recorded for the entire world from 1970 to 1997. This unique database was originally collected by the Pinkerton Global Intelligence Service (PGIS).

Because the PGIS database was designed to document every known terrorist event across countries over time, we can examine the total number of different types of terrorist events by specific date and geographical region. To the best of our knowledge this is the most comprehensive open source data set on terrorism that has ever been available to researchers. PGIS trained their employees to identify and code terrorism incidents from a variety of sources, including wire services (especially Reuters and the Foreign Broadcast Information Service), U.S. State Department reports, other U.S. and foreign government reports, U.S. and foreign newspapers, information provided by PGIS offices around the world, occasional inputs from such special interests as organized political opposition groups, and data furnished by PGIS clients and other individuals in both official and private capacities.

S. Mehrotra et al. (Eds.): ISI 2006, LNCS 3975, pp. 407–419, 2006.

While this is the only database of this sort, it has both strengths and weaknesses which are reviewed below. Strengths include its broad definition of terrorism and its longitudinal structure. Weaknesses of the database include potential media bias and misinformation, lack of information beyond incident specific details alone, and missing data from lost cards (data for the year 1993 were lost by PGIS in an office move). Finally, as we discovered cases that were missing from PGIS, we added them to the data and changed the name from PGIS to the Global Terrorism Database (GTD).

## 2   Building a Global Terrorism Database

Although the research literature on terrorism has expanded dramatically since the 1970s (for reviews, see [1], [13], [16], [18]), the number of studies based on systematic empirical analysis is surprisingly limited. In their encyclopedic review of political terrorism, Schmid and Jongman [19:177] identify more than 6,000 published works but point out that much of the research is "impressionistic, superficial (and offers) ... far-reaching generalizations on the basis of episodal evidence."

One of the main reasons for this lack of cutting-edge empirical analysis on terrorism is the low quality of available statistical data. While several organizations now maintain databases on terrorist incidents,[1] these data sources face at least three serious limitations. First, most of the existing data sources use extremely narrow definitions of terrorism. For example, although the U.S. State Department [21:3] provides what is probably the most widely-cited data set on terrorism currently available, the State Department definition of terrorism is limited to "politically motivated violence" and thus excludes terrorist acts that are instead motivated by religious, economic, or social goals.

Second, because much of the data on terrorism is collected by government entities, definitions and counting rules are inevitably influenced by political considerations. Thus, the U.S. State Department did not count as terrorism actions taken by the Contras in Nicaragua. By contrast, after the 1972 Munich Olympics massacre in which eleven Israeli athletes were killed, representatives from a group of Arab, African and Asian nations successfully derailed United Nations action by arguing that "people who struggle to liberate themselves from foreign oppression and exploitation have the right to use all methods at their disposal, including force" [8:31].

And finally and most importantly, even though instances of domestic terrorism[2] greatly outnumber instances of international terrorism, domestic terrorism is excluded from all existing publicly available databases. In short, maintaining an artificial separation between domestic and international terrorist events impedes full understanding of terrorism and ultimately weakens counterterrorism efforts.

---

[1]  These include the U.S. State Department [23], the Jaffee Center for Strategic Studies in Tel Aviv [6], the RAND Corporation [9], the ITERATE database[13], [14], and the Monterey Institute of International Studies [20].

[2]  We use the term "domestic terrorism" throughout to signify terrorism where the perpetrator and target were nationals from the same country and the attack was perpetrated within the boundaries of their country.

## 3  The Original PGIS Database

To address this lack of empirical data, we coded and verified a previously unavailable data set composed of 67,165 terrorist events recorded for the entire world from 1970 to 1997. This unique database was originally collected by the Pinkerton Global Intelligence Service (PGIS). The collectors of the PGIS database aimed to record every major known terrorist event across nations and over time. This format allows us to examine the total number of different types of terrorist events by date and by geographical region. The database contains nine unique event types; seven of which were defined *a priori* by PGIS, including bombing, assassination, facility attack, hijacking, kidnapping, assault, and maiming. PGIS later added two categories, arson and mass disruption, to fit unique cases they found during data collection.

To the best of our knowledge this is the most comprehensive open source data set on terrorism events that has ever been available to researchers. There are at least four main reasons for this. First, unlike most other databases on terrorism, the PGIS data include political, as well as religious, economic, and social acts of terrorism. Second, because the PGIS data were collected by a private business rather than a government entity, the data collectors were under no pressure to exclude some terrorist acts because of political considerations. Third, unlike any other publicly available database the PGIS data includes both instances of domestic and international terrorism starting from 1970. And finally, the PGIS data collection efforts are remarkable in that they were able to develop and apply a similar data collection strategy for a 28-year period.

## 4  Evaluating the PGIS Data

Although every effort was made, from data entry eligibility requirements and applicant screening to extensive data verification and cleaning, to ensure that our coding of the PGIS data was as complete and accurate as possible, nevertheless, the resulting database has both strengths and weakness—many of which were beyond our control. Strengths of the database include its broad definition of terrorism and its longitudinal structure. Weaknesses of the database include potential media bias and misinformation, lack of information beyond incident specific details alone, and missing data from a set of cards that were lost during an office move of PGIS. We review some of these strengths and weaknesses in the next section of this report.

### 4.1  Database Strengths

In reviewing our work on these data since 2002, we believe that the database has four major strengths. First, the PGIS data are unique in that they included domestic as well as international terrorist events from the beginning of data collection. This is the major reason why the PGIS data set is so much larger than any other currently available open source databases. In a review, Alex Schmid [18] identified 9 major databases that count terrorist events, and reports that each of these databases contains less than 15 percent of the number of incidents included in the PGIS data. Second, PGIS had an unusually sustained and cohesive data collection effort. Thus, the PGIS data collection efforts were supervised by only two main managers over the 27 years spanned by the data collection effort. We believe that this contributes to the reliability of the PGIS data. Third, we feel that there are advantages in the fact that the PGIS data were collected not be a government entity but by a private business enterprise. This meant that PGIS was under few political pressures in terms of how it classified the data being collected. And finally, the definition of terrorism employed by the original PGIS data collectors was exceptionally broad. Definitions of terrorism are a complex issue for researchers in this area.

A major reason that we were drawn to the PGIS data is that the definition of terrorism it employed throughout the data collection period is especially inclusive, "...the threatened or actual use of illegal force and violence to attain a political, economic, religious or social goal through fear, coercion or intimidation." Where the U.S. State Department defines terrorism as "...premeditated, politically motivated violence perpetrated against noncombatants targeted by subnational groups or clandestine agents, usually intended to influence an audience." Unlike the State Department, whose mandate is to focus on international terrorism (i.e., that involving the interests and/or nationals of more than one country), the PGIS data are not limited to international incidents. To underscore the importance of this difference consider that two of the most noteworthy terrorist events of the 1990s—the March 1995 nerve gas attack on the Tokyo subway system and the April 1995 bombing of the federal office building in Oklahoma City, both lack any known foreign involvement and hence were purely acts of domestic terrorism.

Based on coding rules originally developed in 1970, the persons responsible for collecting the PGIS database sought to exclude criminal acts that appeared to be devoid of any political or ideological motivation and also acts arising from open combat between opposing armed forces, both regular and irregular. The data coders also excluded actions taken by governments in the legitimate exercise of their authority, even when such actions were denounced by domestic and/or foreign critics as acts of "state terrorism." However, they included violent acts that were not officially sanctioned by government, even in cases where many observers believed that the government was openly tolerating the violent actions.

In sum, we regard the fact that these data were collected by a private corporation for a business purpose as an important advantage over other data sets currently available. Because the goal of the data collection was to provide risk assessment to corporate customers, the database was designed to err on the side of inclusiveness. While there is at present no universally accepted definition of terrorism, the definition used to generate the PGIS data is among the most comprehensive that we have been able to identify.

### 4.2   Weaknesses of Open Source Terrorism Databases

But while the PGIS data has some important strengths, we also recognize that it also has important weaknesses that need to be understood when drawing conclusions from the data. Three types of weaknesses are especially important. First, all the major open source terrorism databases (ITERATE, MIPT-RAND and PGIS) rely on data culled from news sources, thus they are likely biased toward the most newsworthy forms of terrorism [6]. Although the PGIS database includes events that were prevented by authorities, it is certain that some potential terrorist attacks never came to the attention of the media and are thus excluded. A related issue is that the PGIS database includes incidents covered by the media where the perpetrator remains unidentified. Without information concerning the perpetrator it may be difficult to accurately classify the incident as terrorism, since the definition relies on the motive of the attacker. Finally, various media accounts of similar terrorist incidents may contain conflicting information. Without measures of reliability in news reporting, it is difficult for researchers to discern which source supplies the most accurate account.

The second issue is that the dataset lacks information on other important issues associated with each terrorism incident. Open source databases, including the one created by PGIS also lack information on the "psychological characteristics, recruitment, and careers of members of terrorist movements" [9:28]. There are also no "broadly-based data sets with coded information on the outcome of terrorist campaigns or on government responses to episodes of domestic terrorism" [9:28]. Of course, the lack of data on terrorist groups is mainly explained by their clandestine nature. The media also tends to focus on terrorism employed by non-governmental insurgents rather than state terrorism. Overall, the reason for the large quantity of information on the characteristics of sub-state terrorism incidents is because this information is more readily available from media sources. Thus, it is important to recognize that the data captured in open source terrorism databases are limited and are appropriate for only certain types of studies.

Finally, for unknown reasons, most of the original data for the year 1993 were lost prior to our acquiring the dataset. We are currently working to replace that missing data. Also, during the process of verifying the PGIS data with other sources, we found that PGIS were unsystematically missing some cases. When the source of missing information was deemed reliable, we added the incident to PGIS and documented the original source. Because this changes the database, and because Pinkerton's corporate offices are no longer affiliated with the data, we changed the name from PGIS to the Global Terrorism Database (GTD).

## 5   A First Look at International and Domestic Global Terrorism, 1970 – 1997

Now we present an overview of international and domestic terrorism worldwide. Between 1970 and 1997 (excluding 1993), the GTD records 69,088 terrorism incidents[3]. Figure 1 contrasts the pattern of terrorism according to GTD with that of RAND, which only includes international incidents. Most striking is the vast difference in magnitude between the two data bases. If we were to exclusively focus on international terrorism, we would miss information on more than 61,000 incidents. In fact, as we shall see later, many groups began by attacking targets within their own country before expanding to international terrorism.

---

[3] This figure is based on the available GTD as of February 17, 2006. Since the database is continuously evolving, the numbers may change over time as new sources are integrated into the existing database.

**Terrorism Frequencies by Source**

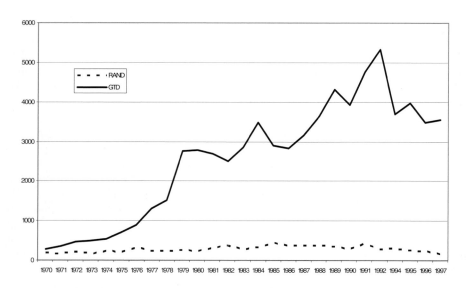

**Fig. 1.** Terrorism Trends over Time According to RAND and GTD

Looking exclusively at the pattern of terrorism from the GTD, we see that terrorism had increased rather steadily to a peak in 1992 with 5,324 events worldwide. Up through 1976 attacks by terrorist attacks were relatively infrequent, with fewer than 1,000 incidents each year. In 1977, incidents rose from 885 to 1,306. From 1978 to 1979 we see evidence that events nearly doubled rising to 2,745 from 1,526. The number of terrorist events continues a broad increase until 1992, with smaller peaks in 1984, at almost 3,500 incidents, and 1989, with about 4,300 events. After the global peak in 1992, the number of terrorist incidents declines to approximately 3,500 incidents at the end of the data collection period in 1997.

To better understand the distribution of terrorism events and lethality, we calculated the distribution of incidents and fatalities according to their region.[4] Figure 2 shows that more terrorism and terrorism-related fatalities occur in Latin America than in any other region. In fact, Latin America is attacked nearly twice as often as any other region of the world more than seven times as often as Sub-Sahara Africa and nearly forty times that of North America.[5] Europe and Asia are nearly tied at second, each accounting for about 20 percent of the world's total terrorism events (21.03 and 18.14 percent, respectively). The Mid-East/North Africa region follows with less than 15 percent (13.14) of the incidents, and Sub-Saharan Africa and North America account for the fewest terrorism events (5.79 and 1.68 percent, respectively).

---

[4] The composition of countries within each region was determined by PGIS.
[5] Mexico is counted as Latin America instead of North America.

Incidents and Fatalities by Region

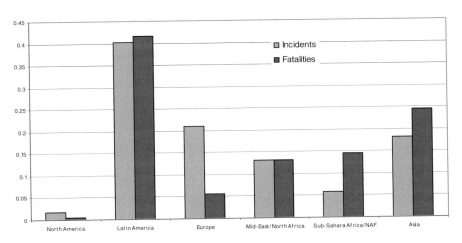

**Fig. 2.** Incidents and Fatalities by Region

Figure 2 also shows that the distribution of fatalities by region differs from that of the incidents. While Latin America remains the leader in fatalities as well as in the proportion of attacks, Asia has the second highest percentage of fatalities by region, accounting for nearly 25 percent of all terrorism-related fatalities (24.56). Figure 2 also reveals that while Europe is second in the proportion of attacks, it suffers relatively few fatalities as a result of these incidents, averaging only 0.53 deaths per incident (See Table 1). This rate is especially low compared to that for Sub-Saharan Africa which averages 5 deaths for every terrorism attack. Thus, while the Sub-Saharan African region accounts for a relatively small proportion of total terrorist attacks during this period, when there were attacks in this region, they tended to be deadlier. The reasons for these differences remain to be explained, although part of the explanation may simply be ready and proximate access to medical care across regions.

**Table 1.** The Average Number of Fatalties per Terrorism Attack

| Region | Fatalities per Attack |
|---|---|
| North America | 0.55 |
| Latin America | 2.06 |
| Europe | 0.53 |
| Mid-East, North Africa | 2.00 |
| Sub-Saharan Africa | 5.00 |
| Asia | 2.70 |

We turn now to the distribution of terrorism activity for each region over time. Figure 3 disaggregates the trend line of Figure 1 to show which regions are driving each portion of the trend from 1970 through 1997. If we were to examine this graph from 1970 until 1978, the story would be that terrorism is largely a European problem, with evidence of it becoming a growing issue in Latin America. After 1978, Europe peaks at over 1,000 incident in 1979 and then drops to an average of 550 incidents a year. Latin America, on the other hand continues rise after 1978 and peaks in 1984 with over 2,100 incidents. After 1984, Latin America continues to average about 1,400 a year with large fluctuations. Most interesting is the fairly steep drop that bottoms out in 1995 at 515 incidents. The steady increase in the overall world-wide terrorism rates are driven by the relatively recent increase in the frequency of attacks in Asia and Sub-Saharan Africa. Figure 3 also shows that compared to other regions, North America has experienced a relatively small proportion of terrorist attacks during this period.

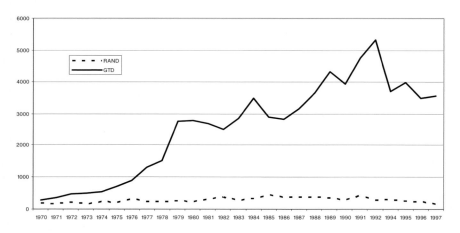

**Fig. 3.** Terrorism Activity over Time by Region

Not only does the GTD provide information about the frequency of attacks, but it allows us to examine the distribution of terrorist tactics. In an analysis not shown, we examine the types of terrorist tactics by region. While the five most common tactics (i.e., assassinations, bombing, facility attacks, hijacking and kidnapping) were relatively common in all six regions, there were substantial differences in the distribution of terrorist tactics.

Theses patterns may be partly due to risk management strategies. Since the GTD documents each incident we can aggregate to any level. We demonstrate the value of examining sub-national patterns in the next two figures. In figures 4 and 5, we disaggregate the trend by the most active groups. We also include the trend line for incidents where the perpetrating group is unrecorded. This comparison in Figure 4

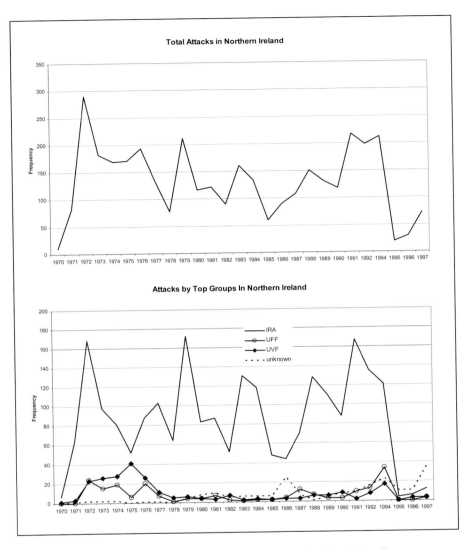

**Fig. 4.** Terrorist Attacks over Time in Northern Ireland for Select Groups

demonstrates that the pattern of terrorism in Northern Ireland is largely driven by the activities of the Irish Republican Army (IRA). Peak years for the IRA were 1972, 1979, 1983, 1988, and 1991, which form the peaks for terrorism in Northern Ireland overall. The two second most active groups, the Ulster Freedom Fighters (UFF) and the Ulster Volunteer Force (UVF) have demonstratively lower rates of attack (totals equal 203 and 251, respectively compared to 2,299 for the IRA).

Figure 5 presents the trends for four groups in the United States as well as that for events where no group claims responsibility. Aside from events perpetrated by an unknown group, most of the U.S. terrorism trends appear to be accounted for by the anti-abortion activists, the Armed Forces of Puerto Rican National Liberation (FALN), the New World Liberation Front (NWLF), and the Jewish Defense League (JDL). Attacks by FALN, NWLF, and JDL were most common between 1970 and 1980. Since then, most activity seems to be driven by the anti-abortion movement.

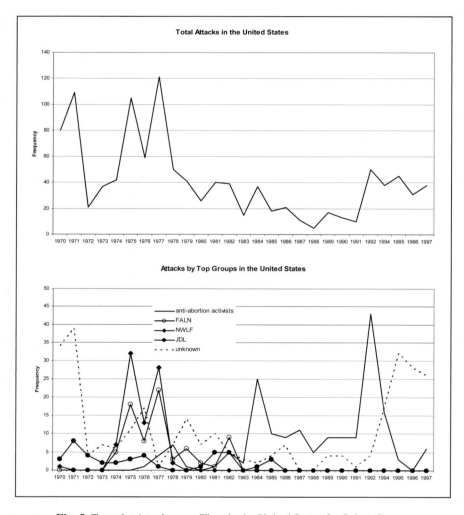

**Fig. 5.** Terrorist Attacks over Time in the United States for Select Groups

## 6  Summary of Current and Future Projects USing GTD

Several projects have been conducted using portions of the GTD. We summarize these below.

## 6.1   Testing a Rational Choice Model of Airline Hijackings

Our study of global aerial hijackings was recently published in <u>Criminology</u> [4]. Although we mostly use data from the Federal Aviation Administration (FAA), this paper demonstrates the strength of using incident based terrorism, like that in the GTD for assessing policy effects.    Our results support the contagion view that hijacking rates significantly increase after a series of hijackings closely-clustered in time—but only when these attempts were successful.    Finally, we found that the policy interventions examined here significantly decreased the likelihood of non-terrorist but not terrorist hijackings.

For this paper we developed a database that combines information from the GTD, the FAA, and RAND-MPIT.    Based on these sources, we were able to develop a database of 1,101 attempted aerial hijackings that occurred around the world from 1931 to 2003.    The GTD data were especially critical for allowing us to classify whether specific aerial hijackings were conducted by terrorist organizations.

## 6.2   Is Counter Terrorism Counterproductive?  Northern Ireland 1969–1992

This second project is still underway, and uses a similar methodology to the above hijacking paper.  In this case, however, we use data exclusively from the GTD.[6]  In it, we examine 3,328 terrorist attacks perpetrated by Northern Irish groups between 1969 and 1992, classifying them as either nationalist or loyalist.  We develop two theoretical perspectives that predict opposing impact of counter terrorist actions on future terrorist strikes. The dominant rational choice perspective suggests that government intervention will decrease terrorist strikes by increasing the costs of future strikes.  By contrast, a legitimacy perspective suggests that counter terrorist retaliation may actually increase future terrorist strikes by undermining the legitimacy of governmental regimes. We identify six major British counter terrorist interventions for the years spanned by the data.   Since loyalists generally support the British government, we expect the nationalists to be more sensitive to the British interventions. We use Cox proportional hazard models to estimate the impact of these interventions on the likelihood of future terrorist attacks.  In five of the six cases examined, we find the strongest support for legitimacy arguments:   government intervention resulted in *increased* activity for Nationalist organizations.  Overall, the results support the conclusion that counter terrorism, especially when it involves the military, may actually increase the risk of additional terrorist strikes.  We discuss the implications for future research and policy.

## 6.3   The Impact of Terrorism on Italian Employment and Business Activity

In this research we use the GTD to assess the economic consequences of terrorism on changes in the number of firms and employment in Italian providences from 1985 to 1997.  We use panel data methods and find that in the year following a terrorism attack, the number of firms in the providences is significantly reduced.  Similarly,

---

[6] Recall that we supplemented the original PGIS data to create the new GTD.  The Northern Ireland data from GTD include sources other than PGIS, such as the Conflict Archive on the Internet (CAIN, http://cain.ulst.ac.uk/).

employment also drops in the year following a terrorist attack. This decrease is mostly attributed to reductions in growth rates of births and expanding firms, significantly reducing the number of firms the following year.

# 7  Conclusion

We have introduced the newly developed Global Terrorism Database that was predominantly compiled from a private source and is the only terrorism database that includes both international and domestic incidents over an extended period of time. We presented a brief description of global terrorism and then described three analyses that relied heavily on the GTD data. Yet, this only begins to describe the analytical potential of the GTD. We have well over a dozen projects with new ideas exponentially forming. For example, we are currently geocoding the data to use geographic mapping techniques to display spatial and temporal patterns of terrorist activity. Our major goal here is to create regional and world-wide maps depicting numbers and rates of terrorist events around the world. Yet, we also are actively assessing the geographic distributions of localized activity. One current project focuses on terrorism attacks in Spain to identify hot spots, temporal changes in the spatial distribution of incidents, and tests models of diffusion. We have also merged the GTD data with other sources to estimate the effects of political, economic, and social indicators on terrorism outcomes. Because the data are longitudinal we can also examine how terrorism contributes to political, economic, and social changes for a country or region.

And finally, additional future projects can further explore the likely non-linear patterns of terrorist events by considering concepts explaining the acceleration or deceleration of activity. For instance, Schelling [17] shows "white flight" behaves as a tipping point phenomena such that when a given neighborhood reaches a particular concentration of African Americans, white flight increases inevitability and precipitously. Applied here, tipping points could be described as that critical point in a region when periodic terrorist activity accelerates to high frequencies of heavily concentrated violence. Other concepts worth exploring are threshold models [7], [22], contagion effects [3], [11], epidemic theories [3], diffusion models [2], and bandwagon effects [7] (for review, see [10]).

# References

1. Babkina, A.M. (1998). Terrorism: An Annotated Bibliography. Commack, NY: Nova Science Publishers.
2. Burt, R. S. (1987). "Social Contagion and Innovation: Cohesion Versus Structural Equivalence" American Journal of Sociology 92:1287-1335.
3. Crane, J. (1991). "The Epidemic Theory of Ghettos and Neighborhood Effects on Dropping Out and Teenage Childbearing" American Journal of Sociology 96:1126-1159.
4. Dugan, L., LaFree, G. Piquero, A.: Testing a Rational Choice Model of Airline Hijackings. Criminology (2005) 43:1031-1066
5. Fairchild, E. and H.R. Dammer (2001). Comparative Criminal Justice Systems. Belmont, CA: Wadsworth /Thomson Learning.

6. Fowler, W. W. (1981). Terrorism Databases: A Comparison of Missions, Methods and Systems. RAND publication, Santa Monica CA.

7. Granovetter, M. (1978). "Threshold Models of Collective Behavior" American Journal of Sociology 9:166-179.

8. Hoffman, B. (1998). Inside Terrorism. New York, NY: Columbia University Press.

9. Jongman, A.J. (1993). "Trends in International and Domestic Terrorism in Western Europe, 1968-88," Pp. 26-76 In Western Responses to Terrorism, edited by A. P. Schmid and R.D. Crelinsten. London: Frank Cass.

10. LaFree, G. (1999). "Declining Violent Crime Rates in the 1990s: Predicting Crime Booms and Busts." Annual Review of Sociology 25:145-68.

11. Loftin, C. (1986). "Assaultive Violence as a Contagious Social Process" Bulletin of the New York Academy of Medicine 62:550-555.

12. Mickolus, E. F. (1991). Terrorism, 1988-1991: A Chronology of Events and a Selectively Annotated Bibliography. Boulder, CO: Westview Press.

13. Mickolus, E. F. (1982). International Terrorism: Attributes of Terrorist Events, 1968-1977. (ITERATE 2). Ann Arbor, MI: Inter-University Consortium for Political and Social Research.

14. Mickolus, E.F., T. Sandler, J.M. Murdock, and P. Fleming (1993). International Terrorism: Attributes of Terrorist Events 1988-91 (ITERATE 4). Dunn Loring, VA: Vineyard Software.

15. Mickolus, E.F. and S.L. Simmons (1997). Terrorism, 1992-1995: A Chronology of Events and a Selectively Annotated Bibliography. Westport, CT: Greenwood Press.

16. Prunkun, H. W. (1995). Shadow of Death: An Analytical Bibliography on Political Violence, terrorism, and Low-Intensity Conflict. Lanham, MD: Scarecrow Press.

17. Schelling, T.C. (1971). "Dynamic Models of Segregation" Journal of Mathematical Sociology 1:143-186.

18. Schmid, A.P. (1992). "Terrorism and Democracy." Terrorism and Political Violence 4:14-25.

19. Schmid, A.P. and A.J. Jongman (1988). Political Terrorism: A New Guide to Actors, Authors, Concepts, Databases, Theories and Literature. Amsterdam: North-Holland Publishing Company.

20. Tucker, J.B. (1999). "Historical Trends Related to Bioterrorism: An Empirical Analysis." Emerging Infectious Disease 5:498-504.

21. United States Department of State (2001). "Introduction: Patterns of Global Terrorism, 2000." http://www.state.gov/s/ct/rls/pgtr.

22. Wallace, R. (1991). "Social Distintegration and the Spread of AIDS: Threshold for Propagation along 'Sociogeographic' Networks" Social Science & Medicine 33:115-1162.

# Computational Modeling and Experimental Validation of Aviation Security Procedures

Uwe Glässer, Sarah Rastkar, and Mona Vajihollahi

Software Technology Lab
School of Computing Science, Simon Fraser University
Burnaby, B.C., Canada
{glaesser, srastkar, mvajihol}@cs.sfu.ca

**Abstract.** Security of civil aviation has become a major concern in recent years, leading to a variety of protective measures related to airport and aircraft security to be established by regional, national and international authorities. We propose a novel computational approach to checking consistency, coherence and completeness of procedural security requirements defined by aviation security guidelines. To deal with uncertainty, we use probabilistic modeling techniques, combining *abstract state machine* modeling with *symbolic model checking*.

## 1  Introduction

Civil aviation security encompasses a variety of protective measures related to airport and aircraft security which collectively aim at safeguarding airports, aircrafts and air traffic control against unlawful events. Striving to eliminate potential vulnerabilities as far as possible, a key concern is the question: *Do these measures ultimately provide adequate protection?*

Critical checks of aviation security are one way of providing useful feedback for enhancing and improving protective measures. However, empirical techniques and real-world experiments have their limitations, making any exhaustive testing virtually impossible to do. So what are more feasible alternatives? Arguably, there is a lack of analytical means for reasoning about the effectiveness of critical security measures, such as procedures and routines for airport passenger screening, checked baggage screening, and likewise of measures for air cargo security. Hence, we propose here the use of computational methods and tools for analyzing and validating procedural security models as an effective means to cope with the notorious problem of establishing the consistency and completeness of aviation security guidelines. We restrict on security of civil aviation.

In principle, security measures for civil aviation are regulated by regional, national and international standards and recommended practices, e.g. [1, 2]. Such documents specify requirements for procedures and routines, informally, in terms of natural language—typically in the form of rules that have to be followed in order to conform with established standards (see Sect. 3.1 for examples of such rules). Due to the very nature of natural language, informal requirements make

S. Mehrotra et al. (Eds.): ISI 2006, LNCS 3975, pp. 420–431, 2006.
© Springer-Verlag Berlin Heidelberg 2006

it difficult to identify and eliminate hidden deficiencies and weaknesses[1], potentially causing severe misinterpretations that can result in security holes with fatal consequences. Additionally, validation and verification of resulting properties by computational means require a well defined computational framework as a prerequisite for machine assisted inspection of models through computer simulation (testing) and/or symbolic execution (verification).

We propose here a novel approach to computational modeling and experimental validation of aviation security, building on a structured mathematical framework for the construction of models derived from aviation security guidelines. Behavioral aspects of security procedures and routines are formalized in abstract computational terms, making the resulting properties checkable by machine assisted validation techniques. We therefore combine *abstract state machine* (ASM) specification techniques [3] with symbolic *model checking* (MC) [4]. More specifically, we use a probabilistic variant of the asynchronous ASM computation model in combination with probabilistic MC techniques [5] as a computational framework for establishing the consistency, coherence, and completeness of procedural security requirements. The main purpose of this work is to provide a practical instrument and a tool for experimental studies on the effectiveness of security procedures and routines with the intention to improve existing standards and practices by identifying potential deficiencies and weaknesses.

Security mechanisms rely to some non-negligible extend on assumptions that involve uncertainty. For instance, screening measures for baggage, like x-ray or hand search, can identify an unlawful object in a certain baggage item with a relatively high probability, especially when the two measures are combined. However, depending on a number of human and technical factors, an object may escape the attention of the operator of the x-ray machine and also pass a hand search performed afterward. In the presence of such real-world phenomena, probabilistic modeling techniques provide a rational choice. We reflect this fact in our models by including probabilistic aspects, as will be illustrated by examples.

Related to our work is a European project called EDEMOI [6]. The approach presented in [6] is based on transforming UML graphical models into formal notations such as B or Z. Unlike our approach, it does not consider probabilistic aspects caused by the inherent uncertainty of security procedures.

The paper is structured as follows. Section 2 outlines our approach and describes the context of this work. Section 3 presents our probabilistic ASM model of airport security procedures. Section 4 addresses probabilistic model checking of the model and provides some results, and Section 5 concludes the paper.

## 2   Background

This section briefly outlines the technical background and motivates the chosen formal framework, avoiding technical details that are well documented in the standard literature on abstract state machines and model checking.

---

[1] Frequent problems are accidental ambiguities, loose ends, and logical inconsistencies.

## 2.1   Aviation Security Guidelines

International, regional and national authorities have devised a series of standards that specify various procedures and security measures to be implemented to ensure the security of civil aviation. The International Civil Aviation Organization (ICAO) provides guidelines at the international level which form Annex 17 to the Convention on International Civil Aviation [1].

In order to synchronize the operations among the countries in a region, regional authorities also introduce security standards and regulations. For instance, recognizing the fact that Annex 17 provides minimum standards to ensure the security of civil aviation, the European Parliament and the Council of the European Union have approved a set of regulations for establishing common rules in the field of aviation security.

The international and regional standards must be implemented by all contracting states involved in civil aviation, and are usually refined to capture the national laws of each country, forming national standards for civil aviation.

## 2.2   Abstract State Machines

Abstract state machines [3] are known for their versatility in computational and semantic modeling of virtually all kinds of sequential, parallel and distributed systems. Applications have been studied extensively by researchers in academia and industry for more than 15 years with the intention to bridge the gap between formal and empirical approaches [7]. Building on extensive experience in a variety of areas, spanning from modeling distributed embedded systems [8] and industrial standards, e.g. the ITU-T standard for SDL [9], to applications in computational criminology [10], there is a solid methodological foundation for building *ASM ground models* [3]. Intuitively, a ground model is considered a 'blueprint' of the key functional requirements that need to be established in a precise and reliable form, genuinely reflecting an intuitive understanding of the system under study [11]. The underlying abstraction principles directly support concurrent and reactive behavior as well as timing aspects. We will illustrate the ASM modeling paradigm by means of examples[2].

## 2.3   Probabilistic Model Checking

Modeling airport security procedures requires to deal with the probabilistic behavior which many parts of an airport exhibit. For instance, the screening equipment and the operators involved in the screening process introduce a degree of uncertainty and unreliability to the system. In fact, there is no guarantee that an operator of an x-ray machine will always identify every unlawful object in the baggage being screened under all possible circumstances. To capture such cases, we extend the original ASM definition by integrating probabilistic modeling techniques. The resulting *Probabilistic ASMs* model stochastic properties of a system and its constituent components in terms of probabilistic functions embedded into the guards of ASM state transition rules.

---

[2] See also the many references at the ASM Web site at www.eecs.umich.edu/gasm.

We first build an abstract computational model of typical airport security procedures described in terms of a probabilistic ASM. The construction of the model itself can already reveal logical inconsistencies and potential weaknesses in the security measures. In the next step, we apply a *model checking* (MC) tool for analyzing model parameters and checking the consistency and completeness of the model. Model checking [4] is a computational method to automatically verify properties of a system given in the form of a formal specification. Specifically, one can use MC to verify the conformance of security procedures to the existing standards or to validate the consistency and completeness of standards and guidelines. Some system properties can be analyzed by conventional model checking techniques (e.g. 'every passenger must pass a security checkpoint to enter a security restricted area'). However, there are also properties that are dependent on probabilistic procedures. For instance, one may be interested in analyzing properties such as the following one: 'the probability of any unauthorized unlawful object being on board an aircraft is negligible'.

Conventional MC techniques only enable the checking of properties like 'never ever there can be any unauthorized unlawful object on board an aircraft', which obviously does not hold for any given airport, due to the probabilistic nature of security procedures. However, one can use existing *probabilistic model checking* (PMC) [5] techniques to analyze these properties. PMC is a relatively recent development which aims to apply automatic verification techniques to probabilistic systems.[3] In addition to constructing a finite-state model of the system, as performed in conventional MC, PMC includes information about the likelihood of making state transitions.

We use a probabilistic model checker called PRISM which has been already applied to a wide range of real-life systems [12, 13]. To apply the probabilistic model checker to our probabilistic ASM model, we transform the ASM model to the input language of the model checker (PRISM) using the algorithm presented in [14]. Using a probabilistic model checker one can analyze a set of quantitative properties. One advantage of such a quantitative analysis is that the results can be plotted as graphs that can be inspected for trends and anomalies related to reliability, consistency, completeness, or even the performance of the model. This approach is discussed in more detail in Sect. 4.

## 3   Airport Security Model

In this section, we present an ASM ground model of the screening procedure for a hypothetical airport built upon the ICAO standard [1] and the European civil aviation security standard [2]. First, a model is built at a high level of abstraction capturing the general requirements provided by [1]. In the next step, this model is then refined using the more specific European guidelines. Since the standards and recommendations provided by ICAO have to be followed at the international level by all the member countries, building a ground model based

---

[3] PMC techniques combine traversal of the underlying state transition graph with numerical solution methods.

on [1] provides the general framework for further refining the model according to 'any' more specific guidelines. In this paper, we have chosen to use the European standard for further refinements, simply because it is publicly available.

### 3.1   Airport Security Guidelines

This section provides an overview of the principal rules/guidelines provided by [1] and [2] to ensure civil aviation security.

**Civil Aviation Security.** Our work focuses on Preventive Security Measures outlined in Chapter 4 of [1]. The objective is *"to prevent weapons, explosives, or any other dangerous devices which may be used to commit an act of unlawful interference, the carriage or bearing of which is not authorized, from being introduced, by any means whatsoever, on board an aircraft engaged in international civil aviation."* [1, Sect. 4.1] In this paper, we mainly consider the guidelines for measures relating to hold baggage[4] to further exemplify our approach.

Each Contracting State shall establish measures to ensure that [1, Sect. 4.4]:

- *Hold baggage is subjected to appropriate security controls prior to being loaded into an aircraft engaged in international civil aviation operations.* (4.4.1)
- *Operators when providing service from that State do not transport the baggage of passengers who are not on board the aircraft unless that baggage is subjected to appropriate security control which may include screening.* (4.4.3)
- *Originating hold baggage intended to be carried in an aircraft engaged in international civil aviation operation is screened prior to being loaded into the aircraft.* (4.4.8)

The guidelines and rules provided in [1] form the general framework for our ground model of airport security procedures.

**European Regulation.** We regard the European standard as a source for clarifying and refining the guidelines outlined in [1], providing a more detailed and practical view of the security measures. As such, it proved to be an asset in understanding the airport security process flow and, at the same time, showed the complexity of such a process.

In this paper, we focus on the regulations regarding hold baggage [2, Sect. 5]. The European standard clearly defines "hold baggage" as "baggage intended for carriage in the hold of an aircraft." The security measures related to hold baggage are classified into three groups: (1) Reconciliation of Hold Baggage; (2) Screening of Hold Baggage; (3) Protection of Hold Baggage. Here, we use the rules provided for screening of hold baggage to refine the ground model of [1]. For instance, the following rule is defined for screening accompanied hold baggage[5]:

---

[4] A precise definition of hold baggage is not provided in [1]. Here, we assume it is the baggage intended for carriage in the hold of an aircraft, as defined in [2].

[5] Accompanied hold baggage is defined as "baggage accepted for carriage in the hold of an aircraft, on which the passenger who checked it in is on-board."[2, Sect. 1]

*All items of accompanied hold baggage (both originating and transfer hold baggage, unless previously screened to the standard detailed in this Annex) shall be screened by one of the following methods before being loaded onto an aircraft:*

- *hand search; or*
- *conventional x-ray equipment with at least 10% of screened baggage also being subjected to either: hand search; or EDS or EDDS or PEDS[6]; or ...*

## 3.2   Abstract State Machine Model

The ASM ground model presented here captures the process flow for ensuring civil aviation security as outlined in [1, Sect. 4]. We define a domain ENTITY that contains all the entities in the system security of which must be ensured. This includes passengers, cabin baggage, and hold baggage.

---

ENTITIY ≡ PASSENGER ∪ BAGGAGE
BAGGAGE ≡ CABIN_BAGGAGE ∪ HOLD_BAGGAGE

---

Each entity has to follow the required security procedure before boarding the aircraft. As discussed in Sect. 3.1, Annex 17 [1] only provides a set of rules describing the required security measures for each type of entities; no architectural view or further description of the security procedures is provided in the document. However, after close examination of the standard, and in the process of requirement elicitation in order to build the model, we extracted an architectural view to the security procedure that provides an abstract flow model for all the entities in the system. In this view, the abstract security flow model is applied to all the entities subjected to security controls. We define the flow model in terms of a *control-state abstract state machine*[7] as shown in Fig. 1.

From the time an entity enters the airport, to the time it leaves the airport by plane, it goes through different *modes* as represented by *control states*. When the entity enters the airport it starts with the *checkIn* mode, where it has to go through the check-in procedure as modeled by the Check_In_Machine. When completed, the mode switches to the *secControl* mode where the required security measures are invoked by the Sec_Control_Machine. If the security control procedure is completed successfully, the mode switches to the *protection* mode, where it is protected from any "unauthorized interference". On the other hand, if the security control fails, the mode switches to the *special* mode. The *special* mode is designed to capture such exceptions and special cases where the routine security flow is interrupted. The entity stays in the *protection* mode, unless

---

[6] EDS: Explosive Detection System, EDDS: Explosive Device Detection System, PEDS: Primary Explosive Detection System [2, Sect. 1].

[7] Control state ASMs represent "a normal form for UML activity diagrams and allow the designer to define machines which below the main control structure of finite state machines provide synchronous parallelism and the possibility to manipulate data structures".[3]

boarding is started or the protection is violated; i.e. an unauthorized contact occurs. The violation is captured in the *special* mode, whereas if the boarding is started without any violation, the mode is changed to *preBoarding*. After additional security checks are performed by the PreBoarding_Machine, the mode is changed to *boarding*. Once the entity is *onBoard*, final security checks are performed in the OnBoard_Machine. For instance, before the plane takes off, Rule 4.4.3 (see Sect. 3.1) states that if the passenger of a piece of baggage is not on board of the aircraft, the baggage must not be transported unless it is subjected to appropriate security controls. Once the plane is ready to take off, the mode is changed to *ready4TakeOff*. At this point, the entity is removed from the system and the mode is changed to *finished*.

In the following sections we focus on the security control procedure for hold baggage and describe how it is refined using the European regulations of [2].

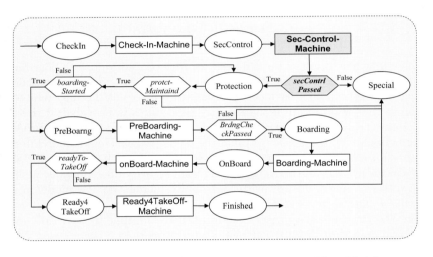

**Fig. 1.** Control-State ASM for Airport Security Flow Model

**Security Control Machine.** The security control machine (highlighted in Fig. 1) is refined to Sec_Control_Machine$_{passCabin}$ and Sec_Control_Machine$_{holdBag}$ to capture specific measures for each type of entity.

Annex 17 [1] clearly states that the contracting state must ensure that hold baggage is subjected to appropriate security controls, regardless whether it is transfer or originating baggage [1, Rules 4.4.1 and 4.4.6]. More specifically, originating hold baggage must be screened prior to being loaded into the aircraft [1, Rule 4.4.8]. It also states that if hold baggage is not *accompanied* by the passenger, it is subjected to appropriate security controls which may include screening [1, Rule 4.4.3]. However, Annex 17 does not clearly differentiate between the screening of accompanied and unaccompanied hold baggage. The European standard, on the other hand, provides two different procedures for screening accompanied and unaccompanied hold baggage [2, Sect. 5]. Therefore, we formalize the security control procedure for the hold baggage as follows.

---

**Sec_Control_Machine**$_{holdBag}(h : \text{HOLD\_BAGGAGE}) \equiv$
  **if** $accompanied(h)$ **then**
    Screen$_{accompanied}(h)$
  **else**
    Screen$_{unaccompanied}(h)$

---

**Screening.** We further use the guidelines provided by the Council of European Union to refine the screening procedure. The Screen$_{accompanied}$ rule presented above is refined to capture the requirements for screening accompanied hold baggage (see Sect. 3.1). The baggage goes through a set of internal modes which determine whether or not it passes the security controls. The control-state ASM for screening of accompanied hold baggage is shown in Fig. 2.

It is important to note that the main objective of the screening process is to determine the faith of the hold baggage in the flow model of Fig. 1; i.e. before the screening operation is finished (and the machine enters the *done* mode), the value of the *secContrlPassed* function (highlighted in Fig. 1) is determined. This function is used in the airport security flow model to decide whether the entity can enter the *protection* mode, or it should switch to the *special* mode. For a complete specification of the ground model and its refinements we refer to [15]. As example, we provide here the definition of the function highlighted in Fig. 2.

The European standard requires 10% of the hold baggage that is screened with a conventional x-ray machine to be subjected to re-screening (see Sect. 3.1 and [2, Sect. 5.2]); i.e., if the type of the equipment used for screening a piece of hold baggage is conventional x-ray, with a probability of 0.1, additional screening is required. Thus, the *additnlScreenReq* function is defined as follows.

---

$additnlScreenReq(h) \equiv$
    $equipType(screenEquip(h)) = conXRay \wedge randomSearch(randomSearchProb)$
**where**
  $randomSearchProb = 0.1$
  // $h$ is a piece of hold baggage
  // $screenEquip$ identifies the equipment with which $h$ has been screened
  // $equipType$ identifies the type of a screening equipment $e$

---

The probabilistic nature of the function is captured by a *monitored* function[8], called *randomSearch*, which follows the use of probabilistic ASMs as described in Sect. 2.2. The function *randomSearch(p)* returns *true* with a probability of $p$.

---

[8] Monitored functions are dynamic functions which are read but not updated by an ASM and directly updatable only by the environment.

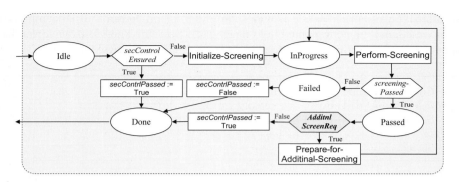

**Fig. 2.** Control-State ASM for Screening of Accompanied Hold Baggage

## 4   Verification

In this section, we explain how probabilistic model checking, and in particular PRISM, can be used to analyze the airport model presented in Sect. 3.2.

First, we have to decide on a probabilistic modeling formalism. PRISM directly supports three types of probabilistic models, which are all variants of Markov chains with discrete states, namely: discrete-time Markov chains, Markov decision processes, and continuous-time Markov chains. We use discrete-time Markov chains (DTMCs) for modeling procedural security within the airport. In DTMCs, time steps and the probabilities of transitions are both discrete. For details on the underlying theory, we refer to [5].

The next step is to transform our ASM model to the input language of PRISM. The transformation uses the mapping algorithm proposed in [14] to transform ASM models to the input language of the SMV model checker.[9] Here, we focus on the hold baggage security flow model presented in Sect. 3.2. The resulting DTMC models the flow of one piece of hold baggage in the airport from the check-in point until the aircraft takes off.

The basic components of PRISM's input language are modules and variables. Each module contains a number of local variables. The values of these variables, at any given time, constitute the state of the module. The behavior of each module is described by a set of commands. Each machine defined in the ASM model is mapped to a module in the PRISM input language. For example, in the *secControl* module, one of the commands is as follows:

```
mode = secControl & accompanied & !originating & screeningEnsured
& isScreened = screeningType1 -> mode' = protection;
```

This command states that accompanied (`accompanied`), transfer (`!original`) hold baggage which has been screened (`isScreened = screeningType1`) according to the standard (`screeningEnsured`) and is currently in the *secControl* mode (`mode = secControl`) immediately enters the *protection* mode (`mode' = protection`) and does not need to undergo further screening.

---

[9] As the PRISM/SMV languages are similar, the algorithm needs only minor changes.

Another example is the following command which formalizes the fact that conventional x-ray equipment can identify unlawful objects with a certain probability (conXRayProb). Consequently, hold baggage containing unlawful objects may pass the screening (screeningStatus' = passed) without being identified with a probability of $1 -$ conXRayProb.

```
mode = secControl & screeningStatus = inProgress &
hasUnlawfulObj & screeningEquip = conXRay ->
conXRayProb:(screeningStatus' = failed) +
(1-conXRayProb):(screeningStatus' = passed);
```

Probabilistic Computational Tree Logic (PCTL) is used to specify properties for DTMCs. Using PCTL, it is possible to either determine if a probability satisfies a given bound or to obtain the actual probability value. In the latter case, one can compute a range of values to identify trends. For instance, there are two ways to analyze the probability of a piece of hold baggage containing unlawful objects being on board an aircraft. One way is to check if this probability is below some pre-specified threshold:

```
"init" => P<=threshold [ true U mode=onBoard & hasUnlawfulObj ],
```

where 'init' is a label to check the property in the initial state and [ true U mode=onBoard & hasUnlawfulObj ] is a path formula stating 'eventually a piece of hold baggage containing unlawful objects ends up on board the aircraft.'
The other option is to compute the actual value of $P$:

```
P=? [ true U mode=onBoard & hasUnlawfulObj ]    (prop1)
```

We have applied the PRISM model checker to our hold baggage security flow model (comprising 4529 states) to analyze some sample properties. Some of the results are presented here to show how probabilistic model checking can be used to investigate and explore the effect of different probabilistic parameters on selected security properties and, hence, on the overall security of the system.

Based on the values of probabilistic parameters, a subset of which is presented in Table 1, PRISM produced the following result when analyzing prop1:

```
P[ true U mode=onBoard & hasUnlawfulObj ] = 0.029
```

**Table 1.** The values of some probabilistic parameters of the system in the experiment

| Parameter | Description | Value |
|---|---|---|
| hasUnlawfulObjProb | Probability of having unlawful objects | 0.2 |
| originatingProb | Prob. of being originating (vs. transfer or transit) | 0.5 |
| accompaniedProb | Probability of being accompanied | 0.8 |
| screeningEnsuredProb | Prob. of having been screened according to standard | 0.8 |
| randomSearchProb | Probability of being screened again randomly | 0.1 |
| conXRayProb | The accuracy of conventional x-ray | 0.6 |

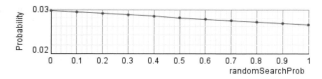

**Fig. 3.** Analysis of *prop1* depending on `randomSearchProb` (`rSP`)

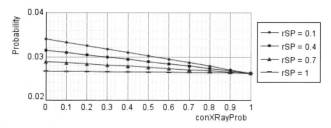

**Fig. 4.** Analysis of *prop1* depending on `conXRayProb` for different fixed values of `rSP`

To inspect *prop1* for trends, we assign different values to `randomSearchProb` ranging between 0.0 and 1.0 and compute the probability of the property in each case (see Fig. 3). On the other hand, by assigning different values to `randomSearchProb`, we can illustrate how the probability that the property holds changes with the value of `conXRayProb`. The diagram in Fig. 4 shows that when the probability of re-screening accompanied hold baggage (`randomSearchProb`) increases, the accuracy of conventional x-ray (`conXRayProb`) has less effect on the probability of the security property *prop1*.

The results show how combining probabilistic ASMs with PMC can be used as a practical tool for inspecting security properties and ensuring the quality of security procedures within airports.

## 5    Conclusion

Formalization of informal requirements is a common approach to deal with the inherent ambiguity and impreciseness of natural language and also a prerequisite for validation and verification of system models by computational means. We combine probabilistic variants of two well established formal techniques, abstract state machines and model checking, for analyzing key properties of aviation security models. The abstract computational framework allows to systematically reason about the effectiveness and to check the logical consistency, coherence and completeness of procedural security requirements.

This paper aims at presenting a novel approach to computational modeling and experimental validation of airport security procedures and routines, exemplifying the basic concepts by means of simple yet meaningful examples. For a comprehensive technical description of our aviation security model, specifically screening of hold baggage, we refer to our technical report [15]. Based on extensive experience with modeling real-life distributed systems as abstract machine models, we can say that our modeling approach is scalable to capture complex procedural requirements defined by aviation security guidelines.

We intend to test our approach by further refining and extending the ground model illustrated here, capturing relevant properties of more detailed security plans in close collaboration with aviation security authorities. We will also explore different ways of how to benefit from the probabilistic nature of modeling and validation for dealing with uncertainty.

# References

1. International Civil Aviation Organization: Annex 17 to the Convention on International Civil Aviation: Standards and Recommended Practices - Security (2002)
2. The European Parliament and the Council of the European Union: Regulation (EC) No 2320/2002 of the European Parliament and of the Council - Establishing Common Rules in the Field of Civil Aviation Security (2002)
3. Börger, E., Stärk, R.: Abstract State Machines: A Method for High-Level System Design and Analysis. Springer-Verlag (2003)
4. Clarke, E.M., Grumberg, O., Peled, D.A.: Model Checking. MIT Press (2000)
5. Rutten, J., Kwiatkowska, M., Norman, G., Parker, D.: Mathematical Techniques for Analyzing Concurrent and Probabilistic Systems, P. Panangaden and F. van Breugel (eds.). Volume 23 of CRM Monograph Series. American Mathematical Society (2004)
6. Laleau, R., Vignes, S., Ledru, Y., Lemoine, M., Bert, D., Donzeau-Gouge, V., Dubois, C., Peureux, F.: Application of Requirements Analysis Techniques to the Analysis of Civil Aviation Security Standards. In: Proc. of the First Intl. Workshop on Situational Requirements Engineering Processes (SREP'05), France (2005)
7. Farahbod, R., Glässer, U.: Semantic Blueprints of Discrete Dynamic Systems: Challenges and Needs in Computational Modeling of Complex Behavior. In: Proc. 6th International Heinz Nixdorf Symposium, Heinz Nixdorf Institute (2006)
8. U. Glässer and Y. Gurevich and M. Veanes: Abstract Communication Model for Distributed Systems. IEEE Trans. on Soft. Eng. **30**(7) (2004) 458–472
9. Glässer, U., Gotzhein, R., Prinz, A.: The Formal Semantics of SDL-2000: Status and Perspectives. Comput. Networks **42**(3) (2003) 343–358
10. Brantingham, P.L., Kinney, B., Glässer, U., Singh, K., Vajihollahi, M.: A Computational Model for Simulating Spatial Aspects of Crime in Urban Environments. In Jamshidi, M., ed.: Proceedings of 2005 IEEE International Conference on Systems, Man and Cybernetics, IEEE (2005) 3667–74
11. Börger, E.: The ASM Ground Model Method as a Foundation for Requirements Engineering. In: Verification: Theory and Practice. (2003) 145–160
12. Hinton, A., Kwiatkowska, M., Norman, G., Parker, D.: PRISM: A Tool for Automatic Verification of Probabilistic Systems. In: Proc. 12th International Conference on Tools and Algorithms for the Construction and Analysis of Systems. (2006)
13. PRISM: (PRISM Web Site) http://www.cs.bham.ac.uk/~dxp/prism.
14. Del Castillo, G., Winter, K.: Model Checking Support for the ASM High-Level Language. In Graf, S., Schwartzbach, M., eds.: Proceedings of the 6th International Conference TACAS 2000. Volume 1785 of LNCS., Springer-Verlag (2000) 331–346
15. Glässer, U., Rastkar, S., Vajihollahi, M.: Computational Modeling and Experimental Validation of Aviation Security Procedures. Technical Report SFU-CMPT-TR-2006-02, Simon Fraser University (2006)

# Intelligent Face Recognition Using Feature Averaging

Adnan Khashman and Akram A. Garad

Electrical & Electronic Engineering Department, Near East University, North Cyprus
amk@neu.edu.tr, akram_garad@yahoo.com

**Abstract.** Over the past four years there has been a marginal increase in research on developing advanced information technologies that can be efficiently used for national and international security in our war against terrorism. The list of wanted persons who are still free is getting larger, however, in most cases there is a database containing their face images and this can be used in the development of face recognition systems. A human face is an extremely complex object with features that can vary over time, sometimes very rapidly. This paper presents a fast intelligent face recognition system that uses essential face features averaging and a neural network to identify multi-expression faces. A real life application using this method is implemented on 180 images of 30 persons. Experimental results suggest that this simple but efficient system performs well, thus providing a fast intelligent system for recognizing faces with different expressions.

## 1 Introduction

Biometrics technology is rapidly being adopted in a wide variety of security applications such as electronic and physical access control, homeland security, and defense. Face recognition is an important application in biometrics and has lately been thoroughly investigated [1]. There are many methods to solve the face recognition problem such as Geometric Approach and Template Matching [2], Principle Component Analysis (PCA) [3], Linear Discriminant Analysis (LDA) [4] and Independent Component Analysis (ICA) [5]. PCA and LDA are considered as linear subspace learning algorithms and focus on the global structure of the Euclidean space. ICA is a statistical method for transforming an observed multidimensional random vector into its components that are statistically as independent from each other as possible.

An intelligent face recognition system which is feature-based must deal with three basic problems: detection of the human face in an image, extraction of the essential features of the facial image; and finally the classification. Classification can be implemented using back propagation neural networks which have been successfully used as classifiers for various pattern recognition applications [6].

The aim of the work that is presented in this paper is to develop a fast intelligent face recognition system that recognizes multi-expression faces. The suggested method uses a back propagation neural network and essential face features (eyes, nose and mouth) from different face expressions (natural, smiley, sad and surprised). The averages of these features are determined and presented to the neural network as

S. Mehrotra et al. (Eds.): ISI 2006, LNCS 3975, pp. 432–439, 2006.

pattern vectors. The trained neural network identifies the persons regardless of their different face expressions by learning approximations (via averaging) of the essential face features. The features (eyes, nose and mouth) change according to the expressions. The use of four expressions (natural, smiley, sad and surprised) provides sufficient data for training the neural network to identify the persons.

The developed system is implemented using 180 face images representing 30 persons with 6 different expressions (4 training and 2 testing expressions) for each, and successful results have been achieved. The structure of the paper is as follows: Section 2 provides a brief explanation of the face image databases. Section 3 describes the developed method in details showing face image preprocessing, feature averaging and neural network implementation. Section 4 presents the results of training and testing the neural network using the face image databases. Finally, section 5 concludes the work and provides suggestions for further work.

## 2  Face Databases

There are two databases which will be used for the implementation of the developed intelligent face recognition system. Firstly, our own face database which contains 90 images of 15 persons. Each person has six different face expression images captured and resized to (100x100) pixels, thus resulting in 90 face images in the same resolution and lighting condition. Figure 1 shows the faces of the 15 persons from our database, and an example of a person's six different expressions.

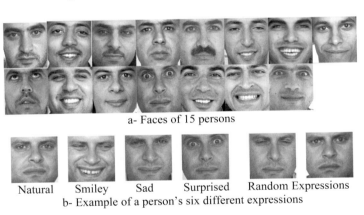

a- Faces of 15 persons

Natural    Smiley    Sad    Surprised    Random Expressions
b- Example of a person's six different expressions

**Fig. 1.** Faces and expressions from our face database

Secondly, our proposed intelligent face recognition system will be implemented using the ORL face database [7]. For implementation and comparison purposes, 90 images from the ORL face database of 15 persons with six different expressions for each will be used. Figure 2 shows the faces of the 15 persons from ORL database, and an example of a person's six different expressions.

A total number of 180 face images of 30 persons with different expressions will be used for the implementation of the proposed intelligent face recognition system. Four out of the six expressions (natural, smiley, sad and surprised) are specifically used for training the neural network within system. The remaining two face expressions are random expressions and will be used together with the four training face expressions (without averaging) to test the trained neural network.

Averaging is applied only during the neural network training phase where the four facial expressions (natural, smiley, sad and surprised) images are reduced to one face image per person by averaging the essential features (eyes, nose, and mouth) separately, thus providing 30 averaged face images for training the neural network. Generalizing or testing the neural network will be implemented using the six facial expressions without the averaging process, thus providing 180 face images for testing the trained neural network.

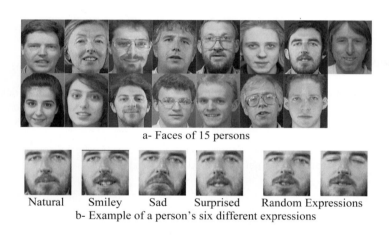

a- Faces of 15 persons

Natural     Smiley     Sad     Surprised     Random Expressions

b- Example of a person's six different expressions

**Fig. 2.** Faces  and expressions from ORL face database [7]

## 3     Intelligent Face Recognition System

The implementation of recognition system comprises two phases: firstly, training the neural network using an approximation of four specific facial expressions which is achieved by averaging the essential features, and secondly testing or generalizing the neural network using the six different expressions without averaging. The block diagram of the proposed intelligent face recognition system is shown in Figure 3. However, before presenting the training or testing images to the network, image preprocessing must be applied in order to reduce the amount of data thus providing a faster recognition system while presenting the neural network with sufficient data representation of each face to achieve meaningful learning.

There are 180 face images of 30 persons with six expressions for each. Training the neural network uses 120 images (which will be averaged to 30 images) representing the 15 persons with four specific expressions. The remaining 60 images of the 15 persons with random different expressions are used together with the 120 training images (prior to averaging) for generalizing the trained neural network, as can be seen in Figure 4, thus resulting in 180 face images for testing.

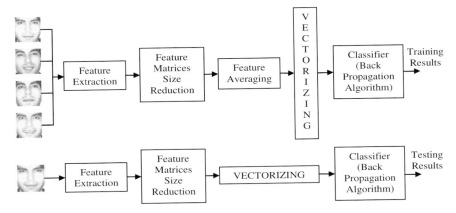

**Fig. 3.** General architecture of the intelligent face recognition system

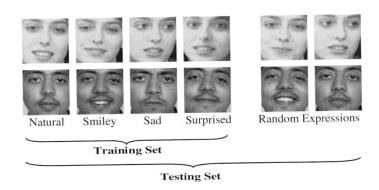

Natural     Smiley     Sad     Surprised          Random Expressions

**Training Set**

**Testing Set**

**Fig. 4.** Examples of training and testing face images

## 3.1   Feature Extraction and Training Face Averaging

Face images preprocessing, prior to training or testing, involves the following stages: Firstly, the main features of the face (eyes, nose and mouth) are manually extracted using Photoshop for each facial expression of each subject as shown in Figure 5 and Figure 6. Secondly, the dimensions of each feature are reduced by averaging. The right eye, left eye, nose and mouth dimensions will be reduced to (5 x 10) pixels, (5 x 10) pixels, (7 x 10) pixels and (6 x 17) pixels respectively. Thus, the output matrices dimension after the averaging process will be 1/3 of the input matrices; for example, the 15x30 pixels input matrix will be after averaging 5x10 pixels.

Thirdly, and this is applied only in the training phase, the 120 training images are reduced to 30 averaged images by taking the average for each feature in the four specific expressions (natural, smiley, sad and surprised) for each subject.

Finally, the averaged extracted features are represented as (272x1) pixel vectors, which will be presented to the input layer of neural network.

**Fig. 5.** Extracted features from different expressions

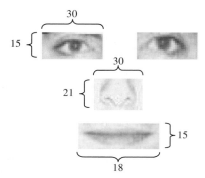

**Fig. 6.** Extracted features dimensions in pixels

## 3.2 Neural Network

The back propagation algorithm is used for the implementation of the proposed intelligent face recognition system, due to its simplicity and efficiency in solving pattern recognition problems [8].

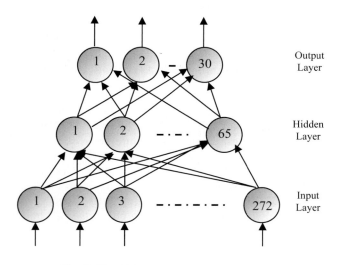

**Fig. 7.** Classifying Neural Network Topology

The neural network comprises an input layer with 272 neurons that carry the values of the averaged extracted features, a hidden layer with 65 neurons and an output layer with 30 neurons which is the number of persons. Figure 7 shows the back propagation neural network design.

The implementation of a neural network consists of training and testing. In this work a total of 180 face images are used and correspond to 30 persons with six different facial expressions for each. For training the neural network 120 face images with the specific expressions, shown in Figure 4, are averaged using the proposed method in section 3.1 and thus reduced to 30 averaged face images that represent approximation of different expressions of the 30 persons.

Testing the trained neural network involves using the remaining 60 face images with random expressions in addition to the 120 training set without averaging.

## 4   Results and Analysis

The neural network learnt and converged after 3188 iterations and within 265 seconds, whereas the running time for the generalized neural network after training and using one forward pass was 0.032 seconds. These results were obtained using a 1.6 GHz PC with 256 MB of RAM, Windows XP OS and Matlab 6.5 software. Table 1 lists the final parameters of the successfully trained neural network. A training time of 265 seconds is fast considering the number of training images and the technical specifications of the computer used. This short training time has been achieved by the novel method of reducing the face data via averaging selected essential face features for training, while maintaining meaningful learning of the neural network. The intelligent face recognition system correctly recognized all averaged face images in the training set as would be expected yielding a 100% recognition rate for all 30 persons.

The intelligent face recognition system was tested using 180 face images which contain different face expressions that were not exposed to the neural network before; 90 images from our face database, and 90 images from the ORL database. All 90 face

**Table 1.** Final Parameters of Trained Neural Network

| | |
|---|---|
| Number of Input Neurons | 272 |
| Number of Hidden Neurons | 65 |
| Number of Output Neurons | 30 |
| Learning Coefficient | 0.0495 |
| Momentum Coefficient | 0.41 |
| Minimum Error | 0.001 |
| Training Iterations | 3188 |
| Training Time | 265 Seconds |

images in our database were correctly identified yielding 100% recognition rate with 91.8 % recognition accuracy, whereas, 84 out of the 90 images from the ORL database were correctly identified yielding 93.3 % recognition rate with 86.8 % recognition accuracy. In total the system recognized 174 out of the available 180 faces achieving 96.7 % correct recognition rate with 89.3 % accuracy.

The processing times were as follows: feature extraction and averaging (7.5 seconds), training the neural network (265 seconds) and running the trained neural network (0.032 seconds). The recognition rates, recognition accuracy and running time of the trained system are shown in Table 2. The robustness, flexibility and speed of this novel intelligent face recognition system have been demonstrated through this application.

**Table 2.** Recognition Rates, Accuracy and Run Time of Recognition System

| Database | Own | ORL | Total |
|---|---|---|---|
| Recognition Rate | (90/90) 100 % | (84/90) 93.3 % | (174/180) 96.7 % |
| Recognition Accuracy | 91.8 % | 86.8 % | 89.3 % |
| Recognition Time | | 0.032 seconds | |

## 5   Conclusion

An intelligent face recognition system is proposed in this paper. The successfully implemented system can be used in a wide variety of security applications such as electronic and physical access control, and homeland security. The novel method uses essential face feature-averaging and neural network classification. The essential features in a face (eyes, nose and mouth) can be used for identifying faces with different expressions. Although the feature pattern values (pixel values) may change with the change of facial expression, the use of averaged-features of a face with four expressions provides the neural network with an approximated understanding of the identity and is found to be sufficient for training a neural network to recognize that face with any expression. The successful implementation of the proposed method was shown throughout a real life implementation using 30 face images showing six different expressions for each.

The use of averaging to reduce the amount of training/testing image data prior to neural network implementation provided reduction in computational cost while maintaining sufficient data for meaningful neural network learning. The overall processing times that include image preprocessing and neural network implementation were 272.5 seconds for training and 0.032 seconds for neural recognition.

Future work includes implementing the developed method using different and larger face databases and comparing the results with currently used face recognition methods. Additionally, partially obstructed faces will be used for testing a trained neural network.

# References

1. Li, S.Z., Jain, A.K. (Eds.): Handbook of Face Recognition, Springer-Verlag, New York (2005)
2. Brunelli, R., Poggio, T.: Face Recognition: Features versus Templates. IEEE Transactions on Pattern Analysis and Machine Intelligence 15 (1993) 1042-1052
3. Turk, M., Pentland, A.: Eignefaces for Recognition. Journal of Cognitive Neuroscience, Vol. 3 (1991) 72-86
4. Belhumeur, P., Hespanha, J., Kriegman, D.: Eigenfaces vs. Fisherfaces: Face Recognition using class specific linear projection. In Proc. ECCV (1996) 45-58
5. Vasilescu, M.A.O., Terzopoulos, D.: Multilinear Image Analysis for Facial Recognition, Proceedings of International Conference on Pattern Recognition (ICPR 2002)
6. Khashman, A., Sekeroglu, B.: Multi-Banknote Identification Using a Single Neural Network, Lecture Notes on Computer Science, Vol. 3708. Springer-Verlag (2005) 123-129
7. Cambridge University, Olivetti Research Laboratory face database, http://www.uk.research.att.com/facedatabase.html
8. Haykin, S.: Neural Networks: A Comprehensive Foundation, Prentice Hall, Upper Saddle River, NJ (1999)

# Multi-perspective Video Analysis of Persons and Vehicles for Enhanced Situational Awareness*

Sangho Park and Mohan M. Trivedi

Computer Vision and Robotics Research Laboratory
University of California at San Diego, La Jolla, CA, USA
{parks, mtrivedi}@ucsd.edu

**Abstract.** This paper presents a multi-perspective vision-based analysis of people and vehicle activities for the enhancement of situational awareness. Multiple perspectives provide a useful invariant feature of object in image, i.e., the footage area on the ground. Moving objects are detected in image domain, and tracking results of the objects are represented in projection domain using planar homography. Spatio-temporal relationships between human and vehicle tracks are categorized to safe or unsafe situation depending on site context such as walkway and driveway locations. Semantic-level information of the situation is achieved with the anticipation of possible directions of near-future tracks using piecewise velocity history. Crowd density is estimated from the footage in homography plane. Experimental data show promising results. Our framework can be applied to broad range of situational awareness for emergency response, disaster prevention, human interactions in structured environments, and crowd movement analysis in wide-view areas.

## 1   Introduction and Motivation

There has been a growing interest in the society and industry to make sensor-based systems enhance the safety and efficiency of human inhabited environments. Enhanced situational awareness is one of the key issues in developing intelligent infrastructures for safer environments. In order to develop automatic situational awareness system, it is important to understand how people interact with each other and with the environment itself. It will be useful to detect, represent and estimate what kind of events are occurring or about to occur in the monitored site. Pedestrian safety and crowd behavior analysis are good examples.

In this paper, we present a methodology for multi-perspective vision-based analysis of human interactivity with other persons and vehicles for enhanced situational awareness. It belongs to more general research problems of analyzing and recognizing human behavior in active environments. We present our methodology in the context of pedestrian safety and crowd monitoring domain.

---

* This research was supported in part by the NSF RESCUE ITR-Project and US DoD Technical Support Work Group (TSWG).

S. Mehrotra et al. (Eds.): ISI 2006, LNCS 3975, pp. 440–451, 2006.

Several research issues have been addressed in the context of behavior analysis when visual modality is used as the main source of information. First of all, the vision-based system is required to distinguish pedestrians versus vehicles and their typical movement patterns, respectively. Detection of invariant features from raw data is critical for the purpose. It is also desirable to locate each moving objects (i.e., persons or vehicles) and to effectively map them on the world coordinate system of the site of interest. Extraction and formation of semantic information from raw video signal is at the heart of the *situational awareness* of the system.

There has been active research effort for vision-based analysis of human activity in computer vision including video surveillance, human-computer interaction, virtual reality, choreography, and medicine. Reviews of general research on vision-based understanding of human motion can be found in [1, 3].

Most of outdoor human monitoring systems have been developed under certain specific environmental contexts: i.e., specific time, place, and activity scenarios involved in the situation [4, 5, 9]. Examplar surveillance systems have been either based on track analysis [6, 8, 10] or body analysis [4]. Track-level analysis is usually applied to wide-area surveillance of multiple moving vehicles / pedestrians in open space such as a parking lot or a pedestrian plaza. In some wide-area surveillance situations, coarse representation of human body in terms of a moving bounding box or an ellipse may be enough for tracking [6]. Other researchers have applied more detailed representation of a human body such as a moving region or a blob [8, 10]. Velastin et al. [10] estimated optical flow to compute the motion direction of pedestrians in subway environments. Body-level analysis usually focuses on more detailed activity analysis of individual persons.

Another important categorization of examplar systems is related to indoor vs. outdoor setup. Comparing to indoor environments, outdoor environments have a lot of environmental variations such as weather change, time shift from morning to evening, moving backgrounds, etc. Outdoor surveillance systems have to deal with those variations, and robustness is still an issue in outdoor surveillance. Most of the outdoor surveillance systems apply track analysis due to the limited image resolution, because the wide field of view (FOV) for outdoor surveillance usually limits the resolution of person appearance to relatively low-resolution images. One of the recent developments in video surveillance is the usage of distributed system to cover multiple monitored scenes with various FOV's. Most of the research mentioned above mainly focuses on recognition of human activity, i.e., human-human interactions. Recognition of human-machine interaction in outdoor environments such as human-vehicle interaction has not been actively addressed. This paper presents a new framework to analyze human activity and interaction with vehicles as well as other humans for the enhancement of automatic situational awareness.

The rest of the paper is organized as follows: Section 2 summarizes our approach to the problem of vision-based transportation safety. Section 3 articulates new concepts and methods for spatio-temporal analysis of tracks. Section 4 explains the site modeling and sensor distribution in a real-world environment.

Section 5 describes the method to track multiple moving objects. Section 6 shows the representation of tracked objects in a world coordinate systems. Experimental results and concluding remarks follow in Sections 7 and 8, respectively.

## 2    System Overview

Our system uses multiple cameras with different perspectives and analyzes the visual information at multiple levels. At gross level, we represent each moving object as a trajectory point of the center of gravity of the object. Track of the moving object is formed along the video sequence. At detailed level, we represent the object in terms of its footage area on the ground in order to estimate the invariant size of the object. We observe that the approximate size of the object's footage area is invariant to translation and rotation, unless the object falls or flips over. Planar homography is used to locate the object's footage position on the world coordinate system. At semantic level, the interaction among persons and vehicles is analyzed. Contextual information including site model and activity scenario is integrated at the semantic level. The concepts of *spatio-temporal interaction boundary* and *time to collide* are introduced to represent and predict various interaction patterns among moving objects.

Foreground moving objects are detected and segmented by background subtraction. Tracking of each object is performed by data association of foreground object appearances between consecutive frames using a constrained expectation-maximization (EM) learning method. Image appearance of the same object varies significantly according to camera perspectives as shown in Fig. 1. Therefore, even though the tracker keeps following the same object, it does not classify the object category into vehicle or person. For the reliable classification of object types, we need to estimate the invariant size of the object. We rectify the images and

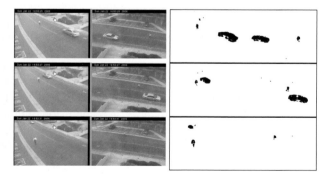

**Fig. 1.** Perspective effect on image appearance. The same object appears very different at different time frames.

map the objects to the world coordinate system using planar homography. We estimate the footage area and location of an object in the world coordinate system by using multiple-view geometry. Fig. 2 depicts the process of estimating

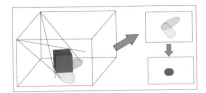

**Fig. 2.** Schematic diagrams for footage area estimation using multiple planar homography. Multiple views of the same object are projected by planar homography, and the intersection of the projected images are used as the object's footage region on the ground.

the footage area. Multiple views of the same object are transformed by planar homography and the intersection of the projected images are used as the footage region of the object on the ground.

Planar homography assumes all the pixels lie on the same plane (i.e., the ground plane in 3D world.) Pixels that violate this assumption result in mapping to a skewed location on the projection plane. By intersecting multiple projection maps of the same object, we can estimate the object's common footage region that observes the assumption. In order to reduce the false estimation of the footage region possibly caused by other adjacent objects, we compare the color histograms of the raw image regions in the multiple views using back-projection of the homography. Bhattacharyya distance measure is used to compare the histogram profiles.

Moving object's true velocity (i.e., speed and direction) in 3D world coordinate system is estimated at the projection plane. The velocity of a moving object determines the object's reaching boundary in a given time. This reaching boundary defines the *spatio-temporal interaction boundary* of the object. If there exists a foreign object at the vicinity of a moving object, the estimation of *time to collide* becomes important; the time of arrival or the time to collide has significant implication regarding safety in transportation systems. In the next section, we discuss the spatio-temporal analysis of tracks.

## 3   Track Analysis in Spatio-temporal Domain

The spatio-temporal characteristics of the interaction boundary provides a useful tool to analyze human-human interactions as well as human-vehicle interactions in terms of time, velocity, and distance as described below.

It is observed that the distance $x$ that can be reached within time $t$ is proportional to velocity $v$ according to dynamics as formulated in Eqn. 1. This implies that, with higher velocity, the range of impact of interaction can reach farther within a given time period.

$$x = v \times t \tag{1}$$

where $v$ has directional component.

Humans are subconsciously aware of this fact, and anticipate the consequence of speed with respect to safety. In the case of human movement, the direction of motion is ambiguous due to the possibility of agile body motion. Therefore, we make the directionality broader, resulting in a circular interaction boundary. It means that we model the interaction boundary as a circular shape with radius proportional to track velocity. In circular interaction boundary, the velocity $v$ is replaced by speed $|v|$ and the reaching distance is represented in terms of distance $|x|$. In the case of vehicle movement, the direction of motion would be more deterministic depending on the driver's intent. Therefore, it would be more realistic to shape the interaction boundary of a vehicle more directional depending on velocity. In the current paper, we assume the circular boundary for both humans and vehicles for simplicity.

The spatio-temporal interaction boundary can be categorized into *interaction potential* from *interaction region*. Both concepts are expressed in terms of spatial boundary that surrounds a moving object, but the former is related to anticipatory interaction, while the latter indicates actual interaction.

We derive the effective radius of *interaction potential*, $r_p$, of a moving object:

$$r_p \approx |v| \times t \tag{2}$$

We model the radial shape of the interaction potential as a probability distribution function (PDF) in terms of a 2D Gaussian distribution, $R = N(\mu, \sigma)$, truncated by the circle of radius $r_p$. The actual parameters of the PDF can be learned with training data. A similar formulation of pedestrian's moving directionality was proposed by Antonini and Bierlairein [2]. However, their method using manual tracking is computed on image plane from a single perspective and is perspective-dependent, whereas our approach is computed on projection plane using planar homography and is view-independent.

As seen above, the spatial and temporal analysis of tracks are highly correlated. We will present more details about the spatio-temporal analysis at track-level modeling of human/vehicle activity in later sections in this paper. The significance and connotation of a specific human track pattern depends on the site context: driveway, walkway, crowded area, etc. The relation between human track patterns and site context is mediated by policy, by which we mean which activity needs to be regulated/monitored and which activity is allowed. In this paper, we are interested in the combination of spatial and temporal relations in the site context as summarized in Table 1. The table on the left shows the *spatial* site context of human activity, while the table on the right shows the *temporal* site context of interactivity between two objects. A person may stay, walk, or run at different sites such as walkway, driveway, or specific region of interest (ROI) at a bus-stop area or a building entrance zone. $\bigcirc$, $\triangle$, and $\times$ denote normal, cautious, and abnormal track patterns, respectively. Cautious or abnormal pattern at a specific ROI depends on the duration of stay and the site context. *Interaction region* is the actual boundary in which interaction between two objects occurs. We define the interaction region between two objects (i.e., person or vehicle) to be the intersection of the two interaction potentials.

Diagrams for the track-level analysis of human activity and interactivity are shown in Fig. 3. The figures from the left to the right show a track in 3D spatio-temporal space in xyt dimensions, the track's interaction potential boundary in

**Table 1.** Track vs. site context. ◯, △, and × denote normal, cautious, and abnormal track patterns, respectively. Cautious or abnormal pattern at a specific ROI depends on duration of stay and site context.

| person<br>site | stay | walk | run |
|---|---|---|---|
| walkway | ◯ | ◯ | × |
| driveway | × | ◯ | ◯ |
| ROI | ◯, × | ◯ | × |

| object 1<br>object 2 | stay | slow | fast |
|---|---|---|---|
| stay | ◯ | ◯ | △ |
| slow | ◯ | △ | × |
| fast | △ | × | × |

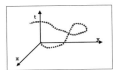 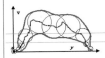 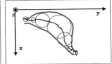 

**Fig. 3.** Schematic diagrams for trajectory analysis in spatio-temporal space. Circles represent interaction potential boundaries at a given space/time. Red curves represent the envelopes of the interaction boundary along tracks.

velocity (v) vs. spatial (y) dimension, planar view of the track and interaction potential in space (x vs. y axis), and the interaction duration between two tracks depicted by the rectangle along a time line, respectively.

The main focus on moving-person interactions in this paper is regarding the macro-level concepts such as *approach, pass by, depart*, etc. This kind of interactions is characterized by short duration of the interaction period.

## 4  Distributed Sensor Placements and Site Model

Environmental context, especially spatial environment, can be represented by site modeling. Various approaches are possible depending on the available site information. If the 3D structural information is available, we can build a 3D CAD model of the site, which is useful for representing important structures such as buildings and roads. The merit of 3D CAD model is that it provides actual 3D world coordinate systems for the site. But this modeling usually requires multiple cameras and accurate camera calibration. If the site is mainly composed of a flat ground plane, then we can build a planar homography. The advantage of homography-based modeling is that it provides perspective-compensated plan view of the site. It may require multiple cameras with overlapped field of view (FOV). If the site is arbitrarily complex or spatial configuration is ambiguous from camera view, we can still manually assign region of interest (ROI) for specific interest regions. Most of the single camera-based 2D site modeling falls in this category. The advantage of 2D site modeling is that it is flexible and

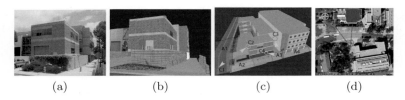

(a)                    (b)                    (c)                    (d)

**Fig. 4.** The real testbed of the current system: Actual building (a),its 3D site model (b), camera placements (C1-C4) with viewing directions to areas (A1-A4) (c), and Area-1 (A1) in yellow in the satellite image (d), respectively

simple. Some ambiguity is inevitable due to occlusion, perspective distortion of the view, etc.

We have built an intelligent infrastructure (called 'smart space') with the combination of the above modeling options to generate a heterogeneous site model of an actual building in Fig. 4 (a) which is located in the satellite image in Fig. 4 (d). A 3D CAD model is made and texture-mapped based on architectural data about the building structure and floor plans (Fig. 4 (a), (b).) Four cameras are mounted on specific locations of the building to cover surrounding roads (Fig. 4 (c)). Camera placements are indicated by (C1-C4) with viewing directions and the corresponding view areas (A1-A4). Cameras 1 and 2 view Area-1, Camera-3 views Area-3, and Camera-4 views Area-4, respectively. This paper focuses on Area-1 viewed from Cameras 1 and 2. Area-1 viewed from C1 and C2 is shown in yellow in Fig. 4 (d); straight lines depict the camera fields of view, and the yellow rectangular region corresponds to the planar homography result in Fig. 5 (c). (See the upper right panel in Fig. 6 for another example of the homography mapping.)

## 5   Tracking of Multiple Objects

Vision-based tracking of multiple objects starts from the processing of foreground segmentation. We use the frame differencing technique with posterior morphological operation for the segmented foreground.

At track-level, the multi-object tracking uses bounding boxes and 2D Gaussian representations of foreground regions. As the objects translate, the Gaussian parameters are updated along the sequence in a frame-by-frame manner. Updating these Gaussian parameters along the sequence amounts to tracking the objects moving in the 2D image frames. The expectation maximization (EM) based updating of the 2D Gaussian representation effectively keeps track of grouping and splitting between objects. However, the usual EM-based update is not reliable under severe occlusions or long time grouping and it can be caught in a local minimum in the parameter space. We overcome this problem by constraining the EM process according to each objects' track history and velocity limitations. At detaile level, the color distribution of the foreground regions are represented by Gaussian mixture model and trained by Expectation-Maximization (EM) learning algorithm. Multiple coherent image patches (called blobs) are formed within the segmented foreground regions and are represented by the Gaussian mixture model. The details of the tracking algorithm is explained in our previous paper in [7].

## 6   Planar Homography Mapping

The geometric registration of a camera viewpoint is performed using a homography mapping $H$ from a set of 4 matching points between image coordinate system (i.e., $[x_i, y_i], i \in \{1, 4\}$)) and the world coordinate system (i.e., $[x_i', y_i'], i \in \{1, 4\}$)). The perspective parameters correspond to a null space of the matrix A (given in Eqn. 3 ) and are estimated using SVD of A.

$$AH = \begin{bmatrix} x_1 & y_1 & 1 & 0 & 0 & 0 & -x_1'x_1 & -x_1'y_1 & -x_1' \\ 0 & 0 & 0 & x_1 & y_1 & 1 & -y_1'x_1 & -y_1'y_1 & -y_1' \\ x_2 & y_2 & 1 & 0 & 0 & 0 & -x_2'x_2 & -x_2'y_2 & -x_2' \\ 0 & 0 & 0 & x_2 & y_2 & 1 & -y_2'x_2 & -y_2'y_2 & -y_2' \\ x_3 & y_3 & 1 & 0 & 0 & 0 & -x_3'x_3 & -x_3'y_3 & -x_3' \\ 0 & 0 & 0 & x_3 & y_3 & 1 & -y_3'x_3 & -y_3'y_3 & -y_3' \\ x_4 & y_4 & 1 & 0 & 0 & 0 & -x_4'x_4 & -x_4'y_4 & -x_4' \\ 0 & 0 & 0 & x_4 & y_4 & 1 & -y_4'x_4 & -y_4'y_4 & -y_4' \end{bmatrix} \begin{bmatrix} h_{11} \\ h_{12} \\ h_{13} \\ h_{21} \\ h_{22} \\ h_{23} \\ h_{31} \\ h_{32} \\ h_{33} \end{bmatrix} = \begin{bmatrix} 0 \\ 0 \\ 0 \\ 0 \\ 0 \\ 0 \\ 0 \\ 0 \\ 0 \end{bmatrix} \quad (3)$$

If we denote $H_2^1$ as the homography from view 2 to 1, we can register multiple cameras by series of concatenated homographies given in Eqn. 4.

$$H_m^n = H_{n+1}^n H_{n+2}^{n+1} \ldots H_{m-1}^{m-2} H_m^{m-1} \quad (4)$$

In the current system, we map points in view 1, $P_1$, and points in view 2, $P_2$, to a common corresponding point in the virtual view, $P_v$, by homography matrices $H_1^v$ and $H_2^v$, respectively. The coordinate system of the virtual view is specified by the 3D CAD model in Fig. 4.

$$P_1^v = H_1^v P_1 \quad (5)$$
$$P_2^v = H_2^v H_2 \quad (6)$$

$P_1^v$ and $P_2^v$ are then averaged.

## 7   Experiments

We have tested our system with video data captured at area A1 in Fig. 4 during different day times for several days. Two cameras C1 and C2 were used to capture the views. Images in Fig. 5 (a)(b) are example views from camera C1 and C2 with detected persons, respectively, and the homography-based registration result is shown in (c). The green and red regions in (c) are user-defined walkway and driveway for site contextualization. The ground truth for the image registration is obtained from satellite imagery in Fig. 4 (d).

(a)                    (b)                        (c)

**Fig. 5.** View registration of Area-1 (A1) in Fig. 4 using the planar homography

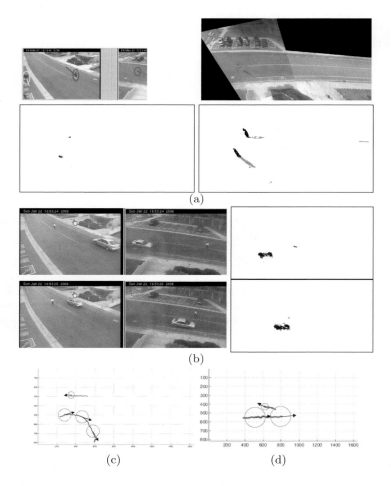

(a)

(b)

(c)                                (d)

**Fig. 6.** Estimation of interaction patterns of moving objects with different velocities using the homography-mapped footage regions in the projection planes. Walking person in green plot vs. skateboarding person in red plot (a)(c). Walking person in green plot vs. driving car in red plot (b)(d).

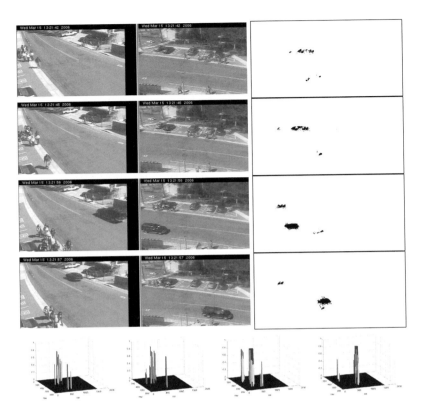

**Fig. 7.** Dynamic density estimation of crowds and moving vehicles captured at 0, 3, 14, and 15 seconds, respectively. PDFs correspond to the homography maps.

Fig. 6 shows the estimation of interaction patterns between different moving objects captured on a cloudy day. The interaction patterns are analyzed using the tracks of the homography-mapped footage regions in the projection plane corresponding to the region of interest in Fig. 4 (d). In Fig. 6 (a), the images starting clockwise from upper left panel show that multiple views of the site with two detected persons in circle, homography projection plane map of the two views, overlay of the two projections of foreground regions (not shadow!), and the footage areas of each person obtained from the overlay, respectively. Fig. 6 (c) shows two simultaneous tracks of (a): a walking person's track in green and a skateboarding person's track in red in different speeds. Piecewise velocities are represented by arrows, and spatio-temporal interaction potentials are denoted by gray circles at each moment. The absence of overlap between the two tracks' interaction potentials successfully indicates that the monitored scene is in safe situation. In Fig. 6 (b), the images on the upper and lower rows show the raw input views and the detected footage regions in projection plane at different moments.

Fig. 6 (d) shows two simultaneous tracks of (b): a walking person's track in green and a moving vehicle's track in red. The person's proximity to the big interaction potentials (denoted by gray circles) of the vehicle properly indicates the danger of a possible hit.

Our systems' site context information also includes various statistics computed on the fly for crowd density plot, pedestrian flow directions, vehicle traffic histogram, etc. In wide-view open area, counting individuals may not be possible or robust especially when the site is crowded. Therefore, it would be more useful to estimate the detected objects' density, range, and moving velocity in the world coordinate system using the footage areas for each group of objects. Fig. 7 shows our estimation of dynamic density patterns of crowds and moving vehicles observed on a sunny day. Each row in Fig. 7 shows multi-perspective image frames, and the moving objects' detected footage regions mapped on homography plane. The upper four rows show the scene change in terms of spatial distribution of moving objects. The last row shows the probability density functions (PDFs) of crowdiness of the upper four rows. The PDFs were estimated by dividing the homography plane inherently into grid regions and computing the density of the footage pixels in each grid cell. The density patterns and their dynamic changes provide the information about how each region of the monitored site is occupied by people or vehicles for how many frames and how they interact. The information provides enhanced situational awareness.

From the tested experimental site, it is observed that the driveway is sporadically occupied by fast moving high-density large blobs classified to vehicles, whereas the pedestrian walkways are frequently occupied by slow-moving sparse blobs classified to moving crowds. This empirical observation supports our framework for the spatio-temporal analysis of site context in Table 1.

## 8   Conclusion

In this paper we have presented a multi-perspective vision-based analysis framework to estimate human and vehicle activities for enhanced situational awareness. Planar homography using multiple perspectives provides invariant estimation of footage area of viewed objects for object classification. Moving objects' tracks are robustly estimated with the footage regions in the world coordinate system. Spatio-temporal interrelationship between human and vehicle tracks is capitalized in terms of different combinations of track vs. site context such as walkway and driveway. The concepts of *interaction boundary* and *time to collide* of each moving objects are introduced to build semanticcally meaningful situational awareness. We demonstrated experimental evaluation of our method using pedestrian safety and disaster anticipation applications. Our multi-perspective vision system and the multi-level analysis framework can be applied to broader domains including emergency response, human interactions in structured environments, and crowd movement analysis in wide-view sites.

# References

1. J.K. Aggarwal and Q. Cai. Human motion analysis: a review. *Computer Vision and Image Understanding*, 73(3):295–304, 1999.
2. Antonini G and Bierlaire M. Capturing interactions in pedestrian walking behavior in a discrete choice framework. *Transportation Research Part B*, September 2005.
3. D. Gavrila. The visual analysis of human movement: a survey. *Computer Vision and Image Understanding*, 73(1):82–98, 1999.
4. I. Haritaoglu, D. Harwood, and L. S. Davis. W4: Real-time surveillance of people and their activities. *IEEE transactions on Pattern Analysis and Machine Intelligence*, 22(8):797–808, August 2000.
5. Stephen J. McKenna, Sumer Jabri, Zoran Duric, and Harry Wechsler. Tracking interacting people. In *4th IEEE International Conference on Automatic Face and Gesture Recognition (FG 2000)*, pages 348–353, 2000.
6. N. M. Oliver, B. Rosario, and A. P. Pentland. A Bayesian Computer Vision System for Modeling Human Interactions. *IEEE Trans. Pattern Analysis and Machine Intelligence*, 22(8):831–843, August 2000.
7. S. Park and M. M. Trivedi. A track-based human movement analysis and privacy protection system adaptive to environmental contexts. In *IEEE International Conference on Advanced Video and Signal based Surveillance*, Como, Italy, 2005.
8. P. Remagnino, A.I. Shihab, and G.A. Jones. Distributed intelligence for multi-camera visual surveillance. *Pattern Recognition: Special Issue on Agent-based Computer Vision*, 37(4):675–689, 2004.
9. M. M. Trivedi, T. Gandhi, and K. Huang. Distributed interactive video arrays for event capture and enhanced situational awareness. *IEEE Intelligent Systems, Special Issue on Artificial Intelligence for Homeland Security*, September 2005.
10. S.A. Velastin, B.A. Boghossian, B. Lo, J. Sun, and M.A. Vicencio-Silva. Prismatica: Toward ambient intelligence in public transport environments. *IEEE Transactions on Systems, Man, and Cybernetics -Part A*, 35(1):164–182, 2005.

# Database Security Protection Via Inference Detection*

Yu Chen and Wesley W. Chu

Computer Science Department
University of California, Los Angeles, CA 90095
{chenyu, wwc}@cs.ucla.edu

**Abstract.** Access control mechanisms are commonly used to provide control over who may access sensitive information. However, malicious users can exploit the correlation among the data and infer sensitive information from a series of seemingly innocuous data access. In this paper, we proposed a detection system that utilizes both the user's current query and past query log to determine if the current query answer can infer sensitive information. This detection system is being extended to the cases of multiple collaborative users based on the query history of all the users and their collaborative levels for specific sensitive information.

## 1  Introduction

Access control mechanisms are commonly used to protect users from the divulgence of sensitive information in data sources. However, such techniques are insufficient because malicious users may access a series of innocuous data, and from the received answers, the malicious users may employ inference techniques to derive sensitive information.

Database inferences have previously been studied. Delugach and Hinke [DH96] and Garvey et al. [GLQ92] developed approaches that use schema level knowledge for inference detection at database design time. However, Yip et al. has pointed out the inadequacy of schema level inference detection, and he identifies six types of inference rules from data level [YL98]. An inference controller prototype was developed to handle inferences during query processing. Rule-based inference strategies were applied in this prototype to protect the security [TFC93]. Furthermore, to provide scalable inference in large systems, feasible inference channels that are based on query and database schema are generated to guide the data inference [CCH94].

In this paper, we propose to develop an inference detection system that resides at the central directory site. The system keeps track of users' query history and when a new query is posed, all the channels where sensitive information can be inferred will be identified. If the probability to infer sensitive information exceeds a pre-specified threshold, the current query request will then be denied. Further, we analyze user social relations to detect collaborative inference attacks.

---

* This research is supported by NSF grant number IIS-03113283.

S. Mehrotra et al. (Eds.): ISI 2006, LNCS 3975, pp. 452–458, 2006.

## 2  The Inference Framework

As shown in Figure 1, the proposed inference detection system consists of three modules:

The *Knowledge Acquisition* module extracts data dependency knowledge, data schema knowledge and domain semantic knowledge. Based on the database schema and the data sources, we can extract data dependency between attributes in entities. Domain semantic knowledge can be derived by specific constraints and rules.

The *Semantic Inference Model (SIM)* is a data model that combines data schema, dependency and semantic knowledge. The model links related attributes and entities as well as semantic knowledge needed for data inference. Therefore SIM represents all the possible relationships among the attributes of the data sources. A *Semantic Inference Graph (SIG)* can be constructed by instantiating the entities and attributes in the SIM. For a given query, the SIG provides inference channels for inferring sensitive information.

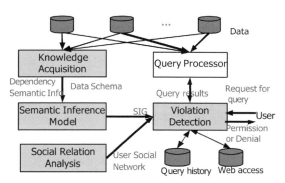

Based on the inference channels derived from the SIG, the *Violation Detection* module combines the new query request with the request log, and it checks to see if the current request exceeds the pre-specified threshold of information leakage. If there is collaboration according to social relation analysis, the *Violation Detection* module will decide whether to answer the current query based on the acquired knowledge among the malicious group members and their social relation to the current user.

**Fig. 1.** The framework for an Inference Detection System

## 3  Knowledge Acquisition for Data Inference

Since users may pose queries and acquire knowledge from different sources, we need to construct a model for the detection system to track the users' inference intention. The semantic inference model requires the system to acquire the following knowledge.

*Data Dependency*: Data dependency represents causal relationships and correlations between attribute values. Let $E_i$ be entity $i$, $e_i$ be the instance of $E_i$, A and B be attributes of $E_i$. We use conditional probability $p_{ij}=Pr(B=b_i|A=a_j)$ as a parameter to represent the data dependency from B to A. Data dependency can be divided into two types: *dependency-within-entity* and *dependency-between-related-entities*. Let A and B be two attributes in an entity E. If B depends on A, then for all the instances of E, the value of attribute B depends on the value of attribute A. In this case, we say A and B are dependent within entity. Let A be an attribute in entity $E_1$, B be an attribute in

$E_2$, and $E_1$ and $E_2$ are related by R, which is a relation that can derived from database schema.

*Database Schema*: In relational databases, database designers use data definition language to define data schema. The owners of the entities specify the primary key and foreign key pairs. Such pairing represents a relationship between two entities. If entity $E_1$ has primary key *pk*, entity $E_2$ has foreign key *fk*, and $e_1.pk=e_2.fk$, then dependency-between-related-entities from attribute A (in $e_1$) to attribute B (in $e_2$) can be derived.

*Domain-Specific Semantic Knowledge*: For a given database, there are certain semantic relationships among attributes and/or entities which can be represented by the constraints for the attribute values. Since users often pose query with semantic constraints, domain-specific semantic knowledge is needed to transform these constraints into non-semantic terms for query processing [CYC96]. Therefore, such semantic knowledge needs to be acquired and should play a part in the data inference. Semantic knowledge among attributes is not defined in the database and may vary with context. We can acquire the corresponding set of semantic knowledge based on the set of semantic queries posed by the users. Based on queries, we can extract semantic knowledge and integrate it into the Semantic Inference Model.

## 4   Semantic Inference Model

The Semantic Inference Model (SIM) represents dependent and semantic relationships among attributes of all the entities in the information system. As shown in Figure 2, the related attributes (nodes) are connected by links that represent their relationships. There are three types of relation links:

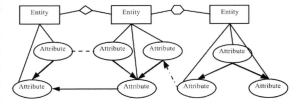

**Fig. 2.** A Semantic Inference Model. Entities are interconnected by schema relations and semantic relations. The related attributes (nodes) are connected by their data dependency, schema and semantic links.

*Dependency link* connects dependent attributes within the same entity or related entities.

*Schema link* connects an attribute of the primary key to the corresponding attribute of the foreign key in the related entities.

*Semantic link* connects attributes with a specific semantic relation. The specific semantic relation (e.g., "can land") can be obtained from the domain knowledge or by mining the data sources. The set of candidate semantic relations can be derived from the set of semantic queries.

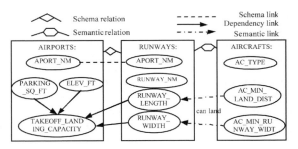

**Fig. 3.** A Semantic Inference Model example for Airports, Runways and Aircraft

## 4.1  Semantic Inference Model Reduction

It is desirable for us to simplify the SIM model by reducing the number of redundant links. A SIM consists of linking related attributes (structure) and their corresponding conditional probabilities (parameters). To reduce the model complexity, we generate a set of candidate structures with their corresponding parameters, and select the one that best matches the data sources [FGK96, GTK01, GFK01].

## 4.2  Semantic Inference Graph

To perform inference at the instance level, we instantiate the SIM with specific entity instances and generate a semantic inference graph (SIG). Each node in the SIG represents an attribute for a specific instance. Related attributes are then connected via instance-level dependency links, instance-level schema links and instance-level semantic links. As a result, the SIG represents all the instance-level inference channels in the SIM.

*Instance-level dependency link:* When a SIM is instantiated, the dependency-within-entity is transformed to dependency-within-instance in the SIG. Similarly, the dependency-between-related-entities in the SIM is transformed to dependency between two attributes in the related instances. This type of dependency is preserved only if two instances are related by the instantiated schema link.

*Instance-level schema link:* The schema links between entities in SIM represent "key, foreign-key" pairs. At instance level, if the value of the primary key of an instance $e_1$ is equal to the value of the corresponding foreign key in the other instance $e_2$, which can be represented as $R(e_1, e_2)$, then connecting these two attributes will represent the schema link at the instance level. Otherwise, these two attributes are not connected.

*Instance-level semantic link evaluation:* The semantic inference from a source node to a target node can be evaluated as follows. If the semantic relation between the source and the target node is unknown or if the value of the source node is unknown, then the source and target node are independent. When the semantic relationship is known, the conditional probability table of the target node is updated with the known semantic relationship.

## 4.3  Evaluating Inference in Semantic Inference Graph

For a given SIG, there are many feasible inference channels that can be formed via linking the set of dependent attributes. Therefore, we propose to map the SIG to a Bayesian network to reduce the computational complexity in evaluating users' inference probability for the sensitive attributes.

For any given node in a Bayesian network, if the value of its parent node(s) is known, then the node is independent of all its non-descending nodes in the network [Pea88]. This independence condition greatly reduces the complexity in computing the joint probability of nodes in the network. More specifically, let $x_i$ be the value of the node $X_i$, $pa_i$ be the values of the parent nodes of $X_i$, then $P(x_i|pa_i)$ denotes the conditional probability of $x_i$ given $pa_i$ where $i=1,2,...,n$. Thus, the joint probability of the variables $x_i$ is reduced to the product of $P(x_i \mid pa_i)$:

$P(x_1,\ldots,x_n) = \prod_i P(x_i | pa_i)$ (Equation (1)). The probability for users to infer the sensitive node $S=s$ given known evidences $D_i=d_i$, $i=1, 2,\ldots, n$ is: $P(s | d_1, d_2 \ldots, d_n) = P(s, d_1, d_2 \ldots, d_n)/P(d_1, d_2 \ldots, d_n)$ (Equation (2)), which can be further computed using Equation (1). Thus, the probability of inferring a sensitive node can be computed from the conditional probabilities in the Bayesian network. Many algorithms have been developed to efficiently perform such calculations [Dec96, JLO90].

Probabilistic Relational Model (PRM) is an extension of Bayesian network that integrates schema knowledge from relational data sources [FGK99, GTK01, GFK01]. Specifically, in PRM an attribute can have two distinct types of parent-child dependencies: *dependency-within-entity* and *dependency-between-related-entities*, which matches the two types of dependency links in the SIM. Since the semantic links in SIM are similar to dependency links, we can convert each SIM to a PRM-based model. The corresponding Bayesian network can be generated after instantiating the model to instance level. Thus, for a given network, the probability of inferring a specific sensitive attribute can be evaluated via efficient Bayesian inference algorithms. In our test bed, we use SamIam [Sam], a comprehensive Bayesian network tool developed by the Automated Reasoning Group at UCLA, to carry out the inference calculation.

## 5   Inference Violation Detection

Semantic inference graphs provide an integrated view of the relationships among data attributes, which can be used to detect inference violation for sensitive nodes. In such a graph, the values of the attributes are set according to the answers of the previous posted queries. Based on the list of queries and the user who posted these queries, the value of the inference will be modified accordingly. If the current query answer can infer the sensitive information greater than the pre-specified threshold, then the request for accessing the query answer will be denied.

Consider our previous example, let the TAKEOFF_LANDING_CAPACITY of any airport be the sensitive attribute, and it should not be inferred with probability greater than 70%. If the user has known that:

1. Aircraft C-5 can land in airport LAX runway r1.
2. C-5 has "aircraft_min_ land_dist = long"and "aircraft_min_runway_width = wide." Then this user is able to infer the sensitive attribute LAX's "TAKEOFF_LANDING_ CAPACITY=large" via Equation (2) and (1) with probability 58.30%. Now if the same user poses another query about the "Parking_sq_ft of LAX", and if this query is answered ("LAX_Parking_Sq_Ft=large"), then the probability of inferring "LAX_TAKEOFF_ LANDING_CAPACITY=large" will increase to 71.50%, which is higher than the pre-specified threshold. Thus, this query request should be denied.

We are currently extending our inference violation detection system from a single user to multiple user cases, where users may collaborate with each other to jointly infer sensitive data. We propose to employ a user social network to model the relationships among cell members for deriving their collaborative inference. A social network is a graph structure that represents the relationship among the user population. The edges of the network represent the influence level of one user to another. Such a network can be constructed from the answers of questionnaires such as those used in security clearances, personal profiles and interviews. For a given specific task, the amount of information that flows from one user to another depends on how close their relationships are. Thus, the collaborative inference for a specific task can be derived by tracking and combining each user's query history together with their collaborative levels from the user social network.

## 6 Conclusion

We proposed a technique to prevent users to infer sensitive information from a series of seemingly innocuous queries. Based on the data dependency, the database schema and the semantic knowledge, we constructed a semantic inference model (SIM) that links all the related attributes and thus, represent all possible inference channels from any attributes to the set of pre-assigned sensitive attributes. The SIM is then instantiated by specific instances and reduced to a semantic inference graph (SIG) for inference violation detection to control query access. To reduce computation complexity for inference, the SIG can be mapped into a Bayesian network. Available Bayesian network tool can then be used for evaluating the inference probability along the inference channels. When a user poses a query, the detection system will examine his/her past query log and calculate the probability of inferring sensitive information from answering this posed query. The query request will be denied if it can infer sensitive information with probability exceeding the pre-specified threshold. We are currently extending the detection system to multiple collaborative users based on query history of all the users as well as their social relations.

## References

[CCH94]  Wesley W. Chu, Qiming Chen and Andy Y. Hwang. "Query Answering via Cooperative Data Inference." *Journal of Intelligent Information Systems* (JIIS), Volume 3(1): 57-87, 1994.

[CYC96]  Wesley W. Chu, Hua Yang, Kuorong Chiang, Michael Minock, Gladys Chow, and Chris Larson. "CoBase: A Scalable and Extensible Cooperative Information System." *Journal of Intelligence Information Systems* (JIIS). Vol6, 1996, Kluwer Academic Publishers, Boston, Mass.

[Dec96]  Rina Dechter. "Bucket elimination: A unifying framework for probabilistic inference." In *Proc. of the 12th Conference on Uncertainty in Artificial Intelligence (UAI)*, pages 211-219, 1996.

[DH96]   H. S. Delugach and T. H. Hinke. "Wizard: A Database Inference Analysis and Detection System." In *IEEE Trans Knowledge and Data Engeneering*, vol. 8, no. 1, 1996. pp. 56-66.

[FGK99]  N. Friedman, L. Getoor, D. Koller and A. Pfeffer. "Learning Probabilistic Relational Models." *Proceedings of the 16th International Joint Conference on Artificial Intelligence (IJCAI)*, Stockholm, Sweden, August 1999, pages 1300--1307.

[GLQ92] T.D. Garvey, T.F. Lunt, X. Quain, and M. Stickel, "Toward a Tool to Detect and Eliminate Inference Problems in the Design of Multilevel Databases." *6th Annual IFIP WG 11.3 Working Conference on Data and Applications Security*, 1992.

[GTK01] L. Getoor, B. Taskar, and D. Koller. "Selectivity Estimation using Probabilistic Relational Models." *Proceedings of the ACM SIGMOD Conference*, 2001.

[GFK01] Z. Getoor, N. Friedman, D. Koller, and A. Pfeffer. "Learning Probabilistic Relational Models." *Relational Data Mining*, S. Dzeroski and N. Lavrac, Eds., Springer-Verlag, 2001.

[JLO90] F. V. Jensen, S.L. Lauritzen, and K.G. Olesen. "Bayesian updating in recursive graphical models by local computation." *Computational Statistics Quarterly*, 4:269-282, 1990.

[Pea88] Judea Pearl. "Probabilistic Reasoning in Intelligence Systems." Morgan Kaufmann, 1988.

[Sam] SamIam by Automated Reasoning Group, UCLA. http://reasoning.cs.ucla.edu/samiam/

[TFC93] Bhavani M. Thuraisingham, William Ford, M. Collins, and J. O'Keeffe. "Design and Implementation of a Database Inference Controller." *Data Knowl. Eng.* 11(3), page 271, 1993.

[YL98] Raymond W. Yip, and Karl N. Levitt. "Data Level Inference Detection in Database Systems." PCSFW: *Proceedings of the 11th Computer Security Foundations Workshop*, 1998.

# An Embedded Bayesian Network Hidden Markov Model for Digital Forensics

Olivier De Vel [1], Nianjun Liu [2], Terry Caelli [2], and Tiberio S. Caetano[2]

[1] Defence Science & Technology Organisation (DSTO), Australia
olivier.devel@dsto.defence.gov.au
[2] National ICT Australia (NICTA)
{nianjun.liu, terry.caelli, tiberio.caetano}@nicta.com.au

**Abstract.** In the paper we combine a Bayesian Network model for encoding forensic evidence during a given time interval with a Hidden Markov Model (EBN-HMM) for tracking and predicting the degree of criminal activity as it evolves over time. The model is evaluated with 500 randomly produced digital forensic scenarios and two specific forensic cases. The experimental results indicate that the model fits well with expert classification of forensic data. Such initial results point out the potential of such Dynamical Bayesian Network methods for the analysis of digital forensic data.

## 1 Forensics Evidence and Its Temporal Metadata Structure

Digital forensic evidence corresponds to the dataset used to decide whether a crime has been committed and can provide a link between a crime and its victim or a crime and its perpetrator [1]. The evidence can be sourced from storage devices (disks, discs etc.), networks (e.g., packet data, routing tables, logs), embedded digital systems (mobile phones, PDAs), telecommunications traffic, and so on. Evidence not only includes the content of a forensic entity but also meta-data associated with the entity such as, the document tracking history, timestamps, users, authors etc. Of particular interest to digital forensic investigations are conditions where the evidence is available in the form of forensic entities (eg., a MS Word document, an email message, a web page that was browsed etc.) that are generally time-stamped (eg., time-stamps for document files, cached web pages etc.) and attributed (eg., name of the document author). Some of these entities may be related to one or more other forensic entities (*eg.,* the topic of the contents of a web page and of an email may be the same). In such cases forensic evidence is rich in content, meta-data and relations in which evidence instances are linked together in a complex temporal directed multi-graph.

Many research groups are working in inducing graphs from text documents – some of which are working in the temporal domain [2] but few of them induce the graphs from a combination of text data (sourced from documents, emails etc.) and the rich set of meta-data (time-stamps, sender/receivers, etc.) that we obtain in digital forensics. However, to accomplish this we need to develop a taxonomy that encompasses both the text data and meta-data in a temporal context.

S. Mehrotra et al. (Eds.): ISI 2006, LNCS 3975, pp. 459 – 465, 2006.

The major objective of digital forensic investigations is to extract unusual and interesting events and their causal relationships. Our paper focuses on the analysis of the metadata, the extraction of forensic evidence along a time sequence or timeline, building up a Bayesian network to model interactions between different forensic evidence and then applying the proposed EBN-HMM model — Embedding Bayesian Network Hidden Markov Model for summarizing, learning, inference and interpreting possible criminal activities. The fundamental tasks are to estimate typical digital crime scenario models from data and to infer the most likely criminal acts given current observations and past criminal activities.

## 2  Evidence Extraction Along a Time Sequence and Classification

The example forensic case we deal with in this paper is a synthetic industrial IP leakage scenario. There are two principal suspects ("Tricia", a manager, and "Arthur", a system admistrator and software engineer) involved in this case. There are three computers (two PCs, one each belonging to Tricia and Arthur, and one server named "womboyn") in two different locations. Multiple parallel threads of activities are happening in this case including, a) an unanticipated company restructure (with a document being emailed anonymously prior to the fact), b) non work-related activities, and c) submarine code (the IP) being leaked to a rival company. The end-game is to identify the innocent or criminal party and then identify the sequence of events that lead to identifying the perpetrator of the IP leakage. This is summarized as a graph of observation objects (with time attributes) from which one has to induce the causal graph of events/activities. The forensic data come from three sources. The first consists of email messages including all of the suspects' emails: sending, receiving, deleting, and draft, etc., during a specific period. The second source of data is the web browsing dataset having attributes such as directories, file type, file name, timestamps, etc, which are extracted from the internet cache folder. The third data set is related to file systems, event logs, document files, etc.

Forensic data and their relations are quite complex, even if these data are encountered on a single computer host system where the data could be sourced from webpage cache, emails, event logs,  file systems, chat room records and registries. For examples, web pages have URL addresses, images, topic(s), time-stamps, etc. We summarize and simplify the forensic actions being eight nodes and their interactions as shown in Figure 2. "User" is the first Node (labelled N1), the "LogServer" node (N2) includes who logged into the server, the "Browseweb" node (N3) describes when and what web page is being browsed etc. The nodes of "ReadEmail"(N4) and "SendEmail" (N8) correspond to when, who and what topics are transmitted through emails. The nodes for "DownloadSoftware"(N5), "InstallApp"(N6) and "ExecuteApp" (N7) programs indicate when and which programs are being downloaded and executed.

According to the eight nodes of forensic actions, all of the forensic data extracted and stored were summarised in the temporal domain. The temporal domain is partitioned into ten convenient time intervals (T1 to T10), where each time interval corresponds to one or more days of case activities. Table 1 is a sample analysis of one suspect's (Tricia) email messages, showing activities in her emails sent.

**Table 1.** An example of a suspect's (Tricia) email outbox analysis over ten time intervals

| Time | Date | Quantity | Event brief descriptions |
|---|---|---|---|
| T1 | 8-10/01/2003 | 5 | Contacts Marvin in the rival company. |
| T2 | 11/01/2003 | 1 | Tries to have a dinner with Marvin and other staff of the rival company. |
| T3 | 14/01/2003 | 0 | |
| T4 | 15/01/2003 | 3 | Work-related activities. |
| T5 | 16/01/2003 | 2 | Tricia is thinking about Marvin's suggestion and would like to continue the conversation. |
| T6 | 17/01/2003 | 3 | Push Arthur to finish the report, tense relation exists with Arthur. |
| T7 | 18-20/01/2003 | 0 | |
| T8 | 21/01/2003 | 0 | |
| T9 | 22/01/2003 | 2 | Email to Marvin saying "Got it", got what? Once again, pushes Arthur to finish the report, which again shows the tense relation with her colleague Arthur. |
| T10 | 23/01/2003 | 1 | Work-related activities |

**Table 2.** Ten degrees of suspiciousness event probabilities (T(p), F(p): see text for details)

| Suspiciousness Degree | T | T - | T -- | T --- | T ---- | F ---- | F --- | F -- | F - | F |
|---|---|---|---|---|---|---|---|---|---|---|
| Probability | 0 | 0.1 | 0.25 | 0.35 | 0.5 | 0.6 | 0.7 | 0.8 | 0.9 | 1 |

**Table 3.** Suspiciousness event probabilities for a sample of Tricia's actions

| | N1 | N2 | N3 | N4 | N5 | N6 | N7 | N8 |
|---|---|---|---|---|---|---|---|---|
| T1 | T | | T | T | | T | | T--- |
| T2 | T | | T--- | T | | | | T---- |
| T3 | T | | T | T | | | T | |
| T4 | T | | T | F-- | | | T | T |
| T5 | F-- | | T--- | F-- | F | | | F-- |
| T6 | T | | | | | | | T- |
| T7 | | | | | | | | |
| T8 | T | | | F---- | F | | F | |
| T9 | | | T | F-- | | F | F- | F- |
| T10 | T | | T--- | T | | | | T |

Actions are labelled to a suspiciousness probability according to a table of suspiciousness degree varying from normal to abnormal (see Table 2).

Using Table 2, we map the forensic events of suspects to suspiciousness probabilities. Table 3 shows this for Tricia's action set over the ten time intervals.

## 3   EBN-HMM Model for Forensic Evidence

The EBN-HMM model — Embedded Bayesian Network Hidden Markov Model, is examined here since it has the advantages of coping with incomplete observation data and reduced uncertainty. The EBN-HMM model applies one of the popular Dynamical Bayesian Networks, Hidden Markov Models [3], for modelling temporal relations in the Bayesian Net (BNet) [4]. That is, the BNet defines the structure of the observations that occur in given intervals and the HMM defines the evolution of the criminal activity over time by the association of specific observation variable values with different degree of criminal activity. That is, the hidden nodes correspond to the "degree of criminality" which is conditioned on both its present (*t*) observation and the state at the previous time (*t-1*) as shown in Fig. 1.

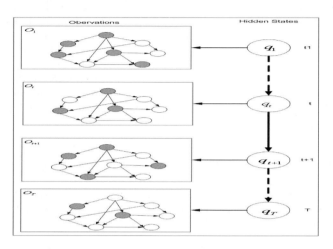

**Fig. 1.** EBN-HMM: Hidden Markov Model embedded Bayesian Network observation model

In this specific EBN-HMM model, observations are modelled by a Bayesian Net. We refer to this BNet as the Bayesian Forensic Evidence Network Model (BFENM) in Figure 2 to represent the users' forensic evidence and relations. The Conditional Probability Tables (CPT) was empirically obtained observations. Fig. 2 also presents

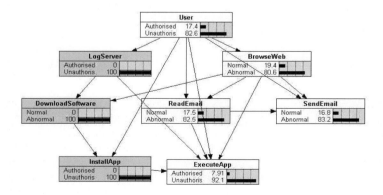

**Fig. 2.** The proposed BFENM model for modelling forensic evidence

a sample of the probability distribution during a specific time interval. There are three observable nodes (shaded) and five hidden ones in the net. Node logServer's probability is 0.0 (0%), which means unauthorised logging on. A zero probability for the Node DownloadSoftware represents downloading unauthorised software, files,etc. The same representation applies to Node installApp as well. After inference, the probabilities of the other five nodes are obtained. The node "User"'s probability is 0.174 (17.4%), which means the user is more likely to be an unauthorised user.

Training and testing data were obtained from a large number of forensic cases produced by Monte Carlo sampling of an expert-provided observation BNet (BFENM) to produce 5,000 samples for training and testing with the addition random selection of observations occurring at any given node so that we could simulate missing observations. At each interval, the data consisted of a vector of eight dimensions, resulting in 5,000 eight-dimensional vectors, and therefore, 500 scenarios over 10 time intervals. K-means vector quantization [5] was applied to clustering discrete resulting in 16 clusters (symbols). The Baum-Welch [3] and supervised training algorithms were used for training the HMMs from annotated (interpreted for degree of suspiciousness) datasets over time.

## 4   A Specific Forensic Case Study

After extracting and labelling the forensic evidence along the timeline when events happened, Table 4 shows the observables and inferred probabilities obtained in the temporal domain for suspect Tricia. A table for Arthur table was also computed.

**Table 4.** Suspect Tricia's probabilities (in percentages) for observed and inferred actions

|     | N1  | N2  | N3  | N4  | N5  | N6  | N7  | N8  |
|-----|-----|-----|-----|-----|-----|-----|-----|-----|
| T1  | 100 | 88  | 100 | 100 | 89  | 100 | 93  | 0   |
| T2  | 100 | 80  | 100 | 100 | 78  | 79  | 84  | 0   |
| T3  | 100 | 86  | 100 | 100 | 85  | 89  | 100 | 80  |
| T4  | 100 | 85  | 100 | 0   | 83  | 86  | 100 | 100 |
| T5  | 0   | 26  | 0   | 0   | 0   | 10  | 5   | 0   |
| T6  | 100 | 80  | 86  | 83  | 73  | 77  | 77  | 100 |
| T7  | 50  | 60  | 40  | 37  | 45  | 47  | 40  | 35  |
| T8  | 100 | 53  | 20  | 0   | 0   | 35  | 0   | 24  |
| T9  | 15  | 28  | 100 | 0   | 28  | 0   | 0   | 0   |
| T10 | 100 | 80  | 0   | 100 | 40  | 60  | 62  | 100 |

We then applied the complete EBN-HMM model to process the Tricia and Arthur datasets and, in particular, the Viterbi (Dynamic Programming) algorithm [6] to determine the most likely type of suspicious activity associated with observations. Important decision-based results are shown in Figures 3a and 3b for Tricia and Arthur. Here, the grey bars correspond to high degrees of suspicion with Tricia having four grey bars and Arthur only one. Arthur's one occured at T9 where, in fact, there were no suspicious observations at that time, a grey bar only represents warning that the evidence had accumulated to infer that state. One conclusion from this is that Tricia is possibly the criminal party and Arthur is more likely innocent (although he was doing non-work related, but not criminal, activities). Fig. 3a is an example of a sequence of events that could lead to identifying the perpetrator of the IP leakage.

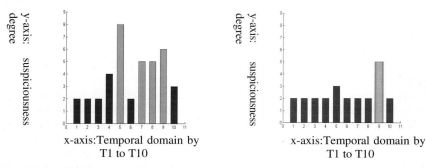

Fig. 3. (a) Tricia's evolution of criminal activity over time (T1-T10)

Fig. 3. (b) Arthur's evolution of criminal activity over time (T1-T10)

Upon further analysis of a graph of observation objects (with time attributes), we found that there were a few important events  relating to Tricia's activities during time intervals T5, T8, and T9 that may point to Tricia's culpability. During T5, Tricia had been undertaking unauthorised log-ins into the womboyn server (perhaps she discovered the restructure document) and had browsed non work-related websites. She had been downloading, installing and executing unauthorised software (the anonymous emailer). During interval T8, she downloaded files from the company server (eg, the restructure document) and transferred the IP code from her PC onto removable media (floppy disk), as well as browsed non work-related websites. During T9, Tricia emailed Marvin (in the rival company) "Got it" (presumably the IP which she would eventually pass onto him) and proceeded to anonymously email the re-structure document to all staff. These events would need to be investigated to confirm (or refute) her culpability (eg, how did she get access to the IP?).

## 5   Conclusions

The proposed approach allows us to model both the dependencies between different digital forensic evidence and how evidence evolves over time to infer specific levels of suspiciousness or criminal activity. Experimental results on the sampling data with 5,00 scenarios and with two specific synthetic forensic cases strongly suggest the model performs well and is comparable to expert decision making. It remains to be seen how it performs with additional real field-data in known criminal cases and how it could be deployed as a decision-support technology. Certainly such dynamical Bayesian Network models all assume that decision making is made in accord to in-ferred probabilities of dependent events and underlying hidden variables and this, as such, needs further exploration.

# Acknowledgement

The authors would like to thank Dr Jason Bobbin (DSTO) and Dr. Warren Jin (CSIRO). Financial support from DSTO and NICTA are gratefully acknowledged.

# References

1. Casey, Eoghan, "Digital Evidence and Computer Crime: Forensic Science", *Computer and the Internet,* Academic Press, 2000.
2. C. Apte, F. Damerau, "Automated learning of decision rules for text categorization", *ACM Transactions on Information Systems*, Vol 12, No.3, pp.233-251, 1994.
3. L. R. Rabiner, "A tutorial on Hidden Markov Models and selected applications in speech recognition". *Proc. of the IEEE*, 77(2):257–286, 1989.
4. F. V. Jensen. *Bayesian Networks and Decision Graphs.* Springer-Verlag, 2001.
5. Y. Linde, A. Buzo, and R.M. Gray, "An algorithm for vector quantizer design", *IEEE Transactions on. Communications,* vol 28, pp. 84-95, Jan 1980.
6. G.D. Forney, "The Viterbi algorithm", *Proc.IEEE*, vol 61, pp.268-278, Mar 1973.

# Entity Workspace: An Evidence File That Aids Memory, Inference, and Reading

Eric A. Bier[1], Edward W. Ishak[2], and Ed Chi[1]

[1] Palo Alto Research Center, Inc., 3333 Coyote Hill Road, Palo Alto, CA 94304, USA
{bier, echi}@parc.com
[2] Columbia University, Department of Computer Science, 1214 Amsterdam Ave., 450 CS
Bldg, New York, NY 10027, USA
ishak@cs.columbia.edu

**Abstract.** An intelligence analyst often needs to keep track of more facts than can be held in human memory. As a result, analysts use a notebook or evidence file to record facts learned so far. In practice, the evidence file is often an electronic document into which text snippets and hand-typed notes are placed. While this kind of evidence file is easy to read and edit, it provides little help for making sense of the captured information. We describe Entity Workspace, a tool designed to be used in place of a traditional evidence file. Entity Workspace combines user interface and entity extraction technologies to build up an explicit model of important entities (people, places, organizations, phone numbers, etc.) and their relationships. Using this model, it helps the analyst find and re-find facts rapidly, notice connections between entities, and identify good documents and entities to explore next.

## 1 The Need for a Better Evidence File

An intelligence analyst working on a case may encounter hundreds of documents, each containing any number of facts relevant to the case. The number of facts can quickly become too large to be held in human memory alone. For this reason, analysts record the facts in a notebook or *evidence file*, which is often an electronic document into which the analyst places text snippets and hand-typed notes about the case.

Electronic documents are suitable for use as evidence files because they are easy to edit and read, hold both text and pictures, support full text search, and are easy to re-purpose for the final report. However, as used today, electronic documents offer little help in making sense of the facts captured in them. Although the system knows that the analyst has selected certain pieces of text, it does not know which entities mentioned in this text are important, nor how they relate to each other.

We describe a software evidence file called *Entity Workspace* that helps the analyst explicitly represent information about relevant entities and their relationships. Entities of interest to intelligence analysts include people, places, organizations, telephone numbers, addresses, weapons, bank accounts, and so on. With this information, Entity Workspace offers several kinds of assistance. In particular, Entity Workspace helps the analyst: (1) re-find important facts quickly, usually without the need for explicit

S. Mehrotra et al. (Eds.): ISI 2006, LNCS 3975, pp. 466–472, 2006.

searching or querying; (2) "connect the dots," by visualizing relationships between entities, supporting inference tasks; (3) discover new information, by recommending entities and documents to study next based on previously investigated entities; and (4) read quickly through new documents, by highlighting key terms automatically.

Entity Workspace can provide this kind of assistance to analysts because it builds up a model of documents, entities, and relationships that we call the *Document-and-Entity Graph*. The analyst does not directly view or edit this graph. It is constructed automatically as a side effect of organizing information in the workspace.

We will describe the Entity Workspace tool, how it supports and accelerates the analytical process, and present some concluding remarks and related work.

## 2   Snap-Together Knowledge

The tool that we describe here, *Entity Workspace*, consists of four panels that display different kinds of information relevant to intelligence analysis.  These panels, shown in Fig. 1, are called Workspace, System Suggestions, Entity Inspector, and Trails. The *Workspace Panel* is the focus of this paper. It allows the analyst to edit representations of entities, documents, and their relationships. The *System Suggestions Panel* shows all entities represented in the workspace, ordered according to how closely related each is to high-interest objects. The top of this panel displays a document page object ("CIA Report 04 p.1") representing the page that is currently open for reading.The *Entity Inspector Panel* displays information about the currently selected entity, including its name, aliases, documents that mention it, and other entities that appear in

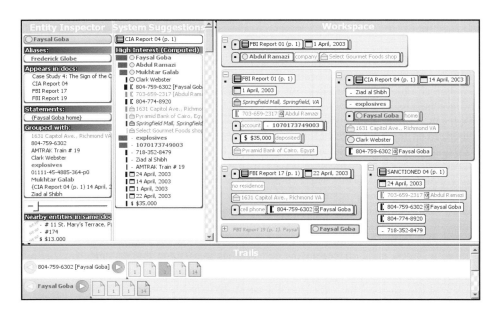

**Fig. 1.** The four panels of the Entity Workspace tool

the same statements, groups or documents with it. Finally, the *Trails Panel* displays icons representing documents in which the entity appears; icons appear in different colors and patterns to distinguish documents that have already been read or have been marked as high interest. Entity Workspace works together with the CorpusView document corpus browser [2], which provides an overview of the analyst's document collection and displays documents with important information highlighted.

Entity Workspace enables analysts to rapidly capture the names of important entities and their relationships. This is done using the Workspace Panel (or simply "the workspace"), as follows: Upon finding a relevant fact in a document, the analyst may capture that fact by copying entities from the document into the workspace using traditional copy-and-paste or other methods described below. Consider the (fictitious) report in Fig. 2, a report drawn from "The Sign of the Crescent," an intelligence analysis tutorial by Frank Hughes, a professor at the Joint Military Intelligence College. Important entities in this report, such as dates, people, account numbers, businesses, and phone numbers, are highlighted. If relevant, the analyst records them.

Each entity recorded in the workspace becomes a separate visual object, an *entity object*, which can be dragged and positioned. A small icon at the left end of each entity indicates its type, if known. A circle icon indicates a person, a house icon indicates a place, a calendar icon indicates a date, and so on.

The analyst can also add an unrestricted text string, called a *comment object*, to act as a label, relationship name, category, or general comment. A comment object is created by copying text from a document or typing. The upper right of Fig. 1 shows six comment objects, including those labeled "company", "account", and "deposited". Comments look like entities, but have no icon and have gray text and a gray border.

Finally, an analyst can add a *document page object*, representing a page in the document collection. Examples of these in Fig. 1 have labels beginning with "FBI Report", "CIA Report", or "SANCTIONED". They can be dragged into the workspace from the Entity Inspector or System Suggestions Panels. They are also added automatically by some functions to record where a given fact was discovered. Clicking on a document page object causes its corresponding page to be displayed.

When an object is placed in close vertical proximity to another object, a new composite object is created, called an *entity group*, containing both original objects. A group can contain any number of objects and is displayed as a rounded rectangle large enough to fit them all. Each group displays a collapse button in the upper left corner (to request a condensed view). Placing objects together in a group indicates that they are related to each other in some way. For example, the orange right middle group in Fig. 1 indicates that Faysal Goba is connected to explosives and other entities.

The analyst indicates a stronger relationship between two objects by dragging one object in close horizontal proximity to another. Our system then creates a new composite object, called an *entity statement* containing both objects. A statement can contain any number of objects and is shown visually by placing the objects side-by-side with "book end" shapes to the left and right of them and an underline below them. Statements can be placed in groups as shown in several groups in Fig. 1.

An object can appear in the workspace any number of times. An object can appear in multiple groups, in multiple statements, both in and out of groups, and in and out of statements. Each appearance is called an *instance*. Multiple instances of an object are used to express its relationships to any number of other objects in multiple contexts.

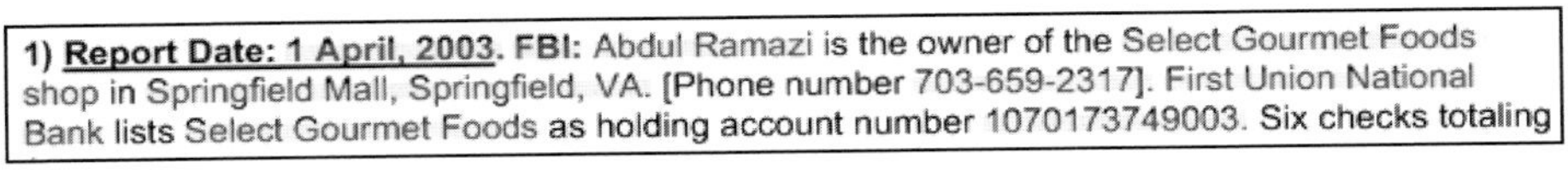

1) **Report Date: 1 April, 2003**. FBI: Abdul Ramazi is the owner of the Select Gourmet Foods shop in Springfield Mall, Springfield, VA. [Phone number 703-659-2317]. First Union National Bank lists Select Gourmet Foods as holding account number 1070173749003. Six checks totaling

**Fig. 2.** A fictitious FBI report that mentions a person, a company, and several other entities

Some objects are so closely related that the analyst may wish to ensure they are always displayed together. This can be done with a "coupling command". For example, the analyst may couple a phone number to its owner's name. Thereafter, every current and future instance of this phone number will appear followed by a link icon and the name, like the phone number linked to "Faysal Goba" in Fig. 1.

Each entity in the workspace is associated with a number, from 1 to 4, that indicates the degree to which that entity is of interest to the analyst. The display properties of an entity, such as color and typeface, are varied based on this *degree of interest*. Clicking on the icon in each entity cycles through the interest values.

To capture the number of entities needed in analysis, we supply faster ways to record entities than copy-and-paste. One of our techniques, *entity quick click*, is described elsewhere [3]. We summarize it here, and describe its modification for intelligence analysis. With this technique, the system runs an information extraction algorithm over each document to be displayed to find entities such as person names, company names, telephone numbers, and so on. When the document is displayed to the analyst, these entity phrases are highlighted, as in Fig. 2. Next, the analyst presses a modifier key (e.g., Shift) to initiate entity quick click mode. Then, the analyst clicks on a desired phrase. A new entity group is created containing a new entity with that phrase and a document page object corresponding to the page in which the analyst just clicked. By holding down modifier keys (e.g., Shift and Control), the analyst can add the selected phrase as a comment instead of an entity. At one click per entity or comment, analysts can build up an entity workspace quickly.

As the workspace grows from the addition of entities, statements, and groups, the system creates a data structure, called the *Document-and-Entity Graph* or *DE Graph*, to represent the relationships indicated by the arrangement of objects. The DE Graph is an undirected graph whose nodes are entity objects and document page objects. A weighted edge is placed in the DE Graph between any two related objects if they (1) are coupled, (2) belong in the same statement, (3) belong to the same group, or (4) are mentioned near each other in one or more documents. The edge weights are assigned according to the closeness of the relationship; the previous sentence lists these relationships in decreasing order of closeness. For example, edges joining objects that share a statement are weighted more heavily than edges joining objects that share a group.

Given this weighted graph, we compute closeness scores that describe how related entities are to each other. This method is based on computational models of *Spreading Activation* [1] used in the study of relevancy in human memory. The system uses this computation over the DE Graph to provide the analyst with memory aids, recommendations, inference aids, and support for reading, as described below.

# 3   Improving Memory, Inference, and Reading

As soon as an analyst has recorded some information into the workspace, the system can help the analyst in remembering facts, making inferences, and finding new information more rapidly. These capabilities are described next.

Entity Workspace uses the DE Graph and the panels described above to help the analyst remember what has already been learned. In particular, each visible entity serves as a reminder of what has already been encountered. Each statement and group represents one or more relationships between the entities. When the analyst selects an entity, all instances of that entity in the Workspace Panel highlight in orange, as do all groups containing an instance of that entity. Fig. 1 shows an example, where "Faysal Goba" is the selected entity. By examining the other entities in the highlighted groups, the analyst is quickly reminded of direct links to the selected entity. Also, the Entity Inspector Panel summarizes all of the directly linked information about the selected entity, and the Trails Panel lists all document pages that mention the entity.

Our system helps the analyst discover direct and indirect connections between entities. For example, when two entities are *coupled* using the coupling operation, the analyst can see connections between entities that require synthesizing information from multiple sources. For example, say that the analyst is recording information from a document describing a phone call from number X to number Y. If the analyst has previously coupled the phone numbers to persons A and B respectively, the resulting entity group will immediately display the names of both people, allowing the analyst to infer that A has called B.

A second tool helps find any known connections between persons C and D when the analyst *selects both entities*. The system then displays the two selected entities with distinctive colors, say orange and magenta. Each group that contains only one entity is highlighted in its corresponding color. Groups mentioning *both* entities are highlighted in a third color, green, such that the analyst can rapidly find those groups that contain information that relates the two selected entities to each other.

A third tool helps the analyst view all entities connected to a given entity by paths of length two. In this case, the analyst activates the *Highlight Linked Entities* operation. This highlights the selected entity and all entities that are directly linked to it, while dimming all other entities. By looking at dimmed entities that are in the same group with any highlighted entity, the analyst can see immediately the entities that are at most two links away from the selected entity.

Entity Workspace supports an analyst's reading processes in three ways by providing: (1) recommendations on entities to examine, (2) reading recommendation trails that enable rapid reading through all of the documents on a topic, and (3) keyword highlighting within each document to aid skimming.

The System Suggestions Panel rank orders all entities as a way of recommending entities that are worth further attention. Each entity's rating is determined using a spreading activation algorithm over the DE Graph. The initial activation of each node is based on the degree-of-interest score set on the corresponding entity by the analyst.

Whenever the analyst selects one or more entities, the system constructs a query and runs it against every document in the analyst's document collection. The resulting rank ordered document list is then displayed in the Trails Panel next to the query text.

The analyst can then visit all of the document pages in the trail, in turn, much as one would flip through a stack of paper documents to skim for important facts.

As each document is displayed, words and phrases in the document are highlighted automatically: entities found by the entity extractor in yellow, and phrases with a high degree of interest in a more salient red. Finally, the system gives a distinctive appearance to phrases that match the current search query.

## 4  Conclusions and Related Work

Entity Workspace is a compromise. It is designed to elicit more information from analysts, so it can provide more assistance, while requiring little additional effort. Thus, while we might have it ask the analyst to specify more details about entity relationships, we resist this temptation to keep effort low. This tradeoff appears to work well. With little extra effort, the analyst provides enough information to allow our user interface tools to support memory, inference, and reading.

The design of Entity Workspace has been influenced by interactions with four intelligence analysts. While results have been informal, these sessions have given us confidence in an approach based on recognized entities and in snap-together knowledge, quick click copying of entities, and entity coupling to aid inference. We are currently hardening this technology for use on real analytical tasks.

Our work on Entity Workspace builds on recent work related to recording evidence, spatial hypertext, automatic highlighting, and automating inference. Like the Sandbox component of Oculus nSpace [7] our tool gathers evidence into a work area. Like Good's spatial hypertext system, Niagara [6], our tool uses spatial proximity to automatically group evidence. Like ScentHighlights [4], our system automatically highlights words to aid skimming and reading. Our system builds up a graph of linked evidence like that used in the subgraph isomorphism approach described by Coffman et. al [5]. Our system differs from the previous interactive tools by providing snap-together knowledge, a rapid method for capturing and structuring entity information. It differs from other graph-based approaches by using the graph both to support automated inference and to support interactive techniques that help guide the analyst while leaving the analyst in control.

This research was funded in part by the Advanced Research and Development Activity NIMD and ARIVA programs (MDA904-03-C-0404).

## References

1. Anderson, J. R., Pirolli, P. L.  Spread of Activation. *Journal of Experimental Psychology: Learning, Memory and Cognition*, 10 (1984): pages 791—798.
2. Bier, E., Good, L., Popat, K., and Newberger, A. A document corpus browser for in-depth reading. *Proceedings of the Joint Conference on Digital Libraries (JCDL)*, 2004, 87-96
3. Bier, E. A., Ishak, E. W., and Chi, E. Entity quick click: rapid text copying based on automatic entity extraction. In the *Extended Abstracts of the Conference on Human Factors in Computing Systems* (CHI 2006), 2006.  In press.

4. Chi, E. H., Hong, L., Gumbrecht, M., Card, S. K. ScentHighlights: highlighting conceptually-related sentences during reading. *Proceedings of the 10th International Conference on Intelligent User Interfaces*, 2005, pages 272-274.
5. Coffman, T., Greenblatt, S., and Marcus, S. Graph-based technologies for intelligence analysis. *Communications of the. ACM*, Volume 47, Number 3 (Mar. 2004), pages 45-47.
6. Good, L. E., *Zoomable User Interfaces for the Authoring and Delivery of Slide Presentations*. Ph.D. dissertation, Department of Computer Science, University of Maryland, October 27, 2003. http://hdl.handle.net/1903/262
7. Wright, W., Schroh, D., Proulx, P., Skaburskis, A., and Cort, B. Advances in nSpace – the sandbox for analysis. Poster at the 2005 International Conference on Intelligence Analysis.

# Strategic Intelligence Analysis: From Information Processing to Meaning-Making

Yair Neuman, Liran Elihay, Meni Adler,
Yoav Goldberg, and Amir Viner

The Laboratory for the Interdisciplinary Study of Symbolic Process
Ben-Gurion University of the Negev, Israel
yneuman@bgu.ac.il

**Abstract.** Strategic intelligence involves the efforts to understand the "Big Picture" emerging from data sources. Concerning textual data, this process involves the extraction of meaning from textual information. In this paper we present a new methodology for meaning extraction from news articles. This methodology is based on the gradual construction of visual maps from processed textual information. The methodology is not a substitute for meaning-making by human agents but combines computational power with human evaluation and provides a tool for identifying emerging patterns of meaning.

## 1 Introduction

Information science and information technology have been shown to be indispensable for national security and intelligence analysis. However, one should realize that there are two different and complementary axes of information: "The syntactic axis concerns the formal representation of information in a digital code. The semiotic axis concerns the *meaning* of information for interpreting agents as this information appears in the analogical mode" ([6]). While the first axis has been intensively studied and formalized in information sciences, the second axis has been almost exclusively studied by other fields such as Semiotics ([10]), the study of signs and signification, and Pragmatics ([5]), the branch of linguistics dealing with language use in context. The need for a meaning-based information analysis is evident in strategic intelligence that aims to provide officials with the "*big picture*". Our aim is to present a novel methodology for meaning-based analysis of texts for strategic intelligence. The methodology leans on insights gained from studying meaning-making in various domains such as political rhetoric ([4], [7], [9]), and computational linguistics ([6]), and from the interdisciplinary background of the authors. Due to space limits, we present only the general outlines of the methodology without dwelling on technical details.

When trying to understand a text, whether a political speech or a newspaper article the reader faces a cognitive problem: The text is *linearly* organized as a string of linguistic signs. However, in order to understand the text he has to map it into an *associative* network in his mind. If we adopt the theoretical position that meaning emerges as a global property from an interconnected network of signs/concepts ([10], [11]), then the analyzer of a given text should cope with the cognitive burden of

S. Mehrotra et al. (Eds.): ISI 2006, LNCS 3975, pp. 473 – 478, 2006.

extracting an associative network from a linear text. This task is cognitively demanding and the logic governing the process is not self-evident. It was argued by Neuman and Muchnick ([8]) that this problem is to a certain extent solvable if the linear text is mapped into a network of signs characterized by scale-free topology ([1], [2]) in which few signs have the highest connectivity to other signs. By analyzing political speeches and news articles Neuman and Muchnick ([8]) exposed a scale-free topology of the texts. A text organized as a scale-free network of signs has 3 main benefits that may guide its representation in the human mind. These benefits will be exploited in the suggested methodology. First, the text is organized around just a few hubs (i.e., its organizing concepts) that function as coordinates for understanding the whole text. Second, scale-free networks are constructed through the dynamics of *preferential attachment* ([2]). The dynamics of preferential attachment is such that a new concept/sign/node entering the text/network is more likely to attach to one of the hubs/organizing concepts. Therefore, it is the topology that directs the linkage of new entering concepts. These dynamics load the new entering concepts with meaning by associating them with few existing hubs. This is an important characteristic in the cognitive economy of mapping a linear text into an associative semiotic network. Third, the hubs do not only get their meaning from the context of their associated nodes. By playing the role of a "magnet" for other concepts, through the dynamics of preferential attachment, they also create the context for their own interpretation. In other words, the hubs are interpreted by their surrounding context and recursively provide the context for the interpretation of their associative nodes.

## 2   Extracting Meaning from Texts

### 2.1   The Data

As data we used all the news articles (N = 800) of the online monthly English-language Palestinian newspaper: *Palestine Times*. The newspaper appears in 104 volumes from 1997 to 2006. The newspaper is targeted to a Western and educated English speaking audience. As any communicative text, this political newspaper aims to provide its readers with a certain representation of the world. In this context, uncovering hidden patterns of meaning in the newspaper's articles may be of great relevance for intelligence analysis seeking to understand the way Palestinians appeal to the Western audience with regard to key issues such as the American involvement in Iraq.

### 2.2   The Methodology

The suggested methodology is built around several phases. At the first step a news article is segmented to sentences. The components of a sentence are classified with Part-of-Speech tagging. Only nouns, corresponding to concepts, were included in this phase. The nouns were cleaned for singular/plural and for noun-compounds. For each article we created a network. The nouns were represented as nodes and co-occurrence of nouns in a given sentence was used to establish a link/edge between the nodes. We found that the networks have a scale-free topology with only a few nouns having the greatest degree of connection. For each news article we ranked the nouns according to their connectivity and the 5 highest ranking nouns were identified as hubs. The criterion of 5 hubs is arbitrary, but justified by the lower limit of the working memory. We considered these hubs as the basic organizing concepts of the text. It was found that at least one of the hubs appeared in the title of the article or in the opening paragraph. This finding is not surprising because it is known that in news articles most newsworthy information comes first. In the next step, we used a heuristic we call "hubs first." For each article we identified the first sentence in which one (or more) of the hubs appeared, removed this hub/s from our list, and continued searching for the next sentence in which one (or more) of the remaining hubs appeared. This process was repeated until the list was exhausted. The sentences we extracted are *context sentences* for the interpretation of a hub and were stored in a data bank for queries with the hub's name as an index. The "hubs first" heuristic is at the core of our methodology and produces valuable information for diagnosis and prediction that cannot be discussed here. We will illustrate the methodology with regard to the hub "IRAQ". Let's assume that we would like to understand the way in which the issue of Iraq is represented by the Palestinian newspaper to its audience. As we will show, an interesting pattern emerges from the analysis. Iraq appears as a hub in 8 news articles dated from March 2000 to October 2004. We organized these articles chronologically and for each article extracted (1) the hubs and (2) the context-sentences. For example, consider the first news article in which the hub "IRAQ" appears. The hubs are: <u>Iraq</u>, <u>Palestinians</u>, <u>Government</u>, <u>Land</u> and <u>Plan</u>. According to the "hubs first" heuristics the context-sentences are (the hubs are underlined):

S1: America presses for resettling refugees in <u>Iraq</u>

S2: An Iraqi opposition leader has disclosed that the Iraqi <u>government</u>, under pressure from the United States, was considering a <u>plan</u> whereby a million Palestinian refugees would be settled in Western <u>Iraq</u>.

S3: According to an article written by Sa'ad Farage, President of "The Iraqi Activists," a Washington based organization, the <u>government</u> of Saddam Hussein was giving out signals suggesting that it was receptive and open to the idea of settling <u>Palestinians</u> in <u>Iraq</u>.

S4: Among the signals, he wrote, was a recent Iraqi decree allowing <u>Palestinians</u> living in <u>Iraq</u>—around 62,000—to own <u>land</u> and property in <u>Iraq</u>.

Next we represent each sentence as a list that includes the hub(s) that appears in that sentence. In addition, drawing on Hoey's theory of lexical cohesion ([3]), if in a sentence there is a lexical item that establishes a link to a lexical item from the previous sentence (as a repetition, synonym etc.) then it is added to the list and semantically condensed. For example, the first sentence includes the noun "America" and the second includes "United States". Therefore, "America" is added to the list. The nouns are organized in the list in the order of presentation in the sentence as follows: L1: America, Palestinians, Iraq; L2: government, America, Plan, Palestinians, Iraq; L3: government, Palestinians, Iraq; L4: signals, Palestinians, Iraq, land, Iraq. By Using a Graphical User Interface, the next step is to map the lists onto a single network in which each noun is mapped to a node. A relation between two nodes is established if the nouns co-occur in a sentence. The relations are labeled

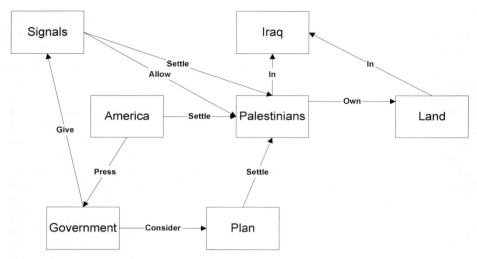

**Fig. 1.** The network of the first article

according to well-defined instructions. The direction of the link is determined by the question whether the second or the first nouns are the subject of the relation. The network of the first article is as follows:

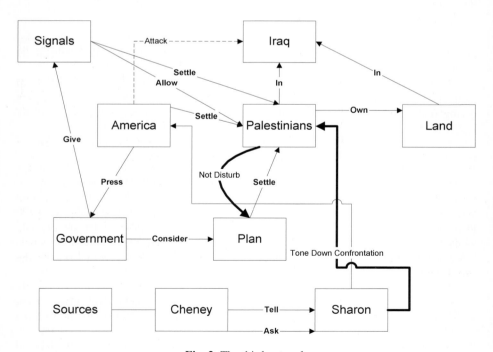

**Fig. 2.** The third network

The same process is applied to the next articles in the chronological order of their appearance and maps are added to the original map. For example, the third news article was published in April 2002 and it includes the following hubs: Iraq, Sharon, Cheney, Palestinians, and Sources. From this article we extracted the following context sentences: S1: <u>Cheney</u> tells <u>Sharon</u> U.S. wants to attack <u>Iraq</u> for Israel's sake. S2: According to Israeli <u>sources</u> quoted by the Israeli state-run radio on 20 March, <u>Cheney</u> asked Sharon to "tone down" the confrontation with the <u>Palestinians</u> so as not to disrupt or disturb American plans *vis-à-vis* <u>Iraq</u>. We created the lists and mapped them onto the network as follows, where the bold/dashed lines indicate the new important paths:

What is interesting to notice is that in this phase of the evolving network we can observe an *emerging pattern of meaning*: America not only plans to settle Palestinian refugees in Iraq (as we noticed in network 1) or to attack Iraq for "Israel's sake." An interesting link is established between Cheney's request from Sharon to "tone down the confrontation with the Palestinians" and the US plan. Cheney asks Sharon not to disturb the US from actualizing its plan. What is the plan? The plan, as indicated in the first network, is to resettle Palestinian refugees in Iraq. This interpretation makes sense in the context of the first sentence saying that "U.S. wants to attack Iraq for Israel's sake." The attack is for "Israel's sake" because it will solve the Palestinian problem through transfer of Palestinians to Iraq! This emerging *conspiracy theory* is further supported by the analysis of the other articles.

## 3  Conclusions and Further Work

The methodology we present is preliminary, and we are working to maximize its computational power. These efforts take into account the difficulty of accommodating noise as the analysis unfolds and some other inevitable difficulties. The system is currently being refined and tested on other corpuses. Nevertheless, one should remember that the difficulty of extracting the "Big Picture" is not a technical one. The flood of information facing the analyzer is the major barrier to seeing the "forest." In this context, the extraction of meaning from information involves a process of abstraction in which information is necessarily lost ([12]) in favor of the big picture. We may conclude that a computational tool for meaning extraction should be guided by an "oblivion algorithm" that will filter the irrelevant information in the system. Such an algorithm is currently not at hand and computational theories of abstraction and meaning-making are currently far from being applicable to strategic intelligence analysis. We may conclude by suggesting that the great challenge of intelligence analysis and informatics is exactly in developing tools that support meaning-based information analysis by scaffolding a movement from the micro level of data to the macro level of meaning.

## References

1. Barabasi, A, L. *Linked*, Perseus, 2002.
2. Barabasi, A. L., Albert, R., *Emergence of Scaling in Random Networks*, Science, Vol. 286, 1999, pp. 509-512.

3. Hoey, M. *Patterns of Lexis in Text*, Oxford University Press, 1991.
4. Liebersohn, Y., Neuman, Y., Bekerman, Z., *Oh Baby, it's Hard for Me to Say I'm Sorry: Public Apologetic Speech and Cultural Rhetorical Resources*, Journal of Pragmatics, Vol. 36, 2004, pp. 921-944.
5. Mey, J. L. *Pragmatics: An Introduction*, Blackwell, 2002.
6. Neuman, Y. *A Theory of Meaning*, Information Sciences, Vol. 176, 2006, pp. 1435-1449.
7. Neuman, Y., Levi, M., *Blood and Chocolate: A Rhetorical Approach to Fear Appeal.* Journal of Language and Social Psychology, Vol. 29, 2003, pp. 29-46.
8. Neuman, Y., Muchnick, L. *On the Small-World of Political Rhetoric*, Submitted.
9. Neuman, Y., Tabak, I. *Inconsistency as an Interactional Problem: A lesson from Political Rhetoric*, Journal of Psycholinguistic Research, Vol. 32, 2003, pp. 251-267.
10. Sebeok, T. A., and Danesi, M. *Forms of Meaning*, Mouton de Gruyter, 2000.
11. Sigman, M., Cecci, G. A. *Global Organization of the Wordnet Lexicon*, PNAS, Vol. 99, 2002, pp. 1742-1747.
12. Zucker, J-D. *A Grounded Theory of Abstraction in Artificial Intelligence*, Phil. Trans. R. Soc. Lond. B, Vol. 358, 2003, pp. 1293-1309.

# A Multi-layer Naïve Bayes Model for Approximate Identity Matching

G. Alan Wang, Hsinchun Chen, and Homa Atabakhsh

University of Arizona, Department of Management Information Systems,
1130 E. Helen St., Tucson, AZ 85721, U.S.A.
{gang, hchen, homa}@eller.arizona.edu

**Abstract.** Identity management is critical to various governmental practices ranging from providing citizens services to enforcing homeland security. The task of searching for a specific identity is difficult because multiple identity representations may exist due to issues related to unintentional errors and intentional deception. We propose a Naïve Bayes identity matching model that improves existing techniques in terms of effectiveness. Experiments show that our proposed model performs significantly better than the exact-match based technique and achieves higher precision than the record comparison technique. In addition, our model greatly reduces the efforts of manually labeling training instances by employing a semi-supervised learning approach. This training method outperforms both fully supervised and unsupervised learning. With a training dataset that only contains 30% labeled instances, our model achieves a performance comparable to that of a fully supervised learning.

## 1 Introduction

Many governmental agencies manage identity information for various purposes ranging from providing citizens services to enforcing homeland security. Identity verification is a common practice for them and is used to verify whether a person is who he/she claims to be. As digital government purportedly leads to increased integration and interoperability among agencies, identity verification becomes a key to tying together customers from different agency systems and achieving integration. In the wake of 9/11 terrorist attacks, this issue became one of the critical issues related to national security. The ability to validate identity is expected to help post-event investigation as well as to prevent future tragedies.

Identity verification, however, is a surprisingly complex problem [1]. First, the lack of a reliable unique identifier across different agencies makes the task non trivial. Moreover, identity information is not always reliable and is subject to unintentional errors and intentional fraud [2]. Existing identity verification techniques are not adequate in solving the problems mentioned above.

In this research we intend to propose an advanced identity matching technique that requires less or no human intervention. In section 2 we discuss possible identity problems and review existing identity matching techniques. We propose a Naïve-Bayes model for approximate identity matching in section 3. We describe our

S. Mehrotra et al. (Eds.): ISI 2006, LNCS 3975, pp. 479–484, 2006.

experimental design and report the results and discussions in section 4. We summarize our findings and provide future directions in the last section.

## 2  Literature Review

An identity is a set of characteristic features that distinguish a person from others. Identity information, however, is unreliable due to various reasons. First, unintentional errors often occur in data management processes such as data entry, storage and transformation. A study showed that the data error rate in typical enterprises could be as high as 30% [3]. Second, identity information sometimes is subject to intentional deception, especially the identities of criminals or terrorists who are known to use false identities to mislead police investigations [4].

### 2.1  Identity Matching Techniques

To the best of our knowledge, there are few solutions proposed for the problem of identity matching. Marshall et al. [5] provided an exact-value matching technique for law enforcement applications. Two identities are considered matching only if their first names, last names, and DOB values are identical. However, as identity information is unreliable, it is possible that identities referring to the same person have disagreeing values. Wang et al. [4] proposed a record comparison algorithm to detect deceptive identities. Given two identities, the algorithm first computes a similarity rating for the value-pair of each individual identity feature. Assuming features are equally important in making a matching decision, all similarity ratings are combined into an overall similarity rating. The two identities being compared are considered matching when the overall similarity rating is greater than a threshold. A supervised training process is required to determine the threshold. However, supervised training requires experts to manually generate a training dataset. This manual process can be very time-consuming and inefficient.

General entity matching techniques have been studied in the area of database. Ravikumar and Cohen [6] proposed a three-layer hierarchical graphical model, in which a layer of latent variables was added between the binary matching decision variable and feature similarity ratings (Figure 1). The model structure captures the intuition that a match decision made for a record pair is often dependent on matching decisions on features rather than similarity ratings of features. Experiments showed that this approach with unsupervised learning achieved performance comparable to that of fully supervised learning methods. Although effective, this approach has the following disadvantages. First, unsupervised learning is not always preferable because unlabeled data alone often are not sufficient for training because there is no information about class labels [7]. The model is also subject to overfitting the noisy training data [6]. Second, the computational complexity of this approach is high because it allows dependencies between latent variables [8]. Moreover, the three-layer architecture may limit the ability to capture more complex matching heuristics. For example, a matching decision made for a pair of names may depend on the matching decisions of first name and surname. An extra layer of latent variable would be necessary in this case.

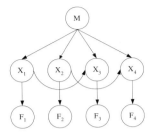

**Fig. 1.** A three-layer hierarchical graphical model

# 3   A Multi-layer Naïve Bayes Model

Based on the three-layer hierarchical graphical model, we propose a multi-layer Naïve Bayes model (Figure 2) by removing the dependencies between latent variables and allowing the capture of complex matching heuristics.

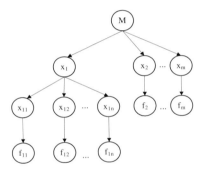

**Fig. 2.** A multi-layer Naïve Bayes model

Let $I$ be an identity record represented as a vector of $m$ feature values. Given a pair of identities $I_a$ and $I_b$, a comparison vector $F$ consists of similarity ratings computed for the value-pairs of $m$ features: $F=\{f_1, f_2, ..., f_m\}$. A binary-valued node $x_i$ is defined as a latent matching variable for the feature $f_i$ $(1 \leq i \leq m)$. The value of the match-class variable $M$ is dependent on $x_i$. The removal of the dependencies between latent variables makes this model a Naïve Bayes model, the computational complexity of which should be greatly reduced. In addition, our proposed model allows more than three layers in order to determine matching decisions for complex features (e.g., name). In these cases, a latent matching variable $x_i$ may have its own latent matching variables $x_{i1}$, $x_{i2}$, ..., $x_{in}$ for the $n$ sub components (e.g., first name, surname).

According to a previous case study on identity problems [2], matching values in name, DOB, ID numbers, and address indicate matching decisions in most cases. We propose a multi-layer Naïve Bayes model for identity matching by incorporating the four features.

The overall framework we propose consists of a training process and a testing process. Given a training dataset, the training process estimates the parameters of the proposed model. Given a pair of identities with an unknown matching decision, the testing process infers the probability that the identity pair is matched using the trained model. Figure 3 illustrates both training and testing processes.

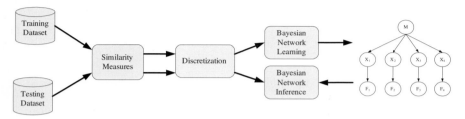

**Fig. 3.** A framework for identity matching

## 4   Experiments

In this section we report an evaluation of our proposed model using real law enforcement data. We first describe our experimental dataset and performance measures used in our study. We then summarize our experimental findings.

### 4.1   Dataset and Performance Metrics

We randomly drew 200 unique identity records out of the 2.4 million records stored in the Tucson Police Department (TPD) database. We considered them to be "suspects" for whom we were trying to find matching identities in the database. Given the huge amount of identity records in the TPD, it is nearly impossible to manually find matching identity records. We used the identity matching approach developed by Wang et al. [4] to compute a similarity score when comparing each "suspect" against every identity record in the database. For each suspect, we chose the top ten most possible matches that had the highest similarity scores. The training dataset was generated by comparing each suspect's primary identity against each of its possible matches. A police veteran manually verified each comparison and labeled it with either "match" or "not a match."

We consider identity matching as a classification problem. We measured the performance of our proposed model using the following three measures: recall, precision, and F-measure. Those measures are widely used in information retrieval.

$$\text{Recall} = \frac{\text{True Positive}}{\text{True Positive} + \text{False Negative}} \qquad (1)$$

$$\text{Precision} = \frac{\text{True Positive}}{\text{True Positive} + \text{False Positive}} \qquad (2)$$

$$\text{F-measure} = \frac{2 * \text{Precision} * \text{Recall}}{\text{Precision} + \text{Recall}} \qquad (3)$$

## 4.2 Experimental Results

In our experiments we compared the performance of our proposed model to that of other existing identity matching techniques, namely the exact-match based technique [5] and the record comparison algorithm [4]. We also evaluated the performance differences of our model in three different learning modes: supervised, semi-supervised, and unsupervised learning. The following four hypotheses were tested in our experiments.

*H1.*  The Naïve Bayes model can achieve a higher F-measure than the exact-match based technique.

*H2.*  The Naïve Bayes model can achieve a higher F-measure than the record comparison algorithm.

*H3.*  The Naïve Bayes model with semi-supervised learning can achieve an F-measure comparable to that with supervised learning.

*H4.*  The Naïve Bayes model with semi-supervised learning can achieve a higher F-measure than that with unsupervised learning.

*H1* was supported. The proposed Naïve Bayes model with either supervised, semi-supervised, or unsupervised learning, performed significantly better than the exact-match technique ($p$-values<0.001 in paired $t$-tests). The exact-match technique suffered from a low recall caused by those matching identities with disagreed name or DOB values.

*H2* was not supported. The Naïve Bayes model with supervised or semi-supervised learning did not perform significantly better than the record comparison algorithm ($p$-value>0.3). However, the Naïve Bayes model achieved statistically higher precision than the weighted-sum technique. The semi-supervised Naïve Bayes model is superior because it can achieve comparable performance overall with only 10% training instances labeled.

*H3* was supported. With varied percentages of unlabeled training instances, the multi-layer Naïve Bayes model with semi-supervised learning achieved F-measures ranging from 0.7017 to 0.7983 (Figure 6). When the percentage was less than or equal to 70%, the F-measure performance of the semi-supervised learning was not statistically different from that of the supervised learning (p-value>0.05).

*H4* was supported. The Naïve Bayes model with unsupervised learning achieved low F-measures (0.5528) for identity matching. Statistical $t$-tests showed that unsupervised learning significantly underperformed semi-supervised learning at all levels ($p$-values < 0.001).

## 5  Conclusions

Identity information is critical to various organizational practices ranging from customer relationship management to crime investigation. The task of searching for a specific identity is difficult because multiple identity representations may exist due to issues such as errors and deception. In this paper we proposed a probabilistic Naïve Bayes model that improved existing identity matching techniques in terms of effectiveness.

In the future we intend to develop an identity matching tool that supports various decision making processes involving identity information. Such a system can be used in identity management systems in various domains.

## Acknowledgements

This project has primarily been funded by the following grants:

National Science Foundation, Digital Government Program, "COPLINK Center: Social Network Analysis and Identity Deception Detection for Law Enforcement and Homeland Security," (IIS-0429364), September 2003-August 2006.

Department of Homeland Security (DHS), "BorderSafe: Cross Jurisdictional Information Sharing, Analysis, and Visualization," September 2003-August 2005.

## References

1. Camp, J. Identity in Digital Government. In: proceedings of 2003 Civic Scenario Workshop: An Event of the Kennedy School of Government. Cambridge, MA 02138 (2003)
2. Wang, G.A., Atabakhsh, H., Petersen, T., Chen, H.: Discovering Identity Problems: A Case Study. Lecture Notes in Computer Science 3495 (2005) 368-373
3. Redman, T.C.: The Impact of Poor Data Quality on the Typical Enterprises. Communications of the ACM 41(3) (1998) 79-82
4. Wang, G., Chen, H., Atabakhsh, H.: Automatically Detecting Deceptive Criminal Identities. Communications of the ACM 47(3) (2004) 71-76
5. Marshall, B., Kaza, S., Xu, J., Atabakhsh, H., Petersen, T., Violette, C., Chen, H. Cross-Jurisdictional criminal activity networks to support border and transportation security. In: proceedings of 7th Annual IEEE Conference on Intelligent Transportation Systems (ITSC 2004). Washington, D.C. (2004)
6. Ravikumar, P., Cohen, W.W. A Hierarchical Graphical Model for Record Linkage. In: proceedings of 20th Conference on Uncertainty in Artificial Intelligence (UAI '04). Banff Park Lodge, Banff, Canada (2004)
7. Nigam, K., McCallum, A.K., Thrun, S., Mitchell, T.: Text Classification from Labeled and Unlabeled Documents using EM. Machine Learning 39 (2000) 103-134
8. Winkler, W.E. Methods for Record Linkage and Bayesian Networks. In: proceedings of Section on Survey Research Methods, American Statistical Association. Alexandria, Virginia (2002)

# Towards Optimal Police Patrol Routes
# with Genetic Algorithms

Danilo Reis, Adriano Melo, André L.V. Coelho, and Vasco Furtado

Master Program in Applied Informatics (MIA)
Center of Technological Sciences (CCT)
UNIFOR – University of Fortaleza
Av. Washington Soares 1321, 60811-905
Fortaleza – Brazil
danilo.reis@fujitec.com.br, aanmelo@hotmail.com,
{acoelho, vasco}@unifor.br

**Abstract.** It is quite consensual that police patrolling can be regarded as one of the best well-known practices for implementing public-safety preventive policies towards the combat of an assortment of urban crimes. However, the specification of successful police patrol routes is by no means a trivial task to pursue, mainly when one considers large demographic areas. In this work, we present the first results achieved with GAPatrol, a novel evolutionary multiagent-based simulation tool devised to assist police managers in the design of effective police patrol route strategies. One particular aspect investigated here relates to the GAPatrol's facility to automatically discover crime hotspots, that is, high-crime-density regions (or targets) that deserve to be better covered by routine patrol surveillance. In order to testify the potentialities of the novel approach in such regard, simulation results related to two scenarios of study over the same artificial urban territory are presented and discussed here.

## 1 Introduction

Police patrolling is an important instrument for implementing preventive strategies towards the combat of criminal activities in urban centers, mainly those involving violence aspects (such as bank robbery, theft, armed robbery, gang fighting, drug dealing, environmental degradation, and kidnapping). An underlying hypothesis of such preventive work is that, by knowing where the occurrences of crime are currently happening and the reasons associated with such, it is possible to make a more optimized distribution of the police resources available to control the overall crime rates.

In fact, place-oriented crime prevention strategies have been the focus of much research study in the last decades, centering, in a way or another, on the concept of "crime hotspots" [3][6]. The main point argued in this theory is that crime is not spread evenly across urban landscapes; rather, it clumps in some relatively small places (that usually generate more than half of all criminal events) and is totally absent in others. Hotspots refer to those high-crime-density areas (targets) that deserve to be better controlled by routine patrol surveillance or other more specific police actions.

Usually, the discovery and analysis of such hotspots are done iteratively by the construction of visual maps, which allow the association of the types of hotspots with

S. Mehrotra et al. (Eds.): ISI 2006, LNCS 3975, pp. 485–491, 2006.

their crime patterns and possible police actions. Moreover, simple-to-apply statistical tests can reveal a prior understanding of what should be expected to be found in a hotspot map, even before the map has been created. Tests for clustering are particularly important. However, analysts may waste valuable time in their attempts to create a crime hotspot map if a test fails to reveal that some clusters (hotspots) exist in the analyzed data. Indeed, different mapping and statistical techniques have revealed the different applications to which they are suited and demonstrated that they have pros and cons with respect to the mapping outputs/results they generate. One consensus that has emerged in this sense is that identifying hotspots requires multiple complementary techniques, since no single method is good enough for all circumstances.

With this in mind, in this paper, we present GAPatrol, a novel evolutionary multiagent-based simulation tool devised to assist police managers in the design of effective police patrol route strategies. As the specification of these patrol routing strategies is intimately associated with the discovery of hotspots, our claim is that such decision-support tool provides an alternative, automatic means for the delimitation and characterization of important crime hotspots that may exist or appear over a real demographic region of interest. The conceptualization of GAPatrol was directly inspired by the increasing trend of hybridizing multiagent systems (MAS) [7] with evolutionary algorithms (EAs) [1], in such a way as to combine their positive and complementary properties [5]. Moreover, it correlates with other prominent research studies that have recently been conducted in the public-safety domain by making use of the theoretical/empirical resources made available by multiagent-based simulation systems [2][4].

In order to testify the potentialities of the GAPatrol approach in uncovering crime hotspots, simulation experiments related to alternative scenarios of study over the same artificial urban territory have been conducted, and some preliminary results are presented and discussed in the following. This is done after characterizing the entities comprising the simulated urban society in focus and some configuration issues related to the adopted multiagent simulation environment, as well as briefly conveying some important details about the evolutionary engine behind GAPatrol.

## 2  GAPatrol

The entities that take part in our simulated multiagent society are described as follows. There is a set of $NP = 6$ police teams available, each one associated with a patrol route passing through some special locations of the urban territory considered. There is no distinction, in terms of skills, between the police officers allotted to the different police teams. We also assume that the teams patrol intermittently and the speed of their patrol cars are the same, meaning that the time spent by a given team in a given location will depend solely on the size of its route. However, routes can overlap and/or share common points of surveillance. The special locations to be patrolled are referred to here as targets, which can be differentiated with respect to the type of commercial/entertainment establishment they represent (like drugstores, banks, gas stations, lottery houses, squares, and malls). In all, there are $NT = 41$ targets in the territory.

Besides, there is a set of $NC = 15$ criminals representing the actors that frequently try to commit the crimes. Each criminal is endowed with a limited sight of the environment, measured in terms of grid cells. For instance, with a vision of 1,000 meters, if each cell has 100-meter sides, the radius of the criminal's sight will be 10 square cells around him/herself. We assume that there is no chance of having a criminal being arrested and jailed, meaning that the number of criminals is always constant. Each criminal offender has a personality, which, in turn, determines the types of places he/she more frequently selects as targets for committing crimes. Moreover, the personality can vary over time, passing from novice to intermediate to dangerous, according to the success of the criminal in committing crimes. For each pair (type of personality, type of target), there is a certain probability for committing a crime, as showed in Table 1. The underlying logic is that a dangerous criminal has a higher probability to seek out banks than a novice, for instance, aiming at obtaining higher returns in money and due to his/her higher level of expertise.

**Table 1.** Probability of approaching a target for different types of criminal personalities

|              | Square | Drugstore | Lottery | Gas Station | Mall | Bank |
|--------------|--------|-----------|---------|-------------|------|------|
| Novice       | 50%    | 30%       | 20%     | 0%          | 0%   | 0%   |
| Intermediate | 20%    | 30%       | 30%     | 20%         | 0%   | 0%   |
| Dangerous    | 10%    | 15%       | 15%     | 10%         | 15%  | 35%  |

Having probabilistically selected the next type of target, it is assumed that the criminal has the knowledge necessary to localize the closest exemplar target on the map, moving straight towards such point. The time expended to reach the target is calculated based on the speed of the criminal and the distance to the target. The shortest period of motion, considering all *NC* criminals, is taken as a reference, so that the criminals are allowed to move only during this time period. Finally, the decision whether or not to commit a crime is made based on the existence of one or more police teams within the radius of the criminal's sight. If the offender decides to not commit a crime, then he/she will select a new target to approach, leaving the current location. Otherwise, we assume that a crime will be simply committed.

GAPatrol's multiagent engine runs atop the Repast simulation environment [2]. Each set of routes designed by a GAPatrol chromosome (see below) gives rise to a series of simulation executions in order to evaluate the crime prevention performance of such set of routes. Each simulation instance runs 3,000 ticks, which would roughly correspond to one month of real-life events.

The evolutionary engine of GAPatrol is based on Genetic Algorithms (GAs) [1], a metaheuristics that complies with the Darwinian theory of evolution by natural selection to efficiently design (quasi-)optimal solutions to complicated search problems. Such metaheuristics maintain a population of individuals, which represent plausible solutions to the target problem and evolve over time through a process of competition and controlled variation. The more adapted an individual is to its environment (i.e., the solution is to the problem), the more likely will such individual be exploited for generating novel individuals. In order to distinguish between adapted and non-adapted individuals, a score function (known as fitness function) should be properly specified beforehand in a manner as to reflect the main restrictions imposed by the problem.

In this paper, a customized GA model is employed for the design of effective police patrol routing strategies, making direct use, for this purpose, of the multiagent engine described earlier. Due to the dynamism implied by the criminals' non-deterministic behavior, this may be viewed as a challenging problem to be coped with by GAs. In what follows, we describe the main components of the GAPatrol evolutionary engine.

Each individual in the evolutionary process represents a set of patrol routes, each route associated with a given patrol team. By this way, the number of routes is pre-fixed. However, the length of each route and the targets it may include are defined adaptively, therefore allowing the overlapping of routes through the crossing of their sub-routes or through the sharing of targets. There is no need that a target be covered by at least one route, which means that the evolutionary process is free to concentrate on those targets that seem to deserve better police patrolling attention (hotspots), if this might be the case. Each individual should be interpreted as a sequence of pairs of indices, the first one representing a police team and the other referencing a target. A binary codification of the chromosomes is employed for such purpose.

As the main objective of this study is to find a set of patrol routes that minimizes the number of crime occurrences in a given area, a straightforward fitness function that was adopted for the evaluation of the individuals is the inverse of the number of crimes. This fitness function is further modified by a fitness scaling mapping operator, so as to better discriminate between the individuals' capabilities and to prevent the premature convergence problem [1]. In each execution of GAPatrol, the initial population of route sets is randomly created according to a uniform distribution over the values of all genes (i.e., bits of the individuals). The fitness value of each individual is calculated taking as basis the average number of crimes achieved in $NS = 10$ executions of the multiagent engine. After that, according to the roulette wheel selection operator [1], some individuals are recruited for mating (via the crossover operator) and producing offspring. The latter may serve as targets for the simple mutation operator. Finally, the current best individuals (from both parents and offspring) are selected deterministically for comprising the next GAPatrol's generation. This process is repeated until a stopping criterion is satisfied, namely that a certain number of generations are reached. Then, the best individuals (sets of patrol routes) produced across all generations are presented to the police managers as the (quasi-) optimal solution to the considered simulation scenario, allowing them to provide visual analysis of the characteristics underlying these most effective sets of patrol routes and the hotspots they have discovered.

## 3 Results and Discussion

In order to evaluate the performance of the GAPatrol approach while tackling the problem of hotspots localization, some simulation experiments were carried out and their results are briefly presented here having as basis two distinct scenarios defined over a simulated urban environment that mimics a well-known neighborhood of Fortaleza, Brazil. In such study, the GA metaparameters were set arbitrarily as follows [1]: 95% as crossover rate, 5% as mutation rate, population size of 30 individuals, and 100 as the maximum number of iterations. Since the criminals begin the simulations as novices, the points that should be targeted more frequently by them are drugstores, squares, and lotteries. Figure 1 presents the physical disposition of all 41 targets over the environment as well as the points of departure of the criminals in the two scenarios. The first scenario was devised as a controlled scenario where the points of departure were localized strategically in the middle of the four quadrants of the environment, facilitating in the recognition of the hotspots. Conversely, in the second scenario, the criminals start out from a unique source, forcing them to initially roam out around the area, which leads to a more dispersed distribution of the hotspots.

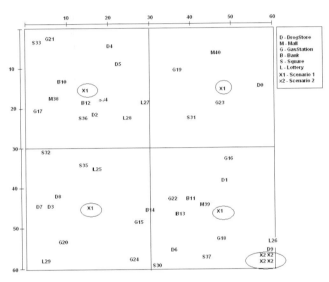

**Fig. 1.** Physical location of the targets (in terms of grid squares) and points of departure of the criminals in both scenarios of study

**Table 2.** GAPatrol's best sets of routes for both scenarios, and the types of targets ranked according to the frequency of visitation by the routes—the higher the frequency of a type, the higher the chance that its associated points are hotspots. Targets with higher probabilities to be hotspots are highlighted.

| | Team1 | Team2 | Team3 | Team4 | Team5 | Team6 | Target Type(%) | | #Crimes |
|---|---|---|---|---|---|---|---|---|---|
| Scenario1 | 34 | 36 | 19, 27, 22, 4, 14 | 24, **14**, 2 , 39, 4, 0, 31, 24, 5, 2, **28**, 26, 28 | 28 | 25, 2, 35, 12, 27, 1, 3, 38, 36, 31, 17 | Drugstore | 22.6 | 135 |
| | | | | | | | Gas Station | 22.6 | |
| | | | | | | | Square | 19.4 | |
| | | | | | | | Lottery | 16.1 | |
| | | | | | | | Banks | 12.9 | |
| | | | | | | | Mall | 6.4 | |
| Scenario 2 | 35, 28, 8, 31 | 2, 36 | 5, 15, 3, 25, 19, 14, 25, 12, 22, 8, 25 | 28, 19, 7, 35, 25 | 34 | 25, 31, 10, 27, 31, 17, 12, 21, 14 | Gas Station | 22.3 | 445 |
| | | | | | | | Square | 22.3 | |
| | | | | | | | Drugstore | 18.2 | |
| | | | | | | | Lottery | 18.2 | |
| | | | | | | | Banks | 15.0 | |
| | | | | | | | Mall | 0 | |

Table 2 brings the configuration of the best sets of routes achieved for both scenarios, indicating the types of targets they concentrate on mostly. It was easy to notice that GAPatrol could identify well, in both scenarios, the targets that are best candidates for being considered as hotspots: either GAPatrol has allocated a patrol team permanently at those points or they appear twice or more times in any route of the set. Moreover, as in both scenarios fifty percent of the patrolled targets are drugstores, squares or lotteries, it is easy to perceive that GAPatrol could somehow "learn" the behavior of the non-expert criminals by allocating more police resources for monitoring those types of places and then not allowing that the criminals become experts.

Finally, by analyzing the behavior of the best individuals of each generation of all GAPatrol executions, we could notice that this sort of hotspot elicitation was indeed very important for giving rise to effective sets of patrol routes at the end of the evolutionary process. Indeed, in the first generations, most of the hotspots were not yet localized by most of the competing sets of routes (GA individuals), which, in turn, tended to be rich in length (i.e. trying to encompass as much points as possible and not focusing on those that were indeed most important). Fig. 2 provides a pictorial illustration of one execution of GAPatrol, ratifying our arguments.

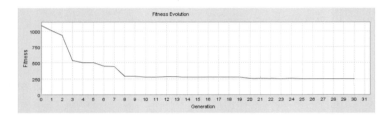

**Fig. 2.** GAPatrol evolutionary process: decreasing in fitness due to hotspots discovery

As future work, we plan to provide a more thorough account on the properties and characteristics underlying the best sets of routes achieved with GAPatrol. A spatial analysis of the routes is also in course, and soon the criminals shall be endowed with capabilities to learn how to better spot their points of attack.

## Acknowledgements

CNPq/Funcap sponsored the third author through the DCR grant n° 23661-04.

## References

[1]   T. Bäck, D. Fogel, Z. Michalewicz. The Handbook of Evolutionary Computation, Oxford University Press, New York, 1997.
[2]   N. Collier. Repast: An extensible framework for agent simulation. Available in http://repast.sourceforge.net, 2003.
[3]   L. Sherman, P. Gartin, and M. Buerger. Hot spots of predatory crime: Routine activities and the criminology of place, Criminology 27:27-56, 1989.

[4]  J.S. Sichman, F. Bousquet, and P. Davidsson (Eds.). Multi-Agent-Based Simulation II, Third International Workshop (MABS 2002), LNAI 2581, Springer, Berlin, 2003.

[5]  R. Smith and C. Bonacina. Evolutionary computation as a paradigm for engineering emergent behaviour in multi-agent systems, in: Plekhanova, V. (Ed.), Intelligent Agent Software Engineering, pp. 118-136, Idea Group, 2002.

[6]  D. Weisburd, L. Maher, and L. Sherman. Contrasting crime general and crime specific theory: The case of hot spots of crime, Advances in Criminological Theory, vol. 4, New Brunswick, NJ: Transaction Press, 1992.

[7]  G. Weiss (Ed.). Multiagent Systems: A Modern Approach to Distributed Artificial Intelligence, The MIT Press, 1999.

# SemanticSpy: Suspect Tracking Using Semantic Data in a Multimedia Environment

Amit Mathew, Amit Sheth, and Leonidas Deligiannidis

Department of Computer Science University of Georgia, Athens, Georgia 30602, USA
{mathew, amit, ldeligia}@cs.uga.edu

**Abstract.** In this paper we describe SemanticSpy, a tool for tracking suspects and their activities around the globe. Using an RDF data store and a three-dimensional multimedia environment, SemanticSpy is able to bring semantic information to life. SemanticSpy utilizes a blend of semantic information and a media-rich environment that can display images, 3D models, and documents, and can play audio clips to give the user the ability to analyze information using the different types of media. We believe that this will help law enforcement officials gain insight into a suspect's behavior and give them the power to avert the next major crime or terrorist attack. Finally, we describe SemanticSpy's architecture and explain its advantages over other information environments.

## 1 Introduction

In this age of international terrorism and global drug smuggling rings, it is apparent that there is a need for law enforcement and counter-terrorism agencies to track the movement and activities of suspects around the world. The Semantic Web [1] can aid in this effort because it allows relationships among entities to be represented in a manner that is both human- and machine-processable. Relationships are a vital aspect of criminal and terrorist organization analysis because such organizations are composed of relationships among members, relationships among events, and so on. Furthermore, Semantic Web technologies, like RDF (Resource Description Framework) [7], provide a suitable format for metadata. Metadata is important whenever details matter: we don't just want to know that a meeting occurred, we also want to know who was involved, where it happened, and how it took place.

The number of relationships and amount of metadata generated from tracking a suspect can easily overwhelm security officials. SemanticSpy offers a way to harness this abundance of data and visualize it in a variety of ways. Phone conversations can be played, photographs of a suspect's meeting can be viewed, and a 3D model of the car a suspect is driving can be shown. With the help of semantic-enhanced data and interactivity, SemanticSpy can potentially allow an analyst to piece together seemingly trivial details to help forestall an act of terrorism.

## 2 Motivations

The two major features of SemanticSpy that differentiate it from existing tools are its use of semantic data and its rich multimedia environment. The value of these two features and how they benefit the user are discussed next.

S. Mehrotra et al. (Eds.): ISI 2006, LNCS 3975, pp. 492–497, 2006.

## 2.1  Advantages of Semantic Data

Semantic data has many advantages over data stored in a traditional database, but the two key aspects are its emphasis on relationships among entities and its use of metadata. Relationships are important in many aspects [9]. One is the idea of human networks and its relationship to organized crime, terrorism, and other illicit activities. Suspects participating in illegal activities often are part of social networks that need to be analyzed to determine leadership and level of involvement. Furthermore, relationships are important when trying to anticipate a suspect's actions. For example, a suspect may have a relationship to a chemical plant which may be legitimate (if the suspect is a chemical engineer) or not (if the suspect is investigating using hazardous materials for malevolent purposes). Explicit semantics afforded by named relationships in Semantic Web representations provide better quality of analysis and insight than what is possible by simple graphs with unnamed edges as used in many earlier approaches that study such networks.

The second important aspect of the Semantic Web is the utilization of metadata. Metadata is often treated as a side effect or unnecessary detail in traditional settings, but for intelligence agencies, metadata can make the difference in catching a criminal. Metadata allows a user to detect relationships that would otherwise go unnoticed. For example, the fact that two seemingly unrelated people are traveling in a car may be innocuous. However, the fact they are traveling in the two cars with registrations belonging to the same person or persons in the same group may be important.

Use of such tools presupposes extensive capability for metadata extraction from heterogeneous data of the type discussed in [10].

## 2.2  Advantages of a Multimedia Environment

The main advantage that a multimedia environment offers over a traditional single media environment is that it allows the user to benefit from the strengths of each media type. Text allows the system to convey precise data to the user. In SemanticSpy, text is used mainly to show metadata about suspects and activities. Some types of information naturally occur in an audio format, such as phone calls or other recorded conversations. Although conversations can be transcribed to text, audio provides additional information through voice intonation and volume. Images are useful for showing photographs and frames from video (which may come from surveillance videos) and are a form of media where humans perform better than computers in comparing between two samples. Three-dimensional models are useful for conveying spatial information, such as the plan for the interior of a plane, and give security professionals more actionable information. For example, a 3D model of the car that suspected terrorists are driving may reveal a hidden compartment where a bomb may be placed.

# 3  Functionality

SemanticSpy offers several different predefined views that aid in the tracking of suspects. These include the suspect view, the activity view, and the global view. The suspect view, shown in the upper right corner of Figure 1, shows a list of suspects that can be selected for tracking. In this figure, the suspects are taken from the list of the FBI's ten most wanted criminals [3]. Notice that the suspects' names are accompanied by their photographs, which allows security officials to see a suspect and possibly recognize the suspect in another picture. The suspect view also shows additional information about the suspect, like their physical features. The list of suspects can be scrolled through, with the currently tracked suspect shown on the top. Once a suspect is selected, the user can choose a date and see the suspect's activities on that date. In this figure, March 5, 2005, is chosen. When a day on which a suspect has been involved in some activity is selected, information for that day is shown in the activity view on the left side.

The activity view shows the type of activity that occurred and its associated metadata. Currently, SemanticSpy supports three types of activities: travel, meetings, and phone calls; more activities are under development. The different types of activities can have different types of metadata. For example, a travel activity can detail the type of travel used, whether it be by air, sea, or land. If the suspect traveled by air, the airline's flight number, and an image or model of the airplane they traveled in can be shown. In Figure 1, a 3D model of a plane is shown with the flight the suspect took on that day. If the suspect traveled by a rental car, information about the rental car company can be shown. Each travel activity is associated with two geographic points, the point of departure and point of arrival. These points are shown in the global view, shown in the center of Figure 1.

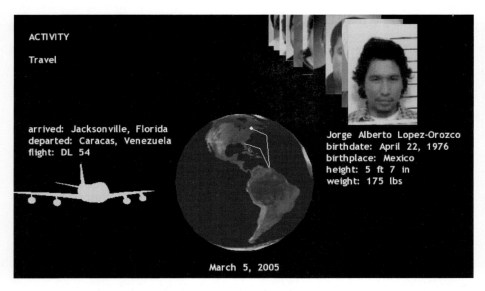

**Fig. 1.** A screenshot of SemanticSpy

The global view is made of a three-dimensional sphere, textured with an image of the earth displayed with terrain. The global view is helpful in several ways. It allows users to absorb information "at a glance." For example, in Figure 1, a user can find the details of each of the suspect's trips, but from the image in the global view it is immediately clear that a suspect traveled first from somewhere in North America to somewhere in South America, and later back to North America. This easy access to general information prevents the user from being overloaded by information, and allows them to more likely notice the information that can stop an international criminal. The currently active points are highlighted in red, while points of previous travel are highlighted in yellow. The point-plotting feature is not restricted to travel. It can be used to communicate any relationship between two points, such as a phone call between parties in two different locations. Another helpful feature of the map is that it shows the topographical information of the Earth. This is helpful because a user may notice a suspect traveling to suspicious terrain, such as a desert.

The other types of activities supported by SemanticSpy are meetings and phone calls. Meetings are displayed with a single geographic point, an optional photograph of the meeting area if one is available, and relevant metadata, like who was present at a particular meeting. The other type of supported activity is phone conversations. Phone calls can be accompanied by an audio recording of the conversation and information about the phone call, like who was called and from what number. All these elements can be used to gain insight into the motivations of a suspect's actions.

A typical use case starts with a user selecting a suspect that may be involved in planning a terrorist attack. The user may then choose a date from a month ago to see the suspect's previous travels and activities. The user may choose to drill down on one of those activities, like playing a recorded phone conversation between the current suspect of interest and another unknown person, or viewing the people involved in a meeting with the suspect of interest.

## 4 Architecture

SemanticSpy's architecture, as seen in Fig. 2, is separated into two major components: the front-end visualization system and the back-end RDF data store. The visualization system is powered by MAGE [8], a high-performance game and virtual reality engine that supports simulation and visualization tasks. MAGE supports the viewing of 3D models, 2D images, and audio, while still maintaining interactive framerates. MAGE also has a scripted material system, making it easy to update suspects' photographs or 3D models on-the-fly.

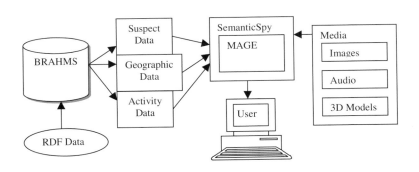

**Fig. 2.** A diagram of SemanticSpy's architecture

BRAHMS [5], developed in the LSDIS lab, is used as SemanticSpy's RDF data store. BRAHMS is a main-memory system that is very fast, making it an appropriate choice for a real-time visualization system. The points on the globe that mark the suspects' travel are determined by GPS coordinates in the RDF input file. The GPS coordinates are converted to Cartesian coordinates and plotted on the globe. The lines connecting the points show the different legs of a suspect's journey.

## 5   Related Work

Much of the work done in Semantic Web visualization today is in the area of graph visualizations, especially of large ontologies. However, there exists some work dealing with Semantic information in a spatial context. Themescape [11] provides topographical maps that show the relations among different types of documents. Ghinea et al [4] use spatial data in the context of the human body to study back pain. SemanticSpy builds upon these research works by combining geospatial visualization and Semantic Web technologies to support suspect tracking. GIS-type visualization applications that predate the Semantic Web have also been developed. For example, Eick [2] developed a method for visualizing communication networks using a three-dimensional globe that contains nodes connected with lines. Eick's work interestingly gives meaning to the thickness and color of the lines that connect the nodes.

## 6   Future Work and Conclusions

The development of SemanticSpy has opened up the possibility for productive future research. SemanticSpy can be extended with more types of multimedia (e.g., video), and more types of activities, such as job interviews, emails and other documents, and social gatherings. Also, the global visualization system can be extended to support zooming and satellite views. Another direction we wish to explore is to move SemanticSpy to a virtual environment to see if an immersive environment improves the user's ability to process information. Finally, we wish to harness Semantic Web technologies to intelligently extract related suspects from a large dataset for viewing in SemanticSpy, using connections based on financial transactions and social networks [6].

SemanticSpy allows law enforcement officials to view information about suspects in new and powerful ways by using a multimedia-rich environment to capitalize on humans' powerful senses and pattern recognition abilities. Furthermore, SemanticSpy is an experimental tool for visualizing semantic information in new ways, by creating domain-specific visualizations that empower analysts to detect important relationships, which facilitate their investigative tasks.

**Acknowledgements.** The authors would like to thank Maciej Janik for his assistance with the BRAHMS system. We would also like to thank Boanerges Aleman-Meza, Angela Maduko, and other members of the Large Scale Distributed Information Systems Lab at the University of Georgia who provided valuable feedback during the development of SemanticSpy.

# References

1. T. Berners-Lee, J. Hendler, and O. Lassila. "The Semantic Web," *Scientific American*, May 2001.
2. S.G. Eick. "Aspects of Network Visualization," *Computer Graphics and Applications* 16(2), 69-72, 1996.
3. FBI's Ten Most Wanted, http://www.fbi.gov/mostwant/topten/fugitives/fugitives.htm
4. G. Ghinea and D. Gill. "Using Scalable Vector Graphics and Geographical Information Systems in a Back Pain Study," Visualizing the Semantic Web, Springer 2002, pp. 180 – 197.
5. M. Janik and K. Kochut. "BRAHMS: A WorkBench RDF Store And High Performance Memory System for Semantic Association Discovery," *Fourth International Semantic Web Conference ISWC 2005*, Galway, Ireland, 6-10 November 2005.
6. V. Krebs, "Mapping Networks of Terrorist Cells," *Connections*, 24(3): 43-52, 2002.
7. O. Lassila and R. R. Swick. "Resource Description Framework (RDF) model and syntax specification," W3C Recommendation, Feb. 1999.    http://www.w3.org/TR/REC-rdf-syntax/
8. A. Mathew and L. Deligiannidis. "MAGE-VR: A Software Framework for Virtual Reality Application Development," *Proc. of The 2005 International Conference on Modeling, Simulation and Visualization Methods*, pp. 191-197, June 2005.
9. A. Sheth, I. Budak Arpinar, and V. Kashyap, "Relationships at the Heart of Semantic Web: Modeling, Discovering, and Exploiting Complex Semantic Relationships," Enhancing the Power of the Internet Studies in Fuzziness and Soft Computing, M. Nikravesh, B. Azvin, R. Yager and L. Zadeh, Springer-Verlag, 2003, pp. 63-94
10. A. Sheth, C. Bertram, D. Avant, B. Hammond, K. Kochut, Y. Warke, Managing Semantic Content for the Web, IEEE Internet Computing, July/August 2002, pp. 80-87.
11. ThemeScape Product Suite, Cartia Inc, http://www.cartia.com/

# A Framework for Exploring Gray Web Forums: Analysis of Forum-Based Communities in Taiwan

Jau-Hwang Wang[1], Tianjun Fu[2], Hong-Ming Lin[1], and Hsinchun Chen[2]

[1] Department of Information Management, Central Police University,
56 Shu-Ren Road, Ta-Kang, Kwei-Shan, Tao-Yuan, Taiwan, ROC 333
jwang@mail.cpu.edu.tw, im933090@sun4.cpu.edu.tw
[2] Department of Management Information Systems,
The University of Arizona, Tucson, AZ 85721, USA
futj@email.arizona.edu, hchen@eller.arizona.edu

**Abstract.** This paper examines the "Gray Web Forums" in Taiwan. We study their characteristics and develop an analysis framework for assisting investigations on forum communities. Based on the statistical data collected from online forums, we found that the relationship between a posting and its responses is highly correlated to the forum nature. In addition, hot threads extracted based on the proposed metric can be used to assist analysts in identifying illegal or inappropriate contents. Furthermore, members' roles and activities in a virtual community can be identified by member level analysis.

## 1 Introduction

Nowadays, computers and computer networks are not only used as tools for processing information, but also have become a new medium to share and access information online. For example, bulletin board systems, internet relay chat systems, and I-phone systems, are all integrated with the WWW and provide various communication channels for individuals to exchange information beyond the limits of time and space. Consequently, our society is in a state of transformation toward a "virtual society," where people's daily activities, such as shopping, getting services, and sharing information, can be accomplished without face-to-face contact with others.

Although the internet has enabled global businesses to flourish, it also allows criminals to make acquaintance of victims, acquiring them and eventually committing crimes. For example, just a few years ago, a National Taipei University student was found dead and wrapped in a luggage box dumped on a street corner by his "net friend," whom he met on a homosexual online forum. Today, many teenagers continue making friends through online activities, such as exchanging e-mails and playing internet video games, without having any physical interaction. The lack of physical interactions leaves few observable trails for parents and makes them less informed on their children's social activities. Just recently, two teenagers in Taiwan who got acquainted through an internet chat room committed suicide together. The breaking news astonished both the two families as well as the Taiwan society.

The advance of computer forensics has shown that online activities often create electronic trails [1]. For examples, bulletin board messages are stored in system

S. Mehrotra et al. (Eds.): ISI 2006, LNCS 3975, pp. 498–503, 2006.
© Springer-Verlag Berlin Heidelberg 2006

archives, and e-mail messages are stored in mail servers or clients. Although archives in private storage can be acquired for analysis only under proper authorization, the information stored in public archives can be retrieved for analysis when necessary. After the 911 disaster, the FBI has shifted the reactive or post crime investigation paradigm to proactive investigation [2]. Thus, precrime investigation and data analysis are of critical importance to mitigate the negative effects of online activities. Although the collection and analysis of "dark web" sites have been under intensive investigations ([3], [4], [5], [6], [7]), only few researches addressed the issue of deriving crime leads or detecting symptoms of crimes from online archives. Wang, et al, conducted a study to gather illegal web sites using special search mechanisms [8]. Dringus, et al., used data mining to discover and build alternative representations for asynchronous education forums [9]. However, no research has been done on gathering crime leads from forum archives. This paper examines the "Gray Web Forums" in Taiwan and develops an analysis framework for assisting investigation on "gray" forums. The organization of this paper is as follows: Section 2 introduces the Gray Web Forum and its implication and challenges on crime investigation. Section 3 describes the framework for exploring Gray Web Forums. Section 4 gives conclusions and the future work.

## 2  Gray Web Forum-Based Communities

A forum is defined as *the computer-mediated medium for the open discussion of subjects of public interest* [10]. Forum members basically have three types of operations:

1. View existing postings.
2. Reply to an existing posting.
3. Start a new topic (also called a thread) of discussion.

"Postings" are messages that are sent to a forum for public viewing. Forum members may respond to existing postings or create a new topic. A group of postings related to the same topic are called a "thread." Detailed forum descriptions can be found in [10].

Communities are characterized by common interests, frequent interaction, and identification [11]. Internet forum members discuss on a certain topic, seek support from members, exchange information by postings, and are identified by e-mail addresses. Thus internet forums are perfect platforms for the formation of virtual communities. However, due to the anonymity and lack of observability, unscrupulous individuals may exploit internet forums for illegal activities. The *Gray Web Forum-based Virtual Community is* defined as: *the community formed through internet forums, which focused on topics that might potentially encourage biased, offensive, or disruptive behaviors and may disturb the society or threaten the public safety*. Such forums may cover topics such as pirated CDs, gambling, spiritualism, and so on. For examples, members of pirated CD forums may share music CDs without proper licensing; gambling forum members may provide hyperlinks to online gambling web sites; spiritualism forums may misguide teenagers and encourage disruptive behaviors.

Investigations on Gray Web Forums are difficult. Firstly, most forum postings are not indexed and thus can not be detected by search engines. Secondly, internet forums are highly distributed and their huge quantity prohibits effective coverage by manual investigations. Thirdly, a thread of discussion may cause numerous postings or sub-threads and the duration of each thread can be very long, which make manual investigations time consuming and highly inefficient. Finally, access control mechanisms adopted by forums may introduce obstacles for effective/efficient investigation.

## 3   A Framework for Gray Web Forum Analysis

### 3.1   Research Design

The framework for Gray Web forum analysis mainly consists of four components, as shown in Figure 1 below:

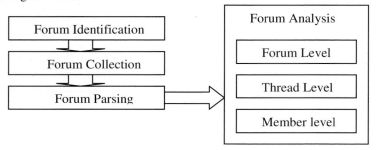

**Fig. 1.** The Gray Web Forum Analysis Framework

Forum identification is to identify Gray Web Forums based on the knowledge of domain experts. Forum collection is to spider the web pages in forums or boards that have been identified. Forum parsing is to extract useful content, such as the number of threads, the number of members, the duration and distribution of threads, and the frequency as well as the volume of postings. Forum analysis can be divided into three levels: forum, thread, and member levels. Forum level analysis is to provide a broad overview for the forums; thread level analysis is to identify *hot or influential threads*; and member level analysis is to segment members into different categories and identify their roles. Furthermore, forum members can be classified as *initiators*, *active members*, and *followers*. Initiators are those who create threads of discussion. Active members have both high frequency of participation and a large volume of postings. Finally, followers have high frequency of participation but a small volume of postings.

### 3.2   Forum Level Analysis

Several representatives of Taiwan Gray Web forums are shown in Table 1.

**Table 1.** Selected Gray Web Forums in Taiwan

| FID* | URLs | Type |
|------|------|------|
| 1 | http://bbs.a35.info/thread.php?fid=486 | Pirated CD |
| 2 | http://oie.idv.tw/cgi-bin/bbs/forums.cgi?forum=1 | Gambling |
| 3 | http://www.525.idv.tw/bbs/cg-ibin/forums.cgi?forum=9 | Sentimentalism |
| 4 | http://www.helzone.com/vbb/forumdisplay.php?f=38 | Spiritualism |

*Forum Identification Number.

Forum 1 provides its members with illegal software and pirated CDs. Forum 2 releases gambling information. Forum 3 allows its members to share and discuss sentimental essays. Forum 4 consists of threads discussing superstitious subjects. The results of forum level analysis are shown in Table 2.

**Table 2.** Overview of the Gray Web Forum Collection

| FID | Type | Threads | Postings | Size(Mb) | Members |
|-----|------|---------|----------|----------|---------|
| 1 | Pirated CDs | 252 | 7749 | 32.2 | **3013** |
| 2 | Gambling | 515 | **31128** | **292** | 539 |
| 3 | Sentimentalism | **1396** | 4452 | 62.8 | 463 |
| 4 | Spiritualism | 434 | 2415 | 41.4 | 228 |

Both Forums 1 and 2 adopt similar access control mechanisms, which only allow members to view the contents of a posting after they have replied a message to the posting. The first postings of many threads in these two forums often contain URL links to pirated CDs or important gambling information, which cannot be viewed unless a viewer replies to them. Therefore, members have to post short/simple message, such as "I want to see it," in order to view the posting. Both Forums 1 and 2 have a high post-per-thread value. However, the average number of postings per member in Forum 1 is 2.6, which is much less than 56.5 in Forum 2. It is because gamblers often reply to as many threads as possible, while people who search for pirated CDs only reply to threads of interest. Forum 3 has 1396 threads but each thread only contains 3.2 postings on average. However, the average number of thread postings in Forum 2 is 60.4. Again, this is because gamblers tend to reply to more threads to gather gambling information.

### 3.3  Thread Level Analysis

*Hot* or *influential threads* are threads which statistically have longer duration, more members, more active members, and more postings in numbers and volumes. The following metric is used to calculate scores for every thread in each forum.

$$\textbf{Thread Score} = F_{norm}(N_p) \times F_{norm}(V_t) \times F_{norm}(D_t) \times F_{norm}(N_{am}) \times F_{norm}(N_m)$$

Where $N_p$ is the number of postings, $V_t$ is the volume of postings, $D_t$ is the duration, $N_{am}$ is number of active members, and $N_m$ is the number of members in a thread. The function $F_{norm}()$ is used to normalize each variable to a range of [0,1]. Note that we classify members who have more than one posting as active members. The hottest threads in each forum and their statistics and topics are shown in Table 3.

Among these threads, Thread 4 has the potential to attract depressed teenagers, who are contemplating suicide. Some robbery cases have also been reported among people who were involved in the hottest thread of Forum 3. We believe such analysis can be used to assist analysts in identifying biased activities.

**Table 3.** The Hottest Threads from Each of the Four Forums

| TID * | Type | Postings | Volume (char) | Dura-tion (day) | Mem-bers | Active Mem-bers |
|---|---|---|---|---|---|---|
| 1 | Pirated CDs | 469 | 7219 | 69 | 462 | 7 |
| 2 | Gambling | 211 | 4132 | 4** | 186 | 25 |
| 3 | Sentimentalism | 91 | 9628 | 118 | 16 | 6 |
| 4 | Spiritualism | 88 | 5295 | 962 | 67 | 8 |

| TID | Topics |
|---|---|
| 1 | Pornography websites recommendation (reply needed to view the content ) |
| 2 | Lottery recommendation (made by an experienced member) |
| 3 | A true story about "network love" |
| 4 | What will you do if you know you will die tomorrow? |

\* Thread Identification Number.
\*\*4 days is in fact a long time for a typical thread in the gambling forum.

### 3.4  Member Level Analysis

Table 4 provides the percentage of members who have initiated new threads. The percentages of members who have never created a thread in Forum 1 (99.3%) and Forum 2 (88.5%) are higher than those of the other two forums. This is because that only a small portion of members in Forum1 and Forum 2 have the valuable information, such as pirated CDs or lottery analysis results. Therefore, most members in gambling forums and pirated CD forums are followers. However, members in senti-mentalism and spiritualism forums tend to publish their own thoughts. Consequently the percentages of posting initiators are higher. The table also shows that most members in Forum 3 are willing to share their feelings online. Besides the fact that senti-mentalism is a more common topic, internet forums are also becoming popular venues for people to share their feelings with strangers. Forum 4 is similar to Forums 1 and 2; however, the percentages of members who have created 1 thread (11.4%) and who have created 2-9 threads in Forum 4 (7.9%) are much higher.

**Table 4.** Percentage of Members Who Have Created New Threads

| FID | Type | Number of threads members created | | | | | | |
|---|---|---|---|---|---|---|---|---|
| | | 0 | 1 | 2-9 | 10-29 | 30-49 | 50-99 | >=100 |
| 1 | Pirated CDs | 99.3% | 0.3% | 0.2% | 0.1% | 0.1% | 0% | 0% |
| 2 | Gambling | 88.5% | 4.5% | 3.9% | 2.6% | 0.4% | 0.2% | 0% |
| 3 | Sentimentalism | 10.6% | 40.6% | 44.1% | 3.2% | 0.9% | 0.6% | 0% |
| 4 | Spiritualism | 77.6% | 11.4% | 7.9% | 2.2% | 0.4% | 0% | 0.4% |

## 4  Conclusions and Future Work

This paper introduced the concept of Gray Web Forums. We developed a framework and analyzed four Gray Web Forums in Taiwan. Gambling forum members reply to as many threads as possible to gather gambling information; while people searching for pirated CDs or illegal software reply only to related threads of interest. Hot thread analysis can be used to assist in manual analysis to identify inappropriate contents. In addition, member level analysis can be used to identify members' roles in virtual communities. Although we were able to find some interesting results, we are far from pinpointing to specific threads or postings with offensive contents. Furthermore, barriers introduced by forum access control also need to be addressed in the future.

## Acknowledgements

This research was supported in part by grants: NSC 94-2213-E-015-002, Taiwan, and the Fulbright Visiting Scholar Grant: 68429239, USA. The authors would also like to thank the Artificial Intelligence Laboratory, Department of Management Information Systems, University of Arizona, for providing space and facilities for the research visit.

## References

1. Wang, J. H.: *Cyber Forensics – Issues and Approaches*, book chapter in book: Managing Cyber Threats: Issues, Approaches and Challenge, edited by Kumar, et al, Kluwer Academic Publishers, 2005.
2. Mena, J.: *Investigative Data Mining for Security and Criminal Detection*, Butterworth Heinemann, 2003.
3. Zhou, Y., Reid, E., Qin, J., Lai, G., Chen, H.: *U.S. Domestic Extremist Groups on the Web: Link and Content Analysis,* IEEE Intelligent Systems, Special Issue on Artificial Intelligence for National and Homeland Security, Vol. 20, Issue 5, 2005, pp. 44-51.
4. Chen, H.: *The Terrorism Knowledge Portal: Advanced Methodologies for Collecting and Analyzing Information from the Dark Web and Terrorism Research Resources*, presented at the Sandia National Laboratories, August 14 2003.
5. Elison, W.: *Netwar: Studying Rebels on the Internet*, The Social Studies 91, pp 127-131, 2000.
6. Tsfati, Y. and Weimann, G.: *www.terrorism.com: Terror on the Internet*, Studies in Conflict & Terrorism 25, pp 317-332, 2002.
7. Weimann, G.: *www.terrorism.net: How Modern Terrorism Uses the Internet*, Special Report 116, U.S. Institute of Peace, http://usip.org/pubs, 2004.
8. Wang, J. H., et al.: *A study of Automatic Search System on Cyber Crimes*, Research Report to Telecommunication Bureau, Ministry of Traffic and Communication, Taiwan, 1999.
9. Dringus, L. P. and Ellis, T.: *Using Data Mining as a Strategy for Assessing Asynchronous Discussion Forums*, Computer & Education 45, pp141-160, 2004.
10. Spaceman: http://www.vbulletin.com/forum/showthread.php?t=32329, 2001.
11. Bock, W.: *Christmas, Communities, and Cyberspace*,
12. http://www.bockinfo.com/docs/community.htm , 2001

# Detecting Deception in Person-of-Interest Statements

Christie Fuller, David P. Biros, Mark Adkins, Judee K. Burgoon,
Jay F. Nunamaker Jr., and Steven Coulon

Spears School of Business, Oklahoma State University, Stillwater, OK 74078, USA
{Christie.Fuller, David.Biros}@okstate.edu,
{madkins, jburgoon, jnunamaker, scoulon}@cmi.arizona.edu

**Abstract.** Most humans cannot detect lies at a rate better than chance. Alternative
methods of deception detection may increase accuracy, but are intrusive, do not
offer immediate feedback, or may not be useful in all situations. Automated
classification methods have been suggested as an alternative to address these
issues, but few studies have tested their utility with real-world, high-stakes
statements. The current paper reports preliminary results from classification of
actual security police investigations collected under high stakes and proposes
stages for conducting future analyses.

## 1 Introduction

Deception has previously been defined as "a message knowingly transmitted by a
sender to foster a false belief or conclusion by the receiver" [1]. Despite thousands of
years of attempting to detect deception [2], humans have not proven to be very
capable lie detectors, as most are not able to detect lies at a rate better than chance [3].
Only a few groups of professionals, such as secret service agents, exceed chance
levels, reaching accuracy levels as high as 73% [4].

Several alternate methods exist for deception detection including the polygraph,
Statement Validity Analysis, and Reality Monitoring [3]. However, these methods are
intrusive or fail to provide immediate feedback. Accurate, non-invasive methods are
needed to address the shortcomings of existing deception detection methods.
Automated classification methods have been introduced into deception research as a
possible alternative [5, 6]. The focus of the current research is to develop a classifier
for analysis of written statements. The classifier is trained and tested on a corpus of
actual statements concerning transgressions.

## 2 Background

A number of deception theories can be used to guide a systematic analysis of
linguistic information as it relates to deception [6]. Interpersonal deception theory
(IDT) [1] focuses on the interaction between participants in a communicative act.
Although it was intended to be more applicable to oral deception than written
statements, its emphasis on the strategic nature of communication underscores the
importance of considering how and why people manage the information in the
messages they produce.

S. Mehrotra et al. (Eds.): ISI 2006, LNCS 3975, pp. 504–509, 2006.

A component of IDT, information management [7], proposes dimensions of message manipulation similar to information manipulation theory (IMT) [8]. Relevant features of these perspectives that lend themselves to automated analysis include quantity of message units such as words or sentences; qualitative content features such as amount of details; clarity, including specificity of language or presence of uncertainty terms; and personalization, such as use of personal pronouns.

IDT has been applied in multiple, text-based studies. For example, Zhou, Burgoon, Twitchell, Qin and Nunamaker [5] argued that IDT can be used in leaner mediated channels and utilized IDT in the analysis of four classification methods of deception in written statements. They organized linguistic indicators into the following categories: *quantity, specificity, affect, expressivity, diversity, complexity, uncertainty, informality, and nonimmediacy.* In [9], IDT was used as the framework to guide an examination of dynamic changes in text-based deception. Based on these previous investigations, potential deception indicators from the Zhou et al. categorization scheme were selected to classify written statements from criminal investigations as truthful or deceptive.

# 3   Method

An important issue in text-based message analysis is the extent to which results generated from laboratory data and collected under low stakes conditions are generalizable to actual deceptive messages collected under high stakes conditions. The current investigation addressed this issue by analyzing person-of-interest statements related to criminal incidents.

## 3.1   Message Feature Mining

Message feature mining, [10] was used to classify the documents as truthful or deceptive. This process has two main steps: extracting features and classification. Key aspects of the feature extraction phase are choosing appropriate features, or cues, and calculating those features over desired text portions. Key components of the classification phase are data preparation, choosing an appropriate classifier, and training and testing the model.

General Architecture for Text Engineering (GATE) [11] is the primary tool that was used for the feature extraction step. Two main features of GATE are language resources, such as corpora and ontologies, and processing resources, such as tokenizers and part-of-speech taggers. Waikato Environment for Knowledge Analysis (WEKA) [12] was utilized for the classification step. GATE and WEKA are both open-source Java-based programs. While GATE already includes processing resources to accommodate some of the cues to deception, it can be modified to incorporate additional cues. Further, GATE includes the WEKA wrapper class. This facilitates the use of the two programs in combination to conduct message feature mining. We combined WEKA and GATE into a program called the Agent99 Analyzer (A99A).

## 3.2  Data Collection

A pilot study was accomplished on a set of 18 criminal incident statements provided by an Air Force investigative service. Statements were taken from cases that occurred within the last few years and were determined to be truthful or deceptive by the polygraph division of the investigative service. The subject wrote the statement due to a criminal investigation. For deceptive statements, the investigators found additional evidence to suggest the subject was lying and ordered a polygraph. Under polygraph the deceivers recanted their statements, thus confirming that the original accountings of the incidents were lies. The polygraph also confirmed the veracity of the truthful statements.

A classification model using those criminal incident statements achieved accuracy of 72% [13]. A99A was deemed feasible and effective. Some minor adjustments were made to the processes before the multi-phased main experiment to be reported here commenced.

Currently, this study is in Phase One of three planned phases. In Phase One, 307 known truthful and deceptive statements have been collected and codified to train A99A. The data for this study include criminal incident statements from 2002 to the present, collected in cooperation with Security Forces Squadron personnel from two military bases. Criminal incident statements are official reports written by a subject or witness in an investigation. In some cases, individuals involved in incidents have lied on their incidents in an attempt to avoid prosecution for an incident. The attempted deception is discovered by security forces personnel during their investigation of the incident. They are known as "false official statements".

False official statements provide invaluable data for this study. Unlike mock lies, they are confirmed deceptive statements where the deceiver attempted to avoid prosecution in a criminal incident (or the deceiver was aiding and abetting another's attempt to avoid prosecution). Ground truth for truthful statements is established where the evidence or eventual outcome of the case supports the person's statement. Standardized procedures were used to transcribe the statements in preparation for automatic classification.

Text-based modeling needs a large sample size relative to number of indicators; therefore, it is prudent to prune the possible set of predictors to a smaller "best' set. A series of $t$-tests identified the 17 discriminating variables noted in Table 1 below. Though the data set currently has many more truthful than deceptive statements, these results show that the predictors are largely consistent for both the full sample (N = 307) of statements and a reduced sample (N = 82) consisting of equal numbers of truthful and deceptive statements.

To analyze the balanced set of 41 truthful and 41 deceptive statements with A99A, a neural network model was implemented using WEKA for classifying the statements as truthful or deceptive. Preliminary results produced a 72 percent overall accuracy on the balanced data set of 82 statements. A99A had a 68.3% success rate at identifying deceptive statements and a 75.6 % success rate at identifying truthful statements, for an overall accuracy of 71.95%.

**Table 1.** Significant Discriminating Variables

| CATEGORY | VARIABLE | SIGNICANT IN FULL SAMPLE (N=307) | SIGNIFICANT IN BALANCED SAMPLE ( N = 82) | Deceptive > Truthful | Truthful > Deceptive |
|---|---|---|---|---|---|
| Quantity | Word count | * | * | * | |
| | Verb count | * | * | * | |
| | Sentence count | * | * | * | |
| Specificity | Modifier count | * | * | * | |
| | Affect ratio | * | * | * | |
| | Sensory ratio | * | * | | * |
| Diversity | Lexical diversity | * | * | | * |
| | Redundancy | * | | * | |
| | Content word diversity | * | * | | * |
| Personalization | Non-self references | * | * | * | |
| | 2nd person pronouns | | * | * | |
| | Other References | * | * | * | |
| | Group pronouns | * | * | * | |
| Nonimmediacy | Immediacy terms | * | * | * | |
| | Spatial far terms | * | * | | * |
| | Temporal nonimmediacy | * | * | * | |
| | Passive voice | * | | | * |

Phase One, the calibration phase, will continue until a balanced data set of 200 statements has been assessed by A99A. This sample size is based on neural network heuristics for achieving generalizable results [14]. Five to ten statements will be needed per weight in the neural network. Based on estimated network size, a balanced sample size of 200 statements has been deemed sufficient.

Once complete, Phase Two, the testing phase, will begin. In this phase A99A will run parallel to the security force incident investigations. A99A will review statements and make predictions of their veracity, but this will be accomplished in a blind study. The security forces will not receive the A99A predictions nor will A99A know the outcome of the security force investigations. At the end of this period, the two methods will be compared.

Phase Three, the final phase, will see A99A used in a predictive mode. Incident statements will be processed through A99A before security forces personnel investigate the incident. It is hoped that the analyzer will decrease the amount of time the SF personnel must spend on each incident.

## 4   Expected Results and Implications of Study

Previous studies in automated detection of 'mock lies' have achieved accuracy levels of approximately 80% [5]. A pilot study using criminal incident statements achieved accuracy of 72% [13]. However, the sample size for the pilot study was only 18 statements. The current study has matched this accuracy rate. As sample size increases and the set of cues included is refined, it is anticipated that accuracy will improve. The cues found to be significant in this study are drawn from a larger set that has been developed in previous research. These cues may not be significant in all contexts. However, if significance of these cues can be replicated and verified within the domain of criminal interrogations, this could be an important finding [8].

It is anticipated that the classifier developed by this study may eventually be used by military personnel to augment current investigative tools, such as the polygraph. This tool might be useful in a situation when an investigator would like to quickly determine from a group of statements which statement might be deceptive. Another suggested use of this is for secondary screening interviews within transportation systems [15]. Given the cost, intrusiveness, and lengthy process associated with other forms of deception detection, we believe our approach will provide military and civilian law enforcement entities a useful tool to facilitate their investigations.

## References

1. Buller, D.B., Burgoon, J.K.: Interpersonal Deception Theory. Communication Theory. 6 (1996) 203-242
2. Trovillo, P.V.: A History of Lie Detection. Journal of Criminal Law & Criminology. 29 (1939) 848-881
3. Vrij, A., Edward, K., Roberts, K.P., Bull, R.: Detecting Deceit Via Analysis of Verbal and Nonverbal Behavior. Journal of Nonverbal Behavior. 24 (2000) 239-263
4. Ekman, P., O'Sullivan, M., Frank, M.G.: A Few Can Catch a Liar. Psychological Science. 10 (1999) 263-265
5. Zhou, L., Burgoon, J.K., Twitchell, D.P., Qin, T., Nunamaker Jr, J.F.: A Comparison of Classification Methods for Predicting Deception in Computer-Mediated Communication. Journal of Management Information Systems. 20 (2004) 139-163
6. Zhou, L., Burgoon, J.K., Nunamaker, J.F., Twitchell, D.:, Automating Linguistics-Based Cues for Detecting Deception in Text-Based Asynchronous Computer-Mediated Communications. Group Decision and Negotiation. 13 (2004) 81-106
7. Zuckerman, M., DePaulo, B.M., Rosenthal, R.:Verbal and Nonverbal Communication of Deception. In: Berkowitz, L (ed.): Advances in Experimental Social Psychology. Academic Press, New York (1981) 1-59

8. DePaulo, B.M., Lindsay, J.J., Malone, B.E., Muhlenbruck, L., Charlton, K., Cooper, H.: Cues to Deception. Psychological Bulletin. 129 (2003) 74-118

9. Zuckerman, M., Driver, R.E.: Telling Lies: Verbal and Nonverbal Correlates of Deception. In Multichannel Intergration of Nonverbal Behavior. 1987, Erlbaum: Hillsdale, NJ.

10. Adkins, M. Twitchell, D.P., Burgoon, J.K., Nunamaker Jr, J.F.: Advances in Automated Deception Detection in Text-based Computer-mediated Communication. In: Enabling Technologies for Simulation Science VIII. (2004)

11. Cunningham, H.: GATE, a General Architecture for Text Engineering. Computers and the Humanities. 36 (2002) 223-254

12. Witten, I.H., Frank, E.: Data Mining: Practical Machine Learning Tools and Techniques with Java. Morgan Kaufman, San Francisco (2000)

13. Twitchell, D., Biros, D.P., Forsgren, N., Burgoon, J.K., Nunamaker, Jr, J.F.: Assessing the Veracity of Criminal and Detainee Statements: A Study of Real-World Data. In: 2005 International Conference on Intelligence Analysis (2005)

14. Sarle, W.: What are Cross-Validation and Bootstrapping? [cited 2005; Available from: http://www.faqs.org/faqs/aifaq/neural-nets/part3/section-12.html. (2004)

15. Twitchell, D., Jensen, M.L., Burgoon, J.K., Nunamaker, Jr, J.F.: Detecting deception insecondary screening interviews using linguistic analysis. In Proceedings of The 7th International IEEE Conference on Intelligent Transportation Systems. (2004) 118-123

# Personal Information Management (PIM) for Intelligence Analysis

Antonio Badia

University of Louisville, Louisville KY 40292, USA
abadia@louisville.edu
http://date.spd.louisville.edu/

**Abstract.** The concept of Personal Information Management (PIM) is currently a hot topic of research. Some of the ideas being discussed under this topic have a long history, and they are relevant to the work of intelligence analysts. Hence, the intelligence community should pay attention to the developments in this area. In this position paper we examine the concept of PIM, point out some issues that are relevant to intelligence work, and discuss some areas of research that PIMs should address in order to be even more relevant to the Intelligence Community.

## 1   Introduction

The concept of Personal Information Management (PIM) is currently a hot topic of research ([17]). While there is no universal definition of PIM, several research groups are working under that umbrella on related projects ([11, 12]). Many ideas considered under this label have a long history; for instance, search tools rely heavily on Information Retrieval techniques and show similarities with Web search engines. As another example, the need for *information integration* has a deep tradition and is a complex issue that has been investigated in the past in other contexts ([8]). While not a completely new idea, PIMs are the point of encounter in the evolution of several trends: tools (appointment managers, to-do lists, calendars,...); hardware (new digital gadgets: PDA, smart phones); ideas ("record everything" / "digital memories", "compute anywhere"); and, most importantly, needs: in a data-intensive, information-rich world, we sometimes fail to find what we're looking for, even though we know *it's in there, somewhere.*

The idea of PIM is not directed to a specific set of users, and may be beneficial to a large segment of the population, since it emphasizes simple, intuitive access to information. In fact, many projects clearly have in mind non-expert users. However, professionals that deal with information processing tasks stand to benefit the most of the ideas proposed. In this sense, Intelligence Analysis can benefit considerably from some of the proposals currently being developed. In this position paper, we argue that indeed PIM ideas and tools can carry valuable support for Intelligence Analysis tasks and therefore the Intelligence Community should pay close attention to developments in the area, as PIMs may become useful tools for Intelligence analysts (the benefit may be mutual,

S. Mehrotra et al. (Eds.): ISI 2006, LNCS 3975, pp. 510–515, 2006.

as Intelligence analysts may provide PIM researchers with ideas and challenges based on their experience). At the same time, we argue that some special characteristics of Intelligence Analysis are not well covered by current research, and therefore specific topics need to be addressed in order to make valuable contributions to Intelligence tasks. We propose a list of such topics and discuss their impact. Finally, we close with some conclusions.

## 2  Personal Information Management (PIM)

We cannot give a good description of PIM in such a short space, especially since there is no uniform, universal notion of PIM. However, most research in the area can be seen as focusing on the study of information-related activities: gathering (through search or other means), organizing (in directories or otherwise), maintaining and retrieving information ([13]). There is an emphasis on activities that are related to everyday tasks, that is, the information-related activities are performed with a particular goal in mind, and is done in the context of day-to-day processes. For instance, organization and retrieval of e-mail messages is an important activity. Another important aspect is the integration of heterogeneous data. Current window-based interfaces depend on the binding of documents to applications, causing different pieces of information (say, those in a spreadsheet, versus those in a document, or those in a database) to be accessed through different applications. Relating data across applications, although supported on a primitive level by current tools, is cumbersome and does not allow for cross-document analysis. The overall goal of PIM is to "always have the right information in the right place, in the right form, and of sufficient completeness and quality to meet our current needs" ([13]).

Some of the key concepts in PIM are ([11]):

- The system should be able to manipulate any kind of data, no matter what application created it or how it was acquired (cross-application scope).
- The system should be able to deal with data that evolves over time, either in content or structure ("life-long data management"). This implies a need to deal with cumulative collections that may grow considerably in size. This in turn generates a need to store efficiently and flexibly.
- Data items do not exist in isolation, they should be associated (linked, correlated) with others. Ideally, the system creates associations of different types for the user. At least some of these associations support *data integration*, that is, identifying identical or overlapping data items as such.
- Because the system wants to connect items for the user, and the data changes and evolves, the system should ideally adapt to and learn about the user, perhaps using machine learning and statistical techniques.
- Keeping everything is not enough (may in fact make things worse); *making everything visible* is what matters ([7]). The ultimate goal is to *find it*, no matter what we remember about it, when and how we stored it (even if we forgot about it!) This generates the need for powerful and flexible search (by recollection, by correlation, by detail, by metadata). As an example,

when trying to locate an old picture or email, we may search by content (we remember that the photo contains a sunset, or that the email is about lunch today), metadata (the photo was taken in town, the email is from 2 days ago), context (the photo was taken in Bermudas, the email was a communication in the context of a project), association (the photo was taken while in vacation, the email is from the same person who called yesterday). The most advanced research deals with *Proactive Information Gathering* (also called *Finding Without Searching*) ([7]): the idea is to analyze the current user context, identify her information needs, and automatically generate queries. Note that this approach may help find information that the user forgot about.

While not all systems deal with all these characteristics, most researchers seem to agree that these are all desirable characteristics for a PIM ([10]).

## 3    PIM for Intelligence Analysis

We argue that work on PIM is relevant to the Intelligence analyst. The task of such a person can be described as the gathering, analysis and evaluation of data ([1, 2, 16]). The amount of data available has been growing considerably in the last few years; more refined sensor architectures, the availability and relevance of large volumes of *open source* data, and other factors have contributed to this increase in quantity. The *gathering* step has been greatly facilitated by advances in networking and tools like Web search engines. Together with this, the degree of *heterogeneity* has also increased markedly. Heterogeneity in this context refers to the differences in structure or meaning of the data: the same information may be structured in several ways (for instance, in natural language in a document and as an entry in a database); even if structured in the same ways, it may be presented in different ways: two different documents may refer to the same event using different vocabulary, or describe two (perhaps overlapping) aspects of the same event. This fact greatly complicates the second and third steps in the analyst work, *analysis* and *evaluation*. In intelligence work, it is often necessary to check facts, determine their source and judge their relevance, completeness and trustworthiness. Having evidence for the same event scattered across multiple sources adds to the challenge. Finally, when evaluating (which includes summarizing the distilled information, interpreting it and assigning it a degree of credibility), one should be able to integrate all bits and pieces of information necessary, regardless of format or origin, to make an overall assessment (that takes into account the number and quality of sources).

The concept of PIM is especially well suited to intelligence analysis, for several reasons. First, the tasks that PIM seeks to support (gathering, organizing, maintaining information in support of everyday activities) is a perfect fit to the everyday activity of an intelligence analyst. Second, PIM aims at providing support to the above tasks through various ideas: the emphasis of data integration helps in dealing with heterogeneity, as does the idea of cross-application scope; flexible search helps in the analysis phase, both in finding the right bits and in making connections (the famous "connect the dots" phase). Thus, one can conclude that a PIM system (or a suite of PIM tools) would be highly valuable for the Intelligence analyst. The goal of having the right information in the right place at the right time should be very appealing to the Intelligence analyst.

## 4   What PIM Is Missing: A Wish List

While we have argued that PIM is very relevant for Intelligence Analysis, current state of the art still does not provide functionality that we consider necessary to support Intelligence work. In particular, we put forth the following needs:

**Support for Querying as an Iterative, Interactive Process:** most PIM concentrate on providing *search* capabilities, leaving aside traditional *querying* of data sources, i.e. using SQL against a database. However, it is clear that both actions are part of a continuum: both are tools that support data analysis. Thus, both activities should be fully integrated. In doing so, lessons from early research must be applied -and the most important lesson, probably, is the fact that search/querying is an *iterative, interactive* process. It is rare that users start with a clear and crisply defined goal in mind, or that they know exactly how to search for what they want (i.e. they know the exact keywords, or they know the exact directory or data source that contains all relevant data). Thus, as searching is expanded to mix with querying, we must make sure that we respect the characteristics of this process. While one may argue that this is an important but generic capability, we argue that it is especially important in Intelligence work, since many times data analysis implies an *exploration* of the data. During this process, hypothesis may be developed, tested, discarded or changed; the analyst may pursue several possible scenarios (*what-if* analysis), and explore alternative explanations for some situations. This is not to say that this not a useful capability in other fields -but it is central to Intelligence work.

**Support for Ongoing Monitoring:** a large part of warning intelligence rests on keeping track of an ongoing situation, finding clues that will set the alarm before the crisis occurs ([16]). Thus, as new data and information are acquired, one would like the new to be connected to the old and any changes to be reflected in events under scrutiny. PIMs do aim at linking data, and seamlessly incorporating new data into a general repository ([11, 12]). However, what is missing is the ability to define arbitrary events that the system should keep an eye on, as well the ability of having the system, on its own, determine that some events are of interest. Current research on *stream analysis and mining* ([5, 6]) is very relevant here, but it is still in a state of fast change and has not been integrated into PIMs yet.

**Support for Groupwork:** analysts rarely work on total isolation. Groups must be formed, many times dynamically, for complex tasks. Some initial research in reported in [9], where the concept of PIM is extended to GIM (Group Information Management). This is a step in the right direction; however, much work remains to be done. In particular, in the context of Intelligence analysis one must support several ways to collaborate, from *selective sharing* of information (i.e.

the analyst decides what can be shared) to *total search* (i.e. search engines are allowed full access to all the information from all the participants in a group). Moreover, support for information integration, already mentioned above as a key component of PIMs, must be leveraged to the group level. This adds another degree of difficulty to this already complex task.

**Support for Workflow:** Intelligence analysts try to follow processes in their work. This is due to several facts: it is not necessary only to come up with some conclusions, but also be able to show how such conclusions were reached, what evidence supports them, and what other alternatives there may be; and given that data may be incomplete, unreliable and even contradictory, it is necessary to examine available evidence in a methodical manner. As steps are taken, it is necessary to keep the links between data, hypothesis, supporting evidence, and conclusions. Drilling down to detail, backward and forward analysis through the chain of evidence, structuring of arguments, all should be supported. Note that we are talking at the *individual level*; however, as pointed out in the previous point, many times the analyst is working as part of the team. In such a situation, there usually is a division of concerns, each participant working on a certain *role* that is related to others; this must also be supported by workflow tools, in order to facilitate teamwork and collaboration. Thus, workflow tools are needed at two levels, team and individual.

**Support for Security:** security is used here to refer to the overall need to protect sensitive and classified material while at the same time making sure that the right people has access to the right information. This is a delicate and difficult balancing act, with which the Intelligence Community is constantly struggling. Even though there has been research in this area ([14]), more remains to be done before a system can be deployed in real intelligence work.

A crucial point to be understood is the *possibilities* of the concept. While PIMs may not have all the characteristics needed by a good Intelligence analysis tool, what makes the concept so promising is that PIMs are in a very good position to *become* such a tool. Their emphasis on across-application capabilities, data linking, and flexible organization and search provide the right foundation for a highly useful system. While some current tools may do some things well (some special-purpose software for Intelligence analysis, for instance, has support for Intelligence workflow), they are proprietary and usually cannot talk to each other. Hence, most of what they lack may be very hard to integrate into the system. PIMs, on the other hand, make minimal commitments to a particular data model and minimal assumptions about the data itself, and therefore are more open to expansion and customization.

## 5   Conclusion

We have examined the concept of PIM and argued that many of the ideas involved are relevant to Intelligence tasks. We have then proposed some further research directions that could make this concept even more relevant to the

Intelligence Community. By examining points of contact between PIM and Intelligence analysis, we hope to stimulate research in the area that will be useful to the Intelligence Community, as well as involve the Intelligence Community in the research and development of the concept.

**Acknowledgment.** The author wants to thank the anonymous reviewers for their useful feedback.

# References

1. *A Consumer's Guide to Intelligence*, Washington, DC, CIA Public Affairs Staff, 1995.
2. *A Compendium of Analytic Tradecraft Notes*, Washington DC, CIA, Directorate of Intelligence, 1997.
3. Baeza-Yates, R. and Ribeiro-Neto, B. *Modern Information Retrieval*, Addison-Wesley and ACM Press, 1999.
4. Cuttrell, E., Dumais, S. and Teevan, J. *Searching to Eliminate Personal Information Systems*, in [17].
5. Demers, A., Gehrke, J. and Riedewald, M. *The Architecture of the Cornell Knowledge Broker*, in Proc. Second Symposium on Intelligence and Security Informatics (ISI-2004), 2004.
6. Dobra, A., Garofalakis, M., Gehrke, J. and Rastogi, R. *Processing Complex Aggregate Queries over Data Streams*, In Proceedings of the 2002 ACM SIGMOD International Conference on Management of Data, 2002.
7. Dumais, S., Cuttrell, E., Sarin, R. and Horvitz, E. *Implicit Queries for Contextualized Search*, in Proceedings of the International Conference on Research and Development in Information Retrieval, ACM Press, New York, 2004.
8. Elmagarmid, A., Rusinkiewicz, M. and Sheth, A. eds. *Heterogeneous and Autonomous Database Systems*, Morgan Kaufmann, San Francisco, CA, USA, 1999.
9. Erickson, T. *From PIM to GIM: Personal Information Management in Group Contexts*, in [17]
10. Franklin, M., Halevy, A. and Maier, D. *From Databases to Dataspaces: A New Abstraction for Information Management*, SIGMOD Record, 34(4), December 2005, pages 27-33.
11. Halevy, A. *Semex: A Platform for Personal Information Management and Integration*, presentation available online at http://www.cs.washington.edu/homes/alon/.
12. Haystack project, http://haystack.csail.mit.edu/home.html.
13. Jones, W. *A Review Of Personal Information Management*, IS-TR-2005-11-01, The Information School Technical Repository, University of Washington.
14. Karat, C.M., Brodie, C. and Karat, J. *Usable Privacy and Security for Personal Information Management*, in [17].
15. Karger, D. and Jones, W. *Data Unification in Personal Information Management*, in [17].
16. Krizan, L. *Intelligence Essentials for Everyone*, Occasional Paper n. 6, Joint Military Intelligence College, Washington DC, 1999.
17. Teevan, J., Jones, W. and Bederson, B. editors, *Personal Information Management*, Communications of the ACM, v. 49, n. 1, January 2006.

# Synergy: A Policy-Driven, Trust-Aware Information Dissemination Framework

Ragib Hasan and Marianne Winslett

Department of Computer Science,
University of Illinois at Urbana-Champaign*
rhasan@cs.uiuc.edu, winslett@cs.uiuc.edu

**Abstract.** Information dissemination is of vital importance in today's information-centric world. However, controlling the flow of information across multiple security domains is a problem. Most of the current solutions rely on prior knowledge of the users for authorization, which does not scale well. Also, many information sources have dynamic access control policies, which are hard to satisfy under existing schemes. In this paper, we present *Synergy*, a general purpose information sharing framework that uses *trust negotiation* to implement scalable authorization in an open environment. Synergy provides an abstraction for the information sources and consumers to accommodate new trust-aware systems as well as legacy systems. We also present a practical disaster management application that uses this framework.

## 1 Introduction

Information is the key to today's world. Sharing information across security domains has become necessary, as the need for inter-operability increases. This brings forward inter-domain authorization issues. Traditional authorization techniques are not applicable in the large-scale open nature of the Internet. Another issue is trust: how the resource owners in open systems can trust the clients trying to access those resources. Authorization in such situations needs to be dynamic and content-triggered. It is simply not possible to predict who may need to access the system, and therefore arrange user accounts for those clients. This calls for a policy-based authorization infrastructure that allows negotiated access to resources.

Recently, attribute-based authorization schemes like *trust negotiation* have emerged as a solution to the scalable authorization problem. Trust negotiation uses unforgeable digital credentials that can be automatically verified. Resource owners set up policies regarding resource access, and negotiate with clients to establish trust gradually in a monotonic and bilateral manner. This brings the advantage and scalability of real life into the realm of computing. However, it is difficult to change existing protocols to enable legacy applications to use trust

---

* This research was sponsored by NSF Award number 0331707 and 0331690 to the RESCUE project.

S. Mehrotra et al. (Eds.): ISI 2006, LNCS 3975, pp. 516–521, 2006.

negotiation. To solve this, we present *Synergy*, a policy-driven trust-aware framework that enables negotiated dissemination of information across multiple security domains. Synergy decouples the information producers and consumers by acting as a medium for transfer of information. The information producers and information consumers are abstracted to allow usage of legacy applications. The producers and consumers do not require any knowledge of the authorization or trust establishment details. Information is exchanged in a platform/application-independent manner, allowing the information producers and consumers to agree on any format. Synergy's approach improves on the traditional authorization approach in several aspects: first, it is highly scalable; the servers do not have to store per-client information, or any pre-existing relationship with the clients. Second, authorization and access control are dynamic, and fine-grained. Third, trust is bilateral; both the client and the server need to satisfy each other's policies. And finally, it can be integrated into existing information sharing infrastructures with minimal or no changes to legacy applications.

The rest of this paper is organized as follows: in Sect. 2, we discuss briefly the related work. Sect. 3 presents the overview of the Synergy infrastructure. We highlight VisiRescue, an application prototype information sharing, in Sect. 4. Finally, we conclude and discuss future directions in Sect. 5.

## 2  Related Work

In this section, we examine the related work on authorization in open systems. In attribute-based authorization, user attributes, rather than identity, are used for authorization. Trust negotiation is an iterative process that can establish trust among strangers through the gradual discovery of credentials [17]. Entities possess attributes, represented by unforgeable digital credentials, such as X.509 attribute certificates, Kerberos tickets, etc. [3]. Several systems have been built using TrustBuilder [17] as the agent for trust negotiation. For example, Traust [12] is a generic authorization service built using TrustBuilder. It uses trust negotiation for providing access to both legacy and newer services. While Synergy shares many of the mechanisms used in Traust, it builds on Traust's authorization services to provide an infrastructure for sharing information through decoupling of the information sources and consumers.

PolicyMaker [5] and Keynote [4] are two early trust management systems that are based on capabilities, but are restricted to a closed system. Trust-X [2] is a peer-to-peer framework. which uses an XML-based policy language, X-TNL. Cassandra [1] is a trust management system that uses Datalog. The RT family of role-based trust languages [13] use an extension of SPKI/SDSI. In [6], a formal framework for policy-based access regulation and information disclosure is presented. Interactive access control strategies for trust negotiation are discussed in [11]. In principle, any of these can be used as the trust agent of Synergy.

Shibboleth [15] is an attribute-based authorization system for quasi-open systems. It uses SAML assertions [10], and requires federations among organizational security domains. While it also uses attributes, it is different from trust negotiation in several aspects. Trust negotiation does not require a federated structure, but Shibboleth is heavily dependent on the notion of pre-established organizational relationships. Shibboleth also has a very limited access control decision-making capability [7], while trust negotiation can enable fine-grained, dynamic authorization. Synergy takes advantage of trust negotiation and hence does not require the federated relationship that Shibboleth has to establish.

## 3   System Overview

In this section, we present an overview of the Synergy framework, the resource access protocol, and the interaction between this framework and the trust negotiation agents from TrustBuilder [17]. Fig. 1 shows the components of Synergy.

### 3.1   Components

Synergy uses a client-server framework consisting of the following components: information producers, servers, clients, consumers, and trust agents. The *information producer* component is an abstraction of the resources, e.g. a wind sensor. The framework does not specify the content or the nature of the resource. The *information servers* act as front-ends for the resources. Each security domain needs to have one or more servers handling its resources. Rather than keeping per-client states, the servers maintain time-stamped access tokens, issued to a client when it satisfies the access policy. The *information clients* interact with the servers. After getting the information, the clients transfer it to the *information consumer*, which is an abstraction of the end-application. We ensure modularity by separating the trust and policy-awareness from the clients and servers. The *trust agents* negotiate trust between a server and a client. The server instructs the client to invoke its trust agent to obtain an authorization token.

### 3.2   Mode of Operation

The client operates in three main phases: *initiation, resource discovery*, and *resource access*. During initiation, it establishes contact with the server, and sends initiation messages. During resource discovery, the client discovers the list of resources served by the server. Finally, in resource access phase, it retrieves the resources from the server. Any resource requiring an establishment of trust triggers a trust negotiation session, using the trust agents. The server's operation consists of two phases: *initiation*, and *resource access control*. During initiation, the server listens for client requests. During resource access control, the server responds to the client requests or commands. If the client's request does not have the authorization token, the token has expired, or the token is incorrect for the type of access requested, the server instructs the client to obtain a token using the trust agents. The *Resource Access Protocol* [8] is used for client-server communication. Each resource is represented by a resource type, a resource name, and an XML definition of the resource contents.

### 3.3    Implementation

Synergy is implemented using about 1100 lines of commented Java code. We used TrustBuilder as the trust agent. For specification of access policies, we use the IBM Trust Policy Language (TPL) [9] which is currently supported by TrustBuilder [17]. This has the advantage of being monotonic, sufficiently expressive, and simple enough for automated processing [16]. Synergy currently supports digital credentials in the form of X.509 Certificates. More details of the implementation can be found in [8].

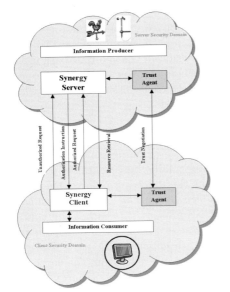

**Fig. 1.** Components of Synergy

**Fig. 2.** Screenshot of VisiRescue front-end

## 4    VisiRescue Application Prototype

In this section, we present an application prototype built on top of Synergy. This prototype, named *VisiRescue*, is a situational awareness system. We built it for possible use in an Emergency Operations Center (EOC), as part of the Responding to Crises and Unexpected Events (RESCUE) initiative[14].

### 4.1    Overview

Situational awareness is important in disaster management. To get information for, say, a wind storm, sensors and cameras can be deployed around the city. However, outside access to these resources may be restricted due to privacy concerns. For example, the mall owners are not likely to allow police to monitor the mall's security cameras all the time, except for emergencies. Traditional authorization schemes would require scaling to a large number of heterogeneous organizations and setting up *a priori* relationships with them. Also, schemes like Shibboleth [15], would require coalitions. We argue that the Synergy framework is appropriate here, because each of the resource owners can set access policies to allow attribute-based authorization. Also, Synergy is lightweight, and can be retro-fitted to almost any legacy system.

The information produced by the sensors of VisiRescue map to information producer module of Synergy. A server collecting information from sensors map to the Synergy servers. The aggregator client that runs at the EOC and updates the geo-databases maps to the Synergy client. Finally, ArcGIS display or the Google map interface correspond to the information consumer component. A daemon periodically invokes the Synergy client, which negotiates access to the sensors. The daemon updates the retrieved information in the geo-database used by ArcGIS. We use a loosely defined XML based scheme for resource information. A screenshot of the front-end is shown in Fig. 2. Next, we discuss a usage scenario.

### 4.2   Usage Scenario

Here, a shopping mall provides access to surveillance cameras via the Synergy servers. For brevity, we present the policies informally here. Sample policies written in TPL can be found in [8]. The mall has the following policy: *Access to video feeds from the surveillance cameras is given only when the requester has the following characteristics: a) The requester is affiliated with either the police department or the fire department, b) The requester is a certified first responder, and c) The fire department provides proof of a fire alarm at the mall*. During an emergency, first responders at the EOC can request a feed from the cameras by clicking the camera icon in the VisiRescue GIS display. The Synergy client will try to access the feed, and may need to perform a trust negotiation session to satisfy the mall's policies. To do so, it will have to provide proof of having the three attributes specified in the policy. On success, the server provides a temporary, limited usage URL for the video feed, which the end-application can use to access the video.

## 5   Conclusions and Future Work

In this paper, we have presented an information sharing architecture for large scale open systems. The decoupling of the information sources and consumers from the dissemination framework and the authorization mechanism enables Synergy to adapt to different scenarios with the minimal management overhead. The application prototype, VisiRescue, shows the advantage of this approach in practical situations. Our ultimate goal is to have a distributed set of servers and trust agents with increased fault tolerance and robustness. We plan to build a full-fledged prototype application, such as VisiRescue, for possible deployment in real-life. The robustness of Synergy against different types of attacks also needs to be explored. A detailed security analysis using formal security models may also be done in order to analyze and protect against vulnerabilities.

# References

[1] M. Becker and P. Sewell. Cassandra: Distributed access control policies with tunable expressiveness. In *5th IEEE Intl. Workshop on Policies for Distributed Systems and Networks*, 2004.

[2] E. Bertino, E. Ferrari, and A. C. Squicciarini. Trust-X: A peer-to-peer framework for trust establishment. *IEEE Trans. on Knowledge and Data Engineering*, 16(7), 2004.

[3] E. Bina, R. McCool, V. Jones, and M. Winslett. Secure access to data over the internet. In *Proc. of the 3rd Intl. Conf. on Parallel and Distributed Information Systems*, 1994.

[4] M. Blaze, J. Feigenbaum, and A. D. Keromytis. KeyNote: Trust management for public-key infrastructures. *Lecture Notes in Computer Science*, 1550, 1999.

[5] M. Blaze, J. Feigenbaum, and J. Lacey. Decentralized trust management. In *Proc. IEEE Symp. on Security and Privacy*, 1996.

[6] P. Bonatti and P. Samarati. Regulating service access and information release on the web. In *Proc. of the 7th ACM Conf. on Computer and Communications Security*, 2000.

[7] D. Chadwick, S. Otenko, W. Xu, and Z. Wu. Adding distributed trust management to Shibboleth. In *Proc. of the 4th Annual PKI Workshop*. NIST, 2005.

[8] R. Hasan. *Synergy: A Policy-driven, Trust-aware Information Dissemination Framework*. Masters Thesis, Dept. of Computer Science, University of Illinois at Urbana-Champaign, 2005.

[9] A. Herzberg, Y. Mass, J. Michaeli, Y. Ravid, and D. Naor. Access control meets public key infrastructure, or: Assigning roles to strangers. In *Proc. of the IEEE Symp. on Security and Privacy*, 2000.

[10] J. Hughes, E. Maler, H. Lockhart, T. Wisniewki, P. Mishra, and N. Ragouzis. Technical overview of the OASIS security assertion markup language (SAML) v1.1. *OASIS Open*, 2004.

[11] H. Koshutanski and F. Massacci. An interactive trust management and negotiation scheme. In *Proc. of the 1st Intl. Workshop on Formal Aspects in Security and Trust*, 2004.

[12] A. Lee. *Traust: A Trust Negotiation Based Authorization Service for Open Systems*. Masters Thesis, Dept. of Computer Science, University of Illinois at Urbana-Champaign, 2005.

[13] N. Li, J. Mitchell, and W. Winsborough. Design of a role-based trust management framework. In *Proc. of the IEEE Symp. on Security and Privacy*, 2002.

[14] RESCUE Project. The RESCUE Project website. http://www.itr-rescue.org.

[15] T. Scavo, S. Cantor, and N. Dors. Shibboleth architecture technical overview. http://shibboleth.internet2.edu/docs/draft-mace-shibboleth-tech-overview-latest.pdf, 2005.

[16] K. Seamons, M. Winslett, T. Yu, B. Smith, E. Child, J. Jacobson, H. Mills, and L. Yu. Requirements for policy languages for trust negotiation. In *3rd IEEE Intl. Workshop on Policies for Distributed Systems and Networks*, 2002.

[17] M. Winslett, T. Yu, K. E. Seamons, A. Hess, J. Jacobson, R. Jarvis, B. Smith, and L. Yu. Negotiating trust on the web. *IEEE Internet Computing*, 6(6), 2002.

# Sanitization of Databases for Refined Privacy Trade-Offs

Ahmed HajYasien, Vladimir Estivill-Castro, and Rodney Topor

IIIS, Griffith University, Australia

**Abstract.** In this paper, we propose a new heuristic algorithm called the QIBC algorithm that improves the privacy of sensitive knowledge (as itemsets) by blocking more inference channels. We show that the existing sanitizing algorithms for such task have fundamental drawbacks. We show that previous methods remove more knowledge than necessary for unjustified reasons or heuristically attempt to remove the minimum frequent non-sensitive knowledge but leave open inference channels that lead to discovery of hidden sensitive knowledge. We formalize the refined problem and prove it is NP-hard. Finally, experimental results show the practicality of the new QIBC algorithm.

## 1 Introduction

Data mining promises to discover unknown information. Whether the data is personal or corporate data, data mining offers the potential to reveal what others regard as private. Thus, there is a need to protect private knowledge during the data mining process. This challenge is called privacy preserving data mining [5, 8]. Privacy preserving data mining allows individuals or parties to share knowledge without disclosing what is considered private. This paper works on sanitizing the database in order to hide a set of sensitive itemsets specified by the database owners. It will offer an improved sanitizing algorithm. We lack the space here to prove the corresponding problem is NP-hard, which justifies the heuristic nature of our algorithm. Typically sanitizing involves processing a database to produce another one so that sensitive itemsets are now hidden.

The task of mining association rules over market basket data [2] is considered a core knowledge discovery activity. Association rule mining provides a useful mechanism for discovering correlations among items belonging to customer transactions in a market basket database. Let $D$ be the database of transactions and $J = \{J_1, ..., J_n\}$ be the set of items. A transaction $T$ includes one or more items in $J$. An association rule has the form $X \rightarrow Y$, where $X$ and $Y$ are non-empty sets of items such that $X \cap Y = \emptyset$. A set of items is called an itemset, while $X$ is called the antecedent. The support $sprt_D(x)$ of an item (or itemset) $x$ is the percentage of transactions from $D$ in which that item or itemset occurs in the database. The confidence or strength $c$ for an association rule $X \rightarrow Y$ is the ratio of the number of transactions that contain $X \cup Y$ to the number of transactions that contain $X$. An itemset $X \subseteq J$ is frequent if at least a fraction

S. Mehrotra et al. (Eds.): ISI 2006, LNCS 3975, pp. 522–528, 2006.

$s$ of the transaction in a database contains $X$. Frequent itemsets are important because they are the building block to obtain association rules.

Parties would release data at different levels because they aim at keeping some patterns private. Patterns represent different forms of correlation between items in a database. In our paper the focus is on patterns as itemsets. *Sensitive itemsets* are all the itemsets that are not to be disclosed to others. While no sensitive itemset is to become public, the non-sensitive itemsets are to be released. One could keep all itemsets private, but this would not share any knowledge. The aim is to release as many non-sensitive itemsets while keeping sensitive itemsets private. This is an effort to balance privacy with knowledge discovery. It seems that discovery of itemsets is in conflict with hiding sensitive data. *Sanitizing algorithms* take (as input) a database $D$ and modify it to produce (as output) a database $D'$ where mining for rules will not show sensitive itemsets. The alternative scenario is to remove the sensitive itemsets from the set of frequent itemsets and publish the rest. This scenario implies that a database $D$ does not need to be published. The problem (in both scenarios) is that sensitive knowledge can be inferred from non-sensitive knowledge through direct or indirect inference channels. **This paper focuses on the problem in the first scenario where a database $D'$ is to be published.**

## 2   Drawbacks of Previous Methods

Both, data-sharing techniques and pattern-sharing techniques face another challenge. That is, blocking as much inference channels to sensitive patterns as possible. Inference is defined as "the reasoning involved in drawing a conclusion or making a logical judgement on the basis of circumstantial evidence and prior conclusions rather than on the basis of direct observation" [1]. Farkas et al. [6] offers a good inference survey paper for more information. Frequent itemsets have an anti-monotonicity property; that is, if $X$ is frequent, all its subsets are frequent, and if $X$ is not frequent, none of its supersets are frequent. Therefore, it is sound inference to conclude that $XZ$ is frequent because $XYZ$ is frequent. This has been called the "backward inference attack" [9].

But the "forward inference attack" [9] consists of concluding that $XYZ$ is frequent from knowledge like "$XY, YZ$, and $XZ$ are frequent". This is not sound inference. It has been suggested one must [9] hide one of $XY, YZ$, or $XZ$ in order to hide $XYZ$; however, this is unnecessary (it is usually possible to hide $XYZ$ while all of $XY, YZ$, and $XZ$ remain frequent). In huge databases, forcing to hide at least one subset among the $k-1$ subsets of a $k$-itemset results in hiding many non-sensitive itemsets unnecessarily. This demonstrates that the method by Oliveira et al. [9] removes more itemsets than necessary for unjustified reasons.

An adversary that uses systematically the "forward inference attack" in huge databases will find unlimited possibilities and reach many wrongful conclusions. Nevertheless, we argue that an adversary with knowledge that (in a sanitized database) $XY, YZ$ and $XZ$ are frequent may use the "forward inference attack" with much better success if $XYZ$ is just below the privacy support threshold. This is the drawback of the method by Atallah et al. [3] that heuristically attempts to remove the minimum non-sensitive itemsets but leaves open this inference channel. Atallah et al. proposed an (item restriction)-based algorithm to sanitize data in order to hide sensitive itemsets. The algorithm works on a set of sensitive itemsets in a one-by-one fashion. The algorithm lowers the support of these sensitive itemsets just below a given privacy support threshold, and therefore, is open to a "forward inference attack" if the adversary knows the security threshold (which will usually be the case).

## 3    Statement of the Problem

Formally, the problem receives as inputs a database $D$ and a privacy support threshold $\sigma$. Let $F(D, \sigma)$ be the set of frequent itemsets with support $\sigma$ in $D$. We are also given $B \subseteq F$ as the set of sensitive itemsets that must be hidden based on some privacy/security policy. The set $Sup(B) = B \cup \{X | \exists b \in B \text{ and } b \subset X\}$ is considered also sensitive because sensitive itemsets cannot be subsets of non-sensitive itemsets. The task is to lower the support of the itemsets in $B$ below $\sigma$ and keep the impact on the non-sensitive itemsets $A = F(D, \sigma) \setminus Sup(B)$ at a minimum. The question then is how far below $\sigma$ should we lower the support of itemsets in $B$? We discussed in the previous section why it is not enough to lower the support of the itemsets in $B$ just below $\sigma$.

In addition, the security level is different from one user to another. That is why the best one to answer the question "how far below?" are users themselves. The lower the support of sensitive itemsets below $\sigma$, the higher the possibility of lowering the support of other itemsets that are not sensitive. Naturally, we would not be addressing this problem if it was not in the context of knowledge sharing. Thus, it is necessary that as many as possible of these non-sensitive itemsets appear as frequent itemsets above $\sigma$. In other words, the more changes that hide non-sensitive itemsets, the less beneficial for knowledge sharing the database becomes. How many database changes can the user trade off for privacy (blocking inference channels)? This question summarizes the problem. Even though, a variant of the problem have been explored before by Atallah et al. [3], such variant did not allow the user to specify security levels and control this trade off. The task is to come up with algorithms that interact with users and allow them to customize security levels.

To lower the confidence of success from a forward inference attack, we specify within the problem that the user must be able to specify, for each sensitive itemset, how many other non-sensitive itemsets with support below $\sigma$ shall be among those candidates that may be confused as frequent. Our statement of the problem quantifies this using a confusion value $l_b$ supplied by the user (one value $l_b$ for each sensitive itemset $b \in B$). Not only sensitive itemsets will have support less than $\sigma$ but the value $l_b \in N \cup 0$ specifies that for each sensitive itemset $b \in B$, the new database $D'$ will have at least $l_b$ or more non-sensitive itemsets with equal or higher support that $B$ and with support less than $\sigma$. Because we will later discuss the theoretical complexity of the problem, it is important to understand the inputs as well as what constitutes a solution. We now provide the formal description of the problem.

**The** DEEP HIDE ITEMSETS **Problem:**
**Input:** A set of transactions $T$ in a database $D$, a privacy support threshold $\sigma$ and a set of sensitive itemsets $B$ with a value $l_b$ assigned to each itemset $b \in B$ (each $b \in B$ is frequent with at least threshold $\sigma$ in $D$, i.e. $sprt_D(b) \geq \sigma$, $\forall b \in B$).
**Solution:** A sanitized database $D'$ where
**Condition 1** for each $b \in B$, there are $l_b$ or more non-sensitive itemsets
$\quad y \in A = F(D, \sigma) \setminus Sup(B)$ such that $sprt_{D'}(b) \leq sprt_{D'}(y) < \sigma$, and
**Condition 2** the number of itemsets in $y \in A$ so that $sprt_{D'}(y) \leq \sigma$ is
$\quad$ minimum (i.e. the impact on non-sensitive itemsets is minimum).

It is quite delicate to prove this problem is NP-Hard.

# 4   Heuristic Algorithm to Solve the DEEPLY HIDE ITEMSETS

Our process to solve this problem has two phases. In Phase 1, the input to the privacy process is defined. In particular, the user provides a privacy threshold $\sigma$. The targeted database $D$ is mined and the set $F(D, \sigma)$ of frequent itemsets is extracted. Then the user specifies sensitive itemsets $B$. The algorithm removes all supersets of a set in $B$ because if we want to hide an itemset, then the supersets of that itemset must be also hidden (in a sense we find the smallest $B$ so that $Sup(B) = Sup(B')$ if $B'$ was the original list of sensitive itemsets). In Phase 1, we also compute the size (cardinality) $\|b\|$ and set $T_D(b) \subset T$ of transactions in D that support $b$, for each frequent itemset $b \in B$. Then, we sort the sensitive itemsets in ascending order by cardinality first then by support (size-$k$ contains the frequent itemsets of size $k$ where $k$ is the number of items in the itemset). One by one, the user specifies $l_b$ for each sensitive itemset. Users may specify a larger $l_b$ value for higher sensitivity of that itemset. Note that as a result of Phase 1 we have a data structure that can, given a sensitive itemsets $b \in B$, retrieve $T_{D'}(b)$, $\|b\|$, and $sprt_{D'}(b)$ (initially, $D' = D$, $T_{D'}(b) = T_D(b)$, and $sprt_{D'}(b) = sprt_D(b)$).

Phase 2 applies the QIBC algorithm. The algorithm in Fig. 1 takes as input the set of transactions in a targeted database $D$, the set $B$ of sensitive itemsets, and set of non-sensitive itemsets. Then, the algorithm takes the sensitive itemsets one by one. The strategy we follow in the experiments in this paper is we start

---

**procedure** Quantified Inference Block Channel (QIBC) Algorithm
1. **for** each $b \in B$
$\quad$ 1.1 **while**   Condition 1 is not satisfied for $b$
$\quad\quad$ 1.1.1 Greedily find frequent 2-itemset $b' \subset b$.
$\quad\quad$ 1.1.2 Let $T(b', A)$ the transactions in $T_{D'}(b')$ that affects the minimum number of 2-itemsets.
$\quad\quad$ 1.1.3 Set the two items in $b'$ to nil in $T(b', A)$.
$\quad\quad$ 1.1.4 Update $T_{D'}(b)$, $\|b\|$, and $sprt_{D'}(b)$

**Fig. 1.** The QIBC Algorithm

with the sensitive itemsets with the smallest cardinality. If there are more than one $b \in B$ with the same cardinality we rank them by support, and select next the itemset with highest support. The algorithm enters a loop where we follow the same methodology of the algorithm by Attalah *et al.* [3] to greedily find a 2-itemset to eliminate items from transactions. This consists of finding the $(k-1)$-frequent itemset of highest support that is a subset of a current $k$-itemset. We start with $b \in B$ as the top $k$-itemset; that is, the algorithm finds a path in the lattice of frequent itemsets, from $b \in B$ to a 2-itemset, where every child in the path is the smaller proper subset with highest support among the proper subsets of cardinality one less. Then, the database of transactions is updated with items removed from those specific transactions.

## 5    Experimental Results and Comparison

In order to evaluate the practicality of the QIBC algorithm, we will compare its results with the results of the earlier heuristic algorithm [3]. We will call their heuristic algorithm ABEIV (based on the first letter of the last name of the authors). These experiments confirm that our algorithm offers a higher security level while essentially has no overhead w.r.t the ABEIV algorithm. This is because the main cost in both algorithms is finding the frequent itemsets.

The experiments are based on the first $20,000$ transactions from the "Frequent Itemset Mining Dataset Repository". The dataset is available in KDD-nuggets and was donated by T. Brijs. It includes sales transactions acquired from a fully-automated convenience store over a period of 5.5 months [4]. We used the "Apriori algorithm" [7] to obtain the frequent itemsets. We performed the experiments with three different privacy support thresholds ($\sigma = 5\%, \sigma = 4\%, \sigma = 3\%$). From among the frequent itemsets, we chose three itemsets randomly (one from among the size-2 itemsets and two from among the size-3 itemsets) to be considered as sensitive itemsets. We also set a value $l_b = 6$ to hide size-2 sensitive itemsets and a value $l_b = 2$ to hide size-3 sensitive itemsets.

We ran the experiment 10 times for each privacy support threshold with different random selection of size-2 and size-3 itemsets among the itemsets (in this way we are sure we are not selecting favorable instances of the DEEP HIDE ITEMSETS problem). We apply the QIBC algorithm to each combination of sensitive itemsets. Fig. 2 shows the percentage of the frequent non-sensitive itemsets affected by the execution of the algorithm. Since we have 10 instances of the DEEP HIDE ITEMSETS problem, we labeled them Run 1 to Run 10.

We observe that during the 10 runs with 5% privacy support threshold, QIBC has no more impact (on non-sensitive itemsets) than ABEIV on 6 occasions while on the other 4 it impacts less than 7% more. Thus, QIBC is closing the open inference channel 60% of the time with no penalty of hiding non-sensitive itemsets. If it incurs some cost on hiding non-sensitive itemsets, this is less than 7% of those to be made public. If we lower the privacy support threshold to 4%, still 60% of the time the QIBC incurs no impact on non-sensitive itemsets, and it reduces the impact to less than 5% when it hides itemsets that shall be public.

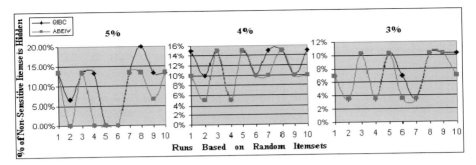

**Fig. 2.** The QIBC Algorithm vs The ABEIV Algorithm

When the privacy threshold is 3%, the results improve to 8 out of 10 runs in which QIBC has no penalty, and in those two runs that hide something public, this is less than 4% of the non-sensitive itemsets.

We conclude, sometimes the QIBC algorithm pays a higher price but it is reasonable for the sake of blocking the inference channel of forward attacks left open by the ABEIV algorithm.

These results were expected as discussed before. We want to emphasize the fact that usually more security means paying a higher price. The price in our case is sacrificing non-sensitive itemsets to ensure less confidence on forward attack.

## 6    Conclusion

We reviewed algorithms that hide sensitive patterns by sanitizing datasets and we showed their drawbacks. The proposed QIBC algorithm solved the problems and shortcomings in these algorithms. The QIBC algorithm added a very important feature that did not exist in the other algorithms. The QIBC algorithm allows users to customize their own levels of security. The QIBC algorithm adds this flexibility with a reasonable cost and blocking more inference channels.

## Acknowledgement

We thank Floris Geerts for helpful conversations on the topic of this paper.

## References

1. Dictionary.com. http://dictionary.reference.com/.
2. R. Agrawal, T. Imielinski, and A. Swami. Mining association rules between sets of items in large databases. In *Proc. of the ACM SIGMOD Conference on Management of Data*, pages 207–216, Washington D.C., USA, May 1993.
3. M. Atallah, E. Bertino, A. Elmagarmid, M. Ibrahim, and V. Verykios. Disclosure limitation of sensitive rules. In *Proc. of 1999 IEEE Knowledge and Data Engineering Exchange Workshop (KDEX'99)*, pages 45–52, Chicago, IL., November 1999.

4. T. Brijs, G. Swinnen, K. Vanhoof, and G. Wets. Using association rules for product assortment decisions: A case study. In *Knowledge Discovery and Data Mining*, pages 254–260, 1999.
5. C. Clifton, M. Kantarcioglu, and J. Vaidya. Defining privacy for data mining. In *Proc. of the National Science Foundation Workshop on Next Generation Data Mining*, pages 126–133, Baltimore, MD, USA, November 2002.
6. C. Farkas and S. Jajodia. The inference problem: a survey. In *Proc. of the ACM SIGKDD Explorations Newsletter*, volume 4, pages 6–11, New York, NY, USA, December 2002. ACM Press.
7. J. Han and M. *Data Mining:Concepts and Techniques*. 2001.
8. Y Lindell and Pinkas B. Privacy preserving data mining. In M. Bellare, editor, *Proceedings of CRYPTO-00 Advances in Cyptology*, pages 36–54, Santa Barbara, California, USA, August 20-24 2000.
9. S.R.M. Oliveira, O.R. Zaiane, and Y. Saygin. Secure association rule sharing. In *Proc. of the 8th PAKDD Conference*, pages 74–85, Sydney, Australia, May 2004. Springer Verlag Lecture Notes in Artificial Intelligence 3056.

# Access Control Requirements for Preventing Insider Threats

Joon S. Park[1] and Joseph Giordano[2]

[1] Syracuse University, Syracuse, NY 13244-4100, USA
jspark@syr.edu
http://istprojects.syr.edu/~jspark
[2] Information Directorate, Air Force Research Laboratory (AFRL),
Rome, NY 13441-4505, USA

**Abstract.** Today the Intelligence Community (IC) has faced increasing challenges of insider threats. It is generally accepted that the cost of insider threats exceeds that of outsider threats. Although the currently available access control approaches have a great potential for preventing insider threats, there are still critical obstacles to be solved, especially in large-scale computing environments. In this paper we discuss those requirements with respect to scalability, granularity, and context-awareness. For each requirement we discussed related problems, techniques, and basic approaches to the corresponding countermeasures. Detailed solutions and implementations are not described in this paper.

## 1 Introduction

Sensitive organizations such as the Intelligence Community (IC) have faced increasing challenges of insider threats because insiders are not always friends, but can be significant threats to the corporate assets [1, 2, 3, 4]. Therefore, access control mechanisms become most critical when we need resource-sharing services in the large-scale computing environments of sensitive organizations.

Since the initial proposals on enforcing protection and access control in computer security by Lampson [5] and Graham and Denning [6], considerable evolutions and developments of many access control models have come about over the last three decades. Based on the two proposals, Harrison et al. developed the HRU model [7] that introduced the subject-object paradigm of access control generally for multi-user operating systems and led to the development of the typed access matrix (TAM) model [8]. Bell et al. introduced the Bell-LaPadula model [9], Sandhu et al. formalized the Role-Based Access Control (RBAC [10, 11, 12]) model, and Thomas et al. developed the task-based authorization control (TBAC [13]) model. There are many other works in access control with safety analysis [14, 15, 16] and logic programming [17, 18, 19]. However, due to the advent of newly-developed and integrated systems in large-scale computing environments and their dynamically changing contexts, people began to consider moving towards more advanced access control paradigms that could be paced

S. Mehrotra et al. (Eds.): ISI 2006, LNCS 3975, pp. 529–534, 2006.

with rapidly changing computer technologies, especially for homeland security related applications that are usually large and integrated.

Although the currently available access control approaches have a great potential for providing more reliable access control services, there are still critical obstacles to be solved, especially in large-scale, dynamic computing environments. The lack of sophisticated access control mechanisms in such environments has become a serious constraint for preventing insider threats, which are critical challenges to the IC. To overcome these limitations, in this paper we discuss those requirements with respect to scalability, granularity, and situation-aware (we call this active) decision. Detailed solutions are not described in this particular paper. We focus on large-scale computing environments within a sensitive organization.

## 2    Scalable Access Control

Current IT systems have become more complex and better integrated with other systems. Usually, a large distributed system supports many users in various contexts from different organizations. Machines may run in heterogeneous environments under different policies. Different users, or even the same user, require different privileges based on their current contexts and constraints, which may change dynamically. Obviously, the complexity of the security factors in IT systems is increasing, which brings a serious scalability problem to security services and management. This becomes even more critical if multiple organizations are involved in the same collaborative enterprise. Some users may have common functionality in one application, while each user may be involved in multiple applications. Users privileges need to be in synch with their contexts in the enterprise as users join or leave the corresponding community.

The least privileges need to be assigned to the proper users at the right time. The complexity and large scale of access control demands an efficient mechanism to deal with such issues as which user has what privileges for which contents under what conditions. A conventional identity-based approach may suffice for this purpose if the application is small and involves a limited number of users, and if privilege assignments to users are stable. However, in a large-scale system that supports many users from different organizations requiring different kinds of privileges, the identity-based approach would be severely inefficient and too complicated to manage because the direct mapping between users and privileges is transitory.

Furthermore, in a collaborative project, each organization does not necessary know the identities of users from other organizations who are involved in the project. The organization could share user databases and recognize users from other organizations, but this also brings a security risk to the organization because it exposes the data of all users to a third party, while only some of those users in the organization are involved in the collaborative project. Even though the risk may be reduced by setting up a dedicated database only for participating users and sharing it with other project members, it raises the management overhead because the assignment of users to job functionalities in projects changes constantly, which makes it difficult to update and synchronize such temporary databases. Therefore, more scalable access control approaches, especially for large systems, are needed for preventing insider threats.

As a possible solution, we may need to consider a role-based approach. Role-Based Access Control (RBAC) has proven to be an effective way to address the scalability problem [10, 11, 12]. The main idea of RBAC is to separate users from privileges by linking users with privileges through their roles. Since Permission-Role Assignment (PRA) is more stable, compared to User-Role Assignment (URA), RBAC reduces the management workload by avoiding direct mapping between users and privileges. An RBAC system makes access control decisions based on users job functions (roles) instead of on their identities. This provides a scalable access control mechanism to the system and resolves the scalability problem. In order to provide RBAC to an access-controlled computing environment, we need to securely transfer each user's role information to check for allotted permissions to access contents. In our previous work we identified the User-Pull and Server-Pull architectures and the support mechanisms for securely obtaining role information from the role server using secure cookies and smart certificates [20, 21, 22]. Recently, we introduced an approach of role-based user-profile analysis for scalable and accurate insider-anomaly detection [23, 24].

## 3   Fine-Grained Access Control

We could enhance the scalability in access control simply by increasing control granularity. For instance, if there are many resources (e.g., files where each file includes multiple fields), a file-level security mechanism is more scalable than a field-level security mechanism. However, the file-level security mechanism is too coarse when we need different security services for different fields in the same file. Typically, an intelligence application deals with a wide variety of contents. Some of these contents might have multiple sub-contents or fields and require different levels of access control to all or part of the fields in the contents. However, the control granularity in most of the conventional access control mechanisms is at the file level (e.g., entire document). This coarse-grained control mechanism offers insufficient services for providing fine-grained information protection for sub-contents or fields within a file.

Technically, for instance, a document such as an XML (Extensible Markup Language) file can contain both actual contents (e.g., intelligence information) and their metadata (e.g., support information [25, 26, 27, 28]). The contents and metadata may also be stored in separate files and linked via URIs (Uniform Resource Identifiers). In either case, it is imperative to control the contents as well as metadata with fine granularity, so that we can ensure a user has access to the only necessary portion in the contents and metadata, avoiding over-privileges.

For this purpose we could consider cryptographic access control by using field encryption as done in DBMS and in previous XML work [29, 30]. However, this approach may not be scalable in a large application because each field has to be encrypted and decrypted by the corresponding key and the entire document that contains multiple fields encrypted by different keys is transferred to the users even if they need access to only particular fields in the document. Basically, a user can obtain the entire document and can decrypt some of those fields in the document based on the keys that the user has. Therefore, this approach allows malicious insiders to collect more information to break the unauthorized fields because it transfers the unnecessary fields that are encrypted for other users. It also increases the complexity with key management.

Without fine granularity, it is hard to provide to users the least-privilege principal, a fundamental approach to make a system more secure, but we should not ignore scalability. Therefore, we need fine-grained access control mechanisms that are still scalable in a large application.

## 4    Active Access Control (AAC)

Most of the currently available access control mechanisms make decisions on predefined sets of rules. They typically use a static mechanism and are known for their non-changeable, one-time decision-making capability. Once a set of privileges is assigned to a user, the user can typically utilize those privileges in another context for any purpose desired. The user's context change is not considered. Once a user is authenticated, that user is allowed to use his or her privileges in different contexts until log-out. For example, if a user, Alice, is assigned to an administrative role, and she needs non-administrative job activities such as Web searching for her own purpose, her administrative role in this case should be considered to be over-privileged, which allows her to abuse her privileges intentionally or unintentionally. Actually, this kind of privilege abuse is a serious insider threat in sensitive organizations. Furthermore, conventional access control approaches do not consider the user's current computing environment, but simply make an access control decision based on the high-level policy.

However, what if the users current operational environment is not secure enough to fulfill some of the assigned privileges? For instance, if a user is using a wireless connection in a public cafeteria, that user should not be allowed to use sensitive administrative privileges (although those privileges are assigned by the organizational policy), while allowed to use those sensitive privileges if she is using a secure connection in her office. To solve this kind of problem, we should provide continuous and dynamic access control beyond the initial access control decision. We call it *active access control*.

While some research efforts do address access control mechanisms for dynamic computing environments, they are still relatively static, compared with our requirement. Furthermore, most of them are identity-based approaches that are not scalable for a large, distributed system. To provide active access control we should consider not only the static attributes but also the dynamic attributes of the users and the current computing environments, which can change even in the same session, such as the current location. Furthermore, we should also define the priority order of those attributes that varies in different organizations and systems. The weight reflects the importance of the attribute. For instance, the Location attribute can be the most important attribute in one application for its access control decision, while the Time attribute may be the most important attribute in another application.

## 5  Conclusions

In this paper we analyzed the requirements in conventional access control mechanisms for preventing insider threats, with respect to scalability, granularity, and context-awareness. For each requirement we discussed related problems, techniques, and basic approaches to the corresponding countermeasures. Detailed solutions and implementations are not described in this paper.

## Acknowledgment

This research is supported in part by the US Air Force Research Laboratory (AFRL)/Griffiss Institute for Information Assurance and the DoD Intergovernmental Personnel Act (IPA) mobility program for Dr. Joon S. Park.

## References

1. Anderson, R.H.: Research and development initiatives focused on preventing, detecting, and responding to insider misuse of critical defense information systems. In: Workshop at RAND, Santa Monica, CA (1999)
2. Brackney, R.C., Anderson, R.H.: Understanding the insider threat. In: ARDA (The Advanced Research and Development Activity) Workshop. (2004)
3. Hayden, M.V.: The insider threat to U.S. government information systems. Technical report, National Security Telecommunications and Information Systems Security Committee (NSTISSAM) (1999) INFOSEC 1-99.
4. Park, J.S., Costello, K.P., Neven, T.M., Diosomito, J.A.: A composite RBAC approach for large, complex organizations. In: the 9th ACM Symposium on Access Control Models and Technologies (SACMAT), Yorktown Heights, NY (2004)
5. Lamson, B.W.: Protection. In: the 5th Princeton Symposium in Information Sciences and Systems, Princeton University, NJ (1971) 437–443
6. Graham, G.S., Denning, P.: Protection principles and practice. In: AFIPS Spring Joint Computer Conference, Montvaler, NJ (1972)
7. Harrison, M.H., Ruzzo, W.L., Ullman, J.D.: Protection in operating systems. Communications of the ACM 19(8) (1976) 461–471
8. Sandhu, R.S.: The typed access matrix model. In: IEEE Symposium on Research in Security and Privacy, Oakland, CA (1992) 122–136
9. Bell, D., Lapadula, L.: Secure computer systems: Mathematical foundations. Technical report, The MITRE Corporation, Bedford, MA (1973) MTR-2547.
10. Ferraiolo, D.F., Sandhu, R.S., Gavrila, S., Kuhn, D.R., Chandramouli, R.: Proposed nist standard for role-based access control. ACM Transactions on Information and System Security (TISSEC) 4(3) (2001) 224–274

11. National Institute of Standards and Technology (NIST): The economic impact of role-based access control. (2002) Planning Report 02-1.
12. Sandhu, R., Coyne, E., Feinstein, H., Youman, C.: Role-based access control models. IEEE Computer **29**(2) (1996)
13. Thomas, R.K., Sandhu, R.S.: Task-based authorization control (TBAC): A family of models for active and enterprise-oriented authorization management. In: IFIP WG11.3 Workshop on Database Security, Vancouver, Canada (1997)
14. Ammann, P., Sandhu, R.S.: The extended schematic protection model. Journal of Computer Security **1**(3-4) (1992) 335–383
15. Li, N., Mitchell, J.C., Winsborough, W.H.: Beyond proof-of-compliance: Safety and availability analysis in trust management. In: IEEE Symposium on Research in Security and Privacy, Oakland, CA (2003) 123–139
16. Minsky, N.H.: Selective and locally controlled transport of privileges. ACM Transactions on Programming Languages and Systems **6**(4) (1984) 573–602
17. Bertino, E., Catania, B., Ferrari, E., Perlasca, P.: A logical framework for reasoning about access control models. ACM Transactions on Information and System Security (TISSEC) **6**(1) (2003) 71–127
18. Bertino, E., Jajodia, S., Samarati, P.: A flexible authorization mechanism for relational data management systems. ACM Transactions on Information and System Security (TISSEC) **17**(2) (1999) 101–140
19. Jajodia, S., Samarati, P., Subrahmanian, V.S.: A logical language for expressing authorizations. In: IEEE Symposium on Research in Security and Privacy, Oakland, CA (1997) 31–42
20. Park, J.S., Sandhu, R.: RBAC on the web by smart certificates. In: the 4th ACM Workshop on Role-Based Access Control (RBAC), Fairfax, VA (1999)
21. Park, J.S., Sandhu, R., Ahn, G.J.: Role-based access control on the web. ACM Transactions on Information and System Security (TISSEC) **4**(1) (2001) 207–226
22. Park, J.S., Sandhu, R., Ghanta, S.: RBAC on the Web by secure cookies. In: the 13th IFIP WG 11.3 Working Conference on Database Security, Seattle, WA (1999)
23. Park, J.S., Giordano, J.: Role-based profile analysis for scalable and accurate insider-anomaly detection. In: IEEE Workshop on Information Assurance (WIA), Phoenix, AZ (2006)
24. Park, J.S., Ho, S.M.: Composite role-based monitoring (CRBM) for countering insider threats. In: Symposium on Intelligence and Security Informatics (ISI), Tucson, AZ (2004)
25. Berners-Lee, T., Hendler, J., Lassila, O.: The semantic web. Scientific American **284**(5) (2001) 34–43
26. Hendler, J., Berners-Lee, T., Miller, E.: Integrating applications on the semantic web. Journal of the Institute of Electrical Engineers of Japan **122**(10) (2002) 676–680
27. Lassila, O.: Web metadata: A matter of semantics. IEEE Internet Computing **2**(4) (1998) 30–47
28. Park, J.S.: Towards secure collaboration on the semantic web. ACM Computers and Society **32**(6) (2003)
29. Bertino, E., Ferrari, E.: Secure and selective dissemination of XML documents. ACM Transactions on Information and System Security (TISSEC) **5**(3) (2002) 290–331
30. Bertino, E., Ferrari, E., Squicciarini, A.C.: Trust-X: A peer-to-peer framework for trust establishment. IEEE Transactions on Knowledge and Data Engineering **16**(7) (2004) 827–842

# Venn Diagram Construction of Internet Chatroom Conversations

James F. McCarthy and Mukkai S. Krishnamoorthy[*]

Department of Computer Science
Rensselaer Polytechnic Institute
110 8th Street, Troy, NY 12180, USA

**Abstract.** Venn Diagrams are used to depict relationships between subsets of a set of items. In this paper we will discuss the methods we use to render these Diagrams on a plane. Algorithms to both place members of subsets and render the curves of the Diagram will be presented. We close with discussion of results and application to chatroom conversation analysis.

## 1 Introduction

The Venn Diagram is an esoteric member of the field of mathematics. While elementary education covers them to teach relationships and most mathematics professors will accept the diagrams as acceptable answers in courses based on set and/or probability theory, very few people have ever seen or contemplated a diagram of 5 curves or more. In fact, only recently has the largest symmetric Diagram known, with 11 curves, been constructed. Our intention in this paper is to use computer science techniques used to construct displays to understand Venn Diagrams for further study.

### 1.1 Definition of a Venn Diagram

Grunbaum[6] defined a Venn Diagram by first defining an independent family.

> Let $C = C_1, C_2, \ldots, C_n$ be a collection of simple closed curves drawn in the plane. We say the collection $C$ is an independent family if the intersection of $X = X_1, X_2, \ldots, X_n$ is nonempty where $X_i$ is either the interior of $C_i$ or the exterior of $C_i$. If each intersection is connected and $\mid X \mid$ is finite then we can say $C$ is a Venn Diagram.

Ruskey[10] points out that the limit on $\mid X \mid$ is usually assumed in literature but rarely explicitly specified. An $n$-Venn Diagram is a Venn Diagram with $n = \mid C \mid$.

[*] This research is supported by NSF ITR Award #0324947 and NSF ACT Award #0442154.

## 1.2   Exploration of Current Research

Current research has been worked on extending Venn Diagrams to larger Diagrams. Winkler[11] conjectured that every simple $n$-Venn Diagram is extendible to a simple $n+1$ Diagram. Grunbaum[7] modified this to apply to all $n$-Venn Diagrams, and Chilakimarri, Hamburger, and Pippert[2][3] proved this right and theorized that Venn Diagrams are currently extendible only if the Planar Radual Graph of the Diagram is Hamiltonian. Hamburger[8] is credited with being the first to construct the first symmetric 11-Venn Diagram. An extremely good summary of research in this area was written by Ruskey[10].

**Fig. 1.** 3-Venn Diagram by the Force-Directed Algorithm

## 2   Visualization

In order to represent the diagram, we had to evaluate what properties of the diagram to highlight and how we would represent these using current computer graphics methods. Typically, mathematics has addressed Venn Diagrams by their curves only and not the underlying theory that the entire space of the Venn Graph $V(\mathscr{F})$ represents a set of elements and the relationships between selected subsets of that set. We decided to counter current research and highlight this almost exclusively as it serves as an easier method for understanding what a Venn Diagram essentially is. As a result, we were faced with discussing methods for representing elements in the Graph both as nodes in a graph $G(V, E)$ and members in a Set $S$ with selected subsets.

### 2.1   Node and Subset Representation

Upon reflection, we decided that each element in the Graph must be represented as a node that can be manipulated in the plane on which we are drawing our diagram. We describe the algorithms to place the nodes in this manner later in the paper.

To represent a subset, we determined the upper right and lower left corner of the entire subset coverage area based on the locations of the nodes in the subset and found the center of the line connecting these two corners. Using a radius equal to half the distance of this diagonal plus a few coordinates for error, we ended up with a properly placed curve.

The dynamic creation of Ellipse drawing and rendering was based upon a Bresenham algorithm [9] that rendered an Ellipse with the major axis oriented along the x-axis and the minor axis oriented along the y-axis. This allows us to render the ellipse properly, but we must rotate the shape to properly fit all nodes that we are encompassing. We decided to use the node that was furthest from the midpoint, or center, of the nodes in the set we were rendering. Since that node most likely defined $a$, we can attempt to rotate the point $(0, a)$ to the node's location and get a good fit for the ellipse. We determined the angle of rotation by:

$$\theta = \pi + \arctan \frac{n_y - c_y}{n_x - c_x}$$

where $n$ is the node, $c$ is the center of the ellipse of set $S$, and $n \varepsilon S$.

## 2.2 Intersection Checking

We use a property first noted by Chilakimarri, Hamburger, and Pippert[3] to check whether or not a Venn Diagram has the proper number of subsets. In their paper, they theorized that since a Venn Diagram $V(\mathscr{F})$ is a planar graph, then Euler's equation $V - E + F = 2$ holds for $V(\mathscr{F})$. They then take it a step further to derive that $V = 2n - 2$ for all $V(\mathscr{F})$. Here, if we have a set C that contains all curves in $V(\mathscr{F})$, then $n = |C|$. It is important to point out here that in a Venn Diagram, the set V does not refer to the nodes that we have been discussing but instead represents all intersections that may exist for a graph. So, we now know that $V(\mathscr{F})$ should have $2n - 2$ intersections to be valid.

## 2.3 Subset Manipulation

We have found through our research that it is possible to specify input to our algorithms that may not coincide with the traditional set elements of an n-Venn Diagram. The 4-Venn Diagram is an excellent example of this problem. This Diagram is known as the smallest Diagram without an existing simple Venn Diagram. In fact, due to the rule [10] that specifies that simple Venn Diagrams exist only when n is prime, there will never be a simple 4-Venn Diagram. Only 2 possible 4-Venn Diagrams are really known to exist [7].

Figure 2 is the most recent attempt at a 4-Venn Diagram. This implementation uses an ellipse to create one of the diagrams specified by Grunbaum [7].

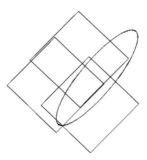

**Fig. 2.** 4-Venn Diagram attempt

Because the ellipse is used in place of one of the squares, it should be possible to achieve all of the necessary intersections. However, the placement of the ellipse is quite precise and as yet it has not been possible to render it properly. While it is now possible to achieve all of the necessary intersections of 2 subsets, it is challenging to ensure all intersections of 3 subsets are present as well.

## 3    Algorithms

We must discuss the various algorithms used in our research. The Force Directed algorithm is established as a very good approach to drawing a graph of vertices. The Weighted-Distance Algorithm attempts to use a different method to place nodes in the proper subsets.

The Force-Directed algorithm, first proposed by Fruchterman and Reingold[5], creates a physical simulation that moves nodes around our painting canvas until the algorithm has finished. It uses a temperature value to control the movement of individual nodes. The temperature function used in our implementation is

$$Temperature = \left( \frac{\frac{L}{2D}}{1 + e^{t - \frac{8}{5}}} \right)$$

where $D$ is the arbitrary area constant, $t$ is the current iteration count and $L = D* \mid S \mid$ where $S$ is the set of all nodes. $D$ is manipulated by the user to test out different values, but a typical default that we used in testing was 20. Our implementation gained these values from research done by Erlingsson and Krishnamoorthy[4]. The algorithm is also notorious for a complexity $O(n^2)$ derived from the fact that each node repels every other node in each iteration.

The Weighted-Distance algorithm attempts to place nodes on a grid rather than through a graph and allow for a more reliable creation of an accurate Venn Diagram. The algorithm allows each node to determine the grid distance from every other node and then one of the nine squares in its immediate area to move to (including staying in place). The algorithm uses a weight that is placed on each possible move as follows:

$$Weight = (C_b * d_b{}^{E_b}) + (C_g * d_g{}^{E_g})$$

where the C is a constant, E is an exponent, d is the total distance for each type of node, b refers to "bad" nodes (they don't share a subset with the current node), and g refers to "good" nodes (they share a subset with the current node). When finished, the node then chooses the move with the smallest weight.

There are a few points that we can use to compare the two algorithms. The Force Directed node requires a force calculation between every node, whereas the Weighted Distance algorithm only calculates a Euclidean distance between these nodes. Since distance is much easier to calculate (and may not change between iterations), this benefits the Weighted Distance approach. Also, Weighted Distance limits the range of movement that a node can have in one iteration, while the Force Directed implementation sums up all forces and moves the node once all calculations are finished. Finally, neither algorithm has a set termination point. This is to be determined by the implementation.

# 4    Application to Chatroom Analysis

In coordination with Acar[1], we have been attempting to recently take chatroom conversation analysis and visualize it as a Venn Diagram. While most of the data we have used so far has not been cleaned by the chatroom tensors, we believe that our representations have painted an accurate picture of the range of subjects that may occur in a chatroom and how the subjects relate to each other.

## 4.1    Collection of Data

The collection of the conversations that were used for this operation were outside of the research performed by Acar[1]. The methods used were similar to previous research, however no automation was involved. Manual collection was conducted because the data was only needed for visualization testing and it was felt this method was sufficient to satisfy those needs.

Once data was collected from the chatroom, it was entered into an XML file format that helped maintain the data in a universal format. This file basically treated the group of chatroom participants as the global set for the Venn Diagram. The conversation topics were the subsets and each user who spoke about that topic was considered a subset element. This allowed the depiction of how different groups interacted and exactly who was talking to whom about what.

## 4.2    Discussion of Findings

Several interesting results were depicted by the diagrams that were rendered using the chatroom conversations. An interesting phenomenon was the presence of sub-conversations. These conversations occur when a group of people are talking about one thing and then two or more people in this group talk to themselves about something different. There are two things we could possibly deduce from this. Either the sub-conversants are changing the topic and someone did not follow along or possibly the conversants are debating something related to the larger topic at hand.

In Fig. 3, there are specific separations in the conversations that are present. The fact that there are no less than three groups of people talking shows that there was a disjunction in the subject matter. It should be noted that the example has nodes that are not necessarily taking part in any conversation except their own. Usually these people are those who ask questions that aren't answered. However, we shouldn't rule these people out of the dynamic altogether. For instance, if a network of automated clients are sitting in a room waiting for an order, a human being might join the room, say something, and then leave and the let the automated clients do their work. These clients sometimes say things so that it looks as though the chatroom is legitimate, but upon closer reflection

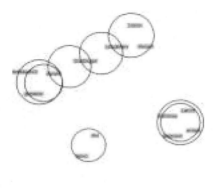

**Fig. 3.** Chatroom visualization example

it is easy to see that the conversation is irrelevant. So, we shouldn't ignore these singletons just because no one is talking to them. They could be giving a signal and the concentration of conversations could be used as a distraction from this.

## 5    Conclusion

We have presented a framework for the automatic generation of Venn Diagrams based on set relationships. Further analysis of our algorithms will find that they are quite flexible to the given problem and, with a little more work, will reliably generate the necessary graphs. The general goal here is to produce diagrams with little or no background in the mathematics that direct them.

The Venn Diagram is unique as a visualization tool for explaining relationships between sets of data. Investigation into dynamic creation of these diagrams can help more effectively use them to express our data in methods that catch the attention of the viewer. While they may not be the best in all situations, when the emphasis of relationships in data is necessary there are few tools that can quickly and aesthetically support findings and provide insight like the Venn Diagram.

## References

1. Acar, E., Camtepe, S., Krishnamoorthy, M., and Yener, B. *Modeling and Multi-way Analysis of Chatroom Tensors*, IEEE Symposium on Intelligence and Security Informatics, May 2005.
2. Chilakamarri, K.B., Hamburger P., and Pippert R.E.: *Hamilton Cycles in Planar Graphs and Venn Diagrams*, Journal of Combinatorial Theory (Series B), 67 (1996) 296-303.
3. Chilakamarri, Kiran, Hamburger, Peter, and Pippert, Raymond E: *Venn diagrams and planar graphs*, Geometriae Dedicata, 62 (1996) 73-91.
4. Erlingsson, Ulfar and Krishnamoorthy, Mukkai: *Interactive Graph Drawing on the World Wide Web*, Technical Report 96-13, Department of Computer Science, Rensselaer Polytechnic Institute, Troy, NY, 1996.

5. Fruchterman, T.M.J, and Reingold, E.M.: *Graph Drawing by Force-Directed Placement*, Software - Practic and Experience, 21(11), (1991) 1129-1164.
6. Grunbaum, Branko: *Venn diagrams and Independent Families of Sets*, Mathematics Magazine, 48 (Jan-Feb 1975) 12-23.
7. Grunbaum, Branko: *Venn Diagrams II, Geombinatorics*, Volume II, Issue 2, (1992) 25-32.
8. Hamburger, Peter: *Doodles and Doilies*, manuscript, 2000.
9. Kennedy, John: *A Fast Bresenham Type Algorithm For Drawing Ellipses*, http://homepage.smc.edu/kennedy_john/BELIPSE.PDF
10. Ruskey, Frank: *A Survey of Venn Diagrams*, Electronic Journal of Combinatorics, 1996, http://www.combinatorics.org/Surveys/ds5/VennEJC.html
11. Winkler, Peter: *Venn diagrams: Some observations and an open problem*, Congressus Numerantium, 45 (1984) 267-274.

# Spatial-Temporal Cross-Correlation Analysis: A New Measure and a Case Study in Infectious Disease Informatics

Jian Ma, Daniel Zeng, and Hsinchun Chen

Department of Management Information Systems, The University of Arizona
1130 E. Helen Street, Tucson, AZ 85721-0108
{jma, zeng, hchen}@eller.arizona.edu

**Abstract.** This paper aims to develop a new statistical measure to identify significant correlations among multiple events with spatial and temporal components. This new measure, $K(r,t)$, is defined by adding the temporal dimension to Ripley's $K(r)$ function. Empirical studies show that the use of $K(r,t)$ can lead to a more discriminating and flexible spatial-temporal data analysis framework. This measure also helps identify the causal events whose occurrences induce those of other events.

## 1 Introduction

Spatial-temporal data analysis plays an important role in many security informatics applications. Current practices in analyzing data with spatial and temporal components focus on one type of data event [1, 2]. In this paper, we aim to develop an analysis approach that can assess spatial-temporal correlations among multiple data streams.

One of the widely adopted concepts for correlation analysis is Ripley's $K(r)$ function which focuses mostly on spatial data [3, 4]. In order to analyze datasets with both spatial and temporal components, we extend $K(r)$ by adding a temporal parameter $t$. Through a case study based on a real-world infectious disease dataset, we conclude that this extended spatial-temporal definition $K(r,t)$ provides more discriminating power than $K(r)$ function. In addition, this extended definition can be used to discover causal events whose occurrences induce those of other events.

The remainder of this paper is structured as follows. In Section 2 we introduce $K(r)$ and $K(r,t)$ functions. Section 3 summarizes an empirical study to evaluate $K(r,t)$. We conclude in Section 4 by reviewing our findings and proposing potential avenues of future research.

## 2 Ripley's $K(r)$ Function and Its Spatial-Temporal Extension

In the area of spatial-temporal data analysis, data observations may belong to one or multiple events. Auto-correlation analysis considers one event while cross-correlation

S. Mehrotra et al. (Eds.): ISI 2006, LNCS 3975, pp. 542–547, 2006.
© Springer-Verlag Berlin Heidelberg 2006

analyzes the relationship across two events [4]. Our research is focused on the analysis of spatial-temporal cross-correlations. In this section, we first introduce Ripley's $K(r)$ function and then present its spatial-temporal extension.

## 2.1  Ripley's $K(r)$ Function

Ripley's $K(r)$ function is mainly used to describe the correlation between two completely mapped spatial point processes in a predefined study area. Applications include spatial patterns of trees [5], bird nests [6], and disease cases [7]. Various theoretical aspects of $K(r)$ are extensively discussed in books by Ripley [4], and Dixon [8]. Specifically, Ripley's $K(r)$ function is given as

$$K_{ij}(r) = \lambda_j^{-1} E[\text{Number of Event } j \text{ observations within distance } r \quad (1)$$
$$\text{of a randomly chosen Event } i \text{ observation}]$$

[3], where $\lambda_j$ is the density of event $j$. The higher the $K(r)$ value, the stronger the correlation is. When $i = j$, the value of $K(r)$ indicates the auto-correlative magnitude.

While $K(r)$ function has been proven effective in discovering spatial cross-correlations, it does not include the temporal component. By ignoring temporal effects, $K(r)$ function has two effects that may lead to wrong conclusions. The first effect is what we refer to as the "aggregate effect" which may overlook significant correlations. A typical correlated scenario in infectious disease informatics is that a disease observation has an effect to trigger other observations in a short period of time. As time progresses, such effect deceases in intensity and disappears eventually. The average intensity over the entire time span is "diluted" by the absence of observations at other time periods. As a result, the estimated value of $K(r)$ may not be high enough to signify a significant correlation.

The second effect, the "backward shadow effect", may falsely signal meaningless correlations. For a given observation $i_m$, we assume that there are many observations in the neighborhood prior to the time of $i_m$, and few after $i_m$. Since $K(r)$ does not differentiate the observations occurred before or after the time of $i_m$, the abundance of previously-occurred observations will shadow the absence of observations after the time of $i_m$. As a result, a significant correlation is identified. Note that this conclusion is not necessarily meaningful because the correlation is built on the assumption that previous observations can be affected by an observation occurred later.

## 2.2  $K(r,t)$ Function with Temporal Considerations

To analyze spatial-temporal correlation, we propose a new measure $K(r,t)$ that extends Ripley's $K(r)$ function by explicitly taking into consideration the occurring times of observations. We intend to reduce the aggregate effect by eliminating the observations that satisfy the spatial restriction but occur at far-apart time periods. Depending on whether or not allowing the assumption that previous observations can be affected by observations occurred later, we can choose to eliminate the backward shadow effect. Two-tail time effect considers observations occurred both *before* and *after* the time of the interest. The one-tail time effect considers the observations *after* a certain time. Equations (2) and (3) show the unbiased estimations of the one- and two-tail $K(r,t)$, respectively.

$$\widehat{K}_{ij}(r,t) = \frac{1}{\hat{\lambda}_i \hat{\lambda}_j AT} \sum_{i_m} \sum_{j_n} w(i_m, j_n) I(d_{i_m, j_n} < r \text{ and } 0 \le t_{j_n} - t_{i_m} < t) \tag{2}$$

$$\widehat{K}_{ij}(r,t) = \frac{1}{\hat{\lambda}_i \hat{\lambda}_j AT} \sum_{i_m} \sum_{j_n} w(i_m, j_n) I(d_{i_m, j_n} < r \text{ and } -t < t_{j_n} - t_{i_m} < t) \tag{3}$$

In the above estimations, $r$ and $t$ are independent variables representing the distance and time window respectively; A is the study area; T is the entire time span of the observations; $i_m$ is the $m$-th observation of event $i$; $\hat{\lambda}_j$ is the number of observations of event $j/AT$; $d_{i_m, j_n}$ is the distance between $i_m$ and $j_n$; $t_{j_n}$ is the occurring time of $j_n$; $I(x)$ is an indicator variable whose value is 1 when x is true and 0 otherwise; and $w(i_m, j_n)$ takes into account of the edge effect [3].

We observe that $\widehat{K}_{ij}(r,t)$ is a monotonically increasing function with respected to the radius $r$ and time $t$. The minimum of the function value is 0 and the maximum is the product of the study area A and time span T. When the time window $t$ is set to be greater than the time span T, the two-tailed $K(r,t)$ provides no more restriction than $K(r)$ and the ratio between their values given the same $r$ differs by a constant T.

# 3   A Case Study Using an Infectious Disease Dataset

We evaluate $K(r,t)$ function using a real-world dataset from infectious disease informatics. We intend to evaluate whether and to what extent $K(r,t)$ is able to reveal detailed correlative relationships among spatial-temporal data events and how it is different from $K(r)$ function for analysis purposes. Furthermore, by manipulating the one-tail time effect, we intend to study how $K(r,t)$ can help discover the causal events whose occurrences induce those of other events.

## 3.1   Dataset and Data Analysis Procedure

The dataset is from the dead bird reporting and mosquito surveillance system in Los Angeles County, California, with a time span of 162 days from May to September, 2004. There are four types of events in total, namely, Dead birds with Positive results on West Nile Virus (WNV) detection, Mosquitoes with Positive WNV detection, Mosquitoes with Negative WNV detection, and Mosquito Treatments performed by public health clerks. We denote them as DBP, MosP, MosN, and MosTr, respectively.

After identifying the area and the time span of the dataset, we chose multiple combinations of $r$ and $t$ to perform our analysis. The values of $r$ are represented by the percentage of the average of the length and the width of the study area.

To evaluate the cross-correlation between two events without the impact of auto-correlations of each event, we compute $K_{ij}(r,t) - K_{jj}(r,t)$ [6] . We then employ random labeling simulation 200 times to evaluate the correlation significance [8]. Specifically, we combine the observations of event $i$ and $j$, then randomly assign event type to every observation without changing the number of observations that each event originally has. If the value of $K_{ij}(r,t) - K_{jj}(r,t)$ calculated from real data is higher than 195 values (97.5%) calculated from random labeling simulations, we conclude that events $i$ and $j$ are significantly correlated under such $r$ and $t$, and that event type $i$ is the causal event whose occurrences induce those of event type $j$.

The $K(r)$ function is also computed following the similar procedure as a base line to $K(r,t)$. Although we have tested both one- and two-tail time effects, we only report the results using one-tail time effect.

## 3.2    Results and Discussions

To compare $K(r,t)$ and $K(r)$, we are particularly interested in the effects of time restrictions. (Other effects are left for future discussion.) We summarize our findings below.

1) We observe that as $t$ increases, more event pairs are found to be significantly correlated. When $t$ is set to be 6 days or less, no significant correlations are discovered. When $t$ equals 9 days and $r$ is larger than 26.25%, there appears the first correlated event pair, MosTr-MosN. Specifically, MosTr is the causal event that induces MosN. When we set $t$ to 30 days, DbP-MosN is found to be correlated. When $t$ is set to be 60 days or greater, two more pairs are found: MosTr-MosP and DbP-MosP. That is, MosTr and DbP induce MosN and MosP.

2) More importantly, when comparing the results obtained by $K(r,t)$ and $K(r)$, we observe that those two methods provide different correlated event pairs. $K(r)$ ignores the time restriction and shows four pairs of events with high correlations. Those four pairs are: MosTr-MosN, DbP-MosN, MosTr-MosP, and MosTr-DbP. When compared with the four pairs found by $K(r,t)$ with $t$ greater than 60 days, the difference is that $K(r)$ reports MosTr-DbP and does not report DbP-MosP. As shown in Figures 1(a) - (d), these differences between the results of $K(r,t)$ and $K(r)$ are substantial and meaningful, especially for MosTr-DbP. This is due to the backward shadow effect. The reason why $K(r)$ does not report DbP-MosP is because of the aggregate effect.

The difference between $K(r,t)$ and $K(r)$ demonstrates that in many cases $K(r)$ function is a measure that may be exceedingly aggregated to reveal the nature of detailed correlations. The time restriction is necessary to explore the real correlative

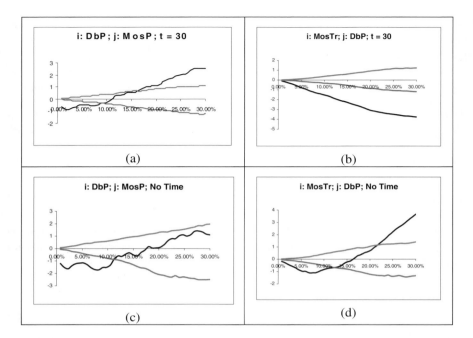

**Fig. 1.** Selected analysis results based on the dead bird and mosquito surveillance dataset. All x-axes are radius; all y-axes are $K_{ij}(r,t) - K_{jj}(r,t)$ . The cone shape bands are formed by 2.5% and 97.5% quantiles estimated from 200 random labeling simulations.

relationships among events. $K(r,t)$ excludes the backward shadow effect if $t$ is set to be one-tailed. It will also reduce the aggregate effect if $t$ is set to be more restrictive.

## 4   Conclusions and Future Research

Spatial-temporal data analysis presents a key challenge in many security informatics related applications. The identification of significant correlative relations among multiple data events with spatial and temporal components is of great importance to security informatics practitioners. This paper introduces a new measure, $K(r,t)$, extending Ripley's $K(r)$ function, a commonly used spatial correlation analysis measure. The new measure is evaluated using a public health dataset. The result indicates that the proposed new measure is more discriminating when compared to Ripley's $K(r)$ function and provides the ability to identify the causal events. The additional restriction of the time window also provides the users with the flexibility to choose the suitable aggregation level to reveal specific correlations.

Our future research is targeted at deriving analytical properties of the $K(r,t)$ function, conducting a more comprehensive empirical evaluation, and reducing the computational effort associated with the $K(r,t)$ calculations.

# Acknowledgment

Research reported in this paper was supported in part by the National Science Foundation through Grant #IIS-0428241. The second author is also affiliated with the Key Lab of Complex Systems and Intelligence Science, Chinese Academy of Sciences, and was supported in part by a grant for open research projects (ORP-0303) from the Chinese Academy of Sciences and a grant (60573078) from the National Science Foundation of China. We wish to thank Dr. Cecil Lynch for providing the dataset used in this study and related discussions. We also thank Mr. Wei Chang and other members of the NSF-funded BioPortal project for informative and constructive discussions.

# References

[1]   W. Chang, D. Zeng, and H. Chen, "A Novel Spatio-Temporal Data Analysis Approach based on Prospective Support Vector Clustering," in the Proceedings of 15th Annual Workshop on Information Technologies and Systems, Las Vegas, Nevada, 2005.

[2]   M. Kulldorff, "Prospective time periodic geographical disease surveillance using a scan statistic," *Journal of the Royal Statistical Society Series a-Statistics in Society*, vol. 164, pp. 61-72, 2001.

[3]   B. D. Ripley, "Second-Order Analysis of Stationary Point Processes," *Journal of Applied Probability*, vol. 13, pp. 255-266, 1976.

[4]   B. D. Ripley, *Spatial Statistics*. New York: Wiley, 1981.

[5]   D. Stoyan and A. Penttinen, "Recent applications of point process methods in forestry statistics," *Statistical Science*, vol. 15, pp. 61-78, 2000.

[6]   K. F. Gaines, A. L. Bryan, and P. M. Dixon, "The effects of drought on foraging habitat selection of breeding Wood Storks in coastal Georgia," *Waterbirds*, vol. 23, pp. 64-73, 2000.

[7]   P. J. Diggle and A. G. Chetwynd, "Second-Order Analysis of Spatial Clustering for Inhomogeneous Populations," *Biometrics*, vol. 47, pp. 1155-1163, 1991.

[8]   P. M. Dixon, "Ripley's K function," in *Encyclopedia of Environmetrics*, vol. 3, L. John Wiley & Sons, Ed. Chichester, 2002, pp. 1796–1803.

# Integration of Instance-Based Learning and Text Mining for Identification of Potential Virus/Bacterium as Bio-terrorism Weapons*

Xiaohua Hu[1], Xiaodan Zhang[1], Daniel Wu[1], Xiaohua Zhou[1] , and Peter Rumm[2]

[1] College of Information Science and Technology, Drexel University,
Philadelphia, PA 19104
{thu, xzhang, daniel.wu, xiaohua.zhou}@cis.drexel.edu
[2] School of Public Health, Drexel University, Philadelphia, PA 19104
pdr26@drexel.edu

**Abstract.** There are some viruses and bacteria that have been identified as bioterrorism weapons. However, there are a lot other viruses and bacteria that can be potential bioterrorism weapons. A system that can automatically suggest potential bioterrorism weapons will help laypeople to discover these suspicious viruses and bacteria. In this paper we apply instance-based learning & text mining approach to identify candidate viruses and bacteria as potential bio-terrorism weapons from biomedical literature. We first take text mining approach to identify topical terms of existed viruses (bacteria) from PubMed separately. Then, we use the term lists as instances to build matrices with the remaining viruses (bacteria) to discover how much the term lists describe the remaining viruses (bacteria). Next, we build a algorithm to rank all remaining viruses (bacteria). We suspect that the higher the ranking of the virus (bacterium) is, the more suspicious they will be potential bio-terrorism weapon. Our findings are intended as a guide to the virus and bacterium literature to support further studies that might then lead to appropriate defense and public health measures.

## 1 Introduction

Terrorist attack concerns many people in the world. Biological agent is one of five categories of terrorist weapons. For certain biological agents, the potential for devastating casualties is very high. The anthrax mail attack in October, 2001 terrorism caused 23 cases of anthrax-related illness and 5 deaths. Due to the widespread availability of agents, widespread knowledge of production methodologies, and potential dissemination devices, bioterrorism can be very cute for now and future. Because it is very difficult for laypeople diagnose and recognize most of the diseases caused by biological weapons, we need surveillance systems to keep an eye on potential uses of such biological weapons [1]. In this paper, we propose an instance based learning method to discover biological agents as potential Bioterrorism Weapons (BW).

---

* This work is supported partially by the NSF Career grant IIS 0448023 and NSF 0514679 and PA Dept of Health Tobacco Formula Grants.

S. Mehrotra et al. (Eds.): ISI 2006, LNCS 3975, pp. 548–553, 2006.

Before discovering potential BW, it's reasonable to study the characteristics of biological agents identified by human experts as BW. Some human experts have generalized some criteria for identifying virus and bacteria. The more detail is in section 3. However, it's hard for human being to map all the viruses and bacteria one by one to these criteria. Moreover, the list is compiled manually, requiring extensive specialized human resources and time. Because the biological agents such as viruses are evolving through mutations, biological or chemical change, some biological substances have the potential to turn into deadly virus through chemical/genetic/biological reaction, there should be an automatic approach to keep track of existing suspicious viruses and to discover new viruses as potential weapons. We expect that it would be very useful to identify those biological substances and take precaution actions or measurements. For better studying the characteristics of existed biological agents as BW, we use a text mining approach to extract topical MeSH terms from them. This is an exhaustive approach, so we believe that the topical MeSH terms we extract are very representative of the particular BW collection. Then, we use this discovered terms to build a term biological agent matrix from which we check how much these terms can be topical terms for the remaining biological agents. Later, we use the combination of these terms to rank each remaining biological agent. In the end, we get a top ranked term list that can be used as key words for human experts to examine the remaining biological agents. The most important is that we generate a biological agent as potential BW ranked by the extracted terms from the existed biological agents. We suspect that the higher rank the biological agent, the more it can become potential BW.

## 2   Related Works

The problem of mining implicit knowledge/information from biomedical literature was exemplified by Dr. Swanson's pioneering work on Raynaud disease/fish-oil discovery in 1986 [5]. Back then, the Raynaud disease had no known cause or cure, and the goal of his literature-based discovery was to uncover novel suggestions for how Raynaud disease might be caused, and how it might be treated. He found from biomedical literature that Raynaud disease is a peripheral circulatory disorder aggravated by high platelet aggregation, high blood viscosity and vasoconstriction. In another separate set of literature on fish oils, he found out the ingestion of fish oil can reduce these phenomena. But no single article from both sets in the biomedical literature mentions Raynaud and fish oil together in 1986. Putting these two separate literatures together, Swanson hypothesized that fish oil may be beneficial to people suffering from Raynaud disease [5] [6]. This novel hypothesis was later clinically confirmed by DiGiacomo in 1989 [2]. Later on [4] Dr. Swanson extended his methods to search literature for potential virus. But the biggest limitation of his methods is that, only 3 properties/criteria of a virus are used as search key word and the semantic information is ignored in the search procedure. In this paper, we present a novel biomedical literature mining algorithms based on this philosophy with significant extensions. Our objective is to extend the existing known virus list compiled by CDC or bacterium recognized by domain experts as BTW to other viruses/ bacteria that might have similar characteristics. We thus hypothesize that viruses/bacteria that have been researched with respect to the characteristics possessed by existing viruses are leading candidates for extending the virus/bacterium lists. Our findings are intended as a guide to the according literature to support further studies that might then lead to appropriate defense and public health measures.

## 3   Background of Virus and Bacterium

Before initiating suspicious viruses and bacteria mining systems, we should identify what biological agents could be used as biological weapons.

### 3.1   Virus

Geissler identified and summarized 13 criteria (shown in Table 1) to identify biological warfare agents as viruses [3]. Based on the criteria, he compiled 21 viruses. Figure 1 lists the 21 virus names in MeSH terms. The viruses in Figure 1 meet some of the criteria described in Table 1.

| | |
|---|---|
| ▪ Hemorrhagic Fever Virus, Crimean-Congo | ▪ Encephalitis Virus, Eastern Equine |
| ▪ Lymphocytic choriomeningitis virus | ▪ Encephalitis Virus, Japanese |
| ▪ Encephalitis Virus, Venezuelan Equine | ▪ Encephalitis Viruses, Tick-Borne |
| ▪ Encephalitis Virus, Western Equine | ▪ Encephalitis Virus, St. Louis |

| | | |
|---|---|---|
| ▪ Arenaviruses, New World | ▪ Chikungunya virus | ▪ Hepatitis A virus |
| ▪ Marburg-like Viruses | ▪ Dengue Virus | ▪ Orthomyxoviridae |
| ▪ Rift Valley fever virus | ▪ Ebola-like Viruses | ▪ Junin virus |
| ▪ Yellow fever virus | ▪ Hantaan virus | ▪ Lassa virus |
| | | ▪ Variola virus |

**Fig. 1.** Geissler's 21 Viruses

Based on the criteria, government agencies such as CDC and the Department of Homeland Security compile and monitor viruses which are known to be dangerous in bio-terrorism.

### 3.2   Bacterium

There are known 13 bacteria that can cause deadly disease. For example, anthrax is an acute infectious disease caused by the spore-forming bacterium Bacillus anthracis. Anthrax most commonly occurs in wild and domestic lower vertebrates (cattle, sheep, goats, camels, antelopes, and other herbivores), but it can also occur in humans when they are exposed to infected animals or to tissue from infected animals or when anthrax spores are used as a bioterrorist weapon. Q fever is a zoonotic disease caused by Coxiella burnetii, a species of bacteria that is distributed globally. Coxiella burnetii is a highly infectious agent that is rather resistant to heat and drying. It can become airborne and inhaled by humans. A single C. burnetii organism may cause disease in a susceptible person. This agent could be developed for use in biological warfare and is considered a potential terrorist threat. For other deadly diseases caused by bacteria, please refer table 1.

**Table 1.** Bacteria used in biological warfare

| Bacteria name (caused disease) | Bacteria name (caused disease) |
| --- | --- |
| Bacillus anthracis (authrax) | Francisella tularensis (tularemia) |
| Clostridium botulinum (botulism) | Burkholderia mallei, Burkholderia pseudomallei (glanders) |
| Brucella melitensis, Brucella abortus, Brucella suis (brucellosis) | Coxiella burnetti (Q fever) |
| Vibrio cholerae (cholera) | Salmonella (Salmonellosis, typhoid fever) |
| Yersinia pestis (plague) | Shigella dysenteriae (shigellosis) |

## 4   Method

MedMeSH Summarizer [8] summarizes a group of genes by filtering the biomedical literature and assigning relevant keywords describing the functionality of a group of genes. Each Gene cluster contains $N$ genes, while each gene has a set of terms associated with it. A co-occurrence matrix is thus built, with number of citations associated with the gene and containing the mesh term as the cell value. Based on this matrix and some statistical information, they made overall relevance ranking for all the terms describing the topic of certain cluster of genes. There are 630 bacteria defined in PubMed database. We found it quite reasonable to extract topical terms for known 13 bacteria and then use these terms to look for suspicious remaining bacteria.

- **Normalized Term Bacterium Matrix**

$$\tilde{f}_{ij} = F_{ij} / (\sum_{i=1}^{M} F_{ij})^{\alpha} \ (0 \leq \alpha \leq 1) \tag{1}$$

where $F_{ij}$ is a term by bacteria matrix. It means that how many PUBMED documents retrieved by bacterium j contains term i.

- **Relevance Ranking**

1. Cluster Topics (Major): Terms occur in most bacteria with high frequency. Criterion $R1$: Rank the MeSH terms by decreasing order of the means $\mu_j$.

2. Cluster Topics (Minor): Terms occur in most bacteria with low frequency. Compute $\sigma_i = \sqrt{(\sum_{j=1}^{N}(\tilde{f}_{ij} - \mu_i)^2)/N}$. Criterion $R2$: Rank the MeSH terms by decreasing order of the ratios $\mu_j / \sigma_i$'s.

3. Particular Topics: Terms occur in a few bacteria with high frequency. Criterion $R3$: Rank the MeSH terms by decreasing order of the ratios $\sigma_i^2 / \mu_j$'s.

4. Each MeSH term in $\Omega$ is ranked based on each of the above three criteria. The terms were then given an overall relevance rank $R$ where:

$$R = wR_1 + ((1-w)/2)R_2 + ((1-w)/2)R_3 \tag{2}$$

The weight parameter in formula ② has been assigned so that the major topics are given weight $w$ being the most important set of terms in providing a summary of the cluster. The remaining weight $1 - w$ is divided equally between the minor topics and the particular topics. In our system, w is set to 0.5 because we look for more topical terms of the whole bacteria cluster.

- **Procedure of Algorithm**
  1. Submit query "bacteria name [major]" to the pubmed and download Mesh term after applying stop word list for each biological agent. We download documents of 13 existing bacteria. Our stop word list is composed of MeSH terms extracted from PubMed documents (1994-2004) by their overall usage. For example, some MeSH term without biomedical meaning is used very frequently such as "Government Supported".
  2. Build a normalized matrix (①) of terms by bacterium (13 bacteria).
  3. Rank all the terms according to formula② and pick top k terms.
  4. Download the documents of the remaining 617 bacteria. And use terms above to build a matrix of terms by bacteria (617 bacteria) (①).
  5. Let the rank value of term be $R_i$. We use formula $R^B = \sum_{i=1}^{M} \tilde{f}_{ij} \times R_i$ to rank each bacterium.

## 5  Experimental Results

We apply our method to two data sets: viruses and bacteria. As for space, we only list the result of bacteria. Table 2 displays the top ranked bacteria by $R^B$ criteria.

**Table 2.** Ranked bacterium

|    | Top 1-10 | weight |    | Top 11-20 | weight |
|----|----------|--------|----|-----------|--------|
| 1  | Clostridium tetani | 38.8 | 11 | Brucellaceae | 23.68 |
| 2  | Erysipelothrix | 36.96 | 12 | Campylobacter fetus | 22.74 |
| 3  | Coxiellaceae | 31.57 | 13 | Yersinia enterocolitica | 21.95 |
| 4  | Sarcina | 31.27 | 14 | Bacillus thuringiensis | 21.24 |
| 5  | Yersinia pseudotuberculosis | 28.16 | 15 | Pediococcus | 21.2 |
| 6  | Atypical Bacterial | 26.41 | 16 | Mycobacterium bovis | 20.36 |
| 7  | Corynebacterium diphtheriae | 26.22 | 17 | Proteus vulgaris | 20.23 |
| 8  | Photobacterium | 26.13 | 18 | Haemophilus influenzae-b | 19.89 |
| 9  | Brucella | 24.9 | 19 | Nocardia asteroides | 19.88 |
| 10 | Haemophilus ducreyi | 24.69 | 20 | Bacillus megaterium | 19.69 |

## 6  Potential Significance for Public Health and Homeland Security

This work is critical to public health and homeland security. Our nation is spending alone this year just in disbursements to states, terrorities and local health over a billion dollars to prepare for terrorism including such efforts as building public health capacity, disease surveillance and laboratory notification. [9] However, without the ability to prioritize these resources which have improved public health capacity and laboratory capacity we cannot further improve both national and international preparedness efforts [10]. In 1999 the Department of Defense was involved in building a directory of known emerging infectious diseases and laboratory tests worldwide and identified approximately 40 high threat agents for bio-terrorism including many of the hemorrhagic viruses [11]. However since that time we have had the emergence of SARS, Avian Flu virus and many other threats to the public health. We must be prepared and without continued work such as this to identify additional threats, the preparedness efforts may fall short.

# References

1. SdfsdfBüchen-Osmond C. Taxonomy and Classification of Viruses. In: Manual of Clinical Microbiology, ASM Press, Washington DC, 8th ed, Vol 2, p. 1217-1226, 2003
2. DiGiacome, R.A, Kremer, J.M. and Shah, D.M. Fish oil dietary supplementation is patients with Raynaud's phenomenon: A double-blind, controlled, prospective study, American Journal of Medicine, 158-164m, 8, 1989.
3. Geissler, E. (Ed.), Biological and toxin weapons today, Oxford, UK: SIPRI (1986)
4. Swanson, DR, Smalheiser NR, & Bookstein A. Information discovery from complementary literatures: categorizing viruses as potential weapons. JASIST 52(10): 797-812 , 2001
5. Swanson, DR., Fish-oil, Raynaud's Syndrome, and undiscovered public knowledge. Perspectives in Biology and Medicine 30(1), 7-18, 1986
6. Swanson, DR., Undiscovered public knowledge. Libr. Q. 56(2), pp. 103-118 1986
7. Hu X., I. Yoo. P. Rumm, M. Atwood., Mining Candidate Viruses as Potential Bio-Terrorism Weapons from Biomedical Literature, in 2005 IEEE International Conference on Intelligence and Security Informatics (IEEE ISI-2005), Atlanta, Georgia, May 19-20, 2005
8. P. Kankar, S. Adak, A. Sarkar, K. Murari, K. and G. Sharma. "MedMeSH Summarizer: Text Mining for Gene Clusters", in the Proceedings of the Second SIAM International Conference on Data Mining, Arlington, VA, 2002
9. Guidance on cooperative agreements from the U.S. Department of Health and Human Services, Centers for Disease Control and Prevention and the Human Resource Service Administration. Accessible at www.bt.cdc.gov
10. Rumm P.D. Bioterrorism preparedness: potential threats remain.  Am J Public Health. 2005 Mar;95(3):372 (comment on previous article)
11. Rumm P, Gaydos J, Mansfield J and Kelley P, A Department of Defense (DOD) Virtual Public Health Laboratory Directory, *Mil Med*, 2000;Jul,165-Supp. 2):73.

# An Info-Gap Approach to Policy Selection for Bio-terror Response

Anna Yoffe[1] and Yakov Ben-Haim[2]

[1] Faculty of Mechanical Engineering, Technion,
32000 Haifa, Israel
annay@tx.technion.ac.il
[2] Yitzhak Moda'i Chair in Technology and Economics,
Faculty of Mechanical Engineering, Technion,
32000 Haifa, Israel
yakov@technion.ac.il

**Abstract.** Bio-terror events are accompanied by severe uncertainty: great disparity between the best available data and models, and the actual course of events. We model this uncertainty with non-probabilistic information-gap models of uncertainty. This paper focuses on info-gaps in epidemiological models, in particular, info-gaps in the rate of infection. robustness to uncertainty is defined as a function of the required critical morbidity resulting from the attack. We show how preferences among available interventions are deduced from the robustness function. We demonstrate the irrevocable trade-off between robustness and demanded performance, and show that best-estimated performance has zero robustness. Finally, we present a theorem concerning the reversal of preferences between available interventions, and illustrate it with a numerical example.

## 1 Introduction and Motivation

The constant threat of bio-terror attacks on civilian populations in recent years has emphasized the importance of mathematical models as policy planning tools [1] – [5]. Due to the paucity of accurate scientific knowledge about the mechanisms underlying the dynamics of bio-terror events, attempts to model them will inevitably include a wide range of hypothetical premises and assumptions about the unknown. A careful decision maker should therefore treat results that are provided by conventional mathematical models skeptically, keeping in mind that no model accurately reflects unknown future occurrences, even more so due to the severe lack of reliable information.

When developing models to support a decision process, the uncertainties — the information gaps — should be carefully identified and incorporated into the models. The aim of this paper is to present a new methodology, info-gap decision theory, in mathematical modeling of highly uncertain phenomena, such as the aftermath of a bio-terror attack. Info-gap theory provides a new option-ranking criterion that allows the decision makers to evaluate the robustness of their decisions to uncertainty, and also to assess the possibility of better than anticipated outcomes that the uncertainty may favor us with.

Probabilistic and statistical tools are suitable when the underlying processes are understood and stable. Info-gap decision theory, on the contrary, is most useful when decisions of high significance must be made in unique situations of high uncertainty.

## 2    Epidemic Model from an Info-Gap Point of View

Info-gap theory was invented and developed to provide decision makers with analytical tools that help establish preferences and to assess risks and opportunities when there is a severe lack of reliable information [6]. To outline the basic principles of info-gap theory and its applications in the field of defense against bioterrorism, we consider a simple epidemic model adopted from [7].

The model represents a spread of some highly infectious but not lethal disease, assuming that the total population of size $N$ consists of susceptibles, $x(t)$ and infectives, $y(t)$. Infectives remain in contact with susceptibles for all time $t \geq 0$. Once a susceptible is infected, he becomes an infective and remains in that state. The susceptibles and infectives mix homogeneously with rate $\beta$, and in absence of intervention, according to this model, all the individuals in the population eventually become infected (at $t = \infty$ in equation (3)).

The equations describing the epidemic are:

$$x(t) + y(t) = N, t \geq 0 \tag{1}$$

$$\frac{dy}{dt} = \beta xy = \beta(N - y)y \tag{2}$$

were $\beta$ and $N$ are constant. Solving equation (2) we get:

$$y(t, \beta) = \frac{y_0 N}{y_0 + (N - y_0)\exp(-\beta N t)} \tag{3}$$

were $y_o$ is the initial size of infected population at the beginning of the event, i.e at time $t = 0$.

In this simple model we view the $\beta$ and $N$ as decision parameters, i.e. response strategies may be formulated in terms of their influence on $\beta$ and $N$. For example, timely announcement of an event may, for better or worse, affect the infection rate $\beta$. Different quarantine or vaccination policies may regulate the population size, $N$. The actual impact of policy interventions on outcomes is highly uncertain. By defining the notions of robustness of uncertain effects on $\beta$ and $N$, we will establish the preference ranking on the available policies.

## 3    Modeling the Uncertainty

A wise decision making process not only should rely upon available knowledge, but also must not ignore the absence of information, as if all we know is all there is. Info-gap theory views uncertainty as an unbounded family of nested sets of all possible events, and supplies a mechanism of incorporating this into the mathematical models.

To illustrate this we formulate here a simple model of uncertainty in the pair-wise rate of infection $\beta$.

Say we have a conjecture that the nominal pair-wise rate of infection varies over time in the following manner: It has a constant value, until time $t_a$, at which the announcement of a terrorist attack in public and other possible preventive measures take place. As a result the pair-wise rate of infection is expected to decline, but in an uncertain manner, i.e.:

$$\bar{\beta}(t) = \begin{cases} \bar{\beta} & \text{if } 0 \leq t \leq t_a \\ \bar{\beta} + \bar{\delta}t & \text{else} \end{cases} \tag{4}$$

and $\bar{\beta}$ and $\bar{\delta} < 0$ are constant. Since the real infection rate $\beta(t)$ is not known, we assume that it may differ from the conjectured rate of infection $\bar{\beta}(t)$, such that the relative error does not exceed some unknown "horizon" of uncertainty $\alpha \geq 0$. Here $\alpha$ is unbounded in its value, and thus admits all possible relative errors. The appropriate info-gap model would be an unbounded family of nested sets:

$$U(\alpha, \bar{\beta}(t)) = \left\{ \beta(t) : \left| \frac{\beta(t) - \bar{\beta}(t)}{\bar{\beta}(t)} \right| \leq \alpha, \beta(t) > 0 \right\}, \alpha \geq 0. \tag{5}$$

Note that if we take $t_a = \infty$, i.e. we don't announce the attack, we get that our conjectured infection rate is constant over time, $\bar{\beta}(t) = \bar{\beta}$.

## 4    Making Robust Decisions

Perfectly optimal solutions cannot be identified with highly imperfect models. We suggest looking for robust satisfactory decisions instead of optimal ones. But what is a robust decision? How does one measure robustness? Info-gap theory is well equipped to answer these questions. The evaluation of robustness to uncertainty is done by the means of the *robustness function* that expresses the greatest level of uncertainty at which failure cannot occur.

To be more specific, consider the demand that the size of the infected population, $y(t_c, \beta(t))$, at some time $t_c$ such that $t_a < t_c$, does not exceed some critical value $Y_c$. Solving equation (2) with $\beta = \beta(t)$ and using our nominal function $\bar{\beta}(t)$ we may estimate that at time $t_c$ infected population size is:

$$y(t_c, \bar{\beta}(t)) = \frac{y_0 N}{y_0 + (N - y_0) \exp\left[ -N(\bar{\beta}t_c - \bar{\delta}(t_c^2 - t_a^2)/2) \right]} \tag{6}$$

Since the function $\bar{\beta}(t)$ is most possibly wrong, the result in equation (6) is hardly reliable and therefore is not a good basis for choosing policy interventions which influence $\bar{\beta}(t)$ or $N$. In the following subsections we introduce the notion of robustness to uncertainty in $\bar{\beta}(t)$ by defining and calculating the robustness function. Through this example we show how the robustness function enables us to measure the reliability of policy interventions, make the adequate preferences and view the unavoidable trade-offs in demands and expectations vs. robustness to uncertainty.

## 4.1   Definition and Calculation of the Robustness Function

The robustness to uncertainty in $\bar{\beta}(t)$ is the greatest horizon of uncertainty $\alpha$, up to which all possible functions $\beta(t)$ satisfy the requirement that at time $t_c$ the infected population size is not greater than $Y_c$:

$$\widehat{\alpha}(Y_c, \bar{\beta}(t)) = \max \left\{ \alpha : \left( \max_{\beta(t) \in U(\alpha, \bar{\beta}(t))} y(t_c, \beta(t)) \right) \leq Y_c \right\} \tag{7}$$

After some calculations we get:

$$\widehat{\alpha}(Y_c, \bar{\beta}(t)) = \begin{cases} 0 & , \; 0 \leq Y_c \leq y(t_c, \bar{\beta}(t)) \\ \frac{1}{N(\beta t_c - \delta(t_c^2 - t_a^2)/2)} \ln\left(\frac{Y_c(N-y_0)}{y_0(N-Y_c)}\right) - 1 & , \; y(t_c, \beta(t)) < Y_c < N \\ \infty & , \; N \leq Y_c \end{cases} \tag{8}$$

where $t_a \leq t_c$.

It is easily seen from equation (8) that decreasing $t_a$ we increase the value of robustness function, confirming our intuition that the earlier we intervene the greater would be our chances that at time $t_c$ the size of infected population will not exceed some critical infection volume $Y_c$.

## 4.2   Basic Properties and Applications of the Robustness Function

Here we outline the basic properties of robustness function, which are also clearly seen from the graphs of robustness functions, in Fig. 1:

Substituting $Y_c = y(t_c, \bar{\beta}(t))$ in equation (8) we get

$$\widehat{\alpha}(y(t_c, \bar{\beta}(t)), \bar{\beta}(t)) = 0 \tag{9}$$

This means that obtaining morbidity as low as the estimated value, $y(t_c, \bar{\beta}(t))$, has no robustness to error in the estimate $\bar{\beta}(t)$. This result is very natural: since the parameter $\bar{\beta}(t)$ is an approximation, and sometimes even a guess, we cannot expect the prediction $y(t_c, \bar{\beta}(t))$ to be reliably realized.

The robustness function $\widehat{\alpha}(Y_c, \bar{\beta}(t))$ is increasing as a function of $Y_c$ and $\lim_{Y_c \to N} \widehat{\alpha}(Y_c, \bar{\beta}(t)) = \infty$. This suggests that in order to gain robustness, one must accept poorer outcomes, i.e. to be content with higher values of critical infection $Y_c$. This property expresses the trade-off between demands and robustness to uncertainty: If high demands (small $Y_c$) are required then only low robustness (small $\widehat{\alpha}$) can be achieved.

If we view $\widehat{\alpha}$ at fixed critical infection volume $Y_c$, we can choose strategies that effect the parameters $N, \bar{\beta}$ and $t_a$ in such a way that they maximize the robustness function. (Actually this is exactly what we argued in (2) when suggesting early announcement.)

When we have several strategies that we need to compare we may use the robustness function to establish the necessary preference. Obviously we would prefer policies that imply greater robustness to uncertainty. In (4.3) we discuss in more detail the essence of this preference ranking.

## 4.3   Crossing of Robustness Curves for Constant $\beta$

In this section we will consider the case when the epidemic is not announced, i.e. $\bar{\beta}(t) = \bar{\beta}$. One of the essential parts in info-gap analysis is the establishment of existence of crossing of different robustness functions (as functions of $Y_c$ and different values of decision parameters). If two robustness curves cross at some value $y^*$ of $Y_c$ then we have a reverse of preferences: Decisions that had high robustness at higher demands, $Y_c < y^*$, become less robust at weaker demands, $Y_c > y^*$. To illustrate this we state without proof here a proposition that assures existence of crossing for robustness functions in our simple epidemic model. We then discuss the possible implications.

**Proposition 1.** *For any given pair $(\bar{\beta}_1, N_1)$ there exist a pair $(\bar{\beta}_2, N_2)$ and a value $y^*$ such that $y_c(\bar{\beta}_1, N_1) < y_c(\bar{\beta}_2, N_2) < y^* < N_2 < N_1$ and $\widehat{\alpha}(y^*, \bar{\beta}_1, N_1) = \widehat{\alpha}(y^*, \bar{\beta}_2, N_2)$.*

Consider a bio-terror attack on a city with a population size $N_1$ and initial estimated infection rate estimate $\bar{\beta}_1$. We can study our preferences among available interventions based on proposition 1 which is illustrated in fig. 2. Let $y^*$ denote the infection volume at which the robustness curves cross, as illustrated in the figure. If we are willing to accept an infection volume larger than $y^*$ at time $t_c$, then fig. 2 shows that we are more robust with interventions which are manifested in $\bar{\beta}_2$ and $N_2$. Greater robustness implies greater preference, so we prefer $\bar{\beta}_2$ and $N_2$ over $\bar{\beta}_1$ and $N_1$. Note that this preference is different from the preference based on the best-estimated infection rates.

On the other hand, if we require that the infection volume at time $t_c$ be less than $y^*$, then we are more robust with interventions $\bar{\beta}_1$ and $N_1$ and hence prefer the corresponding interventions. Succinctly:

$$(\bar{\beta}_2, N_2) \succ (\bar{\beta}_1, N_1) \quad \text{if and only if} \quad Y_c > y^* \tag{10}$$

We note, however, that robustness trades-off against performance, implying that performance-requirement as strict as $Y_c < y^*$ entails very low robustness.

Alternatively, we can establish preferences in terms of required robustness rather than required infection volume. Let $\widehat{\alpha}^*$ denote the value of robustness at which the curves cross in fig. 2. If robustness at least as large as $\widehat{\alpha}^*$ is required, then we prefer $\bar{\beta}_2$ and $N_2$; otherwise we prefer $\bar{\beta}_1$ and $N_1$.

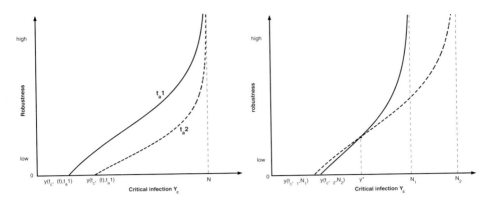

**Fig. 1.** Robustness function versus critical infection volume. Comparing different announcement times $t_a 1 < t_a 2$.

**Fig. 2.** Robustness function versus critical infection volume. Comparing different decision parameters $(\bar{\beta}, N)$.

## 5   Future Research

A natural extension to our work will be moving from a simple epidemic model, which is illustrative but not realistic, to a more hard-nosed epidemiological model. In particular we intend to apply the Info-gap methodology to study the model presented by Kaplan and Wein [1].

**Acknowledgement.** This paper was written with the partial support of the Jewish Institute of Medical Research, Houston, Texas (AY), and the Abramson Family Center for the Future of Health (YBH).

## References

1. E.H. Kaplan, D.L. Craft, L.M. Wein: Analyzing bioterror response logistics: the case of smallpox. *Mathematical Biosciences*, 185 (2003), pp. 33-72.
2. M. E. Halloran, I. M. Longini, Jr., A. Nizam, and Y.Yang: Containing bioterrorist smallpox, *Science*, 298 (2002), pp. 1428-1432.
3. J. Walden, E.H. Kaplan: Estimating Time and Size of Bioterror Attack, *Emerging Infectious Diseases*, Vol. 10, No. 7, July 2004.
4. L. J. Moffitt, J. K. Stranlund, B. C. Field: Inspections to Avert Terrorism: Robustness Under Severe Uncertainty, *Journal of Homeland Security and Emergency Management*, (2005).
5. F. Ellis McKenzie: Smallpox Models as Policy Tools, *Emerging Infectious Diseases*, Vol. 10, No. 11, November, 2004.
6. Y. Ben-Haim: *Information-gap Decision Theory: Decisions Under Severe Uncertainty*, Academic Press, London, 2001.
7. D. J. Daley and J. Gani: *Epidemic Modeling: An Introduction*, Cambridge studies in mathematical biology: 15, 1999.

# Fighting Fear of a Bioterrorism Event with Information Technology: Real-World Examples and Opportunities

David A. Bray and Benn R. Konsynski

Emory University, 1300 Clifton Road
Atlanta, GA 30322
david_bray@bus.emory.edu, benn_konsynski@bus.emory.edu
http://userwww.service.emory.edu/~dbray

**Abstract.** The proximate objective behind a bioterrorism event is to cause fear, with morbidity or mortality as secondary effects. Information technology must empower professionals to respond rapidly and effectively. This paper links detection and identification of a bioterrorism event with opportunities for information technology to aid such efforts, drawing specifically from real-world uses of technology with the Bioterrorism Preparedness and Response Program at the U.S. Centers for Disease Control and Prevention (CDC) from 2000 to the present. Information technology challenges and innovations will be highlighted, as well as lessons learned from the program's response to the anthrax attacks in 2001 and Severe Acute Respiratory Syndrome in 2003.

## 1 Introduction

The U.S. Department of Health and Human Services (DHHS) defines bioterrorism as the use or threatened use of biological agents or toxins against civilians, with the objective of causing fear, illness, or death. A bioterrorism event is said to have occurred regardless whether a disease agent has been released or a hoax has been performed. The role of fear is central to a bioterrorism event; if the sole intention was to cause death, there are much easier ways to cause a mass casualty situation [8].

Why is fear connected strongly with a bioterrorism event? Primarily it is the fear of the unknown, the invisible, and the undetectable that makes the fear of bioterrorism so potent. Since it is difficult to prove with certainty that unknown agents or toxins are not present within a specific building or area, this uncertainty adds to the cycle of fear. Lastly, the self-centric nature of humans causes most individuals to assume that they, personally, may have been exposed to the unseen agent or toxin and should expect to be presenting symptoms at any moment, often causing them to exhibit irrational behaviors [6, 7].

Consequentially, there exists the potential for instigators of a possible bioterrorism event instead to simply prompt the fear associated with such an event, without enlisting the causal disease agent(s). Through electronic global communications, including emails, blogs, and wikis, triggering the spread of erroneous information as to the occurrence of possible bioterrorism event is possible. Government officials at the local, state, and Federal levels would be forced not only to quickly calm public

S. Mehrotra et al. (Eds.): ISI 2006, LNCS 3975, pp. 560–565, 2006.
© Springer-Verlag Berlin Heidelberg 2006

concerns, but also to rapidly sort out truth from fiction to discern whether or not any real disease agent(s) had been released and if so, which ones.

If technology is to help with bioterrorism response, it needs to not only address mitigation of civilian illnesses and deaths, but also help to manage individual and societal fears springing from the real or threatened occurrence of such an event. Timely integration of data at the local, state, and Federal levels can serve as a foundation for biothreat assessment. This foundation in turn, serves to develop a better context for action thresholds related to emergency response, public health decisions, and communications. Fear of the unknown can be overcome with quantified, actionable information.

## 2 Epidemiological Detection of Bioterrorism Events

The first possible detection scenario of a bioterrorism event involves sentinel indicators, where a figurative red flag is raised. The second possible detection scenario includes syndromic surveillance, where a set of odd trends is observed prompting professionals to suspect a possible bioterrorism event. It is important to note that syndromic surveillance differs from active surveillance efforts in that syndromic surveillance is probabilistic and not necessarily definitive in its detection capability – an anomalous event may be associated with other human diseases or behaviors unrelated to bioterrorism or an acute infectious disease outbreak [1].

During the anthrax events of 2001, at the peak of media attention, several key metropolitan health departments opted to establish daily active surveillance efforts in their jurisdiction. While such surveillance efforts increased the likelihood of rapidly identifying additional anthrax-exposure cases, they were also prohibitively expensive to continue long-term past the start of January 2002. In contrast, syndromic surveillance establishes a baseline of activity from an associated data source over a period of time. Analyses of different data sources (e.g. 911 calls, hospital data, school absenteeism data, over the counter drug sales) can be combined for enhanced sensitivity. However, in terms of information technology, syndromic surveillance requires ongoing, routine monitoring of incoming data streams from these data sources; likewise, it requires that these data streams exist in the first place [4].

The anthrax events of 2001 provided a few insights regarding current public health detection capabilities. Prior to such events, most assessments of a bioterrorism event were focused on mass-casualty scenarios. Targeted, limited exposure to a bioterrorism agent was not considered a highly probable scenario, nor was the possibility of contamination of mailed letters through the postal sorting process. In retrospect, syndromic surveillance would not have succeeded at detecting the small number of dispersed cases of intentional exposure to *B. anthracis* in the general population. Conversely, as the anthrax events historically demonstrated in the initial weeks, clinicians themselves were not necessarily all on alert for the possibility that their patients could have been exposed to *B. anthracis* [4, 6].

Neither method of syndromic surveillance nor detection via astute clinicians would have succeeded at rapidly identifying the initial cases of disease associated with the anthrax events of 2001. Fortunately, confirmatory laboratory tests did help with determining exposure status. Further, once a national alert was raised via targeted communications to public health departments and hospital facilities, the value of detection in the anthrax events of 2001 narrowed to becoming mostly dependent on clinicians to diagnose exposure status in patients and provide treatment.

## 3   The Role of Information Technology with Detection

How then, can information technology help with the detection of a bioterrorism event, either overt or covert, in a rapid, cost-effective manner?

Foremost, technology efforts can help detection efforts by advocating standards in electronic reporting of collected epidemiological data and results at the local, state, and Federal levels. Moreover, information technology can advocate standards in the routing and security of data. Solutions are needed to address the replication and reconciliation of locally stored data with de-identified data routed to state or Federal partners. While local and state health departments may be allowed to collect data containing personal identifiers, other state and Federal partners, under the Health Insurance Portability and Accountability Act of 1996 (HIPAA), explicitly may be required not to store or access such personal data [5, 8].

As such, while data should be shared electronically among local, state, and Federal partners during a suspected bioterrorism event, locally stored data when sent to external partners outside of the state collecting the data must be stripped of such identifiers. This poses a problem if the data, at a later date, are updated in the local data store, and said data store needs to inform other partners of the update. What unique identifier is shared among all partners at the local, state, and Federal level, that cannot be linked back to personally identifying data yet allows for such reconciliation to occur? To date, acceptable solutions to this challenge remain elusive [1].

The problem of preserving linkages also occurs if a Federal partner adds associated data to a de-identified data record of an individual and then wishes to send the updated data back to the originating data store – by what mechanism is the updated data to be reconciled with the personally identifying data stored at the local level? How will Federal partners eliminate duplicate data collection if personal identifiers cannot be collected? Further, if two states have data on the same individual, yet cannot share personal identifiers either among themselves, state to state, or with the Federal government – how then is the data to be identified referring to the same, singular individual and thus linked? Attempts to explore these legal and technological challenges continue [1, 3].

The Bioterrorism Preparedness and Response Program (BPRP) at CDC served as a key coordinator and responder to the anthrax attacks in 2001 and Severe Acute Respiratory Syndrome (SARS) in 2003. Since 2000, the program has invested technology resources into an aberration detection solution known as the Early Aberration Reporting System (EARS). The EARS tool was developed to facilitate the analysis of public health surveillance data and is capable of generating either web-based reports or specialized views of analyzed data for suspected bioterrorism or public health emergency. The EARS tool provides users with the choice of applying three content-neutral, aberration detection methods.

BPRP also has provided "drop-in" surveillance assistance for high profile events, chiefly via site-specific implementations of the EARS tool and other tools. Such events require linking to different data streams specific to a locale, and have included the 1999 World Trade Organization Meeting in Seattle, the 2001 Democratic National Convention, and the 2001 Super Bowl.

## 4  Laboratory Identification of Bioterrorism Disease Agents

As part of the "Continuation Guidance for Cooperative Agreement on Public Health Preparedness and Response for Bioterrorism", the CDC has distributed Federal funds to the states to increase the capability of public health labs to isolate, identify, and handle biological agents safely. This funding effort was part of a larger effort known as the Laboratory Response Network (LRN) [2, 6].

The LRN serves as a network of labs prepared to respond to biological and chemical terrorism, and includes state and local public health, veterinary, military, and international labs. All state public health labs are included in the LRN, several local public health and military labs are included additionally. National labs include the CDC and the U.S. Army Medical Research Institute for Infectious Diseases (USAMRIID), both of which possess biosafety level four containment facilities and thus are capable of handling highly infectious agents. The LRN represents a partnership that includes the Association of Public Health Laboratories (APHL), the CDC, U.S. Department of Defense, the Federal Bureau of Investigation, and other collaborating entities. The CDC provides Federal funds to the states through cooperative funding; likewise, DHS provides funding for specific LRN activities. States are entrusted with forming connections between sentinel labs and confirmatory labs [7].

LRN sentinel labs represent the thousands of hospital-based and commercial labs that receive specimens for testing during routine patient care. LRN confirmatory reference labs possess, at a minimum, biosafety level two containment facilities. The LRN has focused on providing rapid lab technologies capable of delivering test results within a minimal period of time (e.g. polymerase chain-reaction techniques, time-resolved fluorescent antibody stainings). Current testing times associated with such technologies range from one to six hours, compared to a traditional bacterial or viral culture, which can take three to seven days for a test result. Since its launch, the LRN has been involved with the anthrax events of 2001, the SARS events of 2003, and the ricin events of 2003-2004. The LRN has also supported numerous other responses to small events, suspected threats, and other public health emergencies [2, 8].

LRN confirmatory lab tests differ from commercial lab tests, as the routing of electronic tests requests and electronic lab test results is not a tightly coupled relationship, but rather a loosely coupled relationship. For such tests, a hospital or clinical facility may begin by requesting a lab test to be performed, and route such an electronic test request to the nearest lab. That lab may be able to do only an initial set of tests before the specimen/sample must be routed to another lab with the equipment and approved facilities capable of continuing the confirmatory testing. This sequence may continue for multiple partners exchanging test requests and returning additional test results.

Given the sensitivity of confirmatory lab test results, as tests are completed, all labs involved may not only have to provide electronic lab test results back to the hospital or clinical facility, but also to their state health department. Their state health department may request that the CDC or other Federal partners do additional confirmatory testing or genomic sub-typing to characterize in detail the specimen/sample.

The net result of this chain of activities is a loosely coupled relationship among multiple entities at the local, state, and Federal levels. Further, some of the entities may be in separate states, raising concerns about transmission of personal identifiers and other sensitive data elements across state lines.

## 5   The Role of Information Technology with Identification

For lab test results, it is essential that linkages between lab specimens/samples collected at the local level be maintained at the state and Federal levels. Database collisions may occur if a lab assigns an identifier to a specimen/sample that has already been assigned by a separate lab, thus rendering the identifier non-unique. Further, similar to detection efforts, locally stored public health data must be stripped of such identifiers when sent to partners who should not have access to specific personal identifiers. However, when lab test results are returned, the results may need to be reconciled with the case history of a patient, presenting a challenging task [3, 6].

Since 2000, BPRP has championed the need for the ability of the LRN member labs to report lab test results electronically. A few states have managed internally to reach agreement as to a common set of standards locally, but externally states are not in agreement. Public health has already attempted some efforts to generate standards, including the National Electronic Disease Surveillance System (NEDSS). NEDSS, however, was designed for disease reporting and surveillance, and its initial design stages did not incorporate specific elements for bioterrorism preparedness and response, nor did the design account for the loosely coupled chain of partners associated with such a response [2, 5].

Thus attention to date has been focused on working with the states themselves to identify a set of standards connecting public health departments, the LRN labs, and possibly hospital electronic data systems for epidemiological surveillance and electronic laboratory reporting. Such efforts are centered on expanding the set of standards contained in Health Level Seven (HL7) to incorporate elements of public health importance. To be of value for bioterrorism preparedness and response, electronic collection of test requests and results requires ongoing, routine monitoring of incoming data streams from laboratory data sources.

The need for electronic laboratory reporting for bioterrorism preparedness and response was demonstrated by the anthrax events of 2001. From October to December 2001, the LRN tested over 121,710 environmental samples nationally. This figure amounts to an estimated one million individual tests total. These collected results demonstrated that the LRN had succeeded in its goal of preparedness and response, as 94% of the samples were tested either by the LRN public health labs or the LRN military labs with the U.S. Department of Defense. Had the CDC been forced to handle the entire volume of the requested lab tests alone, it ostensibly would have been an over-capacity situation.

# 6  Closing Thoughts

What is needed for bioterrorism response is not too different from what is needed for most of public health. Relatively inexpensive, iterative technology solutions are preferable. Public health, including bioterrorism response, has limited resources to dedicate to information technology. Information technology can, must, and is empowering public health professionals to respond quickly and effectively to a bioterrorism event, specifically with regard to detection of possible biological agents and rapid laboratory identification at the local, state, and Federal levels.

# References

1. Centers for Disease Control and Prevention, 2002 Supplemental Guidance, Technical Review Criteria Focus Area B (Atlanta, GA: 2002)
2. Centers for Disease Control and Prevention, 2002 Supplemental Guidance, Technical Review Criteria Focus Area C (Atlanta, GA: 2002)
3. Institute of Medicine, Learning from SARS: Preparing for the Next Disease Outbreak. Workshop Summary (Washington, DC: Jan 2004)
4. Morbidity and Mortality Weekly Report, Evaluation of B. anthracis Contamination Inside the Brentwood Mail Processing and Distribution Center, MMWR 50 (Atlanta, GA: 2001)
5. RAND Science and Technology Policy Institute, A Framework for Information Technology Infrastructure for Bioterrorism, Results of the 1st Summit (Washington, DC: Dec 2001)
6. U.S. General Accounting Office, Bioterrorism: Preparedness Varied Across State and Local Jurisdictions, GAO-03-373 (Washington, DC: April 2003)
7. U.S. General Accounting Office, Homeland Security: New Department Could Improve Coordination but Transferring Control of Certain Public Health Programs Raises Concerns, GAO-02-954T (Washington, DC: July 2002)
8. U.S. General Accounting Office, Infectious Disease Outbreaks: Bioterrorism Preparedness Efforts Have Improved Public Health Response Capacity, but Gaps Remain, GAO-03-654T (Washington, DC: April 2003)

# Covering Based Granular Computing for Conflict Analysis

William Zhu[1,2,3] and Fei-Yue Wang[3,4]

[1] College of Information Engineering, Jiangxi Normal University, Nanchang, China
[2] Department of Computer Sciences, The University of Auckland, New Zealand
[3] The Key Laboratory of Complex Systems and Intelligent Science,
Institute of Automation, The Chinese Academy of Sciences, Beijing 100080, China
[4] SIE Department, The University of Arizona, Tucson, AZ 85721, USA
fzhu009@ec.auckland.ac.nz, feiyue@sie.arizona.edu

**Abstract.** Conflicts are widespread in our society owing to the scarcity of physical resources, different cultures and religions. The Chinese Wall security policy is a conflicts model originally proposed by Brewer and Nash for information access control. The rapid development of intelligence and security informatics prompts us to revisit this policy and we use granular computing based on covering rough set theory to study the problems of conflicts of interest in database access security. This new method catches the IAR(in ally with relation) more accurately. It also has potential application to issues in intelligence and security informatics such as information sharing policy and governance.

## 1 Introduction

Conflicts are ubiquitous phenomena in every level of our society, from intrapersonal to global, and they are also typical in mechanical systems, electronic systems, software systems, and other systems. In order to deal with a conflict constructively, it first needs to be understood. As a result, conflict analysis and resolution plays an important role in business, political and lawsuits disputes, military operations, national security, and etc. Many models and methods have been proposed and investigated [1, 2, 3, 4, 5, 6].

The rapid development of intelligence and security informatics reflects the importance of conflict analysis and resolution, and also provides a realistic area for application of conflict analysis. One of the aims of intelligence and security informatics is to find conflict phenomena inundated in enormous data and propose resolutions to them [5, 7, 8, 9].

There are various models and techniques for analysis of conflicts using graph theory, topology, differential equations, and others [1, 3, 4]. Pawlak explored analysis of conflicts based on ideas of rough set theory [3, 4], a tool to conceptualize, organize and analyse various types of data in data mining. In Pawlak's model, some issues of conflicts are chosen and the agents taking part in the dispute are asked to specify their standings: conflict, alliance, or neutrality.

S. Mehrotra et al. (Eds.): ISI 2006, LNCS 3975, pp. 566–571, 2006.

In [10, 11, 12, 13, 14], Lin used granular computing, a label of many methodologies in artificial intelligence such as fuzzy set theory, rough set theory, etc, to study a model of conflict analysis called the Chinese Walls Security Policy, a prototype originally proposed by Brewer and Nash [15] to build an impenetrable firewall, called the Chinese Wall, between datasets of competing companies. The basic idea behind the Chinese Walls Security Policy is to establish suitable walls between datasets such that no person is allowed to get access to information on the wrong side of the wall.

In this paper, we propose a model of granular computing based on general coverings [16, 17, 18] and apply it to conflict analysis. The remainder of this paper is organized as follows: Section 2 introduces a conflict analysis model, the Chinese Wall security policy, and a solution to it based on binary relation by Lin. In Section 3, we use coverings based granular computing to study the Chinese Wall security policy. We point out coverings are more reasonable than binary relations for modeling the Chinese Wall security policy, and we define enemy datasets and alliance datasets for every dataset to capture the conflict of interest. Through examples, the simple Chinese Wall security policy is expatiated. This paper concludes in section 4.

## 2   Chinese Wall Security Policy

The ubiquity of conflicts in our society means that support is demanded not only by decision-makers, but also by mediators, who propose resolutions, and policy-makers who determine the structures within which conflicts are to be resolved. Various models and techniques for analysis of conflicts have been proposed to cope with problems of interest conflicts.

The Chinese Wall security policy is a commercial security policy model proposed and formally formulated by Brewer and Nash [15] to diminish the dominance of military security thinking in computer security, especially the Bell-LaPadula(BLP) model. In the BLP model, access to data is constrained by attributes of data involved, while in this new model, access to data is restricted by "conflict of interest classes" and the history of his previous access. In another word, access to a dataset is only granted to a person, called a subject, if the dataset, called an object,

a) is in the same company dataset as an object already accessed by that subject, i.e. within the Wall, or
b) belong to an entirely different conflict of interest class.

For example, to a consultant of a consulting firm which serves for companies A, B, C, and D, if A and B do the same business, say insurance, A and B are in conflict of interest. The consultant has the freedom to choose to read the documents of A or B, but as soon as he reads the documents of A, he is not allowed to read the documents of B, otherwise his consulting is not fair for either A or B. This seminal idea has drawn attention of others researchers [5, 10, 11, 12, 13, 14].

## 2.1   Lin's Model

Lin pointed out that, though Brewer and Nash's model was a great idea, it was based on an incorrect assumption that corporate data can be partitioned into mutually disjoint conflict of interest classes, thus, Lin formulated a modified model, called the aggressive Chinese Wall Security Policy model and studied this model through granular computing [10, 11, 12, 13, 14], which is a label of techniques and tools which make use of granules in the process of problem solving and involves various research fields in artificial intelligence, machine learning, etc. In Lin's model, two core concepts are CIR(Conflict of Interest Relation) and IAR(In Ally with Relation). In Brewer and Nash's model, CIR is an equivalence relation, but, as said by Lin, it is not always true. CIR-classes are not a partition but a covering of corporate data. Lin uses the binary relation to describe such a covering, but as shown in the next section, covering itself is a better tool.

Lin reformulated axioms for CIR and defined IAR as a complement of CIR. The axioms of CIR are:

CIR-1:  CIR is symmetric.
CIR-2:  CIR is anti-reflexive.
CIR-3:  CIR is anti-transitive.

In this way, IAR, the complement of CIR, is an equivalence relation.

This model has potential applications to the malicious Trojan horse problem in certain discretionary access control model.

## 3   Covering Based Solution

While Lin's model is sound for some situations, it is not valid for some other cases. For example, IAR is not necessarily an equivalence relation. A friend of one of our friends is not necessarily our friend. Among axioms CIR-1, CIR-2, CIR-3, only CIR-1 is necessary. A covering model is more reasonable to capture the conflict of interest relation since a covering holds the symmetric property intrinsically.

Let $U$ be all objects, **CIC** a covering of $U$ where, $\forall K \in \mathbf{C}$, objects in $K$ are in conflict with each other. We also call such a covering **CIC** a conflict of interest clusters(CIC) to distinguish it from the conflict of interest classes, which are a partition in Brewer and Nash's model. Under this covering, the enemy set of $x \in U$ is defined as $enemy(x) = \overline{\{x\}} - \{x\} = \cup\{K \in \mathbf{C} | x \in K\} - \{x\}$. If a subject has accessed an object $x$, he is not allowed to access any object in $enemy(x)$. Accordingly, the ally set of $x$ is defined as $ally(x) = U - enemy(x)$. As a binary relation on $U$, $IAR$ can be defined as follow. $IAR = \{(x,y) | y \in ally(x)\}$. In this covering based model, access is only granted if the object requested:

a) is in the same company dataset as an object already accessed by that subject, i.e. within the Wall, or
b) does not belong to a conflict of interest cluster in which any object has been accessed.

**Table 1.** A Conflict of Interest Relation

| COMPANY | COMPANY |
|---------|---------|
| A | B |
| A | C |
| A | E |
| B | A |
| B | C |
| C | A |
| C | B |
| C | D |
| C | E |
| D | C |
| D | E |
| E | A |
| E | C |
| E | D |
| E | G |
| F | G |
| G | F |

Through sets $enemy(x)$ and $ally(x)$, access policy can be rephrased as follows: Assuming $x_1, \ldots, x_m$ are all objects a subject has already accessed, a new access to object $o$ request from this subject is only granted if $o$ is not in $enemy(x_1) \cup \ldots \cup enemy(x_m)$. In other words, $o$ is in $ally(x_1) \cap \ldots \cap ally(x_m)$.

*Example 1 (enemy(x) and ally(x)).* Suppose a consulting firm, say CONSULT, works for the following companies: A, B, C, D, E, F, and G. The conflicts of interest are as in Table 1, then **CIC**= $\{K_1, K_2, K_3, K_4, K_5\}$ where $K_1 = \{A, B, C\}$, $K_2 = \{C, D, E\}$, $K_3 = \{A, E\}$, $K_4 = \{E, G\}$, and $K_5 = \{F, G\}$.

The enemy sets are as follows.
$enemy(A) = \{B, C, E\}$, $enemy(B) = \{A, C\}$, $enemy(C) = \{A, B, D, E\}$, $enemy(D) = \{C, E\}$, $enemy(E) = \{A, C, D, G\}$, $enemy(F) = \{G\}$, and $enemy(G) = \{E, F\}$.

The ally sets are as follows.
$ally(A) = \{A, D, F, G\}$, $ally(B) = \{B, D, E, F, G\}$, $ally(C) = \{C, F, G\}$, $ally(D) = \{A, B, D, F, G\}$, $ally(E) = \{B, E, F\}$, ally(F)=$\{A, B, C, D, E, F\}$, and $ally(G) = \{A, B, C, D, G\}$.

*Example 2 (Chinese Wall security policy).* Suppose the conflicts of interest relation is the same as the above example. The Chinese Wall security policy is as follows. At start, a consultant from CONSULT can choose any object(dataset) to access. As soon as he got access to a dataset, for example, of company A, he is not allowed to get access to a dataset of company B, C, and E from $enemy(A)$, but he still can get access to datasets of company A, D, F, and G from $ally(A)$. After he got access to datasets of company A and G, he is not allowed to get access to datasets of company B, C, E, and F from $enemy(A) \cup enemy(G)$, but he is still allowed to access to datasets of company A, D, and G from $ally(A) \cap ally(G)$. After he chose to access a dataset of company, he is not allowed to get access to any dataset from other company, except those he already accessed, i. e. datasets of company A, D, and G.

## 4   Conclusions

We use covering based granular computing to formulate a covering based Chinese Wall security policy model for conflict analysis in information sharing to prevent insider threats. It is a more suitable model than an equivalence relation based one to capture the "in ally with" relationship between datasets. This model has potential applications to model security policy for criminal and intelligence information sharing, to constructing agents and collaborative systems for intelligence, to information sharing policy and governance, and to privacy, security, and civil liberties issues.

## References

1. Pawlak, Z.: On conflicts. International Journal of ManMachine Studies **21** (1984) 127–134
2. Pawlak, Z.: Analysis of conflicts. In: Joint Conference of Information Science. (1997) 350–352
3. Pawlak, Z.: An inquiry into anatomy of conflicts. Journal of Information Sciences **109** (1998) 65–78
4. Pawlak, Z.: Some remarks on conflict analysis. European Journal of Operational Research **166** (2005) 649–654
5. Xia, Z., Jiang, Y., Zhong, Y., , Zhang, S.: A novel policy and information flow security model for active network. In: ISI 2004, LNCS. Volume 3073. (2004) 42–55
6. Hughes, E., Kazura, A., Rosenthal, A.: Policy-based information sharing with semantics. In: ISI 2004. Volume 3073 of LNCS. (2004) 508–509
7. Radlauer, D.: Incident and casualty databases as a tool for understanding low-intensity conflicts. In: ISI 2005. Volume 3495 of LNCS. (2005) 153–170
8. Aleman-Meza, B., Eavenson, P.B.M., Palaniswami, D., Sheth, A.: An ontological approach to the document access problem of insider threat. In: ISI 2005. Volume 3495 of LNCS. (2005) 486–491
9. Bobeica, M., Jeral, J.P., CliveGarciaBest: A study of "root causes of conflict" using latent semantic analysis. In: ISI 2005. Volume 3495 of LNCS. (2005) 595–596
10. Lin, T.Y.: Chinese walls security policy - an aggresive model. In: Proc. 5th Annual International Computer Software and Applications Conference. (1989) 282–289
11. Lin, T.Y.: Chinese walls security model and conflict analysis. In: Proc. 24th Annual International Computer Software and Applications Conference. (2000) 122–127
12. Lin, T.Y.: Granular computing on binary relations-analysis of conflict and chinese wall security policy. In: Rough Sets and Current Trends in Computing. Volume 2475 of LNAI. (2002) 296–299
13. Lin, T.Y.: Placing the chinese walls on the boundary of conflicts. In: Proc. 26th Annual International Computer Software and Applications Conference. (2002) 966–971

14. Lin, T.Y.: Granular computing - structures, representations, and applications. In: LNAI. Volume 2639. (2003) 16–24
15. Brewer, D., Nash, M.: The chinese wall security policy. In: IEEE Symposium on Security and Privacy. (1989) 206–214
16. Zhu, F.: On covering generalized rough sets. Master's thesis, The Universite of Arizona, Tucson, Arizona, USA (2002)
17. Zhu, W., Wang, F.Y.: Reduction and axiomization of covering generalized rough sets. Information Sciences **152** (2003) 217–230
18. Zhu, W., Wang, F.Y.: Relationships among three types of covering rough sets. In: IEEE GrC 2006, to appear. (2006)

# Hybrid Modeling for Large-Scale Worm Propagation Simulations

Eul Gyu Im[1], Jung Taek Seo[2], Dong-Soo Kim[2],
Yong Ho Song[1], and Yongsu Park[1]

[1] College of Information and Communications
Hanyang University, Seoul, 133-791
{imeg, yhsong, yongsu}@hanyang.ac.kr
[2] National Security Research Institute
Daejeon, 305-350, Republic of Korea
{seojt, iskim}@etri.re.kr

**Abstract.** Internet becomes more and more popular, and most companies and institutes use web services for e-business and many other purposes. As results, Internet and web services become core infrastructure for a company or an institute. With the explosion of Internet, the occurrence of cyber terrorism has grown very rapidly. It is difficult to find and close all security flaws in a computer system that is connected to a network. Internet worms take advantages of these security flaws, and attack a large number of hosts with self-propagating techniques. To study and analyze internet worms, one of the most feasible ways is to use simulations. It is quite challenging to simulate very large-scale worm attacks. In this paper, we propose a hybrid model for large-scale worm propagation simulations.

**Keywords:** Network modeling, Internet incidents, Internet worms, simulation.

## 1  Introduction

As Internet popularity grows explosively, so does the number of cyber incidents. Since most of computer systems have vulnerabilities and it is difficult to close all security holes in a computer system, some attackers may be able to find a way to penetrate the system [1]. Recently, instead of targeting specific hosts, attackers develop Internet worms that can spread to computers in all over the world. Examples of worms include CodeRed, Nimda, Slammer, and Blaster [2]. Since those worms can attack a large number of systems, it is difficult to evaluate and analyze damages caused by these kinds of worms through experiments.

One of the best feasible ways to study effects of worms is to use simulations. However, simulating the effects of large-scale worm infections on infrastructure is quite challenging because of the following: 1) a worm gives rise to an inherently large-scale phenomenon, and requires the model to be of appropriate scale to correctly model the propagation dynamics; 2) with few exceptions, most worms have propagated over time scales of hours to days [3, 4].

S. Mehrotra et al. (Eds.): ISI 2006, LNCS 3975, pp. 572–577, 2006.

To reduce burdens of simulators, various models were proposed, e.g. the fluid model [5], the epidemic model [3], and so on. The model we proposed here combines modeling at multiple levels of abstraction in order to be both detailed enough to generate realistic packet traffic, and efficient enough to model a worm spreading through the Internet.

The rest of paper is organized as follows: Section 2 addressed related work. Our proposed model is explained in Section 3, and the Slammer worm example is explained in Section 4, followed by conclusions and future directions in Section 5.

## 2   Related Work

Network security simulation is widely used to understand cyber attacks and defense mechanisms, their impact analysis, and traffic patterns because it is difficult to study them by experimenting such dangerous and large-scale attacks in the real environments. IAS (Internet Attack Simulator) proposed by Mostow, et al. [6] was the first simulator, and several scenarios are simulated using IAS. The simulations on password sniffing attacks and effects of firewall systems are reported in [7]. Simulation is also used to estimate traffics by changing the network topology [8,9]. However, these simulators have limitations to represent the real-world network environments and configuration, and realistic security scenarios [4]. For example, as we mentioned above, the existing simulators are not scalable enough to simulate Internet attacks and defense mechanisms in a large-scale network.

Michael Liljenstam et al. [3] simulated CodeRed v2 and the Slammer worm using SSFnet [10], and compared the simulated results with real traffic data collected by the Chemical Abstract Service (CAS). They adopted the epidemic model that is originally used in biology to express virus infections. They divided networks into two kinds: macroscopic networks and microscopic networks. Worm propagation in macroscopic networks are expressed with an epidemic model, and traffics in microscopic networks are simulated normally. One of the problems with this approach is that data exchanges between macroscopic networks and microscopic networks are quite limited.

Fluid models have been shown to be effective in modeling large-scale IP networks. Yu Gu et al. [5] presented a hybrid simulation method that maintains the performance advantage of fluid models while providing detailed packet level information for selected packet traffic flows. A problem with this approach is that traffics caused by selected packet traffic flows are not updated in the fluid model. For example, the slammer worm caused traffics of backbone networks to be increased a lot instead of increasing only selected packet traffic flows.

H. Kim et al. [11] incorporated network calculus based models in simulating TCP/IP networks. With these models they tries to improve packet-level simulation where each packet generates some events and servers must process each packet and its event. They tried to reduce the number of packets to be processed, assuming that traffic patterns are uniform. However, in case of worm simulations, traffic patterns keep changing and the proposed models may generate incorrect results.

## 3    Our Proposed Hybrid Model

To solve the problems of previous work and to model worm propagations more precisely, we propose a hybrid network model for worm simulations. Our proposed model has four major parts, as shown in Figure 1: packet networks, fluid networks, epidemic networks, and traffic collector/generator.

One of the key advantages of our proposed model is to capture interactions between backbone network and other network. Previous approaches represent models for well-known worms, such as CodeRed worm, and they did not express interactions between leaf node worm traffic and backbone traffic. However, in these days, worm traffic increases dramatically in a very short period of time, and worm propagation is limited by capacity of network. The model proposed in this paper provides feedback mechanisms from worm simulated networks to modeled backbone networks, and these mechanisms can reflect real-world worm traffics more precisely.

To reduce simulation overheads of Internet worm simulations, we designed a new model based on the following assumptions and rationales:

- A worm can spread to a very large number of hosts.
- A worm can saturate backbone network with worm traffic, and worm propagation can be limited by network bandwidth.
- A worm is propagated through a large number of backbone nodes.

Figure 1 shows network configuration of our proposed hybrid modeling. Our model has three major parts: fluid networks, epidemic networks, and packet networks.

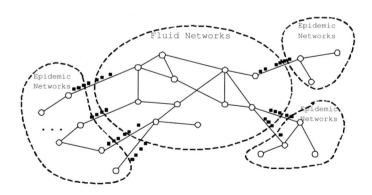

**Fig. 1.** A Hybrid Network Model for Worm Simulations

### 3.1    Fluid Networks

To improve scalability and maintainability, backbone networks grouped into several fluid model nodes. In other words, network nodes, probably backbone nodes, with similar characteristics are modeled into a single fluid model node, and different fluid model nodes have different packet delays, drop rates, and so on.

A fluid model node encompasses a set of actual network nodes and each set is disjoint with the other sets. Characteristics of a fluid model node will be determined mostly by one or two bottlenecked nodes, and these characteristics are updated with traffics generated from the traffic generator as well as epidemic networks. The fluid model in this paper is modified from one proposed by [5].

The arrival rate of the $i_{th}$ traffic flow arrived at a link $l$ on time $t$ can be defined as follows:

$$a_i^l(t) = \begin{cases} \frac{W_i(t)}{R_i(t)}, & l = l_1 \\ d_i^{l_{j-1}}(t - r_{l_{j-1}}), & l = l_j, 2 \le j \le h_i \end{cases}$$

where $W_i(t)$ is the size of TCP windows on time $t$, $R_i(t)$ is round trip time, $d_t^l(t)$ is departure rate at link $l$ on time $t$, $r_l$ is transmission delay at link $l$, and $h_i$ is the length of the $i_{th}$ flow.

The departure rate of the $i_{th}$ traffic flow departed at a link $l$ on time $t$ can be defined as follows:

$$d_t^l(t) = \begin{cases} a_i^l(t), & q_l(t) = 0 \\ \frac{a_i^l(t)}{T_{worm}^l + \sum_k a_k^l(t)} c_l, & q_l(t) > 0 \end{cases}$$

where $c_l$ is a capacity of the link $l$, $T_{worm}^l$ is worm traffic reached to the link $l$, and $q_l(t)$ is the queue length. $T_{worm}^l$ can be calculated using the number of infected hosts, the amount of traffic per each infected host, and the portion of outgoing traffic from an intranet. Therefore, $T_{worm}^l$ can be used to represent interactions from the epidemic network.

The packet drop rate of the link $l$ on time $t$ can be calculated as follows:

$$p^l(D,t) = \begin{cases} 0, & c_l > T_{worm}^l + \sum_k a_k^l(t) \\ \frac{(T_{worm}^l + \sum_k a_k^l(t)) - c_l}{T_{worm}^l + \sum_k a_k^l(t)}, & otherwise \end{cases}$$

### 3.2 Epidemic Networks

The epidemic networks, quite similar to one proposed by Liljenstam et al. [3], simplify simulations of worm infections in each hosts. We slightly modified the epidemic networks to get inputs from packet simulated networks. The packet networks provide the epidemic networks with data such as worm infection rates, traffics generated by worms, etc. The information about outgoing packets from the epidemic networks is sent to the fluid networks.

In the epidemic model, a host is in one of three states: *susceptible, infected,* and *removed.* The changes among these states can be defined as follows, modified from [3]:

$$\frac{ds(t)}{dt} = -\beta' s(t)i(t)$$

$$\frac{di(t)}{dt} = \beta' s(t)i(t) - \gamma i(t)$$

$$\frac{dr(t)}{dt} = \gamma i(t)$$

where $s(t)$ is the number of susceptible hosts at time $t$, $i(t)$ is the number of infected hosts at time $t$, $r(t)$ is the number of removed hosts at time $t$, $\beta'$ is an infection parameter which determines the speed of worm propagations, and $\gamma$ is a removal parameter which determines the speed of worm removals. When $\beta'$ is calculated, the packet drop rate calculated by the fluid model is applied so that results from the fluid model is allowed to affect the epidemic model.

## 4    Example: Slammer Worm Simulation

Figure 2 shows the number of infected hosts with two cases: one without interaction between worm traffic and backbone traffic, and the other with interactions. As we can see here, when we simulate the worm with interactions enabled, the number of infected hosts grows slower than the other case. In this simulation, we did not consider any removal parameters, so that we can clearly shows the interactions.

If interactions between worm traffic and backbone traffic are applied, the packet drop rate increases more slowly than the other case.

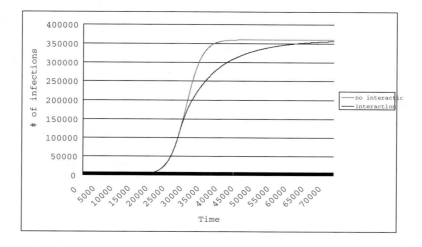

**Fig. 2.** The number of infected hosts

# 5 Conclusions and Future Directions

With the explosion of Internet, the occurrence of cyber terrorism has grown very rapidly. Internet worms take advantages of security flaws in a system, and attack a large number of hosts with self-propagating techniques.

This paper proposed a hybrid model that is scalable enough to simulate large-scale worms while dynamically reflecting increases of network traffics caused by worms. Our proposed hybrid model uses the fluid model to model backbone traffic and the epidemic model to model worm propagation. Considering trends of flash worm propagation, we need to consider effects caused by increases of backbone traffic when we try to simulate a worm. Our paper represents a first step into considering backbone traffic when a worm is simulated or modeled.

As future directions, we will do more experiments with various worms to show the correctness of the model.

# References

1. Lala, C., Panda, B.: Evaluating damage from cyber attacks: A model and analysis. IEEE Transactions on Systems, Man and Cybernetics **31** (2001) 300–310
2. Center, C.C.: CERT advisories, http://www.cert.org/advisories/. (2004)
3. Liljenstam, M., Nicol, D.M., Berk, V.H., Gray, R.S.: Simulating realistic network worm traffic for worm warning system design and testing. In: Proceedings of the 2003 ACM workshop on Rapid Malcode, ACM Press (2003) 24–33
4. Yun, J.B., Park, E.K., Im, E.G., In., H.P.: A scalable, ordered scenario-based network security simulator. In: Proceedings of the AsianSim 2004. Also in LNAI vol. 3398. (2004)
5. Gu, Y., Liu, Y., Towsley, D.: On integrating fluid models with packet simulation. In: Proceedings of the IEEE INFOCOM. (2004)
6. Mostow, J.R., Roberts, J.D., Bott, J.: Integration of an internet attack simulator in an HLA environment. In: Proceedings of the 2001 IEEE Workshop on Information Assurance and Security, West Point, NY (2001)
7. Donald Welch, Greg Conti, J.M.: A framework for an information warfare simulation. In: Proceedings of the 2001 IEEE Workshop on Information Assurance and Security, West Point, NY (2001)
8. Breslau, L., Estrin, D., Fall, K., Floyd, S., Heidemann, J., Helmy, A., Huang, P., McCanne, S., Varadhan, K., Xu, Y., Yu, H.: Advances in network simulation. IEEE Computer **33** (2000) 59–67 Expanded version available as USC TR 99-702b.
9. Technology, O.: Opnet modeler (2001)
10. SSFnet. SSF Research Network, http://www. ssfnet. org/. (2004)
11. Kim, H., Hou, J.C.: Network calculus based simulation for tcp congestion control: Theorems, implementation and evaluation. In: Proceedings of the IEEE INFOCOM. (2004) 2844–2855

# Worm Traffic Modeling for Network Performance Analysis*

Yufeng Chen[1], Yabo Dong[1], Dongming Lu[1], Yunhe Pan[1], and Honglan Lao[2]

[1] College of Computer Science and Technology,
Zhejiang University, Hangzhou, 310027, P.R. China
{xztcyfnew, dongyb, ldm, panyh}@zju.edu.cn
[2] Department of Electrical Engineering, University of Southern California,
Los Angeles, CA 90089-2564, USA
hlao@usc.edu

**Abstract.** Worm research depends on simulation to a large degree due to worm propagation characters. In worm simulation, worm traffic generation is the base to analyze influences of worm traffic on network. The popular Random Constant Spread (RCS) model ignores the burstiness of "latency-limited" worm traffic, which will cause underestimation of the influences. According to worm scan behaviors, the Periodic Burst Scanning (PBS) model is proposed to model "latency-limited" worm traffic. Simulation results show that network performance decreases much more with PBS model than that with RCS model.

## 1 Introduction

Worms have been one of the most serious threats to Internet security due to the significant damage and fast spread. Worm research depends on simulation to a large degree. With worm simulation, the propagation dynamics can be shown up and the network performance can be analyzed, which are helpful to worm containment. If we know the influence, we can take corresponding actions. Due to the importance of local worm detection for controlling worm propagation [1], we focus on the impact of local worms on local network. Here local worms mean worm hosts within a local network. The impacts include packet loss, link utilization and self-similarity of traffic. Self-similarity is the nature of traffic [2] and has considerable impact on network [3].

Worm traffic generation is a key consideration in worm simulation. There are two ways to generate worm traffic. The first is to simulate the real worm attack behaviors, and the other is to generate traffic with worm traffic model. The first one generates worm traffic at a very small granularity [4], however, along with high computation cost. The second can statistically describe the scanning behaviors of worm, which is more suitable for large-scale worm simulation. The Random Constant Spread (RCS)

* This work is supported by a grant from the Zhejiang Provincial Natural Science Foundation (No. Y104437), Science and Technology Program of Zhejiang Province (No. 2005C33034), Science and Technology Program of Hubei Provincial Department of Education (No. D200523007, D200623002). The NLANR CodeRed data used in this paper was collected by the NLANR Measurement and Network Analysis Group (NLANR/MNA) with funding under the National Science Foundation cooperative agreement nos. ANI-0129677 (2002) and ANI-9807479 (1998).

S. Mehrotra et al. (Eds.): ISI 2006, LNCS 3975, pp. 578–583, 2006.

model [5] is the most popular worm traffic model, which assumes a worm host generates traffic with constant rate, i.e., the average rate of worm scanning traffic at a rather large time scale, such as one second. RCS model can describe the traffic characters of "bandwidth-limited" worms who send scans limited only by the capacity of infected computer or network [5]. While for "latency-limited" worms who send scans limited by the latency of connection requests [5], the model will ignore the burstiness. "Latency-limited" worm, such as CodeRed, sends out cluster scans and waits for responses of destination hosts. If there are no responses, "latency-limited" worms will send out retransmission packets after timeout. We can find that there is burstiness, which has bad influence on network. The influence of "latency-limited" worm traffic can not be shown up using RCS model, thus, we need a new traffic model of "latency-limited" worm to analyze the influence on network performance.

In this paper, we focus on local network to estimate influence of local worm traffic on network. Thus, we can test local worm detection and response measures with simulation. To balance the accuracy and efficiency in local worm simulation, we use the mixed abstraction level simulation method [6] as a framework. The framework is composed of two parts: the local network and other part. The statistical worm traffic model for "latency-limited" worm is used to generate local worm traffic and the analytical SIR model of worm propagation is used to describe worm propagation of other part in the Internet. This paper is organized as follows. In Section 2, we propose a worm traffic model for "latency-limited" worm and analyze the network performance in Section 3. In Section 4, the conclusions and future work are presented.

## 2 Periodic Burst Traffic Model for "Latency-Limited" Worm

The dataset for worm traffic modeling is CodeRed (http://pma.nlanr.net/Special), provided by the NLANR Measurement and Network Analysis Group (NLANR/MNA). The scanning traffic of the local worm host, denoted as C1, is shown in Fig. 1.

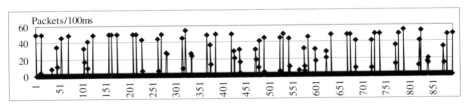

**Fig. 1.** Scanning traffic of C1. The traffics possess periodic burstiness due to the scanning pattern of "latency-limited" worms.

Every connection of C1 initiated by a thread is composed of three packets: the initial SYN packet, the retransmitted SYN packet after 3 seconds timeout and the RST packet after 0.5 second to end the connection. For one thread, the time between connections is 1 second. Thus, for every connection, the cycle is 4.5 seconds and the inner three cycles are 3, 0.5 and 1 seconds. The empirical inner cycles for connections of C1 are 3.3, 0.6 and 1.1 seconds. The differences between the empirical times and definition of TCP protocol is caused by the timer of OS. The number of cluster scans is 50, which shows that the worm is a CodeRed variant worm. We can model the "latency-limited" worm traffic as $(clusterNum, cycle1, cycle2, \ldots, cycleN)$, where $clusterNum$ means the number of new cluster scans, and $cycle1 \sim cycleN$ define the inner cycles of each connection. We call the model Periodic Burst Scanning traffic (PBS) model. For the CodeRed variant worm, the traffic model is $Code\operatorname{Re}dVar = (50, 3, 0.5, 1)$. For C1, the traffic sent within a cycle are $clusterNum^* N = 50^* 3 = 150$ packets, where $N$ is the number of inner cycles of each connection. The traffic is different from the number of scans used to analyze the worm propagation, which is equal to $clusterNum$. When estimating the influence of worm traffic, we should consider the traffic sent by worm host. Based on the framework proposed in [6], we validate the PBS model with simulation of CodeRed 2. The PBS model is $Code\operatorname{Re}d2 = (100, 3, 6, 12)$, where the cycle is 21 seconds. The simulating topology is shown in Fig. 2. Traffic sample time is 1 second.

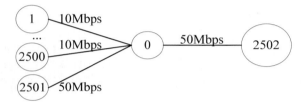

**Fig. 2.** Simulating topology. Nodes 1~2501 denote local network hosts and node 2502 the external network. Node 1~2500 generate worm traffic. The parameters for SIR model are same as that in [6]: the population of susceptible $N = 380,000$ and the scan rate $\sigma = 5.65$ scans/s. We use method in [7] to generate background traffic at node 2501. To validate the PBS model, the background traffic at node 2501 is not generated in this simulation.

The traffic from link 0 to 2502 means the worm traffic, shown in Fig. 3.

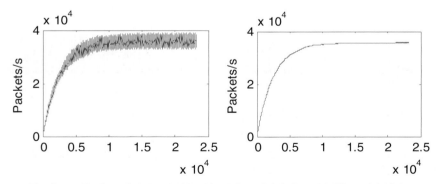

**Fig. 3.** Traffic from link 0 to 2502 with PBS model (left) and RCS model (right)

The average traffic with PBS model is same as that with RCS model, which shows that PBS model is valid. However, traffic with PBS model is more fluctuant due to the burstiness of "latency-limited" worm traffic.

# 3   Influence of Worm Traffic on Network Performance

To compare the influence of PBS traffic and RCS traffic on network performance, we simulate two cases, one for network traffic and the other for host traffic.

## 3.1   Influence of Periodic Burst Scanning Worm Traffic on Network Traffic

In this case, background traffic is generated at node 2501 in Fig. 2. The link utilize-tion is 30% and the self-similarity is 0.8. If all 2500 susceptible local machines are infected, the average link utilization of worm traffic is $2500*300/21*40*8/50000000*100\% = 22.86\%$, where 40 is packet size (Bytes). To-tally, the link utilization is 52.86%. It seems that worm traffic will not influence background traffic much. However, for PBS model, results show much difference. The total and background traffic from node 0 to 2502 are shown in Fig. 4 and Fig. 5.

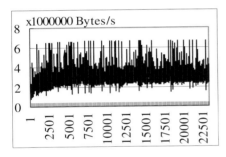 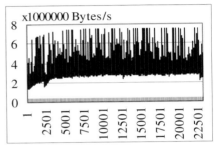

**Fig. 4.** The total traffic from node 0 to 2502. The traffic with PBS model (left) shows more fluctuant than that with RCS model (right) due to the packet loss caused by burst worm traffic.

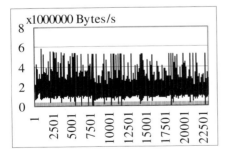 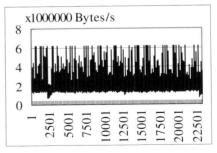

**Fig. 5.** The background traffic from node 0 to 2502. The background traffic is influenced more by worm traffic with PBS model (left) than that with RCS model (right).

The traffic decrease and fluctuation with PBS model are due to packet loss caused by the burstiness of "latency-limited" worm traffic. The packet loss of background traffic from node 0 to 2502 is 2449816 with PBS model, which is 25.5 times higher than that with RCS model. The influence of worm traffic on network performance is underes-timated with RCS model. When we compare the self-similarity of traffic from node 0 to

2502, we find that the difference is not obvious. The reason is that the traffic from node 0 to 2502 is rescaled at node 0, which decease the bursiness of traffic.

## 3.2   Influence of Periodic Burst Scanning Worm Traffic on Host Traffic

For host case, we simulate a worm similar to CodeRed 2 with the only difference of 300 *clusterNum*. Traffic sample time is 100ms. The topology is shown in Fig. 6.

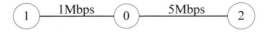

**Fig. 6.** Simulating topology. Background traffic and worm traffic are generated at node 1. For background traffic, the link utilization is 30% and the self-similarity is 0.8.

With PBS and RCS models, the worm traffic and background traffic from node 1 to 0 are shown in Fig. 7 and Fig. 8.

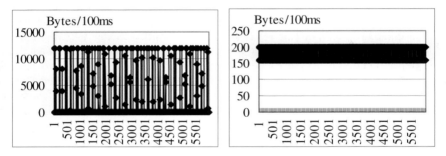

**Fig. 7.** Worm traffics from node 1 to 0 with PBS (left) and RCS (right) models. Due to the time schedule of NS2, the traffic with RCS model shows like a band, not a line.

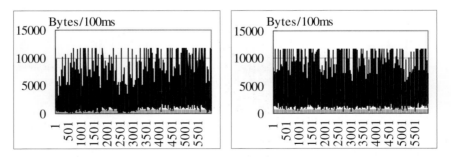

**Fig. 8.** Background traffics from node 1 to 0 with PBS (left) and RCS (right) models. For PBS model, the traffic shows more fluctuant.

With three simulation runs, for RCS model, there are no packet losses, and the mean link utilization is 29.37%, very close to the configured value. While for PBS model, packet loss occurs although the link utilization of worm traffic is only

$900/21*40*8/1000000*100\% = 1.37\%$ , and the numbers of lost packets are 568, 453 and 638. The burst PBS worm traffic induces packet loss, which makes the transmission control react. The result of the transmission control is the decrease of link utilization of background traffic. The mean decrease is 15.7% compared with the configured value. Further, the burst PBS traffic can influence the self-similarity of background traffic. The mean values of self-similarity of background traffic for PBS model are 7.4% larger than configuration, which means the network performance will decrease. While for RCS model, the values of self-similarity remains almost the same as configuration. Also, we can obtain the similar results with comparison of self-similarity of total traffic. The bandwidth of link 1 to 0 is 1Mbps, which is the popular configuration of ADSL. If we increase the bandwidth to 10Mbps, we can get similar results. The "latency-limited" worm traffic can influence network and host traffic much, which can not be represented with RCS model.

## 4  Conclusions and Future Work

In this paper, we investigated the influence of "latency-limited" worm traffic on network focusing on local network. We modeled the worm traffic with Periodic Burst Scanning model according to the scan behaviors. The influences on network and host traffic were analyzed with simulation. Compared with the popular RCS worm traffic model, the simulation results of packet loss, link utilization and self-similarity showed that network performance decreased much with PBS model. We concluded that the RCS worm traffic model underestimated the influence of worm traffic on network. The future works will include: 1) the influence of worm traffic to multi-fractal character of network traffic; 2) the QoS control when worms break out.

## References

[1]  Nicholas Weaver, Dan Ellis, Stuart Staniford, Vern Paxson. Worms vs. perimeters: the case for HardLANs. Proc. of Hot Interconnects, 2004.http://www.icir. org/vern/ papers/hardlans.hot-inter04.pdf

[2]  Kihong Park, Walter Willinger, Editors. Self-Similar Network Traffic and Performance Evaluation. John Wiley & Sons, New York, 2000.

[3]  Ashok Erramilli,  Onuttom Narayan, Walter Willinger. Experimental queueing analysis with long-range dependent packet traffic. IEEE/ACM Transactions on Networking, 1996, 4(2): 209 - 223

[4]  Arno Wagner, Thomas Dübendorfer, Bernhard Plattner, Roman Hiestand. Experiences with worm propagation simulations. Proc. of ACM workshop on Rapid Malcode, 2003, p34-41.

[5]  David Moore, Vern Paxson, Stefan Savage, Colleen Shannon, Stuart Staniford, Nicholas Weaver. Inside the slammer worm. IEEE Security and Privacy, 2003, 1(4): p33-39.

[6]  Michael Liljenstam, David M. Nicol, Vincent H. Berk, Robert S. Gray. Simulating realistic network worm traffic for worm warning system design and testing. Proc. of the ACM Workshop on Rapid Malcode, 2003, p24-33.

[7]  Yufeng Chen, Yabo Dong, Dongming Lu, Yunhe Pan. A Simulating Method for TCP Aggregated Traffic of Large Scale Network. Journal on Communications, 2006, 27(2): 100-106.

# Analysis of Abnormalities of Worm Traffic for Obtaining Worm Detection Vectors*

Zhengtao Xiang[1], Yufeng Chen[2], Yabo Dong[2], and Honglan Lao[3]

[1] Computer Center, Hubei Automotive Industries Institute,
Shiyan, 442002, P.R. China
syxiang2000@163.com
[2] College of Computer Science and Technology, Zhejiang University,
Hangzhou, 310027, P.R. China
{xztcyfnew, dongyb}@zju.edu.cn
[3] Department of Electrical Engineering, University of Southern California,
Los Angeles, CA 90089-2564, USA
hlao@usc.edu

**Abstract.** Scanning traffic is the majority of worm traffic. Gaining deep insight into worm traffic can do much help in detecting worm hosts. The distributions of vectors related with First Contact Connections (FCC) of legitimate hosts and worm hosts are analyzed. The vectors are arrival interval, request size, response size, duration and RTT. Distributions of these vectors of worm traffic show abnormalities of the lack of heavy-tailed character, which is hold by that of legitimate traffic. Besides high probability of failed FCC, arrival interval and request size can be used as additional vectors.

## 1  Introduction

Worms brought heavy damages to the Internet, such as CodeRed, SQL slammer, Blaster and Sasser worms. There are two kinds of worms [1] according to scanning constraints: "latency-limited" and "bandwidth-limited" worms. The former sends scans limited by the latency of connection requests, and the latter sends scans as fast as quickly, which only is limited by the capacity of infected computer or network. Due to huge losses, effective worm detection raises attention for controlling worm propagation. Because detection of local worms is important to control worm propagation, we focus on the abnormalities of traffic generated by local worm host.

For unknown worms, anomaly detection methods are appropriate. However, vectors of recent worm detection methods come from qualitative analysis of worm behavior. Virus throttle system [2] used the observations that worm host established high volume

---

* This work is supported by a grant from Science and Technology Program of Hubei Provincial Department of Education (No. D200523007, D200623002). The NLANR BellLabs-I, Auckland-VI, CodeRed and Slammer data used in this paper were collected by the NLANR Measurement and Network Analysis Group (NLANR/MNA) with funding under the National Science Foundation cooperative agreement nos. ANI-0129677 (2002) and ANI-9807479 (1998).

S. Mehrotra et al. (Eds.): ISI 2006, LNCS 3975, pp. 584–589, 2006.

of new connections. Robertson et al [3] and Bakos et al [4] configured thresholds of failed new connections to detect worm hosts. Reverse Sequential Hypothesis Tests method [5] was proposed based on the high probability of failed First Contact Connection (FCC) for worm hosts. FCCs are connections whose responders are hosts with which the initiator (a given source IP) has not previously communicated. Such vector-based methods face problems of high false positives.

We need more effective detection vectors for local worm detection. We know that worm traffic possesses less self-similarity than that of legitimate host [6]. However, the computation complexity of self-similarity limits the real-time application. In this paper, we try to find out worm detection vectors according to the causations of self-similarity, which is the superposition of many ON/OFF sources whose ON or OFF periods exhibit heavy-tailed property [7]. Because connections compose traffic, we regard connections as ON/OFF sources and investigate the heavy-tailed properties of vectors related with connections. In practice, heavy-tailed properties of vectors related with FCCs are analyzed because worms try to infect all susceptible machines, which implies that most connections sent by a worm host are FCCs.

## 2 Traffic Characters of Legitimate and Worm Hosts

The datasets including BellLabs-I, Auckland-VI, CodeRed and Slammer, are all provided by the NLANR Measurement and Network Analysis Group (NLANR/MNA, http://pma.nlanr.net/Traces/long/). We pick up four legitimate hosts from the former two datasets, denoted as B_High, B_Low and A_High, A_Low, where High or Low represent high or low link utilization. We choose four worm hosts from the latter two datasets, denoted as C1, C1 and S1, S2. The four worms are representations of "latency-limited" and "bandwidth-limited" worms, respectively.

### 2.1 Heavy-Tailed Distribution

If a random variable follows heavy-tailed distribution, the distribution decays slower than exponential. A distribution is defined as heavy-tailed [8] if

$$\overline{F}(x) = P[X > x] \sim x^{-\alpha}, \text{ as } x \to \infty, 0 < \alpha \tag{1}$$

The simplest heavy-tailed distribution is Pareto distribution, with Complementary Cumulative Distribution Function (CCDF) as

$$\overline{F}(x) = (k/x)^{\alpha} \tag{2}$$

$\alpha$ is shape parameter, denoting the tail thickness. If $\alpha \leq 2$, the distribution has infinite variance. When plotted on log-log axes, the curve of CCDF appears linear.

Another important distribution is Weibull distribution with CCDF as

$$\overline{F}(x) = e^{-(x/\eta)^{\beta}} \tag{3}$$

If the shape parameter $\beta < 1$, Weibull distribution is heavy-tailed. Weibull distribution has better fitness with connection arrival [9].

## 2.2  Distributions of Vectors of FCC

The vectors related with FCC include arrival interval, request size, response size, duration and RTT (Round Trip Time). Request size means the bytes sent by initiator of the connection, while response size means the bytes sent by responder. Duration means the time that the connection lasts. For legitimate hosts, the CCDFs of the above vectors are plotted on log-log axes. While for worm hosts, only the CCDFs of arrival interval of FCC are plotted on log-log axes. CCDFs of other vectors are plotted on the original coordinate axes due to the concentration of probability mass.

### 2.2.1  Distributions of Arrival Interval of FCC

The log-log CCDFs of arrival interval of FCC of the eight hosts are shown in Fig. 1. The arrival intervals of legitimate hosts follow Weibull distribution. The shape parameters $\beta$ that best fit the measured CCDFs are all less than 1. While for worm hosts, because worm hosts try to infect as many machines as possible and initiate FCCs automatically, the CCDFs show much difference.

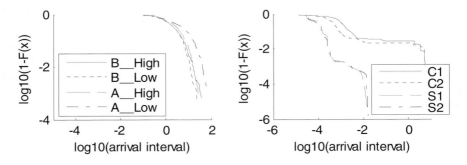

**Fig. 1.** CCDFs of arrival interval of FCC

Legitimate hosts have large-span arrival interval, and most intervals are more than hundreds of milliseconds. The order of magnitude of arrival interval is not surprising because mean visual reaction times of human beings are 180-200 milliseconds [10]. While for worm hosts, the time span is rather small, and most interval are less than 100 milliseconds. And there are horizontal lines in the CCDFs for C1 and C2. The lines are caused by the timeout. For Slammer, there is no latency, and thus the curves of CCDFs are rather continuous.

### 2.2.2  Distributions of Request Size and Response Size of FCC

The CCDFs of request size and response size of FCC of the eight hosts are shown in Fig. 2. The tails of the CCDFs of request size and response size of legitimate hosts show linear, which means that the two vectors follow Pareto distribution. The shape parameters $\alpha$ for fitness are all less than 2, which means the request and response sizes have infinite variance contributing to high variability. While for worm hosts, the values of request size concentrate into few numbers, which means the request size follows constant distribution

$P[X = x] = 1$. The values of request size of C1 and C2 concentrate into 44, 84, 88 or 128 due to the different retransmission stages. While for S1 and S2, the value of request size of FCC is 404 because there is only one packet with size of 404 Bytes in one FCC.

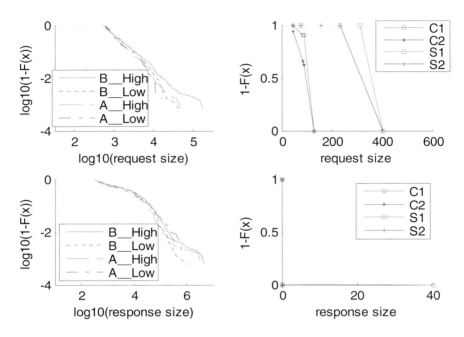

**Fig. 2.** CCDFs of request size and response size of FCC

The values of response size of the four worm hosts are almost zero, which means almost all FCCs failed. The failed connections means the responders do not exist, or are not active, or are not listening on the corresponding port. For "latency-limited" worms, the request belongs to protocol data, which is hard to be changed. While for "band-width-limited" worms, the request belongs to application data, which can be changed by worm program. With regard to response size, "latency-limited" worms can not change the values because response belongs to protocol data, and for "band-width-limited" worms, the response size can hardly be changed because they send scans without requiring responses.

### 2.2.3  Distributions of Duration and RTT of FCC

The CCDFs of duration and RTT of FCC of the eight hosts are shown in Fig. 3. The tails of CCDFs of duration and RTT of legitimate hosts show linear, too. The two vectors also follow Pareto distribution. Although some of the shape parameters are greater than 2, the distributions decay slower than exponential. While for worm hosts, the CCDFs of duration of C1 and C2 are ladder-like, which is also caused by the different retransmission stages. For S1 and S2, because the initiators of almost all FCCs send only one packet with size of 404 Bytes, thus the duration is computed as the transmission time, which concentrates in one point. And because almost all FCCs fail with no responses of destination hosts, the RTT is computed with configured timeout, 30 seconds.

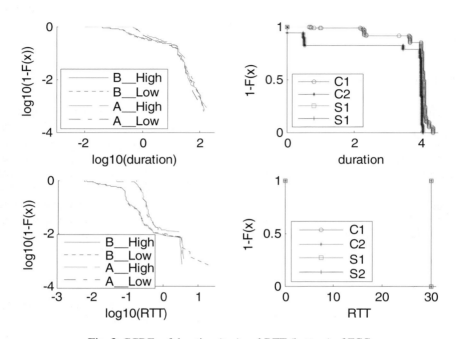

**Fig. 3.** CCDFs of duration (top) and RTT (bottom) of FCC

Same as request size, duration can hardly be changed by "latency-limited" worms, while can be changed by "bandwidth-limited" worms. And, neither "latency-limited" worms nor "bandwidth-limited" worms can change RTT.

## 3   Discussions of Abnormalities of Worm Traffic

Generally, the abnormalities of response size, duration and RTT of FCC are related with high probability of failed FCC. To simplify worm detection, we can substitute failed probability of FCC for the three vectors. Failed probability of FCC can be used as general worm detection vector. To decide an FCC is successful or failed, we can set the timeout according to the values of RTT of FCCs of legitimate hosts, which are less than 1 second.

However, detection methods with the only vector must face problems of high false positives rate. We need other detection vectors. Arrival interval is a candidate. Worm hosts can hardly send FCCs with arrival interval following the same heavy-tailed distribution as that of legitimate hosts. If worms try to evade detection with slow scans, stealthy scans or scans whose arrival interval follows heavy-tailed distribution, the propagation of worms will be slowed down, which will destroy the goals of worms. Thus, arrival interval can be used as an additional detection vector. Also, request size can be another candidate. However, the ability that worms change the vector decides the applicability. For "latency-limited" worms, request size can be used as detection vector, while for "bandwidth-limited" worms, the vector may induce false negatives if this kind of worm changes request size deliberately.

## 4   Conclusions and Future Works

Worm detection needs effective detection vectors. The vectors of recent worm detection methods come from qualitative analysis of worm behavior, which may induce high false positives rate. In this paper, the distributions of vectors related with FCC are analyzed. Besides high probability of failed FCC, two vectors can be used as additional vectors, which are arrival interval and request size. Arrival interval is a general vector to detect "latency-limited" and "bandwidth-limited" worms, while request size is applicable to "latency-limited" worms. The future works include: 1) investigate suitable detection algorithms with detections vectors proposed in this paper; 2) develop worm containments methods according to the vectors.

## References

[1] David Moore, Vern Paxson, Stefan Savage, Colleen Shannon, Stuart Staniford, Nicholas Weaver. Inside the slammer worm. IEEE Security and Privacy, 2003, 1(4): p33-39.
[2] Jamie Twycross, Matthew M. Williamson. Implementing and testing a virus throttle. Proc. of the 12th USENIX Security Symposium, 2003, p285-294.
[3] Seth Robertson, Eric V. Siegel, Matt Miller, Salvatore J. Stolfo. Surveillance detection in high bandwidth environments. Proc. of DARPA DISCEX III Conference, 2003, p130-139.
[4] George Bakos, Vincent H. Berk. Early detection of internet worm activity by metering ICMP destination unreachable messages. Proc. of SPIE - The International Society for Optical Engineering, v 4708, 2002, p33-42.
[5] Stuart E. Schechter, Jaeyeon Jung, Arthur W. Berger. Fast detection of scanning worm infections. Proc. of The Seventh International Symposium on Recent Advances in Intrusion Detection, 2004, p59-81.
[6] Yufeng Chen, Yabo Dong, Dongming Lu, Zhengtao Xiang. Research of characteristics of worm traffic. Proc. of Intelligence and Security Informatics, Lecture Notes in Computer Science, v3073, 2004, p518-519.
[7] Walter Willinger, Murad S. Taqqu, Robert Sherman, Daniel V. Wilson. Self-Similarity Through High-Variability: Statistical Analysis of Ethernet LAN Traffic at the Source Level. Net-working, IEEE/ACM Transactions on, 1997, 5(1): 71-86.
[8] Mark E. Crovella, Azer Bestavros. Self-similarity in World Wide Web traffic: evidence and possible causes. Networking, IEEE/ACM Transactions on, 1997, 5(6): 835-846.
[9] Anja Feldmann. Characteristics of TCP connection arrivals. Technical report, 1998. http://www.net.in.tum.de/~anja/feldmann/papers/ss_conn.ps
[10] Bob Kosinski, John Cummings. The scientific method: an introduction using reaction time. Proce. of the 20th Workshop/Conference of the Association for Biology Laboratory Education (ABLE), 1999, v20, p63-84.

# A Two-Tier Intrusion Detection System
# for Mobile Ad Hoc Networks – A Friend Approach

Shukor Abd Razak[1], Steven Furnell[1], Nathan Clarke[1], and Phillip Brooke[2]

[1] Network Research Group, School of Computing, Communications & Electronics,
University of Plymouth, Plymouth, United Kingdom
info@network-research-group.org
[2] School of Computing, University of Teesside, Middlesbrough, United Kingdom
P.J.Brooke@tees.ac.uk

**Abstract.** Existing Intrusion Detection Systems (IDS) in Mobile Ad Hoc Network (MANET) environments suffer from many problems because of the inherent characteristics of the network. Limited audit data, along with the problems faced in achieving global detection and response mechanisms, creates challenges for establishing reliable IDS for MANETs. In this paper, several scenarios are investigated where a 'friend' concept has been applied to solve MANET problems. This same concept is applied to a new IDS framework, and discussion is presented into how it can help in minimizing the problems that are faced in existing IDS. The key advantages of this two-tier IDS framework are its ability to detect intrusion at an early stage of such behaviour in the network, and its capability to minimize the impact of colluding blackmail attackers in the systems.

## 1 Introduction

MANET is a computer network that combines the capabilities of peer-to-peer, wireless, and mobile network technologies and has been used to support communications in various environments such as in military and disaster relief operations [1]. It has several unique characteristics that make it differ from other types of computer networks. It operates in a fully distributed fashion without the aid of a central authority, has random network topologies, and uses wireless links for communications. Since the conception of MANET several security measures, concepts and architectures have been proposed to counter many of the inherent security concerns the network topology introduces. However, most of these are focused upon prevention mechanisms to protect MANET from external attackers. It is suggested that by employing an IDS as a second line of defense could be very useful whenever prevention mechanisms failed to protect the network. In this paper, two important issues in MANET IDS are discussed: what is the best way to detect intrusions in a collaborative fashion; and how to minimize the impacts of blackmail attacks/false accusations. This paper proposes a new IDS framework for MANET to provide solutions for such problems.

The paper proceeds to provide some background of a friend concept in small world phenomenon and discusses how it can be applied in a MANET environment. Section 3 summarizes some existing work in MANET security, which is related to

S. Mehrotra et al. (Eds.): ISI 2006, LNCS 3975, pp. 590–595, 2006.

the concept of friend, and Section 4 outlines some of the important features of a two-tier IDS framework.

## 2  Friends as Short Cut in Ad Hoc Networks

The small world phenomenon is a concept that suggests any two individuals, selected randomly from almost anywhere on the planet, are connected via a chain of no more than six acquaintances. Milgram [2] conducted an experiment in which he sent 60 letters to various recruits in Wichita, Kansas who were asked to forward the letter to the wife of a divinity student living at Cambridge, Massachusetts. The letters could only be forwarded by hand to personal acquaintances (directly or through friend of a friend) who they thought might be able to reach the recipient. Milgram claimed that he has proved the concept when 3 out of 60 letters that he sent reached the recipients but neglected to say about the low (i.e. 5%) chain completion percentage. However, his experiment has motivated other researchers to investigate more on this concept, such as in the Internet context, as observed by Adamic [3]. In his study, he suggested that the World Wide Web is a 'small world' in a sense that all the sites are highly clustered yet the path length between them is small. Helmy [4] established a relationship between the small world concept and wireless networks. Simulations result from his study proved that by adding a few 'short cut' nodes in the wireless networks, the degree of separation between nodes could be decreased drastically. One question emerging from this study is how to select few 'short cut' nodes in an autonomous, fully distributed, and self-organized ad hoc network. The author proposed the concept of *contacts*, which will act as short cuts to transform the wireless network into a small world. However, the author did not discuss how these *contacts* can be made available in the system, and this problem remains an open issue.

The concept of 'friends' has been introduced in MANET environments to solve many problems, especially those that relate to security issues. One of the common assumptions made by researchers to create friend relationships is that each node must be known to each other in a real world before they can establish a friend relationship in MANET environment. Based upon the concept that a friend in the real world is also a friend in the MANET, along with the concept of six degree separations between friends in real world, we propose a two-tier IDS framework for MANET to investigate how we can benefit from these concepts. Several previous works that make use of 'friendship' concept are discussed in the next section followed by the details of the proposed IDS framework in Section 4.

## 3  Related Work

Establishing a security association between nodes is very important because without it, secret information such as users' personal information or network information might be passed to unauthorized parties. One way to establish security associations is by deploying an encryption mechanism (e.g. private/public key system). Each message will be encrypted with the recipient's public key so that it can be decrypted using the corresponding private key. While this system could work perfectly well in wired networks, where there exists a central server to manage and to distribute the public keys of each node, the same scenario does not apply in MANET. Since we cannot assume the existence of a central authority to manage and distribute the keys, it seems impossible for each node to know the public keys of others without having a physical contact. However, this problem can be eased with the help of friends as suggested by Capkun et al. [5]. They suggested that each node is capable of establishing a security association with another anonymous node in the system by requesting a recommendation from friends. Friend nodes in their system are nodes that one has physically met in a real world. With a recommendation from a friend, a trustworthiness level for an anonymous node can be determined, thus a security association between two anonymous nodes can be established without the need of a physical contact in a real world.

In a real world, when we apply for a job, usually we are required to supply the employer with names of referees, who know about our background, capabilities and enthusiasm, and may also be used for security purposes. The same concept has been applied in a MANET environment, as proposed by Weimerskirch and Thonet [6]. Their concept is somewhat similar to the work proposed in [5] where recommendation from a friend is needed to authenticate an anonymous node in the system. However, in their system, the anonymous node will supply a few names as its references so that its trustworthiness can be judged.

In another scenario, a friend concept has been used to prevent node selfishness in the routing mechanism. In a MANET, nodes might sometimes refuse to participate in network operations in order to save their own limited resources. As mentioned in [7], nodes can be forced to participate in network operations in two ways; either penalizing them for not cooperating, or rewarding them for their participation. However, this mechanism creates unfairness especially for the nodes that are located outside the 'busy' area. Nodes need credits to send their own packets in the network and the only way to gain credits is by forwarding others' packets. However, for nodes located outside the 'busy' area, the chances for them to be selected in a packet forwarding process are low, and this will make it difficult for them to gain more credits. Miranda and Rodrigues [8] suggest a solution for this problem by using a friend concept. They proposed a concept of selective forwarding, where each node will only participate in a packet forwarding process if the packets come from, or need to be sent to, one of its friends. Each node will advertise to others about its friend list so that it cannot be accused for not forwarding other nodes' packets that are not in its friend list.

## 4   A Two-Tier IDS for Mobile Ad Hoc Networks

A two-tier hybrid IDS for MANET is a novel IDS architecture proposed to improve the efficiency of existing MANET IDS architectures with the help of friend nodes. The main idea of the proposed system is to provide a reliable IDS that can detect any intrusion attempts and at the same time reduce the number of false alarms raised in the system.

## 4.1  System Components

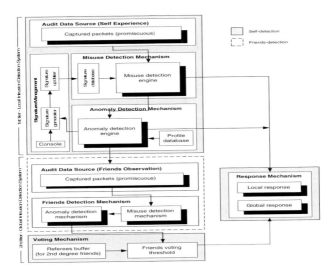

**Fig. 1.** Conceptual framework of the two-tier hybrid IDS for MANET

**Real Time Audit Data Source.** In the proposed architecture, two audit data sources have been identified as appropriate to detect intrusive activities in the networks. Any network operations initiated by, or having a direct connection with the participating nodes (source, destination, and all the intermediate nodes) are classified as self-experience audit data. Neighbours that are close to the participating nodes are also able to capture the overheard network activities using a promiscuous mode. This kind of audit data is known as friends' observation audit data in the proposed framework.

**Misuse Detection Mechanism.** This module comprises a misuse detection engine to detect activities that match the attack signatures as stored in the signature database. At the initial stage, the attack database might only cover a few attack signatures, but as time goes by, with the aid of the anomaly detection mechanism and the signature management module, the attack signature database will reach its maturity level and thus be able to detect more attacks.

**Anomaly Detection Mechanism.** Attacks that cannot be detected by a misuse detection mechanism will be passed here for further investigation. The failure of detecting the attacks could be because of the attack signature database is still immature or could be because of insufficient evidence. The anomaly detection mechanism applied here is similar to the existing techniques proposed by previous researchers, and its main components include an anomaly detection engine and a profile database.

**Signature Management.** This module completes the feedback loop by enabling a dynamic update to the misuse detection mechanism. The signature generator automatically generates the attack signature each time the anomaly detection mechanism successfully identifies deviation from normal user/system profiles.

**Friends Detection Mechanism.** Any suspicious activity that was unsuccessfully detected as intrusive by the misuse and anomaly detection mechanisms in local detection will be further investigated with the help of friends. First degree friends are nodes in the networks that have a direct connection with the source node (i.e. the node that initiates the global detection process). Nodes in the network will have a direct connection to each other if they are friends in a real world. On the other hand, second degree friends are nodes in the networks that do not have a direct connection to the source node. First degree friends can participate in the global detection process without any problem because their identity can be verified by the source node. However, source node might only have a few first degree friends especially at the early stage of its participation in the networks. As a result, a global detection mechanism might take a longer time to complete or might not be completed because of the insufficient number of first degree friends' reports received. For that reason, second degree friends' reports can be accepted to speed up the detection process. However, since second degree friends are the indirect friends to the source node and their identity cannot be directly verified, a referee (a node that has first degree relationships with both the source and the second degree node) is needed to verify the second degree node's identity. Reports from both first and second degree friends are equal in weight and will be counted by a voting mechanism. Once the reports reached the preset threshold limit, the response mechanism will be triggered.

**Response Mechanism.** A local response unit will raise an alarm to alert the local user about the detected intrusive activity. The intrusion alarm then will be broadcasted to the other nodes in the networks to make them aware about the existence of intrusive nodes. However, to avoid false accusations, only alarms received from first degree friends can be accepted.

### 4.2   Friends' Role in Two-Tier IDS

**Speed Up the Detection Process.** Cooperative detection could speed up the detection process but this method is vulnerable to packet modification attacks. Friend detection mechanism in the two-tier IDS can ease this problem as each node in the system will carry out the detection process based on its own local audit data, and will only share the result of the decision whether the suspicious node is malicious or not.

**Minimizing the Risk of Cooperative Blackmail Attacks.** The problem of blackmail attack has been discussed in [9], and the authors suggested that a voting mechanism could ease the problem. However, a voting mechanism could only be used to protect the network from a single blackmail attacker, but not a cooperative blackmail attack. A friend mechanism is capable of minimizing the risk of such problems as only detection results from friends can be accepted in the proposed system. In case of there being a lot of blackmail attackers, the immunity of a friend mechanism can be strengthened by increasing the number of positive detection results that must be gathered from friends before any suspicious activity can be confirmed intrusive.

**Reliable Global Response Mechanism.** Broadcasting intrusion alerts is a big challenge in a MANET because each node is anonymous to others, and there is always a possibility that some of the alerts are not genuine (i.e. broadcasted by attackers). The reliability of a global response mechanism can be increased with the help of friend nodes. Since each node is only interested in the alerts that came from its friends, all other alerts (including the fake ones) will be dropped. This will solve the false accusation problem caused by the fake alerts in the system.

## 5  Conclusion

In this paper, a new IDS framework for MANET environments based upon the concept of a friend in a small world phenomenon has been proposed. Current anomaly detection mechanisms as proposed in previous work make the detection process longer, as the system needs to gather sufficient evidence before a decision can be made against any suspicious activity. In another scenario, existing techniques for global detection suffer from the potential for blackmail attackers and false accusations. The proposed two-tier IDS framework has been designed to overcome these issues with the help of friend nodes. For future work, simulations will be carried out to investigate the performance of the proposed IDS framework in various MANET scenarios. It is hypothesized that with the introduction of friend nodes, the impacts of the IDS problems mentioned earlier can be minimized.

## References

1. F. Stajano, and R. Anderson. The Resurrecting Duckling: Security Issues for Ad-Hoc Wireless Networks. In Proc. of the 7th Int. Workshop on Security Protocols, LNCS, vol. 1796, pp172-194, 1999.
2. S. Milgram. The Small World Problem. Psychology Today, pp60-67, May, 1967.
3. L. Adamic. The Small World Web. In Proc. of Eur. Conf. on Digital Libraries (ECDL), pp443-452, September, 1999.
4. A. Helmy. Small Worlds in Wireless Networks. IEEE Communications Letters. Vol. 7, No. 10, October, 2003.
5. S. Capkun, J.-P. Hubaux, and L. Buttyan. Mobility Helps Security in Ad Hoc Networks. In Proc. of MobiHoc'03, Annapolis, Maryland, USA, pp46-56, June, 2003.
6. A. Weimerskirch, and G. Thonet. A Distributed Light-Weight Authentication Model for Ad-Hoc Networks. In Proc. of 4th International Conference on Information Security and Cryptology (ICISC 2001), pp341-354, Seoul, South Korea, December, 2001.
7. B. Raghavan, and A.C. Snoeren. Priority Forwarding in Ad Hoc Networks with Self-Interested Parties. Workshop on Economics of Peer-to-Peer Systems, Berkeley, USA, May, 2003.
8. H. Miranda, and L. Rodrigues. Friends and Foes: Preventing Selfishness in Open Mobile Ad Hoc Networks. In Proc. of the First International Workshop on Mobile Distributed Computing (MDC'03), USA, 2003.
9. Y. Zhang, W. Lee, and Y.-A. Huang. Intrusion Detection Techniques for Mobile Wireless Networks. Journal of Wireless Networks, Vol. 9, No. 5, pp545-556, 2003.

# Distributing the Cost of Securing a Transportation Infrastructure*

Sudarshan S. Chawathe

Computer Science Department
University of Maine
Orono, Maine 04469, USA
chaw@cs.umaine.edu
http://www.cs.umaine.edu/chaw/

**Abstract.** We address the problem of fairly distributing the cost of system-wide improvements to the security of a transportation infrastructure over the beneficiaries. We present a framework that models transportation links and the emergence (magnitude and frequency) and propagation of threats. The cost-distribution is based on a weighted sum that characterizes the expected reduction in the vulnerability of a site as a result of the security improvements.

## 1   Introduction

Securing the transportation infrastructure to protect it from hostile agents is an increasingly important task that is the subject of much recent work. No matter what strategy one uses for improving the security of the infrastructure, there are substantial and varied costs related to personnel, equipment, impediments to traffic, loss of revenue due to slow or rerouted traffic, etc. Once such costs have been determined, an important question is how they are borne by the typically numerous parties involved in the infrastructure. Indeed, lack of agreement on such division of costs has been the topic of much political controversy and threatens to derail initiatives for securing the transportation infrastructure.

For example, consider a proposal to implement additional checkpoints on some highways of a regional network and to disallow hazardous-material carriers on certain routes. Such actions incur the obvious direct costs associated with setting up checkpoints and enforcing new regulations. However, there are also indirect costs such as noise, pollution, and danger of rerouted hazardous-material carriers. Further, additional checkpoints may lead to congestion which may result in loss of business in the affected areas. It is not surprising, then, that even modest proposals that affect the functioning of the transportation infrastructure often elicit strong protests.

Given the increased awareness of security, it is likely that major disagreement is not about whether additional security is necessary, but rather about who

* This work was supported in part by the U.S. National Science Foundation with grants IIS-9984296, IIS-0081860, and CNS-0426683.

S. Mehrotra et al. (Eds.): ISI 2006, LNCS 3975, pp. 596–601, 2006.

should shoulder what portion of its cost. In this paper, we present a model of the costs and benefits of improvements to transportation-infrastructure security. Using this model, we can determine a cost distribution that has a sound basis and is thus likely to be considered fair by the concerned parties.

## 2   Model

We model a network of transportation links using a graph whose vertices represent locations of interest, or simply intersections, and whose edges represent links. A link $(i, j)$ between locations $i$ and $j$ permits, in general, travel both from $i$ to $j$ as well as from $j$ to $i$. However, travel in these two directions is modeled using separate parameters, as described below. Figure 1 on page 598 suggests a small transportation network modeled in this manner.

One-way links do not pose a problem to this model. The disallowed direction may simply be assigned a very low probability of traversal. A nonzero probability of traversal in the disallowed direction of a one-way link, such as a one-way street, may often model the link more accurately than a zero probability because, for example, it is quite likely that agents perpetrating an attack do not hold traffic regulations in high regard.

Threats may originate at any vertex of the graph representing the transportation network. Threats that originate at locations on a link between two vertices, such as a rail link between two stations, are modeled by inserting an additional vertex between those vertices. In other words, locations at which threats originate are, by definition, locations of interest and are therefore modeled using vertices in the graph.

We use two parameters to describe threats originating at a vertex $i$: a *magnitude* $m_i$ and a *frequency* $f_i$. Intuitively, the magnitude represents the seriousness of a threat, modeling quantities such as the amount of damage and the affected area. The frequency indicates how often a threat is likely to materialize at $i$. Our methods do not depend on any particular interpretation of these parameters. Further, our work uses these parameters only in conjunction, as the product $m_i f_i$, which represents the expected magnitude, per unit time, of a threat originating at vertex $i$. Determining appropriate values for $m_i$, $f_i$, and the other parameters of our model is an important problem, but not one that is the focus of this paper. Our focus is on how such data, once obtained, may be used to allocate system-wide costs of securing the transportation network.

When a threat appears at a location in the network, it may either be executed at that location or be transported to another location using one of the links. A threat may appear at a location either because it originates at that location, as described earlier, or because it traversed a link from another location to that location. We use $e_i$ to denote the probability that a threat appearing at a location is executed at that location. More precisely, the *probability of execution* $e_i$ is the conditional probability of a threat executing at $i$ given that it has appeared at $i$. Similarly, we use $t_{ij}$ to denote the conditional *probability of traversal* from $i$ to $j$, given a threat appearing at $i$. In general, $t_{ij}$ and $t_{ji}$ are not the same. Let us use

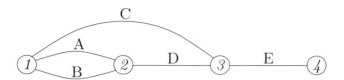

**Fig. 1.** A network of transportation links used by the running example

nbd($i$) to denote the *neighborhood* of $i$, i.e., the set of vertices that are the targets of links from $i$. Since $e_i$ and $t_{ij}$ represent probabilities we must have the following for every vertex $i$ in the graph: $e_i + \sum_{j \in \mathrm{nbd}(i)} t_{ij} \leq 1$ . However, the terms on the left-hand side of this inequality need not sum to one because the threat may disappear (e.g., a planned attack may be abandoned).

We denote the cost of improving the security on link $(i, j)$ by $c_{ij}$. The resulting (lower) link traversal probability is denoted by $t'_{ij}$. Finally, we define $s_{ij} = 1 - t_{ij}$ and $s'_{ij} = 1 - t'_{ij}$ for notational convenience.

## 3   Vulnerabilities

The model of Section 2 allows us to quantify the *vulnerability* of each location of interest. Intuitively, the vulnerability of a location of interest is the expected magnitude of a threat executed at that location. In order to keep the calculations simple, we henceforth assume that a threat is executed at its intended target (location of interest) as soon as it arrives at that target. That is, we may restrict our attention to traversals that do not visit any vertex more than once (acyclic paths). It is conceptually easy to do away with this assumption by using the steady-state distribution obtained by interpreting the graph of Section 2 as a Markov process [1].

Figure 1 suggests a small transportation network that we shall use as a running example. The four locations of interest are identified by the numbers within the circles: $V = \{1, 2, 3, 4\}$. The five links are identified by the letters above each link: $L = \{A, B, C, D, E\}$. The magnitude and frequency of a threat originating at vertex 1 are 1024 and 4, respectively, so that $f_1 m_1 = 4096$. (The numbers are chosen to minimize fractions in the calculations that follow but nothing in our model depends on such carefully chosen values.) For all other vertices in this example, $f_i m_i = 0$. That is, a nontrivial threat originates only at vertex 1. We use an execution probability of $1/4$ at each vertex. That is, $e_i = 1/4$ for all $i \in [1, 4]$. Traversal probabilities for all links (in either direction) are uniformly $1/4$. That is, for all $i, j \in [1, 4]$, $i \neq j$, we have $t_{ij} = t_{ji} = 1/4$ (and thus $s_{ij} = s_{ji} = 3/4$). We may verify that these values satisfy $e_i + \sum_{j \in \mathrm{nbd}(i)} t_{ij} \leq 1$ for all vertices $i$ in our example.

By a slight abuse of notation, we shall use the link identifiers, such as A and B, to denote both the links themselves and traversals of those links. More precisely, given a link $X = (i, j)$ with $i < j$, a traversal from $i$ to $j$ is denoted by $X$ while a traversal from $j$ to $i$ is denoted by $X'$. Paths are denoted by concatenating these labels for the traversals, in sequence. Thus, given Figure 1, $AD$ denotes a path from vertex 1 to vertex 3 via vertex 2, while $A'CE$ denotes a path from vertex 2 to vertex 4 via vertices 1 and 3. Further, we use $\overline{X}$ to denote a non-traversal from $i$ to $j$, and similarly $\overline{X}'$ to denote a non-traversal from $j$ to $i$.

Let us now calculate the vulnerability of vertex 3. Since there is only one origin of threats (vertex 1) in our example, the vulnerability of any other vertex in our example depends only on the paths leading to that vertex from vertex 1. A threat from vertex 1 may arrive at vertex 3 either directly, using link C, or via vertex 2, by using either of links A and B followed by link D. Therefore, we may calculate the probability of a threat from vertex 1 arriving at vertex 3 as follows.

$$P(((A \text{ or } B) \text{ and } D) \text{ or } C) = 1 - P(\overline{(((A \vee B) \wedge D) \vee C)})$$
$$= 1 - P(\overline{C})(1 - (1 - P(\overline{A})P(\overline{B}))P(\overline{D}))$$

Using our notation for the traversal probabilities from Section 2, we have the following expression for the vulnerability of vertex 3:

$$v_3 = m_1 f_1 (1 - s_C (1 - (1 - s_A s_B) t_D)) \qquad (1)$$

Substituting the parameter values from our running example yields

$$v_3 = 1024 \cdot 4 \cdot (1 - (1/4)(1 - (1 - (3/4)(3/4))(1/4)) = 1360$$

The interpretation of this number depends on the interpretation used in assigning values to the parameters $m_1$ and $f_1$. For instance, if $m_1$ represents the number of persons affected by a bomb and if $f_1$ represents the number of times a year such a bomb is expected to originate at site 1, then 1360 is the expected number of people affected yearly by the bomb, given our model. However, our work is equally applicable to any other interpretation that fits our model described in Section 2.

The above calculations are based on the state of the transportation network before any security improvements are made, i.e., the base state. In general, the vulnerability $v_i$ of vertex $i$ depends on the set of links on which security improvements have been made. Therefore, we use $v_i(S)$ to denote the vulnerability of $i$ given a set $S$ of improved links. The left-hand side of Equation 1 is expressed as $v_3(\emptyset)$ in this notation, which we shall henceforth use.

Continuing our running example (Figure 1), suppose that improving the security of a link halves the probability of traversal. Recall that we have traversal probabilities $t_{ij} = 1/4$ for all $i, j \in [1, 4]$, $i \neq j$. Using the notation of Section 2, we have, for all $i, j \in [1, 4]$, $i \neq j$, $t'_{ij} = 1/8$ and $s'_{ij} = 7/8$.

We may calculate $v_3(S)$ for all $S \subseteq L$ using Equation 1 by substituting $s_A$, $s_B$, $s_C$, and $t_D$ with, respectively, $s'_A$, $s'_B$, $s'_C$, and $t'_D$ depending on whether $A$, $B$, $C$, and $D$ (respectively) belong to $S$. For $S = \{A, C\}$, substituting $s'_A$ for $s_A$ and $s'_C$ for $s_C$ yields the following:

$$v_3(\{A, C\}) = m_1 f_1 (1 - s'_C (1 - (1 - s'_A s_B) t_D))$$
$$= 1024 \cdot 4 \cdot (1 - (7/8)(1 - (7/8)(3/4))(1/4)) = 820$$

**Table 1.** Vulnerability of vertex 3 of Figure 1 (page 598) for different sets of improved links, based on the discussion in Section 3

| Improved set $S$ | Vulnerability $v_3(S)$ |
|---|---:|
| $\emptyset$, $\{E\}$ | 1360 |
| $\{A\}$, $\{A, E\}$ | 1288 |
| $\{B\}$, $\{B, E\}$ | 1288 |
| $\{C\}$, $\{C, E\}$ | 904 |
| $\{D\}$, $\{D, E\}$ | 1192 |
| $\{A, B\}$, $\{A, B, E\}$ | 1204 |
| $\{A, C\}$, $\{A, C, E\}$ | 820 |
| $\{A, D\}$, $\{A, D, E\}$ | 1156 |
| $\{B, C\}$, $\{B, C, E\}$ | 820 |
| $\{B, D\}$, $\{B, D, E\}$ | 1156 |
| $\{C, D\}$, $\{C, D, E\}$ | 708 |
| $\{A, B, C\}$, $\{A, B, C, E\}$ | 722 |
| $\{A, B, D\}$, $\{A, B, D, E\}$ | 1114 |
| $\{A, C, D\}$, $\{A, C, D, E\}$ | 666 |
| $\{B, C, D\}$, $\{B, C, D, E\}$ | 666 |
| $\{A, B, C, D\}$, $\{A, B, C, D, E\}$ | 617 |

The result of such calculations for all subsets $S$ in our running example summarized in Table 1. There is no origin of a threat at vertex 4 in our example. Therefore, as indicated by Equation 1, link $E$ is immaterial for calculating the vulnerability of vertex 3. This fact explains the two sets in the first column of each row of Table 1.

The benefit of improving the security of a link is, in general, different for each the vertex. A fair scheme for distributing the cost of improving links over the vertices in the network reflects these differing benefits using the above framework. We defer the details of the distribution scheme to a forthcoming paper.

## 4   Related Work

While our work abstracts away some of the details of how various model parameters are determined, such determination is nevertheless very important and forms the basis of our model by providing the important parameters. For example, Shao presents a method for allocating redundant resources for disaster-recovery planning [2]. Similarly, recent work by Park et al. may be used to determine the vulnerabilities of nodes in a computer-network infrastructure [3]. Sinai discusses how work in the social and behavioral sciences may be applied to model and assess threats of terrorism [4]. Such work is key to determining the parameters, such as threat magnitude and frequency, used by our model in this paper. Information resources such as the MIPT system described by Ellis provide a means for efficiently accessing a variety of information necessary for threat assessment [5]. A similar effort in the context of the spread of infectious diseases is described by Zeng et al. [6]. Park and Ho describe a method for addressing insider threats [7], which are an important category of threats in any environment, including the one in this paper. Lin et al.'s user-acceptance study based on the COPLINK system [8] highlights the importance of solutions that make a compelling case for acceptance, which is also one of the motivations of our work in this paper. Xu et al. present a method to analyze and visualize criminal networks, focusing on dynamics [9]. Introducing the dynamic element into our model in this paper is an interesting avenue for further work.

# References

1. Breiman, L.: Probability. Society for Industrial and Applied Mathematics (1992)
2. Shao, B.B.M.: Optimal redundancy allocation for disaster recovery planning in the network economy. In: Proceedings of the Symposium on Intelligence and Security Informatics (ISI). Volume 3073 of Lecture Notes in Computer Science (LNCS)., Tucson, Arizona (2004) 484–491
3. Park, E., Seo, J.T., Im, E.G., Lee, C.W.: Vulnerability analysis and evaluation within an intranet. In: Proceedings of the Symposium on Intelligence and Security Informatics (ISI). Volume 3073 of Lecture Notes in Computer Science (LNCS)., Tucson, Arizona (2004) 514–515
4. Sinai, J.: Utilizing the social and behavioral sciences to assess, model, forecast and preemptively respond to terrorism. In: Proceedings of the Symposium on Intelligence and Security Informatics (ISI). Volume 3073 of Lecture Notes in Computer Science (LNCS)., Tucson, Arizona (2004) 531–533
5. Ellis III, J.O.: MIPT: Sharing terrorism information resources. In: Proceedings of the Symposium on Intelligence and Security Informatics (ISI). Volume 3073 of Lecture Notes in Computer Science (LNCS)., Tucson, Arizona (2004) 520–525
6. Zeng, D., Chen, H., Tseng, C., Larson, C., Eidson, M., Gotham, I., Lynch, C., Ascher, M.: West nile virus and botulism portal: A case study in infectious disease informatics. In: Proceedings of the Symposium on Intelligence and Security Informatics (ISI). Volume 3073 of Lecture Notes in Computer Science (LNCS)., Tucson, Arizona (2004) 28–41
7. Park, J.S., Ho, S.M.: Composite role-based monitoring (CRBM) for countering insider threats. In: Proceedings of the Symposium on Intelligence and Security Informatics (ISI). Volume 3073 of Lecture Notes in Computer Science (LNCS)., Tucson, Arizona (2004) 201–213
8. Lin, C., Hu, P.J., Chen, H., Schroeder, J.: Technology implementation management in law enforcement: COPLINK system usability and user acceptance evaluations. In: Proceedings of the National Conference on Digital Government Research, Boston, Massachusetts (2003)
9. Xu, J., Marshall, B., Kaza, S., Chen, H.: Analyzing and visualizing criminal network dynamics: A case study. In: Proceedings of the Symposium on Intelligence and Security Informatics (ISI). Volume 3073 of Lecture Notes in Computer Science (LNCS)., Tucson, Arizona (2004) 359–377

# Multi-document Summarization for Terrorism Information Extraction

Fu Lee Wang[1], Christopher C. Yang[2], and Xiaodong Shi[2]

[1] Department of Computer Science, City University of Hong Kong, Hong Kong SAR, China
flwang@cityu.edu.hk
[2] Department of Systems Engineering and Engineering Management,
The Chinese University of Hong Kong, Shatin, Hong Kong SAR, China
{yang, xdshi}@se.cuhk.edu.hk

**Abstract.** Counterterrorism is one of the major challenges to the society. In order to flight again the terrorists, it is very important to have a through understanding of the terrorism incidents. However, it is impossible for a human to read all the information related to a terrorism incident because of the large volume of information. Summarization technique is urgently required for analysis of terrorism incident. In this work, we propose a multi-document summarization system to extract the critical information from terrorism incidents. News stories of a terrorism incident are organized into a hierarchical tree structure. Fractal summarization model is employed to generate a summary for all the news stories. Experimental results show that our system can effectively extract the most important information for the incident.

## 1 Introduction

After September 11th of 2001, the public realized that terrorist attacks are threatening us anywhere over the world. In order to flight against the terrorists effectively, it is important to build a knowledge base of terrorism. However, there is a large volume of information related to a terrorism incident. It is impossible for a human to digest all the information. The problem of information-overloading can be reduced by automatic summarization. Research in this area is very essential for counterterrorism.

Many summarization models have been proposed [5, 6]. Traditionally, summarization system considers a document as a sequence of sentences. They calculate the significance of sentences. The most significant sentences are then extracted and concatenated as a summary. It was shown that the document structure is important in both automatic summarization [1] and human abstraction [2]. The fractal summarization was proposed based on hierarchical structure of document [11]. Experiment results showed that fractal summarization is a promising summarization technique.

Summarization has been extended to multi-document summarization [7]. Given a set of flat-structured documents, the summarization system identifies the similarities among the documents. The sentences are extracted based on their similarity measurement. However, there is not a trivial way to organize a set of flat-structured documents into a hierarchical tree structure. This paper investigates the impact of different hierarchical structure to the summarization technique. Experiments are conducted on

S. Mehrotra et al. (Eds.): ISI 2006, LNCS 3975, pp. 602–608, 2006.

terrorism incidents to determine how the summarization techniques perform in extracting the terrorism information from a set of documents.

## 2  Fractal Summarization Model

The information overloading problem can be solved by automatic summarization. A lot of summarization models have been developed. Traditional automatic summarization is the selection of sentences from the source based on their significance to the document [6]. The thematic, location and heading are the most widely used features.

A large document can be represented as a tree structure with several levels. At the lower abstraction level of a document, more specific information can be obtained. Studies of human abstraction had shown that the human abstractors extract the topic sentences according to the document structure [1, 2]. Fractal summarization model was proposed to generate summary based on the hierarchical structure of the document and fractal theory [11]. The detail algorithm is shown as follow:

```
Fractal Summarization Algorithm
    1. Calculate the Sentence Quota of the summary.
    2. Divide the document into range blocks and transform the document into fractal tree.
    3. Set the current node to the root of the fractal tree.
    4. Repeat
    4.1  For each child node under current node,
             Calculate the fractal value of child node.
    4.2  Allocate Quota to child nodes in proportion to fractal values.
    4.3    For each child nodes,
           If the quota is less than threshold value
                   Select the sentences in the range block by extraction
        Else
                   Set the current node to the child node
                   Repeat Step 5.1, 5.2, 5.3
    5. Until all the child nodes under current node are processed
```

In fractal summarization, the document is partitioned and transformed into a hierarchical tree structure according to its document structure. For each node, the system calculates the Range-block Significance Score by summing up sentence significance scores under the range-block. The fractal value of the root node is 1, and it is prorogated to other nodes directly proportional to its significance score. Then, the system calculates the number of sentences to be extracted according to the compression ratio. The number of sentences is assigned to the root of document tree as the quota of sentences. The quota is allocated to child-nodes by propagation directly proportional to the fractal value of the child-nodes. The quota is then iteratively allocated to child-nodes of child-nodes until the quota allocated is less than a threshold value and the range-block can be transformed to some topic sentences.

The fractal values of the nodes in the hierarchical fractal structure are computed based on the traditional salient features. To fully utilize the fractal structure of document, the traditional salient features are fractalized as follows:

- It is believed that a term carries different weight in different location of a full-length document [3]. In fractal summarization, the *tfidf* of a term in a range block is defined as proportional to the term frequency within a range-block and inversely proportional to the frequency of range-block containing the term.

- Fractal summarization calculates the location weight based on which document-level we are looking at. We calculate the location weight for a range-block, all sentences inside a range-block will receive same location weight.
- At different abstraction level, some headings should be hidden and some headings are emphasized. Moreover, the significance of the heading is inversely proportional to its distance from the sentence. Propagation of fractal value [4] is a promising approach to calculate the heading weight for a sentence.

Our experiments showed that the fractal summarization model produces a summary with a wider coverage of information subtopic than traditional (non-hierarchical) summarization model. The precision of fractal summarization model outperforms the traditional summarization significantly at 99% confidence level [11].

## 3 Hierarchical Structure of News Stories for Terrorism Incident

To prevent a terrorism incident, it is very important to have a through understanding of the incident. However, analysis of the incident is infeasible without help of summarization tools because of a large number of documents. Multi-document summarization systems have been developed for flat-structured documents. Advanced technique is required for analysis of structured documents.

Typically, multi-document summarization systems consider the documents as individual documents in a flat-structure [7]. However, a set of news stories related to a terrorism incident has a more complicated structure. A timestamp is associated with each news story. The distribution of news stories is not uniform along the timeline. Moreover, the news stories can be classified into event topics [12], and the number of news stories is not uniform in all events. As a result, a more advance multi-document summarization system is required for analysis of news stories of terrorism incidents.

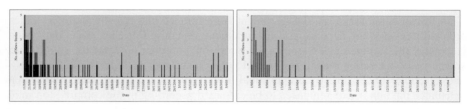

(a) "Madrid Train Bombing"          (b) "Beslan School Hostage Crisis"

**Fig. 1.** Distribution of News Stories of Terrorist Attack Incident vs. Time

In order to have an insight understanding of terrorism incidents, two terrorist attack incidents have been analyzed. Related news stories have been collected from the CNN.com. In the figures of distribution of news stories against time (Fig. 1), obvious peaks can be identified at the beginning of each incident. The peak is caused by a large number of news stories soon after the burst of the incident. Then, the number

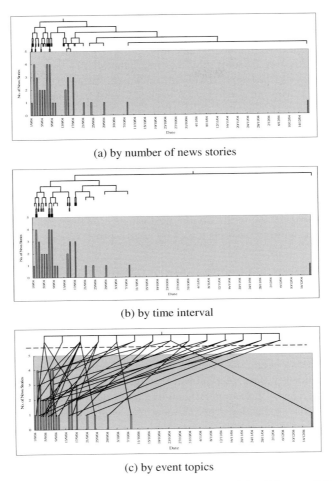

(a) by number of news stories

(b) by time interval

(c) by event topics

**Fig. 2.** Example of Different Hieratical Structures ("Beslan School Hostage Crisis" Incident)

of news stories decreases as time goes by. As shown in Fig. 1, the "Madrid train bombing" has a more long-term impact. Therefore, 115 news stories continually appear more than one year. However, the "Beslan school hostage crisis" has only a short-term impact, 36 news stories appear in the first month, and then it remains silent for about two month until last story in the third month.

It has been shown that the document structure is important in summarization [1, 2]. Therefore, the news stories are organized into a hierarchical tree. Taking consideration of the temporal and semantic information of news stories, we have investigated three alternatives:

1. The news stories are organized by the number of stories (Fig. 2a). Our previous result showed that a good summary must extract information distributively [11]. Moreover, when an author writes a document he distributes information evenly

into sections. Therefore, we consider all stories equally significant and they are evenly distributed into a tree structure. We propose to organize the tree such that the nodes at same depth contain same number of news articles.

2. The news stories are organized by the time interval (Fig. 2b). Temporal text mining technique has been applied to multi-document summarization [8]. Summarization of news stories are generated for each period of fixed number of days, then an overall summary is generated. We propose to organize news stories in a tree such that each child represents an equal and non-overlapping interval.

The news stories are organized by the event topics (Fig. 2c). The research of information retrieval focus on detecting of event topics of news stories [12]. A good summary must extract information from each event topics [10]. Recent research in automatic summarization proposes to classify the documents into document set before summarization [9]. Therefore, we propose to organize by event topics. As the accuracy of event topic detection affects the performance of the summarization directly, the stories are clustered into events topics by human professional in advance.

## 4   Impact of Hierarchical Structure to Summarization

News stories of a terrorism incident can be organized into different hierarchical structures (Figure 2). Experiments are conducted to investigate the impact of hierarchical structure to the performance of automatic summarization. The results show that classification of news stories by event topics achieves the best performance.

Experiments have been conduced on previous two terrorism incidents. The news stories are organized in three hierarchical structures as previous section. As there are relatively more children in the hierarchical tree by event topics, in order to have a fair comparison, we have considered hierarchical tree with different number of children for first two structures in addition to binary tree. Fractal summarization model is then applied to summarize these two incidents.

The fractal summarization for news stories is very similar to the fractal summarization of large text document, only some minor modifications are required to demonstrate the characteristic of the news stories.

– First, there is no heading for the internal node in the tree. As a result, the heading feature will only be considered at the news headings of individual news stories and the theme of the incident.
– The location feature in traditional summarization assumes that the text unit in the beginning or ending is more important. The news stories inside a node of news tree are considered as equally significant. Therefore, the location feature is not considered during summarization of news stories.

As the high-compression ratio abstracting is more useful, the news stories in our experiment are summarized with 5% compression ratio. To measure the precisions, the summaries generated by machine are compared with abstracts composed by human professional by gold standard [5]. The precision of a summary is calculated as the percentage of sentences selected by human professional (Table 1).

**Table 1.** Precision of Summarization with Different Hierarchical Stucture

| Incident | By Number of News Stories | | | By Time Interval | | | By Event Topics |
| --- | --- | --- | --- | --- | --- | --- | --- |
| | Degree-2 | Degree-3 | Degree-4 | Degree-2 | Degree-3 | Degree-4 | |
| Madrid Train Bombing | 62.1% | 58.9% | 63.2% | 58.9% | 58.9% | 55.8% | 71.6% |
| Beslan School Hostage Crisis | 58.7% | 56.5% | 60.9% | 56.5% | 63.0% | 58.7% | 82.6% |

When an author writes a large document with a lot of information, he groups similar information into same sections [2]. Therefore, classification of news stories into event topics simulates the process of an author writing a large document. It gives a more natural classification of the news stories. However, the classifications of news stories by number of news stories and by time interval partition the news stories by brute force. The themes among stories are not preserved. Therefore, the precision of summaries of news stories with hierarchical structure by event topics is significantly higher than the other two (Table 1).

News stories in hierarchical structure classified by number of stories and by time interval are both organized by their order along the timeline. Therefore, there is not much difference among two structures, and their precisions are similar (Table 1). On the other hand, there is no significant difference among the precisions for different degrees (Table 1). Changing the degree will not change the intra-stories relationship; they are still organized by time ordering. It will only change the amount of information inside each node. The fractal summarization model calculates the significance of each node by the amount of information inside the node, and the quotas are assigned accordingly. However, organizing news stories into hierarchical structure by event topics makes a fundamental change in the organization. As observed in the experiment, there is a substantial improvement in the precision.

Moreover, it is believed that a good summary must cover as many topics as possible and the redundant information within a topic must be eliminated [10]. If the news stories are organized into hierarchical tree by event topics, the fractal summarization extracts sentences distributively among the event topics. It also ensures that the most significant node will not dominate the summary. A more balanced quota among event topics can eliminate the possibility of redundant information as well. The fractal summarization model summaries a large document in the similar way as a human abstractor. Therefore, it is promising technique to summarize multiple documents.

## 5 Conclusion

Automatic summarization of multiple news stories is very useful to extract terrorism information from a large volume of information. Three hierarchical structures of news stories have been investigated in this paper. Experimental results show that the summarization of news stories with hierarchical structure classified by event topics outperforms the other two structures. The fractal summarization model together with hierarchical structure classified by event topics becomes a promising multi-document summarization system for multiple news stories. This novel approach provides an essential analytical tool for terrorism incident.

# References

1. Endres-Niggemeyer B. et al., How to implement a naturalistic model of abstracting: Four core working steps of an expert abstractor. Info. Proc. & Manag., 31(5):631-674, 1995.
2. Glaser B.G. et al., The discovery of grounded theory. Aldine de Gruyter, NY, 1967.
3. Hearst M. Subtopic structuring for full-length document access. SIGIR'93, 56-68, 1993.
4. Koike H. Fractal Views: A fractal-based method for controlling information display. ACM Tran. on Information Systems, 13(3), 305-323, 1995.
5. Kupiec J. et al. A trainable document summarizer. SIGIR'95, 68-73, 1995.
6. Luhn H.P. The automatic creation of literature abstracts. IBM J R&D, 159-165, 1958.
7. McKeown K.R. et al., Columbia multidocument summarization: Approach and evaluation. Document Understanding Conference (DUC01), 2001.
8. McKeown K.R. et al., Tracking and summarizing news on a daily basis with columbia's newsblaster. Human Language Technology Conference, 2002.
9. Nobata C. et al., A summarization system with categorization of document sets, Third NTCIR Workshop, 2003.
10. Nomoto T. et al., A new approach to unsupervised text summarization, SIGIR'01, 2001.
11. Yang C.C. et al., Fractal summarization: Summarization based on fractal theory, SIGIR 2003, Toronto, 2003.
12. Yang Y. et al., Learning approaches for detecting and tracking news events. Intelligent Information Retrieval, July 1999, 32-43, 1999.

# Rational Choice Deterrence and Israeli Counter-Terrorism

Don Radlauer

Associate, Institute for Counter-Terrorism, Interdisciplinary Center, Herzliya

**Abstract.** Deterrence is the "holy grail" of counter-terrorism: a strategy that offers the promise of reducing or eliminating terror attacks at minimal cost. Israel's experience has shown, however, that while many tactics have been promoted as deterrents, very few have actually worked. As claimed deterrence can be used to justify retributive policies that are unjust or simply unwise, it is important to apply careful thought before implementing such policies.

## 1 Introduction

Nations targeted by terrorist campaigns are in a difficult position: while they must respond to terror attacks, there is no obvious "correct" response. Passively absorbing attacks is not an attractive policy option, particularly for democracies, where public dissatisfaction affects government decision-making. However; the alternatives to passive victimhood are often controversial, expensive, and inconvenient – and sometimes ineffective as well.

Thus, the "holy grail" of counter-terrorism is deterrence. If enough potential terrorists can be convinced that carrying out attacks is a bad idea, all the massive investment in target-hardening, security checks, and other means of reducing terrorism will no longer be necessary. The risk, however, is that retributive policies justified as deterrents may be ineffective or even counter-productive.

Israel has been confronted by one of the world's longest terrorist campaigns, and over the years its leaders have tried in many ways to find ways of deterring terrorists. Israel thus provides an excellent case-study for examining the potentials and pitfalls of deterrence as a counter-terrorism strategy.

## 2 Rational Choice – A Theory of Deterrence

In modern criminology, the most widely accepted model for understanding deterrence is the Rational Choice Theory. According to Rational Choice, potential criminals are best understood as rational actors who weigh the costs and risks involved in committing a crime against the potential benefits of the crime. If punishment is swift, severe, and certain, few people will choose to disobey the law even if the potential illicit gain is substantial; but if punishment is uncertain, slow, or minimal, breaking the law can be seen as worthwhile even if the potential rewards are modest.

S. Mehrotra et al. (Eds.): ISI 2006, LNCS 3975, pp. 609–614, 2006.

At its most simplistic, Rational Choice Theory would seem to hold out the potential for creating precise mathematical formulae which would yield the correct punishment to deter any given crime. Reality, of course, is not so straightforward. Potential criminals do indeed weigh the risks, costs, and benefits before deciding on a course of action; but the factors they include in their intuitive calculations go far beyond the value of stolen goods and the income that would be lost due to imprisonment. So while it seems reasonable to expect people's decision-making to be rational given their goals, beliefs, circumstances, social milieu, and so on, it can be very difficult to describe these factors accurately enough to create precisely "correct" deterrence.

Even though Rational Choice Theory cannot tell us precisely what will constitute an adequate minimum penalty to deter a particular crime, it can certainly explain the general effectiveness of punishment in deterring premeditated crime. In fact, without Rational Choice Theory or something much like it, the concept of deterrence would make no sense at all.

### 2.1 Is Terrorism a Rational Choice?

Given the nature of today's terrorism – particularly suicide terrorism – it is easy to label terrorists as irrational. Were terrorists truly irrational, it would be pointless to seek to deter terrorism – since deterrence requires a rational actor who can change his mind in order to avoid punishment. In fact, though, there is no convincing reason to consider even suicidal terrorists to be irrational; extensive studies have failed to show any psychopathology associated with suicide terrorism.[1] Further, terror attacks – particularly the "high-quality" attacks that result in many casualties – are not carried out impulsively, but are the result of long, meticulous planning, preparation, and indoctrination. The fact is that potential suicide terrorists have changed their minds about carrying out an attack at all stages of the process, showing that even the "craziest" terrorists have the ability and opportunity to make decisions based upon rational considerations.

The question is not whether Rational Choice Theory applies to terrorism; but rather, what strategies for creating deterrence against terrorism might be effective, and at what cost. The most obvious criterion of effectiveness is whether a particular strategy has been shown to work in the real world. For the most part, reality is too complex to yield unambiguous answers. Accordingly, we must look at deterrence from a theoretical as well as historical standpoint.

## 3  Individual Deterrence

Terrorism is seldom a purely personal affair. While attacks are ultimately carried out by individuals, these perpetrators have been recruited, trained, indoctrinated, equipped, and delivered to their target by organizations that have their own agendas and concerns. Further, terror attacks take place in a national and community context.

---

[1] See for example, Ariel Merari. The Profile of the Modern Terrorist. In Post-Modern Terrorism: Trends, Scenarios and Future Threats. Transaction Publishers ( 2006).

So to analyze the potential for deterring terrorism, we need to examine how deterrence works – and fails – at all three levels.

## 3.1  Deterring the Suicide Terrorist

The terrorist who has no thought of escape, who seeks only to find the most damaging place and time to detonate his explosives, is very difficult to intercept once he has begun the final approach to his target. Clearly, suicide terrorists are a prime target for deterrence. At the same time, they present one of the most obvious challenges to a retaliatory strategy: by the time any retaliation can be carried out, they are already dead.

Since punishing the guilty is clearly impossible in this case, the only remaining option for creating deterrence is to punish the innocent. Such punishments can range from the mild to the draconian; the challenge for policy-makers is to balance the obvious injustice of punishing people who have done nothing (or very little) wrong against the benefits that effective deterrence would provide.

Israel's response to the challenge of deterring suicide terrorists was the demolition of the terrorist's family home. This policy attempted to capitalize on the terrorist's presumed reluctance to see his relatives made homeless; however, a military investigating commission determined in early 2005 that these demolitions had never had any significant deterrent effect on suicide terrorism. Home demolitions are unlikely to work as a general deterrent because they oppose transcendent benefits (furthering the terrorist's national cause, enjoying the eternal pleasures of Paradise, and even automatic entry to Paradise for one's relatives) with a mere economic punishment. Since his family house is likely to be replaced by the Palestinian Authority or foreign donors, and families of "*shahids*" receive special pensions and the like, the potential suicide bomber is likely to feel that "martyrdom" is an acceptably good deal even if his family's house is demolished.

At the same time as it failed to deter suicide terrorists, Israel's home-demolition policy damaged its international standing, caused internal dissention, and if anything increased Palestinian motivation to carry out terror attacks.

All of this does not mean that such deterrence is impossible to achieve. It is easy to imagine retaliatory policies that would create effective deterrence against suicide terrorism – for example, killing the terrorist's parents rather than destroying their house. However, such policies would be so flagrantly unjust that they would never be acceptable to the Israeli public, much less the international community. We can generalize these observations as follows: *Any policy of retaliation intended to deter suicide terrorism is likely to be either too weak to have any appreciable deterrent effect, or too harsh to be acceptable to the citizens of a democracy and the international community.*

## 3.2  Imprisonment as an Individual Deterrent

Arrest and imprisonment are the most common punishments for ordinary criminal behavior – but even for "normal" criminals, the deterrent effect of prison is somewhat uneven. To the extent that prison works as a deterrent to crime (as opposed to being simply a means of keeping the criminal off the streets for a while), it does so either because it interferes with the individual's family or social life, keeps him from earning a living, or carries a social stigma.

None of these applies to Palestinian terrorists imprisoned in Israel. Their families receive stipends to make up for their missing income; they are treated as heroes when they return home; and their release *en masse* is a standard demand of the Palestinian leadership in all negotiations with Israel. These factors do not completely negate the deterrent effect of imprisonment, but they certainly do reduce it.

### 3.3 "Targeted Killing" as an Individual Deterrent

Terror-organization leaders, recruiters, bomb-makers, and other functionaries present another attractive target for deterrence. Actions taken against these terrorists, unlike retaliation against relatives of suicide terrorists, are reasonably defensible from a moral and political standpoint. Further, unlike retaliation against the innocent for suicide attacks, actions against living terrorists serve a tactical as well as a deterrent purpose.

"Targeted killings" ought to be an effective deterrent. Death is a severe enough punishment to give most people pause, and members of terror organizations other than those being groomed to carry out suicide attacks are not known for being suicidal themselves.[2] However, three factors reduce the deterrent effect of "targeted killings":

- Since "targeted killings" of terror-group leaders and functionaries are not, in general, a response to specific terror attacks, their value as an individual deterrent is somewhat limited. The possible victim of a "targeted killing" cannot avoid his death by refraining from carrying out a particular attack; he must renounce terrorism entirely and resign from his organization, or else try to turn his organization's policy against terrorism. Either of these courses of action could well carry its own serious risks.
- Terrorists – particularly those who work with explosives – become accustomed to a high degree of risk. For a policy of "targeted killings" to be effective as an individual deterrent, the probability of being killed in this manner must be quite high.
- For various political reasons, the use of "targeted killings" tends to be rather sporadic. Since deterrence is best created by swift, severe, and certain punishment, "targeted killings" that are undertaken only occasionally do not have the impact that they otherwise might – especially given terrorists' acceptance of high risk.

Given the political costs of "targeted killings", it would appear that this tactic is best used either very selectively against especially high-value targets, or else as part of a concerted and intense campaign as described below.

## 4  Organizational Deterrence

While organizations are composed of individuals, they act in many ways as independent entities, with collective interests that do not necessarily correspond to the

---

[2] It has often been noted that terror-organization leaders and functionaries never carry out suicide attacks; neither, in general, do their close relatives.

personal interest of any particular member of the organization. In several ways, the terror organization is an attractive target for deterrence:

- Unlike individual terrorists who may be indoctrinated to accept or even welcome "martyrdom", terror organizations resist their own dissolution. There is no afterlife for organizations, and thus even religiously-motivated terror groups consistently pursue their earthly interests.
- Terror organizations, especially those with a traditional hierarchical structure, tend to react in rational, predictable ways. The leaders of such organizations tend to be rather "professional" in their outlook; this means that they will act to preserve their organization's interests even when this means making ideological compromises.
- Given sufficient motivation, the leadership of a traditional terror organization is capable of changing the organization's tactics and even calling a halt to attacks.

At the same time, there are challenges facing a terror organization that decides to change its ways in response to the threat of punishment:

- Terror groups derive much of their "street" legitimacy from the attacks they carry out. To cease to carry out attacks is to risk losing popular support.
- If the leadership of a terror organization decides to abandon terrorism, there is a possibility that part of the organization's membership will split off and form a new, violent splinter group. For deterrence at the organizational level to be fully effective, the organization's leadership must be sufficiently strong to persuade the rank and file to follow its new policies.
- If the organization's leadership decides to abandon terrorism permanently, they have to find a new role for the organization or face its dissolution. Organizations that have been in the "terror business" for years find it difficult to reinvent themselves as purely political or social organizations.

## 4.1  Organizational vs. Individual Deterrence

Just as terror organizations have goals that are different from the goals of any particular individual, they also have different vulnerabilities. Organizations do not "feel pain" or other emotions; they generally react much more cold-bloodedly than individuals do. On the other hand, organizations need a constant supply of money and other material resources, as well as recruits, in order to survive. If any of these processes are sufficiently disrupted, an organization can lose its effectiveness or even disintegrate.

The most obvious strategy for deterring terror organizations is to deprive them of key personnel. Imprisonment may be effective in this regard, but it is often very difficult to capture senior leaders of terror organizations; Israel has generally found it easier to kill terror-group leaders than to arrest them.

A number of countries confronting terror campaigns have attempted to use a "decapitation" strategy, on the assumption that taking out the top leader of a terror organization will cause it to collapse. This has seldom worked. Most terror groups do not rely on one leader's personality to survive, and can promote second-rank leaders to fill positions left open by "decapitation" attempts or other sporadic attacks on their leadership. A more effective strategy appears to be a focused campaign of "targeted killings" designed to eliminate enough senior operatives of a terror organization in a short enough time that the orderly process of promotion can no longer function effectively; if enough holes in the hierarchy open up at the same time, only relatively junior personnel lacking experience and reputation will be available to take over the leadership of the organization. Israel adopted this strategy in early 2004, killing Sheikh Ahmed Yassin and then Abdel Aziz Rantisi less than a month later. While Hamas has not disappeared or even renounced terrorism, the organization has behaved much more cautiously since these killings than it did previously.

While a strategy of deterrence based on the threat of aggressive attacks on a terror organization's leadership can be effective against a traditionally-structured group like Hamas, it is less likely to work well against more chaotic, decentralized groups or "leaderless resistance" movements. Further, there is a risk that effective deterrence of traditional terror organizations may actually encourage the growth of these non-traditional terror movements.

## 5 Conclusions

Deterrence has been a long-standing goal of Israeli counter-terrorism; and yet, despite many years' experience, Israel has not had very many successes in deterring terror attacks. Many of the strategies ostensibly designed to create deterrence are ineffective; subjected to analysis, they are rather obviously doomed to failure. The fact that some of these strategies have been pursued for years despite their high political cost and the lack of any good reason to believe that they would work suggests that claimed "deterrence" may sometimes be a way of rationalizing revenge.

The only strategy that shows real promise in creating effective deterrence against terrorism is to threaten terror organizations directly – not merely by sporadically attacking "key figures", but by mounting a concerted attack on their entire leadership structure. While this approach is far from a panacea, it appears to work against traditionally-structured hierarchical terror organizations, which have been responsible for most anti-Israel terrorism. Whether such an approach is effective against terrorist networks like the Global Jihad is questionable, however.

# Content Analysis of Jihadi Extremist Groups' Videos

Arab Salem, Edna Reid, and Hsinchun Chen

Department of Management Information Systems, The University of Arizona,
Tucson, AZ 85721, USA
{asalem, reide, hchen}@email.arizona.edu

**Abstract.** This paper presents an exploratory study of jihadi extremist groups'
videos using content analysis and a multimedia coding tool to explore the types
of videos, groups' modus operandi, and production features. The videos convey
messages powerful enough to mobilize members, sympathizers, and even new
recruits to launch attacks that will once again be captured and disseminated via
the Internet. The content collection and analysis of the groups' videos can help
policy makers, intelligence analysts, and researchers better understand the
groups' terror campaigns and modus operandi, and help suggest counter-
intelligence strategies and tactics for troop training.

## 1 Introduction

In recent years, web-hosted audio and video clips have become a powerful and robust
information platform and communication medium for jihadi extremist groups
(henceforth referred to as extremist groups) This has been made possible by
technological advances and the decreasing cost and size, ease of use, and
sophistication of video capturing and editing technology have made web-hosted audio
and video clips a powerful and robust information platform and communication
medium for jihadi extremist groups (henceforth referred to as extremist groups).
Extremist groups have become independent and prolific producers of multimedia
artifacts. Multimedia resources are widely used to spread and gain wider acceptance
of radical ideologies, raise funds, and show real results based on their view of justice.
This exploratory study analyzes extremist groups' Arabic videos and constructs a
coding scheme for examining the types of video, groups' modus operandi, and
production features. This study is part of a larger effort called the Dark Web Portal
research project that exploits automatic methodologies for collecting and analyzing
extremist groups' web-based artifacts to support research communities.

## 2 Related Work

In this section, we review trends in extremist groups' videos, approaches for
organizing and analyzing extremist videos, and video content analysis.

**Extremist Groups' Usage of Videos.** Several studies [3, 4, 7] describe the diversity
of extremist groups' videos in terms of language, size, format, and purpose. Some of

S. Mehrotra et al. (Eds.): ISI 2006, LNCS 3975, pp. 615 – 620, 2006.

the videos are mirrored hundreds of times on the web within a matter of days. According to Berger [3] the vast majority of the videos are simple, amateur productions filmed with handheld cameras or video cell phones. Videos a) are a powerful and easy way to communicate messages quickly; b) are a cost-effective means to produce lots of information in a short amount of time; and c) can provide persuasive action, vivid images, and sound to reach viewer's emotions.

**Collections of Extremist Videos.** Several organizations collect and analyze extremist groups' videos. The most notable organizations are IntelCenter (60 volumes), Intelwire.com (208 titles), SITE Institute (400 titles), and Global Terror Alert (134 titles). Most of the organizations analyze the videos and generate report; while the Artificial Intelligence (AI) Lab at the University of Arizona expands on this approach and collects videos using a systematic spidering and performs research using web content and link analysis. The AI Lab's Dark Web video collection contains 346 titles from the 6th batch collected in November 2005.

**Content Analysis of Videos.** Extremist groups' videos contain massive amounts of information that is useful for analyzing the types of violence [1], trends in groups' operations [13], leadership styles, and networks [7]. There is a wealth of content analysis studies of violence in television programs, video games [9], and music videos [10]. However, in-depth studies of the videos such as patterns of the groups involved, types of violence, modus operandi (e.g., targets, weapons, locations), and sophistication of videos are not available. Content analysis is a methodology for making inferences by objectively and systematically identifying specific characteristics of messages [6]. Automated content analysis approaches such as the Movie Content Analysis [12] and the Informedia Digital Video Library [14] projects are needed to extract structural and semantic content from the videos for use in terrorism research. A systematic exploration of the content of the videos is therefore in order.

## 3   Methodology

By using the video as a unit of analysis we aim to answer the following two research questions:

1. What types of video, groups' modus operandi, and production features are identified in extremist groups' videos?
2. How are the videos used by the extremist groups?

The content analysis process includes several steps: sample selection, constructing and assessing the coding scheme reliability, design of a coding tool (Multimedia Coding Tool), coding the videos, and analysis of results.

**Sample Collection.** We used a collection development approach used by Chen et al. [4] in their Dark Web portal project. For the sixth batch we collected 346 video files, totaling 73 hours and 45 minutes of video. From this collection we identified Arabic videos that were produced by extremist groups or their sympathizers in Iraq, and then randomly picked 20 videos.

**Coding Tool and Scheme.** The coding scheme is based on features of videos, terrorism ontologies [5, 11], the IntelCenter's video categorization [8], and the (narrowly scoped) domain of videos produced by extremist groups. The process of refining the scheme was incremental in nature.

**Table 1.** Coding Scheme

| Content Category | Content Feature | Description |
|---|---|---|
| **Class 1. Types of Video (Violent Attacks)** | | |
| Attack | Planning, Statement, Target, Weapon used (e.g., bombing) | attacks except hostage taking & suicide bombing |
| Hostage Taking | Captive's name, Nationality, Demand, Execution, Negotiation, Statement | Person held against his/her will |
| Suicide Bombing | Method, Suicider's name, Suicider's nationality, Statement, Target | Attack leads to a certain death of the attacker |
| **Class 1. Types of Video (Others)** | | |
| Message | Tribute, Leader Statement, Newsletter | Statement by extremists |
| Education | Instruction, Training | Documenting training |
| **Class 2. Content Properties** | | |
| Victim | Name, Nationality, Civilian/Military | Injury or loss of life |
| Date of Attack | Hijri Calendar, Julian Calendar | Reported attack date |
| Location | City, County, District, Town, Country | Location of depicted event |
| Target of threat | Person, Organization, Country | Threatened entity |
| **Class 3. Groups** | | |
| Extremist group | Name, Sub-group, Media agency | Group involved |
| **Class 4. Expressions** | | |
| Quotation | Religious quotation, Violent quotation | Quotation used |
| Reference to Media | Arab Media, Western Media | Mention of media |
| **Class 5. Production** | | |
| Production Feature | Title, Sound, Visual, URL, Multiclip | Video feature |

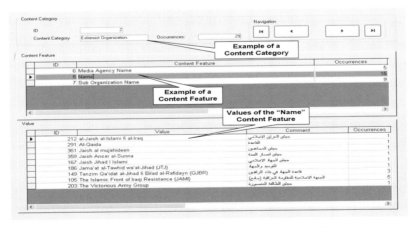

**Fig. 1.** MCT Interface for Coding Extremist Group's Videos

Table 1 summarizes the coding scheme, arranged into class, content category, content feature, and description. The first four classes focus on the types of video such as violent attacks and others, the content properties, groups involved, and expressions. Production is the last class, which includes the technical features of the video. Each class is subdivided into content category and feature that capture specific aspects of the videos.

We designed a Multimedia Coding Tool (MCT) that allows the coder to record his observations in a systematic and structured manner. The MCT manages the coding scheme and supports database query. Fig. 1 displays the MCT interface for coding videos. To validate our coding scheme, we performed an intercoder reliability (ICR) test.

## 4   Results

We analyzed the content of 20 videos. The average length of the sample videos was 3 minutes and 6 seconds. The videos are often filmed in real-time, instructive (take the viewer inside the planning and attack execution processes including scenes of the different weapons and skills required for their operations), low quality, and appeal to diverse audiences through use of Arabic and English subtitles. The plots are simple (focus on few goals such as to destroy the enemy's tankers), versatile (can be used for training, fundraising, motivational sessions), persuasive (display actors' emotions and dedication), succinct, and targeted (producers have complete control over the message and sequence of events).

**Types of Video.** The videos were organized into two categories: violent attacks and others. The violent attack video was the most frequently identified (18 videos out of 20) and some included planning sessions with maps, diagrams, and logistic preparations (13 attack, 4 suicide bombing, 1 hostage taking). The remaining 2 videos are leader messages.

**Groups and Modus Operandi.** We found 9 unique groups who took credit for the videos. In 5 videos the groups did not identify themselves. Two Iraqi insurgency groups, the Islamic Front of Iraqi Resistance (JAMI) and the Tanzim Qa'idat al-Jihad (QJBR), produced a total of eight videos that were in our sample. Extremist groups, such as Tanzim Qa'idat al-Jihad (led by Abu Musab al-Zarqawi), produced videos which included planning meetings (with maps, diagrams, and logistic preparations) before bombings. Scenes provide emotional and spiritual support by showing

**Fig. 2.** RPG Attack to Disturb a Supply Line

**Fig. 3.** Al Qaeda Video with English Subtitles

hugging, greeting, and praying together. Our results show that 60% of the targets are Western military humvees, cargo convoys, and other vehicles. Other targets include military bases (25%), military facilities such as barracks (10%), and infantry soldiers (5%). Most attacks occur in the Sunni triangle. Roadside bombs and RPGs (rocket propelled grenades) are the most common types of weapons utilized. These results are compatible with media reports on the Iraqi insurgency. Fig. 2 provides a snapshot from a video of someone shooting an RPG.

**Production Features.** A range of production patterns, from amateurish to professional, were identified. In addition, diverse visual production patterns were identified such as the use of subtitles, the groups' logos, background hymns (with/without music), and leaders' speeches. "Al-Sahab" (Al Qaeda's media agency) delivered a professionally produced video of a message from Bin Laden (see Fig. 3). The production quality and English subtitles suggest that the video is directed towards a worldwide audience. Ideologies and customs identified in the videos were consistent with real-world activities. For example, hymns in Tanzim Qa'idat al-Jihad's (QJBR) videos were not accompanied by musical instruments, abiding by the strict stance on the use of such instruments in Salafi jihad ideology. In summary, the videos convey messages that we believe are powerful enough to mobilize members, sympathizers, and even new recruits to launch attacks that will once again be filmed and disseminated via the Internet.

## 5  Conclusion

In this study, we conducted an exploratory analysis of 20 Arabic extremist groups' videos and designed a Multimedia Coding Tool (MCT) as well as a coding scheme for examining the content. We identified types of videos, extremist groups, modus operandi, and video production features.

Because extremist groups' video collections will continue to grow, a system for automatic extraction of structural (e.g., subtitles, images) and semantic content (e.g., weapons, target locations) is needed. Therefore, we need to expand our efforts to analyze video content by creating collaborations with research teams in the automated video content analysis domains [12, 14].

The results of this research are relevant for our Dark Web project, in that they provide a glimpse into some of the challenges of analyzing Arabic extremist groups' videos. Because this study was limited to a sample of 20 Arabic video clips, future studies of this kind should endeavor to enlarge the sample and verify if similar results are found. Further research should also be done to provide insights into extremist groups' operations and diffusion of multimedia.

## Acknowledgement

This research has been supported in part by the following grants:

- DHS/CNRI, "BorderSafe Initiative," October 2003-March 2005.
- NSF/ITR, "COPLINK Center for Intelligence and Security Informatics – A Crime Data Mining Approach to Developing Border Safe Research," EIA-0326348, September 2003-August 2005.

We would like to thank all of the staff of the Artificial Intelligence Lab at the University of Arizona who contributed to the project, in particular Wei Xi, Homa Atabakhsh, Cathy Larson, Chun-Ju Tseng, and Shing Ka Wu.

# References

1. Aikat, D. (2004). "Streaming Violent Genres Online: Visual Images in Music Videos on BET.com, Country.com, MTV.com, VH1.com." Popular Music and Society 27.
2. Becker, A. (2005). Technology and Terror: the New Modus Operandi. Frontline. Washington, D.C., PBS.
3. Berger, J. M. (2005). Short Primer on Terrorist Videos. Intelfiles, Alexandria, Virginia. http://www.intelfiles.com
4. Chen, H., J. Qin, et al. (2004). Dark Web Portal: Collecting and Analyzing the Presence of Domestic and International Terrorist Groups on the Web. IEEE Intelligence Transportation Conference, Washington, D.C., IEEE.
5. Guitonni, A., A. Boury-Brisset, et al. (2002). Automatic Documents Analyzer and Classifier. 7th International Command and Control Research and Technology Symposium, Quebec.
6. Holsti, O. R. (1969). Content Analysis for the Social Sciences and Humanities. Reading, Addison-Wesley.
7. IntelCenter (2004). Al Qaeda Videos & 3rd 9-11 Anniversary v1.0. IntelCenter, Alexandria, Virginia. http://www.intelcenter.com
8. IntelCenter (2005). Evolution of Jihad Video, v1.0. IntelCenter, Alexandria, Virginia.
9. Lachlan, K., M. S, Stacy L., et al. (2003). Popular Video Games: Assessing the Amount and Context of Violence. Annual Meeting of the National Communication Association, Seattle, Washington.
10. Makris, G. (1999). Searching for Violence on the Internet: an Exploratory Analysis of MTV Online Music Video Clips, North Carolina Chapel Hill.
11. Mannes, A. and J. Golbeck (2005). Building a Terrorism Ontology. ISWC Workshop on Ontology Patterns for the Semantic Web.
12. MOCA (2005). Overview: Movie Content Analysis Project (MoCA). Univ. Mannheim. Mannheim.
13. SITE (2004a). Jaish Ansar al Sunah Insurgency Group in Iraq Issues a Clarification Statement and Video Regarding the Blessed Attack Against the American Base in Mosul. SITE Institute. Washington, D.C.
14. Wactlar, H. (2000). Informedia: Search and Summarization in the Video Medium. Proceedings of Imagina 2000 Conference, January 31-Februrary 2, 2000, Monaco, France.

# Exploring the Dark Side of the Web: Collection and Analysis of U.S. Extremist Online Forums

Yilu Zhou, Jialun Qin, Guanpi Lai, Edna Reid, and Hsinchun Chen

Department of Management Information Systems, The University of Arizona
Tucson, AZ 85721, USA
{yilu, qin, guanpi}@email.arizona.edu,
{ednareid, hchen}@eller.arizona.edu

**Abstract.** Contents in extremist online forums are invaluable data sources for extremism research. In this study, we propose a systematic Web mining approach to collecting and monitoring extremist forums. Our proposed approach identifies extremist forums from various resources, addresses practical issues faced by researchers and experts in the extremist forum collection process. Such collection provides a foundation for quantitative forum analysis. Using the proposed approach, we created a collection of 110 U.S. domestic extremist forums containing more than 640,000 documents. The collection building results demonstrate the effectiveness and feasibility of our approach. Furthermore, the extremist forum collection we created could serve as an invaluable data source to enable a better understanding of the extremism movements.

## 1 Introduction

Previous studies provided an abundance of illustrations of how computer-mediated communication (CMC) tools were used by extremist organizations to support their activities [3, 5]. Contents generated by extremist organizations' use of online CMC tools, especially online forums, provide snapshots of their activities, communications patterns, and ongoing developments. They could serve as invaluable data sources for researchers to better study extremist movements. However, due to problems such as information overload and the covert nature of extremism, no systematic methodologies have been developed for collection and analysis of extremists' Internet usage.

To address these research gaps, in this research, we propose a systematic Web mining approach to collecting, monitoring, and analyzing extremist online forums. We discuss in detail the primary issues in extremist forum collection and how to address them. We also report the preliminary results of a case study where we built a U.S. domestic extremist forum collection using the proposed approach to demonstrate its effectiveness and feasibility.

The remainder of the paper is structured as follows. In section 2, we briefly review relevant research in extremists' exploitation of the Internet. In section 3, we describe the proposed extremist forum collection approach. In section 4, we present the preliminary results of a case study with U.S. domestic extremist forum collection. In the last section, we conclude this paper and provide future recommendations.

S. Mehrotra et al. (Eds.): ISI 2006, LNCS 3975, pp. 621–626, 2006.

## 2   Literature Review

### 2.1   U.S. Domestic Extremists and the Internet

U.S. domestic extremist groups have continuously exploited technology to enhance their operations. Stormfront.org, a neo-Nazi's Web site set up in 1995, is considered the first major domestic "hate site" on the Internet [5]. Nowadays, extremist groups have established a significant presence on the Internet with several hundred multimedia Web sites, online chat rooms, online forums [4].

The dynamic contents in extremist forums and chat rooms could serve as invaluable data sources for extremism research. However, chat rooms are difficult to monitor, because chatting history is often not preserved after chatting sessions are over. Forums retain all communication messages for users to view and reply at a later time. Thus, forums are of special interest to us because of their rich information and accessibility.

### 2.2   Existing Studies on Extremists' Use of the Internet

Research on extremist groups' use of the Internet is in its early stages [2, 4]. Table 1 identifies several studies that used various methodologies to explore a range of research questions about domestic extremist groups' exploitation of Internet technology.

**Table 1.** Summary of Research on Domestic Extremist Groups' Use of the Internet

| Methodology | Finding |
|---|---|
| Observation | Whine [5] traced of the early usages of the Internet by extremists and identified patterns of usage of USENET, bulletin boards, and Web sites. |
| Content Analysis | Bunt [1] analyzed Islamic Web sites and found that those sites formed part of a religious conceptual framework to inspire and motivate followers. |
| Content & Link Analysis | Burris et al. [2] found hyperlinks provided a accurate representation of inter-organizational structure among related organizations. |
| Content & Link Analysis | Zhou et al. [6] used a semi-automated approach in mining U.S. extremist Web sites. They performed link structure analysis and content analysis to facilitate understanding of extremists' virtual communities. |

Except for our previous research on U.S. extremist Web sites, most of the studies identified in Table 1 involved manual processes for monitoring and collecting extremist Web site and forum data. Due to the inefficiency of manual approaches and complexity of forums monitoring, the scope of these studies was limited. None of these studies resulted in a comprehensive extremist forum testbed for large-scale in-depth analysis.

## 3   Proposed Approach

To effectively and efficiently collect and analyze extremist forum contents, we propose a systematic Web mining approach that combines expert knowledge and automatic Web mining techniques to monitor and collect extremist forums. As shown in Figure 1, our proposed approach contains three major steps: forum identification, forum collection and parsing, and forum analysis. In the following sub-sections, we discuss the propose approach in detail.

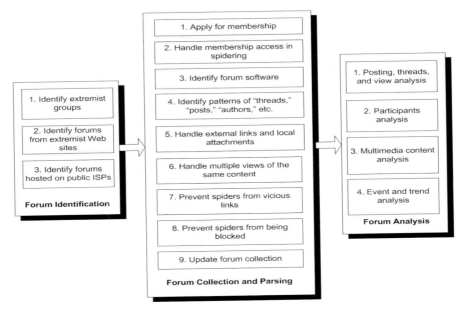

**Fig. 1.** A Web Mining Approach to Monitoring and Collecting Extremist Forums

## 3.1 Forum Identification

The identification of extremist forums is complicated by the fact that the Dark Web is covert and hidden away from general public. To ensure the quality of the collection, we identify extremist forums in the following three steps:

*1) Identify extremist groups.* We start the forum identification process by identifying the groups that are considered by authoritative sources as extremist groups. The sources include government agency reports (e.g., U.S. State Department reports, etc.), authoritative organization reports (e.g., UN Security Council reports, etc.), and studies published by terrorism research centers. Information such as group names, leader names, and jargons are identified to create an extremist keyword lexicon for use in the next steps.

*2) Identify forums from extremist Web sites.* In order to identify extremist forums, we first manually identify an initial set of terrorist group Web sites (called seed Web sites) from two sources: first, from authoritative sources used in the first step; second, from querying major online search engines with the extremist keyword lexicon. We expand the initial set of Web sites by extracting their out-links and back-links. We then identify and record forum entries from the expanded set of extremist Web sites.

*3) Identify forums hosted on public ISPs.* Besides forums on extremists' own Web sites, many extremist forums are hosted on public ISP servers such as Yahoo! Groups and Google Groups. We identify a list of these popular public ISPs and search for relevant forums using the extremist domain lexicon. By browsing through the messages of the forums returned from our search, relevant extremists' forums can be extracted.

The forums identified from both extremist Web sites and public ISP servers are filtered by domain experts to make sure that irrelevant or bogus forums do not make way into our final collection.

## 3.2   Forum Collection and Parsing

We proposed to use an automatic Web spidering approach to address the low efficiency problems of traditional manual forum collection approaches. Traditional Web crawling techniques cannot be directly applied in our case due to the defensive and diverse nature of extremist forums. To address these problems, we collect extremist forum documents in the following nine steps.

*1) Apply for forum membership and handle access in spidering.* Most extremist forums require membership to access. We manually send the application request to extremist forum masters as a curious neophyte. Once the application is approved, we use the user name and password to manually access the forums for the first time. Our access information is then stored in Internet cookies on our local computers. Then, we direct our spider program to use the cookies to access the forum contents.

*2) Handle different forum software.* Extremist forums are implemented using different forum software packages. The spider program needs to use different set of parameters to access those packages. We have created parameter templates for 12 most popular forums packages (e.g., vBulletin, ezboard, etc.) such that our spider program can generate parameters required by the corresponding forum packages. We also created parsers for each of the 12 popular forum such that our spider program can correctly extract thread information such as title, author, and post date, from the messages in different types of forums.

*3) Handle external links, local attachments, and multiple views.* Attachments posted by forum participants in their messages are very important. We set up our spider program to not only download textual messages, but also download multimedia documents, archive documents (e.g., ZIP files, etc.), and other non-standard files (files with extension names not recognizable by Windows operating system). Forums sometimes support views of the same message. These redundant documents need to be filtered based on the URL patterns to keep the collection concise.

*4) Prevent Spiders from Vicious Links.* Some forums may contain hyperlinks that trap a spider program in a loop (e.g. calendars, forum internal search engines, etc.). If the spidering process does not finish in a reasonable time, we need to examine the spidering log and exclude the vicious links from future spidering process.

*5) Prevent Spiders from Being Blocked.* We need to set a random time delay between hits and make the spider program mimic human browsing behaviors such that it will not be blocked by the forum servers. Some forums only allow specific types of Web browsers to access their contents. We need to set up the spider program such that it mimics a certain Web browser to access the target forums.

*6) Update Forum Collection.* Forum contents are constantly being updated. The spider program needs to revisit the target forums periodically to download new threads and posts.

Once the terrorist/extremist forum collection is built, automatic Web mining and text mining techniques can be applied to the collection to identify the characteristics of active participants and listeners, analyze the number and types of multimedia files posted, and analyze the correlation between forum activities and major world events. Results of such analysis can facilitate researchers' in-depth analysis on those forums.

# 4   Case Study: A U.S. Domestic Extremist Forum Collection

In order to test the proposed approach, we conducted a case study in which we collected and analyzed contents from major U.S. domestic extremist forums. We believe that Web-based research on domestic extremist groups should prove valuable for supplementing and improving studies on domestic extremist movements.

Following the proposed approach, we started our forum collection process by identifying U.S. extremist groups from authoritative sources. We referred to the authoritative sources and identified 224 U.S. domestic extremist groups. Using the information of these groups as queries, we searched major search engines and public ISP servers for additional extremist forums. After the expansion and filter steps, we identified a total of 110 extremist forums of which 18 are hosted on extremist Web sites, 31 are hosted on Google Groups, 47 are hosted Yahoo! Groups, nine are hosted on MSN Groups, and five are hosted on AOL groups.

After obtaining membership for the password-protected forums, we spidered documents from the identified extremist forums. Table 2 is a summary of the number and volume of different types of documents we downloaded from the extremist forums.

**Table 2.** Summary of Document Types in the Forum Collection

|  | Stand Alone Forums | | Public ISP Forums | |
|---|---|---|---|---|
|  | # of Files | Volume (Bytes) | # of Files | Volume (Bytes) |
| Total | 116,419 | 7.7G | 524,652 | 20G |
| Textual Files | 93,655 | 6.5G | 350,046 | 10.7G |
| Multimedia Files | 21,518 | 1.1G | 6,511 | 1.3G |
| Non-Standard Files | 1,246 | 45M | 168,095 | 9G |

As we can see from Table 2, our collection contains not only textual files, but also rich multimedia files and non-standard files. The non-standard files on extremist forums could be encrypted materials that were deliberately made inaccessible for normal software. Such rich contents could be used for various analysis purposes, such as hot topic analysis, time-series analysis, authorship analysis, and social network analysis.

## 5  Conclusions and Future Directions

In this study, we proposed a systematic Web mining approach to monitoring and collecting information from extremist forums. Using the proposed approach, we created a U.S. domestic extremist forums collection containing more than 600,000 multimedia documents. The comprehensiveness and quality of this collection demonstrated the effectiveness and feasibility of the proposed approach. Furthermore, this collection could serve as an invaluable data source for extremism research.

We have several future directions to pursue. First, we plan to get feedback from more domain experts to further improve the proposed approach. Second, we plan to apply our approach in case studies of larger scale. Third, we plan to explore more advanced machine learning and natural language processing techniques in the context of extremist forum analysis.

## Acknowledgements

This research has been supported in part by the following grants:

- NSF, "COPLINK Center: Information & Knowledge Management for Law Enforcement," July 2000-September 2005.
- DHS/CNRI, "BorderSafe Initiative," October 2003-March 2005.

We also thank all anonymous domain experts who have contributed to the projects.

## References

1. Bunt, G. R.: Islam In The Digital Age: E-Jihad, Online Fatwas and Cyber Islamic Environments. Pluto Press, London (2003)
2. Burris, V., Smith, E. Strahm, A.: White Supremacist Networks on the Internet, Sociological Focus, 33(2) (2003) 215-235
3. Dennings, D. E: Information Operations and Terrorism. (2004)
4. Gustavson, A. T., Sherkat, D.E.: Elucidating the Web of Hate: the Ideological Structuring of Network Ties Among Right Wing Hate Groups on the Internet, Annual Meetings of the American Sociological Association (2004)
5. Whine, M.: Far Right on the Internet, Governance of Cyberspace. B. Loader, ed., London Routledge (1997)
6. Zhou, Y., Reid, E., Qin, J., Chen, H., Lai, G.: US Domestic Extremist Groups on the Web:Link and Content Analysis, IEEE Intelligent Systems 20(5) (2005) 44-51

# Fast Pedestrian Detection Using Color Information

Y.W. Xu[1,2], X.B. Cao[1,2], H. Qiao[3], and F.Y. Wang[3]

[1] Department of Computer Science and Technology,
University of Science and Technology of China, Hefei, 230026, P.R. China
[2] Anhui Province Key Laboratory of Software in Computing and Communication,
Hefei, 230026, P.R. China
ywxu@mail.ustc.edu.cn, xbcao@ustc.edu.cn
[3] Institute of Automation, Chinese Academy of Sciences, Beijing, 10080, P.R. China
hong.qiao@mail.ia.ac.cn, feiyue@sie.arizona.edu

**Abstract.** In a pedestrian detection system, the application of color information can increase the detection rate; however, the detection speed will be slowed down a lot. This paper presents a fast pedestrian detection method using color information. It firstly scans a pair of sequential gray-scale frames to select candidates using both appearance and motion features; and then uses information of each color channel (RGB) to do a further confirmation with support vector machine based classifiers. Compared with pedestrian detection systems that only use gray-scale information, the system using our method has almost the same detection speed; at the same time, it also gets a better detection rate and false-positive rate. The experiment in a pedestrian detection system with a single optical camera proves the effectiveness of our method.

## 1  Introduction

The existing optical camera based pedestrian detection systems (PDS) usually throw away color information and only deal with gray-scale images [1], [2], since the computing cost is too large to process color images.

However, in practice, sometimes it is hard to distinguish a pedestrian from the background after the color information has been washed out, because the pedestrian will be hidden into the background in the gray-scale image of the same scene. Therefore only using gray-scale information to detect pedestrian will lead to low detection rate and high false positive rate.

There are just a few existing PDS systems use color information to detect pedestrians. For example, Constantine Papageorgiou and Tomaso Poggio proposed an object detection system which can be trained to detect pedestrians [3]. The system is mainly based on a trainable support vector machine (SVM) classifier using color information. However, they detected pedestrians with an extremely low speed at about 20 minutes per frame.

In this paper, we propose a fast method to detect pedestrians using color information. The detection procedure comprises two steps: First, candidates are selected from a pair of sequential gray-scale frames using a statistical learning classifier. Second, information of three color channels (RGB) is used for further confirmation. Compared

S. Mehrotra et al. (Eds.): ISI 2006, LNCS 3975, pp. 627–632, 2006.
© Springer-Verlag Berlin Heidelberg 2006

with similar systems, such as [3], ours has a much higher detection speed of 10 fps; meanwhile, pedestrians can be detected in different dimension.

The remainder of this paper is arranged as follows: Section 2 and 3 describe the detection and training procedures, separately. Section 4 introduces the experimental design and results. Section 5 concludes this paper.

## 2   Procedure of Detection

There are three main parts in our detection procedure: a preprocessing module, a statistical learning based classifier and a SVM based classifier. As shown in Fig. 1 (in the left half), each detection round can be described as follows:

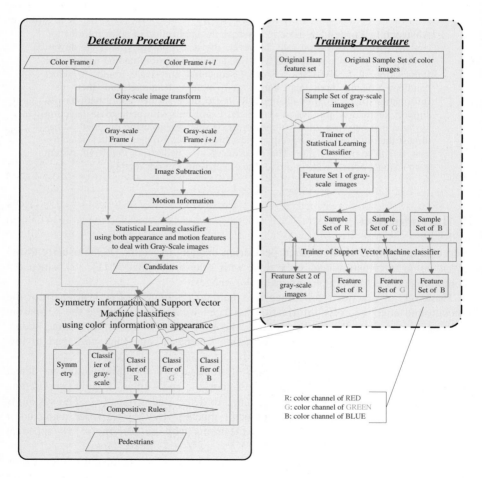

**Fig. 1.** Detection and training procedures our method

Step1 (preprocessing): Transform two sequential color frames into gray-scale images and then apply image subtraction technique to get motion information. Furthermore, in order to speed up the detection process, a particular region of the original frame pair, the region of interest (ROI) which is a rectangular region in which pedestrians might be in danger, is the only one dealt with.

Step2 (candidate selection): Apply zoom-image and slide-window techniques to perform exhaustive search over the ROI at every scale. Then for each window, a statistical learning classifier is designed to recognize whether there is a human body in it. These candidates will be further confirmed in the next step.

Step3 (accurate confirmation): Use three color-information-based SVM classifiers and one gray-scale-information-based SVM classifier as well as symmetrical character to do an accurate confirmation. Each of the SVM based classifiers is trained separately with its own training set using SVM$^{light}$ algorithm [4]. As shown in Fig. 1, these five modules (classifiers of R, G, B, gray-scale and symmetry) work together to finish the task of accurate detection.

## 3   Procedure of Training

The right half of Fig. 1 shows the training procedure of our system. As to gray-scale images, we apply AdaBoost algorithm [2], [5] and SVM algorithm [3], [4], [6], [7] to train two different classifiers. We also trained three other classifiers for three color channels (RGB). Symmetry of pedestrian is considered to assist detection, too.

We use color images so that the system will be able to take advantage of the most visually significant information in the three color channels (RGB) that gets washed out in gray-scale images of the same scene.

For example, as shown in Fig. 2, we can image that a pedestrian in red (RGB (180,0,0)) walks along the street, the color of the background is green (RGB(0,30,0)) and blue (RGB(0,0,60)). In this kind of situation, the pedestrian can not be found out if only using gray-scale information because he/she hides into the background; in contrast, he/she can be easily found out with red color information.

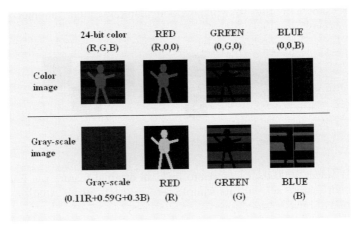

**Fig. 2.** Samples of color images and gray-scale images

## 3.1  Sample Sets

For a classifier, various high quality samples are very important. In all, we make 3600 positive sample pairs and 3000 high-quality negative sample pairs from great amount of videos in real city traffic. Here high-quality means that these negative samples are very similar to human body, such as trees and so on. We also produce a large number of negative sample pairs (about 1,000,000 pairs) automatically.

In order to get gray-scale sample set, we only need to transform the original color samples to gray-scale ones. We can also conveniently get sample set of the each color channel (RGB) in similar way (See in Fig. 2).

All of the gray-scale samples are used to train the statistical learning classifier, while only high-quality negative sample pairs and the false positive sample pairs out of statistical learning classifier are used to train the SVM classifier of gray-scale. The classifier of each color channel is trained with its own sample set.

## 3.2  Feature Extraction

Motion information can be obtained by subtracting two consecutive frames in gray-scale. For example, Δ in Fig. 3 contains motion information.

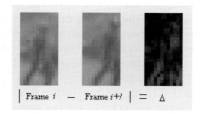

**Fig. 3.** Motion information obtainment

Five kinds of appearance features which are selected for the statistical learning classifier are shown in Fig. 4; while motion features contain another kind with a single dark rectangle.

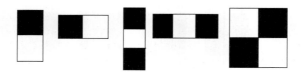

**Fig. 4.** Five kinds of appearance features

We firstly select 5000 haar features to form an original feature set. Each classifier selects its own feature set with its sample set separately using AdaBoost algorithm [2], [5] instead of random selection.

### 3.3  Training of Each Classifier

Different kinds of classifiers aim at different purposes; therefore, each classifier is trained separately with its own target.

The statistical learning classifier is designed to be a cascaded structure. It is made up of seven layers. Appearance features are used in the first five cascades and motion features are adopted in the other two.

The statistical learning classifier is trained by applying AdaBoost algorithm [2], [5]. Within training, false negative rate should be as low as possible and the number of features selected should be as fewer as possible, therefore the detection speed can be accelerated.

The four SVM based classifiers are trained to have a high positive rate and a low false positive rate. SVM$^{light}$ algorithm [4] was used to train the classifiers.

## 4  Experiments

In order to validate the detection ability of our method, we carried out several tests on a Pentium IV 2.8G computer with 512M DDR RAM.

With the slide window size of 32×16 (pixel × pixel), the average result of pedestrian detection for eight verification videos is listed in Table 1. The test videos were captured at a 320×240 resolution with 30fps on a moving vehicle in real city traffic environment and the vehicle speed is 40 km/h in average. Each video has 450 frames (15 seconds). The dimension of ROI is 240×120 (pixel × pixel).

**Table 1.** System performance with/without color information

| System performance in average | Only use gray-scale information | Use both gray-scale information and color information |
|---|---|---|
| Detection rate | 80.2% | 87.3% |
| False positive rate | 0. 7% | 0.05% |
| Detection speed | 10.3 fps | 10.1 fps |

Table 1 indicates that:

(1) To our cascaded architecture, the system with/without color information both gets good performance comparing to other typical single-camera-based PDS systems only using gray-scale information. With videos of real city traffic, the detection speed is about 10 fps in average, and the detection rate reaches to more than 80%; whilst the false positive is no more than 0.7%.

- D.M. Gavrila proposed a vehicular PDS with a single optical camera, and it use gray-scale images and binary images to detect pedestrians. Its false positive rate is 15 % and false negative rate is 10% at a detection speed of 1 fps with a dual-Pentium 450 MHz. [1]
- Fengliang Xu et al. designed a single infrared camera based PDS. His PDS has an unstable detection rate between 26% and 94% with an average false positive rate of 2.6%. Its detection speed is 40 seconds per frame. [7]

(2) The application of color information increases the detection ability/rate and reduces the false positive rate compared with that only uses gray-scale information. At the same time, the detection speed of using color information is almost the same as that of only using gray-scale information, because classification with color information only applies on the small amount of selected candidates.

## 5  Conclusions

This paper proposed a fast pedestrian detection method using color information. It is suit for low-cost PDS system based on cheap optical cameras. With color information we can increase the detection rate without more time cost.

Comparing with similar pedestrian detection method using color information [6], our method has the following features:

(1) With zoom-image technique we can detect pedestrian in different dimension.
(2) Our method is much faster than theirs; hence it is more suitable for a real-time vehicular pedestrian detection.

## Acknowledgement

This work was supported by National Natural Science Foundation of China (60204009), and Open Foundation of The Key Laboratory of Complex Systems and Intelligence Science, Chinese Academy of Sciences (20040104).

## References

1. D.M. Gavrila: Pedestrian detection from a moving vehicle. European Conference on Computer Vision (ECCV), (2000) 37–49
2. Paul Viola, Michael Jones, Daniel Snow: Detecting Pedestrians Using Patterns of Motion and Appearance. International Conference on Computer Vision (ICCV), Vol.2. (2003)734–741
3. Papageorgiou, C., Poggio, T.: Trainable pedestrian detection. International Conference on Image Processing, Vol.4. (1999) 35–39
4. T. Joachims: Making large-scale SVM learning practical, in Advances  in Kernel Methods – Support Vector Learning. B. Schölkopf, C. J. C. Burges, A. J. Smola, Eds. Cambridge. MA: MIT Press (1998)
5. Paul Viola, Michael Jones: Robust Real-Time Face Detection. International Journal of Computer Vision, Vol.57. (2004) 137–154
6. Zhang X.G.: Introduction to statistical learning theory and support vector machines. Acta Automatica Sinica, Vol.26. (2000) 32–42
7. Fengliang Xu, Xia Liu, Kikuo Fujimura: Pedestrian Detection and Tracking with Night Vision. IEEE Transaction on Intelligent Transportation Systems, Vol.6. (2005) 63–71

# SG-Robot: CDMA Network-Operated Mobile Robot for Security Guard at Home

Je-Goon Ryu[1], Se-Kee Kil[2], Hyeon-Min Shim[2], Sang-Moo Lee[3],
Eung-Hyuk Lee[4], and Seung-Hong Hong[2]

[1] Intelligent Healthcare Research Center, Bucheon-City, Korea
doctory@empal.com
[2] Dept. of Electronic Engineering, Inha Univ., Incheon, Korea
kclips@hanmail.net, elecage@paran.com, shhong@inha.ac.kr
[3] Division for Advanced Robot Technology, KITECH, Korea
lsm@kitech.re.kr
[4] Dept. of Electronic Engineering, Korea Polytechnic Univ., Gyeonggi-Do, Korea
ehlee@kpu.ac.kr

**Abstract.** The paradigm of robot which performs specific tasks remotely has changed into intelligent robot to perform public and individual tasks. Especially, in the robot and security industry, security guard robot provides a variety of information to the user and achieves its duty through the Web. The communication technique for these telepresence robots takes charge of the probability of various services in the robot industry. Last year, the interface for telepresence robot has developed over the Web or RF between robots, but these systems have the demerits of limited distance or geographical limit to be established to an internet link. In this paper, we propose the SG-Robot(*Security Guard Robot*) that can be operated and conduct surveillance of the environment around itself anytime/anywhere using CDMA networking. SG-Robot was able to solve those problems, conduct the surveillance task and communicate between multi SG-Robot and users over the CDMA2000-1x communication network efficiently.

## 1 Introduction

Various intelligent robot control solutions can be observed in various fields around our life. Telepresence robot has been also utilized with the guard robot, as using internet. As broadband internet and CDMA communication networking are being used nation-widely in Korea, Korea has advanced infrastructure to utilize robots through wireless communication solutions. So, more derived and more intelligent applications can be added to the existing functionalities of robots by using CDMA communication solution in robot industry.

Web-based tele-operation interfaces for robots have been developed and have gained serious interest over the last few years. Three of the earlier systems are the Mercury Project installed in 1994[1], Austria's Tele-robot on the Web[2], which came on-line nearly at the same time, and the Tele-Garden[3], which replaced the Mercury robot in 1995. While the Mercury robot and the Tele-Garden allow the Web user to

S. Mehrotra et al. (Eds.): ISI 2006, LNCS 3975, pp. 633–638, 2006.

perform different types of digging tasks, such as excavation of artifacts as well as watering and seeding flowers, the Tele-robot on the Web gives Web users the opportunity to build complex structures from toy blocks.

Mobile robots which can be controlled over the Web provide exclusive remote control to a single person or provide queues to schedule user requests. KhepOnTheWeb[4] is a typical representative of mobile robots with a Web interface. Users can give elementary movement actions to the robots and observe them using several Web-cameras. Xavier[5] was probably the first mobile robot which operates in a populated office building controlled through the Web. Xavier can be advised by Web users to move to an office and to tell a knock-knock joke after arrival. Cyberguard[6] is a mobile security robot marketed by Cybermotion. The aim of Cyberguard is to patrol indoor building areas for intruders, fires and chemical threats.

Telepresence robots are typically equipped with a video camera, a microphone, and a wireless transmitter that enables it to send signals to an internet connection. But, these systems have the demerits of geographical limit, requiring it to be operated in the environment with an established internet link. Current intelligent robots applied with image processing technology also has inferior product value because it uses low price level CMOS type cameras only, which have low frame rate and low image quality when encoding, and the function of transferring images wirelessly is still missing and only viewing images through PC from robot is provided now.

Therefore, this paper purposes to combine robot solution with mobile communication technology and develop security guard robot utilizing CDMA communication infrastructure and image processing technology.

## 2  System Configuration

The SG-Robot project, a research and development activity entitled "Tele-operated robot using CDMA networking", introduces a new communication interface approach to telepresence and security surveillance of robot at home or at outdoor. The user is offered the capability to remotely issue commands to navigate a specific place.

SG-Robot is characterized by differential drive, turret drive for turning body without driving the wheels, communication interface and various sensors. The sensory equipment includes auditory, vision, ultrasonic, and IR scanner sensors, which allow the robot to behave autonomously and to observe the environment around it.

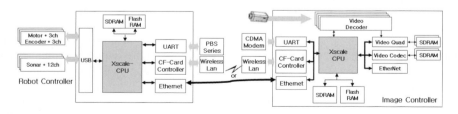

**Fig. 1.** Architecture of SG-Robot

Figure 1 represents the architecture of the developed SG-Robot. The controller of SG-Robot entirely consists of the image controller and the robot controller. Each controller exchanges command data through the wireless adhoc LAN. The reason of that is to easily establish the image controller for other robot systems. The robot controller is divided into three branches by function: communication, sensory, and drive function. And the image controller is divided into two parts by function: internal/external communication and image processing function. The image controller directly communicates with mobile phone through the CDMA modem placed in robot system. Received/transmitted packets are streaming images and robot control commands. Input images through a camera placed in front of the SG-Robot are compressed with the QCIF size and transmitted to mobile phone by CDMA modem using CDMA2000-1x network. Image controller allows data to be sent to mobile phone, after CDMA modem connects to the relay server.

Figure 2(a) shows mobile phone for controlling SG-Robot. CDMA mobile phone has two functions for controlling SG-Robot. First, it can display streaming images. When a camera is used for SG-Robot, motion picture data need to be transferred to mobile phone through the CDMA network. CDMA2000-1x network has very low bit rate of the bandwidth. Due to the mismatch between the data rates of the CDMA network and the motion picture, data compression should be performed before the transmission from the mobile phone. Image controller of the SG-Robot provides MPEG-4 and JPEG compression of the motion picture. As mobile phone has low capacity memory, the baseline JPEG compressing methods are used in image coding over CDMA network. Next, mobile phone allows user to control SG-Robot. SG-Robot is operated by pushing the buttons. Therefore, a user can monitor the environment around SG-Robot and control to navigate it through the LCD screen of mobile phone.

The CDMA Modem in SG-Robot access to wireless network with PPP Protocol based on Mobile IP. For continuing connection between SG-Robot and mobile phone, relay server needs to be established. Multi SG-Robots and users can be also constructed in this configuration. The relay server allows multi users to access to SG-Robot in accordance with their permission degree. In the whole SG-Robot configuration, a relay strategy is designed to increase the system efficiency and to satisfy the isochronous requirements of showing motion pictures and providing command control of SG-Robot to multi users. Figure 2(b) shows the relay server for connection management.

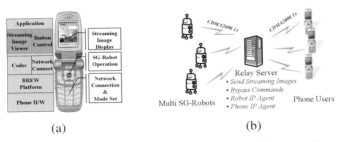

(a)                                      (b)

**Fig. 2.** Mobile phone for controlling SG-Robot and Relay server for connection management

## 3   Implementation

The objectives of SG-Robot are to guard home or public places, to inform user of the state of emergency, and to be controlled for specific mission. To accomplish these objectives, robot controller uses the RTAI (Real Time Application Interface) to provide real-time performance with embedded Linux. It provides a high-performance real-time kernel which supports both deadline and highest-priority-first scheduling.

Sensor-based robotic systems contain both general and special purpose hardware, and thus the development of applications tends to be a very tedious and time consuming task. In the SG-Robot system, obstacle avoiding behavior, various robot motion, efficient user interface, communication interface, and system fail check are easily implemented by using multitasking function, intertask communication mechanism, and real-time runtime libraries of RTAI.

Figure 3(a) and 3(b) show the implemented framework in this system. The framework for the SG-Robot controller consists of 5 layers, such as hardware layer, firmware layer, task layer, thread layer, and GUI layer. Especially, in the thread layer and task layer, data share uses the shared memory and data transfer uses the FIFO. Each thread communicates with each other using the message event.

Data interface of this robot framework was designed with similarly a nervous system and memory system of human. As SG-Robot simultaneously processes the command of user and the navigation procedure, it can guarantee a high efficiency and stability the designed system. PBS series and sonar array is updated each 200ms, and odometry is only updated each 100ms. After gained sensor data is stored in shared memory, free navigation thread and find obstacle thread reprocess the information to avoid obstacle and to navigate to specific goal.

Multi-threads in framework for image controller also have the soft real-time performance. Captured image information is updated each 100ms and stored in Queue. At the same time, face recognition thread conducts the process to find who was known through comparing with sample face in DB, and CDMA communication thread sends the captured images in queue to mobile phone.

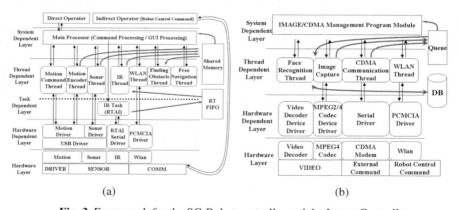

(a)                                         (b)

**Fig. 3.** Framework for the SG-Robot controller and the Image Controller

## 4   Experiments and Result

To evaluate the designed system, we measure the transmission rate of motion pictures and command data in the office environment.

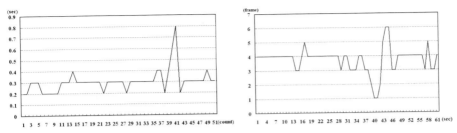

**Fig. 4.** Response time of robot control command and Transmission rate of streaming image to the mobile phone

Figure 4 represents the response time of the robot after being issued the command by mobile phone and the transmission rate of streaming images from a camera in the robot to mobile phone. In general, the average response time was 0.3~0.4ms. But, the response time takes about 1sec from time to time, due to the irregular wave interference or the spatial characteristics. The image transmission rate is 4~5frame/sec. Sometimes, it was also delayed about 2~3frames by the same reason. Figure 5 shows the scene which streaming images are transferred from camera in front of SG-Robot to mobile phone, when user operates the SG-Robot by mobile phone. Through the LCD screen displaying the images, user could recognize the scene and operate the robot to other place.

**Fig. 5.** Images transmitted to mobile robot as the SG-Robot moves

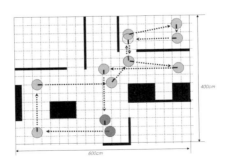

**Fig. 6.** SG-Robot navigation operated by the mobile phone of the user

Figure 6 represents the navigated path when the user at outdoors operates the SG-Robot located in modeling house in an indoor environment. We obtained a rate of 95% of successive control during conducted experiments. The successive rate is calculated using an experimental time and the time that is subtracted by delay time due to irregular wave interference. In this experiment, the operator could control the SG-Robot to navigate to a specific place through the LCD screen of mobile phone.

## 5  Conclusion

We have created a telepresence robot that allows SG-Robot to be operated by mobile phone through CDMA network. The outcomes of this study can be utilized for intelligent service robot and URC (Ubiquitous Robotic Companion) industries and will be considered to be a valuable technology to apply robot technology to mobile communication.

## References

1. K.Goldberg, S. Gentner, C.Sutter, J. Wiegley, and B. Farzin, The mercury project: A feasibility study for online robots. An Introduction to Online Robots, MIT Press, 2002.
2. K.Goldberg, J. Santarromana, G. Bekey, S. Gentner, R. Moris, J. Wiegley, and E. Berger, "The telegarden", Proc. of  ACM SIGGRAPH, 1995.
3. K. Taylor and J. Trevelyan, "A telerobot on the World Wide Web", Proc. of the 1995 National Conference of the Australian Robot Association, 1995.
4. W. Burgard and D. Schulz, "Robust visualization for web-based control of mobile robot", K. Goldberg and R. Siegwart, editors, Robots on the Web: Physical interaction through the Internet, MIT-Press, 2001.
5. F.Dellaert, W.Burgard, D.Fox, and S. Thrun, "Using the condensation algorithm for robust, vision-based mobile robot localization", Proc. of the IEEE Conference on Computer Vision and Pattern Recognition, CVPR, 1999.
6. Nikolaos A. Massios and Frans Voorbraak, "Issues in Surveillance", March, 1998.
7. Fischer, America Calling: A Social History of the Telephone to 1940, University of California Press. 1992.
8. W. Burgard, P. Trahanias, D. Hahnel, M. Moors, D. Schulz, and H. Baltzakis, A. Argyros, "TOURBOT and WebFAIR : Web-Operated Mobile Robots for Tele-Presence in Populated Exhibitions", Fullday workshop in Robots In Exhibitions, IEEE/RSJ Conf. IROS'2, 2002.
9. T. Tomizawa, A. Ohya, and S.Yuta, "Book Browsing System using an Autonomous Mobile Robot Teleoperated via the Internet", Proceeding of IROS, 2002.
10. W. Burgard, P. Trahanias, D. Hahnel, M. Moors, D. Schulz, and H. Baltzakis, A. Argyros, "Tele-presence in Populated Exhibitions through Web-operated Mobile Robots", AUTONOMOUS ROBOTS, Kluwer academic publisher, Vol. 15-3, 2003, pp.299.
11. E.Paulos and J. Canny, " Ubiquitous Tele-embodiment: Applications and Implications", International Journal of Human Computer Studies, Academic Press, Vol. 46-6, 1997, pp 861.

# Design of Syntactical Morphological and Semantical Analyzer (SMSA) for Processing Arabic Texts

Samar Mouti[1] and Fadel Sukkar[2]

[1] University of Aleppo, Faculty of Informatics Engineering, Aleppo, Syria
samarmouti@hotmail.com
[2] University of Boston, Cognitive and Neural Systems Department, 677 Beacon Street,
Boston, MA 02215, USA
fadelsuk@cns.bu.edu

**Abstract.** This research describes an ongoing expert system developed for Natural Language Processing (NLP), and presents an approach for Arabic language manipulation, which integrates Syntactical Morphological and Semantical Analyzer (SMSA). Informational goal of SMSA is processing Arabic language from its inductive database, which is organized without dictionary.

Search engine is built up as a high performance linguistic engine that facilitates analyses of written texts in Arabic language, performs full linguistic processing on text, and generates robust parser for Arabic sentences. Learned knowledge is represented in form of rules and facts. Reasoning and inference are accredited to aid grammar induction containing syntactical, morphological and semantical rules, which are conducive towards language processing.

Arabic sentences are divided into two main parts: statement sentence and composition sentence. In turn, statement sentence is divided into a noun, verbal, and conditional sentences. Composition sentence is splited up into imperative and expletive composition. Words are divided into two parts: possession and functional words, also verbs and nouns are sorted in semantical groups.

Programming language Visual Prolog 6.1 is used. Database is built up to save Arabic sentences frames as facts. Facts of noun and verbal sentence are written as the following form:

```
sentn2 ("Adverb" "ظرف" , "Subject" "مبتدأ" ).
sentn2          ("Detached Nominative Pronoun" " ضمير
رفع منفصل" ,"Predicate" "خبر" ).
    sentv2 ("Subject" "فعل" , "Intransitive Verb"
"فاعل لازم").
    sentv2 ("Transitive Verb" "فعل متعد" , "Object"
"مفعول به").
```

Grammar of Arabic language are represented as rules. For example:

$$\text{Sentence} = \text{word1}(X) + \text{word2}(Y)$$

Rules are applied on this sentence as follows:

If X="Subject" And Y="Predicate" Then slot of nominatives is called.
If X="Past Verb" And Y="Subject" Then slot of accusatives is called.

S. Mehrotra et al. (Eds.): ISI 2006, LNCS 3975, pp. 639–641, 2006.

Inductive algorithms associated with both database and gramatical rules involve a test methodology for building databases. Learned knowledge is principal in the expert system SMSA, Inductive learning is used to make decisions. Many rules are implemented for reasoning and inference using a segmentation algorithm based on forward and backward maximum matching, together with a database, each Arabic sentence is represented in a sequence of Arabic words.

Search engine is built up to reach for the best goal from possible solutions. Inductive learning is particularly suitable to this context, where design system can be generated in an automated method. Collection of labeled data is built up, related rules are formed to make accurate predictions on future data, and to obtain reasoning and inference. Mechanism of search engine is designed to serve expert system to deal with text, it depends on Arabic language rules.

Syntactical analyzer is designed to analyze the sentence into primitive elements (words), specify number of words available in each sentence (length of sentence), and find possible frames of the sentence as a noun or verbal phrase, and reach correct parsing of sentence in especial cases. Morphological analyzer is accredited to divide word to separate letters, strip word from extra letters, suffix and prefix, and find suitable weight. Semantical analyzer is built up to select correct frame for this sentence using group of semantical rules, and reach correct parsing and vowellation of sentence.

Each sentence in Arabic language may be grammatically accepted but semantically not accepted. Role of the semantical analyzer comes to refuse wrong sentences that are not correct in the meaning, just like: the sentence (كتب الطالب الماء) (The student wrote the water) is refused, because of the verb (write) can never be related to the word (water) at all. This verb is completely related to the nouns that can be written (lesson, homework, etc). So, semantical analyzer examines the third word, and finds whether it belongs to the group that can be related to the verb (write), if it does not belong to it, then it is rejected.

When a sentence is entered to the expert system SMSA, it is analyzed using rules, search engine through reasoning and inference connections between database and SMSA to search on possible frames. Correct frame is reached after a series of executive procedures of words of sentence. For example, noun sentence is inserted:

"The sun is rising today" (الشمس مشرقة اليوم)

After being subjected to analysis, the words of this sentence are defined :

```
List= ["الـشمس","مـشرقة","الـيـوم"]  [today , rising , sun]
Length of this sentence is defined: Number of words= 3
```

Possibilities at parsing this sentence are appeared as form:

الــشمس مـشرقـة الـيـوم = مـبـتـدأ + خـبر + جـار ومجـرور

```
The sun is rising today =subject+predicate+prepositional
```

الــشمس مـشرقـة الـيـوم = مـبـتـدأ + خـبر + ظرف

```
The sun is rising today = subject + predicate + adverb
. . . . . . . . . . . . . . . . . . . . . . .
```

Basic rules are applied on each word of sentence to choose the correct parsing through the search engine mechanism:

- First word is a prepositional, a separated personal pronoun, an adverb or an interpreted infinitive is excluded.
- Second word is an adjective is excluded, because the adjective rules can not be applied on the word (مشرقة) (rising).
- Third word (اليوم) (today) belongs to the adverbs group, so one frame is found for the correct parsing of sentence:

الشمس مشرقة اليوم = مبتدأ + خبر + ظرف

```
The sun is rising today = subject + predicate + adverb
```

Morphological analyzer strips words from defined article "ال" to find the suitable weights, then complete vowellation of sentence is reached:

الشَمْسُ مُشْرِقَةُ الـيَـوْمَ "The sun is rising today"

Semantical analyzer exams Semantical groups of words, these groups are suitable, so this sentence is accepted semantically.

Experiment with the SMSA showed positive results in parsing and vowellation. Results thus far are encouraging. Ambiguity in Arabic language due to the inconsistent use or absence of vowellation, which should also be resolved in order to properly parsing of a given text. One of the most difficult tasks is determining true meaning of text, and semantic meaning of a sentence.

Arabic language is a particularly challenging language for computer analysis, especially in data processing applications. Revolutionary applications of AI are currently in use around the world, recent advances in this application will lead to many more applications.

# Using Author Topic to Detect Insider Threats from Email Traffic*

James S. Okolica[1], Gilbert L. Peterson[2], and Robert F. Mills[3]

Air Force Institute of Technology, AFIT/ENG, Bldg 641 RM 220, 2950 Hobson Way,
Wright Patterson AFB, OH 45433-7765, USA
{james.okolica, gilbert.peterson, robert.mills}@afit.edu

**Abstract.** Despite a technology bias which focuses on external electronic threats, insiders pose the greatest threat to commercial and government organizations. One means of preventing insider theft is by stopping potential insiders from becoming actual thieves. In most cases, individuals do not begin work at an organization with the intent of doing harm. Instead, over time something changes resulting in their becoming an insider threat. By detecting warning signs it is possible to discover potential insiders before they become actual insiders. Using the Author Topic [1] clustering algorithm, we discern employees interests from their daily emails. These interests provide a means to create two social networks that are used to locate potential insiders by finding individuals who either (1) feel alienated from the organization (a key warning sign of a possible disgruntled worker) or (2) have a hidden interest in a sensitive( e.g. proprietary or classified) topic. In both cases, this is revealed when someone demonstrates an interest in a topic but does not share that interest with anyone in the organization.

The dataset used for this research is the Enron email corpus. Unlike most organizations, Enron has a known whistleblower, Sherron Watkins, who was considered an insider threat by her boss, Andy Fastow, who was engaged in the illegal business practices [2]. The first step of the research resolves the Enron email into a collection of stemmed words and frequency counts (i.e. the number of times each word and each individual occurs in each email). These frequency counts are then fed into Author Topic producing four probability distributions: the probability of a word given a topic ($p(w|z)$), the probability of an individual given a topic ($p(u|z)$), the probability of a topic ($p(z)$) and the probability of a topic given a document ($p(z|d)$). The second step creates two social networks for each topic. The first, the implicit interest network, is constructed by linking individuals who have shown an interest in the topic. An individual has an interest in a topic if the conditional probability for an individual ($p(u|z)$) is 1.64 standard deviations above average conditional probability for that topic. The second, the explicit email network, is constructed by linking individuals who have passed an email related to that topic. An email is considered to be related to a topic if the conditional

---

* The views expressed in this article are those of the authors and do not reflect the official policy or position of the United States Air Force, Department of Defense, or the U.S. Government.

S. Mehrotra et al. (Eds.): ISI 2006, LNCS 3975, pp. 642–643, 2006.

probability for that email ($p(d|z)$) is 1.64 standard deviations above average conditional probability for that topic. Individuals who have links in the implicit interest network but not the explicit email network and classified as having a clandestine interest in that topic.

In looking for potential insiders using the Enron dataset, the first step is selecting the social networks related to a sensitive topic. For this investigation, this topic concerns the off-book partnerships called the Raptors. Four topics emerge with a non-zero conditional probability for the word "raptor". The next step is checking which individuals have clandestine interests in these topics. These individuals have a link in the implicit interest network but none in the explicit email network. This reduces the list of potential insiders from over 34,000 to 71. This process is then repeated using the topics that concern socializing in order to determine which employees may be feeling alienated. Since there is no clear word that defines socializing, several words are used including *dinner, drink, fun, tonight, love, weekend, family* and *game*. Two topics emerge with a non-zero probability for all of these words. When the individuals with clandestine interests in socializing are compared with individuals with a clandestine interest in the off-book partnerships, only three individuals emerge with a clandestine interest in both. Sherron Watkins is one of the three individuals.

Author Topic emerges from this research as an effective tool at revealing potential insiders by datamining email. The topics generated by Author Topic are easily identifiable both based on the most probable words as well as the most probable individuals. In addition, Author Topic effectively reveals Sherron Watkins as a potential insider by flagging both her interest in the Raptor topic as well as her failure to communicate that interest via email to any of her colleagues. However, it is one thing to show that the signs existed that an individual was an insider after the fact. What is needed is to show that Author Topic would have revealed her before the fact. The analysis shows this as well since Sherron Watkins is one of only 3 individuals (out of a possible 34,000) with both a clandestine interest in the Raptor topic and a clandestine interest in socializing. If there was cause for concern that someone might leak information about the Raptors, this analysis would have generated, prior to the leak, a short list of people to pay closer attention to.

# References

1. Rosen-Zvi, Michal and Thomas Griffiths and Mark Steyvers and Padhraic Smyth. "The Author-Topic Model for Authors and Documents". *Proceedings of the 20th Conference on Uncertainty in Artificial Intelligence*. 487-494, 2004.
2. McLean, Bethany and Peter Elkind. *The Smartest Guys in the Room*. Penguin Group (USA), New York, NY, 2003.

# Digitized Forensic Investigation at P2P Copyright Controversy, Infringement[*]

Da-Yu Kao[1], Shiuh-Jeng Wang[2,**], and Frank Fu-Yuan Huang[1]

[1] Department of Crime Prevention and Correction, Central Police University,
Taoyuan, Taiwan 333
[2] Department of Information Management, Central Police University,
Taoyuan, Taiwan 333
sjwang_fsu@yahoo.com

**Abstract.** In recent decades, copyright violations have been moving into the criminal realm. This paper focuses on one fictitious P2P model, and discusses whether it contributes to the crime of copyright infringement for being involved in dealing with the distribution of digital content. After the perspective of digitized forensic investigation in the action research and the whole control mechanism, the facts show that a commercial server has full control over the P2P model.

**Keywords:** Copyright Protection, P2P Model, Cyber-crime, Digital Content, Forensic Analysis.

## 1 Introduction

P2P networks exist for searching and downloading files. Before that can happen, the IP address of the intended destination is required, prior to or at the moment of downloading the file. To battle the problem, efficient investigations of local authorities are required in response to the increase of violations.

## 2 Arguments on P2P Model

Some P2P networks shared files of popular but copyrighted material, duplicated in a variety of digital formats. The sharing of these copies is illegal in most jurisdictions. This situation poses a great potential threat to the rather recent online copyright protection laws, even though some decisions are still pending. In order to prevent the public from finding out the true facts, the accused company, saying defendant, had been providing irrelevant information in an anti-forensics manner. This paper outlines the

[*] This work was supported in part by National Science Council in R.O.C. under Grant No. NSC 93-2213-E-015-001.
[**] Correspondence author.

S. Mehrotra et al. (Eds.): ISI 2006, LNCS 3975, pp. 644–646, 2006.
© Springer-Verlag Berlin Heidelberg 2006

perspective in the manner of forensic investigation to resolve the arguments offering to the court as a key reference at determining the sentence.

# 3  Digitized Forensic Investigation

In response to the demands of digitized forensic investigation coping with digital IT society, there have been three categories developed, referred to the investigations of digitized analyses of media analysis, code analysis and network analysis [1]. In this paper, however, the forensic investigation is presented in two ways, action research and the whole control mechanism in our case assumptions, respectively, where the former one is discussed in the view-point of the investigators as well as the criminals [2] and the latter one is in terms of identification authentication, index scheme and account record.

## 3.1  Action Research: Two Four-Step Spiral Phases

This paper uses the action research method for the following question: what kind of roles do servers play in this cyber event? To reach the fact in P2P copyright infringement, a model of spiral is proposed in this paper. The first phase focuses on the normal operation of this system, and the second phase uses the suggested examination of management technicians.

The operations and functions of the 'X' program have undergone frequent fine-tuning to maximize the company's profitability. Once the 'X' program runs, a number of peer links are established. If the 'X' program is not executed, the defined process will not run, and the specified TCP port is also not established. The communication between the client and the server can be controlled or monitored by program design. To turn uncompromising beginnings into effective endings is what allows researchers to improve the action and explore the results through a process of iteration. Once we blocked the access to certain IP addresses and entered the account password, we found that this project would take the last access IP information temporarily stored in its cache memory, and at that point one could search files without paying but could not swap files. When the client does not have the latest client IP list, prior membership verification is required to conduct a file swap. When all computers at last-log-in client IP list are off-line, a file search operation would yield no result on the computer screen.

## 3.2  The Whole Control Mechanism

On any commercial P2P model, the control mechanism is one of the most crucial parts for managers, and the server always plays a primary role. Many P2P models inevitably employ a client-server architecture to perform search, manage, or other operation. Identification authentication means that the server controls verification. An index scheme connotes that the server provides on-line peers, consisting of IP address, specified directory, and sharing files. These three components are essential to connect and operate smoothly with peers. Any virtual-dollar balance information found on the server supposedly should be regarded as part of the account record.

## 4   Conclusions

Using the perspective of digitized forensic investigation proposed in this paper will further assist the law to make a clearer case study in respect to the suspect in the P2P case. A more precise perspective for determining the violations is pointed out. As a result, a structured report indicating all possible violations in this P2P model operation will be supplied to the court as a key reference for determining the sentence.

## References

[1] Digital Forensics Research Workshop, "A Road Map for Digital Forensics Research," http://www.ijde.org/archives/02_fall_art2.html, 2001.
[2] Levy E. and Arce I., "Criminals become Tech Savvy," IEEE Security and Privacy, Vol. 2, No. 2, 2004.

# On Off-Topic Web Browsing

Nazli Goharian, Alana Platt, and Ophir Frieder

Information Retrieval Laboratory, Illinois Institute of Technology
{goharian, platt, frieder}@ir.iit.edu

## 1 The Problem

For many, accessing files (documents in our context) from the web is a daily activity. The web has de facto become the "first place" to find information. For example, for many of the on-line community, Wikipedia is becoming the de facto first source of information, namely, the encyclopedia of choice. This reliance on web content, however, has introduced new problems for employers, namely, their employees are simply "browsing away" their time. To combat this perceived waste of time, some employers simply block access to the web for their employees. However, by blocking employee web access, the employers eliminate a valuable information resource, one that can potentially help employees accomplish their assigned activities.

We propose a compromise in which employers define a *user profile* for each employee or employee group. This profile defines the legitimate employee or employee group scope of interest. Given such a profile, mechanisms that detect misuse (off-topic browsing) can monitor employees searching for non-assigned topics.

Traditionally, misuse was detected based on violations of *access rights*. That is, for every file, a list of users that can access the file was maintained, and only the users on such a list were allowed access to the file. Alternatively, but equivalently, for each user, a list of allowed files was established, and the user could only access those files.

If one simply mapped an access list approach onto the web domain, one could limit the user to only a set of URLs with misuse defined as any access to any other URLs. Clearly, such an approach, however, is nonsensical for many reasons including:

- File content is ignored; rather only a file's location is taken into account;
- Multiple URLs can point to the same location; hence, an accessed URL not appearing on the access list, namely indicating misuse, might actually be equivalent to a URL that appears on the list, indicating legitimate use;
- New files appear daily; hence the access list will continuously be outdated.

To account for file content rather than location, in [1, 2], we presented approaches based on information retrieval processing techniques, such as relevance feedback and clustering that detected off-topic searches. Later, we enhanced the work on the relevance feedback approach [3] and likewise developed a supervised classifier that capitalized on training data to improve detection accuracy [4]. We apply those efforts herein.

## 2 Investigating a Potential Solution

Misuse detection techniques can be partitioned into two categories: system and content-based approaches. System based approaches *learn* normal user characteristics for

S. Mehrotra et al. (Eds.): ISI 2006, LNCS 3975, pp. 647–649, 2006.
© Springer-Verlag Berlin Heidelberg 2006

such items as typing accuracy, frequency of certain operating systems commands, average number of mouse clicks per minute, frequency of access to a given set of files, etc. and compare these characteristics to the present user. Significant deviation from normal usage results in an alarm. Content-based approaches verify that the content accessed matches a valid scope of interest as represented by a *user profile*.

**Table 1.** Results from the clustering & relevance feedback with and without training data

|           | Clustering Results (w/o training data) | Relevance Feedback (w/o training data) | Relevance Feedback (with training data) |
|-----------|:--------------:|:--------------:|:--------------:|
| **Recall**    | 89.8 % | 97.3 % | 97.3 % |
| **Precision** | 83.5 % | 75.7 % | 83.4 % |

In the context of information systems, content-based detection schemes, user profiles generally consist of terms and phrases that accurately portray the topic of interest of the user. These profiles can either be assigned or learned. For example, QUIET [6] supports the creation of *vocabularies* that represent a domain, or in our context, profiles. Whether the user profiles are created or assigned, they represent the valid scope of interest, and queries or responses not matching the defined valid scope result in an alarm.

We evaluate three content-based detection methods for search applications. All approaches are based on either strictly information retrieval utilities, namely, relevance feedback and clustering, or also on data mining operations. In all three approaches, a user profile is defined, and results are matched against the profile. If a sufficiently high percentage of returned documents do not match the profile, namely, have a similarity measure coefficient that indicates that they are irrelevant to the profile, an alarm is indicated. The system administrator is notified of the alarm and processes it as appropriate.

The first approach clusters the returned documents and retains the documents corresponding to the largest two clusters [5]. Our assumption is that if these documents correspond to misuse, then the query is off-topic.

The second approach evaluates selected terms from returned documents, namely relevance feedback terms. These terms are matched against the user profile; if a sufficiently high percentage of these terms do not match the user profile, an alarm is set.

Finally, the third approach is identical to the second approach with the exception that a classifier is trained to aid in the detection. As shown in the table above, the detection accuracy of this approach outperforms the rest. Unfortunately, in the web environment, obtaining a representative and stable training set is not always possible; hence we used the publicly available test collection described in [3]. In such cases, if one favors the rate of detection then the relevance feedback approach is selected. Otherwise, if the reduction of false positives is at a premium, namely detection accuracy, then the clustering approach is selected. Our future goal is to combine (fuse) both the relevance feedback and the clustering approaches to yield a system that sustains both a high rate of misuse detection with a low rate of false alarm.

# References

1. R. Cathey, L. Ma, N. Goharian, and D. Grossman, "Misuse Detection for Information Retrieval Systems," ACM Conf. of Inform. & Knowledge Management (CIKM), Nov 2003.
2. Frieder, et al, "Detection of Misuse of Authorized Access in an Information Retrieval System," US Patent# 09/929,094, filed August 14, 2001
3. N. Goharian & L. Ma, "Query Length Impact on Misuse Detection in Information Retrieval Systems," ACM 20th Symp. on Applied Computing (SAC), March 2005.
4. N. Goharian, L. Ma, and C. Meyers, "Detecting Misuse of Information Retrieval Systems Using Data Mining Techniques," IEEE ISI, May 2005.
5. N. Goharian & A. Platt, "Detection Using Clustering Query Results," IEEE ISI, May 2006.
6. M. Knepper, K. Fox, and O. Frieder, "Query Improvement Elevation Technique (QUIET)," Intelligence Analysis, May 2005.

# Mining Weighted Sequential Patterns Based on Length-Decreasing Support Constraints

Unil Yun, John J. Leggett, and TeongJoo Ong

Computer Science, Texas A&M University
College station, TX 77843, USA
{yunei, leggett, teongjoo}@cs.tamu.edu

**Abstract.** We suggest an efficient weighted sequential pattern mining algorithm with length decreasing support constraints. Our approach is to push weight constraints and length decreasing support constraints to improve performance.

## 1  Introduction

Data mining has become an important task with broad application. Algorithms for sequential pattern mining have been extensively developed such as general sequential pattern mining, closed sequential pattern mining, constraint-based sequential pattern mining, multi-dimensional sequence pattern mining, sequence mining in a noisy environment, biological sequence mining, incremental sequence mining and sequence indexing. More efficient mining algorithms have recently been suggested. Specifically, sequential pattern growth based approaches have been developed which mine the complete set of frequent sequential patterns using a prefix projection growth method that reduces the search space without generating all candidates. The mined patterns can be used in various applications such as Biomedical and DNA data analysis, and Web access pattern analysis.

Two main concerns exist for sequential pattern mining in the real world. The first concern is that sequential patterns and items within sequential patterns have been treated uniformly, but real sequences have different importance. For this reason, weighted frequent pattern mining [2, 3] and weighted sequential pattern mining algorithms [4] have been suggested. The items within a sequence are given different weights in the sequence database. The support of each pattern is usually decreased as the length of a pattern is increased, but weight has a different characteristic. A pattern which has low weight may obtain a higher weight after adding an item, so it is not guaranteed to keep the downward closure property. For instance, assume that a minimum support is 3, the support of a pattern, <A> is 2, the support of a pattern, <AB> is also 2, the weight of pattern <A> is 1 and the weight of  pattern <B> is 2. The weighted support of pattern <A> is 2 and the weighted support of pattern "<AB>" is 3. We can not prune pattern <A> even though the weighted support (2) of pattern <A> is less than the minimum support (3) because the weighted support of the pattern <AB> is equal to the minimum support and the pattern <AB> is a weighted sequential pattern. Therefore, the algorithm focuses on satisfying the downward closure property.

S. Mehrotra et al. (Eds.): ISI 2006, LNCS 3975, pp. 650–651, 2006.

As a second concern, most of the previous mining algorithms are based on a constant minimum support threshold, irrespective of the length of the discovered patterns. The key observation here is that long sequential patterns can be interesting even though their support is low and short patterns can be interesting if they have high support. SLPMiner [1] for sequential pattern mining has addressed these issues. The downward closure property can not be used with length decreasing support constraints. For this reason, the smallest valid extension (SVE) property was introduced to prune the search space. The weight constraint and the length decreasing support constraint are key factors, but no mining algorithm considers both constraints. In this paper, we re-examine two basic but interesting constraints, a weight constraint and a length decreasing support constraint and suggest weighted sequential pattern mining based on length decreasing constraints. Our main approach is to push weight constraints and length decreasing support constraints into the projected pattern growth approach. In future work, this approach will be combined with pruning techniques suggested in other algorithms using length decreasing support constraints.

## 2  Discussion

The sequential order in a sequence database is important in many situations. In huge datasets, extracting valuable sequential patterns is not easy work. Previous sequential pattern mining algorithms use the same priority for each pattern or sequence. The number of sequential patterns becomes huge as the minimum support becomes lower so it is difficult for users to find more important sequential patterns. Applying weights is effective and efficient to not only generate more important sequential patterns but also adjust the number of sequential patterns. Specifically, it is more effective to apply weight constraints to sequential pattern mining with lower minimum support. Many opportunities exist to apply weight based sequential pattern mining.

## References

[1]  Masakazu, Seno and George Karypis, *SLPMiner: An Algorithm for Finding Frequent Sequential Patterns Using Length-Decreasing Support Constraints*, ICDM'02.
[2]  Unil Yun, John J. Leggett, *WFIM: Weighted Frequent Itemset Mining with a weight range and a minimum weight*, SDM'05, April 2005.
[3]  Unil Yun, John J. Leggett, *WLPMiner: Weighted Frequent Pattern Mining with Length-decreasing support constraints*, PAKDD'05, May 2005.
[4]  Unil Yun, John J. Leggett, WSpan: Weighted Sequential pattern mining in large sequence databases, IEEE IS'06.

# Intelligence Analysis Using High Resolution Displays

Timothy Buennemeyer, John Booker, Andrew Sabri, and Chris North

The Bradley Department of Electrical and Computer Engineering,
and The Center for Human-Computer Interaction, Department of Computer Science
Virginia Polytechnic Institute and State University, Blacksburg, Virginia 24061 USA
{timb, jobooker, plastk, north}@vt.edu

Intelligence analysis is a difficult task that involves mining complex datasets for clues. Distinguishing between evidence of suspicious activity and background noise is complicated, as is making connections between events, people, and other evidence. While algorithms to parse, extract, and make connections between data are important to this field, at some point the data must be interpreted by human users. Information visualization allows people to employ their innate visual strengths to gain insights about data and is necessary to effectively understand both raw data and the filtered output of algorithms.

While there are many barriers to effective intelligence analysis, based on related research and our own experience we focused our efforts on the following problems:

1. Viewing geospatial and temporal data simultaneously is difficult; however, it is desirable to do so in order to identify "geotemporal" relationships that might show movement trends or where a terrorist plot might culminate into an attack.
2. Intelligence data is often displayed with multiple views overlaid with numerous data points, connections, and details. This data can overwhelm the display space of a single monitor.
3. Maintaining context within large datasets is challenging because it is mentally demanding to remember what was seen previously, where it was, and its potential relationship to current information.

We developed a prototypical *Gigapixel Intelligence Analysis Navigation Tool* (GIANT) to solve to these problems. GIANT (Fig. 1) was developed in C++ with the OpenGL and QT 4.0 libraries on a Linux platform. It included a geospatial view that contained nodes mapped to their actual latitude and longitude coordinates on a mercator map projection, a timeline view, and an interface specifically designed for a large tiled display. The code was designed to run on a 12-node Linux cluster with 24 LCD monitors (two monitors per server), which used Distributed Multihead X and Chromium. A MySQL database server operated as the backend, and was populated with data from "The Sign of the Crescent," a case study from the Joint Military Intelligence College used to train intelligence analysts. This supporting architecture (Fig. 2) satisfied the performance, quality of service, data storage, reliability, and rapid access time requirements needed to support our visualization.

We used node-linking techniques similar to the type often employed to represent social networks, and a geospatial visualization that placed nodes overtop of a map in their appropriate positions. The "geotemporal" problem was addressed by mapping activity age to the opacity of the edges between nodes. Each activity type was assigned its own color (for example a crime was red) so the older the link was, the

S. Mehrotra et al. (Eds.): ISI 2006, LNCS 3975, pp. 652–653, 2006.
© Springer-Verlag Berlin Heidelberg 2006

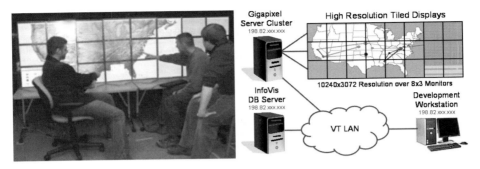

**Fig. 1.** GIANT's 3x1 meter display          **Fig. 2.** Implemented system architecture

more transparent that color became. We also included a separate timeline view, however the edge opacity allowed a basic understanding of event ordering without requiring users to divide their focus between views.

We addressed the remaining problems by using a high resolution tiled display. While the traditional visualization mantra of overview first, zoom and filter, and details on demand still applied to GIANT, the increased pixel count allowed us to display both a larger overview and more details, even with multiple views. Using a single monitor would cause us to lose either 96% (23 of the 24 screens) of the detail and/or overview, leaving no extra room to display both views concurrently.

The increased pixel count also allowed us to avoid traditional information visualization navigation strategies such as panning and zooming, overview + detail, and focus + context, and their associated problems with maintaining context. Even though nodes occluded each other in highly active areas, the visualization still allowed examination of individual details without the use of a zoom. Instead we dispersed the nodes around their original location, and anchored them back home with a white line. Since the map was stationary, users were able to exploit their spatial memory to maintain context about where earlier clues were located.

We also realized that traditional interface design methods fail when transferred directly to a large display. When working with a screen space that is physically large, we found that controls had to be near the user's focus and appropriately sized. A typical slider interface configuration for a single monitor would use the entire display width. In our large display, this translated to a three meter slider positioned half a meter below the data that users were focused on. For this reason we used direct manipulation when possible and a floating window that contained other filters. These features of GIANT gave users the ability to quickly interact with and analyze data so that they could make intelligence-related knowledge discoveries.

Tiled displays, such as the one presented in this paper, show great potential for intelligence analysis. Our preliminary evaluation provided positive results, which appear promising for future experimentation and system development. Analysts need visualizations that provide multiple views of large datasets, allow rapid access to details, and preserve the context of data. We expect that the GIANT system will satisfy these visualization requirements and are eager to compare and demonstrate its effectiveness at solving intelligence analysis problems against other visualizations developed for a range of displays.

# Privacy Preserving Mining of Global Association Rules on Distributed Dataset

Huizhang Shen[1], Jidi Zhao[1], and Ruipu Yao[2]

[1] Institute of System Engineering, Shanghai Jiao Tong University,
200052, Shanghai, China
{Hzshen, Judyzhao33}@sjtu.edu.cn
[2] School of Information Engineering, Tianjin University of Commerce,
300134, Tianjin, China
Yaoruipu@yahoo.com.cn

The issue of maintaining privacy in data mining has attracted considerable attention over the last few years. In this paper, we continue the investigation of the techniques of distorting data in developing data mining techniques without compromising customer privacy and present a privacy preserving data mining algorithm for finding frequent itemsets and mining association rules on distributed data allocated at different sites. Experimental results show that such a distortion approach can provide high privacy of individual information and at the same time acquire a high level of accuracy in the mining result.

We assume a scenario of mining association rules in distributed environments as follows: a transaction database $DB(=DB_1 \cup DB_2 \cup \cdots \cup DB_n)$ is horizontally partitioned among $n$ sites. An itemset $X$ has local support count of $X_{.supi}$ at site $S_i$ ($1 \leqslant i \leqslant n$) if $X_{.supi}$ of the transactions contains $X$. The global support count of $X$ is given as $X_{.sup} = \sum X_{.supi}$. An itemset $X$ is globally supported if $X_{.sup} \geqslant S_{min} * \sum |DB_i|$, where $S_{min}$ is the user-defined minimum support. Global confidence of a rule can be given as $\{X \cup Y\}_{.sup} / X_{.sup}$. The set of frequent itemsets consists of all $k$-itemsets that are globally supported. Thus the objective of distributed association rule mining is to find the set of frequent itemsets and the support counts for these itemsets and, based on this, generate association rules with the minimum support and minimum confidence.

Markov chains can be applied to privacy preserving data mining, in which a Markov state corresponds to a frequent $k$-itemset $X_i$. Let $M = \{X_1, X_2, \cdots, X_m\}$ be a set of itemsets and $P_M$ be the itemset transition probability matrix of $M$ subject to (1) $p_{kl} \geqslant 0$, (2) $\forall k\ (1 \leq k \leq m)$, $\sum_{l=1}^{m} p_{kl} = 1$, where $p_{kl}$ is the probability with which itemset $X_k$ transits to itemset $X_l$. In the algorithm presented in later section, we generate the distorted data value from a transaction by randomly transiting each given itemset in it.

We denote the distorted set of $k$-itemsets, obtained with a distortion probability matrix $P_M$, as $D$. Let $S^M(X_1, X_2, \cdots, X_m)$ be the vector of expected support of itemsets on $M$ and $S^D(X_1, X_2, \cdots, X_m)$ be the vector of support of itemsets on $D$. We have $S^M(X_1, X_2, \cdots, X_m) = S^D(X_1, X_2, \cdots, X_m) * P_M^{-1}$ where $P_M^{-1}$ is the inverse matrix of $P_M$.

In a probabilistic distortion approach, we may have errors in the estimated supports of frequent itemsets with the reported values being either larger or smaller than the actual supports. This kind of error is qualified as the metric of *Support Error* which

S. Mehrotra et al. (Eds.): ISI 2006, LNCS 3975, pp. 654–656, 2006.

reflects the average relative error in the reconstructed support values for those item-sets that are correctly identified to be frequent. Errors in support estimation can also result in errors in the identification of the frequent itemsets. It is quite likely that for an itemset slightly above $S_{min}$ that one of its subsets will have recovered support below $S_{min}$. The itemset will be discarded from the candidate set due to a key property of Apriori algorithm that if itemsets is a frequent itemset, all of its subsets must have supports larger than $S_{min}$. It will become especially an issue when the $S_{min}$ setting is such that the support of a number of itemsets lies very close to this threshold value. This kind of error is measured by the metric of *Identification Error*, which reflects the percentage error in identifying frequent itemsets. Hence, to reduce such errors in frequent itemset identification, we discard only those itemsets whose recovered support is smaller than a candidate limit, given as $S_{min}*(1 - \sigma)$, for candidate set generation. Here $\sigma$ is a reduction coefficient.

The distributed association rule mining algorithm, given the global minimum support, the global minimum confidence and the reduction coefficient, works as follows.

Let $k=1$, let the candidate set be all the single items included in the dataset. Repeat the following steps until no itemset left in the candidate set. {(1) The common site broadcasts the transition probability matrix for $k$-itemsets included in the candidate set. (2) Each site generates its local frequent $k$-itemsets using Apriori-like algorithm. To each transaction located in its local dataset, it finds out the frequent itemsets included in this transaction and distorts them with the distortion approach and sends the distorted data to the common site. (3) The first site gets some "fake" itemsets randomly choosing from the predefined set of fake itemsets, adds them to its local frequent set of $k$-itemsets, and then sends its local frequent set (not the real one at this time) to the second site. The second site adds its local frequent set, the real one without fake itemsets, to the set it gets, deletes the duplicated itemsets, and sends the set to the third site. The third and other sites do the similar work till the set is sent back to the first site. The first site removes the random fake itemsets from the set and thus gets the global candidate set. And then the global candidate set is sent to the common site for data mining. (4) The common site reads the distorted dataset from all the sites and scans it to compute all the supports for each $k$-itemset in the global candidate set. (5) The common site recovers the supports on the original dataset for each $k$-itemset in the global candidate set using above support recovery equation. (6) The common site discards every itemset whose support is below its candidate limit. (7) The common site saves for output only those $k$-itemsets and their supports whose recovered support is at least $S_{min}$. (8) The common site forms all possible $(k+1)$-itemsets such that all their $k$-subsets are among the remaning itemsets generated in step(6). Let these $(k+1)$-itemsets be the new candidate set. (9) Let $k=k+1$.} The common site finds out all the association rules with all the saved itemsets and their supports, given the user-specified global minimum confidence.

We carry out the evaluation of the new algorithm on a synthetic dataset which was generated from the IBM Almaden generator. Experimental results show that providing high accuracy and at the same time preventing exact or partial disclosure of individual information are conflicting objectives and the tradeoff between privacy and accuracy is sensitive to the transition matrix. Appropriate transition matrix must be chosen to achieve the goal of acquiring plausible values for both privacy level and accuracy. Future research involves the combination of probabilistic approach and cryptographic approach to get better performance for privacy preserving mining.

# CC-GiST: Cache Conscious-Generalized Search Tree for Supporting Various Fast Intelligent Applications

Won-Sik Kim[1], Woong-Kee Loh[2], and Wook-Shin Han[1],[*]

[1] Department of Communication Engineering
Kyungpook National University, Korea
`wskim@www-db.knu.ac.kr, wshan@knu.ac.kr`
[2] Department of Computer Science
Korea Advanced Institute of Science and Technology (KAIST), Korea
`woong@mozart.kaist.ac.kr`

According to the advance of technologies, the speed gap between CPU and main memory is getting larger every year. Due to the speed gap, it was perceived important to make the most use of the cache residing between CPU and main memory, and there have been a lot of research efforts on this issue. Among those is the research on cache conscious trees for reducing the cost for accessing main memory indexes. Cache conscious trees were designed to cause as few cache misses as possible based on the characteristics of the cache. The most widely known cache conscious trees are the $CSB^+$-tree, the pkB-tree, and the CR-tree. Since it is costly and error-prone to implement every cache conscious tree separately, we need a new systematic approach. An analogous approach was made for the disk based indexes. The Generalized Search Tree (GiST) was proposed as a framework for development of disk based indexes. The GiST basically provides the common features for disk based balanced search trees. Hence, when developing a disk based index using the GiST, only the features specific to the index need to be implemented. However, the GiST has the weakness that it cannot be efficiently used for main memory indexes because it was originally designed for the disk based indexes.

In this paper, we propose the Cache Conscious-Generalized Search Tree (CC-GiST) by extending the GiST to be cache conscious. By analyzing the techniques used by the existing cache conscious trees, we derive two generalized techniques that can be applied to any cache conscious trees: the pointer compression and the key compression techniques. The CC-GiST incorporates the techniques in extending the disk based GiST. The *pointer compression* technique in cache conscious trees reduces the number of pointers in an internal node. It removes a subset of $n$ pointers $\mathsf{ptr}_i$ $(1 \leq i \leq n)$ in the internal node, and stores the child node (pointed by a pointer $\mathsf{ptr}_j$ that is not removed) along with the subsequent child nodes (originally pointed by the pointers $\mathsf{ptr}_{j+1}$, $\mathsf{ptr}_{j+2}$, ... that are removed) physically consecutively in the same segment. The *key compression* technique in cache conscious trees reduces the size of a key so that $Len(Compress(\mathsf{BaseKey}_i, \mathsf{Key}_i)) \leq Len(\mathsf{Key}_i)$ holds, where $\mathsf{Key}_i$ is the $i$-th key in a node, and $\mathsf{BaseKey}_i$

---

[*] Corresponding author.

S. Mehrotra et al. (Eds.): ISI 2006, LNCS 3975, pp. 657–658, 2006.

is the base key used for compression and decompression of $Key_i$. The function *Compress* returns the compressed key of $Key_i$ using $BaseKey_i$, and the function *Len* returns the size of a key.

The CC-GiST provides three classes of methods: the pointer methods, the key methods, and the tree methods. The pointer and the tree methods are common to all the cache conscious trees and are basically provided by the CC-GiST, while the key methods should be implemented separately for each of cache conscious trees. The objects stored in the CC-GiST can be of any data type as in the GiST. The pointer methods are a set of functions to implement the pointer compression technique. Although each cache conscious tree uses its own specific pointer compression technique, the only thing needed to be done to implement the tree using the CC-GiST is to set the flag IsFixedSizeSegment and the variable MaxNumOfNodesInSegment appropriately. Pointer compression is automatically performed in the CC-GiST according to these values. The key methods are a set of functions to implement the key processing algorithms including the key compression technique. Since each cache conscious tree uses its own specific key processing algorithm, the key methods should be implemented to fully reflect the features of the target tree. The tree methods provide the search, insert, and delete functions that are common to all the cache conscious trees. When developing a cache conscious tree using the CC-GiST, the tree methods can be used as provided by the CC-GiST without any additional implementation. Hence, it is very efficient and systematic to develop a cache conscious tree using the CC-GiST. We completely rewrote the tree methods of the disk based GiST to be cache conscious.

The CSB$^+$-tree, the pkB-tree, and the CR-tree can be implemented using the proposed CC-GiST. Specifically, users need to specify the key methods and set a few flags and variables for each tree. We analyzed the performance of the CC-GiST by comparing the performance of the cache conscious trees implemented using the CC-GiST with the existing cache conscious trees. Given the node size, the performance of the cache conscious trees is inversely proportional to the average number of entries in a node. The less the number of entries is, the more probably the cache misses are incurred, which causes the increase of main memory accesses and thus the performance degradation of the cache conscious tress. Therefore, the existing cache conscious trees tried to increase the number of entries in a node using the pointer and the key compression techniques. We compared the number of entries in an internal node in the cache conscious trees implemented using the CC-GiST with those in the existing cache conscious trees. As the result of our analysis, the CC-GiST has the negligible overhead for supporting all the existing cache conscious trees in a single framework, and the performance of the tree is almost unaffected.

## Acknowledgement

This work was supported by Korea Research Foundation Grant (KRF-2003-003-D00347).

# KD³ Scheme for Privacy Preserving Data Mining

Peng Zhang, Yunhai Tong, Shiwei Tang, and Dongqing Yang

School of Electronics Engineering and Computer Science
Peking University, Beijing, 100871, China
{pengzhang, yhtong, tsw, dqyang}@pku.edu.cn

Privacy preserving data mining is a novel research direction. The main objective is to develop algorithms for modifying the original data in some way, so that the private information remains private even fter the mining process.

Agrawal and Srikant first proposed a scheme for privacy preserving data mining using random perturbation [1]. Then, Rizvi and Haritsa presented a scheme called MASK to mine associations with secrecy constraints [2]; Du and Zhan proposed an approach to conduct privacy preserving decision tree building [3]. A methodology for hiding knowledge in database was also presented and applied to classification and association rule mining [4]. However, all those approaches are different in their frameworks and processes. Only can they deal with a special data type, a given mining algorithm, and one kind of the attribute of private information.

In this paper, we present a new KD³ (Knowledge Discovery in Distorted Database) scheme for privacy preserving data mining that is shown in Fig. 1. In a general data mining process, the result $X$ is directly discovered from a database $D$. However, in practice, maybe there is some private information in $D$. Therefore, the database $D$ must be distorted to set up a published database $D$' in which the private information is protected well enough. Then, we can reconstruct the original feature $F$ from $D$' through a reconstructing method, and make use of a mining method $M$ to discover result $X$' from $D$' with feature $F$. The result $X$' should be as close as possible to the real result $X$. The data distorting method, the feature reconstructing method, and the mining algorithm are all designed and implemented based on a consistent privacy preserving strategy. The whole KD³ process consists of the following six steps:

- Data analysis: The first step is to analyze the original database $D$ to identify the private information that needs to be protected, as well as its type, size, and scale.
- Privacy preserving strategy (parameters) selection: The second step is to select a strategy and a set of parameters according to the data analyzing result. This is the key step. The data provider and the data miner must confer to find out a reasonable trade-off between privacy preservation and data usability. Then, the following steps will be instructed by the strategy as well as the selected parameters.
- Data distortion: The third step is to preserve the private information in the original database $D$ by data distortion according to the privacy preserving strategy selected in the second step. The main distorting methods include data transformation, data discretization, data hiding, data sampling, and adding noise to the original data.
- Feature reconstruction: The main purpose of the former three steps is to preserve private information. From this step, our primary intention is to discover patterns and rules from the distorted database $D$' generated in the third step. The fourth step

S. Mehrotra et al. (Eds.): ISI 2006, LNCS 3975, pp. 659–661, 2006.
© Springer-Verlag Berlin Heidelberg 2006

is to reconstruct the original feature $F$ according to the privacy preserving strategy for the following mining process.

- Data mining: The fifth step is to design a mining method $M$ modified from the original method according to the privacy preserving strategy, and then mine the distorted database $D$' with the reconstructed feature $F$.
- Result generation: The final step is to generate the result $X$'.

The former three steps are mainly performed by data providers, and the latter three steps are mostly accomplished by data miners. $KD^3$ scheme has a clear process and independent modules. It is also of outstanding applicability in data distribution, data type, data mining algorithm, and the attribute of private information. We have already implemented privacy preserving classification [5] and association rule mining [6] based on $KD^3$ scheme, and validated it by experiments. We also plan to apply $KD^3$ scheme to protect private knowledge such as sensitive association rules.

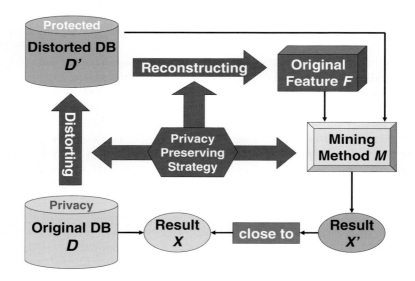

**Fig. 1.** $KD^3$ Scheme

# References

1. R. Agrawal and R. Srikant. Privacy-Preserving Data Mining. In Proceedings of the ACM SIGMOD Conference on Management of Data, 2000.
2. S. J. Rizvi and J. R. Haritsa. Maintaining Data Privacy in Association Rule Mining. In Proceedings of the 28th International Conference on Very Large Data Bases, 2002.
3. W. Du and Z. Zhan. Using Randomized Response Techniques for Privacy-Preserving Data Mining. In Proceedings of the 9th ACM SIGKDD International Conference on Knowledge Discovery and Data Mining, 2003.
4. T. Johnsten and V. V. Raghavan. A Methodology for Hiding Knowledge in Databases. In Proceedings of the IEEE ICDM Workshop on Privacy, Security and Data Mining, 2002.

5. P. Zhang, Y. Tong, S. Tang, and D. Yang. Privacy Preserving Naive Bayes Classification. In Proceedings of ADMA05, LNAI 3584, 2005.
6. P. Zhang, Y. Tong, S. Tang, and D. Yang. Mining Association Rules from Distorted Data for Privacy Preservation. In Proceedings of KES05, LNAI 3683, 2005.

# Using Logic Programming to Detect Deception on the Basis of Actions

James D. Jones

Computer Science
Angelo State University
james.d.jones@acm.org

**Abstract.** Software which can perform generalized, high-level reasoning with respect to the detection of deception is needed, is quite difficult to produce, and is absent from the arsenal of tools available to practitioners and researchers in this field. The author has produced such a program which reasons within the confines of a simple espionage scenario. This program provides the general architecture needed by our desired software. Significant work is still needed to mature this generalized architecture into a feasible tool. That work would include making the program far more robust (handling more varied and more complicated situations), increasing the knowledge base (in the vein of "common sense reasoning"), applying the architecture to many more scenarios, and generalizing the lessons learned from those scenarios. The goal of all this work is to develop an architecture which can automatically detect deception in a wide variety of contexts.

The work presented here attempts to detect deception on the basis of actions. This is in sharp contrast with current approaches which detect deception on the basis of physiological factors, and on the basis of verbal and non-verbal queues. Software based on our architecture should be able to predict consequences of actions, and predict future actions. Further, in the light of uncertainty, multiple views of the world can be maintained simultaneously. (In the presence of uncertainty, the ability to postulate different ways that the world could be is very important. Not only can we represent different ways of perceiving the world, but we can also reason about those differences.)

An agent architecture is used to represent agents (or entities), their interrelationships, and their actions. These details are represented in a very formal logic programming paradigm, called Answer Set Programming, which is more clearly specified as A-Prolog. The inference engine used is SMODELS

We are also using a specific action language formalism. This formalism allows us to reason about prerequisites to actions, consequences of actions, co-requisites of actions, mutual exclusivity of actions, and sequences of actions. It also allows us to represent and reason about time. We can predict future actions on the basis of observations. One method of detecting deception is the fact that present observations may not match our earlier predictions. Predicting future actions allows us to identify potential opportunities for deception.

A very simple problem has been designed to demonstrate these techniques. In this simple scenario, there are 3 persons. Those 3 persons are agents, and potentially, double agents. The only actions these agents can perform are communicating messages. Our task is to identify that deception has occurred when these communications are inconsistent with present beliefs, or when they are inconsistent with each other.

S. Mehrotra et al. (Eds.): ISI 2006, LNCS 3975, pp. 662 – 663, 2006.

To test this program, it is run under four different scenarios. The first scenario is a state of equilibrium: the world operates as normal, there are no contradictions, and there are no suspicions of deception. In this case, the program performs as desired, and there is no deception identified. That is, there are no "false positives".

The second scenario is that an agent communicates some information which is mutually exclusive with beliefs of the system. Since the system does not have any reason to doubt its own beliefs, the best explanation for this state of affairs is that the agent must be lying. Hence, the agent is a double agent. Deception has been detected.

In the third scenario, we have two agents which communicate information which is contradictory with each other. We have a contradiction, and we have no reason to believe one agent over the other. Either one agent is lying, or the other agent is lying. (We do not consider the case where both agents are lying. A bias that has purposefully been built into the system is that of a minimalist view: we have the smallest set of beliefs that we are forced to have with respect to set inclusion. In our example, this means that we have one liar instead of two liars.) The problem is: which agent is the liar? Since we do not have information to prefer the word of one agent over the other, we maintain two views of the world: one in which one agent is lying, and another in which the other agent is lying. We accept both views with equal veracity.

In the final scenario, we have the same contradiction between the two agents. We also have a third agent who is communicating information contradictory to the first agent. The second agent and the third agent are in contradiction to the first agent. Either the first agent is lying, or the second and third agents are lying. We have purposefully built in an additional bias: fewer liars are preferred over more liars. (This is dramatically different than the above bias.) Without this bias, we would again have two views of the world: one in which the first agent is lying, and the other in which the other two agents are lying. (Both of these views are "minimal" with respect to set inclusion, and adhere to the semantics of logic programs.) If we allowed this to happen, we would again have to accept both views as equally plausible. We could certainly do this. However, we have chosen to introduce the additional bias that fewer liars are preferred to more liars. Therefore, the system maintains only one view of the world: that the first agent is lying. What is important about this last scenario is not only that we introduced this additional bias, but more importantly, we have resolved the uncertainty introduced by having two views of the world (induced by the previous scenario) by the introduction of additional information. The additional information helped us to narrow the range of possibilities, such that we could definitively conclude which agent was lying.

Many enhancements can be made to our approach. We could more thoroughly understand contradictions (for example, to distinguish between mistakes and lies). We could also enhance the software to log observations, and to learn patterns of communication (specific to each agent). The patterns that would be looked for include not only frequency of discrepancies, but also some possible intent or motive behind the discrepancy. Another enhancement would be to provide for a very complex arsenal of actions which interrelate with each other. We could also make predictions about future actions. A significant arena of enhancement would be in defining and addressing more forms of deception.

# Intelligent Information Retrieval Tools for Police

Nishant Kumar[1], Jan De Beer[2], Jan Vanthienen[1], and Marie-Francine Moens[2]

[1] Research Center for Management Informatics,
Katholieke Universiteit Leuven, Belgium
{nishant.kumar, jan.vanthienen}@econ.kuleuven.be
[2] Legal Informatics and Information Retrieval group,
Katholieke Universiteit Leuven, Belgium
{jan.debeer, marie-france.moens}@law.kuleuven.be

**Abstract.** Intelligent information retrieval tools can help intelligence and security agencies to retrieve and exploit relevant information from unstructured information sources and give them insight into the criminal behavior and networks, in order to fight crime more efficiently and effectively. This article aims at analysing off-the-shelf information extraction tools on their applicability and competency for such applications.

## 1 Introduction

With increasing volume of crime data, intelligence and security agencies across the world need intelligent support systems which can help them to retrieve and exploit relevant information and give them insight into the criminal behavior and networks, in order to fight crime more efficiently and effectively. The unstructured information (e-mails, reports, web pages, etc.), representing the bulk of all information, poses a great challenge in automation.

Many of the IR tools available today provide good and fast solution to the retrieval problems (retrieval, querying, structuring, visualization, extraction, etc.). But it is also very difficult to know which of these tools are most effective for a given application. We report our work on the evaluation of 10 tools, shortlisted from a market selection of 23 tools, under the INFO-NS [1] project for the Belgian Federal Police.

## 2 Evaluation Method

We identified several user profiles, their functional requirements and priorities and generalized them over user profiles to five high-level *use cases*, namely (free text search, Metadata Search, Classification, Named Entity Extraction and Entity Linking). For each of these use cases, we compiled a detailed evaluation form based on sound evaluation frameworks, covering three crucial aspects of assessment, Conformity[1], Quality, and Technical.

We tested the use cases on multilingual document collection containing more than half a million real-life case reports, in Dutch and French, encoded in the MS Word file format.

[1] Visit AGORA at http://www.belspo.be/belspo/fedra/prog.asp?l=en&COD=AG

S. Mehrotra et al. (Eds.): ISI 2006, LNCS 3975, pp. 664–665, 2006.

# 3   Evaluation Results

**Free Text Search:** The proprietary fuzzy matching algorithm of one tool gave excellent results on most of the variation types considered, whereas the use of the Soundex ([2]) and edit distance ([3]) operators as provided by most other tools proved to be ill-suited for most variation types. Moreover, neither Soundex nor edit distance copes well with word reorderings, e.g. as with person names.

On relevance ranking ([4]) one tool consistently produced well-ranked result lists (on a scale from 0 to 100, baseline+30 up to +70) and whereas other tools clearly showed variable scores.

**Metadata Search:** Standard document attributes (such as url, title, author, date, size), when available, are automatically imported by the tools. Most information retrieval tools also derive a static summary simply by extracting the most salient sentences or phrases from the text.

**Named Entity Extraction:** IR tools support NE extraction ([5]) on common entity types person names, organisations, locations, and time instances. Results show high precision, up to 97%, on the most common entity types, while recall is very poor, less than 50%.

# 4   Conclusions and Future Directions

This evaluation of tools has given us the impression that without a careful consideration of functional requirements and integrating a good human computer interaction feature these tools might prove to be of less fruitful. We have also found that the tools lack support for cross lingual search, an important aspect in a trilingual country like Belgium. While in case of entity extraction and classification most of the tools work on keyword matching, which does not give the right contextual result and therefore decreases the relevancy factor and also they lack support for noisy texts.

# References

[1] N. Kumar, J. De Beer, J. Vanthienen, and M.-F. Moens, "Multi-criteria evaluation of information retrieval tools," in *Proceedings of the 8th International Conference on Enterprise Information Systems(ICEIS)*, 2006.
[2] R. Russell and M. Odell, "Soundex," Patent 01 261 167, 1918.
[3] V. I. Levenshtein, "Binary codes capable of correcting deletions, insertions and reversals," *Doklady Akademii Nauk SSSR*, vol. 163, no. 4, pp. 845–848, 1965.
[4] C. Buckley and E. M. Voorhees, "Retrieval evaluation with incomplete information," in *Proceedings of the ACM SIGIR Annual International Conference on Information Retrieval*, vol. 27, July 2004.
[5] M. Chau, J. J. Xu, and H. Chen, "Extracting meaningful entities from police narrative reports," in *Proceedings of the International Conference on Intelligence Analysis*, 2005.

# Evaluation of Information Retrieval and Text Mining Tools on Automatic Named Entity Extraction

Nishant Kumar[1], Jan De Beer[2], Jan Vanthienen[1], and Marie-Francine Moens[2]

[1] Research Center for Management Informatics,
Katholieke Universiteit Leuven, Belgium
{nishant.kumar, jan.vanthienen}@econ.kuleuven.be
[2] Legal Informatics and Information Retrieval group,
Katholieke Universiteit Leuven, Belgium
{jan.debeer, marie-france.moens}@law.kuleuven.be

**Abstract.** We will report evaluation of Automatic Named Entity Extraction feature of IR tools on Dutch, French, and English text. The aim is to analyze the competency of off-the-shelf information extraction tools in recognizing entity types including person, organization, location, vehicle, time, & currency from unstructured text. Within such an evaluation one can compare the effectiveness of different approaches for identifying named entities.

## 1   Introduction

Named Entity Extraction, a subfield of information extraction, also known as NE Recognition (NER), is to recognize structured information, such as proper names (person, location and organization), date & time, and numerical values (currency and percentage) from natural language text. It has also been extended to identify other patterns, such as email addresses, and URLs. We test named entity extraction from text in the context of the INFO-NS [1] project.

We report our work on 4 commercial IR tools[2], which utilises NER techniques to identify meaningful entities from unstructured text. Named entity recognition constitutes a basic operation in the structuring of texts. Its automation within the Belgian Federal Police would tremendously aid operational analysts in the coding (schematisation) of criminal cases, sometimes covering hundreds of pages that otherwise would have to be skimmed manually for the discovery of entities of interest.

## 2   Evaluation Method

A set of 6 police narrative reports (2 from each language, Dutch, French & English) has been used as the test bed. A human experimenter manually identifies all entities of interest. We do this testing to measure the tools on conformity ([1])

---

[1] Visit AGORA at http://www.belspo.be/belspo/fedra/prog.asp?l=en&COD=AG
[2] Due to contractual obligations the names has not been disclosed.

S. Mehrotra et al. (Eds.): ISI 2006, LNCS 3975, pp. 666–667, 2006.

and qualitative criteria. We used standard measures of evaluation, namely precision, recall, and the F-measure ([2]) to assess the tools. We treat misalignment between extracted entity mentions and a golden standard of manually extracted mentions consistently in favor of the tools. For example, the extracted entity "Congo" is equated with the full entity name " Republic of congo", when the latter is present in the text.

## 3   Evaluation Results

| Tools | Tool-A | Tool-B | Tool-C | Tool-D |
|---|---|---|---|---|
| Precision | 0.944 | 0.718 | 0.976 | 0.959 |
| Recall | 0.440 | 0.145 | 0.397 | 0.681 |
| F-measure | 0.601 | 0.241 | 0.564 | 0.797 |

Results show high precision on the most common entity types (persons, organisations, locations), up to 97%. Recall is very poor however, less than 50%.

## 4   Conclusions and Future Directions

The evaluated tools rely largely on human editable dictionaries and work on keyword matching, which does not give the right contextual result and therefore decreases the relevancy factor. Some IE tools provide human editable and expandable rule sets. A rule is a simple regular expression, but can be extended to incorporate lexical analysis of the source text and the context of entity may be used to trigger recognition of their type. We also mention the problem of ambiguity, resulting in errors, mostly when it comes to determine the entity type (e.g. locations or organisation named after persons).

From these findings we may assume that the use of dictionaries and/or rule sets, both are limited in scope and in their tolerance towards typographical, compositional, and other kinds of observed variations.

Also none of the evaluated tools offers a learning approach to automated entity recognition, whereas the academic community has made much progress in this field ([3]). An equally important line of research is the extraction of entities within noisy texts ([4]).

## References

[1] N. Kumar, J. De Beer, J. Vanthienen, and M.-F. Moens, "Multi-criteria evaluation of information retrieval tools," in *Proceedings of the 8th International Conference on Enterprise Information Systems(ICEIS)*, 2006.
[2] C. J. Van Rijsbergen, *Information Retrieval*, 2nd ed.   Butterworths London, 1979.
[3] M.-F. Moens, *Information Extraction: Algorithms and Prospects in a Retrieval Context*.   Springer-Verlag, 2006.
[4] M. Chau, J. J. Xu, and H. Chen, "Extracting meaningful entities from police narrative reports," in *Proceedings of the International Conference on Intelligence Analysis*, 2005.

# A Child's Story to Illustrate Automated Reasoning Systems Using Opportunity and History

James D. Jones[1], Hemant Joshi[2], Umit Topaloglu[2], and Eric Nelson[2]

[1] Department of Computer Science
Angelo State University
james.d.jones@acm.org
[2] Department of Computer Science
University of Arkansas at Little Rock

**Abstract.** The primary author has performed previous work to create generalized, high-level reasoning software to identify deception on the basis of actions. The work here is to apply that software architecture to an entirely different domain. The original domain was an espionage scenario, and detected deception when communications were in conflict. This present domain is reasoning about a child's story to determine who is lying about the theft of some objects. Applying the previous work to a different domain is an attempt to demonstrate the generality of the architecture. It is also an attempt to further generalize the software, and to formalize additional "common sense" strategies in the detection of deception.

This software detects deception on the basis of actions. This is in sharp contrast with present approaches that detect deception based on physiological factors, as well as on verbal and non-verbal cues. Our approach models agents and their actions in a logic programming framework using a theory of agents, a theory of actions, and a theory of reasoning with respect to time. As a test case, a children's mystery is analyzed and implemented. The goal of the story is to identify who stole some items. The software correctly reasons about who the potential suspects are, and ultimately, correctly identifies the chief culprit. Further, it can correctly introspect with regard to previously held beliefs. The program we have developed is able to mimic the thought processes and conclusions of a police investigation.

To demonstrate our approach, we have created a scenario loosely based upon a child's book. The basic idea of the story is that a bat is missing, and the goal is to identify who stole the bat. The flow of the story is as follows. There is a practice at the beginning of the story. A particular baseball bat is missing, and presumed stolen. Everyone present at that practice is a suspect in the theft of the bat. There is a subsequent practice at which a glove becomes missing. Everyone present at that subsequent practice is a suspect in the theft of the glove. At this point, there are two separate, but partially overlapping lists of suspects. At a later time, someone is discovered in possession of the glove. That person is assumed to have stolen the glove, and hence, the most likely person to have stolen the bat, since he was a suspect in the theft of both items. The events of our story occur over time. Our program can correctly represent and reason about these events.

S. Mehrotra et al. (Eds.): ISI 2006, LNCS 3975, pp. 668–670, 2006.

The events in the story are sequential with respect to time and so the experiments were performed in incremental fashion. They are presented here as four distinct executions. However, each execution completely subsumes the previous exectuion. As such, each execution contains all the results of the earlier executions.

Execution 1 is trivial, but is necessary to demonstrate that our program reasons correctly, and does not enter the arena with unfair predispositions. The results of this execution tell us that there are no items missing, and hence no suspects.

Subsequently, a practice occurs (execution 2.) There are four persons present at this practice. A bat becomes missing, and is assumed stolen. Those present at the practice are assumed to be suspects. Obviously, the owner of the bat is not a suspect. Therefore, there are three suspects in the theft of the bat. The program correctly identifies those persons.

Our third execution takes place at a subsequent practice. There are five persons present at this practice: the same four persons that were present at the previous practice, plus one more person. The significant event that happens at this practice is that a glove is missing, and assumed stolen. There are four suspects in the theft of the glove. Again, the owner of the glove is not a suspect in the theft of the glove. The program correctly identifies who these suspects are, as well as correctly maintaining the suspects in the earlier theft.

For our final execution, a specific individual is caught in possession of the glove. That person is therefore presumed to have stolen the glove. Further, that person is also presumed to be the chief suspect in the stealing of the bat since that person is also a suspect in that theft. The other two suspects in the theft of the bat still remain suspects in that theft. However, the person who is identified as having stolen the glove rises to the top of the list of the suspects in the theft of the bat. That person is the chief suspect, and is the only chief suspect in the theft of the bat. If something happened such that that person was no longer considered the chief suspect, then the two remaining suspects would resurface as primary suspects. The program correctly performs these inferences, matching our intuition.

We have seen the ability of the program to reason with available, incomplete information. It correctly models our intuition. However, there are three very significant avenues by which this software could be enhanced. First, we could more closely employ an already well established theory of actions. Following this theory more closely, our actions could be more complicated. In addition, our actions could have prerequisites, and consequences. Certain actions could happen in parallel, and other actions could be mutually exclusive. We could predict the consequences of actions, and we could predict future actions.

Another significant enhancement would be to follow the tri-axis of police investigations. That is, that suspects should have the means, motive, and opportunity. In our scenario here, we ignored the first two (means and motive), and we trivialized the latter (opportunity.) In our case, we considered that those who were present at practice had opportunity. What if someone was at practice, but was in the concession stand the entire time (meaning that they were nowhere near the bat)? This introduces the idea of degree of opportunity. Or, what about the opportunity a car rider may have had? (That is, someone who rode in the car with the owner and her bat, but who did not attend practice.) This expands our definition of opportunity.

Another enhancement would be to apply this software to solve other mysteries. This pursuit would highlight other considerations. Further, the overlap between scenarios may identify opportunities for more general approaches.

# Detection Using Clustering Query Results

Nazli Goharian and Alana Platt

Information Retrieval Laboratory, Computer Science Department,
Illinois Institute of Technology
goharian@ir.iit.edu, platt@ir.iit.edu

**Abstract.** Previously, we proposed techniques to detect the misuse of search systems using predominantly *relevance feedback* based techniques. Although the approaches developed achieved high detection rate, they did so with a relatively high rate of false alarm. We now present a *clustering query results* based approach. This approach supports a higher precision, i.e., lower false alarm rate, with only a modest compromise on detection rate, namely recall.

## 1 Introduction

We expand our misuse detection efforts, the most recent of which is described in [1]. Like in previous efforts, the first phase defines a user profile, and the second phase detects potential misuse by comparing a user's search results against his/her profile. We did not modify the first phase, but the second phase now clusters query results, whereas previously, this detection phase was based on relevance feedback.

Our relevance feedback based efforts focused on detection rate (recall) possibly at the expense of detection accuracy (precision). Our clustering approach improves precision but with a modest degradation of recall. Our future efforts will focus on fusing both approaches to yield a higher level of combined recall and precision, namely a high F-measure.

## 2 Detection Using Query Result Clustering

Briefly, the approach is as follows. A query is issued. The returned results are clustered, and a set of clusters is retained. Hierarchical clustering is used for better accuracy, as the number of items to be clustered is small. Cluster selection algorithms are listed in Table 1.

**Table 1.** Cluster Selection Methods

| Algorithms | Definition |
|---|---|
| CR1a | Keeping the largest cluster |
| CR1b | Keeping the cluster with the highest similarity to the query |
| CR2a | Keeping the two largest clusters |
| CR2b | Keeping the largest cluster, and the second or third largest cluster, based on which is more similar to the query |

S. Mehrotra et al. (Eds.): ISI 2006, LNCS 3975, pp. 671–673, 2006.

**Table 2.** Long / Tolerant

| Algorithm | Precision | Recall |
|---|---|---|
| CR1a | 87.35 | 83.24 |
| CR1b | 86.13 | 81.73 |
| CR2a | 88.63 | 83.74 |
| CR2b | 88.38 | 84.38 |

**Table 3.** Long / Stringent

| Algorithm | Precision | Recall |
|---|---|---|
| CR1a | 78.43 | 91.25 |
| CR1b | 76.63 | 91.96 |
| CR2a | 78.48 | 92.76 |
| CR2b | 78.69 | 93.20 |

**Table 4.** Short / Tolerant

| Algorithm | Precision | Recall |
|---|---|---|
| CR1a | 81.96 | 85.61 |
| CR1b | 79.81 | 84.11 |
| CR2a | 83.50 | 85.50 |
| CR2b | 82.53 | 86.83 |

**Table 5.** Short / Stringent

| Algorithm | Precision | Recall |
|---|---|---|
| CR1a | 72.39 | 91.04 |
| CR1b | 71.14 | 90.88 |
| CR2a | 74.50 | 91.30 |
| CR2b | 73.61 | 92.64 |

Regardless which cluster selection approach is used, the top $t$ ($tfnidf$ based) terms from each document within the selected clusters defines the user's actual search intent. If the profile and terms are not sufficiently similar (given a threshold), then potential misuse exists.

## 3 Experimentation

Since no benchmark collection exists, we once again used our TREC-based test collection that we made publicly available and described in our prior efforts. Likewise, we again evaluated both short and long queries and stringent and tolerant detection configurations.

Our results are presented in Tables 2-5. Our initial experiment (CR1a) involved only the largest cluster. While our initial results were promising, we were unsure if keeping a cluster based solely on size was the best way to determine the best documents. We next tried a method (CR1b) that computes the centroid of each cluster, and compares it to the query. This proved to be a worse way to detect misuse as precision and recall dropped for both the stringent and tolerant evaluation plans. The only exception to this pattern was that the recall of the descriptive query in the stringent mode improved slightly. As our focus is to improve precision without significantly worsening the recall, we chose CR1a.

We then evaluated the effect of using more clusters to detect misuse. Our next method (CR2a) was similar to (CR1a), except that it keeps the two largest clusters rather than only the top cluster. This resulted in an improvement over (CR1a) in precision and recall, both for the stringent and tolerant evaluation plans. Since keeping two clusters was an improvement, we expanded our experimentation using two clusters. Our next method (CR2b) retains the largest cluster and the second or third largest, based on which cluster has a greater similarity to the query. The observed performance of (CR2b) was equivalent to (CR2a). We thus concluded that using two clusters outperforms using one cluster. Future experiments will consist of a larger number of retained clusters and using more sophisticated ranking measures.

# Reference

1. N. Goharian, L. Ma: On Off-Topic Access Detection In Information Systems, ACM 14th Conference on Information and Knowledge Management (CIKM) Nov 2005.

# Application of Latent Semantic Indexing in Generating Graphs of Terrorist Networks

R.B. Bradford

SAIC, Reston, VA
bradfordr@saic.com

## 1 Introduction

Understanding networks of connections among individuals is an important element of counterterrorism analysis. Determining nodes and links for such networks is one of the most labor-intensive aspects of counterterrorism analysis. This paper presents an automated approach for generating and displaying an initial estimate of nodes and links relevant to a chosen topic. This work combines the use of entity extraction and latent semantic indexing (LSI).

## 2 Experimental Procedure

This investigation employed a test collection of 158,492 English-language news articles from the time period 2002 to 2003. The text of the articles was pre-processed using the LingPipe entity extraction software. Identified entity names were treated as units in creating an LSI representation space for these documents. The LSI space was created using version 2.6.2 of the text analytics software from Content Analyst Company, using log entropy weighting and 300 dimensions. A brief document describing the Salafist Group for Call and Combat (GSPC) was used as a seed query.

## 3 Results

Figure 1 depicts a link chart directly generated from the relationship information represented in the LSI space, drawn using TouchGraph. This chart was generated by connecting all names that simultaneously satisfied two criteria:

- The angle between their representation vector in the LSI space and that for the GSPC text query had a cosine greater than .5.
- The angle between their representation vector and the vector for one of the other names had a cosine greater than .8.

This graph provides a good representation of connections within this terrorist group, as reflected in the test collection. All of the relationships shown in the chart are meaningful. Abou Doha, who has the largest number of connections (ten), was the senior representative of the GSPC in Europe at the time of the articles. Abu Qutada the spiritual leader for the GSPC in Europe, was closely associated with him. Djamel Beghal was the leader of a GSPC cell and Kamel Daoudi was his principal aide in that

S. Mehrotra et al. (Eds.): ISI 2006, LNCS 3975, pp. 674–675, 2006.
© Springer-Verlag Berlin Heidelberg 2006

cell.  Mabrouk Echiker, Meroine Berrahal, Laurent Mourad, and Yacine Akhnouche were members of the GSPC cell in Frankfurt. Brahim Yadel was closely associated with these other individuals. Hassan Hattab interacted with the European elements of the GSPC primarily through Doha and Qutada. Richard Reid and Rachid Ramda received support from the GSPC but apparently were not members of it.

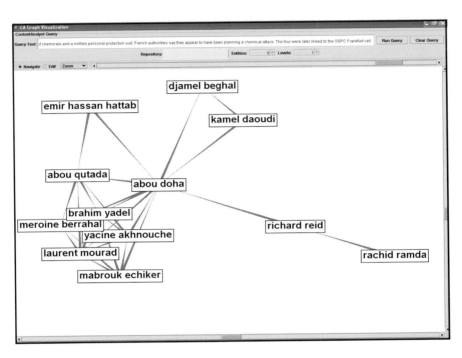

**Fig. 1.** Link chart for GSPC generated using cosine thresholds of .5 and .8

## 4   Conclusion

The experiment reported here demonstrates that the LSI technique, combined with entity extraction, can be used to support terrorist network analysis based on large collections of real-world documents. Identified relationships represent the aggregate implications of high-order associations. Thus, although the specific nature of each association is not derived, the links can reflect quite subtle relationships. Of particular interest is that, using the cross-lingual capabilities of LSI, documents in multiple languages can be analyzed simultaneously. In fact, the relationship information contained in foreign-language documents can be exploited in creating graphs using the method described here without having to translate any of the foreign-language text.

# Mining the Acceleration-Like Association Rules[*]

Dechang Pi, Xiaolin Qin , and Wangfeng Gu

College of Information Science and Technology,
Nanjing University of Aeronautics and Astronautics,
Yudao Street 29, Nanjing, Jiangsu, 210016, P.R. China
{dc.pi, qinxcs}@nuaa.edu.cn

**Abstract.** A new rule called Acceleration-like Association Rule that denotes the evolving direction of rules is proposed by analyzing the changes of the support and confidence in the primitive dataset and the increment dataset. Although this kind of rules can't be strong in the final rule set, they can decide the developing trend of the rule. Experiment with the UCI datasets shows that our algorithm can efficiently discover this kind of rules which are very useful for decision, including criminal symptom analysis and terrorism forecasting.

## 1 Introduction

Many of current algorithms are based on a hypothesis that global pattern to be studied should be kept constant. But rules mined previously in the updated dataset may be inconsistent with the past rules when dataset is updated [1-4]. S.Zhang [2] presented an aggregation and maintenance algorithm for association rules based on cardinality. Illumined by S.Zhang's view, we present our novel idea and its mining algorithm.

## 2 Concept of Acceleration-Like Association Rule

One company has been dealing with selling household appliances for many years. The sale of air-conditioner in South China has been very good during recent years. This company found a strong rule in its dataset with Apriori-like algorithm:

Area="South China" and goods="air-conditioner" $\Rightarrow$ sale="much"

Moreover, if we add statistical data of sale in the past year to the dataset of previous years, the same rule can be found too. Because of continuous rain in the past year, the sale of air-conditioner dropped evidently. We only analyze the dataset of last year and find that this rule is not valid anymore. Is this rule strong on earth? We believe that this kind of knowledge is valuable.

It is assumed that D is a dataset, S the rule set of D, D+ the increment dataset, S+ the rule set of D+, $W_1$ and $W_2$ the weights of D and D+ respectively. To reflect this change of support and confidence of rules with the data increment, we adopt the competitive set CS, which is introduced in [2]. In the meantime, suppose $r \in$ S+ is a rule.

---

[*] This research is supported by the Aeronautical Science Foundation of China under Grant No. 02F52033 and the Hi-Tech Research Project of Jiangsu province under Grant No. BG2004005.

S. Mehrotra et al. (Eds.): ISI 2006, LNCS 3975, pp. 676–677, 2006.

(1) If $r \in CS \cap S+$, r is not only a strong rule in D+ but also a candidate rule in D. The total measure degree of rule r, support(r) in $D \cup D+$ and confidence(r) in $D \cup D+$ may be greater than or equal to the thresholds Minsup and Minconf respectively. If rule r meets the following conditions,

support(r) in D+ > Minsup                   confidence(r) in D+ > Minconf

support(r) in $D \cup D+$ < Minsup                   confidence(r) in $D \cup D+$ < Minconf,

rule r must be positive, just like the acceleration is greater than zero. The reason is that r "stands out" in the increment dataset D+ although r is unable to become strong in the final dataset.

(2) If $r \in S \cap CS+$, rule r belongs to the strong rules of D and the candidate rules of D+. If rule r meets the following conditions,

support(r) in D > Minsup                   confidence(r) in D > Minconf

support(r) in $D \cup D+$ < Minsup                   confidence(r) in $D \cup D+$ < Minconf

rule r is negative, just like the acceleration is less than zero. Current algorithms cannot cope with this two type of rules and will delete them from the rule set S.

## 3  Experiment

Experiment was conducted on the UCI vote dataset. Firstly, the first 350 records of vote dataset were taken as original dataset while the following 85 records as increment dataset. The minimum support and minimum confidence are the same. Four positive and five negative rules were discovered. A positive example is

if  mx-missile = n  then  religious-groups-in-schools = y

Secondly, the first 235 records were taken as original dataset while the following 200 records as increment dataset. Only four negative ones were gotten.

Thirdly, the first 135 records were taken as original dataset while the following 300 records as the increment dataset. Only five negative ones were discovered.

Compared with the lookup rules of the entire dataset, our algorithm always results in better outcomes whether the size of increment data is less than, greater than or equal to that of original data.

## References

1. D. Cheung, J. Han, V. Ng and C. Wong, Maintenance of discovered association rules in large databases: an incremental updating technique. 12th IEEE ICDE, 1996, pp106-114.
2. S.Zhang, Aggregation and maintenance for database mining. Intelligent Data Analysis, 3 (1999): 475-490
3. Vijay Raghavan and Alaaeldin Hafez . Dynamic Data Mining. IEA/AIE 2000, LNAI 1821, pp. 220-229, 2000.
4. Wan-Jui Lee and Shie-Jue Lee. An Efficient Mining Method for Incremental Updation in Large Databases. IDEAL 2003, LNCS 2690, pp. 630–637, 2003.

# Analyzing Social Networks in E-Mail with Rich Syntactic Features

Paul Thompson and Wei Zhang

Department of Computer Science
Dartmouth College
Hanover, NH 03755

Social network analysis has emerged as a key technique in countering crime and terrorism. The Enron e-mail dataset, originally made public and posted to the web by the Federal Energy Regulatory Commission during its investigation, consists of around half a million e-mails among several thousand individuals. It is valuable in the sense that it is perhaps the only real e-mail dataset that is accessible to the research community. This paper presents preliminary results of an analysis of the Enron e-mail dataset based on a variation of the Author-Recipient-Topic (ART) model [1]. The GR-ART model described here uses grammatical relations as features, rather than bags of words. It is our hypothesis that using grammatical relations as features will provide a more useful model of authors, topics, and recipients than will the use of words alone. This research complements earlier research by one of the authors in applying information extraction techniques to cross-document named entity co-reference [2].

The ART model is based on several earlier models, including Latent Dirichlet Allocation (LDA) [3] and the Author-Topic (AT) model [4]. LDA is a generative probabilistic model of a corpus, where each document is represented by a mixture of latent topics and each topic is characterized by a multinomial distribution over words. AT can model the message content for a specific topic in order to decide how likely it is that a new message is about this topic. The ART model is an extension of the AT model. It is a Bayesian network that models message content over the relation links in a social network, which consists of all the senders and recipients of all the messages. ART extends the author modeling in AT to author-recipient pairs. For each message, the sender is observed and each of the message's recipients is also observed. The probability of a corpus in ART model is the product of the marginal probabilities of single documents.

Carroll et al. [5] proposed an annotation scheme, in which each sentence in the corpus is marked-up with a set of grammatical relations (GRs), specifying the syntactic dependency that holds between each head and its dependent. This approach is implemented in the Robust Accurate Statistical Parsing (RASP) software.

Our proposed GR-ART model uses grammatical relations in place of words as in the ART, AT, and LDA models. Grammatical relations are substantial forms of syntactic features and syntactic features encode some semantic information. By introducing grammatical relations into these models, it is expected that more semantic information can be extracted from the text and the underlying social

S. Mehrotra et al. (Eds.): ISI 2006, LNCS 3975, pp. 678–679, 2006.

network can be better modeled. The RASP-ART model uses Gibbs sampling to construct an author-topic matrix and a GR (Grammar Relation)-topic matrix.

One of the goals of this study is to analyze the distribution of authors for any specific topic (and vice versa), and find those most related to that topic. On the other hand, the pair-wise relationship between authors, based on the similarity of their topic distributions, is also of interest. If two authors have very similar topic distributions over all of their email, they can be considered role-equivalent. Results from this study are still being analyzed. It is not yet possible to confirm the hypothesis that grammatical relations will yield better performance than bags of words. However, early analysis suggests that one further extension of the ART model could be to investigate the topic distributions of senders and recipients separately. This could help to detect discrepancies of people's activities when they serve in different roles, and to reveal more complicated social relationships beyond those shown by the current study. To the best of our knowledge, a suitable methodology has not yet been developed for analyzing social networks in the context of e-mail corpora. Research reported to date has been exploratory.

# References

1. McCallum, A., Corrada-Emmanuel, A., Wang, X.: The author-recipient-topic model for topic and role discovery in social networks: Experiments with enron and academic email. Technical Report UM-CS-2004-096, UMass Amherst (2004)
2. Patman, F., Thompson, P.: Names: A new frontier in text mining. [6] 27–38
3. Blei, D., Ng, A., Jordan, M.: Latent Dirichlet allocation. Journal of Machine Learning Research **3** (2003) 993–1022
4. Steyvers, M., Smyth, P., Rosen-Ziv, M., Griffiths, T.: Probabilistic author-topic models for information discovery. In: Proceedings of the Tenth ACM SIGKDD International Conference on Knowledge Discovery and Data Mining, Seattle, Washington (2004)
5. Carroll, J., Briscoe, E., Sanfilippo, A.: Parser evaluation: a survey and a new proposal. In: Proceedings of the 1st International Conference on Language Resources and Evaluation, Granada, Spain (1998) 447–454
6. Chen, H., Miranda, R., Zeng, D.D., Demchak, C.C., Schroeder, J., Madhusudan, T., eds.: Intelligence and Security Informatics, First NSF/NIJ Symposium, ISI 2003, Tucson, AZ, USA, June 2-3, 2003, Proceedings. In Chen, H., Miranda, R., Zeng, D.D., Demchak, C.C., Schroeder, J., Madhusudan, T., eds.: ISI. Volume 2665 of Lecture Notes in Computer Science., Springer (2003)

# E-mail Traffic Analysis Using Visualisation and Decision Trees

Mark Jyn-Huey Lim[1], Michael Negnevitsky[1], and Jacky Hartnett[2]

[1] School of Engineering, University of Tasmania, Australia
{mjlim, Michael.Negnevitsky}@utas.edu.au
[2] School of Engineering, University of Tasmania, Australia
J.Hartnett@utas.edu.au

Intelligence analysts at law enforcement agencies face a difficult task with efficiently monitoring and analysing the electronic communications of suspected criminals and terrorists. Firstly there are thousands of accounts to search through and enormous amounts of data to process, in order to search for accounts exhibiting certain kinds of suspicious behaviour that may indicate the presence of possible criminal or terrorist suspects. Secondly, while suspicious accounts are being monitored the intelligence analyst needs to be alerted when the suspicious accounts start exhibiting "unusual" or "abnormal" communication behaviour, indicating the occurrence of criminal or terrorist communication activities. Such alerts need to clearly show the analyst what type of "abnormal" behaviour is occurring so that the analyst can determine whether to further investigate the behaviour of the suspicious account or dismiss the alert. Our work focuses on traffic analysis of e-mail communications, by investigating different Artificial Intelligence (A.I.) or machine learning techniques to determine whether they are capable of assisting an analyst in searching for suspicious e-mail accounts and monitoring those accounts for "unusual" or "abnormal" communication behaviour.

There are few works that have been published on behaviour profiling the communication traffic of e-mail users. Work has been completed by Columbia University [1], where they developed an Email Mining Toolkit (EMT) system for profiling the communication traffic behaviour of e-mail users. Their system creates a set of behaviour profile models of each e-mail user and checks the recent behaviour of e-mail accounts to determine whether there has been any "abnormal" changes from the user's behaviour profile. Behaviour profile models used on each user were: 24-hour behaviour profile, frequency of communication with recipients, and group communication models. In our work, we take a different approach by focusing more on classifying e-mail accounts based on particular types of e-mail traffic behaviour characteristics (e.g. speed of replies, delays between e-mails sent, no. of e-mails sent per week), rather than building a set of behaviour profile models for each e-mail user and checking for deviations from the profile.

The system we are currently developing is the e-mail traffic analyser system, shown in Figure 1. The e-mail traffic analyser system has been developed using a modular approach, utilising freely available programs developed by other researchers (GUESS, TimeSearcher, and WEKA) as well as developing our own

S. Mehrotra et al. (Eds.): ISI 2006, LNCS 3975, pp. 680–681, 2006.

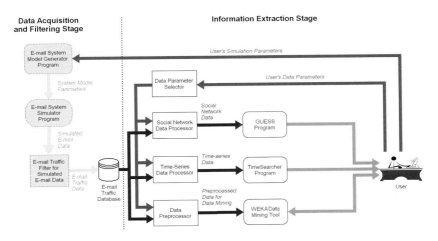

**Fig. 1.** The e-mail traffic analyser system

components. This approach allows us to quickly build up the system using available components rather than building each component individually.

Data is input into an e-mail traffic database by filtering the e-mail traffic generated by our simulated e-mail system [2]. The simulation model allows us to input different types of behaviour profiles for each e-mail client in the e-mail system, so that each e-mail client exhibits different e-mail traffic behaviour according to the behaviour profile assigned. Using this approach, we at least know what kind of behaviour is present in the data and are able to verify that the A.I. or machine learning technique is detecting the correct type of behaviour, as opposed to obtaining real e-mail data and not knowing what type of behaviour is present.

Visualisation of the e-mail traffic data is provided by the TimeSearcher and GUESS programs to aid the user in observing the relationships and patterns found in the e-mail traffic data, through the use of time-series and social network visualisation. Classification of e-mail accounts is performed using the J4.8 decision tree algorithm provided by the WEKA program. Our studies so far have found we can use decision trees to classify e-mail accounts based on the types of "unusual" behaviour exhibited by e-mail clients in the simulated e-mail system.

# References

1. Stolfo, S.J., Hershkop, S., Wang, K., Nimeskern, O., Hu, C.W.: Behavior profiling of email. In: Intelligence and Security Informatics, Proceedings. Volume 2665 of Lecture Notes in Computer Science. SPRINGER-VERLAG BERLIN, Berlin (2003) 74–90
2. Lim, M.J.H., Negnevitsky, M., Hartnett, J.: Personality trait based simulation model of the e-mail system. International Journal of Network Security **3**(2) (2006) 164–182

# Advanced Patterns and Matches in Link Analysis*

Michael Wolverton, Ian Harrison, John Lowrance,
Andres Rodriguez, and Jerome Thomere

SRI International
333 Ravenswood Ave
Menlo Park, California 94025
lastname@ai.sri.com

**Abstract.** The Link Analysis Workbench (LAW) is a tool for detecting and monitoring situations of interest using inexact matching of graphical patterns. Here we describe some recent advances to LAW: incorporating hierarchy, cardinality, disjunction, and constraints in the pattern language and similarity metric, and a flexible, user-friendly interface for displaying matching data. These capabilities support analysts in rapidly exploring and understanding large, incomplete relational data sets.

The Link Analysis Workbench (LAW) is designed to help intelligence analysts find instances in the world of generic scenarios comprised of combinations of events and facts about players involved in those events. This problem requires more than a simple database querying capability because of ambiguity and uncertainty within the intelligence process—noisy and incomplete data, etc. To deal with these problems and to meet the additional requirement of understandability, LAW uses an intuitive pattern language based on *semantic graphs*, along with a simple *similarity metric*, based on graph edit distance, that supports the retrieval and ranking of inexact matches. The core of LAW is described in [1]. Here, we summarize some advances to the pattern language, matcher, and user interface made since that earlier paper.

*Hierarchical Patterns and Cardinality Constraints.* LAW's Graph Edit Model (GEM) pattern language allows patterns to be composed and combined hierarchically, so that one pattern can be a subpattern of another. Figure 1(a) shows a hierarchical pattern. A subpattern is connected to its parent pattern through *interface nodes*—the oval-shaped nodes of Figure 1(a)—which allow a parent pattern and subpattern to share an identical entity. Each subpattern has its own set of inexact match criteria with respect to the graph edit distance metric. A subpattern may also have an associated cardinality constraint, indicating minimum or maximum numbers of matches of that subpattern—e.g., "three or more meetings." Multiple matches to subpatterns with cardinality constraints will be aggregated within a given match of the parent pattern. Hierarchy and cardinality provide expected advantages in understandability, modularity, and expressive power, and they also provide surprising efficiency benefits. See [2] for details.

---

* This research was supported under Air Force Research Laboratory (AFRL) contract number F30602-01-C-0193.

S. Mehrotra et al. (Eds.): ISI 2006, LNCS 3975, pp. 682–683, 2006.

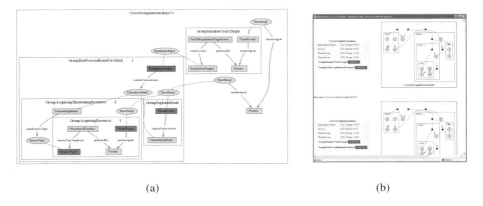

(a)                                                      (b)

**Fig. 1.** Two images from the LAW interface: (a) a hierarchical pattern with cardinality constraints, and (b) the display of match results

*Disjunction.* Disjunctive subpatterns indicate multiple alternative ways of achieving a condition within a pattern. As with hierarchical patterns, each disjunct is attached to its parent graph through interface nodes. One interesting benefit of disjunction is that it allows the formulation of recursive patterns, which can be used to specify, for example, arbitrary-length paths of repeating nodes and links.

*Constraints.* GEM supports constraints between attributes on one or more nodes. Constraints may specify, for example, that the amount of a transfer is $10,000 or more, or that one event occurs before another one. A constraint in GEM is treated the same as any other relation between nodes with respect to the similarity metric. That is, a constraint may be soft, with an associated cost in edit distance if it is not met.

*Results Display.* Figure 1(b) shows one of LAW's match results displays. The display shows, for each match, a thumbnail version of the pattern depicting missing and partially matching elements (right side), along with textual descriptions of the pattern roles played by elements in the data (left side). The analyst can expand any subpattern in the display to see a similar table for the sub-match. In addition, to make sense of large numbers of matches, the analyst can bring up an alternate view of the match set: a table showing only the main nodes as columns. He can then sort and regroup matches according to any particular node.

# References

1. Wolverton, M., Berry, P., Harrison, I., Lowrance, J., Morley, D., Rodriguez, A., Ruspini, E., Thomere, J.: LAW: A workbench for approximate pattern matching in relational data. In: The Fifteenth Innovative Applications of Artificial Intelligence Conference (IAAI-03). (2003)
2. Wolverton, M., Thomere, J.: The role of higher-order constructs in the inexact matching of semantic graphs. In: Proceedings of the AAAI Workshop on Link Analysis. (2005)

# A Flexible Context-Aware Authorization Framework for Mediation Systems

Li Yang[1], Joseph M. Kizza[1], and Raimund K. Ege[2]

[1] University of Tennessee at Chattanooga, Chattanooga TN 37403, USA
[2] Florida Interantionlal University, Miami FL 33199

**Abstract.** Security is a critical concern for mediator-based data integration among heterogeneous data sources. This paper provides a modeling and architectural solution to the problem of mediation security that addresses the security challenges including context-awareness, semantic heterogeneity, and multiple security policy specification. A generic, extensible modeling method for the security policies in mediation systems is presented. A series of authorization constraints are identified based on the relationship on the different security components in the mediation systems. Moreover, we enforce the flexible access control to mediation systems while providing uniform access for heterogeneous data sources.

**Keywords:** Mediation, security, access control, constraints.

## 1 Flexible Context-Aware Authorization Specification for Mediation Systems

We use subject *subj* to denote those entities for which authorization permission can be specified. i.e subjects are therefore users, groups, and roles. And object *obj* refers to entities on which authorization can be specified, i.e. objects and object schemas. The context *cxt* is used to denote the context-related information, i.e. environmental information or relationship defined on the subjects and objects. The context information can be captured either by environmental sensors or by accessing data sources or user credentials. Constrained authorization is an authorization followed by a set of Literals. A constrained authorization is defined as $(< subj >, < obj >, < sign > < op >, < level >) \leftarrow (L_1 \& \dots \& L_n)$
Each $L_i$ is a predefined predicate, i.e., $in, dirin, typeof$. The permission $(< subj >, < obj >, < op >, < level >)$ is granted when all predicates after $\leftarrow$ are *true*.

We now categorize and enumerate a variety of constraints that have been identified as the relationship over the entities in the mediation data system $(O, S, OP, C, OA, SA)$. The authorization constraints denoted by the predicates are illustrated as follows:

1. context-based constraints, the authorization is decided by either a certain property of the *user* or a specific property of the environment, i.e, time.
2. subject-based constraints are used to define the relationship betwen subjects, i.e., hierarchical, exclusive. The security policies could be propagated along the subject hierarchy.

S. Mehrotra et al. (Eds.): ISI 2006, LNCS 3975, pp. 684–685, 2006.

3. object-based constraints could be a subset of $O$, the set of objects, or of $T$, the set of types. They can be employed to defined the hierarchical or exclusive relationship between two objects.
4. operation-based constraints are defined to define the relationship between operations, i.e., exclusive relationship.
5. history-based constraints prvent the user from obtaining the sensitive data by data mining.
6. information-flow constraints prevent the inforamtion flowing from high sensitive level to low sensitive level.
7. semantic mapping constraints can enforce the propagation of security specification from the global level to the local source level.

## 2   Authorization Enforcement Architecture

Our architecture assumes that access is requested by a user (subject), possible playing a role. The authorization enforcement architecture is designed to check whether the authorization can be derived by the access control module from the authorization rules. The authorization enforcement architecture is composed of the following modules: Access control module who receives the requests for authorization decisions from the user; Policy Locator module who is activated for the specific request; Policy locator (0 or more) module who locate(s) and evaluates applicable policies by calling the constraint services; Constraint service (0 or more) module who is/are called by policy locators to evaluate the constraints specified in the constrained authorizations; Dynamic attribute manager (0 or more) module who is/are called to to evaluate the individual authorization constraint; and Decision Combinator who resolves conflicts and makes decision.

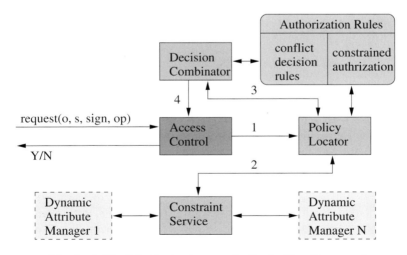

**Fig. 1.** A Flexible Context-aware Authorization Framework

# Continuous Authentication by Keystroke Dynamics Using Committee Machines

Sergio Roberto de Lima e Silva Filho and Mauro Roisenberg

Informatics and Statistics Dept.
Federal University of Santa Catarina
P.O. Box 476 Campus Trindade 88040-900
Florianopolis, SC, Brazil
{sergio, mauro}@inf.ufsc.br
http://www.inf.ufsc.br/

## 1   Introduction

Current authentication mechanisms have a barely addressed problem: they only authenticate a user at the login procedure. If a user leaves the desk without logging out or locking computer session, an intruder has an occasion to use the system.

This paper proposes an authentication methodology that is both inexpensive and non-intrusive and authenticates users continuously while using a computer keyboard. The proposed methodology uses neural networks committee machines to recognize user's typing pattern, which is a biometric behavioral characteristic. The continuous authentication prevents potential attacks when user leaves the desk without logging out or locking computer session. Some experiments are done to evaluate and calibrate the authentication committee.

## 2   Methodology

The methodology proposed to authenticate users by keystroke dynamics can be divided into 2 steps: collecting data and modeling user template; and collecting data and classifying data to authenticate or to deny a user. In this study, we used as a structure representing users template a framework of ANNs grouped in a committee machine as can be seen in figure 1.

In order to represent each user template, a set of 13 ANNs sharing same topology are trained individually. The weights of this combination of ANNs become each user template. In the authentication step, data to be analyzed are presented to each network previously trained and a combination of all those ANNs outputs will decide whether the user is a valid one or is an intruder.

To provide training for the proposed committee machine, data from true user training set are presented as valid to each ANN. Accordingly, to each ANN invalid data set will be all other users training sets.

In order to define whether a given sample is valid or not, two variable thresholds were determined in the combination of committee machines. The first one

S. Mehrotra et al. (Eds.): ISI 2006, LNCS 3975, pp. 686–687, 2006.

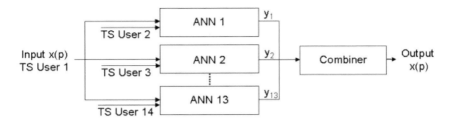

**Fig. 1.** Committee machine framework with the user 1 template

indicates which must be the minimum percentage of digraphs classified as valid ones by the committee machine. The second variable threshold is related to the number of ANNs that must classify data as valid.

## 3   Experiments and Results

In order to check proposed methodology performance some experiments were performed. These experiments used proposed committee machine to represent user template and user classification. In one of the experiments, thresholds are variable to each user committee machine classifier. The best results shown that a 0% FAR and a 0.15% FRR can be achieved, what was an excellent success rate when compared with other authentication methods. Other feature of the methodology is that new users can be easily added to the system, without the need to re-train all the Neural Networks.

## 4   Conclusions

From this study we can conclude that is possible to develop a secure, inexpensive, and continuous authentication method by behavioral characteristics of keystroke dynamics, using committee machines as classifiers.

Using ANNs in an adaptation of committee machines, the results obtained make possible to classify a user as true or intruder with accuracy comparable with other studies about the subject. From those results we can conclude that system effectiveness is improved using distinct thresholds for each user. Many studies in this research area show the need to re-training ANNs whenever a new user is added to the system as a major negative factor of using ANNs for authentication. This is the primary contribution of this study, because using committee machines there is no such need to re-train ANNs, we only have to train the ANNs that will constitute that user's committee machine and a new ANN for the committee machines of all the other users.

# A Flexible and Scalable Access Control for Ubiquitous Computing Environments[*]

Le Xuan Hung, Nguyen Ngoc Diep, Yonil Zhung, Sungyoung Lee[**],
and Young-Koo Lee

Department of Computer Engineering, Kyung Hee University, Korea
{lxhung, nndiep, zhungs, sylee}@oslab.khu.ac.kr, yklee@khu.ac.kr

The *ubiquity* and *invisibility* characteristics of ubiquitous computing (*ubicomp*) arise many security problems, especially in the field of access control. Some important issues that are needed to be addressed in access control design are: (1) Ubicomp environment is composed of huge amount of entities. Therefore, determination of access rights must be based on *role* or *group of role*, instead of individuals. (2) The *context* (e.g. user's location, user's need, etc) changes dynamically over time. Hence authorization of user's accessibility is required to be based on such contextual information for proper enforcement of the required policies. (3) Users may not know what credentials are to be provided to access a specific service. In that case, the delivery service must support some interaction mechanism to explicitly acquire necessary credentials from users. (4) Numerous entities, roaming across different domains in ubiquitous network, are usually unknown to the local system. Access control should be based on the notion of trust to grant privileges in such circumstances. Lots of works have been done in the area of access control. Most of them have followed any of the four main approaches: Role-based Access Control (RBAC), Policy-based Access Control (PBAC), Context-based Access Control (CBAC), and Trust-based Access Control (TBAC). However, each of these approaches itself can not fulfill such security requirements of ubicomp. Hence we propose a Hybrid Access Control (HAC) model to tackle the problems of these approaches while taking their major advantages. HAC is hybrid of RBAC, PBAC, CBAC, and TBAC.

**Architecture:** HAC consists of *Trust Calculator (TC), Context Provider (CP), Policy Manager (PM), Role Manager (RM),* and *Access Control Manager (ACM).* Trust Calculator is responsible for calculating trust value on principal P (user). Context Provider provides *user's context* (UC) and *system's context* (SC) to ACM. Policy Manager maintains *system policies* and *service policies.* System policy deals with the permission over resource access on the system level. Service policy is local policy of each service. It defines what actions can be performed on the services and who are authorized to perform them. Role Manager stores *roles* in hierarchical structure. Fig 1 depicts the workflow of HAC including three major operations: *deduction, abduction,* and *trust comparison.* When a user sends a service request ($R_S$) to the ACM along with his credentials ($C_P$), the ACM firstly perform *deduction* operation (step 1,

---

[*] This work is financially supported by the Ministry of Education and Human Resources Development(MODE), the Ministry of Commerce, Industry and Energy(MOCIE), and the Ministry of Labor(MOLAB) through the fostering project of the Lab of Excellency.

[**] Corresponding author.

S. Mehrotra et al. (Eds.): ISI 2006, LNCS 3975, pp. 688–689, 2006.
© Springer-Verlag Berlin Heidelberg 2006

written in the circle). It evaluates the service request by using policy rules from Policy Manager and context (*UC, SC*) from Context Provider, and it makes a decision whether this request is permitted or not. If the service request is not allowed due to limited privileges of his credentials, the system will pass this request to *abduction* operation. By checking the request and system policies, the abduction operation finds the minimum additional credentials ($C_m$) that the user must provide in order to get access permission. This additional credential requirement is sent to the user (step 2). If the user provides such credentials, then there is no problem for him to access the resource (step 3). If the user is unknown to the system or he is not able to provide required credentials, Trust Calculator computes trust value on this principal ($T_V$) based on recommendations of other principals, history of its interaction with the system, and other factors. It then passes this value to Trust Comparison (step 5). If the trust value exceeds the predefined trust value of given service/resource, he will be permitted to access to that service/resource, otherwise the access is denied. After that, ACM sends a feedback to Trust Calculator to update interaction information (step 6).

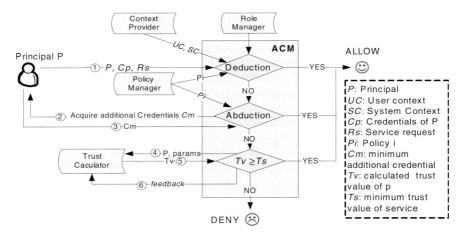

**Fig. 1.** Flow of Hybrid Access Control

By adopting role hierarchical structure, HAC can reduce the complexity and cost of security administration. HAC also uses context in design of principal to dynamically assign and adapt permissions to users. Whenever the context changes, role of user is also changed accordingly. By doing this, HAC provides flexible, convenient, and high secure accessing to resource. *Deduction* and *Abduction* are two fundamental operations that support users to specify the required credential for accessing the resource. These deal with the problem that a user usually does not have prior knowledge of required credentials to access certain resources. Moreover, trust management is involved as the final operation to deal with the problems of *uncertainty* between different domains. By applying trust, we want to provide as many services as possible to *unknown* users even though they can not show necessary credentials. Though HAC was introduced as a promising approach for ubicomp, it is not a complete security model. There are many works that we are still working on such as defining access control policy and integrating risk analysis.

# A Parallel System Strategy of Evaluation and Forecasting for Security Information with Artificial Society

Dalei Guo[1] and Shuming Tang[2]

[1] Institute of Automation,
The Chinese Academy of Sciences, P.O. Box 2728, Beijing 100080, P.R. China
dalei.guo@ia.ac.cn
[2] The Automation Institute of Shandong Academy of Sciences, Jinan 250014, P.R. China
sharron@gmail.com

## 1 Introduction

Analysis, evaluation and forecast for the collection, memory and management of information play an important role in the research and engineering application of intelligence and security informatics. Theoretically speaking, the developed science and technology have already well-founded for decision and strategy of ISI. For example, all the production, consumption, distributing and reserves of the energy of the country or worldwide could be searched, tracked and resisted dynamic in virtue of the information analysis, such as petroleum, forest and coal and so on. Whereas, greats of impacts still remain extremely difficult among key issues in ISI research. Such as the incapability of repeated or re-constructed of the situation, or the impossibility of reducing and simplifying the experiments to acquire the necessary data and so on, all these factors awfully obstacle the new advanced process of ISI research. Specially, the project attempts to build a parallel system support for ISI decision analysis and support based on a newly developed computational theory with the artificial societies and computational experiments.

## 2 Methodology

In artificial societies, the computers are assumed as social labs that could generate the relationship between the artificial human and the societal through autonomous programming. Base on this concept, to some extents, the accuracy of real systems is no longer the only criterion for model construction. Instead, the artificial model begins to turn into an alternative of a real system or an equivalent to the reality. That is to say, once the artificial mode of the natural system was created and put under the real, simulative situations or their mixed environments, we could inspect, detect, analyze and comprehend their interplay including the influence factors of the artificial mode and real events by the method of emergence. Thus, artificial societies provide a valid measure and effective mode for depicting and generating the real performance.

A parallel system consists of a real system and an artificial system, which could be linked in different means of operations. Actually, whatever mathematical modeling or computational simulating even virtual reality, are all the instances that use parallel

S. Mehrotra et al. (Eds.): ISI 2006, LNCS 3975, pp. 690–691, 2006.

theory to design and analyze. Then, the characteristics and the relationship of the reality and the artificial system could be compared and detected according to parallel systems. Hence, the parallel systems of the real system and artificial system provide the support to evaluate, forecast, manage and control for ISI research and analysis. Moreover, various concepts and methods developed in adaptive control can be used in operations of parallel systems.

This study attempts to build a large-scale energy platform, consisted of energy demand of the worldwide, the policy and its possible sequent, or the dynamic deduction of the energy situation with artificial society and parallel system. In order to verify the methodology of ISI research, greats of experiments are necessary for the energy parallel system under artificial societies. As we known, in reality, for many problems in ISI, it is commonly very difficult, costly and sometimes impossible to study concerned objects through active and controlled experiments. But the computational experiment is an alternative and complement to actual physical experiments. Computational experiments are natural applications of artificial systems too. Various techniques in experiment design and statistical analysis can be applied here directly.

In short, the parallel system provides the methodologies evaluation and forecast with artificial societies and computational experiments for security intelligence.

**Acknowledgments.** This support has been supported in part by the National Natural Science Foundation of China (Grants 60334020, 60573078 and 50505049).

# References

1. H. Chen, F. Y. Wang, D. Zeng. Intelligence and security informatics for homeland security: information, communication and transportation, IEEE Transaction on Intelligent Transportation Systems, 2004, v. 5, n4: 329-341
2. Hsinchun Chen and Fei-Yue Wang, "Artificial Intelligence for Homeland Security", IEEE Intelligent Systems, Vol. 20, Issue 5, 2005, pp. 12-16.
3. Y. Y. Yao, Fei-Yue Wang ☐J. Wang,, D. Zeng " Rule + Exception Strategies for Security Information Analysis" , IEEE Intelligent Systems, Vol. 20, Issue 5, 2005, pp. 52-57.
4. H. Chen, F.-Y. Wang, and D. Zeng "Intelligence and Security informatics for Homeland Security: Information, Communication and Transportation", IEEE Trans. Intelligent Transportation Systems, Vol. 5, No. 4, 2004, pp. 329-341.

# Identifying Information Provenance in Support of Intelligence Analysis, Sharing, and Protection[*]

Terrance Goan, Emi Fujioka, Ryan Kaneshiro, and Lynn Gasch

Stottler Henke Associates, Inc.
1107 NE 45th St., Suite 310, Seattle, WA 98105
{goan, emifuji, ryank, lynng}@stottlerhenke.com

## 1 Introduction

In recent years, it has become clear that our ability to create vast information assets far outstrips our ability to exploit and protect them. The Intelligence Community faces particularly significant information management challenges as they seek to: improve information awareness amongst analysts; improve the reliability of intelligence; safely share information with warfighters and allies; and root out malicious insiders. One means to mitigating these challenges is to provide reliable knowledge of the provenance (i.e., lineage) of documents. This knowledge would allow, for instance, analysts to identify source information underpinning an intelligence report.

There are two primary approaches to establishing information provenance. First, we might seek to develop information systems or processes that track (through metadata) the source of data imported into new intelligence products. Unfortunately, information system heterogeneity makes such an approach largely impractical.

The more attractive alternative is to recover provenance knowledge as required by users. This approach is exemplified by plagiarism detection tools. The most common approach employed by these systems is to calculate and compare compact document fingerprints by hashing select substrings. Unfortunately these approaches are only effective when documents are near-duplicates [3]. The commercial Turnitin plagiarism detection service utilizes a different approach – relying on detecting long strings of words shared by co-derived documents. Regrettably this tactic is susceptible to errors when faced with heavily edited text or shared (but inconsequential) boilerplate text.

## 2 Efficiently and Accurately Identifying Text Provenance

In order to support new Intelligence Community applications and to overcome the shortcomings of past approaches, we have developed a new approach that enables the scalable comparison of the full text of documents. Fundamental to our InfoTracker system is the concept of a suffix tree [2]. Our contribution is in the development of a means to detect derivative text (and thereby information provenance) even when overlaps are much less pervasive than assumed by previous approaches.

---

[*] This work was supported by the ARDA/DTO Advanced Information Assurance program under contract NBCHC030077.

S. Mehrotra et al. (Eds.): ISI 2006, LNCS 3975, pp. 692–693, 2006.

We accomplish this by contrasting two distinct corpora, one composed of documents of interest (e.g., intelligence reports) and the other composed of background knowledge made up of, for instance, hundreds of thousands of randomly selected Web documents. By analyzing string overlaps in the light of general language usage, InfoTracker is better able to judge the likelihood that text strings could be produced independently. In other words, while previous approaches exploit the rareness of long strings (e.g., eight words or more), InfoTracker can exploit its greater knowledge of common text patterns to recognize much shorter strings of text that are likely co-derived. This allows InfoTracker to succeed in a number of situations where past approaches would fail including identifying co-derivative relationships between paraphrases or between documents processed with different Optical Character Recognition (OCR) systems (each of which generates its own errors).

Enabling this new capability is a data structure based on String B-Trees [1], which is disk resident and allows incremental updating. Our approach also scales well – with the size of the index being linear in the size of the corpus, and document updates to the index and query parsing both being linear in the length of the new input.

## 3  Applications

In our poster and accompanying software demonstration we will provide details of our approach and describe how InfoTracker can be profitably employed in a wide variety of applications of import to the Intelligence Community. Some of these include:

- Identifying documents underpinning integrated intelligence products. This would allow analysts to independently verify and more easily reuse component data.
- Detecting malicious insiders. Infotracker can detect attempts to place classified material within documents with unclassified labels for exfiltration.
- Facilitating legitimate declassification. We have found, unexpectedly, that InfoTracker can effectively track the contents of short text redactions, and thereby improve the accuracy, consistency, and efficiency of future declassification tasks.
- Data spill recovery. Methods for identifying derivative text could be extremely helpful in determining where accidentally released intelligence has reached.

## References

1. Ferragina, P. and Grossi, R. "The String B-Tree: A New Data Structure for String Search in External Memory and its Applications." Journal of the ACM 46(2):236-280 (1999).
2. Gusfield, D. Algorithms on strings, trees, and sequences: computer science and computational biology, Cambridge University Press (1997).
3. Hoad, T. & Zobel, J. "Methods for identifying versioned and plagiarized documents," JASIST 54(3), 203-215 (2003).

# Intelligence Use of Unstructured Data in a Data Warehouse Environment

Jim Wakefield

The Greentree Group
jwakefield@greentreegroup.com

## 1 Introduction

In today's environment, analysts in all intelligence disciplines spend much of their time performing research and producing results, with a minimal amount of time dedicated to analysis. By changing current analysis, the amount of time dedicated to performing research and reporting results can be dramatically minimized. This allows more time for in-depth analysis of actionable information and better overall knowledge management being provided to the statesman and the war-fighter.

The world's data is generally comprised within two categories:

- Structured Data, which is tabular and easily works within row/column formats such as names, places, numbers, dates, etc.
- Unstructured Data, which is just about every type of information, not listed above, to include pictures, satellite images, signals, documents, e-mails, fingerprints, medical images, audio files, etc.

The Greentree Group has been developing a capability to remove obstacles associated with manipulation and analysis of unstructured data. We are now applying this technology to the task of transforming unstructured data into structured data and performing rapid analysis to determine correlations. The result is a high performance system that provides detailed answers to complex situations with sub-second response time on multi-petabyte data sets.

Recognizing the extraordinary business application potential of this implementation we have been maturing and expanding this data storage and mining technique directed at image mapping applications.

## 2 Image Mapping

In automating the procedure in which computers interpret pictures, we utilize a method of computational analysis known as Wavelet Analysis. Wavelet Analysis offers a mathematical means of detecting patterns within images. Not only do Wavelets provide computational analysis, but they also formulate excellent compression algorithms, which allow complex computer images to be stored digitally in a drastically compressed format, thus reducing storage, memory and CPU processing requirements. In essence, Wavelets provide a way to compute and visualize higher levels of information from seemingly random data streams and store the images in a compressed format. Identical images will have identical Wavelet Signatures. Yet, very similar images will still have different Signatures. It is possible to use the signatures to detect and locate differences

S. Mehrotra et al. (Eds.): ISI 2006, LNCS 3975, pp. 694–695, 2006.

between images of similar content because the signatures include location dependant information. Potential image comparison applications include:

- Photos/Satellite Imagery/Aerial Photography (JPEGs, TIFs, GIFs, etc.):
- Automated image recognition (Tanks, SCUDS, facial, etc.)
- Trend analysis over time
- Signal analysis (Automated signal recognition/comparison and noise removal)

The following examples were produced by sampling matches based on 1,100 images. **The results, based on over 1.2 million possibilities, were returned in subsecond response time on a relatively small test platform.**

The two LANDSAT images below are of the same land mass. Due to the position filtering, the location of the similarities is overcome and the two images were considered close matches due to the strong signatures that the land masses generate.

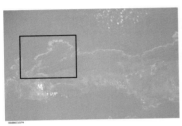 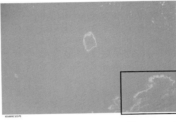

Rank: 1 of 1,100
Difference: 18.98

Trend analysis based on "triggers" automates the tedious task for analysts to determine when changes occur in an area of interest:

Rank: 1 of 1,100
Difference 9.05

## 3  Future Capabilities

It is believed that further research on tuning the algorithm will yield better matching capability and performance. Areas for continued development include:

- Integrated image recognition; the ability to analyze satellite images to automatically find certain military equipment or discern a T-72 tank from a haystack.
- In database processing to parallelize the signature generation.
- Other areas yet to be identified by customer requirements.

For intelligence agencies, this technology represents a paradigm shift in intelligence gathering and enables agencies to rapidly make educated decisions and gain a tactical advantage.

# An Evolutionary Approach in Threats Detection for Distributed Security Defence Systems

C. Onwubiko and A.P. Lenaghan

Networking and Communications Group, Faculty of Computing, Information Systems and
Mathematics, Kingston University, Kingston Upon Thames, KT1 2EE, UK
{k0327645, A.Lenaghan}@kingston.ac.uk

**Abstract.** A security defence framework is proposed that offers capabilities for
distributed sensing of security threats, centralised analysis and coordinated
response. The centralised analysis component of the framework uses graph and
evolutionary computing techniques to analyse distributed threats perceived in
the network.

**Keywords:** security defence framework, genetic algorithms, security threats.

## 1 Introduction

A new paradigm in security defence is envisaged where distributed defence mechanisms
are required with the potential to provide distributed threat detection, centralised
analysis and coordinated countermeasures to perceived threats to networks. A
distributed security infrastructure operates across the whole network. And distributed
solutions offer three significant advantages over point solutions, namely, their abilities
to: (i) Collate information about threats across a population of hosts rather than an
individual host; (ii) Analyse threats across a population of hosts rather than a part of the
network; and (iii) Coordinate the deployment or reconfiguration of multiple
countermeasures across a network.

## 2 Proposed Security Defence Framework

Emerging security threats are shown to be distributed and coordinated [1]; while
existing defence mechanisms defend in isolation. We propose a new security defence
paradigm – *"Sensor, Analysis and Response"* (SAR) that offer potentials for
distributed defence mechanisms to computer network systems. The SAR approach
provides capabilities for distributed sensing of threats, centralised analyses and
coordinated responses to perceived threats on the network. And also offers extension
mechanisms to cooperate human countermeasures in its analysis of threats, which
relies on *security spaces* [2] for communicating security information among security
components (sensors, analysers and responders) in the framework (see fig. 1).

    The proposed logical framework defines 4 types of component; sensor components
that contribute evidence about security related events, analysis components that
implement autonomous software agents capable of analysing evidence, an abstract

S. Mehrotra et al. (Eds.): ISI 2006, LNCS 3975, pp. 696–698, 2006.

"security space" through which sensor and analysis components communicate, and finally, response components implement countermeasures and can be configured to protect networks. The requirements for the framework are to offer mechanisms to: (i) distribute sensors in the network to gather security threats; and to correlate and normalise threat incidences; providing secure distributed network monitoring capabilities; (ii) provide appropriate and expressive representation of security threats; (iii) provide "centralised" analyse of threats - integrated and real-time - that assists defence mechanisms in decision making; (iv) provide appropriate and coordinated countermeasures to perceived threats; (v) provide *cooperation* with human expertise.

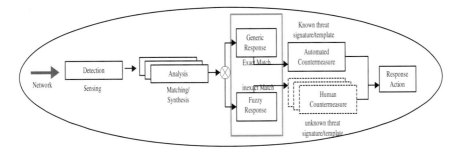

**Fig. 1.** Conceptualised Operations in the Framework

## 3 Experiment and Analysis of Result

A network simulator model (ns-2) is used to sense security threats in a midsize network. Threats gathered are processed using a graph library –GraphML [3], and codify from subgraph problem to genetic algorithms (GA). We represent node of the graphs as genes in a chromosome, while the corresponding pair of node in the subgraph (fig. 2) represents position. By pairing chromosomes for each graph we obtain an initial population $N$=20. String permutation crossover, translocation mutation and elitism all utilised to evolve concrete security threats at the $7^{th}$ iteration (fig. 3) with a crossover and mutation rate of ($p_c = 0.5$) and ($p_m = 0.001$) respectively.

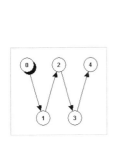

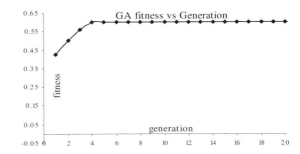

**Fig.2.** Subgraph (template graph)

**Fig. 3.** Representation of fitness of the best individual in a given generation

# 4  Conclusion

Our proposed framework offers capabilities to detecting emerging threats by distributing security sensors across the network that communicate threats evidences to the analysis component. The analysis component analyses these evidences to inform appropriate countermeasures to perceived threats on the whole network. Although we used graph and genetic algorithms in our analysis; however, other analysis techniques can be utilised in the framework.

# References

[1]  S. Braynov and M. Jadliwala (2003) "Representation and Analysis of Coordinated Attacks", *Proc. of FMSE'03, Washington DC, USA, October 30, 2003*
[2]  Lenaghan, C. Onwubiko, L. Hebbes and R.R. Malyan (2005), "Security spaces for Protecting Users of Wireless Public Hotspots", *Proc. of the IEEE - EUROCON 2005*
[3]  GraphML – "Graph Markup Language", http://graphml.graphdrawing.org/

# Classification of Threats
# Via a Multi-sensor Security Portal

Amar Singh and Lawrence Holder

Department of Computer Science and Engineering,
University of Texas at Arlington,
Arlington, TX 76019, USA
amar.singh@uta.edu, holder@cse.uta.edu
http://prodigy.uta.edu, http://www.cse.uta.edu/~holder

Classification of threats has always been a major security decision issue when a person walks through a security portal. To classify threat by combining data from multiple sensors like Millimeter Wave (MMW) imagery and Multi-zone Metal Detector is proposed and studied. Decisions made according to data from multiple sensors are analyzed. We present results for processing the fused sensor data and study the performance of several learning algorithms on this task. Usually the decision is being made based on single types of sensors, e.g., pulse induction metal detectors. We wish to identify the threats which are not determined by metal detectors alone.

There are numerous papers in the literature on the conventional way of fusing data from multiple sensors. The focus has been to identify the kind, shape, and location of weapons; whereas, the concern is to determine if a person is a threat or not irrespective of what object is being carried.

In this paper, we propose a decision technique based on a multi sensor security portal. The decision is made by a classifier, which is learned based on the vector level fused data from multiple sensors. We show an improvement in performance of a security portal at detecting threats by combining multiple sensors.

Currently, our portal consists of a walk-through pin-point metal detector (MD) sensor and a millimeter-wave (MMW) imagery sensor. Results in this paper are based on the fusion of the MD and MMW sensors, but we also plan to incorporate additional sensors like infrared cameras and vapor trace detectors.

To keep the data as low level as possible with no intervention of human knowledge in the form of image processing, pixel-level fusion techniques have been used. We averaged to a factor of 25 to reduce an image from 200 x 200 to 8 x 8. Two Millimeter Wave Images are taken of a person, one of the upper half (Figure 1- First from left) and another of the lower half (Figure 1- Second from left). The metal detector gives sensor values for 19 different zones of the archway through which a person passes (Figure 1- Third from left). Emulating a real-life scenario the set of sensors were placed in a room operating at room temperature.

Our model is provided profiles for training purpose. Each profile represents a sample case of a person passing through the portal. Information given as a profile includes the upper body MMW image, lower body MMW image, 19 metal detector zone readings and a possible classification. The combination of the MMW and MD sensor

S. Mehrotra et al. (Eds.): ISI 2006, LNCS 3975, pp. 699 – 700, 2006.

values is given to the learning algorithm. The learning algorithm finds classifiers capable of distinguishing threats from non-threats. The knowledge gained by the learning algorithm based on the training data is then used for prediction on the testing dataset.

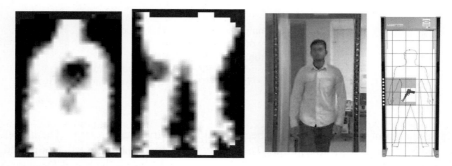

**Fig. 1.** First from left: Millimeter Wave Image of person carrying suspicious object on their upper chest. Second from left: Millimeter Wave Image of person carrying suspicious object on their right thigh. Third from left: Person walking through Pin-point Metal Detector. Fourth from left: Lights getting illuminated when person carries gun.

Various learning algorithms were used to classify the profiles. For conducting the experiments we used the Weka (The Waikato Environment for Knowledge Analysis) data mining tool. Among the classifiers used was Decision trees (J48), Multi-layer perceptron (MLP), and SMO (Sequential Minimal Optimization). The table below presents the percentage of test cases correctly classified for the various algorithms. Using both sensors outperforms either sensor individually.

|  | J48 | SMO | MLP |
|---|---|---|---|
| Both sensors | 90.32 % | 97.58 % | 95.96 % |
| Only MMW Image | 77.41 % | 87.90 % | 85.48 % |
| Only Metal Detector | 88.71 % | 75.8 % | 83.87 % |

Until now, threats have been detected in a person based on a single sensor or based on multiple sensors for identifying the object a person is carrying. The idea of using multiple sensors has shown better accuracy as compared to a single sensor looking at the results of all the algorithms above. Furthermore, various other sensors can be introduced to augment the sensor data.

# Exploring the Detection Process: Integrating Judgment and Outcome Decomposition

Ignacio J. Martinez-Moyano,[1] Eliot H. Rich,[2] and Stephen H. Conrad[3]

[1] Argonne National Laboratory
imartinez@anl.gov
[2] University at Albany
e.rich@albany.edu
[3] Sandia National Laboratories
shconra@sandia.gov

**Detection Processes.** In detection processes, decision making includes comparing indicators with thresholds that determine the preferred course of action. The prototypical detection problem deals with identification of elements that belong to a class when mixed with elements that do not belong to it. In our model, we integrate elements from social judgment theory *SJT* (Brunswik, 1943) (e.g., lens model of judgment analysis) and signal detection theory *SDT* (Green & Swets, 1966) using the system dynamics framework (Forrester, 1961; Sterman, 2000) to further the understanding of detection processes.

*SJT* evolved from Brunswik's (1943) probabilistic functionalist psychology coupled with multiple correlation and regression-based statistical analysis (Hammond & Stewart, 2001). The decomposition of judgment is the central focus of this theory but fails to explore outcomes derived from decisions following the judgment. On the other hand, although *SDT* fails to address the mechanisms of judgment that lead to a selection, the theory offers a mechanism to understand uncertainty and decompose outcome into four categories: true positives, true negatives, false positives, and false negatives. Integrating these theories might lead to a better understanding of the integrated selection-detection problem in a holistic manner.

**Detection Model.** The detection model has three basic sectors: judgment, decision making, and threshold setting. The sectors are interconnected through one major feedback mechanism that leads to the adjustment of the decision threshold over time. Numerical simulation is used to explore the model under various conditions.

In the model, we use a three-cue structure to determine distal variable (the phenomenon to be detected) behavior. In addition, an error term captures the inherent unpredictability of the environment. Cues are formulated as independent stochastic variables. Judges generate judgments based on a noisy signal of the information cues, judge bias, and judge reliability (modeled as a stochastic variable).

Events and actions are modeled by comparing their values with a criterion threshold (definition of what constitutes an event) and a decision threshold, respectively. Decomposition of the judgment process, and of the threshold-setting mechanism, allows for the identification of different sources of error: poor judgment and poor decision-threshold setting. In the model, outcome feedback (knowledge of the results) is used to modify the decision threshold as a result of the influence (based on a fixed payoff matrix) of the four types of outcomes in the decision process.

S. Mehrotra et al. (Eds.): ISI 2006, LNCS 3975, pp. 701–703, 2006.
© Springer-Verlag Berlin Heidelberg 2006

The model was parameterized to create a base-case run that captures the case in which a conservative judge selects a cautious decision threshold and applies it consistently as a decision policy. In this case, however, the judge has neither perfect information (measurement error exists) nor the correct judgment weights. Four additional scenarios are simulated: perfect information, perfect judgment weights, perfectly consistent judgment, and a combined case of the previous conditions. The environment, in all cases, is 80% predictable (see Table 1 for the results).

**Table 1.** Numerical Simulation Output

| Modified Erev et al 1995 Payoff with 40 Events (TP+FN) and 400 Judgments | Fixed (F) | Dynamic (D) | Perfect Info (F) | Perfect Info (D) | Perfect Weights (F) | Perfect Weights (D) | Consistent Judge (F) | Consistent Judge (D) | Combined (F) | Combined (D) |
|---|---|---|---|---|---|---|---|---|---|---|
| True Positives | 26 | 31 | 20 | 31 | 30 | 34 | 22 | 31 | 39 | 37 |
| False Negatives | 14 | 9 | 20 | 9 | 10 | 6 | 18 | 9 | 1 | 3 |
| False Positives | 190 | 243 | 193 | 269 | 179 | 226 | 168 | 229 | 162 | 170 |
| True Negatives | 169 | 116 | 166 | 90 | 180 | 133 | 191 | 130 | 197 | 189 |
| Actions (TP + FP) | 216 | 274 | 213 | 300 | 209 | 260 | 190 | 260 | 201 | 207 |
| Number of Errors (FP + FN) | 204 | 252 | 213 | 278 | 189 | 232 | 186 | 238 | 163 | 173 |
| Non-Events (TN+FP) | 359 | 359 | 359 | 359 | 359 | 359 | 359 | 359 | 359 | 359 |
| Sensitivity (TP/Total Events) | 65.00% | 77.50% | 50.00% | 77.50% | 75.00% | 85.00% | 55.00% | 77.50% | 97.50% | 92.50% |
| Specificity (TN/Total Non-Events) | 47.08% | 32.31% | 46.24% | 25.07% | 50.14% | 37.05% | 53.20% | 36.21% | 54.87% | 52.65% |

The simulated detection process, even when very efficient in detecting events (sensitivity of 97.5% and 92.5% in the combined case), is not efficient in defining a threshold that could eliminate errors. (An optimal level can be found as a function of the payoff structure of the detection problem. Different payoff structures will yield different optimal decision cutoff levels.)

**Conclusions and Future Research.** Combining judgment decomposition and outcome decomposition in a single dynamic framework seems promising to increase understanding of selection-detection processes. A number of problems and opportunities are associated with the approach taken in this research as theory integration is a delicate enterprise in itself. The research presented here still requires refinement of the structure of the model and exploration of current decision threshold adjustment behavioral theories (see Erev, 1998). Additionally, data need to be collected to identify descriptive time series to continue with the process of confidence building. The creation of such an integrated model of judgment and decision making for detection problems can provide additional help in understanding the implications and complications of these processes in complex situations.

**Acknowledgments.** Work supported by the U.S. Department of Homeland Security.

# References

Brunswik, E. 1943. Organismic achievement and environmental probability. *Psychological Review*, 50: 255-272.

Erev, I. 1998. Signal detection by human observers: A cutoff reinforcement learning model of categorization decisions under uncertainty. *Psychological Review*, 105: 280-298.

Forrester, J. W. 1961. *Industrial Dynamics*. Cambridge MA: Productivity Press.

Green, D. M., & Swets, J. A. 1966. *Signal Detection Theory and Psychophysics*. New York: John Wiley.

Hammond, K. R., & Stewart, T. R. (Eds.). 2001. *The Essential Brunswik: Beginnings, Explications, Applications*. Oxford: Oxford University Press.

Sterman, J. D. 2000. *Business Dynamics: Systems Thinking and Modeling for a Complex World*. Boston MA: Irwin McGraw-Hill.

# Issues in Merging Internet Autonomous Systems for Emergency Communications

Selwyn Russell[1,2,*]

[1] School of Software Engineering and Data Communications
Queensland University of Technology, Brisbane, Australia
`S.Russell@qut.edu.au`
[2] National ICT Australia Ltd. Queensland Laboratory, Brisbane, Australia

## Extended Abstract

The Internet has certain properties which make it the first choice for communications during an emergency. Experiences during the Kobe earthquake in 1995 indicated that the Internet was more resilient than other networks [1]. Fault tolerance and fault recovery were basic DARPA requirements [2]. The lack of a central controller or base station (as used in the two way radio systems often used by emergency handling teams) eliminates a potential critical point of failure.

In a large developed area, there will be numerous TCP/IP networks installed: fiber, copper, wireless, and cable. Internet connectivity is typically provided through communications carriers which operate for profit. Over the past few decades, governments have encouraged or caused, e.g. through privatisation of a government utility, increasing numbers of suppliers of communications services. In a region, the larger utilities and enterprises provide their own networks, each individually registered with the Internet authorities as an Autonomous System (AS). These competing networks normally operate independently, with common gateway points where traffic is passed from one carrier to another. In a time of a large scale emergency in the area, these independent networks provide a basis for a fault tolerant network with good capacity and compatibility with many other networks and user devices. Even though a single network may not be fault tolerant, the diversity and duplication of links and nodes of the combined individual infrastructures are the correct components to form an adaptive network suitable for the situation. The difficulty of course is in merging the independent competing networks into a single collaborative network.

During a large scale emergency traffic behaves quite differently from normal times. The emergency recovery team needs a communication network with capabilities and configurations which have a very different profile from everyday communications networks, to avoid network overload from enquiry bursts and to favour emergency management traffic. Ideally, this temporary network would involve a merger of all commercial networks in the area which at other times

* National ICT Australia is funded by the Australian Government's Backing Australia's Ability initiative, in part through the Australian Research Council.

are competitive. Merging networks involves reconfiguration of significant nodes throughout the individual ASes. For large networks, care is needed to ensure inefficiencies and manual errors are not introduced, resulting in a single temporary AS which is inferior to the original arrangement.

To function as a single composite network, the routing tables of at least the gateway routers need to be modified so the networks co-operate and share the loads, and give priority to traffic to/from emergency services devices. Current router software is based on the assumption of a stable network with only small and incremental changes. During an emergency, speed and accuracy are vital, but at those times there is more chance of human error. To simplify communications management throughout a region, it is desirable to be able to describe the ideal network behaviour at that time in a high level policy style specification, and to have the relevant network components automatically reconfigured in accordance with the regional specification.

To accomplish this goal, management must be able to simply specify a complete and unambiguous high level policy for the communications network, and accomplish this act in times of stress and time pressure with a minimum of delay. An RFC on policies for routing first appeared in 1989 and languages for policy specification were used in RIPE-81 in 1993 [3]. Further work has been done, e.g. [4], relating to the control of traffic through transit networks, but we conclude they are not the type of policies or policy description languages needed during an emergency.

As well as the technical difficulties involved in merging networks, there are numerous non-technical barriers, such as commercial secrets, privacy, legal liability, and policies. If the the ASes are highly competitive, commercially sensitive information on operational details might be difficult to obtain, and there is the risk of incompatible equipment, formats, databases or support systems.

In future work we will investigate in more detail requirements for solutions and ways to meet them [5].

# References

1. Yoichi Shinoda, Tomomitsu Baba, Nobuhiko Tada, Akira Kato, and Jun Murai, "Forethought and Hindsight: Experiences from the First Internet Disaster Drill", 1996, INET 1996. Accessed 24 November 2005.
2. Internet Society, "A Brief History of the Internet and Related Networks", Tech. Rep., Internet Society, Oct. 2005.
3. T. Bates, E. Gerich, L. Joncheray, J-M. Jouanigot, D. Karrenberg, and M. Terpstra. J. Yu, "Representation of IP Routing Policies in a Routing Registry (ripe-81++)", Mar. 1995, RFC 1786 and RIPE-181.
4. C. Alaettinoglu, C. Villamizar, E. Gerich, D. Kessens, D. Meyer, T. Bates, D. Karrenberg, and M. Terpstra, "Routing Policy Specification Language (RPSL)", June 1999, RFC 2622; Obsoletes: 2280.
5. Selwyn Russell and Peter Croll, "A Project for the Synthesis of Composite TCP/IP Networks During Emergencies", in *AusCERT2006*.

# CWME: A Framework of Group Support System for Emergency Responses

Yaodong Li, Huiguang He, Baihua Xiao, Chunheng Wang, and Feiyue Wang

Institute of Automation, Chinese Academy of Sciences Beijing 100080, China
{yaodong.li, huiguang.he, baihua.xiao,
chunheng.wang, feiyue.wang}@ia.ac.cn

## Background

As the world becomes more and more interconnected and complex, the emergent events, such as terrorist acts, infectious diseases and natural disasters challenge the rapid response ability of the public and the governments more and more. In general, emergency responses always involve so many complex problems that it beyond the decision capacity of a single person or organization. To meet this challenge, some new approaches of decision support for emergency responses need to be discovered. In this paper, a framework of this type of system, CWME, is introduced. It's based on the theories for Open Complex Giant Systems [1]. The key point of this system is to synthesize the intelligence of experts, the high performance of computers and data, information to understand the problems comprehensively and to make better decisions.

## Overview of CWME System and Its Working Process

Faced more and more complex problems related to the social systems, ecological systems and etc., many scientists try to find innovative ways to study these problems in an unified framework. In the early 1990s, Prof. Tsein and his colleagues summarized their experiences in the fields of seminar, $C^3I$ and warfare simulation, information & intelligence technologies, man-computer cooperated intelligent systems, etc. and proposed a methodology, Hall for Workshop of Meta-synthetic Engineering (HWME), to deal with these complex problems. Sponsored by the National Natural Science Foundation of China (NSFC), we have successfully build a prototype of HWME, called Cyberspace for Workshop of Meta-synthetic Engineering (CWME)[2], which is considered a appropriate platform for decision support for emergency responses.

CWME is a distributed group support system. It consists of three parts: a discussion center, a data center and an information/knowledge center. The three centers are interconnected by the Internet. They form a cyberspace on the Internet. Data, information, knowledge, models, model building tools and other resources related to emergency responses can be added to the platform at ordinary times. When an emergent event happens, experts (maybe in different locations) that are familiar to the fields affected by the event are invited to login CWME via the Internet. Each expert can study the situation and propose the solution with the aid of data, model and other computerized tools supplied by CWME. While, different experts can exchange their

S. Mehrotra et al. (Eds.): ISI 2006, LNCS 3975, pp. 706 – 707, 2006.

ideas and knowledge via the discussion center, which provides effective interaction, dialog and consensus tools to improve the quality of group support.

The general process of group support for emergency responses in CWME is as follows: 1) Experts discuss the situation rapidly and propose an initial response draft; 2) Each expert examines the draft from the point of view of his/her field. The intelligence and security informatics technologies and tools [3-5] always play an important role in this step; 3) Experts discuss, argue and modify the initial draft. Data, models and other tools are often utilized to prove their opinions; 4) Experts evaluate the modified draft through discussion and calculation; 5) If the draft doesn't satisfy the group, experts may return to step 1. They will consider the situation again and repeat step 2 - 5. 6) If the draft is OK, experts submit the draft to decision maker to response the emergent event. And the group support process ends.

In CWME, the data center, the information/knowledge center, in addition to the discussion center, make up a virtual collaborative workspace. An initial draft can be rapidly proposed by experts from their experiences, conjecture and intuition. And then the draft will be quantitatively evaluated with the aid of computers' high performance. Information and knowledge stored in computers and experts' brains help experts obtain sound solution in the whole process. Thus, the experts, the computers and the information/knowledge bases form a giant man-computer cooperated intelligent system. Different members of the system play different roles. They work together and complement each other to accelerate the speed of decision making, and to improve the quality of decision, which are extremely important for emergency responses.

**Acknowledgments.** This work is supported in part by NSFC (Grant 60573078, 60334020, 60302016) and Beijing NSF (Grant 4042024).

# References

1. T. S. Tsein, R. W. Dai, J. Y. Yu. "A New Scientific Field: Open Complex Giant Systems and Its Methodology", Ziran Zazhi, 1990, 13(1):3-10.
2. R. W. Dai, Y. D. Li. Researches on Hall for Workshop of Meta-synthetic Engineering and System Complexity, Complex Systems and Complex Science, 2004, 1(4):1-24.
3. Hsinchun Chen and Fei-Yue Wang, "Artificial Intelligence for Homeland Security", IEEE Intelligent Systems, Vol. 20, Issue 5, 2005, pp. 12-16.
4. Y. Y. Yao, Fei-Yue Wang , J. Wang,, D. Zeng " Rule + Exception Strategies for Security Information Analysis" , IEEE Intelligent Systems, Vol. 20, Issue 5, 2005, pp. 52-57.
5. H. Chen, F.-Y. Wang, and D. Zeng "Intelligence and Security informatics for Homeland Security: Information, Communication and Transportation", IEEE Trans. Intelligent Transportation Systems, Vol. 5, No. 4, 2004, pp. 329-341.

# Abnormal Detection Algorithm Based on Match Range Model

Jungan Chen

Zhejiang Wanli University
Ningbo, Zhejiang, 315100, China
friendcen21@hotmail.com

Two main techniques used to build Intrusion Detection System (IDS), abnormal detection and misuse detection, have their own strengths and limitations respectively. It implies that an effective IDS should employ an abnormal detector and a misuse detector in parallel. While the human immune system (HIS) distinguishes previously known and unknown pathogens from human body via its own passive layers which are called natural immune systems and adaptive immune systems. Natural immune system is akin to the misuse detector of IDS and adaptive immune system is similar to the abnormal detector. Inspired from adaptive immune system, Negative Selection Algorithm (NSA) is applied to abnormal detection. But NSA can not generate dynamic detectors changed with nonselves. Inspired from affinity maturation, Dynamic Negative Selection Algorithm Based on Affinity Maturation (DNSA-AM), where NSA is used to delete detectors which detect any selves, is proposed and can be adapted to the change of nonselves. Match rule with the match threshold (r) is one of the most important components in NSA and DNSA-AM. 'r' is related to selves and must be set at first. So DNSA-AM can not be adapted to the change of selves.

In Human Immune System, T-cells maturation goes through two processes, positive and negative selection. Positive selection requires T-cells to recognize self cells with lower affinity, while T- cells must not recognize self cells with higher affinity in negative selection. Based on this principle, there is a range between lower affinity and higher affinity. So a match range model with selfmin, selfmax is proposed in this work. Selfmin is the minimal distance between detector and selves. Selfmax is the maximal distance. The range between selfmin and selfmax is belonged to the self space. Based on this model, a new match rule called range-match rule is proposed. i.e., when the distance is bigger than selfmax or smaller than selfmin, a nonself is detected. One detector with selfmax, selfmin will not detect any selves because the distance between detector and selves must be in the range between selfmax and selfmin. So the function of setting selfmax, selfmin of one detector could be equal to the function of NSA. In this work, Dynamic Negative Selection Algorithm Based on Match Range Model (DNSA-MRM) is proposed. It is tested by simulation experiment for anomaly detection and compared with DNSA-AM. The results show that DNSA-MRM is more effective than DNSA-AM with following characters:

**Self-adapted Match Range:** In DNSA-MRM, range-match rule is used, NSA is replaced by the process of setting the value of selfmax,selfmin. There is no match threshold but match range. Match range can be adapted to the change of selves because the value of selfmax and selfmin is evaluated by selves.

S. Mehrotra et al. (Eds.): ISI 2006, LNCS 3975, pp. 708 – 710, 2006.

**Less Time Complexity:** DNSA-MRM with range-match rule executes more effectively than DNSA-AM with r-match rule because the detected range of one detector with match range is always wider than the detector with r. So there is less time complexity in DNSA-MRM.

Otherwise, DNSA-MRM has other characters:

**DetectionSpeed changed with AttackSpeed:** Some parameters is defines as following:    Speed = the number of nonselves / the number of generations;

DetectionSpeed = the number of nonselves detected / generation spended;

AttackSpeed = m / n; (the number of nonselves m in every n generations)

In Fig.1, the slope of curve is 1/DetectionSpeed, so the steeper slope means the lower detection speed. In the second fig, the slope of curve is lead to stable when the AttackSpeed is not smaller than 4/5, i.e., the maxim detection speed is reached, which means system is running in full power. When the AttackSpeed is smaller than 4/5, the slope of curve is becoming big, i.e., the detection speed is becoming slow with AttackSpeed, which means that system is not running in full power. In first fig, when AttackSpeed changed with time, the slope of curve changed, which means that running power of the system is changed with AttackSpeed. In a word, running power of the system or detection speed is changed with AttackSpeed. Also, it is shown that DNSA-MRM can detect new unknown nonselves quickly, which reflects the effective function of adaptive immune system.

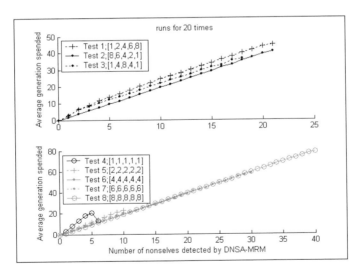

**Fig. 1.** Results of Detection Speed: Random generated string is used. The length of detector is 64, a=0.95, β=1-a=0.05, MaxGeneration is 250, the number of selves is 1000, the number of detectors is 200. In the legend, Test 1:[1,2,4,6,8] means that the number of nonselves happened in [0,5,10,15,20]$^{th}$ generation is [1,2,4,6,8].

**Learning:** With the stimulation of nonselves, DNSA-MRM will produce detectors with higher fitness. Some detectors will survive for a long time because of the stimulation of the same or similar nonselves repeatedly, so the patterns of nonselves will be remembered, which called 'memory' or 'learning'. Learning can accelerate the DetetctionSpeed just like the secondary response in immune system.

# Experimental Validation and Analysis of an Intelligent Detection and Response Strategy to False Positives and Network Attacks

Emmanuel Hooper

Information Security Group, University of London,
Royal Holloway,
Egham, Surrey, TW20 OEX, UK
manny.hooper@gmail.com, ehooper@aya.yale.edu

**Abstract.** Intrusion Detection Systems (IDSs) and security tools are used to monitor potential attacks in network infrastructures. The IDSs and tools trigger alerts of potential attacks in networks. However, most of these alerts are false positives. The high volumes of false positives makes manually analysis of alerts difficult and inefficient. In this paper we present a novel approach for efficient intelligent detection and response to suspect packets and benign false positives. The intelligent strategy consists of Network Quarantine Channels (NQCs) with multiple zones for isolation and interaction with the suspect packets in real-time. We propose multiple feedback methods to enhance the capability of the IDS to detect threats and benign attacks. We describe new techniques for feeding the results of the NQC to the IDS. These approaches are effective in responding to benign and attack packets.

## 1 Introduction

The motivation for the NQCs is the reduction of false positives through the diversion of suspicious packets to separate and multiple channels in the NQC. Each NQC channel analyzes different attack types, categories or subcategories. This enables the NQC-based IDS to respond appropriately to benign and malicious traffic. The problem is that many IDSs have high levels of false positives [10, 8]. Furthermore, unsuitable adaptive rules and honeypots [1] have limitations, since they depend on these same logs from the IDS or firewalls [9, 7, 5] or signatures on the IDS [4, 6].

## 2 An Overview of the Approach

The approach for solving the problem of benign and suspected network traffic consists of generating false network responses to suspect packets at the perimeter to obtain more information about the source of the suspect packets and the intentions of that source. The responses supply reply conditions desired by the suspect

S. Mehrotra et al. (Eds.): ISI 2006, LNCS 3975, pp. 711–714, 2006.

source packet. This results in the suspect packet providing more packets with information on the connection's identity. An overview of the architecture for an intelligent detection and response strategy through NQCs is shown in Figure 1. The NQC approach improves on existing solutions including adaptive rules, honeypots and other administrative interventions [2]. It performes the roles of the administrator in the automatic separation and analysis of benign traffic. The difference from honeypots [3] is that this approach includes interaction with the IDS, feedbacks methods to the IDS and detailed analysis of connection types. Honeypots do not include interaction with the IDS, feedbacks to the IDS [11]. The NQCs responds to all suspicious traffic and after interactive responses and analysis, send feedback messages to the IDS to filter out all benign traffic. This includes traffic with internal IP addresses, which have commonly known alerts. Those with external IP addresses are re-directed to the NQC zones for analysis of their attributes, including the protocols, applications, categories and subcategories.

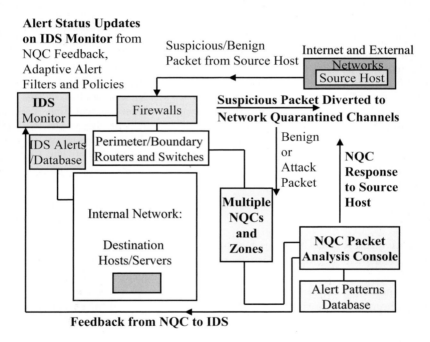

**Fig. 1.** Overview of Network Quarantined Channels for Analysis and Response to Attacks and Intrusions

The communication between the NQC and the IDS consists of feedback methods. The effects of these feedback methods on the effectiveness of the proposed approach are as follows. The first approach involves direct communication from the NQC to the IDS database using message flags. If the alert is benign, it is subsequently removed from the alert view of the IDS, and this reduces the number of false positives. The second approach involves communication from the NQC to the IDS using adaptive rules in the IDS Alert Filter. The filter rules specify that the benign packets should be filtered from the IDS alert monitor, and this also reduces false positives. The third approach involves communication to the IDS using adaptive rules in the IDS alert policies. The policy rules state that the source IP address and destination, port and packet type should be denied access to the destination host. This means the packet does not generate any further alerts on the IDS monitor, which also reduces false positives. The final approach consists of a combination of all three actions simultaneously. The advantage of simultaneous action is that the effect is immediate. Since the IDS requires time to update the policies and filters, a flag message is faster.

## 3    Experimental Results

The method involves the diversion of suspected network attacks to the quarantined channels and zones. This is followed by sending responses to the suspicious packets, which appear as valid return packets to the potential attacker. This results in further packets from the attacker, which if they persist, are directed to subsequent zones for additional responses. These interactive responses are repeated until the identity of the source and the nature of the attack types, category or subcategories have been determined in the NQCs so that an appropriate response can be applied to the suspicious packet. The results for suspicious connections in the multiple NQC channels and zones are as follows. The patterns of the suspicious packets were detected as attacks in different channels of the NQC. Initially this was detected by the IDS in the DMZ and diverted to the quarantined zones for response and further analysis by the IDS sensors, using the attack patterns analysis console. The normal packet did not trigger an IDS alert at the DMZ. The suspicious but benign connections alerted on the IDS as suspicious protocol and application anomalies, but proved to be actually benign. Reduction of false positives and misclassifications through the NQC channels result in accuracy in detection for appropriate and relevant response. This approach has proven effective in both architecture and methodology so that effective countermeasures can be taken to curtail misclassifications and false positives through effective intelligent real-time response. The attack was diverted for containment and analysis and stored in the database for subsequent analysis. Once the attack type was determined, the attack was denied access to the network via TCP disconnection and resets, etc.

## 4    Conclusion

The development of an intelligent detection and response strategy involving NQCs resulted in the reduction of false positives in network attacks. The feedback methods of the results of the NQC to the IDS, including flags, were used to distinguish normal benign packets from attack packets for appropriate automatic real-time responses. This reduced manual administrative interventions, misdirected efforts and the time given to false positives. Furthermore, the feedback methods enhanced intrusion detection capabilities and responses to suspicious packets through the reduction of false positives.

# References

1. T. Bowen, D. Chee, and M. Segal. Building survivable systems: An integrated approach based on intrusion detection and damage containment. In *IEEE Proceedings of the DARPA Information Survivability Conference and Exposition*, volume II of II, pages 84–999, 2000.
2. Jason Crampton and G. Loizou. Administrative scope: A foundation for role-based administrative models. *ACM Transactions on Information and System Security*, 6(2):201–231, July 2003.
3. John Levine, Richard La Bella, Henry Owen, D. Contis, and Brian Culver. The use of honeypots to detect exploited systems across large enterprise networks. In *Proceedings of the 2003 IEEE Workshop on Information Assurance*. IEEE Computer Society Press, 2003.
4. R. Lippmann, S. Webster, and D. Stetson. The effect of identifying vulnerabilities and patching software on the utility of network intrusion detection. *Computer Networks: The International Journal of Computer and Telecommunications Networking*, Volume 2516 of Lecture Notes in Computer Science:307–326, 2002.
5. M.V. Mahoney and P.K. Chan. An analysis of the 1999 DARPA Lincoln Laboratory evaluation data for network anomaly detection. In *Recent Advances in Intrusion Detection (RAID2003)*, volume 2820 of Lecture Notes in Computer Science, pages 220–237. Springer-Verlag, 2003.
6. S. Manganaris, M. Christensen, D. Zerkle, and K. Hermiz. A data mining analysis of RTID alarms. *Computer Networks: The International Journal of Computer and Telecommunications Networking*, 34:571–577, 2000.
7. B. Morin, L. Me, H. Debar, and M. Ducasse. M2D2: A formal data model for IDS alert correlation. In *Recent Advances in Intrusion Detection (RAID2002)*, volume 2515 of Lecture Notes in Computer Science, pages 115–137. Springer-Verlag, 2002.
8. Network Associates. NAI Intruvert IDS: 1200, 2600 and 4000 Series, 2004. Santa Clara, CA, USA.
9. V. Paxson. Bro: A system for detecting network intruders in real-time. In *Computer Networks*, volume 31, pages 2435–2463, 1999.
10. Leonid Portnoy, Eleazer Eskin, and Sal Solfo. Intrusion detection with unlabelled data using clustering. In *Proceedings of ACM CSS Workshop on Data Mining Applied to Security (DMSA-2001)*, pages 76–105, 2001.
11. T. H. Project. Know your enemy sebek. 2003. The Honeynet Project, http://project.honeynet.org/papers/sebek.pdf.

# A PCA-LVQ Model for Intrusion Alert Analysis

Jing-Xin Wang, Zhi-Ying Wang, and Kui Dai

Computer School, National University of Defense Technology, Changsha, China
wjx_eagle@163.com

**Abstract.** We present a PCA-LVQ model and a balanced-training method for efficient intrusion alert analysis. For the connection records in the 1999 DARPA intrusion dataset, we firstly get a dimension-reduced dataset through Principal Component Analysis (PCA). Then, we use the Learning Vector Quantization (LVQ) neural network to perform intrusion alert clustering on the purified intrusion dataset. The experiment results show that the PCA-LVQ model and the balanced-training method are effective: the time costs can be shortened about by three times, and the accuracy of detection can be elevated to a higher level, especially for the U2R and R2L alerts.

## 1 Introduction

Although often used as the benchmark for intrusion alert analysis, the 1999 DARPA intrusion dataset includes large volume of inessential information. The existence of these insignificant information will result in some adverse scenarios. So, in our opinion, to operate directly on the rough intrusion dataset is not an optimal method.

We propose a new hybrid method for intrusion alert analysis. We call it PCA-LVQ method. Concretely speaking, we first preprocess the rough intrusion dataset by performing principal component analysis. Then, we will use the learning vector quantization neural network to analyze the connection records in the purified intrusion dataset. By this PCA-LVQ method, we aim at obtaining the higher accuracy of detection with the lowered system performance costs than before. We will verify this method through some experiments.

## 2 Intrusion Dataset and Principal Component Analysis

The intrusion dataset includes 39 attack types, 22 of which appear in both the training dataset and the test dataset, and other attack types appear only in the test dataset. All these attack types can be categorized into 4 classes, i.e. R2L, DOS, U2R and Probing. Both the attack types and the normal traffic are represented by the connection records, and each connection record consists of 41 features.

PCA is a useful technique for dimension reduction and multivariate analysis [1].Limited to the length, we will not describe it in detail. Through PCA and security domain knowledge, we select 12 key features to represent the connection records. Thus, the purified intrusion dataset is a finite set of the 12-dimension Euclidean space, $R_{CR}^{12}$, which will be analyzed by the learning vector quantization neural network.

S. Mehrotra et al. (Eds.): ISI 2006, LNCS 3975, pp. 715–716, 2006.

## 3  Alert Clustering Using LVQ

LVQ is a supervised competitive neural network model. By using pre-assigned cluster labels to the training samples, it can maximize correct data classification [2]. In the training phase, by using modified LVQ algorithm, the Euclidean space $R_{CR}^{12}$ will be divided into 5 subspace, $R_{Normal}^{12}, R_{Probing}^{12}, R_{DOS}^{12}, R_{U2R}^{12}$ and $R_{R2L}^{12}$, each subspace is  also called a cluster center. Then, in the test phase, given a connection record $CR$ as the input of the LVQ neural network, it will be categorized into one of $\{R_{Normal}^{12}, R_{Probing}^{12}, R_{DOS}^{12}, R_{U2R}^{12}, R_{R2L}^{12}\}$. More formally, we describe the problem as follows:

Given codebook $C = \{Y_{Normal}, Y_{Probing}, Y_{DOS}, Y_{U2R}, Y_{R2L} | Y \in R^{12}\}$ and the input vector $\overline{X}$ to be clustered, LVQ will look for a certain codeword $Y$ from $C$ and stipulate the correctness of the following expression: $\{Y \in C \wedge \forall Y' \in C \Rightarrow \|Y - \overline{X}\| \leq \|Y' - \overline{X}\|\}$.

## 4  Experiment Results and Conclusion

Our method has been verified through experiments. We use the LVQ model in the experiment 1 and PCA-LVQ model in the experiment 2. In both the experiments, we adopt our modified LVQ algorithm and balanced-training method. From the experiment 1, we can see that our method has higher clustering accuracy rate than other research [3,4], especially for the U2R and R2L alerts (from less than 5% to more than 60%). Through the experiment 2, the overall clustering accuracy rate can be increased farther, which shows that the PCA-LVQ model is effective. Besides, the time cost can be shortened about by three times.

As a whole, the major contribution of our work includes the betterment of the LVQ algorithm, the balanced-training method and the first application of the PCA-LVQ model on intrusion alert analysis. The experiments showed that our method is correct and efficient for intrusion alert analysis.

## References

[1] E. Oja. Neural Networks, principal components, and subspaces, International Journal ofNeural Systems, vol.1, no.1, pp 61-68, 1989.
[2] Teuvo Kohonen Jussi Hynninen, Jari Kangas. LVQ_PAK: The Learning Vector Quantization Program Package. Techinical report, 1996.
[3] Y. Bouzida, S. Gombault. EigenConnections to Intrusion Detection, Proceedings of the 19th IFIP International Information Security Conference, August  2004.
[4] Manikantan Ramadas. Detecting Anomalous Network Traffic with Self-Organizing Maps. Master's thesis, Ohio University, Mar 2003.

# A Formalized Taxonomy of DDoS Attacks Based on Similarity

Jian Kang, Yuan Zhang, and Jiu-bin Ju

Department of Computer Science & Technology,
Jilin University, Changchun, 130012, China
kj885788@gmail.com

Distributed Denial of Service (DDoS) attacks have posed an immense threat to the Internet. Various DDoS attack tools and their late editions come to the fore and DDoS field rapidly becomes more and more complex. In order to understand and deal with DDoS attacks, it is of great significance to classify them. Thus, a formalized and scalable taxonomy is needed, and in this paper, the taxonomy is proposed as follows:

The basic idea of the taxonomy is to use Hierarchical Clustered method to classify various DDoS attacks based on similarity. It is necessary to abstractly describe attacks for problem formulation and to measure distance between different attacks for clustering analysis.

In order to make problem formulation, we extract features of DDoS attacks and build a Binary Weighted Tree based on these features. First, select comparable and representative features [1][2](such as topologies of attacks network, types of attack flood, IP spoof, etc.) to compose a feature set, and of course, this set is scalable. Second, build a tree corresponding with a feature. And to the tree, encode its edges. The binary code string's length of the edges connecting the node and its children is $\lceil \log_2 n \rceil$ , and $n$ is the number of the node's children. The binary code strings of these edges in turn are the first $n$ strings from $00\ldots 0$ to $11\ldots 1$. Then, assign weight for each node based on their weightiness. For example, Fig 1 shows the tree of Exploit Weakness. To each attack, we could record one's information about the path it passed in the tree using a sequence of three-tuple, and each three-tuple is $(name, code, weight)$. Here $name$ is the name of the node; $code$ is encoding string of the edge connecting the node with its parent; $weight$ is the weight of the node in the tree. In addition, set weights for different features because they play different role in the clustering process. In this way, DDoS attacks could be abstractly described for problem formulation.

We use similarity to measure the difference between attacks, and in this paper similarity is defined as the reciprocal of the distance between attacks. So the problem now is how to get that distance. There are two steps: First, to each feature, calculate the distance between two attacks. Here is the algorithm: According to the sequences of three-tuples of the two attacks, compare each $code$ of three-tuples in different sequences one by one . Till the first

S. Mehrotra et al. (Eds.): ISI 2006, LNCS 3975, pp. 717–719, 2006.

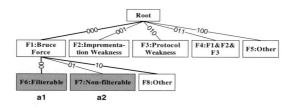

**Fig. 1.** Binary Weighted Tree of Exploit Weakness

different codes, we can choose the *weight* of this node as the value of the distance. Second, sum the distances with weight corresponding to the features, and the sum is the final distance between two attacks. For instance, Fig 1 shows the paths that attacks $a1$ and $a2$ pass through the tree of Exploit Weakness. The sequences of three-tuples can be formed as (here we have assigned the weights):

$a1 : (BruceForce, 000, 1), (Filterable, 00, 2)$

$a2 : (BruceForce, 000, 1), (Non - filterable, 01, 2)$

According to the algorithm mentioned above, to Exploit Weakness feature, the distance between $a1$ and $a2$ is 2.

Finally, we can use Hierarchical Clustered method to classify various DDoS attacks. Suppose there are $n$ attacks, the process are as follows:

STEP1: calculate similarities between twain of the $n$ attack samples, and record them as a similarity matrix;

STEP2: construct $n$ classes, each attacks is one class;

STEP3: find out the greatest element from the similarity matrix, and merge the two classes whose similarity is the greatest. If there is more than one greatest element, merge the ecorresponding classes simultaneously;

STEP4: calculate the similarities between the new class and each of the classes currently, and update the similarity matrix. If the number of classes is one, skip to STEP5, or else, skip to STEP3;

STEP5: make the clustering pedigree graph according to the process above;

STEP6: set Threshold, get the number of the classes and divide the attack samples into classes.

To test and evaluate our taxonomy, we have performed a series of experiments with 12 real DDoS attacks. The result shows that our taxonomy is valid not only to the attacks currently known and their different editions, but also to the derivatives based on known attacks.

The abstract and formalized taxonomy proposed in this paper is important to the development of realistic models of DDoS simulation and experimentation. In addition, this taxonomy can be used for performing attacks detection and analyzing as a Plug-in, and can also be packaged as an automated tool to aid in rapid response to DDoS attacks.

# References

1. Jelena. Mirkovic, J. Martin, P. Reiher: A Taxonomy of DDoS Attacks and DDoS Defense Mechanims. UCLA CSD Technical Report CSD-TR-020018.
2. A. Hussain, J. Heideman, C. Papadopoulos: A Framework for Classifying Denial of Service Attacks. In proceedings of SIGCOMM'03, , Karlsruhe, Germany (2003)

# Practical Intrusion Detection Using Genetic-Clustering

Chien-Chuan Lin and Ming-Shi Wang

Department of Engineering Science, National Cheng Kung University,
No. 1, Ta-Hsueh Road, Tainan 70101, Taiwan
n9893106@mail.ncku.edu.tw, mswang@mail.ncku.edu.tw

Filtering and classifying features of attack traffic is a crucial issue for network security applications such as intrusion detection systems (IDS). In this research, a genetic-clustering algorithm has been developed to detect and classify the data instances collected from IDS into normal or attack clusters automatically. The proposed algorithm can obtain the optimal clustering solution based on the minimum within-cluster distance (WCD) and maximum between-cluster distance (BCD). The advantages of the proposed algorithm are increasing the DR(Detection Rate), reducing the process time, decreasing the FNR(False Negative Rate) and also identify new attack traffics. The proposed algorithm is consisted of two phases, training phase and testing phase, and used the dataset generated from the 1999 KDD Cup dataset.

The Training Phase Steps: 1. Data Normalization: source data were normalized as unbiased data; 2. Encode Chromosome: encoded the normalized data set into the format of genetic algorithm; 3. Initialization Population: produced the first generation population; 4. Termination Conditions: defined a termination condition such as while (t != MG and r != RB) {... }, where MG is maximum generation, RB=MG/m, m is a given number and 1<m<MG ; 5. Fitness Function: WCD was defined as equation(1). BCD was defined as equation(2). The optimal classification must satisfy the condition max(BCD/WCD). The fitness function is given by equation(3). This fitness function is utilized as the evaluation tool for population selection; 6. Evaluation: evaluated each population and selected the best elitist one. The elitist of current generation would be replaced if a fitter member existed at its next generation; 7. Crossover: this work adopted the one-point crossover mechanism. The total number of members of P(t), the population of current generation, to be executed by crossover procedure is PN×PCR, where PN is number of population, PCR is probability of crossover; 8. Mutation: altered the selected chromosome from original chromosome to TGM(The Global Mean) or TFM(The Farthest Mean). Figure 1 shows the main procedures of Training Phase. The Testing Phase: according to the results of Training Phase, Testing Phase labels each instance as attack or normal. Figure 2 shows the Testing Phase main steps.

$$WCD = \sum_{j=1}^{K}(\sum_{i=1}^{n}D(x_{ij}, m_j)) \text{ , where n is the number of instances in cluster j.} \tag{1}$$

$$BCD = \sum_{i=1}^{k} D(m_i, (\sum_{i=1}^{k} m_i)/k), \text{ where mi is the mean of cluster i.} \tag{2}$$

$$F(P(t)) = \max(BCD(P_i(t))/WCD(P_i(t))), \text{ where i = 1, 2, ..., PN.} \tag{3}$$

S. Mehrotra et al. (Eds.): ISI 2006, LNCS 3975, pp. 720–721, 2006.
© Springer-Verlag Berlin Heidelberg 2006

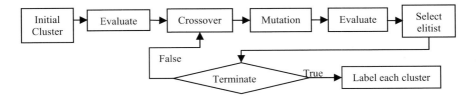

**Fig. 1.** The procedures flowchart of Training Phase

**Fig. 2.** The procedures flowchart of Testing Phase

The Training data set has 4500 instances that include 3967 normal and 533 attack instances; Testing data set has 1000 instances that include 884 normal and 116 attack instances. The parameters for the following experiment were set as follows: population = 20; MG = 200 and 300; RB = MG/10; K(the number of cluster) = 2,3,...,30; the probability of crossover = 0.6 and probability of mutation = 0.05; NR(Normal Rate, the rate of normal instances at a cluster) are 0.8, 0.9 and 0.95. Table 1 is our main experimental results. Table 1 lists the optimal result of DR and FNR; we can determine that the optimal result for system future work. The training phase is a time-consuming process, and the processing time depends on the source instances, the number of population and the number of clusters. The response time of testing phase is shorter than training phase, and is dependent on the testing data set and the value K, which determines the response time. The lower the value of K takes the shorter the response time.

**Table 1.** The optimal result of DR and FNR

| MG | NR | DR(%) | FNR(%) | K |
|----|------|-------|--------|----|
| 200 | 0.8 | 94.10 | 3.45 | 15 |
| | 0.9 | 94.40 | 3.45 | 30 |
| | 0.95 | 94.10 | 3.45 | 13 |
| 300 | 0.8 | 95.10 | 3.45 | 18 |
| | 0.9 | 93.90 | 3.45 | 30 |
| | 0.95 | 94.20 | 3.45 | 23 |

This investigation presented a solution to detect, classify and analyze IDS datasets and obtain high DR and low FNR of IDS, and also get the optimal solution for the number of clusters, the best means of clusters, NR and MG. Experimental results demonstrate that the optimal DR is greater than 95%; the FNR is lower than 3.5%. Hence, the new approach is feasible for IDS, and can be applied to any IDS.

# An Ontology-Based Network Intrusion Detection System: A User-Oriented Approach

Shao-Shin Hung[1] and Damon Shing-Min Liu[2]

Department of Computer Science and Information Engineering
National Chung Cheng University
Chiayi, Taiwan 621, Republic of China
{hss, damon}@cs.ccu.edu.tw

**Abstract.** In this paper, a new approach is suggested for designing and developing an intrusion detection application where the domain expertise is used for generating it more easily. This approach uses ontologies as a way of grasping the knowledge of a domain, expressing the intrusion detection system much more in terms of the end users domain, generating the intrusion detection more easily and performing intelligent reasoning. Experimental results show that our anomaly detection techniques are very promising and are successful in automatically detecting intrusions at very low false alarm rate compared with several important traditional classification techniques.

## 1 Introduction

Undercoffer et al. [4] have defined the ontology for intrusion detection. Our approach can be seen as a more intelligent way of designing an intrusion detection application. The rest of this paper is organized as follows. Section 2 discusses the relevant aspects of detecting intrusion. Section 3 overviews our techniques applied on the detecting intrusion and the idea behind our approach. Our results and analysis are presented in Section 4. Conclusions and future works are presented in Section 5.

## 2 Related Works

There are mainly four types of intrusion detection techniques: anomaly detection [5], misuse detection [3], data mining [5].and ontology-based system [4].

## 3 Our Ontology-Based Intrusion Detection Model

Our approach is divided into three phases, namely, a specification phase, a mapping phase and a generation phase. We have prototyped the logic portion of our system using *DAMLJessKB* [1] reasoning system.

S. Mehrotra et al. (Eds.): ISI 2006, LNCS 3975, pp. 722–723, 2006.

## 4  Our Results and Analysis

Our experimental dataset was the KDD Cup 1999 Data [2], which contained a wide variety of intrusions simulated in a military network environment. The simulated attacks fell in one of the following four categories: (1) DOS; (2) R2L; (3) U2R; and (4) Probing. The *hit rate* (HT) is the ration of the number of hits to the total number of the truly intrusive data records. The *false alarm rate* (FAR) is the ration of false alarms to the total number of the truly normal data records. Experimental results are presented in Table 1.

**Table 1.**  PD, HT and FAR for various algorithms

|         |     | DoS    | U2R    | R2L       | Probing   |
|---------|-----|--------|--------|-----------|-----------|
| K-means | PD  | 0.8912 | 0.9813 | 0.1415    | 0.0636    |
|         | HT  | 0.8978 | 0.8991 | 0.8914    | 0.9001    |
|         | FAR | 0.0042 | 0.0039 | 0.0052    | 0.0011    |
| NEA     | PD  | 0.8923 | 0.9713 | 0.024     | 0.0342    |
|         | HT  | 0.8813 | 0.9021 | 0.8979    | 0.8993    |
|         | FAR | 0.0054 | 0.0036 | 6.20E-06  | 1.20E-04  |
| C4.5    | PD  | 0.8131 | 0.9789 | 0.0187    | 0.0565    |
|         | HT  | 0.8679 | 0.9002 | 0.8928    | 0.9032    |
|         | FAR | 0.0073 | 0.0032 | 2.60E-05  | 5.30E-05  |
| Ours    | PD  | 0.9012 | 0.9867 | 0.1502    | 0.0601    |
|         | HT  | 0.9028 | 0.9189 | 0.9214    | 0.9267    |
|         | FAR | 0.0037 | 0.0029 | 2.71E-06  | 5.27E-05  |

## 5  Conclusions and Future Works

Our approach allows user to model an intrusion detection application at the conceptual level and in terms of concepts from the application domain. This is realized by using a Domain Ontology, which captures the domain knowledge. Simulation results demonstrated that for four given attack categories the ontology-based mode performed better.

## References

1. DAMLJessKB (2002). Available at: http://edge.cs.drexel.edu/assemblies/software/damljesskb/, October
2. Lee, W. S., Stolfo, J., Mok, K.W.: Data Mining in Work Flow Environments: Experiences in Intrusion Detection. Proceedings of the 1999 Conference on Knowledge Discovery and Data mining (KDD-99) (1999) 253-262
3. Reddyl, Y.B., Guha, R.: Intrusion Detection using Data Mining Techniques. Artificial Intelligence and Applications (AIA-2004), (2004) 232-241
4. Undercoffer, J., Pinkston, J., Joshi, A., Finin, T. A: Target-Centric Ontology for Intrusion Detection. In IJCAI Workshop on Ontologies and Distributed Systems (IJCAI'03), August, 2003.
5. Kumar, S., Spafford, E.H.: A Software Architecture to Support Misuse Intrusion Detection. Proceedings of the 18th National Information Security Conference (1995) 194-204.

# Design and Implementation of FPGA Based High-Performance Intrusion Detection System

Byoung-Koo Kim, Young-Jun Heo, and Jin-Tae Oh

Security Gateway System Team, Electronics and Telecommunications Research Institute,
Gajeong-dong, Yuseong-gu, Daejeon, 305-700, Korea
{bkkim05, yjheo, showme}@etri.re.kr

**Abstract.** As network technology presses forward, Gigabit Ethernet has become the actual standard for large network installations. Therefore, it is necessary to research on security analysis mechanism, which is capable to process high traffic volume over the high-speed network. This paper proposes FPGA based high-performance IDS to detect and respond variant attacks on high-speed links. Most of all, It is possible through the pattern matching function and heuristic analysis function that is processed in FPGA Logic. In other words, we focus on the network intrusion detection mechanism applied in high-speed network.

## 1 Introduction

As a response to increased threats, many Network based Intrusion Detection Systems(NIDSs) have been developed to serve as a last line of defense in the overall protection scheme of a computer system[1]. However, existing NIDSs have problems of a lowering of performance as ever, such as bottleneck, overhead in collecting and analyzing data in a specific component. Therefore, the effort of performing NIDS on high-speed links has been the focus of much debate in the intrusion detection community[2]. And, there is an emerging need for security analysis techniques that can keep up with the increased network throughput. This paper proposes high-performance IDS to detect and respond attacks on the high-speed network. It is possible through the function that is processed in FPGA(Field Programmable Gate Array) Logic. So, our proposed system has hardware architecture that can provide efficient way to detect and respond variant attack behaviors on high-speed and high volume large-scale network.

## 2 FPGA-Based High-Performance Intrusion Detection System

Our system is aimed at real-time network-based intrusion detection based on misuse detection approach. For instruction detection on high-speed links, our system has three FPGA Chips. One is ATIE(Anomaly Traffic Inspection Engine) FPGA Chip for wire-speed packet forwarding and blocking, another is PPE(Pre-Processing Engine) FPGA Chip for packet preprocessing, and the other is IDE(Intrusion Detection

S. Mehrotra et al. (Eds.): ISI 2006, LNCS 3975, pp. 724–725, 2006.
© Springer-Verlag Berlin Heidelberg 2006

Engine) FPGA Chip for high-performance intrusion detection. The detection mechanism of our system is mainly run on IDE FPGA Chip. This chip has three detection mechanisms.

First, header lookup mechanism is performed by flexible header combination lookup algorithm. This algorithm compares pre-defined header related rule-sets with header information of incoming packets. If the incoming packet is matched with existing header patterns, 256bits match result is sent to payload matching logic and traffic volume based heuristic analysis logic. Second, payload matching mechanism is performed by linked word based store-less running search algorithm. This algorithm uses the pattern reconstruction technique. Reconstruction pattern length has boundary of size5 or 7 because of the limit of block memory in FPGA Chip. Also, this algorithm uses the spectrum dispersion technique. The spectrum dispersion technique is method to calculate unique hash values about reconstructed patterns. Through these operations, our system performs the pattern matching operation without lowing of performance and packet loss. Finally, traffic volume based analysis mechanism is performed by traffic volume based heuristic analysis algorithm. This mechanism generates alert message by traffic volume within time threshold. Through this mechanism, our system is capable of detecting the DoS and Port-scan attacks such as TCP syn flooding attack, UDP Bomb, SYN/ACK/XMAS Port-scans, and so forth.

## 3   Conclusions and Future Work

In this paper, we designed the architecture of our system that performs the real-time traffic analysis and intrusion detection on high-speed links, and proposed the detection mechanism in FPGA-based reconfiguring hardware that supports more efficient intrusion detection. Also, we have developed the prototype of our system for the analysis of the traffic carried by a Gigabit link. In future, we will go and consider on system performance, availability, faults-tolerance test with prototype. Also, we will keep up our efforts for improvement in performance of detection mechanism on high-speed links. Finally, we will implement and expand our designed system and give more effort to demonstrate effectiveness of our system.

## References

1. Kruegel, C., Valeur, F., Vigna, G. and Kemmerer, R. "Stateful intrusion detection for high-speed networks", In Proceedings of the IEEE Symposium on Security and Privacy, pp. 266-274, 2002.
2. M. Roesch. "Snort-Lightweight Intrusion Detection for Networks". In Proceedings of the USENIX LISA '99 Conference, November, 1999.

# Anomaly Detection of Excessive Network Traffic Based on Ratio and Volume Analysis

Hyun Joo Kim, Jung C. Na, and Jong S. Jang

Network Security Department Electronics and Telecommunications Research Institute
161 Gajeong-Dong, Yuseong-Gu, Daejeon, 305-350, Korea
{khj63353, njc, jsjang}@etri.re.kr

**Abstract.** Recent attacks typically cause not only traffic congestion but also network failure exhausting network bandwidth, router processing capacity using the abnormal traffic or excessive network traffic, so that they can have an extremely large impact on the public network. Therefore we propose the detection mechanism of network traffic anomalies. This mechanism analyzes flow data based on the statistical anomaly detection, which supports the two analysis method- ratio based analysis and volume based analysis and correlates the results from these two models.

## 1 Introduction

Today's attack usually targets on a public network because the damage of the public network attack is far stronger than an enterprise network or systems attack and the speed of its propagation is far faster. It can cause not only traffic congestion but also network failure using the abnormal traffic or excessive network traffic. Therefore focusing on the traffic anomalies with the excessive abnormal network traffic, we developed the Security Management System (SMS) which can provide detecting, diagnosing, and responding to anomalies in real-time. SMS diagnoses the network state analyzing security alerts from network security equipments such as IDS and firewall and flow data from the measuring equip. such as Netflow of Cisco, and it takes the response actions to mitigate and treat the security threat. However in this paper, we introduce the only detection mechanism of network traffic anomalies.

## 2 Anomaly Detection of Excessive Network Traffic

We analyze flow data based on not signature based detection but anomaly detection and support the two analysis method-ratio based analysis and volume based analysis and correlate the results from these two models to solve the problems of each model and reduce the false-positive error. Firstly we collect and analyze the network flow data from Cisco Netflows periodically according to the characteristic parameter for analysis. Then considering the analysis count, traffic learning period and threshold calculated from two analysis models, our detection mechanism decides and reports the network traffic abnormal state and profiles the normal state with the normal traffic

S. Mehrotra et al. (Eds.): ISI 2006, LNCS 3975, pp. 726–727, 2006.
© Springer-Verlag Berlin Heidelberg 2006

data to determine the normal/abnormal state of network. Also we provide the severity level to the manager to response to the threat.

Our detection system uses exponential smoothing model and population proportion testing model for each volume and ratio based analysis. To know the traffic analysis mechanism of our SMS applied exponential model, refer to the paper [2].

$$T_i(t+1) = T_v(t, t+1) / T_{total}(t, t+1) \tag{1}$$

$$\mu = N \mu + T_i(t+1) / N+1, \quad \sigma^2 = \beta \sigma^2 + (1-\beta) \{ T_i(t) - \mu \}^2, \quad \sigma = \sqrt{\sigma 2} \tag{2}$$

$$Threshold = \mu + z_\alpha \, \sigma \tag{3}$$

Formula (1)~(3) shows some formulas of proportion testing. $T_i(t+1)$: rate of specific traffic at time t+1, $T_v(t, t+1)$: volume of specific traffic, $T_{total}(t,t+1)$: total traffic volume at time t+1. $\mu$, $\sigma$: mean and deviation of standard distribution, $\beta$: exponential constant(0.02: the larger $\beta$ is, the more fluctuant the threshold is). $N$: sample size (number of analysis period), $Z_\alpha$: level of significance. In formula (3), we finally calculate the ratio based threshold, which is used as a means of detecting the traffic anomalies and updated continually by $\mu$ and $\sigma$ updated with the normal state values.

## 3  Conclusion

In this paper, we present the anomaly detection mechanism for detecting excessive network traffic based on correlation model using both ratio-based analysis model and volume-based analysis model. The result of our anomaly detection can be used to manage a network in combination with the security response policy, thereby we can provide an automatic detection and response. Also because our mechanism integrates and analyzes the traffics of not the private network but all managed networks, it can detect more quickly abnormal situations such as network performance degradation, traffic congestion, etc., in the initial step of network attack.

## References

1. P. Barford, J. Kline, et al, "A Signal Analysis of Network Traffic Anomalies", in Proceedings of ACM SIGCOMM Internet Measurement Workshop, France, November 2002.
2. S.H. Lee, H.J. Kim, J.C.Na et al., "Abnormal Traffic Detection and Its Implementation", ICACT2005 , Feb. 21~23, 2005
3. S.S Kim, A.L Narasimha Reddy, M. Vannucci, "Detecting Traffic Anomalies at the Source through aggregate analysis of packet header data", TAMU-ECE-2003-03, 2003
4. P.Barford, D. Plonka, "Characteristics of network traffic flow anomalies;' in Proceedings of ACM SIGCOMM Internet Measurement Workshop, Francisco, CA, November 2001.

# Detecting Anomalies in Cargo Using Graph Properties

William Eberle and Lawrence Holder

Department of Computer Science and Engineering
University of Texas at Arlington
Box 19015, Arlington, TX 76019-0015
{eberle, holder}@cse.uta.edu

The ability to mine relational data has become important in several domains (e.g., counter-terrorism), and a graph-based representation of this data has proven useful in detecting various relational, structural patterns [1]. Here, we analyze the use of *graph properties* as a method for uncovering anomalies in data represented as a graph.

**Graph Properties.** While our initial research examined many of the basic graph properties, only a few of them proved to be insightful as to the structure of a graph for anomaly detection purposes. For the *average shortest path length L*, we used the Floyd-Warshall all-pairs algorithm. For a measurement of *density*, we chose to use a definition that is commonly used when defining social networks [4]. For *connectedness*, we used a definition that Broder et al. [2] defined in their paper. For some of the more complex graph properties, we investigated two measurements. First, there is the maximum *eigenvalue* of a graph [5]. Another, which was used in identifying e-mail "spammers", is the *graph clustering coefficient* [3].

**Synthetic Results.** For each of our tests, we created 6 different graph size types consisting of approximately 35, 100, 400, 1000, and 2000 vertices, and another being a dense graph of 100 vertices and 1000 edges. For each of these increment sizes, we created 30 non-anomalous graphs. We then generated 30 anomalous graphs for each of the graph types and for each of the following structural anomalies: add substructure, remove substructure, move edge, and add isolated substructure. The *density* of small graphs lessens when an anomalous substructure is connected to existing vertices in the graph. This makes sense, as the ratio of actual vertices and edges to the number of *possible* pairs would increase, resulting in a lower density. This also explains why the density of graphs that contain *isolated* substructures is less, due to containing unconnected vertices. Also, the removal of a substructure results in a wide deviation in the density measurement. The *connectedness* of the smaller graphs varies for each of the different types of anomalies. The insertion and isolation anomalies result in lower values, and insertion of an isolated substructure has an even greater variation on the measurement. The same behavior is also found in dense graphs. Changes in the *clustering coefficient* on smaller graphs are only evident for inserted isolated anomalous substructures and the anomaly of moved edges. This variance, because of the moved edges, is significant due to the way the deviation changes. As the graphs get larger, the distribution still holds, but the coefficient of the graphs with moved edges increases significantly. The *average path length* and *eigenvalue* metrics behave similarly to the above metrics, except that they are better indicators of inserted substructures and moved edges.

S. Mehrotra et al. (Eds.): ISI 2006, LNCS 3975, pp. 728–730, 2006.
© Springer-Verlag Berlin Heidelberg 2006

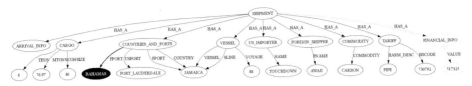

**Fig. 1.** Graph representation of cargo and anomaly (insertion in bold, removals as dotted lines)

**Cargo Results.** This data set consists of cargo shipments that represent imported items from foreign countries to the U.S. The anomalies that we introduced into the cargo data consist of two scenarios. The first anomaly represents drug smuggling [6], whereby the perpetrators attempt to smuggle the contraband into the U.S. without disclosing some financial information about the shipment. Also, an extra port was traversed in-route. While the shipment looked for the most part like containers of toys, food, and bicycles from Jamaica, there were a couple of structural alterations. Fig. 1 shows a graphical representation of a shipment (as a substructure in the entire graph) that contains the anomaly. For the second anomaly representing an arms shipment [7], similar to the first anomaly, there is certain manifest information not consistent with other similar (but legal) shipments. In addition, the original port of departure (in this case, China) is removed from the manifest. Again, these are all structural changes in the graph representation of the cargo data.

For both of these anomalies, there are no significant deviations displayed using the average shortest path or eigenvalue metrics. However, there are visible differences for the density, connectedness and clustering coefficient measurements. Another encouraging metric that can be used is the *combination* of individual measurements to provide a clearer view. For instance, when combining the density, connectedness and clustering coefficient measurements, we get values for the drug smuggling and arms shipment scenarios that clearly indicate anomalies. Similar results are evident when applying different combinations on the synthetic data sets.

**Conclusion.** We show that differences in graph properties between normal graphs and those intentionally altered can detect anomalies. While the changes vary based on the type of modification, they can be combined to clarify what is occurring, as was shown in the results from the issue of analyzing cargo containers for illegal, and possibly terrorist-related, shipments.

# References

1. Holder, L., Cook, D., Coble, J., and Mukherjee, M.: Graph-Based Relational Learning with Application to Security. Fundamenta Informaticae Special Issue on Mining Graphs, Trees and Sequences, Vol. 66, Number 1-2. (2005) 83-101
2. Broder, A. et al.: Graph Structure in the Web. Computer Networks. Vol. 33. (2000) 309-320
3. Boykin, P. and Roychowdhury, V.: Leveraging Social Networks to Fight Spam. IEEE Computer, April 2005, Vol. 38, Number 4. (2005) 61-67
4. Scott, J.: Social Network Analysis: A Handbook. SAGE Publications, Second Edition. (2000) 72-78

5. Chung, F., Lu, L., and Vu, V.: Eigenvalues of Random Power Law Graphs. Annals of Combinatorics 7, 2003. (2003) 21-33
6. U.S. Customs Service: 1,754 Pounds of Marijuana Seized in Cargo Container at Port Everglades. November 6, 2000. (http://www.cbp.gov/hot-new/pressrel/2000/1106-01.htm)
7. Mae Dey Newsletter: Customs Seizes Weapons. Vol. 23, Issue 4, August/September (2003)

# Design of a Reliable Hardware Stack to Defend Against Frame Pointer Overwrite Attacks

Yongsu Park, Yong Ho Song, and Eul Gyu Im

The College of Information and Communications, Hanyang University,
17 Haengdang-dong, Seongdong-gu, Seoul 133-791, Korea
{yongsu, yhsong, imeg}@hanyang.ac.kr

**Keywords:** computer security, buffer overflow attack, computer architecture.

## 1 Introduction

Currently, a buffer overflow attack is one of the most serious and widely utilized attacks in computer systems. Defense methods against this attack can be classified as three: compiler modification, system software modification, and hardware modification. Among them, most of the cases, hardware modification methods aim at detecting or tolerating alternation of return addresses in the memory stack. However, to the best of our knowledge, the previous methods cannot defend against frame pointer overwrite attacks, where an adversary can control the execution at his/her will by modifying the saved frame pointers in the stack. In this extended abstract, we present a new reliable hardware stack to detect alternation of saved frame pointers as well as return addresses.

## 2 Frame Pointer Overwrite Attack

First, we explain the frame pointer overwrite attack [1]. Assume that a vulnerable code has a local buffer and performs strcpy() function to copy the input parameter string into this buffer. The activation record (a. k. a. stack frame) consists of local variables (where that buffer resides in), a saved frame pointer, and a return address. If an adversary can overflow the buffer with a large parameter string during strcpy() operation, he/she can overwrite the saved frame pointer (detailed procedure is in [1]), which can be used to control the execution flow at his/her will. To the best of our knowledge, there is no hardware based scheme to defend against this attack, which is motivation of our work.

## 3 Proposed Method

In this section we describe the proposed hardware stack. This stack resides in the CPU, has the fixed size, and supports overflow/underflow detection facilities. The stored value is a set of 3-tuple: <saved frame pointer, stack pointer, return address>. Fig. 1 shows the structure of the hardware stack.

S. Mehrotra et al. (Eds.): ISI 2006, LNCS 3975, pp. 731–732, 2006.

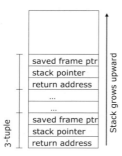

**Fig. 1.** Hardware stack in the proposed scheme

When the call instruction is executed, a 3-tuple is pushed into the hardware stack and when the ret instruction is executed, the 3-tuple is popped. Detailed description is as follows.

1. **call instruction execution:** First, the return address and the value of stack pointer %esp are stored into the hardware stack. Then, the original call operation is performed (the return address is stored in the memory stack and the instruction pointer %eip is set to the starting address of the callee function). After the call instruction is executed, the CPU observes the fetched instructions until 'pushl %ebp' appears. If so, after that command is executed, the hardware stack stores the value of %ebp (= the saved frame pointer) and completes storing the 3-tuple.

2. **ret instruction execution:** When the CPU fetches 'popl %ebp', it triggers a certain internal status bit. This status bit is turned off when the value of the register %ebp is changed (by instructions addl/movl/incl, etc). In the case of the execution of 'ret', if that internal bit is on, the CPU compares the value of %ebp with the saved frame pointer in the hardware stack. If two values are identical, then the CPU performs the following 2 comparisons: the saved stack pointer in the hardware stack and the value of the register %esp, the return address in the hardware stack and the return address in the memory stack. If they are identical to each other, the CPU executes the ret instruction. Otherwise, it terminates the execution and raises an exception.

## 4   Conclusion

We have designed a new hardware stack, which contains 3-tuples <return address, stack pointer, frame pointer> to defend against both the stack smashing attack and the frame pointer overwrite attack. Our scheme can be viewed as an approach to increase trustworthiness as well as to enhance security of the systems to be protected.

## Reference

1. klog. The Frame Pointer Overwrite, Phrack Magazine, Vol. 9, Issue 5, 1999.

# Email Worm Detection Using Naïve Bayes and Support Vector Machine

Mohammad M. Masud[1], Latifur Khan[1], and Ehab Al-Shaer[2]

[1] Department of Computer Science, The University of Texas at Dallas,
Richardson, Texas
{mmm058000, lkhan}@utdallas.edu
[2] School of Computer Science, Telecommunications and Information Systems
DePaul University, Chicago, IL
ehab@cti.depaul.edu

## 1 Introduction

Email worm, as the name implies, spreads through infected email messages. The worm may be carried by attachment, or the email may contain links to an infected website. When the user opens the attachment, or clicks the link, the host is immediately infected. Email worms use the vulnerability of the email software of the host machine and sends infected emails to the addresses stored in the address book. In this way, new machines get infected. Examples of email worms are "W32.mydoom.M@mm", "W32.Zafi.d", "W32.LoveGate.w", "W32.Mytob.c", and so on. Worms do a lot of harm to computers and people. They can clog the network traffic, cause damage to the system and make the system unstable or even unusable.

There has been a significant amount of research going on to combat worms. The traditional way of dealing with a known worm is to apply signature based detection. But the problem with this approach is that it involves significant amount of human intervention and it may take long time (from days to weeks) to discover the signature. Since worms can propagate very fast, there should be a much faster way to detect them before any damage is done.

This research work deals with the problem of detecting new email worms without discovering their signatures. Thus, we are concerned with automatic (i.e., without any human intervention) and efficient detection of novel worms. Our work is inspired by Martin et. al.'s two-layer approach [1] to detect novel worms. In this approach different features of the email (e.g.: no. of chars in body etc) are extracted and the email is classified as clean or infected based on these features. Their goal is to reduce both the false positive and false negative rate. To achieve this, they employ two classifiers in series. The first classifier in the series is Support Vector Machine (SVM), which works as a novelty detector. The next classifier in the series is Naïve Bayes (NB). They report a very high accuracy, leading to very low false positive and false negative rate on the data set. But the problem with their experiment is that it does not apply a balanced data set to test the accuracy , nor does it report any cross validation result. Our contributions to this research work are as follows: First, we apply a NB classifier and an SVM classifier and compare their individual performance with SVM + NB series implementation. We have shown that both NB and SVM alone gives better accuracy than the combined method. So, we claim that one of the layers of the two-layer

S. Mehrotra et al. (Eds.): ISI 2006, LNCS 3975, pp. 733–734, 2006.

approach is redundant. Second, we rearranged the data set so that it becomes more balanced. We then divide the data set into two portions: one containing only known worms (and some clean emails), the other containing only novel worm. Then we apply a three-fold cross validation on the first portion of the data set, and test the accuracy on the novel worms on each of the learned classifiers.

## 2   Results

Table 1 reports the accuracy of the cross validation and novel detection for each data set. The cross validation accuracy is shown under the column *accuracy* and the accuracy of detecting novel worms is shown under the column *novel detection accuracy*. Each worm at the row heading is the novel worm for that data set. We have shown that either NB or SVM alone is more effective than the SVM+NB series method. For example, in the last row of table 1, we report the overall accuracy of these methods, and notice that the novel detection accuracy of NB and SVM are much higher than that of NB+SVM. The choice between NB and SVM is in fact a trade off between simplicity and accuracy. When optimum accuracy is a premium, we should prefer SVM, on the other hand, NB can be trained much faster than SVM and very easily implemented, but sacrificing accuracy up to a certain amount.

**Table 1.** Comparison of accuracy of different classifiers on the worm data set

| Worm Type | NB | | SVM | | SVM+NB | |
|---|---|---|---|---|---|---|
| | Accuracy (%) | Novel detection Accuracy (%) | Accuracy (%) | Novel detection Accuracy (%) | Accuracy (%) | Novel detection Accuracy (%) |
| **mydoom.m** | 99.42 | 21.72 | 99.58 | 94.03 | 99.38 | 21.06 |
| **sobig.f** | 99.11 | 97.01 | 99.77 | 97.01 | 99.27 | 96.52 |
| **Netsky.d** | 99.15 | 97.01 | 99.69 | 65.01 | 99.19 | 64.02 |
| **mydoom.u** | 99.11 | 97.01 | 99.69 | 96.19 | 99.19 | 96.19 |
| **bagle.f** | 99.27 | 97.01 | 99.61 | 98.01 | 99.31 | 95.52 |
| **bubbleboy** | 99.19 | 0 | 99.65 | 0 | 99.31 | 0 |
| **Overall** | 99.21 | 68.29 | 99.67 | 75.04 | 99.28 | 62.22 |

## Reference

1. Steve Martin, Anil Sewani, Blaine Nelson, Karl Chen Anthony D. Joseph. A Two-Layer Approach for Novel Email Worm Detection. URL: http://www.cs.berkeley.edu/~anil/papers/SRUTI_submitted.pdf

# An Anomaly Detection Algorithm for Detecting Attacks in Wireless Sensor Networks*

Tran Van Phuong, Le Xuan Hung, Seong Jin Cho, Young-Koo Lee,
and Sungyoung Lee

Computer Engineering Dept. Kyung Hee University
449-701 Suwon, Republic of Korea
{tvphuong, lxhung, sycho}@oslab.khu.ac.kr,
yklee@khu.ac.kr, sylee@oslab.khu.ac.kr

Wireless sensor networks (WSNs) consisting of thousands of sensor nodes have many potential applications nowadays from temperature, light monitoring in a smart house to detecting enemy's movement in a battle field. In most cases, sensor networks are deployed in open and unprotected environments so it is very attractive to adversaries. Although some preventive mechanisms were proposed and installed, they do not guarantee the security of sensor networks one hundred percent. Thus, it is necessary to have some mechanisms of intrusion detection as a second protecting wall to prevent intruders from causing damages to the networks.

A lot of work has been done on Intrusion Detection System (IDS) for traditional wired networks so far. However, it is not appropriate to apply directly IDSs in wired networks into sensor networks because of unique characteristics of sensor networks. From the intrusion detection viewpoint, the main challenges in sensor networks are their flexible network topologies, lack of concentration points where traffic can be analyzed and the most important, sensor resource constraints. In this paper, we proposed another approach to detect intrusion in sensor networks by using Cumulative Sum algorithm (CuSum) to detect anomalies based on statistical information of packets in the networks. The network is considered under attacks if any abrupt change of one of these features is reported.

**Proposed Algorithm:** Some of the most common attacks in sensor networks include: wormhole, blackhole, HELLO flood attack, Jamming, ... Most of them focus on vulnerabilities of routing protocols. To realize the anomaly characteristics of these attacks, we divide them into three major categories: (1) attracting other nodes to send their traffic to a compromised node, (2) causing collision to disrupt sensor network and (3) exhausting a node's resources by sending many packets to the target. It is straightforward to see that attacks in each category makes the network traffic deviated from that in normal condition in different ways. If the network is under attacks in the first category, traffic to some nodes (compromised nodes) will be suddenly increased. Attacks in the second category will raise the number of packet collision and attacks in the third category is realized by the increasing amount of outgoing traffic related to one node. Therefore, we can detect attacks in sensor networks by monitoring these

---

* This work was supported by IITA Professorship for Visiting Faculty Position in Korea from Ministry of Information and Communications. Dr. Young-Koo Lee is the corresponding author.

S. Mehrotra et al. (Eds.): ISI 2006, LNCS 3975, pp. 735–736, 2006.

anomalies. They are the changes in (1) the number of incoming packets to a node, (2) the number of collisions associated with packets sent by a node and (3) the number of outgoing packets from a node.

In order to detect these changes, we use the non-parametric CUSUM algorithm which is used to detect the change of mean value of a random sequence based on the cumulative effect of the changes made in the sequence. Our algorithm is described briefly as following:

```
all CuSum = 0
n = 0
repeat
    n = n + 1
        for each neighbor i do
            CuSum(inc i) : = (CuSum(inc i) + Xn(inc i))⁺
            CuSum(out i) : = (CuSum(out i) + Xn(out i))⁺
            if any CuSum > Its Threshold then
                    Signal attack indication
        end for
        CuSum(collision)    :    =    (CuSum(collision)    +
Xn(collision))⁺
        if CuSum(collision) > Its Threshold then
            Signal attack indication
until Finished
```

where n is the $n^{th}$ sampling period. Xn(inc i) means the number of incoming packets of $i^{th}$ neighbor in the $n^{th}$ sampling period. Xn(out i) means the number of outgoing packets of $i^{th}$ neighbor. Xn(collision) means the number of collision packets of the monitor node in the $n^{th}$ sampling period.

Our algorithm is very light-weight and powerful to detect abrupt changes in a random sequence. Suppose that the monitor node in the network has k neighbors, the algorithm 2 shows us that the complexity in each step (each sampling period) is O(k). In common sensor networks, k is often less than 10 so the monitor node just needs to do some basic operations in each sampling period. Besides, little amount of memory resource is required for some counters. So this solution adapts well to memory and computational power constraints of wireless sensor networks.

**Intrusion Detection model:** Because of the lack of central point to collect data, our Intrusion Detection System is distributed. That means some nodes, called monitor nodes, will be installed Intrusion Detection Agents to protect themselves and their neighbors (called monitored node). Monitor nodes are selected so that every node in the network is monitored by at least one monitor node. One node can be monitored by several monitor nodes. There is a trade off between security level and resources. The more monitor nodes, the higher security level.

# A New Methodology of Analyzing Security Vulnerability for Network Services

Yong Ho Song, Jung Min Park, Yongsu Park, and Eul Gyu Im

College of Information and Communications, Hanyang University, Seoul, Korea
{yhsong, jmpark, yongsu, imeg}@hanyang.ac.kr

The explosively increasing use of Internet has brought to the emergence and dissemination of new network worms and viruses. The techniques exploited by those malicious software codes become so sophisticated that even newly updated anti-virus engines often fail to detect the existence of the codes successfully. One of the security defects in network services often exploited by the codes is the vulnerability due to buffer overflow [1].

Considering the potential damages that could arise from such security attacks, it is desirable to detect security vulnerabilities of the services in advance and take preventive measures to deal with the problems. The precise identification of service defects in security usually requires the thorough inspection of software source codes. However, in many cases the codes are considered as a valuable property of developers, not open to the public.

Many techniques have been proposed to address this problem [1][2]. One of the well-known techniques is *fuzzing* which repeatedly makes a large number of subroutine calls to a suspected target service with varying input parameters exceeding a presumed upper bound in length or size. In this technique, service malfunction or abnormal execution behavior is considered as a clue to the existence of buffer overflow vulnerability in target service. However, this technique has two limitations: first, the *upper bound* of input parameters is difficult to determine, second, abnormal behavior of fuzzed service provides no clue on the precise location of security defects.

This paper proposes a new methodology to analyze security vulnerability of executable binaries for stack overflow attacks. The proposed technique consists of two different mechanisms, called *runtime stack frame analysis (RSFA)* and *return address check (RAC)*, adding to existing fuzzing mechanisms to lift the limitations above.

The RSFA measures the size of stack frame at the beginning of every subroutine execution. The stack frame of a called subroutine contains both a return address and subroutine-local variables. Considering that stack overflow attacks often alter return addresses in stack via improperly-sized string copy operation, the measured size of stack frame could be considered as an upper bound of input parameters. One of the difficulties associated with RSFA is that a given input parameter may be indirectly used by other child subroutines called in a nested fashion. In this case, all the stack frames of child subroutines must be measured and the maximum of them should be chosen as upper bound of input parameters.

In order to identify the existence of successful attack, the RAC mechanism generates a log data containing a pair of return addresses for each function, one saved on procedure call and the other saved on return. The log is examined off-line after the

S. Mehrotra et al. (Eds.): ISI 2006, LNCS 3975, pp. 737–738, 2006.
© Springer-Verlag Berlin Heidelberg 2006

completion of service execution to check whether each pair of return addresses is matched. The automated log generation eliminates unnecessary user intervention to service execution, which enhances analysis productivity. For generating a log, the RAC sets breakpoints on the first instruction and the last (return) instructions of each subroutine and records program execution states including return addresses into the log on each breakpoint trigger. In RISCs, all the instructions are aligned in memory, which helps to identify those instructions. However, in CISCs, the instructions vary in length depending upon their type, which makes it difficult to precisely identify the locations of call and return instructions before executing them.

Both RSFA and RAC works together to determine whether and where the security vulnerability exists. The RSFA effectively contributes to the reduction of the time to check vulnerability by finding upper bounds on input parameter for each subroutine and the RAC provides evidence of vulnerability instead of presuming existence of vulnerability from service crash or misbehavior.

The proposed technique works in two stages. The first is the RSFA stage where the service under inspection runs with a set of arbitrarily chosen inputs. This stage measures the frame size for the subroutines invoked during execution. The second is the RAC stage where the log of system states including return addresses is created.

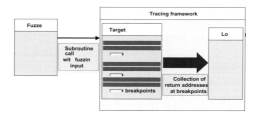

**Fig. 1.** The proposed runtime analysis framework

In this work, a tracing framework based on a Windows-based debugging tool, called *dum(b)ug*, has been developed to trace calls to the subroutines exported at a header of the Windows PE file format. The framework includes a parser for executable files in Windows PE format, a breakpoint manager, a partial disassembler, and a thread handler. One of the limitations in the current implementation of the framework is that only exported subroutines of target services in .dll files can be traced. It is because the address information is available at the PE header only for exported subroutines. Through the experiments, it is observed that this framework is effective in using fuzzing techniques for vulnerability analysis with less time overheads and more accuracy, particularly when only execution binaries are available.

## References

1. Pheonoelit, *Bug Hunting (Vulnerability finding methods in Windows 32 environments compared)*, http://www.phenoelit.de/stuff/Bugs.pdf
2. Goran Begic, *An Introduction to Runtime Analysis with Rational PurifyPlus*, Rational Software, December 2002

# Using One-Time Password Based Authentication for Wireless IP Network

Binod Vaidya[1], SangDuck Lee[2], Eung-Kon Kim[3], and SeungJo Han[2]

[1] Dept. of Electronics & Computer Eng., Tribhuvan Univ., Nepal
bvaidya@ioe.edu.np
[2] Dept. of Information & Communication Eng., Chosun Univ., Korea
dandylsd@hanmail.net, sjbhan@chosun.ac.kr
[3] Dept. of Computer Science, Sunchon National Univ., Korea
kek@sunchon.ac.kr

**Abstract.** Wireless IP Networks have gained popularity in ubiquitous environment, providing users mobility and flexibility in accessing information. Existing solutions for wireless LAN networks have been exposed to security vulnerabilities. The further widespread deployment of wireless LANs, however, depends on whether secure networking can be achieved. In this poster, we envisage a simple authentication scheme using one-time password protocol for IEEE 802.11 wireless LAN. [*]

## Extended Abstract

Wireless IP Networks have gained popularity in ubiquitous environment, providing users mobility and flexibility in accessing information. Existing solutions for wireless LAN networks have been exposed to security vulnerabilities. The freedom and mobility that wireless LANs promise also present some serious security challenges. The further widespread deployment of wireless LANs, however, depends on whether secure networking can be achieved. Major security measures provided for IEEE 802.11 WLAN are Wired Equivalent Privacy (WEP), Wi-Fi Protected Access (WPA) and IEEE 802.11i.

Lamport proposed a One-time password (OTP) /hash-chaining technique, which has been used in many applications. The S/KEY authentication system is designed to provide users with OTPs which can be used to control user access to remote hosts. OTP system provides protections against passive eavesdropping and replay attacks.

There is a desire to increase the security and performance of authentication mechanisms due to strong user authentication, protection of user credentials, mutual authentication and generation of session keys. As demand for strong user authentication grows, OTP based authentication tends to become more common. We propose a simple scheme for implementing authentication scheme based on hash function. The authentication protocol is proposed to solve the weak authentication and security flaw problem of WEP in 802.11 WLAN. There are four phases in proposed authentication scheme.

[*] This study was supported (in part) by research funds from Chosun University 2005.

S. Mehrotra et al. (Eds.): ISI 2006, LNCS 3975, pp. 739–740, 2006.
© Springer-Verlag Berlin Heidelberg 2006

## Phase 0: Discovery phase

In the discovery phase, the client (STA) and Access Point (AP) locate each other and discover each other's capabilities. IEEE 802.11 provides integrated discovery support utilizing Beacon frames, allowing the STA to determine capabilities of AP.

## Phase 1: OTP authentication phase

The authentication phase begins once the STA and AP discover each other. This phase always includes OTP authentication. In this phase, the STA authenticates itself as a legal member for a particular AP. On receiving AP's request message, a STA sends $\{ID_C\|Y_C\|H(ID_C, A)\}$. Then the AP sends $\{ID_A\|ID_C\}$ to the server. Depending on $ID_C$, the server examines $PW_C, SB$, and client's privacy key ($K_C$) from user's database, and generates a new stream bits ($SB_N$) and $A$. The $ID_C$ and $SB_N$ are encrypted with $K_C$ producing $E_{K_C}(ID_C\|SB_N)$, which in turn along with $ID_C$, and $A$ are encrypted by server with symmetric cryptosystem to get $E_{AS}(ID_C\|A\|E_{K_C}(ID_C\|SB_N))$. This message is send to the AP. Then the AP computes and verifies $H(ID_C, A)$ between the client and the server. If true, it will send authentication success frame $\{ID_C\|Y_A\|E_{K_C}(ID_C\|SB_N)\}$ to the STA. The STA accomplishes authentication procedure, then it sends $\{ID_C\|H(SB_N)\}$ to the server through the AP to update client's database in the server. The STA and the AP apply $Y_A$ or $Y_C$ to generate a session key ($K$), then the STA sends $\{ID_C\|E_K(otp\|ctr\|ID_C)\}$ to the AP. The AP responds with $\{ID_C\|H(otp, ctr)\}$ to the STA.

## Phase 2: Secure key exchange phase

The Secure key exchange phase begins after the completion of OTP authentication. The phase 2 is used to negotiate a new secret key between the STA and the AP. In this phase, a message authentication code (MAC) is added to each packet and then is encrypted together, and the receiver should check the MAC. The STA sends $\{ID_C\|E_K(otp_{I+1}\|H(otp_I, ctr, ID_C))\}$ to AP. It should be noted that $H(opt_{I+1})$ is equal to $otp_I$ and $K$ is session key by OTP authentication phase. The AP checks the MAC and $ID_C$ by checking if $H(opt_{I+1})$ is equal to $otp_I$. If this is true, the STA is a legal member. It will replace $otp_I$ by $opt_{I+1}$ and decrease the counter by 1. And AP transmits $H(otp_I, ctr)$ to STA. The STA checks hash value and decreases the counter by 1.

## Phase 3: Refreshing OTP phases

When the counter decreases to zero, the STA should change its OTP, otherwise the AP has the right to prohibit the STA from using its services. The STA sends its $\{ID_C\|E_K(otp_{I+1}\|otp_N\|ctr_N, H(otp_{I+1}, otp_N, ctr_N, ID_C))\}$ to AP. The AP verifies the MAC and $otp_{I+1}$ (check $H(otp_{I+1})$ is equal to $otp_I$). If this is true, the STA is a legal member, and AP replaces $otp_I$ by $otp_N$ and resets $ctr$ to $ctr_N$. Then the AP sends $\{ID_C\|H(otp_I, ctr)\}$ to the STA. The STA checks his ID and the hash value.

# Experimental Study on Wireless Sensor Network Security*

Taekyoung Kwon and Sang-ho Park

Dept. of Computer Engineering, Sejong University, Seoul, 143-747, Korea
tkwon@sejong.ac.kr

**Abstract.** The emergence of wireless sensor networks should allow for entirely new kinds of infrastructure in the ubiquitous computing environments while physical attacks will be new concerns. We study security of wireless sensor networks with experiments on physical capture attacks.

## 1 Introduction

A wireless sensor network (WSN) is composed of a large number of sensor nodes for covering wide area through multi-hop connections, and has various kinds of applications including environmental monitoring, industrial monitoring, safety and security services, military system, health-care services, etc. The mission critical applications of WSNs make security and privacy functions required. However, one of the major obstacles to securing the WSNs is a possible physical capture attack, while the economically viable sensor nodes are severely constrained in their capabilities. Since the sensor nodes are deployed in an unattended or even hostile fashion, they can readily be captured and memory-dumped by adversaries, while this is not the easy case in the conventional computer networks. In this work, we study the security of WSNs with experiments on such physical capture attacks. We then discuss several methods for mitigating those weaknesses.

## 2 Sensor Nodes

Sensor nodes are small low-powered devices which are constrained in their computation, communication, and storage capabilities. They may sense around themselves and communicate over wireless channels, but within short ranges. They also tend to fall into the sleep mode for saving their power. Therefore, it is not easy to add security functions to sensor nodes. For our experimental study, we choose the Mica2 mote produced by Crossbow, Inc [1]. The Mica2 mote is composed of Atmel ATmega128L AVR RISC CPU (8-bit, upto 7.37MHz), 128KB program memory, 4KB SRAM, and 512KB flash memory. It also has a 51-pin Hirose connector (DF9-51P-1V) for connecting to sensor and programming boards. This connector is needed for customization and further update of

---

* This research was supported by the MIC (Ministry of Information and Communication), Korea, under the ITRC (Information Technology Research Center) support program supervised by the IITA (Institute of Information Technology Assessment).

S. Mehrotra et al. (Eds.): ISI 2006, LNCS 3975, pp. 741–743, 2006.

the sensor nodes. The most recent advances in the mote technologies come from Intel's IMote2 in which X-Scale MPU (PXA-271 or 3) is incorporated along with various I/O connectors including mini USB ports [2]. We believe the given external ports may attract the adversaries for physical capture attacks while the tamper-resistant packaging of each sensor node is still far from practice.

## 3    Experiments on Physical Attacks

We let Mica2 equipped with the Berkeley TinySec link security architecture which uses Skipjack as block cipher and CBC-MAC for message authentication, respectively. TinySec utilizes 16-byte secret keys that must be stored in `.tinyos_keyfile`, and supports 29-byte packets for TinyOS. We get a default key, 94C68C9E275F6572C2603B5D15DA9868, when compiling TinySec as underlined in Figure 1-(a). Thus, the secret key will be stored in program memory.

(a) TinySec Compilation (TINYSEC_KEY=0x94, ... , 0x68)

(b) Quick Memory Dump Using UISP Software

| type | length | address | data | checksum |

(c) Motorola S−Record Structure

S1134D707DABBA83010101010**94C68C9E275F6553**
S1134D80**72C2603B5D15DA9868**00FFFFFFFFFFFFF0A

(d) Obtained S-Records

**Fig. 1.** TinySec Compilation and Memory Dump

Among the deployed nodes, an attacker could capture one and connect through the 51-pin port or JTAG pins. This is classified as a physical attack. As depicted in Figure 1-(b), the UISP software is simply utilized for memory dump through the serial port of MIB 510 programming board to which the captured node is engaged via the 51-pin connector. Then we could obtain the Motorola s-records in text as depicted in (c) and (d). It took only 33 seconds. In this experiment, we could see easily that the secret key (bold characters in (d)) is disclosed simply by removing type, length, address, and checksum fields in the obtained s-records.

## 4    Risk Analysis and Discussion

Sensor nodes are vulnerable to physical attacks since simple memory dump can be conducted in short time. These weaknesses may affect the security of future infrastructure severely, while lots of them are overlooked in many security schemes today. For example, ZigBee Alliance wants its residential mode in which the secret key is similarly pre-installed only within program memory [3]. Dynamic key establishment schemes should even store secret keys in flash memory for robustness, while it can be dumped through JTAG ports. Conclusively, we recommend to develop and utilize location-aware schemes for security of WSNs, e.g., [4], and to exploit wisely the velocity and movement sensing capabilities of sensor boards for the purpose. We will show and discuss more details in our poster.

# References

1. Crossbow technology, Inc. URL: http://www.xbow.com.
2. IMote2, http://www.intel.com/research/downloads/imote_overview.pdf, 2005
3. ZigBee Specification Ver. 1.0, http://www.zigbee.org, 2005
4. D. Huang, M. Mehta, D. Medhi, and L. Harn, "Location-aware Key Management Scheme for Wireless Sensor Networks," in *Proc. of the 1st ACM workshop on Security of ad-hoc and sensor networks (SASN'04)*, pp. 29-42, Oct. 2004.

# Terrorist Database: A Bangladesh Study

Abu Md. Zafor Alam[1] and Sajjad Waheed[2]

[1] Faculty of Computer Science & Engineering,
Daffodil International University, 102 - Shukrabad, Dhaka-1207
zafor767@aitlbd.net
[2] Dept. of ICT, Maulana Vhasani University, Tangail,
sajad302@yahoo.com

**Abstract.** The Terrorism today is transnational in scope, reach, and presence, and this is perhaps its greatest source of power. Terrorist acts are planned and perpetrated by collections of loosely organized people operating in shadowy networks that are difficult to define and identify. They move freely throughout the world, hide when necessary, and exploit safe harbors proffered by rogue entities. They find unpunished and oftentimes unidentifiable sponsorship and support, operate in small independent cells, strike infrequently, and utilize weapons of mass effect and the media's response in an attempt to influence governments.

Identifying terrorists and terrorist cells whose identities and whereabouts we do not always know is difficult. Equally difficult is detecting and preempting terrorists engaged in adverse actions and plots against the U.S. Terrorism is considered a low-intensity/low-density form of warfare; however, terrorist plots and activities will leave an information signature, albeit not one that is easily detected.

One result of the increasing number of terrorist attacks throughout the world as well as the seemingly frequent release of new viruses or worms has been the realization that better mechanisms need to be developed to share information.

Now we are giving the data about the incidents of bomb blasts in Bangladesh for last few years. The data are arranges in the order of, date of incident, place of incident, target, weapon used and number of death/injury.

01. 17 Aug 2005,63 districts of Bangladesh,To scare public and to establish their presence, 459 Home-made bombs, 2/100.
02. 27 Jan 2005, Boidder Bazaar / Habiganj, Shah AMS Kibria, Former Finance Minister and Foreign Secretary, Grenade, 5/70.
03. 9 Sep 2004, Chittagong, Noapara / Jessore, Takerhat / Joypurhat, To scare public with bombs, 4 bombs, 800gm explosive material, 1 / 0.
04. 21 Aug 2004, Dhaka, key leaders of opposition political party, Grenade & gun shot19/300.
05. 27 Jun 2004, Khulna, Killing of Humayun Kabir, Editor of a regional daily news paper, Bomb1/0.
06. 21 May 2004, Shrine of Shah Jalal/Sylhet, The British High Commissioner, Grenade, 3/50.
07. 21 Feb 2004, Fulbaria / Mymensingh, Rally on Language Movement day, Bomb recovered from water tank, Not reported

S. Mehrotra et al. (Eds.): ISI 2006, LNCS 3975, pp. 744 – 745, 2006.
© Springer-Verlag Berlin Heidelberg 2006

08. 28 Jan 2004, Golakandi / Narayangonj, Visitors to a traditional winter fair, Bomb, 2/20.
09. 12 Jan 2004, Shrine of Shah Jalal / Sylhet, Religious congregation, Bomb, 5/50.
10. 11 Mar 2003, Khulna, Attack on police, Series bomb blast, 2/2.
11. 1 Mar 2003, Khulna, People visiting international Trade fair, Bomb, 1/10.
12. 17 Jan 2003, Shrine of Pagla Pir / Shakhipore, Tangail, Village carnival, Bomb, 7/20.
13. 6 Dec 2002, Four Cinema Halls / Mymensigh, Viewers who came to enjoy cinema on Eid holidays, Time bombs, 18/300.
14. 26 Sep 2001, Political party's meeting / Sunamgonj, Attendees of the meeting, Bomb, 4/0.
15. 23 Sep 2001, Bagerhat, Election Campaign rally.
16. 16 Jun 2001, Nrayangonj, A political party's district office, People gathered in the office building for election preparations, 22/50.
17. 3 June 2001, Baniarchar / Gopalgonj, Religious congregation, Time bomb, 10/25.
18. 14 Apr 2001, Ramna Park / Dhaka, People celebrating Bengali New Year, Remote control bombs, 11/22.
19. 20 Jan 2001, Dhaka, Opposition political party meeting and rally, Explosive implement underneath the earth, 7/50.
20. 20 Jan 2001, Dhaka, Opposition party rally, Government supporters hurled bombs, 0/30.
21. 20 Jul 2001, Kotalipara / Gopalgonj, Attempt to assassinate the then Prime minister, Two heavy bombs were planted at the helipad, not printed.
22. 8 Oct 1999, Holy prayer hall / Khulna, People gathered for saying prayer, Bomb, 8/0.
23. 6 Mar 1999, Jessore, Cultural conference, Explosives underneath the earth, 10/100.

Terrorism neither can be eradicated from the country over night nor can a single agency combat it. It demands integrated effort from all related private and public agencies. Government cannot alone handle the issue single handedly. So we should all come forward to prevent this terrorism to live better and peaceful life.

# Terrorist Organizations and Effects of Terrorism in Bangladesh

Abu Md. Zafor Alam[1], Abu Md. Siddique Alam[2], and Mahjabeen Khan[3]

[1] Dept. Of Computer Science, Daffodil International University,
102 Shukrabad, Dhaka
zafor767@aitlbd.net
[2] Captain, Serving in Bangladesh Army, Comilla Cantonment, Comilla
siddique_lm@yahoo.com
[3] Dept. Of CSE & CIS, Saint Jones University, New York, U.S.A
mkhan06@yahoo.com

**Abstract.** This paper will discuss terrorism in general term in Bangladesh. Study also makes an endeavor to find out the relation of international and regional terrorism in present perspective. In the early phase of the paper, we described about the terrorist organizations in Bangladesh. There after, in the paper will focus on the effects of terrorism in our social environment in Bangladesh. We show the bad impacts of terrorism in out society. Terrorism is a great threats for any country and we all should try to overcome from this burden.

So far none has been able to define terrorism in a manner that could be universally acceptable. Most dictionaries describe terrorism as an act of frightening or intimidating individuals, populations or even governments. In the negative sense, the word defines heartless and evil-minded individuals and organizations with no perceived moral compass. In a more positive light, self-sacrificing freedom fighters will to give life or limb for a noble cause. For the personal gain terrorism has become a new culture to our society in the recent past. Poor governance, unhealthy political environment, extreme poverty etc has resulted the present deteriorating law and order situation in which the normal citizens no longer can expect a peaceful state of mind. Although, there is no declared ideological or political terrorist groups operating in the country, but the country is today besieged with acts of terrorism mostly by day- to-day political hood looms and criminals.

Linkup of Bangladeshi terrorist group with international terrorist organization is yet a matter of controversy. Whatever may be the form or pattern of terrorism in Bangladesh, the causes are many and multi dimensional. The vital causes of terrorism are poverty, corruption and political instability. Ethnic and religious differences, drug, weak law enforcing agencies, violence in print and audio-visual media etc promote the terrorist activities.

The government has identified as well as 11 Islami fundamentalist group in the country and 48 camps of this fundamentalist group. Those are : Jamatul Mujahidin, Party of Allah (Allah'r Dal), Al Queda, Harkatul Jihad, Taliban Cadre, Islamic Ain Bastobayan Committee, Sarbahara.

Some of the affected area for terrorism are: Effects on the National Security, Psychological Impact, Effect on Politics, Effect on Economy, Effect on Education, Social Insecurity.

S. Mehrotra et al. (Eds.): ISI 2006, LNCS 3975, pp. 746–747, 2006.

An in depth study reveals that, poverty, political instability and corruption are the prime causes of terrorism in our country. There are other causes, which also contribute substantially for the growth of terrorism. However, the widely talked issue i.e. religious terrorism has negligible influence in overall perspective. There is some sympathetic group for the Taliban or Al Queda or believer of Islamic Jihad, but they do not fall under terrorist categories. Some external force and hostile media are portraying the existence of terrorism in Bangladesh for their interest. However, those could not be proved. Though terrorism in true sense is not prevailing in the country, but the society has become vulnerable to any kind of terrorism due to poverty, political instability and other causes. For Bangladesh to curb the movement potentials a thorough corrective drive in the field of politics is the first step that would ensure developing a healthy political atmosphere guided by the educated class. The confidence of the deprived class will have to be restored. The market economy will have to be controlled so that people can have equal access to the market in terms of purchasing power. The political unity in case of national interest has to be maintained and corruption free administrations with effective law enforcing agencies have to surface. The youth force will have to be directed towards the correct path with opportunities to flourish in the life. The religious and cultural values and social ethics are to be infused in the national character. Proper religious education must be ensured in every level of the society to curb the rise of fundamentalism. The ruling party and the administration must be made accountable to the people. The national electronic and print media should be made free to express neutral views and help keep a balance in the society. Armed forces may play a significant role to combat terrorism. At regional level SAARC may also play vital role to combat cross border terrorism. Finally, What is essential is a general awareness, a holistic and proactive approach towards solving the problems; only then the country can possibly avoid falling prey to terrorism.

# Decider.Track, a Revolutionary Cyber-Tracker for Antiterrorist Fight

Dr Martine Naillon[1], Prefect Jean-François di Chiara[2],
Bruno Eude[3], and Christian Amathieux[4]

[1] Co-Mining® Technology, 12 avenue de Verdun 92330 Sceaux France
naillon@comining.org
http://www.comining.org
[2] French Interior Ministry, INHES ,3 avenue du Stade de France - 93210 St-Denis France
jean-francois.dichiara@interieur.gouv.fr
http://www.inhes.interieur.gouv.fr/index.php
[3] CompleTel, Tour Ariane 5, place de la pyramide 92088 La Défense France
b.eude@completel.fr
http://www.completel.fr
[4] Emergence Consulting, 12 Leedon Height #03-02 Singapore 26 79 35
christian@amathieux.com

**Abstract.** *decider.track, dt"*, is a unique proprietary and *"Electronic Neurotransmitter"* technology which literally mimics both the conscious and intuitive reasoning of humans - *hunch decisions.* "dt" is a *"Portable Distributed Object"*(PDO®) based on the unique world wide patented Co-Mining® technological breakthrough, which acts as "mobile intelligence", travelling in the global cyberspace to link information distributed in space and in time.

## 1 Introduction

*decider.track ("dt")* with *Co-Mining*® inside tracks, day and night, disparate events and relates them to discover abnormalities. It can link relevant global information distributed in international intelligence services data bases around the world, to track dangerous people, or terrorists. It has the ability to decode the invisible bias introduced by the human subjectivity of operators when they are under the pressure of continuous, sometimes contradictory and overwhelming, global information flows.

*"dt"* is a revolutionary, unique AI technology, originating from European civil and Defence industries, with 150 industrial R&D person-years in advanced cognitive sciences, [1] to [5]. Nowadays developed by Co-Mining® Technology, it has become a mature technology patented world-wide[6], a complementary proposal for *Net Centric Operations* applied in Defence, Global Security and Global Finance [7].

## 2 Global Security Need

In high-risk environments where human lives or where large sums of money are at stake - such as those related to homeland or global security and finance - decision processes can last several months and require successions of *micro-decisions* and

S. Mehrotra et al. (Eds.): ISI 2006, LNCS 3975, pp. 748–749, 2006.

requests which require the police or finance investigations. The greatest difficulties for humans, more than finding the right information at the right time, is to make the *right requests in the right data bases.* How does one link an event which occurred a few months or years before, somewhere on the planet or in the city, with a new fact currently observed by a secret service? How does one know that an observed radicalist had been arrested previously in another country, not for terrorist actions but merely for delinquency and that his biometry is already somewhere in police files?

To handle this *Information Sharing Need,* the concept of *Net Centric Operations (NCO)* is based on huge shared data bases which are exploding in size due to the amount of *meta data required,* which reflect the   heterogeneity of   levels of perception.

## 3   Technical Description

Compared to the current NCO with metadata, the brain-like Co-Mining® technology provides the users with private cognitive agents, analogous to "cerebral lobes" (ref www.comining.com) embedded with the user private decisional rules to process his/her private data. "dt", the *"Portable Distributed Object"(PDO®),* analogous to *"Electronic neurotransmitter",* makes the linkages between the different private data bases. The *revolutionary feature* is that *dt is not a mobile agent,* dt is *a mobile information moving with a request,* remotely controlled by the service who discovered the first suspect elements about an individual or event. Part of those cerebral-like agents have embedded *data, text or image miners,* which act as sensors enabling them to extract *locally* in real time significant information that dt links *globally*; thus, dt solution is complementary with the current information extraction technologies. Co-Mining® mimics human reasoning but better than human, it interweaves collective human reasoning, retracing it in the so called *"Co-Mining® decisional track".*

## References

1. Naillon, M., Theeten, J.B.: Neural approach for TV image compression using a Hopfield type neural network. IEEE, Neural Processing Systems (1988)
2. Naillon, M.: Eco-systemic theory and application to the future Defence systems. DASSAULT AVIATION. Internal Report, DGT 48268  (1992)
3. Naillon, M., Atlan, L., Bonnet, J: Learning reactive strategies using genetic programming. Application to Job-Shop scheduling. FLAIRS, Springer (1994)
4. Naillon, M.: Active vision in satellite scene analysis. SAIRAS'94, Jet Propulsion Laboratories, USA (1994)
5. Naillon, M., Innovation strategy for Communication and Information Systems, Note MN-CB/TH/001-French Ministry of Defense (1996)
6. Naillon, M.: Method for monitoring a decision-making process when pursuing an objective in economical, technical and organizational field, US Patent, No. 09/443 371(1999), Europe No.°00 402 875.9 (2000)
7. Naillon, M.: Co-Mining® technology, a new generation of Command and Control Systems from aerospace surveillance to global financial intelligence AAA 1st International CS2E Conference, France (2004)

# The Role of Information Superiority in the Global War on Terrorism

Annette Sobel

USAF, National Guard Bureau, Director of Intelligence

## 1 Introduction

Organizational agility, thoughtful purpose in information/intelligence-sharing and collaboration, speed of action and decision-making are critical elements to winning the War on Terrorism. These elements define the guidance of the Chairman of the Joint Chiefs of Staff, General Peter Pace, United States Marine Corps. The role of each element should be considered in the knowledge discovery process and a focused, yet adaptive, approach should be adopted in the effort toward terrorist/extremist early cueing, identification, and warning.

Terrorism is recognized internationally as premeditated, politically motivated violence perpetrated against noncombatant targets. Hence, the War on Terrorism must include strategies that address nontraditional approaches to winning war. These approaches include information superiority through information/intelligence-sharing and analytic collaboration. In addition, they must consider development and maturation of long-term, sustainable networks of like-minded individuals and entities committed to countering terrorism and extremism.

The field of information operations and, optimally, information superiority leading to superior decision-making, is a broad discipline which includes non-kinetic and non-traditional options for waging war. Integration of information and analysis leading to "fused" assessments and analytic products is a strategic pillar in this War. Fusion enables clarity of mission and purpose, efficient and effective mechanisms to optimize resources, and produces highly credible and targeted "actionable intelligence" for tactical operations. In contrast, strategic intelligence leads to warning, anticipation of surprise, and potential courses-of-action for pre-emption, and is one of the primary goals of long-term information superiority. The critical importance of information superiority has been appreciated for centuries:

> *"Now the reason the enlightened prince and the wise general conquer the enemy whenever they move and their achievements surpass those of ordinary men is foreknowledge."*
> *-Sun Tzu*

## 2 Establishing the Networks

Asymmetry of information may be achieved through development and implementation of broad information/intelligence-sharing networks. These networks must

S. Mehrotra et al. (Eds.): ISI 2006, LNCS 3975, pp. 750–752, 2006.
© Springer-Verlag Berlin Heidelberg 2006

include global government, private and academic sectors, and in many ways should mirror the threats imposed by terrorist organizations. Only through this worldwide networking may realistic strategies leading to successful tactical plans may be achieved in a timely, decisive manner.

The first step in developing an effective network is defining the relevant and credible information sources that may be employed. When considering open-source (i.e., publicly available information sources), one of the first steps is development of a rapid validation, cueing, analytic, and dissemination process. The private and academic sectors work quite effectively in these collaborative and competitive arenas, utilizing effective business, intellectual property, and financial models, and standards imposed by peer-review processes.

Next, global standards of intelligence reporting and early warning are essential to ensure integrity of this process. Clearly stated, prioritized requirements for information-on-demand impose challenges and organizational stresses on this process, hence the need for clearly predefined objectives, prioritized essential elements of information/intelligences (EEIs), and "triggers". Contextual triggers are the core to this analysis and reporting process. This collaborative process must be developed with the full participation of policy and decision-makers at all levels, and structure must be imposed that supports the reality of real-world operations, to include legal and cultural constraints, in the War on Terrorism.

The private and federal sectors are especially equipped to lead the information/intelligence-sharing tasks of critical infrastructure situation awareness (SA) and vulnerability assessment. National and international SA are achieved through government and military partnerships at all levels with the private and academic sectors.

The special task of science and technology intelligence (S&TI) and prevention of technologic surprise must be achieved through government-private-academic partnerships. World markets drive the opportunities for technologic surprise and academic environments are the grist for those partnerships and developmental efforts. S&TI is of critical importance due to its driving force within national security capability.

Once the networks for collaboration have been defined and partnerships are implemented, the roles and responsibilities of requesting information/intelligence (RFI process) must be agreed upon. The RFI process is most effective when formalized procedures have been agreed upon for standing and ad hoc (more urgent, situation-driven) requirements.

## 3  Summary

As previously stated, global networks for information/intelligence collaboration ultimately lead to clarity of mission and purpose, and produce focused intelligence products enabling effective operations. Information operations assist in shaping the security environment, fostering accurate assessments of the significance and "actionability" of the derived intelligence products. Ultimately, the contextual inferences of these products depend on the ability of organizations to integrate technology, systems, and people. These products are critically important for driving policy and operational plans at the state, local, national and international levels. As global networks for collaboration in the War on Terrorism are established, their agility, clarity of mission and purpose, speed of action and effective decision-making will be metrics of their success.

# A Trust-Based Security Architecture for Ubiquitous Computing Systems*

Le Xuan Hung, Pho Duc Giang, Yonil Zhung,
Tran Van Phuong, Sungyoung Lee**, and Young-Koo Lee

Department of Computer Engineering, Kyung Hee University, Korea
{lxhung, pdgiang, zhungs, tvphuong, sylee}@oslab.khu.ac.kr,
yklee@khu.ac.kr

Ubiquitous Computing (*ubicomp*) is a revolution of computing paradigm that promises to have a profound affect on the way we interact with computers, devices, physical spaces and other people. Traditional authentication and access control which has been applied to stand-alone computers and small networks are not adequate to ubicomp technology. Instead, we need a new security model that is based on notion of trust to support cross-domain interactions and collaborations. This means that ubicomp environments involves the interaction, coordination, and cooperation of numerous, casually accessible, and often invisible computing devices. Authenticating the identity certificate of a previous unknown user does not provide any access control information. Simple authentication and access control are only effective if the system knows in advance which users are going to access the system and what their access rights are. Security information in different domains is subject to inconsistent interpretations in such open, distributed environment. In order to fulfill these security requirements of ubicomp, in this paper we present USEC, A Trust-based Security Infrastructure, for securing ubicomp systems. USEC is being developed for CAMUS[1]. It is composed of seven major components: *hybrid access control, entity recognition, trust/risk management, intrusion detection, privacy control,* and *home firewall.* Our objective is to provide a lightweight infrastructure with sufficient security services that tackles most security problems in ubicomp systems.

Entity Recognition is a novel authentication technology for ubicomp paradigm. In USEC architecture, Pluggable Entity Recognition Module (PRM) supports flexibly various devices such as Smart Badges, iButtons, Smart Watchs, PDAs. This component integrates different type of authentications, ranging from conventional authentication approaches (Username/Password, PKI, Kerberos, etc) to emerging identity recognition technology. Trust/Risk Management provides trust value to the Access Control Manager. It supports trust collaborations and interactions among roaming entities. By modeling trust relationships in smart spaces environments, unknown entities from different domains can interact, request services and resources from a given domain in secure and privacy manner. Risk evaluator and Trust calculator cooperate with each other to support making decision. Hybrid Access

---

* This work is financially supported by the Ministry of Education and Human Resources Development(MODE), the Ministry of Commerce, Industry and Energy(MOCIE), and the Ministry of Labor(MOLAB) through the fostering project of the Lab of Excellency.
** Corresponding author.
[1] CAMUS: Context-Awareness Middleware for Ubiquitous Computing Systems.

S. Mehrotra et al. (Eds.): ISI 2006, LNCS 3975, pp. 753–754, 2006.

Control (HAC) is the core part of USEC infrastructure. This is hybrid of Role-based (RBAC), Policy-based (PBAC), Context-based (CBAC) and Trust-based Access Control (TBAC) to solve different shortcomings of those approaches. HAC is critical to preserve confidentiality and integrity. Conventionally, the condition of confidentiality requires that only authorized users can read information, and the condition of integrity requires that only authorized users can alter information and in authorized ways. In USEC, HAC extends scopes of users by using Trust/Risk Management. Privacy Control is integral part in this convenient but obtrusive environment. It provides *location privacy, anonymous connections* and *confidentiality* of information to users. In USEC infrastructure, we also integrate Home Firewall to protect smart space against potential outside attackers. Intrusion Detection System is deployed in order to defend against unauthorized access and who has legitimate access to the system but abuse privileges. In ubiquitous environments, this usually occurs due to ubiquity and wireless communication of the systems. In the sensor network layer, USEC provides a lightweight cryptography mechanism in order maintain secure communication among sensors and between sensors and context-aware systems. Trust/Risk Management, Intrusion Detection System, Home Firewall, and Sensor Network Security are together supports Entity Recognition. Fig 1 shows the relationships and interactions among these components.

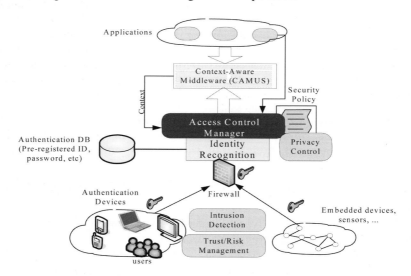

**Fig. 1.** USEC architecture and its component interactions

Currently, we have completed deploying a smart environment by CAMUS in our RTMM Lab. This environment facilitates professors, students and staffs of our Lab to work and research as well as to entertain. We also are completing USEC framework to support security for this environment. USEC is component-based architecture and can support various ubicomp systems. After accomplishing in this environment, we will extend to other systems/environments such as parking spaces, airports, and hospitals. We believe that USEC will also fulfill security requirements in such systems/environments.

# A Trust Model for Uncertain Interactions in Ubiquitous Environments*

Le Xuan Hung, Hassan Jammeel, Seong Jin Cho, Yuan Weiwei,
Young-Koo Lee[**], and Sungyoung Lee

Department of Computer Engineering,
Kyung Hee University, Korea
{lxhung, hassan, babebear, weiwei}@oslab.khu.ac.kr,
yklee@khu.ac.kr, sylee@oslab.khu.ac.kr

The notion of trust has played an important role in ubiquitous computing (*ubicomp*). It supports uncertain interactions and collaborations between mobile entities. Most of previous work on trust did not attach enough importance to uncertainty. Besides, these works draw a general picture without any detailed computational model. In this paper, we present a trust model based on the vectors of trust values including *peer recommendation, confidence, history of past interaction,* and *time-based evaluation.*

Whenever two principals want to interact, they should be able to evaluate the amount of trust on each other using some evaluation metric. This metric should include the recommendations of other principals that had past experiences with these principals; the more the experiences, the higher the weight of these recommendations. Also, the interacting principals' past experiences with each other should obviously have a say in this evaluation. First, we define some basic notions:

**Definition 1.** The *trust vector* of principal $Q_i$ is defined as:

$$\overrightarrow{Q_i} = \left( t_{Q_i,Q_1}, t_{Q_i,Q_2}, \ldots, t_{Q_i,Q_{i-1}}, t_{Q_i,Q_{i+1}}, \ldots, t_{Q_i,Q_n} \right)$$

where *trust value* of $Q_i$ on $Q_k$: $t_{Q_i,Q_k} = NULL$ if they have NOT interacted before ($i \neq k$).

**Definition 2.** The *peer set* of a principal $Q_i$ denoted by $S_{Q_i}$ is the set of all those principals $Q$, such that $t_{Q_i,Q} \neq NULL$.

**Definition 3.** The *common peer vectors* of $Q_i$ with $Q_j$ are defined as:

$$\overrightarrow{C}_{Q_i,Q} = \left( t_{Q_i,Q_{k_1}}, t_{Q_i,Q_{k_2}}, \ldots, t_{Q_i,Q_{k_m}} \right), \text{ and } \overrightarrow{C}_{Q,Q_i} = \left( t_{Q_{k_1},Q_i}, t_{Q_{k_2},Q_i}, \ldots, t_{Q_{k_m},Q_i} \right)$$

where $\left\{ Q_{k_1}, Q_{k_2}, \ldots, Q_{k_m} \right\} = S_{Q_i} \cap S_{Q_j}$.

---

[*] This work was supported by IITA Professorship for Visiting Faculty Positions in Korea from Ministry of Information and Communications.
[**] Corresponding author.

S. Mehrotra et al. (Eds.): ISI 2006, LNCS 3975, pp. 755 – 757, 2006.

Now, our evaluation metrics are precisely developed as following:

**Peer Recommendation:** Suppose there are $n$ principals in the system: $Q_1, Q_2,...,Q_n$. Each principle has a trust value for any other principal it interacted with before. The *common peer vectors* of $Q_i$ with $Q_j$ are defined as:

$$\vec{C}_{Q_i,Q} = \left(t_{Q_i,Q_{k_1}}, t_{Q_i,Q_{k_2}},...,t_{Q_i,Q_{k_m}}\right), \text{and } \vec{C}_{Q,Q_i} = \left(t_{Q_{k_1},Q_i}, t_{Q_{k_2},Q_i},...,t_{Q_{k_m},Q_i}\right)$$

where $\left\{Q_{k_1}, Q_{k_2},...,Q_{k_m}\right\} = S_{Q_i} \cap S_{Q_j}$.

The *peer recommendation* for the interaction with $Q_j$ to $Q_i$ is defined as:

$$PR_{Q_i,Q_j} = \begin{cases} \left|\left(\vec{C}_{Q_i,Q} \bullet \vec{C}_{Q,Q_j}\right)\right|/m & , S_{Q_i} \cap S_{Q_j} \neq \phi \\ 0 & , S_{Q_i} \cap S_{Q_j} = \phi \end{cases} \text{ where, } \begin{array}{l} m = \left|S_{Q_i} \cap S_{Q_j}\right|, \text{and} \\ \vec{C}_{Q_i,Q} \bullet \vec{C}_{Q,Q_i} \text{ is the dot product} \end{array}$$

**Confidence:** Let $I_{Q_i}$ and $I_{Q_j}$ denote the total number of interactions of principals $Q_i$ and $Q_j$ with all the principals in $S_{Q_i} \cap S_{Q_j}$. The *confidence* (*CF*) on the *PR* value for $Q_i$ and $Q_j$ as:

$$CF_{Q_i,Q_j} = \frac{1}{2}\left(f(m) + f\left(I_{Q_i}\right)\right), \quad CF_{Q_j,Q_i} = \frac{1}{2}\left(f(m) + f\left(I_{Q_j}\right)\right)$$

where $f(x) = 1 - 1/(x+\alpha)$, we choose such *f(x)* since it approaches 1 as $x$ becomes bigger, and $\alpha$ is an adjustable positive constant and can be tuned accordingly.

**History of Past Interactions:** The *Past Interaction Evaluation* (*PI*) of $Q_j$ as calculated by $Q_i$ is defined as:

$$PI_{Q_i,Q_j} = 1 - 1/(h_{Q_i,Q_j} + 1) = f\left(h_{Q_i,Q_j}\right), \alpha = 1 .$$

where $h_{Q_i,Q_j} = \max\left\{w_S SI_{Q_i,Q_j} - w_U UI_{Q_i,Q_j}, 0\right\}$ ($w_S$ and $w_U$ are positive numbers; the corresponding weights of $SI_{Q_i,Q_j}$ and $UI_{Q_i,Q_j}$).

**Time Based Evaluation:** Intuitively, very old experiences of peers should have less weight in peer recommendation over new ones. Let $\tau_{P,Q}$ denotes the time stamp between $P$ and $Q$, $\Delta\tau$ denotes the threshold time interval, and $\tau$ denotes the moment that $Q_i$ and $Q_j$ decide to interact. The time based evaluation (*TE*) for both $Q_i$ and

$Q_j$ as: $TE_{Q_i,Q_j} = m/\left(\sum_{l=1}^{m}\left\lceil \Delta\tau_{Q_j,Q_{k_l}}/\Delta\tau \right\rceil\right)$, and $TE_{Q_j,Q_i} = m/\left(\sum_{l=1}^{m}\left\lceil \Delta\tau_{Q_i,Q_{k_l}}/\Delta\tau \right\rceil\right)$

where $\Delta\tau_{X,Y} = \tau - \tau_{X,Y}$.

**Trust Evaluation Metric:** Based on the aforementioned metrics, we are now ready to describe our trust evaluation metric. The trust metric is defined as a weighted arithmetic mean of *PR*, *CF*, *TE*, and *PI*. More precisely, the trust between two principals $Q_i$ and $Q_j$ who want to interact can be calculated as:

$$t_{Q_i,Q_j} = \left\{ w_1\left(PR_{Q_i,Q_j}\right)\left(CF_{Q_i,Q_j} + TE_{Q_i,Q_j}\right)/2 + w_2\left(PI_{Q_i,Q_j}\right)\right\} / \left(\sum_{i=1}^{2} w_i\right)$$

where $w_i \in N$ and they can be adjusted to a suitable value if more weight is to be given to a specific metric.

The calculation of the trust depends upon the recommendation of peer entities common to the entities which are weighted according to the number of past interactions and the time of last interaction. The model can calculate trust between two entities in situations both in which there is past experience among the interacting entities and in which the two entities are communicating for the first time. Several tuning parameters are suggested which can be adjusted to meet the security requirement of a distributed system. A highly secure system can adjust these parameters such that only a few entities with very high reputation and recommendation are allowed to perform requested actions.

# A Multiclass Classifier to Detect Pedestrians and Acquire Their Moving Styles

D. Chen[1, 2], X.B. Cao[1, 2], H. Qiao[3], and F.Y. Wang[3]

[1] Department of Computer Science and Technology,
University of Science and Technology of China,
Hefei, 230026, P.R. China
[2] Anhui Province Key Laboratory of Software in Computing and Communication,
Hefei, 230026, P.R. China
dchen4@mail.ustc.edu.cn, xbcao@ustc.edu.cn
[3] Institute of Automation, Chinese Academy of Sciences,
Beijing, 10080, P.R. China
hong.qiao@mail.ia.ac.cn, feiyue@sie.arizona.edu

**Abstract.** In a pedestrian detection system, to discover the intention of a pedestrian and warn the driver, it is necessary to obtain the pedestrian's main moving style. In this paper, an efficient multiclass classifier is presented to detect pedestrians and classify their moving style simultaneously. The multiclass classifier composes of three two-class classifiers and each of them is trained with a SVM algorithm. Experiments based on a single camera pedestrian detection system show that the multiclass classifier has an acceptable detection rate; at the same time, it can judge whether a pedestrian is walking along the road or across the road.

## 1 Introduction

The final purpose of a pedestrian detection system (PDS) is to reduce pedestrian-vehicle related injure. To achieve this requirement, it is not enough to detect a pedestrian merely; one more important work is to obtain the pedestrian's moving style. However, most of existing systems use a two-class classifier and do not care about the pedestrian's moving style [1], [2].

In this paper, we propose a multiclass classifier to detect pedestrians and classify their moving style simultaneously. Since the states of across/along the road are the most important moving styles, our classifier divides a candidate into three classes: pedestrian across the road, pedestrian along the road and non-pedestrian.

## 2 The Multiclass Classifier Structure

Since solving this multiclass classification problem with a single classifier will lead to a huge optimization problem, we combine three two-class classifiers to construct a multiclass classifier. Each classifier is trained with a SVM algorithm [3], [4]. The structure of the multiclass classifier is shown in Fig. 1.

S. Mehrotra et al. (Eds.): ISI 2006, LNCS 3975, pp. 758–759, 2006.

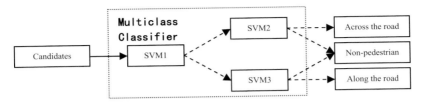

**Fig. 1.** The structure of the multiclass classifier

When a candidate is asked to be classified, it will be sent to SVM1 firstly. If it is classified as a pedestrian across the road, SVM2 is used to determine whether it is a pedestrian across the road or non-pedestrian. Otherwise, it is classified as a pedestrian along the road, and then SVM3 is used to determine whether it is a pedestrian along the road or a non-pedestrian. Therefore each candidate will be classified twice until it is finally verified.

The multiclass classifier has the following advantages: (1) it has higher classification ability; (2) it can get pedestrian's moving style, whilst the time cost increases not too much.

## 3 Experiments

We experiment on a single optical camera PDS. In the multiclass SVM classifier, each two-class classifier has much less support vectors and features than a single classifier for all type of pedestrians.

The multiclass classifier gets average detection rate of 89.6% and false positive rate of 0.13%. When pedestrians are detected correctly, the average detection rate of moving style is 96.4%.

In conclusion, replacing a single classifier with our multiclass classifier do not have significant penalty on detection speed; meanwhile, a higher detection rate and the moving style information can be obtained.

## References

1. T. Evgeniou, C. Papageorgiou, T. Poggio: A trainable pedestrian detection system, IEEE Intelligent Vehicles Symposium, Stuttgart, Germany, Oct. (1998) 241–246
2. Fengliang Xu, Xia Liu, and Kikuo Fujimura: Pedestrian Detection and Tracking With Night Vision, IEEE Transactions on Intelligent Transportation System, Vol. 6, No.1, (2005) 63–71
3. Zhang XG: Introduction to statistical learning theory and support vector machines, Acta Automatica Sinica, Vol. 26, No. 1, (2000) 32–42
4. T. Joachims: Making large-scale SVM learning practical, in Advances in Kernel Methods — Support Vector Learning, B. Schölkopf, C. J. C. Burges, and A. J. Smola, Eds. Cambridge, MA: MIT Press, 1998.

# A Home Firewall Solution for Securing Smart Spaces

Pho Duc Giang, Le Xuan Hung, Yonil Zhung,
Sungyoung Lee, and Young-Koo Lee

Computer Engineering Department, Kyung Hee University, Korea
{pdgiang, lxhung, zhungs, sylee}@oslab.khu.ac.kr,
yklee@khu.ac.kr

In Ubiquitous Computing environments, service servers play a central role of actively gathering situation information to detect changes in context to provide appropriate functions for users. However, they also raise concerns related to security and privacy. It is the dynamism and mobility absolutely necessary for smart spaces that can yield extra chances for attackers to exploit vulnerabilities in the system invisibly. From a server-centric viewpoint, researchers must find techniques to reduce the security risks as much as possible from these servers. Firewall technology is a logical approach that can help them accomplish this troublesome task. In this paper, we propose a new concept of context-aware host-based firewall called *Home Firewall*[1], to protect the central server deploying our current context-aware middleware, namely Context-Aware Middleware for Ubiquitous computing Systems (CAMUS), from suspicious actions. The idea is established on host-based firewalls to filter off malicious context-aware and command packets in/out the service server.

**Threats to the Central Server:** One of the most severe security threats to the server coming from wireless sensor networks is base station spoofing. The wireless sensor networks often collect and relay data to the server via a gateway or base station. An attacker gain unauthorized access to the environment by making it appear that a malicious message has come from the base station by spoofing the IP and/or the MAC address of that machine. Therefore, instead of sending the control packets to the base station, i.e., to turn the surveillance camera and alarm system on, to alert strangers breaking into the house, the server delivered messages to the hacker's machine. Moreover, dangers to the main server coming from wireless networks are wireless device compromise. We can take a visual example by supposing that the home owner joins his laptop into an unprotected network already infected with viruses, worms, or Trojan horses at his office, his laptop is then infected with the kind of plague. Later, he brings the laptop into his home network, a protected environment, and connecting to the central server through the Wireless Access Point (WAP). In this case, packets from his laptop are sent to the servers without any verification and they are thus free to corrupt the entire system. Also, risk to the principle server resulting from applications or services implemented on the system can be exploited by attackers because they miss crucial security patches. Once these programs are compromised,

---

[1] This work is financially supported by the Ministry of Education and Human Resource Development (MODE), the Ministry of Commerce, Industry and Energy (MOCIE), and the Ministry of Labor (MOLAB) through the fostering project of the Lab of Excellency. Dr. Sungyoung Lee is the corresponding author.

S. Mehrotra et al. (Eds.): ISI 2006, LNCS 3975, pp. 760–761, 2006.
© Springer-Verlag Berlin Heidelberg 2006

the system control right will be taken over by hackers. Our server may be planted viruses, opened back doors for serving the intruder's remote control demands.

**Our Proposed Methodology:** We present our basic design of the Home Firewall in the smart home infrastructure described in Fig.1.

In our approach, the Home Firewall contains MAC Address Refining (MAR) module. This module is responsible for real-time selecting trusted MAC addresses of available confident base stations in the space for preventing base station spoofing attack. The selected addresses are maintained in an admission list. The MAR module periodically sends a RARP (Reverse Address Resolution Protocol) packet to each address in the list. The function of RARP is mapping a MAC address into an IP address. Following this, Reverse ARP should reply one IP address for one network device. If multiple IP addresses return, it means that the MAC address is being exploited by more than one device.

The firewall manages all the transactions between the user's mobile devices and the central server. If the WAP and/or user's mobile device are compromised, attackers still have no way to change the behavior of our server since they don't know the username/password to change the firewall policies. Our policy, i.e., was set to turn the camera system on from 11P.M to 6A.M. Therefore, malicious control packets that want to improperly turn the system off at that time will be dropped by the firewall.

The Home Firewall also helps preventing other server's programs from being compromised by stopping common hacker's reconnaissance port scanning techniques. In order to defend our server from these kinds of potential threats, such as ICMP scanning, TCP scanning, UDP scanning, we deploy an anti-scanning security policy. Our firewall will prohibit the ICMP replying packets for preventing ICMP scanning technique and deny the ICMP Port Unreachable packets transmitted back to an attacker for protecting UDP scanning probe. For detecting the TCP scanning signature, we might say that if there are more than 5 SYN packet attempts to non-listening ports in one minute, an alarm SMS message should be automatically triggered to the user's cell phone.

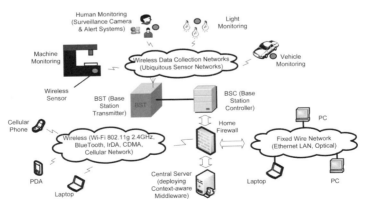

**Fig. 1.** A smart space with Home Firewall support

# The Security Performance Evaluation of Digital Watermarking

Xinhong Zhang[1], Shejiao Li[2], and Fan Zhang[2]

[1] Department of Computer Center, Henan University,
Kaifeng 475001, P.R. China
`hnkfzxh@163.com`
[2] College of Computer & Information Engineering, Henan University,
Kaifeng 475001, P.R. China
`zhangfan@vip.sohu.com`

Digital watermarking technique is one of the powerful tools for the protection of intellectual property rights (IPR). Recently, many new watermarking algorithms have been proposed, at the same time, many new watermarking attack algorithms also have been proposed. The research of attacks and anti-attacks algorithms will help us find more effective watermarking or information hiding algorithms.

Recently, some watermark algorithms have been proposed which can resist several geometrical transform attack and StirMark attack etc. We give a simple analysis to the anti-attack in the difference stages of digital watermark respectively, the design stage, the embedded stage and the examination stage.

1. The watermark design. In the watermark design stage, the complicated degree of the watermarking algorithms and embedded quantity will bring a great influence on the robustness of watermarking system. Some watermarking algorithms resist the watermarking attacks by the sacrifice of capacity and operating speed. The different extraction methods also have certain influence to the anti-attack of the watermark. For example, the blind examination system can resist the attack of IBM. Moreover, choosing a complicated watermark or a bigger private key capacity can improve the anti-attack ability of the watermarking system.

2. The watermark embedded. It is a good way to resist the watermarking attack that embedding as many as watermark information will keep the invisibility of watermark. In the spectral domain watermark system, the watermark information should be distributed on the all space. The watermark information should be embedded in the most important part of the source data to raise the watermark robustness, for example the edge area of the image, the medium low frequency bands of the DCT, and the low frequency bands of the DWT etc. The embedded watermark signal energy in the frequency domain can distribute to all pixels in the spectral domain, the anti-attack ability in the frequency domains is better than it in the spectral domain. Moreover, the watermarking algorithms in the frequency domains have a good performance to resist the images compressing, the quantization of images and the noise. Fourier-Melline transform is a kind of Fourier transformation in polar coordinates system. The watermarking algorithms in the Fourier-Melline transform domains have a good RST robustness.

S. Mehrotra et al. (Eds.): ISI 2006, LNCS 3975, pp. 762–763, 2006.

3. The watermark examination. In the blind watermarking system, it is very important to improve the correlation test algorithms. In order to resist several geometrical transform attacks, recently, the invariant moments, the relative moments and the additional registration patterns are proposed to detect and recover the geometrical attacks. When the energy-efficient watermarks satisfy a power-spectrum condition (PSC), the watermark's power spectrum should be directly proportionate to the original signals. PSC-compliant watermarking has a good robustness performance. The watermarking algorithms based on local vector quantization and double color channels can resist the StirMark attacks. Some papers analyze the watermark estimate problems based on image de-noise. They assume that the original image subject to the non-stationary Caussian distribution or globally generalized Gaussian distribution, the noises subject to Caussian distribution. And they try to find the area that more suits for hiding the watermark information. In the IBM attacks, the best solution is to establish a registration center and detect the Time Stamp coming from the third organization.

Just like the attackers can combine various attack methods, the watermark anti-attack can also combine different anti-attack methods to resist the attacks. Moreover, we can combine the software and hardware together and the method of combining the robust watermarking to the fragile watermarking.

A watermark algorithm may be sensitive to a special attack. Sometimes attackers may use various methods to attack. The watermark algorithms that can resist all of attacks do not exist currently. With the fast development of watermarking, we badly need a perfect benchmark. It will accelerate and promote the technical development of watermarking.

The benchmark for watermarking is a standard platform that provides an objective comparison of watermarking techniques, and evaluates their performance with respect to watermarking applications. In the digital watermark system, the benchmark is a program set that includes a series of watermarking attacks algorithms. Familiar benchmarks include StirMark, Checkmark, Certimark and Optimark.

In recent years, the new watermark algorithms usually have a good performance of robustness to the watermarking attack. Removal attack is not a great threat to them. The synchronization attack become a main attack methods. A good watermarking attack should make use of the local and overall prosperities of the image in the spectral domain and the frequency domain. But recently, the vision models cannot reach the requirements of the watermark algorithms. If a more accurate and practical vision models, which satisfy the HVS prosperities, are proposed, it will bring forth an important influence on either watermarking algorithms or attacks algorithms.

# A Novel Key Release Scheme from Biometrics

Ong Thian Song, Andrew B.J. Teoh and David C.L. Ngo

Faculty of Information Science and Technology, Multimedia University
Jalan Ayer Keroh Lama, 75450 Melaka, Malaysia
{tsong, bjteoh, david.ngo}@mmu.edu.my

In this paper, we introduce a novel method to secure cryptographic private key binding and retrieving from fingerprint data using BioHash[1][2], Reed-Solomon error code (RSC)[3] and the thresholded secret sharing scheme[4]. Figure 1 illustrates the schematic diagram of the proposed scheme. Firstly, we generate cancelable biometrics features from fingerprint data through BioHashing and encode the resulting hash. From the encoded BioHash, we formulate the process of cryptographic private key, $\kappa$ binding and retrieving with the following steps:

$$\textit{Key Binding} \qquad : \quad b_c \oplus \kappa = \gamma \tag{1}$$

$$\textit{Key Retrieval} \qquad : \quad \gamma \oplus b_c^{'} = \kappa^{'} \tag{2}$$

where $\gamma$ is called Biokey, $b_c$ and $b_c^{'}$ refer to the encoded BioHash (gallery sample) and decoded BioHash (probe sample) respectively, while $\oplus$ denotes bitwise XOR operation.

The use of BioHash as the mixing process provides the one-way transformation and deters exact recovery of the biometrics features from compromised hashes and stolen token. Besides, we incorporate RSC acts as an error correction step to correct the bit disparity between the gallery and probe sample of BioHash. The core processes in both (1) and (2) are securely protected by thresholded secret sharing, i.e., our private key protection involved the process of using threshold scheme to construct the sharing of $(t, n)$ secret. We design $t=2$ with the simple linear polynomial of two secret share $(2, l_t)$ thresholding scheme as follow:

a) one share associated with BioHash ($b$)
b) one share associated with key serialization ($k$)

The above configurations constitute a rigorous 2 of $l_t$ threshold system with $l_t$ the number $b$ of a particular user. The construction of such secret sharing scheme provides an extra secure protection layer to private key besides one-way transformation of BioHashing, as knowledge of any one of the above share $(t-1)$ leaves the key completely undetermined.

We use FVC2002 [5] fingerprint database in our experimental analysis to examine the retrievable of private key from Biokey, i.e, $\kappa = \kappa^{'}$. We define False Acceptance Rate (FAR) as the percentage of unauthorized attempts of imposter users to retrieve the key that are accepted, while the False Rejection Rate (FRR) is the percentage of authorized attempts to retrieve the key by a genuine user that is rejected. From our analysis, we determine that RSC decoder (15,9) is the best threshold that can correct the bit disparity with the minimal error rate of 0.0272 in $b$. Table 1 tabulates the

S. Mehrotra et al. (Eds.): ISI 2006, LNCS 3975, pp. 764 – 765, 2006.
© Springer-Verlag Berlin Heidelberg 2006

FAR-FRR analysis on the three database set, DB1, 2 and 3 respectively and the empirical results confirms that the proposed scheme could retrieve error free key reliably from the genuine samples up to a 99.8% success rate, and completely detering imposter users from unauthorized access to the secret key, with FAR = 0% and FRR = 0.12% respectively.

**Table 1.** FAR-FRR Performance Analysis on DB1,2 and 3 based on decoder (15,9)

| *Database* | *FAR (%)* | *FRR (%)* |
|:---:|:---:|:---:|
| DB1 | 0 | 0.12 |
| DB2 | 0 | 1.01 |
| DB3 | 0 | 1.35 |

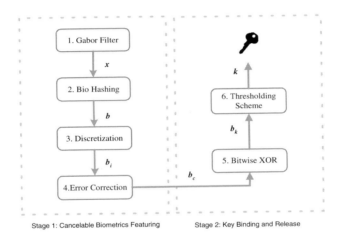

Stage 1: Cancelable Biometrics Featuring          Stage 2: Key Binding and Release

**Fig. 1.** Proposed Private Key Release Scheme

# References

[1] Goh, A. & Ngo, D.C.L.:Computation of Cryptographic Keys from Face Biometrics, 7th IFIP CMS 2003, Torino, LNCS 2828, (2003) pp. 1-13
[2] Andrew T.B.J., David N.C.L and Alwyn G.: Biohashing: Two Factor Authentication Featuring Fingerprint Data And Tokenised Random Number. Pattern Recognition, Vol 37, Issue 11. (2004) 2245-2255.
[3] Reed I.S and Solomon G.: RS codes over certain finite fields. Journal of SIAM, Vol.8 No.2. (1960) 300-304
[4] Shamir, A.: How to share a secret. Communications of the ACM. Vol.22 No.1. (1979). 612–613.
[5] FVC 2002, http://bias.csr.unibo.it/fvc2002/

# Matching Images of Never-Before-Seen Individuals in Large Law Enforcement Databases

Olcay Kursun[1], Kenneth M. Reynolds[2], and Oleg Favorov[3]

[1] Department of Engineering Technology
[2] Department of Criminal Justice and Legal Studies
University of Central Florida, Orlando, FL 32816
{okursun, kreynold}@mail.ucf.edu
[3] Department of Biomedical Engineering
University of North Carolina, Chapel Hill, NC 2759
favorov@bme.unc.edu

**Abstract.** A method is developed for extraction of robust human facial features that can be used on never-before-seen individuals in homeland security tasks such as human tracking or matching photos of dead against missing individuals (e.g. recent Asian tsunami aftermath).

One of the central goals of face-processing research is to identify informative high-order facial features that can effectively characterize and distinguish human faces independent of variations of viewing conditions, such as, for example, viewing angle, illumination, or facial expression. Such features constitute hidden factors – they are variables that are present in face images, but hidden in the spatial patterns of pixels across the image and require computational extraction. Due to lack of knowledge of such features, classical face recognition deals only with known individuals. In most cases, a separate classifier will be developed for each known individual to discriminate it from other known individuals. These classifiers will be less likely to come up with good generalization with small number of training samples. Our approach is to search for invariants by concurrently exposing SINBAD cell to different images of the same individual, thus forcing it to discover some higher-order variable that does not change across different images of the same individuals.

Lately face recognition for real-world applications focuses on no human intervention during all phases; training (learning), recognition, insertion of new face classes (individuals). Scalable approaches not requiring constant overhead of extra training with addition of new individuals have recently been particularly demanded for applications such as in criminology and homeland security. Another consequential demand is compression of the visual input. Robust facial features that are valid for never-before-seen individuals make all these possible. Once they are learnt, no more training is needed, recognition becomes much easier, and adding a new class only requires feature values to be stored, which will also accomplish good compression.

For example, after the recent tsunami in Asia, we learnt that an application was needed in Sri Lanka to match photos of dead bodies with photos provided by relatives of lost people. Offender tracking is just another possibility as a homeland security

S. Mehrotra et al. (Eds.): ISI 2006, LNCS 3975, pp. 766–767, 2006.

application; for example, suppose we have collected photos of persons who committed crimes or behaved suspiciously, the task might be to match these photos with photos of passengers taken at times of boarding airplanes. We hope that our approach will be very useful in these types of tracking applications (see Fig. 1). Face-matching can also help in duplicate record elimination (e.g., the confidence in merging/purging distinct records can also be based on face-matching as well as matching records based on name, address, date of birth, race, sex, and so on...).

**Fig. 1.** Two exemplary images from our simulation database. Only robust high-level features make it possible to compare two face images.

One of the major advantages of our research is that we have a working test-bed to experiment with (FINDER – the Florida Integrated Network for Data Exchange and Retrieval). FINDER has been a highly successful project in the state of Florida that has addressed effectively the security and privacy issues that relate to information sharing between over 120 law enforcement agencies. It is operated as a partnership between the University of Central Florida and the law-enforcement agencies in Florida sharing data – referred to as the Law Enforcement Data Sharing Consortium. Detailed information about the organization of the data sharing consortium and the FINDER software is available at http://finder.ucf.edu.

We have already demonstrated the usefulness of SINBAD approach in a variety of fields, including metabolomics, natural images, and face recognition. After we have obtained top face recognition accuracies, we moved towards this much more difficult problem of matching faces of unknown individuals. We obtained very high accuracy in this task as well. We are ready to deploy our method in a real-world application: FINDER.

# Author Index

# Lecture Notes in Computer Science

For information about Vols. 1–3896

please contact your bookseller or Springer